INTERACTIVE CASEBOOK SERIES[SM]

WILLS, TRUSTS, AND ESTATES

A Contemporary Approach

Lloyd Bonfield

PROFESSOR OF LAW
NEW YORK LAW SCHOOL
VISITING PROFESSOR OF LAW
UNIVERSITY OF IOWA
COLLEGE OF LAW

Joanna L. Grossman

ELLEN K. SOLENDER ENDOWED CHAIR IN WOMEN AND THE LAW
PROFESSOR OF LAW
SMU DEDMAN SCHOOL OF LAW

William P. LaPiana

RITA AND JOSEPH SOLOMON PROFESSOR OF WILLS, TRUSTS, AND ESTATES
NEW YORK LAW SCHOOL

WEST
ACADEMIC
PUBLISHING

Interactive Casebook Series is a servicemark registered in the U.S. Patent and Trademark Office.

© 2019 LEG, Inc. d/b/a West Academic
    444 Cedar Street, Suite 700
    St. Paul, MN 55101
    1-877-888-1330

West, West Academic Publishing, and West Academic are trademarks of West Publishing Corporation, used under license.

Printed in the United States of America

ISBN: 978-0-314-19958-4

In memory of my parents, Libby and Joseph Bonfield,
and my parents-in-law, Elisa Viani and Luigi Musumarra
—L.B.

For the thousands of students I have taught,
many of whom have come to accept that
inheritance law is "actually" interesting
—J.L.G.

To the memory of our colleague
Pamela R. Champine
Skilled Practitioner, Creative Scholar, Dedicated Teacher
—W.P.LaP. and L.B.

Preface

Law professors often begin an upper-division elective course like Wills, Trusts, and Estates by justifying students allocating a valuable slot in their otherwise crammed academic schedule to study the subject matter. This Preface is not an attempt to pre-empt that interesting discourse, but to provide some defense, some *raison d'être*, for your selection of Wills, Trusts, and Estates (or whichever permutation of that title your faculty's curriculum committee has chosen to give this course). No doubt, like snowflakes, no two professorial presentations are alike; there are as many modes of attack as there are faculty members. What follows is a non-exclusive list of justifications that we have offered in nearly a century (collectively) of teaching the course.

The first is that you will discover when the ink on the parchment of your diploma is not yet dry, and perhaps even before it is printed, advice will be sought from you on 'estate planning issues.' This is so whether you ever advertise your knowledge of inheritance law or ever touch a related case in your practice. If your parents or grandparents have furnished capital for your academic career, they will expect some return in the form of free (or at the very least cut-price) legal advice. Be prepared for a litany of questions: do I need a will?; can I avoid inheritance taxes?; can I disinherit my children Tom and Sally (or even you?) Such questions are not limited to these possible 'investors' in your legal career: any relationship will do. Even friends (Facebook or otherwise) and acquaintances will solicit and expect advice. Never read this book on a crowded airplane. Your neighbor may, particularly if the flight is long, delayed, or bumpy, solicit estate planning advice, if he or she surmises that you may have even a modicum of expertise in the field.

A more serious justification, perhaps, is that this is a course in the process of **property** transmission. While you may be taking courses in your final two years that supplement what you learned in introductory Constitutional Law, Contracts or Civil Procedure, upper-level property courses (save perhaps Real Estate Transactions and Intellectual Property) have all but disappeared from the curriculum. Wills, Trusts, and Estates is a survivor. Taking this course will reinforce what you learned or should have learned in first-year Property, which will serve you well for the MBE portion of the bar exam as well as for your future career as a lawyer.

Let's return to the bar examination. Many students think that they cannot pass it without taking a course in Wills, Trusts, and Estates. At least one of the authors is evidence to the contrary. Let's face it: you can't take every course that is covered on the bar. You must be selective. Wills, Trusts, and Estates is one of those courses that is often heavily tested on the bar (and remember it supplements and reinforces Property Law which most definitely is on the bar). It is one of the subjects on the new Uniform Bar Examination that is rapidly becoming, well, uniform, in the jurisdictions. You don't NEED to take a course in Wills, Trusts, and Estates to pass the bar. But if you do take one, that portion of the bar will be smoother sailing.

Another reason is historical and cultural: you are joining a time-honored profession. Wills, Trusts and Estates was a subject with which all lawyers in the not-to-distant past had significant acquaintance. Estate planning was a far more significant tranche of law practice than it is in our own time, particularly in what is now fondly called 'Big Law.' The vocabulary and doctrine that you will learn in Wills, Trusts, and Estates was imbibed by your forebears. Not being able to state the rule against perpetuities by heart or know the difference between a vested remainder subject to divestment and a contingent remainder was unheard of a generation ago. By taking the course, and grappling with the sometimes hairsplitting distinctions that are part of the law of Wills, Trusts, and Estates, you will provide continuity between and amongst generations of lawyers.

Wills, Trusts, and Estates is also a subject of great, if underappreciated, social importance. Inheritance is a significant driver of class and opportunity in our society, and the rules governing inheritance affect individuals, families, and society as a whole in significant ways.

Finally, for those not bound for 'Big Law,' Wills, Trusts, and Estates is an important component of a general practice. The client who asks you to draft a contract, structure a modest real estate deal, or divorce him or her might also require a will or trust. Never (well almost never) turn down business. One need not specialize in the area to practice therein. Taking this course will prepare you to plan an estate, perhaps not that of Messrs. Bezos, Buffett, or Gates, but the folks who are likely to inhabit your waiting room.

So we have persuaded you to remain enrolled and not return this volume from whence it came. You've made the right decision: it's a great course. What distinguishes this book from the myriad other tomes that cover Wills, Trusts, and Estates? What we have tried to produce is a user-friendly book that comprehensively covers the subject matter, but recognizes that the treatise-like format of most casebooks is daunting to the student. Most law students ignore the lengthy notes and law review articles after the case parsing the subject matter covered in the principle case, be it holding or dictum. By and large, we have eschewed references to them. To be honest, when was the last time you chased up a note case or law review article buried in the small print after the principal case? We do not want to discourage you from further research, but we are well aware that you possess the practical tools to find supplementary readings if you are so inclined. What we (and your professor) will expect from you is that you read (not skim) the more manageable assignment carefully, think about the succinct questions and observations made in the text boxes, so that when you come to class you will be ready, willing, and able to engage with your colleagues. Being prepared and alert in the classroom is still the most efficient means by which to learn the law. This casebook intends to provide the wherewithal.

The authors would like to acknowledge the assistance of Lisa Martina Bonfield (J.D. Tulane, 2011) for her efforts in correcting the final proofs.

Lloyd Bonfield
New York Law School

Joanna L. Grossman
SMU Dedman School of Law

William P. LaPiana
New York Law School

June 2019

Summary of Contents

Table of Contents

Table of Cases

The principal cases are in bold type.

WILLS, TRUSTS, AND ESTATES

A Contemporary Approach

PART I

Introduction

CHAPTER 1

The Vocabulary of Wills and Trusts

3 -22

A. Introduction to the Process of Property Transmission

Sweeping generalizations about the way human beings live are generally misleading and often plainly erroneous. Nevertheless, one is on relatively safe ground in asserting that men and women are not indifferent to what happens to their property after they die. The old saw "You can't take it with you" is certainly true, but it is also correct that one can maintain considerable control over the disposition of property after his or her death. This course is an introduction to the law that governs the passage of property at death and the mechanisms that govern it.

The subject of this volume, the process of property transmission, is a complex one, and many of its complications come from the affection that individuals have for property and its centrality to human life. Sir William Blackstone wrote:

> There is nothing which so generally strikes the imagination, and engages the affections of mankind, as the right of property; or that sole and despotic dominion which one man claims and exercises over the external things of the world, in total exclusion of the right of any other individual in the universe.[1]

Human beings have been dying after having accumulated property for a very long time. There is no natural or inherent process for dictating where it goes after the owner's death. Most legal systems, however, have created structures for governing the process of property transmission. Much of the history of English law (from which much American law is derived) and the legal profession reflects a struggle born from the counterpoised interests between property owners and the English crown (or royal government) to control the transmission of wealth from one generation to the next. One of the consequences of this long history is that many contemporary concepts and doctrines have roots in a past that is very different from the world in which we currently live. The law of property, therefore, is a frequent target of reformers who clearly see a gap between its core principles and the demands of contemporary society.

As to the acts that govern the process of property transmission (primarily gifts, wills, and trusts), reform-minded lawyers and legislators in the last third of the twentieth century have

---

1   Blackstone's Commentaries on the Laws of England, Book 2, Chapter 1, p.2 (1766).

3

succeeded in transforming much of that law. Bear in mind that the law governing the process of property transmission is state-specific. Much of this law is statutory, but even the common law that is still relevant differs from state to state. Reform has been uneven. Regardless it has proceeded apace; the law observed here is decidedly dynamic rather than static. Understanding why this change has been successful is an important part of grasping the relationship between society and the law it produces.

The topic of property transmission is also complicated by the variety of ways in which one can control the disposition of one's property after death. Many non-lawyers believe that the will is the exclusive means by which the intergenerational transfer of wealth is governed. That supposition is perfectly reasonable given the importance of the will in popular culture, which is, of course, a reflection of its significance in the law. Indeed, for a very long time the only way to pass property at death, other than to hand property over to individuals while the owner was on the deathbed, was to make a valid will. Other mechanisms of transfer now exist, which will be explored in turn.

"To pass property at death" is an odd-sounding phrase, but it accurately describes what a will does—it disposes of the property that the decedent owns at death and which is held by her absolutely, and therefore is "orphaned;" it has "nowhere to go." Understanding the devolution of this property, what the law refers to as *"probate property"* or *"the probate estate,"* is crucial, and a grasp of the legal definition of these terms is basic to understanding the law of wills and trusts.

B. Distinguishing the "Probate Estate" and "Non-Probate Property"

Probate property is property owned by the decedent at death that is not held in a form in which its disposition has already been directed. As noted above, such property is "orphaned" in the sense that it requires the owner's action to transfer it, but the owner is no longer capable of doing so. For example, recall first-year Property: law students are probably familiar with property held in co-tenancy: the ubiquitous bank accounts held in "joint tenancy with right of survivorship," where the sum on deposit passes to the surviving joint tenant after the death of the deceased joint tenant by operation of law. Passage of this property at the first co-owner's death is determined by the way it was held during his life. Transfer to the surviving co-owner is automatic, triggered by the death of the first joint owner. Likewise, much real property is held in this form of ownership, particularly among spouses. But, as we shall observe, the modest joint tenancy is in the contemporary world merely the tip of a much larger iceberg of property owned by an individual, but where the disposition has already been directed at her death. The following discussion, however, provides examples of the issues raised by property held by solely by an owner at death. Note especially the vocabulary employed; generations of lawyers have been highly paid because they have mastered it.

1. Probate Property

First, consider *real property*. Generally, real property can be conveyed only by deed. The holder of title to the property must sign the deed as grantor. If the owner is dead, there is no one who can execute the deed. Thus title can be conveyed only if there is someone who succeeds to the dead owner's rights. That person is the *"personal representative"* of the deceased owner's estate. A personal representative named in a will is an *"executor."* If the decedent did not leave a will, the person designated by statute to be personal representative is the *"administrator"* of the *"intestate estate."* The personal representative might also be deemed an *"administrator"* for a testate estate if the will did not designate an executor.

Second, there are other types of property in which ownership is registered in the name of an individual, and therefore requires the registered owner to sign a document in order to make a transfer. Motor vehicles are a good example, as are stocks and bonds. Even if stocks and bonds are held in a brokerage account, if the decedent is the only person who can give instructions regarding sales and purchases, then the account is "orphaned" at death like real property exclusively in the name of the decedent. A checking account in which the decedent alone could write checks is another example.

Finally, consider the decedent's *tangible personal property*, or, more colloquially, the decedent's "stuff." This includes furniture, decorations, jewelry, artwork, books, clothing, and, yes, the ubiquitous laptop, and various genre of items coveted by the owner. Such property can only be transferred by its owner, and when she is no longer amongst us, it likewise comes under the control of the personal representative of the decedent's estate. That said, the law in many states directs that at least some personal property pass automatically to a surviving spouse and children. Note again, while this book deals with the law of property transmission, that law is state law, and particularities exist from one jurisdiction to another.

Not all property passes at death. The process of property transmission is generally undertaken over time, hence the term process, rather than manifested by a single event. A person, of course, can always make a gift of her property during life, and what is given away during life will not be part of the probate estate at death. So we have what appears to be a strict dichotomy: either owner gives her property away while alive, or she holds on to it until death and writes a will that bequeaths her probate estate to beneficiaries and names someone (the executor) to carry out those transfers. Any attempt to make a gift at death through any sort of device other than a will is *"an invalid testamentary (or will) substitute."*

Of course, every statement of black letter law has its exceptions and often they come close to swallowing the rule. That is certainly the case with the law we are investigating here. For a very long time, there have been exceptions to the rule that "only a will can make a gift at death," but, as exceptions often do, they were limited in at least one very important way. There has been an increase in the quantity and forms of *non-probate property*, property transferable at death without the use of a will. Some forms give the person receiving the property after the death of the owner some interest in the property while the owner was still alive; others do not, making the resemblance to wills more obvious.

2. Non-Probate Property

In many situations, property passes at the owner's death untouched by a will or the rules of intestacy. Property that fits this description is deemed "*non-probate property.*" One sort of *non-probate property* you should already be familiar with from your property course is, as we have noted above, *joint tenancy property.* When a joint tenant dies, the surviving joint tenant becomes the sole owner and can transfer the property under his or her signature alone. (Yes, there can be multiple joint tenants, but we will limit ourselves to two-person joint tenancies for now.) Therefore, if a married couple own their residence as joint tenants with rights of survivorship, when one spouse dies, the surviving spouse becomes sole owner by right of survivorship. Thus, in our parlance, joint tenancy property is not "orphaned;" the decedent's signature is not necessary to make a valid deed to transfer the property. The same analysis applies to *tenancies by the entirety*, a particular form of joint estate in real property held by spouses available in some jurisdictions. Of course, all sorts of property can be jointly held with rights of survivorship like joint checking accounts, jointly held brokerage accounts, and jointly held investment accounts. It is possible to buy shares in a mutual fund, have the investment held in an account with the company that manages the fund, and title the account in joint names with right of survivorship.

Do not abandon knowledge painfully acquired in your property course. Remember, while both joint tenants are alive, either can sever the joint tenancy and turn it into a tenancy in common, which has no rights of survivorship. This is not the case with a tenancy by the entirety which, while the spouses are alive can only be ended by dissolving the marriage. In many states, this is also true of joint accounts between spouses. Consider the transmission options open to A, who owns Blackacre in fee simple. A would like B to own Blackacre after A's death. A can write a will that gives Blackacre to B. Alternatively, A can deed the property to a straw person who then would deed Blackacre to A and B as joint tenants with right of survivorship. If A does indeed die before B, B will be the sole owner of Blackacre. Under both strategies, B has a fee simple interest in Blackacre following A's death. What is the difference between the two strategies? Danger lurks in the latter. If B is aware of the transfer, B can unilaterally sever and own one-half of Blackacre as tenant in common with A, and perhaps force a partition. But B's choice may ultimately be shortsighted. If the tenancy in common is not ended while A and B are alive, the interest in Blackacre belonging to the first to die is her own probate property, and can be disposed of by her will. There may be a price for A or for B to pay in order to avoid probate: the owner may find herself losing full control over the property during her life; B's action to sever may cause her to lose the other undivided one-half should A predecease B.

A similar result transpires upon the creation of a legal life estate in land. Suppose A wants to continue to hold possessory rights in the whole of Blackacre and wishes to avoid the prospect of potential severance. As an alternative, A could convey Blackacre to B, and, in the deed, reserve a life estate in Blackacre. At A's death, the life estate terminates, and B owns Blackacre in fee simple. Once again, however, A does not have sole control of Blackacre. B owns the remainder interest and fee simple title to Blackacre is divided between A and B along the proverbial plane of time. While there is no need for a will, A has given up sole ownership of Blackacre.

Another way to create non-probate property that more closely resembles the disposition of property by will (and is of much more recent vintage than joint tenancies and life estates) is to name a beneficiary of property that is the subject of a contract between the owner and some other entity. The naming of a beneficiary in a contractual arrangement is called in our trade is often called a '*will substitute*.' In contemporary America, the quantum of wealth held in such arrangements with "*payable on death*" ("P.O.D.") provisions is enormous and likely exceeds in value all holdings of probate property. Perhaps the most common contemporary example, and the oldest, is a life insurance policy. The owner of the policy (usually the insured) can designate a beneficiary to receive the death benefit under the policy directly from the insurance company when the insured dies. The insurance contract dictates the receipt of the insurance benefits, and a will plays no role in the outcome, even if it purports to bequeath the policy proceeds. Other sorts of property that commonly have beneficiary designations include Individual Retirement Accounts (IRAs), pension accounts, certain kinds of bank accounts, as well as, securities and brokerage accounts, which hold a bewildering diversity of financial investments. Indeed, as we will observe later in detail, almost any sort of contractual arrangement can be structured so that the property involved will be paid to someone on the death of the owner.

With respect to control, what is the effect of structuring property ownership through these 'non-probate' arrangements? Like a will, which we shall see is revocable, the owner of the property in a '*will substitute*' almost always retains complete control of it during life and will usually retain the ability to change the beneficiary until death. Like the beneficiary of a bequest in a will, the beneficiary of a will substitute has no choate interest in the property until the death of the owner. Revocation of the beneficiary designation in a *will substitute*, however, may require some particularized process. There are usually three parties to these arrangements: the owner, the entity holding the property (the insurance company, the bank where the payable on death account is held, the custodian of the IRA or 401(k) plan, the administrator of a pension account) and the beneficiary who will take directly from the entity when the owner dies.

But today the creation of non-probate property through the use of contracts is overshadowed by yet another '*will substitute*.' It is possible, though usually not practical, to hold only non-probate property by using a '*revocable living trust* or "lifetime" trust. The central feature of this type of trust is that it is created by a living person rather than in a will. We will study trusts in detail, but at this juncture, let us rehearse only the basic structure and operation of a trust.

First, a definition: *a trust is a device for separating the legal and the equitable ownership of property*. A concise definition, but what does it mean? Any person who is competent can create a trust by transferring title to property to a "*trustee*." The transaction results in a bifurcation of interests. The trustee manages the property (called the "*trust corpus*" or "*trust principal*") according to the instructions of the creator of the trust, which are almost always (and always should be) set forth in a written instrument. The creator of the trust also designates the persons for whose benefit the trustee will manage the property; these persons are the "*beneficiaries*." The trustee has title to the trust property, and property law therefore regards the trustee as the "owner" of the trust corpus. Proper drafting of the trust will ensure that there will always be a trustee, and therefore in a very real sense the trustee, the holder of legal title (as opposed to the creator) will never die. Therefore, trust property avoids probate at the death of the creator of the trust. The terms of the trust dictates how property shall be transferred at the owner's death or at other designated points in time. Finally, trustees, like executors and administrators, are "*fiduciaries*." The legal title to property that the fiduciary holds must be used solely in the interests of the beneficiaries who, for purposes of the use and enjoyment of the trust property, are the equitable owners of the property. Each state has statutory law governing the obligations of fiduciaries and there is also extensive common law that regulates their behavior.

[handwritten margin notes: fiduciary, trust, faith, fidelity, obligation]

Of course our treatment above depicts only a broad outline of trust law. The important point for you to appreciate as we focus initially on the will is that the trust is merely one weapon (to use a military metaphor) in a broader arsenal at the disposal of the estate planner. At this juncture, you should understand that it is possible, though perhaps not always advisable, to use a trust to render much or even all of a client's property non-probate property.

3. Comparing Probate and Non-Probate Transfers

Let us return to the will. Consider again the basic workings of a will. Recall that the will gives instructions about what is to be done with the decedent's probate assets after death and gives the responsibility for carrying out those instructions to the executor. A will does not take effect until death, so a decedent's relationship with probate property is unchanged while the decedent is alive. At the decedent's death, the executor will collect the now-orphaned property and distribute it to the named beneficiaries. A decedent can change his or her mind at any time and amend the will or revoke it and write a new one. Whimsy is one advantage that the will has over every form of non-probate property transaction that we have discussed up to now. Wills can be altered or revoked more simply than most *will substitutes* (although there are rules), and while trust creators can stipulate that the trust is revocable (and specify the manner of revocation), more formality may be required. Designation of a beneficiary by contract through the use of a *will substitute* is all well and good, but every asset is subject to its own contract. Those wanting to make extensive changes in the beneficiary designations have to contact each bank, brokerage house, insurance company, IRA and 401(k) custodian, and the parties to all the other contracts; each entity may impose different requirements for changing or revoking beneficiary designations.

Property owners may not want to deal with the third party needed to create a *will substitute*. However, in such a case, an owner of property may create a self-settled trust of probate assets property by transferring title (or possession if the property does not pass through the transfer of title documents) to a trustee and retaining a life interest in the income produced by the property. The creator may constitute herself the exclusive beneficiary of the trust during her life, while at the same time designating the persons who are to be beneficiaries after her death, but nevertheless retain the power to change the trust in any way and even to revoke it completely. A creator may also constitute herself trustee. (Should she do so she ought to name someone as "*successor trustee*" who will become trustee after her death.)

This particular form of revocable trust is the functional equivalent of a will. Observe carefully the interests created. Suppose a trust's creator uses the following terms: "I am the only person who benefits from my property while I'm alive, and I can at any time change my mind about who is to benefit from my property after I die and make those changes effective by changing one document, the trust instrument." When the creator dies, *none of the property in the trust is "orphaned" because the office of trustee does not die and the trustee is the legal owner of the trust property.* Even if the creator is the trustee, the successor trustee simply takes over and makes sure that whatever the creator wanted done with the property is done.

Once again, unsurprisingly, there is a difference between the law of trusts and the law of wills that prevents the revocable lifetime trust from being a perfect *will substitute.* As previously discussed, a will has absolutely no effect during the decedent's life, except, as we will see, to revoke an existing will. The beneficiaries named in the will have no interest whatsoever in the probate property. The beneficiaries have only *"expectancies,"* which are not property rights. *'expectancy'*

Conversely, the beneficiaries of a revocable living trust do have an interest in the trust property under the law of trusts. Admittedly, those interests may be of little or no practical economic value so long as the creator of the trust can revoke it. Yet if the creator of the trust cannot revoke the trust because he or she has lost capacity to do so, the interests of the beneficiaries gain some value, and they certainly should be able to protect those interests. We will spend some time investigating the rights of beneficiaries of a revocable living trust, but for now just remember that the existence of those rights in a trust is an important difference between wills and revocable living trusts.

The existence of a beneficiary's property interests in a revocable living trust does detract from the fact that if a property owner can somehow transfer to the trustee title (and possession) to all of her probate property, a will becomes superfluous. As a practical matter, however, it is often not possible (or perhaps wise) to add every single property interest owned to a revocable trust. There is yet another wrinkle to estate planning that we shall explore in more detail: one may link together a living trust and a will, which will add or *"pour-over"* all the will-maker's probate property at death into the trust, augmenting the corpus. For now, however, it is enough to understand that the revocable living trust, like a life insurance policy, a P.O.D. account, or a joint ownership with right of survivorship arrangement, is a substitute for a will and is a means of turning a wide variety of property into a non-probate form.

C. What Is Probate?

The word *"probate"* appears frequently in these materials. What is the legal definition of the term? In fact, the term is frequently used in a number of contexts. In the past, the term simply meant proof—the deceased's last will was probated when it was proved according to applicable procedures. So probate was a process and not simply an event. It so remains. If a person dies with a will, the process begins with proving that the will is indeed the decedent's last will, and that it is valid: that the decedent was mentally competent, made the will of his or her own volition and not under duress, and the document has been executed with the required statutory formalities. Probate is also the legal process by which a *personal representative* named in the will (usually called the executor of the decedent's estate) attains legal recognition. Most property owners do not execute wills. If they do not, or the will is deemed invalid, they die *"intestate."* A process (sometimes called "administration" but similar in process to probate for a will) begins with the appropriate order empowering an administrator—the counterpart of the executor—to deal with the decedent's probate property. A decedent with a valid will that does not successfully give away the entire estate could be said to die *"partially intestate."*

1. The Probate Process

The probate process usually takes place in a specialized court, which might have any number of names—probate court, widows' and orphans' court, or surrogate's court, to name a few. The entire process described below takes place under the authority of this type of court. Once the personal representative qualifies, the first job is to collect the decedent's probate property. Then the decedent's debts are paid from the property, any taxes due are calculated and paid, and finally the property is distributed to the beneficiaries of the will or the persons designated under the intestacy statute. We will examine each of these aspects of the probate process in turn.

a) Qualifying a Personal Representative

This discussion will presume the decedent died with a will (or *"testate"*) rather than without a will (*intestate*). Usually, the executor nominated therein will bring the will to the appropriate court for probate. That statement sounds terribly abstract because it is. Probate procedures vary greatly among the jurisdictions that comprise the United States. The term "jurisdictions," of course, includes the States, the District of Columbia, the Commonwealth of Puerto Rico, the Territory of the Virgin Islands, and the Commonwealth of the Marianas, as well as Guam. In other words, the law of wills and, in particular, probate practice is local law, not federal law.

With that caveat, it is safe to say that most United States jurisdictions use one of two types of probate. *"Common* (or *simple*) *form probate"* is the equivalent of an *ex parte* proceeding: only one side appears. In a common form probate, that one side is the proponent of the will. The executor nominated in the will offers the will for probate in the appropriate jurisdiction in the will-maker's domicile. Executor proves the decedent's signature on the will, and the judge or other probate official authorizes him or her to begin her duties as personal representative. The only notice given to those who might have an objection to the validity of the will is published notice. If no one comes forward to make an objection (usually called a *"caveat"*) within the prescribed period of time (almost never more than one year from publication) the validity of the will is beyond legal challenge. Most jurisdictions recognize common form probate.

Some jurisdictions also recognize *"solemn form probate."* In some states, most prominently New York, the only way to qualify as a personal representative is through solemn form probate.

Solemn form probate is a proceeding before a court that begins with notice to persons who have an interest in the estate. The proponent of the will (again, usually the executor nominated in the will) begins the proceeding with a form of pleading, called a *"petition,"* which asks the court to admit the will to probate and to issue process (give notice) to those persons who have an interest in opposing admission of the will. Who are those persons? In almost all cases, they are those who would take the probate property if the decedent had died without a will; in other words, the *"heirs"* or *"next-of-kin"* designated by the particular state's intestacy statute. Process (in New York this form of process is called a *"citation"*) must be properly served so that the interested parties are likely to have notice of their opportunity to appear in court on the *return date* stated in the process. If no objections are made at that time the judge admits the will to probate and the personal representative's work begins. If objections (for example, regarding the will's validity) are made, probate becomes a contested proceeding and proceeds in most ways strikingly similar to any other lawsuit; it is carried on in conformity with the governing procedural law.

As you can imagine, solemn form probate can be time-consuming and expensive, especially if a search must be made for the persons who must be cited. Complications in opening probate, however, are not the only source of delay. In some states, once the executor qualifies, the court continues to supervise his or her conduct in administering the estate, often requiring the personal representative to return frequently to court for permission to carry out necessary tasks or to report on acts undertaken. California is notorious for what is generally regarded as burdensome supervision of executors. On the other hand, although New York requires that the executor qualify through solemn form probate, once the will is admitted to probate he or she is free to carry out his or her duties without the need to return to court to seek permission or approval until administration of the estate is complete absent special circumstances (for example, an executor needs permission to carry on a business belonging to the estate).

Whatever the rules governing the supervision of executors, most jurisdictions supervise administrators of intestate estates more closely. Executors are selected by the will-maker. The probate court appoints the administrator, and usually in accordance with a statute that prescribes who may qualify as an administrator. Priority is given to a surviving spouse, followed by parents or children; in their absence, more remote relatives may qualify. If no one on the statutory list qualifies, every jurisdiction has a public official who is the administrator of last resort. (States cannot constitutionally prefer male relatives over female relatives. *(Reed v. Reed*, 404 U.S. 71 (1971))).

Once the personal representative qualifies, the court grants *"letters testamentary"* to an executor and *"letters of administration"* to an administrator. These documents are the official evidence of the personal representative's authority. The personal representative will then obtain certificates from the court stating that letters have been issued. These certificates will be presented to anyone who requires legally sufficient evidence (e.g., the bank where the decedent held an account) of the personal representative's authority to deal with the decedent's probate property.

b) Collecting the Probate Property

Armed with the certificates, the personal representative collects the deceased's probate property. Sometimes collection is literal: the personal representative may withdraw all funds in a bank account and open an account in the name of the personal representative (an *estate account*). Sometimes the personal representative may only need to change the title to property. For example, the decedent's brokerage account could be re-titled in the name of the personal representative. In such cases, ownership reflects that the personal representative owns the property "as personal representative;" styling ownership in this manner shows clearly that the property in the account is not the property of the personal representative in his own right, but rather is property held by the personal representative on behalf of the decedent's estate. For real property held in the name of the deceased, title can be transferred by the personal representative by executing a deed directly to the beneficiaries, or if necessary, to the personal representative herself as representative.

Sometimes collection of property by the personal representative is informal. Consider the decedent's tangible personal property. If the property is located in the decedent's residence, the personal representative may need only to make sure the contents are distributed to the beneficiaries of the estate. Alternatively, the personal representative may contribute some of it to charity or sell some of it in a yard sale (or even online). The personal representative will not usually need to show evidence of qualification, but of course she is still legally responsible for the property. If the personal representative donates the decedent's clothing to a charitable agency such as Goodwill or the St. Vincent de Paul Society, it is unlikely that anyone at the agency will ask for proof that the person making the donation has title to the property. However, the personal representative must obtain a receipt as proof of the proper disposition of the property.

What's That?

Provenance is the term used to describe where a work of art came from It's the equivalent of a chain of title for real property.

Not all tangible personal property can be handled so informally. If the decedent owned a valuable work of art, for example, anyone purchasing the piece will want to make sure of its *provenance*. The purchaser will certainly want to see proof of the personal representative's authority.

c) Paying Debts

Once the probate estate has been inventoried and collected, the personal representative must pay the decedent's debts. If the decedent's property is insufficient to pay the debts, the creditors are simply out of luck. Generally, only the probate estate is liable for the decedent's debts, although we will see that some non-probate property, especially property in a revocable living trust, can be liable for debts if the probate estate is insufficient. Spouses can sometimes be held liable for certain kind of debts, such as medical expenses, but the law varies tremendously from state to state.

The procedure involved in paying debts is extremely important. Every jurisdiction has a statute of limitations applicable to creditors of a decedent's estate. Unless the claim is presented within the prescribed period, the debt is barred. The need for such a statute should be obvious; without it, the fiduciary could never wind up the decedent's financial affairs and distribute the estate to named beneficiaries. Usually the period for presenting claims is no longer than a year, although as a matter of due process, the personal representative should seek out known and easily discoverable creditors. (*See Tulsa Professional Collection Services, Inc. v. Pope*, 485 U.S. 478 (1988)).

d) Paying Taxes

The decedent's final income taxes must be paid from the estate, and the estate is also liable for any estate or inheritance taxes. The threshold for liability for federal estate tax is high: in 2019 it is $11,400,000, and this figure adjusts upward annually for inflation. The exempt amount covers lifetime gifts made by the decedent as well as those made at death. The federal estate tax only applies, therefore, where a decedent's "taxable estate" exceeds this threshold. The "taxable estate" is, generally, the decedent's property (both probate and non-probate) minus various deductions for debts, expenses, and gifts to charity and a surviving spouse. With such a high threshold it is perhaps no surprise that it is estimated that only about .02% of all estates in 2019 will be subject to federal estate tax.

Several states have their own taxes on the transmission of property at death. Exempt amounts, tax rates, and procedures for payment differ, but they will generally kick in at a lower amount than the federal tax. It is the personal representative's responsibility to determine whether the decedent's estate is taxable, to file the appropriate returns, and to pay the tax. If the personal representative does not perform these tasks, or if no personal representative qualifies, the tax law places the obligation to determine if tax is due, and to pay it, on those who receive the estate's property.

e) Distributing the Probate Property and Closing the Estate

Once expenses and taxes have been paid, the personal representative distributes the probate property to the beneficiaries under the decedent's will or to the heirs of an intestate estate. Once the property has been distributed, the personal representative's task is over, except for "closing" the estate, which may be done in a number of ways. Administrators generally must report to the court in which they qualified to demonstrate that they have completed their tasks and present for approval a complete record of what how they have distributed the estate's property. This submission is called an "*accounting*." Executors generally have a greater range of choices. An executor can present an accounting to the estate's beneficiaries and ask them to sign a formal approval of the accounting. The executor can also submit the accounting to the appropriate court, ask that process issue to those interested in the estate. The executor may then ask the court to issue a decree approving the accounting, thereby releasing the executor from further liability. This "*judicial accounting*" provides the greatest protection to an executor, but obviously involves greater time and expense than an accounting presented only to the beneficiaries.

The following problem should help you to determine whether you have grasped the distinction between probate and non-probate property.

Problem 1-1

David Drake is a new client who wants you to plan his estate. He is unmarried and has no descendants. His parents are dead, and his only living close relatives are his brother, Donald Drake, who is married, and Donald's four living children. David wants all his property to go to Donald's children on his death. David's assets are as follows:

- brokerage account, value $2,000,000; the account is in David's sole name

- condominium apartment, value $1,250,000; David is the sole owner of the condo

- house in the country, value $350,000; David is the sole owner of the house

- insurance policy on his life, death benefit $250,000; David owns the policy and the beneficiaries are Donald's four children in equal shares

- 401(k) account, value $1,500,000; the beneficiaries are Donald's four children in equal shares

- tangible personal property: an automobile, clothes, furnishings, household goods, books, a computer, stereo equipment, CDs and DVDs, two televisions, total value uncertain.

(a) What items are in David's probate estate?

Now consider the various mechanisms that have been introduce to allow David to pass his estate to his chosen beneficiaries.

Practice Pointer

The role of the estate planner is to present the client with options taking into account the client's economic and familial circumstances and his distributional preferences. The estate planner begins with asking questions to ferret out the information required to provide estate planning strategies.

(b) Can David either execute a will or create a revocable living trust? If he creates the trust, do you yet have a sense of which items should be added to the trust?

(c) Will the administration of David's estate be carried out in a different way if he creates a trust rather than a will, or even if he does neither and dies intestate? If the pattern he chooses mirrors that of the intestate succession statute, should he bother to write a will or execute a trust instrument?

(d) How would your answer be different if David were married but had no children and the beneficiary of items #4 and #5 were his spouse with his nieces and nephews as contingent beneficiaries (that is, they would take if David's spouse did not survive him)?

f) Some Additional Law

Problem 1-1 shows that at this early juncture, you do not know everything you need to know in order to make a decision about whether David should write a will or create a revocable trust. One threshold issue, particularly in the minds of clients, is the comparative costs of the various strategies.

One aspect of the cost of the process of property transmission is the legal charges involved in creating the appropriate documents. Fees vary widely, but generally speaking, it may cost somewhat more to have a lawyer draft a revocable living trust than it does to have the same lawyer draft a will. In addition, there are almost always legal fees involved in transferring property into the trust. For example, a lawyer will draft the deed that conveys the summer house and the condo from David to David-as-trustee. That said, there will be similar costs after his death if David chooses to write a will.

Both the will and trust occasion further costs: the trustee's or executor's *commissions*. Trustees and executors (who are *fiduciaries*) are entitled to compensation the amount of which is sometimes set by statute. For example, observe New York's schedule of executor's fees (SCPA 2307(1)) for 2019:

Rate Table	Cumulative Maximum Commission
5% on the first $100,000	$5,000
4% on the next $200,000	$13,000
3% on the next $700,000	$33,000
2.5% on the next $4,000,000	$133,000
2% on all amounts over $5,000,000	Unlimited

The maximum commission on an estate of $1,000,000 is $33,000 and, on a $5,000,000 estate, it is $133,000. The testator can waive commissions or set his own rates in the will or trust.

Commissions for trustees are more complicated. Again, using New York as an example, trustees are entitled to a default commission of 1% of all sums paid out of the trust (not including income earned by the trust) and to annual commissions of $10.40 per $1,000 on the first $400,000 in the trust, $4.50 per $1,000 on the next $600,000 and $3.00 per $1,000 on all the rest above $1,000,000 (SCPA 2709). Assuming the successor trustee of a $1,000,000 revocable living trust simply distributes the trust to the beneficiaries after the death of the creator of the trust, the total commission would be $10,000 in "paying out" commissions and a single annual commission of $6,860 for a total of $16,860.

In addition, an executor or trustee is likely to have to hire a lawyer to help with administering the estate or trust. The lawyer's fee is paid out of the trust or estate. While it is impossible to provide clear guidance on the approximate level of these fees, especially if it is necessary to prepare an estate tax return, the fees for an estate and a trust are likely to be comparable in the long run. If there are fees to be paid to change the title on assets, they will be paid when those assets are titled in the name of the trustee, or when they are titled in the names of the beneficiaries of the will.

There will be filing fees for the probate proceeding, a cost which in some cases may amount to many hundreds of dollars. There is no comparable expense for a revocable living trust, although if the trustee or the executor wishes to have a formal accounting there will be filing fees then as well.

g) A Note on Statutes

Much of the law in this field has deep common law roots and is still common law. The various jurisdictions in the United States differ in how much of this law is codified. In the mid-twentieth century, however, the National Conference of Commissioners on Uniform State Laws (now known as the Uniform Law Commission, or ULC) became active in the area of wills and trusts and eventually produced two influential uniform acts: the Uniform Probate Code (UPC) and the Uniform Trust Code (UTC). In the last two decades of the twentieth century, the ULC members working on the uniform acts were also highly influential in writing the American Law Institute's Third Series of Restatements of the Law of Property (Wills and Other Donative Transfers) and Trusts. The close working relationship between ULC and the American Law Institute has increased the impact of the UPC and UTC. The former has greatly influenced statutes throughout the United States and the latter, although relatively new, seems to be on the way to becoming even more influential.

The statutes of most states can be found in what is usually called the "probate code" and the "trust code." Terms do vary, however. The relevant New York statutes, for example, can be found in two titles of the "Consolidated Laws": The Estates, Powers and Trusts Law (EPTL) and the Surrogate's Court Procedure Act (SCPA). (In spite of its title, there is a good deal of substantive law in the SCPA, but most of the provisions that touch on the topics in these materials are found in the EPTL). California has its Probate Code; Florida its Probate Code and Trust Code (Title 42 of the Florida Statutes); Texas its Probate Code and a Trust Code (Title 9 of the Property Code). The lesson is that not only do state laws differ in substance but also in organization. It can be very useful to flip through the hard copy of the code book to get a sense of the relevant set of statutes in a particular state.

2. Some More Vocabulary

The preceding material introduced some of the vocabulary from the world of trusts and estates. There are a few more words with which you should become familiar.

a) "Will Words"

The phrase "*last will and testament*" is probably familiar. Like many of the terms in this area of law, it has a complicated history. The transmission of land was far more complicated, and until the enactment of the Statute of Wills of 1540, real property could not be transmitted by will. Most land passed through inter vivos settlements remarkably similar to trusts. Still, there was a role for wills. The validity of all wills was determined by probate courts which were largely ecclesiastical courts. Real property was *devised* by will to a *devisee* while personal property was the subject of a *legacy* or *bequest* to a *legatee*. After the enactment of the Statute of Frauds of 1677, separate rules governed the validity of wills of real property and personal property until the Wills Act of 1837 created a unified set of requirements. Disputes over the construction of wills were litigated in two separate courts: royal courts dealt with land and church courts with personal property. Church courts' jurisdiction over probate was abolished by statute in 1857, and replaced the following year with Probate Registries.

Church courts never existed in the United States (though they were at work in some of the colonies), and legal differences between transmission at death of real property and of personal property are of almost no significance today. It is correct to refer to a "will" and to the "beneficiary" of the will (although the Uniform Probate Code uses the term "devisee" for all will beneficiaries and "devise" for all gifts in wills). It is equally acceptable to use the verb "to give" to refer to dispositions under a will and to refer to what is given as a gift under the will. If you do use both "devise" and "bequeath," however, make sure you use them correctly, using the former to refer to real property and the latter to personal property. When learning the law of any particular state, pay attention to the words used in the applicable statutes and cases.

There is one aspect of the history that is still of great importance. All legal proceedings respecting trusts and most matters respecting wills sound in equity rather than law. In the modern world, jury trials of contested matters are often not available. We will consider this at greater length later on in these materials.

Another vocabulary matter has to do with the gender of nouns. Very few English words have different forms to refer to men and women; actor/actress and waiter/waitress are probably the only ones in common use, and increasingly one sees "actor" and "waitperson" used to describe both men and women. *Executrix* (plural *executrices*), the feminine form of executor and *administratrix* (plural *administratrices*), the feminine form of administrator, are still sometimes used, but ever less frequently. However, the terms do appear in some of the cases that have been selected. In our discussion in these materials, we will use executor and administrator to refer to both genders, as this is becoming the preferred approach.

b) "Trust Words"

There are two terms related to trusts which need to be introduced at the beginning: *principal* and *income*. *Principal* refers to the property that is held in the trust. As mentioned previously, it is also sometimes referred to as the *corpus* of the trust or as the trust *res*. It is the property the trustee must manage. *Income* is what the principal produces. While there is an elaborate law distinguishing between principal and income in the surprisingly numerous close cases, most of the time identifying income is simple. Rent produced by real property held in trust is income, as are dividends paid by equities held in the trust and the interest paid by bonds or other debt instruments. In many trusts, income may be distributed to one or more beneficiaries, while principal may be distributed to the income beneficiaries or to different beneficiaries. Often, income is to be distributed at regular intervals while principal is not distributed until termination of the trust.

c) "Family Words"

You might think that there is little especially "legal" about words that describe family relationships. We all know what "father," "mother," "brother," "sister," and similar words mean, although we shall see that the legal relationships these words describe are not as simply defined as they once were. There is one group of terms, however, that often causes confusion. A person's *issue*, *lineal descendants*, and *descendants* all mean the same thing: all of the persons who trace their ancestry back to that person. For example, you are the issue, a descendant, and a lineal descendant of your parents, your grandparents, your great-grandparents, and all of your more remote ancestors.

Note that "issue" is an odd sort of noun; it is both singular and plural. It can designate a single person (The Prince of Wales is Queen Elizabeth II's issue) and many persons (Queen Victoria's issue include many members of European royalty). If a testator refers in his or her will to "my issue," that is a reference to children, grandchildren, great-grandchildren and all more remote descendants. Thus, while "children" are "issue," "issue" includes persons more distantly related than children.

Another related term is *collateral relative* or *collateral heirs*. Your collateral relatives are those related to you through any of your ancestors but not in your direct line of descent. If you have brothers and sisters they are your collateral relatives or simply "collaterals." Your aunts, uncles, cousins and their descendants are also your collateral relatives. In other words, your collateral relatives are your relatives who are not your issue.

3. Small Estates

As the foregoing discussion suggests, for estates with only a modest amount of assets, the cost to probate a will or to open an intestate administration would quickly consume the bulk of the estate. Many states have simplified pro-

Go Online

For a link to the small estates statutes of all the states, click on http://small-estates.uslegal.com.

cedures for collecting relatively small sums belonging to a decedent. Section 3–1201 of the Uniform Probate Code requires anyone indebted to the decedent to pay a person claiming to be a successor of the decedent upon presentation of a proper affidavit. The affidavit must state that the total value of the entire estate does not exceed $25,000 (the suggested amount; states enacting the provision can of course enact a different number), that 30 days have elapsed since the decedent's death, no probate proceeding is pending, and that the person claiming the asset is indeed entitled to it. Debts owed to the decedent include all sorts of accounts that belong to the decedent. The checking account for these purposes is a debt owed by the bank to its creditor, the depositor. Most states have similar provisions, some based on the UPC, but they vary widely in their details. The value of a "small estate" differs, as one might imagine, and in some states real property may be subject to these simplified rules. Many states also have special provisions for transferring title to cars when a probate proceeding would not otherwise be necessary.

D. Reflections on the Law of Wills and Trusts

Let us think more theoretically upon the law upon whose study we have embarked. This course builds upon a number of themes that you probably grappled with in your first-year Property course. Foremost is that property consists not only of a bundle of rights to its use and enjoyment, but also of a set of limitations upon its exploitation. The dominion over property is often not as despotic as Blackstone posited above. A landowner may usually develop her property but she cannot, for example, build a nuclear power plant in a residential neighborhood.

Another broad theme that you have previously visited is that property law can be quite specific in directing the means by which it can be transferred. The law controls the way holders of interests in property can convey them to others, even gratuitously, even though often the transaction involves family members and is frequently between generations (parents, children, and grandchildren). As we shall see, the law is not always forgiving when the 'hoops' and 'hurdles' stipulated for will or trust validity are ignored, or somehow compliance with them is wanting.

> **Go Online**
>
> For the complete text of Blackstone's *Commentaries on the Laws of England,* 1st ed. http://avalon.law.yale.edu/subject_menus/blackstone.asp. And for a portrait of the great man: http://en.wikipedia.org/wiki/File:Sir_William_Blackstone_from_NPG.jpg.

Let us begin our study of case law with a simple narrative of an attempt at property transmission, that of a soldier in the World War II who, though young and with plans for his future, contemplates his death in battle.

Wescott v. First & Citizens Nat'l Bank

40 S.E.2d 461 (N.C. 1946)

The question presented by the defendants' appeal is whether the facts found by the trial judge, which were unquestioned, were sufficient to constitute an express trust in favor of the plaintiff with respect to the deposits made in defendant Bank by the deceased soldier.

Ulysses C. Robbins was a sergeant in the United States Army serving in 1945 in Italy in a Quartermaster Truck Company. During this time deposits were made by him and accepted by the Bank pursuant to instructions contained in a typewritten letter from Robbins to the Bank, dated Italy, January 15, 1945, in which letter Robbins stated he had heretofore sent to his grandfather, the plaintiff Wescott, residing in Elizabeth City, sums of money to be deposited 'in one of the banks in the city, for me.' Robbins further wrote the Bank: 'I wish to establish an account with your Bank. * * * Please deposit the money that I will send regularly to this account. I would like to make this an 'in trust for' account so I am the only person who can withdraw from it. In case I become deceased I would like to make an agreement with you so as to make my beneficiary my grandfather, whose name and address is stated above, eligible to receive the money only after I have been deceased for five years.' The deposits were credited on the books of the Bank in name of 'Sgt. Ulysses C. Robbins, Quartermaster Truck Co.' The deposits to the last date, June 9, 1945, totaled $6900.

Food for Thought

Is there no right in natural law to dispose of your property? Is there no constitutional guarantee? Why is the form of a will regulated by statute?

The record further shows that on February 24, 1945, plaintiff Wescott deposited in savings account in defendant Bank $800, which had been sent by Robbins to the plaintiff to be deposited. This was placed by the Bank to the credit of 'Ulysses C. Robbins, deceased, by Ulysses S. Wescott, Agt'.

[On] January 22, 1945, Robbins wrote to plaintiff from Italy as follows: 'I sent some money to the bank awhile back for my bank account. I didn't know whether I already had it in my name or yours, however I started it in my name. I made an agreement if something should happen to me my money would not be payable to my beneficiary until five (5) years after the war. I plan to use this money for my business after the war and why the five years is anything could happen. I could be reported dead and then not be dead. I have a good partner for my business and some day I hope you will meet him. I want to go back to school after the war and study business and law. I am planning on letting the Government send me there and if nothing happens I intend to go to N. Y. U. New York University. Of course this is just my future dreams and I guess every soldier has them.'

The Adjutant General of U. S. Army reported to the plaintiff that Ulysses C. Robbins was killed in Italy June 19, 1945, as result of injuries incurred while driving a government vehicle. The death of Ulysses C. Robbins was a fact admitted by all parties, and so found by the court.

Upon the death of Robbins the fund became immediately available either for the plaintiff or for the defendant administrator for distribution to the next of kin.

Neither of the letters of Robbins was offered or proven in the manner and form prescribed by the statutes so as to constitute a valid disposition of the property to take effect after his death, and therefore may not be regarded as affording basis for awarding the fund to the plaintiff on that ground. G.S. s 31–3; G.S. s 31–26. The right to dispose of property by will is conferred and regulated by statute *Paul v. Davenport,* 217 N.C. 154, 7 S.E.2d 352; *In re Perry,* 193 N.C. 397, 137 S.E. 145.

Nor may these letters be held to create a trust in favor of the plaintiff enforceable in a court of equity. An express trust has been defined as 'a fiduciary relationship with respect to property, subjecting the person by whom the property is held to equitable duties to deal with the property for the benefit of another person, which arises as a result of a manifestation of an intention to create it.' 1 Restatement Law of Trusts, 6. The term signifies the relationship resulting from the equitable ownership of property in one person entitling him to certain duties on the part of another person holding the legal title. 54 Am. Jur. 21. To constitute this relationship there must be a transfer of the title by the donor or settlor for the benefit of another. *Coon v. Stanley,* 230 Mo.App. 524, 94 S.W.2d 96. The gift must be executed rather than executory upon a contingency. *Cazallis v. Ingraham,* 119 Me. 240, 110 A. 359.

Here the essentials of an express trust are lacking. There was no evidence of a transfer or assignment of a present beneficial interest in the fund deposited in the defendant Bank. There was only evidence of a desire that in the event of the depositor's death the grandfather should be the beneficiary. That was the only sense in which the words 'beneficiary' or 'in trust for' were used, and these were coupled with express directions to the Bank that the depositor should remain the sole owner of the deposits, and that they were intended for his own use and benefit. He declared that only in the event of his own death should the plaintiff become 'eligible' to receive this money. The Bank so understood, and placed the deposits to the credit of Ulysses C. Robbins. The letters of Robbins evidence a desire only to secure for his own use the money he was sending back from overseas, and do not seem to contain definite expression of purpose or intention thereby to make a testamentary disposition of the fund. No present beneficial interest was conveyed. *Coon v. Stanley,* supra.

Nor is the evidence sufficient to show a gift inter vivos or causa mortis (a deathbed transfer). *Buffaloe v. Barnes,* 226 N.C. 313, 38 S.E.2d 222. Nor are there here any facts which would give rise to the inference of family settlement justifying the disposition of the fund to the plaintiff. *Reynolds v. Reynolds,* 208 N.C. 578, 182 S.E. 341. The fund should be turned over to the defendant administrator of Ulysses C. Robbins for disposition according to law.

On defendants' appeal the judgment is reversed.

Points for Discussion

1. *Wescott* illustrates that in North Carolina during the period (and in much of modern America even to this day) the law governing property transmission is strictly (some might say formalistically) applied. One might even argue that the key to understanding the outcome in the cases involving wills, trusts and estates is to discover to whom the owner wanted the property to pass, eliminate that individual from consideration, and select another claimant. *Wescott* may be cited as an example. Assuming that the letters excerpted in the opinion were actually written by Sgt. Robbins, do you have any doubt that at the time he wrote the letters the intention of Sgt. Robbins was the following: the bank should pay the money in the account over to him upon demand during his life; if he should be reported to have died in the war, the bank should hold the funds in his account for five years thereafter, and then pay the balance on deposit over to Grandpa Wescott? What interests were served by thwarting his clearly expressed intent?

2. In endeavoring to give effect to the 'estate plan' crafted in the letters, the court considers each of three modes of gratuitous transfers: a will, a trust, and a gift. As the court notes, wills are the creature of the legislature: state law governs the requirements for a document to be valid as a will. Neither letter was witnessed. Suppose each was, would the will be valid? Should the court have been more forgiving? Why didn't Sgt. Robbins follow the legal rules for passing along his property?

3. For a will to be valid, its maker must have 'testamentary intent' at the time the document is executed: she must be thinking 'I am making my will . . .' Are you satisfied that while Sgt. Robbins was writing the letters, he believed that he was making his will?

4. What about a trust? In the letter to the bank, Sgt. Wescott indicated that he wanted to set up 'an in trust for account.' The court employs the definition of a trust in the Restatement of Trusts Sec 6. Why don't the two letters combined create a trust? What does the court mean when it indicates that Sgt. Robbins intended to confer a benefit on Grandpa Wescott rather than to create a trust?

5. This casebook gives little attention to inter vivos gifts. For a transaction to be a completed gift, Sgt. Robbins would have to have delivered the property. Could the sending of the letter be construed as constructive delivery?

6. Unlike most gifts, gifts *causa mortis*, transfers made on the deathbed, are revocable if the donor survives.

1.   Limitations on the Power to Control the Process of Property Transmission

Sergeant Robbins wanted to circumvent the rules of intestate succession, but failed. It is likely that his intent was to make a bequest to take effect five years after his death, but the court held that he did not properly create the legal instruments necessary to effectuate his testamentary intent. The advantages to dying with a valid will or trust in place is that it allows the property owner to choose his or her distributees, those who will succeed to his or her property at death. The testator can also place conditions on the receipt of property. But how much? The following case is an excellent example of how much control the testator can exert from the grave and how little the living can sometimes do to evade the control of "the dead hand."

Shapira v. Union National Bank

315 N.E.2d 825 (Ohio 1974)

HENDERSON, JUDGE.

This is an action for a declaratory judgment and the construction of the will of David Shapira, M.D., who died April 13, 1973, a resident of this county. By agreement of the parties, the case has been submitted upon the pleadings and the exhibit.

The portions of the will in controversy are as follows:

> 'Item VIII. All the rest, residue and remainder of my estate, real and personal, of every kind and description and wheresoever situated, which I may own or have the right to dispose of at the time of my decease, I give, devise and bequeath to my three (3) beloved children, to wit: Ruth Shapira Aharoni, of

> **Take Note**
>
> Daniel Shapira is suing the bank because the bank is the executor of his father's will. Once having accepted the appointment as executor, the bank must defend the will against attack.

> Tel Aviv, Israel, or wherever she may reside at the time of my death; to my son Daniel Jacob Shapira, and to my son Mark Benjamin Simon Shapira in equal shares, with the following qualifications: * * *

> '(b) My son Daniel Jacob Shapira should receive his share of the bequest only, if he is married at the time of my death to a Jewish girl whose both parents were Jewish. In the event that at the time of my death he is not married to a Jewish girl whose both parents were Jewish, then his share of this bequest should be kept by my executor for a period of not longer than seven (7) years and if my said son Daniel Jacob gets married within the seven year period to a Jewish girl whose both parents were Jewish, my executor is hereby instructed to turn over his share of my bequest to him. In the event, however, that my said son Daniel Jacob is unmarried within the seven (7) years after my death to a Jewish girl whose both parents were Jewish, or if he is married to a non Jewish girl, then his share of my estate, as provided in item 8 above should go to The State of Israel, absolutely.'

The provision for the testator's other son Mark, is conditioned substantially similarly. Daniel Jacob Shapira, the plaintiff, alleges that the condition upon his inheritance is unconstitutional, contrary to public policy and unenforceable because of its unreasonableness, and that he should be given his bequest free of the restriction. Daniel is 21 years of age, unmarried and a student at Youngstown State University.

What's That?

An executory devise or legacy is a future interest that becomes possessory on a contingency unlike most gifts in a will, which give the beneficiary possession of the property on the testator's death.

The provision in controversy is an executory devise or legacy, under which vesting of the estate of Daniel Jacob Shapira or the State of Israel is not intended to take place necessarily at the death of the testator, but rather conditionally, at a time not later than seven years after the testator's death. The executory aspect of the provision, though rather unusual, does not render it invalid.

CONSTITUTIONALITY

Plaintiff's argument that the condition in question violates constitutional safeguards is based upon the premise that the right to marry is protected by the Fourteenth Amendment to the Constitution of the United States. In Meyer v. Nebraska, holding unconstitutional a state statute prohibiting the teaching of languages other than English, the court stated that the Fourteenth Amendment denotes the right to marry among other basic rights. In Skinner v. Oklahoma, holding unconstitutional a state statute providing for the sterilization of certain habitual criminals, the court stated that marriage and procreation are fundamental to the very existence and survival of the race. In Loving v. Virginia, the court held unconstitutional as violative of the Equal Protection and Due Process Clauses of the Fourteenth Amendment an antimiscegenation statute under which a black person and a white person were convicted for marrying. . . . In its opinion the United States Supreme Court made the following statements:

'There can be no doubt that restricting the freedom to marry solely because of racial classifications violates the central meaning of the Equal Protection Clause.

' * * * The freedom to marry has long been recognized as one of the vital personal rights essential to the orderly pursuit of happiness by free men.

'Marriage is one of the 'basic civil rights of man,' fundamental to our very existence and survival. * * * The Fourteenth Amendment requires that the freedom of choice to marry not be restricted by invidious racial discriminations. Under our Constitution, the freedom to marry, or not marry, a person of another race resides with the individual and cannot be infringed by the State.'

From the foregoing, it appears clear, as plaintiff contends, that the right to marry is constitutionally protected from restrictive state legislative action. Plaintiff submits, then, that under the doctrine of Shelley v. Kraemer (1948), 334 U.S. 1, 68 S.Ct. 836, 92 L.Ed. 1161, the constitutional protection of the Fourteenth Amendment is extended from direct state legislative action to the enforcement by state judicial proceedings of private provisions restricting the right to marry. Plaintiff contends that a judgment of this court upholding the condition restricting marriage would, under Shelley v. Kraemer, constitute state action prohibited by the Fourteenth Amendment as much as a state statute.

In Shelley v. Kraemer the United States Supreme Court held that the action of the states to which the Fourteenth Amendment has reference includes action of state courts and state judicial officials. Prior to this decision the court had invalidated city ordinances which denied blacks the right to live in white neighborhoods. In Shelley v. Kraemer owners of neighboring properties sought to enjoin blacks from occupying properties which they had bought, but which were subjected to privately executed restrictions against use or occupation by any persons except those of the Caucasian race. Chief Justice Vinson noted, in the course of his opinion at page 13, 68 S.Ct. at page 842: 'These are cases in which the purposes of the agreements were secured only by judicial enforcement by state courts of the restrictive terms of the agreements.'

In the case at bar, this court is not being asked to enforce any restriction upon Daniel Jacob Shapira's constitutional right to marry. Rather, this court is being asked to enforce the testator's restriction upon his son's inheritance. If the facts and circumstances of this case were such that the aid of this court were sought to enjoin Daniel's marrying a non-Jewish girl, then the doctrine of Shelley v. Kraemer would be applicable, but not, it is believed, upon the facts as they are.

Counsel for plaintiff asserts, however, that his position with respect to the applicability of Shelley v. Kraemer to this case is fortified by two later decisions of the United States Supreme Court: Evans v. Newton (1966), 382 U.S. 296, and Pennsylvania v. Board of Directors of City Trusts of the City of Philadelphia (1957), 353 U.S. 230.

Evans v. Newton involved land willed in trust to the mayor and city council of Macon, Georgia, as a park for white people only, and to be controlled by a white board of managers. To avoid the city's having to enforce racial segregation in the park, the city officials resigned as trustees and private individuals were installed. The court held that such successor trustees, even though private individuals, became agencies or instrumentalities of the state and subject to the Fourteenth Amendment by reason of their exercising powers or carrying on functions governmental in nature. The following comment of Justice Douglas seems revealing: 'If a testator wanted to leave a school or center for the use of one race only and in no way implicated the State in the supervision, control, or management of that facility, we assume arguendo that no constitutional difficulty would be encountered.' 382 U.S. 300, 86 S.Ct. 489.

Food for Thought

The court certainly has neatly distinguished the cases. However, has the court correctly applied the spirit of *Shelley*?

The case of Pennsylvania v. Board, as the full title, above, suggests, is a case in which money was left by will to the city of Philadelphia in trust for a college to admit poor white male orphans. The court held that the board which operated the college was an agency of the state of Pennsylvania, and that, therefore, its refusal to admit the plaintiffs because they were negroes was discrimination by the state forbidden by the Fourteenth Amendment.

So, in neither Evans v. Newton nor Pennsylvania v. Board was the doctrine of the earlier Shelley v. Kraemer applied or extended. Both of them involved restrictive actions by state governing agencies, in one case with respect to a park, in the other case with respect to a college. Although both the park and the college were founded upon testamentary gifts, the state action struck down by the court was not the judicial completion of the gifts, but rather the subsequent enforcement of the racial restrictions by the public management.

Basically, the right to receive property by will is a creature of the law, and is not a natural right or one guaranteed or protected by either the Ohio or the United States constitution. It is a fundamental rule of law in Ohio that a testator may legally entirely disinherit his children. This would seem to demonstrate that, from a constitutional standpoint, a testator may restrict a child's inheritance. The court concludes, therefore, that the upholding and enforcement of the provisions of Dr. Shapira's will conditioning the bequests to his sons upon their marrying Jewish girls does not offend the Constitution of Ohio or of the United States.

PUBLIC POLICY

The condition that Daniel's share should be 'turned over to him if he should marry a Jewish girl whose both parents were Jewish' constitutes a partial restraint upon marriage. If the condition were that the beneficiary not marry anyone, the restraint would be general or total, and, at least in the case of a first marriage, would be held to be contrary to public policy and void. A partial restraint of marriage which imposes only reasonable restrictions is valid, and not contrary to public policy. The great weight of authority in the United States is that gifts conditioned upon the beneficiary's marrying within a particular religious class or faith are reasonable. * * *

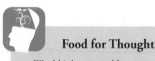

Food for Thought

Would it be reasonable to permit a restriction requiring that Daniel marry a person of the opposite sex? Or of the same sex? Does "reasonable" have a role here?

Plaintiff contends, however, that in Ohio a condition such as the one in this case is void as against the public policy of this state. In Ohio, as elsewhere, a testator may not attach a condition to a gift which is in violation of public policy. There can be no question about the soundness of plaintiff's position that the public policy of Ohio favors freedom of religion and that it is guaranteed by Section 7, Article I of the Ohio Constitution, providing that 'all men have a natural and indefeasible right to worship Almighty God according to the dictates of their own conscience.' Plaintiff's position that the free choice of religious practice cannot be circumscribed or controlled by contract is substantiated by Hackett v. Hackett (C.A. Lucas 1958), 78 Ohio Law Abs. 485, 150 N.E.2d 431. This case held that a covenant in a separation agreement, incorporated in a divorce decree, that the mother would rear a daughter in the Roman Catholic faith was unenforceable. However, the controversial condition in the case at bar is a partial restraint upon marriage and not a covenant to restrain the freedom of religious practice; and, of course, this court is not being asked to hold the plaintiff in contempt for failing to marry a Jewish girl of Jewish parentage.

Counsel contends that if 'Dr. David Shapira, during his life, had tried to impose upon his son those restrictions set out in his Will he would have violated the public policy of Ohio as shown in Hackett v. Hackett. The public policy is equally violated by the restrictions Dr. Shapira has placed on his son by his Will.' This would be true, by analogy, if Dr. Shapira, in his lifetime, had tried to force his son to marry a Jewish girl as the condition of a completed gift. But it is not true that if Dr. Shapira had agreed to make his son an inter-vivos gift if he married a Jewish girl within seven years, that his son could have forced him to make the gift free of the condition.

It is noted, furthermore, in this connection, that the courts of Pennsylvania distinguish between testamentary gifts conditioned upon the religious faith of the beneficiary and those conditioned upon marriage to persons of a particular religious faith. In In re Clayton's Estate, supra (13 Pa.D. & C. 413), the court upheld a gift of a life estate conditioned upon the beneficiary's not marrying a woman of the Catholic faith. In its opinion the court distinguishes the earlier case of Drace v. Klinedinst (1922), 275 Pa. 266, 118 A. 907, in which a life estate willed to grandchildren, provided they remained faithful to a particular religion, was held to violate the public policy of Pennsylvania. In Clayton's Estate, the court said that the condition concerning marriage did not affect the faith of the beneficiary, and that the condition, operating only on the choice of a wife, was too remote to be regarded as coercive of religious faith.

But counsel relies upon an Ohio case much more nearly in point, that of Moses v. Zook (C.A. Wayne 1934), 18 Ohio Law Abs. 373. This case involves a will in which the testatrix gave the income of her residual estate in trust to her niece and nephews for two years and then the remainder to them. Item twelve provides as follows: 'If any of my nieces or nephews should marry outside of the Protestant Faith, then they shall not receive any part of my estate devised or bequeathed to them.' The will contained no gift over upon violation of the marriage condition. The holding of the trial court was that item twelve was null and void as being against public policy and the seven other items of the will should be administered as specified in detail by the court. There is nothing in the reported opinion to show to what extent, if at all, the question of public policy was in issue or contested in the trial court; only one of the several other unrelated holdings of the trial court (not including the public policy holding) was assigned as error; and although the Court of Appeals adopted the unexcepted-to holdings of the trial court, there is no citation of authorities or discussion concerning the public policy question itself. The case was apparently not appealed to the Supreme Court, and no other cases in Ohio have been cited or found. Moses v. Zook differs in its facts in not containing a gift over upon breach of the condition, and appears not to have been a sufficiently litigated or reasoned establishment of the public policy of Ohio which this court should be obliged to follow.

The only cases cited by plaintiff's counsel in accord with the holding in Moses v. Zook are some English cases and one American decision. In England the courts have held that partial restrictions upon marriage to persons not of the Jewish faith, or of Jewish parentage, were not contrary to public policy or invalid. Other cases in England, however, have invalidated forfeitures of similarly conditioned provisions for children upon the basis of uncertainty or indefiniteness. Since the foregoing decisions, a later English case has upheld a condition precedent that a granddaughter-beneficiary marry a person of Jewish faith and the child of

Jewish parents. The court distinguished the cases cited above as not applicable to a condition precedent under which the legatee must qualify for the gift by marrying as specified, and there was found to be no difficulty with indefiniteness where the legatee married unquestionably outside the Jewish faith.

The American case cited by plaintiff is that of Maddox v. Maddox (1854), 52 Va. (11 Grattain's) 804. The testator in this case willed a remainder to his niece if she remain a member of the Society of Friends. When the niece arrived at a marriageable age there were but five or six unmarried men of the society in the neighborhood in which she lived. She married a non-member and thus lost her own membership. The court held the condition to be an unreasonable restraint upon marriage and void, and that there being no gift over upon breach of the condition, the condition was in terrorem, and did not avoid the bequest. It can be seen that while the court considered the testamentary condition to be a restraint upon marriage, it was primarily one in restraint of religious faith. The court said that with the small number of eligible bachelors in the area the condition would have operated as a virtual prohibition of the niece's marrying, and that she could not be expected to 'go abroad' in search of a helpmate or to be subjected to the chance of being sought after by a stranger. The court distinguished the facts of its case from those in England upholding conditions upon marriage by observing that England was 'already overstocked with inhabitants' while this country had 'an unbounded extent of territory, a large portion of which is yet unsettled, and in which increase of population is one of the main elements of national prosperity.' The other ground upon which the Virginia court rested its decision, that the condition was in terrorem because of the absence of a gift over, is clearly not applicable to the case at bar, even if it were in accord with Ohio law, because of the gift over to the State of Israel contained in the Shapira will.

In arguing for the applicability of the Maddox v. Maddox test of reasonableness to the case at bar, counsel for the plaintiff asserts that the number of eligible Jewish females in this county would be an extremely small minority of the total population especially as compared with the comparatively much greater number in New York, whence have come many of the cases comprising the weight of authority upholding the validity of such clauses. There are no census figures in evidence. While this court could probably take judicial notice of the fact that the Jewish community is a minor, though important segment of our total local population, nevertheless the court is by no means justified in judicial knowledge that there is an insufficient number of eligible young ladies of Jewish parentage in this area from which Daniel would have a reasonable latitude of choice. And of course, Daniel is not at all confined in his choice to residents of this county, which is a very different circumstance in this day of travel by plane and freeway and communication by telephone, from the horse and buggy days of the 1854 Maddox v. Maddox decision. Consequently, the decision does not appear to be an appropriate yardstick of reasonableness under modern living conditions.

It's Latin to Me

In terrorem: In order to frighten: to serve as a warning; describes a provision of a will aimed at coercing the behavior of a beneficiary by threatening to take away the beneficiary's gift if the beneficiary acts or doesn't act in a specified way.

Plaintiff's counsel contends that the Shapira will falls within the principle of Fineman v. Central National Bank (1961), 87 Ohio Law Abs. 236, 175 N.E.2d 837, 18 O.O.2d 33, holding that the public policy of Ohio does not countenance a bequest or device conditioned on the beneficiary's obtaining a separation or divorce from his wife. Counsel argues that the Shapira condition would encourage the beneficiary to marry a qualified girl just to receive the bequest, and then to divorce her afterward. This possibility seems too remote to be a pertinent application of the policy against bequests conditioned upon divorce. Most other authorities agree with Fineman v. Bank that as a general proposition, a testamentary gift effective only on condition that the recipient divorce or separate from his or her spouse is against public policy and invalid. But no authorities have been found extending the principle to support plaintiff's position. Indeed, in measuring the reasonableness of the condition in question, both the father and the court should be able to assume that the son's motive would be proper. And surely the son should not gain the advantage of the avoidance of the condition by the possibility of his own impropriety.

Finally, counsel urges that the Shapira condition tends to pressure Daniel, by the reward of money, to marry within seven years without opportunity for mature reflection, and jeopardizes his college education. It seems to the court, on the contrary, that the seven year time limit would be a most reasonable grace period, and one which would give the son ample opportunity for exhaustive reflection and fulfillment of the condition without constraint or oppression. Daniel is no more being 'blackmailed into a marriage by immediate financial gain,' as suggested by counsel, than would be the beneficiary of a living gift or conveyance upon consideration of a future marriage-an arrangement which has long been sanctioned by the courts of this state. Thompson.

In the opinion of this court, the provision made by the testator for the benefit of the State of Israel upon breach or failure of the condition is most significant for two reasons. First, it distinguishes this case from the bare forfeitures in Moses v. Zook, and in Maddox v. Maddox (including the technical in terrorem objection), and, in a way, from the vagueness and indefiniteness doctrine of some of the English cases. Second, and of greater importance, it demonstrates the depth of the testator's conviction. His purpose was not merely a negative one designed to punish his son for not carrying out his wishes. His unmistakable testamentary plan was that his possessions be used to encourage the preservation of the Jewish faith and blood, hopefully through his sons, but, if not, then through the State of Israel. Whether this judgment was wise is not for this court to determine. But it is the duty of this court to honor the testator's intention within the limitations of law and of public policy. The prerogative granted to a testator by the laws of this state to dispose of his estate according to his conscience is entitled to as much judicial protection and enforcement as the prerogative of a beneficiary to receive an inheritance.

It is the conclusion of this court that public policy should not, and does not preclude the fulfillment of Dr. Shapira's purpose, and that in accordance with the weight of authority in this country, the conditions contained in his will are reasonable restrictions upon marriage, and valid.

Points for Discussion

1. Some practical matters

What happens to Daniel's share of his father's residuary estate while we're waiting seven years to see if Daniel marries the right woman? If you think that the executor is responsible for the one-third of the residuary estate conditionally given to Daniel you are correct. The executor will have to keep that amount invested (in what, do you imagine?) so it produces income and be ready to hand the property over to Daniel or to the State of Israel depending on whether or not Daniel marries a woman who meets the criterion set forth in his father's will. That means, of course, that the executor, Union National Bank, might have to keep at it for the full seven years to determine whether Daniel has complied with his father's wishes. Why would the bank take on such an onerous obligation? Granted it is receiving commissions, but doesn't this particular will ask a good deal of the executor? Also, how does the State of Israel know about the potential gift? Every probate system requires some sort of notice to those named in the will.

2. Making sure Dr. Shapira's will withstands challenge

Dr. Shapira's lawyer did an excellent job of drafting a will that would withstand attack. Think about the following: A Roman Catholic testator conditions his daughter's bequest on her marrying a man "who is a practicing Roman Catholic." Or a Presbyterian testator conditions his son's bequest on his marrying a woman "who is a faithful Presbyterian." Are those conditions enforceable?

Why is it important that the property that would otherwise go to Daniel Shapira is given to the State of Israel if Daniel does not fulfill the condition? Why is the court so sure that seven years is a reasonable time for Daniel to marry the right person? Why *seven* years? Would five or six or eight have been as acceptable?

3. Your responsibility as a lawyer

Assume that you have written several wills over the years for Dr. Shapira and he comes to you asking for a new will that disinherits Daniel unless he marries a Jewish woman. Would you write the will? Why does Dr. Shapira want to condition Daniel's bequest on his marrying a Jewish woman both of whose parents are Jewish?

4. Further developments

Religious restrictions on marriage became a current question in 2008 when the intermediate Illinois appellate court held over a strong dissent that a religious restriction on marriage invalid "because it seriously interferes with and limits the rights of individuals to marry a person of their own choosing." *In re Estate of Feinberg*, 383 Ill.App.3d 992, 891 N.E.2d 549 (Ill.App. 1 Dist. 2008). The court relied on Illinois precedents which conditioned gifts on the ending of the beneficiary's marriage by divorce or death and on Restatement (Third) of Trusts § 29, *cmt. j.* A concurring opinion noted that the dissent cites only two cases less than fifty years old (one of them is *Shapira*) and the cases that are cited rely on the First and Second

Restatements of Trusts. The concurrence concludes that religiously oriented restraints on marriage were once considered reasonable but Restatement (Third) of Trusts shows that it is no longer appropriate to enforce them. The case was appealed to the Illinois Supreme Court, which reversed in an opinion which is difficult to summarize. Although it makes some broad statements about the acceptability of religious conditions on marriage, and expressly rejects the position of Restatement (Third) of Trusts, the holding is quite narrow. The opinion seems to have been carefully crafted to gain unanimous support from the state's highest court. *In re Estate of Feinberg*, 235 Ill.2d 256, 919 N.E.2d 888 (2009).

Test Your Knowledge

To assess your understanding of the material in this chapter, click here to take a quiz.

CHAPTER 2

Planning an Estate:
Ward's Estate Plan

Introductory casebooks on wills and trusts serve many purposes. While the focus of most of the chapters is upon the substantive law of wills and trusts, the seemingly endless litany of statutes, cases, Restatement provisions and the like that follows, what lawyers in this area actually do is plan estates: they draft wills and trusts. Sadly, you cannot write a will until you have a client, and you cannot have a client until you pass the bar. So at this point in your legal career, all we can do is provide you with an hypothetical client with an estate to plan. Happily, being hypothetical, any errors that you may initially make will not be actionable.

So, please, Meet the Cleavers.

Who amongst us needs introduction to the Cleavers: Ward, June, Wally (and of course) the Beaver. This typical 1950s American family lives comfortably in Hollywood, lodged in a film vault. In that era, they were presented to the country as the 'typical' middle-class nuclear family. Ward and June were married once, and only to each other. They had children, but again only with each other. It was, after all, the 1950s, when a narrative of American life was being recast after the war. Our heroes are Ward (age 50) and June (age 45). Our Ward has a respectable while collar job, though it is not clear his area of expertise. Our June is a respectable home-maker. She saw Ward off in the morning after having served him (and the boys) breakfast. On his return, after a hard day's work, June, impeccably dressed and coiffed, met him at the door, a delicious dinner already on its way to the table. By that time, she had already righted whatever mischief that the boys had generated.

While the Cleaver nuclear family may still exist somewhere in modern America, economic realities have altered so we have taken some modest license in recasting the Cleavers as principals in our 'estate planning' problem: June is now employed as a part-time realtor. Ward's job has been modernized; and he is a software designer earning $120,000 per year. June receives a salary of $1000 a month plus commissions. Their combined income after taxes and benefit contributions (alas, June receives no benefits—but Ward's job includes the full panoply of subsidized employee benefits including pension matching, health insurance, long-term disability, and life insurance) is $7,500 per month. The Cleavers have agreed that all of June's commissions (sadly modest given the current real estate market) should be directed into a savings account to pay the inevitable tuition fees. Given what we know about the boys, Wally (age 16) and the Beaver (age 13), they may not be scholarship candidates.

A little more about the family circumstances of the Cleavers. Both the Cleavers have parents living, Ward a mom, and June a dad. Each is in good health, and economically self-sufficient. Someday Ward and June might each receive a modest inheritance from either or both. At this point, they are relieved that each is not a burden on Ward and June's modest resources. Because both Ward and June each have a sibling, any inheritance would be divided. Ward's brother Ken has two daughters whom Ward adores. Because he has been more economically successful than his brother, he feels the need from time to time to be generous to his nieces Beth and Andrea. June has a sister Amy, who is married with two children. Both Amy and her husband, Brian are successful doctors. June has two nieces.

Ward's college roommate is a lawyer: real estate, not wills and trusts. But on his last swing through the film vault he drafted the following document for Ward. June's is the mirror image, but it excludes Items four and five. Let's consider its terms.

WILL OF WARD CLEAVER

I, Ward Cleaver, declare this to be my Last Will, and Testament, and by this document do revoke any and all other testamentary instruments that I have made at any time during my life.

Item One—I direct that my just debts be paid by my executor. I also direct that the costs of my funeral and estate administration costs be paid from my estate as soon as is practical.

Item Two—I appoint my wife June to be executrix of my estate, and I direct that she serve without bond. If she predeceases me or otherwise fails to qualify, I nominate our dear family friend Fred Rutherford as executor. I appoint my trusted attorney Professor LJ Grouchfield to serve as overseer of this will. If in Prof. Grouchfield's judgment, it is necessary to remove an executor for any reason, I empower him to so. He shall then serve as executor of this my last will. All executors nominated herein shall serve without bond.

Item Three—I empower my executor, or any administrator appointed by the court, to sell or otherwise transfer all personal property and convey all real estate without court order.

Item Four—I give, devise, and bequeath the sum of $10,000 to each of my nieces and nephews living at my death. If any niece and nephew living at my death is under the age of 18 at the time of my death, I direct that my executor open a Uniform Gifts to Minors account in the First National Bank of Cleaver City in the name of that minor niece and nephew with the niece and nephew's father or mother to serve as custodian. It is my desire that they use this bequest to travel to Europe on their 'Junior Year Abroad.'

Item Five—I give, devise, and bequeath the my gold Omega watch that I received on the anniversary of twenty-fifth year of employment at Software Designers Inc. to my protégé David Griff.

Item Six—All the rest residue and remainder of my estate, I give, devise, and bequeath to my beloved wife June Cleaver. If she does not survive me, I give, devise, and bequeath all the rest residue and remainder of my estate to my children.

Item Seven—In the event my wife June does not survive me, I nominate as legal guardians of my children my brother Kenneth Cleaver and his wife Dianne Cleaver.

In witness thereof, I sign this last will being of sound and disposing mind.

Ward Cleaver

Joe Witness

Jane Witness

Let us consider each will provision sequentially.

Item One—Like many of us, Ward wants to exit this life owing nothing to anybody. Is that the reason why his will contains a 'just debts' clause? Prof. Grouchfield, on the other hand, is less noble: what is the point of dying if you can't stiff your creditors? Will all his debts be eradicated merely by dying and executing a will that does not contain a clause directing his executor pay his debts? By the way, what is the meaning of the term 'just debt?' Are there any 'unjust debts?' Does it differ from a 'debt?' Consider the following debts, and whether they would be paid absent a 'just debts' clause.

1. The mortgage on his residence held in joint tenancy with June. Both are listed as borrowers on the mortgage documents.

2. Ward's doctor submitted a bill dated July 4, 1976 for $500 for an x-ray. The jurisdiction has a three-year statute of limitations for contract claims.

3. Ward has been playing poker with the 'boys' for months. He is a big loser and owes Fred Rutherford $1000 on last week's final hand.

4. State inheritance taxes of $8,000 are levied.

Item Two—Husbands have been naming their wives executrices and the reverse for centuries. Can you think of any reason why one would not want to select a spouse? Maybe your answer will be more informed if we consider the role of that office. What exactly does the executor execute? Under what circumstances might June not be able to serve as executrix? Does it make sense to nominate his friend as alternate executor? Why not his brother, Kenneth, or his lawyer, Grouchfield? Suppose Ward was 75 and Wally and the Beaver were adults? Would your advice to Ward differ? Overseer is an odd term to find in a will. In the English poor law, an overseer was one who managed parish poor relief. Its negative connotation was furthered by its use as term for men who managed plantations. What does an overseer of a will oversee? What is the meaning of the term phrase 'shall serve without bond' in the last sentence?

Item Three—Every item or word or phrase in a will should be there for a purpose. Why might an executrix require the powers elaborated in this clause? Absent the provision, would the executrix have to petition the court to transfer land, or withdraw cash from an account in Ward's name, or sell some of his shares in Apple?

Item Four—Ward has only one brother who has been less economically successful than he is. He has remembered his nieces generously on their birthdays. Does it make sense to make bequests to all his nieces and nephews alive at his death, or just to Beth and Andrea? Is it fair to exclude nieces and nephews born after his death? Does he need to be 'fair?' Might there be a perpetuities issue? Should he stipulate where the bequest should be deposited? Must they use the cash to squander their junior year at a European university? What if they decide the future is in Asia. What if a child decides to become a health care professional and does not enter a university?

Item Five—How does this bequest differ from the cash bequest to his nieces and nephews? What happens if the watch is stolen, or otherwise cannot be located at the death of Ward?

Item Six—Ward leaves all his property to June if she survives him, and if she does not, the property passes to his children. Sounds good? Has Ward thought through the pattern of distribution or is he just 'shooting from the hip'? Is there any reason why June should not receive all his property outright? What if Wally predeceases Ward or they die together, and Wally is married with a young son, Ward, Jr.?

Item Seven—June dies first or the pair die in a car accident. Suppose Uncle Ken and Aunt Dianne live in Florida. Will a Cleaver City court ship the children 'down south?' Does it matter that the executor is located in Cleaver City and the kids in Florida? If the boys are still boys (minors), in what legal form will the money be held?

Asset Profile of the Cleavers

Tangible Personal Property

In common with most married couples, the Cleavers have a house festooned with valuable items: paintings, furniture, souvenirs, and so on. Others, however, might refer to these precious items as 'junk.'

- **Fair market value: $10,000 at a stretch**

Ward has been generous in decking June out with gold, diamonds and pearls.

- **Fair market value: $25,000**

Ward owns a 1996 blue Jeep Cherokee.

- **Fair market value: $1,500**

June owns a 2009 green Jeep Grand Cherokee

- **Fair market value: $15,000 market value**

Ward has been collecting 19th century books on British Birds. He has approximately 4 sets of first editions.

- **Fair market value: $10,000**

Real Estate

For the past twenty years, Ward and June have owned in joint tenancy with right of survivorship a split-level house on a quarter-acre in a suburb of a major American city.

- **Fair market value: $350,000**

A number of years ago, June inherited a small house in warmer climes from her Uncle Martin. Title is held in her own name.

- **Fair market value: $150,000**

Bank Accounts

"Checking:" Each month both Ward and June's salaries are directly deposited in a checking account in the First National Bank of Cleaver City. So each month approximately $7,500 enters. But it exits by month's end. Both Ward and June are signatories and therefore can draw checks on the account. June, a real 'techie,' pays many bills online.

- **Fair market value: $2,000**

"Savings:" Given the poor yields generated by Certificates of Deposit, Ward and June have decided to keep surplus cash (the occasional month when there is a surplus in the checking account) in an Internet Savings Account yielding 1.40%. Given that rate of return they are probably fortunate in having somewhere in the neighborhood of $5,000 in the account held by Ward and June in joint tenancy with right of survivorship.

- **Fair market value: $5,000**

Payment on Death Account: A few years ago Ward received a bonus from his employer of $10,000 and purchased two ($5,000 each) ten year Certificates of Deposit. One is in the name of 'Ward Cleaver payable on death to Andrea Cleaver,' and the other 'Ward Cleaver payable on death to Beth Cleaver'

- **Fair market value: $14,000**

Brokerage Accounts

Ward and June have modest investments in the market which they hold in an Infidelity Ultra Service Account. The account is held in joint tenancy with right of survivorship. In it they own four individual stocks, two stock mutual funds and three TIPS US Treasury Bonds:

Individual Stocks

50 Shares of Apple	$350 per share	$17,500
100 Shares of GE	$20	2,000
100 Shares Pfizer	$20	2,000
100 Shares of IBM	$160	16,000
		$37,500

Stock Mutual Funds

1000 shares Trojan Horse Index Fund	$82.50 per share	82,500
1000 shares Trojan Horse Consumer Staples	$42.50	42,500
		$125,000

TIPS U.S. Treasury Bonds

$25,000	2%	Maturity 1/1/2015	29,000
$25,000	1.75%	1/1/2020	31,000
$25,000	1.85%	1/1/2025	28,000
			$88,000

TOTALS

	$250,500

Retirement Benefits

Ward has about $900,000 in a 401k. At current rates, he could purchase a joint and survivor annuity for that would pay the Cleaver couple $40,000 per year. Should Ward die before June, he has directed that his pension rights pass to June.

Each has about $100,000 in Individual retirement Accounts. Each has named Wally and the Beaver as the beneficiaries.

Life Insurance

Ward has a Life Insurance policy provided to him by his employer at two times his salary—now $240,000. He has named June his beneficiary if she survives him, to Wally and the Beaver share and share alike, if she does not.

Test Your Knowledge

To assess your understanding of the material in this chapter, click here to take a quiz.

PART II

Wills

CHAPTER 3

Wills: Doctrines Dealing with the Testator

A page of history ...

In the past wills were more likely to be written *in extremis*, on the death bed, than is the case today.[1] Moreover, they were often dictated by the dying person to anyone who was literate, a cleric, a merchant, or a friend, rather than a 'lawyer.' Informality was permitted. An oral recitation could stand as a will, and wills in the hand of the testator were valid without any attestation. With the adoption of the Statute of Frauds (1677), oral wills remained valid for estates under 20 pounds but could no longer be used to transmit land. Probate was bifurcated: a writing witnessed by 3 or 4 credible witnesses was required to transmit land, but oral and holographic wills still were available to pass personal property.

Even before the Statute of Frauds was adopted, there was also a mental requirement for wills to be valid. In order to be valid, wills required the will-maker to be of 'sound mind,' and frequently the wills themselves often so proclaim. But what did that mean? The law often defined it the negative. Henry Swinburne, whose wrote a treatise on wills in the reign of Elizabeth I defined sound mind, by enumerating those individuals who lacked it: 'mad folks and lunatic persons;' 'Idiots;' 'older men;' 'Of him that is drunke;' and 'Of him that is at the very point of Death.'[2]

Some attempts were thereafter made to refine the law of mental capacity, by pondering the human being's ability to reason. Likewise, the seventeenth century saw a growth of interest in England in 'diseases of the mind.' Because property rights in England were vested in individuals and rights to succeed to a person' property by family members was

---

1   For a history of will-making, and in particular the question of testamentary capacity, see Lloyd Bonfield, Devising, Dying, and Dispute: Probate Litigation in Early Modern England (2012), pp. 81–108.

2   Henry Swinburne, A Brief Treatise of Testaments and Last Wills (Garland Reprint of 1590 edition, 1978), pp. 36–42, 61–64.

subrogated to the person right to dispose thereof. Only in extreme cases should capacity to direct the devolution of property by removed. The ability to govern the transmission of property, according to John Locke should only be withdrawn from those 'through defects that might happen out of the ordinary course of nature . . . any one comes not to such a degree of reason . . . he is never capable of being a free man, he is never let loose to the disposure of his own will.'[3]

Writing at the same time, John Ayliffe, another commentator on the law of property noted that will-making "ought to be executed in *humano modo*: but a human Act cannot be executed by him that hath not sufficient Judgement and Will to make a Testament."[4] Reason and volition, judgment and will: the will-maker must have the mental presence both to appreciate that the act undertaken directed the transmission of property upon death and to be able to construct a logical pattern of disposition. He provided an example of how sound mind might be measured. It was not 'sufficient' that the testator 'answer to usual and ordinary questions;' rather he or she 'ought to have disposing Memory . . . to make a Disposition of his Estate with Reason and Understanding, and such a Memory is called a sound and perfect Mind or Memory.'[5] Other commentators set the bar less high; as William Sheppard put it, only 'mean' understanding was sufficient, 'of the middle sort between a wise man and a fool.'[6] A later discourse on sound mind agreed, noting that 'the law will not scrutinize into the depth of a man's capacity, particularly after his death,' and conceded that an individual need only 'conduct himself in the common course of life' to execute a valid testamentary act. The rather low threshold was justified, because to hold otherwise 'might be opening a wide door to support pretensions of fraud or imposition on the testator.'[7]

A. Capacity

This historical exegesis set forth, perhaps at unnecessary length, retain vitality in the modern conceptualization of mental capacity. A similar malleable standard, elegantly expressed but difficult to apply in the case of a particular will-maker, continues to be used.

The objective aspect of the test for capacity is the testator's age. The testator must be an adult, that is, eighteen years of age and of sound mind (§ UPC 2–501 and NY EPTL § 3–1.1).

Ponder the following provision of the Restatement which is the a modern formulation of the requisite mental faculties that constitutes sound mind:

---

3   Ian Shapiro, ed. The Two Treatises on Government and a Letter on Toleration, Book II, sec 59 (2003).

4   John Ayliffe, *Paregon Juris Anglicani* or a Commentary By Way of Supplement to the Canon and Constitutions of the Church of England (1724), pp. 530–31.

5   Ibid., p. 533.

6   William Sheppard, Touchstone of Common Assurances, p. 389.

7   A Familiar Plan and Easy Explanation of the Law of Wills and Codicils (London, 1785), p. 16.

Restatement Third, Property (Wills and Donative Transfers) § 8.1(b)

If the donative transfer is in the form of a will . . . the testator . . . must be capable of knowing and understanding in a general way the nature and extent of his or her property, the natural objects of his or her bounty, and the disposition that he or she is making of that property, and must also be capable of relating these elements to one another and forming an orderly desire regarding the disposition of the property.

It should be noted that these requirements, sometimes referred to as capacities, are not demanding. It is usually said that the mental capacity needed to make a valid will is less than that required to make a gift during life. It is also less than the capacity needed to enter a binding contract, buy or sell land, or fend off an involuntary guardianship. Why? Generally the only important legal act that requires less mental capacity is marrying. Marriage is a fundamental right and cannot be subject to burdensome requirements, although marriages are occasionally voided for lack of capacity. The application of these tests or requirements to any particular case, however, is often far from clear.

> **Make the Connection**
>
> Note the procedural "flow" in will contests. It obtains in most of the cases that follow.

The diagnosis and understanding of Alzheimer's disease has had an effect upon mental capacity cases. Consider the following case.

Wilson v. Lane

614 S.E.2d 88 (Ga. 2005)

FLETCHER, CHIEF JUSTICE.

After Executrix Katherine Lane offered Jewel Jones Greer's 1997 last will and testament for probate, Floyd Wilson filed a caveat, challenging Greer's testamentary capacity. A Jasper County Superior Court jury found that Greer lacked testamentary capacity at the time she executed her will, but the trial court granted Lane's motion for judgment notwithstanding the verdict. Wilson appeals. Because we agree that there was no evidence to show that Greer lacked testamentary capacity, we affirm.

A person is mentally capable to make a will if she "has sufficient intellect to enable [her] to have a decided and rational desire as to the disposition of [her] property . . ." In this case, the propounders introduced evidence that the will in question distributed Greer's property equally to seventeen beneficiaries, sixteen of whom are blood-relatives to Greer. The only non-relative beneficiary is Katherine Lane, who spent much of her time caring for Greer before her death in 2000. The drafting attorney testified that in his opinion, at the time the 1997 will was signed, Greer was mentally competent, and that she emphatically selected every beneficiary named in the will. Numerous other friends and acquaintances also testified that Greer had a clear mind at the time the will was signed.

Thus, the propounders established a presumption that Greer possessed testamentary capacity. The caveators, however, never presented any evidence whatsoever showing that Greer was incapable of forming a decided and rational desire as to the disposition of her property, even when the evidence is examined in the light most favorable to their case.

Food for Thought

Does the presumption and the requirement that caveators must refuse it make sense to you? What is their strategy in overcoming the presumption. Read on!

The caveators challenged Greer's capacity by showing that she was eccentric, aged, and peculiar in the last years of her life. They presented testimony that she had an irrational fear of flooding in her house, that she had trouble dressing and bathing herself, and that she unnecessarily called the fire department to report a non-existent fire. But "[t]he law does not withhold from the aged, the feeble, the weak-minded, the capricious, the notionate, the right to make a will, provided such person has a decided and rational desire as to the disposition of his property." Although perhaps persuasive to a jury, "eccentric habits and absurd beliefs do not establish testamentary incapacity."

All that is required to sustain the will is proof that Greer was capable of forming a certain rational desire with respect to the disposition of her assets.

In addition to Greer's eccentric habits, the caveators also introduced evidence of a guardianship petition filed for Greer a few months after the will was executed, the testimony of an expert witness, and a letter written by Greer's physician. None of that evidence, however, was sufficient to deprive Greer of her right to make a valid will, as none of it showed that she was incapable of forming a rational desire as to the disposition of her property.

The expert admitted that he had never examined Greer, and that his testimony was based solely on a cursory review of some of Greer's medical files. Further, he was equivocal in his testimony, stating only that "it appears that she was in some form of the early to middle stages of a dementia of the Alzheimer's type." Regardless of the stigma associated with the term "Alzheimer's," however, that testimony does not show how Greer would have been unable to form a rational desire regarding the disposition of her assets. Indeed, the expert offered no explanation of how her supposed condition would affect her competency to make a valid will.

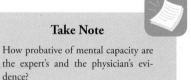

Take Note

How probative of mental capacity are the expert's and the physician's evidence?

The testimony of Greer's physician also failed to show how she lacked testamentary capacity. In 1996, the physician wrote a letter stating that Greer "was legally blind and suffered from senile dementia . . ." But the doctor testified that he was "not sure whether she had senile dementia at the time or not, even though I wrote that." He stated further that he only wrote the letter to try and assist Greer in obtaining help with her telephone bill because she had been having trouble with her eyes. In any event, a vague reference to "senile dementia" cannot eliminate testamentary capacity. If it could, it would undermine societal confidence in the validity and sanctity of our testamentary system.

Finally, as the dissent points out, Lane filed a guardianship petition in 1998, after the will was executed, proclaiming that Greer was no longer capable of managing her own affairs alone. According to the testimony, however, the petition was filed solely in order to satisfy the Department of Family and Children Services' concerns regarding Greer's ability to continue living on her own, and thus to allow Greer to remain in her home. Even if Greer's inability to live alone existed at the time the will was executed, which was not proven by any evidence, that fact bears no relation to her ability to form a rational desire regarding the disposition of her assets.

Food for Thought

The issue of mental capacity was submitted to the jury. Should this crucial question be one of fact determined by a jury? Might a member of the jury be wondering who will disinherit him or her?

In Brumbelow v. Hopkins, the caveators challenged a will by showing that the testator was of unsound mind, including a physician's testimony that a few days before the will's execution, the testator's "mind was not good." But this Court ruled that the evidence was insufficient to deprive the testator of the "valuable right" to make a will, as allowing it to do so would undermine "certainty and uniformity in the administration of justice." Accordingly, this Court ruled that the jury verdict to the contrary should have been set aside.

Take Note

Note similarities between procedural matters in will contests with those of other civil actions.

Similarly, in this case, no testimony, expert or otherwise, was offered to establish that at the time the will was executed, Greer suffered from a form of dementia sufficient in form or extent to render her unable to form a decided and rational desire regarding the disposition of her assets. Notwithstanding the dissent's attempt to piece together "the totality of the evidence," none of the evidence, either alone or in combination, provided any proof that Greer lacked testamentary capacity, as that term is defined in this State. At most, there was evidence that Greer was an eccentric woman whose mental health declined towards the end of her life. Accordingly, the evidence demanded a verdict upholding the validity of the will, and the trial court was correct to reverse the jury's contrary verdict.

Judgment affirmed.

CARLEY, JUSTICE, dissenting.

I agree that the evidence in this case would have authorized a finding that Ms. Greer possessed the requisite testamentary capacity when she executed a will in September of 1997. However, the jury found that she lacked such capacity, and we must decide whether the evidence supports that finding. I submit that, when the evidence is construed most strongly in support of the jury's verdict in favor of the Caveators, it authorized the finding that Ms. Greer did not have sufficient intellect to enable her to make a decided and rational determination concerning the disposition of her estate. Therefore, I dissent to the affirmance of the trial court's grant of the Propounder's motion for judgment notwithstanding the verdict.

When considering the grant of a motion for judgment n.o.v., "[t]he appellate standard of review . . . is whether the evidence, with all reasonable deductions therefrom, demanded a verdict contrary to that returned by the factfinder. [Cits.]" (Emphasis supplied.) Bagley v. Robertson, 265 Ga. 144, 145, 454 S.E.2d 478 (1995).

A judgment n.o.v. . . . is authorized when there can be only one reasonable conclusion as to the proper judgment; if there is any evidentiary basis for the jury's verdict, viewing the evidence most favorably to the party who secured the verdict, it is . . . error to [grant] the motion.

> ### Make the Connection
>
> What is the nub of the dissenting judge's quibble? It is substantive (that she lacked capacity) or procedural (the court is operating beyond its mandate in reviewing a jury verdict)?

[Cit.] The fact that Ms. Greer was elderly, sickly, eccentric or forgetful does not authorize a finding that she lacked the necessary testamentary capacity to make a valid will.

However, evidence that, as the result of her age or health, her mental condition had deteriorated to the extent that she was unable to form a decided and rational desire regarding the disposition of her property will authorize a finding that the instrument she executed is invalid. See Stanley v. Stanley, 277 Ga. 798, 596 S.E.2d 138 (2004) (will invalid where testator suffered from "severe dementia"); Horton v. Horton, 268 Ga. 846(1), 492 S.E.2d 872 (1997) (will invalid where testatrix suffered from "underlying dementia").

"Evidence of incapacity at a reasonable time prior to and subsequent to a will's execution creates an issue of fact as to capacity at the time of execution. [Cit.]" Sullivan v. Sullivan, 273 Ga. 130, 131(1), 539 S.E.2d 120 (2000). Because the jury found that Ms. Greer lacked testamentary capacity, "[o]nly the testimony favorable to [the] Caveator[s] need be considered, because the sole question before us is whether there is sufficient evidence to sustain the jury's verdict. [Cit.]" Horton v. Horton, supra at 847(1), 492 S.E.2d 872. Here, the Caveators presented expert medical opinion testimony showing that, at the time Ms. Greer executed the will, "she was in some form of the early to middle stages of a dementia of the Alzheimer's type." A year earlier, her own physician had expressed his belief that she exhibited "senile dementia. . . ." In January of 1998, a petition was filed which alleged that Ms. Greer was an "incapacitated" adult and sought the appointment of a guardian. This petition for guardianship was supported by the affidavit of her doctor, who stated his opinion that she had "dementia-Alzheimer's type," that she suffered from "poor memory, poor judgment, [was] difficult to reason with," and that she was "incapacitated on a permanent basis." The physician's affidavit also indicated that Ms. Greer was in present need of a guardian for both her person and her property. With regard to the guardianship of her person, the doctor noted that she "lacks sufficient understanding or capacity to make significant responsible decisions concerning . . . her person or is incapable of communicating such decisions." As for the guardianship of her property, the physician indicated that she was "incapable of managing . . . her estate, and [her] property . . . will be wasted or dissipated unless proper management is provided. . . ." The Caveator's expert testified that, if, as Ms. Greer's own doctor expressed in his affidavit, she was:

> having profound problems in one month where [she] would be considered incapacitated or needing a guardian then you would be able to go backwards for a number of months, probably up to a year or two, at least, and say that [she] was having some sort of problem with [her] thinking.

It was only four months between the time she signed the instrument tendered for admission into probate and the petition alleging that she was "permanently incapacitated" due to "dementia" based upon Alzheimer's disease. In addition to the expert medical opinion evidence showing that Ms. Greer suffered from dementia attributable to Alzheimer's disease shortly before, during and shortly after the time she executed the will, the Caveators introduced evidence which was indicative of the extent to which her mental acuity had been impaired. She had an irrational fear that her home was being flooded. She even refused to get into the bathtub, and insisted on sponge baths. Visitors to her home:

> couldn't flush the commode, couldn't really run the water in her kitchen sink. . . . [S]he had a phobia of water and when you went to [visit her] you dare not go in the commode, use the bathroom, you didn't cut on the water to get a drink of water or anything so you just had to sit.

There was additional evidence showing that in mid-December of 1997, only three months after executing the will, Ms. Greer was disoriented as to time and, believing that it was March, she was unaware that Christmas was imminent. She did not know her own social security number. She had a list of first names and telephone numbers, but could not provide last names for any of those on that list. As the majority notes, she called the fire department to report a non-existent fire.

"[A] court must allow the issue of testamentary capacity to go to the jury when there is a genuine conflict in the evidence regarding the testator's state of mind. [Cit.]" Murchison v. Smith, 270 Ga. 169, 172, 508 S.E.2d 641 (1998). Here, the testimony introduced by [C]aveators covering a reasonable period of time before and after the time of the execution of the will constitute[s] a genuine conflict in the evidence regarding the state of the [testatrix's] mind on the date [s]he signed the will from which inferences could be drawn by a jury establishing a lack of the requisite mental capacity. [Cits.] Mallis v. Miltiades, 241 Ga. 404, 405, 245 S.E.2d 655 (1978). While no single element of the Caveators' proof, standing alone, might otherwise be a sufficient predicate for invalidating Ms. Greer's will, when the totality of the evidence as to her mental condition during the relevant time period is considered, a jury certainly would be authorized to find that she suffered from serious dementia. If the evidence supports such a finding, then the jury was authorized to return a verdict holding that she lacked the requisite testamentary capacity. See Stanley v. Stanley, supra; Horton v. Horton, supra. Since the evidence supports the jury's verdict in favor of the Caveators, the trial court erred in granting the Propounder's motion for judgment n.o.v.

Points for Discussion

1. Capacity as a legal concept

Testamentary capacity is a legal concept. While it is almost certainly professional malpractice to write a will for a person who the drafter knows to be incompetent, the decision about capacity is one the drafter must make on legal, not medical, criteria. Of course, if a challenge to the will is anticipated, the careful attorney will arrange for an appropriate medical examination of the testator, or perhaps several examinations over time in order to bolster the case for finding that the testator possessed the requisite degree of capacity. There is much interest in creating better ways to measure capacity for various purposes, and one can expect measurements of testamentary capacity to become more sophisticated. ⚜

2. Why bother with a capacity test?

Consider who the requirement of mental capacity protected in the last case. Who is injured if someone who "doesn't know what he's doing" writes a will which is admitted to probate—the testator or the "natural objects" of the testator's bounty?

3. Eccentricity is not lack of capacity

Eccentric behavior is usually insufficient to set aside a will on the grounds of a lack of capacity. Mr. Wright's will is an example: amongst the endearing acts Mr. Wright undertook, he gives neighbors fish soaked in kerosene, offers to buy household effects not for sale, tells people that he sends them turkeys for gifts which they never receive, collects paper flowers from the rubbish and pastes them on rose bushes, leaves his house half-clad. Even the scrivener and the two witnesses thereto agree that he was not of sound mind. The court refused to set aside the will. "Testamentary capacity cannot be destroyed by showing a few isolated acts, foibles, idiosyncrasies, moral or mental irregularities or departures from the normal unless they directly bear upon or have influenced the testamentary act." *In re Estate of Wright,* 60 P. 2d 434 (Cal. 1936). Why is the burden of persuasion such that in lay terms a person must be 'crazy' to set aside a will on the grounds of a lack of capacity? Does this explain why the recitation of the Ms. Greer's personal cleanliness and housekeeping skills though relevant were not controlling?

4. A policy reason?

What about policy? Is the standard lenient because holding otherwise would provide too much of an incentive to persons who would receive more through intestacy than under a will to contest on capacity grounds?

5. How much capacity is enough?

Depends why you're asking. Consider the following case: Professor Grouchfield is placed under a conservatorship. Thereafter, he enters into a contract to produce a casebook, executes a deed to sell his house, and writes his will. Which legal acts will be valid? In *Lee v. Lee,* 337 So. 2d 713 (Miss. 1976), the court held that a deed and a contract that he entered into while under guardianship were void, but that his will was valid. Thus the oft quoted refrain: it takes less capacity to execute a will than it does to undertake almost any other legal act. But what if he got married and wrote a will on the same day? A court might well invalidate the will but not the marriage, which requires even less capacity.

B. Insane Delusion

Ms. Greer and Mr. Wright were elderly and were to varying degrees acting oddly. The contention by the contestants of their wills was that they lacked mental capacity because their intellect was weakened. There was some suggestion of mental illness in *Wilson*: Alzheimer's or dementia. In some cases in which a mental disease is said to affect a disposition or dispositions in the will, the contestant may allege an insane delusion. Though a legal concept rather than a medical one, the focus is often a specific medical diagnosis, the overt symptoms of a disease, diminished mental awareness or eccentricities,

Restatement (Third) of Property (Wills and Donative Transfers) § 8.1, comment s

Insane delusion. An insane delusion is a belief that is so against the evidence and reason that is must be the product of derangement. A belief resulting from a process of reasoning from existing facts is not an insane delusion, even though the reasoning is imperfect or the conclusion illogical. Mere eccentricity does not constitute an insane delusion.

A person who suffers from an insane delusion is not necessarily deprived of capacity to make a donative transfer. A particular donative transfer is invalid, however, to the extent that it was the product of an insane delusion.

How subjective is the standard? Do you think the standard was employed correctly in the following case:

In re Strittmater's Estate

53 A.2d 205 (N.J. 1947)

The opinion of VICE ORDINARY BIGELOW follows:

This is an appeal from a decree of the Essex County Orphans' Court admitting to probate the will of Louisa F. Strittmater. Appellants challenge the decree on the ground that testatrix was insane.

> ### Food for Thought
>
> Where does the burden of proof and persuasion fall? If she was able to interact with bankers and lawyers (presumably male), should the court not presume that a document that combined the legal and financial aspects of her affairs was not the product of sound mind?

The only medical witness was Dr. Sarah D. Smalley, a general practitioner who was Miss Strittmater's physician all her adult life. In her opinion, decedent suffered from paranoia of the Bleuler type of split personality. The factual evidence justifies the conclusion. But I regret not having had the benefit of an analysis of the data by a specialist in diseases of the brain.

The deceased never married. Born in 1896, she lived with her parents until their death about 1928, and seems to have had a normal childhood. She was devoted to both her parents and they to her. Her admiration and love of her parents persisted after their death to 1934, at least. Yet four years later she wrote: "My father was a corrupt, vicious, and unintelligent savage, a typical specimen of the majority of his sex. Blast his wormstinking carcass and his whole damn breed." And in 1943, she inscribed on a photograph of her mother "That Moronic she-devil that was my mother."

> ### Food for Thought
>
> Why the need for an expert in diseases of the mind?

Numerous memoranda and comments written by decedent on the margins of books constitute the chief evidence of her mental condition. Most of them are dated in 1935, when she was 40 years old. But there are enough in later years to indicate no change in her condition. The Master who heard the case in the court below, found that the proofs demonstrated 'incontrovertibly her morbid aversion to men' and 'feminism to a neurotic extreme.' This characterization seems to me not strong enough. She regarded men as a class with an insane hatred. She looked forward to the day when women would bear children without the aid of men, and all males would be put to death at birth. Decedent's inward life, disclosed by what she wrote, found an occasional outlet such as the incident of the smashing of the clock, the killing of the pet kitten, vile language,

> ### What's That?
>
> The expert conducted a psychiatric autopsy. Would you want your personality deconstructed based upon your scribbling in the margins of books?

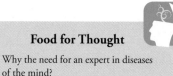
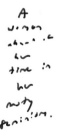

etc. On the other hand,—and I suppose this is the split personality,—Miss Strittmater, in her dealings with her lawyer, Mr. Semel, over a period of several years, and with her bank, to cite only two examples, was entirely reasonable and normal.

Decedent, in 1925, became a member of the New Jersey branch of the National Women's Party. From 1939 to 1941, and perhaps later, she worked as a volunteer one day a week in the New York office, filing papers, etc. During this period, she spoke of leaving her estate to the Party. On October 31, 1944, she executed her last will, carrying this intention into effect. A month later, December 6, she died. Her only relatives were some cousins of whom she saw very little during the last few years of her life.

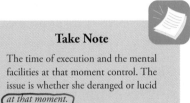

Take Note

The time of execution and the mental facilities at that moment control. The issue is whether she deranged or lucid *at that moment.*

The question is whether Miss Strittmater's will is the product of her insanity. Her disease seems to have become well developed by 1936. In August of that year she wrote, "It remains for feministic organizations like the National Women's Party, to make exposure of women's 'protectors' and 'lovers' for what their vicious and contemptible selves are." She had been a member of the Women's Party for eleven years at that time, but the evidence does not show that she had taken great interest in it. I think it was her paranoiac condition, especially her insane delusions about the male, that led her to leave her estate to the National Women's Party. The result is that the probate should be set aside.

COLIE, JUSTICE, and WELLS, JUDGE, dissenting. PER CURIAM.

The decree under review will be affirmed for the reasons stated in the opinion of VICE ORDINARY BIGELOW.

For affirmance: THE CHIEF JUSTICE, JUSTICES BODINE, DONGES, HEHER, WACHENFELD, and EASTWOOD, and JUDGES DILL, FREUND, McGEEHAN, and McLEAN.

Here's how the New York Court of Appeals applied the concept:

Matter of Honigman

168 N.E.2d 676 (N.Y. 1960)

DYE, JUDGE.

Frank Honigman died May 4, 1956, survived by his wife, Florence. By a purported last will and testament, executed April 3, 1956, just one month before his death, he gave $5,000 to each of three named grandnieces, and cut off his wife with a life use of her minimum statutory share plus $2,500, with direction to pay the principal upon her death to his surviving brothers and sisters and to the descendants of any predeceased brother or sister, per stirpes. The remaining one half of his estate was bequeathed in equal shares to his surviving brothers and sisters and to the descendants of any predeceased brother or sister, per stirpes, some of whom resided in Germany.

We'll discuss the meaning of these terms in the notes below. Suffice it to say that he left her the minimum amount that he was allowed under then-existing New York law.

When the will was offered for probate in Surrogate's Court, Queens County, the widow Florence filed objections. A trial was had on framed issues, only one of which survived for determination by the jury, namely: 'At the time of the execution of the paper offered for probate was the said Frank Honigman of sound and disposing mind and memory?' The jury answered in the negative, and the Surrogate then made a decree denying probate to the will.

Upon an appeal to the Appellate Division, Second Department, the Surrogate's decree was reversed upon the law and the facts, and probate was directed. Inconsistent findings of fact were reversed and new findings substituted. We read this record as containing more than enough competent proof to warrant submitting to the jury the issue of decedent's testamentary capacity. By the same token the proof amply supports the jury findings, implicit in the verdict, that the testator, at the time he made his will, was suffering from an unwarranted and insane delusion that his wife was unfaithful to him, which condition affected the disposition made in the will. The record is replete with testimony, supplied by a large number of disinterested persons, that for quite some time before his death the testator had publicly and repeatedly told friends and strangers alike that he believed his wife was unfaithful, often using obscene and abusive language. Such manifestations of suspicion were quite unaccountable, coming as they did after nearly 40 years of a childless yet, to all outward appearances, a congenial and harmonious marriage, which had begun in 1916. During the intervening time they had worked together in the successful management, operation and ownership of various restaurants, bars and grills and, by their joint efforts of thrift and industry, had accumulated the substantial fortune now at stake.

Food for Thought

Another example of 'jury nullification' of an estate plan.

The decedent and his wife retired from business in 1945 because of decedent's failing health. In the few years that followed he underwent a number of operations, including a prostatectomy in 1951, and an operation for cancer of the large bowel in 1954, when decedent was approximately 70 years of age.

From about this time, he began volubly to express his belief that Mrs. Honigman was unfaithful to him. This suspicion became an obsession with him, although all of the witnesses agreed that the deceased was normal and rational in other respects. Seemingly aware of his mental state, he once mentioned that he was 'sick in the head' ('Mich krank gelassen in den Kopf'), and that 'I know there is something wrong with me' in response to a light reference to his mental condition. In December, 1955 he went to Europe, a trip Mrs. Honigman learned of in a letter sent from Idlewild Airport after he had departed, and while there he visited a doctor. Upon his return he went to a psychiatrist who Mr. Honigman said 'could not help' him. Finally, he went to a chiropractor with whom he was extremely satisfied.

On March 21, 1956, shortly after his return from Europe, Mr. Honigman instructed his attorney to prepare the will in question. He never again joined Mrs. Honigman in the marital home.

To offset and contradict this showing of irrational obsession the proponents adduced proof which, it is said, furnished a reasonable basis for decedent's belief, and which, when taken with other factors, made his testamentary disposition understandable. Briefly, this proof related to four incidents. One concerned an anniversary card sent by Mr. Krauss, a mutual acquaintance and friend of many years, bearing a printed message of congratulation in sweetly sentimental phraseology. Because it was addressed to the wife alone and not received on the anniversary date, Mr. Honigman viewed it as confirmatory of his suspicion. Then there was the reference to a letter which it is claimed contained prejudicial matter but just what it was is not before us, because the letter was not produced in evidence and its contents were not established. There was also proof to show that whenever the house telephone rang Mrs. Honigman would answer it. From this Mr. Honigman drew added support for his suspicion that she was having an affair with Mr. Krauss. Mr. Honigman became so upset about it that for the last two years of

Food for Thought

Is the actual issue of marital fidelity not relevant? If Mr. Honigman's hunch was correct, was he suffering from a delusion?

their marriage he positively forbade her to answer the telephone. Another allegedly significant happening was an occasion when Mrs. Honigman asked the decedent as he was leaving the house what time she might expect him to return. This aroused his suspicion. He secreted himself at a vantage point in a nearby park and watched his home. He saw Mr. Krauss enter and, later, when he confronted his wife with knowledge of this incident, she allegedly asked him for a divorce. This incident was taken entirely from a statement made by Mr. Honigman to one of the witnesses. Mrs. Honigman flatly denied all of it. Their verdict shows that the jury evidently believed the objectant. Under the circumstances, we cannot say that this was wrong. The jury had the right to disregard the proponents' proof, or to go so far as to hold that such trivia afforded even additional grounds for decedent's irrational and unwarranted belief. The issue we must bear in mind is not whether Mrs. Honigman was unfaithful, but whether Mr. Honigman had any reasonable basis for believing that she was.

In a very early case we defined the applicable test as follows: 'If a person persistently believes supposed facts, which have no real existence except in his perverted imagination, and against all evidence and probability, and conducts himself, however logically, upon the assumption of their existence, he is, so far as they are concerned, under a morbid delusion; and delusion in that sense is insanity. Such a person is essentially mad or insane on those subjects, though on other subjects he may reason, act and speak like a sensible man.' (American Seamen's Friend Soc. v. Hopper, 33 N.Y. 619, 624–625.)

It is true that the burden of proving testamentary incapacity is a difficult one to carry (Dobie v. Armstrong, 160 N.Y. 584, 55 N.E. 302), but when an objectant has gone forward, as Mrs. Honigman surely has, with evidence reflecting the operation of the testator's mind, it is the proponents' duty to provide a basis for the alleged delusion. We cannot conclude that as a matter of law they have performed this duty successfully. When, in the light of all the circumstances surrounding a long and happy marriage such as this, the husband publicly and repeatedly expresses suspicions of his wife's unfaithfulness; of misbehaving herself in a most unseemly fashion, by hiding male callers in the cellar of her own home, in various closets, and under the bed; of hauling men from the street up to her second-story bedroom by use of bed sheets; of making contacts over the household telephone; and of passing a clandestine note through the fence on her brother's property and when he claims to have heard noises which he believed to be men running about his home, but which he had not investigated, and which he could not verify the courts should have no hesitation in placing the issue of sanity in the jury's hands. To hold to the contrary would be to take from the jury its traditional function of passing on the facts.

The statute referred to is the so-called "dead man rule": the lips of the deceased are sealed regarding the transaction, so too should be those of the living. In common with some (many? or most?) evidence rules it is riddled with exceptions.

Clapp v. Fullerton, 34 N.Y. 190, is not controlling in the circumstances of this case. There, the decedent had not expressed his suspicion of the infidelity of his first wife, who had died 45 years earlier, until after the making of the will, and even then he did so casually and discreetly. His belief was based on a statement made by the wife during her last illness, while she was in a state of delirium. Here, on the other hand, Mr. Honigman persisted over a long period of time in telling his suspicions to anyone who would listen to him, friends and strangers alike. That such belief was an obsession with him was clearly established by a preponderance of concededly competent evidence and, prima facie, there was presented a question of fact as to whether it affected the will he made shortly before his death.

The proponents argue that, even if decedent was indeed laboring under a delusion, the existence of other reasons for the disposition he chose is enough to support the validity of the instrument as a will. The other reasons are, first, the size of Mrs. Honigman's independent fortune, and, second, the financial need of his residuary legatees. These reasons, as well as his belief in his wife's infidelity, decedent expressed to his own attorney. We dispelled a similar contention in American Seamen's Friend Soc. v. Hopper, supra, where we held that a will was bad when its 'dispository provisions were or might have been caused or affected by the delusion' (emphasis supplied). The dictum of Matter of Nicholas' Will, never approved by this court, is erroneous insofar as it points to the contrary. . . .

The order appealed from should be reversed and a new trial granted, with costs to abide the event.

FULD, JUDGE (dissenting).

I am willing to assume that the proof demonstrates that the testator's belief that his wife was unfaithful was completely groundless and unjust. However, that is not enough; it does not follow from this fact that the testator suffered from such a delusion as to stamp him mentally defective or as lacking in capacity to make a will.

'To sustain the allegation,' this court wrote in the Clapp case, 34 N.Y. 190, 197, 'it is not sufficient to show that his suspicion in this respect was not well founded. It is quite apparent, from the evidence, that his distrust of the fidelity of his wife was really groundless and unjust; but it does not follow that his doubts evince a condition of lunacy. The right of a testator to dispose of his estate, depends neither on the justice of his prejudices nor the soundness of his reasoning. He may do what he will with his own; and if there be no defect of testamentary capacity, and no undue influence or fraud, the law gives effect to his will, though its provisions are unreasonable and unjust.'

> **Food for Thought**
>
> Why is the dissent also convinced that Mrs. H was faithful? And that Mr. H's suspicions were groundless? Would you be concerned if your spouse received an anniversary card on a date other than that of your marriage, and which you didn't send? ✏

As a matter of fact, in the case before us, a goodly portion of the widow's testimony bearing on her husband's alleged delusion should have been excluded, as the court itself notes, by reason of section 347 of the Civil Practice Act. And, of course, if such testimony had not been received in evidence, a number of items of proof upon which the widow relies would not have been available, with the consequence that the record would have contained even less basis for her claim of delusion.

Moreover, I share the Appellate Division's view that other and sound reasons, quite apart from the alleged decision, existed for the disposition made by the testator. Indeed, he himself had declared that his wife had enough money and he wanted to take care of his brothers and sisters living in Europe.

In short, the evidence adduced utterly failed to prove that the testator was suffering from an insane delusion or lacked testamentary capacity. The Appellate Division was eminently correct in concluding that there was no issue of fact for the jury's consideration and in directing the entry of a decree admitting the will to probate. Its order should be affirmed.

> **Practice Pointer**
>
> Under these circumstances, should the estate planner been more cautious?

DESMOND, C.J., and FROESSEL and BURKE, JJ., concur with DYE, J.; FULD, J., dissents in an opinion in which VAN VOORHIS and FOSTER, JJ., concur. Order reversed, etc.

———————

Points for Discussion

1. *Was Louisa Strittmater ill?*

What was the mental illness from which Louisa Strittmater suffered and, according to the court, caused her odd behavior? Can you think of a different explanation for Louisa Strittmater's behavior? Regardless of whether the Restatement was applied, do you think that the outcome would be the same if this case came before a court in the twenty-first century rather than the mid-twentieth?

2. *Did Ms. Strittmater exclude the natural objects of her bounty?*

It was conceded that she had little contact with her relatives (some cousins) and was dedicated to the National Women's party. Can a cause or organization be the natural objects of a will-maker's bounty? Must family always be considered the most appropriate devisees?

3. *What was Ms. Strittmater's state of mind at the time the will was executed?*

Assuming *arguendo* the suffered from an insane delusion, the morbid hatred of men, is it clear that at the time the will was executed the will reflected that delusion. After all, it was conceded by the Vice Ordinary that she was at times 'normal'. How can we be sure the will was not executed in the course of what is call a lucid interval?

4. *Consequences of the invalidity of Mr. Honigman's will*

If Mr. Honigman's will is not admitted to probate, he would die intestate. At the time of Mr. Honigman's death, New York's intestacy statute provided that if a person died intestate, and was married and had left no issue, the estate was distributed one-half to the surviving spouse and one-half *to the issue of the decedent's parents*. Given the governing statute, how would Mr. Honigman's probate estate have been distributed if the will is denied probate? Would the outcome be different under the governing statute of your jurisdiction?

5. *Why Mr. Honigman's will gave Mrs. Honigman the life income interest in a trust*

Mr. Honigman's will gave Mrs. Honigman the minimum amount necessary to prevent her from exercising her rights as a surviving spouse to a share of the deceased spouse's estate. As we will see in detail in a subsequent section, the lone person one cannot disinherit is a surviving spouse because a surviving spouse can set aside the dispositive plan by a process known as "election." At the time of Mr. Honigman's death the minimum to which a surviving spouse was entitled under the "elective share" was one-half the decedent's property. However, only $2500 of that one-half had to be given outright to the surviving spouse; the remainder could be placed in a trust from which the surviving spouse had to receive all the income for life.

The current New York statute (EPTL § 5–1.1–A) requires that the minimum amount, which is measured differently from the earlier statutes (and differs in other jurisdictions), must pass outright to the surviving spouse.

6. *An unexpressed ground for the majority opinion in* Honigman?

Would your view of whether the case was decided correctly be affected by the source of Mr. Honigman's property? Suppose his estate consisted entirely of assets traceable to saving and investment of salary he received as an employee of a business enterprise? To an inheritance he received from his parents? Would it make a difference if Mrs. Honigman had never worked outside the home? If she had worked outside the home and had assets in her name alone traceable to saving and investment of her earnings? Are any of these changed facts relevant to the question of whether Mr. Honigman suffered from an insane delusion and that the delusion impacted his estate plan?

C. Undue Influence

A page of history . . .

While the will-maker's state of mind was also relevant with respect to a contest on the grounds of undue influence, it is the conduct of others that is the focus of inquiry. An individualistic notion of property ownership mandates that a valid will represent the volition of the will-maker, and not that of another. Thus, whether another individual coerced the will-maker into directing dispositions in the testamentary act is at issue, in particular whether pressure to influence the will-maker was sufficiently extensive so as to overwhelm his or her volition, thereby substituting another person's testamentary preferences for that of the will-maker.[8] Then as now, because an individual with a less than robust mental state might be susceptible to the influence of others, the grounds of undue influence and testamentary capacity were often linked. Swinburne, the lawyer cited as authority above, noted that:

> those in extremitie . . . therefore are readie to answere (yea) to anie question almost, that they may be quiet: which advantage, craftie and covetous persons knowing very well, are then most busie, and doo labour with toothe and naile to, to procure the sicke person to yield to their demands.[9]

Accordingly, if a person of 'weak judgment and easie to be perswaded' gave an individual a large bequest, undue influence might be suspected. Likewise, when a testator in a

---

8   The classic discussion in American law is Ashbel Gulliver and Catherine Tilson, 'Classification of Gratuitous Transfers,' 51 Yale L.J., 1–39 (1941).

9   Ibid., p. 63.

weakened condition was under the 'government' or control of the persuader it might be present.[10] Then as now, undue influence, whether control by another overwhelmed the volition of the testator, was (and remains in modern law) difficult to delineate.[11] Swinburne opined that 'fair and flattering speeches to move the will-maker' which led to a bequest was not immoderate, and would not therefore invalidate a will. On the other hand, if the will-maker was in a weakened position and friends 'press him much and so wrest words from him, especially if it be in advantage of them,' the will was 'very suspicious.'[12] Accordingly, it was recognized that those who were ill at the time a will was executed might be willing to yield to the "desires of another person . . . to be at quiet and rest."[13]

The application undue influence to the reality of modern will-making is very difficult to discern. In one sense, every testamentary disposition is the result of some influence. Wills are seldom written to make gifts to individuals or organizations unknown to the testator. The key, of course, is figuring out what sort of influence is "undue." The Restatement formulation is widely accepted (the Restatement is generalizing about all donative transfers so "donor" includes "testator"):

Restatement (Third) of Property (Wills and Other Donative Transfers) § 8.3(b)

A donative transfer is procured by undue influence if the wrongdoer exerted such influence over the donor that it overcame the donor's free will and caused the donor to make a donative transfer that the donor would not otherwise have made.

As you might imagine, proving a case of undue influence can be difficult. Evidence will almost certainly be circumstantial. Restatement § 8.3 comment *e* says that a person objecting to the admission to probate of a will on grounds of undue influence will prevail in the absence of direct evidence if he or she can prove

- That the testator was "susceptible" to undue influence,

- That the person alleged to have exercised undue influence had an opportunity to do so,

- That the person alleged to have exercised undue influence "had a disposition to exercise undue influence", and

---

10   Ibid., pp. 242–43.

11   For a recent treatment in American law, see Melanie Leslie, 'The Myth of Testamentary Freedom,' <u>Arizona Law Review</u> vol. 38, pp. 235–90.

12   Sheppard, <u>Touchstone</u>, p. 399.

13   George Meriton, <u>The Parson's Monitor consisting of Such Cases and Matter as principally concern the Clergy</u> (London, 1681), p.29.

- That the will or part of the will appears to be the result of the alleged undue influence.

Clearly, a party trying to keep a will from being admitted to probate on the ground of undue influence will be grateful for a presumption that works in his or her favor. Just such a presumption usually arises when, in the words of Restatement (Third) of Property § 8.3 comment *f*, the alleged wrongdoer had a "confidential relationship" with the testator "and there were suspicious circumstances surrounding the preparation, formulation, or execution" of the will.

Comment *g* to § 8.3 then explains what a "confidential relationship" is. According to the Restatement, they come in three categories. The first, **fiduciary relationships**, arise "from a settled category of fiduciary obligation" such as that between attorney and client or trustee and beneficiary or the agent under a power of attorney and the principal for whom the agent acts. The quality that links all these relationships together is the fiduciary's obligation to put the needs and interests of the other person before the fiduciary's own. Whether such a relationship exists is a matter of law.

Whether or not either of the other categories exists in a given situation is a question of fact. The second, **reliant relationships**, exists when the testator relies on the assumed expertise and good faith of the alleged wrongdoer. Examples are the relationship between a financial advisor and a customer or between doctor and patient or between a member of the clergy and a parishioner. The third, **dominant-subservient relationships**, exists when the testator is unable to care for him or herself and needs the other person to furnish requisite aid. The Restatement provides as examples the relationship "between a hired caregiver and an ill or feeble" testator or between "an adult child and an ill or feeble parent." Generally, courts seem to be increasingly more willing to expand the scope of the "confidential relationship" concept. Some of the impetus for this expansion is probably due to increased awareness of the dependency of so many elderly on assistance from individuals other than family members (although family members certainly can exercise undue influence). Remember, however, that family relationships, including the parent-child relationship, do not give rise to confidential relationships without the existence of the sort of relationships the Restatement classification describes.

The second branch of the analysis that can give rise to a presumption of undue influence is the existence of suspicious circumstances. Restatement (Third) of Property § 8.3 comment *h* offers the following list of so-called suspicious circumstances which where they exist gives rise to an inference of abuse of the confidential relationship. The list is extensive:

- The extent to which the testator was in a weakened condition, physically, mentally or both and thus susceptible to undue influence

- The extent to which the alleged wrongdoer participated in the preparation or procurement of the will

- Whether the donor received independent advice from an attorney or from other competent and disinterested advisors in preparing the will

- Whether the will was prepared in secrecy or haste

- Whether the testator's attitude towards others had changed by reason of the relationship with the alleged wrongdoer

- Whether there is a "decided discrepancy" between a new and previous wills of the testator

- Whether there was a continuity of purpose running through former wills indicating a "settled intent" in the testator's plans for disposing of his or her property

- Whether the disposition of the probate estate made by the will "is such that a reasonable person would regard it as unnatural, unjust, or unfair, for example, whether the disposition abruptly and without apparent reason disinherited a faithful and deserving family member.

According to the Restatement, once the presumption of undue influence is established, the burden of going forward shifts to the person or persons offering the will for probate (the proponents). What does not shift is the burden of persuasion. What that means is that even if the presumption exists, the persons objecting to the will are entitled to summary judgment *only* if the proponents do not bring forward any evidence of rebut the presumption.

Points for Discussion

1. *The law of undue influence is not uniform*

Whether the existence of the presumption makes it easier or not to "prove" undue influence is not an easy question to answer, and the law of every state does not neatly match up with the Restatement's analysis of the question. Most notably, the distinction between shifting the burden of going forward (sometimes known as the burden of production) with evidence to prove the elements of undue influence is not always the law. After a Florida case (*Estate of Carpenter*, 253 So.2d 697 (Fla. 1971)) stated that the existence of the presumption of undue influence shifted only the burden of going forward, the legislature overruled the case by amending Fla. Stat. Ann. § 733.107(2): "The presumption of undue influence implements public policy against abuse of fiduciary or confidential relationships and is therefore a presumption shifting the burden of proof . . . ."

2. *California's experiment with codification*

The complications of the basic legal structure applying to undue influence claims and the growing concerns about influence of hired caregivers has led California to codify a good deal of the law of undue influence. The statutes have been changed somewhat since their first enactment with the latest version, below, effective January 1, 2011:

California Probate Code § 21380

(a)   A provision of an instrument making a donative transfer to any of the following persons is presumed to be the product of fraud or undue influence:

    (1)   The person who drafted the instrument.

    (2)   A person in a fiduciary relationship with the transferor who transcribed the instrument or caused it to be transcribed.

    (3)   A care custodian of a transferor who is a dependent adult, but only if the instrument was executed during the period in which the care custodian provided services to the transferor, or within 90 days before or after that period.

    (4)   A person who is related by blood or affinity, within the third degree, to any person described in paragraphs (1) to (3), inclusive.

    (5)   A cohabitant or employee of any person described in paragraphs (1) to (3), inclusive.

    (6)   A partner, shareholder, or employee of a law firm in which a person described in paragraph (1) or (2) has an ownership interest.

(b)   The presumption created by this section is a presumption affecting the burden of proof. The presumption may be rebutted by proving, by clear and convincing evidence, that the donative transfer was not the product of fraud or undue influence.

(c)   Notwithstanding subdivision (b), with respect to a donative transfer to the person who drafted the donative instrument, or to a person who is related to, or associated with, the drafter as described in paragraph (4), (5), or (6) of subdivision (a), the presumption created by this section is conclusive.

(d)   If a beneficiary is unsuccessful in rebutting the presumption, the beneficiary shall bear all costs of the proceeding, including reasonable attorney's fees.

If a gift is indeed the product of undue influence, the instrument creating the gift operates as if the person who received the gift died before the donor (in the case of a will, the testator), without a spouse, domestic partner, or issue (Cal. Prob. Code § 21386). (When we study the rules relating to lapse of bequests hereinafter, the gift will fail and remedial statutes designed to prevent that result will not apply.) At first glance, the California statute seems decidedly punitive. Not only must the presumption be rebutted by clear and convincing evidence, but when it comes to the drafter of the "donative instrument" (which of course includes a will), as well as persons related to or associated with the drafter, the presumption is conclusive. Note, too, that if the beneficiary of the will attempts to rebut the presumption but fails, the unsuccessful beneficiary is charged with the prevailing parties "reasonable attorney's fees." This provision is usually regarded as a strong disincentive to contest a will, and at the very least will make a settlement with the parties opposing the will a most attractive alternative.

There are statutory exceptions to the rules of § 21380. Examples are when the gift is to a relative or "cohabitant" of the testator: the document is drafted by a relative or "cohabitant;" the gift is to charity; in most circumstances if the gift is worth $5000 or less; or if the will was executed outside of California by someone not a resident of California at the time of execution.

There is also a statutory provision, Probate Code § 21384, for exempting the gift from the operation of § 21380 by review of the will (or other document) by an "independent attorney who counsels the transferor, out of the presence of any heir or proposed beneficiary, about the nature and consequences of the intended transfer, including the effect of the intended transfer on the transferor's heirs and on any beneficiary of a prior donative instrument, attempts to determine if the intended transfer is the result of fraud or undue influence", and then signs a "Certificate of Independent Review" (the form of which is also included in § 21384). Keep these provisions in mind as you read the following cases.

3. Attorney as beneficiary

As observed in California Probate Code § 21380, some jurisdictions, at least, take a very dim view of lawyers who draft wills in which they (and perhaps persons associated with them) are beneficiaries. Although the California statute is unusual, there is both case law and principles of professional responsibility that apply. Consider the following provision:

Model Rule of Professional Responsibility (MRPC) 1.8(c)

A lawyer shall not solicit any substantial gift from a client, including a testamentary gift, or prepare on behalf of a client an instrument giving the lawyer or a person related to the lawyer any substantial gift, unless the lawyer or other recipient of the gift is related to the client. For purposes of this paragraph, related persons include a spouse, child, grandchild, parent, grandparent or other relative or individual with whom the lawyer or the client maintains a close, familial relationship.

Note the exception for gifts from relatives, an exception also carved out in the California statute. Even in such cases, care must be taken not to appear to take advantage of the relationship between the testator and the lawyer. The Commentaries on the Model Rules prepared by the American College of Trust and Estate Counsel (ACTEC) offer the very sensible observation that "the lawyer should exercise special care" if the gift left to the lawyer is "disproportionately large" compared to gifts made to those who are equally related to the testator.

Go Online

To consult the ACTEC *Commentaries*: https://actecfoundation.org/trust-and-estate-professional-resources/professional-conduct-rules-for-trust-and-estate-practitioners/.

For example, consider a lawyer who is the niece of a childless widowed aunt. Suppose under the law of intestacy, aunt's heirs would be six nieces and nephews, including the lawyer. Would it be problematic if all the nieces and nephews share the estate equally? But what if the lawyer drafts a will that limits one-half of aunt's probate estate to her and divides the other half equally among the other five nieces and nephews? Exercising "special care" may mean that a lawyer should not draft the will in which she receives property in excess of an equal share as those beneficiaries related in the same degree to the testator.

"Solicit," of course, has a well-established meaning, but it may be very difficult to explain that a gift was not "solicited" but rather was the idea of the testator without prompting by the scrivener. In New York, *Matter of Putnam*, 177 N.E. 399 (N.Y. 1931), has long been authority for the rule that any gift in a will to the lawyer who drafted the will raises a presumption of undue influence on the part of the lawyer. The New York Surrogate's Courts regularly require attorneys who receive gifts in wills to rebut the presumption in a proceeding before the court known as a "Putnam hearing." Not every such gift results in a hearing: the attorney who writes her spouse's will giving everything to herself is not going to have to justify herself to the court (except in the most egregious circumstances). Likewise, a will in which a lawyer who receives a gift the value of which is quite small compared to the size of the estate is usually not subject to a hearing. On the other hand, the lawyer in our example in the previous paragraph (who leaves herself a bequest that exceeds the amounts of her cousins) might very well find herself having to explain her aunt's favoritism.

4. Attorney as executor

Aside from the more sensitive issue of a bequest to the attorney/scrivener, is it appropriate for an attorney to receive compensation as executor of a will and a legal fee for representing the executor? In New York, for example, the compensation of the executor (the executor's commission) is set by statute (SCPA 2307) but legal fees are not. The amount of the lawyer's fee, however, is ultimately controlled by the Surrogate's Court. In some states, the legal fee is also set by statute. Whether the statutes set the compensation or not, one can regard (perhaps pejoratively) an attorney serving as executor and as counsel to the executor as engaging in "double dipping." In order to limit the possibilities for abuse, New York's SCPA 2307–a requires that an attorney provide certain information to a testator when the attorney prepares a will in which the attorney is nominated as executor. The statute provides a form for disclosing the required information. The testator must be informed that generally anyone can serve as executor, that any person serving as executor, including an attorney, is entitled to statutory commissions, and that any attorney, including the attorney/executor who provides legal services to the executor is entitled to just and reasonable compensation. Absent the proper acknowledgment of disclosure of this information in a writing separate from the will, the attorney/executor is entitled only to one-half of the statutory commission.

The New York statute codifies what probably most commentators would agree is best practice when a client asks the scrivener to be executor or trustee, statute or no statute. The ACTEC *Commentaries* to MRPC 1.7, which deals with conflicts of interest, state that a lawyer is free to accept designation as a fiduciary so long as the client is properly informed which means "the client is provided with information regarding the role and duties of the fiduciary, the ability of a lay person to serve as fiduciary, with legal and other professional assistance, and the comparative costs of appointing the lawyer or another person or institution as fiduciary."

Consider the following two cases. They both to add texture to the interplay between the formulation of the *law* of undue influence to the *facts* of a particular will execution, and query whether the scrivener should have been better prepared to resist a challenge on the grounds of undue influence.

In re Will of Moses

227 So. 2d 829 (Miss. 1969)

SMITH, JUSTICE:

Mrs. Fannie Traylor Moses died on February 6, 1967. An instrument, dated December 23, 1957 and purporting to be her last will and testament, was duly admitted to probate in common form in the Chancery Court of the First Judicial District of Hinds County. Thereafter, on February 14, 1967, appellant, Clarence H. Holland, an attorney at law, not related to Mrs. Moses, filed a petition in that court tendering for probate in solemn form, as the true last will and testament of Mrs. Moses, a document dated May 26, 1964, under the terms of which he would take virtually her entire estate. This document contained a clause revoking former wills and Holland's petition prayed that the earlier probate of the 1957 will be set aside.

The beneficiaries under the 1957 will (the principal beneficiary was an elder sister of Mrs. Moses) responded to Holland's petition, denied that the document tendered by him was Mrs. Moses' will, and asserted, among other things, that it was (1) the product of Holland's undue influence upon her, (2) that at the time of its signing, Mrs. Moses lacked testamentary capacity, and, (3) that the 1957 will was Mrs. Moses' true last will and testament and its probate should be confirmed. By cross bill, respondents prayed that Holland's apparent ownership of an interest in certain real estate had been procured by undue influence and that it should be cancelled as a cloud upon the title of Mrs. Moses, the true owner.

By agreement, the case was heard by the chancellor without a jury.

A brief summary of facts found by the chancellor and upon which he based his conclusion that the presumption was not overcome, follows: Mrs. Moses died at the age of 57 years, leaving an estate valued at $125,000. She had lost three husbands in less than 20 years. Throughout the latter years of her life her health became seriously impaired. She suffered from serious heart trouble and cancer had required the surgical removal of one of her breasts. For 6 or 7 years preceding her death she was an alcoholic. On several occasions Mrs. Moses had declared her intention of making an elder sister her testamentary beneficiary. She had once lived with this sister and was grateful for the many kindnesses shown her. Mrs. Moses' will of December 23, 1957 did, in fact, bequeath the bulk of her estate to this sister.

The exact date on which Holland entered Mrs. Moses' life is unclear. There is a suggestion that she had met him as early as 1951. Their personal relationship became what the chancellor, somewhat inaccurately, characterized, as one of 'dubious' morality. The record, however, leaves no doubt as to its nature. Soon after the death of Mrs. Moses' last husband, Holland, although 15 years her junior, began seeing Mrs. Moses with marked regularity, there having been testimony to the effect that he attended her almost daily. Holland was an attorney and in that capacity represented Mrs. Moses. She declared that he was not only her attorney but her 'boyfriend' as well. On August 22, 1961, a date during the period in which the evidence shows that Holland was Mrs. Moses' attorney, she executed a document purporting to be her will. This instrument was drawn by an attorney with whom Holland was then associated and shared offices, and was typed by a secretary who served them both. It was witnessed by Holland's associate and their secretary. In addition to other testamentary dispositions, this document undertook to bequeath to Holland 'my wedding ring, my diamond solitaire ring and my three gold bracelets containing twenty-five (25) pearls each.' In it Holland is referred to as 'my good friend.' The validity of this document is not an issue in the present case.

After Mrs. Moses died, the 1964 will was brought forward by another attorney, also an associate of Holland, who said that it had entrusted to him by Mrs. Moses, together with other papers, for safekeeping. He distinguished his relation with Holland from that of a partner, saying that he and Holland only occupied offices together and shared facilities and expenses in the practice of law. He also stated that he saw Mrs. Moses on an 'average' of once a week, most often in the company of Holland.

> **Take Note**
>
> Burden shifted to proponent even though he appears to have given no legal advice regarding the will.

Throughout this period, Mrs. Moses was a frequent visitor at Holland's office, and there is ample evidence to support the chancellor's finding that there existed a continuing fiduciary relationship between Mrs. Moses and Holland, as her attorney. . . .

The evidence supports the chancellor's finding that the confidential or fiduciary relationship which existed between Mrs. Moses and Holland, her attorney, was a subsisting and continuing relationship, having begun before the making by Mrs. Moses of the will of August 22, 1961, under the terms of which her jewelry had been bequeathed to Holland, and having ended only with Mrs. Moses' death. Moreover, its effect was enhanced by the fact that throughout this period, Holland was in almost daily attendance upon Mrs. Moses on terms of the utmost intimacy. There

> **Food for Thought**
>
> Do you know more about the life and times of Fanny Moses than is necessary to resolve the case?

was strong evidence that this aging woman, seriously ill, disfigured by surgery, and hopelessly addicted to alcoholic excesses, was completely bemused by the constant and amorous attentions of Holland, a man 15 years her junior. There was testimony too indicating that she entertained the pathetic hope that he might marry her. Although the evidence was not without conflict and was, in some of its aspects, circumstantial, it was sufficient to support the finding that the relationship existed on May 26, 1964, the date of the will tendered for probate by Holland.

The chancellor's factual finding of the existence of this relationship on that date is supported by evidence and is not manifestly wrong. Moreover, he was correct in his conclusion of law that such relationship gave rise to a presumption of undue influence which could be overcome only by evidence that, in making the 1964 will, Mrs. Moses had acted upon the independent advice and counsel of one entirely devoted to her interest.

Appellant takes the position that there was undisputed evidence that Mrs. Moses, in making the 1964 will, did, in fact, have such advice and counsel. He relies upon the testimony of the attorney in whose office that document was prepared to support his assertion. This attorney was and is a reputable and respected member of the bar, who had no prior connection with Holland and no knowledge of Mrs. Moses' relationship with him. He had never seen nor represented Mrs. Moses previously and never represented her afterward. He was acquainted with Holland and was aware that Holland was a lawyer.

A brief summary of his testimony, with respect to the writing of the will, follows: Mrs. Moses had telephoned him for an appointment and had come alone to his office on March 31, 1964. She was not intoxicated and in his opinion knew what she was doing. He asked her about her property and 'marital background.' He did this in order, he said, to advise her as to possible renunciation by a husband. She was also asked if she had children in order to determine whether she wished to 'pretermit them.' As she had neither husband nor children this subject was pursued no further. He asked as to the values of various items of property in order to consider possible tax problems. He told her it would be better if she had more accurate descriptions of the several items of real and personal property comprising her estate. No further 'advice or counsel' was given her.

On some later date, Mrs. Moses sent in (the attorney did not think she came personally and in any event he did not see her), some tax receipts for purposes of supplying property descriptions. He prepared the will and mailed a draft to her. Upon receiving it, she telephoned that he had made a mistake in the devise of certain realty, in that he had provided that a relatively low valued property should go to Holland rather than a substantially more valuable property which she said she wanted Holland to have. He rewrote the will, making this change, and mailed it to her, as revised, on May 21, 1964. On the one occasion when he saw Mrs. Moses, there were no questions and no discussion of any kind as to Holland being preferred to the exclusion of her blood relatives. Nor was there any inquiry or discussion as to a possible client-attorney relationship with Holland. The attorney-draftsman wrote the will according to Mrs. Moses' instructions and said that he had 'no interest in' how she disposed of her property. He testified 'I try to draw the will to suit their purposes and if she (Mrs. Moses) wanted to leave him (Holland) everything she had, that was her business as far as I was concerned. I was trying to represent her in putting on paper in her will her desires, and it didn't matter to me to whom she left it * * * I couldn't have cared less.'

Practice Pointer

Surprising? After all, the scrivener had no personal interest in the will or affinity for Holland. Why should he have had an interest in the terms of the disposition? That said, in retrospect, should he have sensed a potential contest and prepared a record accordingly?

When Mrs. Moses returned to the office to execute the will, the attorney was not there and it was witnessed by two secretaries. . . . One of these secretaries, coincidentally, had written and witnessed the 1961 will when working for Holland and his associate. The attorney's testimony supports the chancellor's finding that nowhere in the conversations with Mrs. Moses was there touched upon in any way the proposed testamentary disposition whereby preference was to be given a nonrelative to the exclusion of her blood relatives. There was no discussion of her relationship with Holland, nor as to who her legal heirs might be, nor as to their relationship to her, after it was discovered that she had neither a husband nor children. It is clear from his own testimony that, in writing the will, the attorney-draftsman, did no more than write down, according to the forms of law, what Mrs. Moses told him. There was no meaningful independent advice or counsel touching upon the area in question and it is manifest that the role of the attorney in writing the will, as it relates to the present issue, was little more than that of scrivener. The chancellor was justified in holding that this did not meet the burden nor overcome the presumption. The sexual morality of the personal relationship is not an issue. However, the intimate nature of this relationship is relevant to the present inquiry to the extent that its existence, under the circumstances, warranted an inference of undue influence, extending and augmenting that which flowed from the attorney-client relationship. Particularly is this true when viewed in the light of evidence indicating its employment for the personal aggrandizement of Holland. For that purpose, it was properly taken into consideration by the chancellor.

The rule that where a fiduciary relationship has been established, a presumption of undue influence arises, is not limited to holographs, nor confined to wills otherwise prepared by the testator himself. It encompasses with equal force wills written for the testator by a third person. There is no sound reason supporting the view that a testator, whose will has become subservient to the undue influence of another, is purged of the effects of that influence merely because the desired testamentary document is prepared by an attorney who knows nothing of the antecedent circumstances.

Take Note

The gentleman protested too much? If "sexual morality" wasn't an issue, the court need not have raised it.

The chancellor was justified in finding that the physical absence of Holland during Mrs. Moses' brief visit to the office of the attorney who wrote the will did not suffice to abate or destroy the presumption of undue influence.

The chancellor was the judge of the credibility of the witnesses and the weight and worth of their testimony. Moreover, as trier of facts, it was for him to resolve conflicts and to interpret evidence where it was susceptible of more than one reasonable interpretation. It was also his prerogative to draw reasonable inferences from facts proved. As said in Croft, supra, '(The only positive and affirmative proof required is of facts and circumstances from which the undue influence may be reasonably inferred.' This Court, in passing upon the sufficiency of the evidence to support the factual findings of the chancellor, must accept as true all that the evidence proved or reasonably tended to prove, together with all reasonable inferences to be drawn from it, supporting such findings.

Viewed in the light of the above rules, it cannot be said that chancellor was manifestly wrong in finding that Holland occupied a dual fiduciary relationship with respect to Mrs. Moses, both conventional and actual, attended by suspicious circumstances as set forth in his opinion, which gave rise to a presumption of undue influence in the production of the 1964 will, nor that he was manifestly wrong in finding that this presumption was not overcome by 'clearest proof' that in making and executing the will Mrs. Moses acted upon her 'own volition and upon the fullest deliberation,' or upon independent advice and counsel of one wholly devoted to her interest.

BRADY, PATTERSON, INZER and ROBERTSON, JJ., dissent.

ROBERTSON, JUSTICE (dissenting):

Mrs. Fannie T. Moses was 54 years of age when she executed her last will and testament on May 26, 1964, leaving most of her considerable estate to Clarence H. Holland, her good friend, but a man fifteen years her junior. She had been married three times, and each of these marriages was dissolved by the death of her husband. Holland's friendship with Mrs. Moses dated back to the days of her second husband, Robert L. Dickson. He was also a friend of her third husband, Walter Moses.

She was the active manager of commercial property in the heart of Jackson, four apartment buildings containing ten rental units, and a 480-acre farm until the day of her death. All of the witnesses conceded that she was a good businesswoman, maintaining and repairing her properties with promptness and dispatch, and paying her bills promptly so that she would get the cash discount. She was a strong personality and pursued her own course, even though her manner of living did at times embarrass her sisters and estranged her from them.

There is no proof in this voluminous record that Holland ever did or said anything to Mrs. Moses about devising her property to anybody, much less him. It is conceded that in the absence of the presumption of undue influence that there is no basis to support a finding that Holland exercised undue influence over Mrs. Moses. This being true, the first question to be decided is whether the presumption of undue influence arises under the circumstances of this case.

It is my opinion that the presumption did not arise. The fact, alone, that a confidential relationship existed between Holland and Mrs. Moses is not sufficient to give rise to the presumption of undue influence in a will case. . . .

Take Note

The dissenting judge feels no compulsion to present a detailed narrative of Ms. Moses' life.

It was not contended in this case that Holland was in any way actively concerned with the preparation or execution of the will. Appellees rely solely upon the finding of the chancellor that there were suspicious circumstances. However, the suspicious circumstances listed by the chancellor in his opinion had nothing whatsoever to do with the preparation or execution of the will. These were remote antecedent circumstances having to do with the meretricious relationship of the parties, and the fact that at times Mrs. Moses drank to excess and could be termed an alcoholic, but there is no proof in this long record that her use of alcohol affected her will power or her ability to look after her extensive real estate holdings. It is common knowledge that many persons who could be termed alcoholics, own, operate and manage large business enterprises with success. The fact that she chose to leave most of her property to the man she loved in preference to her sisters and brother is not such an unnatural disposition of her property as to render it invalid.

In this case, there were no suspicious circumstances surrounding the preparation or execution of the will, and in my opinion the chancellor was wrong in so holding. However, even if it be conceded that the presumption of undue influence did arise, this presumption was overcome by clear and convincing evidence of good faith, full knowledge and independent consent and advice.

When she got ready to make her will she called Honorable Dan H. Shell for an appointment. Shell did not know her, although he remembered that he had handled a land transaction for her third husband, Walter Moses, some years before. Shell had been in the active practice of law in Jackson since 1945; he was an experienced attorney with a large and varied practice.

> **Practice Pointer**
>
> Had Dan Shell actually tried to counsel Ms. Moses on the proper disposition of her money, what would have been her likely response? How quickly would she have been out the door?

The majority was indeed hard put to find fault with his actions on behalf of his client. It is easy for us who are removed from the active practice of law to criticize our brethren who are 'on the firing line.' The question is, did he do all that was reasonably required of him to represent his client in the preparation of her will. He was not required to be perfect, nor was he required to meet a standard of exact precision. He ascertained that Mrs. Moses was competent to make a will; he satisfied himself that she was acting of her own free will and accord, and that she was disposing of her property exactly as she wished and intended. No more is required.

There is not one iota of testimony in this voluminous record that Clarence Holland even knew of this will, much less that he participated in the preparation or execution of it. The evidence is all to the contrary. The evidence is undisputed that she executed her last will after the fullest deliberation, with full knowledge of what she was doing, and with the independent consent and advice of an experienced and competent attorney whose sole purpose was to advise with her and prepare her will exactly as she wanted it.

In January 1967, about one month before her death and some two years and eight months after she had made her will, she called W. R. Patterson, an experienced, reliable and honorable attorney who was a friend of hers, and asked him to come by her home for a few minutes. Patterson testified:

> 'She said, 'Well, the reason I called you out here is that I've got an envelope here with all of my important papers in it, and that includes my last will and testament,'

and says, 'I would like to leave them with you if you've got a place to lock them up in your desk somewhere there in your office.' ' * * * (A)ND she said, 'Now, Dan Shell drew my will for me two or three years ago,' and she says, 'It's exactly like I want it,' and says, 'I had to go to his office two or three times to get it the way I wanted it, but this is the way I want it, and if anything happens to me I want you to take all these papers and give them to Dan,' and she says, 'He'll know what to do with them." (Emphasis added).

What else could she have done? She met all the tests that this Court and other courts have carefully outlined and delineated. The majority opinion says that this still was not enough, that there were 'suspicious circumstances' and 'antecedent agencies', but even these were not connected in any shape, form or fashion with the preparation or execution of her will. They had to do with her love life and her drinking habits and propensities.

If full knowledge, deliberate and voluntary action, and independent consent and advice have not been proved in this case, then they just cannot be proved. We should be bound by the uncontracted testimony in the record; we should not go completely outside the record and guess, speculate and surmise as to what happened.

I think that the judgment of the lower court should be reversed and the last will and testament of Fannie T. Moses executed on May 26, 1964, admitted to probate in solemn form.

Lipper v. Weslow

369 S.W.2d 698 (Tex. App. 1963)

McDonald, Chief Justice.

This is a contest of the will of Mrs. Sophie Block, on the ground of undue influence. Plaintiffs, Julian Weslow, Jr., Julia Weslow Fortson and Alice Weslow Sale, are the 3 grandchildren of Mrs. Block by a deceased son; defendants are Mrs. Block's 2 surviving children, G. Frank Lipper and Irene Lipper Dover (half-brother and half-sister of plaintiff's deceased father). (The will left the estate of testatrix to her 2 children, defendants herein; and left nothing to her grandchildren by the deceased son, plaintiffs herein). Trial was to a jury, which found that Mrs. Block's will, signed by her on January 30, 1956, was procured by undue influence on the part of the proponent, Frank Lipper. The trial court entered judgment on the verdict, setting aside the will.

Take Note

Yet another jury rewriting a deceased will-maker's estate plan.

Defendants appeal, contending there is no evidence, or insufficient evidence, to support the finding that the will was procured by undue influence.

Testatrix was married 3 times. Of her first marriage she had one son, Julian Weslow, (who died in 1949), who was father of plaintiffs herein. After the death of her first husband testatrix married a Mr. Lipper. Defendants are the 2 children of their marriage. After Mr. Lipper's death, testatrix married Max Block. There were no children born of this marriage. Max Block died several months after the death of testatrix.

On 30 January, 1956, Sophie Block executed the will in controversy. Such will was prepared by defendant, Frank Lipper, an attorney, one of the beneficiaries of the will, and Independent Executor of the will. The will was witnessed by 2 former business associates of Mr. Block. Pertinent provisions of the will are summarized as follows:

'That I, Mrs. Sophie Block, * * * do make, publish and declare this my last will and testament, hereby revoking all other wills by me heretofore made.'

1, 2, 3 and 4.

(Provide for payment of debts; for burial in Beth Israel Cemetery; and for minor bequests to a servant, and to an old folks' home.)

5.

(Devises the bulk of testatrix's estate to her 2 children, Mrs. Irene Lipper Dover and Frank Lipper (defendants herein), share and share alike).

6.

States that $7000. previously advanced to Mrs. Irene Lipper Dover, and $9300. previously advanced to Frank Lipper be taken into consideration in the final settlement of the estate; and cancels such amounts 'that I gave or advanced to my deceased son, Julian.'

7.

Appoints G. Frank Lipper Independent Executor of the estate without bond.

8.

Provides that if any legatee contests testatrix's will or the will of her husband, Max Block, that they forfeit all benefits under the will.

Take Note

A no contest clause, the effects of which we explain at the end of the case.

9.

My son, Julian A. Weslow, died on August 6, 1949, and I want to explain why I have not provided anything under this will for my daughter-in-law, Bernice Weslow, widow of my deceased son, Julian, and her children, Julian A. Weslow, Jr., Alice Weslow Sale, and Julia Weslow Fortson, and I want to go into sufficient detail in explaining my relationship in past years with my said son's widow and his children, before mentioned, and it is my desire to record such relationship so that there will be no question as to my feelings in the matter or any thought or suggestion that my children, Irene Lipper Dover and G. Frank Lipper, or my husband, Max, may have influenced me in any manner in the execution of this will. During the time that my said son, Julian, was living, the attitude of his wife, Bernice, was at times, pleasant and friendly, but the majority of the years when my said son, Julian, was living, her attitude towards me and my husband, Max, was unfriendly and frequently months would pass when she was not in my home and I did not hear from her. When my said son, Julian, was living he was treated the same as I treated my other children; and, my husband, Max, and I gave to each of our children a home and various sums of money from time to time to help in taking care of medical expenses, other unusual expenses, as well as outright gifts. Since my said son Julian's death, his widow, Bernice, and all of her children have shown a most unfriendly and distant attitude towards me, my husband, Max, and my 2 children G. Frank Lipper and Irene Lipper Dover, which attitude I cannot reconcile as I have shown them many kindnesses since they have been members of my family, and their continued unfriendly attitude towards me, my husband, Max, and my said children has hurt me deeply in my declining years, for my life would have been much happier if they had shown a disposition to want to be a part of the family and enter into a normal family relationship that usually exists with a daughter-in-law and grandchildren and great grandchildren. I have not seen my grandson, Julian A. Weslow, Jr. in several years, neither have I heard from him. My granddaughter, Alice Weslow Sale, I have not seen in several years and I have not heard from her, but I heard a report some months ago that she was now living in California and has since married William G. Sale. My granddaughter, Julia Weslow Fortson, wife of Ben Fortson, I have not seen in several years and I was told that she had a child born to her sometime in December 1952, and I have not seen the child or heard from my said granddaughter, Julia, up to this writing, and was informed by a friend that Julia has had another child recently and is now living in Louisiana, having moved from Houston; and needless to say, my said daughter-in-law, Bernice, widow of my deceased son, Julian, I have not seen in several years as she has taken little or no interest in me or my husband, Max, since the death of my son, Julian, with the exception that Christmas a year ago, if I remember correctly, she sent some flowers, which I acknowledged, and I believe she has sent some greeting cards on some occasions prior to that time. My said daughter-in-law, Bernice Weslow, has expressed to me, on several occasions, an intense hatred for my son, G. Frank Lipper, and my daughter, Irene Lipper Dover, which I cannot understand, as my said children have always shown her and her children every consideration when possible, and have expressed a desire to be friendly with her, and them. My said children, G. Frank Lipper, and Irene Lipper Dover, have

Take Note

The statement of justification. Persuasive? Does it sound like it came from the pen of Sophie? Or perhaps elsewhere?

at all times been attentive to me and my husband, Max, especially during the past few years when we have not been well. I will be 82 years old in June of this year and my husband, Max, will be 80 years of age in October of this year, and we have both been in failing health for the past few years and rarely leave our home, and appreciate any attention that is given us, and my husband, Max, and I cannot understand the unfriendly and distant attitude of Bernice Weslow, Widow of my said son, Julian, and his children, before mentioned.'

10.

(Concerns personal belongings already disposed of.)

'In Testimony Whereof, I have hereunto signed my name * * *. '(S) Sophie Block'

(Here follows attestation clause and signature of the 2 witnesses.)

The record reflects that the will in question was executed 22 days before testatrix died at the age of 81 years. By its terms, it disinherits the children of testatrix's son, who died in 1949. Defendant, Frank Lipper, gets a larger share than would have been the case if the plaintiffs were not disinherited. Defendant Lipper is a lawyer, and is admittedly the scrivener or the will. There is evidence that defendant Lipper bore malice against his dead half-brother. He lived next door to testatrix, and had a key to her house. The will was not read to testatrix prior to the time she signed same, and she had no discussion with anyone at the time she executed it. There is evidence that the recitations in the will that Bernice Weslow and her children were unfriendly, and never came about testatrix, were untrue. There is also evidence that the Weslows sent testatrix greeting cards and flowers from 1946 through 1954, more times than stated in the will.

Food for Thought

Consider the testimony of these witnesses. Which testimony strikes you as the strongest evidence of her intent to disinherit the Weslow grandkids?

Plaintiffs offered no direct evidence pertaining to the making and execution of the will on January 30, 1956, and admittedly rely wholly upon circumstantial evidence of undue influence to support the verdict.

All of the evidence is that testatrix was of sound mind at the time of the execution of the will; that she was a person of strong will; that she was in good physical health for her age; and that she was in fact physically active to the day of her death. Mrs. Weslow's husband died in 1949; and after 1952 the Weslows came about testatrix less often than before.

The witness Lyda Friberg, who worked at the home of testatrix from 1949 to 1952, testified that in *1952* she had a conversation with Bernice Weslow in which Mrs. Weslow told her if her children didn't get their inheritance she would 'sue them through every court in the Union'; that she told testatrix about this conversation, and that testatrix told her 'she would have those wills fixed up so there would be no court business', and that she wasn't going to 'leave them (the Weslows), a dime.' The foregoing was prior to the execution of the will on January 30, 1956.

Subsequent to the execution of the will, testatrix had a conversation with her sister, Mrs. Levy. Mrs. Levy testified:

'Q. Who did she say she was leaving her property to?

'A. She was leaving it to her son and her daughter.

'Q. What else did she say about the rest of her kin, if anything?

'A. Well she said that Julian's children had been very ugly to her; that they never showed her any attention whatever; they married and she didn't know they were married; they had children and they didn't let her know. After Julian passed away, she never saw any of the family at all. They never came to see her.

'Q. Did she make any statement?

'A. Yes, she did. When she passed away, she didn't want to leave them anything; that they did nothing for her when she was living.'

Shortly before she passed away, Testatrix told Mrs. Augusta Roos that she was going to leave her property to her 2 children, and further:

'Q. Did she give any reason for it?

'A. Yes. She said that Bernice had never been very nice to her and the children never were over.'

Again, subsequent to the making of her will, testatrix talked with Effie Landry, her maid. Mrs. Landry testified:

'Q. Did Mrs. Block on any occasion ever tell you anything about what was contained in her will.

'A. Yes.

'Q. What did she tell you about that?

'A. She said she wasn't leaving the Weslow children anything.'

The only question presented is whether there is any evidence of undue influence. The test of undue influence is whether such control was exercised over the mind of the testatrix as to overcome her free agency and free will and to substitute the will of another so as to cause the testatrix to do what she would not otherwise have done but for such control.

The evidence here establishes that testatrix was 81 years of age at the time of the execution of her will; that her son, defendant Lipper, who is a lawyer, wrote the will for her upon her instruction; that defendant Lipper bore malice against his deceased half-brother (father of plaintiffs); that defendant Lipper lived next door to his mother and had a key to her home; that the will as written gave defendant Lipper a larger share of testatrix's estate than he would otherwise have received; that while testatrix had no discussion with anyone at the time she executed the will, she told the witness Friberg, prior to executing the will, that she was not going to leave anything to the Weslows; and subsequent to the execution of the will she told the witnesses Mrs. Levy, Mrs. Roos, and Mrs. Landry that she had not left the Weslows anything, and the reason why. The will likewise states the reasons for testatrix's action. The testatrix, although 81 years of age, was of sound mind and strong will; and in excellent physical health. There is evidence that the recitations in testatrix's will about the number of times the Weslows sent cards and flowers were incorrect, to the extent that cards and flowers were in fact sent oftener than such will recites.

The contestants established a confidential relationship, the opportunity, and perhaps a motive for undue influence by defendant Lipper. Proof of this type simply sets the stage. Contestants must go forward and prove in some fashion that the will as written resulted from the defendant Lipper substituting his mind and will for that of the testatrix. Here the will and the circumstances might raise suspicion, but it does not supply proof of the vital facts of undue influence—the substitution of a plan of testamentary disposition by another as the will of the testatrix. Boyer v. Pool, supra.

All of the evidence reflected that testatrix, although 81 years of age, was of sound mind; of strong will; and in excellent physical condition. Moreover, subsequent to the execution of the will she told 3 disinterested witnesses what she had done with her property in her will, and the reason therefor. A person of sound mind has the legal right to dispose of his property as he wishes, with the burden on those attacking the disposition to prove that it was the product of undue influence.

Testatrix's will did make an unnatural disposition of her property in the sense that it preferred her 2 children over the grandchildren by a deceased son. However, the record contains an explanation from testatrix herself as to why she chose to do such. She had a right to do as she did, whether we think she was justified or not.

Plaintiffs contend that the record supports an inference that testatrix failed to receive the cards and flowers sent to her, or in the alternative that she failed to know she received same, due to conduct of defendant Lipper. Here again, defendant Lipper had the opportunity to prevent testatrix from receiving cards or flowers from the Weslows, but we think there is no evidence of probative

Food for Thought

Might the result have differed if the burden had shifted to the proponents?

force to support the conclusion that he in fact did such. Moreover, the will itself reflected that *some* cards and flowers were in fact received by the testatrix, the dispute in this particular area, going to the number of times that such were sent, rather than to the fact that any were sent.

We conclude there is no evidence of probative force to support the verdict of the jury. The cause is reversed and rendered for defendant.

TIREY, J., not participating on account of illness.

Points for Discussion

1. *The right result?*

Do the facts and the outcome of the case incline you towards burden shifting upon a showing of a confidential relationship? Were sufficient suspicious circumstances in play to satisfy the Restatement's standard? Are they any suspicious circumstances in *Moses*?

2. *Evidence*

From your reading of the evidence, had you been on the jury would you have found undue influence in *Lipper*? What evidence might have been available to the jury and not to the appeals court?

3. *Planning for a contest—I*

While Frank may not have been the most artful estate planner, he rightly sensed a contest. Were you to grade his performance on protecting the dispositions in Mom's will, what marks would he obtain? Consider the following:

Food for Thought

How would you have resolved the case in *Lipper* had you been on the court?

How persuasive was Sophie Block's statement in paragraph 9? Would it have been more effective if her sentiments were expressed in language that we are more accustomed to hearing from the mouth of an elderly grandmother? Does your grandmother refer to her son, your dad or uncle, as 'my said son?' Might one rightly conclude that if Frank wrote that passage, perhaps he wrote the dispositive provisions as well? Consider other strategies to state justification for disinheritance, a hand-written note, a video-tape, would they have been more effective, or would they also have provided the basis for a contest? Might such a strategy encourage a contest by an heir so maligned simply for the purposes of vindication of reputation?

How effective is the recital of things the Weslow children did not do? If it can be shown that Sophie believed that they had not done things they had done, might there be the basis for a contest based on insane delusion? Consider the result in *Levin v. Levin*, 60 So.3d 1116 (Fla. Ct. App. 2011) where a daughter opposed probate of mother's will, alleging lack of testamentary capacity, undue influence by her brother, and insane delusion. Proponent prevailed at trial. On appeal, the Florida intermediate appellate court affirmed the finding that testator had the required capacity and that the will was not the product of undue influence, but reversed and remanded on the issue of insane delusion. The record, including the recording of the will execution, showed that the testator stated she had not seen her daughter in many years (the exact number of years varied from statement to statement) and also showed that the daughter had visited her mother several times during those years, most recently fifteen months before execution of the will. Because the trial court never made a finding on the issue of insane delusion, the appellate court remanded for findings on this issue after a review of the record or an evidentiary hearing at the trial court's discretion.

4. Planning for a contest—II

Consider again the majority in *Moses* and their opinion about what Dan Shell should have done in counseling his client. Do you see a similarity with the requirements of the California Probate Code § 21384 discussed on page 64? Would the California statutory scheme apply to the wills of Fanny Moses or of Sophie Block? If the majority opinion in Moses states the law of Mississippi, does every lawyer who drafts a will for a Mississippi have to create the equivalent of a California "certificate of independent review"? Is that good policy?

5. No contest clauses

Another strategy Frank employed to forestall a will contest was the no-contest clause (also called *in terrorem* clauses) in paragraph 8. The clause directs that should a beneficiary under the will contest the will, that beneficiary forfeits the bequest thereunder. What loss did the Weslows incur by contesting the will Frank drafted? None. Frank did not bait the trap. Some modest bequest to the grandchildren might have made the Weslows think twice about contesting the will. Not all jurisdictions recognize no-contest clauses. Other jurisdictions follow the UPC §§ 2–517 and 3–905 and the Restatement (Third) of Property, Wills and Other Donative Transfer § 8.5, which do not enforce the clause if there is probable cause for the contestant to pursue an action to set aside the will. Contrast the UPC with New York's more nuanced and less liberal approach. Since the likely contestants of a will are the intestate heirs, do the varying approaches to no-contest in the jurisdictions suggest considerable divergence in the willingness to respect testamentary freedom against the claims of family members?

UPC § 2–517. Penalty clause for contest

A provision in a will purporting to penalize an interested person for contesting the will or instituting other proceedings relating to the estate is unenforceable if probable cause exists for instituting proceedings.

New York Estates, Powers, and Trusts Law § 3–3.5(b)

(b)　A condition, designed to prevent a disposition from taking effect in case the will is contested by the beneficiary, is operative despite the presence or absence of probable cause for such contest, subject to the following:

　(1)　Such a condition is not breached by a contest to establish that the will is a forgery or that it was revoked by a later will, provided that such contest is based on probable cause.

　(2)　An infant or incompetent may affirmatively oppose the probate of a will without forfeiting any benefit thereunder.

　(3)　The following conduct, singly or in the aggregate, shall not result in the forfeiture of any benefit under the will:

(A)   The assertion of an objection to the jurisdiction of the court in which the will was offered for probate.

(B)   The disclosure to any of the parties or to the court of any information relating to any document offered for probate as a last will, or relevant to the probate proceeding.

(C)   A refusal or failure to join in a petition for the probate of a document as a last will, or to execute a consent to, or waiver of notice of a probate proceeding.

(D)   The preliminary examination, under SCPA 1404 [which allows someone who is considering but has not yet begun a proceeding to challenge admission of a will to probate to conduct discovery], of a proponent's witnesses, the person who prepared the will, the nominated executors and the proponents in a probate proceeding and, upon application to the court based upon special circumstances, any person whose examination the court determines may provide information with respect to the validity of the will that is of substantial importance or relevance to a decision to file objections to the will.

(E)   The institution of, or the joining or acquiescence in a proceeding for the construction of a will or any provision thereof.

Practice Planning Problem

As the *Moses* case illustrates, a non-traditional relationship may also spark a contest between family members and the partner of a property-owner. It is frequently mused in the T and E professoriate that had gender roles not been reversed, that is had Fanny been Frank Moses and Clarence, Clare Holland, the court might have been less inclined to find undue influence. Do similar prejudices apply to same-sex couples?

Fraud and Duress

Fraud is a tort. Its elements as applied to the procuring of a will or a testamentary disposition are generally articulated as follows:

1.   A misrepresentation of a fact or the law;

2.   Made with intent to deceive;

3.   For the purposes of inducing a disposition;

4.   That actually deceives the testator and influences a testamentary act.

Take, for example, the following hypothetical in which fraud in the inducement may be present. Aunt Rebecca, unmarried and without children, had eight siblings, all of whom had children. Adam was the one who exhibited the most concern for her well-being and is her sole beneficiary under her will. Aunt Rebecca's health takes a turn for the worst. Nephew Lloyd comes to visit her, and when she asks him if he has seen Adam. Lloyd, who had never been fond of Adam, tells her that Adam will not be visiting for some time because he has entered a drug detox program. She tells Lloyd "In that case, I shall change my will and divide the estate amongst all my nieces and nephews." She institutes the changes the next day, and dies. In fact, Adam's employer has transferred him to San Francisco. Has Lloyd procured his proportional bequest (and/or thwarted Adam's) by fraud?

This hypothetical illustrates *fraud in the inducement* to make or change a will or some provision thereof. The first element is present, misrepresentation of a fact with the statement that Adam is in a detox program. But what about the others? Absent some justification, other than with the intent to deceive, why are false statements made? So element two can be assumed. What about the 'purpose:' can it likewise be presumed? If the speaker understands that his statement has induced a change in a testamentary plan, may we infer that his intent was to prompt such action?

In *Puckett v. Krida,* 1994 WL 475863 (Tenn. App.), the will-maker's nurses were found to have done the following:

> "Defendants, either individually or collectively, made false statements to the deceased and concealed facts from her. The deceased was led to believe that her family wasted her money. When the defendants arrived in the deceased's life, her greatest fear was going to a nursing home. The evidence shows that these defendants suddenly began to exert control over the deceased by listening in on her telephone conversations and by deluding her into believing that her family intended to place her in a nursing home. Once this fear was planted, defendants fostered and nurtured it until the deceased firmly opposed those formerly most dear to her. The deceased was told by the defendants that her niece was wasting or misappropriating funds and was reimbursing herself for airline expenses and to rent fancy cars. Defendants told the deceased that her niece was wasting money and that the deceased would be left penniless. The defendants offered no proof to refute these statements, and the trial court found that Jean Law, the deceased's niece, kept meticulous records. When the defendants accepted employment to provide around-the-clock care for the deceased, they entered into a fiduciary or confidential relationship with her, and the defendant Krida assumed additional fiduciary obligations under the unrestricted power of attorney she obtained.

> " 'Since frauds are generally secret [they] have to be tracked by the footprints, marks, and signs made by the perpetrators and discovered by the light of the attending facts and circumstances.' *Henry R. Gibson, Gibson's Suits in Chancery,* § 448 (William H. Inman, ed., 7th ed.1988)."

The court concluded that an inference of fraud was justified.

A second type of fraud is ***fraud in the execution***, where the individual who signs her will does not understand the nature or the document. So I stand outside Arthur Ashe Stadium and ask Venus Williams for an autograph. She obliges. I am careful that she signs at the bottom of the page. I then add dispositions (to me!!) and have it witnessed. Other than one based upon fraud, is there another argument that might be successfully used to deny probate?

While fraud is a tort that deceives the mind, ***duress*** generally involves physical coercion. The classic case is the saga of Mary Lyon and Father Divine.

Latham v. Father Divine

85 N.E. 2d 168 (N.Y. 1949)

DESMOND, JUDGE.

The amended complaint herein has, in response to a motion under rule 106 of the Rules of Civil Practice, been dismissed for insufficiency. Its principal allegations are these: plaintiffs are first cousins, but not distributees, of Mary Sheldon Lyon, who died in October, 1946, leaving a will, executed in 1943, which gave almost her whole estate to defendant Father Divine, leader of a religious cult, and to two corporate defendants in some way connected with that cult, and to an individual defendant (Patience Budd) said to be one of Father Divine's active followers; that said will has been, after a contest instituted by distributees, probated under a compromise agreement with the distributees, by the terms of which agreement, to which plaintiffs were not parties, the defendants just above referred to will receive a large sum from the estate; that after the making of said will, decedent on several occasions expressed 'a desire and a determination to revoke the said will, and to execute a new will by which the plaintiffs would receive a substantial portion of the estate', 'that shortly prior to the death of the deceased she had

> **Go Online**
>
> To learn more about this charismatic religious leader: http://peacemission.info/father-divine/.

certain attorneys draft a new will in which the plaintiffs were named as legatees for a very substantial amount, totaling approximately $350,000'; that 'by reason of the said false representations, the said undue influence and the said physical force' certain of the defendants 'prevented the deceased from executing the said new Will'; that, shortly before decedent's death, decedent again expressed her determination to execute the proposed new will which favored plaintiffs, and that defendants 'thereupon conspired to kill, and did kill, the deceased by means of a surgical operation performed by a doctor engaged by the defendants without the consent or knowledge of any of the relatives of the deceased.'

Nothing is better settled than that, on such a motion as this, all the averments of the attacked pleading are taken as true. For present purposes, then, we have a case where one possessed of a large property and having already made a will leaving it to certain persons, expressed an intent to make a new testament to contain legacies to other persons, attempted to carry out that intention by having a new will drawn which contained a large legacy to those others, but was, by means of misrepresentations, undue influence, force, and indeed, murder, prevented, by the beneficiaries named in the existing will, from signing the new one.

Plaintiffs say that those facts, if proven, would entitle them to a judicial declaration, which their prayer for judgment demands, that defendants, taking under the already probated will, hold what they have so taken as constructive trustees for plaintiffs, whom decedent wished to, tried to, and was kept from, benefiting.

We find in New York no decision directly answering the question as to whether or not the allegations above summarized state a case for relief in equity. But reliable texts, and cases elsewhere, see 98 A.L.R. 474 et seq., answer it in the affirmative. Leading writers, 3 Scott on Trusts, pp. 2371–2376; 3 Bogert on Trusts and Trustees, part 1, ss 473–474, 498, 499; 1. Perry on Trusts and Trustees (7th ed.), pp. 265, 371, in one form or another, state the law of the subject to be about as it is expressed in comment *i* under section 184 of the Restatement of the Law of Restitution:

> **What's That?**
>
> A constructive trust is an equitable remedy to avoid Father Divine's unjust enrichment if he were to take the bequest under the will absolutely.

"Preventing revocation of will and making new will. Where a devisee or legatee under a will already executed prevents the testator by fraud, duress or undue influence from revoking the will and executing a new will in favor of another or from making a codicil, so that the testator dies leaving the original will in force, the devisee or legatee holds the property thus acquired upon a constructive trust for the intended devisee or legatee."

A frequently-cited case is Ransdel v. Moore, 153 Ind. 393, at pages 407–408, 53 N.E. 767, at page 771, 53 L.R.A. 753, where, with listing of many authorities, the rule is given thus: 'when an heir or devisee in a will prevents the testator from providing for one for whom he would have provided but for the interference of the heir or devisee, such heir or devisee will be deemed a trustee, by operation of law, of the property, real or personal, received by him from the testator's estate, to the amount or extent that the defrauded party would have received had not the intention of the deceased been interfered with.

This rule applies also when an heir prevents the making of a will or deed in favor of another, and thereby inherits the property that would otherwise have been given such other person.' To the same effect, see 4 Page on Wills (3d ed.), p. 961.

> **Food for Thought**
>
> Why is a constructive trust "necessary" in this case? Why not let the property pass to the testatrix's heirs by intestate succession?

While there is no New York case decreeing a constructive trust on the exact facts alleged here, there are several decisions in this court which, we think, suggest such a result and none which forbids it. Matter of O'Hara's Will, 95 N.Y. 403, 47 Am. Rep. 53; Trustees of Amherst College v. Ritch,

151 N.Y. 282, 45N.E. 876, 37 L.R.A. 305; Edson v. Bartow, 154 N.Y. 199, 48 N.E. 541, and Ahrens v. Jones, 169 N.Y. 555, 62 N.E. 666, 88 Am. St. Rep. 620, which need not be closely analyzed here as to their facts, all announce, in one form or another, the rule that, where a legatee has taken property under a will, after agreeing outside the will, to devote that property to a purpose intended and declared by the testator, equity will enforce a constructive trust to effectuate that purpose, lest there be a fraud on the testator. In Williams v. Fitch, 18 N.Y. 546, a similar result was achieved in a suit for money had and received.

In each of those four cases first above cited in this paragraph, the particular fraud consisted of the legatees' failure or refusal to carry out the testator's designs, after tacitly or expressly promising so to do. But we do not think that a breach of such an engagement is the only kind of fraud which will impel equity to action. A constructive trust will be erected whenever necessary to satisfy the demands of justice. Since a constructive trust is merely 'the formula through which the conscience of equity finds expression'. . . its applicability is limited only by the inventiveness of men who find new ways to enrich themselves unjustly by grasping what should not belong to them.

Nothing short of true and complete justice satisfies equity, and, always assuming these allegations to be true, there seems no way of achieving total justice except by the procedure used here.

The Appellate Division held that Hutchins v. Hutchins, 7 Hill 104, distinguished, decided by the Supreme Court, our predecessor, in 1845, was a bar to the maintenance of this suit. Hutchins v. Hutchins, supra, was a suit at law, dismissed for insufficiency in the days when law suits and equity causes had to be brought in different tribunals; the law court could give nothing but a judgment for damages, see discussion in 41 Harv. L. Rev., 313, supra. Testator Hutchins' son, named in an earlier will, charged that defendant had, by fraud, caused his father to revoke that will and execute a new one, disinheriting plaintiff. The court sustained a demurrer to the complaint, on the ground that the earlier will gave the son no title, interest or estate in his father's assets and no more than a hope or expectancy, the loss of which was too theoretical and tenuous a deprivation to serve as a basis for the award of damages. See, also, Simar v. Canaday, 53 N.Y. 298, 302, 303, 13 Am. Rep. 523. Plaintiffs' disappointed hopes in the present case, held the Appellate Division, were similarly lacking in substance. But disappointed hopes and unrealized expectations were all that the secretly intended beneficiaries, not named in the wills, had in Matter of O'Hara's Will, supra; Trustees of Amherst College v. Ritch, supra and Edson v. Bartow, supra, but that in itself was not enough to prevent the creation of constructive trusts in their favor. Hutchins v. Hutchins, supra, it seems, holds only this: that in a suit at law there must, as a basis for damages, be an invasion of a common-law right. To use that same standard in a suit for the declaration and enforcement of a constructive trust would be to deny and destroy the whole equitable theory of constructive trusts.

Food for Thought

Is the policy of the Statute of Frauds/Wills eviscerated if the property can ultimately pass to the plaintiffs by oral testimony of the decedent's testamentary desires?

Nor do we agree that anything in the Decedent Estate Law, Consol. Laws, c. 13, s 1 et seq., or the

Statute of Frauds stands in the way of recovery herein. This is not a proceeding to probate or establish the will which plaintiffs say testatrix was prevented from signing, nor is it an attempt to accomplish a revocation of the earlier will as were Matter of Evans' Will, 113 App.Div. 373, 98 N.Y.S. 1042 and Matter of McGill's Will, 229 N.Y. 405, 411, 128 N.E. 194, 195, 196. The will Mary Sheldon Lyon did sign has been probated and plaintiffs are not contesting, but proceeding on, that probate, trying to reach property which has effectively passed thereunder. See Ahrens v. Jones, 169 N.Y. 555, 561, 62 N.E. 666, 667, 668, 88 Am. St. Rep. 620, supra. Nor is this a suit to enforce an agreement to make a will or create a trust or any other promise by decedent, . . . This complaint does not say that decedent or defendants, promised plaintiffs anything or that defendants made any promise to decedent. The story is, simply, that defendants by force and fraud, kept the testatrix from making a will in favor of plaintiffs. We cannot say, as matter of law, that no constructive trust can arise therefrom.

The ultimate determinations in Matter of O'Hara's Will, supra and Edson v. Bartow, supra, that the estates went to testators' distributees do not help defendants here, since, after the theory of constructive trust had been indorsed by this court in those cases, the distributees won out in the end, but only because the secret trusts intended by the two testators were, in each case, of kinds forbidden by statutes.

We do not agree with appellants that Riggs v. Palmer, 115 N.Y. 506, 22 N.E. 188, 5 L.R.A. 340, 12 Am .St. Rep. 819, completely controls our decision here. That was the famous case where a grandson, overeager to get the remainder interest set up for him in his grandfather's will, murdered his grandsire. After the will had been probated, two daughters of the testator who, under the will, would take if the grandson should predecease testator, sued and got judgment decreeing a constructive trust in their favor. It may be, as respondents assert, that the application of Riggs v. Palmer, supra, here would benefit not plaintiffs, but this testator's distributees. We need not pass on that now. But Riggs v. Palmer, supra, is generally helpful to appellant, since it forbade the grandson profiting by his own wrong in connection with a will; and, despite an already probated will and the Decedent Estate Law, Riggs v. Palmer, supra, used the device or formula of constructive trust to right the attempted wrong, and prevent unjust enrichment.

* * * *

The judgment of the Appellate Division, insofar as it dismissed the complaint herein, should be reversed, and the order of Special Term affirmed, with costs in this court and in the Appellate Division.

LOUGHRAN, C.J., and CONWAY and FULD, JJ., concur with DESMOND, J.

LEWIS and DYE, JJ., dissent and vote for affirmance upon the grounds stated by VAUGHAN, J., writing for the Appellate Division.

Point for Discussion

1. Constructive trusts

Up to this point we have not discussed trusts in detail. What is the legal nature of the constructive trust? Trusts are created to further estate planning goals, facilitating the process of property transmission, and in particular, intergenerational transfer. The constructive trust, on the other hand, is an equitable remedy. It allows a court of equity to consider done, as the equitable maxim notes, what ought to be done. The use and enjoyment of Mary Lyon's property (if the plaintiffs' contentions can be proved) ought to pass to them rather than to Father Divine. But the will leaving property to Father Divine is a valid will. How can a court of conscience reconcile the competing interests? The oft quoted words of Judge Cardozo assist:

> "constructive trust is the formula through which the conscience of equity finds expression. When property has been acquired in such circumstances that the holder of the legal title may not in good conscience retain the beneficial interest, equity converts him into a trustee." *Beatty v. Guggenheim Exploration Co.*, 122 N.E. 378, 380 (N.Y. 1919).

The constructive trust as an equitable remedy will appear at several other junctures in this book.

Test Your Knowledge

To assess your understanding of the material in this chapter, click here to take a quiz.

CHAPTER 4

Wills: Doctrines Dealing with the Document

87-113

A. Formalities of Execution: Signature and Witnessing

A page of history . . .

The history of will-making extends about as far back in time as do written records addressing property-ownership. The Romans had wills, as did the Germanic tribes who replaced them over much of continental Europe in the course of the six centuries after the fall of Rome. In Anglo-Saxon England, both oral and written wills were made, the former were often reduced to writing.

The process of property transmission through testation has always contained an element of trust. After all, wills take effect at death: after the property owner was able to attend to the mechanics of transfer personally. Clerics, often present at the death bed, became involved in will-making and the enforcement of bequests because they were regarded (perhaps) as more trustworthy than the laity. Another justification for clerical intervention was because wills often contained bequests for the now-departed individual's soul. Thus the clergy had an interest in making sure that the provisions were observed.

Over the nine centuries after the Norman Conquest (1066 and all that), the process of will-making slowly became secularized. The arduous journey need not trouble the post-modern American law student, because American probate law and process was secularized by the time of the revolution. Probate remained in church courts in England until the middle of the nineteenth century, and vestiges of its vocabulary and processes remain. For example, the particular title for a probate court judge in New York, the surrogate, is derived from ecclesiastical law where a lay person probated wills as a representative or 'surrogate' of the bishop who had jurisdiction to prove wills and administer estates in his name. But more than nomenclature survived. Much of the modern substantive law of wills, for example, the standards for mental capacity and undue influence, were forged in the church courts.

The secularization of society eventually led to legislative mandates that established requirements of due execution of wills: first in the Statute of Frauds (1677) for bequests of land; and then in the Statute of Wills (1837) where the rules of due execution for both personal property and wills were unified. Many American states cast their own statutes of due execution of wills with identical or striking similar requirements. These formalities were not fashioned in a jurisprudential vacuum. The rules were thought to protect the process of property transmission by will.

This historical introduction is calculated to remind the modern American law student that the contemporary will is the creation of the legislature, and the substantive law of wills is controlled in part by statute and therefore can vary by jurisdiction. That said, the specifics are variations on a theme. There is also more in common among the statutes.

For More Information

Generations of law students have been directed to the lucid exposition describing the ritual, evidentiary and protective functions that the formalities of will-making perform by Ashbel G. Gulliver and Catherine J. Tilson, *Classification of Gratuitous Transfers,* 51 Yale L. J. 1–10 (1941).

It should not surprise you that will formalities which have been adopted have been treated with great reverence over the centuries. Because the will has legal validity due to "positive law," that is, statutes, precise adherence to the statutes' dictates has long been required. The advantage of such strict adherence to the formalities is that a bright line is created. Most of the time a document either is a will or it is not; there is far less room for argument, and therefore (at least presumably) far less need for litigation. Another way to look at this approach to will-making is that strict adherence to the formalities of due execution actually makes dispositions easier and more secure for testators. If they comply with the formalities they *know* that the documents they intend to be wills will be given legal effect as wills. If the document was not created with requisite formality, it is likely the now-deceased did not regard the document as a will. Thus, adherence to the formalities of due execution allow the property owner can rest easy, with the knowledge that the document which does not comply with the formalities cannot be regarded as a will, and will not govern the process of property transmission of his or her estate. (Of course, a document may not be admissible to probate for other reasons, as we will see.)

Creating a bright line rule can also benefit society. Commentators have long argued that the need to proceed in a formal, precise, ritualistic way impresses on testators the importance of what

Go Online

A straightforward means of accessing the law governing property transmission in your jurisdiction is through the Cornell Legal Information Institute https://www.law.cornell.edu/wex/table_probate.

they are doing. Because the formalities of creating a valid will are relatively demanding, it can be argued that testators are thus led to think carefully about what they are doing and are discouraged from acting in an off-hand or thoughtless manner in configuring their estate plan. Society benefits because property is distributed after the owner's death in a considered way. Exactly how society benefits, however, is not so easy to articulate, beyond the bland statement that considered actions are better than those undertaken in haste. The disadvantages of close attention to the formalities are equally well known. Most of those disadvantages can be summed up in the simple statement that demanding undeviating fulfillment of formalities frustrates intent. Just as the process of property transmission can be furthered by formality, it can also be thwarted by rigid adherence to complex rules.

1. Formalities and Realities

The application of the formalities of the statute of due execution of wills can in some cases lead to what some might regard as unsatisfactory results. Consider this case:

Stevens v. Casdorph

508 S.E.2d 610 (W. Va. 1998)

PER CURIAM:

The plaintiffs below and appellants herein Janet Sue Lanham Stevens, Peggy Lanham Salisbury, Betty Jean Bayes, and Patricia Miller Moyers (hereinafter collectively referred to as the "Stevenses") appeal a summary judgment ruling for the defendants by the Circuit Court of Kanawha County. The Stevenses instituted this action against Patricia Eileen Casdorph and Paul Douglas Casdorph, individually and as executor of the estate of Homer Haskell Miller, defendants below and appellees herein (hereinafter referred to as "Casdorphs"), for the purpose of challenging the will of Homer Haskell Miller. The circuit court granted the Casdorphs' cross-motion for summary judgment. On appeal, this Court is asked to reverse the trial court's ruling. Following a review of the parties' arguments, the record, and the pertinent authorities, we reverse the decision of the Circuit Court of Kanawha County.

Who are the plaintiffs and how did this dispute over a will come to be decided by the West Virginia Supreme Court? Most will contests are commenced by an heir who would take a larger share of the deceased's estate through intestate succession than if the will was given effect. The process differs by jurisdictions, but works like this: executors offer the will for probate; plaintiffs, as heirs, were served notice of the probate; unhappy with the deceased's treatment, they filed an action to set aside the will, litigation in which they prevailed; executors appealed. We find ourselves in the highest court in the jurisdiction where compliance with the statutory mandate will finally be considered.

I. FACTUAL BACKGROUND

On May 28, 1996, the Casdorphs took Mr. Homer Haskell Miller to Shawnee Bank in Dunbar, West Virginia, so that he could execute his will.[1] Once at the bank, Mr. Miller asked Debra Pauley, a bank employee and public notary, to witness the execution of his will. After Mr. Miller signed the will, Ms. Pauley took the will to two other bank employees, Judith Waldron and Reba McGinn, for the purpose of having each of them sign the will as witnesses. Both Ms. Waldron and Ms. McGinn signed the will. However, Ms. Waldron and Ms. McGinn testified during their depositions that they did not actually see Mr. Miller place his signature on the will. Further, it is undisputed that Mr. Miller did not accompany Ms. Pauley to the separate work areas of Ms. Waldron and Ms. McGinn.

Mr. Miller died on July 28, 1996. The last will and testament of Mr. Miller, which named Mr. Paul Casdorph[2] as executor, left the bulk of his estate to the Casdorphs.[3] The Stevenses, nieces of Mr. Miller, filed the instant action to set aside the will. The Stevenses asserted in their complaint that Mr. Miller's will was not executed according to the requirements set forth in W.Va.Code § 41–1–3 (1995).[4] After some discovery, all parties moved for summary judgment. The circuit court denied the Stevenses' motion for summary judgment, but granted the Casdorphs' cross motion for summary judgment. From this ruling, the Stevenses appeal to this Court.

II. STANDARD OF REVIEW

This Court has held that "[a] circuit court's entry of summary judgment is reviewed de novo." Syl. pt. 1, *Painter v. Peavy*, 451 S.E.2d 755 (W. Va. 1994). In syllabus point 5 of *Wilkinson v. Searls*, 155 W.Va. 475, 184 S.E.2d 735 (1971), we indicated that "[a] motion for a summary judgment should be granted if the pleadings, exhibits and discovery depositions upon which the motion is submitted for decision disclose that the case involves no genuine issue as to any material fact and that the party who made the motion is entitled to a judgment as a matter of law." ....

Make the Connection

Though probate procedure in some jurisdictions is governed by a separate set of procedural rules, others follow the same procedure and utilize terms similar to those that you learned in your course in Civ. Pro.

III. DISCUSSION

The Stevenses' contention is simple. They argue that all evidence indicates that Mr. Miller's will was not properly executed. Therefore, the will

---

1 Mr. Miller was elderly and confined to a wheelchair.

2 Paul Casdorph was a nephew of Mr. Miller.

3 Mr. Miller's probated estate exceeded $400,000.00. The will devised $80,000.00 to Frank Paul Smith, a nephew of Mr. Miller. The remainder of the estate was left to the Casdorphs.

4 As heirs, the Stevenses would be entitled to recover from Mr. Miller's estate under the intestate laws if his will is set aside as invalidly executed.

should be voided. The procedural requirements at issue are contained in W.Va.Code § 41–1–3 (1997). The statute reads:

No will shall be valid unless it be in writing and signed by the testator, or by some other person in his presence and by his direction, in such manner as to make it manifest that the name is intended as a signature; and moreover, unless it be wholly in the handwriting of the testator, *the signature shall be made or the will acknowledged by him in the presence of at least two competent witnesses, present at the same time; and such witnesses shall subscribe the will in the presence of the testator, and of each other,* but no form of attestation shall be necessary. (Emphasis added.)

Go Online

Find the statute that governs the execution of wills in your jurisdiction and learn its requirements.

The relevant requirements of the above statute calls for a testator to sign his/her will or acknowledge such will in the presence of at least two witnesses at the same time, and such witnesses must sign the will in the presence of the testator and each other. In the instant proceeding the Stevenses assert, and the evidence supports, that Ms. McGinn and Ms. Waldron did not actually witness Mr. Miller signing his will. Mr. Miller made no acknowledgment of his signature on the will to either Ms. McGinn or Ms. Waldron. Likewise, Mr. Miller did not

Take Note

What does the requirement of being in the "presence" of the testator mean? Is it related to physical proximity; must the testator and the witnesses be within a certain finite distance? Or perhaps it means conscious presence: that each of the parties observed and understood the significance of the acts the others were undertaking? Exactly what are the witnesses witnessing?

observe Ms. McGinn and Ms. Waldron sign his will as witnesses. Additionally, neither Ms. McGinn nor Ms. Waldron acknowledged to Mr. Miller that their signatures were on the will. It is also undisputed that Ms. McGinn and Ms. Waldron did not actually witness each other sign the will, nor did they acknowledge to each other that they had signed Mr. Miller's will. Despite the evidentiary lack of compliance with W.Va.Code § 41–1–3, the Casdorphs argue that there was substantial compliance with the statute's requirements, insofar as everyone involved with the will knew what was occurring. The trial court found

that there was substantial compliance with the statute because everyone knew why Mr. Miller was at the bank. The trial court further concluded there was no evidence of fraud, coercion or undue influence. Based upon the foregoing, the trial court concluded that the will should not be voided even though the technical aspects of W.Va.Code § 41–1–3 were not followed.

Our analysis begins by noting that "[t]he law favors testacy over intestacy." Syl. pt. 8, *In re Teubert's Estate,* 171 W.Va. 226, 298 S.E.2d 456 (1982).

Food for Thought

Courts repeat over and over again the principle that testacy is favored over intestacy. Any idea why?

However, we clearly held in syllabus point 1 of *Black v. Maxwell*, 131 W.Va. 247, 46 S.E.2d 804 (1948), that "[t]estamentary intent and a written instrument, executed in the manner provided by [W.Va.Code § 41–1–3], existing concurrently, are essential to the creation of a valid will." *Black* establishes that mere intent by a testator to execute a written will is insufficient. The actual execution of a written will must also comply with the dictates of W.Va.Code § 41–1–3. The Casdorphs seek to have this Court establish an exception to the technical requirements of the statute. In *Wade v. Wade*, 119 W.Va. 596, 195 S.E. 339 (1938), this Court permitted a narrow exception to the stringent requirements of the W.Va.Code § 41–1–3. This narrow exception is embodied in syllabus point 1 of *Wade*:

> Where a testator acknowledges a will and his signature thereto in the presence of two competent witnesses, one of whom then subscribes his name, the other or first witness, having already subscribed the will in the presence of the testator but out of the presence of the second witness, may acknowledge his signature in the presence of the testator and the second witness, and such acknowledgment, if there be no indicia of fraud or misunderstanding in the proceeding, will be deemed a signing by the first witness within the requirement of Code, 41–1–3, that the witnesses must subscribe their names in the presence of the testator and of each other.

See Brammer v. Taylor, 175 W.Va. 728, 730 n. 1, 338 S.E.2d 207, 215 n. 1 (1985), ("[T]he witnesses' acknowledgment of their signatures . . . in the presence of the testator [and in the presence of each other] is tantamount to and will be deemed a 'signing' or 'subscribing' in the presence of those persons").

Practice Pointer

If you had drafted Mr. Miller's will, how would you have handled its due execution?

Wade stands for the proposition that if a witness acknowledges his/her signature on a will in the physical presence of the other subscribing witness *and the testator*, then the will is properly witnessed within the terms of W.Va.Code § 41–1–3. In this case, none of the parties signed or acknowledged their signatures in the presence of each other. This case meets neither the narrow exception of *Wade* nor the specific provisions of W.Va. Code § 41–1–3.

IV. CONCLUSION

In view of the foregoing, we grant the relief sought in this appeal and reverse the circuit court's order granting the Casdorphs' cross-motion for summary judgment. Reversed.

Workman, Justice, dissenting:

The majority once more takes a very technocratic approach to the law, slavishly worshiping form over substance. In so doing, they not only create a harsh and inequitable result wholly contrary to the indisputable intent of Mr. Homer Haskell Miller, but also a rule of law that is against the spirit and intent of our whole body of law relating to the making of wills.

There is absolutely no claim of incapacity or fraud or undue influence, nor any allegation by any party that Mr. Miller did not consciously, intentionally, and with full legal capacity convey his property as specified in his will. The challenge to the will is based solely upon the allegation that Mr. Miller did not comply with the requirement of West Virginia Code 41–1–3 that the signature shall be made or the will acknowledged by the testator in the presence of at least two competent witnesses, present at the same time. The lower court, in its very thorough findings of fact, indicated that Mr. Miller had been transported to the bank by his nephew Mr. Casdorph and the nephew's wife. Mr. Miller, disabled and confined to a wheelchair, was a shareholder in the Shawnee Bank in Dunbar, West Virginia, with whom all those present were personally familiar. When Mr. Miller executed his will in the bank lobby, the typed will was placed on Ms. Pauley's desk, and Mr. Miller instructed Ms. Pauley that he wished to have his will signed, witnessed, and acknowledged. After Mr. Miller's signature had been placed upon the will with Ms. Pauley watching, Ms. Pauley walked the will over to the tellers' area in the same small lobby of the bank. Ms. Pauley explained that Mr. Miller wanted Ms. Waldron to sign the will as a witness. The same process was used to obtain the signature of Ms. McGinn. Sitting in his wheelchair, Mr. Miller did not move from Ms. Pauley's desk during the process of obtaining the witness signatures. The lower court concluded that the will was valid and that Ms. Waldron and Ms. McGinn signed and acknowledged the will "in the presence" of Mr. Miller.

In *Wade v. Wade,* 119 W.Va. 596, 195 S.E. 339 (1938), we addressed the validity of a will challenged for such technicalities[4] and observed that "a narrow, rigid construction of the statute should not be allowed to stand in the way of right and justice, or be permitted to defeat a testator's disposition of his property." 119 W.Va. at 599, 195 S.E. at 340–341. We upheld the validity of the challenged will in *Wade,* noting that "each case must rest on its own facts and circumstances to which the court must look to determine whether there was a subscribing by the witnesses in the presence of the testator; that substantial compliance with the statute is all that is required. . . ." *Id.* at 599, 195 S.E. at 340. A contrary result, we emphasized, "would be based on illiberal and inflexible construction of the statute, giving preeminence to letter and not to spirit, and resulting in the thwarting of the intentions of testators even under circumstances where no possibility of fraud or impropriety exists." *Id.* at 600, 195 S.E. at 341.

The majority's conclusion is precisely what was envisioned and forewarned in 1938 by the drafters of the *Wade* opinion: illiberal and inflexible construction, giving preeminence to the

---

4   We concluded as follows in syllabus point one of *Wade*:

Where a testator acknowledges a will and his signature thereto in the presence of two competent witnesses, one of whom then subscribes his name, the other or first witness, having already subscribed the will in the presence of the testator but out of the presence of the second witness, may acknowledge his signature in the presence of the testator and the second witness, and such acknowledgment, if there be no indicia of fraud or misunderstanding in the proceeding, will be deemed a signing by the first witness within the requirement of Code, 41–1–3, that the witnesses must subscribe their names in the presence of the testator and of each other.

letter of the law and ignoring the spirit of the entire body of testamentary law, resulting in the thwarting of Mr. Miller's unequivocal wishes. In *In re Estate of Staff,* 125 Or. 288, 266 P. 630 (1928), the court encountered an argument that the attesting witness had not signed the will in the presence of the testator. The evidence demonstrated that the witnesses had signed the document at the request of the testator, and the court reasoned:

> While it is the duty of the court[s] to observe carefully the spirit and intent of the statute, they will not adopt a strained and technical construction to defeat a will where the capacity and intention is plain and where by fair and reasonable intendment the statute may be held to have been complied with, and such is the case here.

Id. at 298, 266 P. 630.

We also specified, in syllabus point two of *Wade,* that "[w]hether witnesses to a will have subscribed the same in the presence of the testator and of each other, as required by statute, is a question of fact to be determined in each case from the circumstances thereof." Summary judgment is inappropriate where there is a dispute regarding the conclusions to be drawn from evidentiary facts. *Williams v. Precision Coil, Inc.,* 194 W.Va. 52, 59, 459 S.E.2d 329,336. Thus, the majority could have legitimately concluded that summary judgment was inappropriate and that the issue of compliance with the statute was a question of fact to be determined by the jury. I could have accepted such reasoning far more readily than that employed by the majority in its swift eradication of Mr. Miller's legal right to convey his estate in the manner of his own conscious choosing.

The majority strains the logical definition of "in the presence" as used in the operative statute. The legal concept of "presence" in this context encompasses far more than simply watching the signing of the will, which is the technical, narrow interpretation of the word apparently relied upon by the majority. Where the attestation of the will by the witnesses occurred within the same room as the testator, there is, at the very minimum, prima facie evidence that the attestation occurred within the "presence" of the testator.

In re Demaris' Estate, 166 Or. 36, 110 P.2d 571 (1941), involved a challenge to a will signed by a very ill gentleman, witnessed in another room by a physician and his wife thirty minutes after the testator signed the will. The court grappled with the question of whether the witnesses had complied with the statutory requirement that the witnesses sign in the presence of the testator. *Id.* at 39–40, 110 P.2d at 572. The court rejected a strict interpretation of the language of the statute, recognizing that the purpose of requiring the presence of the witnesses was to protect a testator against substitution and fraud. *Id.* at 62, 110 P.2d at 581. Rather, the court determined that "presence" did not demand that the witnesses sign within the sight of the testator, if other senses would enable the testator to know that the witnesses were near and to understand what the witnesses were doing. *Id.* The court concluded that "the circumstances repel any thought of fraud and speak cogently of the integrity of the instrument under review. The signatures of all three persons are conceded. The circumstances of the attestation are free from dispute." 166 Or. at 74, 110 P.2d at 586.

To hold the will invalid on a strictly technical flaw would "be to observe the letter of the statute as interpreted strictly, and fail to give heed to the statute's obvious purpose. Thus, the statute would be turned against those for whose protection it had been written." 166 Or. at 76, 110 P.2d at 586.

The majority embraces the line of least resistance. The easy, most convenient answer is to say that the formal, technical requirements have not been met and that the will is therefore invalid. End of inquiry. Yet that result is patently absurd. That manner of statutory application is inconsistent with the underlying purposes of the statute. Where a statute is enacted to protect and sanctify the execution of a will to prevent substitution or fraud, this Court's application of that statute should further such underlying policy, not impede it. When, in our efforts to strictly apply legislative language, we abandon common sense and reason in favor of technicalities, we are the ones committing the injustice.

I am authorized to state that JUSTICE MAYNARD joins in this dissent.

Points for Discussion

1. Formality and intent

The majority and the dissent differ most strikingly in their approach to the need for adherence to formality. Mr. Miller's estate plan seems to play second fiddle. If the question was not did the will execution comply with the statute but rather is there any doubt that Mr. Miller intended the document offer for probate to be his would the majority have admitted the will to probate?

Considering that the purpose of the witnessing requirement is to satisfy the ritual (understands that he is undertaking a legal act), evidentiary (that document offered for probate is the one Miller executed) and protective (that Miller was acting of his own volition), functions which is the appropriate question to control the outcome? What purpose is served by refusing to probate the will? Is it simply enough to say the law is the law?

2. What went wrong?

With what formality did Mr. Miller's will actually fail to comply? If the purpose of the rules is to produce a will that manifests the testamentary intent of Mr. Miller, how significant was the lapse in form? Tragic?

3. What does presence mean?

Mr. Miller may not have been in the presence of the witnesses to his will at the time they signed the document? The word "presence" alone typically is interpreted to mean in the line of sight—that the observer could see the specified act if she chose to look. Can a will be witnessed over the phone? Consider the following scenario: client consults with lawyer; lawyer brings the document to client's house where client signs the will, and the lawyer witnesses it immediately thereafter; lawyer brings the will back to his office, places the will on his secretary's desk, with both the client's and lawyer's signature visible; secretary calls client, and client asks secretary to witness the will; secretary does so. Is the execution valid under a statute like the West Virginia statute in *Stevens*? Or the following: client is ill in bed; partner and associate bring the will to the client who signs it; partner and associate move to a desk in the same room where they sign as witnesses; at the time client is in bed looking at the ceiling. Valid execution? Would it matter is the desk was in another room? *Estate of Fisher*, 886 A. 2d 996 (N. H. 2005). The presence requirement has long been controversial. When the Wills Act (1837) was adopted, much consideration was given to the issue in Parliamentary debates, partly because the Statute of Frauds took a different approach to presence.

4. What is a signature?

In *Stevens* there is no question that Miller signed the will. Suppose he was too infirmed to do so, and could only make an X. Would that mark meet the signature requirement? Note also that in most jurisdictions the testator can request another to sign to validate the document. Why must an individual sign a will? Does it have something to do with authentication? Finality of intention?

5. State variations

Whether a will is validly executed depends upon the particular requirements for due execution in individual states. Many states are modeled on the English Wills Act of 1837, excerpted below. Some have been amended to be more lenient like the UPC, also below. How would the *Stevens* case be resolved under either of these statutes? Note the more exacting requirements for due execution of wills in New York, which seems to go beyond the West Virginia statute in crafting formalities.

English Wills Act of 1837

[N]o will shall be valid unless it shall be in writing and executed in manner hereinafter mentioned; . . . it shall be signed at the foot or end thereof by the testator, or by some other person in his presence and by his direction; and such signature shall be made or acknowledged by the testator in the presence of two or more witnesses present at the same time, and such witnesses shall attest and shall subscribe the will in the presence of the testator, but no form of attestation shall be necessary.

UPC § 2–502

    (a)   Except as provided in subsection (b) and in Sections 2–503, 2–506, and 2–513, a will must be:

        (1)   in writing;

        (2)   signed by the testator or in the testator's name by some other individual in the testator's conscious presence and by the testator's direction; and

(3) either:

    (A) signed by at least two individuals, each of whom signed within a reasonable time after he [or she] witnessed either the signing of the will as described in paragraph (2) or the testator's acknowledgment of that signature or acknowledgment of the will; or.

    (B) acknowledged by the testator before a notary public or other individual authorized by law to take acknowledgments.

(b) A will that does not comply with subsection (a) is valid as a holographic will, whether or not witnessed, if the signature and material portions of the document are in the testator's handwriting.

(c) Intent that the document constitute the testator's will can be established by extrinsic evidence, including, for holographic wills, portions of the document that are not in the testator's handwriting.

Note the additional requirements under New York law. Any idea why? How would Stevens be decided under New York law, and the law of your jurisdiction.

New York Estates, Powers, and Trusts Law § 3–2.1. Execution and Attestation of Wills; Formal Requirements

(a) Except for nuncupative and holographic wills authorized by 3–2.2, every will must be in writing, and executed and attested in the following manner:

    (1) It shall be signed at the end thereof by the testator or, in the name of the testator, by another person in his presence and by his direction, subject to the following:

        (A) The presence of any matter following the testator's signature, appearing on the will at the time of its execution, shall not invalidate such matter preceding the signature as appeared on the will at the time of its execution, except that such matter preceding the signature shall not be given effect, in the discretion of the surrogate, if it is so incomplete as not to be readily comprehensible without the aid of matter which follows the signature, or if to give effect to such matter preceding the signature would subvert the testator's general plan for the disposition and administration of his estate.

        (B) No effect shall be given to any matter, other than the attestation clause, which follows the signature of the testator, or to any matter preceding such signature which was added subsequently to the execution of the will.

        (C) Any person who signs the testator's name to the will, as provided in subparagraph (1), shall sign his own name and affix his residence address to the will but shall not be counted as one of the necessary attesting witnesses to the will. A will lacking the signature of the person signing the testator's name shall not be given effect; provided, however, the failure of the person signing the testator's name to affix his address shall not affect the validity of the will.

(2)   The signature of the testator shall be affixed to the will in the presence of each of the attesting witnesses, or shall be acknowledged by the testator to each of them to have been affixed by him or by his direction. The testator may either sign in the presence of, or acknowledge his signature to each attesting witness separately.

(3)   The testator shall, at some time during the ceremony or ceremonies of execution and attestation, declare to each of the attesting witnesses that the instrument to which his signature has been affixed is his will.

(4)   There shall be at least two attesting witnesses, who shall, within one thirty-day period, both attest the testator's signature, as affixed or acknowledged in their presence, and at the request of the testator, sign their names and affix their residence addresses at the end of the will. There shall be a rebuttable presumption that the thirty-day requirement of the preceding sentence has been fulfilled. The failure of a witness to affix his address shall not affect the validity of the will.

(b)   The procedure for the execution and attestation of wills need not be followed in the precise order set forth in paragraph (a) so long as all the requisite formalities are observed during a period of time in which, satisfactorily to the surrogate, the ceremony or ceremonies of execution and attestation continue.

What result would transpire in *Stevens* under each of the above statutes?

Mr. Miller's will was certainly executed with significant (if insufficient) formality. The same cannot be said in the *Slack* case. Read the case carefully. What does it tell you about adherence to formality. And what differing views do the majority and minority hold in defining legal words of art like "attest" and "presence"?

Slack v. Truitt

791 A.2d 129 (Md. 2002)

Argued before BELL, C.J., and ELDRIDGE, RAKER, WILNER, CATHELL, HARRELL, and BATTAGLIA, JJ.

RAKER, J.

This is an appeal concerning the probate of a purported will. The question we must decide is whether a will signed by the testator outside the presence of witnesses should have been admitted to probate despite the fact that one of the witnesses did not know it was a will and cannot recall seeing the testator's signature on the instrument. The Orphans' Court and the Circuit Court for Cecil County denied the admission of the will to probate. Both courts denied probate because the testator, Dale Slack, failed to acknowledge to the witnesses that the will was his own instrument. The Court of Special Appeals reversed. 768 A.2d 715 (Md. 2001). We shall affirm the Court of Special Appeals.

On July 5, 1999, Dale Slack, testator, went to the house of his neighbor, Dorothy Morgan, and asked her to sign a one-page handwritten document. On the bottom left hand side of the page, following the words "Witnessed By," Slack had reserved a space for witnesses' signatures. Slack did not tell Morgan that the document was a will, nor did he draw her attention to his signature. Morgan testified that the neighborhood had been having problems with development, and she thought Slack was asking her to sign a petition. Morgan also testified that she could not recall whether Slack had signed the document prior to asking her to sign it. When asked whether she saw Slack's signature, Morgan stated, "I didn't notice. I didn't even look that long." She explained: "I don't recall seeing it. Like I said, I didn't look at the paper that well. I just signed my name. That was it."

Approximately five minutes after Ms. Morgan signed the will, Slack returned to Morgan's house and asked Morgan's daughter, Sandra Bradley, to sign it. As before, Slack did not disclose that the document was his will and did not draw Ms. Bradley's attention to his signature. Nonetheless, Bradley, unlike her mother, was able to remember that Slack had signed the document before she affixed her signature.

> **Food for Thought**
>
> Assume *arguendo* that the will was signed by the testator and the witnesses, were the functions of those formalities satisfied?

Approximately two hours after seeking Morgan and Bradley's signatures, Slack committed suicide. In the will signed by Morgan and Bradley, Slack had written, *inter alia:*

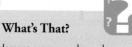

Food for Thought

Wills that appear regularly executed (signed and witnessed) are presumed valid. Why is that?

"To Michael Truitt who is the closest I've ever had to a son I leave all my fishing & camping gear and one third of all monetary holdings.

* * *

Terri Truitt is to receive *all* my rings & other jewelry. She will finally [sic] get the rings if she wants them or not. * * *

This Court granted Clinton Slack's petition for writ of certiorari, *Slack v. Truitt,* 364 Md. 534, 774 A.2d 408 (2001), to answer the following questions:

1. In a case in which a will is signed outside of the presence of the witnesses, must the testator either declare the document to be his will, or acknowledge his signature, to obtain a valid attestation pursuant to Estates & Trusts Article, § 4–102?

2. Whether a valid attestation requires that a witness sign a document as a witness?

What's That?

Acknowledgment means that the person making the will, the testator, makes the witnesses understand that the signature on the will is indeed the testator's. Some definitions of acknowledgment of the signature on the will require the witnesses to see the actual signature.

Maryland Code (1957, 2001 Rep. Vol., 2001 Supp.) § 4–102 of the Estates and Trusts Article addresses the statutory requirements relating to the execution of wills in Maryland. The statute states, in pertinent part, as follows:

"Except as provided in §§ 4–103[3] and 4–104[4], every will shall be (1) in writing, (2) signed by the testator . . . and (3) attested and signed by two or more credible witnesses in the presence of the testator."

What's That?

Attestation is the witnesses' verification that an instrument has been executed in their presence according to the formalities required by law. In other words, it's a statement that the statutory formalities have been met.

It is uncontested that Dale Slack handwrote his will and signed it. Likewise, there is no question that Morgan and Bradley, the witnesses, signed the will in Dale Slack's presence. Therefore, the question before us is whether the will properly was attested, and, if not, whether it may nonetheless be admitted to probate.

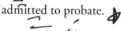

---

3   Section 4–103 addresses holographic wills signed by a person in the armed forces.

4   Section 4–104 addresses wills made outside the State of Maryland.

This Court has recognized that a presumption of due execution attaches to a will that contains the testator's signature and an attestation clause signed by the witnesses. . . .

We have held that once the presumption attaches, the burden of proof is on the caveator to show by clear and convincing evidence that the facts stated in the attestation clause are untrue.

When the presumption of due execution attaches to a will, a court may look to surrounding circumstances to determine whether the will should be admitted to probate in the face of testimony from witnesses who swear that the formalities of the statute were not met. In *Van Meter,* this Court addressed the presumption of due execution of a will that included an attestation clause and on its face bore every indicia of proper execution. We found that the attestation clause, signed by two witnesses, raised a presumption that the will was executed in accordance with the law, and the presumption could only be overcome by clear and convincing evidence that the facts stated in the attestation clause were not true. *Van Meter,* 183 Md. at 618, 39 A.2d at 754 (1944). In light of the presumption, we reversed the Orphans' Court's refusal to admit the will to probate even though one of the witnesses who signed the attestation clause testified that he did not sign his name in the testator's presence. *Id.* at 617, 39 A.2d at 754. We also noted that "[t]he court views such contradictory testimony with great caution and scans it with grave suspicion. . . ." *Id.*

* * *

This Court has not addressed the question of whether the presumption of due execution arises notwithstanding the absence of an attestation clause. In *Mead v. Trustees of the Presbyterian Church,* 229 Ill. 526, 82 N.E. 371 (1907), the Supreme Court of Illinois reviewed a will that contained no attestation clause but was signed by the testator and two witnesses. Neither witness could recall anything about the circumstances under which they had signed the writing. The court held that, under certain circumstances, an attestation clause was not necessary to give rise to the presumption of validity:

> **Take Note**
>
> Why has the primary issue considered by the court morphed to 'attestation'?

"In this case . . . the witness Boswell wrote immediately after his name the word 'witness,' which shows clearly he understood that he was witnessing the execution of the instrument which he had signed as a witness, and the marks 'following the name of Paul and appearing immediately underneath the word 'witness,' show that witness also understood he was signing as a witness to the execution of the instrument. It was not necessary that a formal attestation clause reciting all the facts necessary to a correct execution of the will be added to the instrument to make it a valid will."

* * *

We agree with the reasoning of those courts that hold that an attestation clause is not the *sine qua non* of the presumption of due execution. The will in the case *sub judice* bears on its face every indicia of due execution. It consists of a single page, written entirely in the testator's handwriting, and bearing the signature of the testator and two witnesses. The two witnesses, in the presence of the testator, signed beneath the words "Witnessed By." The testator's signature, which the second witness saw, was nearly adjacent to the signatures of the witnesses. Finally, the testator asked each witness to sign the paper without preventing them from reading it. The presumption of due execution attaches to such a will.

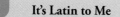

It's Latin to Me

Sub judice means under judgment or before the court.

Petitioner challenges the will on the basis that the will was not properly attested to by the witnesses. Petitioner points out that the witnesses did not see the testator sign the will and the first witness, Ms. Morgan, did not know she was signing a will and cannot remember whether Slack had signed the piece of paper he handed to her. As a result, petitioner argues, the will was not properly attested.

This Court has defined attestation of a will as "the act of witnesses in seeing that those things exist and are done which the statute requires." *Van Meter,* 183 Md. at 619, 39 A.2d at 755. Addressing the attestation of a will in *McIntyre,* this Court stated:

> "The attestation of the will is the act of the witnesses in seeing that those things exist and are done which the attestation clause declares were done and which the statute requires. After the witnesses so attest the will and subscribe their names, the statute is complied with. As the attestation clause, as such, preserves in permanent form a record of the facts attending the execution of the will and is *prima facie* evidence of the facts therein stated, the burden of proof is upon the *caveators* to show by clear and convincing evidence that the facts therein stated are not true."

McIntyre, 205 Md. at 421, 109 A.2d at 72. In *Casson v. Swogell,* 304 Md. 641, 500 A.2d 1031 (1985), we noted that "[t]o fulfill the requirement that a testator request a witness sign a document it is not necessary that the witness know it is a will." *Id.* at 654, 500 A.2d at 1038. We held that where the testator signs a will in front of the witnesses, proper attestation does not require that the testator inform the witnesses that they are signing a will. *Id.* at 656, 500 A.2d at 1039. We observed, however, that where the testator has signed a will *outside* of the presence of the witnesses, the testator must *acknowledge* his signature before the witnesses or declare the document to be his will.[8] *Id.* at 655, 500 A.2d at 1038.

---

8   The acknowledgment requirement has a long history. In *Casson v. Swogell,* 304 Md. 641, 500 A.2d 1031 (1985), we quoted from a leading English case, *White v. Trustees of the British Museum,* 6 Bing. 310 (1829), which states:

> "It has been held in so many cases that it must now be taken to be settled law, that it is unnecessary for the testator actually to sign the will in the presence of the three witnesses who subscribe to the same; but that any acknowledgment before the witnesses that it is his signature, or any declaration before them that it is his will, is equivalent to an actual signature in their presence, and makes the attestation and subscription of the witnesses complete."

Id. at 318, 500 A.2d 1031.

In acknowledging the will to the witnesses as his or her act, the testator need not "verbally declare the instrument to be his will, if his conduct, or the paper itself, apprises the witnesses of that fact." *Woodstock College,* 129 Md. at 680, 99 A. at 964. Thus, a testator need not acknowledge a will or signature orally; acknowledgment can be accomplished by conduct alone.

In the case *sub judice,* the Court of Special Appeals in discussing the acknowledgment require-ment, noted that the basic purpose of the acknowledgment requirement is to force "testators to manifest in some way: 'this is my document, the one I want you to sign.' " *Truitt,* 137 Md.App. at 366, 768 A.2d at 719. The court concluded that Slack satisfied the requirement by "handing them [the witnesses] a document in his own handwriting and asking them with apparent authority to sign it." *Id.* at 367, 768 A.2d at 719.

Before turning to the issue of Morgan's attestation, we find that the lower courts did not err in finding that the testator acknowledged his signature to Bradley. While Slack did not verbally draw Bradley's attention to his signature, he wrote the instrument in such a fashion that Bradley, in discussing the will, was later able to testify, "I looked down and saw the date written under his name and copied it from there." The testator, by his conduct, drew Bradley's attention to his signature, thereby acknowledging the will as his act. Bradley saw the testator's signature on the instrument and thus, her attestation was sufficient.

The issue of Morgan's attestation is more difficult. She testified that she did not know that the paper she was signing was a will, and could not remember whether she saw Slack's signature on the document. She testified that she thought it was a neighborhood petition. Moreover, it cannot be determined whether Slack acknowledged his signature to Morgan because Morgan cannot recall whether she saw his signature. As we have discussed, once it has been shown that a writing has been signed by the testator and attested and signed by two credible witnesses in the presence of the testator, there is a presumption of due execution. The question, then, is whether, under these circumstances, the presumption of due execution has been overcome by clear and convincing evidence.

It is important to recognize that Ms. Morgan did not testify that the testator had not signed the document. She simply could not remember seeing his signature. As the Court of Special Appeals observed, "while she could not recall seeing Slack's signature on the paper, she also could not certify that Slack did not sign the paper before he gave it to her." *Truitt,* 137 Md.App. at 366–67, 768 A.2d at 719. Morgan's failure to remember whether Slack had signed his will, or her failure to look at the document she signed, does not suggest that the testator had not signed the will prior Morgan's signing it. Her failure to remember the signature is just that, a failure to remember.

This Court and most other state courts consistently have found that a witness' inability to remember certain events should not overcome the presumption of due execution. *See Woodstock College of Baltimore County,* 129 Md. 675, 99 A. 962 (involving a witness who signed an attestation clause but later stated that he was not told, and therefore could not swear, that the paper was a will); *In re Carey's Estate,* 56 Colo. 77, 136 P. 1175 (1913) ("A will, duly attested upon its face, the signatures to which are all genuine, may be admitted to probate, although none of the subscribing witnesses are able to swear, from recollection, that the formalities required by the statute were complied with. . . ."); *In re Christenson's Estate,* 128 Minn. 17, 150 N.W. 213 (1914) (stating that "[w]e know of no rule of law which makes the probate of a will depend upon the recollection, or even the veracity of a subscribing witness."); *In re Pitcairn's Estate,* 6 Cal.2d 730, 59 P.2d 90 (noting that the authorities have clearly recognized that where witnesses are unable to testify or recollect, it is proper to apply the presumption of due execution).

The text writers make clear that "[a] presumption which arises out of proof of the genuineness of the signature of the testator and the subscribing witnesses is not overcome by the fact that the subscribing witnesses, or those whose evidence can be obtained, do not remember the facts of the execution." 3 WILLIAM J. BOWE & DOUGLAS H. PARKER, PAGE ON THE LAW OF WILLS § 29.22, at 451–52. "If the subscribing witnesses identify their signatures, but have no recollection of having attested the instrument, or of the circumstances of execution, the presumption that it was properly executed will prevail in the absence of clear and satisfactory proof to the contrary." *Id.* at 453.

The reasoning behind these cases is that if subscribing witnesses were required to recollect all the formalities prescribed by statutory requirements, few wills would be immune to attack, particularly after the passage of many years. In *Mead v. Trustees of the Presbyterian Church,* the Supreme Court of Illinois addressed the will of the testator, Mead Holmes. The will contained no attestation clause but was subscribed by two witnesses, both of whom signed their name following the word "witnesses." *Mead,* 82 N.E. at 372. The court recounted the first witness' testimony as follows:

> "[H]is signature was attached to the instrument; that he had no doubt but that he signed said instrument as an attesting witness at the request of Mead Holmes and in the presence of Mead Holmes and C.E. Paul [the second witness], but that he had no recollection of the transaction."

Id. The second witness also testified that he could not recollect certain facts:

> "[H]is genuine signature was attached to the instrument shown him, which purported to be the will of Mead Holmes, and that he signed said instrument at the request of Mead Holmes . . . but that he had no recollection of anything that was said at the time he signed the instrument, or whether Boswell [the first witness] was present at the time he signed the same or not."

Id. Although the will contained no attestation clause and the witnesses could not recollect whether it was properly executed, the court found that the witnesses' lapse of memory was not a sufficient basis for denying probate to a will that facially bore every indicia of validity. The court stated:

> "In this case, while there was no attestation clause attached to the instrument reciting all the acts necessary to be done that the will might be legally executed, we think the evidence found in this record clearly supplies the presumption arising from the presence of an attestation clause, and that there can be no question in the unbiased mind but that the instrument admitted to probate was duly executed by

Mead Holmes as and for his last will, in the presence of Boswell and Paul, who signed the same as attesting witnesses. The instrument was in the handwriting of Mead Holmes. It was therefore impossible that a spurious will was foisted upon him. It was found among his private papers after his death, duly signed and witnessed, which showed he considered it a valid will. The objects of his bounty designated in the instrument were persons and objects which had received his most tender consideration and thoughtful care in life, and there is nothing lacking in the evidence to show a legal execution of the will, save that the attesting witnesses, by lapse of time, could not recollect the facts surrounding the execution of the instrument by Mead Holmes as his last will and testament. To lay down as a rule of law that the failure of the attesting witnesses to recollect all the facts surrounding the execution of a will would defeat its probate, would be, in many instances, to defeat the probate of wills where there is no reasonable question but that they were executed by the testator or testatrix with all the formalities required by law, which is in conflict with the decisions of this and many other courts of last resort."

> **Food for Thought**
>
> Is the majority court merely indicating that they believe that Slack believed that the document was a valid will, or that the will complied with the formalities of due execution? There is a difference.

Id. at 373–74 (Citations omitted).

Finally, this Court has long held that the purpose of Maryland Code (1957, 2001 Repl. Vol., 2001 Supp.) § 4–102 of the Estates and Trusts Article was to remove uncertainty in the making of wills and to prevent the practice of imposition and fraud upon testators. *See Shane v. Wooley,* 138 Md. 75, 113 A. 652 (1921); *see also* 1 PHILIP L. SYKES, MARYLAND PRACTICE § 15, at 24–25 (1956) (noting that the "statute was passed to remove uncertainty in the making of wills and to prevent the practice of imposition and fraud upon testators.").

The circumstances in the case *sub judice* do not suggest that there was any fraud worked upon the testator. The will was found in testator's home after his death, duly signed and witnessed; this shows that the testator thought it was a valid will. The inability of a witness to remember the facts surrounding the execution of the instrument is insufficient to overcome the presumption of due execution. Accordingly, we hold that there is not clear and convincing evidence to overcome the presumption of due execution that attaches to the will, and, therefore, the will was entitled to probate as a validly executed will.

JUDGMENT OF THE COURT OF SPECIAL APPEALS AFFIRMED. COSTS TO BE PAID BY PETITIONER.

BATTAGLIA, J., dissents.

Battaglia, J., dissenting.

I respectfully dissent.

I differ from the majority in its definition of what constitutes sufficient proof of attestation or conversely, what standard of proof for lack of attestation must be met by the caveators to a document that does not bear an attestation clause, purporting to be a will under Section 4–102 of the Estates and Trusts Article of the Maryland Code (1974, 2001 Repl. Vol.). In so doing, I agree with the Orphans' Court and the Circuit Court for Cecil County that the testator, who signed the will outside of the presence of the witnesses to the instrument, failed to acknowledge that the document was his own instrument when he asked the witnesses to sign it, thus rendering the will invalid under Maryland law.

* * *

In support of its holding admitting Dale Slack's will to probate, the majority emphasizes the genuineness of the testator's and witnesses' signatures. If proof of the genuineness of the signatures of the testator and the witnesses alone were deemed sufficient to establish the validity of the will, the statutory requirement that the will be "attested" would be rendered useless. *See* Md. Code, § 4–102 (requiring that a will be "*attested and signed* by two or more credible witnesses in the presence of the testator") (emphasis added). Therefore, in cases where the testator has signed a will *which does not contain an attestation clause* outside of the presence of the attesting witnesses, I believe that the practice more in keeping with our case law and the statutory requirements of Section 4–102 would be for the court to evaluate the totality of the circumstances surrounding the execution of the document in order to determine if the will should properly be admitted to probate. Thus, the caveator would have to prove by a preponderance of the evidence that the execution of the will did not meet the statutory requirements for valid execution as set forth in Section 4–102 of the Estates and Trusts Article. In so doing, proof of the genuineness of the signatures of the testator and the witnesses could be significant factors in determining the validity of the will, which may be overcome by a finding that the caveator has demonstrated by a preponderance of the evidence that the statutory requirements were not met.

In the present circumstances, Dale Slack did not tell the people whose signatures appear on the will that they were "attesting" to his will. Rather, the first witness to sign the will, Dorothy Morgan, testified that Slack requested that she sign a paper for him. Morgan testified that she believed she was signing a neighborhood petition rather than a will belonging to Slack, and that she did not see his signature on the document when she signed it. As such, the circumstances indicate that Ms. Morgan could not have attested to the will as required by Section 4–102.

The second witness, Sandra Bradley, testified that Slack hurriedly requested her signature on a "piece of paper." Although Bradley did acknowledge that she saw Slack's signature on the document, she testified that she neither knew the document to be of Slack's creation, nor knew that it was a will. Bradley's testimony regarding her recognizing Slack's signature may be sufficient to validate the will, but the statute clearly states that attestation and signatures are required of "*two or more* credible witnesses" in order to satisfy the elements of a valid will. Md. Code, § 4–102 of the Estates and Trusts Article.

I believe that the Orphans' Court and the Circuit Court for Cecil County appropriately weighed the evidence set forth by petitioner and quite reasonably concluded that the statutory requirements had not been met. For example, in denying the will's admission to probate, the circuit court balanced the evidence put before it, stating, "[i]n applying equity to this situation, of course, the court cannot be ignorant of the very specific statutory law that applies in this case which I have already recited, as well as the interpretative cases rendered within the State and other jurisdictions recognized by the State, such as England's law." While it was not necessary for Mr. Slack to verbally instruct the witnesses that the paper he wished for them to sign was his *will,* the statute's mandate that the will be attested and signed by two witnesses requires that, in the absence of signing the will in their presence, the testator must apprize the witnesses of the fact that they are attesting to the validity of the execution of *the testator's document,* either through the testator's conduct or through the contents of the instrument itself. *See Van Meter,* at 617, 39 A.2d at 754. Although Dale Slack's document contained valid signatures of the testator and two witnesses, such proof is insufficient to countermand the evidence supplied by petitioner that the statutory formalities for valid execution of a will were not met. For the foregoing reasons, the Orphans' Court and the Circuit Court for Cecil County properly declined to admit the will to probate. Accordingly, I would reverse the decision of the Court of Special Appeals.

Points for Discussion

1. What is an attestation clause anyway?

The *Slack* case illustrates that conforming to the requirements of due execution is not always a straightforward matter. There are various strategies the scrivener can employ to avoid a will contest. A will that contains an attestation clause will be presumed to have been duly executed. What is an attestation clause? It is a block of text that follows the testator's signature (which is formally known as the *testimonium*). The attestation clause recites the performance of the main features of the execution ceremony. Here is typical example of both clauses:

IN WITNESS WHEREOF, I have signed my name this _____ day of _____, 20__

_____(L.S.)

Name of Testator

The foregoing instrument was signed, published and declared by _____, the testator, to be (his *or* her) last will and testament, in our presence, and we, at (his *or* her) request and in (his *or* her) presence, and in the presence of each other have hereunto subscribed our names as witnesses this _____ day of _____, 20__.

Some observations: First, the "(L.S.)" at the end of the signature line. The letters are the first letters of two Latin words that translate as "place of the seal." The testator's personal seal would have been impressed in wax at the end of the signature line. Today, of course, the seal is an anachronism, but the past lives on in quaint little things like the "(L.S.)."

Second, note that this sample attestation clause describes an execution ceremony far more formal than that required by most modern statutes and indeed fulfills the requirements of the strictest of statutes. Being overly strict is not inadvisable because the enhanced formality noted supports an assumption that the will complied with a less rigorous statute. Of course, the execution ceremony should correspond to what is recited in the attestation clause. Some attestation clauses specify that the clause was read aloud to the testator before the witnesses signed. Whether or not to include such a provision is really a matter of personal preference. It adds little or nothing to the effectiveness of the clause, but so doing lends an air of greater solemnity to the proceedings. Some attestation clauses recite the number of pages in the will ("The foregoing instrument, consisting of X pages, . . .") Such a statement may help to insure the integrity of the document, but as we will see, there are other ways to make sure that the will is properly "integrated."

Third, most courts presume that a document that conforms to the formalities of due execution required by statute is valid. Additionally, some states, for example, New York, have long had an another presumption of valid execution: Where the attorney who drafted the will supervises the execution, "there is a presumption of regularity in all respects." (*Matter of Spinello*, 291 A.D.2d 406 (N.Y. App. 2002))

2. *The self-proving affidavit*

The cautious scrivener might also include a *self-proving affidavit,* an affidavit made by the witnesses (and sometimes by the testator as well) which recites the facts of the execution ceremony and which is conclusive proof of those facts. If a self-proving affidavit accompanies the will, there usually is no need to find the witnesses at the time the will is offered for probate to have them testify or swear in an affidavit to the facts of the execution ceremony.

The form that follows is the one used in New York. The form of self-proving affidavits varies among jurisdictions. The Uniform Probate Code in § 2–504 provides two ways to create a self-proved will. One is by attaching to the will an affidavit made by the testator and the witnesses and attached to the will; the other incorporates the affidavit into the attestation clause. No matter what form the affidavit takes, it is an important tool for making probate simpler. This affidavit probably satisfies the requirements of all jurisdictions, including those that adhere to the UPC.

STATE OF NEW YORK   )

) :.ss:

COUNTY OF NEW YORK   )

_____, residing at _____, _____, and _____, residing at _____, _____ each being duly sworn, deposes and says:

We witnessed the execution of the Will of [*testator's name*], dated the ___ day of _____ 20__, consisting of [*number*] (*X*) pages. The Will was executed at _____, New York, New York, under the supervision of [*name of attorney*], an attorney-at-law licensed to practice in [the State of New York *or other* jurisdiction] This affidavit is made at the request of the Testator.

The Testator in our presence subscribed her name to the Will at the end, and, at the time of making such subscription, published and declared the Will to be her Last Will and Testament; we then, at the Testator's request and in her presence and in the presence of each other, signed our names as subscribing witnesses.

The Testator at the time of such execution was more than 18 years of age and, in our opinion, of sound mind, memory, and understanding, and not acting under any restraint or in any respect incompetent to make a Will.

The Testator indicated to us that she had read the Will, knew its contents, and indicated that the provisions of the Will expressed the manner in which she desired her estate to be administered and distributed.

The Testator could write and converse in the English language, and was suffering from no defect of sight, hearing or speech, or from any physical or mental impairment which would affect her capacity to make a valid Will.

The Testator signed only one original instrument and the will was not executed in counterparts.

_____

_____

Sworn to before me this _____ day of ___, 20____

_____

Notary Public

3. Witness competence

A page of history . . .

Though it seems odd to the modern mind, parties to litigation in the past, even criminal defendants, in England were not permitted to give evidence under oath, the notion being that they might be tempted to lie, and therefore jeopardize their souls for transitory advantage in a law suit.

The Statute of Frauds (1677) required a will to be witnessed by three or four credible witnesses. Credible was an ambiguous term, and much discussion was given to whether it should be required of witnesses in the Wills Act of 1837. It mattered because the testator might not be certain of the past conduct of his or her witnesses. Those convicted of crimes were not deemed to be credible, as well as, those of dubious moral character. There was also concern with whether a witness could be disinterested in the transaction if he or she received a bequest under the will. As disabilities were removed, and parties became free to testify, subject to cross-examination, and the fact-finders were permitted to determine their veracity, so too modern law has relaxed the requirements that a witness to wills not receive a bequest thereunder.

But old law disappears slowly. While no jurisdiction invalidates the will if there are not two disinterested witnesses, not all jurisdictions accept interested witnesses as does the Uniform Probate Code, which states "the signing of a will by an interested witness does not invalidate the will or any provision of it." sec 2–505 (b).

Some jurisdictions, for example, New York, have a witnessing statute that purges gifts to witnesses in certain circumstances: the gift is not given effect unless there are two other disinterested witnesses to the will.

New York Estates, Powers, and Trusts Law § 3–3.2. Witness Who Is Also Beneficiary

(a) An attesting witness to a will to whom a beneficial disposition or appointment of property is made is a competent witness and compellable to testify respecting the execution of such will as if no such disposition or appointment had been made, subject to the following:

(1) Any such disposition or appointment made to an attesting witness is void unless there are, at the time of execution and attestation, at least two other attesting witnesses to the will who receive no beneficial disposition or appointment thereunder.

(2)   Subject to subparagraph (1), any such disposition or appointment to an attesting witness is effective unless the will cannot be proved without the testimony of such witness, in which case the disposition or appointment is void.

(3)   Any attesting witness whose disposition is void hereunder, who would be a distributee if the will were not established, is entitled to receive so much of his intestate share as does not exceed the value of the disposition made to him in the will, such share to be recovered as follows:

(A)   In case the void disposition becomes part of the residuary disposition, from the residuary disposition only.

(B)   In case the void disposition passes in intestacy, ratably from the distributees who succeed to such interest. For this purpose, the void disposition shall be distributed under 4–1.1 as though the attesting witness is not a distributee.

(b)   The provisions of this section apply to witnesses to a nuncupative will authorized by 3–2.2.

The idea behind EPTL § 3–3.2 and similar statutes in other jurisdictions is that someone who receives a benefit under the will should not be relied on to be 'testify' about what happened at the execution ceremony, and they can be "made honest" by removing any incentive to lie by "purging" the witness of the gift under the will. Whether or not this "cure" is good psychology is open to question.

The complications caused by EPTL § 3–3.2 and similar statutes is illustrated by the following case:

Matter of Morea

645 N.Y.S.2d 1022 (Surrogate's Ct. 1996)

LEE L. HOLZMAN, J.

In this uncontested proceeding to probate a will dated December 2, 1991, the issue presented is whether the bequest to decedent's friend George Buonaroba is void under EPTL 3–3.2 in light of the fact that he was one of the three attesting witnesses and that decedent's son Kevin, whose legacy under the will is less than his intestate share as one of decedent's six surviving children, was also one of the attesting witnesses. The third attesting witness does not receive any disposition or appointment under the will.

EPTL 3–3.2(a)(1) provides that an attesting witness to a will to whom a beneficial disposition is made is a competent witness who can be compelled to testify with respect to the execution of such will but that the disposition to the attesting witness is void "unless there are, at the time of execution and attestation, at least two other attesting witnesses to the will who receive no beneficial disposition or appointment thereunder." The purpose of the statute is to preserve the maker's testamentary scheme to at least some extent by making all attesting witnesses competent while preserving the integrity of the process of will executions by removing the possibility that attesting witnesses who receive a disposition under the will might give false testimony in support of the will to protect their legacies (*Matter of Walters*, 285 N.Y. 158; *Matter of Fracht*, 94 Misc. 2d 664).

Food for Thought

Why is that? Are New Yorkers inherently more dishonest? Part of our agenda here is to consider the wisdom of the substantive law and whether is it ripe for reform. Should the finder of fact make the determination? Can the law simply rely on capacity, undue influence and fraud to make certain that there is no interference in the process of testation?

The Legislature, in effect, has concluded that the public good is served by requiring that a few innocent attesting witnesses forfeit their legacies so that the validity of a greater number of wills might not be suspect by dint of a beneficiary under the will being one of the attesting witnesses whose testimony is required to probate the will. New York's law on this subject has been criticized as creating "a most unfortunate conclusive presumption that a beneficiary under a will who also served as an attesting witness should be dramatically and summarily punished" (Turano, 1994 Supp Practice Commentaries, McKinney's Cons Laws of NY, Book 17B, EPTL 3–3.2, 1996 Pocket Part, at 80). This "conclusive presumption" is not the law in those States that have enacted the Uniform Probate Code nor is it the law in most jurisdictions.

Here, decedent's son, Kevin, does not forfeit his legacy as a result of being both an attesting witness and a beneficiary because EPTL 3–3.2(a)(3) permits him, as a distributee, to receive the lesser of his intestate share or his legacy under the will. However, since the attesting witness, George Buonaroba, is not a distributee of the decedent, it must be determined whether the bequest to him of one eighth of decedent's tangible personal property "that is not otherwise disposed through Paragraph Second" is void under EPTL 3–3.2.

In light of the policy that statutes are to be construed to carry out the over-all legislative intent and to avoid injustice or hardship (*Matter of Jacob*, 86 N.Y. 2d 651, 667), neither the spirit nor the letter of EPTL 3–3.2 requires that George Buonaroba forfeit, through no fault of his own, the legacy that decedent wanted him to receive. The objective of EPTL 3–3.2 that there be at least two attesting witnesses who have nothing to gain by the admission of the will to probate is fulfilled in this matter by the one witness who receives no disposition or appointment and by decedent's son Kevin, who, although he received a bequest under the will, is actually adversely affected by the admission of the will to probate because his intestate share would be greater than his bequest. Considering that the first definition of the word "beneficial" in Webster's Dictionary (New Twentieth Century Unabridged Second Edition) is "advantageous", it is concluded that, although Kevin received a disposition under the will, it was not beneficial to him to the extent that he would have received a larger inheritance if he testified against the validity of the will and the instrument were denied probate. Consequently, the disposition to George Buonaroba is not void under EPTL 3–3.2(a)(1) because there are at least two other witnesses to the will who receive no beneficial disposition thereunder. That this interpretation is reflected by the provisions of EPTL 3–3.2(a)(3) which permit a distributee who is an attesting witness to receive the legacy whenever its value is less than the intestate share of the witness.

In conclusion, regardless of whether one agrees with New York's minority rule mandating that a legacy to an attesting witness is void in the absence of two disinterested witnesses, there is no need to stretch that rule to fit the facts of this case. Inasmuch as the court is satisfied that the will was duly executed in accordance with the statutory formalities and that the testatrix at the time of executing it was in all respects competent to make a will and not under any restraint, a decree has been entered admitting the will to probate as a will valid to pass property, including the legacy to George Buonaroba.

> ### Take Note
>
> A riddle. Doesn't interest attach at the time of execution? How can a will with an interested witness be executed with testamentary formalities under EPTL § 3–2.2?

Points for Discussion

1. What does it mean to be "interested"?

Let's consider the term 'interested." Are the following interested witnesses:

1. the will leaves a bequest to a witness's spouse, should the bequest be purged? Connecticut's statute so directs. *See* CGSA § 45a–258

2. the dean of your law school witness a will executed by an alum in which a substantial disposition made in favor of her *alma mater.*

3. a person nominated as executor or trustee in the will. *See Matter of Fracht,* 94 Misc.2d 664, 405 N.Y.S.2d 222 (Sur. Ct. Bronx Co. 1978).

2. Integration

What should a will look like? What papers constitute the deceased's will? Neither question, though seemingly obvious is entirely frivolous. Because both deliberation and due execution are required, it should not be surprising that the internal integrity of the document itself is important.

The first legal doctrine discussed is "integration."

Restatement Third, Property (Wills and Donative Transfers) § 3.5

To be treated as part of a will, a page or other writing must be present when the will is executed and must be intended to be part of the will.

So all the papers present at the time of execution are covered by the due execution of a single page. The best way to insure that there is no question that all the pages of the will were present when the execution ceremony took place is to make sure that the pages are physically connected. As comment *b* to § 3.5 of the Restatement notes, although physical connection is not required, "[p]hysical connection does, however, support an inference that the physically connected pages . . . were present at the time of execution and that they were intended to be part of the will." The method of physical connection can be elaborate—some offices still thread a ribbon through the top of the pages of the will, fasten the ends of the ribbon over the "(L.S.)" and cover them with a paper or even wax seal—or very simple. Staples will do just fine. If the will is stapled, however, it is imperative that the staples are never removed. The resulting holes will raise suspicion that the will was tampered with after execution.

Practice Pointer

While tying the will may look elegant, there are disadvantages. Many probate courts now scan wills that are offered for probate and that will require the clerk to break the seal and untie the will. Staples are more and more the better choice.

In New York's Surrogate's Courts, for example, the proponent of a will introduced for probate that has staple holes showing staples have been removed will be required to do an "affidavit of staples" explaining the circumstances. For example, take this real life incident. The testator's child and nominated executor had possession of the will. With only good intentions, the child removed the staples from the will in order to facilitate making photocopies and then re-stapled the will. The child's affidavit explained it all, but of course delayed the probate proceeding.

There are additional steps that can be taken to ensure there is no question about the integration of the document. A simple footer stating that the current page is "Page X of Y pages" followed by a line on which the testator writes his or her initials before signing the will is a helpful precaution. Some attorneys ask the witnesses to initial each page of the will, but most would regard that as an excess of caution. Some attorneys also include a recitation of the number of pages in the will in the attestation clause as noted above.

Another way to demonstrate that the separate pages of the will are an integration is what the Restatement calls "internal coherence." Comment *c* to § 3.5 states: "Internal coherence is present if the pages or other writings appear to be part of a single document. This inference can arise, for example, if the sentences from one page to the next appear to be a continuum, or if the pages of provisions appear to be a continuum or are numbered sequentially." Techniques fostering internal coherence include making sure that the last sentence on every page runs over to the next and that at least two (and preferably) more lines of text appear on the page that contains the testimonium and attestation clauses. Accomplishing these formatting tricks with modern word processing programs sometimes requires a good deal of patience, but the time invested is worth it.

Last but not least, the testator and the witnesses (and the notary if there is a self-proving affidavit) should all use the same pen. Just like staple holes, different colored inks can raise suspicions.

The following case illustrates what may happen in the absence of a stapler:

In re Estate of Beale

113 N.W.2d 380 (Wisc. 1962)

* * *

It cannot be questioned that on June 16 or 17, 1959, Professor Beale dictated a 14 page Document in the form of a last will, revoking all prior wills; that his secretary typed the original will, with three carbon copies, and delivered all of them to him in loose leaf form the afternoon of June 20th; that Beale was in New York City at the home of a friend, a professor of Columbia University, on the evening of June 21st and on that evening he exhibited 'a pile' of sheets of paper and declared to his three friends that this was his will and desired them to witness his will; that they saw him sign the sheet which was on top of the pile and that immediately thereafter, at his request, they signed as witnesses in his presence and in the presence of each other; that the place where they put their signatures was immediately below the usual testamentary clause declaring this to be Professor Beale's will; that none of the witnesses paid any detailed attention to the number of pages in the pile nor could they identify later any of the pages except the one where they had written their names; that when all four participants had signed, Beale put all papers in his briefcase and the meeting ended.

It is uncontradicted that on the next day, or shortly thereafter, Beale and his two sons left by plane for Moscow; that a few days after June 21st Mrs. Burleigh, Beale's secretary, received a letter from him on Columbia University note paper, bearing date June 21, 1959, mailed in New York or in London on a day not given; that the letter asked Mrs. Burleigh to make several changes in pages 12 and 13 of the will which she had previously typed, to carry out marginal penciled notes in Beale's handwriting on those pages; that enclosed with the letter were the original pages 12 and 13; that Mrs. Burleigh made the alterations as directed and mailed them back to him in Moscow; that these pages were later found in a sealed envelope addressed to Beale in Beale's handwriting and mailed from London, England to him at his Madison address.

There is nothing legally invalid in the execution of a will because the separate pages of the will have not been fastened together. It is a requirement, though, that all the pages be present at the time of execution.

Thompson on Wills (3rd Ed.), sec. 124, page 197, states:

> ' * * * It is not necessary that they [the witnesses] see or examine all the pages of the will to see that all the sheets of paper were in place when the will was executed.
> * * * ' Citing In Re Sleeper's Appeal, 129 Maine 194, 151 Atl. 150, 71 A.L.R. 518.

In Sleeper's Appeal, supra, the court stated:

> ' * * * nor is it essential that the witnesses should see and examine all the pages of a will at the time of execution, if the court is satisfied, from other evidence or the circumstances surrounding the execution, that all the sheets of paper offered for probate **385 were present at the time of execution. * * *

2 Page on Wills (Bowe-Parker Revision), sec. 19.147, page 277, is to the same effect, citing Sleeper's Appeal, supra, and 11 B. U .L. Rev. 148; 5 Temp. L. Q. 152; 17 La. L. Rev. 69; and 40 Yale L.J. 144.

In the case at bar the witnesses are unable to say whether or not the 14 pages were on the table before them when, on June 21st, they signed the last page. The determination then, comes down to the reasonable inferences to be drawn from the established facts. Appellant relies on the undisputed fact that two pages of the will were received in Madison within a few days following June 21st, enclosed in a letter dated June 21st. And appellant infers that those two pages had already been sent off to Madison when, late in the evening of June 21st, the testator and witnesses signed the last page.

Food for Thought

The court seems to think that the inference they draw is the most likely, but not the only one. What alternative inference can you suggest?

On the other hand, the trial court put weight on the fact that all 14 original pages are clearly identified and legible as they were dictated by Beale before the corrections or amendments. This intact original was handed to Beale by his secretary and was taken by him to New York. The very next day Beale presented 'a pile' of papers to his witnesses and declared that such papers were his will. It is not impossible or improbable that Beale was speaking the truth and the pile of pages were the complete 14 page will, as the trial court found. The fact that Beale sent off two pages to Mrs. Burleigh with a letter dated June 21st may raise an inference that Beale did this before he went to the party and he had there only the remaining pages, which he falsely declared to be his will. Certainly that is not the only permissible inference. When Beale and his friends had signed the will and he had gathered up the pages and departed June 21st was not over; Beale could still have written the letter, less than 100 words, on that date after the party and enclosed with it pages 12 and 13. There is no evidence at all of when the letter and the pages were mailed and there is some evidence that they were mailed in London. . . .

[The court affirmed the judgment of the trial court that Professor Beale's will consisted of 14 pages, including the uncorrected versions of pages 12 and 13.]

3. Incorporation by reference

The doctrine of incorporation by reference creates an exception to the requirements of the will execution statutes, by allowing unexecuted documents to be brought into the deceased will. The UPC § 2–510 provides:

> Any writing in existence when a will is executed may be incorporated by reference if the language of the will manifests this intent and describes the writing sufficiently to permit its identification.

Thus if a will refers to a writing, not present at the time of execution, but one that is in existence at the time the will is executed and the writing referenced can be identified with reasonable certainty, the writing becomes part of the will (is incorporated therein) and is effective to dispose of property at the testator's death. More frequently than you might imagine, testators write wills which instruct the executor to make distributions according to the directions contained in a letter or in some other writing that the testator has made. Why might a will-maker wish to incorporate an extraneous document? Privacy. Although witnesses to a will need not see its contents, a probated will is a public record. Perhaps one reason for referring to documents outside the will is the desire to keep the contents of the writing secret from other beneficiaries of the will. Generally, while a writing incorporated by reference is part of the will it need not be offered for probate and is not part of the public record (*See* Restatement (Third) Property (Wills and Other Donative Transfers), § 3.6, comment *h*.) so a bequest to a "special friend" may be engineered without notoriety. There is also convenience. The following case illustrates both the convenience and the potential dangers of relying on incorporation by reference.

Clark v. Greenhalge

582 N.E.2d 949 (Mass. 1991)

NOLAN, JUSTICE.

We consider in this case whether a probate judge correctly concluded that specific, written bequests of personal property contained in a notebook maintained by a testatrix were incorporated by reference into the terms of the testatrix's will.

We set forth the relevant facts as found by the probate judge. The testatrix, Helen Nesmith, duly executed a will in 1977, which named her cousin, Frederic T. Greenhalge, II, as executor of her estate. The will further identified Greendale as the principal beneficiary of the estate, entitling him to receive all of Helen Nesmith's tangible personal property upon her death except those items which she "designate[d] by a memorandum left by [her] and known to [Greenhalge], or in accordance with [her] known wishes," to be given to others living at the time of her death. Among Helen Nesmith's possessions was a large oil painting of a farm scene signed by T.H. Muckley and dated 1833. The value of the painting, as assessed for estate tax purposes, was $1,800.00.

In 1972, Greenhalge assisted Helen Nesmith in drafting a document entitled "MEMORAN-DUM" and identified as "a list of items of personal property prepared with Miss Helen Nesmith upon September 5, 1972, for the guidance of myself in the distribution of personal tangible property." This list consisted of forty-nine specific bequests of Ms. Nesmith's tangible personal property. In 1976, Helen Nesmith modified the 1972 list by interlineations, additions and deletions. Neither edition of the list involved a bequest of the farm scene painting.

> ### Practice Pointer
>
> Is it wise to appoint as executor an individual who is to receive all personal property save items specifically noted in collateral writings and perhaps even by oral direction? Does the strategy create just too great an incentive to "forget" the will-maker's directions?

Ms. Nesmith kept a plastic-covered notebook in the drawer of a desk in her study. She periodically made entries in this notebook, which bore the title "List to be given Helen Nesmith 1979." One such entry read: "Ginny Clark farm picture hanging over fireplace. Ma's room." Imogene Conway and Joan Dragoumanos, Ms. Nesmith's private home care nurses knew of the existence of the notebook and had observed Helen Nesmith write in it. On several occasions, Helen Nesmith orally expressed to these nurses her intentions regarding the disposition of particular pieces of her property upon her death, including the farm scene painting. Helen Nesmith told Conway and Dragoumanos that the farm scene painting was to be given to Virginia Clark, upon Helen Nesmith's death.

Virginia Clark and Helen Nesmith first became acquainted in or about 1940. The women lived next door to each other for approximately ten years (1945 through 1955), during which time they enjoyed a close friendship. The Nesmith-Clark friendship remained constant through the years. In more recent years, Ms. Clark frequently spent time at Ms. Nesmith's home, often visiting Helen Nesmith while she rested in the room which originally was her mother's bedroom. The farm scene painting hung in this room above the fireplace. Virginia Clark openly admired the picture.

> ### Practice Pointer
>
> Given the testator's whimsy, should the scrivener have just written an entirely new document? When to redraft in entirety and when to use a codicil is a judgment call. Helen Nesmith often alluded to the fact that Ms. Clark someday would own the farm scene painting.

According to Ms. Clark, sometime during either January or February of 1980, Helen Nesmith told Ms. Clark that the farm scene painting would belong to Ms. Clark after Helen Nesmith's death. Helen Nesmith then mentioned to Virginia Clark that she would record this gift in a book she kept for the purpose of memorializing her wishes with respect to the disposition of certain of her belongings. After that conversation, Ms. Nesmith executed two codicils to her

1977 will: one on May 30, 1980, and a second on October 23, 1980. The codicils amended certain bequests and deleted others, while ratifying the will in all other respects.

Greenhalge received Helen Nesmith's notebook on or shortly after January 28, 1986, the date of Ms. Nesmith's death. Thereafter, Greenhalge, as executor, distributed Ms. Nesmith's property in accordance with the will as amended, the 1972 memorandum as amended in 1976, and certain of the provisions contained in the notebook. Greenhalge refused, however, to deliver the farm scene painting to Virginia Clark because the painting interested him and he wanted to keep it. Mr. Greenhalge claimed that he was not bound to give effect to the expressions of Helen Nesmith's wishes and intentions stated in the notebook, particularly as to the disposition of the farm scene painting. Notwithstanding this opinion, Greenhalge distributed to himself all of the property bequeathed to him in the notebook. Ms. Clark thereafter commenced an action against Mr. Greenhalge seeking to compel him to deliver the farm scene painting to her.

The probate judge found that Helen Nesmith wanted Ms. Clark to have the farm scene painting. The judge concluded that Helen Nesmith's notebook qualified as a "memorandum" of her known wishes with respect to the distribution of her tangible personal property, within the meaning of Article Fifth of Helen Nesmith's will. The judge further found that the notebook was in existence at the time of the execution of the 1980 codicils, which ratified the language of Article Fifth in its entirety. Based on these findings, the judge ruled that the notebook was incorporated by reference into the terms of the will. Newton v. Seaman's Friend Soc'y, 130 Mass. 91, 93 (1881). The judge awarded the painting to Ms. Clark.

> ### Take Note
>
> Greenhalge must really have wanted that painting to pursue the case through three courts! Or were there also other items in the notebook in question that he coveted?

The Appeals Court affirmed the probate judge's decision in an unpublished memorandum and order, 30 Mass. App. Ct. 1109, 570 N.E.2d 184 (1991). We allowed the appellee's petition for further appellate review and now hold that the probate judge correctly awarded the painting to Ms. Clark.

A properly executed will may incorporate by reference into its provisions any "document or paper not so executed and witnessed, whether the paper referred to be in the form of . . . a mere list or memorandum, . . . if it was in existence at the time of the execution of the will, and is identified by clear and satisfactory proof as the paper referred to therein." Newton v. Seaman's Friend Soc'y, supra at 93. The parties agree that the document entitled "memorandum," dated 1972 and amended in 1976, was in existence as of the date of the execution of Helen Nesmith's will. The parties further agree that this document is a memorandum regarding the distribution of certain items of Helen Nesmith's tangible personal

> ### Food for Thought
>
> What about grammar? The will makes reference to a memorandum (singular) not memoranda (plural)?

property upon her death, as identified in Article Fifth of her will. There is no dispute, therefore, that the 1972 memorandum was incorporated by reference into the terms of the will. Newton, supra.

The parties do not agree, however, as to whether the documentation contained in the notebook, dated 1979, similarly was incorporated into the will through the language of Article Fifth. Greenhalge advances several arguments to support his contention that the purported bequest of the farm scene painting written in the notebook was not incorporated into the will and thus fails as a testamentary devise. The points raised by Greenhalge in this regard are not persuasive. First, Greenhalge contends that the judge wrongly concluded that the notebook could be considered a "memorandum" within the meaning of Article Fifth, because it is not specifically identified as a "memorandum." Such a literal interpretation of the language and meaning of Article Fifth is not appropriate.

"The 'cardinal rule in the interpretation of wills, to which all other rules must bend, is that the intention of the testator shall prevail, provided it is consistent with the rules of law.'" Boston Safe Deposit & Trust Co. v. Park, 307 Mass. 255, 259, 29 N.E.2d 977 (1940), quoting McCurdy v. McCallum, 186 Mass. 464, 469, 72 N.E. 75 (1904). The intent of the testator is ascertained through consideration of "the language which [the testatrix] has used to express [her] testamentary designs," Taft v. Stearns, 234 Mass. 273, 277, 125 N.E. 570 (1920), as well as the circumstances existing at the time of the execution of the will. Boston Safe Deposit & Trust Co., supra 307 Mass. at 259, 29 N.E.2d 977, and cases cited. The circumstances existing at the time of the execution of a codicil to a will are equally relevant, because the codicil serves to ratify the language in the will which has not been altered or affected by the terms of the codicil. See Taft, supra 234 Mass. at 275–277, 125 N.E. 570.

Applying these principles in the present case, it appears clear that Helen Nesmith intended by the language used in Article Fifth of her will to retain the right to alter and amend the bequests of tangible personal property in her will, without having to amend formally the will. The text of Article Fifth provides a mechanism by which Helen Nesmith could accomplish the result she desired; i.e., by expressing her wishes "in a memorandum." The statements in the notebook unquestionably reflect Helen Nesmith's exercise of her retained right to restructure the distribution of her tangible personal property upon her death. That the notebook is not entitled "memorandum" is of no consequence, since its apparent purpose is consistent with that of a memorandum under Article Fifth: It is a written instrument which is intended to guide Greenhalge in "distribut[ing] such of [Helen Nesmith's] tangible personal property to and among . . . persons [who] are living at the time of her decease." In this connection, the distinction between the notebook and "a memorandum" is illusory. The appellant acknowledges that the subject documentation in the notebook establishes that Helen Nesmith wanted Virginia Clark to receive the farm scene painting upon Ms. Nesmith's death. The appellant argues, however, that the notebook cannot take effect as a testamentary instrument under Article Fifth, because the language of Article Fifth limits its application to "a" memorandum, or the 1972 memorandum. We reject this strict construction of Article Fifth. The language of Article Fifth does not preclude the existence of more than one memorandum which serves the intended purpose of that article. As previously suggested, the phrase "a memorandum" in Article Fifth appears as an expression of the manner in which Helen Nesmith could exercise her right to alter her will after its execution, but it does not denote a requirement that she do so within a particular format. To construe narrowly Article Fifth and to exclude the possibility that Helen Nesmith drafted the notebook contents as "a memorandum" under that Article, would undermine our long-standing policy of interpreting wills in a manner which best carries out the known wishes of the testatrix. See Boston Safe Deposit & Trust Co., supra. The evidence supports the conclusion that Helen Nesmith intended that the bequests in her notebook be accorded the same power and effect as those contained in the 1972 memorandum under Article Fifth. We conclude, therefore, that the judge properly accepted the notebook as a memorandum of Helen Nesmith's known wishes as referenced in Article Fifth of her will. The appellant also contends that the judge erred in finding that Helen Nesmith intended to incorporate the notebook into her will, since the evidence established, at most, that she intended to bequeath the painting to Clark, and not that she intended to incorporate the notebook into her will. Our review of the judge's findings on this point, which is limited to a consideration of whether such findings are "clearly erroneous," proves the appellant argument to be without merit. First Pa. Mortgage Trust v. Dorchester Sav. Bank, 395 Mass. 614, 621, 481 N.E.2d 1132 (1985). The judge found that Helen Nesmith drafted the notebook contents with the expectation that Greenhalge would distribute the property accordingly.

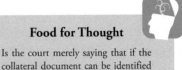

Food for Thought

Is the court merely saying that if the collateral document can be identified from the description in the will, the "specific identification" requirement is met?

The judge further found that the notebook was in existence on the dates Helen Nesmith executed the codicils to her will, which affirmed the language of Article Fifth, and that it thereby was incorporated into the will pursuant to the language and spirit of Article Fifth. It is clear that the judge fairly construed the evidence in reaching the determination that Helen Nesmith intended the notebook to serve as a memorandum of her wishes as contemplated under Article Fifth of her will.

Take Note

Had the codicil not been executed would the gifts in the notebook have been valid? Would some requirement of incorporation not have been met? The doctrine of republication by codicil rode to the rescue because it acts to re-date the will as of the date of the codicil. More on that doctrine in the Points for Discussion.

Lastly, the appellant complains that the notebook fails to meet the specific requirements of a memorandum under Article Fifth of the will, because it was not "known to him" until after Helen Nesmith's death. For this reason, Greenhalge states that the judge improperly ruled that the notebook was incorporated into the will. One of Helen Nesmith's nurses testified, however, that Greenhalge was aware of the notebook and its contents, and that he at no time made an effort to determine the validity of the bequest of the farm scene painting to Virginia Clark as stated therein. There is ample support in the record, therefore, to support the judge's conclusion that the notebook met the criteria set forth in Article Fifth regarding memoranda.

We note, as did the Appeals Court, that "one who seeks equity must do equity and that a court will not permit its equitable powers to be employed to accomplish an injustice." Pitts v. Halifax Country Club, Inc., 19 Mass. App. Ct. 525, 533, 476 N.E.2d 222 (1985). To this point, we remark that Greenhalge' s conduct in handling this controversy fell short of the standard imposed by common social norms, not to mention the standard of conduct attending his fiduciary responsibility as executor, particularly with respect to his selective distribution of Helen Nesmith's assets. We can discern no reason in the record as to why this matter had to proceed along the protracted and costly route that it did.

Judgment affirmed.

Points for Discussion

1. *The scope of the doctrine*

Most jurisdictions accept the doctrine of incorporation by reference. New York, Connecticut, and Louisiana are said to be the holdouts. In Booth v. Baptist Church, 28 N.E. 238 (N.Y. 1891) New York's highest court rejected the doctrine of incorporation by reference. There have been a few New York cases that have found exceptions to that blanket disapproval (although some of them certainly can be seen as applications of the doctrine of acts of independent significance, which we will address below) and there are a few statutory exceptions, the most important dealing with wills that make gifts to existing trusts which we will discuss when we discuss the use of revocable trusts as will substitutes. What is clear is that the use of a document outside the will to dispose of personal property is not possible under New York law. What policy reasons support this minority view? Can you imagine a scenario in which the doctrine is used to augment a will's dispositions by a third party? Could Greenhalge have created his own notebook revoking the gift of the farm painting in the notebook to Ms. Clark and limiting it to himself? Does the potential for fraud outweigh the utility of incorporation to the testator?

2. *Republication by codicil*

One of the difficulties faced by Virginia Clark in her quest to obtain the farm scene painting from her friend's estate is the chronology of events. Remember that if a document is to be incorporated into a will the document must be in existence when the will is executed. If you read the opinion in *Clark* carefully you will note that the notebook which contained the entry giving Ms. Clark the painting is dated 1979 and that Ms. Nesmith's will was executed in 1977. Helen Nesmith executed codicils to her will in 1980, codicils which changed some provisions of her will but not Article Fifth which made reference to the "memorandum." The codicils are of the greatest importance because of the rule that executing a codicil to a will is regarded as a re-executing of the existing will; more properly, execution of the codicil *republishes* the existing will. It re-dates the existing will as of the date of the republication. In *Clark*, this rule really saves the day for Ms. Clark—Ms. Nesmith's will is deemed to be executed when the codicils were executed. The trial court found that the notebook and the entries in it were in existence when the codicils were executed. Because the will was republished when the codicils were executed the notebook was indeed in "existence" when the will was executed and could be incorporated by reference into the will.

3. The problem of the "stuff"

Ms. Nesmith, in common with many other individuals, was particularly concerned with the passage of individual items of tangible personal property to her friends and relatives as mementos. She believed that she could update her wishes after the execution of her will by way of her notebook. Her testamentary goal was saved by the subsequent execution of her two codicils. In the absence of such a document, the scrivener might have to draft a lengthy will, resorting to frequent codicils if the client wishes to update the list. If scrivener asks the client to have a list with client when the will is executed, it can be integrated into the will or incorporated by reference. But neither of these doctrines permit the list to be updated. If the list is changed after the execution of the will the alterations will not be given effect, unless of course (as in *Greenhalge*) a codicil is executed.

Of course, one cannot count on a codicil coming to the rescue, so the drafters of the UPC decided to accommodate the statute to what they saw as reality. (Take the time to read the Comment to UPC § 2–513 to learn how the provision has evolved and to see the drafting suggestion.)

UPC § 2–513

Whether or not the provisions relating to holographic wills apply, a will may refer to a written statement or list to dispose of items of tangible personal property not otherwise specifically disposed of by the will, other than money. To be admissible under this section as evidence of the intended disposition, the writing must be signed by the testator and must describe the items and the devisees with reasonable certainty. The writing may be referred to as one to be in existence at the time of the testator's death; it may be prepared before or after the execution of the will; it may be altered by the testator after its preparation; and it may be a writing that has no significance apart from its effect on the dispositions made by the will.

Comment

"Purpose and Scope of Revision. As part of the broader policy of effectuating a testator's intent and of relaxing formalities of execution, this section permits a testator to refer in his or her will to a separate document disposing of tangible personality other than money. The pre-1990 version precluded the disposition of "evidences of indebtedness, documents of title, and securities, and property used in a trade or business." These limitations are deleted in the revised version, partly to remove a source of confusion in the pre-1990 version, which arose because evidences of indebtedness, documents of title, and securities are not items of tangible personal property to begin with, and partly to permit the disposition of a broader range of items of tangible personal property.

"The language "items of tangible personal property" does not require that the separate document specifically itemize each item of tangible personal property covered. The only requirement is that the document describe the items covered "with reasonable certainty." Consequently, a document referring to "all my tangible personal property other than money" or to "all my tangible personal property located in my office" or using similar catch-all type of language would normally be sufficient.

"The separate document disposing of an item or items of tangible personal property may be prepared after execution of the will, so would not come within Section 2–510 on incorporation by reference. It may even be altered from time to time. The only requirement is that the document be signed by the testator. The pre-1990 version of this section gave effect to an unsigned document if it was in the testator's handwriting. The revisions remove the language giving effect to such an unsigned document. The purpose is to prevent a mere handwritten draft from becoming effective without sufficient indication that the testator intended it to be effective. The signature requirement is designed to prevent mere drafts from becoming effective against the testator's wishes. An unsigned document could still be given effect under Section 2–503, however, if the proponent could carry the burden of proving by clear and convincing evidence that the testator intended the document to be effective.

"The typical case covered by this section would be a list of personal effects and the persons whom the decedent desired to take specified items.

"**Sample Clause.** Section 2–513 might be utilized by a clause in the decedent's will such as the following:

"I might leave a written statement or list disposing of items of tangible personal property. If I do and if my written statement or list is found and is identified as such by my Personal Representative no later than 30 days after the probate of this will, then my written statement or list is to be given effect to the extent authorized by law and is to take precedence over any contrary devise or devises of the same item or items of property in this will.

"Section 2–513 only authorizes disposition of tangible personal property "not otherwise specifically disposed of by the will." The sample clause above is consistent with this restriction. By providing that the written statement or list takes precedence over any contrary devise in the will, a contrary devise is made conditional upon the written statement or list not contradicting it; if the written statement or list does contradict a devise in the will, the will does not otherwise specifically dispose of the property.

"If, however, the clause in the testator's will does not provide that the written statement or list is to take precedence over any contrary devise in the will (or contain a provision having similar effect), then the written statement or list is ineffective to the extent it purports to dispose of items of property that were otherwise specifically disposed of by the will.""

4. *When you can't use incorporation by reference or UPC § 2–513*

A client domiciled in New York comes to you with a long list of personal property, some of it quite valuable, and a list of almost the same length of persons who are to receive specific items. How should the matter be handled to carry out client's wishes? If incorporation by reference is not an option, what doctrine remains? How might the will execution ceremony be configured.

5. *Acts of independent significance*

In addition to bringing unexecuted documents into the client's will through the concept of integration and incorporation by reference, the will may make a 'geographical' reference. Suppose your client keeps stock certificates and bonds, the family silver, and some jewelry in his or her safe deposit box, and yes, perhaps the odd wad of 'Franklins.' The doctrine of facts of independent significance permits the court to give testamentary effect to an extrinsic fact where that fact has some significance apart from the testator's will. A bequest to "the beneficiaries named in my brother's will at the time of his death," for example, would be valid under this doctrine. Or a gift to "the students enrolled in my Trusts & Estates class during the last semester in which I teach" would also be valid. How far are courts willing to stretch this doctrine?

The plan is to leave the contents to a favorite niece and nephew. You are asked to draft the will which has a provision that the "contents of my safe deposit box to my niece Prunella and my nephew Nigel." But at what point in time are the contents ascertained for distribution to the beneficiaries at client's death? There are two competing moments: the time of the execution of the will; or at client's death? If you choose the former, how can the contents be ascertained (unless of course of there is reference to each article in the will—in which case incorporation by reference obtains). Other 'space' may be devised, for example, the contents of my "center desk drawer" (such devises are often called devises of the contents of a container), "my safe deposit box," or perhaps "my house and contents."

In any case, since the devise is generic, and if it is interpreted as "the contents" at death, there may have been a change in the bequest from the of will execution. Each time client adds or takes out an item, it is tantamount to an alteration in the bequest, a "codicil," and one which has not been made with testamentary formality.

So what is the problem? Hark back to the reasons for requiring testamentary formality. Primary among them: to protect against fraud. Suppose Uncle Scrooge has a desk with three side drawers. He devises the contents of the top to his nephew Huey; the center to nephew Lewey, and the bottom to Dewey. Dewey knows of the arrangement. After Scrooge's death, there is a disproportionate share of property in Dewey's drawer. Was he more highly regarded by Scrooge, or did he merely get to his uncle's house first and move things around?

Courts have been lenient and permitted such bequests under the doctrine of independent significance on the grounds that the designations are not exclusively testamentary. The constant movement in and out of the space is said to have significance apart from the deceased estate plan. But how can the probate court know that? Convenience is the justification, and the property is, after all, that of the will-maker. If the will-maker wants to assume the risk of fraud . . .

6. Will custody

What should be done with the executed will? Clearly, the will must be kept safe and must also be accessible to the executor or another when the testator dies so it can be expeditiously offered for probate. The single worst place is usually the most intuitive: the testator's safe deposit box, the repository of client's other legal documents. The reason why it is the least sensible repository is that the box will be sealed at the testator's death and usually can be entered only by the executor of the will, who cannot be ascertained or appointed until the will is probated—you get the idea. If the box has to be opened to search for the will, a court order will usually be necessary. So common is this problem that in New York Article 20 of the SCPA is devoted to "Proceeding to Open Safe Deposit Box" (although there is only one substantive section, § 2003).

What other will custody options are there? The executor's safe deposit box might be a good idea so long as someone makes sure to retrieve the will should the executor predecease the testator. In some states, including New York, the courts may accept wills for safekeeping. Surrogate's Courts certainly do so, although especially in metropolitan New York City there may be a fee involved. But ours is a mobile society; what if will-maker migrates to warmer climes? How about the attorney-drafter—can she retain the will for safekeeping? At one time, this course was thought to raise a serious question of professional ethics. There was a strong body of opinion that retaining a client's will was an impermissible way of soliciting business by leaving the client with the impression that he or she had to return to the lawyer when the client wanted to revise her estate plan or when her heirs wanted to probate the will. Moreover, retention by the scrivener might lead the executor to choose that lawyer to probate the document. Today there is no doubt that providing safekeeping for clients' will is permissible (at least almost everywhere). Large law firms will store their clients' wills, usually in a footlocker sized safe deposit box in a bank. Safekeeping of all sorts of documents has become a more prominent concern since the destruction of the World Trade Center in the terrorist attacks of September 11, 2001. At least one law firm in the Trade Center kept its clients' wills in the offices, and of course, all were lost. As we will see a lost will can be probated, but safekeeping has become more critical than ever.

Retaining clients' wills for safekeeping can be difficult for a sole practitioner. When a sole practitioner retires or dies, what is to become of the wills he or she has been keeping for clients, some of whom may have had later wills written by other attorneys? The Trusts and Estates Section of the New York State Bar has long been working on finding a solution along the lines of a state-wide depository for such "orphan" wills. Expense, not surprisingly, is a major obstacle.

The testator is entitled, of course, to the original will if he or she requests it and is equally entitled to a copy. It is possible to carefully photocopy the executed will, but far easier is to simply "conform" a copy. To conform a copy means to hand print (or type) the information added to the will at the time of execution (signatures and addresses principally), preceding a signature with "S/." If Joseph Green had signed as witness or testator the conformed copy would show: "S/Joseph Green" on the appropriate signature line. If the testator, Joseph Green again, has initialed the page number footer the copy of the first page would show: "Page 1 of 1 S/J.G." and so forth for each page of the will.

Executing multiple copies, so that both lawyer and client have originals is not a good idea. The client may believe, wrongly in many states, that he or she can alter the will through interlineations and handwritten (holographic additions). In those states that allow either or both, the potential for litigation increases if the two duly executed documents are offered with inconsistent provisions.

B. The Decline of the Formalities and the Rise of the Curative Doctrines

A page of history . . .

The premise underscoring strict compliance with will execution statutes was straightforward. Courts did not investigate the subjective intent of the will-maker, but merely concluded that if he or she intended a document to be a will he or she would comply with the formalities. Thus when faced with a non-conforming document, the court conclusively presumed that it was not intended to be a will. Logic is the backbone of the law!

The above-proffered reasoning seems less compelling in modern law where, as we have observed, arguments have been made (though not always accepted) against strict enforcement of any sort of formalities. Formalism may frustrate intent. A concrete example is the *Stevens* case. There is no doubt, or at least only the slightest, that Mr. Miller intended the document to be his will, yet it is not entitled to probate because of a fault in execution that does not really speak at all to the testator's intent.

Likewise, there was little or no potential for fraud in the execution ceremony as carried out. In short, Mr. Miller's testamentary volition was thwarted because the rules channeling testamentary expression draws the bright line too far to one end of the spectrum of possible situations: in application the rules are over "overbroad." This situation has led to two doctrinal developments, or rather the application of two familiar legal concepts, to the statute of wills: *substantial compliance*; and the *harmless error rule.* Before we examine these two doctrines, bear in mind that even courts in New York, where the judiciary is not prone to fiddling with legislative direction, rules can be malleable, *reformation* on the grounds of mistake may be used to achieve the same end.

1. Reformation

Matter of Snide

418 N.E.2d 656 (N.Y. 1981)

OPINION OF THE COURT

WACHTLER, JUDGE.

This case involves the admissibility of a will to probate. The facts are simply stated and are not in dispute. Harvey Snide, the decedent, and his wife, Rose Snide, intending to execute mutual wills at a common execution ceremony, each executed by mistake the will intended for the other. There are no other issues concerning the required formalities of execution (see EPTL 3–2.1), nor is there any question of the decedent Harvey Snide's testamentary capacity, or his intention and belief that he was signing his last will and testament. Except for the obvious differences in the names of the donors and beneficiaries on the wills, they were in all other respects identical.

The proponent of the will, Rose Snide, offered the instrument Harvey actually signed for probate. The Surrogate, 96 Misc.2d 513, 409 N.Y.S.2d 204 decreed that it could be admitted, and further that it could be reformed to substitute the name "Harvey" wherever the name "Rose" appeared, and the name "Rose" wherever the name "Harvey" appeared. The Appellate Division, 426 N.Y.S.2d 155, 74 A.D.2d 930 reversed on the law, and held under a line of lower court cases dating back into the 1800's, that such an instrument may not be admitted to probate. We would reverse.

> **What's That?**
>
> The Snides executed "mutual wills," (also known as "reciprocal wills"), two wills usually executed by husband and wife which each contain a devise to the surviving spouse, with the same distribution pattern of distribution to take effect at the death of the surviving spouse so that no matter what the order of death the same beneficiaries (usually their descendants) receive their estate.

It is clear from the record, and the parties do not dispute the conclusion, that this is a case of a genuine mistake. It occurred through the presentment of the wills to Harvey and Rose in envelopes, with the envelope marked for each containing the will intended for the other. The attorney, the attesting witnesses, and Harvey and Rose, all proceeding with the execution ceremony without anyone taking care to read the front pages, or even the attestation clauses of the wills, either of which would have indicated the error.

Harvey Snide is survived by his widow and three children, two of whom have reached the age of

> **FYI**
>
> Rewriting the will in this way is an equitable remedy called the reformation of a will, where dispositive provisions are altered by judicial fiat.

majority. These elder children have executed waivers and have consented to the admission of the instrument to probate. The minor child, however, is represented by a guardian ad litem who refuses to make such a concession. The reason for the guardian's objection is apparent. Because the will of Harvey would pass the entire estate to Rose, the operation of the intestacy statute (EPTL 4–1.1) after a denial of probate is the only way in which the minor child will receive a present share of the estate.

The gist of the objectant's argument is that Harvey Snide lacked the required testamentary intent because he never intended to execute the document he actually signed. This argument is not novel, and in the few American cases on point it has been the basis for the denial of probate (see Nelson v. McDonald, 61 Hun. 406, 16 N.Y.S. 273; Matter of Cutler, Sur., 58 N.Y.S.2d 604;

> **Practice Pointer**
>
> As you can see from the citations, similar 'switches' have occurred with some frequency. How can the scrivener avoid the embarrassment?

Matter of Bacon, 165 Misc. 259, 300 N.Y.S. 920; see, also, Matter of Pavlinko, 394 Pa. 564, 148 A.2d 528; Matter of Goettel, 184 Misc. 155, 55 N.Y.S.2d 61). However, cases from other common-law jurisdictions have taken a different view of the matter, and we think the view they espouse is more sound (Matter of Brander, 4 Dom. L. Rep. 688 (1952); Guardian, Trust & Executor's Co. of New Zealand v. Inwood, 65 N. Z. L. Rep. 614 (1946) (New Zealand); see Wills, 107 U. of Pa .L. Rev. 1237, 1239–1240; Kennedy, Wills-Mistake-Husband and Wife Executing Wills Drawn for Each Other Probate of Husband's Will With Substitutions, 31 Can. Bar. Rev. 185).

Of course it is essential to the validity of a will that the testator was possessed of testamentary intent (Matter of May, 241 N.Y. 1, 148 N.E. 770; 64 N. Y. Jur., Wills, s 11; see EPTL 1–2.18), however, we decline the formalistic view that this intent attaches irrevocably to the document prepared, rather than the testamentary scheme it reflects. Certainly, had a carbon copy been substituted for the ribbon copy the testator intended to sign, it could not be seriously contended that the testator's intent should be frustrated (Matter of Epstein, Sur., 136 N.Y.S.2d 884, see 81 ALR2d 1112, 1120–1121). Here the situation is similar. Although Harvey mistakenly signed the will prepared for his wife, it is significant that the dispositive provisions in both wills, except for the names, were identical

Moreover, the significance of the only variance between the two instruments is fully explained by consideration of the documents together, as well as in the undisputed surrounding circumstances. Under such facts it would indeed be ironic if not perverse to state that because what has occurred is so obvious, and what was intended so clear, we must act to nullify rather than sustain this testamentary scheme. The instrument in question was undoubtedly genuine, and it was executed in the manner required by the statute. Under these circumstances it was properly admitted to probate (see Matter of Pascal, 309 N.Y. 108, 113–114, 127 N.E.2d 835).

In reaching this conclusion we do not disregard settled principles, nor are we unmindful of the evils which the formalities of will execution are designed to avoid; namely, fraud and mistake. To be sure, full illumination of the nature of Harvey's testamentary scheme is dependent in part on proof outside of the will itself. However, this is a very unusual case, and the nature of the additional proof should not be ignored. Not only did the two instruments constitute reciprocal elements of a unified testamentary plan, they both were executed with statutory formality, including the same attesting witnesses, at a contemporaneous execution ceremony. There is absolutely no danger of fraud, and the refusal to read these wills together would serve merely to unnecessarily expand formalism, without any corresponding benefit. On these narrow facts we decline this unjust course.

> **Food for Thought**
>
> Arguably this is an easy case; do easy cases make good law?

Nor can we share the fears of the dissent that our holding will be the first step in the exercise of judicial imagination relating to the reformation of wills. Again, we are dealing here solely with identical mutual wills both simultaneously executed with statutory formality.

For the reasons we have stated, the order of the Appellate Division should be reversed, and the matter remitted to that court for a review of the facts.

Jones, Judge (dissenting).

I agree with the Appellate Division that the Surrogate's Court had no authority to reform the decedent's will and am of the conviction that the willingness of the majority in an appealing case to depart from what has been consistent precedent in the courts of the United States and England will prove troublesome in the future. This is indeed an instance of the old adage that hard cases make bad law.

Our analysis must start with the recognition that any statute of wills (now articulated in this State at EPTL 3–2.1) operates frequently to frustrate the identifiable dispositive intentions of the decedent. It is never sufficient under our law that the decedent's wishes be clearly established; our statute, like those of most other common-law

> **Food for Thought**
>
>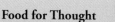
>
> Exactly how did a court, probating the will signed by Harry, take cognizance of Harry's will signed by Rose?

jurisdictions, mandates with but a few specific exceptions that the wishes of the decedent be memorialized with prescribed formality. The statutes historically have been designed for the protection of testators, particularly against fraudulent changes in or additions to wills. "(W)hile often it may happen that a will truly expressing the intention of the testator is denied probate for failure of proper execution, it is better that this should happen under a proper construction of the statute than that the individual case should be permitted to weaken those provisions intended to protect testators generally from fraudulent alterations of their wills" (64 N.Y. Jur., Wills, s 198, p. 348).

Next it must be recognized that what is admitted to probate is a paper writing, a single integrated instrument (codicils are considered integral components of the decedent's "will"). We are not concerned on admission to probate with the substantive content of the will; our attention must be focused on the paper writing itself. As to that, there can be no doubt whatsoever that Harvey Snide did not intend as his will the only document that he signed on August 13, 1970.

Until the ruling of the Surrogate of Hamilton County in this case, the application of these principles in the past had uniformly been held in our courts to preclude the admission to probate of a paper writing that the decedent unquestionably intended to execute when he and another were making mutual wills but where, through unmistakable inadvertence, each signed the will drawn for the other. Nor had our courts blinkingly invoked a doctrine of equitable reformation to reach the same end. (Nelson v. McDonald, 61 Hun. 406, 16 N.Y.S. 273; Matter of Bacon, 165 Misc. 259, 300 N.Y.S. 920; Matter of Egner, Sur., 112 N.Y.S.2d 568; Matter of Cutler, Sur., 58 N.Y.S.2d 604; subsequently, contra, Matter of Iovino, NYLJ, April 16, 1980, p. 14, col. 5 (an uncontested case).)

On the basis of commendably thorough world-wide research, counsel for appellant has uncovered a total of 17 available reported cases involving mutual wills mistakenly signed by the wrong testator. Six cases arise in New York, two in Pennsylvania, three in England, one in New Zealand and five in Canada. With the exception of the two recent Surrogate's decisions (Snide and Iovino) relief was denied in the cases from New York, Pennsylvania and England. The courts that have applied the traditional doctrines have not hesitated, however, to express regret at judicial inability to remedy the evident blunder. Relief was granted in the six cases from the British Commonwealth. In these cases it appears that the court has been moved by the transparency of the obvious error and the egregious frustration of undisputed intention which would ensue from failure to correct that error.

Under doctrines both of judicial responsibility not to allow the prospect of unfortunate consequence in an individual case to twist the application of unquestioned substantive legal principle and of stare decisis, I perceive no jurisprudential justification to reach out for the disposition adopted by the majority. Not only do I find a lack of rigorous judicial reasoning in this result; more important, I fear an inability to contain the logical consequences of this decision in the future. Thus, why should the result be any different where, although the two wills are markedly different in content, it is equally clear that there has been an erroneous contemporaneous cross-signing by the two would-be testators, or where the scrivener has prepared several drafts for a single client and it is established beyond all doubt that the wrong draft has been mistakenly signed? Nor need imagination stop there.

Take Note

Is there any possibility that the document signed by Rose admitted to explain the disposition in the will offered for probate did *not* contain Harry's desired depository plan?

For the reasons stated, I would adhere to the precedents, and affirm the order of the Appellate Division.

JASEN, FUCHSBERG and MEYER, JJ., concur with WACHTLER, J.

JONES, J., dissents and votes to affirm in a separate opinion in which COOKE, C.J., and GABRIELLI, J., concur.

Order reversed, with costs to all parties appearing separately and filing separate briefs payable out of the estate, and the matter remitted to the Appellate Division, Third Department, for further proceedings in accordance with the opinion herein.

—————————

2. Substantial Compliance

In addition to reformation, there are two other so-called curative doctrines. What are they curing? A will that does not comply with statutory mandates on due execution. The first doctrine is *substantial compliance*, or, "close enough is good enough." You should be familiar with this concept from studying the law of contracts. Many substantial compliance cases involve situations where the witnesses, or perhaps the testator, sign the self-proving affidavit rather than at the appropriate places in the attestation clause. An example of the application of substantial compliance in this context is *In re Will of Ranney*, 124 N.J. 1, 589 A.2d 1339 (1991). There the testator signed the will and the separate self-proving affidavit, but the witnesses signed only the affidavit and not the will itself. The intermediate appellate court held that the affidavit was part of the will and that therefore the witnesses' signatures appeared on the will and the will was duly executed. The New Jersey Supreme Court overruled the lower court, holding that the affidavit was separate from and not part of the will. Nevertheless it remanded the case directing that the trial court proceed with solemn form probate, and if the court was then satisfied "that the execution of the will substantially complies with the statutory requirements" the will should be admitted to probate:

> **Make the Connection**
>
> How good a fit is the borrowing? In contracts, the application usually deals with performance issues. The issue in wills situations is compliance with statutory mandates.

> "Substantial compliance is a functional rule designed to cure the inequity caused by the "harsh and relentless formalism" of the law of wills. * * * The underlying rationale is that the finding of a formal defect should lead not to automatic invalidity, but to a further inquiry: does the noncomplying document express the decedent's testamentary intent, and does its form sufficiently approximate Wills Act formality to enable the court to conclude that it serves the purposes of the Wills Act? . . . .

> "Legislative history confirms that N.J.S.A. 3B:3–2 was enacted to free will execution from the ritualism of pre-Code law and to prevent technical defects from invalidating otherwise valid wills. Senate Judiciary Committee Public Hearing on Uniform Probate Code Bills at 20 (comments of Harrison Durand) (reduction of statutory formalities meant to prevent failure of testamentary plans); see In re Estate of Peters, supra, 107 N.J. at 272 n. 2, 526 A.2d 1005 (noting that former statute often resulted in wills being refused probate because some formality not followed). Generally, when strict construction would frustrate the purposes of the statute, the spirit of the law should control over its letter. New Jersey Builders, Owners & Managers Ass'n v. Blair, 60 N.J. 330, 338, 288 A.2d 855 (1972). Accordingly, we

believe that the Legislature did not intend that a will should be denied probate because the witnesses signed in the wrong place.

"The execution of a last will and testament, however, remains a solemn event. A careful practitioner will still observe the formalities surrounding the execution of wills. When formal defects occur, proponents should prove by clear and convincing evidence that the will substantially complies with statutory requirements. See Uniform Probate Code, supra, § 2–503; Restatement, supra, § 33.1 comment *g*. Our adoption of the doctrine of substantial compliance should not be construed as an invitation either to carelessness or chicanery. The purpose of the doctrine is to remove procedural peccadillos as a bar to probate.

"Furthermore, . . . a subsequently-signed self-proving affidavit serves a unique function in the probate of wills. We are reluctant to permit the signatures on such an affidavit both to validate the execution of the will and to render the will self-proving. Accordingly, if the witnesses, with the intent to attest, sign a self-proving affidavit, but do not sign the will or an attestation clause, clear and convincing evidence of their intent should be adduced to establish substantial compliance with the statute. For that reason, probate in these circumstances should proceed in solemn form. See N.J.S.A. 3B:3–23; R. 4:84–1. Probate in solemn form, which is an added precaution to assure proof of valid execution, may be initiated on an order to show cause, R. 4:84–1(b), and need not unduly delay probate of a qualified will. The record suggests that the proffered instrument is the will of Russell Ranney, that he signed it voluntarily, that Schuster and Stout signed the self-proving affidavit at Russell's request, and that they witnessed his signature. Furthermore, Betty has certified that Russell executed the will and that she is unaware of the existence of any other will. Before us, however, her attorney questions whether Russell "actually signed" the will.

"If, after conducting a hearing in solemn form, the trial court is satisfied that the execution of the will substantially complies with the statutory requirements, it may reinstate the judgment of the Surrogate admitting the will to probate."

Before becoming too staunch an advocate for the adoption of the doctrine of substantial compliance, consider that applying the doctrine to will execution statutes creates the problem of deciding how close is indeed 'close enough.' Signatures of witnesses appearing only on the self-proving affidavit and not the will present perhaps the easiest case, even though in signing an affidavit which does not truthfully recount what occurred at the execution ceremony suggests that the witnesses have technically perjured themselves. Recall that the affidavit attests to a legal act, the signature of witnesses on the will itself, that had not taken place. In a case like *Ranney*, the court may simply be making allowances for the possibility of confusion during a complicated and often emotionally fraught ritual.

In 1990, the UPC was amended to address the situation the New Jersey Supreme Court faced in *Ranney*. UPC § 5–504(c) states: "A signature affixed to a self-proving affidavit attached to a will is considered a signature affixed to the will, if necessary to prove the will's due execution."

You should realize the novelty of *Ranney* is its use of substantial compliance to possibly excuse strict compliance with so fundamental a requirement as the witnesses signing the will. Courts in states like New York which have the reputation of demanding strict adherence to the statutory formalities of execution have occasionally bent the rules of due execution.

Take Note

The devil is in the detail. In jurisdictions (like New Jersey) where the requirements are minimal anyway, how frequently will you not have actual compliance?

Specifically, the New York Appellate Division for the Fourth Department (an intermediate appellate court) has stated that "substantial compliance with those requirements [the publication requirement of EPTL § 3–2.1(a)(3) and the attesting witness requirements of § 3–2.1(a)(4), specifically the requirement that the testator request that the witnesses sign] is sufficient." (*Matter of Frank*, 249 A.D.2d 893 (N.Y. App. 1998)).

3.   The Harmless Error Rule (a.k.a. the Dispensing Power)

The second curative doctrine, and the one adopted by the current UPC (largely because substantial compliance rarely was actually implemented by courts to validate defectively executed wills), is the harmless error rule. Unlike substantial compliance, which asks the question were the formalities observed closely enough to those mandated by statute, the harmless error rule focuses on the will-maker's subjective belief in the validity of the testamentary act that fails to conform to the letter of the statutory formalities. The question posed is "did the will-maker believe that the document was her will?" The doctrines are not dissimilar, and their use may be supported by the same evidence: we may be more confident that the will-maker believed her will was a valid testamentary document if the formalities observed approximated (came close enough to) statutory mandates.

UPC § 2–503. Harmless Error

Although a document or writing added upon a document was not executed in compliance with Section 2–502, the document or writing is treated as if it has been executed in compliance with that section if the proponent of the document or writing established by clear and convincing evidence that the decedent intended the document or writing to constitute (i) the decedent's will, (ii) a partial or complete revocation of the will, (iii) an addition to or an alternation of the will, or (iv) a partial or complete revival of his [or her] formerly revoked will or of a formerly revoked portion of the will.

Observe its application in the following case.

In re Estate of Hall

310 Mont. 486, 51 P.3d 1134 (2002)

JUSTICE JIM REGNIER delivered the Opinion of the Court.

James Mylen Hall ("Jim") died on October 23, 1998. At the time of his death, he was 75 years old and lived in Cascade County, Montana. His wife, Betty Lou Hall ("Betty"), and two daughters from a previous marriage, Sandra Kay Ault ("Sandra") and Charlotte Rae Hall ("Charlotte"), survived him.

Jim first executed a will on April 18, 1984 (the "Original Will"). Approximately thirteen years later, Jim and Betty's attorney, Ross Cannon, transmitted to them a draft of a joint will (the "Joint Will"). On June 4, 1997, Jim and Betty met at Cannon's office to discuss the draft. After making several changes, Jim and Betty apparently agreed on the terms of the Joint Will. Jim and Betty were prepared to execute the Joint Will once Cannon sent them a final version.

At the conclusion of the meeting, however, Jim asked Cannon if the draft could stand as a will until Cannon sent them a final version. Cannon said that it would be valid if Jim and Betty executed the draft and he notarized it. Betty testified that no one else was in the office at the time to serve as an attesting witness. Jim and Betty, therefore, proceeded to sign the Joint Will and Cannon notarized it without anyone else present.

> **Practice Pointer**
>
> Is there a lesson to be learned here? Or, would you like to be the lawyer in this case?

When they returned home from the meeting, Jim apparently told Betty to tear up the Original Will, which Betty did. After Jim's death, Betty applied to informally probate the Joint Will. Sandra objected to the informal probate and requested formal probate of the Original Will.

On August 9, 2001, Judge McKittrick heard the will contest. He issued the Order admitting the Joint Will to probate on August 27, 2001. Sandra appealed.

Sandra argues that the judicial interpretation and construction of a will are questions of law. This appeal, however, does not involve interpreting or constructing a will. The dispositive issue is whether the District Court properly admitted the disputed will to probate. Determining whether a court properly admitted a will involves both questions of law and fact. *See In re Estate of Brooks* (1996), 279 Mont. 516, 519, 927 P.2d 1024, 1026. In *Brooks,* we described our standard as follows:

> "We will not disturb a district court's findings of fact unless they are clearly erroneous. A court's findings are clearly erroneous if they are not supported by substantial credible evidence, the court has misapprehended the effect of the evidence, or our review of the record convinces us that a mistake has been committed. We

review a district court's conclusions of law to determine whether the interpretation of the law is correct. [Citations omitted.]"

Brooks, 279 Mont. at 519, 927 P.2d at 1026.

Did the District Court err in admitting the Joint Will to formal probate?

> **Food for Thought**
>
> Is the contestant trying to suggest that failure to comply with the rules of due execution is evidence that testamentary intent was not present at the time of the botched execution? Or perhaps that the document was really intended only to be a draft?

In contested cases, the proponent of a will must establish that the testator duly executed the will. *See* § 72–3–310, MCA; *Brooks,* 279 Mont. at 519, 927 P.2d at 1026. For a will to be valid, two people typically must witness the testator signing the will and then sign the will themselves. *See* § 72–2–522(1)(c), MCA. If two individuals do not properly witness the document, § 72–2–523, MCA, provides that the document may still be treated as if it had been executed under certain circumstances. One such circumstance is if the proponent of the document establishes by clear and convincing evidence that the decedent intended the document to be the decedent's will. *See* § 72–2–523, MCA; *Brooks,* 279 Mont. at 522, 927 P.2d at 1027.

Sandra urges this Court not to use § 72–2–523, MCA, "to circumvent the statute requiring two witnesses to the execution of a will." Jim and Betty's failure to use witnesses, according to Sandra, was not an innocent omission on their part. She also expresses concern that the improperly witnessed Joint Will materially altered a long-standing agreement to divide the property. She primarily argues, however, that the Joint Will should be invalid as a matter of law because no one properly witnessed it.

Sandra does not dispute any of the court's factual findings. She argues only that Betty testified that she and Jim had not executed the will even after they had signed it. In making this argument, she points to the following testimony:

Question: Do you know if [Jim] gave [Sandra and Charlotte] a copy of the new will?

Answer: I don't believe he did, no.

Question: Do you know why?

Answer: Well, I guess because we didn't have the completed draft without all the scribbles on it.

Question: So he thought that will was not good yet?

Answer: No, he was sure it was good, but he didn't give it to the girls. And we didn't give it to my son. We didn't give it to anybody.

Question: Why?

Answer: Because it wasn't completely finished the way Ross was going to finish it.

This testimony may suggest that Betty believed that the Joint Will was not in a final form because of "all the scribbles on it." Nevertheless, she immediately goes on to state that she believed the will was good. When asked if it were Jim's and her intent for the Joint Will to stand as a will until they executed another one, she responded, "Yes, it was." The court could reasonably interpret this testimony to mean that Jim and Betty expected the Joint Will to stand as a will until Cannon provided one in a cleaner, more final form. Sandra points to no other evidence that suggests that Jim did not intend for the Joint Will to be his will.

For these reasons, we conclude that the District Court did not err in admitting the Joint Will into final probate. Because Jim directed Betty to destroy the Original Will, we also conclude that the District Court did not err in finding that these acts were acts of revocation of the Original Will under § 72–2–527, MCA.

Affirmed.

Points for Discussion

1. Harmless error and restatement third

The "harmless error" rule of UPC § 2–503 is a statement in statutory form of the principle enunciated in Restatement (Third) of Property (Wills and Donative Transfers) § 3.3. The commentary to the Restatement section discusses the history and the willingness on the part of courts to relax formal requirements for the execution of wills.

2. What are the "curative doctrines" really about?

Are the two curative doctrines really doctrinally distinct? Do courts ask the same or different questions in applying each of these rules? For example, does the majority opinion in the *Snide* case mean that the harmless error rule is part of the common law of New York? Or is the case authority for "reformation" in cases where the testator's error is so obvious that there is no danger of fraud or imposition? Is the harmless error rule easier to satisfy than is substantial compliance? Consider the following:

1. Would *Matter of Snide* and *Matter of Hall* be decided the same way using substantial compliance?

2. How would *Slack v. Truitt* be decided using substantial compliance? Harmless error (assume that UPC § 2–503 applies)?

3. Would *Stevens v. Casdorph* be decided differently using substantial compliance? Harmless error (assume that UPC § 2–503 applies)?

4. How would substantial compliance and harmless error (UPC § 2–503) apply to the "execution over the phone" and the "testator in bed" hypos following *Stevens*?

5.   Would substantial compliance or harmless error allow a court to treat as the valid the two disputed pages of Prof. Beale's will (pages 115–116)?

3. Is there anything left of the formalities?

What is the point of having statutory formalities of execution which are not difficult to satisfy and then bending them?

4. And how do we know anyway?

Finally, how can courts ever be sure of what a now-deceased person actually thought at the time of the supposed will execution or thereafter?

5. The witness who signs after the testator's death

Suppose a will is offered for probate in which a person who was present at the time the testator signed the will, but did not sign the will as an attesting witness is asked to sign the will as witness after the testator's death. If the relevant statute requires the witnesses to sign in the "presence" of the testator like NY EPTL § 3–2.1(a)(2) it is easy to decide that the answer is "no." As we've seen, however, UPC § 2–502 does not have such a requirement. Not surprisingly, once states began to adopt the UPC provision, the question of whether postdeath signing by the witnesses could satisfy the statute did not have an easy answer. In *Estate of Peters,* 526 A.2d 1005 (N.J. 1987) the New Jersey Supreme Court said the witnesses must sign within a "reasonable time" of witnessing the testator sign or acknowledge her signature and that while the signing could occur after the testator's death, the 18 months that elapsed between the testator's death and the witnesses' signing the will in *Peters* was unreasonable. (Interestingly, the court refused to consider substantial compliance, as position it reversed in *Ranney.*)

The Colorado Supreme Court rejected the holding in *Peters* and held that the witnesses must sign before the testator's death, period. (*Estate of Royal,* 836 P.2d 1236 (Colo. 1992)). (By that time the UPC execution statute had been amended to require that the witnesses sign within a reasonable time of witnessing the testator's signature or acknowledgment of that signature and the official comment was also amended to state that the reasonable time requirement "could be satisfied even if the witnesses sign after the testator's death," but Colorado had not adopted the amended version of the statute.)

In 2006, the supreme courts of California and Idaho both addressed the question. In *Estate of Saueressig,* 136 P.3d 201 (Cal. 2006), the court refused to probate a will that bore the notarized signature of the testator but no signatures of witnesses. The testator brought his will to a Mail Boxes, Etc. store and asked the proprietor, Ms. Shin, to notarize his signature on the will. After the testator's death, the proprietor's husband, who was present when his wife notarized Mr. Saueressig's signature, offered to sign the will as the second witness (the signature of the notary would then be considered the signature of a witness), stating that he had heard Mr. Saueressig request that Ms. Shin notarize his will, that he had seen Mr. Saueressig sign a document which he understood to be Mr. Saueressig's will, and had seen Ms. Shin notarize Mr. Saueressig's signature on the will. The court analyzed in great detail the legislature's removal from the will execution statute of the requirement that the witnesses sign in the presence of the testator. It held first that the removal did not authorize post-mortem witnessing, and second that sound policy forbade it. The court did not mention substantial compliance, and noted that the legislature had not adopted the harmless error rule.

In *Estate of Miller*, 1149 P.3d 840 (Idaho 2006), the court also ignored both substantial compliance and the harmless error rule and admitted a post-mortem attested will on the grounds that the statute itself did not prohibit a witness signing after the death of the testator. The testator brought his will to his bank where a bank officer notarized his signature. The testator was accompanied by the sole beneficiary of the will who witnesses the signing and the notarization. The testator died four years later and on advice of counsel the beneficiary signed the will as a witness.

"The issue in this case is whether Miller's will was validly executed under Idaho law. Idaho Code § 15–2–502 provides insofar as is relevant, "[E]very will shall be in writing signed by the testator . . ., and shall be signed by at least two (2) persons each of whom witnessed either the signing or the testator's acknowledgment of the signature or of the will." The statute is not ambiguous. It does not impose any requirement as to when the witnesses must sign the will. There is no question that the will in this case complies with the requirements of the statute. The will was in writing, it was signed by Miller, two persons witnessed that signing, and both of those witnesses signed the will."

"The only issue is whether this Court should follow other courts in adding an additional requirement that the witnesses must sign within a reasonable time after witnessing or at least before the testator's death. We will not do so."

"It is the province of the legislature to set the standards for the execution of a will. *Miller v. Miller*, 99 Idaho 850, 590 P.2d 577 (1979). From 1887 until the adoption of Idaho's version of the Uniform Probate Code in 1971, Idaho law had more stringent requirements for a valid will. Section 5727 of the Revised Statutes of Idaho Territory (1887) provided:

> Every will, other than a nuncupative will, must be in writing, and every will, other than an [h]olographic will and a nuncupative will, but be executed and attested as follows:
>
> 1. It must be subscribed at the end thereof by the testator himself, or some person in his presence and by his direction must subscribe his name thereto;
>
> 2. The subscription must be made in the presence of the attesting witnesses or be acknowledged by the testator to them, to have been made by him or by his authority;
>
> 3. The testator must, at the time of subscribing or acknowledging the same, declare to the attesting witnesses that the instrument is his will; and

4.   There must be two attesting witnesses, each of whom must sign his name as a witness, at the end of the will, at the testator's request, and in his presence.

Under this statute, the witnesses were required to sign their names "at the testator's request, and in his presence."

> **Food for Thought**
>
> Hark back to the function of formalities: ritual, evidentiary, and protective. Are they satisfied in cases like *Miller*?

"The legislature did not retain that requirement when it adopted Idaho Code § 15–2–502. The comment to the official text of § 15–2–502 states, "The formalities for execution of a witnessed will have been reduced to a minimum. . . . The intent is to validate wills which meet the minimal formalities of the statute."

"The legislature obviously knew the changes it was making to the execution requirements of a valid will when it adopted Idaho Code § 15–2–502. Had it desired to include a provision specifying when the witnesses must sign, it could have done so. It could have required that they sign in the presence of the testator, as did Idaho law from 1887 until 1971. It could have required that they sign within a reasonable time after witnessing. It could have required that they at least sign prior to the death of the testator. It did not impose either these or any other requirements as to when the witnesses must sign."

Would it be correct to say that old fashioned legal formalism rather than newer-fangled curative doctrines seems to have saved Mr. Miller's testamentary designs!

6. Applications of the harmless error statute

Colorado has enacted the harmless error rule of UPC § 2–503 (C.R.S.A. § 15–11–503(1)), with an additional requirement that the offered document be signed or acknowledged by the decedent as his or her will (C.R.S.A. § 15–11–503(2)). In *Estate of Wiltfong*, 148 P.3d 465 (Colo. App. 2006), the court admitted to probate a birthday card containing a typed letter decedent had signed. The letter expressed decedent's wish that if anything should ever happen to him, everything he owned should go to proponent, the person offering the "will" for probate. The letter also stated that proponent, their pets, and an aunt were his only family, and "everyone else is dead to me." Decedent told proponent and the friends that the letter represented his wishes. He died from a heart attack the following year. The court held that the statute does not require that the decedent declare that a signed document is a will and therefore remanded the matter for a determination of whether clear and convincing evidence showed that the decedent intended the document to be his will.

New Jersey has also enacted the harmless error rule (N.J.S.A. 3B:3–3; identical to UPC § 2–503). In *Matter of Macool*, 2 A.3d 1258 (N.J. App.Div. 2010), the New Jersey intermediate appellate court denied probate of a draft will which the testator never saw. She died only an hour or so after visiting her lawyer to discuss the will. The lawyer produced a draft, but death came before the client could return to the lawyer's office. The court found that the facts clearly showed that the document was indeed a draft and that it was impossible to know whether the document expressed the decedent's intent. The court held that, for a document to be admitted to probate under the statute, the proponent must show by clear and convincing evidence that the decedent reviewed the document and gave his or her "final assent" to it. The court went on to construe the statute and stated that it did not require the document be signed by the testator. Under the New Jersey court's reading of UPC § 2–503, would the will in *Hall* be admitted to probate?

C. Holographic Wills

Wills that are valid because they are executed in conformity with the jurisdiction's due execution statute are usually referred to as attested wills. UPC § 2–502(b), reproduced above, also recognizes as valid a will that is not properly attested by witnesses so long as the signature of the testator and "material portions of the document" are in the testator's handwriting. Such wills are called *holographic* wills: handwritten. About one-half of the states recognize holographic wills. New York is one of the states that generally does not recognize holographic wills, but it makes an exception for holographs and nuncupative (oral) wills made by members of the armed forces and those accompanying an armed force actually engaged in military service during a war, be it declared or undeclared, and mariners at sea. Such wills are generally valid only for a limited period of time (EPTL § 3–2.2).

A page of history . . .

Roman law recognized holographic wills, and therefore recognized when Roman law was codified in continental Europe. Thus, in the United States, holographs were recognized in west where the influence of Spanish law was greatest (Louisiana, Texas, Arizona, New Mexico, and California). English law, developed in the church courts also recognized holographic wills of land until the Statute of Frauds (1677) and of personalty until the Statute of Wills (1837). Indeed, nuncupative will were also probated, until the respective Statutes of Frauds and Wills required attested wills. In the United States, a scattered population and an absence of lawyers probably led to the recognition of these "home-made wills." Early holographic will statutes required that the entire document be handwritten and usually that it be dated and signed at the end by the testator.

The UPC has greatly influenced modern statutes many of which require, as does § 2–502(b), that only "material provisions" need be in the testator's handwriting. (See the brief discussion of the history of the statutes in Restatement Third, Property (Wills and Donative Transfers) § 3.2, comment *a*.)

In re Estate of Kuralt

15 P.3d 931 (Mont. 2000)

To summarize [the facts], Charles Kuralt and Elizabeth Shannon maintained a long term and intimate personal relationship. Kuralt and Shannon desired to keep their relationship secret, and were so successful in doing so that even though Kuralt's wife, Petie, knew that Kuralt owned property in Montana, she was unaware, prior to Kuralt's untimely death, of his relationship with Shannon.

Over the nearly 30-year course of their relationship, Kuralt and Shannon saw each other regularly and maintained contact by phone and mail. Kuralt was the primary source of financial support for Shannon and established close, personal relationships with Shannon's three children. Kuralt provided financial support for a joint business venture managed by Shannon and transferred a home in Ireland to Shannon as a gift.

> **Go Online**
>
> To learn more about one of the twentieth century's most travelled journalists: https://museumtv.past-perfectonline.com/byperson?keyword=Kuralt%2C+Charles.

In 1985, Kuralt purchased a 20-acre parcel of property along the Big Hole River in Madison County, near Twin Bridges, Montana. Kuralt and Shannon constructed a cabin on this 20-acre parcel. In 1987, Kuralt purchased two additional parcels along the Big Hole which adjoined the original 20-acre parcel. These two additional parcels, one upstream and one downstream of the cabin, created a parcel of approximately 90 acres and are the primary subject of this appeal. . . .

On May 3, 1989, Kuralt executed a holographic will which stated as follows:

> May 3, 1989
>
> In the event of my death, I bequeath to Patricia Elizabeth Shannon all my interest in land, buildings, furnishings and personal belongings on Burma Road, Twin Bridges, Montana.
>
> Charles Kuralt
>
> 34 Bank St.
>
> New York, N.Y. 10014

Although Kuralt mailed a copy of this holographic will to Shannon, he subsequently executed a formal will on May 4, 1994, in New York City. This Last Will and Testament, prepared with the assistance of counsel, does not specifically mention any of the real property owned by Kuralt. The beneficiaries of Kuralt's Last Will and Testament were his wife, Petie, and the Kuralt's two children.

> **Food for Thought**
>
> Does the choice of language used by Kuralt (a man who made his living with words) suggest that this document was to have testamentary effect? Compare the language in the June 18, 1997 letter with the language of the document of May 3, 1989.

Neither Shannon nor her children are named as beneficiaries in Kuralt's formal will. Shannon had no knowledge of the formal will until the commencement of these proceedings.

On April 9, 1997, Kuralt deeded his interest in the original 20-acre parcel with the cabin to Shannon. The transaction was disguised as a sale. However, Kuralt supplied the "purchase" price for the 20-acre parcel to Shannon prior to the transfer. After the deed to the 20-acre parcel was filed, Shannon sent Kuralt, at his request, a blank buy-sell real estate form so that the remaining 90 acres along the Big Hole could be conveyed to Shannon in a similar manner. Apparently, it was again Kuralt's intention to provide the purchase price. The second transaction was to take place in September 1997 when Shannon, her son, and Kuralt agreed to meet at the Montana cabin. Kuralt, however, became suddenly ill and entered a New York hospital on June 18, 1997. On that same date, Kuralt wrote the letter to Shannon which is now at the center of the current dispute:

June 18, 1997

Dear Pat—

Something is terribly wrong with me and they can't figure out what. After cat-scans and a variety of cardiograms, they agree it's not lung cancer or heart trouble or blood clot. So they're putting me in the hospital today to concentrate on infectious diseases. I am getting worse, barely able to get out of bed, but still have high hopes for recovery . . . if only I can get a diagnosis! Curiouser and curiouser! I'll keep you informed. I'll have the lawyer visit the hospital to be sure you inherit the rest of the place in MT. if it comes to that.

I send love to you & [your youngest daughter,] Shannon. Hope things are better there! Love,

C.

Enclosed with this letter were two checks made payable to Shannon, one for $8000 and the other for $9000. Kuralt did not seek the assistance of an attorney to devise the remaining 90 acres of Big Hole land to Shannon. Therefore, when Kuralt died unexpectedly, Shannon sought to probate the letter of June 18, 1997, as a valid holographic codicil to Kuralt's formal 1994 will.

Practice Pointer

How might Kuralt have accomplished his desire to give Shannon the Montana property? Obviously, his do-it-yourself estate planning strategy was less than optimal.

The Estate opposed Shannon's Petition for Ancillary Probate based on its contention that the June 18, 1997 letter expressed only a future intent to make a will. The District Court granted partial summary judgment for the Estate on May 26, 1998. Shannon appealed from the District Court order which granted partial summary judgment to the Estate. This Court, in Kuralt I, reversed the District Court and remanded the case for trial in order to resolve disputed issues of material fact. Following an abbreviated evidentiary hearing, the District Court issued its Findings and Order. The District Court held that the June 18, 1997 letter was a valid holographic codicil to Kuralt's formal will of May 4, 1994 and accordingly entered judgment in favor of Shannon. The Estate now appeals from that order and judgment.

* * *

The Estate contends that the District Court made legal errors which led to a mistaken conclusion about Kuralt's intent concerning the disposition of his Montana property. The Estate argues that the District Court failed to recognize the legal effect of the 1994 will and therefore erroneously found that Kuralt, after his May 3, 1989 holographic will, had an uninterrupted intent to transfer the Montana property to Shannon. The Estate further argues that Kuralt's 1994 formal will revoked all prior wills, both expressly and by inconsistency. This manifest change of intention, according to the Estate, should have led the District Court to the conclusion that Kuralt did not intend to transfer the Montana property to Shannon upon his death.

* * *

What's That?

Aren't two probates excessive even for a prominent person like Charles Kuralt? The fact that he owned land in Montana required probate there to pass title to Shannon or to the beneficiaries under the New York will. Because real estate is always governed by the law of its situs the executor (or administrator) must receive letters testamentary from a court in the state where the real estate is located.

The record supports the District Court's finding that the June 18, 1997 letter expressed Kuralt's intent to effect a posthumous transfer of his Montana property to Shannon. Kuralt and Shannon enjoyed a long, close personal relationship which continued up to the last letter Kuralt wrote Shannon on June 18, 1997, in which he enclosed checks to her in the amounts of $8000 and $9000. Likewise, Kuralt and Shannon's children had a long, family-like relationship which included significant financial support.

The District Court focused on the last few months of Kuralt's life to find that the letter demonstrated his testamentary intent. The conveyance of the 20-acre parcel for no real consideration and extrinsic evidence that Kuralt intended to convey the remainder of the Montana property to Shannon in a similar fashion provides substantial factual support for the District Court's determination that Kuralt intended that Shannon have the rest of the Montana property.

The June 18, 1997 letter expressed Kuralt's desire that Shannon inherit the remainder of the Montana property. That Kuralt wrote the letter in extremis is supported by the fact that he died two weeks later. Although Kuralt intended to transfer the remaining land to Shannon, he was reluctant to consult a lawyer to formalize his intent because he wanted to keep their relationship secret. Finally, the use of the term "inherit" underlined by Kuralt reflected his intention to make a posthumous disposition of the property. Therefore, the District Court's findings are supported by substantial evidence and are not clearly erroneous.

Accordingly, we conclude that the District Court did not err when it found that the letter dated June 18, 1997 expressed a present testamentary intent to transfer property in Madison County to Patricia Shannon.

* * *

The Estate contends that the District Court erred when it held that the June 18, 1997 letter was a valid codicil, because by definition a codicil must refer to a previous will or must itself be a valid will. Because the District Court held that the June 18, 1997 letter was a codicil without analyzing how the letter affected the provisions of the 1994 will, the Estate contends that the District Court erred and that it improperly deprived the parties of a chance to be heard on this issue.

However, we agree with the District Court's conclusion that the June 18, 1997 holograph was a codicil to Kuralt's 1994 formal will. Admittedly, the June 18, 1997 letter met the threshold requirements for a valid holographic will. Kuralt I, ¶ 3. Moreover, the letter was a codicil as a matter of law because it made a specific bequest of the Montana property and did not purport to bequeath the entirety of the estate. See Official Comments to § 72–2–527, MCA ("when the second will does

> **Food for Thought**
>
> But doesn't the will do more than express an *intention* to transfer property—that's the contestant's point. It is the document that transfers property albeit in the future. Did Kuralt think he needed another document?

not make a complete disposition of the testator's estate, the second will is more in the nature of a codicil to the first will"). The District Court was therefore correct when it concluded that the June 18, 1997 letter was a codicil. Furthermore, we see no evidence that the Estate had any less opportunity to argue this issue in the District Court than it has had on appeal. Accordingly, we affirm the judgment of the District Court.

Points for Discussion

1. Problems relating to holographic wills and codicils

1. Determined to change her will, testator handwrites a letter to her lawyer, describing the changes she wants made. She mails the letter but on the way home from the post office is killed in a traffic accident. The lawyer receives the letter in due course. Can the letter be probated as a holographic will or codicil (amendment to a will)?

2. Mr. Kimmel writes by hand a rambling letter addressed to two of his children in which he describes work on the farm and the weather. After writing that he may or may not come to visit his children during Christmas holidays (the letter is dated December 12) and other matters like the proper pickling of pork he writes:

> I have some very valuable papers I want you to keep fore me so if enny thing happens all the scock money in the 3 Bank liberty lones Post office stamps and my home on Horner St goes to George Darl & Irvin Kepp this letter lock it up it may help you out.

. . . . .

Mr. Kimmel signed the letter "Father." He died later that day having mailed the letter in the morning. Can the letter be admitted to probate as a holographic will? *See In re Kimmel's Estate*, 278 Pa. 435, 1123 A. 405 (1924).

2. Will forms

Can printed will forms (or print outs from the internet) be probated as valid holographs? In a will form, the boiler-plate language of a will is printed, and the will-maker fills in the date, executor, beneficiaries and the like. If the printed will is witnessed, there is no issue: it is validly executed will. But what if it is not? Can the filled-in blanks on the form signature be admitted to probate as a holographic will? The will-maker clearly expects the printed material to be a part of the will—she intends to incorporate the printed language. In some states that intention is sufficient to deny probate as a holograph. Other states would ignore the writing, consider it surplusage, if the material provisions of the will are in the handwriting of the will-maker. Remember testamentary intent is a material provision in a will. So if the handwriting contains no words indicating that the document is a will, and testamentary intent can only be found in the printed language, the form will might be denied probate.

Form will cases go both ways. But the conflict revolves about the willingness or unwillingness to read the handwritten words in the context of the words on the printed form. For example, *Estate of Johnson*, 630 P.2d 1031 (Ariz. App. 1972) held that handwriting that named the testator's children, followed by a fraction, and the words "of my estate" did not meet the "material provisions" requirement. The argument the other way, of course, is that the word "estate" written on a pre-printed will form can only mean property owned at death and clearly indicates that the writer intends the document to be a will. The question is one of reading words in their context. Certainly the word "estate" has many meanings, but which one is intended when the word is written on a will form? In the case, the court noted an earlier case (*Estate of Blake v. Benza*, 587 P.2d 271 (Ariz. App. 1981) in which the handwritten word "estate" was sufficient to indicate testamentary intent where it was accompanied by the words "save this." The Arizona courts may have relented. In *Estate of Muder* 765 P. 2d 997 (Ariz. 1998) the Arizona Supreme Court admitted a will form that was signed and notarized conceding that:

> We hold that a testator who uses a preprinted form, and in his own handwriting fills in the blanks by designating his beneficiaries and apportioning his estate among them and signs it, has created a valid holographic will. Such handwritten provisions may draw testamentary context from both the printed and the handwritten language on the form. We see no need to ignore the preprinted words when the testator clearly did not. . .'

The issue might not finally be resolved. Two dissenting judges regarded the expansive reading of the holographic will statute's mandate that the signature and material provisions be in the hand of the will-maker as "more mischievous than helpful."

As noted above, the relevant UPC provision, § 2–502(b) requires that a will is valid as a holograph "if the signature and material portions of the document are in the testator's handwriting." The language was changed from "material provisions" in order to allow the probate of printed will forms. The official comment to the section, in fact, states that the fact that the words "I give, devise and bequeath to" at printed on the form does not prevent the document from being a holographic will so long "the testator fills out the remaining portion of the dispositive provision in his own hand." In addition, UPC § 2–502(c) expressly allows intent to be proved from those portions of the document not in the testator's handwriting.

D. Note on Conditional Wills

Mr. Kimmel's letter included the phrase "if enny thing happens." Testators sometimes associate making their wills with an event such as going on a journey or having surgery. Sometimes the will is written in such a way as to make it possible to conclude that the will is to be effective only if the condition is fulfilled by returning from the particular journey or not recovering from the surgery. Courts usually interpret such language as not setting forth a true condition but rather as showing the event that focused the testator's attention on the need for writing a will. These cases reflect the strong presumption that having written a will the testator does not intended to die intestate whenever death comes. *See* Eaton v. Brown, 193 U.S. 411 (1904), where the holographic will stated "I am going on a journey and may not return. If I do not, I leave everything to my adopted son." In an opinion by Justice Oliver Wendell Holmes, the United States Supreme Court held that the will was entitled to probate even though the testator died sometime after returning from the journey mentioned in the will.

> **Make the Connection**
>
> What is the United States Supreme Court doing deciding a probate case?

True conditional wills do exist, however. A modern example is In re Estate of Perez, 155 S.W.3d 599 (Tex.App.—San Antonio 2004) where the will stated "because I am sick and waiting for a [sic] heart surgery, and providing ahead of any emergency, I make the following disposition to be fulfilled in case my death occurs during the surgery . . . ." The testator survived the surgery and died sometime after while residing with his sister. The intermediate Texas appellate court reversed the trial court's admission of the will to probate holding that the testator intended the will to be effective only if he died during surgery.

> **Practice Pointer**
>
> Should a client be advised to create an "estate plan" based on a single impending event? How would you respond to a client in a situation like Perez?

E. Contractual Wills

Contracts and wills do not easily partner. Wills and contracts interact in two ways. First there is a contract *to make a will*. Such contracts often involve an elderly person promising a younger person, often a relative, to make a will in the young person's favor if he or she moves in with the elderly person and provides care and companionship. "Come live with your old grandma and I'll leave you the farm when I die." When the will isn't executed as was promised, the disappointed promisee sues if he or she has performed. If the contract can be proved and if the promisee has fulfilled the bargain, often a *quantum meruit* recovery is possible. (See the comment to the UPC § 2–514, reproduced below). To enforce the contract, it must of course be a valid one. Contracts between spouses, who owe each other a duty of support, are not valid. Fulfilling a legally required obligation cannot be consideration for a contract.

The other sort of contract that commonly gets tangled up with wills is a contract *not to revoke* a will. While the above mentioned scenario, a promise to devise in return for services can result in the execution of a will, and a promise not to revoke might be expressed or implied, the classic situation in which contracts to devise appear involves a "later in life" marriage where one or the other (or both) husband and wife have children by their prior marriages. Though the estate planning strategy may be to ensure that the survivor is well cared for, there may be a countervailing concern about children from the previous marriage. The couple might want to regard all their property as a single "pot" and provide that all the children share equally; alternatively, they may wish that each set of children only inherit from only their natural parent, and not share in the property left by the stepparent. In the first scenario (which may also be employed where the family is nuclear and not blended) the couple writes *reciprocal* or *mutual wills* in which each spouse leaves the entire estate to the survivor, and on the death of the second to die, the property is given to all the children or all the descendants by representation (perhaps one-half to each side of the family or equally to all the children or some variation on equal treatment). Alternatively, the couple can write a *joint will,* a single will for two persons. The will, signed by both spouses, leaves all property to the survivor and on the survivor's death to the children just as does a mutual will. The issue that such a strategy raises is whether the mutual wills or the joint will was made pursuant to an expressed or implied promise by the survivor that he or she not revoke or alter the will after one of the spouses dies.

Many jurisdictions once enforced a presumption that joint wills and even mutual wills, at least between spouses, had been executed pursuant to a contract. Modern statutes like UPC § 2–514 require that a contract involving a testamentary gift be in writing and signed by the promisor.

UPC § 2–514. Contracts concerning succession

A contract to make a will or devise, or not to revoke a will or devise, or to die intestate, if executed after the effective date of this [article], may be established only by (i) provisions of a will stating material provisions of the contract, (ii) an express reference in a will to a contract and extrinsic evidence provision the terms of the contract, or (iii) a writing signed by the decedent evidencing the contract. The execution of a joint will or mutual wills does not create a presumption of a contract not to revoke the will or wills.

It is fair to say that such contracts are not favored by the courts, in part because of the problems that can arise after the death of the first testator as the following case illustrates:

Matter of Murray

84 A.D.3d 106 (N.Y. App. Div. 2011)

BELEN, J.

[Decedent, Sandra Murray, and her husband, Jerome Murray, executed a joint will which gave the entire estate of the first to die to the survivor as well as property over which either of the spouses had "power of disposal, whether owned jointly or severally." The will also stated that it was "forever binding" and could be revoked or modified only by a writing signed by both parties and executed with testamentary formalities. This provision made the will unalterable after the death of the first spouse to die and made the will contractual under New York EPTL 13–2.1 which requires that a contract to make or not to revoke a joint can be established only by an express statement in the will. The decedent and her husband divorced 8 years after execution of the joint will (and after some 50 years of marriage). Some months before the divorce they had reaffirmed the joint will in a Marital Settlement Agreement which was incorporated into the judgment of divorce. The agreement stated that neither party would revoke the joint will and granted sole title to one condominium (the Boca Raton condominium) owned by the couple to husband and title to the other condominium owned by the couple (the Roslyn condominium) to decedent.

Decedent then created an irrevocable trust of which she and her son-in-law Ivan were trustees and conveyed title to the Roslyn condominium to the trustees. The trust terms stated that on decedent's death the condominium is to be distributed as the decedent should direct in her will to one of more of her ex-husband, her descendants and spouses of her descendants. This is a power of appointment which we will examine in Chapter 5. In 2007 she executed a will which did nothing but exercise her power of appointment by directing the trustee of the trust to distribute the Roslyn condominium in equal shares to her and her ex-husband's four children and which stated that it was not intended to modify or revoke the joint will.]

Following the decedent's death on June 14, 2008, Jerome filed a petition for the probate of the joint will. On June 30, 2008, Jerome applied for preliminary letters testamentary to be issued to him, which the Surrogate's Court granted in an order dated July 15, 2008. On August 12, 2008, Jerome, as the preliminary executor of the decedent's estate, commenced a turnover proceeding pursuant to SCPA 2103 against, among others, his daughter, Karen, and her husband, Ivan (hereinafter together the Klines), seeking, inter alia, to direct Ivan, as trustee of the trust, to execute and deliver the deed to the Roslyn condominium to the decedent's estate.

In their answer to Jerome's petition, the Klines alleged, among other things, that the Roslyn condominium was no longer a part of the probate estate, as a will is not effective until the death of the testator, and that neither the joint will nor the 2007 will prohibited the decedent from making inter vivos gifts or transferring property during her lifetime. Thereafter, on August 25, 2008, Ivan, as trustee of the trust, commenced a proceeding for the probate of the 2007 will.

On September 5, 2008, the Klines filed objections to Jerome's appointment as executor of the decedent's estate. The Klines alleged that the decedent had already transferred her ownership interest in the Roslyn condominium to the trust on June 2, 2006, and, therefore, the property was neither a part of the decedent's probate estate nor subject to the terms of the joint will that Jerome propounded for probate. The Klines also alleged that Jerome had an "unwaivable . . . . conflict of interest" that prevented him from administering the decedent's estate according to her 2007 will and, if the Surrogate's Court would allow Jerome to act as the decedent's executor regardless, his letters should be limited and he should be required to post a bond.

On September 18, 2008, Jerome filed objections to Ivan's petition for probate, claiming that the terms of the 2007 will violated the joint will and, therefore, the 2007 will should not be admitted to probate. On October 10, 2008, Jerome moved for summary judgment (1) dismissing Ivan's petition for the probate of the 2007 will, (2) dismissing the Klines' objections to his appointment as executor, and (3) on the petition in the turnover proceeding against the Klines, i.e., to direct Ivan to execute and deliver the deed to the Roslyn condominium to the decedent's estate.

Also on October 10, 2008, the Klines cross-moved for summary judgment (1) dismissing the turnover proceeding insofar as asserted against them on the ground that any property the decedent had either transferred during her lifetime to the trust, including the Roslyn condominium, or given to Karen, was not part of the probate estate, (2) dismissing Jerome's objections to Ivan's petition for the probate of the 2007 will, and (3) on their petition for the probate of the 2007 will.

In opposition to the cross motion, Jerome argued that although Jerome's and the decedent's estate plan did not restrict either of them from using or selling their assets during their lifetimes, it did restrict the manner in which they could dispose of their assets upon their deaths. Among other things, he stressed that Article "SECOND" of the joint will provided that upon the death of the first of them,

> "the entire estate of the one dying first and all property of which she or he has power
> of disposal, whether owned jointly or severally, is hereby given to the survivor."

The terms of Article "SECOND" of the joint will therefore create two categories of property that passed to the survivor, (1) any property comprising "the entire estate of the one dying first," and (2) "all property of which [the decedent or Jerome] has [the] power of disposal." Jerome asserted that even accepting the Klines' argument that the decedent transferred title to the Roslyn condominium to the trust, thereby placing such property outside the first category created by Article "SECOND" of the joint will, such property was nevertheless encompassed by the second category created by Article "SECOND" of the joint will. Specifically, Jerome asserted that because the decedent, pursuant to the trust document, retained upon her death the power of appointment regarding the disposal of the Roslyn condominium, and exercised such power in her 2007 will by directing that upon her death, the trust was to convey such property to their four children, in equal shares, the decedent retained power of disposal over the Roslyn condominium. Accordingly, because the decedent retained power of disposal over the Roslyn condominium, the 2007 will was, in effect, a nullity, because it did not exercise the decedent's power of appointment in favor of Jerome, as required by Article "SECOND" of the joint will and, accordingly, that branch of the Klines' cross motion which was for summary judgment on their petition for the probate of the 2007 will should be denied.

In a decision dated March 17, 2009, the Surrogate's Court found that Jerome was entitled to summary judgment on the petition in the turnover proceeding "to the extent of a direction that Ivan as co-trustee reconvey the [Roslyn condominium] to the estate." The Surrogate's Court held that Jerome was entitled to summary judgment on the petition for the probate of the joint will, dismissing the Klines' objections to Jerome's appointment as executor, and dismissing Ivan's petition for the probate of the 2007 will.

In an order dated June 17, 2009, the Surrogate's Court, in effect, granted Jerome's petition for the probate of the joint will and, in effect, granted that branch of Jerome's motion which was for summary judgment on the petition in the turnover proceeding, directing Ivan, as trustee of the trust, to execute and deliver the deed to the Roslyn condominium to Jerome, as executor of the decedent's estate. The Surrogate's Court also, in effect, granted those branches of Jerome's motion which were for summary judgment dismissing the Klines' objections to his appointment as executor, as well as Ivan's petition for the probate of the 2007 will.

By decree also dated June 17, 2009, the Surrogate's Court admitted the joint will to probate, denied admission of the 2007 will to probate, dismissed the Klines' objections to Jerome's appointment as executor of the decedent's estate, revoked Jerome's preliminary letters testamentary, and directed that letters testamentary be issued to Jerome.

> **Make the Connection**
>
> The Surrogate's Court disposes of all of the controversy on summary judgment, neatly showing how the meaning of a will can be a matter of law for the court.

The Klines appeal from so much of the decree as dismissed their objections to Jerome's appointment as executor of the decedent's estate and denied Ivan's petition for the probate of the 2007 will, and from so much of the order as awarded Jerome summary judgment on the petition in the turnover proceeding, and as, in effect, awarded Jerome summary judgment dismissing their objections to Jerome's appointment as executor and dismissing Ivan's petition for the probate of the 2007 will.

The Surrogate's Court found that Jerome established his prima facie entitlement to judgment as a matter of law based on Article "SECOND" of the joint will, which, it indicated, granted "all property of which she or he has power of disposal" to the surviving spouse upon the other's death. The Surrogate's Court determined that regardless of whether the decedent had transferred her ownership interest in the Roslyn condominium to the trust, such property was subject to the terms of Article "SECOND" of the joint will because she retained the power of appointment pursuant to the trust document and the "power of disposal" pursuant to the 2007 will over the Roslyn condominium. As such, the decedent was bound by the terms of the joint will and could only bequeath title to the Roslyn condominium to Jerome. Since the decedent's testamentary disposition in her 2007 will violated the terms of the joint will, the Surrogate's Court determined that Jerome was entitled to summary judgment on the petition in the turnover proceeding and, accordingly, directed Ivan to execute and deliver the deed to the Roslyn condominium. We agree with that determination.

A turnover proceeding is exactly that; a proceeding asking the court to require someone who has possession of property belonging to the decedent's estate to turn it over to the personal representative.

In a turnover proceeding pursuant to SCPA article 21, to be entitled to summary judgment, the petitioner must make a prima facie showing that the subject property belonged to the decedent at the time of his or her death (*see Matter of Coviello*, 78 AD3d 696, 698; *Matter of Rappaport*, 66 AD3d 1032; *Matter of Kelligrew*, 63 AD3d 1064, 1065).

To meet his burden, Jerome relies on Article "SECOND" of the joint will, which provides, in pertinent part, that upon the death of the decedent or Jerome, "the entire estate of the one dying first and all property of which she or he *has power of disposal, whether owned jointly or severally*," will be given to the survivor (emphasis added). Jerome argues that the decedent's power of appointment set forth in Article II, Section B, of the trust document demonstrated that she retained "power of disposal" over the Roslyn condominium and, thus, pursuant to Article "SECOND" of the joint will, he is entitled to that property.

"A validly executed joint will is a proper and legally tenable means of effecting a testamentary disposition of property" (*Matter of Covert*, 97 NY2d 68, 73–74; *see Glass v Battista*, 43 NY2d 620, 623–624; *Matter of Diez*, 50 NY 88). Generally, "a will is inoperative and wholly ineffective until the death of [a] testator" (*Matter of Fabbri*, 2 NY2d 236, 239; *see Blackmon v Estate of Battcock*, 78 NY2d 735, 739 ["(e)ven after due execution of a will, testators also retain unfettered authority to dispose of all property during their lifetimes"]). However, where a joint will is at issue, when one of the testators dies, the survivor is bound by the terms of the joint will and is prohibited

Make the Connection

In this paragraph the court is construing the language of the will to find its meaning as intended by the testator. We'll learn more about construction later on in this chapter.

from making a testamentary disposition or inter vivos gift that would defeat the purpose or plan of the joint will, "for equity would be ill-served if, after one party had honored the agreement, the other party, having reaped its fruit, were at liberty to uproot it" (*Glass v Battista*, 43 NY2d at 624; *see Rastetter v Hoenninger*, 214 NY 66, 73; *cf. Schwartz v Horn*, 31 NY2d 275, 280).

"[T]estamentary instruments are strictly construed so as to give full effect to the testator's clear intent" (*Matter of Covert*, 97 NY2d at 74; *see Matter of Bieley*, 91 NY2d 520, 525; *Matter of White*, 65 AD3d 1255, 1257), "as far as is consonant with principles of law and public policy" (*Matter of Fabbri*, 2 NY2d at 240; *see Matter of Rodrigues*, 33 AD3d 926, 927). The testator's intent "must be gleaned not from a single word or phrase but from a sympathetic reading of the will as an entirety and in view of all the facts and circumstances under which the provisions of the will were framed" (*Matter of Fabbri*, 2 NY2d at 240; *see Matter of Brignole*, 32 AD3d 538; *Matter of Ramdin*, 11 AD3d 698, 699). Thus, "[i]f the court upon reading the will in this setting discerns a dominant purpose or plan of distribution, the individual parts of the will must be read in relation to that purpose and given effect accordingly" (*Matter of Fabbri*, 2 NY2d at 240; *see Matter of Carmer*, 71 NY2d 781, 785–786; *Matter of White*, 65 AD3d 1255, 1257). Notably, this principle of interpretation "is true despite the fact that a literal reading of the portion under construction might yield an inconsistent or contradictory meaning because of the use of awkward language inadvertently or carelessly chosen" (*Matter of Fabbri*, 2 NY2d at 240; *see Matter of Bieley*, 91 NY2d at 525 ["where the entire will manifests a general testamentary scheme, it is the duty of the courts to carry out the testator's purpose, notwithstanding that general rules of interpretation might point to a different result"; internal quotation marks omitted]; *Blackmon v Estate of Battcock*, 78 NY2d at 740 ["In the absence of an express provision in the agreement or factors far more substantial within the four corners of the settlement agreement itself from which a judicial inference could comfortably and properly be drawn, courts should not innovate for parties after the fact"]).

As Jerome correctly concedes, the decedent's ability to dispose of her assets during her lifetime was unfettered by that part of Article "SECOND" of the joint will that bequeathed to the survivor of each of them the "entire estate" of the one to die first. Because the joint will makes no specific bequests, any inter vivos gifts made by the decedent or Jerome would not have necessarily defeated their intent that the survivor receive the entire estate of the first to die (*see Rastetter v Hoenninger*, 214 NY at 73; *cf. Schwartz v Horn*, 31 NY2d at 280). As such, during her lifetime, the decedent could have transferred title to the Roslyn condominium outright or directly to her four children without violating the terms of the joint will (*see Blackmon v Estate of Battcock*, 78 NY2d at 740).

The crux of the parties' dispute then, is that part of Article "SECOND" of the joint will which provides, in pertinent part, that (in addition to receiving title to the entire estate of the first of them to die), the survivor was also to receive title to all property over which Jerome or the decedent, upon his or her death, had "power of disposal, whether owned jointly or severally." The crucial analysis is whether the Klines are correct that any power of disposal over the Roslyn condominium the decedent possessed pursuant to Article II, Section B, of the trust document, is of no moment since she had previously transferred title to such property to the trust and, thus, she no longer owned such property "jointly or severally."

At the time they executed the joint will in 1993, Jerome and the decedent had been married for nearly 43 years. As Jerome and the decedent did not separate until 1997, it is reasonable to infer, as we do, that at the time they executed the joint will, Jerome and the decedent intended to remain married and to bequeath to each other their respective estates as well as all properties over which they retained power of disposal. Given the circumstances in which the joint will was executed—namely, a long-standing marriage— the phrase "whether owned jointly or severally" was not, as the Klines contend, intended to qualify the "power of disposal" phrase, but instead intended to expand the scope of the requisite power of disposal to include properties Jerome and the decedent owned jointly or severally with each other. A sympathetic reading of the entire joint will strengthens our conclusion, as the first testamentary disposition, in Article "SECOND," leaves "the entire estate of the one dying first and all property of which she or he has power of disposal" to the survivor, while the second, in Articles "THIRD" and "FOURTH," bequeathed their respective estates "and all property of which we or either of us has power of disposal" to a Trust to divide the residuary estate into equal shares for Karen and their lawful grandchildren, should they die "at the same time, or as a result of a common accident" (*see Matter of Brignole*, 32 AD3d at 539).

Further, even after Jerome and the decedent had entered into divorce proceedings, they reaffirmed the validity of the joint will in the agreement they executed in December 2000; this strengthens our conclusion that they never strayed from the testamentary disposition set forth in their joint will. We further note that to accept the Klines' argument would ignore the decedent's intent when she executed the joint will in 1993, an intent she reaffirmed when she executed the agreement in December 2000, and improperly substitute[d] it with her intent when she executed the 2007 will (*see Blackmon v Estate of Battcock*, 78 NY2d at 740).

Accordingly, since, in the turnover proceeding, Jerome established that the Roslyn condominium was a part of the decedent's estate because she retained power of disposal over it pursuant to the trust document and, in opposition, the Klines failed to raise a triable issue of fact, the Surrogate's Court properly awarded Jerome summary judgment on the petition in the turnover proceeding.

Turning to Ivan's petition for the probate of the 2007 will, a will must be admitted to probate "[i]f it appears that the will was duly executed and that the testator at the time of executing it was in all respects competent to make a will and not under restraint it must be admitted to probate as a will valid to pass real and personal property" (SCPA 1408[2]; *see Matter of Kumstar*, 66 NY2d 691, 692; *Matter of Imperato*, 67 AD3d 909). Here, the Klines established their prima facie entitlement to judgment as a matter of law by providing an affidavit from the attesting witnesses acknowledging the validity of the 2007 will and its execution.

In opposition, Jerome failed to raise a triable issue of fact. In opposing the Klines' cross motion, Jerome principally contended that the 2007 will should not be admitted to probate because Article "FIFTH" of the joint will specifically provided that it was irrevocable and that the joint will could only be revoked or modified be a writing subscribed by both of them and executed by both of them with the formality of a will (*see* EPTL 13–2.1[b]; *cf. Matter of Lubins*, 250 AD2d 850).

As a general rule, a will is ambulatory in nature and revocable during the life of the testator (*see* EPTL 1–2.19[a]; *Matter of Blackmon v Estate of Battcock*, 78 NY2d at 739; *Tutunjian v Vetzigian*, 299 NY 315, 319; *Matter of Lubins*, 250 AD2d at 851). While individuals may validly surrender their power of revocation, the law requires, as a threshold, a showing of clear and unambiguous evidence of the intent to surrender such right (*see* EPTL 13–2.1[b]; *Matter of Blackmon v Estate of Battcock*, 78 NY2d at 739; *Oursler v Armstrong*, 10 NY2d 385, 392; *Tutunjian v Vetzigian*, 299 NY 320; *Matter of Thompson*, 309 AD2d 1013, 1015; *Matter of Lubins*, 250 AD2d at 851–852; *see also Matter of American Comm. for Weizmann Inst. of Science v Dunn*, 10 NY3d 82, 92). Even if we agree with Jerome that Article "FIFTH" of the joint will satisfies that threshold showing, that article does not preclude admitting the 2007 will to probate, since a will may not be denied probate on the ground that the testator previously "bound himself to a different disposition of [his] property by contract" (*Matter of Higgins*, 264 NY 226, 229 [discussing former Surrogate's Court Act § 144, the predecessor statute to SCPA 1408]; *see* SCPA 1408[2]). Put differently, the enforceability of the terms of a will does not affect the "will's status as a legal instrument" (*Matter of Coffed*, 46 NY2d 514, 519), nor does it determine if the will should be admitted to probate (*id.* at 519). Rather, in light of Article "FIFTH" of the joint will, admitting the 2007 will to probate may render the decedent's estate vulnerable to an action against it by Jerome, for example, seeking to impose a constructive trust upon her estate or for an accounting (*see Matter of Coffed*, 46 NY2d at 519; *Oursler v Armstrong*, 10 NY2d at 391; *Matter of Higgins*, 264 NY at 229–230; *Olin v Lenoci*, 119 AD2d 739).

Since the Klines satisfied their prima facie burden and Jerome did not raise any triable issue of fact in opposition, the Klines were entitled to summary judgment dismissing Jerome's objections to Ivan's petition for the probate of the 2007 will and on their petition for the probate of the 2007 will. We recognize that by being awarded summary judgment in the turnover proceeding, Jerome obtains title to the Roslyn condominium and, thus, the 2007 will is admitted to probate, but its

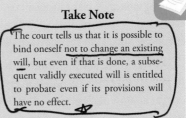

Take Note

The court tells us that it is possible to bind oneself not to change an existing will, but even if that is done, a subsequent validly executed will is entitled to probate even if its provisions will have no effect.

terms are not enforceable, since the sole purpose of the 2007 will was to bequeath the Roslyn condominium to the decedent's four children, including Karen. Ironically, as correctly observed by Jerome, had the decedent simply gifted or even sold the Roslyn condominium during her lifetime, the joint will would not have served as a bar to its transfer.

The Klines' remaining contentions are without merit.

Practice Planning Questions

Your client H and W have entered into a second marriage in the 50s. Each has a set of teenage children from a previous marriage. Prior to their marriage, a lawyer (not you) drafted a joint will which bequeaths all of each spouse's probate property to the survivor and on the death of the second to die leaves the survivor's probate estate one-half to H's descendants and one-half to W's (both H and W have children by prior marriages). Like the joint will in *Murray* the document states that it can be revoked or modified only by a writing signed by both parties and executed with testamentary formalities. They wonder whether in their sixties with children now in their twenties, the current documents provide a sound estate planning strategy.

Consider the following possible scenarios:

1. After H's death, W decides to sell the home in which they had lived and use the proceeds to buy herself a modest condominium apartment to which she takes title as joint tenant with right of survivorship with her son, S. She puts the rest of the proceeds into a joint and survivor brokerage account with her daughter, D. Can H's children prevent D from receiving the account balance by right of survivorship and S from receiving the condominium at W's death and recapture it for W's estate?

2. Suppose instead of a straight forward bank account in joint tenancy, W created a revocable trust with the proceeds, income to herself for life, and at her death all trust property to be distributed to D? She also takes title to the condo as trustee of her revocable trust. What then?

3. Grief-stricken, W's consumption patterns are ratcheted up to compensate. Suppose, W sells the family home and then decides to take a round-the-world cruise in the Captain's suite. H and W never took elaborate vacations and certainly never spent on leisure and entertainment the amount of money W plans to spend on the cruise. Can H's children prevent W from spending money on the cruise, and, more generally, can they somehow prevent W from "squandering" the property subject to the contractual will?

As you might surmise from both the *Murray* case and the problems above, contractual wills probably create more problems than they solve. As we will see, the typical family circumstances that most likely give rise to the thought of contractual will can almost always be better handled by creating a trust to benefit the surviving spouse during his or her lifetime with the trust property to pass on death to the children of the spouse creating the trust.

———————————

F. Revocation of Wills

A page of history . . . .

Henry Swinburne set out a rule in the sixteenth century that obtains today:

> A man may as oft as he will make a new testament even until the last breath neither is there any cautele under the sun to prevent this liberty: but no man can die with two testaments, and therefore the last and newest is in force: so that if there were a thousand testaments, the last of all is the best of all, and maketh void all of the former. (Henry Swinburne, *A Brief Treatise of Testaments and Last Wills* (Garland Reprint of 1590 edition, 1978), pp. 164–5.)

In other words, prior wills are revoked by subsequent wills, but it is not quite that simple in practice.

Given the formalities required by statute to create a valid attested will, it is not surprising that the statutes prescribe significant formalities to be observed in revoking a will. The revocation statutes generally provide that a will may be revoked in two different ways. The first involves some physical act by the testator done to the document such as burning, tearing, canceling, obliterating or destroying the will. Statutes differ on whether the will can be partially revoked by performing the physical act on part of the will. In any event, the physical act must accomplished by the testator with the *intent to revoke.* The second method is to execute a new will that has provisions which are completely or partially inconsistent with an existing will If the new document is not completely inconsistent with the prior will the new document is usually called a *codicil*, which simply means it is an amendment to the prior will and is to be read together with it (although the UPC no longer draws a distinction between a "will" and a "codicil"; both are simply wills). However, if the second will is entirely inconsistent with the existing will, it supplants it. Many such wills have express revocation clauses (see Ward's will in Chapter 2). Like will execution provisions, the statutory will revocation mandates are often followed with a vengeance.

Thompson v. Royal

175 S.E. 748 (Va. 1934)

HUDGINS, J., delivered the opinion of the court.

The only question presented by this record, is whether the will of Mrs. M. Lou Bowen Kroll had been revoked shortly before her death.

The uncontroverted facts are as follows: On the 4th day of September, 1932, Mrs. Kroll signed a will, typewritten on five sheets of legal cap paper; the signature appeared on the last page duly attested by three subscribing witnesses. H. P. Brittain, the executor named in the will, was given possession of the instrument for safe-keeping. A codicil typed on the top third of one sheet of paper dated September 15, 1932, was signed by the testatrix in the presence of two subscribing witnesses. Possession of this instrument was given to Judge S. B. Coulling, the attorney who prepared both documents.

On September 19, 1932, at the request of Mrs. Kroll, Judge Coulling, and Mr. Brittain took the will and the codicil to her home where she told her attorney, in the presence of Mr. Brittain and another, to destroy both. But instead of destroying the papers, at the suggestion of Judge Coulling, she decided to retain them as memoranda, to be used as such in the event she decided to execute a new will. Upon the back of the manuscript cover, which was fastened to the five sheets by metal clasps, in the handwriting of Judge Coulling, signed by Mrs. Kroll, there is the following notation:

> This will null and void and to be only held by H. P. Brittain, instead of being destroyed, as a memorandum for another will if I desire to make same. This 19 Sept 1932
>
> 'M. LOU BOWEN KROLL.

The same notation was made upon the back of the sheet on which the codicil was written, except that the name, S. M. B. Coulling, was substituted for H. P. Brittain; this was likewise signed by Mrs. Kroll.

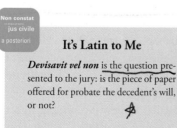

It's Latin to Me

Devisavit vel non is the question presented to the jury: is the piece of paper offered for probate the decedent's will, or not?

Mrs. Kroll died October 2, 1932, leaving numerous nephews and nieces, some of whom were not mentioned in her will, and an estate valued at approximately $200,000. On motion of some of the beneficiaries, the will and codicil were offered for probate. All the interested parties including the heirs at law were convened, and on the issue, devisavit vel non, the jury found that the instruments dated September 4th and 15, 1932, were the last will and testament of Mrs. M. Lou Bowen Kroll. From an order sustaining the verdict and probating the will this writ of error was allowed.

For more than one hundred years, the means by which a duly executed will may be revoked, have been prescribed by statute. These requirements are found in section 5233 of the 1919 Code, the pertinent parts of which read thus:

> No will or codicil, or any part thereof, shall be revoked, unless * * * by a subsequent will or codicil, or by some writing declaring an intention to revoke the same, and executed in the manner in which a will is required to be executed, or by the testator, or some person in his presence and by his direction, cutting, tearing, burning,

obliterating, canceling, or destroying the same, or the signature thereto, with the intent to revoke.

The notations, dated September 19, 1932, are not wholly in the handwriting of the testatrix, nor are her signatures thereto attached attested by subscribing witnesses; hence under the statute they are ineffectual as "some writing declaring an intention to revoke." The faces of the two instruments bear no physical evidence of any cutting, tearing, burning, obliterating, canceling, or destroying. The only contention made by appellants is, that the notation written in the presence, and with the approval, of Mrs. Kroll, on the back of the manuscript cover in the one instance, and on the back of the sheet containing the codicil in the other, constitute "canceling" within the meaning of the statute.

Both parties concede that to effect revocation of a duly executed will, in any of the methods prescribed by statute, two things are necessary: (1) The doing of one of the acts specified, (2) accompanied by the intent to revoke—the animo revocandi. Proof of either, without proof of the other, is insufficient. Malone v. Hobbs, 1 Rob. (40 Va.) 346, 39 Am. Dec. 263; 2 Minor Ins. 925. The proof established the intention to revoke. The entire controversy is confined to the acts used in carrying out that purpose. The testatrix adopted the suggestion of her attorney to revoke her will by written memoranda, admittedly ineffectual as revocations by subsequent writings, but appellants contend the memoranda, in the handwriting of

> **Food for Thought**
>
> Would the outcome have been the same if the testatrix rather than the judge wrote the "notation"?

another, and testatrix's signatures, are sufficient to effect revocation by cancellation. To support this contention appellants cite a number of authorities which hold that the modern definition of cancellation includes, "any act which would destroy, revoke, recall, do away with, overrule, render null and void, the instrument."

Most of the authorities cited, that approve the above, or a similar meaning of the word, were dealing with the cancellation of simple contracts, or other instruments that require little or no formality in execution. However, there is one line of cases which apply this extended meaning of "canceling" to the revocation of wills. The leading case so holding is Warner v. Warner's Estate, 37 Vt. 356. In this case proof of the intent and the act were a notation on the

> **Take Note**
>
> Cancellation first became a means of revoking a will in the English Statute of Frauds (1677). What potential for fraud is averted by requiring that Ms. Kroll rather than Judge Coulling undertake the physical act of cancellation?

same page with, and below the signature of the testator, reading: "This will is hereby cancelled and annulled. In full this the 15th day of March in the year 1859," and written lengthwise on the back of the fourth page of the foolscap paper, upon which no part of the written will appeared, were these words, "Cancelled and is null and void. (Signed) I. Warner." It was held this was sufficient to revoke the will under a statute similar to the one here under consideration.

In Evans' Appeal, 58 Pa. St. 238, the Pennsylvania court approved the reasoning of the Vermont court in Warner v. Warner's Estate, supra, but the force of the opinion is weakened when the facts are considered. It seems that there were lines drawn through two of the three signatures of the testator appearing in the Evans will, and the paper on which material parts of the will were written was torn in four places. It therefore appeared on the face of the instrument, when offered for probate, that there was a sufficient defacement to bring it within the meaning of both obliteration and cancellation. The construction of the statute in Warner v. Warner's Estate, supra, has been criticized by eminent text writers on wills, and the courts in the majority of the states in construing similar statutes have refused to follow the reasoning in that case. (citations omitted)

The above, and other authorities that might be cited, hold that revocation of a will by cancellation within the meaning of the statute, contemplates marks or lines across the written parts of the instrument, or a physical defacement, or some mutilation of the writing itself, with the intent to revoke. If written words are used for the purpose, they must be so placed as to physically affect the written portion of the will, not merely on blank parts of the paper on which the will is written. If the writing intended to be the act of cancelling, does not mutilate, or erase, or deface, or otherwise physically come in contact with any part of written words of the will, it cannot be given any greater weight than a similar writing on a separate sheet of paper, which identifies the will referred to, just as definitely, as does the writing on the back. If a will may be revoked by writing on the back, separable from the will, it may be done by a writing not on the will. This the statute forbids.

Go Online

Avoid Judge Couling's embarrassment and read carefully the revocation statute in your jurisdiction.

The learned trial judge, A. C. Buchanan, in his written opinion, pertinently said: "The statute prescribes certain ways of executing a will, and it must be so executed in order to be valid, regardless of how clear and specific the intent." It also provides certain ways of revoking and it must be done so in order to a valid revocation, regardless of intent. As said in Will of Ladd, 60 Wis. 187, 18 N.W. 734, 50 Am. Rep. at pp. 362–3: "The difficulty with the rule contended for is that it gives to the words written in pencil, although not attested, witnessed, nor executed in the manner prescribed by statute, the same force as though they had been so attested, witnessed and executed, for the purpose of proving that the act of putting the words there was with the 'intention' of revoking the will. It is the language, the expression by written words alone, which is thus sought to be made effectual; whereas the statute in effect declares that such written words shall have no force or effect as such" * * *

The attempted revocation is ineffectual, because testatrix intended to revoke her will by subsequent writings not executed as required by statute, and because it does not in any wise physically obliterate, mutilate, deface, or cancel any written parts of the will.

For the reasons stated, the judgment of the trial court is affirmed.

Since other courts might, like the Virginia court, literally apply the revocation statute, compare two, the UPC and that of New York:

UPC § 2–507

(a)   A will or any part thereof is revoked:

    (1)   by executing a subsequent will that revokes the previous will or part expressly or by inconsistency; or

    (2)   by performing a revocatory act on the will, if the testator performed the act with the intent and for the purpose of revoking the will or part or if another individual performed the act in the testator's conscious presence and by the testator's direction. For purposes of this paragraph, "revocatory act on the will" includes burning, tearing, canceling, obliterating, or destroying the will or any part of it. A burning, tearing, or canceling is a "revocatory act on the will," whether or not the burn, tear, or cancellation touched any of the words on the will.

(b)   If a subsequent will does not expressly revoke a previous will, the execution of the subsequent will wholly revokes the previous will by inconsistency if the testator intended the subsequent will to replace rather than supplement the previous will.

(c)   The testator is presumed to have intended a subsequent will to replace rather than supplement a previous will if the subsequent will makes a complete disposition of the testator's estate. If this presumption arises and is not rebutted by clear and convincing evidence, the previous will is revoked; only the subsequent will is operative on the testator's death.

(d)   The testator is presumed to have intended a subsequent will to supplement rather than replace a previous will if the subsequent will does not make a complete disposition of the testator's estate. If this presumption arises and is not rebutted by clear and convincing evidence, the subsequent will revokes the previous will only to the extent the subsequent will is inconsistent with the previous will; each will is fully operative on the testator's death to the extent they are not inconsistent.

New York Estates, Powers, and Trusts Law § 3–4.1. Revocation of Wills; Effect of Codicils

(a)   Except as otherwise provided in this chapter, a revocation or alteration, if intended by the testator, may be effected in the following manner only:

    (1)   A will or any part thereof may be revoked or altered by:

        (A)   Another will.

        (B)   A writing of the testator clearly indicating an intention to effect such revocation or alteration, executed with the formalities prescribed by this article for the execution and attestation of a will.

(2)   A will may be revoked by:

    (A)   An act of burning, tearing, cutting, cancellation, obliteration, or other mutilation or destruction performed by:

        (i)   The testator.

        (ii)   Another person, in the presence and by the direction of the testator; in which case, the fact that the will was so revoked in the presence and by the direction of the testator shall be proved by at least two witnesses, neither of whom shall be the person who performed the act of revocation.

(b)   In addition to the methods set forth in paragraph (a), a will may be revoked or altered by a nuncupative or holographic declaration of revocation or alteration made in the circumstances prescribed by 3–2.2 by any person therein authorized to make a nuncupative or holographic will. Any such nuncupative declaration of revocation or alteration must be clearly established by at least two witnesses; any such holographic declaration, by an instrument written entirely in the handwriting of the testator, although not executed and attested in accordance with the formalities prescribed by this article for the execution and attestation of a will.

(c)   The revocation of a will, as provided in this section, revokes all codicils thereto.

Points for Discussion

1. Partial revocation

Other than their verbiage, how do these statutes actually differ? Suppose Uncle Scrooge devises $100,000 to Huey, Dewey and Louie share and share alike. When the will is located at his death, the words Huey and Dewey are crossed out. What result under the UPC and in New York? Is partial revocation by physical act, accepted in the UPC, recognized in New York? If not, why not?

2. How much is enough?

Testator writes "This will is void" on the back of the last page of the will and crosses out some of the provisions of the will. Is the will revoked in New York? Under the UPC? The following case should help you answer this question for New York:

Matter of Lewis

360 N.Y.S.2d 761 (Surr. Ct. 1974)

EVANS V. BREWSTER, S.

Submitted for probate is a typewritten will dated April 4, 1974 which contains the signature of the testator and two subscribing witnesses and an attestation clause. The will has a legal back, a portion of which is folded over and covers a small part of the top of the first page.

Upon the folded over portion appears in decedent's handwriting, "This will is void not to be in force Samuel J. Lewis." No date appears. Across the entire first page is an inked "X." On page two and between article III and the provisions thereof and article IV and the provisions thereof, appears in the same handwriting "this Part to be inforced Samuel J. Lewis 5/14/74." The provisions of article V, though still readable, have been stricken by an inked "X" and an inked line under the "X." Article VI has not been touched. Between article VII and the first line thereof are the words in ink "VOID Samuel J. Lewis 5/14/74." Through the provisions of article VII is an inked "X" and in the right hand margin alongside the said article in ink appears, "James to make the [*sic*] choice". An inked line has been drawn through the first line of the provisions of article VIII and only the last word "made" has not been lined out. To the right of said sentence in the margin are the words in ink "VOID Samuel J. Lewis 5/14/74." The last page upon which appear the signatures of the testator and witnesses and the attestation clause has not been altered. Before probate can be decreed, the court must decide whether the will has been revoked in the manner prescribed by EPTL 3–4.1.

Practice Pointer

We may surmise that Mr. Lewis had custody of his will after due execution. Regardless of the outcome of the case, do his doodlings on the document suggest that the will might better be held elsewhere?

A revocation, to be effective, must be made pursuant to statute (*Burnham v. Comfort*, 108 N.Y. 535; *Lovell v. Quitman*, 88 N.Y. 377; *Matter of Evans*, 113 App. Div. 373). It is not within the legitimate power of the courts to circumvent the statutory requirements for the revocation of wills and to accept even a definite intention to perform the prescribed act as a substitution for the act itself. The statute controlling the manner of the revocation of a will is specific and unqualified and is to be strictly construed. Formalities to effect the revocation of a will are necessary to prevent mistake, misrepresentation and fraud (*Matter of McGill*, 229 N.Y. 405). EPTL 3–4.1 describes the methods for revoking wills. Basically they are: (1) by a writing and (2) by an act. While the writing which appears on the top of the first page of the will evidences an intent to effect a revocation, EPTL 3–4.1(a)(1)(B) has not been complied with for the writing, though signed by the testator has not been subscribed by at least two witnesses.

In the light of the facts here, the question then arises as to whether the testator, by his acts, has effected a revocation by cancellation in accordance with EPTL 3–4.1(a)(2)(A). By definition, there can be no such thing as a cancellation of an instrument, either as a physical fact or as a legal inference, unless the instrument itself is in some form defaced or obliterated (*Matter of Akers*, 74 App. Div. 461, affd. 173 N.Y. 620).

FYI

Black's defines cancellation rather circularly—to destroy the force of a legal act. Cancellation usually requires lines through the text of a will; obliteration is defined only as a verb to erase or blot out.

The cases have emphasized the importance of the location of the writing evidencing the revocation indorsed on the will. If there has been no obliteration of the will itself and there is nothing denoting a cancellation other than a writing upon the margin or back of the will, the will has not been canceled (*Matter of Akers, supra*; *Matter of Mulligan*, 40 A.D. 2d 136; *Matter of Miller*, 50 Misc. 70). However, a will is generally held to have been canceled when there have been some words of revocation actually written across the entire will or vital parts thereof (*Matter of Parsons*, 236 N.Y. 580; *Matter of Robinson*, 201 Misc. 439; *Matter of Kutzner*, 173 Misc. 776; *Matter of Barnes*, 76 Misc. 382).

Lines drawn through the signature of the testator or subscribing witnesses result in the effective obliteration of the will. (*Matter of Parsons*, 236 N.Y. 580, *supra*; *Matter of Sax*, 25 Misc 2d 576; *Matter of Weinberger*, 206 Misc. 770; *Matter of Semler*, 176 Misc. 687; *Matter of McCaffrey*, 174 Misc. 162; *Matter of Griffith*, 167 Misc. 366; *Matter of Kuntz*, 140 Misc. 598).

If the markings do not affect the will in its entirety, or a vital part thereof, there is no revocation (*Matter of Tremain*, 169 Misc. 549, affd. 257 App. Div. 996, affd. 282 N.Y. 485).

The fact pattern of the case at bar does not fall precisely under one rule or the other. The will contains no words of revocation written across any vital part. The words "VOID Samuel J. Lewis 5/14/74" affect article VII which merely expresses a wish of the testator to employ a named attorney for the probate of the will. The only other words of revocation are found upon a portion of the legal back at the top of page one and in the margin beside the provision in article VIII. The provision for the appointment of the fiduciaries in article V has been lightly deleted in ink but is still discernible. A single "X" crosses page one. A portion of article II is on page one which bequeaths a business and devises some real property to his wife. Ordinarily, this might be considered a vital portion of the will. Significantly, however, is the language in article III which reads "the foregoing bequest and devise in favor of my said wife "(referring to the disposition in article II on page one) "shall be absolute ". Certainly, if testator had intended to revoke the gift to his wife, he would have also deleted the quoted portion of article III. In addition, testator specifically wrote in ink on page two of his will with reference to articles III and IV containing dispositive provisions, that said provisions would be in force.

The court concludes that the requirements of valid revocation have not been met.

It is possible that the testator intended to make some changes but not revoke the entire will. If so, this intention was not effectuated by decedent's acts. As the changes were made subsequent to execution and unwitnessed, there is a failure to comply with EPTL 3–4.1 and they are wholly ineffective.

The paper writing dated April 4, 1974 is admitted to probate.

Submit decree reciting at length the will in the form in which it existed at the time of execution

---

Points for Discussion

1. *Problems of partial revocation*

Suppose T obliterated a paragraph of her will and dated and signed the will immediately following the paragraph. The signatures of two other persons, followed by their addresses and the same date as that written by the testator appear on the foot of the same page of the will. The will is presented for probate. Should it be entitled to probate? With or without the obliterated paragraph? *See Matter of Litwack*, 827 N.Y.S.2d 582 (N.Y. Sur. Ct. 2006) The court noted that New York allows revocation by a writing executed with the formalities of a will, and regarded the additional section as a codicil to the will. The UPC also allows revocation by such a document by defining "will" to include an instrument that only revokes another will (UPC § 1–301(55)).

2. *Physical act performed by someone other than the testator*

Both statutes require that the testator be present if another person performs the revocatory act at the testator's direction. New York requires two witnesses in addition to the person who performs the act of revocation. But both the New York statute and the UPC allow a will-maker to revoke a will in private. In states that do not permit holographic wills, however, a property owner cannot give effect testamentary designs in private. Why may one revoke a will in solitude but not execute one?

3. *Revocation by inconsistency*

Revocation by inconsistent provisions is recognized in all states but is not always clear cut. Consider the *Kuralt* case set out above. The first holographic will only devised the real property in Montana. Had the testator died before executing the formal will, the rest of the probate estate would have passed in intestacy (a *partial intestacy*). With the execution of the 1994 will, the first holograph was revoked by inconsistency, *even though the 1994 will did not mention the Montana real property.* A revocation occurs because the 1994 will disposed of the residue of the estate, and thus made a complete disposition of the testator's probate property. Of course, if the 1997 letter is indeed a valid holograph, it should be considered a codicil to the 1994 will, and because it disposes of only the Montana realty, it revokes the residuary clause to the extent of the inconsistency. It adds to rather than contradicts the disposition in the 1994 will.

Practice Planning Problem

Suppose Charles Kuralt comes into your office and asks you to draft his will. You ask him if he has an existing will. He responds vaguely. Would you include an express revocation clause? Inclusion of such a clause is a sensible strategy. Even if the new will makes only minor changes in the disposition made in the prior will, the inclusion of such a clause means that there is no doubt that the prior will need not be, and indeed *cannot be,* offered for probate. In short, if the document is to make a disposition of the entire probate estate, include an express revocation clause. If the document really is meant to be a codicil, say so by beginning the document with language like this:

> I, [TESTATOR'S NAME], residing in the City and County and State of New York, hereby declare this to be a [FIRST] codicil to my Will, dated [DATE].

G. The Lost Will

An issue that estate planners face is who should retain custody of an executed will. There are many pitfalls regardless of the choice. Assume that the testator takes possession of the original will (the copy with the original signatures of the testator and witnesses), but after the testator's death the will cannot be found. A lost will can be admitted to probate so long as its contents can be proved and so long as it was not revoked. To probate a lost will, its proponents must confront a long-standing and widely honored presumption of the common law:

Restatement Third, Property (Wills and Donative Transfers) § 4.1, comment *j*

> *Presumption if lost or mutilated will traced to testator's possession.* If a will is traced to the testator's possession and cannot be found after death, there are three plausible explanations for its absence: The testator destroyed it with the intent to revoke; the will was accidentally destroyed or lost; or the will was wrongfully destroyed or suppressed by someone dissatisfied with its terms. Of these plausible explanations, the law presumes that the testator destroyed the will with intent to revoke it.

The comment makes a similar observations about a will on which a revocatory act has been performed (for example, a paragraph has been crossed out). There is a presumption that the testator performed the act with the intent to revoke. Both presumptions are rebuttable, although the level of evidence needed to rebut the presumption is not the same in every jurisdiction. The Restatement does not require clear and convincing evidence. The New York courts, however have long described the presumption as a strong one and put a heavy burden on the proponent of a lost will:

> He who seeks to establish a lost or destroyed will assumes the burden of overcoming this presumption by adequate proof. It is not sufficient for him to show that

persons interested to establish intestacy had an opportunity to destroy the will. He must go further, and show, by facts and circumstances, that the will was actually fraudulently destroyed. (Collyer v. Collyer, 65 Sickles 481, 486, 18 N.E. 110, 112 (N.Y. 1888))

This heavy burden makes the need to safeguard an original will all the more important. Consider the following case and ask whether the lawyer made the correct call regarding will custody.

Harrison v. Bird

621 So.2d 972 (Ala. 1993)

HOUSTON, JUSTICE.

The proponent of a will appeals from a judgment of the Circuit Court of Montgomery County holding that the estate of Daisy Virginia Speer, deceased, should be administered as an intestate estate and confirming the letters of administration granted by the probate court to Mae S. Bird.

The following pertinent facts are undisputed: Daisy Virginia Speer executed a will in November 1989, in which she named Katherine Crapps Harrison as the main beneficiary of her estate. The original of the will was retained by Ms. Speer's attorney and a duplicate original was given to Ms. Harrison. On March 4, 1991, Ms. Speer telephoned her attorney and advised him that she wanted to revoke her will. Thereafter, Ms. Speer's attorney or his secretary, in the presence of each other, tore the will into four pieces. The attorney then wrote Ms. Speer a letter, informing her that he had "revoked" her will as she had instructed and that he was enclosing the pieces of the will so that she could verify that he had torn up the original. In the letter, the attorney specifically stated, "As it now stands, you are without a will."

> **Take Note**
>
> Research before you advise. Though not an implausible shot from the hip, the lawyer's advice on revocation was clearly malpractice.

> **Practice Pointer**
>
> Was the execution of duplicate original wills a good idea? Realize that if there are duplicate originals, those offering the will for probate must account for all of the originals before the court will find that the will has not been revoked.

Ms. Speer died on September 3, 1991. Upon her death, the postmarked letter from her attorney was found among her personal effects, but the four pieces of the will were not found. Thereafter, on September 17, 1991, the Probate Court of Montgomery County granted letters of administration on the estate of Ms. Speer, to Mae S. Bird, a cousin of Ms. Speer. On October 11, 1991, Ms. Harrison filed for probate a document purporting to be the last will and testament of Ms. Speer and naming Ms. Harrison as executrix. On Ms. Bird's petition, the case was removed to the Circuit Court of Montgomery County. Thereafter, Ms. Bird filed an "Answer to Petition to Probate Will and Answer to Petition to Have Administratrix Removed," contesting the will on the grounds that Ms. Speer had revoked her will.

Thereafter, Ms. Bird and Ms. Harrison moved for summary judgments, which the circuit court denied. Upon denying their motions, the circuit court ruled in part (1) that Ms. Speer's will was not lawfully revoked when it was destroyed by her attorney at her direction and with her consent, but not in her presence, see Ala. Code 1975, s 43–8–136(b); (2) that there could be no ratification of the destruction of Ms. Speer's will, which was not accomplished pursuant to the strict requirements of s 43–8–136(b); and (3) that, based on the fact that the pieces of the destroyed will were delivered to Ms. Speer's home but were not found after her death, there arose a presumption that Ms. Speer thereafter revoked the will herself. However, because the trial court found that a genuine issue of material fact existed as to whether Ms. Harrison had rebutted the presumption that Ms. Speer intended to revoke her will even though the duplicate was not destroyed, it held that "this issue must be submitted for trial."

Subsequently, however, based upon the affidavits submitted in support of the motions for summary judgment, the oral testimony, and a finding that the presumption in favor of revocation of Ms. Speer's will had not been rebutted and therefore that the duplicate original will offered for probate by Ms. Harrison was not the last will and testament of Daisy Virginia Speer, the circuit court held that the estate should be administered as an intestate estate and confirmed the letters of administration issued by the probate court to Ms. Bird If the evidence establishes that Ms. Speer had possession of the will before her death, but the will is not found among her personal effects after her death, a presumption arises that she destroyed the will. See Barksdale v. Pendergrass, 294 Ala. 526, 319 So.2d 267 (1975). Furthermore, if she destroys the copy of the will in her possession, a presumption arises that she has revoked her will and all duplicates, even though a duplicate exists that is not in her possession. See Stiles v. Brown, 380 So.2d 792 (Ala.1980); see, also, Snider v. Burks, 84 Ala. 53, 4 So. 225 (1887). However, this presumption of revocation is rebuttable and the burden of rebutting the presumption is on the proponent of the will. See Barksdale, supra.

Food for Thought

Is the presumption more or less irrefutable? What evidence might you find in a case that does indeed refute the presumption? Would you regard the existence of the duplicate original as significant?

Based on the foregoing, we conclude that under the facts of this case there existed a presumption that Ms. Speer destroyed her will and thus revoked it. Therefore, the burden shifted to Ms. Harrison to present sufficient evidence to rebut that presumption-to present sufficient evidence to convince the trier of fact that the absence of the will from Ms. Speer's personal effects after her death was not due to Ms. Speer's destroying and thus revoking the will. See Stiles v. Brown, supra.

From a careful review of the record, we conclude, as did the trial court, that the evidence presented by Ms. Harrison was not sufficient to rebut the presumption that Ms. Speer destroyed her will with the intent to revoke it. We, therefore, affirm the trial court's judgment.

We note Ms. Harrison's argument that under the particular facts of this case, because Ms. Speer's attorney destroyed the will outside of Ms. Speer's presence, "[t]he fact that Ms. Speer may have had possession of the pieces of her will and that such pieces were not found upon her death is not sufficient to invoke the presumption [of revocation] imposed by the trial court." We find that argument to be without merit.

Point for Discussion

Now that Ms. Speer's will can be admitted to probate, its contents are easy to prove: the duplicate original still exists. But what if Ms. Speer had executed only one original copy of her will, as good practice suggests? Then what? Every state has some procedure for proving the contents of a lost will. These procedures are usually a matter of common law, but one state at least, New York, has a statute:

N.Y. Sur. Ct. Proc. Act 1407. Proof of Lost or Destroyed Will

A lost or destroyed will may be admitted to probate only if

1. It is established that the will has not been revoked, and

2. Execution of the will is proved in the manner required for the probate of an existing will, and

3. All of the provisions of the will are clearly and distinctly proved by each of at least two credible witnesses or by a copy or draft of the will proved to be true and complete.

H. Dependent Relative Revocation and Revival

If a testator has only written one will in his or her lifetime and then revokes that will and dies, the result is simple enough: the testator has died intestate. Suppose, however, the will-maker revokes a will with the intention to execute another, but never has the opportunity to execute the second will. Alternatively, the second will have been made but it is assumed it is invalid because of improper due execution. Because revocation combines both a physical act (due execution) with a mental element (the intent to revoke) might one argue that the intent to revoke the initial testamentary plan was **dependent** upon and **relative** to the implementation of the second testamentary document. If a subsequent will is not duly executed, might one argue that the revocation never occurred? This analysis sometimes applied is called dependent relative revocation or DRR. Consider the following case:

Carter v. First United Methodist Church of Albany

271 S.E.2d 493 (Ga. 1980)

NICHOLS, JUSTICE.

The caveator, Luther Reynolds Carter, appeals from judgment entered in the superior court in behalf of the propounder, First United Methodist Church, admitting to probate, as the will of Mildred C. Tipton, an instrument bearing the date of August 21, 1963.

The 1963 instrument, typed and signed in the form of and purporting to be the last will and testament of Mildred C. Tipton, was found among Mrs. Tipton's other personal papers in her dining room chest after her death on February 14, 1979. It was folded together with a handwritten instrument dated May 22, 1978, captioned as her will but unsigned and unwitnessed, purporting to establish a different scheme of distribution of her property. Pencil marks had been made diagonally through the property disposition provisions of the 1963 document and through the name of one of the co-executors.

The superior court found that from time to time prior to her death, Mrs. Tipton had made it known to her attorney that she needed his services in order to change or revise her will, or to make a new will; that at one time she had written out some proposed changes on tablet paper to be suggested to her lawyer when he prepared a new will for her; and that she did not intend to revoke her will by scratching through some of its provisions and by writing out the proposed changes.

The caveator contends in his first two enumerations of error that the will should not have been admitted to probate because it had not been introduced in evidence and the propounder had not proven its execution and the testamentary capacity of the testatrix, or in the alternative had not proven the inaccessibility of the witnesses. The parties stipulated that the 1963 instrument offered for probate had been found among Mrs. Tipton 's records and papers in a drawer of a chest in her dining room, and that the 1963 will was executed by Mrs. Tipton and attested by the witnesses to the will. Proof of matters stipulated was not necessary. The trial court's order specifically refers to the "instrument identified as the Last Will and Testament of Mildred C. Tipton" and to "the markings on the Will." The trial court obviously considered the will to be in evidence. There is no transcript of the proceedings below. This court will presume that the will was in evidence. Aviation Electronics, Inc. v. U. S. Energy Conservation Systems, 242 Ga. 224, 248 S.E.2d 610 (1978); see, General Motors Corp. v. Walker, 244 Ga. 191, 193, 259 S.E.2d 449 (1979). The first two enumerations of error are lacking in merit.

Practice Pointer

Once again danger lurks when turning over a will to a client. What would you have done if an elderly client expressed the desire to change a will that you drafted for her?

The caveator contends in the remaining enumerations of error that the superior court erred in admitting the will to probate because the propounder did not produce any evidence to rebut the statutory presumption of revocation. Code Ann. s 113–404. The case was submitted to the trial court on stipulated facts, and under stipulation that the depositions of Mrs. Tipton's attorney and one of her friends, relating to her intentions, be admitted in evidence. There is no transcript, and the record is sparse as to facts. Each party seems to have felt that the burden of proof properly was to be placed upon the other party and, accordingly, neither made much effort to develop the facts. The issue resolves itself, however, if certain presumptions are placed into proper perspective with each other. "As a general rule, the burden is on a person attacking a paper offered for probate as a will to sustain the grounds of his attack. But by express provision of our statute, where a will has been canceled or obliterated in a material part, a presumption of revocation arises, and the burden is on the propounder to show that no revocation was intended . . . Where the paper is found among the testator's effects, there is also a presumption that he made the cancellations or obliterations . . . It having been shown that the paper offered for probate in this case had been in the custody of the deceased up to the time of his death, the propounder was met with both of the presumptions above alluded to." McIntyre v. McIntyre, 120 Ga. 67, 70, 47 S.E. 501 (1904).

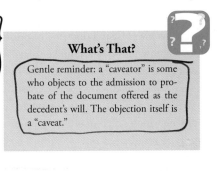

What's That?

Gentle reminder: a "caveator" is some who objects to the admission to probate of the document offered as the decedent's will. The objection itself is a "caveat."

The deposition of Mrs. Tipton's attorney, introduced by stipulation in behalf of the propounder, establishes, without contradiction, that Mrs. Tipton had written out some changes in her will on tablet paper and repeatedly had attempted to get her attorney to change or to revise her will, or to make a new will. The parties stipulated that the two writings, the 1963 will and the 1978 manuscript, were found after her death among her personal effects. No evidence appears in the record, and no contention is made, that Mrs. Tipton did not make the marks on the 1963 will or write the 1978 instrument. The presumption that Mrs. Tipton made the pencil marks and wrote the memorandum of her intentions stands unrebutted. Langan v. Cheshire, 208 Ga. 107, 65 S.E.2d 415 (1951); Porch v. Farmer, 158 Ga. 55, 122 S.E. 557 (1924); Howard v. Hunter, 115 Ga. 357, 41 S.E. 638 (1902). The other presumption, that of absolute revocation, is the focal point of our remaining inquiry.

The statute to which McIntyre refers is Code Ann. s 113–404, which provides, in part, that an intention to revoke the will be presumed from the obliteration or canceling of a material portion of the will. In Georgia, the drawing of pencil lines through provisions of a will is a sufficient "canceling". McIntyre, supra, at p. 70, 47 S.E. 501. The question of whether or not the canceled provision is "material" is one of law. Howard v. Cotten, 223 Ga. 118, 122, 153 S.E.2d 557 (1967). The caveator contends that the propounder introduced no evidence to rebut the statutory presumption of revocation, and the propounder contends that under the doctrine of dependent relative revocation, or conditional revocation, the facts proven give rise to a presumption in favor of the propounder (which the caveator failed to rebut) that

Mrs. Tipton did not intend for her 1963 will to be revoked unless her new dispositions of her property became effective in law. The caveator thus contends that the propounder failed to rebut the presumption of absolute or unconditional revocation, and the propounder contends he rebutted that presumption by evidence giving rise to another presumption, that of conditional revocation, which the caveator failed to rebut.

The doctrine of dependent relative revocation (conditional revocation) has been stated by this court as follows: "It is a doctrine of presumed intention, and has grown up as a result of an effort which courts always make to arrive at the real intention of the testator. Some of the cases appear to go to extreme lengths in the application of this doctrine, and seem to defeat the very intention at which they were seeking to arrive. The doctrine, as we understand it and are willing to apply it, is this: The mere fact that the testator intended to make a new will, or made one which failed of effect, will not alone, in every case, prevent a cancellation or obliteration of a will from operating as a revocation. If it is clear that the cancellation and the making of the new will were parts of one scheme, and the revocation of the old will was so related to the making of the new as to be dependent upon it, then if the new will be not made, or if made is invalid, the old will, though canceled, should be given effect, if its contents can be ascertained in any legal way. But if the old will is once revoked, if the act of revocation is completed, as if the will be totally destroyed by burning and the like, or if any other act is done which evidences an unmistakable intention to revoke, though the will be not totally destroyed, the fact that the testator intended to make a new will, or made one which cannot take effect, counts for nothing. In other words, evidence that the testator intended to make or did actually make a new will, which was inoperative, may throw light on the question of intention to revoke the old one, but it can never revive a will once completely revoked." (Emphasis added.) McIntyre v. McIntyre, 120 Ga. 67, 71, 47 S.E. 501, 503 supra. The doctrine has been recognized and applied by the highest courts of many states. Annos. 62 ALR 1401, 115 ALR 721. It has been the subject of considerable discussion by the text writers. 1 Redfearn, Wills And Administration In Georgia (4th Ed.), p. 188, s 96; Chaffin, Studies In The Georgia Law of Decedent's Estates and Future Interests, pp. 184, 186.

Food for Thought

Why draw the distinction between revocation by physical act and revocation by subsequent writing? Is the latter less equivocal? Does presumed intent figure?

Professor Chaffin is of the opinion that "McIntyre represents a sound approach to the doctrine of dependent relative revocation." He writes that in McIntyre, "The doctrine was correctly perceived to be a rule of presumed intention rather than a rule of substantive law. The court refused to set aside the revocation until evidence bearing on testator's intent, including his oral declarations, was examined in an effort to discern what he would have desired if he had been aware of the true facts." He also concludes, correctly, this court believes, that "Most courts have taken the position that dependent relative revocation is judged by a stricter standard in a situation involving revocation by subsequent instrument as opposed to physical act." He is strongly of the opinion that "if the purpose of the doctrine is to effect testator's intent, there is no point in distinguishing between revocation by physical act and by subsequent instrument." Chaffin, supra, pp. 186–187. This court agrees. In Georgia, the doctrine is one of presumed intention. The principle is the same whether the revocation is by physical act or by subsequent instrument. As this court said of the doctrine in McIntyre, "The matter finally turns upon the intention of the testator, and no mere presumption (that the testator would have preferred the canceled will instead of intestacy) will be allowed to defeat this intention when it has been made to appear." 120 Ga. at 72, 47 S.E. at 504. The reason that the intention of the testator in making the marks or in writing the new instrument is material is that "Joint operation of act and intention is necessary to revoke a will." 120 Ga. at 71, 47 S.E. at 503; Payne v. Payne, 213 Ga. 613, 615, 100 S.E.2d 450 (1957).

In the present case, the testatrix wrote the 1978 instrument which the parties have conceded (by the absence of their contentions) cannot be admitted to probate because it lacks some of the requisites of a will. The propounder says, in effect, if not in express words, that the testatrix would have preferred the property disposition clauses of the 1963 will over the only other alternative intestacy. The caveator contends, in essence, that the testatrix would have preferred intestacy. How stands the record?

The fact that the old will, with pencil lines drawn by Mrs. Tipton through the property disposition provisions, was found among her personal papers folded together with the 1978 writing, that makes a somewhat different disposition of her property, is some evidence tending to establish that "the cancellation and the making of the new will were parts of one scheme, and the revocation of the old will was so related to the making of the new as to be dependent upon it." 120 Ga. at 71, 47 S.E. at 503.

> ### Take Note
>
> The argument about to be made is that had the testatrix realized that the second testamentary plan would not be implemented, she would not have revoked the first: thus the notion of conditional intent to revoke.

This evidence was sufficient to rebut the statutory presumption of revocation (Code Ann. s 113–404) and to give rise to a presumption in favor of the propounder under the doctrine of dependent relative revocation or conditional revocation. McIntyre, supra. The stipulation that these two instruments were found together thus shifted the burden of proof to the caveator to prove, in essence, that Mrs. Tipton would have preferred intestacy.

In McIntyre, the intention of the testator to make a new will was indicated by his having written marginal and attached notes and pencil marks on the will substituting blank lines for the names of persons, items of property, the date of execution, his signature, and the signatures of the witnesses. The new dispositions were not indicated. In McIntyre, the caveator testified that the testator told him, " 'Willie, I have left a pencil memorandum of a will it is not a will I was not able to finish (or complete) it; but I call upon Willie to carry out the provisions of this pencil memorandum.' " In the present case, there is no testimony that the testatrix even told anyone that she had revoked her 1963 will. The cases thus are factually dissimilar. The presumption against intestacy (or in favor of the continued validity of the 1963 will) stands unrebutted in the present case. Cf., Howard v. Cotten, 223 Ga. 118, 123, 153 S.E.2d 557 (1967), in which the testatrix stated her intent to her attorney by saying, "Will you hurry, because, remember, I don't have a will." Cases such as Langan v. Cheshire, 208 Ga. 107, 65 S.E. 415 supra, and Porch v. Farmer, 158 Ga. 55, 122 S.E. 557, supra, are inapposite because they did not involve the doctrine of dependent relative revocation or conditional revocation.

Accordingly, the trial court, as finder of the facts, did not err in admitting the will to probate.

Judgment affirmed.

Points for Discussion

1. DRR: A puzzle with pieces missing

The discussion in *Carter* suggests that a proponent who wishes to promote a will by using the doctrine of dependent relative revocation has to satisfy three requirements. The first is that the proponent must show that revocation of the document was conditional: "I am revoking will 1 because I intend to execute another will or I have already so executed one." The proponent then needs to show that either the proposed substitute will was never executed or its execution was flawed. Finally, proponent needs to demonstrate that that by "revoking the revocation" of the first will the pattern of succession will approximate the will-makers testamentary designs to a greater extent than would transpire by resort to the alternative—intestate succession. Suppose, for example, I as a bird lover execute my will leaving my residuary to the American Audubon Society. Suppose thereafter I learn about the Cornell Ornithology Lab, and I decide to change my will to leave the residuary to the latter. I visit my attorney's office where I draw lines through the signature of my Audubon will. My attorney drafts my second will bequeathing my residuary to the latter. Alas, like with respect to the execution of Mr. Hall's will, there are no witnesses present, so I sign and the attorney notarizes the will. I reside in an unenlightened jurisdiction that accepts neither substantial compliance nor the harmless error rule. My Audubon will is revoked, and my Cornell Lab will has no effect. My nephews Huey, Dewey and Louie, mentioned in neither will, are my intestate heirs. Would this be a case for the application of dependent relative revocation? Does *Carter* support using DRR in this situation? Or are the birds out of luck?

2. DRR and partial revocation by physical act; Changing amounts

How do we know that will-makers whose testamentary designs are thwarted would prefer restoring the revoked will (revoking its revocation) to intestacy? Suppose Donald leaves $5,000 each to his nephews Huey, Dewey and Louie in his will, young ducks who are not his heirs. At his death, the sum $5,000 has a line through it, and $10,000 is written above. Donald resides in jurisdiction that recognizes partial revocation by physical act. Could dependent relative revocation be used to restore the gift of $5,000? If so, what if the interlineated sum is $1,000? Hint: would a will-maker necessarily prefer restoring a gift greater than the interlineated addition to no bequest at all?

3. DRR and revoking an entire will

The choice between the restoration of the will that was revoked and intestate succession is not always a straightforward one. In the following case, the court compared the beneficiaries and concluded that the will that could be restored more approximates the testatrix testamentary designs to a greater extent than did intestacy.

ESTATE OF ALBURN, 118 N.W.2d 919 (Wisc. 1963).

"The plan of testamentary disposition under the two wills was in part as follows: The Milwaukee will contained specific bequests of jewelry and household furnishings to Viola Henkey, the grandniece of testatrix, and directed that any indebtedness owing deceased by Viola Henkey and her husband be deemed satisfied. The residuary clause bequeathed one fourth of the estate to her friend Olga Olson, one fourth to Doris Alburn, one fourth to Lulu Alburn, and one fourth to Viola Henkey. The Kankakee will included a bequest to Olga Olson of 38 shares of stock in the Bank of America National Trust & Savings Association and bequests of jewelry to Lulu and Addie Alburn. The remainder of the estate was bequeathed as follows: four tenths to Lulu Alburn, five tenths to Doris Alburn, and one tenth to Robert Lehmann, brother of testatrix. The Alburns are not related to testatrix but are relatives of her deceased husband. Viola Henkey, although a blood relative of testatrix, is not one of her next-of-kin who would inherit in the event testatrix had died intestate. The next-of-kin consist of four surviving brothers and one sister plus a large number of nieces and nephews of testatrix, the children of four deceased sisters and one deceased brother. Thus under the Milwaukee will, none of the next-of-kin were named as legatees, whereas under the Kankakee will, the only next-of-kin named a legatee was Robert, her brother. His share under the Kankakee will is somewhat less than the one-tenth share of the entire estate which he would receive if testatrix had died intestate. The bulk of the estate under both wills was bequeathed to the Alburns and Olga Olson. There is no evidence of any change of circumstances occurring thereafter that would indicate any reason why testatrix should die intestate and nine tenths of her estate go to next-of-kin not named in either will."

The court was unable to revive (a discussion of the concept follows) the Milwaukee will which the testator believed had been revived by the fact that she had "torn up" the Kankakee will because Wisconsin has a no-revival of revoked wills rule. However, the court restored the Kankakee will because the beneficiaries thereunder *more closely* approximated the desired Milwaukee will than did an intestate distribution. The revocation of the Kankakee will was dependent upon and relative to the revival of the Milwaukee will.

4. Restatement (Third)

The new Restatement recognizes dependent relative revocation, referring to it as the doctrine of "ineffective revocation." Would the application of the following section of the Restatement have upon the two cases discussed above?

Restatement Third, Property (Wills and Other Donative Transfers) § 4.3

(a) A partial or complete revocation of a will is presumptively ineffective if the testator made the revocation:

  (1) in connection with an attempt to achieve a dispositive objective that fails under applicable law, or

  (2) because of a false assumption of law, or because of a false belief about an objective fact, that is either recited in the revoking instrument or established by clear and convincing evidence.

(b) The presumption established in subsection (a) is rebutted if allowing the revocation to remain in effect would be more consistent with the testator's probable intention.

Supposed testator's will makes a bequest of $10,000 to his niece, N. Testator then executes a codicil stating that he is revoking the bequest because he has already made gifts to N. After testator's death, N can show that testator had not in fact made the gifts noted in the codicil. Can a court use the Restatement version of ineffective revocation to restore the bequest? Restatement (Third) of Property (Wills and Other Donative Transfers) § 4.3, Illustration 24 says "no" because the fact of whether or not the gifts were made "is particularly within the testator's knowledge." The Illustration also notes that if testator had taken steps to make such gifts but they had failed "due to some external cause," ineffective revocation could be used to restore the gift in the will.

What if the testator stated in the codicil that the he revoked the gift because N, a member of the armed forces, had died in combat. After testator's death, N, who had not died but was a prisoner of war, was released and returned home. According to Illustrations 21, 22, and 23 to § 4.3 the doctrine is used to restore the gift when the codicil recites the reason for the revocation or that reason is established by extrinsic evidence. A mistake about an "objective fact" can be remedied. The difference between these examples and Illustration 24 is that the latter does involve an objective fact but, as noted, it is one within the testator's knowledge.

Dependent relative revocation might have little application in a state like New York where partial revocation by physical act is not possible. Indeed, the existence of dependent relative revocation as part of New York's common law was in doubt a generation ago, although those doubts have been resolved in favor of the existence of the doctrine. (For a history of DRR in New York see Matter of Collins, 117 Misc.2d 669, 458 N.Y.S.2d 987 (Sur. Ct. Cattaraugus Co. 1982) and more recently, Matter of Sharp, 19 Misc.3d 471, 852 N.Y.S.2d 713 (Sur. Ct. Broome Co. 2008).) Is the outcome in the following case supported by (a)(1) or (a)(2) of Restatement (Third) of Property § 4.3, above, or doesn't it matter?

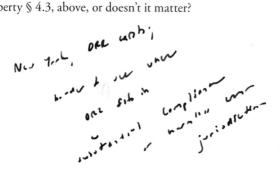

I. Revival

A page of history . . . .

When does a testamentary act have legal effect? Upon execution? At death? Hark back to the Swinburne quote above. What if the testator had a prior will (Will #1) which is revoked by a second will (Will #2), which is then itself revoked? If the individual dies would his or her property pass by intestacy? The implication of Swinburne's exegesis is no. No will is in force until death, and at that moment Will #1 was in existence on the testator's death and the testator's probate estate therefore should pass under the terms of Will #1. This doctrine was changed in England by the Wills Act of 1837 which provided that the execution of Will #2 revoked the Will #1 and the subsequent revocation of Will #2 had no effect on Will #1. It remained revoked unless the testator re-executed it or executed a codicil to the will. New York law follows the Wills Act of 1837. The more modern approach focuses on the will-maker's intent. Will #1 is revoked, but the revocation of Will #2 may *revive* Will #1, that is have effect on the death of the testator, if the testator so intended and manifested that intent in particular fashion. This third rule is the position of Restatement, Third (§ 4.2(a)) and is embodied in UPC § 2–509.

New York Estates, Powers, and Trusts Law § 3–4.6. Revocation or Alteration of Later Will Not to Revive Prior Will

(a) If after executing a will the testator executes a later will which revokes or alters the prior one, a revocation of the later will does not, of itself, revive the prior will or any provision thereof.

(b) A revival of a prior will or of one or more of its provisions may be effected by:

(1) The execution of a codicil which in terms incorporates by reference such prior will or one or more of its provisions.

(2) A writing declaring the revival of such prior will or of one or more of its provisions, which is executed and attested in accordance with the formalities prescribed by this article for the execution and attestation of a will.

(3) A republication of such prior will, whether to the original witnesses or to new witnesses, which shall require a re-execution and re-attestation of the prior will in accordance with the formalities prescribed by 3–2.1.

UPC § 2–509

(a) If a subsequent will that wholly revoked a previous will is thereafter revoked by a revocatory act under Section 2–507(a)(2), the previous will remains revoked unless it is revived. The previous will is revived if it is evident from the circumstances of the revocation of the subsequent will or from the testator's contemporary or subsequent declarations that the testator intended the previous will to take effect as executed.

(b)   If a subsequent will that partly revoked a previous will is thereafter revoked by a revocatory act under Section 2–507(a)(2), a revoked part of the previous will is revived unless it is evident from the circumstances of the revocation of the subsequent will or from the testator's contemporary or subsequent declarations that the testator did not intend the revoked part to take effect as executed.

(c)   If a subsequent will that revoked a previous will in whole or in part is thereafter revoked by another, later, will, the previous will remains revoked in whole or in part, unless it or its revoked part is revived. The previous will or its revoked part is revived to the extent it appears from the terms of the later will that the testator intended the previous will to take effect.

Points for Discussion

1. Comparing the old and new rules for revocation and revival

How exactly does old and new law operate? The UPC is flexible in permitting avenues to revival. Is it an overstatement to say that the above section of the UPC essentially permits an oral will? New York, on the other hand, essentially requires a re-execution of a document to restore the previous document. The three methods of EPTL § 3–4.6(b) all satisfy the ritual, evidentiary, and protective functions that due execution requires. Given the circumstances and consequences of revocation, and the fact patterns that you have gleaned from the cases, which approach to revocation and revival is most sound?

2. How revocation, revival, DRR and holographs all work together

The various rules on revocation and revival create a variety of outcomes depending upon the facts and the jurisdiction. To understand the law that has come from that combination, we first have to think about what happens when a will is partially revoked. Consider the following will which makes several *general bequests* of cash to various beneficiaries, a *specific bequest* of personal property and also contains a residuary clause. The text of these dispositive provisions of the will is as follows. (Bear in mind that the will may (like Ward's will in Chapter 2) contain other provisions including a direction to pay debts, a grant of various powers to the executor, and the nomination of the executor. In addition, the will should have *the testimonium and attestation clauses* and perhaps even a self-proving affidavit.)

I, TERRY A. TESTATOR, residing in the City, County and State of New York, do make, publish, and declare this to be my last will and testament, hereby revoking all wills and codicils heretofore made by me.

* * * * * * * * *

ARTICLE III

I bequeath to the children of my brothers and sisters, that is, my nieces and nephews, who survive me, in equal shares, all tangible personal property (except cash on hand) owned by me at my death and all unearned premiums on policies of insurance insuring said article of personal property against loss by fire, theft, accident or other casualty and also the next proceeds of any claims against any insurance company or person or persons arising out of or connected with any such loss, destruction or damage of any of said property.

ARTICLE IV

A. I give and bequeath ten thousand dollars ($10,000) to my friend Mary Ellen Howard, if she shall survive me, and if she does not this gift shall be added to the gift under Article VI.

B. I give and bequeath fifteen thousand dollars ($15,000) to my sister Susan Sanchez, if she shall survive me, and if she does not this gift shall be added to the gift under Article VI.

C. I give and bequeath twenty thousand dollars ($20,000) to the American Cancer Society

* * * * * * * *

ARTICLE VI

I give, devise, and bequeath all the rest, residue, and remainder of my property, both real and personal, wheresoever situated (but excluding any property over which I may have a power of appointment) ("my residuary estate") as follows:

A. One-half of my residuary estate to the American Red Cross.

B. One-half of my residuary estate in equal shares to the following persons who survive me: Sara Sanchez, Thomas Sanchez, Philip Testator, William Testator, Andrea Testator, and Nelson Newman.

Assume that the will was in Testator's possession and that it is found after Testator's death in the drawer of the decedent's desk along with other important papers. What happens under the following facts:

1. All of clause A of ARTICLE IV is crossed out with a pencil line. What becomes of the gift to Mary Ellen Howard under EPTL § 3–4.1? Under UPC § 2–507?

2. The words "ten thousand dollars" the figures $10,000 in clause A of ARTICLE IV are crossed out and above the figures is written in pencil "$15,000." What becomes of the gift in Clause A under EPTL § 3–4.1? Under UPC § 2–507?

3. Same as #2, but next to the written "$15,000" are the testator's initials. What becomes of the gift in Clause A under EPTL § 3–4.1? Under UPC § 2–507?

4. Same as #1, but written over the crossed out words is "I give Mary Ellen $15,000 instead" and the testator's initials. What becomes of the gift in Clause A under EPTL § 3–4.1? Under UPC § 2–507?

5. In ARTICLE VI the name "Thomas Sanchez" is crossed out with a pencil line. What becomes of the gift to Thomas Sanchez under EPTL § 3–4.1? Under UPC § 2–507?

6. Same as #5 but there is a line drawn from the crossed out name to the written words "Mary Sanchez." Thomas Sanchez died after the will was executed but before the testator's death; Mary Sanchez is Thomas' daughter. How is the residuary estate distributed under EPTL § 3–4.1? Under UPC § 2–507?

7. Do your answers change if you also consider UPC §§ 2–502(b) and 2–503?

The variations on a theme involved in all the questions above illustrate aspects of the law of wills we have already considered, and questions 2 and 6 also illustrate the potential operation of DRR. What questions 2 and 6 have in common is the testator's ineffective attempt to change the gift. If partial revocation by physical act is possible, and the handwritten additions to the will are not sufficient to make an alternative bequest, then the testator has revoked the original bequest and disinherited the beneficiary, even though the testator clearly wants to the beneficiary (or someone close to the beneficiary) to receive some property. Of course, if partial revocation by physical act is not sanctioned, nothing has changed.

In jurisdictions where partial revocation by physical act is permitted, the original bequests in the above example might be restored—"unrevoked"—if that result better fulfills the testator's intent by employing the doctrine of DRR. Consider the gift to Mary Ellen Howard. If the original bequest of $10,000 is revoked and the substitute gift is not valid, then Mary Ellen receives nothing. If the revocation is undone, she will receive $10,000. Since we can be all but certain that the testator wanted her to receive $15,000, the decision is an easy one: restore the $10,000 gift. If the new gift fails, the revocation fails as well.

Should the doctrine apply to the gift to Thomas Sanchez? Assuming the substitute gift is invalid, would the testator prefer the gift to Thomas to fail completely? The answer depends on what will happen to the gift if the revocation is undone. As we will see, in many states, statutes deal with gifts to will beneficiaries who die before the testator. Under many of those statutes, the gift to Thomas, nephew of the testator, will be given to Thomas' issue if Thomas dies before the testator. If that is the result, then undoing the revocation will ensure that Mary at least shares in the gift (depending on whether Thomas has other descendants) and the doctrine will probably be applied.

J. Interpretation or Construction of Wills

{182-206}

A page of history . . .

In the best of all possible worlds, there would never be any question about what the words of a will mean. Scriveners would commit the testamentary intentions of their clients with clarity. Regrettably, there have been lapses in precision, requiring probate courts, past and present, to struggle with questions of will construction for centuries.

The traditional doctrines applicable to will interpretation are relatively easy to state. The first and most important concept is that the intention of the testator controls. That position seems to be very straightforward and comprehensible. Consider this elegantly phrased summary:

> The chief object and purpose of the construction of a will is to discover and carry out the intent of the testator as expressed in the will, and this is the prime duty of the court, and its sole function or province. In other words, the intention of the testator is the prime or paramount consideration, controlling factor or element, main guide in the interpretation of a will, or polestar to guide the court to which the problem is presented in the construction of every will. The intent of the testator in the preparation and execution of the instrument is his or her will, and the law of the case or of the instrument. Such intention when ascertained, governs or must prevail, unless counter to some rule of law or public policy, so that a will must be interpreted so as to effectuate the testator's true intent as expressed in the will. C. J. S Wills § 831.

Yet, though not in absolute contradistinction to the above formulation of the probate court's mission, there is another thread that informs the approach to will construction, the so-called **plain meaning rule**:

> The rule is elementary that the intention of the testator is the polar star which is to guide in the interpretation of all wills, and, when ascertained, effect will be given to it unless it violates some rule of law, or is contrary to public policy. In ascertaining this intention the language used, and the sense in which it is used by the testator, is the primary source of information, as it is the expressed intention of the testator which is sought.

"* * * Generally, ordinary words are to be given their usual and ordinary meanings, and technical words are presumed to have been used in a technical sense." Conrad v. Conrad's Ex'r, 123 Va. 711, 97 S.E. 336, 338. Wallace N. Tiffany, etc. 168 Va. 31, 190 S.E. 101 (Supreme Court of Appeals of Virginia, 1937)

The astronomical or navigational metaphor, the following of polestars, is to direct courts to focus upon the words used in the will and to interpret them in the light of the ordinary meaning of the language used. But not always. There is a qualifier.

> In order to ascertain the actual intent of the settlor or testator, the Court must place itself in his armchair and consider not only the language and scheme of the instrument but also the facts and circumstances with which he was surrounded; and these surrounding facts and circumstances include the condition of his family, the natural objects of his bounty and the amount and character of his property. . . . . Pew Trust, supra, 411 Pa. at 107, 191 A.2d at 405 (citations omitted). In re Estate of Benson, 285 A. 2d 101 (Pa. 1971)

So what seems to begin as an objective quest of what the words employed mean to the reader may turn into a more subjective inquiry into determining what they may have meant to the author, who is, of course, no longer available to be of assistance. Remember too, that traditionally, interpretation and construction are two distinct things:

1.   **Interpretation** involves finding the testator's intent by examining the text of the will in the light of extrinsic evidence.

2.   **Construction** finds meaning by applying to the words of the will rules that have developed over the time by probate courts.

As you can observe from the quote from Corpus Juris Secundum, however, the two terms are not always carefully kept separate. Even so, it is still accurate to say that "interpretation" looks for the testator's actual intent while "construction" finds intent based on rules which may or may not correspond to the testator's intent, if the court could ever determine what intent that was.

Let us begin with a case that sets out the operation of the plain meaning rule, with a vengeance:

Mahoney v. Grainger

186 N.E. 86 (Mass. 1936)

Rugg, Chief Justice.

This is an appeal from a decree of a probate court denying a petition for distribution of a legacy under the will of Helen A. Sullivan among her first cousins who are contended to be her heirs at law. The residuary clause was as follows: 'All the rest and residue of my estate, both real and personal property, I give, demise and bequeath to my heirs at law living at the time of my decease, absolutely to be divided among them equally, share and share alike; provided, however, that the real property which I own at my decease shall not be sold or disposed of until five (5) years after my decease, unless there is not sufficient personal property at the time of my decease to pay my specific legatees; in which case said real property may be sold. The income from said real property during said five (5) years is to be distributed among my heirs at law as I have directed.'

The trial judge made a report of the material facts in substance as follows: The sole heir at law of the testatrix at the time of her death was her maternal aunt, Frances Hawkes Greene, who is still living and who was named in the petition for probate of her will. The will was duly proved and allowed on October 8, 1931, and letters testamentary issued accordingly. The testatrix was a single woman about sixty-four years of age, and had been a school teacher. She always maintained her own home but her relations with her aunt who was her sole heir and with several first cousins were cordial and friendly. In her will she gave general legacies in considerable sums to two of her first cousins. About ten days before her death the testatrix sent for an attorney who found her sick but intelligent about the subjects of their conversation. She told the attorney she wanted to make a will. She gave him instructions as to general pecuniary legacies. In response to the questions 'Whom do you want to leave the rest of your property to? Who are your nearest relations?' she replied 'I've got about twenty-five first cousins * * * let them share it equally.' The attorney then drafted the will and read it to the testatrix and it was executed by her.

> **Practice Pointer**
>
> Good drafting? The language used devises her property to those who would take her estate according to the pattern of —?

> **Take Note**
>
> The plain meaning rule. Extrinsic evidence may be admitted to clarify obscure language. Is the extrinsic evidence here being used to create the ambiguity: what persons were meant to take by the use of the words "heirs at law."

The trial judge ruled that statements of the testatrix 'were admissible only in so far as they tended to give evidence of the material circumstances surrounding the testatrix at the time of the execution of the will; that the words heirs at law were words in common use, susceptible of application to one or many; that when applied to the special circumstances of this case that the testatrix had but one heir, notwithstanding the added words 'to be divided among them equally, share and share alike,' there was no latent ambiguity or equivocation in the will itself which would permit the introduction of the statements of the testatrix to prove her testamentary intention.' Certain first cousins have appealed from the decree dismissing the petition for distribution to them.

There is no doubt as to the meaning of the words 'heirs at law living at the time of my decease' as used in the will. Confessedly they refer alone to the aunt of the testatrix and do not include her cousins. Gilman v. Congregational Home Missionary Society, 276 Mass. 580, 177 N. E. 621; Calder v. Bryant (Mass.) 184 N. E. 440.

A will duly executed and allowed by the court must under the statute of wills (G. L. [Ter. Ed.] c. 191, § 1 et seq.) be accepted as the final expression of the intent of the person executing it. The fact that it was not in conformity to the instructions given to the draftsman who prepared it or that he made a mistake does not authorize a court to reform or alter it or remove it by amendments. The will must be construed as it came from the hands of the testatrix. Polsey v. Newton, 199 Mass. 450, 85 N. E. 574, 15 Ann. Cas. 139. Mistakes in the drafting of the will may be of significance in some circumstances in a trial as to the due execution and allowance of the alleged testamentary instrument. Richardson v. Richards, 226 Mass. 240, 115 N. E. 307. Proof that the legatee actually designated was not the particular person intended by the one executing the will cannot be received to aid in the interpretation of a will. Tucker v. Seaman's Aid Society, 7 Metc. 188, 210. See National Society for the Prevention of Cruelty to Children v. Scottish National Society for the Prevention of Cruelty to Children, [1915] A. C. 207. When the instrument has been proved and allowed as a will oral testimony as to the meaning and purpose of a testator in using language must be rigidly excluded. Sibley v. Maxwell, 203 Mass. 94, 104, 89 N. E. 232; Saucier v. Saucier, 256 Mass. 107, 110, 152 N. E. 95; Calder v. Bryant (Mass.) 184 N. E. 440.

Food for Thought

Why the distinction between admitting extrinsic evidence to demonstrate a mistake in the execution of the will, but not as a guide to will interpretation?

It is only where testamentary language is not clear in its application to facts that evidence may be introduced as to the circumstances under which the testator used that language in order to throw light upon its meaning. Where no doubt exists as to the property bequeathed or the identity of the beneficiary there is no room for extrinsic evidence; the will must stand as written. Barker v. Comins, 110 Mass. 477, 488; Best v. Berry, 189 Mass. 510, 512, 75 N.E. 743, 109 Am. St. Rep. 651.

In the case at bar there is no doubt as to the heirs at law of the testatrix. The aunt alone falls within that description. The cousins are excluded. The circumstance that the plural word 'heirs' was used does not prevent one individual from taking the entire gift. Calder v. Bryant (Mass.) 184 N. E. 440.

Decree affirmed.

Points for Discussion

1. *What does it mean to "reform" a will?*

Suppose the court was amenable to 'reforming' the will. How would the process transpire? The court would admit extrinsic evidence—the scrivener's testimony of the conversation. Is there a reason to exclude it? Might it be unreliable? The will says what the will says and that's it. What would this Massachusetts court do in the situation in *Snide*?

2. Latent and patent ambiguities

If the 'rule' is *no extrinsic evidence should be admitted to explain the meaning of terms in the will*, there is an exception to that rule: *extrinsic evidence should be admitted to explain the meaning of terms in the will*. When do courts use the exception, when the rule? The *Mahoney* court focuses on 'doubt.' Traditionally courts have made a distinction based on the kind of uncertainty the will presented. Words do not have a plain meaning if they are reasonably susceptible to more than one meaning: multiple reasonable interpretations of a word or phrase creates an ambiguity. A distinction was drawn between *latent* and *patent* ambiguities. A patent ambiguity is one that appears on the face of the will. For instance, a residuary clause may give one-quarter of the residuary estate to each of three charities. What happens to the other one-quarter? Or two bequests seem contradictory. In *Succession of Neff*, 716 So.2d 410 (La. App. 1998) the will left the 'disposable portion of my estate' to daughter Karen, while the sixth paragraph left 'my entire estate' to daughters Katherine and Karen.

In both these examples, the confusion arises from mis-expression and the ambiguity is obvious, or patent. Generally, extrinsic evidence is not admitted to correct inartful drafting. One quarter of the residue would pass through intestacy in the first example; the latter as a derogation corrects the former in the second (that is, the estate is divided between Katherine and Karen). What if the expression in the will is not obscure on its face, as in the two previous examples, but becomes unclear in applying the terms of the will to the testator's property or to the beneficiary. These so-called latent ambiguities arise when the perfectly clear words of the will are applied to the facts of the testator's ownership of property or the identities of beneficiaries. Traditionally, extrinsic evidence is admissible to resolve such ambiguities. For example, the testator's will makes a general bequest of a sum of money to "my cousin, H. Jones" and the testator has one cousin named Henry Jones and another named Harold Jones. Should extrinsic evidence be admitted to show that the testator had a closer relationship with one rather than the other? Or suppose the will leaves property to Hank Jones. Again the testator has one cousin named Henry Jones and another named Harold Jones. Should extrinsic evidence be admitted to demonstrate that Hank is a diminutive of Henry? But could extrinsic evidence could also be admitted to show that the will-maker called cousin Harold 'Hank?' In the latter, evidence is routinely admitted under the *personal usage exception* which allows evidence of the will-makers individual expression. Another example: husband's will bequests his residuary to 'Mom.' Alas his mother died many years ago, but he refereed frequently to his wife as 'Mom,' should extrinsic evidence be admitted in this case to demonstrate the testator frequently referred to his wife as 'Mom.' Today, some jurisdictions have collapsed the distinction between latent and potent ambiguities, admitting extrinsic evidence to resolve either type.

3. Another sort of problem of description of a beneficiary

Suppose the residuary clause of a will reads as follows: "I give the rest, residue, and remainder of my estate to the University of Massachusetts." Is that an ambiguous gift because there are four campuses of the University of Massachusetts? Is the ambiguity latent or patent? Should extrinsic evidence be admitted to show that will-maker graduated from UMass Amherst? Suppose she went to Harvard? Would extrinsic evidence of her gift-giving history be admitted to clarify? That she was on the Chancellor's Board of Directors? Perhaps this example explains the aversion to extrinsic evidence. The question of admissibility is reliability? How reliable was the extrinsic evidence that the cousins in *Mahoney v. Grainger* sought to be admitted?

4. Words of wisdom

One need not be a literary critic or deconstructionist to recognize that the meaning of words is never as plain as courts may think. Professor Wigmore, the evidence scholar, rejected ascribing 'absolute' meaning towards individual words as a 'fallacy.' By so doing, courts in his view merely substituted their own interpretation of the meaning of terms in wills for those actually conceived of by the will-maker.

Consider the following case. The bequest as drafted is alarmingly straightforward. Can there really be a doubt as to who was the intended beneficiary?

Matter of Scale

38 A.D.3d 983 (N.Y. App. Div. 2007)

MERCURE, J.

Appeal from an order and decree of the Surrogate's Court of Albany County (Doyle, S.), entered November 18, 2005, which granted petitioner's motion for a determination of the validity, construction and effect of the disposition of certain property contained in decedent's last will and testament.

Frederick A. Scale (hereinafter the testator) died on June 4, 2002. His last will and testament, dated April 3, 2002, was duly admitted to probate on July 30, 2002, and letters testamentary were issued to petitioner, as the named executor. Petitioner seeks a determination of the validity, construction and effect of the disposition of property contained in paragraph 2F of the testator's will, in which the testator devised 10% of his residuary estate to "The Audubon Society of New York State." Both respondent Audubon Society of New York State, Inc. (doing business as Audubon International) (hereinafter the state organization) and respondent National Audubon Society, Inc. (doing business as Audubon New York) (hereinafter the national organization) claim that they were the intended beneficiary.

Finding a latent ambiguity in the clause, Surrogate's Court admitted extrinsic evidence and concluded that the testator intended to make a gift to the national organization. Specifically, the court relied upon an affidavit of the will drafter stating that, although the testator had "quickly, without reservation" stated upon inquiry that he intended to benefit the state organization, the testator was confused and actually intended to benefit the national organization. The state organization now appeals, arguing that Surrogate's Court improperly relied upon the drafter's affidavit and allegations of public confusion regarding the identity of the organizations to create an ambiguity when the will is unambiguous on its face. We agree.

It is well established that "in a will construction proceeding, the search is for the decedent's intent and not for that of the draft[er]" (620 Matter of Cord, 58 N.Y.2d 539, 544, 462 N.Y.S.2d 622, 449 N.E.2d 402 [1983] [citations omitted] [superseded by statute on other grounds]; see Matter of Carmer, 71 N.Y.2d 781, 785, 530 N.Y.S.2d 88, 525 N.E.2d 734 [1988]; Matter of McCabe, 269 A.D.2d 727, 728, 703 N.Y.S.2d 559 [2000]). All rules of interpretation are subordinated to the requirement that we give effect to the testator's dominant purpose or plan for distribution as manifested in the will, and that "task is not furthered by rote ascription of technical meanings to terms regardless of context; instead, 'a sympathetic reading of the will as an entirety' is required" (Matter of Carmer, supra at 785, 530 N.Y.S.2d 88, 525 N.E.2d 734, quoting Matter of Fabbri, 2 N.Y.2d 236, 240, 159 N.Y.S.2d 184, 140 N.E.2d 269 [1957]; see Matter of Bieley,

> **Food for Thought**
>
> After having read this discourse, is the court inclined to a hard and fast application of the plain meaning rule or have they been co-opted by Professor Wigmore?

91 N.Y.2d 520, 525, 673 N.Y.S.2d 38, 695 N.E.2d 1119 [1998]). Nevertheless, the best indicator of the testator's intent is found in the clear and unambiguous language of the will itself and, thus, where no ambiguity exists, "[e]xtrinsic evidence is inadmissible to vary the terms of a will" (Matter of Wickwire, 270 A.D.2d 659, 661, 705 N.Y.S.2d 102 [2000], lv. dismissed, lv. denied 95 N.Y.2d 824, 712 N.Y.S.2d 908, 734 N.E.2d 1209 [2000]; see Matter of Cord, supra at 544, 462 N.Y.S.2d 622, 449 N.E.2d 402; Matter of Goldstein, 46 A.D.2d 449, 450, 363 N.Y.S.2d 147 [1975], affd. 38 N.Y.2d 876, 382 N.Y.S.2d 743, 346 N.E.2d 544 [1976]; see generally W.W.W. Assoc. v. Giancontieri, 77 N.Y.2d 157, 162, 565 N.Y.S.2d 440, 566 N.E.2d 639 [1990]). When two charitable organizations claim to be the beneficiary named in a will, extrinsic evidence is admissible only if an examination " 'of the name[s] of the two corporations and of their general character and purposes as declared by the laws of their creation' " reveals a latent ambiguity (Union Trust Co. of N.Y. v. St. Luke's Hosp., 74 App.Div. 330, 333, 77 N.Y.S. 528 [1902], affd. 175 N.Y. 505, 67 N.E. 1090 [1903], quoting St. Luke's Home for Indigent Christian Females v. Association for Relief of Respectable Aged Indigent Females in City of N.Y., 52 N.Y. 191, 194 [1873]; see Matter of Seabury, 107 Misc. 705, 707–708, 177 N.Y.S. 91 [1919], affd. 191 App.Div. 889, 180 N.Y.S. 952 [1920], affd. sub nom. Matter of Wentworth, 229 N.Y. 636, 129 N.E. 938 [1920]).

Here, the testator's will designated "The Audubon Society of New York State" and "The World Wildlife Fund" as beneficiaries of his residuary estate, with each receiving 10% of the residuary. Although the national organization and the Attorney General in his statutory capacity under EPTL 8–1.1(f) argue that there is no entity named "The Audubon Society of New York State," it is undisputed that the state organization is named "The Audubon Society of New York State, Inc." In our view, the testator's failure to include "Inc." in naming his beneficiary does not render the will ambiguous (see Union Trust Co. of N.Y. v. St. Luke's Hosp., supra at 334, 77 N.Y.S. 528). Moreover, a review of the certificates of incorporation and consolidation of the state and national organizations-as well as their history-reveals that the general character and purpose of both is to promote understanding, conservation and preservation of wildlife, natural resources and the environment through research and public education. Indeed, despite its criticism of the state organization's sustainable development and resource management programs, the national organization concedes that the state organization sponsors a local bird conservation project, the New York Loon Conservation Project. Thus, reading the will as a whole in view of the surrounding "facts and circumstances" (Matter of Fabbri, supra at 240, 159 N.Y.S.2d 184, 140 N.E.2d) and accepting the argument that the will evinces the testator's intent to donate money to charitable entities that benefit both wildlife generally and avian wildlife in particular, there is nothing on the face of the will to support the claim that the testator intended to donate to the national organization, rather than the state organization that he expressly named in the will (see Union Trust Co. of N.Y. v. St. Luke's Hosp., supra at 334, 77 N.Y.S. 528).

Take Note

Both organizations have similar functions and both operate in New York. Which designation should be chosen, their legal name (in which the designation in will more closely tracks the state organization) or the operational designation (in which the designation in will more closely tracks the national)? Is there an exception to the plain meaning rule that could have been used to admit the scrivener's testimony?

We reject the arguments of the national organization and the Attorney General that the use of the phrase "Audubon Society" by many charities creates a latent ambiguity in this will or, presumably, any will in which money is bequeathed to a charity bearing the "Audubon Society" designation. Those parties rely upon the national organization's prior lawsuit commenced against the state organization for unfair competition due to its use of the phrase "Audubon Society," as well as affidavits from two employees of the national organization indicating that there is public confusion over the organizations' names. We note, however, that Supreme Court, New York County (Arber, J.), dismissed the national organization's claims in the prior action. As the court explained in rejecting the national organization's assertion that it had been harmed due to confusion over the similar names, "[courts] . . . must . . . assume that the public will use reasonable intelligence

Practice Pointer

Is there a lesson here? Why was the scrivener speculating? Should the scrivener have enquired further on which bird watchers his client preferred?

and discrimination with reference to the names of corporations with which they are dealing or intend to deal" (Police Conference of N.Y. v. Metropolitan Police Conference of E. N.Y., 66 A.D.2d 441, 445, 414 N.Y.S.2d 748 [1979], affd. 48 N.Y.2d 780, 423 N.Y.S.2d 922, 399 N.E.2d 952 [1979] [internal quotation marks and citation omitted]). Similarly here, we cannot say that the use of the phrase "Audubon Society" by a large number of charities or the allegations of public confusion in the record give rise to a latent ambiguity justifying the admission of "[p]arol evidence . . . to show that the testat[or] did not mean what [he] has said in words" (Dwight v. Fancher, 245 N.Y. 71, 74, 156 N.E. 186 [1927]; see Matter of Lezotte, 108 A.D.2d 1052, 1052–1053, 485 N.Y.S.2d 626 [1985]; Union Trust Co. of N.Y. v. St. Luke's Hosp., supra at 334–335, 77 N.Y.S. 528; cf. Matter of Van Vliet, 224 N.Y. 572, 572, 120 N.E.

877 [1918]; Matter of Patterson, 139 Misc. 872, 874–875, 249 N.Y.S. 441 [1931]; Matter of Seabury, supra at 707–708, 177 N.Y.S. 91).

Accordingly, we agree with the state organization that Surrogate's Court erred in relying upon the affidavit of the will drafter, in which he speculated based upon his discussions with the testator that, notwithstanding the testator's unequivocal statement that he wished to donate to the state organization, the testator actually intended to benefit the national organization. In this regard, we note that "if courts should permit the substitution of the draft[er's] recollection of what the testator told him [or her], for the language of the will itself, the instrument would cease to be the repository of the decedent's testamentary program" (Matter of Storrs, 18 Misc.2d 941, 944, 186 N.Y.S.2d 423 [1959]; see Matter of Campbell, 171 Misc.2d 892, 902–903, 655 N.Y.S.2d 913 [1997]). Rather, as we have previously explained, "extrinsic evidence may not be used in this fashion to create an ambiguity in a will where none [exists]" (Matter of Wickwire, 270 A.D.2d 659, 662, 705 N.Y.S.2d 102 [2000], supra). In short, as the will unambiguously dictates, the legacy must be paid to the state organization expressly named therein.

The state organization's remaining argument has been rendered academic by our decision. ORDERED that the order and decree is reversed, on the law and the facts, with one bill of costs, and matter remitted to the Surrogate's Court of Albany County for further proceedings not inconsistent with this Court's decision.

CARDONA, P.J., CARPINELLO, MUGGLIN and LAHTINEN, JJ., concur.

Points for Discussion

1. More on names of institutions

If the court places itself in the armchair of the will-maker, ought it not be able to ask him or her what organization he or she had in mind, even if that means asking the attorney who drafted the will? Cases in which organizations with similar names claim a bequest, though not common, are not that rare. Courts seem wedded to textual rather than contextual exegesis. In *National Society for the Prevention of Cruelty for Children v. Scottish National Society for the Prevention of Cruelty for Children*, the London-based organization took the bequest, even though the testator, a Scotsman, lived near and was acquainted with the Scottish organization. [1915] A. C. 207. Similarly, a bequest to 'Perry Manor Inc. Pinckneyville, Illinois' went to a Nevada company that at the time of the execution of the will ran a nursing home in the testatrix's home county called 'Perry Manor,' but had sold it to another corporation which continued to call the home 'Perry Manor.' Is it likely that the testator actually wished to benefit a corporation many miles from her home rather than the nursing home she knew? The court thought the scrivener's evidence was 'speculative,' and refused to admit evidence of the executor that had she known of the changed ownership she would have changed her will. *Estate of Smith*, 555 N. E. 2d 1111 (Ill. App. 1990). Would you have been inclined to admit one or the other or both of these morsels of extrinsic evidence? Where is King Solomon when we really need him? Instead of feathering lawyers' nests in all of the above cases, why not divide the pot?

2. Construction versus reformation

In addition to admitting extrinsic evidence to 'explain' (or create) an ambiguity, why not use *reformation* (read re-write) to cope with either mistakes or ambiguities? Restatement Third, Property § 11.3, allows the resolution of ambiguities (defined in § 11.2 as "an uncertainty in meaning that is revealed by the text or by extrinsic evidence other than direct evidence of intention contradicting the plain meaning of the text") according to the testator's intent established by a preponderance of the evidence in § 11.2, and perhaps most controversially, allowing reformation to conform the words to the testator's intent in the following:

Restatement Third, Property (Wills and Donative Transfers) § 12.1

A donative document, though unambiguous, may be reformed to conform the text to the donor's intention if it is established by clear and convincing evidence (1) that a mistake of fact or law, whether in expression or inducement, affected specific terms of the document; and (2) what the donor's intention was. In determining whether these elements have been established by clear and convincing evidence, direct evidence of intention contradicting the plain meaning of the text as well as other evidence of intention may be considered.

These provisions are highly controversial. On the one hand the Restatement can be seen as merely reflecting the general decline in willingness to allow formalities to frustrate the testator's intent. On the other hand, § 12.1 can be read as completely undermining the foundation of the law of wills by making it possible to rewrite testator's estate plan. Whether concern is justified depends upon how much confidence one has that the heightened evidentiary standard (clear and convincing) will limit reformation to appropriate cases. Does this approach remind you of another set of doctrines that can save a will when some mistake has occurred?

The following case is a milestone in the law of reformation of wills. When the Supreme Court of California changes the law this dramatically one must take notice. *Estate of Duke* is the first state supreme court case to adopt the Restatement view of will reformation.

Estate of Irving Duke, Deceased

352 P.3d 863 (Cal. 2015)

Opinion

Cantil-Sakauye, C.J.

Irving Duke prepared a holographic will providing that, upon his death, his wife would inherit his estate and that if he and his wife died at the same time, specific charities would inherit his estate. The handwritten will, however, contained no provision addressing the disposition of his estate if, as occurred here, he lived longer than his wife. The specified charities contend that at the time the testator wrote his will, he specifically intended to provide in his will that the charities would inherit his estate in the event his wife was not alive when he died. The courts below excluded extrinsic evidence of the testator's intent, finding that the will was unambiguous and failed to provide for the circumstance in which his wife predeceased him. Therefore, finding that Duke died intestate, the court entered judgment in favor of the heirs at law, Seymour and Robert Radin.

We granted review to reconsider the historical rule that extrinsic evidence is inadmissible to reform an unambiguous will. We conclude that the categorical bar on reformation of wills is not justified, and we hold that an unambiguous will may be reformed if clear and convincing evidence establishes that the will contains a mistake in the expression of the testator's intent at the time the will was drafted and also establishes the testator's actual specific intent at the time the will was drafted. We further conclude that the charities' theory that the testator actually intended at the time he drafted his will to provide that his estate would pass to the charities in the event his wife was not alive to inherit the estate is sufficiently particularized, with respect to the existence of such a mistake and the testator's intent, that the remedy of reformation is available so long as clear and convincing evidence on both points is demonstrated. Therefore, we will direct this matter to be remanded to the probate court for consideration of whether clear and convincing evidence establishes that such a mistake occurred at the time the will was written and that the testator at that time intended his estate to pass to the charities in the event his wife was not alive to inherit the estate when he died.

> **Take Note**
>
> This paragraph summarizes the opinion, clearly states that the court is setting forth a new rule of law, and explains exactly what it is.

I. FACTS

In 1984, when Irving Duke was 72 years of age, he prepared a holographic will in which he left all of his property to "my beloved wife, Mrs. Beatrice Schecter Duke," who was then 58 years of age. He left to his brother, Harry Duke, "the sum of One dollar." He provided that "[s]hould my wife . . . and I die at the same moment, my estate is to be equally divided—One-half is to be donated to the City of Hope in the name and loving memory of my sister, Mrs. Rose Duke Radin. One-half is to be donated to the Jewish National Fund to plant trees in Israel in the names and loving memory of my mother and father—Bessie and Isaac Duke."

> **Food for Thought**
>
> This is the problematic provision. How should it have been drafted if Mr. Duke had intended to do what the charities contend was his intent?

Irving further provided in his will that "I have intentionally omitted all other persons, whether heirs or otherwise, who are not specifically mentioned herein, and I hereby specifically disinherit all persons whomsoever claiming to be, or who may lawfully be determined to be my heirs at law, except as otherwise mentioned in this will. If any heir, devisee or legatee, or any other person or persons, shall either directly or indirectly, seek to invalidate this will, or any part thereof, then I hereby give and bequeath to such person or persons the sum of one dollar ($1.00) and no more, in lieu of any other share or interest in my estate."

The will appointed Beatrice the executrix of the estate. The only change Irving ever made to his will was the addition, in 1997, of the statement that "[w]e hereby agree that all of our assets are community property." Beatrice died in July 2002, but the will was not changed to select a new executor.

Irving died in November 2007, leaving no spouse or children. In February 2008, a deputy public administrator for the County of Los Angeles obtained the will from Irving's safe deposit box. In March 2008, two charities, the City of Hope (COH) and the Jewish National Fund (JNF), petitioned for probate and for letters of administration. In October 2008, Robert and Seymour Radin (the Radins) filed a petition for determination of entitlement to estate distribution. The Radins are the sons of Irving's sister, Rose Duke Radin, who predeceased Irving. Their petition alleged that they are entitled to the distribution of Irving's estate as Irving's sole intestate heirs.

Make the Connection

Because the nominated executor died before the testator and there was no successor named in the will, the charities petitioned to become administrators and the relatives petitioned for a determination that the estate should be distributed to them, all in accord with California procedures. Remember that the procedures in other states may be different.

The Radins moved for summary judgment. They did not challenge the validity of the will. Instead, they asserted that the estate must pass to Irving's closest surviving intestate heirs, the Radins, because Irving did not predecease Beatrice, nor did Irving and Beatrice "die at the same moment," and there is no provision in the will for disposition of the estate in the event Irving survived Beatrice. In opposition to the motion, COH and JNF offered extrinsic evidence to prove that Irving intended the will to provide that in the event Beatrice was not alive to inherit Irving's estate when Irving died, the estate would be distributed to COH and JNF.

The probate court concluded that the will was not ambiguous, and on that ground, it declined to consider extrinsic evidence of Irving's intent, and granted summary judgment for the Radins.

The Court of Appeal affirmed, based on our opinion in *Estate of Barnes* (1965) 63 Cal.2d 580, 47 Cal. Rptr. 480, 407 P.2d 656 (*Barnes*). In *Barnes,* the testatrix's will provided that all of her property was to go to her husband, and if she and her husband died simultaneously or within two weeks of each other, her entire estate was to go to her nephew, Robert Henderson. Her will included a disinheritance clause, stating that " 'I hereby declare that I have thought of and considered each

Take Note

The trial court's decision rests on the traditional rule limiting the consideration of extrinsic evidence to cases in which the words are ambiguous. Do you regard the language therein as ambiguous or simply consider the disposition incomplete?

and every person who would inherit from me had I died intestate and who is not mentioned in this Will, and I hereby declare that I do not desire to devise or bequeath to such person or persons any sum whatsoever and I hereby disinherit such person or persons." (*Id.* at p. 581, fn. 5, 47 Cal. Rptr. 480, 407 P.2d 656.) The testatrix's husband predeceased her, but she did not alter her will after his death.

When the testatrix died, 13 years after executing the will, she had various heirs at law, but Robert Henderson was not an heir at law because his mother was still alive. In the heirship proceeding, Henderson's mother testified that at the time the will was executed, Henderson frequently visited the testatrix at her home and spent many holidays with her, the two had a close relationship, and the testatrix was fond of him and often introduced him as her son. She also testified that the other relatives did not visit. The trial court found the will ambiguous, admitted the extrinsic evidence, and construed it in favor of Henderson. (*Barnes, supra,* 63 Cal.2d at p. 582, 47 Cal. Rptr. 480, 407 P.2d 656.)

We reversed the judgment. We stated that the extrinsic evidence concerning Henderson's relationship with the testatrix did not assist in interpreting the will. Although that evidence might have explained why the testatrix named Henderson as an alternate beneficiary in the event she died within two weeks of her husband, it shed no light on her intention in the event her husband died years before she did. We further observed that the will made no disposition of her property in the event she outlived her husband by several years, and noted that although a disinheritance clause could prevent a claimant from inheriting under the will, it could not prevent heirs from inheriting pursuant to the statutory rules of intestacy. (*Barnes, supra,* 63 Cal.2d at pp. 582–583, 47 Cal. Rptr. 480, 407 P.2d 656.)

Turning to the will, we acknowledged that "a will is to be construed according to the intention of the testator, and so as to avoid intestacy." (*Barnes, supra,* 63 Cal.2d at p. 583, 47 Cal. Rptr. 480, 407 P.2d 656.) We added, "However, a court may not write a will which the testator did not write." (*Ibid.*) The terms of the testatrix's will reflected that she wanted all of her property to go to her

> **Take Note**
>
> The irresistible force (avoid intestacy) and the immovable object (we don't write wills for testators). Something has to give!

husband, and "also demonstrate[d] an awareness that [if she died within two weeks of her husband] she might well have no further opportunity to designate an alternate, and therefore she named [Henderson]. However, . . . the will is devoid of a provision or suggestion as to testatrix' intent if, as occurred, she was afforded sufficient time to review the will following the death of her husband." (*Ibid.*) We noted that if the absence of a disposition of her property had come to her attention after her husband died, she might have provided that her estate would go to Henderson, or she might have made other provisions. "Under such circumstances any selection by the courts now would be to indulge in forbidden conjecture." (*Id.* at p. 584, 47 Cal. Rptr. 480, 407 P.2d 656.) Finally, we found no " 'dominant dispositive plan' " that might warrant the finding of a gift by implication. (*Ibid.*) Therefore, finding the extrinsic evidence offered no assistance, we reversed the order distributing the estate to Henderson.

The Court of Appeal noted that the will in this case is similar to the will in *Barnes, supra,* 63 Cal.2d 580, 47 Cal. Rptr. 480, 407 P.2d 656. "Just as the court concluded in *Barnes,* Irving's will is not ambiguous. . . . It simply made no disposition whatsoever of the property in the event Irving outlived his wife by several years, as eventually occurred." The Court of Appeal also found the will sufficiently similar to the will in *Barnes* to compel the conclusion that it does not reflect a dominant dispositive plan to leave the estate to JNF and COH. Finally, it rejected the admission of extrinsic evidence because the evidence did not address any ambiguity in the will.

The Court of Appeal added that it was "mindful of the fact that the ultimate disposition of Irving's property . . . does not appear to comport with his testamentary intent. It is clear that [Irving] meant to dispose of his estate through his bequests, first to his wife and, should she predecease him, then to the charities. It is difficult to imagine that after leaving specific gifts to the charities in the names and memories of beloved family members, Irving intended them to take effect only in the event that he and his wife died 'at the same moment.' " It concluded, however, that because the will is unambiguous, *Barnes, supra,* 63 Cal.2d 580, 47 Cal .Rptr. 480, 407 P.2d 656, precluded consideration of the extrinsic evidence.

We granted review to consider whether the rule applied in *Barnes, supra,* 63 Cal.2d 580, 47 Cal. Rptr. 480, 407 P.2d 656, should be reconsidered. For the reasons set forth below, we hold that the categorical bar on reformation of unambiguous wills is not justified and that reformation is permissible if clear and convincing evidence establishes an error in the expression of the testator's intent and establishes the testator's actual specific intent at the time the will was drafted.[2]

II. DISCUSSION

California law allows the admission of extrinsic evidence to establish that a will is ambiguous and to clarify ambiguities in a will. (Prob. Code, § 6111.5; *Estate of Russell* (1968) 69 Cal.2d 200, 206–213, 70 . 561, 444 P.2d 353.) As COH and JNF acknowledge, however, California law does not currently authorize the admission of extrinsic evidence to correct a mistake in a will when the will is unambiguous. (*Estate of Dominici* (1907) 151 Cal. 181, 186, 90 P. 448; *Estate of Page* (1967) 254 Cal.App.2d 702, 719, 62 . 740; 14 Witkin, Summary of Cal. Law (10th ed. 2005) Wills and Probate, § 236, pp. 315–316.) To evaluate whether there are circumstances in which this court should authorize the admission of extrinsic evidence to correct a mistake in an unambiguous will, we first consider whether the Legislature's actions in this field preclude this court from altering the rule. As explained below, a review of the development of the law in California reflects that the Legislature has codified judicial expansions of the admissibility of evidence with respect to a testator's intent, but has not acted in a manner that restricts the authority of courts to develop the common law in this area. Second, we consider whether the common law rule categorically barring the reformation of wills is warranted, in light of the evolution of the law of probate and modern theories of interpretation of writings, and we conclude that categorical bar on reformation is not justified. Third, we consider principles of

---

2   As explained below, a testator's actual specific intent is the particular disposition of assets the testator intended to set forth in the will. (See p. 34, *post.*)

stare decisis, and conclude that a change in the law is warranted to allow the reformation of an unambiguous will when clear and convincing evidence establishes that the will contains a mistake in the expression of the testator's intent at the time the will was executed and also establishes the testator's actual and specific intent at the time the will was executed. Finally, we conclude that the remedy of reformation is potentially available with respect to the theory of mistake articulated by COH and JNF in this case. Therefore, we will direct the case to be remanded for the probate court's consideration of whether clear and convincing evidence establishes that the testator intended, at the time he drafted his will, to provide in his will that his estate was to pass to COH and JNF in the event his wife was not alive at the time the testator died.

A. Statutory and judicial development of the law concerning the admission of extrinsic evidence regarding wills

Beginning with the original Statute of Wills in 1540, statutory law has required that wills be in writing.[3] [citations omitted] The principles governing the interpretation and enforcement of wills, however, have been developed by the courts. [what follows is a careful an detailed history of California statutes dealing with the construction of wills. The discussion supports the following conclusion] . . . .

This history of statutory provisions concerning the admissibility of evidence of a testator's intent reflects that the Legislature has codified legal principles developed by the courts, and has taken steps to ensure that its enactments do not restrict the admissibility of extrinsic evidence beyond the principles established by the courts. Nothing in this history suggests that the Legislature intended to foreclose further judicial developments of the law concerning the admissibility of evidence to discern the testator's intent, and "we see no reason to interpret the legislation as establishing a bar to judicial innovation." (*American Motorcycle Assn. v. Superior Court* (1978) 20 Cal.3d 578, 601, 146. 182, 578 P.2d 899 [California's contribution statutes did not preclude judicial adoption of comparative partial indemnity]; see *Leung v. Verdugo Hills Hospital* (2012) 55 Cal.4th 291, 301, 145 Cal.Rptr.3d 553, 282 P.3d 1250 ["nothing in the statute's legislative history suggests an intent to foreclose the courts from rendering future decisions that would further the statute's main purpose of ameliorating the harshness and the inequity of the common law rule at issue"].) Moreover, it does not appear that the Legislature has addressed the issue of reformation of wills.[9] Therefore, as we did in *Estate of Russell,*

---

3   One exception to the requirement of a writing was the nuncupative will, which could be declared orally by a person who was serving in the military or was ill in his residence, and who was "in actual contemplation, fear, or peril of death." (Civ. Code, former § 1289, subd. 3.) Such a will was valid only with respect to an estate of limited value, and required proof by two witnesses. (*Id.,* subds. 1, 3.)

9   In connection with its 2001 recommendation to the Legislature concerning the admissibility of extrinsic evidence, the California Law Revision Commission noted that its "recommendation does not address or propose to affect the law governing reformation of an instrument to effectuate the intention of the donor in case of mistake or for other cause." (Recommendation on Rules of Construction, supra, 31 Cal. Law Revision Com. Rep. at p. 175.) When the commission's staff conveyed to the commission its 2001 recommendations concerning the rules of construction, which included the recommendation that Probate Code section 21102 be amended to state that it did

supra, 69 Cal.2d 200, 70. 561, 444 P.2d 353, we may continue to develop the law concerning the admissibility of evidence to assist in the determination of the testator's intent when the language of the document is clear on its face.

B. No sound basis exists to forbid the reformation of unambiguous wills in appropriate circumstances

As discussed below, extrinsic evidence is admissible to correct errors in other types of donative documents, even when the donor is deceased. Extrinsic evidence is also admissible to aid in the construction of a will, and in some cases, the resulting "construction" has essentially reformed the will. Extrinsic evidence is also admissible to determine whether a document was intended to be a will, and to prove the contents of a will that has been lost or destroyed. Because extrinsic evidence is not inherently more reliable when admitted for these various purposes than when admitted to correct an error in a will, concerns about the reliability of evidence do not justify a categorical bar on reformation of wills. To the extent categorical resistance to reformation is based instead on a concern that reformed language would not comply with the formalities required by the statute of wills,[10] principles developed in the context of the statute of frauds, which similarly requires a signed writing to evidence specified documents, illustrate that the purposes of the statute of wills are satisfied by the testator's execution of a writing that complies with the statutory requirements. With the statutory purposes satisfied, only the concerns regarding the reliability of evidence might justify a categorical bar on reformation of wills, and those concerns are addressed by imposing a burden of clear and convincing evidence.

In California, extrinsic evidence is generally admissible to correct errors in documents, including donative documents other than wills. [omitted are citations to California cases and statutes making admissible extrinsic evidence to correct errors in contracts, release agreements,

---

not limit the use of extrinsic evidence to determine the transferor's intention, an accompanying staff memorandum stated that "[t]here was general agreement that the Probate Code should eventually address reformation of instruments. However, this should be done carefully in a separate project." (Cal. Law Revision Com., Staff Memorandum 2001–85, Rules of Construction for Trusts (Draft of Recommendation) (Nov. 8, 2001) p. 1.) It further stated that "[w]hether the Commission has the time and resources to undertake such a project immediately is another question." (*Id.* at p. 2.)

10   The statute of wills, or the "Wills Act," refers generically to the formalities required in connection with the execution of a will, which originated with the Statute of Wills under Henry VIII. (32 Hen. VIII, ch. 1 (July 20, 1540); Estate of Carlson (1970) 9 Cal.App.3d 479, 481, 88. 229.) The Legislature, in its first session, enacted a statute of wills, which required a writing signed by the testator or by a person in his presence, and attested at his express direction by two witnesses subscribing their names to the will in his presence. (Stats.1850, ch. 72, § 3, p. 177.) The Civil Code imposed essentially the same requirements (Civ. Code, former § 1276), and also recognized holographic wills, which it defined as "entirely written, dated, and signed by the hand of the testator himself." (Id., former § 1277.)

The Probate Code retains the requirements that a will be signed by the testator and by two witnesses, but it further provides that if it was not executed in compliance with the provisions concerning witnesses, "the will shall be treated as if it was executed in compliance with [those provisions] if the proponent of the will establishes by clear and convincing evidence that, at the time the testator signed the will, the testator intended the will to constitute the testator's will." (Prob. Code, § 6110.) The Probate Code continues to recognize holographic wills, "if the signature and the material provisions are in the handwriting of the testator." (*Id.,* § 6111, subd. (a))

irrevocable trusts, mutual mistake in insurance policy, gift deed, unilateral mistake in an insurance policy, and deeds.]

In addition, California courts have admitted extrinsic evidence to apply to the *construction* of a will to accomplish what is arguably or has the effect of reforming a will. For example, admission of extrinsic evidence that the testator referred to her siblings as the " 'Broude Trust' " allowed the court to correct the testator's error in leaving everything to the " 'Broude Trust Fund' " instead of to her siblings. (*Estate of Glow* (1962) 208 Cal.App.2d 613, 616–617, 25. 416 [evidence of testator's "lay" usage of a technical term is admissible]; see *Estate of Kime* (1983) 144 Cal.App.3d 246, 264, 193. 718 [testator's statements were admissible regarding whether she understood language merely appoint-ing an executor to be effective to designate a beneficiary]; *Estate of Fries* (1963) 221 Cal.App.2d 725, 727–730, 34. 749 [will identified husband as executor but did not identify to whom testatrix bequeathed property; court relied in part on husband's testimony that testatrix said she would give him everything]; *Estate of Karkeet* (1961) 56 Cal.2d 277, 281–283, 14. 664, 363 P.2d 896 [extrinsic evidence was admissible to establish that a will that named the testatrix's good friend as executrix, but made no testamentary disposition,

> **Make the Connection**
>
> The court candidly admits that "con-struction" is a term that covers a mul-titude of interventions related to wills. "Does it differ from Reformation?" How many of the traditional con-structional rules discussed above can be characterized as "reformation"?

was intended to leave the estate to the good friend]; *Estate of Akeley* (1950) 35 Cal.2d 26, 30, 215 P.2d 921 [evidence that testatrix was unmarried, had no relatives, and drafted her will herself was cited in support of ruling that three charities that were each given one-quarter of the residue of the estate would each receive one-third].)

Principles allowing the admission of extrinsic evidence to identify and resolve ambiguities in wills have also been invoked to correct attorneys' drafting errors and thereby to reform wills. For example, in *Estate of Taff* (1976) 63 Cal.App.3d 319, 133. 737, the testatrix directed her attorney to provide that if the testatrix's sister did not survive her, the residue of the estate would go to her sister's children. Her will, however, stated that if her sister predeceased her, the residue would go to " 'my heirs in accordance with the laws of intestate succession.' " (*Id.* at p. 322, 133. 737.) The court found that the extrinsic evidence of the testatrix's instructions to her attorney and statements to her sister "exposed a latent ambiguity, i.e., that when the testatrix used the term 'my heirs' in her will, she intended to exclude the relatives of her predeceased husband, Harry." (*Id.* at p. 325, 133. 737.) Similarly, in *Estate of Anderson, supra,* 56 Cal.App.4th 235, 65 Cal.Rptr.2d 307, a later will expressly revoked all prior wills, but due to attorney error, the later will failed to include a provision exercising a testamentary power of appointment over a portion of a trust. As a result, the later will failed to carry out the testatrix's intent that the half of the trust over which she had a power of appointment go to her daughter rather than to the issue of her late husband. The court held that extrinsic evidence was admissible to determine whether the testatrix intended to revoke the earlier will's provision exercising her power of appointment. (*Id.* at pp. 242–248, 65 Cal.Rptr.2d 307.)

Extrinsic evidence is admissible not only to aid in the construction of a will, but also to determine whether a document was intended to be a will. (*Halldin v. Usher* (1958) 49 Cal.2d 749, 752, 321 P.2d 746 [parol evidence is admissible to prove a document was intended as a will rather than a contract]; *Estate of Sargavak* (1950) 35 Cal.2d 93, 96, 216 P.2d 850 [evidence is admissible to prove a will was executed in jest, as a threat to induce action, under the mistaken belief it was a mortgage, to induce illicit relations, or in response to annoyance from one who seeks to inherit].) In addition, courts have long recognized that extrinsic evidence is admissible to prove that a will has been lost or destroyed, and to prove its contents. (Prob. Code, § 8223; *Swift v. Superior Court* (1952) 39 Cal.2d 358, 247 P.2d 6; *Estate of Flood* (1941) 47 Cal.App.2d 809, 119 P.2d 168; 14 Witkin, Summary of Cal. Law, *supra,* Wills and Probate, §§ 550–551, pp. 630–633.)

Make the Connection

The analogy to contracts is significant. It is often said that contract is swallowing up the law of property—e.g., the traditional law of landlord and tenant supplanted by contract inspired doctrine like the illegal lease and the implied warranty of habitability. Are contract concepts appropriate for use here?

Thus, extrinsic evidence is admitted to correct donative documents other than wills after the donor's death. Moreover, myriad circumstances exist in which California courts appropriately admit evidence to establish a testator's intentions. Because extrinsic evidence is not inherently more reliable when admitted for these various purposes than when admitted to correct an error in a will, Professors John Langbein and Lawrence Waggoner, leading advocates of an extension of the doctrine of reformation to unambiguous wills, conclude that evidentiary concerns do not explain or justify the bar on reformation of wills. In their view, a greater obstacle to reformation has been concern with the formalities required in the execution of a will by the statute of wills. (Langbein & Waggoner, *Reformation of Wills on the Ground of Mistake: Change of Direction in American Law?* (1982) 130 U.Pa.L.Rev. 521, 524–529 (hereafter Langbein and Waggoner).) To overcome the objection that reformed language is unattested, they look to principles related to the statute of frauds.

Like the statute of wills, the statute of frauds requires certain documents to be evidenced by a writing subscribed by the party. If not evidenced by such a writing, a contract subject to the statute of frauds is invalid. (Civ.Code, § 1624.) " 'The primary purpose of the Statute [of Frauds] is evidentiary, to require reliable evidence of the existence and terms of the contract and to prevent enforcement through fraud or perjury of contracts never in fact made.' " (*Sterling v. Taylor* (2007) 40 Cal.4th 757, 766, 55 Cal.Rptr.3d 116, 152 P.3d 420.) Once sufficient written evidence of an agreement is presented, the evidentiary purpose is served, and extrinsic evidence is admissible to clarify ambiguous terms and to reform the writing to correct a mistake, even when the writing

Make the Connection

Where else have we seen the requirement of "clear and convincing evidence" relied on to refute traditional objections to loosening the traditional formalities of the law of wills?

is intended to be a complete and exclusive statement of the parties' agreement. (*Id.* at p. 767, 55 Cal.Rptr.3d 116, 152 P.3d 420; Civ.Code, §§ 1640, 3399; Code Civ. Proc., § 1856, subds. (b), (e); *Hess v. Ford Motor Co., supra,* 27 Cal.4th at pp. 524–525, 117 Cal.Rptr.2d 220, 41 P.3d 46.)

In correcting a contract subject to the statute of frauds, a court is not enforcing an oral contract, but is instead enforcing a written contract in accordance with the parties' actual agreement. To overcome the presumption that the writing is accurate, we have required clear and convincing evidence of a mistake before allowing reformation of a contract. (*Nat. Auto. & Cas. Co. v. Ind. Acc. Com.* (1949) 34 Cal.2d 20, 25, 206 P.2d 841; *Burt v. Los Angeles Olive Growers' Assn.* (1917) 175 Cal. 668, 675, 166 P. 993; *R & B Auto Center, Inc. v. Farmers Group, Inc.* (2006) 140 Cal.App.4th 327, 382, 44 Cal.Rptr.3d 426.)

In contrast to cases involving the statute of frauds, which may or may not involve a party who is deceased, cases arising under the statute of wills always involve a testator who is deceased and therefore cannot explain his or her intentions. We have already recognized, however, in the context of inheritance rights, that imposing a burden of proof by clear and convincing evidence is a means to address evidentiary concerns related to the circumstances that the principal witness is deceased and statutory formalities were not followed. (*Estate of Ford* (2004) 32 Cal.4th 160, 172, 8 Cal.Rptr.3d 541, 82 P.3d 747 [one seeking to inherit based on the doctrine of equitable adoption must meet the clear and convincing evidence standard, in part because the adoptive parent is deceased and can no longer testify, and the relief sought is outside the ordinary course of intestate succession and without the formalities required by the adoption statutes].) In addition, discerning intent in the context of a will is eased by the fact that the court must ascertain only the subjective intent of a single individual. (Langbein & Waggoner, *supra,* 130 U.Pa. L.Rev. at p. 569.) Therefore, the fact that the testator will always be unavailable to testify does not warrant a categorical bar on the admission of extrinsic evidence to reform a will.

Applying the analysis developed with respect to the statute of frauds, Langbein and Waggoner observe, "Whereas an oral will instances total noncompliance with the Wills Act formalities, a duly executed will with a mistakenly rendered term involves high levels of compliance with both the letter and the purpose of the Wills Act formalities. To the extent that a mistake case risks impairing any policy of the Wills Act, it is the *evidentiary* policy that is in question."[13] (Langbein & Waggoner, *supra,*130 U.Pa. L.Rev. at p. 569, italics added.) With respect to evidentiary concerns, the authors advocate that reformation be allowed only in cases of clear and convincing evidence of the alleged mistake and the testator's intent. (*Ibid.*) As noted, we have previously imposed a clear and convincing evidence standard to support a claim of

---

13　The formalities imposed in connection with the execution of a will serve three functions in addition to the evidentiary purpose of establishing the testator's intent. First, the ritual of the formalities serves to warn the testator of the seriousness of the act. Second, the formalities make it more difficult to deceive the testator. Third, the formalities "serve a channeling function, routinizing testation and facilitating relatively inexpensive processing of wills in post-mortem proceedings." (Langbein & Waggoner, *supra,* 130 U.Pa. L.Rev. at p. 529, fn. 27.) These three additional purposes are served regardless of whether evidence is admitted in the probate proceeding regarding a mistake in the will.

inheritance based on equitable adoption. (*Estate of Ford, supra,* 32 Cal.4th 160, 172, 8 Cal. Rptr.3d 541, 82 P.3d 747.)

In cases in which clear and convincing evidence establishes both a mistake in the drafting of the will and the testator's actual and specific intent at the time the will was drafted, it is plain that denying reformation would defeat the testator's intent and result in unjust enrichment of unintended beneficiaries. Given that the paramount concern in construing a will is to determine the subjective intent of the testator (*Estate of Russell, supra,* 69 Cal.2d at p. 205, 70. 561, 444 P.2d 353; 4 Page on Wills (Bowe-Parker rev.2004) § 30.1, p. 2), only significant countervailing considerations can justify a rule categorically denying reformation.

The Radins cite various factors in support of their contention that reformation of wills should never be allowed, some of which we have addressed above. First, they distinguish wills from other written instruments, noting that probate of a will always occurs after the testator's death, whereas contract litigation typically occurs when the parties to the contract are alive, and trust administration "frequently" begins before the testator's death. In addition, anyone may claim to be an intended beneficiary of a will, but the parties to a contract typically are few. We are not persuaded by these arguments in favor of a categorical bar on reformation. As we have noted, the death of a principal witness has not been viewed as a reason to deny reformation in other contexts. Also, although anyone may claim to be an intended beneficiary of a will, an appropriately tailored reformation remedy will alleviate concerns regarding unintended beneficiaries; it is unlikely that there will be many persons who have a connection to a testator and can produce clear and convincing evidence both of a mistake in the drafting of the will at the time the will was written and of the testator's specific intentions concerning the disposition of property. Categorically denying reformation may result in unjust enrichment if there is a mistake of expression in the will, and imposing a burden of clear and convincing evidence of both the existence of the mistake and of the testator's actual and specific intent at the time the will was drafted helps safeguard against baseless allegations. (See *Estate of Ford, supra,* 32 Cal.4th at p. 172, 8 Cal.Rptr.3d 541, 82 P.3d 747 [equitable adoption must meet the clear and convincing evidence standard]; see also *Dillon v. Legg* (1968) 68 Cal.2d 728, 736, 69. 72, 441 P.2d 912 ["the possibility that fraudulent assertions may prompt recovery in isolated cases does not justify a wholesale rejection of the entire class of claims in which that potentiality arises"]; *Notten v. Mensing* (1935) 3 Cal.2d 469, 477, 45 P.2d 198 [acknowledging the strong temptation to fabricate evidence of an oral agreement to leave property to the plaintiff, but concluding that "if such agreement is proved by full, clear and convincing evidence, such agreement should be enforced according to its terms"].)

Second, the Radins express concern that reformation overrides the formalities required to execute a will. The fact that reformation is an available remedy does not relieve a testator of the requirements imposed by the Statute of Wills. (See, § 6111.) Therefore, the formalities continue to serve various functions associated with the rituals of will execution, such as warning the testator of the seriousness of the act and clearly identifying the document as a will. (See fn. 12, *ante.*) To the extent reformation is inconsistent with the formalities' evidentiary purpose of establishing the testator's intent in a writing, the inconsistency is no different from the tension between reformation and the statute of frauds. As explained above, the evidentiary concern is addressed by requiring clear and convincing evidence of a mistake in expression and the testator's actual and specific intent. We should not allow stringent adherence to formalities to obscure the ultimate purpose of the statute of wills, which is to transfer an estate in accordance with the testator's intent.

Third, the Radins assert that allowing reformation in circumstances in which the estate would otherwise pass pursuant to the laws of intestacy constitutes an attack on the laws of intestacy. We disagree. The purpose of reformation is to carry out the wishes of the testator, and the remedy reflects no judgment other than a preference for disposition pursuant to the wishes of the testator. This preference is consistent with the statutory scheme. (See, §§ 6110 [a will that is not properly executed is enforceable if clear and convincing evidence establishes it was intended to constitute the testator's will], 21120 ["Preference is to be given to an interpretation of an instrument that will prevent intestacy or failure of a transfer, rather than one that will result in an intestacy or failure of a transfer"].)

Fourth, the Radins assert that allowing reformation will result in a significant increase in probate litigation and expenses. Claimants have long been entitled, however, to present extrinsic evidence to establish that a will is ambiguous despite the fact that it appears to be unambiguous. (*Estate of Russell, supra,* 69 Cal.2d at pp. 206–213, 70. 561, 444 P.2d 353.) Therefore, probate courts already receive extrinsic evidence of testator intent from claimants attempting to reform a will through the doctrine of ambiguity. (Cf. *Buss v. Superior Court* (1997) 16 Cal.4th 35, 57, 65 Cal.Rptr.2d 366, 939 P.2d 766 [in rejecting the contention that requiring only a preponderance of the evidence to establish an insurer's right to reimbursement will open the floodgates of litigation, the court noted that "the 'floodgates' have been open for quite some time"].) The task of deciding whether the evidence establishes by clear and convincing evidence that a mistake was made in the drafting of the will is a relatively small additional burden, because the court is already evaluating the evidence's probative value to determine the existence of an ambiguity.[14] To the extent additional claims are made that are based on a theory of mistake rather than a theory of ambiguity, the heightened evidentiary standard will help the probate court to filter out weak claims. Finally, fear of additional judicial burdens is not an adequate reason to deny relief that would serve the paramount purpose of distributing property in accordance with the testator's intent. (See *Buss,* at p. 58, 65 Cal.Rptr.2d 366, 939 P.2d 766 [acknowledging that the future might bring more claims for reimbursement, "[b]ut the possible invocation of this right—or any other—is not a sufficient basis for its abrogation or disapproval"]; *Ochoa v. Superior Court* (1985) 39 Cal.3d 159, 171, 216. 661,

Food for Thought

Cal. Prob. Code § 6110 enacts the "harmless error" rule in California. Had the legislature not taken this step, would the court be less inclined to transform the law of reformation?

---

14   These issues are decided by the court; there generally is no right to a jury trial in a will contest. (Probate Code, § 825; 14 Witkin, Summary of Cal. Law, *supra,* Wills and Probate, § 399, pp. 480–481.)

703 P.2d 1 [rejecting a proposed limit on the circumstances in which negligent infliction of emotional distress may be established, despite claim of " 'infinite liability' "].)

Fifth, the Radins discount justifications for allowing reformation in appropriate circumstances. They assert that Probate Code section 6110, subdivision (c)(2), which allows the probate of a will that was not executed in compliance with statutory attestation requirements if clear and convincing evidence establishes that the testator intended the writing to be a will, was not intended to lessen required formalities. Although section 6110 does not reduce the formalities of attestation, it reflects a judgment that the formalities should not be allowed to defeat the testator's intent when clear and convincing evidence satisfies the evidentiary concerns underlying the formalities of the statute of wills. The Radins also reject as a factor in support of a reformation remedy the avoidance of unjust enrichment. They state that no one has a right to inherit, and they recite various facts that they believe reflect that it is more just for Irving's relatives to inherit his estate than for the charities to receive it. If, however, a testator did not intend to devise property to a particular party, that party's receipt of the property as a result of a mistake constitutes unjust enrichment.

In sum, the Radins identify no countervailing considerations that would justify denying reformation if clear and convincing evidence establishes a mistake in the testator's expression of intent and the testator's actual and specific intent at the time the will was drafted.

C. Principles of stare decisis do not compel adherence to precedent in this context

The Radins assert that because the existing rule has withstood the test of time, any change should be left to the Legislature. " 'It is, of course, a fundamental jurisprudential policy that prior applicable precedent usually must be followed even though the case, if considered anew, might be decided differently by the current justices. This policy, known as the doctrine of stare decisis, "is based on the assumption that certainty, predictability and stability in the law are the major objectives of the legal system; i.e., that parties should be able to regulate their conduct and enter into relationships with reasonable assurance of the governing rules of law." [Citation.]' " (*Freeman & Mills, Inc. v. Belcher Oil Co.* (1995) 11 Cal.4th 85, 92–93, 44 Cal.Rptr.2d 420, 900 P.2d 669.) The rule is flexible, however, and it " ' "should not shield court-created error from correction." ' " (*Id.* at p. 93, 44 Cal.Rptr.2d 420, 900 P.2d 669.)

Although allowing reformation of an unambiguous will in appropriate instances will overturn many decades of precedent, we conclude that principles of stare decisis do not compel continued adherence to the rule at issue. The interest in ensuring certainty, predictability, and stability has been undermined by the inconsistent application of the principles applicable to the construction of wills. As noted above, in the course of applying the doctrine that an ambiguous will may be clarified through the admission of extrinsic evidence, courts have essentially reformed wills. (See, e.g., *Estate of Akeley, supra,* 35 Cal.2d at p. 30, 215 P.2d 921; *Estate of Kime, supra,* 144 Cal.App.3d 246, 264, 193. 718; *Estate of Fries, supra,* 221 Cal.App.2d 725, 727–730, 34. 749; *Estate of Glow, supra,* 208 Cal.App.2d 613, 616–617, 25. 416.) The results have been inconsistent, however, depending on whether a court perceives a gap in a will to reflect an ambiguity. (Compare *Estate of Karkeet, supra,* 56 Cal.2d 277, 281–283, 14. 664, 363 P.2d 896 [testatrix named an executrix but did not name any beneficiaries; it was unreasonable to think the decedent intended to make a will and also allow entire estate to escheat to the state; extrinsic evidence was admissible to resolve ambiguity] with *Estate of DeMoulin* (1950) 101 Cal.App.2d 221, 225, 225 P.2d 303 [will left money to children, described residuary, and appointed his spouse executrix, but did not name beneficiary of residuary; extrinsic evidence that scrivener mistakenly omitted provision leaving residuary to spouse was not admissible]; cf. *Estate of White* (1970) 9 Cal.App.3d 194, 201, 87. 881 ["scholarly analysis of the cases interpreting section 105 of the [former] Probate Code has resulted in the justifiable conclusion that it is impossible to determine when the testator's oral declarations would be deemed admissible in any given case"].)

Rather than introducing uncertainty into estate planning, allowing reformation of a will upon a clear and convincing showing of a mistake in expression and the testator's actual and specific intent helps ensure that the testator's affairs are settled as intended. And because the doctrine is relevant only in the context of litigation, and it affects the distribution of an estate only upon a determination by clear and convincing evidence of a mistake in the will and of the testator's actual intent at the time the will was drafted, adoption of the doctrine will not diminish the principles of law that encourage the preparation of well-drafted, properly executed wills. "Precisely because the reformation doctrine is a rule of litigation, no draftsman would plan to rely on it when proper drafting can spare the expense and hazard of litigation." (Langbein & Waggoner, *supra,* 130 U.Pa. L.Rev. at p. 587.)

In addition, the principles we are reconsidering are entirely court created, and the Legislature's inaction does not weigh against allowing reformation. As explained above, the Legislature has followed the courts' lead in adopting more flexible rules concerning the interpretation of wills, and has been attentive to codifying principles established by our cases without barring the continued evolution of the law. Furthermore, the technical requirements applicable to wills have become more flexible, the evidence admissible to interpret wills has been expanded, and existing doctrines concerning the resolution of ambiguities in wills have been stretched to allow the correction of mistakes.

> **Take Note**
>
> An example of the influence the increasing use of nonprobate property, specifically the revocable trust, has on the law of wills. These forms of transfer will be explored in Chapter 10.

Finally, allowing reformation in these circumstances is consistent with the Legislature's efforts to apply the same rules of construction to all donative documents (see, § 21101 et seq.), and will promote fairness in the treatment of estates, regardless of the tools used for estate planning. According to the legislative history of Probate Code section 21101, the State Bar's estate planning, trust, and probate law section sought uniformity of treatment of various instruments because trusts were increasingly being used in lieu of wills. (Assem. Com. on Judiciary, Analysis of Assem. Bill No. 3686 (1993–1994 Reg. Sess.) Apr. 20, 1994, pp. 2–3.) Moreover, allowing reformation of trusts and other instruments, but never of wills, appears to favor those with the means to establish estate plans that avoid probate proceedings, and to deny a remedy with respect to the estates of individuals who effect their plans through traditional testamentary documents. Denying reformation in these circumstances seems particularly harsh with respect to individuals who write wills without the assistance of counsel, and are more likely to overlook flaws in the expression of their intent.

As the Radins note, to date only a few states allow reformation of wills. However, both the Restatement Third of Property and the Uniform Probate Code now support the remedy.[15] The Restatement's reformation provision appeared in the tentative draft of March 1995, and in the final draft issued in 2003. The Uniform Probate Code's provision authorizing the reformation of wills was added in 2008, and five states have adopted that provision.[16] In addition, Washington, which has not adopted the Uniform Probate Code, has provided by statute that an unambiguous will "may be reformed . . . to conform the terms to the intention of the testator" upon clear and convincing evidence of a mistake. (Wash. Rev.Code § 11.96A.125 (2011).) In Connecticut, extrinsic evidence is admissible to prove a scrivener's error in a will, and a correction will be made upon a clear and convincing showing of error. (*Erickson v. Erickson* (1998) 246 Conn. 359, 716 A.2d 92, 98–100.) Courts in New York and New Jersey have also applied a more liberal approach to correcting flaws in wills. (*In re Herceg* (2002) 193 Misc.2d 201, 747 N.Y.S.2d 901, 905 ["it seems logical to this court to choose the path of considering all available evidence as recommended by the *Restatement* in order to achieve the dominant purpose of carrying out the intention of the testator"]; *Engle v. Siegel* (1977) 74 N.J. 287, 377 A.2d 892, 894 [the "doctrine of probable intent" allows consideration of "'competent extrinsic evidence and common human impulses . . . to ascertain and carry out what the testator probably intended should be the disposition if the present situation developed'"].)[17]

For the reasons discussed above, we are persuaded that authorizing the reformation of wills under the circumstances and with the protections discussed above serves the paramount purpose of the law governing wills without compromising the policies underlying the statutory scheme and the common law rules. If a mistake in expression and the testator's actual and specific intent at the time the will was drafted are established by clear and convincing evidence, no

---

15　　Section 12.1 of the Restatement Third of Property states in full: "A donative document, though unambiguous, may be reformed to conform the text to the donor's intention if it is established by clear and convincing evidence (1) that a mistake of fact or law, whether in expression or inducement, affected specific terms of the document; and (2) what the donor's intention was. In determining whether these elements have been established by clear and convincing evidence, direct evidence of intention contradicting the plain meaning of the text as well as other evidence of intention may be considered." (Rest.3d Property, § 12.1, p. 353.)

Section 2–805 of the Uniform Probate Code states in full: "The court may reform the terms of a governing instrument, even if unambiguous, to conform the terms to the transferor's intention if it is proved by clear and convincing evidence what the transferor's intention was and that the terms of the governing instrument were affected by a mistake of fact or law, whether in expression or inducement." (8 pt.1 West's U. Laws Ann.(2013) U. (2008) § 2–805, p. 335.)

16　　Colorado (Colo.Rev.Stat. § 15–11–806); Florida (Fla.Stat. § 732.615); New Mexico (N.M.Stat.Ann. § 45–2–805); North Dakota (N.D. Cent.Code § 30.1–10–05); and Utah (Utah Code Ann. § 75–2–805).

17　　We have no occasion to consider the extent to which the reformation remedies authorized in other jurisdictions or proposed by the Restatement Third of Property and the Uniform Probate Code are similar to the reformation remedy that we authorize in this case.

policy underlying the statute of wills supports a rule that would ignore the testator's intent and unjustly enrich those who would inherit as a result of a mistake. (Cf. *Rowland v. Christian* (1968) 69 Cal.2d 108, 118–119, 70. 97, 443 P.2d 561 [in rejecting common law classifications based on the plaintiff's status as a trespasser, licensee, or invitee with regard to the liability of a possessor of land, the court looked to the "basic policy" that everyone is responsible for injuries caused by his or her negligence in managing property].)

D. The charities have articulated a valid theory that will support reformation if established by clear and convincing evidence

COH and JNF contend that Irving actually intended at the time he wrote his will to provide that his estate would pass to COH and JNF in the event Beatrice was not alive to inherit his estate when he died, but that his intent was inartfully expressed in his will and thus there is a mistake in the will that should be reformed to reflect his intent when the will was drafted. Their contention, if proved by clear and convincing evidence, would support reformation of the will to reflect Irving's actual intent.

First, the alleged mistake concerns Irving's actual intent at the time he wrote the will. As explained above, reformation of a document that is subject to the statute of frauds or the statute of wills entails the enforcement of the written document in a manner that reflects what was intended when the document was prepared. If Irving's only intent

> **Food for Thought**
>
> How certain can we be about what the testator intended at the time the will was written?

at the time he wrote his will was to address the disposition of his estate in the circumstances in which he died before Beatrice or they died simultaneously, his will accurately reflects his intent. In that circumstance, his mistake, if any, would be in failing subsequently to modify the will after Beatrice died, and that mistake would not be related to the will he wrote and that COH and JNF seek to have reformed. (See generally 1 Witkin, Summary of Cal. Law, *supra,* Contracts, § 278, p. 308.)

Second, the alleged mistake and intent are sufficiently specific. The allegations are precise with respect to the error and the remedy: the charities assert Irving specifically intended when he wrote his will to provide that his estate would pass to COH and JNF not only upon the simultaneous death of Irving and Beatrice, as the will expressly states, but also in the event Beatrice was not alive to inherit the estate at the time of his death. Although COH and JNF do not allege that the error was merely clerical, but instead assert that Irving's intent was inartfully expressed, their theory alleges "a mistake in the rendering of terms that the testator has authored or approved. The remedy in such a case has exactly the dimensions of the mistake. The term that the testator intended is restored." (Langbein & Waggoner, *supra,* 130 U.Pa. L.Rev. at pp. 583–584.)

The charities' theory, which sets forth a specific disposition of assets Irving allegedly intended when he wrote his will, distinguishes this case from circumstances in which it is alleged that the testator had a more general intent regarding the disposition of the estate which was not accomplished by the will as written. An example of an error involving general intent would be a case in which a testator intended in his or her will to provide adequate resources to one of the will's beneficiaries to support that beneficiary for a lifetime, but the specific gift set forth in the will proves to be inadequate for that purpose. Thus, that will accurately sets forth the testator's specific intent with respect to the distribution of assets, but due to a mistake with respect to the value of those assets or the needs of the beneficiary, the will fails to effect the testator's intent to provide adequate assets to support the beneficiary. In contrast to cases in which the alleged error is in the rendering of the specific terms intended by the testator, cases in which the alleged error is in failing to accomplish a general intent of the testator would require a court to determine the testator's putative intent: if the testator had known of the mistake, how would the testator have changed the will? The case before us presents only the issue of whether a will may be reformed when extrinsic evidence establishes that the will fails to set forth the actual specific intent of the testator at the time the will was executed, and we express no opinion on the availability of reformation in cases involving claims of general and putative intent.

Take Note

This distinction between particular intent and general intent is critical to the court's analysis and holding.

Finally, for the reasons discussed above, evidence of the testator's intent must be clear and convincing. Among the evidence to be considered is the will itself, but when reformation rather than construction of a will is at issue, the rules of construction, which set forth principles for determining disposition of estate assets where the testator's intention is not reflected in the will (, § 21102), do not apply where extrinsic evidence supplies the missing terms. (Langbein and Waggoner, *supra,* 130 U.Pa. L.Rev. at pp. 579–580.) Other doctrines of interpretation are also supplanted by the remedy of reformation. For example, although the terms of a will may be inadequate alone to establish a dominant dispositive plan that would warrant a gift by implication (see *Estate of Barnes, supra,* 63 Cal.2d at p. 584, 47. 480, 407 P.2d 656; *Brock v. Hall* (1949) 33 Cal.2d 885, 890–892, 206 P.2d 360), those aspects of the will that tend to reflect an intent to make a particular gift should be considered together with the extrinsic evidence of intent to determine whether there is clear and convincing evidence of an intent to make a gift. Similarly, although a disinheritance clause cannot prevent heirs from inheriting pursuant to the statutory rules of intestacy (*Estate of Barnes, supra,* at pp. 582–583, 47. 480, 407 P.2d 656), any intent reflected in such a clause may be relevant when reformation is sought

III. CONCLUSION

We hold that an unambiguous will may be reformed to conform to the testator's intent if clear and convincing evidence establishes that the will contains a mistake in the testator's expression of intent at the time the will was drafted, and also establishes the testator's actual specific intent at the time the will was drafted. We reverse the judgment of the Court of Appeal and remand the matter to the Court of Appeal with directions to remand the case to the trial court for its consideration of extrinsic evidence as authorized by our opinion.

We concur: WERDEGAR, CHIN, CORRIGAN, LIU, CUÉLLAR, and KRUGER, JJ.

Points for Discussion

1. The need for "specific intent"

The court limits its holding regarding the nature of the testator's intent (which must be shown by the clear and convincing extrinsic evidence) by requiring the alleged mistake and intent to be "sufficiently specific." To obtain a more complete understanding of the court's approach consider the important New Jersey case, *Engle v. Siegel*, 74 N.J. 287, 377A.2d 892 (1977) which precedes the principal case: A married couple executed reciprocal wills which left each other's probate estate to the survivor and on the death of the survivor to their children; if neither spouse nor children survived or the testator, spouse and children died in a common disaster, which is what happened, each will directed that each spouse's probate assets would pass one half of the estate to the testator's mother and the other half to the testator's mother-in-law. Only one spouse's mother was living at the time of the death of the testators and their children. Under New Jersey law, both estates passed to the surviving mother of one testator (the mother-in-law of the other). The siblings of the spouse whose mother did not survive sought distribution of one-half of each estate to them. Assume that the testators intended that their respective siblings take one-half of each estate should their mothers not survive, does the holding and rationale of *Duke* support reformation of the wills to accomplish that result? Is there is clear and convincing evidence of such intent?

If *Mahoney v. Granger* (page 182) were litigated today in California, would it be decided differently? How about *Matter of Scale* (page 186)? Or the following situation:

Decedent's will directs her executor to divide her residuary estate "into twenty-five (25) separate equal shares, so that there shall be one (1) such share for each of my nieces and nephews who shall survive me, and one (1) such share for each of my nieces and nephews who shall not survive me but who shall have left a child or children surviving me." At her death decedent was survived by twenty-two blood nieces and nephews (children of her brothers and sisters) and three nieces and nephews by marriage, being the nieces and nephews of her predeceased husband. Is there an ambiguity? If so, is it latent or patent? Regardless, should the court admit the attorney's affidavit that states that the testatrix indicated that she had 25 nieces and nephews? *See In re McHugh*, 810 N.Y.S.2d 635 (Sur. Ct. 2006), where the Surrogate did indeed admit extrinsic evidence, and found that it showed that testator meant to benefit both the children of her siblings and the children of her spouse's siblings.

2. *The need for clear and convincing evidence*

Before its decision in *Duke*, one of the cases the California court cites, *Erickson v. Erickson*, 716 A.2d 92 (Conn. 1998), was generally regarded as the leading case that took a more liberal approach to the reformation of wills. Ronald Erickson executed his will two days before his marriage to Dorothy Mehring. The will gave his residuary estate to Dorothy Mehring if she survived him, which indeed she did. At Mr. Erickson's death, however, a Connecticut statute in force (§ 45a–257 (a), since repealed) provided that a person's marriage revoked that person's existing will unless the will made a provision for the contingency of marriage (the courts had long held that the provision for the marriage must appear in the language of the will without any resort to extrinsic evidence unless the language is ambiguous). Mr. Erickson's will did not, and provision in the will was not ambiguous. The Connecticut Supreme Court held that the statute revoked the will, but remanded the case for trial on the issue of whether clear and convincing evidence showed "there was a scrivener's error that induced the decedent to execute a will that he intended to be valid despite his subsequent marriage."

The court's analysis foreshadowed much of the reasoning in *Estate of Duke*, including the analogies to contract law, the widespread use of extrinsic evidence in other contexts, and a rejection of the argument that the courts would be swamped with litigation. On remand, however, the did not relent. As one commentator described the result:

> "The court found that no such [clear and convincing] evidence existed because both the drafter and the surviving spouse, who testified to this effect, were not credible. The drafter's testimony was discredited because it varied slightly in the course of the proceedings; the surviving spouse's testimony was discredited based on, among other things, evidence that she had failed to check the box on the probate petition indicating that the decedent had married after executing the proffered will."

────────────

Test Your Knowledge

To assess your understanding of the material in this chapter, click here to take a quiz.

CHAPTER 5

Wills: Doctrines Dealing with Beneficiaries

209-59

A. Void and Lapsed Gifts

A page of history...

Probate courts traditionally regarded bequests in a will to a person who is dead at the time the will is executed as void. The logic may be unexceptional. Why would a will-maker confer property on a person who she knew was dead? Why not leave the property to the deceased legatee's heirs, or to the legatees under the deceased's will? Or even another living person who can actually use the property. But one would not be similarly perplexed if a will left property to a person alive at the time the will was executed, but who ultimately predeceased the will-maker. While the will-maker may be expected to know demographics at the time the will is executed, she cannot be expected to predict the future, in particular who might or might not survive her.

Consider the choices that the law could make when a beneficiary predeceases the testator:

Option 1: the bequest fails and passes to the will-maker's residuary or if a residuary bequest it passes to the will-maker's intestate heirs;

Option 2: the bequest passes as if the beneficiary survived then died, thereby passing through beneficiary's estate;

Option 3: the bequest passes to the descendants or issue of the deceased beneficiary;

Option 4: the bequest passes to takers through the pattern of intestate succession mandated by state law.

English and American law initially selected the first option. Where a person named as a beneficiary in a will was alive at the time the will is executed, but died before the testator, the gift was said to *lapse*: it failed, and passed to the will-maker's residuary or if a residuary gift it passed to the will-maker's intestate heirs. However, if there was a substitutionary gift (if A predeceases me to B) in the limitation to the now-deceased beneficiary, it took effect.

A more detailed illustration may be helpful. Refer back to the will of Terry A. Testator (page 179, above). The will (Article IV) contains a general bequest of $10,000 to Mary Ellen Howard, "if she shall survive me and if she does not this gift shall be added to the gift under Article VI [the residuary]"

Go Online

Though perhaps an overstatement, anti-lapse statutes resemble snowflakes, similar but no two seem to be identical. It's worth finding your state's statute.

Regardless of the language conditioning the gift on survival, if Mary Ellen dies before Terry, the $10,000 gift lapses and becomes part of the residuary; that would be the result even without the language directing the gift to the residue if she does not survive the testator. The same rule applies to the specific bequest of the tangible personal property to Terry's nieces and nephews (Article III); if none of them survive Terry, the tangible personal property will pass to the residue. The result is the same if Mary Ellen or all of the nieces and nephews were dead when the will was executed.

Suppose, however, the bequest reads as it does in the aforementioned will. The condition of survival not having been satisfied, the bequest would pass to the alternative beneficiaries.

The lapse principle developed by the courts was probably supported by what judges may have regarded as the probable intent of the will-maker. The gift was considered personal to the beneficiary: if there was no living beneficiary, there was no gift. But modern law has a different vision. Legislatures have passed anti-lapse statutes to trump the lapse principle in some circumstances. What option has the following statute selected?

UPC § 2–603(b). Antilapse; deceased devisee; class gifts

If a devisee fails to survive the testator and is a grandparent, a descendant of a grandparent, or a stepchild of either the testator or the donor of a power of appointment exercised by the testator's will, the following apply:

(1)   Except as provided in paragraph (4), if the devise is not in the form of a class gift and the deceased devisee leaves surviving descendants, a substitute gift is created in the devisee's surviving descendants. They take by representation the property to which the devisee would have been entitled had the devisee survived the testator. . . .

(3)   . . . words of survivorship, such as in a devise to an individual "if he survives me", or in a devise to "my surviving children", are not, in the absence of additional evidence, a sufficient indication of an intent contrary to the application of this section.

Can you break this statute into separate requirements?

Consider the application of a similar anti-lapse statute in the following case:

Ruotolo v. Tietjen

890 A.2d 166 (Conn. 2006)

LAVERY, C.J.

This appeal presents a question of statutory interpretation of General Statutes § 45a–441, our testamentary antilapse statute. The appellant, Kathleen Smaldone, appeals from the judgment of the Superior Court on appeal from the Probate Court, which found the statute inoperative in the present case. We disagree and, accordingly, reverse the judgment of the Superior Court.

> **Take Note**
>
> Connecticut has a very broad or inclusive anti-lapse statute; would the UPC anti-lapse statute above apply to the gift? The anti-lapse statute of your state?

The facts are undisputed. On March 1, 1990, John N. Swanson executed a will. The residuary clause contained therein bequeathed, inter alia, "one-half . . . of [the residue] property to Hazel Brennan of Guilford, Connecticut, if she survives me. . . ." Brennan died on January 2, 2001, seventeen days prior to the testator's death. Brennan was the testator's stepdaughter, a relation encompassed by § 45a–441. The appellant is the child of the deceased legatee, Brennan, and is a residuary legatee in the will, and, thus, was an object of affection of the testator.

On February 9, 2001, the will was admitted to probate. In a memorandum of decision dated April 26, 2002, the Probate Court concluded that, as § 45a–441 "is not operative," the bequest to Brennan lapsed and passed to the intestate estate. The plaintiffs, Fred Ruotolo and Charlene Ruotolo, beneficiaries under the will, filed a motion for appeal to the Superior Court. The Probate Court issued a decree allowing the appeal. The appellant thereafter filed a cross appeal. Following a de novo hearing, the court issued a memorandum of decision affirming the judgment of the Probate Court, and this appeal followed.

The sole issue on appeal is whether the court properly concluded that the antilapse statute does not apply. Section 45a–441 has never been scrutinized by appellate eyes and, thus, presents a question of first impression. Accordingly, our review is plenary. See *Genesky v. East Lyme*, 275 Conn. 246, 252, 881 A.2d 114 (2005).

Pursuant to General Statutes § 1–2z,[3] we consider first the text of § 45a–441 to determine whether it is ambiguous. The statute provides: "When a devisee or legatee, being a child, stepchild, grandchild, brother or sister of the testator, dies before him, and no provision has been made in the will for such contingency, the issue of such devisee or legatee shall take the

---

3   General Statutes § 1–2z provides: "The meaning of a statute shall, in the first instance, be ascertained from the text of the statute itself and its relationship to other statutes. If, after examining such text and considering such relationship, the meaning of such text is plain and unambiguous and does not yield absurd or unworkable results, extratextual evidence of the meaning of the statute shall not be considered."

estate so devised or bequeathed." General Statutes § 45a–441. The bequest in the present case specified "one-half . . . of [the residue] property to Hazel Brennan of Guilford, Connecticut, if she survives me . . . ." Because the bequest contained the condition, "if she survives me," both the Probate Court and the Superior Court concluded that a provision had been made in the will for such contingency. The appellant disagrees, arguing that because the will contained no provision as to the fate of Brennan's share in the event that she predeceased the testator, a provision had not been made in the will for such contingency. Both readings present plausible interpretations of the salient statutory language. In light of that ambiguity, we turn our attention to extratextual evidence to determine its proper meaning. See General Statutes § 1–2z.

"According to our long-standing principles of statutory construction, our fundamental objective is to ascertain and give effect to the intent of the legislature. . . . In determining the intent of a statute, we look to the words of the statute itself, to the legislative history and circumstances surrounding its enactment, to the legislative policy it was designed to implement, and to its relationship to existing legislation and common law principles governing the same general subject matter. . . . In construing a statute, common sense must be used, and courts will assume that the legislature intended to accomplish a reasonable and rational result." (Citation omitted; internal quotation marks omitted.) *Regency Savings Bank v. Westmark Partners*, 70 Conn.App. 341, 345, 798 A.2d 476 (2002). "A legislative act must be read as a whole and construed to give effect to and to harmonize all of its parts." (Internal quotation marks omitted.) *Hayes v. Smith*, 194 Conn. 52, 58, 480 A.2d 425 (1984). In addition, "[w]here the meaning of a statute is in doubt, reference to legislation in other states and jurisdictions which pertains to the same subject matter, persons, things, or relations may be a helpful source of interpretative guidance." (Internal quotation marks omitted.) *Johnson v. Manson*, 196 Conn. 309, 318–19, 493 A.2d 846 (1985), cert. denied, 474 U.S. 1063, 106 S.Ct. 813, 88 L.Ed.2d 787 (1986).

I

HISTORY

At common law, when a named beneficiary under a will predeceased the testator, the share of the deceased beneficiary passed not to his descendants, but rather "lapsed." See 4 W. Bowe & D. Parker, Page on the Law of Wills (Rev. Ed. 2005) § 35.15, p. 645; see also *Clifford v. Cronin*, 97 Conn. 434, 438, 117 A. 489 (1922). Thus, the rule of lapse automatically conditions all devises on the survival of the legatee. "At common law, all legacies, not affected by substitutionary disposition, became intestate estate whenever the legatee died before the testator." *Ackerman v. Hughes*, 11 Conn.Supp. 133, 135 (1942).

As Judge O'Sullivan explained in *Ackerman*, "[s]ome pretty oppressive results were occasioned by these principles which frequently blocked the way for carrying out the testator's expressed intention. These injustices were most significant in those instances where the will provided legacies for close relatives." Id. To prevent such a harsh and presumably unintended result, legislatures of the United States in the late eighteenth century began crafting statutes designed to protect certain devises from lapsing.

In 1783, the Massachusetts legislature enacted the first antilapse statute. It provided: "When a devise of real or personal estate is made to any child or other relation of the testator, and the devisee shall die before the testator, leaving issue who survive the testator, such issue shall take the estate so devised, in the same manner as the devisee would have done, if he had survived the testator; unless a different disposition thereof shall be made or required by the will." 1783 Mass. Acts, ch. 24, § 8, quoted in S. French, "Antilapse Statutes Are Blunt Instruments: A Blueprint for Reform," 37 Hastings L.J. 335, 339 n. 16 (1985). "In 1810, Maryland went even further and adopted a statute that prevented lapse altogether. . . . These two statutes provided the basic models on which all subsequent antilapse statutes have been constructed." S. French, 37 Hastings L.J., supra, 339. In England, the Wills Act of 1837 took antilapse statutes across the Atlantic Ocean, providing that "when there was a devise or bequest to a child or other issue of the testator, and the child or issue predeceased the testator, leaving issue who survived the testator, the devise or bequest should not lapse, 'but shall take effect as if the death of such person had happened immediately after the death of the testator, unless a contrary intention shall appear by the will.' "6 W. Bowe & D. Parker, supra, § 50.10, p. 91. Today, antilapse statutes have been enacted in every state except Louisiana. "[T]he antilapse statutes in effect across the United States vary significantly [and] so much . . . that no typical or 'majority' antilapse statute exists." E. Kimbrough, "Lapsing of Testamentary Gifts, Antilapse Statutes, and the Expansion of Uniform Probate Code Antilapse Protection," 36 Wm. & Mary L.Rev. 269, 271 (1994).

Although varying in scope, all antilapse statutes provide that when a particular devisee predeceases the testator, the devise does not fall into the residue or pass to the testator's heirs by intestacy, but rather descends to the issue of the predeceased devisee. "Although . . . commonly called 'antilapse' statutes, the label is somewhat misleading. Contrary to what the label implies, antilapse statutes do not reverse the common-law rule of lapse because they do not abrogate the law-imposed condition of survivorship. . . . What the statutes actually do is modify the devolution of lapsed devises by providing a statutory substitute gift in the case of specified relatives." E. Halbach, Jr. & L. Waggoner, "The UPC's New Survivorship and Antilapse Provisions," 55 Alb. L.Rev. 1091, 1101 (1992). With that background in mind, we turn our attention to § 45a–441.

> **Food for Thought**
>
> What do you think is the importance of this historical tidbit? Does it help you understand the policy behind anti-lapse statutes? Does it help you understand their application?

II
OUR ANTILAPSE STATUTE

Connecticut's antilapse statute was enacted in 1821 as part of "An Act for the settlement of Estates, testate, intestate, and insolvent." It provided: "Whenever a devisee or legatee in any last will and testament, being a child or grand-child of the testator, shall die before the testator, and no provision shall be made for such contingency, the issue, if any there be, of such devisee or legatee, shall take the estate devised or bequeathed, as the devisee or legatee would have done, had he or she survived the testator; and if there be no such issue, at the time of the testator's death, the estate disposed of by such devise or legacy, shall be considered and treated as intestate estate." General Statutes (1821 Rev.) tit. 32, ch. 1, § 4. The antilapse statute today provides that "[w]hen a devisee or legatee, being a child, stepchild, grandchild, brother or sister of the testator, dies before him, and no provision has been made in the will for such contingency, the issue of such devisee or legatee shall take the estate so devised or bequeathed." General Statutes § 45a–441. Other than adding siblings and stepchildren to the class of applicable devisees and legatees; see Public Acts 1987, No. 87–355, § 2; no substantive change has been made to our antilapse statute since 1821. Moreover, the pertinent language at issue in the present dispute, namely, "*and no provision shall be made for such contingency*," was part of the original 1821 statute and remains unaltered today.

> **Take Note**
>
> The UPC anti-lapse statute would apply to those gifts within its ambit unless there is a substitutionary gift.

Plainly, the purpose underlying our antilapse statute is the prevention of unintended disinheritance. Its passage reflects a legislative determination that, as a matter of public policy, when a testator fails to provide for the possibility that a particular beneficiary might predecease him, the lineal descendants of that beneficiary take the applicable share.

In the years since its enactment, Connecticut courts have stated that the antilapse statute is remedial and should receive a liberal construction. See, e.g., *Clifford v. Cronin*, supra, 97 Conn. at 438, 117 A. 489; *Ackerman v. Hughes*, supra, 11 Conn. Sup. at 135–36. When a dispute arises regarding application of that statute, therefore, the burden rests on the party seeking to deny the statutory protection.

Under Connecticut law, the antilapse statute applies unless a "provision has been made in the will for such contingency . . . ." General Statutes § 45a–441. A review of the antilapse statutes presently in effect in forty-eight other jurisdictions reveals that this language is unique to our statute. It is not disputed that the "contingency" referenced in § 45a–441 is the death of a devisee or legatee prior to that of the testator. What is contested is the proper construction of the "provision has been made in the will" language.

The appellees contend that inclusion of words of survivorship in a will constitutes a provision for such contingency, thereby rendering the antilapse statute inapplicable. Because the bequest in the present case contains the condition "if she survives me," they claim § 45a–441 is inoperative. That simple and seemingly persuasive argument fails, however, on closer examination.

First, it is significant that the language at issue dates back to 1821, the inception of our antilapse statute. The first antilapse statute, enacted in Massachusetts in 1783, provided that it would apply "unless a different disposition thereof shall be made or required by the will." 1783 Mass. Acts, ch. 24, § 8, quoted in S. French, supra, 37 Hastings L.J. 339 n. 16. The Maryland statute enacted in 1810 contained no such condition.[5] Like every other antilapse statute that followed, ours was modeled on those statutes. Today, a majority of jurisdictions contain some variation of the "unless a different disposition thereof" condition.[1]

* * *

Our inquiry into whether words of survivorship evince a contrary intent sufficient to defeat the antilapse statute is guided by the following principles. Antilapse statutes "will apply unless testator's intention to exclude its operation is shown with reasonable certainty." 6 W. Bowe & D. Parker, supra, § 50.11, p. 96. Section 5.5 of the Restatement (Third) of Property, Wills and Other Donative Transfers (1999), addresses antilapse statutes. Comment (f) to that section provides in relevant part: "Antilapse statutes establish a strong rule of construction, designed to carry out presumed intention. They are based on the constructional preference against disinheriting a line of descent . . . . Consequently, these statutes should be given the widest possible sphere of operation and should be defeated only when the trier of fact determines that the testator wanted to disinherit the line of descent headed by the deceased devisee." 1 Restatement (Third), Property, Wills and Other Donative Transfers § 5.5, comment (f), p. 383 (1999). Hence, the burden is on those who seek to deny the statutory protection rather than on those who assert it.

Finally, we are mindful that our statute was enacted to *prevent* operation of the rule of lapse. Our statute is remedial in nature and must be liberally construed. *Clifford v. Cronin*, supra, 97 Conn. at 438, 117 A. 489; *Ackerman v. Hughes*, supra, 11 Conn. Supp. at 135–36. Accordingly, we resolve any doubt in favor of the operation of § 45a–441.

> **Food for Thought**
>
> Why not read their literal English meaning—the gift passes if the beneficiary is alive at the death of the testator.

The bequest at issue states, "one-half . . . of [the residue] property to Hazel Brennan of Guilford, Connecticut, *if she survives me* . . . ." (Emphasis added.) Our task is to determine the significance of those words of survivorship. While the present case is one of first impression in Connecticut, numerous other states have considered the question of whether words of survivorship, such as "if she survives me," demonstrate a contrary intent on the part of the testator sufficient to negate operation of the antilapse statute.

---

5   The Maryland statute provided: "That from and after the passage of this act, no devise, legacy or bequest, shall lapse or fail of taking effect by reason of the death of any devisee or legatee named in any last will or testament, or any codicil thereto, in the life-time of the testator, but every such devise, legacy or bequest, shall have the same effect and operation in law to transfer the right, estate and interest, in the property mentioned in such devise or bequest as if such devisee or legatee had survived the testator." 1810 Md. Laws, ch. 34, § 4, quoted in E. Kimbrough, supra, 36 Wm. & Mary L.Rev. 274 n. 35.

1   A detailed discussion of anti-lapse statutes in other jurisdictions is omitted. —Eds.

III
OTHER AUTHORITY

Whether words of survivorship alone constitute sufficient evidence of a contrary intent on the part of the testator so as to prevent application of the antilapse statute is a question on which sibling authority is split. Some courts have concluded that words of survivorship demonstrate sufficient contrary intent. Illustrative of that line of cases is *Bankers Trust Co. v. Allen*, 257 Iowa 938, 135 N.W.2d 607 (1965). In that case, the Supreme Court of Iowa stated: "The bequest to Mary in Item III is conditioned on her surviving the testator. We have held many times . . . that our antilapse statute . . . does not apply to a bequest so conditioned. . . . This is on the theory that a bequest to one 'if she survives me' manifests an intent that the bequest would lapse if the named beneficiary dies before the testator." (Citations omitted.) Id., at 945, 135 N.W.2d 607.

Underlying that view is the presumption that the testator knowingly and deliberately included the words of survivorship. As one New York court explained: "[T]hese words were used by the testator in a will drawn by an experienced attorney. Some meaning must be attributed to them—and the meaning is clear—that survivorship was a condition precedent to the receipt of the residuary estate. If words were held to be devoid of meaning, then this court would be rewriting the testator's will." *In re Robinson's Will*, supra, at 548, 236 N.Y.S.2d 293. That presumption has pitfalls of its own, however.

Inclusion of words of survivorship provides neither objective evidence that a conversation about § 45a–441 took place nor objective evidence that the testator considered seriously the possibility

Practice Pointer

Are you persuaded by the logic outlined above? Why include those words if survivorship were not required? How would you have drafted the provision to exclude the operation of the statute? Shall we now question all boilerplate provisions in wills?

of nonsurvival or inquired about the meaning of expressions such as "lapsed bequest" and the protections of the antilapse statute. "Because such a survival provision is often boiler-plate form-book language, the testator may not understand that such language could disinherit the line of descent headed by the deceased devisee. When the testator is older than the devisee and hence does not expect the devisee to die first . . . it seems especially unlikely that a provision requiring the devisee to survive the testator was intended to disinherit the devisee's descendants." 1 Restatement (Third), supra, § 5.5, comment (h), p. 385.

At oral argument, counsel for the appellees alleged that inclusion of the words "if she survives me" indicates that the testator intended for the bequest to Brennan to lapse. While plausible, it remains conjecture nonetheless. As one commentary aptly stated: "The argument can reasonably be extended to urge that the use of words of survivorship indicates that the testator considered the possibility of the devisee dying first and intentionally decided not to provide a substitute gift to the devisee's descendants. The negative inference in this argument, however, is speculative. It may or may not accurately reflect reality and actual intention. It is equally plausible that the words of survivorship are in the testator's will merely because, with no such intention, the testator's lawyer used a will form containing words of survivorship. The testator who went to lawyer X and ended up with a will containing devises with a survivorship requirement could by chance have gone to lawyer Y and ended up with a will containing devises with no survivorship requirement—with no different intention on the testator's part from one case to the other." E. Halbach, Jr. & L. Waggoner, supra, 55 Alb. L.Rev. 1112–13. Furthermore, words of survivorship "might very well be no more than a casual duplication of the survivorship requirement imposed by the rule of lapse, with no independent purpose. Thus, they are not necessarily included in the will with the intention of contradicting the objectives of the antilapse statute." Id., 1109–10. As this court recently observed, "[s]peculation and conjecture have no place in appellate review." *Narumanchi v. DeStefano*, 89 Conn.App. 807, 815, 875 A.2d 71 (2005). Put simply, the intent of the testator cannot definitely be discerned on the basis of words of survivorship alone.

If he intended the bequest to lapse, the testator could have explicitly so provided. The testator also could have made an alternative devise, which "indicates a contrary intent, and hence overrides an antilapse statute . . . ." 1 Restatement (Third), supra, § 5.5, comment (g), p. 384; see also E. Halbach, Jr. & L. Waggoner, supra, 55 Alb.L.Rev. 1110 (when actually intended to call for result contrary to antilapse statute, words of survivorship likely to be accompanied by additional language). That the testator did neither in the present case informs our consideration of whether he intended disinheritance.

The argument is further weakened by the fact that, under the interpretation of § 45a–441 provided by the Probate Court and the Superior Court, the result is not merely that Brennan's share lapses; her share passes to the intestate estate. Thus, at its crux, the contention of the appellees asks us to presume that, although not explicitly provided for, the testator *intended* intestacy as to Brennan's share. That argument confounds Connecticut law, which presumes that a testator designed by his will to dispose of his entire estate and to avoid intestacy as to any part of it. In addition, the bequest to Brennan was residuary in nature. "Residuary language expresses an intention to . . . avoid intestacy." *Hechtman v. Savitsky*, 62 Conn.App. 654, 663, 772 A.2d 673 (2001). Indulging in the presumption that the testator intended to avoid intestacy militates against a finding that he intended for Brennan's share to lapse.

> **Food for Thought**
>
> To what extent are these ruminations about the testator's intent relevant? Surely an alternative devise would have clarified, but is there evidence one way or the other on the issue of what should happen to the bequest if the beneficiary predeceased the testator other than the words 'if she survives me?'

Another presumption bears consideration. In *Clifford v. Cronin*, supra, 97 Conn. at 438, 117 A. 489, our Supreme Court, quoting 2 J. Alexander, Commentaries on Wills, § 874, stated that "the testator is presumed to know the law and that his will is drawn accordingly." As one court has noted, however, "[w]ith respect to any individual, the argument of knowledge and approval of the state law is sheer fiction." *Trimble v. Gordon*, 430 U.S. 762, 775 n. 16, 97 S.Ct. 1459, 52

L.Ed.2d 31 (1977). Discounting that observation, the presumption is revealing nevertheless. If we must presume that the testator was aware of our antilapse statute, we must also equally presume that he was aware that it is remedial in nature and provided a liberal construction in Connecticut. In that event, the testator would have known that any ambiguity arising from the probate of his will, absent an express indication to the contrary, would be resolved in favor of operation of the statute.

Alternatively, another line of cases from various jurisdictions concludes that words of survivorship alone are insufficient to defeat an antilapse statute. As the Supreme Court of Appeals of West Virginia stated, "In order to prevent application of the [antilapse] statute . . . a testator must clearly and unequivocally indicate his intent that the statute not apply." *Kubiczky v. Wesbanco Bank Wheeling*, 208 W.Va. 456, 460, 541 S.E.2d 334 (2000) . . . (Further citations omitted)

A similar case is *Detzel v. Nieberding*, 7 Ohio Misc. 262, 219 N.E.2d 327 (Prob.Ct.1966). In *Detzel*, the will provided in relevant part, "To my beloved sister, Mary Detzel, provided she be living at the time of my death . . . ." (Internal quotation marks omitted.) Id., at 263, 219 N.E.2d 327. Mary Detzel predeceased the testator. Id. In considering the operation of Ohio's antilapse statute, the court noted that "[a]ntilapse statutes are remedial and should receive a liberal construction"; id., at 267, 219 N.E.2d 327; echoing a precept shared by Connecticut law. Accordingly, "[a]ll doubts are to be resolved in favor of the operation of the antilapse statute . . . . [T]o render [the] statute inoperative contrary intent of testator must be plainly indicated." (Citations omitted.) Id., at 266–67, 219 N.E.2d 327. The court continued: "To prevent operation of the Ohio antilapse statute when a devise is made to a relative conditioned upon the survival of the testator by the relative, and the relative predeceases the testator leaving issue who survive the testator, it is necessary that the testator, in apt language, make an alternative provision in his will providing that in the event such relative predeceases or fails to survive the testator such devise shall be given to another specifically named or identifiable devisee or devisees." Id., at 274, 219 N.E.2d 327. Although we do not agree that the only way to negate operation of an antilapse statute is by providing an alternate devise, *Detzel* is persuasive nevertheless. *Detzel* has never been reversed, although another Ohio court characterized it as "clearly and completely erroneous." *Shalkhauser v. Beach*, 14 Ohio Misc. 1, 6, 233 N.E.2d 527 (Prob.Ct.1968). The Uniform Probate Code, however, seems to agree with the logic of *Detzel*.

In 1990, a revised Uniform Probate Code was promulgated, which contained a substantially altered antilapse statute. Notably, § 2–603(b)(3) provides that "words of survivorship, such as in a devise to an individual 'if he survives me,' or in a devise to 'my surviving children,' are not, in the absence of additional evidence, a sufficient indication of an intent contrary to the application of this section." Unif. Prob. Code § 2–603(b)(3). The comment to that section explains that this expansion of antilapse protection was necessary because "an antilapse statute is remedial in nature . . . . [T]he remedial character of the statute means that it should be given the widest possible latitude to operate" in considering whether in an individual case there is an indication of a contrary intent sufficiently convincing to defeat the statute. Id., comment. The Restatement Third of Property agrees; see 1 Restatement (Third), *supra*, § 5.5, comment (f),

p. 383; and that proposition is consonant with Connecticut law. In sum, we agree with those jurisdictions that have held that mere words of survivorship do not defeat antilapse statutes.

IV
CONCLUSION

Our antilapse statute was enacted to prevent operation of the rule of lapse and unintended disinheritance. The statute is remedial and receives a liberal construction. Any doubts are resolved in favor of its operation. We therefore conclude that words of survivorship, such as "if she survives me," alone do not constitute a "provision" in the will for the contingency of the death of a beneficiary, as the statute requires, and thus are insufficient to negate operation of § 45a–441. Our conclusion today effectuates the intent of the General Assembly in enacting this remedial statute. Should a testator desire to avoid application of the antilapse statute, the testator must either unequivocally express that intent or simply provide for an alternate bequest. Because the testator in the present case did neither, the protections of the antilapse statute apply. Accordingly, the bequest to Brennan does not lapse, but rather descends to her issue.

The judgment is reversed and the case is remanded for further proceedings consistent with this opinion.

In this opinion the other judges concurred.

Points for Discussion

1. *Overriding the anti-lapse statute*

Remember that in all jurisdictions anti-lapse statutes are default rules. Therefore, the anti-lapse statute will apply only if the will does not make a disposition of the gift in the event of lapse, or in some jurisdictions, include words indicating that the beneficiary must survive the testator.

As the case above indicates, when it comes to anti-lapse statutes, the greatest source of confusion and litigation is the question of whether or not the language of the will "provides otherwise," in other words, whether the terms of the bequest stipulates contrary intent to override the application of the anti-lapse statute. Traditionally, an express requirement of survival is sufficient "providing otherwise" and the anti-lapse statute will not apply to the gift should the beneficiary predecease the testator even if the beneficiary is one of those persons to whom the anti-lapse statute could apply. That is the rule in New York although applying that rule is often far from simple. Consider this language from the will of Frances P. Haines, the meaning of which was litigated in the Supreme Court of Ohio:

> [I give residue of my estate] to Dorothy Landrum, Dixie Lee Polen, Dorothy N. Franklin, Ercil Cutler and George Baker, equally, share and share alike, the same to be theirs absolutely, or to the survivors thereof.

The majority held that the word "survivors" referred to the named beneficiaries; that is, it was a requirement that they survive the testator in order to take under the will and that therefore the will did indeed override the anti-lapse statute. Two justices dissented; one argued that the use of "equally, share and share alike" meant that the testator intended the named individuals to take as individuals, not as a class, and that the use of the word "absolutely" indicated that the testator did not intend to impose a condition of surviving the testator. Since the word "survivors" could refer to those of the five named persons who survive the testator or to the issue of any of the five who do not survive the testator, the use of the word cannot show an intent to override the anti-lapse statute. The second dissenting justice argued because the word "survivors" appeared after the language giving each of the named persons a share of the residuary estate it must have referred to the surviving issue of a named person who predeceased the testator; therefore the language employed could not override the anti-lapse statute. *Polen v. Baker*, 752 N.E.2d 258 (Ohio 2001). Do you agree with the result in *Polen*? Consider the arguments in the dissenting opinions. Which do you find most persuasive?

2. Variations in which beneficiaries are covered by the statute

Many anti-lapse statutes apply the savings provision to relatives of the testator, although they differ in how closely related to the testator those relatives must be. Note that the UPC limits the application of the anti-lapse statute to testator/beneficiaries who are descendants of a grandparent of the testator. New York's anti-lapse statute is of fairly narrow application. Its operation is limited to bequests to the will-maker's issue and siblings. A few states apply the rules of anti-lapse to all beneficiaries without restriction.

New York Estates, Powers, and Trusts Law § 3–3.3. Disposition to issue or brothers or sisters not to lapse

(a)   Unless the will whenever executed provides otherwise:

(2)   Instruments executed on or after September first, nineteen hundred ninety-two. Whenever a testamentary disposition is made to the issue or to a brother or sister of the testator, and such beneficiary dies during the lifetime of the testator leaving issue surviving such testator, such disposition does not lapse but vests in such surviving issue, by representation.

So a gift to my beloved spouse . . . ? My best buddy Carlo . . . ? Why does the anti-lapse statute apply to some beneficiaries but not to others? Why does the ambit of the anti-lapse statute differ by jurisdiction? Are societal cultural norms in play? Do New Yorkers have a different concept of kinship than those who reside in UPC jurisdictions?

3. Who gets the benefit of the anti-lapse statute?

To whom does the saved bequest pass? Almost all statutes provide that lapsed gifts subject to the statute pass to the deceased beneficiary's descendants by representation. The representational scheme is usually the same one applicable to the jurisdiction's intestacy statute. A very few statutes pass the lapsed gift through the deceased beneficiary's estate which means that the lapsed gift passes through the deceased beneficiary's will (usually through the residuary clause because it is highly unlikely that the beneficiary will have made a specific bequest of the gift) or to the deceased beneficiary's heirs if the deceased beneficiary died intestate. Again, do you think one approach is better than the other?

4. Anti-lapse statutes and class gifts

Thus far we've considered the anti-lapse statute only as applied to gifts to named beneficiaries. Suppose the testator leaves a bequest 'to my nieces and nephews.' This is a bequest to a class—beneficiaries named by a group designation. It need not be a group of relations. A bequest to the Beatles is likewise a class gift; likewise my bequest 'to my Wills and Trust students' is a class gift. Survivorship is required, so in the Beatles example, John and George do not take; Ringo and Paul divide the bequest. Only my students who survive me—those there to blow out the candles (the metaphor used—the candles surrounding testator's coffin!!) took a share of the class gift. Most anti-lapse statutes apply to class gifts. The statutes treat the class gift as if it were a series of gifts to the individual members of the class. The share of the gift that would otherwise have gone to a member of the class who predeceases the testator therefore passes to the predeceased class member's descendants, if the class member is within the ambit of the anti-lapse statute. One way of conceptualizing the outcome is to say that the anti-lapse statute trumps the class gift rule. What about the bequest to my students? And the Beatles? Are these two classes within the ambit of the anti-lapse statute? More about class gifts below.

5. The UPC anti-lapse statute and the requirement of survival

The problems attendant on deciding whether or not the words of the will override the anti-lapse statute led the drafters of the UPC to a fairly radical solution. Under UPC § 2–603(b)(3) words of survivorship attached to a gift in a will are not a sufficient indication of the testator's intent that the anti-lapse statute not apply. The only way to override the statute is to make an express disposition of the gift if the beneficiary does not survive the testator. According to the comments to UPC § 2–603, such a disposition includes a direction that if the beneficiary does not survive the testator the gift passes to the residue or a phrase in the residuary clause which expressly states that all lapsed gifts shall pass through the residuary. This provision has been controversial because it overturns fairly well-settled law. The drafters of the UPC justify the change by arguing that the policy embodied in the anti-lapse statute is to enforce the testator's implied intent and that it should yield only to a clear expression of contrary intention. The court in *Ruotolo* adopted the reasoning of the UPC drafters.

Practice Planning Problem

Assume that Frances Haines, the testator whose will is the subject of the *Polen* case, is your client. She tells you that she wants to divide her residuary estate among five people.

a) What do you ask her next?

b) Assume that Ms. Haines tells you that she wants to give her residuary estate only to those of the five named persons who survive her. How would you draft the residuary clause?

c) Assume that Ms. Haines tells you that she wants to give her residuary estate to those of the five named persons who survive her, but if any of them do not survive her she wants the deceased person's share to go to that person's heirs. How would you draft the residuary clause? (Consider how the intestacy statutes provide for a line of descent inheriting the decedent's probate estate.)

---

1. Lapse and the Residuary

What happens if part of the residuary gift lapses? English and American law initially held that the lapsed portion of the residue passes in intestacy. The other residuary beneficiaries, if any, did not take the lapsed portion of the residuary gift. For example, if all of Terry's nieces and nephews named in ARTICLE VI(B) of the will die before Terry, one-half the residue will pass to Terry's heirs. This is the so-called "no residue of a residue" rule. This rule has long been out of favor and is not the law in the great majority of states. The rule is also rejected by Restatement Third, Property (Wills and Donative Transfers), § 5.5, comment *o* ("[T]he *no-residue-of-a-residue rule*, is not followed in modern statutory law, including the Uniform Probate Code, nor in this Restatement." *See* UPC § 2–604(b).). See also:

New York Estates, Powers, and Trusts Law § 3–3.4. No residue of a residue abolished

Whenever a testamentary disposition of property to two or more residuary beneficiaries is ineffective in part, as of the date of the testator's death, and the provisions of 3–3.3 do not apply to such ineffective part of the residuary disposition nor has an alternative disposition thereof been made in the will, such ineffective part shall pass to and vest in the remaining residuary beneficiary or, if there are two or more remaining residuary beneficiaries, in such beneficiaries, ratably, in the proportions that their respective interests in the residuary estate bear to the aggregate of the interests of all remaining beneficiaries in such residuary estate.

In re Estate of McFarland

167 S.W.3d 299 (Tenn. 2005)

WILLIAM M. BARKER, J.

We granted review in this case to determine the appropriate manner of distributing lapsed residuary gifts in a will. Specifically, we are confronted with a holographic will containing a residuary clause which devised percentages of the testatrix's estate to certain named beneficiaries. Three of these beneficiaries predeceased the testatrix, causing their gifts to lapse. Because these beneficiaries also died without issue, the Tennessee anti-lapse statute is not applicable.

Thus, the question presented is whether the lapsed residuary gifts are to be divided among the remaining residuary beneficiaries or pass through intestate succession to the testatrix's heirs at law. The probate court concluded that the lapsed gifts created a partial intestacy, and the lapsed gifts passed to the heirs at law. The Court of Appeals affirmed. Upon review, we affirm the judgment of the Court of Appeals.

Facts

On November 14, 1994, Ms. Merle Jeffers McFarland executed a holographic will. In this will, Ms. McFarland named an administrator for her estate, gave directions regarding her burial, set aside two percent of her estate to provide funds for funeral expenses, and also devised a specific bequest of three thousand dollars to the Tieke-McCullough Cemetery bank fund. The will further directed that the remainder of her estate was to be divided among eighteen named individuals and entities.

Specifically, Ms. McFarland provided in her will that "[t]he rest of the estate I wish to be divided to the following." She then listed the following beneficiaries along with the percentages of her estate devised to each. Her two brothers, Willie Lee Jeffers and Minnis Rankin Jeffers, were each to receive a ten percent share of the residuary estate. Clarence Lee McFarland, Mary Louise McFarland, and Evelyn B. McFarland McCulley were each also devised a ten percent share. Another ten percent share was to be divided equally between the three sons of Clyde E. McFarland. The First United Methodist Church of Bulls Gap received a five percent share. Larry and Virginia Carpenter were to divide a five percent share. A two percent share was devised to the city of Bulls Gap. Another two percent share went to the Tieke-McCullough Cemetery for "mowing and up keep of the cemetery." The Thompson Cancer Center in Knoxville was devised a ten percent share to be used for research, and the University of Tennessee was also to receive ten percent "for scholarships or what they need most." Ms. McFarland granted one percent shares to the Bulls Gap Masonic Lodge and Eastern Star Lodge. Finally, the United Way Fund or any other "worthy charity fund" was devised a two percent share.

On October 12, 2001, seven years after making the will, Ms. McFarland passed away at the age of eighty-four. An administrator was appointed by the trial court, and the will was admitted to probate. However, the administrator subsequently filed a declaratory judgment action seeking the court's guidance as to how the proceeds of the estate were to be distributed. This action was necessitated due to the fact that three of the residuary beneficiaries named in the will, Minnis Rankin Jeffers, Willie Lee Jeffers, and Mary Louise McFarland, had predeceased the testatrix, Ms. McFarland. Also, none of these predeceased beneficiaries had left a surviving spouse or issue. It was therefore uncertain as to how these individuals' shares were to be distributed.

The chancery court, exercising probate jurisdiction, determined that the gifts to each of the three predeceasing beneficiaries had lapsed. Because each had died without leaving surviving issue, Tennessee's anti-lapse statute, Tennessee Code Annotated section 32–3–105 (2001), did not apply. The probate court concluded that these circumstances resulted in a partial intestacy in Ms. Farland's estate. The chancellor also acknowledged that the long-standing common law rule, as announced in *Ford v. Ford*, 31 Tenn. 431 (1852), was that lapsed residuary gifts do not remain as part of the residue of the will to be distributed to remaining beneficiaries, but instead pass by intestate succession to the testator's next of kin. Therefore, the chancellor directed that those shares of the estate devised to the predeceased beneficiaries were to be distributed to Ms. McFarland's heirs at law, rather than being divided among the remaining residuary beneficiaries.

> **Take Note**
>
> The no residue of a residue rule.

The estate administrator filed an interlocutory appeal in the Court of Appeals, where the decision of the probate court was subsequently affirmed. We then granted review. The issue presented is whether the lapsed residuary gifts pass to the testatrix's heirs at law or to the remaining residuary beneficiaries. The estate administrator, along with the remaining residuary beneficiaries, argue that the lapsed gifts should be divided among the remaining residuary beneficiaries in proportion to their interests granted in the will. In opposition, the surviving heirs argue that the lapsed gifts pass by intestate succession.

I. Principles of Will Construction

In construing a will, the cardinal rule is that the Court must attempt to ascertain the intent of the testator and to give effect to that intent unless prohibited by a rule of law or public policy. *Id.* at 150; see *Winningham v. Winningham*, 966 S.W.2d 48, 50 (Tenn.1998). Holographic wills drawn by unskilled drafters are given a liberal construction. *See Garner v. Becton*, 187 Tenn. 34, 212 S.W.2d 890, 891 (Tenn.1948). Nevertheless, the intention of the testator must be ascertained, if at all possible, from the particular words used in the will and from the context, general scope, and purpose of the instrument. *Daugherty v. Daugherty*, 784 S.W.2d 650, 653 (Tenn.1990). The Court "cannot determine the devolution of estates based upon the mere surmise as to the testator's intention." *Pinkerton v. Turman*, 196 Tenn. 448, 268 S.W.2d 347, 350 (Tenn.1954).

The administrator of the estate argues that Ms. McFarland's will manifested a clear preference for those specified beneficiaries rather than for the heirs at law. He argues that Ms. McFarland clearly intended the residuary beneficiaries to receive the remainder of her estate, in its entirety, and to the exclusion of all other persons, including her heirs. The administrator also correctly notes that when a person makes a will there is a presumption that the person did not intend to die intestate as to any part of his or her property. *See* Tenn.Code Ann. § 32–3–101 (2001); In re Walker, 849 S.W.2d 766, 768 (Tenn.1993).

On the other hand, the law requires us to read a will as if it had been executed immediately prior to the testator's death. Tenn.Code Ann. § 32–3–101 (2001); *see also Bell v. Shannon*, 212 Tenn. 28, 367 S.W.2d 761, 766 (Tenn.1963). Furthermore, a person is presumed to be acquainted with applicable rules of law when executing a will. *McCarley v. McCarley*, 210 Tenn. 484, 360 S.W.2d 27, 29 (Tenn.1962). We must presume, therefore, that Ms. McFarland, prior to her death, knew that several of the beneficiaries had predeceased her, and we can further presume that she knew these lapsed gifts would pass by intestate succession to her heirs. Also, there is no evidence in the record that she attempted to redraft or revise her will to provide for an alternative distribution of the lapsed gifts.

Faced with a lack of any clear evidence concerning the testatrix's intent on this point, we are left to apply the general rules governing residuary clauses and lapsed gifts.

> **Take Note**
>
> The idea that the testator knows the law is a dubious proposition when applied to any area of law.

II. General Rules of Property Descent and Distribution

A gift or devise in a will which fails because the beneficiary predeceases the testator is said to lapse. *White v. Kane*, 178 Tenn. 469, 159 S.W.2d 92, 94 (Tenn.1942). To avoid this problem, Tennessee, like many other states, has enacted an "anti-lapse" statute which works to save lapsed gifts for the representatives of the predeceased beneficiary. *Id*. The Tennessee anti-lapse statute provides, in part:

> (a) Whenever the devisee or legatee or any member of a class to which an immediate devise or bequest is made, dies before the testator, or is dead at the making of the will, *leaving issue which survives the testator*, the issue shall take the estate or interest devised or bequeathed which the devisee or legatee or the member of the class, as the case may

> **Take Note**
>
> This is a very broad anti-lapse statute, which would save bequests to John and George for their issue in a class gift to the Beatles.

be, would have taken, had that person survived the testator, unless a different disposition thereof is made or required by the will. Tenn.Code Ann. § 32–3–105 (2001) (emphasis added).

This statute attempts to further the presumed intent of the testator in the absence of any contrary intent expressed through the will. *Weiss v. Broadway Nat'l Bank*, 204 Tenn. 563 322 S.W.2d 427, 432 (Tenn.1959). However, the anti-lapse statute saves the gift only if the predeceased beneficiary has left issue surviving the testator; otherwise, the statute has no application, and the gift lapses. *See Cox v. Sullins*, 181 Tenn. 601, 183 S.W.2d 865, 866 (Tenn.1944).

Another manner of disposing of lapsed gifts is through a will's residuary clause. If the will contains specific gifts or devises of property which lapse, these are deemed to fall into the residue and are disposed of through the provisions of the residuary clause, unless the testator has manifested a contrary intention. *Milligan v. Greeneville Coll.*, 156 Tenn. 495, 2 S.W.2d 90, 93 (Tenn.1928). Yet a particular problem arises when, as in the present case, the anti-lapse statute is inapplicable, and the gift which has lapsed is already a part of the residue. Under such circumstances, the traditional rule, derived from the English common law, is that the lapsed gift falls out of the terms of the will and passes by intestate succession to the testator's heirs at law. *See, e.g., Corbett v. Skaggs*, 111 Kan. 380, 207 P. 819, 820 (Kan.1922); *In re Frolich Estate*,

112 N.H. 320, 295 A.2d 448, 450 (N.H.1972). This rule has, in fact, been the law in Tennessee for the past 153 years, having been adopted in *Ford v. Ford*, 31 Tenn. 431 (1852). This Court held in *Ford* that when "a bequest to several be of the residue, and it fail as to part by reason of lapse, partial revocation, or other cause before stated, such part cannot fall into the remaining residue, but will be undisposed of and go to the next of kin." *Id.* at 435.

Despite its stability in our state, this rule has been much criticized in other jurisdictions and by legal commentators, with the main argument being that the rule defeats the most probable intent of the testator in this situation. Due in part to this criticism, the Uniform Probate Code adopts an alternative rule, often called the "modern" rule, which directs that "if the residue is devised to two or more persons and the share of one of the residuary devisees fails for any reason, his share passes to the other residuary devisee, or to other residuary devisees in proportion to their interests in the residue." Unif. Probate Code § 2–606 (1974). The UPC rule has gained wide-spread support, having been adopted, either by statute or through case law, in the vast majority of other states. By contrast, the common-law or *Ford* rule remains in effect in only a minority of states, including Tennessee.

Nevertheless, although widely abandoned in other jurisdictions, the *Ford* rule cannot fairly be termed either incorrect or illogical. The reasons supporting the modern UPC rule are generally that it more closely comports with the probable intent of the testator and that it avoids partial intestacy. See *In re Slack Trust*, 220 A.2d at 473–74; *Corbett*, 207 P. at 822. However, in our view, it is just as likely that a person would consider the implications of the traditional or *Ford* rule when executing his or her will and thus implicitly intend that lapsed gifts should pass to the heirs, rather than to the remaining residuary beneficiaries. Therefore, neither of the rules is more logically correct than the other. The two divergent rules simply represent two competing schools of thought as to what a testator would most probably desire to happen when a residuary gift lapses.

Food for Thought

Are you surprised by the court's candid acknowledgment that rules of law are sometimes arbitrary?

The *Ford* rule does not result in any obvious injustice or unfairness, and cannot be said to frustrate the intent of the testator. For instance, in the present case, the testatrix devised certain percentages of her residuary estate to eighteen specified parties, and three of these gifts subsequently lapsed. The will gives no indication of how the testatrix preferred these lapsed gifts to be distributed. However, application of the Ford rule results in the testatrix's stated intentions being carried out precisely as she directed with respect to fifteen of the eighteen beneficiaries. Further, the lapsed gifts pass to the most natural objects of her bounty—her heirs, which is a disposition favored under the law. See *Furchtgott v. Young*, 487 S.W.2d 301, 304 (Tenn.1972) (holding that in the absence of an expressed intention to the contrary, " 'a construction will be favored which conforms most nearly to the general laws of inheritance and which will prefer those of the blood of the testator to strangers or to persons not so closely related to the testator' ") (quoting *Davis v. Mitchell* 27 Tenn.App. 182, 178 S.W.2d 889, 913 (Tenn.Ct.App.1944)).

Conversely, application of the modern UPC rule would work to completely redraft the terms of the will, with none of the eighteen bequests being fulfilled exactly as directed by the testatrix.

Although we do not know how the testatrix would have preferred the lapsed gifts to be distributed, she clearly gave considerable thought to the specific percentages of her estate which she allotted to each beneficiary. To enlarge those percentages now, without any evidence that the testatrix intended such an outcome, would, in our opinion, totally frustrate her intentions as stated in the will. Faced with the choice between these two options, we conclude that the *Ford* rule secures the result which most closely comports with the testatrix's stated intentions and is the most just, natural, and reasonable disposition of the property. *See Davis*, 178 S.W.2d at 913 (stating that "such construction will be adopted if possible that will dispose of the property in a just, natural or reasonable manner").

> **Food for Thought**
>
> It is hardly likely that Ms. McFarland relied on the no-residue-of-a-residue rule. Is this conclusion, however, consistent with the court's earlier bald assertion that she is presumed to know the law?

III. Principle of Stare Decisis

Further supporting retention of the common-law *Ford* rule is the principle that whenever a judicial decision, such as *Ford*, "has been submitted to and for some time, acted under, and is not manifestly repugnant to some rule of law of vital importance in the system, it should not lightly be departed from, nor for purposes which are not of the highest value to the community." *Hall v. Skidmore*, 180 Tenn. 23, 171 S.W.2d 274, 276 (Tenn.1943) (internal quotations omitted) overruled on other grounds by *Graves v. Sawyer*, 588 S.W.2d 542 (Tenn.1979). In urging us to abandon the *Ford* rule, appellants cite a general trend toward adoption of the more modern UPC rule, and also argue that the testatrix probably intended for her estate to be divided among the named residuary beneficiaries, to the exclusion of her heirs. Neither argument is sufficiently persuasive or compelling to support overriding a rule of law that has been in effect in this state for far more than a century. The doctrine of stare decisis is "one of commanding importance, giving, as it does, firmness and stability to principles of law." *J.T. Fargason Co. v. Ball*, 128 Tenn. 137, 159 S.W. 221, 222 (Tenn.1913). Stability in the law allows individuals to plan their affairs and to "safely judge of their legal rights." *Id.* Generally, well-settled rules of law will be overturned only when there is obvious error or unreasonableness in the precedent, changes in conditions which render the precedent obsolete, the likelihood that adherence to precedence would cause greater harm to the community than would disregarding stare decisis, or an inconsistency between precedent and a constitutional provision. None of these reasons are evident in the present case.

The power of this Court to overrule former decisions "is very sparingly exercised and only when the reason is compelling." *Edingbourgh v. Sears, Roebuck & Co.*, 206 Tenn. 660, 337 S.W.2d 13, 14 (Tenn.1960). Radical changes in the law are best made by the legislature. *J.T. Fargason Co.*,

159 S.W. at 222. In our view, if our General Assembly determines that the UPC or "modern" rule would better serve the public interest, then it is within its power to adopt it into law, as have many other states. For the time being, we see no compelling reason in the case now before us to overrule the long-standing precedent established in *Ford*. Therefore, we agree with the probate court and the Court of Appeals that the *Ford* rule governs this case, and the lapsed residuary gifts in Ms. McFarland's will pass to her heirs under the laws of intestate succession.

Conclusion

In summary, we hold that the lapsed residuary gifts at issue in this case are not to be divided among the remaining residuary beneficiaries. Rather, the lapsed gifts result in a partial intestacy and therefore pass under the laws of intestate succession to the testatrix's heirs at law.

[The dissent is omitted.]

———

Problems

1. Testator's will gave 4% of her residuary estate to her husband's niece and the rest of the residue in equal shares to testator's sisters, all of whom predeceased testator. This is a New York case, and even New York's very limited anti-lapse statute applies to gifts to the testator's siblings. If descendants of the sisters had survived the testator, how would the residuary estate be distributed? Assuming no descendants of the sisters survive the testator, how would the residuary estate be distributed if the "no residue of a residue" is applied? What if it is not? (*See Matter of Markus*, 591 N.Y.S.2d 35 (App. Div. 1992)) Which result is likely more consistent with will-maker's presumed intent?

2. Testator's will bequeathed his residuary estate of approximately $1,000,000 "in equal shares to be theirs absolutely and forever to my brother, Raymond A. Cathers and my sister Elsie A. Wright, share and share alike." Raymond predeceased the testator and left no surviving issue. Elsie also predeceased the testator, but left three children surviving her. Two other sisters of the testator were not mentioned in the will. They both predeceased testator, and both left surviving children. How would the residuary estate distributed if the applicable anti-lapse statute operates on both lapsed gifts and no-residue-of-a-residue is not the law? (*See Matter of Cathers*, 416 N.Y.S.2d 743 (Surr. Ct. 1979)) (where the Surrogate held that the abolition of the no residue rule gave the brother's share of the residue to his sister and anti-lapse statute then gave both residuary gifts to the sister's issue.)

3. Can you improve on the drafting of disposition in Problem 2, even assuming that the result in the case is consistent with the testator's testamentary designs?

———

B. Class Gifts

Return to Terry Testator's will (page 179), and notice that in Article III the testator bequeaths all tangible personal property to the children of the testator's brothers and sisters, that is, "my nieces and nephews." What happens to the estate if one of the nieces or nephews dies before Terry? You are probably tempted to answer that the deceased beneficiary's share of the gift lapses and passes to the residue. That might be the wrong answer, however, because the gift in Article III might be *a class gift*.

The bequest in Article III could be (and is likely to be) a class gift because it describes the beneficiaries not by name but by reference to class designation, rather than by name: they all are nieces and nephews of the testator. Whether a gift is regarded as a class gift depends on the testator's intent. The language used in Restatement Third, Property (Wills and Donative Transfers) §§ 13.1 and 13.2 clearly shows the slippery nature of the class gift. Section 13.1 defines the class gift as "a disposition to beneficiaries who are described by a group label and are intended to take as a group." To take as a group, in turn, means that the membership of the class can fluctuate (in this case as Terry's siblings produce more offspring and those living die) until the time the class members are entitled to distribution: on distribution the class members who are entitled to take do so on a fractional basis. In addition, "if the terms of the disposition identify the only beneficiaries only by a group label" the disposition is a class gift, unless, of course, "the language or circumstances" indicate that the testator intended the beneficiaries to take as individuals.

Section 13.2 provides more guidance on differentiating a class gift from a gift to individuals. If the testator intends the beneficiaries to take as individuals, that is, only the identified individuals take, the gift is not a class gift. If the language of the gift identifies "the beneficiaries only by name, without any reference to a group label," the gift is not a class gift but one to individuals. If the language of the gift identifies the beneficiaries by a group label and by name or by the number of the beneficiaries "who then fit the group label" the gift is presumed to be to individuals but the presumption is rebutted "if the language or circumstances indicate that the [testator] intended the beneficiaries to take as a group.

Are the gifts in Article III and Article VI(B) of Terry Testator's will class gifts under the Restatement view outlined above? Does it make a difference if the persons mentioned in Article VI(B) are not all of Testator's nieces and nephews? If they are? (Think about "language and circumstances.")

Why have we taken this rather detailed excursion into the world of the class gift when we started out discussing lapse? If the testator has created a class gift, only class members who are living when the gift comes into possession take the gift. For a gift in a will, of course, that means that only class members who survive the testator share in the gift. (Remember, a gift under a will is made at the moment of death, even though it will take time to have the will admitted to probate and even more time to administer the estate and actually make a distribution to the beneficiaries.) A class gift, therefore, does not lapse until, and unless, all the class members die before the gift is to come into possession. If the gift is to individuals, however, the share of any individual who predeceases the time of distribution (once again, for a gift in a will that time is the death of the testator) will lapse.

Problems

1. Read Article III and Article VI(B) of Terry Testator's will yet again. Does it matter if these gifts are class gifts? In other words, what will happen to the gift if a niece or nephew or one of the named persons predeceases Terry?

2. Consider the application of the "no residue of a residue" rule with respect to a will with the following language:

> I give, devise, and bequeath the rest, residue and remainder of my estate, both real and personal and wheresoever situated, to Abel Adams, Beatrice Bond, and Charles Carlton.

How is the residuary estate distributed if Abel Adams predeceases the testator and the "no residue of a residue" rule is the law? If it is not? Does the language create a class gift? In answering this question, consider the following alternative facts;

   a)   The residuary legatees are three of seven cousins of the testator and the testator's heirs are Abel's mother (testator's aunt), Beatrice, Charles' father (testator's uncle), and the other four cousins.

   b)   The residuary legatees are friends of the testator and unrelated to the testator or to each other and if the testator dies intestate the estate will escheat.

   c)   The residuary legatees are siblings, are unrelated to the testator, and the testator's heirs are cousins with whom the testator has had no contact for many years.

———————————————

1.   Adoption and Class Gifts

Point for Discussion

The general rule is that once adopted, a person is totally integrated into the adoptive family and totally separated from the birth family. (These principles are explored in more detail in Chapter 7.) The UPC (and a very few states that have adopted the UPC provisions or have non-uniform statutes) preserves the birth inheritance rights of adopted persons under some circumstances, usually when an adopted parent is a stepparent or relative of a birth parent. The UPC and the few state provisions generally apply the same rules to class gifts in the wills and trusts of birth relatives. For example, Child is adopted by Mother's Sister and her spouse after the death of Mother and Father. Child participates in a gift to "my grandchildren" in the will of Father's father (Child's paternal grandfather).

C. Disclaimers

Recall from your Property course the elements of a gift: intent on the part of the donor, delivery of the subject of the gift, and acceptance by the donee (acceptance of a beneficial gift being presumed). Although it might be thought improbable, donees actually do reject a gifts. What is the result of such a refusal? The property simply remains property of the donor. A beneficiary under a will or trust can also reject a gift. That rejection is usually called a *disclaimer*. Some states use different terms of art. For example, in New York such a rejection is called a *renunciation*.

The existence of two terms reflects distinctions that were once significant but which are now obsolete. There are two principal reasons to disclaim: 1) if the disclaimer is made in conformity with the governing statutes, the rejected property will not be subject to the beneficiary's creditors and 2) the beneficiary will not be making a taxable gift to the persons who receive the property because of the disclaimer.

The tax benefits of a disclaimer can be illustrated by the following example.

Practice Planning Problem

Assume your client is the child of a parent who has recently died intestate and unmarried, survived by three children. Each child has two children living at her parent's death. Under UPC § 2–103 (and under every other intestacy statute in the United States at least), the probate estate is divided equally among the three children. Client would prefer that her share go to her children. If she simply accepts her intestate share and then gives it to her children, she will make a taxable gift for purposes of the federal gift tax (the great majority of states do not have a gift tax). While she may not actually owe gift tax on the gift, making the gift may have some future impact, for example it may lead to gift tax being owed on future gifts or increase the estate tax owed by her estate on her death. If client disclaims her share of the intestate estate within nine months of her parent's death without having accepted any of the property she would otherwise be entitled to, does not direct to whom the property passes, retains no control over the property, and fulfills minor procedural requirements, she will have complied with Internal Revenue Code § 2518 and made a "tax qualified disclaimer," which is not a taxable gift. As far as the tax law is concerned, therefore, she never owned the property, and it passed directly from her parent to whoever receives it. The destination of the disclaimed property is determined by state law, and under every state's disclaimer statute, the property will pass as if child had died immediately before her parent. In that case child's children are heirs and they take child's share by representation. For purposes of distributing our client's parent's estate, the disclaimer means that child is "pretend dead," treated as if the parent predeceased the child.

While there are many details to the operation of state disclaimer statutes, generally the property disclaimed passes as if the disclaimant had died before the disclaimed interest was certain to pass to the disclaimant. For any bequest in a will, and for any property passing in intestacy, of course, the critical moment is the death of the owner of the property.

One detail that you should be able to understand now involves the following situation:

Suppose above client's parent dies intestate, unmarried, and survived by two children, client and her sibling X, and Z, and the only child of a predeceased sibling Y. Client has four children and X has two. Client may wish to disclaim her share of her parent's intestate estate. Assume that the UPC governs. If client does not disclaim, how will her parent's estate be distributed? If she does disclaim?

The other effect of a disclaimer is to keep the disclaimed property out of the hands of creditors of the disclaimant. In the case above, assume client has an outstanding judgment lien against her. In most states, if client makes a valid disclaimer the property passes directly to client's own children from her deceased parent (through her parent's estate) the judgment creditor would have no recourse against the disclaimed property. Why? Client never owned the disclaimed property. The disclaimer is not a transfer by the disclaimant. That said, some states have enacted statutes that subject the disclaimed property to the disclaimant's creditors, often by precluding an insolvent person from making a disclaimer. (*See*, e.g., Fla. Stat. § 739.402(2)(d).)

Even in states that generally recognize a disclaimer as a device for avoiding creditors, the law has begun to treat disclaimers as transfers in certain situations. Consider the following case:

Molloy v. Bane

214 A.D.2d 171 (N.Y. App. Div. 1995)

Before SULLIVAN, J.P., and MILLER, THOMPSON and JOY, JJ.

MILLER, JUSTICE.

The instant appeal presents a collision of two irreconcilable rules of law. On the one hand, there is a generally recognized right to renounce any and all testamentary or intestate distributions, even when to do so would frustrate one's creditors. On the other hand, public aid is limited and should be spent only on the truly needy. Here, we hold that the policy considerations underlying the latter rule are of paramount importance. Accordingly, while one may renounce a testamentary or intestate disposition, such a renunciation is not without its consequences for purpose of calculating eligibility for Medicaid. Therefore, we confirm the determination of the respondent New York State Department of Social Services.

The petitioner Barbara Molloy, now age 56, had lived for most of her life in Suffolk County before moving to Florida. There she suffered a massive cerebral hemorrhage which left her partially paralyzed, unable to speak, and confined to a wheelchair. She was placed in a rehabilitation hospital in New York and was subsequently moved to the respondent Bishop Sherman Episcopalian Nursing Home in Rockland County. She began receiving medical assistance under the Medicaid program in 1989.

In 1991, the petitioner's 18-year-old daughter Jennifer Molloy was killed in a car accident. The respondent Rockland County Department of Social Services (hereinafter the local agency) learned of this event, and believing that the event could result in a potential recovery for wrongful death, requested on three occasions that the petitioner, through her other daughter Karen Buchholz as attorney-in-fact, assign to the local agency her share of Jennifer's estate. There is no dispute

> Don't confuse Medi*caid* with Medi*care*. The former is a joint federal/state program that provides medical services for indigent persons; the latter is a federal program that provides medical services for those over age 65 and is not "means tested."

that Jennifer died intestate and that her estate had no ascertainable value when the assignment was requested. There was no response to the local agency's first two requests. Before receiving the third request, the petitioner filed a renunciation of her interest in the estate with the Surrogate's Court, Suffolk County.

Take Note

To retain eligibility for Medicaid, a recipient must on an ongoing basis 'pursue available resources,' that is take advantage of potential sources of income that would limit state responsibility.

As a result of the petitioner's renunciation, the local agency concluded that the petitioner had failed to cooperate with eligibility requirements by failing to pursue an available resource and by refusing to execute the tendered assignment, in violation of 18 NYCRR 360–2.3(c)(1) and 360–3.2. Upon receipt of the local agency's notice of intent to discontinue medical benefits, the petitioner demanded a hearing. A fair hearing was held before an Administrative Law Judge at which it was established that the petitioner had renounced her interest in Jennifer's estate, and that Jennifer's sole statutory distributee was her father, whom the petitioner had divorced. Karen Buchholz asserted at the fair hearing that the petitioner, who suffers from numerous debilitating maladies, renounced her interest in Jennifer's estate "because she's not healthy enough to endure the trauma of litigation. It'll kill her". No evidence was adduced at the hearing as to the value of the wrongful death claim, the potential recovery to the estate, or the share thereof that the petitioner would have realized but for the renunciation.

After the fair hearing, the New York State Department of Social Services (hereinafter DSS) concluded that the petitioner had, by virtue of her renunciation, violated 18 NYCRR 360–2.3(c)(1), pursuant to which she was obligated to pursue a potential resource. As the decision makes clear, the central issue was one of law, construing DSS regulations as to the effect of the renunciation. The petitioner commenced the instant proceeding pursuant to CPLR article 78, which the Supreme Court transferred to this court for resolution of a perceived substantial evidence question.

We note that this proceeding was improperly transferred to this court. The facts are undisputed, and the only issues raised involve the interpretation of the relevant statutes. The Supreme Court should have thus considered the legal questions raised. However, inasmuch as the record is sufficient to determine these legal issues, we need not remit the matter to the Supreme Court (*see, e.g., Matter of Tutino v. Perales*, 153 A.D.2d 181, 185 n. 3, 550 N.Y.S.2d 21; *Matter of City School Dist. of City of Elmira v. New York State Pub. Employment Relations Bd.*, 144 A.D.2d 35, 536 N.Y.S.2d 214, *affd.* 74 N.Y.2d 395, 547 N.Y.S.2d 820, 547 N.E.2d 75).

The petitioner correctly argues that pursuant to EPTL 2–1.11, a beneficiary of a testamentary or intestate disposition may renounce such a disposition. The effect of a renunciation is as if the recipient had predeceased the decedent (EPTL 2–1.11[d]; *see, Matter of Chadbourne*, 92 Misc.2d 648, 401 N.Y.S.2d 139). The disposition thus never vests in the beneficiary (*see, Matter of Scrivani*, 116 Misc.2d 204, 455 N.Y.S.2d 505). The right to renounce has also been held to exist where the disposition to be renounced is an intestate share of a wrongful death recovery (*see, Matter of Dominguez*, 143 Misc.2d 1010, 541 N.Y.S.2d 934). It is also settled that a renunciation will be honored even when its purpose is to keep the bequest beyond the reach of the creditors of the renouncing party (*see, Matter of Schiffman*, 105 Misc.2d 1029, 430 N.Y.S.2d 229; *Matter of Reimer*, NYLJ, Sept. 13, 1991, at 28, col 2). The policy underlying statutes recognizing a right to renounce are "based upon the concept that no one should be forced to accept an inheritance or a gift, whether [it] comes about by will, inter vivos gift, or operation of a statute" (*Matter of Dominguez*, 143 Misc.2d, at 1013, 541 N.Y.S.2d 934, *supra*; *see also, Albany Hosp. v. Albany Guardian Socy.*, 214 N.Y. 435, 108 N.E. 812).

However, to be balanced against this recognized policy that a gift can be refused, is an equally established policy that public aid is not without limits, and one who receives public aid may not with impunity hide assets that might otherwise be used to pay for their care.

Article XVII, section 1, of the NY Constitution decrees that the care and support of the needy are public concerns which shall be provided for by the State by such means as the Legislature shall determine. Pursuant thereto, the State must discharge an affirmative duty to aid the needy (*see, Tucker v. Toia*, 43 N.Y.2d 1, 400 N.Y.S.2d 728, 371 N.E.2d 449). Who is, and who is not, needy, is determined by reference to the rules found in, among other places, Social Services Law § 366, which governs eligibility for medical assistance. Underlying all eligibility determinations is a basic premise that aid is to be furnished only to the truly needy and the Legislature enjoys great discretion to exclude from aid programs those individuals who have purposely created their own need (*see, Matter of Kircher v. Perales*, 112 A.D.2d 431, 433, 492 N.Y.S.2d 91; *Matter of Flynn v. Bates*, 67 A.D.2d 975, 413 N.Y.S.2d 446).

Viewed from this perspective, the determination under review is clearly not arbitrary and capricious (*see, Matter of Tutino v. Perales*, 153 A.D.2d 181, 550 N.Y.S.2d 21, *supra*) and there is certainly a rational basis for the termination of the petitioner's Medicaid benefits on the ground that she theoretically perpetuated her own neediness by eschewing a potentially viable resource. The petitioner may have a right to renounce an intestate disposition, but if by so doing she creates or perpetuates her status as a needy person, her renunciation is not without its consequences.

Indeed, while the petitioner argues that EPTL 2–1.11 confers upon beneficiaries an *absolute* right to renounce a disposition, the petitioner's characterization of this right as absolute is far too broad. Ordinarily, the owner of an asset has an absolute right to dispose of that asset, be it realty or personalty, as the owner sees fit. However, for purposes of determining need and eligibility for medical assistance, Social Services Law § 366 places conditions on these rights which cannot be accurately characterized as absolute. For example, subdivision 5 of Social Services Law § 366 provides that any transfer of a non-exempt resource within 24 months prior to an application for medical assistance shall be presumed to have been made for the purpose of qualifying for such assistance. Thus, one cannot convey one's home to a child for no value within 24 months prior to applying for medical aid and not have the value of the home included among the assets to be valued for eligibility determinations (*see, e.g., Matter of Farrell v. Perales*, 194 A.D.2d 670, 599 N.Y.S.2d 94; *Matter of Jirak v. Perales*, 125 A.D.2d 569, 509 N.Y.S.2d 638). In the instant case, the petitioner's renunciation of a potentially available asset was the functional equivalent of a transfer of an asset since by refusing to accept it herself, she effectively funneled it to other familial distributees. This potential windfall should no more remain "all in the family" than should the home conveyed for purposes of meeting eligibility standards.

The Appellate Division, Fourth Department, reached a similar conclusion in a case presenting analogous facts. In *Matter of Keuning v. Perales* (190 A.D.2d 1033, 593 N.Y.S.2d 653), a recipient of medical assistance benefits attempted to renounce her intestate share of a wrongful death recovery, of an established value of approximately $4,000, because as she was aware, it would affect her eligibility for further benefits. The court upheld a determination terminating the recipient's benefits because the renunciation was held to constitute an improper transfer of available assets which perpetuated her neediness. As the court observed, a recipient of public assistance is obligated to utilize all available resources to eliminate or reduce the need for public assistance.

> **Food for Thought**
>
> Perhaps the desired result and a worthy exception to the general rule that disclaimers are not transfers, but is it sound doctrinally to say that it is similar to a transfer? After all property law does not consider it a transfer, nor does tax law.

We recognize that there are lower court decisions which implicitly support a contrary result. For example, in *Matter of Dominguez* (143 Misc.2d 1010, 541 N.Y.S.2d 934, *supra*), Surrogate Bloom refused an application by DSS to set aside a renunciation on behalf of a deceased Medicaid recipient, finding that the renunciation was proper to block DSS from recoupment of Medicaid funds paid out for the decedent's care. The thrust of that decision, however, acknowledged the theretofore unrecognized right to renounce a wrongful death recovery. It gave no consideration to the issue at bar, i.e., the interplay between the policies permitting renunciations and the policies prohibiting fraudulent transfers of assets. In *Matter of Schiffman*, 105 Misc.2d 1029, 430 N.Y.S.2d 229, *supra*, the court likewise refused to set aside a renunciation of an intestate disposition which frustrated an attempt by DSS to recoup benefits because, similar to *Matter of Dominguez* (*supra*) the decision focused only on the right to renounce without consideration of the countervailing policy arguments. In *Estate of Arens* (NYLJ, Nov. 6, 1992, at 26, col 2), Surrogate Bloom did expressly countenance a renunciation as not running afoul of the policies limiting public aid for the truly needy. *Estate of Arens*, however, was decided by the Surrogate's Court, Kings County, prior to the contrary holding by the Appellate Division, Fourth Department, in *Matter of Keuning v. Perales*, 190 A.D.2d 1033, 593 N.Y.S.2d 653, supra. In any event, to the extent that the Surrogate's holding in *Estate of Arens* (*supra*) is inconsistent with the present case, it is hereby overruled. We conclude that a renunciation by a recipient of Medicaid must be considered for purposes of determining eligibility (see, *Matter of Keuning v. Perales, supra*; *Matter of Scrivani*, 116 Misc.2d 204, 455 N.Y.S.2d 505, *supra*).

In the instant case, the petitioner's benefits were terminated because she failed to pursue an available resource in violation of 18 NYCRR 360–2.3(c)(1). To the extent that the estate of Jennifer Molloy represented an available source of funds, the petitioner did violate DSS regulations, and EPTL 2–1.11 does not give her carte blanche to renounce potential available resources without impacting upon her eligibility. Furthermore, contrary to the petitioner's contentions, there is no indication in the record that she would in fact be compelled to participate in any wrongful death action to the detriment of her own health. Indeed, if in fact the petitioner could not participate in litigation without jeopardizing her health, any decision terminating her benefits for alleged noncooperation would likely be considered to be arbitrary and capricious (see, *Matter of Community Hosp. at Glen Cove v. D'Elia*, 79 A.D.2d 1025, 435 N.Y.S.2d 329). As a matter of fact, however, it does not appear that the petitioner would be called upon to be a witness or otherwise be forced to participate in any action by Jennifer's estate and thus, the petitioner's cries of incapacity ring particularly hollow. Moreover, if the estate really was valueless as she contended, the petitioner would have lost nothing by executing the requested assignment.

We are not persuaded by the petitioner's contention that because at the time of the renunciation there was no fixed value to the potential resource the petitioner renounced, the determination under review is arbitrary. To conclude that the lack of a fixed value precludes DSS from seeking an assignment ignores the fact that the regulations require the pursuit of *potential* resources.

It should be noted that 18 NYCRR 360–4.4(c)(2)(iii) limits a recipient's period of ineligibility to 30 months from the date of the transfer of an asset or for a period of time proportionate to the value of the asset transferred. Therefore the petitioner may apply to reinstate her eligibility if she is willing to divulge the amount of money recovered by Jennifer's estate and the proportion thereof that would have been payable to the petitioner but for the renunciation. In that event, the petitioner's eligibility will be recomputed.

We have reviewed the petitioner's remaining contentions and find them to be without merit. Accordingly, the determination is confirmed, without costs or disbursements, and the proceeding is dismissed on the merits.

ADJUDGED that the determination is confirmed, without costs or disbursements, and the proceeding is dismissed on the merits.

SULLIVAN, J.P., and THOMPSON and JOY, JJ., concur.

Points for Discussion

1. *Disclaimers and Medicaid*

The reasoning behind the decision in *Molloy* is fairly straightforward. Concern with the increasing cost of Medicaid is nationwide. Oregon's disclaimer statute includes language forbidding a disclaimer the purpose or effect of which is to prevent recovery of money or property under ORS § 411.620 relating to recovery of moneys expended as public assistance in violation of the law (ORS § 105.649). Iowa's statute takes another tack, but to the same end; it provides that a disclaimer is a transfer of assets for purposes of determining eligibility for medical assistance and therefore would preclude the use of disclaimers to enable an individual to qualify for assistance (Iowa Code Ann. § 633E.15).

2. *Another use for a disclaimer*

Test your understanding of *Molloy* by considering the following facts. Brother has been supporting Sister. He is killed in a motor vehicle accident. He is unmarried and has no issue so that his sole heir under the under the applicable intestacy law is his mother. A wrongful death suit is brought against the other motorist. Damages in wrongful death are measured in part by the loss to the decedent's distributees, those who take in an intestate succession. Mother properly renounces all her interest in Brother's estate under a disclaimer statute similar to New York's renunciation (disclaimer) statute, EPTL § 2–1.11 reproduced above. Mother is now "pretend dead," regarded as predeceasing her son and therefore his only distributee is Sister, whose losses from Brother's death are much greater than Mother's because Brother had been supporting her. Are the damages in the wrongful death suit measured by the loss to Mother or the loss to Sister? *See* DeLuca v. Gallo, 222 (N.Y. App. Div. 2001), where the court said that the disclaimer does indeed make Mother pretend dead, Sister is therefore the sole heir, and her losses will measure any recovery in wrongful death. Should the argument that the result in *Molloy* should govern the result in *DeLuca*? What do the two cases have in common?

3. *Disclaimers and federal tax liens*

Does a disclaimer put the property disclaimed beyond the reach of a federal tax lien? The answer from the United States Supreme Court is "no." *Drye v. United States*, 528 U.S. 49 (1999). Is it consistent to treat public and private debts different—allowing a federal tax lien and a state's claim on after-acquired assets of a Medicaid beneficiary, but disallowing claims of private creditors?

[fuckly federal taxes]

D. Statutory Revocation

As we have seen, the testator can revoke a will in a number of different ways. In addition to revocation by physical act or subsequent testamentary document, there are certain situations in which the intent to revoke is presumed to be so obvious that legislatures have written statutes that revoke wills without any action by the testator. These situations usually involve a change in the status of a beneficiary. Recall that *Erickson* involved a Connecticut statute that revoked the testator's will when the testator married, if the will did not provide for the contingency of marriage. Should the testator die without writing a new will, the surviving spouse will receive his or her intestate share. Not every state has such a statute, but surviving spouses are protected in every non-community property state (except Georgia) by the elective share law, which we will soon consider in detail.

One event that will trigger statutory revocation of a will is divorce. Consider the following statute.

UPC § 2–804. Revocation of Probate and Nonprobate Transfers by Divorce; No Revocation by other Changes of Circumstances

(a)   **[Definitions.]** In this section:

    (1)   "Disposition or appointment of property" includes a transfer of an item of property or any other benefit to a beneficiary designated in a governing instrument.

    (2)   "Divorce or annulment" means any divorce or annulment, or any dissolution or declaration of invalidity of a marriage, that would exclude the spouse as a surviving spouse within the meaning of Section 2–802. A decree of separation that does not terminate the status of husband and wife is not a divorce for purposes of this section.

    (3)   "Divorced individual" includes an individual whose marriage has been annulled.

    (4)   "Governing instrument" means a governing instrument executed by the divorced individual before the divorce or annulment of his [or her] marriage to his [or her] former spouse.

    (5)   "Relative of the divorced individual's former spouse" means an individual who is related to the divorced individual's former spouse by blood, adoption, or affinity and who, after the divorce or annulment, is not related to the divorced individual by blood, adoption, or affinity.

    (6)   "Revocable," with respect to a disposition, appointment, provision, or nomination, means one under which the divorced individual, at the time of the divorce or annulment, was alone empowered, by law or under the governing instrument, to cancel the designation in favor of his [or her] former spouse or former spouse's relative, whether or not the divorced individual

was then empowered to designate himself [or herself] in place of his [or her] former spouse or in place of his [or her] former spouse's relative and whether or not the divorced individual then had the capacity to exercise the power.

(b) **[Revocation Upon Divorce.]** Except as provided by the express terms of a governing instrument, a Court Order, or a contract relating to the division of the marital estate made between the divorced individuals before or after the marriage, divorce, or annulment, the divorce or annulment of a marriage:

   (1) revokes any revocable (i) disposition or appointment of property made by a divorced individual to his [or her] former spouse in a governing instrument and any disposition or appointment created by law or in a governing instrument to a relative of the divorced individual's former spouse, (ii) provision in a governing instrument conferring a general or nongeneral power of appointment on the divorced individual's former spouse or on a relative of the divorced individual's former spouse, and (iii) nomination in a governing instrument, nominating a divorced individual's former spouse or a relative of the divorced individual's former spouse to serve in any fiduciary or representative capacity, including a personal representative, executor, trustee, conservator, agent, or guardian; and

   (2) severs the interests of the former spouses in property held by them at the time of the divorce or annulment as joint tenants with the right of survivorship transforming the interests of the former spouses into equal tenancies in common.

(c) **[Effect of Severance.]** A severance under subsection (b)(2) does not affect any third-party interest in property acquired for value and in good faith reliance on an apparent title by survivorship in the survivor of the former spouses unless a writing declaring the severance has been noted, registered, filed, or recorded in records appropriate to the kind and location of the property which are relied upon, in the ordinary course of transactions involving such property, as evidence of ownership.

(d) **[Effect of Revocation.]** Provisions of a governing instrument are given effect as if the former spouse and relatives of the former spouse disclaimed all provisions revoked by this section or, in the case of a revoked nomination in a fiduciary or representative capacity, as if the former spouse and relatives of the former spouse died immediately before the divorce or annulment.

(e) **[Revival if Divorce Nullified.]** Provisions revoked solely by this section are revived by the divorced individual's remarriage to the former spouse or by a nullification of the divorce or annulment.

(f) **[No Revocation for Other Change of Circumstances.]** No change of circumstances other than as described in this section and in Section 2–803 effects a revocation.

Points for Discussion

1. How necessary is the revocation on divorce statute?

Divorce is a change in circumstance in which the intent to revoke is presumed to be so obvious that legislatures have written statutes that revoke wills without any action by the testator. Is this conclusion always warranted? Moreover, divorces often occasion, though not invariably, a settlement that deals with marital property. Why should law intervene create a presumption of revocation rather than merely leave the issue of revocation of a gift to a divorced spouse to private agreement? Bear in mind that the section simply provides a default provision. A will can explicitly state that it 'survives' a divorce, a point for divorce lawyers to investigate.

2. Scope of the revocation on divorce statute; beyond wills

Note, too, that Section (b) speaks of "governing instruments." Thus the UPC revocation statute applies both to wills and non-probate transfers, such as trusts, payment on death designations, and powers of appointment given to the surviving spouse. We will discuss the application of statutory revocation to non-probate transfers in the chapter dealing with non-probate property arrangements. There is a federal aspect to the application of state law revocation on divorce statutes to some non-probate property arrangements which we will also consider when we deal with non-probate property generally.

3. Scope of the revocation on divorce statute; beyond the ex-spouse

Suppose testator's will gives the residuary estate "to my spouse, S, and if my spouse does not survive me, to X, Y, and Z, in equal shares." Testator and S divorce and testator dies without changing the will. X, Y, and Z are S's children by a previous marriage. To whom is testator's residuary estate distributed under the UPC? Does it matter if X, Y and Z are described in the will as "children of my spouse, S"? Suppose testator has children by a previous marriage? Should it?

There is one other event that might affect an otherwise valid will: the birth of children to the testator.

UPC § 2–302. Omitted Children

    (a)   Except as provided in subsection (b), if a testator fails to provide in his [or her] will for any of his [or her] children born or adopted after the execution of the will, the omitted after-born or after-adopted child receives a share in the estate as follows:

        (1)   If the testator had no child living when he [or she] executed the will, an omitted after-born or after-adopted child receives a share in the estate equal in value to that which the child would have received had the testator died intestate, unless the will devised all or substantially all of the estate to the other parent of the omitted child and that other parent survives the testator and is entitled to take under the will.

(2) If the testator had one or more children living when he [or she] executed the will, and the will devised property or an interest in property to one or more of the then-living children, an omitted after-born or after-adopted child is entitled to share in the testator's estate as follows:

(i) The portion of the testator's estate in which the omitted after-born or after-adopted child is entitled to share is limited to devises made to the testator's then-living children under the will.

(ii) The omitted after-born or after-adopted child is entitled to receive the share of the testator's estate, as limited in subparagraph (i), that the child would have received had the testator included all omitted after-born and after-adopted children with the children to whom devises were made under the will and had given an equal share of the estate to each child.

(iii) To the extent feasible, the interest granted an omitted after-born or after-adopted child under this section must be of the same character, whether equitable or legal, present or future, as that devised to the testator's then-living children under the will.

(iv) In satisfying a share provided by this paragraph, devises to the testator's children who were living when the will was executed abate ratably. In abating the devises of the then-living children, the court shall preserve to the maximum extent possible the character of the testamentary plan adopted by the testator.

(b) Neither subsection (a)(1) nor subsection (a)(2) applies if:

(1) it appears from the will that the omission was intentional; or

(2) the testator provided for the omitted after-born or after-adopted child by transfer outside the will and the intent that the transfer be in lieu of a testamentary provision is shown by the testator's statements or is reasonably inferred from the amount of the transfer or other evidence.

(c) If at the time of execution of the will the testator fails to provide in his [or her] will for a living child solely because he [or she] believes the child to be dead, the child is entitled to share in the estate as if the child were an omitted after-born or after-adopted child.

(d) In satisfying a share provided by subsection (a)(1), devises made by the will abate under Section 3–902.

Points for Discussion

1. *Disinheriting one's children*

Under the law of every American state but one, parents can freely disinherit their children and other descendants, regardless of any individual's age or need for support. In Louisiana, children ages 23 and under or those with mental or physical disability have a right of so-called "forced heirship," which can be forfeited if the parent has "just cause" to disinherit at the time of the will's execution. La. Const. art. 12, § 5, art. 1621(A) (2019).

In other states, the only protection is against accidental disinheritance. Like the UPC (excerpted above), most states only protect children who were born or adopted after execution of a parent's will. (The UPC also protects living children who are wrongly believed dead by the parent.) Even then, a will that makes no provision for the afterborn may be untouched if the exclusion of future children appears intentional, or those children have been provided for outside the will. In some states, a child can be protected from accidental disinheritance even if already living at the time the parent executed the will. A so-called "Missouri-type" statute protects children "not named or provided for," while a "Massachusetts-type" statute permits extrinsic evidence to show whether the omission of the child in the will was intentional or not. If a child is determined to be "pretermitted" or forgotten within the applicable statutory definition, the child might be entitled to a share of the parent's estate.

2. *Applying the UPC provision*

Testator's will divides the residuary estate 50% to the surviving spouse and 50% to the testator's three children. About a year after execution of the will, a fourth child is born to testator. Testator later dies without changing the will. Under UPC § 2–302 what, if anything, is the fourth child entitled to under the will? Would it make a difference if the fourth child were adopted by the testator and spouse? If the fourth child were non-marital, that is, not the child of the surviving spouse?

Practice Planning Problem

A parent disinheriting a child is usually a decision taken with ambivalence if not regret. As we have seen in the sections on capacity and undue influence disinheriting 'natural objects' of the will-maker's bounty can spur litigation. How would you respond if client reveals an intention to disinherit?

E. Slayers

Sometimes beneficiaries named in a will just can't wait for the testator to die and decide to accelerate the process. As you might imagine, killing the testator in order to make sure you take under the will (or inherit under the intestacy statute) is not looked upon with favor by society. One is probably on safe ground in asserting that most people would think it immoral to allow the killer (usually referred to as the "slayer") to inherit from or take under the will of the victim. The following case it perhaps the most cited for the proposition that a slayer cannot benefit from the crime.

Riggs v. Palmer

22 N.E. 158 (N.Y. 1889)

EARL, J.

On the 13th day of August, 1880, Francis B. Palmer made his last will and testament, in which he gave small legacies to his two daughters, Mrs. Riggs and Mrs. Preston, the plaintiffs in this action, and the remainder of his estate to his grandson, the defendant Elmer E. Palmer, subject to the support of Susan Palmer, his mother, with a gift over to the two daughters, subject to the support of Mrs. Palmer in case Elmer should survive him and die under age, unmarried, and without any issue. The testator, at the date of his will, owned a farm, and considerable personal property. He was a widower, and thereafter, in March, 1882, he was married to Mrs. Bresee, with whom, before his marriage, he entered into an antenuptial contract, in which it was agreed that in lieu of dower and all other claims upon his estate in case she survived him she should have her support upon his farm during her life, and such support was expressly charged upon the farm. At the date of the will, and subsequently to the death of the testator, Elmer lived with him as a member of his family, and at his death was 16 years old. He knew of the provisions made in his favor in the will, and, that he might prevent his grandfather from revoking such provisions, which he had manifested some intention to do, and to obtain the speedy enjoyment and immediate possession of his property, he willfully murdered him by poisoning him. He now claims the property, and the sole question for our determination is, can he have it?

> **Practice Pointer**
>
> Given the circumstances, was this a reasonable pre-nuptial agreement, even to 21st century eyes?

The defendants say that the testator is dead; that his will was made in due form, and has been admitted to probate; and that therefore it must have effect according to the letter of the law. It is quite true that statutes regulating the making, proof, and effect of wills and the devolution of property, if literally construed, and if their force and effect can in no way and under no circumstances be controlled or modified, give this property to the murderer. The purpose of those statutes was to enable testators to dispose of their estates to the objects of their bounty at death, and to carry into effect their final wishes legally expressed; and in considering and giving effect to them this purpose must be kept in view. It was the intention of the law-makers that the donees in a will should have the property given to them. But it never could have been their intention that a donee who murdered the testator to make the will operative should have any benefit under it. If such a case had been present to their minds, and it had been supposed necessary to make some provision of law to meet it, it cannot be doubted that they would have provided for it. It is a familiar canon of construction that a thing which is within the intention of the makers of a statute is as much within the statute as if it were within the letter; and a thing which is within the letter of the statute is not within the statute unless it be within the intention of the makers. The writers of laws do not always express their intention perfectly, but either exceed it or fall short of it, so that judges are to collect it from probable or rational conjectures only, and this is called 'rational interpretation;' and Rutherford, in his Institutes, (page 420,) says: 'Where we make use of rational interpretation, sometimes we restrain the meaning of the writer so as to take in less, and sometimes we extend or enlarge his meaning so as to take in more, than his words express.' Such a construction ought to be put upon a statute as will best answer the intention which the makers had in view, for *qui haeret in litera, haeret in cortice.* In Bac. Abr. 'Statutes,' 1, 5; Puff. Law Nat. bk. 5, c. 12; Ruth. Inst. 422, 427, and in Smith's Commentaries, 814, many cases are mentioned where it was held that matters embraced in the general words of statutes nevertheless were not within the statutes, because it could not have been the intention of the law-makers that they should be included. They were taken out of the statutes by an equitable construction; and it is said in Bacon: 'By an equitable construction a case not within the letter of a statute is sometimes holden to be within the meaning, because it is within the mischief for which a remedy is provided. The reason for such construction is that the law-makers could not set down every case in express terms. In order to form a right judgment whether a case by within the equity of a statute, it is a good way to suppose the law-maker present, and that you have asked him this question: Did you intend to comprehend this case? Then you must give yourself such answer as you imagine he, being an upright and reasonable man, would have given. If this be that he did mean to comprehend it, you may safely hold the case to be within the equity of the statute; for while you do no more than he would have done, you do not act contrary to the statute, but in conformity thereto.' 9 Bac. Abr. 248. In some cases the letter of a legislative act is restrained by an equitable con-

struction; in others, it is enlarged; in others, the construction is contrary to the letter. The equitable construction which restrains the letter of a statute is defined by Aristotle as frequently quoted in this manner: *Aequitas est correctio legis generaliter latoe qua parte deficit.* If the law-makers could, as to this case, be consulted, would they say that they intended by their general language that the property of a testator or of an ancestor should pass to one who had taken his life for the express purpose of getting his property? In 1 Bl. Comm. 91, the learned author, speaking of the construction of statutes,

> **Non constat**
> **jus civile**
> a posteriori
>
> ### It's Latin to Me
>
> ***aequitas est . . . :*** Equity corrects deficiencies in the general expression of the law. Literally: he who adheres to the letter adheres to the bark or rind. Interpretations of statutes or agreements that focus on language rather than intent should be avoided and are too literal—the intent of the statute should control explications of its meaning.

says: 'If there arise out of them collaterally any absurd consequences manifestly contradictory to common reason, they are with regard to those collateral consequences void. * * * Where some collateral matter arises out of the general words, and happens to be unreasonable, there the judges are in decency to conclude that this consequence was not foreseen by the parliament, and therefore they are at liberty to expound the statute by equity, and only *quoad hoc* disregard it;' and he gives as an illustration, if an act of parliament gives a man power to try all causes that arise within his manor of Dale, yet, if a cause should arise in which he himself is party, the act is construed not to extend to that, because it is unreasonable that any man should determine his own quarrel. There was a statute in Bologna that whoever drew blood in the streets should be severely punished, and yet it was held not to apply to the case of a barber who opened a vein in the street. It is commanded in the Decalogue that no work shall be done upon the Sabbath, and yet giving the command a rational interpretation founded upon its design the Infallible Judge held that it did not prohibit works of necessity, charity, or benevolence on that day.

What could be more unreasonable than to suppose that it was the legislative intention in the general laws passed for the orderly, peaceable, and just devolution of property that they should have operation in favor of one who murdered his ancestor that he might speedily come into the possession of his estate? Such an intention is inconceivable. We need not, therefore, be much troubled by the general language contained in the

> **Food for Thought**
>
> A reasonable conclusion to be drawn from the law of wills? Might the point be better applied to the default rules of intestate succession?

laws. Besides, all laws, as well as all contracts, may be controlled in their operation and effect by general, fundamental maxims of the common law. No one shall be permitted to profit by his own fraud, or to take advantage of his own wrong, or to found any claim upon his own iniquity, or to acquire property by his own crime. These maxims are dictated by public policy, have their foundation in universal law administered in all civilized countries, and have nowhere been superseded by statutes. They were applied in the decision of the case of Insurance Co. v. Armstrong, 117 U. S. 599, 6 Sup. Ct. Rep. 877. There it was held that the person who procured a policy upon the life of another, payable at his death, and then murdered the assured to make the policy payable, could not recover thereon. Mr. Justice FIELD, writing the opinion, said: 'Independently of any proof of the motives of Hunter in obtaining the policy, and even assuming that they were just and proper, he forfeited all rights under it when, to secure its immediate payment, he murdered the assured. It would be a reproach to the jurisprudence of the country if one could recover insurance money payable on the death of a party whose life he had feloniously taken. As well might he recover insurance money upon a building that he had willfully fired.' These maxims, without any statute giving them force or operation, frequently control the effect and nullify the language of wills. A will procured by fraud and deception, like any other instrument, may be decreed void, and set aside; and so a particular portion of a will may be excluded form probate, or held inoperative, if induced by the fraud or undue influence of the person in whose favor it is. Allen v. McPherson, 1 H. L. Cas. 191; Harrison's

Appeal, 48 Conn. 202. So a will may contain provisions which are immoral, irreligious, or against public policy, and they will be held void.

Here there was no certainty that this murderer would survive the testator, or that the testator would not change his will, and there was no certainty that he would get this property if nature was allowed to take its course. He therefore murdered the testator expressly to vest himself with an estate. Under such circumstances, what law, human or divine, will allow him to take the estate and enjoy the fruits of his crime? The will spoke and became operative at the death of the testator. He caused that death, and thus by his crime made it speak and have operation. Shall it speak and operate in his favor? If he had met the testator, and taken his property by force, he would have had no title to it. Shall he acquire title by murdering him? If he had gone to the testator's house, and by force compelled him, or by fraud or undue influence had induced him, to will him his property, the law would not allow him to hold it. But can he give effect and operation to a will by murder, and yet take the property? To answer these questions in the affirmative it seems to me would be a reproach to the jurisprudence of our state, and an offense against public policy. Under the civil law, evolved from the general principles of natural law and justice by many generations of jurisconsults, philosophers, and statesmen, one cannot take property by inheritance or will from an ancestor or benefactor whom he has murdered. Dom. Civil Law, pt. 2, bk. 1, tit. 1, § 3; Code Nap. § 727; Mack. Rom. Law, 530, 550. In the Civil Code of Lower Canada the provisions on the subject in the Code Napoleon have been substantially copied. But, so far as I can find, in no country where the common law prevails has it been deemed important to enact a law to provide for such a case. Our revisers and law-makers were familiar with the civil law, and they did not deem it important to incorporate into our statutes its provisions upon this subject. This is not a *casus omissus*. It was evidently supposed that the maxims of the common law were sufficient to regulate such a case, and that a specific enactment for that purpose was not needed. For the same reasons the defendant Palmer cannot take any of this property as heir. Just before the murder he was not an heir, and it was not certain that he ever would be. He might have died before his grandfather, or might have been disinherited by him. He made himself an heir by the murder, and he seeks to take property as the fruit of his crime. What has before been said as to him as legatee applies to him with equal force as an heir. He cannot vest himself with title by crime. My view of this case does not inflict upon Elmer any greater or other punishment for his crime than the law specifies. It takes from him no property, but simply holds that he shall not acquire property by his crime, and thus be rewarded for its commission.

Our attention is called to Owens v. Owens, 100 N. C. 240, 6 S. E. Rep. 794, as a case quite like this. There a wife had been convicted of being an accessory before the fact to the murder of her husband, and it was held that she was nevertheless entitled to dower. I am unwilling to assent to the doctrine of that case. The statutes provide dower for a wife who has the misfortune to survive her husband, and thus lose his support and protection. It is clear beyond their purpose to make provision for a wife who by her own crime makes herself a widow, and willfully and intentionally deprives herself of the support and protection of her husband. As she might have died before him, and thus never have been his widow, she cannot by her crime vest herself with an estate. The principle which lies at the bottom of the maxim *volenti non fit injuria* should be applied to such a case, and a widow should not, for the purpose of acquiring, as such, property rights, be permitted to allege a widowhood which she has wickedly and intentionally created.

The facts found entitled the plaintiffs to the relief they seek. The error of the referee was in his conclusion of law. Instead of granting a new trial, therefore, I think the proper judgment upon the facts found should be ordered here. The facts have been passed upon twice with the same result,—first upon the trial of Palmer for murder, and then by the referee in this action. We are therefore of opinion that the ends of justice do not require that they should again come in question. The judgment of the general term and that entered upon the report of the referee should therefore be reversed, and judgment should be entered as follows: That Elmer E. Palmer and the administrator be enjoined from using any of the personalty or real estate left by the testator for Elmer's benefit; that the devise and bequest in the will to Elmer be declared ineffective to pass the title to him; that by reason of the crime of murder committed upon the grandfather he is deprived of any interest in the estate left by him; that the plaintiffs are the true owners of the real and personal estate left by the testator, subject to the charge in favor of Elmer's mother and the widow of the testator, under the antenuptial agreement, and that the plaintiffs have costs in all the courts against Elmer.

All concur, except GRAY, J., who reads dissenting opinion, and DANFORTH, J., concurs.

GRAY, J., (*dissenting.*)

This appeal presents an extraordinary state of facts, and the case, in respect of them, I believe, is without precedent in this state. The respondent, a lad of 16 years of age, being aware of the provisions in his grandfather's will, which constituted him the residuary legatee of the testator's estate, caused his death by poison, in 1882. For this crime he was tried, and was convicted of murder in the second degree, and at the time of the commencement of this action he was serving out his sentence in the state reformatory. This action was brought by two of the children of the testator for the purpose of having those provisions of the will in the respondent's favor canceled and annulled. The appellants' argument for a reversal of the judgment, which dismissed their complaint, is that the respondent unlawfully prevented a revocation of the existing will, or a new will from being made, by his crime; and that he terminated the enjoyment by the testator of his property, and effected his own succession to it, by the same crime. They say that to permit the respondent to take the property willed to him would be to permit him to take advantage of his own wrong. To sustain their position the appellants' counsel has submitted an able and elaborate brief, and, if I believed that the decision of the question could be effected by considerations of an equitable nature, I should not hesitate to assent to views which commend themselves to the conscience. But the matter does not lie within the domain of conscience. We are bound by the rigid rules of law, which have been established by the legislature, and within the limits of which the determination of this question is confined. The question we are dealing with is whether a testamentary disposition can be altered, or a will revoked, after the testator's death, through an appeal to the courts, when the legislature has by its enactments prescribed exactly when and how wills may be made, altered, and revoked, and apparently, as it seems to me, when they have been fully complied with, has left no room for the exercise of an equitable jurisdiction by courts over such matters. Modern jurisprudence, in recognizing the right of the individual, under more or less restrictions, to dispose of his property after his death, subjects it to legislative control, both as to extent and as to mode of exercise. Complete freedom of testamentary disposition of one's property has not been and is not the universal rule, as we see from the provisions of the Napoleonic Code, from the systems of jurisprudence in countries which are modeled upon the Roman law, and from the statutes of many of our states. To the statutory restraints which are imposed upon the disposition of one's property by will are added strict and systematic statutory rules for the execution, alteration, and revocation of the will, which must be, at least substantially, if not exactly, followed to insure validity and performance. The reason for the establishment of such rules, we may naturally assume, consists in the purpose to create those safeguards about these grave and important acts which experience has demonstrated to be the wisest and surest. That freedom which is permitted to be exercised in the testamentary disposition of one's estate by the laws of the state is subject to its being exercised in conformity with the regulations of the statutes. The capacity and the power of the individual to dispose of his property after death, and the mode by which that power can be exercised, are matters of which the legislature was assumed the entire control, and has undertaken to regulate with comprehensive particularity.

The appellants' argument is not helped by reference to those rules of the civil law, or to those laws of other governments, by which the heir, or legatee, is excluded from benefit under the testament if he has been convicted of killing, or attempting to kill, the testator. In the absence of such legislation here, the courts are not empowered to institute such a system of remedial justice. The deprivation of the heir of his testamentary succession by the Roman law, when guilty of such a crime, plainly was intended to be in the nature of a punishment imposed upon him. The succession, in such a case of guilt, escheated to the exchequer. See Dom. Civil Law, pt. 2, bk. 1, tit. 1, § 3. I concede that rules of law which annul testamentary provisions made for the benefit of those who have become unworthy of them may be based on principles of equity and of natural justice. It is quite reasonable to suppose that a testator would revoke or alter his will, where his mind has been so angered and changed as to make him unwilling to have his will executed as it stood. But these principles only suggest sufficient reasons for the enactment of laws to meet such cases.

The statutes of this state have prescribed various ways in which a will may be altered or revoked; but the very provision defining the modes of alteration and revocation implies a prohibition of alteration or revocation in any other way. The words of the section of the statute are: 'No will in writing, except in the cases hereinafter mentioned, nor any part thereof, shall be revoked or altered otherwise,' etc. Where, therefore, none of the cases mentioned are met by the facts, and the revocation is not in the way described in the section, the will of the testator is unalterable. I think that a valid will must continue as a will always, unless revoked in the manner provided by the statutes. Mere intention to revoke a will does not have the effect of revocation. The intention to revoke is necessary to constitute the effective revocation of a will, but it must be demonstrated by one of the acts contemplated by the statute. As WOODWORTH, J., said in Dan v. Brown, 4 Cow. 490: 'Revocation is an act of the mind, which must be demonstrated by some outward and visible sign of revocation.' The same learned judge said in that case: 'The rule is that if the testator lets the will stand until he dies, it is his will; if he does not suffer it to do so, it is not his will.' And see Goodright v. Glazier, 4 Burrows, 2512, 2514; Pemberton v. Pemberton, 13 Ves. 290. The finding of fact of the referee that presumably the testator would have altered his will had he known of his grantor's murderous intent cannot affect the question. We may concede it to the fullest extent; but still the cardinal objection is undisposed of,—that the making and the revocation of a will are purely matters of statutory regulation, by which the court is bound in the determination of questions relating to these acts.

Two cases,—in this state and in Kentucky,—at an early day, seem to me to be much in point. Gains v. Gains, 2 A. K. Marsh. 190, was decided by the Kentucky court of appeals in 1820. It was there urged that the testator intended to have destroyed his will, and that he was forcibly prevented from doing so by the defendant in error or devisee; and it was insisted that the will, though not expressly, was thereby virtually, revoked. The court held, as the act concerning wills prescribed the manner in which a will might be revoked, that, as none of the acts evidencing revocation were done, the intention could not be substituted for the act. In that case the will was snatched away, and forcibly retained. In 1854, Surrogate BRADFORD, whose opinions are entitled to the highest consideration, decided the case of Leaycraft v. Simmons, 3 Bradf. Sur. 35. In that case the testator, a man of 89 years of age, desired to make a codicil to his will, in order to enlarge the provisions for his daughter. His son, having the custody of the instrument, and the one to be prejudiced by the change, refused to produce the will at testator's request, for the purpose of alteration. The learned surrogate refers to the provisions of the civil law for such and other cases of unworthy conduct in the heir or legatee, and says: 'Our statute has undertaken to prescribe the mode in which wills can be revoked [citing the statutory provision.] This is the law by which I am governed in passing upon questions touching the revocation of wills. The whole of this subject is now regulated by statute; and a mere intention to revoke, however well authenticated, or however defeated, is not sufficient.' And he held that the will must be admitted to probate. I may refer also to a case in the Pennsylvania courts. In that state the statute prescribed the mode for repealing or altering a will, and in Clingan v. Micheltree, 31 Pa. St. 25, the supreme court of the state held, where a will was kept from destruction by the fraud and misrepresentation of the devisee, that to declare it canceled as against the fraudulent party would be to enlarge the statute.

I cannot find any support for the argument that the respondent's succession to the property should be avoided because of his criminal act, when the laws are silent. Public policy does not demand it; for the demands of public policy are satisfied by the proper execution of the laws and the punishment of the crime. There has been no convention between the testator and his legatee nor is there any such contractual element, in such a disposition of property by a testator, as to impose or imply conditions in the legatee. The appellants' argument practically amounts to this: that, as the legatee has been guilty of a crime, by the commission of which he is placed in a position to sooner receive the benefits of the testamentary provision, his rights to the property should be forfeited, and he should be divested of his estate. To allow their argument to prevail, would involve the diversion by the court of the testator's estate into the hands of persons whom, possibly enough, for all we know, the testator might not have chosen or desired as its recipients. Practically the court is asked to make another will for the testator. The laws do not warrant this judicial action, and mere presumption would not be strong enough to sustain it. But, more than this, to concede the appellants' views would involve the imposition of an additional punishment or penalty upon the respondent. What power or warrant have the courts to add to the respondent's penalties by depriving him of property? The law has punished him for his crime, and we may not say that it was an insufficient punishment. In the trial and punishment of the respondent the law has vindicated itself for the outrage which he committed, and further judicial utterance upon the subject of punishment or deprivation of rights is barred. We may not, in the language of the court in People v. Thornton, 25 Hun, 456, 'enhance the pains, penalties, and forfeitures provided by law for the punishment of crime.' The judgment should be affirmed, with costs.

DANFORTH, J., concurs.

————————

Points for Discussion

1. *Two views of* Riggs?

Which opinion, majority or dissent, strikes you as more legally sound? Morally justified?

2. *Statutory treatment of the slayer*

Most states have codified the "slayer rule," and the UPC has a comprehensive provision in § 2–803. Note that the cancellation of the designation applies to a wide range of non-probate transfers as well as designations in wills. A variety of powers granted to the slayer are also revoked. It also excludes the slayer from taking by intestate succession.

UPC § 2–803. Effect of Homicide on Intestate Succession, Wills, Trusts, Joint Assets, Life Insurance, and Beneficiary Designations

(a) **[Definitions.]** In this section:

(1) "Disposition or appointment of property" includes a transfer of an item of property or any other benefit to a beneficiary designated in a governing instrument.

(2) "Governing instrument" means a governing instrument executed by the decedent.

(3) "Revocable," with respect to a disposition, appointment, provision, or nomination, means one under which the decedent, at the time of or immediately before death, was alone empowered, by law or under the governing instrument, to cancel the designation, in favor of the killer, whether or not the decedent was then empowered to designate himself [or herself] in place of his [or her] killer and whether or not the decedent then had capacity to exercise the power.

(b) **[Forfeiture of Statutory Benefits.]** An individual who feloniously and intentionally kills the decedent forfeits all benefits under this Article with respect to the decedent's estate, including an intestate share, an elective share, an omitted spouse's or child's share, a homestead allowance, exempt property, and a family allowance. If the decedent died intestate, the decedent's intestate estate passes as if the killer disclaimed his [or her] intestate share.

(c) **[Revocation of Benefits Under Governing Instruments.]** The felonious and intentional killing of the decedent:

    (1) revokes any revocable (i) disposition or appointment of property made by the decedent to the killer in a governing instrument, (ii) provision in a governing instrument conferring a general or nongeneral power of appointment on the killer, and (iii) nomination of the killer in a governing instrument, nominating or appointing the killer to serve in any fiduciary or representative capacity, including a personal representative, executor, trustee, or agent; and

    (2) severs the interests of the decedent and killer in property held by them at the time of the killing as joint tenants with the right of survivorship [UPC § 1–201 includes tenancy by the entirety in the definition of joint tenancy with right of survivorship] transforming the interests of the decedent and killer into equal tenancies in common.

(d) **[Effect of Severance.]** A severance under subsection (c)(2) does not affect any third-party interest in property acquired for value and in good faith reliance on an apparent title by survivorship in the killer unless a writing declaring the severance has been noted, registered, filed, or recorded in records appropriate to the kind and location of the property which are relied upon, in the ordinary course of transactions involving such property, as evidence of ownership.

(e) **[Effect of Revocation.]** Provisions of a governing instrument are given effect as if the killer disclaimed all provisions revoked by this section or, in the case of a revoked nomination in a fiduciary or representative capacity, as if the killer predeceased the decedent.

(f) **[Wrongful Acquisition of Property.]** A wrongful acquisition of property or interest by a killer not covered by this section must be treated in accordance with the principle that a killer cannot profit from his [or her] wrong.

(g) **[Felonious and Intentional Killing; How Determined.]** After all right to appeal has been exhausted, a judgment of conviction establishing criminal accountability for the felonious and intentional killing of the decedent conclusively establishes the convicted individual as the decedent's killer for purposes of this section. In the absence of a conviction, the court, upon the petition of an interested person, must determine whether, under the preponderance of evidence standard, the individual would be found criminally accountable for the felonious and intentional killing of the decedent. If the court determines that, under that standard, the individual would be found criminally accountable for the felonious and intentional killing of the decedent, the determination conclusively establishes that individual as the decedent's killer for purposes of this section.

(h) **[Protection of Payors and Other Third Parties.]**

(1) A payor or other third party is not liable for having made a payment or transferred an item of property or any other benefit to a beneficiary designated in a governing instrument affected by an intentional and felonious killing, or for having taken any other action in good faith reliance on the validity of the governing instrument, upon request and satisfactory proof of the decedent's death, before the payor or other third party received written notice of a claimed forfeiture or revocation under this section. A payor or other third party is liable for a payment made or other action taken after the payor or other third party received written notice of a claimed forfeiture or revocation under this section.

(2) Written notice of a claimed forfeiture or revocation under paragraph (1) must be mailed to the payor's or other third party's main office or home by registered or certified mail, return receipt requested, or served upon the payor or other third party in the same manner as a summons in a civil action. Upon receipt of written notice of a claimed forfeiture or revocation under this section, a payor or other third party may pay any amount owed or transfer or deposit any item of property held by it to or with the court having jurisdiction of the probate proceedings relating to the decedent's estate, or if no proceedings have been commenced, to or with the court having jurisdiction of probate proceedings relating to decedents' estates located in the county of the decedent's residence. The court shall hold the funds or item of property and, upon its determination under this section, shall order disbursement in accordance with the determination. Payments, transfers, or deposits made to or with the court discharge the payor or other third party from all claims for the value of amounts paid to or items of property transferred to or deposited with the court.

(i) **[Protection of Bona Fide Purchasers; Personal Liability of Recipient.]**

(1) A person who purchases property for value and without notice, or who receives a payment or other item of property in partial or full satisfaction of a legally enforceable obligation, is neither obligated under this section to return the payment, item of property, or benefit nor is liable under this section for the amount of the payment or the value of the item of property or benefit. But a person who, not for value, receives a payment, item of property, or any other benefit to which the person is not entitled under this section is obligated to return the payment, item of property, or benefit, or is personally liable for the amount of the payment or the value of the item of property or benefit, to the person who is entitled to it under this section.

(2) If this section or any part of this section is preempted by federal law with respect to a payment, an item of property, or any other benefit covered by this section, a person who, not for value, receives the payment, item of property, or any other benefit to which the person is not entitled under this section is obligated to return the payment, item of property, or benefit, or is personally liable for the amount of the payment or the value of the item of property or benefit, to the person who would have been entitled to it were this section or part of this section not preempted.

Note the length of UPC § 2–803. Does that suggest to you that there's a lot more to a workable slayer rule than the principle no one should benefit from their own wrong? In particular, note the rules for non-probate property, the killings to which the statute applies and the degree of proof necessary for the statute to apply. Also, there is considerable attention therein devoted to those who may have received estate property from a slayer. Why?

3. In the absence of a statute

Interestingly enough, New York is one of the few states without a comprehensive statute. The only reference to the slayer rule in the New York statutes is EPTL § 4–1.6 which refers only to joint bank accounts. The statute provides that a joint tenant convicted of first or second degree murder of the other joint tenant is not entitled to "any monies in a joint bank account created or contributed to by the deceased joint tenant, except for those monies contributed by the convicted joint tenant." The statute has been held to apply to a joint brokerage account, see, *Matter of Kiejliches*, 530 (N.Y. App. Div. 2002). In the absence of a comprehensive statute, the courts must face

> **Food for Thought**
>
> We know that killing is wrong. We also know that all killings are not legally the same. Not only does the criminal law classify killings according to the state of mind (*mens rea*) of the slayer but also some killings are completely excused. How culpable does the slayer have to be to be disqualified from taking from the victim? What about the person who helps their terminally ill spouse or partner commit suicide?

questions involving slayers one case at a time. What happens in New York when the slayer and the victim held property as joint tenants with right of survivorship? In *Matter of Covert*, 761 N.E.2d 571 (N.Y. 2001), New York's highest court, the Court of Appeals, held in a case where husband killed wife and then committed suicide, the husband could not succeed to his wife's interest in the jointly held property but neither could he be deprived of his undivided one-half of the property both because the joint tenancy is severable and because other New York law prohibits forfeiture of property as a punishment for crime (NY Civil Rights Law § 79–b). What happens in that situation under UPC § 2–803? What result in New York if the victim and slayer own property as tenants by the entirety?

F.　Protecting the Surviving Spouse: The Elective Share

The discussion of the revocation on marriage statutes noted that most states do not so provide. Are these state's unconcerned with the fate of a surviving spouse—the fact that he or she could be omitted in a will of a deceased spouse? The simple answer is no. With the exception of Georgia, all states have marital property regimes that either prevent disinheritance of a surviving spouse or operate under a community property system.[2]　Common law martial property states treat property owned by spouses like any other property: it belongs to the person who has title. Absent some sort of statutory constraint, a spouse could write a will leaving all of his or her probate estate to someone other than the surviving spouse. That is not the case in community property states where spousal earnings are allocated upon receipt one—half to each spouse. By so doing, there is no need for a post-mortem reconciliation.

A page of history . . .

Community property is the law of eight states: California, Nevada, Washington, Idaho, New Mexico, Arizona, Texas and Louisiana.[3]　These states adopted the regime because their private law was influenced by Spanish and French law, itself influenced by Roman law and Germanic customary law. The practice in the variety of jurisdictions that followed it, past and present, is not entirely uniform. However, it generally regarded that property acquired prior to marriage remained owned by the spouse who held it prior thereto, and gifts and inheritances received during marriage were owned by the spouse to whom they were transferred. However, property earned during marriage was divided into equal shares, held by each spouse individually. Thus the **community** in community property was one of acquests during marriage. While the husband normally retained management powers over acquests, he owned only his half. At the death of each spouse, his or her share could be transferred free of any claim of the other.

In the thirteenth century, England took its separate path creating a 'separate marital property' regime. In common with community property regimes, spouses owned both property brought into the marriage and property inherited during marriage. But they also owned property earned during marriage. There was no community of acquests. Instead, the first partner to die received dower or curtesy in land (and in some areas of England a share of personal property). It should be noted that the principle of coverture obtained during marriage: English law regarded the property of the wife to be controlled

---

2　　The term "marital property" is not necessarily a legal term of art. For example, it has no meaning in New York when used in the context of succession to a deceased spouse's property. Each spouse has his or her own probate estate. As we'll see very shortly, the elective share law is designed to modify that situation. The only meaning of "marital property" in New York is property subject to equitable distribution on divorce.

3　　In addition, Wisconsin has adopted the Uniform Marital Property Act which creates a community property regime for what the statute refers to as "marital property."

by her husband regardless of provenance. Moreover, married women could write wills only with the consent of their husbands. Spinsterhood and widowhood were golden years for women and their property: prior to their union, and after it was terminated by the death of their husbands, women had full control of their property.

The Restatement Third, Property (Wills and Other Donative Transfers), § 9.1, comment *c* explains the situation thusly:

> At early common law, the decedent's surviving spouse was a distributee of personal property under the English Statute of Distribution, but was not an heir to land under the common-law cannons of descent. The widow, instead, was entitled to dower and the widower, if the marriage produced issue, was entitled to curtesy.

Dower gave a surviving widow a life estate in one-third of the inheritable freehold land that her husband held during the marriage. Curtesy gave a surviving widower a life estate in all of the inheritable freehold land that his wife held at any time during overture. The estate in curtesy arose upon birth of issue.

Dower and curtesy have largely been abolished in the United States and replaced by a statutory elective share that accrues to the surviving spouse upon the deceased spouse's death.

1. The Community Property Regime

Under a community property regime, property that the spouses earn and property purchased with that property forms the marital community which on termination of the marriage, by death or divorce, is immediately allocated one-half to each spouse, *no matter how the property is titled*. When a spouse dies, therefore, their one-half the community property already is owned by the surviving spouse. The other half is part of the decedent's probate assets, which passes in intestacy or by the decedent's will.

Property that the spouses bring into the marriage or receive by gift or inheritance during the marriage is separate property (unless it is "transmuted" into community property) and passes at death along with the decedent's half of the community property. The community property states differ on whether the earnings on separate property during the marriage are community (e.g., California) or separate (e.g., Texas).

The details of community property can be quite complex and its interaction with the tax system raises other problems as well. Even this briefest of descriptions, however, should help you understand why community property is widely regarded as a model for dealing with the property relations between spouses. First, community property gives effect to the concept of marriage as an equal economic partnership. It is the marital community that earns income during the marriage regardless of which spouse actually receives compensation. If one spouse never works outside the home for compensation, that spouse still is entitled to half of what the other spouse earns because the spouses are considered a single interrelated economic unit: maintaining the household full-time allows the other spouse to work full-time outside of the home. Second, the longer the marriage lasts, the larger the amount of community property likely to be earned. A marriage of a few years will have only a small community to divide as compared to a marriage lasting decades. The longer the economic partnership, the bigger the partnership "pot" to divide when the partnership ends.

2. Separate Marital Property Regimes

As the Restatement Third, Property (Wills and Other Donative Transfers), § 9.1, comment *c* states, dower and curtesy were abolished in most separate property states in favor of what is now called the elective share. Why? Dower and curtesy applied only to land and were imagined in a society in which an overwhelming proportion of wealth was held in the form of real property. One would not receive dower in 100 shares of Google! Moreover, dower required surveying skills; measuring a third of the land was not always straightforward. And it applied to land that husband was at any time seized; a widow could claim dower in land sold by her husband unless she joined in the sale. Awkward to say the least: need we go on?

Thus the statutory elective share is far more rational in modern society than is dower and curtesy. However, some of the difficulties that have appeared over time are evident when the elective share is compared to community property. Until the relatively recent revision of the UPC elective share, all statutes gave the surviving spouse some fixed share of the deceased spouse's property irrespective of the length of the marriage. A survivor of a partnership of fifty years was entitled to the same portion of the deceased spouse's property as the survivor of a one-year marriage. Second, most early elective share statutes gave the surviving spouse a fixed percentage of the deceased spouse's "estate." That limited the survivor to a portion of the deceased's probate assets. Once again, property law governed: if property was "orphaned" at the spouse's death, it was a probate asset and therefore was included in the calculation of the elective share of the surviving spouse. With the proliferation of forms of non-probate property (a topic addressed in subsequent chapters, but see Ward's Asset profile and our discussion of it in Chapter 2), however, the protection offered the surviving spouse by an elective share limited to the probate estate diminished. As we shall see in the following case, perhaps down to near zero by conscious efforts on the part of a spouse to drain his or her probate estate.

This strategy, to deprive the surviving spouse of the statutory protection mandated by the elective share, has been addressed in different ways by courts and then by legislatures. Initially, some courts found ways to expand the pool of property subject to the elective share beyond the probate estate by scrutinizing the property arrangements created by the deceased spouse. In 1937, seven years after the abolition of dower and curtesy in New York and the adoption of a statutory elective share, the New York Court of Appeals held that a revocable life time trust was includible in the "estate" to which the elective share applied because the degree of control retained by the spouse who created the trust made the trust "illusory." (*Newman v. Dore*, 9 N.E.2d 966 (N.Y. 1937)) Other courts in other states held that trusts and other transfers by a spouse could be included in the deceased probate assets for purposes of calculating the elective share if the transfers were made with the intent to defraud the surviving spouse of his or her elective share rights. Maryland, for example, uses the intent to defraud test and application of which had led to a great deal of litigation, most recently, *Karensky v. Schoukroun*, 959 A.2d 1147 (Md. 2008).

In a truly exhaustive opinion, the Maryland high court concluded that the following factors must be considered in deciding whether or not to invalidate an inter vivos transfer and subject the property involved to the surviving spouse's elective share:

- As a threshold matter, the decedent must retain an interest in or continue to enjoy the property.

- Equitable powers should not be used to second-guess "reasonable and legitimate estate planning arrangements."

Once the court is satisfied it is not undoing legitimate estate planning, the court must consider the extent of control retained by the decedent, the decedent's motives, the transferee's motives, the degree to which the transfer deprives the spouse of property he or she would otherwise take, whether the decedent actually exercised the retained control or to what the extent the decedent actually enjoyed the property, and the family relationship between the decedent and the person or persons benefiting from the *inter vivos* transfer.

As you can see, neither of these two approaches to expanding the pool of property to which elective share rights attach is particularly easy to apply. What evidence might there be of the motives of a spouse who removed property from his probate estate? What made a transfer *illusory*? Was a transfer *illusory* only when the form of transfer altered ownership but did not affect control? Would probate court have to unpackage each complex transfer to make their judgment? Were the two tests discrete? Why would a spouse make an *illusory* transfer if he did not *intend* to deprive his spouse of her elective share?

One way of avoiding the both fruitless search for subjective intent of nasty spouses and the manipulation of ownership rights by crafty lawyers is to adopt the approach of the following case, which simply construes the word "estate" in elective share statutes.

Sullivan v. Burkin

460 N.E.2d 572 (Mass. 1984)

Before HENNESSEY, C.J., and WILKINS, ABRAMS, NOLAN and O'CONNOR, JJ.

WILKINS, JUSTICE.

Mary A. Sullivan, the widow of Ernest G. Sullivan, has exercised her right, under G.L. c. 191, § 15, to take a share of her husband's estate. By this action, she seeks a determination that assets held in an inter vivos trust created by her husband during the marriage should be considered as part of the estate in determining that share. A judge of the Probate Court for the county of Suffolk rejected the widow's claim and entered judgment dismissing the complaint. The widow appealed, and, on July 12, 1983, a panel of the Appeals Court reported the case to this court.

In September, 1973, Ernest G. Sullivan executed a deed of trust under which he transferred real estate to himself as sole trustee. The net income of the trust was payable to him during his life and the trustee was instructed to pay to him all or such part of the principal of the trust estate as he might request in writing from time to time. He retained the right to revoke the trust at any time. On his death, the successor trustee is directed to pay the principal and any undistributed income equally to the defendants, George F. Cronin, Sr., and Harold J. Cronin, if they should survive him, which they did. There were no witnesses to the execution of the deed of trust, but the husband acknowledged his signatures before a notary public, separately, as donor and as trustee.

> **Food for Thought**
>
> Illusory transfer? Intent to defraud Mrs. Sullivan out her of her elective share? Which side, counsel, would you prefer to argue?

The husband died on April 27, 1981, while still trustee of the inter vivos trust. He left a will in which he stated that he "intentionally neglected to make any provision for my wife, Mary A. Sullivan and my grandson, Mark Sullivan." He directed that, after the payment of debts, expenses, and all estate taxes levied by reason of his death, the residue of his estate should be paid over to the trustee of the inter vivos trust. The defendants George F. Cronin, Sr., and Harold J. Cronin were named co-executors of the will. The defendant Burkin is successor trustee of the inter vivos trust. On October 21, 1981, the wife filed a claim, pursuant to G.L. c. 191, § 15, for a portion of the estate.[3]

Although it does not appear in the record, the parties state in their briefs that Ernest G. Sullivan and Mary A. Sullivan had been separated for many years. We do know that in 1962 the wife obtained a court order providing for her temporary support. No final action was taken in that proceeding. The record provides no information about the value of any property owned by the husband at his death or about the value of any assets held in the inter vivos trust. At oral argument, we were advised that the husband owned personal property worth approximately $15,000 at his death and that the only asset in the trust was a house in Boston which was sold after the husband's death for approximately $85,000.

---

3   As relevant to this case, G.L. c. 191, § 15, as appearing in St.1964, c. 288, § 1, provides:
    "The surviving husband or wife of a deceased person . . . within six months after the probate of the will of such deceased, may file in the registry of probate a writing signed by him or by her . . . claiming such portion of the estate of the deceased as he or she is given the right to claim under this section, and if the deceased left issue, he or she shall thereupon take one third of the personal and one third of the real property; . . . except that . . . if he or she would thus take real and personal property to an amount exceeding twenty-five thousand dollars in value, he or she shall receive, in addition to that amount, only

As presented in the complaint, and perhaps as presented to the motion judge, the wife's claim was simply that the inter vivos trust was an invalid testamentary disposition and that the trust assets "constitute assets of the estate" of Ernest G. Sullivan. There is no suggestion that the wife argued initially that, even if the trust were not testamentary, she had a special claim as a widow asserting her rights under G.L. c. 191, § 15. If the wife is correct that the trust was an ineffective testamentary disposition, the trust assets would be part of the husband's probate estate. In that event, we would not have to consider any special consequences of the wife's election under G.L. c. 191, § 15, or, in the words of the Appeals Court, "the present vitality" of *Kerwin v. Donaghy*, 317 Mass. 559, 572, 59 N.E.2d 299 (1945).

We conclude, however, that the trust was not testamentary in character and that the husband effectively created a valid inter vivos trust. Thus, whether the issue was initially involved in this case, we are now presented with the question (which the executors will have to resolve ultimately, in any event) whether the assets of the inter vivos trust are to be considered in determining

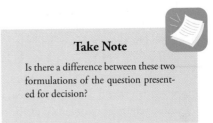

Take Note

Is there a difference between these two formulations of the question presented for decision?

the "portion of the estate of the deceased" (G.L. c. 191, § 15) in which Mary A. Sullivan has rights. We conclude that, in this case, we should adhere to the principles expressed in *Kerwin v. Donaghy, supra*, that deny the surviving spouse any claim against the assets of a valid inter vivos trust created by the deceased spouse, even where the deceased spouse alone retained substantial rights and powers under the trust instrument. For the future, however, as to any inter vivos trust created or amended after the date of this opinion, we announce that the estate of a decedent, for the purposes of G.L. c. 191, § 15, shall include the value of assets held in an inter vivos trust created by the deceased spouse as to which the deceased spouse alone retained the power during his or her life to direct the disposition of those trust assets for his or her benefit, as, for example, by the exercise of a power of appointment or by revocation of the trust. Such a power would be a general power of appointment for Federal estate tax purposes (I.R.C. § 2041(b)(1) [1983]) and a "general power" as defined in the Restatement (Second) of Property § 11.4(1) (Tent. Draft No. 5, 1982).

We consider first whether the inter vivos trust was invalid because it was testamentary. A trust with remainder interests given to others on the settlor's death is not invalid as a testamentary disposition simply because the settlor retained a broad power to modify or revoke the trust,

---

the income during his or her life of the excess of his or her share of such estate above that amount, the personal property to be held in trust and the real property vested in him or her for life, from the death of the deceased. . . . If the real and personal property of the deceased which the surviving husband or wife takes under the foregoing provisions exceeds twenty-five thousand dollars in value, and the surviving husband or wife is to take only twenty-five thousand dollars absolutely, the twenty-five thousand dollars, above given absolutely, shall be paid out of that part of the personal property in which the husband or wife is interested; and if such part is insufficient the deficiency shall, upon the petition of any person interested, be paid from the sale or mortgage in fee, in the manner provided for the payment of debts or legacies, of that part of the real property in which he or she is interested."

the right to receive income, and the right to invade principal during his life. *Ascher v. Cohen*, 333 Mass. 397, 400, 131 N.E.2d 198 (1956); *Leahy v. Old Colony Trust Co.*, 326 Mass. 49, 51, 93 N.E.2d 238 (1950); *Kerwin v. Donaghy*, 317 Mass. 559, 567, 59 N.E.2d 299 (1945); *National Shawmut Bank v. Joy*, 315 Mass. 457, 473–475, 53 N.E.2d 113 (1944); *Kelley v. Snow*, 185 Mass. 288, 298–299, 70 N.E. 89 (1904). The fact that the settlor of such a trust is the sole trustee does not make the trust testamentary. In *National Shawmut Bank v. Joy, supra* 315 Mass. at 476–477, 53 N.E.2d 113, we held that a settlor's reservation of the power to control investments did not impair the validity of a trust and noted that "[i]n *Greeley v. Flynn*, 310 Mass. 23, 36 N.E.2d 394 [1941], the settlor was herself the trustee and had every power of control, including the right to withdraw principal for her own use. Yet the gift over at her death was held valid and not testamentary." We did, however, leave open the question whether such a trust would be testamentary "had the trustees been reduced to passive impotence, or something near it." *Id.* 315 Mass. at 476, 53 N.E.2d 113. We have held an inter vivos trust valid where a settlor, having broad powers to revoke the trust and to demand trust principal, was a cotrustee with a friend (*Ascher v. Cohen, supra* 333 Mass. at 400, 131 N.E.2d 198) or with a bank whose tenure as trustee was at the whim of the settlor (*Leahy v. Old Colony Trust Co., supra* 326 Mass. at 51, 93 N.E.2d 238). In *Theodore v. Theodore*, 356 Mass. 297, 249 N.E.2d 3 (1969), the settlor was the sole trustee of two trusts and had the power to revoke the trusts and to withdraw principal. The court assumed that the trusts were not testamentary simply because of this arrangement. The *Theodore* case involved trust assets transferred to the trust only by third persons. For the purposes of determining whether a trust is testamentary, however, the origin of the assets, totally at the disposal of the settlor once received, should make no difference. *See Gordon v. Feldman*, 359 Mass. 25, 267 N.E.2d 895 (1971), in which the court and the parties implicitly accepted as valid an inter vivos trust in which A conveyed to himself as sole trustee with the power in A to withdraw income and principal. We believe that the law of the Commonwealth is correctly represented by the statement in Restatement (Second) of Trusts § 57, comment *h* (1959), that a trust is "not testamentary and invalid for failure to comply with the requirements of the Statute of Wills merely because the settlor-trustee reserves a beneficial life interest and power to revoke and modify the trust. The fact that as trustee he controls the administration of the trust does not invalidate it."

Make the Connection

Are you convinced that the judiciary is the property forum for making this determination? *Kerwin* was decided many years ago. If the legislature was troubled by its implication for the elective share, didn't it have ample opportunity to correct the problem?

We come then to the question whether, even if the trust was not testamentary on general principles, the widow has special interests which should be recognized. Courts in this country have differed considerably in their reasoning and in their conclusions in passing on this question. See 1 A. Scott, Trusts § 57.5 at 509–511 (3d ed. 1967 & 1983 Supp.); Restatement (Second) of Property-Donative Transfers, Supplement to Tent. Draft No. 5, reporter's note to § 13.7 (1982); Annot., 39 A.L.R.3d 14 (1971), Validity of Inter Vivos Trust Established by One Spouse Which Impairs the Other Spouse's Distributive Share or Other Statutory Rights in Property. In considering this issue at the May, 1982, annual meeting of the American Law Institute the members divided almost evenly on whether a settlor's surviving spouse should have rights, apart from specific statutory rights, with respect to the assets of an inter vivos trust over which the settlor retained a general power of appointment. See Proceedings of the American Law Institute, May, 1982, pp. 59–117; Restatement (Second) of Property-Donative Transfers, Supplement to Tent. Draft No. 5 at 28 (1982).

The rule of *Kerwin v. Donaghy, supra* 317 Mass. at 571, 59 N.E.2d 299, is that "[t]he right of a wife to waive her husband's will, and take, with certain limitations, 'the same portion of the property of the deceased, real and personal, that . . . she would have taken if the deceased had died intestate' (G.L. [Ter.Ed.] c. 191, § 15), does not extend to personal property that has been conveyed by the husband in his lifetime and does not form part of his estate at his death. *Fiske v. Fiske*, 173 Mass. 413, 419, 53 N.E. 916 [1899]. *Shelton v. Sears*, 187 Mass. 455, 73 N.E. 666 [1905]. In this Commonwealth a husband has an absolute right to dispose of any or all of his personal property in his lifetime, without the knowledge or consent of his wife, with the result that it will not form part of his estate for her to share under the statute of distributions (G.L. [Ter. Ed.] c. 190, §§ 1, 2), under his will, or by virtue of a waiver of his will. That is true even though his sole purpose was to disinherit her." In the *Kerwin* case, we applied the rule to deny a surviving spouse the right to reach assets the deceased spouse had placed in an inter vivos trust of which the settlor's daughter by a previous marriage was trustee and over whose assets he had a general power of appointment. The rule of *Kerwin v. Donaghy* has been adhered to in this Commonwealth for almost forty years and was adumbrated even earlier.[5] The bar has been entitled reasonably to rely on that rule in advising clients. In the area of property law, the retroactive invalidation of an established principle is to be undertaken with great caution. *See Boston Safe Deposit & Trust Co. v. Fleming*, 361 Mass. 172, 181–182, 279 N.E.2d 342, appeal dismissed, 409 U.S. 813, 93 S.Ct. 46, 34 L.Ed.2d 69 (1972); *Fiduciary Trust Co. v. Mishou*,

> **Food for Thought**
>
> Why is such a trust, completely under the control of its creator, a valid way to pass property at the death of the creator-trustee? The trust instrument written before death certainly seems to do what a will does. Or does it?

---

5   In early opinions, this court considered an intent to deny inheritance rights to be a ground for invalidating an inter vivos transfer, but in the first part of this century it abandoned that position. Compare Gilson v. Hutchinson, 120 Mass. 27, 28 (1876) (conveyance to a trustee to defraud spouse of her right to dower, invalid), and Brownell v. Briggs, 173 Mass. 529, 533, 54 N.E. 251 (1899) (conveyance to trustee to deprive wife of rights in the husband's property at his death, invalid) with Leonard v. Leonard, 181 Mass. 458, 462, 63 N.E. 1068 (1902) (Holmes, C.J.) (intent to defeat wife's claim not sufficient to invalidate an otherwise valid transaction), Kelley v. Snow, 185 Mass. 288, 299, 70 N.E. 89 (1904) (same), Seaman v. Harmon, 192 Mass. 5, 7, 78 N.E. 301 (1906) (surviving wife had no right to dower in real estate purchased by the husband through a straw to defeat the wife's claim), and Roche v. Brickley, 254 Mass. 584, 588, 150 N.E. 866 (1926) (wife's conveyance to a trustee valid even if she made it to defeat any interest of the husband at her death).

Opinions in this Commonwealth, and generally elsewhere, considering the rights of a surviving spouse to a share in assets transferred by the deceased spouse to an inter vivos trust have analyzed the question on grounds of public policy, as if establishing common law principles. These opinions have not relied in any degree on what the Legislature may have intended by granting a surviving spouse certain rights in the "estate" of a deceased spouse.

321 Mass. 615, 636, 75 N.E.2d 3 (1947). Cf. *Johnson Controls, Inc. v. Bowes*, 381 Mass. 278, 282–283, 409 N.E.2d 185 (1980) (insurance contracts); *Whitinsville Plaza, Inc. v. Kotseas*, 378 Mass. 85, 97–98, 390 N.E.2d 243 (1979) (covenants not to compete made in deeds and leases); *Rosenberg v. Lipnick*, 377 Mass. 666, 667, 389 N.E.2d 385 (1979) (antenuptial agreements); *Tucker v. Badoian*, 376 Mass. 907, 918–919, 384 N.E.2d 1195 (1978) (Kaplan, J., concurring) (relative rights as to the flow of surface water). Contrast as to tort law, *Payton v. Abbott Labs*, 386 Mass. 540, 565–570, 437 N.E.2d 171 (1982). We conclude that, whether or not Ernest G. Sullivan established the inter vivos trust in order to defeat his wife's right to take her statutory share in the assets placed in the trust and even though he had a general power of appointment over the trust assets, Mary A. Sullivan obtained no right to share in the assets of that trust when she made her election under G.L. c. 191, § 15.

We announce for the future that, as to any inter vivos trust created or amended after the date of this opinion, we shall no longer follow the rule announced in *Kerwin v. Donaghy*. There have been significant changes since 1945 in public policy considerations bearing on the right of one spouse to treat his or her property as he or she wishes during marriage. The interests of one spouse in the property of the other have been substantially increased upon the dissolution of a marriage by divorce. We believe that, when a marriage is terminated by the death of one spouse, the rights of the surviving spouse should not be so restricted as they are by the rule in *Kerwin v. Donaghy*. It is neither equitable nor logical to extend to a divorced spouse greater rights in the assets of an inter vivos trust created and controlled by the other spouse than are extended to a spouse who remains married until the death of his or her spouse.

Food for Thought

Why does Mr. Sullivan get a pass? Under what circumstances in the law of wills and trusts should courts avoid retrospective application of revised principles of common law? Is the court interpreting a statute or adopting an amendment to an existing one? Even if Mr. Sullivan relied on existing law, should reliance trump other values?

The rule we now favor would treat as part of "the estate of the deceased" for the purposes of G.L. c. 191, § 15, assets of an inter vivos trust created during the marriage by the deceased spouse over which he or she alone had a general power of appointment, exercisable by deed or by will. This objective test would involve no consideration of the motive or intention of the spouse in creating the trust. We would not need to engage in a determination of "whether the [spouse] has in good faith divested himself [or herself] of ownership of his [or her] property or has made an illusory "transfer" (*Newman v. Dore*, 275 N.Y. 371, 379, 9 N.E.2d 966 [1937]) or with the factual question whether the spouse "intended to surrender complete dominion over the property" (*Staples v. King*, 433 A.2d 407, 411 [Me.1981]). Nor would we have to participate in the rather unsatisfactory process of determining whether the inter vivos trust was, on some standard, "colorable," "fraudulent," or "illusory."

What we have announced as a rule for the future hardly resolves all the problems that may arise. There may be a different rule if some or all of the trust assets were conveyed to such a trust by a third person. Cf. *Theodore v. Theodore*, 356 Mass. 297, 249 N.E.2d 3 (1969). We have not, of course, dealt with a case in which the power of appointment is held jointly with another person. If the surviving spouse assented to the creation of the inter vivos trust, perhaps the rule we announce would not apply. We have not discussed which assets should be used to satisfy a surviving spouse's claim. We have not discussed the question whether a surviving spouse's interest in the intestate estate of a deceased spouse should reflect the value of assets held in an inter vivos trust created by the intestate spouse over which he or she had a general power of appointment. That situation and the one before us, however, do not seem readily distinguishable. See *Schnakenberg v. Schnakenberg*, 262 A.D. 234, 236–237, 28 N.Y.S.2d 841 (N.Y.1941). A general power of appointment over assets in a trust created by a third person is said to present a different situation. Restatement (Second) of Property—Donative Transfers, Supplement to Tent. Draft No. 5, reporter's note to § 13.7 at 29 (1982). Nor have we dealt with other assets not passing by will, such as a trust created before the marriage or insurance policies over which a deceased spouse had control. *Id.* at 30, 38.

The question of the rights of a surviving spouse in the estate of a deceased spouse, using the word "estate" in its broad sense, is one that can best be handled by legislation. See Uniform Probate Code, §§ 2–201, 2–202, 8 U.L.A. 74–75 (1983). See also Uniform Marital Property Act, § 18 (Nat'l Conference of Comm'rs on Uniform State Laws, July, 1983), which adopts the concept of community property as to "marital property." But, until it is, the answers to these problems will "be determined in the usual way through the decisional process." *Tucker v. Badoian*, 376 Mass. 907, 918–919, 384 N.E.2d 1195 (1978) (Kaplan, J., concurring).

We affirm the judgment of the Probate Court dismissing the plaintiff's complaint.

Points for Discussion

1. What does Sullivan mean?

What is the holding of *Sullivan*? Even more importantly, what is the rationale?

To answer those questions we need to ask some preliminary questions. First, the surviving spouse's lawyers offer two reasons why the property in the trust (and remember, that means the property to which the trustee holds legal title) should be subject to her right of election under the Massachusetts statute. The court disposes of the first by upholding the proposition that a person can create a trust while alive, put his or her own property into the trust, be the sole trustee, retain an unlimited power to revoke the trust, and be assured that the property in the trust at death is non-probate property. Such a trust is not an attempt to make a gift at death in a document other than a will and therefore it is not an "invalid testamentary (will) substitute." We will study this law in more detail.

The second arrow in counsel's quiver is the degree of control the deceased spouse has over the trust property. The court analyzes that control by talking about a *"general power of appointment."* We will study powers of appointment in more detail as well, but for now what you need to understand is that a power of appointment is the legal right to direct the holder of legal title to property, usually a trustee, to distribute that property in accordance with the directions of an individual. If the person who has that power to so mandate (the *"donee"* of the power) can tell the person with legal title to give the property to the donee him or herself, then the power is general. Here, Mr. Sullivan can revoke the trust simply by the telling the trustee (who happens to be Mr. Sullivan but if it were not the analysis would not change) to transfer legal title to the property in the trust to Mr. Sullivan in his own right. *What stands between Mr. Sullivan and outright ownership (legal title) of the trust property is simply to ask the trustee to terminate the trust and hand over the property to him.* Perhaps this explains why the court reaches the conclusion it does?

2. *What* Sullivan *leaves unanswered*

And now that you understand the holding and rationale of *Sullivan*, think about the list of property-holding devices that create non-probate property (insurance policies and the now ubiquitous variety of payment on death accounts) the court says it is not addressing. When the Massachusetts Supreme Judicial Court did address one of those situations—the deceased spouse had a general power of appointment over a trust created by the deceased spouse's parent with the parent's property—the Court refused to extend the holding of *Sullivan*. (Bongaards v. Miller, 440 Mass. 10, 793 N.E.2d 335 (2003)). Was that decision consistent with the logic of *Sullivan*? Would you have voted to include the property in the deceased spouse's probate estate for the purposes of calculating the elective share?

3. *Change, statutes, and courts*

Public policy is not immutable. Note that prior to *Kerwin v. Donaghy*, the court was more protective of surviving spouses. What does the ebb and flow of protection for the surviving spouse signify about societal norms? Is the *Sullivan* decision about law or policy? The *Sullivan* court seems cognizant of its role; is the decision the court renders going forward a proper one for the courts or the legislature?

In order to deal with "change" the court must address the thorny issue of judicial construction of statutes based on intent of the legislature. It is a subtle point but extremely important one because it explicates in a sentence one of the great fundamental principles of our legal system. Legislatures make law; courts have the power and duty to apply that law to cases that come before them often by reference to the court's understanding of legislative intent. That said, courts do make law by resolving cases that come before them, and have been known to strain interpretation of statutes by reference to public policy—one definition thereof is what the judge or judges want done or believe society should or would want done. (Consider when reading Surrogate Roth's opinion in *Matter of Martin B.*, Chapter 7.)

The legitimacy of this sort of judicial law making has always been a matter of debate. Sometimes, however, the legislature establishes a comprehensive solution. In some states, including New York, that is exactly what happened. The New York legislature enacted into law a provision by which the elective share applied to the probate estate and to a long list of "testamentary substitutes," transfers by the deceased spouse which had the effect of immediately changing title but postponing the donee's actual enjoyment until the death of the transferor spouse.

Read the following statute. Are you clear about which transfers are called back into the probate estate for the calculation of the elective share?

New York Estates, Powers, and Trusts Law § 5–1.1–A. Right of Election by Surviving Spouse

(a) (1) For purposes of this section, the decedent's estate includes the capital value, as of the decedent's death, of any property described in subparagraph (b)(1)

. . . .

(b) (1) Where a person dies after August thirty-first, nineteen hundred ninety-two and is survived by a spouse who exercises a right of election under paragraph (a), the transactions affected by and property interests of the decedent described in clauses (A) through (H), whether benefiting the surviving spouse or any other person, shall be treated as testamentary substitutes and the capital value thereof, as of the decedent's death, shall be included in the net estate subject to the surviving spouse's elective right except to the extent that the surviving spouse has executed a waiver of release pursuant to paragraph (e) with respect thereto. Notwithstanding the foregoing, a transaction, other than a transaction described in clause (G), that is irrevocable or is revocable only with the consent of a person having a substantial adverse interest (including any such transactions with respect to which the decedent retained a special power of appointment as defined in 10–3.2), will constitute a testamentary substitute only if it is effected after the date of the marriage.

    (A) Gifts causa mortis.

    (B) The aggregate transfers of property (including the transfer, release or relinquishment of any property interest which, but for such transfer, release or relinquishment, would come within the scope of clause (F)), other than gifts causa mortis and transfers coming within the scope of clauses (G) and (H), to or for the benefit of any person, made after August thirty-first, nineteen hundred ninety-two and within one year of the death of the decedent, to the extent that the decedent did not receive adequate and full consideration in money or money's worth for such transfers; provided, however, that any portion of any such transfer that was excludible from taxable gifts pursuant to subsections (b) and (e) of section two thousand five hundred three of the United States Internal Revenue Code, including any amounts excluded as a result of the election by the surviving spouse to treat any such transfer as having been made one half by him or her, shall not be treated as a testamentary substitute.

(C) Money deposited, together with all dividends or interest credited thereon, in a savings account in the name of the decedent in trust for another person, with a banking organization, savings and loan association, foreign banking corporation or organization or bank or savings and loan association organized under the laws of the United States, and remaining on deposit at the date of the decedent's death.

(D) Money deposited after August thirty-first, nineteen hundred sixty-six, together with all dividends or interest credited thereon, in the name of the decedent and another person and payable on death, pursuant to the terms of the deposit or by operation of law, to the survivor, with a banking organization, savings and loan association, foreign banking corporation or organization or bank or savings and loan association organized under the laws of the United States, and remaining on deposit at the date of the decedent's death.

(E) Any disposition of property made by the decedent whereby property, at the date of his or her death, is held (i) by the decedent and another person as joint tenants with a right of survivorship or as tenants by the entirety where the disposition was made after August thirty-first, nineteen hundred sixty-six, or (ii) by the decedent and is payable on his or her death to a person other than the decedent or his or her estate.

(F) Any disposition of property or contractual arrangement made by the decedent, in trust or otherwise, to the extent that the decedent (i) after August thirty-first, nineteen hundred ninety-two, retained for his or her life or for any period not ascertainable without reference to his or her death or for any period which does not in fact end before his or her death the possession or enjoyment of, or the right to income from, the property except to the extent that such disposition or contractual arrangement was for an adequate consideration in money or money's worth; or (ii) at the date of his or her death retained either alone or in conjunction with any other person who does not have a substantial adverse interest, by the express provisions of the disposing instrument, a power to revoke such disposition or a power to consume, invade or dispose of the principal thereof. The provisions of this subparagraph shall not affect the right of any income beneficiary to the income undistributed or accrued at the date of death nor shall they impair or defeat any right which has vested on or before August thirty-first, nineteen hundred ninety-two.

(G) Any money, securities or other property payable under a thrift, savings, retirement, pension, deferred compensation, death benefit, stock bonus or profit-sharing plan, account, arrangement, system or trust, except that with respect to a plan to which subsection (a)(11) of section four hundred one of the United States Internal Revenue Code applies or a defined contribution plan to which such subsection does not apply pursuant to paragraph (B)(iii) thereof, only to the extent of fifty percent of the capital value thereof. Notwithstanding the foregoing, a transaction described herein shall not constitute a testamentary substitute if the decedent designated the beneficiary or beneficiaries of the plan benefits on or before September first, nineteen hundred ninety-two and did not change such beneficiary designation thereafter.

(H) Any interest in property to the extent the passing of the principal thereof to or for the benefit of any person was subject to a presently exercisable general power of appointment, as defined in section two thousand forty-one of the United States Internal Revenue Code, held by the decedent immediately before his or her death or which the decedent, within one year of his or her death, released (except to the extent such release results from a lapse of the power which is not treated as a release pursuant to section two thousand forty-one of the United States Internal Revenue Code) or exercised in favor of any person other than himself or herself or his or her estate.

(I) A transfer of a security to a beneficiary pursuant to part 4 of article 13 of this chapter.[4]

(2) Transactions described in clause (D) or (E) (i) shall be treated as testamentary substitutes in the proportion that the funds on deposit were the property of the decedent immediately before the deposit or the consideration for the property described in clause (E) (i) was furnished by the decedent. The surviving spouse shall have the burden of establishing the proportion of the decedent's contribution; provided, however, that where the surviving spouse is the other party to the transaction, it will be conclusively presumed that the proportion of the decedent's contribution is one-half. For the purpose of this subparagraph, the court may accept such evidence as is relevant and competent, whether or not the person offering such evidence would otherwise be competent to testify.

The drafters of the UPC created a similar list, and the resulting combination of the probate estate and the lifetime transfers is referred to as the "augmented estate," a calculation akin to New York's net estate. Like the New York scheme, the UPC elective share begins with the deceased spouse's probate estate (UPC § 2–204) and includes the decedent's "nonprobate transfers to others" which correspond to the New York statute's "testamentary substitutes." The most prominent difference is that the augmented estate includes the death benefit from life insurance policies on the deceased spouse's life:

---

4   The transfer on death security registration provisions.

UPC § 2–205. Decedent's Nonprobate Transfers to Others

The value of the augmented estate includes the value of the decedent's nonprobate transfers to others, not included under Section 2–204, of any of the following types, in the amount provided respectively for each type of transfer:

(1) Property owned or owned in substance by the decedent immediately before death that passed outside probate at the decedent's death. Property included under this category consists of:

   (i) Property over which the decedent alone, immediately before death, held a presently exercisable general power of appointment. The amount included is the value of the property subject to the power, to the extent the property passed at the decedent's death, by exercise, release, lapse, in default, or otherwise, to or for the benefit of any person other than the decedent's estate or surviving spouse.

   (ii) The decedent's fractional interest in property held by the decedent in joint tenancy with the right of survivorship. The amount included is the value of the decedent's fractional interest, to the extent the fractional interest passed by right of survivorship at the decedent's death to a surviving joint tenant other than the decedent's surviving spouse.

   (iii) The decedent's ownership interest in property or accounts held in POD, TOD, or co-ownership registration with the right of survivorship. The amount included is the value of the decedent's ownership interest, to the extent the decedent's ownership interest passed at the decedent's death to or for the benefit of any person other than the decedent's estate or surviving spouse.

   (iv) Proceeds of insurance, including accidental death benefits, on the life of the decedent, if the decedent owned the insurance policy immediately before death or if and to the extent the decedent alone and immediately before death held a presently exercisable general power of appointment over the policy or its proceeds. The amount included is the value of the proceeds, to the extent they were payable at the decedent's death to or for the benefit of any person other than the decedent's estate or surviving spouse.

(2) Property transferred in any of the following forms by the decedent during marriage:

   (i) Any irrevocable transfer in which the decedent retained the right to the possession or enjoyment of, or to the income from, the property if and to the extent the decedent's right terminated at or continued beyond the decedent's death. The amount included is the value of the fraction of the property to which the decedent's right related, to the extent the fraction of the property passed outside probate to or for the benefit of any person other than the decedent's estate or surviving spouse.

(ii) Any transfer in which the decedent created a power over income or property, exercisable by the decedent alone or in conjunction with any other person, or exercisable by a nonadverse party, to or for the benefit of the decedent, creditors of the decedent, the decedent's estate, or creditors of the decedent's estate. The amount included with respect to a power over property is the value of the property subject to the power, and the amount included with respect to a power over income is the value of the property that produces or produced the income, to the extent the power in either case was exercisable at the decedent's death to or for the benefit of any person other than the decedent's surviving spouse or to the extent the property passed at the decedent's death, by exercise, release, lapse, in default, or otherwise, to or for the benefit of any person other than the decedent's estate or surviving spouse. If the power is a power over both income and property and the preceding sentence produces different amounts, the amount included is the greater amount.

(3) Property that passed during marriage and during the two-year period next preceding the decedent's death as a result of a transfer by the decedent if the transfer was of any of the following types:

(i) Any property that passed as a result of the termination of a right or interest in, or power over, property that would have been included in the augmented estate under paragraph (1)(i), (ii), or (iii), or under paragraph (2), if the right, interest, or power had not terminated until the decedent's death. The amount included is the value of the property that would have been included under those paragraphs if the property were valued at the time the right, interest, or power terminated, and is included only to the extent the property passed upon termination to or for the benefit of any person other than the decedent or the decedent's estate, spouse, or surviving spouse. As used in this subparagraph, "termination," with respect to a right or interest in property, occurs when the right or interest terminated by the terms of the governing instrument or the decedent transferred or relinquished the right or interest, and, with respect to a power over property, occurs when the power terminated by exercise, release, lapse, default, or otherwise, but, with respect to a power described in paragraph (1)(i), "termination" occurs when the power terminated by exercise or release, but not otherwise.

(ii) Any transfer of or relating to an insurance policy on the life of the decedent if the proceeds would have been included in the augmented estate under paragraph (1)(iv) had the transfer not occurred. The amount included is the value of the insurance proceeds to the extent the proceeds were payable at the decedent's death to or for the benefit of any person other than the decedent's estate or surviving spouse.

(iii) any transfer of property, to the extent not otherwise included in the augmented estate, made to or for the benefit of a person other than the decedent's surviving spouse. The amount included is the value of the transferred property to the extent the aggregate transfers to any one donee in either of the two years exceeded $10,000.

The augmented estate also includes the decedent's transfers to the surviving spouse:

UPC § 2–206. Decedent's Nonprobate Transfers to the Surviving Spouse

Excluding property passing to the surviving spouse under the federal Social Security system, the value of the augmented estate includes the value of the decedent's nonprobate transfers to the decedent's surviving spouse, which consist of all property that passed outside probate at the decedent's death from the decedent to the surviving spouse by reason of the decedent's death, including:

(1) the decedent's fractional interest in property held as a joint tenant with the right of survivorship, to the extent that the decedent's fractional interest passed to the surviving spouse as surviving joint tenant,

(2) the decedent's ownership interest in property or accounts held in co-ownership registration with the right of survivorship, to the extent the decedent's ownership interest passed to the surviving spouse as surviving co-owner, and

(3) all other property that would have been included in the augmented estate under Section 2–205(1) or (2) had it passed to or for the benefit of a person other than the decedent's spouse, surviving spouse, the decedent, or the decedent's creditors, estate, or estate creditors.

Practice Planning Problem

Henry and Willa were married for 60 years. Though the marriage was childless, it seemed to be a happy one. Willa and Henry decided to leave their estates to others. Willa was particularly concerned with providing for her infirmed sister Gita; Henry, his nieces Beth and Andrea, daughters of his deceased brother Ralph. Indeed their individual wills direct their property to the stated relatives. Assume they have not agreed to waive their right to elect against their spouse's will, will the amount passing to their beneficiaries be caught by the elective share? Let us begin by observing their individual asset profiles:

Willa's assets include:

(1) house worth $600,000, owned in joint tenancy with Harry; each paid half of the purchase price;

(2) a bank account in her own name worth $300,000;

(3) a POD account to which she made all the deposits worth $100,000 (beneficiary her sister Gita);

(4) a life insurance policy worth $300,000 (beneficiary her sister Gita)

(5) a bank account held jointly with right of survivorship with her sister Gita worth $100,000; Willa has provided all of the funds that have gone into the account.

(6) a joint checking account with Harry which at her death was worth $40,000; Willa made 75% of the deposits into the account.

Harry's assets include:

(1) the house (mentioned in (1) above);

(2) a joint checking account with Harry which at her death was worth $40,000; Willa made 75% of the deposits into the account.

(3) a bank account in his own name worth $20,000;

(4) a bond in his own name that Willa gave him (while she was living) worth $30,000;

(5) a stock portfolio in his own name worth $500,000

(6) unimproved real estate in his own name worth $300,000 which he inherited from his father.

Calculating the elective share is a three-step process:

1. Which items of property are probate assets?

2. To that amount, add items of property that are testamentary substitutes in New York; or are part of the augmented estate under the UPC?

3. Now having established the net estate in New York and the augmented estate in the UPC, calculate the respective shares.

3. Running the Numbers: Calculating the Elective Share

The surviving spouse will not always receive an elective share. Assume that Willa and Henry's most valuable property is a house worth $600,000 held in joint tenancy with right of survivorship. Willa dies first with a will that leaves her entire probate estate to Gita. If Henry's elective share is defined simply as a share of W's probate estate, or even the probate estate plus certain transfers by W to others, H will be able to take a share of the probate estate even though he has already received property from W. We'll see how both the New York statute and the UPC handle this problem.

New York Estates, Powers, and Trusts Law § 5–1.1–A(a)

(2)   The elective share, as used in this paragraph, is the pecuniary amount equal to the greater of (i) fifty thousand dollars or, if the capital value of the net estate is less than fifty thousand dollars, such capital value, or (ii) one third of the net estate. In computing the net estate, debts, administration expenses and reasonable funeral expenses shall be deducted, but all estate taxes shall be disregarded, except that nothing contained herein relieves the surviving spouse from contributing to all such taxes the amounts apportioned against him or her under 2–1.8. . . .

(4)   The share of the testamentary provisions to which the surviving spouse is entitled hereunder (the "net elective share") is his or her elective share, as defined in subparagraphs (1) and (2), reduced by the capital value of any interest which passes absolutely from the decedent to such spouse, or which would have passed absolutely from the decedent to such spouse but was renounced by the spouse, (i) by intestacy, (ii) by testamentary substitute as described in subparagraph (b)(1), or (iii) by disposition under the decedent's last will.

. . . .

(B)   For the purposes of this subparagraph (4), (i) an interest in property shall be deemed to pass other than absolutely from the decedent to the spouse if the interest so passing consists of less than the decedent's entire interest in that property or consists of any interest in a trust or trust equivalent created by the decedent; and (ii) an interest in property shall be deemed to pass absolutely from the decedent to the spouse if it is not deemed to pass other than absolutely.

Thus in calculating the elective share of Henry under New York law, the elective share, 1/3 of the net estate calculated by adding probate assets and testamentary substitutes, is reduced by property passing to the surviving spouse from the deceased spouse: in Willa's case her $300,000 interest in the joint tenancy. Debts, administration expenses and reasonable funeral expenses shall be deducted, but all estate taxes are disregarded. Our calculations do not include these amounts.

Calculating Henry's elective share at Willa's death:

(1)   house worth $600,000, owned in joint tenancy with Harry; each paid half of the purchase price; 300,000

(2)   a bank account in her own name worth $300,000; 300,000

(3)   a POD account to which she made all the deposits worth $100,000 (beneficiary her sister Gita); 100,000

(4)   a life insurance policy worth $300,000 (beneficiary her sister Gita); 0

(5) a bank account held jointly with right of survivorship with her sister Gita worth $100,000; Willa has provided all of the funds that have gone into the account; 100,000

(6) a joint checking account with Harry which at her death was worth $40,000; Willa made 75% of the deposits into the account; 20,000

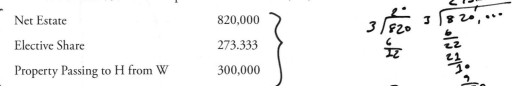

Net Estate   820,000

Elective Share   273.333

Property Passing to H from W   300,000

Because property passing to Henry exceeds his elective share, Henry receives no additional payment from the estate.

Can you run the numbers if Henry died first? Calculating Will's elective share at Henry's death:

(1) the house (mentioned in (1) above); 300,000

(2) a joint checking account with Harry which at her death was worth $40,000; Willa made 75% of the deposits into the account; 20,000

(3) a bond in his own name that Willa gave him (while she was living) worth $30,000; 30,000

(4) a stock portfolio in his own name worth $500,000; 500,000

(5) unimproved real estate in his own name worth $300,000 which he inherited from his father; 300,000

Net estate   1,150,000

Elective share   388,333

Property Passing to W from H   300,000

In this case Henry is entitled to an additional amount 88,333

Having struggled with New York law, let us now turn to the UPC. The UPC elective share, however, has two additional aspects. First, the percentage of the augmented estate that constitutes the elective share depends on the length of the marriage; and second, if the surviving spouse has more assets that the deceased spouse, the survivor will probably have no right to any additional property.

The first provision works through the interaction of UPC §§ 2–202(a) and 2–203(b). The first directs that the elective share amount equals 50% of the value of the "marital-property portion of the augmented estate." The second defines the marital-property portion of the augmented estate on a sliding scale:

UPC § 2–203(b)

If the decedent and the spouse were married to each other:	The percentage [of the augmented estate that is marital property] is:
Less than 1 year	3%
1 year but less than 2 years	6%
2 years but less than 3 years	12%
3 years but less than 4 years	18%
4 years but less than 5 years	24%
5 years but less than 6 years	30%
6 years but less than 7 years	36%
7 years but less than 8 years	42%
8 years but less than 9 years	48%
9 years but less than 10 years	54%
10 years but less than 11 years	60%
11 years but less than 12 years	68%
12 years but less than 13 years	76%
13 years but less than 14 years	84%
14 years but less than 15 years	92%
15 years or more	100%

UPC § 202(b) also provides a minimum elective share in the suggested amount of $75,000.

The second innovation is the result of the calculation of the amount to which the surviving spouse is entitled. UPC § 2–203(a) directs that the decedent's augmented estate (the probate estate plus the non-probate transfers to others and to the surviving spouse) and the surviving spouse's property and nonprobate transfers to others be combined and the percentage taken from the table reproduced above is applied to the combined amount. For example, assume that decedent and surviving spouse had been married for forty years so the percentage is 100%. The decedent's portion of the augmented estate is $300,000 and the surviving spouse's portion is augmented estate is $1,100,000. The total augmented estate is $1,400,000 and the survivor's elective share amount is $700,000 (50% of 100% of $1,400,000). But the survivor already has $1,100,000 of that value which is more than half of $1,400,000 so the surviving spouse does not have a right to any additional property.

Finally, remember that in a community property jurisdiction, the surviving spouse simply owns outright one-half the community on the death of the other spouse. Again, outright ownership is appropriate to a policy that treats the marriage as an equal economic partnership. Some early elective share statutes, however, are based on a support theory. The elective share carried out the policy that requires spouses to support each other by continuing that obligation after death. As first enacted and then revised in the 1960s, the New York statute allowed the elective share right of a surviving spouse to be satisfied by creating a trust of the elective share amount and giving the spouse income from the trust for life, after giving the spouse outright a dollar sum from the trust property. (Remember the provisions of Mr. Honigman's will that satisfied the elective share and thus prevented Mrs. Honigman from electing against the will.)

The New York statute was revised in 1992 and among the changes was the addition of the requirement that the elective share amount pass outright to the surviving spouse. EPTL § 5–1.1–A(a)(4)(B). This is the statutory language that requires the elective share to pass outright to the surviving spouse. Look at it carefully; do you see why, when taken together with EPTL § 5–1.1–A(4) immediately above, it prevents a testator from satisfying the elective share by creating a testamentary trust from which the spouse gets all of the income for life because the value of the income interest, no matter how large, will not count towards satisfying the elective share. This provision was seen as a vindication of the equal economic partnership theory. The UPC also changed its position on the satisfaction of the elective share with an income interest in trust between the original UPC promulgated in 1969 and the 1990 revision. Although the UPC provision is not straightforward, under UPC § 2–209 every interest received from the deceased spouse by the surviving spouse is counted towards the elective share entitlement and that would include the actuarial value of an income interest in a trust. The surviving spouse is not charged with interests the spouse has disclaimed. Therefore, the surviving spouse could disclaim the income interest and take the equivalent value outright.

4. A Bit More on the Elective Share

The preceding material gives you only an introduction to the elective share. Most jurisdictions have considerable case law surrounding the elective share and the procedures for asserting it. The requirement that the elective share amount passes outright to the surviving spouse makes planning for estates large enough to be subject to the estate tax especially complicated. Under both the federal estate tax and many state inheritance taxes, there is an unlimited deduction for property left to a surviving spouse. The deduction can be obtained even if the property is left in trust for the surviving spouse, so long as the surviving spouse is the only beneficiary of the trust during the surviving spouse's life. Of course, property left in trust will not satisfy the elective share, regardless of the extent of its generosity. This makes it more difficult to create a family trust which leaves the elective share to the surviving spouse, and directs that the corpus not expended by the surviving spouse pass to the deceased spouse's children by a prior marriage.

The solution to the problem is to have one's spouse waive the right to the elective share. UPC § 2–213 recognizes a waiver of elective share rights. The UPC requires that the waiver be voluntary and not unconscionable. Until recently, New York courts were relatively unsympathetic to a spouse who tried to set aside a waiver. The cases treated the waiver as any other contract, and set a high bar for proving fraud and unconscionability. All that seemed to change with the following opinion of the Court of Appeals.

Matter of Greiff

703 N.E.2d 752 (N.Y. 1998)

BELLACOSA, JUDGE:

This appeal raises the question whether the special relationship between betrothed parties, when they execute a prenuptial agreement, can warrant a shift of the burden of persuasion bearing on its legality and enforceability. A party challenging the judicial interposition of a prenuptial agreement, used to defeat a right of election, may demonstrate by a preponderance of the evidence that the premarital relationship between the contracting individuals manifested "probable" undue and unfair advantage (*Matter of Gordon v. Bialystoker Ctr. & Bikur Cholim*, 45 N.Y.2d 692, 699–700, 412 N.Y.S.2d 593, 385 N.E.2d 285). In these exceptional circumstances, the burden should fall on the proponent of the prenuptial agreement to show freedom from fraud, deception or undue influence.

The reversal by the Appellate Division of the Surrogate's Court's decree reflects a misapprehension of governing law, in that the Appellate Division reached its conclusion without factoring or finding facts relevant to fixing the evidentiary burden for this kind of case. Thus, this Court should remit for plenary consideration of the particular legal issue, and all others explicitly bypassed but raised at the intermediate level of appellate review.

Appellant Helen Greiff married Herman Greiff in 1988 when they were 65 and 77 years of age, respectively. They had entered into reciprocal prenuptial agreements in which each expressed the usual waiver of the statutory right of election as against the estate of the other. The husband died three months after the marriage, leaving a will that made no provision for his surviving spouse. The will left the entire estate to Mr. Greiff's children from a prior marriage. When Mrs. Greiff filed a petition seeking a statutory elective share of the estate, Mr. Greiff's children countered with the two prenuptial agreements which they claimed precluded Mrs. Greiff from exercising a right of election against her husband's estate (*see*, EPTL 5–1.1[f]).

A trial was held in Surrogate's Court, Kings County, on the issue of the validity and enforceability of the prenuptial agreements. The Surrogate explicitly found that the husband "was in a position of great influence and advantage" in his relationship with his wife-to-be, and that he was able to subordinate her interests, to her prejudice and detriment. The court further determined that the husband "exercised bad faith, unfair and inequitable dealings, undue influence and overreaching when he induced the petitioner to sign the proffered antenuptial agreements," particularly noting that the husband "selected and paid for" the wife's attorney. Predicated on this proof, the credibility of witnesses and the inferences it drew from all the evidence, Surrogate's Court

> **Practice Pointer**
>
> At least the couple had separate counsel. Would it be ethical for a single lawyer to have represented both? Is there a conflict of interest?

invalidated the prenuptial agreements and granted a statutory elective share of decedent's estate to the surviving spouse.

The Appellate Division reversed, on the law, simply declaring that Mrs. Greiff had failed to establish that her execution of the prenuptial agreements was procured through her then-fiancé's fraud or overreaching. This Court granted the widow leave to appeal. We now reverse.

A party seeking to vitiate a contract on the ground of fraud bears the burden of proving the impediment attributable to the proponent seeking enforcement (*see, Matter of Gordon v. Bialystoker Ctr. & Bikur Cholim*, 45 N.Y.2d 692, 698, 412 N.Y.S.2d 593, 385 N.E.2d 285, *supra*). This rubric also applies generally to controversies involving prenuptial agreements (*see, Matter of Phillips'*, 293 N.Y. 483, 488, 58 N.E.2d 504). Indeed, as an incentive toward the strong public policy favoring individuals ordering and deciding their own interests through contractual arrangements, including prenuptial agreements (*see, Matter of Davis'*, 20 N.Y.2d 70, 74, 281 N.Y.S.2d 767, 228 N.E.2d 768; *Matter of Phillips', supra*, at 491, 58 N.E.2d 504; EPTL 5–1.1, formerly Decedent Estate Law § 18), this Court has eschewed subjecting proponents of these agreements to special evidentiary or freighted burdens (*see, Matter of Sunshine*, 40 N.Y.2d 875, 876, 389 N.Y.S.2d 344, 357 N.E.2d 999).

Importantly, however, neither *Sunshine* in 1976 (*supra*) nor *Phillips'* in 1944 (supra) entirely insulates prenuptial agreements from typical contract avoidances. That proposition includes the kind of counterpoint advanced by the surviving spouse in this case to offset her stepchildren's use of the prenuptial agreements against her claim for her statutory elective share (*see, Matter of Davis, supra*, at 76, 281 N.Y.S.2d 767, 228 N.E.2d 768; Rhodes [editor], New York Actions and Remedies, Family Law, Wills and Trusts, Marriage and Dissolution, § 2.10; 3 Lindey, Separation Agreements and Antenuptial Contracts §§ 90.03, 90.06).

This Court has held, in analogous contractual contexts, that where parties to an agreement find or place themselves in a relationship of trust and confidence at the time of execution, a special burden may be shifted to the party in whom the trust is reposed (or to the proponent of the party's interest, as in this case) to disprove fraud or overreaching (*see, e.g., Matter of Gordon v Bialystoker Ctr. & Bikur Cholim, supra*, at 698–699, 412 N.Y.S.2d 593, 385 N.E.2d 285; *Christian v. Christian*, 42 N.Y.2d 63, 72, 396 N.Y.S.2d 817, 365 N.E.2d 849; *Sharp v. Kosmalski*, 40 N.Y.2d 119, 121–122, 386 N.Y.S.2d 72, 351 N.E.2d 721; *see also*, I Farnsworth, Contracts § 4.11, at 452 [2d ed.]).

As an illustration, in *Gordon* (*supra*), the administrator of the decedent's estate challenged the transfer of funds by the decedent, one month before her death, to the nursing home in which she was a patient. The Court restated its applied guidance, as part of the invalidation of the transfer, as follows:

> "Whenever * * * the relations between the contracting parties appear to be of such a character as to render it certain that * * * either on the one side from superior knowledge of the matter derived from a fiduciary relation, or from an overmastering influence, or on the other from weakness, dependence, or trust justifiably reposed, unfair advantage in a transaction is rendered probable, * * * *it is incumbent upon the*

stronger party to show affirmatively that no deception was practiced, no undue influence was used, and that all was fair, open, voluntary and well understood" (*Gordon v Bialystoker Ctr. & Bikur Cholim*, at 698–699, 412 N.Y.S.2d 593, 385 N.E.2d 285 [emphasis added], quoting *Cowee v. Cornell*, 75 N.Y. 91, 99–100).

This enduring, nuanced balance of fair assessment can be applicable in the context of prenuptial agreements (*see, Matter of Sunshine, supra*, at 876, 389 N.Y.S.2d 344, 357 N.E.2d 999; *Matter of Davis', supra*, at 76, 281 N.Y.S.2d 767, 228 N.E.2d 768; *Matter of Phillips', supra*, at 491, 58 N.E.2d 504; *Graham v. Graham*, 143 N.Y. 573, 579–580, 38 N.E. 722).

We emphasize, however, that the burden shift is neither presumptively applicable nor precluded. We eschew absolutist rubrics that might ill serve the interests of fair conflict resolution as between proponents or opponents of these kinds of ordinarily useful agreements.

This Court's role here is to clarify, harmonize and find a happy medium of views reflected in the cases. For example, *Graham* has been read as holding that prenuptial agreements were presumptively fraudulent due to the nature of the relationship between prospective spouses. *Phillips'*, on the other hand, has been urged to suggest that prenuptial agreements may never be subject to burden-shifting regardless of the relationship of the parties at the time of execution and the evidence of their respective conduct.

Graham was decided in 1894 and indicated that prospective spouses stand in a relationship of confidence which necessarily casts doubt on or requires strict scrutiny concerning the validity of an antenuptial agreement. Its outdated premise, however, was that the man "naturally" had disproportionate influence over the woman he was to marry (*Graham v. Graham, supra*, at 580, 38 N.E. 722; *see*, 3 Lindey, Separation Agreements and Antenuptial Contracts § 90.03).

A century later society and law reflect a more progressive view and they now reject the inherent inequality assumption as between men and women, in favor of a fairer, realistic appreciation of cultural and economic realities (*see, e.g.,* Domestic Relations Law § 236[B]; *O'Brien v. O'Brien*, 66 N.Y.2d 576, 498 N.Y.S.2d 743, 489 N.E.2d 712). Indeed, the law starts marital partners off on an equal plane. Thus, whichever spouse contests a prenuptial agreement bears the burden to establish a fact-based, particularized inequality before a proponent of a prenuptial agreement suffers the shift in burden to disprove fraud or overreaching. This rule is less rigid than *Graham's* presumptive equation.

> **Food for Thought**
>
> Has the court adumbrated a standard to determine whether the waiver stands or has it merely required consideration of factors?

Phillips' tugs in the opposite direction from *Graham*. On close and careful analysis, however, *Phillips'* does not upset the balanced set of operating principles we pull together by today's decision. While holding that antenuptial agreements are not enveloped by a presumption of fraud, the Court in *Phillips'* indicated that some extra leverage could arise from the "circumstances in which the agreement was proposed" (*Matter of Phillips', supra*, at 491, 58 N.E.2d 504). This language does not turn its back entirely on *Graham*. Rather, it is generous enough to encompass the unique character of the inchoate bond between prospective spouses—a relationship by its nature permeated with trust, confidence, honesty and reliance. It allows further for a reasonable expectation that these relationships are almost universally beyond the pale of ordinary commercial transactions. Yet, the dispositive tests of legitimacy and enforceability of their prenuptial agreements need not pivot on the legalism or concept of presumptiveness. Instead, a particularized and exceptional scrutiny obtains. ✍

The Appellate Division's approach here did not allow for the calibration and application of these legal principles. Therefore, this Court is satisfied that the most prudent course for the fair resolution of this case is a remittal of the case to that court for its determination. A specific frame of reference for that court should be whether, based on all of the relevant evidence and standards, the nature of the relationship between the couple at the time they executed their prenuptial agreements rose to the level to shift the burden to the proponents of the agreements to prove freedom from fraud, deception or undue influence. Additionally, since the Appellate Division expressly declined to reach other issues raised by the parties in that court, it will now have that opportunity. We note finally that this Court's reversal and remittal reflect and imply no view of or preference concerning the ultimate factual evaluation and fair resolution by the Appellate Division within its plenary intermediate appellate court powers.

Accordingly, the order of the Appellate Division should be reversed, with costs to all parties appearing and filing separate briefs payable out of the estate, and the matter should be remitted to that court for further proceedings in accordance with this opinion.

KAYE, C.J., and SMITH, LEVINE, CIPARICK and WESLEY, JJ., concur.

Order reversed, etc.

Points for Discussion

1. *What* Greiff *changed*

In *Matter of Garbade*, 221 A.D.2d 844 (N.Y. App. Div. 1995), the Appellate Division affirmed the Surrogate's judgment setting aside the surviving spouse's notice of the exercise of the right of election, holding that she was bound by a pre-nuptial waiver, even though, among other facts, she was advised to seek the advice of independent counsel but did not do so. (The agreement involved a waiver by both spouses of their elective share rights and required the husband to maintain a $100,000 life insurance policy with wife as beneficiary, a requirement with which he complied. The future wife was informed of her future husband's net worth of approximately $2,500,000.) Does *Greiff* in any way reverse *Garbade*?

2. *Contracts and waive of elective share rights*

Should contract principles be exhumed to inform decisions in elective share waiver cases? Are the personal aspects of the waiver transaction so different from a typical contract that one can never presume equality of bargaining power? On the other hand, why didn't Ms. Greiff "Just say no"?

Practice Problem

A is engaged to be married. She is far wealthier than her spouse-to-be and would like to get a waiver of elective share rights in exchange for a fixed sum that increases with every five years of marriage. Some of her wealth consists of her shares in a closely-held family business which is notoriously allergic to publicity of any sort. Her parents, who are deeply involved in the business, do not want their future son-in-law to know anything about the business, particularly its value. What steps would you take after the *Greiff* decision to try to make sure the agreement would survive a challenge?

G. The Personal Property Set-Aside

This section on "doctrines which apply to beneficiaries" nears its conclusion. However, we must consider one last matter: statutes that set aside for the decedent's family certain assets which are free from the claims of creditors. Some states, most notably Florida, have generous homestead allowances which allow a residence of any value, no matter how large, to pass free from creditors' claims to family, with a surviving spouse having the preeminent right. UPC § 2–402 creates a modest homestead exemption for decedent's surviving spouse in the suggested amount of $22,500. Some states also allow the appropriate court to make an allowance to the surviving spouse (sometimes including dependent children) out of the assets of the estate which is also exempt from the claims of creditors. UPC § 2–404 allows a "reasonable allowance in money" for the maintenance of a surviving spouse and minor children whom the decedent was obligated to support and did support which cannot be paid for more than a year if the estate is inadequate to pay creditors. Neither of these allowances count against the recipient's intestate share if the decedent dies without a will.

A third type of allowance is a personal property set-aside or exempt property provision. Under UPC § 2–403 the decedent's surviving spouse or if there is no surviving spouse the decedent's surviving children are entitled to household furniture, automobiles, furnishings, appliances, and personal effects exceeding $15,000 in value. This property is exempt from the claims of the decedent's creditors and is in addition to anything passing to the surviving spouse or children in intestacy, under the decedent's will (unless the will provides otherwise), in intestacy or under the elective share. It truly comes "off the top."

Each state will provide a different collection of set-asides with quite disparate total potential values. Regardless of the type or number, however, these support rights are claimed and calculated before anything else is done with the estate. Thus, all other determinations—the elective share, intestate shares, etc.—will be calculated after the value of exempt property has been subtracted from the probate estate.

_____

Test Your Knowledge

To assess your understanding of the material in this chapter, click here to take a quiz.

CHAPTER 6

Wills: Doctrines Dealing with the Property

283-12

A. Ademption

The law dealing with lapse and the anti-lapse statutes illustrates that there is a fairly elaborate law dealing with circumstances in which a beneficiary does not survive the testator. There is also a body of law that deals with situations in which property devised and bequeathed in a will (and therefore owned by the testator at the time of execution) does not 'survive' the testator. By 'survive the testator,' we mean that for a variety of reasons, the property is not part of her probate estate at the time of her death. If property which is mentioned in the will is no longer 'givable,' how does the law deal with that provision in the will? The answer turns on how the law categorizes the devise or bequest.

Consistent with common law classifications, the Restatement Third recognizes four types of bequests and along with the UPC refers to all gifts in wills as devises. Other states, New York, for example, uses the term "dispositions":

Restatement of Property, Third (Wills and Other Donative Transfers) § 5.1

Devises are classified as specific, general, demonstrative, or residuary:

(1) A *specific devise* is a testamentary disposition of a specifically identified asset.

(2) A *general devise* is a testamentary disposition, usually of a specified amount of money or quantity of property, that is payable from the general assets of the estate.

(3) A *demonstrative devise* is a testamentary disposition, usually of a specified amount of money or quantity of property, that is primarily payable from a designated source, but is secondarily payable from the general assets of the estate to the extent that the primary source is insufficient.

(4) A *residuary devise* is a testamentary disposition of property of the testator's net probate estate not disposed by a specific, general, or demonstrative devise.

A **specific bequest** is perhaps the easiest understand: it is simply a bequest of a particular identified item of property. Refer back to Ward's will in Chapter 2. He devised his gold Omega watch to his protégé David Griff. Other examples might include: "my MacBook Air"; "my 2018 Tesla automobile"; "my collection of baseball cards"; "the gold broach I inherited from my grandmother Jane." But what if these items of identifiable property are no longer part of the estate at death? Suppose Ward sells his gold watch? The gift is adeemed: not 'givable' at the time of death, the specific devise is adeemed.

The most common **general bequest** is a sum of money or other fungible property. In the past, wills might leave a basket of oats to a beneficiary. In our monetized society, a bequest of a sum of money is perhaps the most common type of general bequest. However, other forms of fungible property are regarded as a general bequest. For an example, a bequest of a quantity of property, such as "1000 shares of IBM," is also a general bequest. If the property given is not part of the probate estate the executor may have to buy the property in order to fulfill the bequest. If it is not, the executor may satisfy the gift by giving the beneficiary the value on the date of the testator's death of 1000 shares of IBM. Suppose the estate has insufficient cash to purchase the stock, does the executor sell identifiable personal property like the watch to buy the stock?

Do you see why a gift of "my 1000 shares of IBM stock" is a specific bequest, while a gift of "1000 shares of IBM stock" is a general bequest? What happens in the first case if there are no shares of IBM in the estate at the time of death?

Of the four kinds of bequests the demonstrative bequest requires the most explanation. Consider the following case: Father's will includes this bequest: "[I give] the sum of One Thousand ($1,000) Dollars to my beloved daughter, Sylvia Rosner . . . or her heirs. It is my desire that this sum be paid to her out of the butcher store business which I own." Before his death the testator sold the butcher shop. Result? Arguably, because the specified source of the gift is not a part of the decedent's estate, the gift should not take effect: it should not be paid out of other probate assets. The law is to the contrary, however. The result of classifying a bequest as demonstrative is that even if the asset from which the bequest is to be paid does not exist at death, the bequest is still effective. In *Matter of Peters*, 2 Misc.2d 1004, 1005, 224 N.Y.S.2d 305, 307 (Sur. Ct. New York Co. 1962), the Surrogate described the bequest as "almost a classic example of a demonstrative legacy," and held that Ms. Rosner was entitled to the $1,000. Whether or not a bequest is demonstrative is determined by the testator's intent, and the cases are much more sensitive to the specific situations presented than to any definition.

Residuary bequests consist of property that is not subject to specific, general, or demonstrative legacies. It is property that is "left over" in the probate estate.

Consider the following dispositive provisions of the hypothetical testator, Roberta Fone:

> I, ROBERTA FONE, declare this to be my last will and testament and hereby revoke all wills and codicils heretofore made by me.
>
> ARTICLE ONE: I give my diamond engagement ring to my daughter Prunella if she shall survive me;
>
> ARTICLE TWO: I give $100,000 to my son Nigel if he shall survive me;
>
> ARTICLE THREE: I give $100,000 to be raised by the sale of my house at 54 Alpha Terrace to the American Red Cross;
>
> ARTICLE FOUR: I give all the rest, residue and remainder of my property, including any lapsed gifts, to my husband Android.

Can you classify the bequests according to the Restatement's classification scheme?

Suppose Testatrix sells her diamond ring and it is not part of her probate estate at her death? If the subject matter of a specific bequest is not part of the probate estate at the testator's death the gift *adeems*. Some state law classifies regards ademption as an act of revocation by the testator. (New York EPTL § 3–4.3, set forth below and *Matter of Peters*, 2 Misc.2d 1004, 1005, 224 N.Y.S.2d 305, 307 (Sur. Ct. New York Co. 1962). A legal fiction is created: by the transfer of specifically devised property, its owner knew the consequences—the gift would be revoked, the property would not pass to the named beneficiary. But sometimes specifically devised property is destroyed or the will-maker parts with ownership in a non-volitional manner. For example Roberta's ring is stolen; Ward loses his Omega; 54 Alpha Terrace is taken by eminent domain.

The analog to anti-lapse statutes protecting bequests to a wide universe of beneficiaries to limit the lapse principle are ademption statutes that limit the 'damage' to beneficiaries of specifically devised property. Probate law was initially unsympathetic to beneficiaries whose devises and bequests were no longer part of the testator's estate. The UPC is a very broad 'remedial' statute.

Make the Connection

Do you see the analogy with lapse? Lapse applies when the beneficiary is dead; ademption when the specific bequest is no longer property of the deceased.

Probate courts initially developed what is called the *identity rule*, defined by the New York Court of Appeals in terms that are generally applicable: "the legatee takes nothing if the article specifically bequeathed has been given away, lost or destroyed during the testator's lifetime [citations omitted]." (*Matter of Wright*, 7 N.Y.2d 365, 367, 165 N.E.2d 561, 562, 197 N.Y.S.2d 711, 712 (1960)). The identity rule is, therefore, a 'bright line" rule: the specifically devised property is either part of the probate estate or it isn't, and if it isn't the bequest adeems. Like many bright line rules, the identity rule can be pretty ruthless when applied in some situations. Courts have developed doctrines that side-step the rule, modifying its operation by holding that ademption does not occur if the property has undergone *a mere change in form* rather than a change in substance. The question of whether a change is one of form or substance is a question of fact, and not always a straightforward one.

One example should give you an idea of how the mix between the "identity rule" and the "form over substance exception" operates. Testator's will includes a bequest of her mink coat to one friend and of the remainder of her furs to another friend. Does that bequests strike you as specific? Because the coat had become badly worn, testator had the coat restyled into a stole sometime before her death. The worn skins were discarded and those remaining became the stole. In *Matter of Winfield*, 11 Misc.2d 149, 172 N.Y.S.2d 27 (Sur. Ct. New York Co. 1938), the court ruled that the legatee of the coat received the stole, holding that the change was one of form and not substance.

While the fur coat example perhaps seems trivial, ademption can occur whenever there is a specific bequest and seems to be most difficult to apply with specific bequests of financial assets. For example, a bequest of a bank account becomes problematic if the bank merges, changes names and perhaps assigns a new number to the account or if the money in the account is reinvested in a certificate of deposit rather than in another "account." Cases apply the form over substance rule and find that an ademption did not occur.

Even more difficulties are often caused by bequests of a shares in an individual corporation, for example, a bequest in a 2000 will of "1000 shares of Altria." Both Kraft and Phillip Morris International were wholly owned subsidiaries and were spun off. Does the beneficiary of the Altria shares also take the shares in the testator's estate of the other two now independent companies. Suppose the 2010 will leaves 100 shares of Apple which split 7 shares for 1 in 2014. The traditional rule is that a general bequest of securities does not change if there is a stock split, spin off or merger, but a specific bequest does. For example, if the will gives "1000 shares of Apple" and before death the stock splits 7-for-1 so that there are 7000 shares in the probate estate, the general bequest will remain 1000 shares. Were the gift of "my 1000 shares of IBM" the gift would include the shares received as a result of the split (so long as they are in the probate estate). The Restatement Third was changed and rejects the distinction. It gives and gives the legatee of a "specified number of securities" any additional securities acquired by the testator because of the testator's ownership of the described securities—a stock split, spin off or merger occurring after the execution of the will, but not additional shares of the same securities purchased by the testator. (Restatement (Third), Property (Wills and Other Donative Transfers), § 5.

The UPC, as noted above, has drastically altered the identity rule. Note carefully the specific inclusions but also the broad language of (6).

UPC § 2–606. Nonademption of Specific Devises; Unpaid Proceeds of Sale, Condemnation, or Insurance; Sale by Conservator or Agent

A specific devisee has a right to specifically devised property in the testator's estate at the testator's death and to any balance of the purchase price, together with any security agreement, owed by a purchaser at the testator's death by reason of sale of the property;

(1) any amount of a condemnation award for the taking of the property unpaid at death;

(2) any proceeds unpaid at death on fire or casualty insurance on or other recovery for injury to the property;

(3) any property owned by the testator at death and acquired as a result of foreclosure, or obtained in lieu of foreclosure, of the security interest for a specifically devised obligation;

(4) any real property or tangible personal property owned by the testator at death which the testator acquired as a replacement for specifically devised real property or tangible personal property; and

(5) if not covered by paragraphs (1) through (5), a pecuniary devise equal to the value as of its date of disposition of other specifically devised property disposed of during the testator's lifetime but only to the extent it is established that ademption would be inconsistent with the testator's manifested plan of distribution or that at the time the will was made, the date of disposition or otherwise, the testator did not intend ademption of the devise.

(b) If specifically devised property is sold or mortgaged by a conservator or by an agent acting within the authority of a durable power of attorney for an incapacitated principal or a condemnation award, insurance proceeds, or recovery for injury to the property is paid to a conservator or to an agent acting within the authority of a durable power of attorney for an incapacitated principal the specific devisee has the right to a general pecuniary devise equal to the net sale price, the amount of the unpaid loan, the condemnation award, the insurance proceeds, or the recovery.

(c) The right of a specific devisee under subsection (b) is reduced by any right the devisee has under subsection (a).

(d) For the purposes of the references in subsection (b) to a conservator, subsection (b) does not apply if after the sale, mortgage, condemnation, casualty, or recovery, it was adjudicated that the testator's incapacity ceased and the testator survived the adjudication for at least one year.

(e) For the purposes of the references in subsection (b) to an agent acting within the authority of a durable power of attorney an incapacitated principal, (i) "incapacitated principal" means a principal who is an incapacitated person, (ii) no adjudication of incapacity before death is necessary, and (iii) the acts of an agent within the authority of a durable power of attorney are presumed to be for an incapacitated principal.

The UPC, though inclusive, has its limitations. For example, in the first three subsections of (a), the amounts that might represent the value of the property, for example insurance payouts or condemnation awards, must be unpaid at the testator's death. If the funds already have been paid to the testator, say the day before death, the beneficiary will not receive the proceeds. Subsections (4) and (5) look favorably on the possibility that the beneficiary should get property that was purchased or regarded as a substitute. What, then, is the meaning of (6)? Does it reverse the general application of ademption, if the beneficiary can demonstrate that ademption would be inconsistent with the overall estate plan of the deceased? Many states have much narrower exceptions to the ademption rule generally limited to the situations in UPC § 2–606(a)(1) through (4) and (b). See for example New York EPTL §§ 3–4.4, 3–4.5. We'll consider first how the traditional doctrine of ademption works and then consider the innovations embodied in UPC § 2–606(a)(5) and (6).

Let us return to UPC § 2–606(a)(5) and (6). These two provisions move the UPC ademption provisions away from the identity rule towards a more intent based view of the doctrine. This move has been criticized as unnecessarily blurring the bright line of the identity theory beyond the sort of exceptions contained in previous statutory and common law approaches to ademption. The examples given in the comment to UPC § 2–606 involve situations that are fairly clear-cut. An illustration for (a)(5) involves the bequest of "my 1984 Ford." Between the time of the execution of the will and death, the testator had sold the Ford, bought a 1988 Buick, sold the Buick and bought a 1993 Chrysler. The beneficiary of the specific bequest takes the Chrysler since it is a replacement for the Buick. Another example involves the theft of a specifically bequeathed piece of jewelry. The example states that the beneficiary "could likely establish" that testator did not intend the bequest to adeem or that ademption would be inconsistent with "the manifest plan of distribution" and would therefore be entitled to the value of the jewelry. The final example involves the specific bequest of a valuable painting and the subsequent gift of the painting by the testator to a museum. The testator's "deliberate act" of giving the painting away indicates that ademption was intended and unless the beneficiary could come forward with "persuasive evidence" to the contrary the bequest would indeed adeem.

Problems 6-1

1. In the car example described above, would it matter if the testator had sold the Ford and bought a much more expensive car? Assume a Ferrari or a Maserati. Would it influence your answer if between writing the will and buying one of these flashy Italian numbers the testator had won the lottery and "upgraded" her entire lifestyle? Designer everything? Would it matter if the testator's economic position had not changed at all but she had taken a large part of her savings to buy the sports car?

2. At the time of executing his will, testator owns 1000 shares of Apple common stock, which in his will he leaves to his son Nigel in a specific bequest—"I give my 1000 shares of Apple to my son, Nigel." Sometime after executing the will, testator decides that Apple's time in the sun is over, sells the 1000 shares and uses the proceeds to buy equal dollar holdings of Microsoft and Intel for their dividend potential. He does not change his will before he dies. Does Nigel take the shares of Microsoft and Intel under the UPC? In a jurisdiction with the traditional change of form not substance rule? Would your answer change if the will also made a specific bequest of "my 1000 shares of Google" to the testator's daughter, Pippa and gave

the residue to the testator's widow who: alternative 1 is the mother of Nigel and Pippa and alternative 2 is not.

Practice Planning Problems

1. Client has a brokerage account in which he holds shares in ten different companies. Each holding is of approximately the same value. Oddly enough, he is blessed with five nieces and five nephews. He comes to your office with a list of who gets which shares which gives each beneficiary all of the shares in a single company and asks you to draft a codicil. What would your inclination be? Note, for what it's worth, that the decline of the use of paper stock certificates seems to have contributed to a decline in the number of bequests, general or specific, of shares of stock. With most equity investments held in brokerage accounts and given the ease with which securities held in accounts can be bought and sold, fewer testators probably think of making a gift of an investment in a specific company. What do you think of suggesting to your client bequests of a fractional share of the brokerage account to each beneficiary?

2. Regardless of whether or not the identity theory obtains, ademption has the same effect as a revocation of the gift that has 'disappeared.' Revocation requires the intent to revoke. It is perhaps not too far-fetched to argue that disposing of specifically devised property was accompanied by the intent to revoke the gift. Now you are the conservator or guardian (depending on the jurisdiction) of an incapacitated person all of whose personal property has been used to pay the person's expenses. You need to raise cash to pay ongoing expenses. All that is left of the incapacitated person's property is three pieces of real property, which are bequeathed separately one to Huey, a second to Dewey and the third to Louis. Which one you select may not matter to the incapacitated person, and in any event she lacks the capacity to make a choice. Yet there would be consequences for the beneficiary ducklings. What result under the UPC? Given that result what should you as custodian (guardian) do?

B. Abatement

The classification of bequests is also relevant when the executor has to pay the claims against the estate. All of the estate property is subject to those claims as well to payment of taxes and expenses of administration (including "reasonable" funeral expenses). Once specific bequests are satisfied, general bequests are then paid (and one must include demonstrative bequests in the general category if the property or fund from which the bequest was to be paid is adeemed). What property remains passes under the residuary bequest. If the estate does not have sufficient assets to pay all the debts, expenses and taxes and satisfy all the bequests, statutes set forth the order of abatement, that is, they create a hierarchy of bequests. Like most if not all abatement schemes, UPC § 3–902 (a) provides that the residuary abates first. That rule, though doctrinally sound, may mean that the most favored beneficiary (often the case—see, for example, Ward's will) receives no property if, after paying all debts, expenses, and taxes and the specific, general, and demonstrative legacies, there is nothing left. The statutory rule of abatement is a default rule. Subsection (b) allows the will-maker to provide an individualized pattern of abatement of legacies Moreover, the Code allows the probate court to craft an abatement pattern if it feels that to do so is necessary to achieve the testator's estate plan:

> if the testamentary plan or the express or implied purpose of the devise would be defeated by the order of abatement stated in subsection (a), the shares of the distributees abate as may be found necessary to give effect to the intention of the testator.

[handwritten margin note: To give effect to the intent of the testator]

Points for Discussion

1. Does it make sense to abate the residuary bequest first?

Although the default rule of abatement is clear, it can lead to problems in cases in which the residuary bequest is left to the beneficiary that is the most likely object of the testator's bounty: spouse or issue. Unlike the UPC, New York law (EPTL § 13–1.3) specifically allows the statute to be overridden by the *implied* intention of the testator. Proving that intention may be difficult, and it therefore is advisable to draft a document with the possibility of abatement in mind. In addition, at least in New York, the relevant intent is the testator's intent at the time the will was executed. The question is not what the intent would be had the testator considered the situation existing at death. (*See Matter of Smallman*, 138 Misc. 889, 247 N.Y.S. 593 (Sur. Ct. New York Co. 1931).

[handwritten margin note: This is on intestacy twist in the New York law.]

For a case in which the testator's intent did make a difference *see Matter of Volckening*, 75 Misc.2d 221, 347 N.Y.S.2d 521 (Sur. Ct. Kings Co. 1973). The testator's will made specific bequests of shares in a closely held corporation to two trusts, one for each of her daughters and a general bequest of cash to a trust for her third daughter. When the shares increased in value the testator increased the amount of the general bequest. The Surrogate held that all three bequests should abate as if they were all general bequests in light of the testator's intention to treat her three daughters equally.

2. Abatement and estate taxes

While abatement statutes do apply to taxes in general, they usually do not apply to the payment of estate taxes. Rules for the source of payment of estate taxes are usually the subject of a separate statute (in New York, EPTL § 2–1.8).

Practice Planning Problem

Client tells you that he wants to make substantial bequests to a niece and a nephew and to leave the residue to his daughter, his only child. At the time the will is executed Client's assets total about $1,000,000 and the general bequests to the niece and nephew are $150,000 each. Just before Client's death the stock market crashes and at death the probate estate is worth only $500,000. How is the $500,000 distributed? Is there a better way to write the will?

C. Exoneration

At common law the beneficiary of a specific bequest of real or personal property that was encumbered by debt (such as a mortgage) had the right to require the estate to pay off the debt before distributing the property to the beneficiary. The assumption was that the testator would want those secured debts paid off along with all his or her other debts. That rule has been reversed by the UPC (§ 2–607) and in New York (EPTL § 3–3.6).

D. Advancements and Satisfaction

Some gifts during life can have an impact on the distribution of the probate estate after death. At the common law, a lifetime gift to someone who was an heir of the donor at the donor's death reduced his or her intestate share. The logic was that the gift was an advancement, a payment made by the property owner that would be taken into account in calculating the heir's intestate share. The logic supporting the doctrine was that if the amount paid over was not considered the heir who received a pre-mortem share would receive a larger proportion of the intestate estate: her pro rata share plus the sum advanced. But courts began to view the rule as a presumption: the gift was an advancement unless there was evidence of contrary intent. This position made the law of advancements quite complicated, with courts required to ascertain the donor's intent in making the gift. Most modern statutes (note the UPC section below) do not treat any gift as an advancement unless it is accompanied by a writing signed by the donor or perhaps by the donee which states that the gift should be counted against the donee's share of the donor's intestate estate.

A similar doctrine applies to wills. Modern statutes require some acknowledgment in writing that the lifetime gift was meant to be a substitute for the gift in the will.

UPC § 2–109. Advancements

(a)   If an individual dies intestate as to all or a portion of his [or her] estate, property the decedent gave during the decedent's lifetime to an individual who, at the decedent's death, is an heir is treated as an advancement against the heir's intestate share only if (i) the decedent declared in a contemporaneous writing or the heir acknowledged in writing that the gift is an advancement or (ii) the decedent's contemporaneous writing or the heir's written acknowledgment otherwise indicates that the gift is to be taken into account in computing the division and distribution of the decedent's intestate estate.

(b)　For purposes of subsection (a), property advanced is valued as of the time the heir came into possession or enjoyment of the property or as of the time of the decedent's death, whichever first occurs.

(c)　If the recipient of the property fails to survive the decedent, the property is not taken into account in computing the division and distribution of the decedent's intestate estate, unless the decedent's contemporaneous writing provides otherwise.

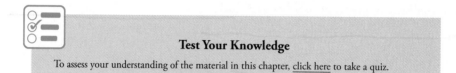

Test Your Knowledge

To assess your understanding of the material in this chapter, click here to take a quiz.

PART III

Intestate Succession

CHAPTER 7

Intestate Succession: An Estate Plan by Operation of Law

Our discussion to this point has dealt primarily with vocabulary. But we have slowly immersed ourselves in estate planning by providing an introduction into the tools of the practitioner. We explored the basic concept of the probate estate and two functions of probate: collecting the decedent's probate assets and paying the decedent's debts and any estate or inheritance taxes that might be due. Once all that work is done, of course, what remains of the estate must go to a new owner and become some other person's property (and perhaps eventually his or her probate property). As we have seen, the property owner can select that person or persons by writing a will or creating a trust; but if there is no will or trust, each state has created a default "estate plan," the property is distributed according to statute in the state of the deceased's domicile. Ultimately, that was how Sgt. Robbins' estate was distributed in the *Wescott* case at the end of Chapter 1. He did not successfully transfer the money in his bank account by will, trust, or gift; his next-of-kin inherited it instead by default.

To die *intestate*, then, is to die without a will, and the *intestacy statute* governs the disposition of an intestate decedent's probate property. Those rules will also come into play when the decedent had a valid will, but did not successfully dispose of all the probate property and thus died partially intestate. Each state has its own intestacy statute which applies to the property of its residents who die without a will. The persons who receive the property are the decedent's *heirs* or *next-of-kin*.

Although intestacy statutes in the United States vary in their details, the basic outlines are similar. Only those who survive the testator qualify as heirs and are entitled to take from the estate. (The legal definition of survival is taken up below.) The preferred heir is the surviving spouse. Usually the surviving spouse receives a specified fraction of the estate and then the spouse and the other heirs divide the remaining probate property. (The modern trend is for the surviving spouse to receive the entire estate or a substantial fraction of

Food for Thought

It's a pretty good guess that most law students do not have wills. What property they have will pass through intestate succession. Is that what you want for your laptop and smartphone? Seriously, at what point in life do you think you should consider writing a will?

it.) Those other heirs, where there is a surviving spouse, are usually limited to the descendants of the decedent. If the decedent has no living descendants, the surviving parents of the decedent are heirs, sometimes entitled to a share even if there is a surviving spouse. In other jurisdictions, all the probate property passes to the surviving spouse, and under the Uniform Probate Code, all the probate property passes to the surviving spouse at least in some circumstances, even if there are surviving descendants of the decedent. Some statutes now account for a greater variety of family forms, changing the share of the surviving spouse, for example, based on whether either the decedent or surviving spouse had children with another.

If the decedent has no surviving spouse or descendants, the statutes begin to vary a bit more, but not if at least one of the decedent's parents is alive. The surviving parent or parents are the sole heirs, but if neither parent survives the decedent, things get more interesting. Before we move on to the law, however, we must pay attention to, surprise, more vocabulary.

A. The Language of Intestacy

Discussions of inheritance in the situation where the decedent is not survived by a spouse or descendants often talk about the *parentelic system*. A "parentela" is a line of descent. The first parentela consists of a person's own descendants. The second parentela is a person's parents and their descendants (other than the person we're considering), and the third parentela is the person's grandparents and their descendants (other than the persons in the first and second parentelas). The third parentela, therefore, consists of the person's grandparents (maternal and paternal), their children (aunts and uncles) and all of the descendants of the aunts and uncles. The first generation of aunts' and uncles' descendants are the person's first cousins, and the next generation are first cousins once removed. Each succeeding generation is simply one more step removed. Confused yet? The following chart might help.

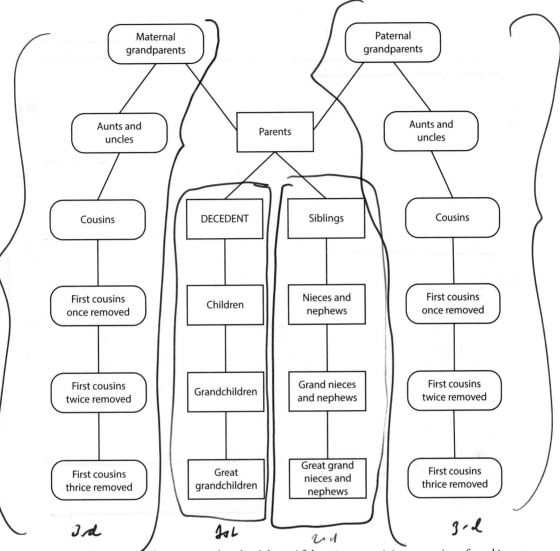

Under a parentelic system, a decedent's heirs (if there is no surviving spouse) are found in the first parentela; if there is no one in the first parentela, heirs are those persons in the second parentela; and if there are no relatives in the second parentela, the heirs are found in the third parentela. Under many intestacy statutes, the search for heirs stops with the third parentela. In other words, no one more distantly related than descendants of the decedent's grandparents are the decedent's heirs. A few intestacy statutes do make relatives in the fourth parentela and beyond heirs if there are not more closely related relatives. Within any parentela, surviving heirs take by representation, a concept that is described in more detail below.

The parentelic system is used by a majority of states. But some use an alternative system called the degree-of-relationship system or the civil law method. This system simply represents a different way of determining a person's closest living relatives—it is based on degrees of relationship between the decedent and the relative. The degrees are calculated by counting the number of "links" between a person and the relative in question. For a relative in the direct line of descent (up or down the line), the degree of relationship is simply the number of steps from the decedent to the relative. For a collateral relative, the degrees are measured by counting from the decedent to the closest common ancestor and then from that ancestor to the relative in question. Your brothers and sisters are related to you in the second degree: there is one "link" from you to your parents and one more link from your parents to your siblings. Your grandparents are also related in the second degree: one link to your parents and another from your parents to your grandparents. Your nieces and nephews are related to you in the third degree—one more link from your siblings to their children—as are your aunts and uncles (first link to parents, second to grandparents, third to the grandparents' children, your aunts and uncles). What degree of relationship to you are your first cousins?

As we have seen, your "first cousins once removed" are the *children of your first cousins*. Who then are your *second cousins*? Your second cousins are the children of your *parents'* first cousins. Those persons, your parents' first cousins, are also your *first cousins once removed*. By this time you have a headache, but try to stay with this. Why are your parents' cousins your first cousins once removed if your first cousin's children are also your first cousins once removed? Because both persons are related to you in the fifth degree. (Try counting the links and you'll see that in both cases they add up to five.) The concept of "removal" for cousins is generational.

Another way to look at it is to consider your relatives who are in your generation. The other descendants of your parents who are the same generation as you are your brothers and sisters. The descendants of your grandparents in your generation are your first cousins; the descendants of your great-grandparents in your generation are your second cousins; and the descendants of your great-great grandparents are your third cousins.

In a degree-counting state, relatives in the closest surviving degree take (or split) the entire estate. Two fourth-degree relatives from different lines would each take half of the estate, but a sole surviving relative in the fourth-degree would take everything even if the decedent left behind a dozen relatives in the fifth degree. Some states begin with degree-counting, but use a parentelic tie breaker so that a relative in a closer line would beat a same-degree relative from a more distant line.

Remember, however, that most modern intestacy statutes do not distribute an intestate estate to relatives more distant that the third parentela. Likewise, in degree-counting states, there is often a cut-off. If a decedent has no living heirs—either no known relatives or none who fall within the statutory cut-off—the intestate estate passes to the state. In that case the estate is said to "*escheat*."

B.   The UPC Intestacy Statute

Now that we have the introduction out of the way, let us look at the Uniform Probate Code's intestacy statute. Your instructor may ask you to compare the UPC's statute to that of your school's home state or perhaps another jurisdiction.

UPC § 2–101. Intestate Estate

(a)　Any part of a decedent's estate not effectively disposed of by will passes by intestate succession to the decedent's heirs as prescribed in this Code, except as modified by the decedent's will.

(b)　A decedent by will may expressly exclude or limit the right of an individual or class to succeed to property of the decedent passing by intestate succession. If that individual or a member of that class survives the decedent, the share of the decedent's intestate estate to which that individual or class would have succeeded passes as if that individual or each member of that class had disclaimed his [or her] intestate share.

UPC § 2–102. Share of Spouse

The intestate share of a decedent's surviving spouse is

(1)　the entire intestate estate if:

　　(i)　no descendant or parent of the decedent survives the decedent; or

　　(ii)　all of the decedent's surviving descendants are also descendants of the surviving spouse and there is no other descendant of the surviving spouse who survives the decedent;

(2)　the first [$300,000], plus three-fourths of any balance of the intestate estate, if no descendant of the decedent survives the decedent, but a parent of the decedent survives the decedent;

(3)　the first [$225,000], plus one-half of any balance of the intestate estate, if all of the decedent's surviving descendants are also descendants of the surviving spouse and the surviving spouse has one or more surviving descendants who are not descendants of the decedent;

(4)　the first [$150,000], plus one-half of any balance of the intestate estate, if one or more of the decedent's surviving descendants are not descendants of the surviving spouse.

UPC § 2–103. Share of Heirs other than Surviving Spouse

Any part of the intestate estate not passing to a decedent's surviving spouse under Section 2–102, or the entire intestate estate if there is no surviving spouse, passes in the following order to the individuals who survive the decedent:

(1)　to the decedent's descendants by representation;

(2)　if there is no surviving descendant, to the decedent's parents equally if both survive, or to the surviving parent;

(3)　if there is no surviving descendant or parent, to the descendants of the decedent's parents or either of them by representation;

(4)   if there is no surviving descendant, parent, or descendant of a parent, but the decedent is survived on both the paternal and maternal sides by one or more grandparents or descendants of grandparents:

   (A)   half to the decedent's paternal grandparents equally if both survive, or to the surviving paternal grandparent, or to the descendants of the decedent's paternal grandparents or either of them if both are deceased, the descendants taking by representation; and

   (B)   half to the decedent's maternal grandparents equally if both survive, or to the surviving maternal grandparent, or to the descendants of the decedent's maternal grandparents or either of them if both are deceased, the descendants taking by representation;

(5)   if there is no surviving descendant, parent, or descendant of a parent, but the decedent is survived by one or more grandparents or descendants of grandparents on the paternal but not the maternal side, or on the maternal but not the paternal side, to the decedent's relatives on the side with one or more surviving members in the manner described in paragraph (4);

(6)   if there is no surviving spouse, descendant, parent, descendant of a parent, grandparent, or descendant of a grandparent, but the intestate decedent had:

   (A)   one deceased spouse who has one or more descendants who survive the decedent, to those descendants by representation; or

   (B)   more than one deceased spouse who has one or more descendants who survive the decedent, the estate is divided into as many equal shares as there are deceased spouses, each share passing to those descendants by representation.

UPC § 2–105. No Taker

If there is no taker under the provisions of this Article, the intestate estate passes to the [state].

Notes

1. Policies shaping spousal inheritance

Can you articulate a justification for the UPC provisions for the surviving spouse (UPC § 2–102)? Why the complications? (Note that the numbers in parentheses are suggestions by the Uniform Law Commission, authors of the UPC; each state legislature will of course make a decision about the proper number.)

A justification for a handsome treatment of the surviving spouse may be a belief that property acquired by the spouse may be the result of joint efforts and that the form of legal ownership the property assumes may mask that reality. So if, in a traditional family of the mid-twentieth century, the husband goes to work and the wife keeps house and raises the family, the husband's salary, though his property, may be regarded as the fruits of spousal division of labor. This is consistent with the way property is treated by most states at the time of divorce.

In most American states, property is owned by the spouses separately during the marriage, but there is a reckoning at the death of the first spouse. However, eight states (Arizona, California, Idaho, Louisiana, Nevada, New Mexico, Texas, and Washington) follow a marital property regime known as community property. A ninth state, Wisconsin, has a marital property law that closely resembles community property. Under a community property regime, income earned by either spouse (and in some states income earned on investments owned by either spouse) and property acquired with that income belongs to the marital community. When one spouse dies, the other spouse is the sole owner of one-half of the community property. The other half is the deceased spouse's share. Thus, in a community property state, the intestacy statute governs a deceased spouse's one-half of the community property and that spouse's separate property (usually property brought to the marriage). Part of our agenda is to survey marital property regimes, but not quite yet.

2. Survival and the problem of simultaneous death

Intestate inheritance is conditioned on survival. It is often obvious whether the taker has outlived the decedent, but sometimes it isn't. The development of travel by car and plane in the twentieth century increased the likelihood of two or more family members dying close in time. The initial response to this problem was the Uniform Simultaneous Death Act (USDA), which was adopted in 1953. It provided a legal definition of survival to be used for all transfers that required such a determination. If sufficient evidence could prove the order of deaths, then the one who lived longer would be deemed to have survived the other. But if there was "no sufficient evidence" on the order of deaths, courts were to assume a different set of facts for each individual's estate. If A and B died close in time, and it could not be determined who died first, then A would be treated as the survivor when distributing A's estate; B would then be treated as the survivor when distributing B's property.

In our Willa and Harry elective share problem in Chapter 5, we posited the death of one spouse, followed by an inheritance, and then the death sometime thereafter of the initial survivor. While such a sequence is likely, it is not inevitable. Let's observe the same scenario with reference instead to the intestacy. Suppose Harry and Willa are out for a drive on the Pacific Coast Highway. Overwhelmed by the beauty, the driver (take your pick) loses control of the car. With them safely strapped inside, it plunges into the ocean, and the couple's bodies are recovered three days later. For the purposes of intestate succession, does who succumbed first to the calamity, Harry or Willa, matter? Perhaps. Suppose Harry has issue from a first marriage, Max. If Harry died before Willa, a spousal intestate share would pass to Willa and increase the size of her estate, which at Willa's death (perhaps minutes or seconds after Harry) passes to Gita (assuming she is her intestate heir—not improbable—Gita is Willa's sister). The remaining property passes to Max; Max's intestate share is reduced by the amount that passed to Willa. However, if Willa died before Harry, even by a split second, a spousal intestate share passes to Harry, and then it devolves to Max. In this scenario, Max's share is increased by the property that would pass to Harry via intestate succession from Willa's estate. So when spouses die in a common disaster, which spouse died first might matter if their intestate heirs are not the same individual. In this situation, under the original USDA, Harry's estate would pass to Max, while Willa's would pass to Gita, or whoever is next in line in her family tree.

Suppose Willa and Harry had mutual wills rather like Harvey and Rose in *In re Snide* (Chapter 4). Harvey intended to leave his property to Rose and the reverse; Rose, if she predeceased Harvey intended to her property to pass to Harvey. But a car crash could also befall them. Would it matter? Refer to the will: do they have a common beneficiary who takes at the death of the survivor? If they do, simultaneous death matters little with respect to the ultimate disposition of the property, though it might have an impact with respect to probate fees. The outcome would be the same in our Ward and June Estate Planning Problem (Chapter 2) because if you assume that June had a will that read like Ward's initial will: the boys would take no matter who died first. The beneficiaries of Ward's and June's Wills (if the spouse does not survive) are the same persons.

So sequencing of death might matter, or it might not. But in cases where it does, like our reconfigured Willa and Harry hypothetical, one or the other claimant might try to prove by forensic evidence who (Harry or Willa) died first. Pardon a gruesome example. Imagine a car stuck on the railway tracks. Harry is driving, Willa to his right in the passenger seat. A train hits the car. If it was moving from the right, the train probably killed Willa first and then nanoseconds later killed Harry. (After all, how long does it take a train to cover the distance between the passenger and driver's seats in an average automobile?) If Harry did die after Willa, his estate could claim an intestate share in Willa's estate. Train heading the other direction? The sequencing of deaths is reversed, and so is the succession. Gruesome litigation might endure if the stakes are sufficiently high.

The hazards of the fact-specific inquiry called for by the "no sufficient evidence" rule are on full display in *Janus v. Tarascewicz*, 482 N.E.2d 418 (Ill. App. 1985), in which two families were forced to relive the tragic deaths of their loved ones due to Tylenol laced with cyanide. In such cases the revised Uniform Simultaneous Death Act of 1993 (incorporated into the Uniform Probate Code) rides to the rescue with a definition of survival that is far easier to implement, yet satisfies the same policy goals.

UPC § 2–104. Requirement of Survival by 120 Hours; Individual in Gestation

(a) For purposes of intestate succession, homestead allowance, and exempt property, and except as otherwise provided in subsection (b), the following rules apply:

(1) An individual born before a decedent's death who fails to survive the decedent by 120 hours is deemed to have predeceased the decedent. If it is not established by clear and convincing evidence that an individual born before a decedent's death survived the decedent by 120 hours, it is deemed that the individual failed to survive for the required period.

· gestation ·

(2) An individual in gestation at a decedent's death is deemed to be living at the decedent's death if the individual lives 120 hours after birth. If it is not established by clear and convincing evidence that an individual in gestation at the decedent's death lived 120 hours after birth, it is deemed that the individual failed to survive for the required period.

So much for simultaneous death and intestacy: what about the possibility of will beneficiaries dying together? The same concerns attach. To remedy, it is not uncommon for the scrivener of a will to draft a requirement that a beneficiary of an interest in the estate survive a certain period of time after the death of the testator to come into possession of a bequest. Why might a testator want a beneficiary to survive the testator's death by some minimum period? First, of course, if the will is drafted so that there is a substitute gift that takes effect if the primary beneficiary does not survive the testator, or survive for the stated period of time, the expressed intent is that the substitute beneficiaries should take if the primary beneficiary really cannot enjoy the property. That the beneficiary cannot do if the beneficiary dies immediately after the testator. Second, if there is no requirement of survival beyond surviving the testator and the primary beneficiary dies shortly after the testator, the property will be subject to the claims of the primary beneficiary's creditors and the expenses of estate administration as well. In short, the property will be administered twice before actually ending up in the hands of persons who can make use of it.

Similar considerations apply to the gift of a remainder interest in a trust. It is not unusual, therefore, for a trust to require that a beneficiary survive the testator by some period of time in order to receive an interest under the trust. In other words, survival for thirty or sixty or ninety days may be inserted in the trust (or will) as a condition precedent to the gift under the provisions of the document. The use of such time periods in trusts seems to be far less common than in wills. Nevertheless, it is a relatively straightforward matter to draft a survival requirement, whether one specific to a particular bequest or gift under a trust or a general requirement applying to all the interests created by an instrument.

That said, the will or trust may not have any provision about what "survival" means and for some non-probate devices, like property held jointly with right of survivorship, it is not possible to draft a provision defining survivorship. The statutory definition of survival is a default rule and yields to a provision in an instrument dealing with survival. Of course, in some instances it is impossible to provide a contrary rule. By definition, the statute must govern survivorship questions in intestate succession and in jointly held property arrangements where it is not possible to specify a survivorship rule.

The Uniform Simultaneous Death Act of 1993 once again provides both a default rule for wills and trusts and rules for jointly held property and other situations where it is not possible to draft language that deals with the possibility. The UPC incorporates the Uniform Simultaneous Death Act provisions in the following section:

UPC § 2–702. Requirement of Survival by 120 Hours

(a) For the purposes of this [code], except as provided in subsection (d) [which allows the governing instrument to override the statute], an individual who is not established by clear and convincing evidence to have survived an event, including the death of another individual, by 120 hours is deemed to have predeceased the event.

(b) Except as provided in subsection (d), for purposes of a provision of a governing instrument that relates to an individual surviving an event, including the death of another individual, an individual who is not established by clear and convincing evidence to have survived the event, by 120 hours is deemed to have predeceased the event.

(c) Except as provided in subsection (d), if (i) it is not established by clear and convincing evidence that one of two co-owners with right of survivorship survived the other co-owner by 120 hours, one-half of the property passes as if one had survived by 120 hours and one-half as if the other had survived by 120 hours and (ii) there are more than two co-owners and it is not established by clear and convincing evidence that at least one of them survived the others by 120 hours, the property passes in the proportion that one bears to the whole number of co-owners. For the purposes of this subsection, "co-owners with right of survivorship" includes joint tenants, tenants by the entireties, and other co-owners of property or accounts held under circumstances that entitles one or more to the whole of the property or account on the death of the other or others.

Subsection (b) applies to wills and trusts which the code lumps together here and in some other places as "governing instruments" along with all sorts of documents that create non-probate property such as "an insurance or annuity policy, account with POD designation, security registered in beneficiary form, transfer on death (hereafter TOD) deed, pension, profit-sharing, retirement, or similar benefit plan, instrument creating or exercising a power of appointment or a power of attorney, or a dispositive, appointive, or nominative instrument of any similar type." This comprehensive list comes from the definition of governing instrument in UPC § 2–201(18). Under the UPC at least, therefore, just about every way to pass property on the death of one person to another living person requires that person to survive the first person by 120 hours unless a governing instrument can and does provide otherwise.

Problem 7-1

Henry and Wanda are a married couple. Wanda had been married before and that marriage ended in divorce. This is Henry's first marriage. Wanda has a child by her first husband, and Henry and Wanda have three children from their marriage. Henry's probate property is valued at $250,000 and Wanda's probate property is also valued at $250,000. How much will each spouse receive under UPC § 2–102 if the other spouse dies intestate? Do you think one result is better than the other?

C. Who Is a Spouse?

There was once a simple answer to the question, "Did the decedent have a surviving spouse?" A person was either married or not. Granted, the marriage might not have been a ceremonial marriage with proper licensing from the state where the marriage took place. Some states still recognize *common law marriage*, a doctrine that provides, roughly, that if a man and a woman hold themselves out as husband and wife, they have the rights and obligations of husband and wife. A common law marriage is sometimes referred to with greater accuracy as a *non-ceremonial marriage*. (Most states that do not recognize common law marriages will recognize a non-ceremonial marriage entered into in a sister state if the requirements of that other jurisdiction were satisfied.)

A married couple legally separated, but not divorced, might not be married for purposes of intestate succession, depending on governing law. The UPC holds otherwise.

UPC § 2–802. Effect of Divorce, Annulment, and Decree of Separation

(a) An individual who is divorced from the decedent or whose marriage to the decedent has been annulled is not a surviving spouse unless, by virtue of a subsequent marriage, he [or she] is married to the decedent at the time of death. A decree of separation that does not terminate the status of husband and wife is not a divorce for purposes of this section.

(b) For purposes of Parts 1, 2, 3, and 4 of this Article, and of Section 3–203, a surviving spouse does not include:

(1) an individual who obtains or consents to a final decree or judgment of divorce from the decedent or an annulment of their marriage, which decree or judgment is not recognized as valid in this State, unless subsequently they participate in a marriage ceremony purporting to marry each to the other or live together as husband and wife;

(2) an individual who, following an invalid decree or judgment of divorce or annulment obtained by the decedent, participates in a marriage ceremony with a third individual; or

(3) an individual who was a party to a valid proceeding concluded by an order purporting to terminate all marital property rights.

Note that under the UPC a final decree or judgment of divorce will prevent the survivor from being regarded as a surviving spouse but a decree of separation does not. Two possible grounds for disqualification in some states, abandonment and refusal to support, are not recognized, perhaps because the question of whether either event has occurred often leads to litigation. That's certainly been the experience in New York, for instance, which recognizes both abandonment and refusal to support as disqualifying a surviving spouse from being legally regarded as a surviving spouse (EPTL § 5–1.2(a) (5), (6)). The legal standard for abandonment has been defined as "desertion of a spouse with intent not to return or with an intent that the marriage should no longer exist." *Matter of Goethie*, 9 Misc.2d 906, 908 (Sur. Ct. Westchester Co. 1957). Questions of refusal to support are also fact specific and the burden of proof is on the party attempting to argue disqualification. Meeting that burden requires showing that the decedent looked to the surviving spouse for support but received none, even though the spouse had the necessary means.

The problems discussed above, however, seem simple in comparison to the years of controversy over the legal recognition of same-sex couples. Massachusetts was the first state to recognize marriages between persons of the same sex, following the decision of the Supreme Judicial Court that to deny a marriage license to a same-sex couple violated the Massachusetts Constitution. (*Goodridge v. Department of Public Health*, 798 N.E.2d 941 (2003)). California followed in 2008, although that development was then reversed by referendum, and a cluster of states legalized same-sex marriage in 2012. But beginning in the mid-1990s, states began to enact statutes and constitutional amendments to ban both the celebration and recognition of same-sex marriage—at the peak of opposition to same-sex marriage, more than forty states had such laws. At the federal level, Congress enacted the Defense of Marriage Act in 1996 in response to the possibility that a decision of the Hawaii Supreme Court might meant that Hawaii would be the first state to allow same-sex couples to marry (it didn't happen). The beginning of the end of the legal puzzle came in 2013, when the United States Supreme Court issued its opinion in *United States v. Windsor*, 570 U.S. 744 (2013), invalidating that section 3 of DOMA which defined marriage for federal purposes as exiting only between a man and a woman. In the wake of *Windsor* the federal government moved quickly to recognize same-sex marriages for federal purposes to the greatest possible extent, whether or not the couple lives in a state that recognizes the marriage as valid, so long as the marriage was valid where it was celebrated. Two years later, the Supreme Court held, in *Obergefell v. Hodges*, 135 S. Ct. 2584 (2015), that same-sex couples had a constitutional right to marry on the same terms as different-sex couples. Although opposition remains in some states, and there have been efforts to undermine the effects of the ruling, *Obergefell* equalized the inheritance rights for same-sex married couples.

D. Children and Parents

If spouses may be disqualified from inheriting through intestate succession, what about children or parents? Should parents who refuse to support their children be disqualified from inheriting from those children? Should children who refuse to support their parents (or mistreat their parents or ignore them) be disqualified from becoming heirs? Compare three statutory approaches to answering those questions:

UPC § 2–114. Parent Barred from Inheriting in Certain Circumstances

(a) A parent is barred from inheriting from or through a child of the parent if:

   (1) the parent's parental rights were terminated and the parent-child relationship was not judicially reestablished; or

   (2) the child died before reaching [18] years of age and there is clear and convincing evidence that immediately before the child's death the parental rights of the parent could have been terminated under law of this state other than this [code] on the basis of nonsupport, abandonment, abuse, neglect, or other actions or inactions of the parent toward the child.

(b) For the purpose of intestate succession from or through the deceased child, a parent who is barred from inheriting under this section is treated as if the parent predeceased the child.

New York Estates, Powers, and Trusts Law § 4–1.4. Disqualification of Parent to Take Intestate Share

(a) No distributive share in the estate of a deceased child shall be allowed to a parent if the parent, while such child is under the age of twenty-one years:

   (1) has failed or refused to provide for the child or has abandoned such child, whether or not such child dies before having attained the age of twenty-one years, unless the parental relationship and duties are subsequently resumed and continue until the death of the child; or

   (2) has been the subject of a proceeding pursuant to section three hundred eighty-four-b of the social services law which:

      (A) resulted in an order terminating parental rights, or

      (B) resulted in an order suspending judgment, in which event the surrogate's court shall make a determination disqualifying the parent on the grounds adjudicated by the family court, if the surrogate's court finds, by a preponderance of the evidence, that the parent, during the period of suspension, failed to comply with the family court order to restore the parent-child relationship.

(b) Subject to the provisions of subdivision eight of section two hundred thirteen of the civil practice law and rules,[1] the provisions of subparagraph one of paragraph (a) of this section shall not apply to a biological parent who places the child for adoption based upon:

   (1) a fraudulent promise, not kept, to arrange for and complete the adoption of such child, or

---

1   The six-year statute of limitations generally applicable to equitable actions. —Eds.

(2)   other fraud or deceit by the person or agency where, before the death of the child, the person or agency fails to arrange for the adoptive placement or petition for the adoption of the child, and fails to comply timely with conditions imposed by the court for the adoption to proceed.

(c)   In the event that a parent or spouse is disqualified from taking a distributive share in the estate of a decedent under this section or 5–1.2, the estate of such decedent shall be distributed in accordance with 4–1.1 as though such spouse or parent had predeceased the decedent.

California Probate Code § 259. Predeceasing a Decedent (2005)

(a)   Any person shall be deemed to have predeceased a decedent to the extent provided in subdivision (c) where all of the following apply:

    (1)   It has been proven by clear and convincing evidence that the person is liable for physical abuse, neglect, or fiduciary abuse of the decedent, who was an elder or dependent adult.

    (2)   The person is found to have acted in bad faith.

    (3)   The person has been found to have been reckless, oppressive, fraudulent, or malicious in the commission of any of these acts upon the decedent.

    (4)   The decedent, at the time those acts occurred and thereafter until the time of his or her death, has been found to have been substantially unable to manage his or her financial resources or to resist fraud or undue influence.

(b)   Any person shall be deemed to have predeceased a decedent to the extent provided in subdivision (c) if that person has been convicted of a violation of Section 236 of the Penal Code or any offense described in Section 368 of the Penal Code.

(c)   Any person found liable under subdivision (a) or convicted under subdivision (b) shall not (1) receive any property, damages, or costs that are awarded to the decedent's estate in an action described in subdivision (a) or (b), whether that person's entitlement is under a will, a trust, or the laws of intestacy; or (2) serve as a fiduciary as defined in Section 39, if the instrument nominating or appointing that person was executed during the period when the decedent was substantially unable to manage his or her financial resources or resist fraud or undue influence. This section shall not apply to a decedent who, at any time following the act or acts described in paragraph (1) of subdivision (a), or the act or acts described in subdivision (b), was substantially able to manage his or her financial resources and to resist fraud or undue influence within the meaning of subdivision (b) of Section 1801 of the Probate Code and subdivision (b) of Section 39 of the Civil Code.

(d)   For purposes of this section, the following definitions shall apply:

(1)   Physical abuse as defined in Section 15610.63 of the Welfare and Institutions Code.

statutes referring to other provisions.

(2)   Neglect as defined in Section 15610.57 of the Welfare and Institutions Code.

> **Take Note**
>
> Unlike the UPC or New York statutes, the California statute applies to *both* intestate and testate succession. Because a person receiving a gift in a will must survive the testator to receive the gift, the provision of the California statute deems the person who has been guilty of neglect to have predeceased the decedent and means that the person loses any gift under the decedent's will.

(3)   False imprisonment as defined in Section 368 of the Penal Code.

(4)   Fiduciary abuse as defined in Section 15610.30 of the Welfare and Institutions Code.

(e)   Nothing in this section shall be construed to prohibit the severance and transfer of an action or proceeding to a separate civil action pursuant to Section 801.

Notes

1. Parents or parents and children?

Only California Probate Code § 259 disqualifies a person from inheriting from or taking under the will of another adult, and the prohibition could easily prevent a child from inheriting (or taking under the will of) a parent regardless of the age at which the neglect occurred. There has been much scholarly discussion of the need for such provisions and, more generally, of linking inheritance (either by intestacy or under a will) to behavior towards the decedent.

For scholarly discussion of behavior-based inheritance, see Anne-Marie Rhodes, *Consequences of Heirs' Misconduct: Moving from Rules to Discretion*, 33 Ohio N.U.L. Rev. 975 (2007); Richard Lewis Brown, *Undeserving Heirs?—The Case of the "Terminated" Parent*, 40 U. Rich. L. Rev. 547 (2006); Linda Kelly Hill, *No-Fault Death: Wedding Inheritance Rights to Family Values*, 94 Ky. L.J. 319 (2005–2006). A now classic article on the Chinese system of rewarding good behavior with inheritance rights is Frances H. Foster, *Towards a Behavior-Based Model of Inheritance? The Chinese Experiment*, 32 U.C. Davis L. Rev. 77 (1998). Think about the problems raised by these disqualification schemes when we discussed the disqualification of slayers in Chapter 5.

2. What makes a good statute?

Note the different standards for disqualification under the three statutes. The UPC ties disqualification to standards articulated in another statute; the California statute sets out a list of tests with a reference to "clear and convincing evidence" (the same standard used by the UPC); the New York statute sets out a standard and refers to other statutes but makes no reference to a standard of proof. Which statute gives the best guidance to lawyers and judges dealing with the problem of disqualification for bad behavior? As a substantive matter, note that the UPC statute disqualifies the parent only if the child dies before a certain age (and suggests 18, the age of majority for most purposes) while the New York statute disqualifies a parent for bad behavior whether the child dies before or after attaining 21 years of age. Which is the better choice? And in thinking about the New York statute, how can a parent resume parental relationship and duties after the child is an adult?

E. Distribution to Descendants and Collateral Relatives: The Idea of Representation

Whatever the legal relationship, the intestate share of the surviving spouse or partner goes to an individual. If you read the UPC intestacy statute carefully, you will notice that all the other possible heirs are described as groups of individuals, or classes: descendants (or issue) of the decedent, or descendants of the decedent's parents or grandparents. All of these classes can have members from more than one generation. The decedent's descendants or issue, for example, could include children, grandchildren, and great-grandchildren. To determine the share of the intestate estate distributable to the members of any given class, statutes embody a concept known as "by representation."

1. The Basics of Representation

It is "by representation" that older generation beneficiaries exclude younger generation beneficiaries. For example, if the decedent dies intestate, survived by a child and the children of the child (the decedent's grandchildren), the intestate share of the decedent's descendants will be distributed only to the child. Another way to consider the position of the grandchildren in this example is that when they trace their relationship to their grandparent on the family tree, their living parent stands between them and their deceased grandparent. And when that parent dies, the children will be first in line—and may very well inherit some of that money the parent inherited from the grandparent.

Unfortunately, calculations are not always so straight forward. What if some children have survived and others have died but left behind surviving children? There are three schemes of representation commonly found in intestacy statutes. They give different results where some descendants of the decedent have died before the decedent. Consider first the person who dies intestate and unmarried and has three children and nine grandchildren. The family tree would look like this.

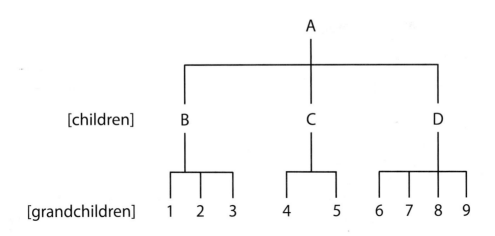

If all of A's children survive A the three living children each inherit one-third of the intestate estate. None of the grandchildren are heirs because when they look up the family tree their parents are alive and standing in the direct line between them and their dead grandparent. A living ascendant always excludes that person's descendants.

If one child (B) predeceases A the two living children, C and D, each inherit one-third of the intestate estate and B's three children each inherit one-ninth, that is, they equally divide the share their parent would have inherited. Again the living ascendant excludes her descendants, but the share of a deceased ancestor is equally divided among her issue.

The results in the examples above are the same in all three systems of representation. The systems first diverge if all of A's children predecease A. Under the system known as *strict per stirpes* (per stirpes means "by the roots") the grandchildren divide up the intestate share their parent would have inherited. The shares are fixed at the closest generation from the decedent, even if there are no survivors in that generation. Therefore 1, 2, and 3 each receive one-ninth of the total estate (one-third of B's one-third share), 4 and 5 each receive one-sixth (one-half of C's one-third share), and 6, 7, 8 and 9 each receive one-twelfth (one-fourth of D's one-third share). The distinguishing feature of strict per stirpes is the attention paid to the family tree. Each branch of the tree, each line of descendants from A, receives the same share of the intestate estate, thus equalizing the treatment of families rather than individuals. In the example above, each family of grandchildren receive the same share of the estate, one-third, but how much each individual grandchild receives depends on how many siblings he or she has.

Under the other two systems, *per capita with representation (modified per stirpes)* and *per capita at each generation*, all the grandchildren will receive exactly the same share of the intestate estate, which here is one-ninth of A's estate. Under both systems, the branches of the family tree begin and division of the intestate estate is made *in the closest generation to the decedent with at least one surviving class member*, with one share set aside for each living descendant in that generation and one share set aside for each deceased descendant who has living descendants of his or her own. In this example, the eldest generation with living members is the grandchild generation and therefore the intestate estate is divided into nine parts and each grandchild takes one part.

These last two systems, per capita with representation (modified per stirpes) and per capita at each generation, differ where there are takers in more than one generation. Per capita at each generation takes the "equally near, equally dear" principle to its fullest extent. Each taker within a generation will end up with the same share as other takers in the same generation. The outcome will be differ, for example, if B and C predecease A but D survives. Under per capita with representation, B's children equally divide the one-third set aside for B, each receiving one-ninth, and C's children equally divide the one-third set aside for C, each receiving one-sixth. Strict per stirpes would give the same result. Again, the shares of families rather than individuals are equalized where the heirs are of different generations. The only difference is where one begins to identify the family that receives a share.

Exam Tip

Add up all the shares in an intestate distribution. If you have done it correctly, the fractions will equal one.

Under per capita at each generation, however, the shares set aside for B and C, *are combined and distributed equally to the heirs in the next generation.* Therefore, all the grandchildren who are heirs (1,2,3,4 and 5) each receive two-fifteenths of the intestate estate. That is, the two-thirds share that would have been paid to B and C are combined and distributed equally among the heirs of B and C. Each of 1, 2, 3, 4, and 5, therefore, gets one-fifth of the two-thirds share, and one-fifth of two-thirds is two-fifteenths. Under this system all the heirs who are of the same generation receive exactly the same share of the intestate estate.

A good method for calculating intestate shares has four steps:

(1) Identify the generation at which to first fix shares based on the survivors in the family tree and the system of representation used in the relevant jurisdiction or instrument;

(2) Count shares within the identified generation, one for each survivor and one for each survivor who leaves behind at least one surviving descendant;

(3) Allocate shares to living takers in the identified generation;

(4) Drop remaining shares to the next generation, either as already fixed under the strict per stirpes or modified per stirpes method or by combining and redividing under the per capita at each generation method.

The UPC uses the latter "per capita at each generation" system. Here's the statutory language that defines the UPC system:

UPC § 2–106. Representation

(a) **[Definitions.]** In this section:

(1) "Deceased descendant," "deceased parent," or "deceased grandparent" means a descendant, parent, or grandparent who either predeceased the decedent or is deemed to have predeceased the decedent under Section 2–104.

(2)   "Surviving descendant" means a descendant who neither predeceased the decedent nor is deemed to have predeceased the decedent under Section 2–104.

(b)   **[Decedent's Descendants.]** If, under Section 2–103(1), a decedent's intestate estate or a part thereof passes "by representation" to the decedent's descendants, the estate or part thereof is divided into as many equal shares as there are (i) surviving descendants in the generation nearest to the decedent which contains one or more surviving descendants and (ii) deceased descendants in the same generation who left surviving descendants, if any. Each surviving descendant in the nearest generation is allocated one share. The remaining shares, if any, are combined and then divided in the same manner among the surviving descendants of the deceased descendants as if the surviving descendants who were allocated a share and their surviving descendants had predeceased the decedent.

(c)   **[Descendants of Parents or Grandparents.]** If, under Section 2–103(3) or (4), a decedent's intestate estate or a part thereof passes "by representation" to the descendants of the decedent's deceased parents or either of them or to the descendants of the decedent's deceased paternal or maternal grandparents or either of them, the estate or part thereof is divided into as many equal shares as there are (i) surviving descendants in the generation nearest the deceased parents or either of them, or the deceased grandparents or either of them, that contains one or more surviving descendants and (ii) deceased descendants in the same generation who left surviving descendants, if any. Each surviving descendant in the nearest generation is allocated one share. The remaining shares, if any, are combined and then divided in the same manner among the surviving descendants of the deceased descendants as if the surviving descendants who were allocated a share and their surviving descendants had predeceased the decedent.

In states that have not enacted the UPC provision, any one of the three representation systems may be in place. In New York, "representation" is defined as per capita in each generation, but "per stirpes" is defined as per capita with representation (modified per stirpes). Here's the statutory language that defines that system:

New York Estates, Powers, and Trusts Law § 1–2.14. Per stirpes

A per stirpes disposition or distribution of property is made to persons who take as issue of a deceased ancestor in the following manner:

The property so passing is divided into as many equal shares as there are (i) surviving issue in the generation nearest to the deceased ancestor which contains one or more surviving issue and (ii) deceased issue in the same generation who left surviving issue, if any. Each surviving member in such nearest generation is allocated one share. The share of a deceased issue in such nearest generation who left surviving issue shall be distributed in the same manner to such issue.

In California, on the other hand, "per stirpes" is defined as strict per stirpes:

California Probate Code § 246. Distribution under a Will, Trust or Other Instrument

(a)   Where a will, trust, or other instrument calls for property to be distributed or taken "in the manner provided in Section 246 of the Probate Code," the property to be distributed shall be divided into as many equal shares as there are living children of the designated ancestor, if any, and deceased children who leave issue then living. Each living child of the designated ancestor is allocated one share, and the share of each deceased child who leaves issue then living is divided in the same manner.

(b)   Unless the will, trust, or other instrument expressly provides otherwise, if an instrument executed on or after January 1, 1986, calls for property to be distributed or taken "per stirpes," "by representation," or "by right of representation," the property shall be distributed in the manner provided in subdivision (a).

(c)   If a will, trust, or other instrument executed before January 1, 1986, calls for property to be distributed or taken "per stirpes," "by representation," or by "right of representation," the property shall be distributed in the manner provided in subdivision (a), absent a contrary intent of the transferor.

Problem 7-2

All of the questions in this Problem 7-2 refer to the family tree below.

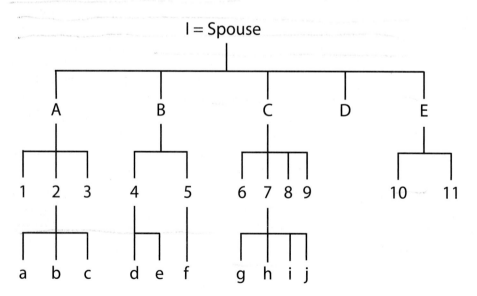

(a) **I** (for Intestate) dies survived by all of the persons on the family tree *except* **Spouse** and **I**'s children, **A** and **B**. How is **I**'s probate estate distributed under each of the three systems of representation?

(b) **I** dies survived by all of the persons on the family tree *except* **Spouse** and **I**'s children **A**, **B**, **C**, **D**, and **E**. How is **I**'s probate estate distributed under each of the three systems of representation?

(c) **I** dies survived by all of the persons on the family tree *except* **Spouse** and **I**'s children **A**, **B**, and **E**. How is **I**'s probate estate distributed under each of the three systems of representation?

(d) **I** dies survived by all of the persons on the family tree *except* **Spouse**, **I**'s children **B** and **C**, and grandchildren **5** and **7**. How is **I**'s probate estate distributed under each of the three systems of representation?

2. Adopted Persons

Until relatively recently, at least as the history of humans is measured, there was no doubt about the identity of the biological parents of any child. The woman who gave birth to the child is the mother and the man who impregnated the woman is the father. *So long as the man and woman were married to each other by the time the child was born*, there was no question, at least under the common law, that the child was the legal child of the couple and could inherit from both of them. Even if the couple divorced, the child was the child of both ex-spouses and could inherit from both. Relatively late in the history of Anglo-American law, the ability to adopt a person into a family was created by legislation. Adoption creates a kinship link—a parent-child relationship between adoptive parent and adopted child. Though anthropologists often refer to it as a "fictive" relationship, lawyers do not. At first, the adopted person was in law the child only of the adopting parents. Other relatives were "strangers to the adoption" and were not related to the adopted person. For example, if H and W adopted C, C was their child and would inherit from them as a child but could not inherit from H or W's parents, from their siblings, or indeed from any other relative of the adoptive parents. Over time, statutes extended the inheritance rights of adopted persons to reflect evolving legal treatment of adoption relationships as substitutionary rather than supplemental. Today, an adopted person is a full member of the families of the adopting parents so that he or she is a grandchild of the adopting parents' parents, a niece or nephew of their siblings and so forth.

The incorporation of the adopted person into the adopting family has as its corollary the complete separation of the adopted person from the birth family. In short, adoptive parents replace birth parents and the adoptive family replaces the birth family. The UPC is illustrative on this point.

UPC § 2–115. Definitions

In this [subpart 2, Parent-Child Relationships]:

. . .

(9)   "Relative" means a grandparent or a descendant of a grandparent.

UPC § 2–118. Parent-child relationship: adoptee and adoptee's adoptive parent or parents

(a)   **[Parent-Child Relationship Between Adoptee and Adoptive Parent or Parents.]** A parent-child relationship exists between an adoptee and the adoptee's adoptive parent or parents.

(b)   **[Individual in Process of Being Adopted by Married Couple; Stepchild in Process of Being Adopted by Stepparent.]** For purposes of subsection (a):

(1)   an individual who is in the process of being adopted by a married couple when one of the spouses dies is treated as adopted by the deceased spouse if the adoption is subsequently granted to the decedent's surviving spouse.

(2)   a child of a genetic parent who is in the process of being adopted by a genetic parent's spouse when the spouse dies is treated as adopted by the deceased spouse if the genetic parent survives the deceased spouse by 120 hours.

(c)   **[Child of Assisted Reproduction or Gestational Child In Process of Being Adopted.]** If, after a parent-child relationship is established between a child of assisted reproduction and a parent under Section 2–120 or between a gestational child and a parent under Section 2–121, the child is in the process of being adopted by the parent's spouse when that spouse dies, the child is treated as adopted by the deceased spouse for purposes of subsection (b)(2).

UPC § 2–119. Parent-child relationship: adoptee and adoptee's genetic parents

(a)   **[Parent-Child Relationship Between Adoptee and Genetic Parents.]** Except as otherwise provided in subsections (b) through (d), a parent-child relationship does not exist between an adoptee and the adoptee's genetic parents.

(b)   **[Stepchild Adopted by Stepparent.]** A parent-child relationship exists between an individual who is adopted by the spouse of either genetic parent and:

(1)   the genetic parent whose spouse adopted the individual; and

(2)   the other genetic parent, but only for purposes of the right of the adoptee or a descendant of the adoptee to inherit from or through the other genetic parent.

(c)   **[Individual Adopted by Relative of a Genetic Parent.]** A parent-child relationship exists between both genetic parents and an individual who is adopted by a relative of a genetic parent, or by the spouse or surviving spouse of a relative of a genetic parent, but only for purposes of the right of the adoptee or a descendant of the adoptee to inherit from or through either genetic parent.

(d)   **[Individual Adopted After Death of Both Genetic Parents.]** A parent-child relationship exists between both genetic parents and an individual who is adopted after the death of both genetic parents, but only for purposes of the right of the adoptee or a descendant of the adoptee to inherit through either genetic parent.

(e)   **[Child of Assisted Reproduction or Gestational Child Who Is Subsequently Adopted.]** If, after a parent-child relationship is established between a child of assisted reproduction and a parent or parents under Section 2–120 or between a gestational child and a parent or parents under Section 2–121, the child is adopted by another or others, the child's parent or parents under Section 2–120 or 2–121 are deemed the child's genetic parent or parents for purposes of this section.

Problem 7-3

H and W die in an accident. W's sister, A, and A's husband, D, adopt H and W's child, C.

(a)   W's mother dies, unmarried survived by A, her other child B, C and D's birth children, X and Y. Who will inherit from W's mother under the UPC?

(b)   H's father dies, unmarried, survived by his daughter E, her children F and G, the two children of another predeceased son, I and J, and C. Under the UPC, who will inherit from H's father?

Problem 7-4

H and W divorce. W marries H2, who adopts H and W's birth children, X, Y, and Z, with the consent of H.

(a)   H dies, unmarried, survived only by W, X, Y, and Z. Who will inherit from H under the UPC?

(b)   H's father dies, survived only by X, Y, and Z. Who will inherit from H's father under the UPC?

(c)   H's sister, his only sibling, dies unmarried, without issue and after the death of H and her parents. Will X, Y, and Z inherit from her?

Practice Planning Problem

A conceives through anonymous sperm donation and gives birth to a child which the law recognizes as hers. Under the law the sperm donor has no parental rights or obligations. A is in a long term committed partnership with B, another woman, who wishes to adopt the child so that both she and A will be the child's parents. How would you advise A and B, assuming the UPC is the applicable law?

———————————

Notes

1. Inheritance by "adopted out" persons

Very few state statutes go as far as UPC § 2–119 in preserving the inheritance rights of adopted out persons. One which preceded the UPC provision by more than 20 years is New York Domestic Relations Law § 117, which closely parallels the UPC provision. Why have such a provision? Should it also apply to gifts in wills to a group (such as "my grandchildren") that include adopted out persons? And why limit it to adoptions by relatives except, at least under the UPC, when the adoption occurs after the death of both genetic (birth) parents?

2. Second parent adoption

Consider Colorado's statute authorizing "second parent adoptions":

Colo. Rev. Stat. Ann. § 19–5–203. Availability for adoption

(1)   A child may be available for adoption only upon . . . .

(d.5)(I) Written and verified consent in a second-parent adoption that the child has a sole legal parent, and the sole legal parent wishes the child to be adopted by a specified second adult.

(II)   In a petition for a second-parent adoption, the court shall require a written home study report prepared by a county department of social services, designated qualified individual, or child placement agency and approved by the department pursuant to section 19–5–207.5(2). If the child of a sole legal parent was adopted by that parent less than six months prior to the filing of an adoption petition by a second prospective parent and if the second prospective parent was included in the home study report that was prepared pursuant to section 19–5–207 for the adoption of the child by the first parent, then that home study report shall be a valid home study report for the purpose of the second parent's adoption. If the filing of a petition for adoption by the second prospective parent occurs six months or more after the adoption by the first parent, a separate home study report shall be required pursuant to section 19–5–207.

The Colorado law overrules the usual result of an adoption: the end of the parent-child relationship between the parent consenting to the adoption and the child. UPC § 2–119(b)(1) is a typical provision preserving the parent-child relationship between the parent consenting to the adoption and the child when the adoptive parent is the spouse of the consenting parent. In the situation addressed by the Colorado statute, the adopting parent is not married to the parent consenting to the adoption, and without some additional law, like the statute, the consenting parent will no longer be the child's parent once the adoption is accomplished. The parent and the prospective parent may be a same-sex couple who was unable to marry prior to 2015 or a different-sex couple who do not wish to marry. In either case, the partner who is a parent can allow the other partner to adopt the parent's child without him or herself severing the parental relationship with the child. The Colorado statute is unusual, but a few states allow second-parent adoption under case law (*see, e.g., Matter of Jacob*, 660 N.E.2d 397 (N.Y. 1995)). The rationale for the court decisions, and almost certainly the policy behind the statute, is "the best interests of the child." What are the material benefits of having two parents?

3. Posthumous Children

Under the common law, the legal existence of a child born alive relates back to the moment of conception. The unborn child is *en ventre sa mere*, a phrase in Law French that translates to "in the mother's womb" or, more colloquially, "belly." The principle is so well accepted that in 1830 a New York court wrote: "It is at this day a well settled rule of law relative to successions, and to most other cases in relation to infants, that a child in ventre sa mere, as to every purpose where it is for the benefit of the child, is to be considered in esse [in being]." *Marsellis v. Thalhimer*, 2 Paige Ch. 35 (1830).

The importance of this doctrine to the distribution of intestate estates involves the birth of a child after the death of its putative father, the *posthumous child*. The traditional common law doctrine includes a rebuttable presumption that a child born to a widow within 280 days (the "average" period of human gestation) is the child of her late husband. The Uniform Parentage Act § 204 sets the period at 300 days. Some state statutes, on the other hand, provide simply that distributees conceived before the decedent's death and born alive thereafter are treated as if they were born during the decedent's lifetime. Presumably the common law presumption then applies in determining whether the child was indeed conceived before the father's death.

In addition to children conceived during the decedent's life and born after the decedent's death, modern technology has enabled posthumous conception using the decedent's gametic material. The inheritance rights of posthumously-conceived children is coming up shortly in this chapter.

4. Non-Marital Children

Up to this point, our discussion has assumed that all children are born to a married couple and therefore there is little ambiguity about whose descendants they are. That assumption, of course, is completely contrary to fact. Non-marital children were certainly known to the common law, but knowledge did not equal respect. The child born outside of marriage was regarded as *filius nullius*—no one's child—and could inherit from no one. This harsh result moderated over time, at first by laws allowing the child to inherit from the mother (after all, how could there be doubt about the identity of the mother) and eventually allowing inheritance from the father, at least where sufficient proof of paternity existed. In the United States these developments, at least with respect to inheritance from the father, were driven by courts applying the equal protection doctrine to the statutes governing inheritance. Eventually, in *Trimble v. Gordon*, 430 U.S. 762 (1977), the United States Supreme Court held that limiting a non-marital child to inheriting from the father only when the father had acknowledged paternity was indeed a violation of the Equal Protection Clause of the Fourteenth Amendment.

Today, the question of paternity has been greatly simplified by the development of technology that allows DNA matching. While no test is ever perfect, courts today almost universally accept the results of DNA testing, which are often stated as giving a 99% probability of paternity. States differ, however, on the circumstances when DNA testing is admissible, and procedural obstacles sometimes prevent proof of biological paternity from being considered or relied upon. States also differ as to whether and when the decedent's remains can be exhumed to provide samples for DNA testing, which can be relevant in inheritance cases where the decedent is the alleged parent. Courts in some states frequently order exhumations for that purpose; in other states courts have been far more reluctant to do so. One of these latter states is New York where the courts almost never allow exhumation for these purposes (*See In re Sekanic*, 229 A.D.2d 76 (N.Y. App. 1997; *In re Janis*, 210 A.D.2d 101 (N.Y. App. 1994). The New York courts, however, have proven to be quite creative in making do without exhumation.

Matter of Nasert

192 Misc.2d 682 (N.Y. Surr. Ct. 2002)

John A. Fusco, S.

In this pending probate proceeding, the decedent died a resident of Richmond County on June 27, 2001, survived by an adopted daughter, Jennifer A. Bragerton (Bragerton), and an alleged nonmarital daughter, Suzanne Manly Knudsen (Knudsen). An instrument purporting to be his last will and testament, dated August 27, 1996, is offered for probate by Bragerton, the nominated executrix and sole beneficiary therein. Knudsen opposes the probate of said instrument; however, before interposing objections she must establish her paternity, thereby giving her standing to object.

A paternity hearing was held pursuant to EPTL 4–1.2 to determine the status of Knudsen as a distributee. At this hearing, decedent's twin brother, Carl W. Nasert, testified on behalf of Knudsen. During his testimony, he offered to make himself available for DNA identification testing, if it would aid the court in determining Knudsen's paternity.

The courts in this jurisdiction first accepted the reliability of DNA fingerprinting in 1988 in criminal matters. In *People v Wesley* (140 Misc 2d 306, 308, *affd* 183 AD2d 75, *affd* 83 NY2d 417), the court stated:

> DNA Fingerprinting is a genetic and molecular biological process that has its basis in the fact that each individual has an entirely unique genetic 'signature,' derived

in turn from the fact that the overall configuration of the DNA, found in every cell in the human body (and for that matter, in every living organism) containing a nucleus—over 99% of the cells of the human body—is different in every individual *except in the case of identical twins.* This fact is not only generally accepted by the scientific community to which it is related, but is uniformly accepted therein. (Emphasis added.)

Since that time DNA testing also has been extended to paternity issues in civil matters (*see, Matter of Baby Girl S.*, 140 Misc 2d 299 [wherein the Surrogate recognized the validity and reliability of DNA testing]). Indeed, EPTL 4–1.2 (a) (2) now provides that a nonmarital child is the legitimate child of his father so that he and his issue inherit from his father if: "(C) paternity has been established by clear and convincing evidence and the father of the child has openly and notoriously acknowledged the child as his own; or (D) a blood genetic marker test had been administered to the father which together with other evidence establishes paternity by clear and convincing evidence."

> ### Food for Thought
>
> How else might the clear and convincing standard be met? What if the decedent and his surviving sibling were fraternal twins? Or the decedent had no siblings but was survived by a marital child? What if the decedent was an only child and had no marital children?

'clear and convincing'

In *Matter of Sandler* (160 Misc 2d 955), the court extended DNA testing to collateral relatives of the decedent. The Surrogate therein pointed out that she had earlier prohibited the exhumation of a putative father's body for the purpose of DNA testing holding that under clause (D) of EPTL 4–1.2 (a) (2) the test had to be administered to the father during his lifetime. However, she found no prohibition against establishing paternity by the DNA testing of the putative paternal grandparents in an effort to provide the "clear and convincing evidence" that is required to establish paternity under clause (C) of EPTL 4–1.2 (a) (2).

The court could find no instance where DNA testing was done on an identical twin to establish paternity of a decedent. Inasmuch as the court, however, was not satisfied that the strict requirements of EPTL 4–1.2 (a) (2) (C) had been met, the court ordered the voluntary testing of Carl W. Nasert, decedent's identical twin, who shares the identical DNA of the decedent.

This testing resulted in a report indicating "[I]f it is true that these brothers are identical twins, and if the child's mother admits to relations with Robert and not Carl, then Robert Nasert cannot be excluded as the biological father of Suzanne B. Manly Knudsen. Based upon the above genetic testing results, the probability of paternity is 99.96%."

Both sides concede that Carl is indeed the identical twin of the decedent. Furthermore, there was uncontroverted testimony that the child's mother had a sexual relationship exclusively with the decedent (and not his brother, Carl) during the critical period of conception.

The court therefore gives great weight to the result of the genetic test report as if the testing had been done on the decedent himself before his demise. Accordingly, the court finds the requirements of clauses (C) and (D) of EPTL 4–1.2 (a) (2) to have been satisfied. Suzanne

Manly Knudsen is determined to be a distributee of Robert Nasert with standing to oppose the probate of the instrument purporting to be his last will and testament. . . .

---

5. Equitable Adoption

Children are of course dependent on adults for survival and sometimes their birth parents cannot or will not care for them and other adults assume the role of parents. Sometimes a formal adoption never takes place even though the child and the foster parents behave toward each other like parents and child. In some relatively narrow circumstances, courts have found that children in this situation are the heirs of the foster parents.

Estate of Ford

82 P.3d 747 (Cal. 2004)

Werdegar, J.

Terrold Bean claims the right to inherit the intestate estate of Arthur Patrick Ford as Ford's equitably adopted son. The superior court denied the claim, and the Court of Appeal affirmed the denial, for lack of clear and convincing evidence that Ford intended to adopt Bean. After reviewing California case law on equitable adoption, we conclude that no equitable adoption is shown unless the parties' conduct and statements clearly and convincingly demonstrate an intent to adopt. We will therefore affirm the judgment of the Court of Appeal.

FACTUAL AND PROCEDURAL BACKGROUND

Born in 1953, Bean was declared a ward of the court and placed in the home of Ford and his wife, Kathleen Ford, as a foster child in 1955. Bean never knew his natural father, whose identity is uncertain, and he was declared free of his mother's control in 1958, at the age of four. Bean lived continuously with Mr. and Mrs. Ford and their natural daughter, Mary Catherine, for about 18 years, until Mrs. Ford's death in 1973, then with Ford and Mary Catherine for another two years, until 1975.

During part of the time Bean lived with the Fords, they cared for other foster children and received a county stipend for doing so. Although the Fords stopped taking in foster children after Mrs. Ford became ill with cancer, they retained custody of Bean. The last two other foster children left the home around the time of Mrs. Ford's death, but Bean, who at 18 years of age could have left, stayed with Ford and Mary Catherine.

Bean knew the Fords were not his natural parents, but as a child he called them "Mommy" and "Daddy," and later "Mom" and "Dad." Joan Malpassi, Mary Catherine's friend since childhood and later administrator of Ford's estate, testified that Bean's relationship with Mary Catherine was "as two siblings" and that the Fords treated Bean "more like Mary rather than a foster son, like a real son was my observation." Mary Catherine later listed Bean as her brother on a life insurance application.

> **Make the Connection**
>
> Equitable principles frequently inform the law of succession to property. But this case involves family law. Why could "fairness" require the court to create an adoption when no adoption took place or was even attempted?

Bean remained involved with Ford and Mary Catherine even after leaving the Ford home and marrying. Ford loaned Bean money to help furnish his new household and later forgave the unpaid part of the debt when Bean's marriage was dissolved. Bean visited Ford and Mary Catherine several times per year both during his marriage and after his divorce. When Ford suffered a disabling stroke in 1989, Mary Catherine conferred with Bean and Malpassi over Ford's care; Ford was placed in a board and care facility where Bean continued to visit him regularly until his death in 2000.

Mary Catherine died in 1999. Bean and Malpassi arranged her funeral. Bean petitioned for Malpassi to be appointed Ford's conservator, and with Malpassi's agreement Bean obtained a power of attorney to take care of Ford's affairs pending establishment of the conservatorship. Bean also administered Mary Catherine's estate, which was distributed to the Ford conservatorship. When a decision was needed as to whether Ford should receive medical life support, Malpassi consulted with Bean in deciding he should. When Ford died, Bean and Malpassi arranged the funeral.

> **Food for Thought**
>
> Is Bean's role in the planning of his foster sister's funeral evidence of an "attempt to adopt" that was somehow thwarted?

The Fords never petitioned to adopt Bean. Mrs. Ford told Barbara Carter, a family friend, that "they wanted to adopt Terry," but she was "under the impression that she could not put in for adoption while he was in the home." She worried that if Bean was removed during the adoption process he might be put in "a foster home that wasn't safe."

Ford's nearest relatives at the time of his death were the two children of his predeceased brother, nephew John J. Ford III and niece Veronica Newbeck. Neither had had any contact with Ford for about 15 years before his death, and neither attended his funeral. John J. Ford III filed a petition to determine entitlement to distribution (Prob.Code, § 11700), listing both himself and Newbeck as heirs. Bean filed a statement of interest claiming entitlement to Ford's entire estate under Probate Code sections 6454 (foster child heirship) and 6455 (equitable adoption) as well as sections 6402, subdivision (a) and 6450.

After trial, the superior court ruled against Bean. Probate Code section 6454's requirement of a legal barrier to adoption was unmet, since the Fords could have adopted Bean after his mother's parental rights were terminated in 1958. The doctrine of equitable adoption, the trial court found, was inapplicable because "there is no evidence that [Ford] ever told [Bean] or anyone else that he wanted to adopt him nor publicly told anyone that [Bean] was his adopted son." There was thus no clear and convincing evidence of "an intent to adopt."

> ### Make the Connection
>
> Is this the point at which fairness enters? Is it more equitable for Bean to inherit rather than the collaterals? If the Fords thought so, why didn't they write wills?

Bean appealed only on the equitable adoption issue. The Court of Appeal affirmed, agreeing with the trial court that equitable adoption must be proven by clear and convincing evidence. Moreover, the reviewing court held, any error by the trial court in this respect would be harmless because the evidence did not support equitable adoption on any standard of proof "for the same reasons articulated by the trial court."

We granted Bean's petition for review.

DISCUSSION

Chapter 2 of part 2 of division 6 of the Probate Code, sections 6450 to 6455, defines the parent-child relationship for purposes of intestate succession. Section 6450, subdivision (b) provides that such a relationship exists between adopting parents and the adopted child. Section 6453, subdivision (a) provides that the relationship exists between a child and a presumptive parent under the Uniform Parentage Act. Section 6454 delineates the circumstances in which a foster parent or stepparent is deemed a parent for the purpose of succession, requiring both a personal relationship beginning during the child's minority and enduring for the child's and parent's joint lifetimes, and a legal barrier but for which the foster parent or stepparent would have adopted the child. (See generally *Estate of Joseph* 949 P.2d 472 (Cal. 1998). Finally, section 6455 provides in full: "Nothing in this chapter affects or limits application of the judicial doctrine of equitable adoption for the benefit of the child or the child's issue." We therefore look to decisional law, rather than statute, for guidance on the equitable adoption doctrine's proper scope and application.

I. Criteria for Equitable Adoption

In its essence, the doctrine of equitable adoption allows a person who was accepted and treated as a natural or adopted child, and as to whom adoption typically was promised or contemplated but never performed, to share in inheritance of the foster parents' property. "The parents of a child turn him over to foster parents who agree to care for him as if he were their own child. Perhaps they also agree to adopt him. They do care for him, support him, educate him, and treat him in all respects as if he were their child, but they never adopt him. Upon their death he seeks to inherit their property on the theory that he should be treated as if he had been adopted. Many courts would honor his claim, at least under some circumstances, characterizing the case as one of equitable adoption, or adoption by estoppel, or virtual adoption, or specific enforcement of a contract to adopt." (Clark, The Law of Domestic Relations in the United States (2d ed.1988) § 20.9, p. 925.) The doctrine is widely applied to allow inheritance from the adoptive parent: at least 27 jurisdictions have so applied the doctrine, while only 10 have declined to recognize it in that context. (Annot., Modern Status of Law as to Equitable Adoption or Adoption by Estoppel (1980) 97 A.L.R.3d 347, § 3.)

A California court first recognized the doctrine, albeit in the atypical context of inheritance *through* the adoptive parent, in *Estate of Grace* (1948) 88 Cal.App.2d 956, 200 P.2d 189. A California couple had taken custody of and raised a Texas girl, Edna Grace, having recorded in Texas a statement that they " 'hereby adopt' " the child, who was to be their heir and " 'a member of our family, with all the rights and privileges as if born to us.' " (*Id.* at p. 957, 200 P.2d 189.) Although Texas adoption law at that time did not recognize inheritance from an adoptive grandparent through an adoptive parent (*id.* at pp. 959–960, 200 P.2d 189), the California court upheld Grace's daughter's entitlement to inherit from her adoptive grandparents as a matter of contract. The parents had offered to adopt Grace and make her a full member of their family, and "[t]he child, by living with them as a member of the family, accepted the offer," creating a contract concluded and performed in California. (*Estate of Grace, supra,* at p. 962, 200 P.2d 189.) Quoting from a treatise, the appellate court noted that " 'the courts, in their effort to protect and promote the welfare of the child, have given effect to a contract to adopt, where it has been fully performed on the part of the child, although it was invalid under the laws where it was made.' " (*Id.* at p. 963, 200 P.2d 189.)

This court decided its only case relating to equitable adoption nine years later. (*Estate of Radovich, supra,* 48 Cal.2d 116, 308 P.2d 14.) The question before us was not whether the child could inherit as an equitable adoptee—a final superior court decree established that he could—but the child's status, for purposes of inheritance taxation, as either the decedent's adopted child or a stranger

> **Food for Thought**
>
> Is there any evidence of a contract in this case? Is it more likely to exist in other cases?

in blood to the decedent. (*Id.* at pp. 118–119, 308 P.2d 14.) The majority took the former view, but its opinion rested on the in rem character of the superior court's probate decree and did not address the contours of the equitable adoption doctrine. (*Id.* at pp. 119–124, 308 P.2d 14.)

Justice Schauer's dissenting opinion, however, addressed the equitable adoption doctrine at some length, concluding the child took solely by virtue of an unperformed contract of adoption and thus as a stranger in blood. (*Estate of Radovich, supra,* 48 Cal.2d at pp. 129–135, 308 P.2d 14 (dis. opn. of Schauer, J.).) Citing sister-state authority, Justice Schauer explained: "When the child takes property in such a case it is as a purchaser by virtue of the contract [citation] and by way of damages or specific performance [citations]. . . . The child shares in the estate of the deceased foster parent *as though* his own child but not as such. In order to do justice and equity, as far as possible, to one who, though having filled the place of a natural born child, through inadvertence or fault has not been legally adopted, the court enforces a contract under which the child is entitled to property, declaring that as a consideration on the part of the foster parents a portion of their property will pass on their death to the child." (*Id.* at p. 130, 308 P.2d 14.)

Although expressed in a dissenting opinion, Justice Schauer's explanation of the doctrine has been widely cited and relied upon by the Courts of Appeal. . . .

In *Estate of Bauer* (1980) 111 Cal.App.3d 554, 168 Cal.Rptr. 743, an inheritance tax case, the court found insufficient evidence of equitable adoption—the child did not live with the asserted parents either as a minor or for any extended time as an adult, and did not assume "any duties normally associated with a parent-child relationship" (*id.* at p. 559, 168 Cal.Rptr. 743)—but aptly summarized the doctrine as it had developed in California: "[E]quitable adoption requires some form of agreement to adopt, coupled with subsequent objective conduct indicating mutual recognition of an adoptive parent and child relationship to such an extent that in equity and good conscience an adoption should be deemed to have taken place." (*Id.* at p. 560, 168 Cal.Rptr. 743.) . . .

As reflected in this summary, California decisions have explained equitable adoption as the specific enforcement of a contract to adopt. Yet it has long been clear that the doctrine, even in California, rested less on ordinary rules of contract law than on considerations of fairness and intent for, as Justice Schauer put it, the child "should have been" adopted and would have been but for the decedent's "inadvertence or fault." (*Estate of Radovich, supra,* 48 Cal.2d at pp. 134, 130, 308 P.2d 14 (dis. opn. of Schauer, J.), italics omitted.) In the earliest case, *Estate of Grace,* the court quoted a New Mexico case explaining why specific performance was an unrealistic description of equitable adoption: " 'A specific performance of a contract to adopt is impossible after the death of the parties who gave the promise. Equity was driven to the fiction that there had been an adoption. That fiction being indulged, the case was not one of specific performance.' " (*Estate of Grace, supra,* 88 Cal.App.2d at pp. 964–965, 200 P.2d 189, quoting *Wooley v. Shell Petroleum Corporation* (1935) 39 N.M. 256, 45 P.2d 927, 931–932.) In both *Estate of Rivolo, supra,* 194 Cal.App.2d 773, 15 Cal.Rptr. 268, and *Estate of Wilson, supra,* 111 Cal.App.3d 242, 168 Cal.Rptr. 533, moreover, the contracts purportedly being enforced were made between foster parents and their minor charges, yet neither court addressed the children's capacity to contract, suggesting, again, that the contract served mainly as evidence of the parties' intent, rather than as an enforceable legal basis for transmission of property.

Bean urges that equitable adoption be viewed not as specific enforcement of a contract to adopt, but as application of an equitable, restitutionary remedy he has identified as quasi-contract or, as his counsel emphasized at oral argument, as an application of equitable estoppel principles. While we have found no decisions articulating a quasi-contract theory, courts in several states have, instead of or in addition to the contract rationale, analyzed equitable adoption as arising from "a broader and vaguer equitable principle of estoppel." (Clark, The Law of Domestic Relations in the United States, *supra,* at p. 926.) Bean argues Mr. Ford's conduct toward him during their long and close relationship estops Ford's estate or heirs at law from denying his status as an equitably adopted child.

For several reasons, we conclude the California law of equitable adoption, which has rested on contract principles, does not recognize an estoppel arising merely from the existence of a familial relationship between the decedent and the claimant. The law of intestate succession is intended to carry out " 'the intent a decedent without a will is most likely to have had.' " (*Estate of Griswold* (2001) 25 Cal.4th 904, 912, 108 Cal.Rptr.2d 165, 24 P.3d 1191.) The existence of a mutually affectionate relationship, without any direct expression by the decedent of an intent to adopt the child or to have him or her treated as a legally adopted child, sheds little light on the decedent's likely intent regarding distribution of property. While a person with whom the decedent had a close, caring and enduring relationship may often be seen as more deserving of inheritance than the heir or heirs at law, whose personal relationships with the decedent may have been, as they were here, attenuated, equitable adoption in California is neither a means of compensating the child for services rendered to the parent nor a device to avoid the unjust enrichment of other, more distant relatives who will succeed to the estate under the intestacy statutes. Absent proof of an intent to adopt, we must follow the statutory law of intestate succession.

In addition, a rule looking to the parties' overall relationship in order to do equity in a given case, rather than to particular expressions of intent to adopt, would necessarily be a vague and subjective one, inconsistently applied, in an area of law where "consistent, bright-line rules" (*Estate of Furia, supra*, 103 Cal.App.4th at p. 6, 126 Cal.Rptr.2d 384) are greatly needed. Such a broad scope for equitable adoption would leave open to competing claims the estate of *any* foster parent or stepparent who treats a foster child or stepchild lovingly and on an equal basis with his or her natural or legally adopted children. A broad doctrine of equitable adoption would also render section 6454, in practice, a virtual nullity, since children meeting the familial-relationship criteria of that statute would necessarily be equitable adoptees as well.

While a California equitable adoption claimant need not prove all the elements of an enforceable contract to adopt, therefore, we conclude the claimant must demonstrate the existence of some direct expression, on the decedent's part, of an intent to adopt the claimant. This intent may be shown, of course, by proof of an unperformed express agreement or promise to adopt. But it may also be demonstrated by proof of other acts or statements directly showing that the decedent intended the child to be, or to be treated as, a legally adopted child, such as an invalid or unconsummated attempt to adopt, the decedent's statement of his or her intent to adopt the child, or the decedent's representation to the claimant or to the community at large that the claimant was the decedent's natural or legally adopted child. (See, e.g., *Estate of Rivolo, supra*, 194 Cal.App.2d at p. 775, 15 Cal.Rptr. 268 [parents who orally promised child she would "be their little girl" later told her and others they had adopted her]; *Estate of Wilson, supra*, 111 Cal. App.3d at p. 248, 168 Cal.Rptr. 533 [petition to adopt filed but dismissed for lack of natural mother's consent]; *Estate of Reid* (1978) 80 Cal.App.3d 185, 188, 145 Cal.Rptr. 451 [written agreement with adult child].)

Thus, in California the doctrine of equitable adoption is a relatively narrow one, applying only to those who "though having filled the place of a natural born child, through inadvertence or fault [have] not been legally adopted," "[where] *the evidence establishes an intent to adopt.*"

(*Estate of Furia, supra*, 103 Cal.App.4th at p. 5, 126 Cal.Rptr.2d 384, italics added.) In addition to a statement or act by the decedent unequivocally evincing the decedent's intent to adopt, the claimant must show the decedent acted consistently with that intent by forming with the claimant a close and enduring familial relationship. That is, in addition to a contract or other direct evidence of the intent to adopt, the evidence must show "objective conduct indicating mutual recognition of an adoptive parent and child relationship to such an extent that in equity and good conscience an adoption should be deemed to have taken place." (*Estate of Bauer, supra*, 111 Cal.App.3d at p. 560, 168 Cal.Rptr. 743.)

II. Standard of Proof of Equitable Adoption

Bean also contends the lower courts erred in applying a standard of clear and convincing proof to the equitable adoption question. We disagree. Most courts that have considered the question require at least clear and convincing evidence in order to prove an equitable adoption. (See Clark, The Law of Domestic Relations in the United States, *supra*, at p. 927; Rein, *supra*, 37 Vand. L.Rev. at p. 780.) Several good reasons support the rule.

First, the claimant in an equitable adoption case is seeking inheritance outside the ordinary statutory course of intestate succession and without the formalities required by the adoption statutes. As the claim's "strength lies in inherent justice" (*Wooley v. Shell Petroleum Corporation, supra*, 45 P.2d at p. 932), the need in justice for this "extraordinary equitable intervention" (Rein, *supra*, 37 Vand. L. Rev. at p. 785) should appear clearly and unequivocally from the facts.

Second, the claim involves a relationship with persons who have died and who can, therefore, no longer testify to their intent. . . .

Finally, too relaxed a standard could create the danger that "a person could not help out a needy child without having a de facto adoption foisted upon him after death." . . .

Evidence Code section 115 provides that the burden of proof in civil cases is a preponderance of the evidence "[e]xcept as otherwise provided by law." The law providing for a higher standard of proof may include decisional law. (*Weiner v. Fleischman* (1991) 54 Cal.3d 476, 483, 286 Cal. Rptr. 40, 816 P.2d 892.) Persuaded by the reasoning of sister-state decisions and commentary, we hold that in order to take as an equitably adopted child from the alleged adoptive parent's intestate estate, the claimant must prove the decedent's intent to adopt by clear and convincing evidence.

CONCLUSION

Although the evidence showed the Fords and Bean enjoyed a close and enduring familial relationship, evidence was totally lacking that the Fords ever made an attempt to adopt Bean or promised or stated their intent to do so; they neither held Bean out to the world as their natural or adopted child (Bean, for example, did not take the Ford name) nor represented to Bean that he was their child. Mrs. Ford's single statement to Barbara Carter was not clear and convincing evidence that Mr. Ford intended Bean to be, or be treated as, his adopted son. Substantial evidence thus supported the trial court, which heard the testimony live and could best assess its credibility and strength, in its finding that intent to adopt, and therefore Bean's claim of equitable adoption, was unproven.

DISPOSITION

The judgment of the Court of Appeal is affirmed.

Notes

1. *Contract or not?*

Some cases take a much less doctrinal approach to situations like that in Ford and focus instead on the relationship between the decedent and the foster child and find that the foster child does inherit from the decedent. *See Welch v. Wilson*, S.E.2d 35 (W. Va. 1999) (clear and convincing evidence that the person claiming equitable adoption enjoyed a status within the decedent's home and family identical to that of a formally adopted child). On the whole those cases are limited to allowing the equitably adopted child to inherit from the foster parents. There are also cases taking a very strict approach to the contract requirement (*See O'Neal v. Wilkes*, 439 S.E.2d 490 (Ga. 1994)).

2. *What should be required?*

If a man and a woman can become a married couple by behaving like a married couple in jurisdictions that recognize non-ceremonial marriages (so-called "common law marriages"), why shouldn't an adult and child become parent and child if they live their lives as if that was their relationship? One way to start thinking about the question is to consider if there are differences between the marriage relationship and the parent and child relationship that justify the distinction.

6. Children of Assisted Reproduction

Technology has greatly diminished the power of the old certainties of parentage. Once, it was possible to be completely certain of the identity of a child's mother: the only candidate for the position was the woman who gave birth to the child. The identity of the father, however might not be so certain. Today, however, the situation is reversed. Genetic testing makes identifying the father, or rather eliminating possible candidates, about as certain as is humanly possible. Advances in *in vitro* fertilization remove the certainty that the woman who gives birth to a child is the child's biological mother. In addition, the storage of gametes (sperm and ova) makes possible posthumous conception.

Woodward v. Commissioner of Social Security

760 N.E.2d 257 (Mass. 2002)

Present: MARSHALL, C.J., GREANEY, IRELAND, SPINA, COWIN, SOSMAN, & CORDY, JJ.

MARSHALL, C.J.

The United States District Court for the District of Massachusetts has certified the following question to this court.

"If a married man and woman arrange for sperm to be withdrawn from the husband for the purpose of artificially impregnating the wife, and the woman is impregnated with that sperm after the man, her husband, has died, will children resulting from such pregnancy enjoy the inheritance rights of natural children under Massachusetts' law of intestate succession?"

We answer the certified question as follows: In certain limited circumstances, a child resulting from posthumous reproduction may enjoy the inheritance rights of "issue" under the Massachusetts intestacy statute. These limited circumstances exist where, as a threshold matter, the surviving parent or the child's other legal representative demonstrates a genetic relationship between the child and the decedent. The survivor or representative must then establish both that the decedent affirmatively consented to posthumous conception and to the support of any resulting child. Even where such circumstances exist, time limitations may preclude commencing a claim for succession rights on behalf of a posthumously conceived child. Because the government has conceded that the timeliness of the wife's paternity action under our intestacy law is irrelevant to her Federal appeal, we do not address that question today.

The United States District Court judge has not asked us to determine whether the circumstances giving rise to succession rights for posthumously conceived children apply here. In addition, she has removed from our consideration the question whether the paternity judgment obtained by the wife in this case was valid. . . .

I

The undisputed facts and relevant procedural history are as follows. In January, 1993, about three and one-half years after they were married, Lauren Woodward and Warren Woodward were informed that the husband had leukemia. At the time, the couple was childless. Advised that the husband's leukemia treatment might leave him sterile, the Woodwards arranged for a quantity of the husband's semen to be medically withdrawn and preserved, in a process commonly known as "sperm banking." The husband then underwent a bone marrow transplant. The treatment was not successful. The husband died in October, 1993, and the wife was appointed administratrix of his estate.

In October, 1995, the wife gave birth to twin girls. The children were conceived through artificial insemination using the husband's preserved semen. In January, 1996, the wife applied for two forms of Social Security survivor benefits: "child's" benefits under 42 U.S.C. § 402(d)(1) (1994 & Supp. V 1999), and "mother's" benefits under 42 U.S.C. § 402(g)(1) (1994).

The Social Security Administration (SSA) rejected the wife's claims on the ground that she had not established that the twins were the husband's "children" within the meaning of the Act. In February, 1996, as she pursued a series of appeals from the SSA decision, the wife filed a "complaint for correction of birth record" in the Probate and Family Court against the clerk of the city of Beverly, seeking to add her deceased husband as the "father" on the twins' birth certificates. In October, 1996, a judge in the Probate and Family Court entered a judgment of paternity and an order to amend both birth certificates declaring the deceased husband to be the children's father. In his judgment of paternity, the Probate Court judge did not make findings of fact, other than to state that he "accepts the [s]tipulations of [v]oluntary [a]cknowledgment of [p]arentage of [the children] . . . executed by [wife] as [m]other, and [the wife], [a]dministratrix of the [e]state of [the husband], for father." See G.L. c. 209C, § 11.

The wife presented the judgment of paternity and the amended birth certificates to the SSA, but the agency remained unpersuaded. A United States administrative law judge, hearing the wife's claims de novo, concluded, among other things, that the children did not qualify for benefits because they "are not entitled to inherit from [the husband] under the Massachusetts intestacy and paternity laws." The appeals council of the SSA affirmed the administrative law judge's decision, which thus became the commissioner's final decision for purposes of judicial review. The wife appealed to the United States District Court for the District of Massachusetts, seeking a declaratory judgment to reverse the commissioner's ruling.

The United States District Court judge certified the above question to this court because "[t]he parties agree that a determination of these children's rights under the law of Massachusetts is dispositive of the case and . . . no directly applicable Massachusetts precedent exists."

> **Take Note**
>
> State family and property law may determine whether or not a person can receive benefits under federal law.

II
A

We have been asked to determine the inheritance rights under Massachusetts law of children conceived from the gametes of a deceased individual and his or her surviving spouse. We have not previously been asked to consider whether our intestacy statute accords inheritance rights to posthumously conceived genetic children. Nor has any American court of last resort considered, in a published opinion, the question of posthumously conceived genetic children's inheritance rights under other States' intestacy laws.

This case presents a narrow set of circumstances, yet the issues it raises are far reaching. Because the law regarding the rights of posthumously conceived children is unsettled, the certified question is understandably broad. Moreover, the parties have articulated extreme positions.

The wife's principal argument is that, by virtue of their genetic connection with the decedent, posthumously conceived children must *always* be permitted to enjoy the inheritance rights of the deceased parent's children under our law of intestate succession. The government's principal argument is that, because posthumously conceived children are not "in being" as of the date of the parent's death, they are *always* barred from enjoying such inheritance rights.

Food for Thought

Why should a court resort to a body of law which had its origins in an era in which posthumous conception would have involved magic rather than science?

Neither party's position is tenable. In this developing and relatively uncharted area of human relations, bright-line rules are not favored unless the applicable statute requires them. The Massachusetts intestacy statute does not. Neither the statute's "posthumous children" provision, see G.L. c. 190, § 8, nor any other provision of our intestacy law limits the class of posthumous children to those in utero at the time of the decedent's death. On the other hand, with the act of procreation now separated from coitus, posthumous reproduction can occur under a variety of conditions that may conflict with the purposes of the intestacy law and implicate other firmly established State and individual interests. We look to our intestacy law to resolve these tensions.

B

We begin our analysis with an overview of Massachusetts intestacy law. In our Commonwealth, the devolution of real and personal property in intestacy is neither a natural nor a constitutional right. It is a privilege conferred by statute. Our intestacy statute "excludes all rules of law which might otherwise be operative. It impliedly repealed all preexisting statutes and supersedes the common law."

Section 1 of the intestacy statute directs that, if a decedent "leaves issue," such "issue" will inherit a fixed portion of his real and personal property, subject to debts and expenses, the rights of the surviving spouse, and other statutory payments not relevant here. See G.L. c. 190, § 1. To answer the certified question, then, we must first determine whether the twins are the "issue" of the husband.

Take Note

"Issue" is a term you will see again and again in your study of wills and trusts. Remember that just as the court says, the term means anyone descended from a particular individual, not just their children.

The intestacy statute does not define "issue." However, in the context of intestacy the term "issue" means all lineal (genetic) descendants, and now includes both marital and nonmarital descendants. The term " '[d]escendants' . . . has long been held to mean persons 'who by consanguinity trace their lineage to the designated ancestor.' "

Turning to "issue" who are the nonmarital children of an intestate, the intestacy statute treats different classes of nonmarital children differently based on the presumed ease of establishing their consanguinity with the deceased parent. A nonmarital child is presumptively the child of his or her mother and is entitled by virtue of this presumption to enjoy inheritance rights as her issue. G.L. c. 190, § 5. However, to enjoy inheritance rights as the issue of a deceased father, a nonmarital child, in the absence of the father's acknowledgment of paternity or marriage to the mother, must obtain a judicial determination that he or she is the father's child. G.L. c. 190, § 7. The general purpose of such a specific adjudication requirement is to ensure that wealth passes from and to the actual family. We held, at a time when the means for establishing the paternity of a child were less certain than they are today, that such disparate treatment between the mother and the father of a child advanced the Legislature's interests in preventing fraudulent claims against the estate and in administering estates in an orderly fashion.

The "posthumous children" provision of the intestacy statute, G.L. c. 190, § 8, is yet another expression of the Legislature's intent to preserve wealth for consanguineous descendants. That section provides that "[p]osthumous children shall be considered as living at the death of their parent." The Legislature, however, has left the term "posthumous children" undefined. The Massachusetts intestacy statute originally made no provision for after-born children. Then in *Hall v. Hancock*, 1834 WL 2638 (1834), in the context of a will contest, this court held that a child who was presumptively in utero as of the date of the decedent's death was a child "in being" as of the date of the decedent's death "in all cases where it will be for the benefit of such child to be so considered." Two years later, the Legislature enacted the "posthumous children" provision of the intestacy statute, bringing that devolution mechanism into conformity with our decision concerning wills. Despite numerous later amendments to our intestacy laws, the "posthumous children" provision has remained essentially unchanged for 165 years.

> **Make the Connection**
>
> Once again we see a statement of the completely statutory nature of the "right" to succeed to the property of the dead.

The Massachusetts intestacy statute thus does not contain an express, affirmative requirement that posthumous children must "be in existence" as of the date of the decedent's death. The Legislature could surely have enacted such a provision had it desired to do so. We must therefore determine whether, under our intestacy law, there is any reason that children conceived after the decedent's death who are the decedent's direct genetic descendants-that is, children who "by consanguinity trace their lineage to the designated ancestor"-may not enjoy the same succession rights as children conceived before the decedent's death who are the decedent's direct genetic descendants.

To answer that question we consider whether and to what extent such children may take as intestate heirs of the deceased genetic parent consistent with the purposes of the intestacy law, and not by any assumptions of the common law. In the absence of express legislative directives, we construe the Legislature's purposes from statutory indicia and judicial decisions in a manner that advances the purposes of the intestacy law.

The question whether posthumously conceived genetic children may enjoy inheritance rights under the intestacy statute implicates three powerful State interests: the best interests of children, the State's interest in the orderly administration of estates, and the reproductive rights of the genetic parent. Our task is to balance and harmonize these interests to effect the Legislature's over-all purposes.

* * *

1. First and foremost we consider the overriding legislative concern to promote the best interests of children. "The protection of minor children, most especially those who may be stigmatized by their 'illegitimate' status . . . has been a hallmark of legislative action and of the jurisprudence of this court." Repeatedly, forcefully, and unequivocally, the Legislature has expressed its will that all children be "entitled to the same rights and protections of the law" regardless of the accidents of their birth. Among the many rights and protections vouchsafed to all children are rights to financial support from their parents and their parents' estates. See G.L. c. 119A, § 1 ("It is the public policy of this commonwealth that dependent children shall be maintained, as completely as possible, from the resources of their parents, thereby relieving or avoiding, at least in part, the burden borne by the citizens of the commonwealth"); G.L. c. 191, § 20 (establishing inheritance rights for pretermitted children); G.L. c. 196, §§ 1–3 (permitting allowances from estate to widows and minor children); G.L. c. 209C, § 14 (permitting paternity claims to be commenced prior to birth). See also G.L. c. 190, §§ 1–3, 5, 7–8 (intestacy rights).

We also consider that some of the assistive reproductive technologies that make posthumous reproduction possible have been widely known and practiced for several decades. In that time, the Legislature has not acted to narrow the broad statutory class of posthumous children to restrict posthumously conceived children from taking in intestacy. Moreover, the Legislature has in great measure affirmatively supported the assistive reproductive technologies that are the only means by which these children can come into being. See G.L. c. 46, § 4B (artificial insemination of married woman). See also G.L. c. 175, § 47H; G.L. c. 176A, § 8K; G.L. c. 176B, § 4J; G.L. c. 176G, § 4 (insurance coverage for infertility treatments). We do not impute to the Legislature the inherently irrational conclusion that assistive reproductive technologies are to be encouraged while a class of children who are the fruit of that technology are to have fewer rights and protections than other children.

In short, we cannot, absent express legislative directive, accept the commissioner's position that the historical context of G.L. c. 190, § 8, dictates as a matter of law that all posthumously conceived children are automatically barred from taking under their deceased donor parent's intestate estate. We have consistently construed statutes to effectuate the Legislature's overriding purpose to promote the welfare of all children, notwithstanding restrictive common-law rules to the contrary. Posthumously conceived children may not come into the world the way the majority of children do. But they are children nonetheless. We may assume that the Legislature intended that such children be "entitled," in so far as possible, "to the same rights and protections of the law" as children conceived before death. See G.L. c. 209C, § 1.

2. However, in the context of our intestacy laws, the best interests of the posthumously conceived child, while of great importance, are not in themselves conclusive. They must be balanced against other important State interests, not the least of which is the protection of children who are alive or conceived before the intestate parent's death. In an era in which serial marriages, serial families, and blended families are not uncommon, according succession rights under our intestacy laws to posthumously conceived children may, in a given case, have the potential to pit child against child and family against family. Any inheritance rights of posthumously conceived children will reduce the intestate share available to children born prior to the decedent's death. See G.L. c. 190, § 3(1). Such considerations, among others, lead us to examine a second important legislative purpose: to provide certainty to heirs and creditors by effecting the orderly, prompt, and accurate administration of intestate estates.

The intestacy statute furthers the Legislature's administrative goals in two principal ways: (1) by requiring certainty of filiation between the decedent and his issue, and (2) by establishing limitations periods for the commencement of claims against the intestate estate. In answering the certified question, we must consider each of these requirements of the intestacy statute in turn.

First, as we have discussed, our intestacy law mandates that, absent the father's acknowledgment of paternity or marriage to the mother, a nonmarital child must obtain a judicial determination of paternity as a prerequisite to succeeding to a portion of the father's intestate estate. Both the United States Supreme Court and this court have long recognized that the State's strong interest in preventing fraudulent claims justifies certain disparate classifications among non-marital children based on the relative difficulty of accurately determining a child's direct lineal ancestor.

Because death ends a marriage, posthumously conceived children are always nonmarital children. And because the parentage of such children can be neither acknowledged nor adjudicated prior to the decedent's death, it follows that, under the intestacy statute, posthumously conceived children must obtain a judgment of paternity as a

> **Food for Thought**
>
> Is this an example of new wine in old bottles? In what sense (if any) are the twins non-marital?

necessary prerequisite to enjoying inheritance rights in the estate of the deceased genetic father. Although modern reproductive technologies will increase the possibility of disputed paternity claims, sophisticated modern testing techniques now make the determination of genetic paternity accurate and reliable. Posthumous maternity is as uncertain until judicially established as is posthumous paternity and neither more nor less difficult to prove. A construction of the intestacy statute that would impose greater burdens on children posthumously conceived from their father's gametes than on children posthumously conceived from their mother's gametes would run afoul of our State and Federal Constitutions, for such classifications would serve no rational State interest.

We now turn to the second way in which the Legislature has met its administrative goals: the establishment of a limitations period for bringing paternity claims against the intestate estate.

Our discussion of this important goal, however, is necessarily circumscribed by the procedural posture of this case and by the terms of the certified question. The certification record discloses that, after one unsuccessful insemination attempt, the wife conceived using her deceased husband's sperm approximately sixteen months after his death. The children were born approximately two years after the husband's death, and the paternity action (in the form of a "complaint for correction of birth record") was filed approximately four months after the children's birth. Both the SSA and the administrative law judge concluded that the wife and the children were not entitled to Social Security survivor benefits because, among other things, the paternity actions were not brought within the one-year period for commencing paternity claims mandated by the intestacy statute. See G.L. c. 190, § 7.

Take Note

The administrative efficiency argument applies to all claims that could be brought against the decedent's estate.

However, in his brief to this court, the commissioner represented that he had informed the United States District Court judge that the wife "had been advised that she need not address" the timeliness issue on appeal in light of a change in Federal regulations. Specifically, the SSA has amended its regulations to read:

> We will not apply any State inheritance law requirement that an action to establish paternity must be taken within a specified period of time measured from the worker's death or the child's birth, or that an action to establish paternity must have been started or completed before the worker's death. . . .

20 C.F.R. § 404.355(b)(2). We understand the commissioner's representation to be a concession that the timeliness of the wife's Massachusetts paternity actions is not relevant to the Federal law question whether the wife's children will be considered the husband's "natural children" for Social Security benefits purposes, and that therefore whatever we say on this issue has no bearing on the wife's Federal action. We also note that the certified question does not specifically address the limitations matter and that, in their briefs to this court, the parties referred to the limitations question only peripherally. See also note 6, *supra*.

Nevertheless, the limitations question is inextricably tied to consideration of the intestacy statute's administrative goals. In the case of posthumously conceived children, the application of the one-year limitations period of G.L. c. 190, § 7 is not clear; it may pose significant burdens on the surviving parent, and consequently on the child. It requires, in effect, that the survivor make a decision to bear children while in the freshness of grieving. It also requires that attempts at conception succeed quickly. Cf. Commentary, Modern Reproductive Technologies: Legal Issues Concerning Cryopreservation and Posthumous Conception, 17 J. Legal Med. 547, 549 (1996) ("It takes an average of seven insemination attempts over 4.4 menstrual cycles to establish pregnancy"). Because the resolution of the time constraints question is not required here, it must await the appropriate case, should one arise.

3. Finally, the question certified to us implicates a third important State interest: to honor the reproductive choices of individuals. We need not address the wife's argument that her reproductive rights would be infringed by denying succession rights to her children under our intestacy law. Nothing in the record even remotely suggests that she was prevented by the State from choosing to conceive children using her deceased husband's semen. The husband's reproductive rights are a more complicated matter.

In *A.Z. v. B.Z.*, 431 Mass. 150, 725 N.E.2d 1051 (2000), we considered certain issues surrounding the disposition of frozen preembryos. A woman sought to enforce written agreements between herself and her former husband. The wife argued that these agreements permitted her to implant frozen preembryos created with the couple's gametes during the marriage, even in the event of their divorce. We declined to enforce the agreements. Persuasive to us, among other factors, was the lack of credible evidence of the husband's "true intention" regarding the disposition of the frozen preembryos, and the changed family circumstance resulting from the couple's divorce. Recognizing that our laws strongly affirm the value of bodily and reproductive integrity, we held that "forced procreation is not an area amenable to judicial enforcement." In short, *A.Z. v. B.Z., supra*, recognized that individuals have a protected right to control the use of their gametes.

Consonant with the principles identified in *A.Z. v. B.Z., supra*, a decedent's silence, or his equivocal indications of a desire to parent posthumously, "ought not to be construed as consent." See Schiff, Arising from the Dead: Challenges of Posthumous Procreation, 75 N.C. L.Rev. 901, 951 (1997). The prospective donor parent must clearly and unequivocally consent not only to posthumous reproduction but also to the support of any resulting child. After the donor-parent's death, the burden rests with the surviving parent, or the posthumously conceived child's other legal representative, to prove the deceased genetic parent's affirmative consent to both requirements for posthumous parentage: posthumous reproduction and the support of any resulting child.

This two-fold consent requirement arises from the nature of alternative reproduction itself. It will not always be the case that a person elects to have his or her gametes medically preserved to create "issue" posthumously. A man, for example, may preserve his semen for myriad reasons, including, among others: to reproduce after recovery from medical treatment, to reproduce after an event that leaves him sterile, or to reproduce when his

> **Practice Pointer**
>
> How should the estate planner deal with the possibility of posthumous children? Should a will or trust specify children to be conceived after death if client has banked his sperm?

spouse has a genetic disorder or otherwise cannot have or safely bear children. That a man has medically preserved his gametes for use by his spouse thus may indicate only that he wished to reproduce after some contingency while he was alive, and not that he consented to the different circumstance of creating a child after his death. Uncertainty as to consent may be compounded by the fact that medically preserved semen can remain viable for up to ten years after it was first extracted, long after the original decision to preserve the semen has passed and when such changed circumstances as divorce, remarriage, and a second family may have intervened. See Banks, Traditional Concepts and Nontraditional Conceptions: Social Security Survivor's Benefits for Posthumously Conceived Children, 32 Loy. L.A. L.Rev. 251, 270 (1999).

Such circumstances demonstrate the inadequacy of a rule that would make the mere genetic tie of the decedent to any posthumously conceived child, or the decedent's mere election to preserve gametes, sufficient to bind his intestate estate for the benefit of any posthumously conceived child. Without evidence that the deceased intestate parent affirmatively consented (1) to the posthumous reproduction and (2) to support any resulting child, a court cannot be assured that the intestacy statute's goal of fraud prevention is satisfied.

As expressed in our intestacy and paternity laws, sound public policy dictates the requirements we have outlined above. Legal parentage imposes substantial obligations on adults for the welfare of children. Where two adults engage in the act of sexual intercourse, it is a matter of common sense and logic, expressed in well-established law, to charge them with parental responsibilities for the child who is the natural, even if unintended, consequence of their actions. Where conception results from a third-party medical procedure using a deceased person's gametes, it is entirely consistent with our laws on children, parentage, and reproductive freedom to place the burden on the surviving parent (or the posthumously conceived child's other legal representative) to demonstrate the genetic relationship of the child to the decedent and that the intestate consented both to reproduce posthumously and to support any resulting child.

* * *

The court in *Woodward* recognized that the legislature rather than the courts might be a preferable forum for resolving the issue of post-mortem children born through reproductive technology. Consider the following approaches, which include two uniform acts, the Restatement (Third) of Property and the California statute, among others.

Restatement (Third) of Property (Wills and Other Donative Transfers) § 2.5 comment *l*

> This Restatement takes the position that, to inherit from the decedent, a child produced from genetic material of the decedent by assisted reproductive technology must be born within a reasonable time after the decedent's death in circumstances indicating that the decedent would have approved of the child's right to inherit.

Uniform Parentage Act § 708 (2017). Parental Status of Deceased Individual

> If an individual who intends to be a parent of a child conceived by assisted reproduction dies during the period between the transfer of the gamete or the embryo and the birth of a child the individual's death does not preclude the establishment of the individual's parentage of the child if the individual otherwise would be a parent of the child under this [Act.]

California Probate Code § 249.5 (2008). Identity of Heirs

For purposes of determining rights to property to be distributed upon the death of a decedent, a child of the decedent conceived and born after the death of the decedent shall be deemed to have been born in the lifetime of the decedent, and after the execution of all of the decedent's testamentary instruments, if the child or his or her representative proves by clear and convincing evidence that all of the following conditions are satisfied:

(a)   The decedent, in writing, specifies that his or her genetic material shall be used for the posthumous conception of a child of the decedent, subject to the following:

(1)   The specification shall be signed by the decedent and dated.

(2)   The specification may be revoked or amended only by a writing, signed by the decedent and dated.

(3)   A person is designated by the decedent to control the use of the genetic material.

(b)   The person designated by the decedent to control the use of the genetic material has given written notice by certified mail, return receipt requested, that the decedent's genetic material was available for the purpose of posthumous conception. The notice shall have been given to a person who has the power to control the distribution of either the decedent's property or death benefits payable by reason of the decedent's death, within four months of the date of issuance of a certificate of the decedent's death or entry of a judgment determining the fact of the decedent's death, whichever event occurs first.

(c)   The child was in utero using the decedent's genetic material and was in utero within two years of the date of issuance of a certificate of the decedent's death or entry of a judgment determining the fact of the decedent's death, whichever event occurs first. This subdivision does not apply to a child who shares all of his or her nuclear genes with the person donating the implanted nucleus as a result of the application of somatic nuclear transfer technology commonly known as human cloning.

UPC § 2–120. Child Conceived by Assisted Reproduction Other Than Child Born to Gestational Carrier

(a)   **[Definitions.]** In this section:

(1)   "Birth mother" means a woman, other than a gestational carrier under Section 2–121, who gives birth to a child of assisted reproduction. The term is not limited to a woman who is the child's genetic mother.

(2)   "Child of assisted reproduction" means a child conceived by means of assisted reproduction by a woman other than a gestational carrier under Section 2–121.

(3) "Third-party donor" means an individual who produces eggs or sperm used for assisted reproduction, whether or not for consideration. The term does not include:

  (A) a husband who provides sperm, or a wife who provides eggs, that are used for assisted reproduction by the wife;

  (B) the birth mother of a child of assisted reproduction; or

  (C) an individual who has been determined under subsection (e) or (f) to have a parent-child relationship with a child of assisted reproduction.

(b) **[Third-Party Donor.]** A parent-child relationship does not exist between a child of assisted reproduction and a third-party donor.

(c) **[Parent-Child Relationship with Birth Mother.]** A parent-child relationship exists between a child of assisted reproduction and the child's birth mother.

(d) **[Parent-Child Relationship with Husband Whose Sperm Were Used During His Lifetime by His Wife for Assisted Reproduction.]** Except as otherwise provided in subsections (i) and (j), a parent-child relationship exists between a child of assisted reproduction and the husband of the child's birth mother if the husband provided the sperm that the birth mother used during his lifetime for assisted reproduction.

(e) **[Birth Certificate: Presumptive Effect.]** A birth certificate identifying an individual other than the birth mother as the other parent of a child of assisted reproduction presumptively establishes a parent-child relationship between the child and that individual.

(f) **[Parent-Child Relationship with Another.]** Except as otherwise provided in subsections (g), (i), and (j), and unless a parent-child relationship is established under subsection (d) or (e), a parent-child relationship exists between a child of assisted reproduction and an individual other than the birth mother who consented to assisted reproduction by the birth mother with intent to be treated as the other parent of the child. Consent to assisted reproduction by the birth mother with intent to be treated as the other parent of the child is established if the individual:

(1) before or after the child's birth, signed a record that, considering all the facts and circumstances, evidences the individual's consent; or

(2) in the absence of a signed record under paragraph (1):

  (A) functioned as a parent of the child no later than two years after the child's birth;

  (B) intended to function as a parent of the child no later than two years after the child's birth but was prevented from carrying out that intent by death, incapacity, or other circumstances; or

(C)   intended to be treated as a parent of a posthumously conceived child, if that intent is established by clear and convincing evidence.

(g)   **[Record Signed More than Two Years after the Birth of the Child: Effect.]** For the purpose of subsection (f)(1), neither an individual who signed a record more than two years after the birth of the child, nor a relative of that individual who is not also a relative of the birth mother, inherits from or through the child unless the individual functioned as a parent of the child before the child reached [18] years of age.

(h)   **[Presumption: Birth Mother Is Married or Surviving Spouse.]** For the purpose of subsection (f)(2), the following rules apply:

(1)   If the birth mother is married and no divorce proceeding is pending, in the absence of clear and convincing evidence to the contrary, her spouse satisfies subsection (f)(2)(A) or (B).

(2)   If the birth mother is a surviving spouse and at her deceased spouse's death no divorce proceeding was pending, in the absence of clear and convincing evidence to the contrary, her deceased spouse satisfies subsection (f)(2)(B) or (C).

(i)   **[Divorce Before Placement of Eggs, Sperm, or Embryos.]** If a married couple is divorced before placement of eggs, sperm, or embryos, a child resulting from the assisted reproduction is not a child of the birth mother's former spouse, unless the former spouse consented in a record that if assisted reproduction were to occur after divorce, the child would be treated as the former spouse's child.

(j)   **[Withdrawal of Consent Before Placement of Eggs, Sperm, or Embryos.]** If, in a record, an individual withdraws consent to assisted reproduction before placement of eggs, sperm, or embryos, a child resulting from the assisted reproduction is not a child of that individual, unless the individual subsequently satisfies subsection (f).

(k)   **[When Posthumously Conceived Child Treated as in Gestation.]** If, under this section, an individual is a parent of a child of assisted reproduction who is conceived after the individual's death, the child is treated as in gestation at the individual's death for purposes of Section 2–104(a)(2) if the child is:

(1)   in utero not later than 36 months after the individual's death; or

(2)   born not later than 45 months after the individual's death.

In *Woodward*, the question was whether a child conceived by assisted reproduction after the death of one of the child's genetic parents could inherit from that parent. As you have learned, children of specified individuals may have rights in trusts created by others or in bequests in wills. What are the rights of posthumously conceived children under wills of and trusts created by persons other than their genetic parents that make a gift to the issue of the genetic parent or to an ancestor of the genetic parent? The answer to that question often involves taking into account the interests of other persons who would be directly affected by a decision on the status of the posthumously conceived person.

In re Martin B.

17 Misc. 3d 198 (N.Y. Surr. Ct. 2007)

Renee R. Roth, J.

This uncontested application for advice and direction in connection with seven trust agreements executed on December 31, 1969, by Martin B. (the Grantor) illustrates one of the new challenges that the law of trusts must address as a result of advances in biotechnology. Specifically, the novel question posed is whether, for these instruments, the terms "issue" and "descendants" include children conceived by means of in vitro fertilization with the cryopreserved semen of the Grantor's son who had died several years prior to such conception.

The relevant facts are briefly stated. Grantor (who was a life income beneficiary of the trusts) died on July 9, 2001, survived by his wife Abigail and their son Lindsay (who has two adult children), but predeceased by his son James, who died of Hodgkin's Lymphoma on January 13, 2001. James, however, after learning of his illness, deposited a sample of his semen at a laboratory with instructions that it be cryopreserved and that, in the event of his death, it be held subject to the directions of his wife Nancy. Although at his death James had no children, three years later Nancy underwent in vitro fertilization with his cryopreserved semen and gave birth on October 15, 2004, to a boy (James Mitchell). Almost two years later, on August 14, 2006, after using the same procedure, she gave birth to another boy (Warren). It is undisputed that these infants, although conceived after the death of James, are the products of his semen.

Although the trust instruments addressed in this proceeding are not entirely identical, for present purposes the differences among them are in all but one respect immaterial. The only relevant difference is that one is expressly governed by the law of New York while the others are governed by the law of the District of Columbia. As a practical matter, however, such difference is not material since neither jurisdiction provides any statutory authority or judicial comment on the question before the court.

All seven instruments give the trustees discretion to sprinkle principal to, and among, Grantor's "issue" during Abigail's life. The instruments also provide that at Abigail's death the principal is to be distributed as she directs under her special testamentary power to appoint to Grantor's "issue" or "descendants" (or to certain other "eligible" appointees). In the absence of such exercise, the principal is to be distributed to or for the benefit of "issue" surviving at the time of such disposition

Take Note

The estate planning strategy employed here is quite common. We will have further occasions to explore alternative distribution patterns.

(James's issue, in the case of certain trusts, and Grantor's issue, in the case of certain other trusts). The trustees have brought this proceeding because under such instruments they are authorized to sprinkle principal to decedent's "issue" and "descendants" and thus need to know whether James's children qualify as members of such classes.

The question thus raised is whether the two infant boys are "descendants" and "issue" for purposes of such provisions although they were conceived several years after the death of James.

Although the particular question presented here arises from recent scientific advances in biotechnology, this is not the first time that the Surrogate's Court has been called upon to consider an issue involving a child conceived through artificial means.

Over three decades ago, Surrogate Nathan R. Sobel addressed one of the earliest legal problems created by the use of artificial insemination as a technique for human reproduction (*Matter of Anonymous*, 74 Misc.2d 99, 345 N.Y.S.2d 430). In that case, the petitioner sought to adopt a child that his wife had conceived, during her prior marriage, through artificial insemination with the sperm of a third-party donor (heterologous insemination). The question before Surrogate Sobel was whether the former husband had standing to object to the adoption. In the course of his analysis, the learned Surrogate predicted that artificial insemination would become increasingly common and would inevitably also complicate the legal landscape in areas other than adoption. Indeed, he specifically forecast that, as a result of such technological advances, "[legal] issues . . . will multiply [in relation to matters such as] intestate succession and will construction" (*id.*, at 100, 345 N.Y.S.2d 430). Surrogate Sobel noted, however, that there was at that point a dearth of statutory or decisional guidance on questions such as the one before him.

The following year New York enacted Domestic Relations Law 73, which recognized the status of a child born to a married couple as a result of heterologous artificial insemination provided that both spouses consented in writing to the procedure, to be performed by a physician. Such statute reflected the evolution of the State's public policy

> **Make the Connection**
>
> Recall the discussion in Chapter 5 of provisions for "after-born" (also known as "pretermitted children").

toward eliminating the distinction between marital and non-marital children in determining family rights. Thus, where a husband executes a written consent (or even in some instances where he has expressed oral consent) to artificial insemination the child is treated as his natural child for all purposes despite the absence of a biological connection between the two (*see e.g.* Scheinkman, Practice Commentaries, McKinney's Con Laws of NY, Book 14, Domestic Relations Law 73, at 309–10).

Surrogate Sobel's predictions in *Anonymous* proved to be prophetic. Some thirty years later, the novel issues generated by scientific developments in the area of assisted human reproduction are perplexing legislators and legal scholars.

Compounding the problem, as the authors of the foregoing studies have observed, decisions and enactments from earlier times-when human reproduction was in all cases a natural and uniform process-do not fit the needs of this more complex era. These new issues, however, are being discussed and in some jurisdictions have been the subject of legislation or judicial decisions. But, as will be discussed below, neither New York nor the District of Columbia, the governing jurisdictions, has a statute directly considering the rights of post-conceived children. In this case legislative action has not kept pace with the progress of science. In the absence of binding authority, courts must turn to less immediate sources for a reflection of the public's evolving attitude toward assisted reproduction-including statutes in other jurisdictions, model codes, scholarly discussions and Restatements of the law.

Go Online

Scott, *A Look at the Rights and Entitlements of Posthumously Conceived Children: No Surefire Way to Tame the Reproductive Wild West*, 52 Emory L.J. 963, 995; Elliott, *Tales of Parenthood from the Crypt: The Predicament of the Posthumously Conceived Child*, 39 Real Prop. Prob. & Tr. J. 47, 50; Mika & Hurst, *One Way to be Born? Legislative Inaction and the Posthumous Child*, 79 Marq. L. Rev. 993.

We turn first to the laws of the governing jurisdictions. At present, the right of a posthumous child to inherit (EPTL 4–1.1[c] [in intestacy]) or as an after-born child under a will (EPTL 5–3.2 [under a will]) is limited to a child conceived during the decedent's lifetime. A recent amendment to section 5–3.2 was specifically intended to make it clear that a post-conceived child is excluded from sharing in the parent's estate as an "after-born" (absent some provision in the will to the contrary, EPTL 5–3.2[b]). Such limitation was intended to ensure certainty in identifying persons interested in an estate and finality in its distribution (*see* Sponsor's Mem, Bill Jacket L 2006, ch 249). It, however, is by its terms applicable only to wills and to "after-borns" who are children of the testators themselves and not children of third parties (*see* Turano, Practice Commentaries, McKinney's Cons Laws of NY, Book 17B, EPTL 5–3.2, at 275). Moreover, the concerns related to winding up a decedent's estate differ from those related to identifying whether a class disposition to a grantor's issue includes a child conceived after the father's death but before the disposition became effective.

With respect to future interests, both the District of Columbia and New York have statutes which ostensibly bear upon the status of a post-conceived child. In the D.C. Code, the one statutory reference to posthumous children appears in section 704 of title 42 which in relevant part provides that, "[w]here a future estate shall be limited to heirs, or issue, or children, posthumous children shall be entitled to take in the same manner as if living at the death of their parent. . . ." New York has a very similar statute, which provides in relevant part that, "[w]here a future estate is limited to children, distributees, heirs or issue, posthumous children are entitled to take in the same manner as if living at the death of their ancestors" (EPTL 6.5–7). In addition, EPTL 2–1.3(2) provides that a posthumous child may share as a member of a class if such child was conceived before the disposition became effective.

Each of the above statutes read literally would allow post-conceived children-who are indisputably "posthumous"-to claim benefits as biological offspring. But such statutes were enacted long before anyone anticipated that children could be conceived after the death of the biological parent. In other words, the respective legislatures presumably contemplated that such provisions would apply only to children *en ventre sa mere* (*see e.g.* Turano, Practice Commentaries, McKinney's Cons Laws of NY, Book 17B, EPTL 6–5.7, at 176).

We turn now to the jurisdictions in which the inheritance rights of a post-conceived child have been directly addressed by the legislatures, namely, Louisiana, California and Florida and to the seven States that have adopted, in part, the Uniform Parentage Act (2000, as amended in 2002) (UPA, discussed below), namely, Delaware, North Dakota, Oklahoma, Texas, Utah, Washington and Wyoming. Although we are concerned here with a male donor, the legislation also covers the use of a woman's eggs (UPA 707).

> **Take Note**
>
> Trust interests may be created so that they vest many years after the death of the creator. In other words, beneficiaries of the trust may come into existence many years after the trust was created.

In Louisiana, a post-conceived child may inherit from his or her father if the father consented in writing to his wife's use of his semen and the child was born within three years of the father's death. But it is noted parenthetically that the statute also allows a person adversely affected to challenge paternity within one year of such child's birth (LA Civil Code 9:391.1).

In order for a post-conceived child to inherit in the State of California, the parent must have consented in writing to the posthumous use of genetic material and designated a person to control its use. Such designee must be given written notice of the designation and the child must have been conceived within two years of decedent's death (CA Probate Code 249.5).

Florida, by contrast, requires a written agreement by the couple and the treating physician for the disposition of their eggs or semen in the event of divorce or death. A post-conceived child may inherit only if the parent explicitly provided for such child under his or her will (FL Stat Ann 742.17).

> **Practice Pointer**
>
> It's not surprising that the trust document is silent on this issue. Given the state of medical knowledge, should the lawyer routinely ask the client about what provisions should be made for posthumously conceived children?

Under the UPA, a man who provides semen, or consents to assisted reproduction by a woman as provided under section 704, with the intent to become a father is the parent of the child who is born as a result (UPA § 703). Under section 704 of the UPA, both the man and the woman must consent in writing to the recognition of the man as the father. The UPA has also addressed the situation where the potential parent dies before the act of assisted reproduction has been performed. In such situation, decedent is the parent of the child if decedent agreed to the use of assisted reproduction after his death (UPA 707).

On a related question, the courts of three States have held that a post-conceived child is entitled to benefits under the Social Security Act: Massachusetts (*Woodward v. Commissioner of Soc. Sec.*, 435 Mass. 536 [2001]), New Jersey (*Matter of Kolacy*, 332 N.J.Super. 593, 753 A.2d

1257[NJ Super. Ct. Ch.Div.2000 (which had enacted an earlier version of the UPA), and Arizona (*Gillett-Netting v. Barnhart*, 371 F.3d 593). All three courts concluded that post-conceived children qualified for such benefits.

> **Food for Thought**
>
> Does this mean that the children are also their father's heirs in intestacy?

As can clearly be seen from all the above, the legislatures and the courts have tried to balance competing interests. On the one hand, certainty and finality are critical to the public interests in the orderly administration of estates. On the other hand, the human desire to have children, albeit by biotechnology, deserves respect, as do the rights of the children born as a result of such scientific advances. To achieve such balance, the statutes, for example, require written consent to the use of genetic material after death and establish a cut-off date by which the child must be conceived. It is noted parenthetically that in this regard an affidavit has been submitted here stating that all of James's cryopreserved sperm has been destroyed, thereby closing the class of his children.

Finally, we turn to the instruments presently before the court. Although it cannot be said that in 1969 the Grantor contemplated that his "issue" or "descendants" would include children who were conceived after his son's death, the absence of specific intent should not necessarily preclude a determination that such children are members of the class of issue. Indeed, it is noted that the Restatement of Property suggests that "[u]nless the language or circumstances indicate that the transferor had a different intention, a child of assisted reproduction [be] treated for class-gift purposes as a child of a person who consented to function as a parent to the child and who functioned in that capacity or was prevented from doing so by an event such as death or incapacity" (Restatement [Third] of Property [Wills and Other Donative Transfers] 14.8 [Tentative Draft No. 4 204]).

The rationale of the Restatement, *Matter of Anonymous* and section 73 of the Domestic Relations Law should be applied here, namely, if an individual considers a child to be his or her own, society through its laws should do so as well. It is noted that a similar rationale was endorsed by our State's highest court with respect to the beneficial interests of adopted children (*Matter of Park*, 15 N.Y.2d 413, 260 N.Y.S.2d 169, 207 N.E.2d 859). Accordingly, in the instant case, these post-conceived infants should be treated as part of their father's family for all purposes. Simply put, where a governing instrument is silent, children born of this new biotechnology with the consent of their parent are entitled to the same rights "for all purposes as those of a natural child".

Although James probably assumed that any children born as a result of the use of his preserved semen would share in his family's trusts, his intention is not controlling here. For purposes of determining the beneficiaries of these trusts, the controlling factor is the Grantor's intent as gleaned from a reading of the trust agreements. Such instruments provide that, upon the death of the Grantor's wife, the trust fund would benefit his sons and their families equally. In view of such overall dispositive scheme, a sympathetic reading of these instruments warrants the conclusion that the Grantor intended all members of his bloodline to receive their share.

Based upon all of the foregoing, it is concluded that James Mitchell and Warren are "issue" and "descendants" for all purposes of these trusts.

As can be seen from all of the above, there is a need for comprehensive legislation to resolve the issues raised by advances in biotechnology. Accordingly, copies of this decision are being sent to the respective Chairs of the Judiciary Committees of the New York State Senate and Assembly.

Decree signed.

Notes

1. *What should be the rule?*

As you can see from Surrogate Roth's candid statement that she will have to look for evidence of "the public's evolving attitude toward assisted reproduction" and "statutes in other jurisdictions, model codes, scholarly discussions and Restatements of the law," New York, like most jurisdictions, had no law on the status of posthumously conceived children. There are some authorities, the most influential of which are set forth after the *Woodward* opinion. How would *Woodward* be decided under each of them? In 2014, New York adopted a law specifically to address the intestate inheritance rights of children conceived after the death of a genetic parent. Under that law, EPTL § 4–1.2, a posthumously conceived child is treated as the genetic parent's child only if the genetic parent executed a formal written instrument not more than seven years before the parent's death that gave express consent for posthumous conception and authorized a person to make decisions about the use of genetic material after death. The law includes a number of rules regarding timing, including, most importantly, that the child must be in utero no later than twenty-four months after the genetic parent's death. What reasons might explain these requirements? As revised in 2008, the UPC provides that a posthumously conceived child is included in a class gift in a will or trust to "children," "issue," or "descendants" if the distribution is occasioned by the genetic parent's death, the child is in utero within 36 months of that date, and the deceased parent consented to the posthumous conception. UPC § 2–705 (2008).

2. *Why now?*

The appearance of cases dealing with posthumous conception does not seem to be the result of recent technological advances. As Surrogate Roth notes in *Martin B*, artificial insemination with preserved semen is a relatively low-tech procedure and has been more or less routinely performed for decades. Why have these cases arisen only relatively recently (the first public notice of these cases involving inheritance rights of posthumously conceived children, all of which concern claims for Social Security benefits, date from the early 1990s)? The impetus in many states for the adoption of posthumous conception inheritance statutes was the Supreme Court's ruling in *Astrue v. Capato*, 566 U.S. 541 (2012), in which it held that a posthumously conceived child is entitled to dependent child benefits only if the child would have been recognized as an intestate distributee of the deceased genetic parent under the law of his home state. This means that children in different states might have different benefits based on nothing other geography. Is this fair? Would it make more sense to develop a federal law that equalized the benefits? Or would that infringe on the rights of states to define family and inheritance relationships?

Problem 7-5

H, aged 32, is severely injured in a motor vehicle accident. He is taken to the nearest hospital emergency room. Informed by police, W arrives at the emergency room while H is still alive but in critical condition, and doctors inform W that H is not expected to survive. W is properly authorized to make decisions about medical treatment for H and using that authority directs the doctors to recover H's semen and preserve it. Shortly after the procedure is successfully completed H dies.

Eight months after H's death, W is artificially inseminated with the H's semen and nine months later W gives birth to a child.

(a)   Will the child be regarded as the H's heir? (Use the authorities above for your answers.)

(b)   Will the child be regarded as the H's child for purposes of a trust created by H's mother for her "descendants?" (Use the authorities above for your answers.)

(c)   Would your answers to (a) and (b) change if W could produce three friends of the couple who were willing to testify under oath that during a conversation about assisted reproduction (occasioned by friends of the couple having a child by in vitro fertilization) H stated that he would be pleased if W could have their child "should anything happen to me"?

7.   Surrogacy: Separation of Genetics and Parenthood

The ability to fertilize ova outside of the body and then implant the resulting zygotes in a woman's uterus completely separates conception from sexual intercourse and makes it possible for the resulting child to have two mothers: a birth mother and a genetic mother.

Two California cases address the problem directly. In *Johnson v. Calvert*, 851 P.2d 776 (Cal. 1993), the California Supreme Court held that a husband and wife who arranged for the implantation of a zygote resulting from the fertilization of the wife's ovum by the husband's sperm (presumably *in vitro*) into the uterus of a surrogate mother pursuant to a valid surrogacy contract were the legal parents of the child born to the surrogate. The court reasoned that having caused the child to be conceived, the married couple intended to be parents:

"We conclude that although [California's enactment of the then current version of the Uniform Parentage Act] recognizes both genetic consanguinity and giving birth as means of establishing a mother and child relationship, when the two means do not coincide in one woman, she who intended to procreate the child—that is, she who intended to bring about the birth of a child that she intended to raise as her own—is the natural mother under California law." [851 P.2d at 882].

Five years later, the California intermediate appellate court reasoned from *Johnson* and the statutes governing artificial insemination to hold that a child genetically unrelated to the surrogate mother who gave birth or to the married (now divorced) couple who entered into the surrogate contract was the child of the persons who arranged for his birth and ordered the former husband to support the child. (*Buzzanca v. Buzzanca*, 72 Cal. Rptr. 2d 280 (Cal. App. 1998)). In 2012, the California legislature codified the longstanding support of surrogacy arrangements, imposing just a few requirements to ensure voluntariness of the arrangement. Cal. Fam. Code § 7962.

While the following case involves a trust instrument rather than the intestacy statute, it shows clearly the legal results of gestational surrogacy even in a state that does not recognize surrogacy contracts involving payments to the surrogate.

Matter of Doe

793 N.Y.S.2d 878 (Surr. Ct. 2005)

EVE PREMINGER, J.

In creating trusts for the benefit of the issue of his eight children, the settlor required that "adoptions shall not be recognized." The court will return to this point later in the opinion. One of the settlor's daughters ("K. Doe") and her husband became the parents of fraternal twins by virtue of a surrogacy arrangement, using an anonymous donor egg, fertilized *in vitro* with the sperm of K. Doe's husband, and carried to term by an unrelated surrogate mother. Petitioners, successors trustees, bring this construction proceeding to determine whether the settlor's exclusion of "adoptions" excludes these children as beneficiaries.

The eight identical *inter vivos* trust instruments, created by the settlor, an attorney, in 1959, required that the net income of each trust be paid to such charitable organizations as appointed by each child until September 1, 1979, after which date the net income of each trust was to be paid to the "issue" or "descendants" of each child. As of December 31, 2001, the issue of five of the settlor's eight children were receiving income from the trusts. The income

> **Non constat** **jus civile** *a posteriori*
>
> ### It's Latin to Me
>
> ***Inter vivos*** means "during life" and refers to a trust created by a living person (also called a lifetime trust). A trust can also be created in a will; such a trust is a testamentary trust.

from the remaining three trusts was being distributed in equal shares *per capita* to the fourteen then-living grandchildren of the settlor as specified by the trust instruments.

As to the twins' birth, K. Doe and her husband arranged for a genetically unrelated surrogate mother in the state of California to be impregnated with the eggs of an anonymous donor fertilized *in vitro* by K. Doe's husband's sperm. After the twins' birth, with consent of the surrogate mother, K. Doe and her husband obtained a Judgment of Parental Relationship from the Superior Court of California to establish them as the twins' sole legal parents.

If the twins are not excluded by the terms of the trust prohibiting recognition of adopted children, they are: 1) income beneficiaries and presumptive remaindermen of the trust created for benefit of the issue of their mother, K. Doe; 2) eligible to receive their per capita share of the income of trusts for two of the settlor's issue who currently have no issue; 3) permissible beneficiaries of the exercise of the lifetime power of appointment reserved to the trustees to make discretionary principal distributions to the settlor's grandchildren; and 4) permissible beneficiaries of the testamentary powers of appointment given to K. Doe and her seven siblings over their respective remainders.

The Court has appointed a guardian *ad litem* for the twins, who argues they should be included, as well as one for the infant grandchildren of the settlor whose interests in the trusts will be affected by this decision, who argues that they should not.

In a construction proceeding, the intent of the settlor controls. (*In re Balsam's Trust*, 58 Misc.2d 672, 677, 296 N.Y.S.2d 969; *see Matter of Buechner*, 226 N.Y. 440, 443, 123 N.E. 741). The reproductive technologies involved in this case in vitro fertilization and gestational surrogacy were established in the 1970s, well after these trusts were settled. It is unlikely that the settlor's views of these methods of reproduction can be discovered. Even if the court were to consider the trusts ambiguous and allow extrinsic evidence on this question, the petitioning trustees candidly state that they know of none. This construction question is thus confined to the language employed in the trusts.

> ### Food for Thought
> If that is the case, why the exclusion of adopted persons?

Looking at that language, one interpretation of the settlor's exclusion of "adoptions" is that he intended to exclude all non-blood relations. However, in examining, as the court must, the document as a whole (*see Matter of Fabbri*, 2 N.Y.2d 236, 240, 159 N.Y.S.2d 184, 140 N.E.2d 269), it is clear that was not his intent. The settlor provided a means for spouses, non-blood relatives, to take under the trusts. Upon the death of a child, the trustees are directed to distribute any remaining trust principal to the settlor's then-living issue, other than the estate of the child, *and the spouse of such issue* in such proportions as the child may designate by will. In default of the child's exercise of the testamentary power of appointment, the remainder is to be distributed to the issue of the child, or in default of such issue, to the settlor's issue per stirpes. Although the possibility of a non-blood relative's taking a portion of the remainder depends on an affirmative exercise of the power of appointment by a child, the settlor contemplated that his non-blood relatives might take a portion of the trust remainder. Similarly, certain trustees are permitted in their discretion to appoint principal to "grandchildren and more remote issue of the Settlor and *spouses of such grandchildren and more remote issue.*" Thus, under the trusts, there is the possibility of a non-blood relation being a beneficiary.

This is the main language in the trusts that bears on this question, and nothing else suggests that the court should extend "adoptions" to include the reproductive technologies at issue in this case. When the settlor excluded "adoptions," it cannot be said that he intended to exclude all means of assisted reproduction; such means of assisted reproduction were not then in existence, and no language in the trusts anticipates technologies relating to birth that may be developed in the future.

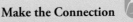

Make the Connection

Isn't adoption a type of low-tech assisted reproduction? Both allow a person to become a parent other than through sexual intercourse.

With some evidence in the trust documents that the settlor did not intend to exclude all non-blood relations, the court turns to the question of whether the California judgment should be considered an adoption, and if not, whether New York should afford it full faith and credit.

Under California law, a judgment of parental relationship is entirely distinct from an adoption proceeding, and the two are governed by different divisions of the California Family Code.

Food for Thought

Must a state give full faith and credit to all judgments involving family law matters?

The Judgment of Parental Relationship obtained by K. Doe and her spouse was entered in a proceeding brought under sections 7630 and 7650 of Division 12 of the California Family Code, which govern the establishment of parental relationships, not adoptions. The judgment declared K. Doe and her husband to be "the sole and legal parents" of the twins and the surrogate mother and her husband to be "strangers in blood" to the twins. The judgment ordered amendment of the twins' birth certificates to list K. Doe as mother and her husband as father. In contrast, California adoptions are governed by division 13 of the California Family Code. California treats these two methods of establishing parental rights as distinct in nature. A California gestational surrogacy arrangement, where, as here, the surrogate mother is implanted with an egg fertilized in vitro, is not subject to the adoption statutes.

It is clear that in California the twins were not adopted, and recognizing this result in New York is appropriate. Surrogacy is not the functional equivalent of adoption. For example, in gestational surrogacies, as here where the birth mother is implanted with a fertilized ovum genetically unrelated to her the basic question of who should be considered the natural mother must be answered in light of the advanced technologies that permit such a procedure. In *Johnson*, California developed an analysis that has become known as the intent test: those who intended to be parents, absent other compelling circumstances, should be considered the parents. Applying that test, the *Johnson* court declared the genetic mother, who intended from the beginning to be the mother, instead of the gestational surrogate mother, to be the natural).

New York also has a separate article, article 8 (§§ 120–124) of the Domestic Relations Law, dealing with surrogate parenting. Unlike California, it forbids recognition of surrogate parenting contracts, and considers them void and unenforceable (Domestic Relations Law § 122). Nonetheless, New York courts entertain petitions for declarations of maternity, and do not require parents to go through an adoption proceeding in cases of in vitro fertilization and gestational surrogacy arrangements and apply the intent test to determine who the "natural mother" is in such an arrangement in the context of a divorce and custody. While the practice commentaries to Domestic Relations Law § 122 state that surrogacy arrangements are "specialized adoption agreements," adoption need not follow a surrogate parenting arrangement, as it does not in California and did not in this case.

Finally, no reasoning justifies a denial of full faith and credit to the California judgment. Where a judgment of a sister state is issued with jurisdiction of all parties, New York must afford it full faith and credit. Although New York forbids enforcement of surrogacy contracts, the enforcement of the contract is not at issue here. More importantly, the legislature did not punish or prejudice the rights of children born from such arrangements. Instead, the statutory scheme explicitly contemplates full and fair proceedings to determine "parental rights, status and obligations" (Domestic Relations Law § 124), notwithstanding the surrogate parenting contract. Although for different reasons, a New York court could have reached the same conclusions as to who the twins' parents are as the California court did, and full faith and credit cannot be denied the California judgment on grounds of some countervailing New York public policy.

Accordingly, the Court holds that the twins are not excluded from the benefits of the John Doe trusts by virtue of the adoption exclusion.

———————————

Notes

1. *Becoming a parent through surrogacy*

As the opinion in *Doe* shows, not every jurisdiction is as favorably disposed to gestational surrogacy as is California. There is perhaps even less "law" relating to the issues raised by surrogacy than there is relating to posthumous conception. When the UPC was amended to add provisions dealing with the latter a section dealing with gestational surrogacy was also added:

UPC § 2–121. Child Born to Gestational Carrier

(a) **[Definitions.]** In this section:

(1) "Gestational agreement" means an enforceable or unenforceable agreement for assisted reproduction in which a woman agrees to carry a child to birth for an intended parent, intended parents, or an individual described in subsection (e).

(2) "Gestational carrier" means a woman who is not an intended parent who gives birth to a child under a gestational agreement. The term is not limited to a woman who is the child's genetic mother.

(3) "Gestational child" means a child born to a gestational carrier under a gestational agreement.

(4) "Intended parent" means an individual who entered into a gestational agreement providing that the individual will be the parent of a child born to a gestational carrier by means of assisted reproduction. The term is not limited to an individual who has a genetic relationship with the child.

(b) **[Court Order Adjudicating Parentage: Effect.]** A parent-child relationship is conclusively established by a court order designating the parent or parents of a gestational child.

(c) **[Gestational Carrier.]** A parent-child relationship between a gestational child and the child's gestational carrier does not exist unless the gestational carrier is:

(1) designated as a parent of the child in a court order described in subsection (b); or

(2) the child's genetic mother and a parent-child relationship does not exist under this section with an individual other than the gestational carrier.

(d) **[Parent-Child Relationship with Intended Parent or Parents.]** In the absence of a court order under subsection (b), a parent-child relationship exists between a gestational child and an intended parent who:

(1) functioned as a parent of the child no later than two years after the child's birth; or

(2) died while the gestational carrier was pregnant if:

(A) there were two intended parents and the other intended parent functioned as a parent of the child no later than two years after the child's birth;

(B) there were two intended parents, the other intended parent also died while the gestational carrier was pregnant, and a relative of either deceased intended parent or the spouse or surviving spouse of a relative of either deceased intended parent functioned as a parent of the child no later than two years after the child's birth; or

(C) there was no other intended parent and a relative of or the spouse or surviving spouse of a relative of the deceased intended parent functioned as a parent of the child no later than two years after the child's birth.

(e) **[Gestational Agreement after Death or Incapacity.]** In the absence of a court order under subsection (b), a parent-child relationship exists between a gestational child and an individual whose sperm or eggs were used after the individual's death or incapacity to conceive a child under a gestational agreement entered into after the individual's death or incapacity if the individual intended to be treated as the parent of the child. The individual's intent may be shown by:

(1) a record signed by the individual which considering all the facts and circumstances evidences the individual's intent; or

(2) other facts and circumstances establishing the individual's intent by clear and convincing evidence.

(f) **[Presumption: Gestational Agreement after Spouse's Death or Incapacity.]** Except as otherwise provided in subsection (g), and unless there is clear and convincing evidence of a contrary intent, an individual is deemed to have intended to be treated as the parent of a gestational child for purposes of subsection (e)(2) if:

(1) the individual, before death or incapacity, deposited the sperm or eggs that were used to conceive the child;

(2) when the individual deposited the sperm or eggs, the individual was married and no divorce proceeding was pending; and

(3) the individual's spouse or surviving spouse functioned as a parent of the child no later than two years after the child's birth.

(g) **[Subsection (f) Presumption Inapplicable.]** The presumption under subsection (f) does not apply if there is:

(1) a court order under subsection (b); or

(2) a signed record that satisfies subsection (e)(1).

(h) **[When Posthumously Conceived Gestational Child Treated as in Gestation.]** If, under this section, an individual is a parent of a gestational child who is conceived after the individual's death, the child is treated as in gestation at the individual's death for purposes of Section 2–104(a)(2) if the child is:

(1) in utero not later than 36 months after the individual's death; or

(2) born not later than 45 months after the individual's death.

(i) **[No Effect on Other Law.]** This section does not affect law of this state other than this [code] regarding the enforceability or validity of a gestational agreement.

Note the parallels between this provision and UPC § 2–120 dealing with children of assisted reproduction. Especially note the treatment of someone who functions or intends to function as a parent. What that means is defined in UPC § 2–115(4):

(4) "Functioned as a parent of the child" means behaving toward a child in a manner consistent with being the child's parent and performing functions that are customarily performed by a parent, including fulfilling parental responsibilities

toward the child, recognizing or holding out the child as the individual's child, materially participating in the child's upbringing, and residing with the child in the same household as a regular member of that household.

The Comment to that section says:

The term "functioned as a parent of the child" is derived from the Restatement (Third) of Property: Wills and Other Donative Transfers. The Reporter's Note No. 4 to § 14.5 of the Restatement lists the following parental functions:

Custodial responsibility refers to physical custodianship and supervision of a child. It usually includes, but does not necessarily require, residential or overnight responsibility.

Decision making responsibility refers to authority for making significant life decisions on behalf of the child, including decisions about the child's education, spiritual guidance, and health care.

Caretaking functions are tasks that involve interaction with the child or that direct, arrange, and supervise the interaction and care provided by others. Caretaking functions include but are not limited to all of the following:

(a) satisfying the nutritional needs of the child, managing the child's bedtime and wake-up routines, caring for the child when sick or injured, being attentive to the child's personal hygiene needs including washing, grooming, and dressing, playing with the child and arranging for recreation, protecting the child's physical safety, and providing transportation;

(b) directing the child's various developmental needs, including the acquisition of motor and language skills, toilet training, self-confidence, and maturation;

(c) providing discipline, giving instruction in manners, assigning and supervising chores, and performing other tasks that attend to the child's needs for behavioral control and self-restraint;

(d) arranging for the child's education, including remedial or special services appropriate to the child's needs and interests, communicating with teachers and counselors, and supervising homework;

(e) helping the child to develop and maintain appropriate interpersonal relationships with peers, siblings, and other family members;

(f) arranging for health-care providers, medical follow-up, and home health care;

(g) providing moral and ethical guidance;

(h) arranging alternative care by a family member, babysitter, or other child-care provider or facility, including investigation of alternatives, communication with providers, and supervision of care.

Parenting functions are tasks that serve the needs of the child or the child's residential family. Parenting functions include caretaking functions, as defined [above], and all of the following additional functions:

> (a) providing economic support;
>
> (b) participating in decision making regarding the child's welfare;
>
> (c) maintaining or improving the family residence, including yard work, and house cleaning;
>
> (d) doing and arranging for financial planning and organization, car repair and maintenance, food and clothing purchases, laundry and dry cleaning, and other tasks supporting the consumption and savings needs of the household;
>
> (e) performing any other functions that are customarily performed by a parent or guardian and that are important to a child's welfare and development.

Ideally, a parent would perform all of the above functions throughout the child's minority. In cases falling short of the ideal, the trier of fact must balance both time and conduct. The question is, did the individual perform sufficient parenting functions over a sufficient period of time to justify concluding that the individual functioned as a parent of the child. Clearly, insubstantial conduct, such as an occasional gift or social contact, would be insufficient. Moreover, merely obeying a child support order would not, by itself, satisfy the requirement. Involuntarily providing support is inconsistent with functioning as a parent of the child.

The context in which the question arises is also relevant. If the question is whether the individual claiming to have functioned as a parent of the child inherits from the child, the court might require more substantial conduct over a more substantial period of time than if the question is whether a child inherits from an individual whom the child claims functioned as his or her parent.

2. Surrogacy under the UPC and what it means to be a parent

What does the UPC approach to the question of who is a parent mean for the doctrine of equitable adoption (which the UPC expressly says does not affect UPC § 2–122)?

8. Stepchildren

Remember that intestacy is a matter of family relationship, even though in the modern world that relationship may be established in different ways. Absent family relationship there is no heirship.

Example: H is killed in an accident and is survived by W and three young children of the marriage. W remarries, and H2 and she together support and raise the children, H2 in every way performing the role of male parent. Unless H2 adopts the children, they are not his heirs.

In California, however, stepchildren do have limited inheritance rights. Under Cal. Prob. Code § 6454, a parent-child relationship exists for purposes of inheritance "from or through" a foster parent or stepparent if the relationship began during the step- or foster child's minority and continued through the joint lifetimes of the persons involved and "it is established by clear and convincing evidence that the foster parent or stepparent would have adopted the person but for a legal barrier." In *Estate of Joseph*, 949 P.2d 472 (Cal. 1998) the California Supreme Court interpreted the statute to require that the legal barrier be in existence throughout the stepparent's lifetime.

Point for Discussion

Would Cal. Prob. Code § 6454 give the children in the **Example** above inheritance rights from H2?

357-51

F. Inheritance by Collateral Relatives

If an intestate decedent has no surviving spouse, issue or parents, the next heirs in line are the descendants (issue) of the decedent's parents—brothers and sisters and their descendants. Once again, these heirs (distributees) are defined as a class and the distribution of property is by representation. If there are no surviving descendants of the decedent's parents, most intestacy statutes, including UPC § 2–103, divide the probate property between the maternal and paternal sides of the family. The intestate estate moves up the family tree and splits in half; surviving grandparents are then the heirs. For example, if the decedent is survived by the maternal grandmother and both paternal grandparents, the maternal grandmother receives one-half the probate estate and the paternal grandparents one-quarter each. Once the property "moves up" the family tree beyond the decedent's parents, under most state statutes and the UPC, the two halves of the probate estate are treated as two separate entities.

New York's intestacy statute, EPTL § 4–1.1(a)(6) and (7) limits inheritance by collateral relatives more strictly than does the UPC. When the issue of the deceased intestate's grandparents are heirs (distributees in New York terminology), the "issue" are defined to be no one more distantly related to the grandparents than their grandchildren, the decedent's first cousins. The first cousins' children (the decedent's first cousins once removed) are heirs only if there is no one more closely related to the decedent living on either side of the family, and if in that case there are no living first cousins once removed, the decedent's estate escheats to the state.

Some states, including California allow collateral kin descended from common great grandparents (and beyond) to inherit, co-called "laughing heirs," because such a distant relation may receive an inheritance from an individual that they have never met. How well do you know your third cousin, once removed, descended from a common great-great grandparent? Has New York gone too far in cutting off inheritance by collaterals? Does the UPC strike the right balance?

Problem 7-6

Consider the following family tree:

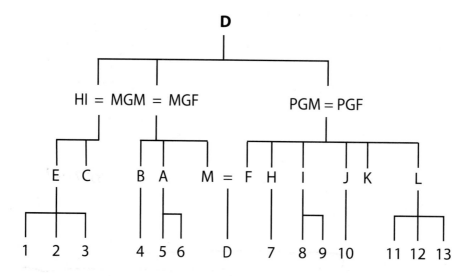

(a) **D**, the decedent, dies intestate, survived by everyone shown on the family tree *except* (that is, the following people have predeceased the decedent): **D**'s parents, **M** and **F**, **D**'s grandparents, **MGM, MGF, PGM,** and **PGF,** aunts and uncles **C, A, H,** and **J,** and cousins **7** and **11**. How is **D**'s probate estate distributed under the UPC intestacy provisions?

(b) How would the distribution change if none of **D**'s paternal first cousins had survived **D**?

(c) **D**, the decedent, dies intestate, survived by everyone shown on the family tree *except* (that is, the following people have predeceased the decedent): **D**'s parents, **M** and **F**, **D**'s grandparents, **MGM, MGF, PGM,** and **PGF,** aunts and uncles **E, C, B, A, H, I, J, K,** and **L,** cousins **1, 2, 3, 4, 5, 7, 8, 9, 10, 11, 12** and **13**. How is **D**'s probate estate distributed under the UPC intestacy provisions?

G. Providing for Minors

It should be clear by now that one reason to write a will is to decide who will receive one's property rather than to allow state intestate succession law to take its course. We will explore the limits on a testator's ability to dispose of property by will in a moment, but first it is important to understand another reason for writing a will: providing for the management of property.

Some persons are not *sui juris*; the law does not allow them to deal with property they may own. The logic of removing the power to control property from individuals, is to protect these persons from errors they might make because of a lack of "capacity" to deal with the world. Adults may be incapacitated to some degree by disability or illness. Persons under eighteen years of age, of course, are minors, and while they certainly can possess property they cannot do much with it, principally because their ability to enter into binding contracts is limited by law in an effort to protect them from exploitation by those with greater experience and apparent authority. The common law has long taken what can be described as a jaded view of human nature, unwilling to trust anyone, even a parent, with unsupervised control of the property of a minor or incapacitated

> **FYI**
>
> A proceeding to authorize an expenditure of guardian's funds will require the preparation of a budget showing the need for the invasion of principal in order to maintain the minor's standard of living or to deal with an emergency or simply an increased need (such as a tuition payment occasioned by a change in schools). At any rate, such proceedings are expensive and payment for everything from court filing costs to the compensation of all the lawyers involved, including the guardian ad litem (a guardian for the purposes of litigation), comes from the guardianship property.

adult, although there are some relatively modern exceptions to that generalization. (From this point on the materials will discuss only minors; incapacitated adults will appear later in the materials on trusts.)

Under UPC § 5–104, if property due a minor does not exceed in value $10,000 it can be paid directly to a parent or other adult who has the "care and custody" of the minor and with whom the minor resides or to a guardian or custodian under the Uniform Transfers to Minors Act or to a financial institution with an account in the name of the minor.

Aside from statutory provisions similar to § 5–104, money that must be distributed outright to a minor must be managed by a court-appointed individual, traditionally called a *guardian of the property* (as opposed to the *guardian of the person*). The UPC refers to the guardian of the property as a *conservator* and limits the term guardian to designate the person who has the responsibility to care for the minor. UPC §§ 5–201 through 5–210 deal with guardianships of minors.

While a conservator under the UPC has broad discretion to invest and spend the minor's property, traditionally the guardian of the property is closely supervised by the appointing court and often is limited to only the safest of investments (insured bank accounts and perhaps government bonds). Perhaps the most important limit, however, is on the guardian of the property's ability to spend. Traditionally the guardian may expend for the minor's benefit only the *income* on the guardianship property. If the income is insufficient and the guardian must dip into the guardianship property, the *principal*, (yes, these terms have the same meaning they have when applied to trusts as explained in Chapter 8), and the appropriate court must approve the use of principal and the amount. Obtaining that approval requires a court proceeding which may very well include the appointment by the court of a lawyer (a *guardian ad litem*, a guardian for purposes of a court proceeding) to represent the interests of the minor. In addition, the guardianship must come to an end when the minor is an adult, generally on attaining eighteen [Probably most parents believe that eighteen is far too young an age at which to be entrusted with managing money.]

The above analysis should lead you to the following guiding principle:

GUARDIANSHIPS OF THE PROPERTY ARE TO BE AVOIDED.

The next question, of course, is what are the alternatives to a guardianship of the property? If the parent dies intestate, the answer is none at all, absent some statutory provision.

Problem 7-7

Parents and their three children are domiciliaries of State A. One of the parents dies intestate at which time the children are 19, 14, and 12 years of age. The probate estate is valued at $500,000. Assume neither parent has any other children.

(a) How is the intestate estate distributed under the UPC?

(b) Is there an advantage to the UPC provision?

Take Note

Remember that if the surviving spouse remarries and then dies before the second spouse, the second spouse may have a claim on the property inherited from the first spouse to die (something we discussed in the materials about the elective share in Chapter 5).

The UPC's intestate succession pattern allocates the entire estate to the surviving spouse so no guardianship is required. If, however, the deceased had a child who was not a child of the survivor, a guardianship would be required. Moreover, many state intestacy statutes allocate a share even in cases in which the children are children of both spouses. Some states, like New York, have a statutory provision which allows any personal representative (including an administrator), trustee, or guardian to transfer property belonging to a minor to a custodial account (described below) even in the absence of a will and even if the will or trust does not authorize such a transfer, provided the amount does not exceed a certain threshold.

If the parent dies testate, however, there are choices that can be made to ensure that the parent's children are properly cared for. Most obviously, perhaps, is to leave all the probate property to the surviving spouse. This might not be the best option if the testator has children by someone other than the surviving spouse, but in many cases it will be the best alternative. That alternative is not available, however, if there is no surviving parent. How likely are children to be orphaned before they reach the age of majority, or even 21? Probably not very, given life expectancy in the contemporary United States, but such a sad event is possible. (Of course, exactly the same principles apply to grandparents who might wish to make testamentary gifts to minor grandchildren.) There are two alternative methods of providing for the management of property given to a minor by will.

First, the will can direct that the executor deposit the property in a *custodial account* under the state's version of the Uniform Gifts to Minor Act (UGMA) or the more up-to-date Uniform Transfers to Minors Act (UTMA) which has been very widely adopted and which we'll summarize here. Any sort of property can be held by a custodian under the statute. Property that has written title is transferred to a custodian by changing the written title. For example, a brokerage account holding securities can be titled "X as custodian for Y under the [name of state] Uniform Transfers to Minors Act." Whether the property has written title or not, all that is necessary is that the property be delivered to the custodian accompanied by an instrument stating that the transferee holds the property as custodian for the named minor. The statute gives a form for the necessary written instrument (UTMA § 9(b)).

The custodian has broad powers to use "so much of the custodial property as the custodian considers advisable for the use and benefit of the minor . . . ." (UTMA § 14(a).) The custodian also has broad discretion in deciding how to invest the property (UTMA § 12(b)). While the custodian must keep records "of all transactions with respect to custodial property" (UTMA § 12(e)), the custodian has no obligation to make a formal accounting to a court of such transactions although a court may order an accounting. The custodianship ends when the minor attains the age of twenty-one years, although it ends at the age of majority (which is usually 18) with regard to property transferred by a fiduciary (personal representative or trustee) other than in accordance with a direction in the will or trust to make the transfer by someone obligated to the minor (UTMA § 20)). A transfer into a custodianship can be made for only one minor and there can be only one custodian (UTMA § 10).

The custodial property belongs to the minor, although the custodian holds title and deals with the property. Any taxable income produced by the custodial property belongs to the minor and must be reported on the minor's income tax returns (or on the minor's parents' return if the minor is under nineteen years of age or twenty-four years of age if the child is a full-time student and can be taken as a dependent on a parent's income tax return).

The second option is to create a *testamentary trust* for the minor children. The child or children are the beneficiaries of the trust. A trust, unlike a custodial account, may have more than one beneficiary. Title is in the trustee and the trust is a taxpayer; that is, the trustee must file income tax returns for the trust. Generally speaking, the beneficiaries pay income tax on whatever taxable income of the trust is distributed to them and the trust pays income tax on whatever is left. The income tax filing requirement makes trusts more expensive to administer than custodial accounts. On the other hand, the creator of the trust has great leeway in determining how the trust property is to be used by the trustee for the beneficiaries. The trust need not end at any particular age and the trustee's general duties and responsibilities, as we will see, are better defined than those of a custodian. In addition, the record keeping requirements applicable to trustees are more demanding than those applicable to a custodian.

We have already addressed the creation of trusts when we discussed Ward's estate plan. In the following materials, we will learn a good deal more about the possibility of crafting a trust to meet specific circumstances faced by the person creating the trust. For now however, you must understand the concept of a testamentary trust. First, remember that a lifetime or inter vivos trust as discussed above is an alternative to writing a will. A testamentary trust, in contrast, is a device for dealing with probate property and is created by a bequest in the testator's will to the trustee of the trust. If the will contains such a bequest, the will should nominate a trustee as well an executor. Once the will is admitted to probate, the trustee receives *letters of trusteeship* analogous to the executor's letters testamentary. Of course, the testamentary trust is irrevocable by the person who created it, although it is possible to give someone else the authority to alter the terms of the trust.

The following is typical language that can be used to create a single testamentary trust for the testator's children:

> All the rest, residue, and remainder of my estate, both real and personal, wheresoever situated (my "residuary estate"), I give, devise, and bequeath to my spouse (name) if (he or she) shall survive me. If my spouse does not survive me and any of my children are under the age of (age at which trust will terminate), I give my residuary estate to my Trustee, hereinafter named, in trust, nevertheless, to hold, administer, and distribute my said residuary estate for the following uses and purposes:

Next follow the actual terms of the trust. We will consider those terms in some detail after we have learned much more about the workings of trusts. A testamentary trust will be created only if the conditions directed in testator's will are fulfilled at death. In the situation we've been discussing the conditions are the failure of the testator's spouse to survive the testator and that at least one of the testator's children is under a stated age. Before the testator's death the trust does not exist.

If the conditions are fulfilled, the trust comes into existence at the moment of the testator's death, although the practicalities of administering the estate will delay the actual setting up of the trust. While the rules involved can be complicated, every jurisdiction has statutory law which insures that the beneficiaries of a testamentary trust begin to benefit from the trust from the moment of the testator's death.

By now, one hopes that any of you studying these materials who have children but who do not have a will are scared silly. But the situation can be worse. Minor children cannot live on their own. They require a *guardian of the person* to act *in loco parentis*. A parent can name a guardian of the person by will in most states (e.g., N.Y. Dom. Rel. L. § 81) and under the UPC (§ 5–202). In the absence of an appointment a court will have to appoint a guardian of the person based on the best interests of the child. It can safely be assumed that few parents wish to surrender such an important decision to a court.

Practice Planning Problem

Unlike an account under the Uniform Transfer to Minors Act, a trust can have more than one beneficiary. Suppose you are the lawyer for a married couple with three young children. Which is the better option for the couple should both parents die while the children are under 21?

A. Direct the surviving spouse's executor to distribute any property passing to a child under the age of 21 to an account under the Uniform Transfer to Minors Act. (The will can name the custodian or allow the executor to select the custodian and even allow the executor to select him or herself.)

B. Create three testamentary trusts, one for each child.

C. Create one testamentary trust for all of the children.

The advantages to dying testate, therefore, are many. They may be summarized by a single word: "flexibility." This flexibility goes far beyond replacing the default rule of the intestacy statute with the testator's own ideas about who receives property. The testator can also place conditions on the receipt of property. Recall *Shapira v. Union National Bank*, 315 N.E.2d 825 (Ohio 1974). The father's will required his sons to marry Jewish women within seven years of the father's death in order to inherit from the estate. That condition was upheld in court as a reasonable, partial restraint on marriage.

Test Your Knowledge

To assess your understanding of the material in this chapter, click here to take a quiz.

PART IV

Will Substitutes

CHAPTER 8

Trusts

357 – 96

A page of history . . .

Just like you can effectively use your computer without understanding the operation of 'Intel core 2 duo inside' one need not be a historian of trusts to draft a family trust. But some historical background is useful to place squarely in mind the function of this splendid legal construct.

Simply put, it is based on a legal fiction that one can separate legal title from beneficial ownership. It is often rehearsed that the Franciscan friars could own no property. How might a wealthy lay benefactor further their cause? Transfer property to William who would hold for the 'use' or benefit of the friars. So far so good. But what if he absconds with the cash or otherwise defaults on his obligation, may the friars sue to protect their interest, and in what forum? Or consider another narrative. Innocent III has called the Third Crusade. Lord Curmudgeon wants to participate. But who will manage his estates in his absence; and who will transmit the property to his family should he die in the Holy Land, assuming he has more elaborate designs for his landed property than the law of dower and primogeniture dictates. Lord Grouchfield is too infirmed to participate. Might Curmudgeon enfeoff Grouchfield to the 'uses' (a medieval term that we can define as 'estate plan" expressed in a separate writing). *Bien sur.* But should wily Grouchfield have second thoughts, how may he be kept honest, particularly since the common law recognizes as evidence of the terms of the transfer the bare deed, and not the collateral written understanding? But if Curmudgeon returns or even if he does not, to what forum can he or his beneficiaries repair to compel Grouchfield to keep his 'trust?'

In medieval England, the chancellor, initially the King's confessor and eventually a royal judge, would entertain on an ad hoc basis cases which came to the royal penitent, and troubled his master's conscience, but for which the legal system offered no redress. The chancellor would order the holder of legal title to perform his trust. Now that there is a remedy, there is a right; and for the ensuing half millennium, chancellors (and their judicial descendants) have been enforcing promises attached to the transfer of property, both real and personal. So regular were these arrangements fashioned, and so routinely were they enforced by the chancellor, that he came to hold a court, the Court of Chancery, and it began to form a substantive law of trusts. The doctrine developed therein continues to inform the enforcement of trusts in our own time.

A. Trust Creation

We have already encountered the law of trusts a number of times in these materials, most prominently in our discussion of Ward's Estate Plan and we shall again in the section on will substitutes in which lifetime trusts figure prominently. Revocable inter vivos or lifetime trusts, like most trusts, are usually (and in some states must be) created through the execution of written instruments which expressly use clear language, words of art, of trust creation. These words transfer legal title to the trust property to a trustee and create beneficial or equitable title in the beneficiary or beneficiaries. These written instruments are of three types:

1. **wills**, which create testamentary trusts;

2. **trust agreements between the creator** (sometimes called settlor) **of the trust and the trustee** (who may be and often is in the case of revocable lifetime trusts intended to be the same person);

3. **self-settled trusts**, declarations of trust by an owner of property who simply declares that he or she holds property as trustee. Such declarations of trust are often used to create revocable lifetime trusts intended to be will substitutes. No matter what type of instrument is used, when properly drafted, the writing creating the trust should leave little doubt, if any, that the person executing the document intends to create a trust.

Example 1: O(wner) executes his will leaving her residuary to T to hold the same in trust for his niece Alyssa and nephew Aaron aged 12 and 10 respectively. According to the terms of the trust, income from the trust should be expended to provide for the health, education and welfare of the children until the corpus is distributed. The distribution of the corpus should occur when the youngest child reaches the age of 25. At that time, the corpus is to be divided between the two children equally.

A testamentary trust has been created which takes effect if and when O's will is probated.

Example 2: O executes a trust instrument in which his 1000 shares of Apple are to be held by T in trust for his niece Alyssa and nephew Aaron aged 12 and 10 respectively. The shares are transferred to T. According to the terms of the trust, income from the trust should be expended to provide for the health, education and welfare of the children until the corpus is distributed. The distribution of the corpus should occur when the youngest child reaches the age of 25. At that time, the corpus is to be divided between the two children equally. O retains the power to amend the terms of the trust or to revoke the instrument entirely.

A revocable lifetime trust has been created through a trust agreement.

Example 3: O executes a trust instrument of his 1000 shares of Apple naming himself as trustee in trust for his niece Alyssa and nephew Aaron aged 12 and 10 respectively. He changes ownership of the shares from O to O as Trustee. According to the terms of the trust, income from the trust should be expended to provide for the health, education and welfare of the children until the corpus is distributed. The distribution of the corpus should occur when the youngest child reaches the age of 25. At that time, the corpus is to be divided between the two children equally. O retains the power to amend the terms of the trust or to revoke the instrument entirely. Same facts as above but O names herself trustee.

A self-settled revocable lifetime trust has been created.

Example 4: Suppose O hands over cash, $500,000 to T and tells him the following: hold this property to support Alyssa and Aaron until they reach 25, then fork over the cash to them. Has a trust been created? O dies one year later. What if T pockets the cash? Can Alyssa or Aaron sue to compel T to perform? Can O's intestate heir and residuary beneficiary Lisa sue?

Flummoxed? Consider the following. Intent rather than any particular form of words employed by the purported creator is what is controlling. As the current Restatement of Trusts puts it, "No particular manner of expression is necessary to manifest the trust intention. Thus, a trust may be created without the settlor's use of words such as 'trust' or 'trustee;' likewise, the fact that a transferor uses the word 'trust' or 'trustee' does not necessarily indicate the intention to create a relationship that constitutes a trust . . . ." (Restatement Third, Trusts § 13, comment *b*). Generally, any conveyance of property by O to another, B, accompanied by some manifestation of the intention that B uses the property for the benefit of others (including B so long as there are other beneficiaries) is sufficient to create a trust. In most jurisdictions oral expressions of intent are sufficient. Under New York law, every lifetime trust must be in writing (EPTL § 7–1.17(a)). What are the likely consequences of New York's position? Would it in Case 4 lead to unjust enrichment? Can you propose a remedy to avoid it?

[handwritten margin note: NY is often very formalistic.]

What is critical in trust creation, however, is that the creator manifest the intent to separate legal (in a trustee) and beneficial (equitable) title (in a beneficiary). Needless to say, any written instrument that is supposed to create a trust should clearly do exactly that. The use of the word "trust," however, is not necessarily enough, as the following case shows:

Matter of Mannara

785 N.Y.S.2d 274 (Surr. Ct. 2004)

Eve Preminger, J.

Petitioner, administrator c.t.a. of the will of Lydia Mannara, has asked the Court to construe the sole dispositive provision of the will and find a valid trust.

What's That?

An administrator c.t.a. [*cum testamento annexo*] is appointed when the executor refuses to serve or does not qualify.

The entire text of the will is:

I, Lydia Mannara, hereby give my power of attorney to my friend, Christodoulas Pelaghias, [sic] I empower him to make decisions concerning my health, life support and any medical arrangements. I hereby appoint him Executor of my last will and testament. I hereby bequeath all of my assets to my two nephews in trust for their education.

The testator executed the will while *in extremis.*

A friend who happened to be visiting the testator the day before her death handwrote the will; and although the friend is an attorney, it is clear from the affidavits of attesting witnesses filed in the probate proceeding that the friend served merely as an amanuensis for the testator who was a layperson.[1]

It's Latin to Me

in extremis: on the death bed

Non constat
jus civile
a posteriori

An "amanuensis" is a person who is employed to take dictation. In this context, it means the friend simply wrote down what the testator said and therefore was not acting as an attorney.

Petitioner, who is testator's sole distributee and father of her infant nephews, contends the will creates two residuary trusts one for the benefit of each nephew and would have the Court imply certain detailed provisions: that the trustees are petitioner and one Hormoz Lashkari, each of whom may designate his own successor trustee, that the trustees may make discretionary payments for the benefit of the beneficiary's education, and that each trust shall terminate when the beneficiary attains the age of twenty-two, with the remainder payable to the beneficiary. Pe-

---

1   Affidavits of the two attesting witnesses filed in the probate proceeding indicate that two friends of the testator's visited her in the hospital the day before her death. The first to arrive asked the testator if she had a will, and learning that she did not, suggested that the second friend, an attorney whose arrival was expected shortly, prepare a will for her. The second friend met with the testator and drafted the document, which she then read aloud to the testator, in the presence of the first friend. The testator requested that the phrase "in trust for their education" be added, the phrase was added, and the testator then approved the terms of the instrument and executed it.

titioner has also provided for the disposition of property in the event a beneficiary dies before attaining the age of twenty-two.

The guardian *ad litem*, appointed to represent the interests of the two nephews, posits that the will creates a "passive" or invalid trust and that the residuary bequest therefore vests directly in her wards.

A trust is a "fiduciary relationship in which one person holds a property interest, subject to an equitable obligation to keep or use that interest for the benefit of another" (Bogert, *The Law of Trusts and Trustees* § 1 [2d ed. rev. 1984]). There are four essential elements of a trust: (1) a designated beneficiary; (2) a designated trustee; (3) a fund or other property sufficiently designated or identified to enable title thereto to pass to the trustee; and (4) actual delivery or legal assignment of the property to the trustee, with the intention of passing legal title to such property to the trustee (*Brown v. Spohr*, 180 N.Y. 201, 209, 73 N.E. 14). No formulaic expression is required to create a trust; not even the words "trust" and "trustee" are mandatory (see *Matter of Leonard*, 218 N.Y. 513, 520, 113 N.E. 491; *Matter of Donohue*, 143 N.Y.S.2d 405, 405–406). Conversely, mere inclusion of the phrase "in trust for" does not effectuate a trust (*Matter of Douglas*, 195 Misc. 661, 665, 89 N.Y.S.2d 498; *Matter of Grauer*, 146 Misc. 469, 471–472, 262 N.Y.S. 368). What matters is the testator's intent to create a trust relationship (*Matter of Babbage*, 201 Misc. 750, 752, 106 N.Y.S.2d 332; *Matter of Santini*, N.Y.L.J., Dec. 12, 1995, at 32, col. 2; *see Matter of Gladstone*, N.Y.L.J., Feb. 18, 1999, at 34, col. 5). The test is objective rather than subjective, a question of manifestation of intent rather than actual intent (*Scott, Trusts* § 2.8 [4th ed. 1987]).

The instant will lacks fundamental attributes of a trust. It neither designates a trustee, nor confers upon anyone who could be construed to be a trustee the duties of managing the fund. Other than the words "in trust for," there is no language that would sustain or give color to the construction of a trust. The testator does not distinguish income from principal, exhibit any conception of a trust remainder, or otherwise provide for the use and duration of the fund in terms which would limit qualitatively or quantitatively her nephews' interest in the property. Certainly, the testator has not manifested an intent to impose upon a transferee of property the equitable duties of holding such property for the benefit of another.

Petitioner claims that, because the will was handwritten by an attorney instead of by the testator, *Matter of Douglas*, 195 Misc. 661, 89 N.Y.S.2d 498, *supra* is not apposite. He is incorrect.

The will in *Matter of Douglas*, 195 Misc. 661, 89 N.Y.S.2d 498, *supra* left property "in trust for" a five-year old boy; the interest could be used for vocal and music lessons, and the principal was to be used for his college education. The testator, however, evinced no intent to create a trust; indeed, the Surrogate determined that the testator contemplated a guardianship rather than a trust. Reasoning that the testator, a layperson, could hardly be expected to distinguish the technical from the colloquial use of the word "trust," the Surrogate found the testator's reference to the beneficiary's education was not a qualification of the bequest, but an expression of the testator's motive for making it (*Matter of Douglas*, 195 Misc. 661, 666, 89 N.Y.S.2d 498, *supra*).

In the instant will, use of the term "in trust for" is as indiscriminate and inadvertent as it was in *Matter of Douglas*, 195 Misc. 661, 89 N.Y.S.2d 498, *supra*, the reference to the education of testator's nephews, an expression of her motivation for the bequest. Like the testator in *Matter of Douglas*, 195 Misc. 661, 89 N.Y.S.2d 498, *supra*, she contemplated a guardianship rather than a trust.

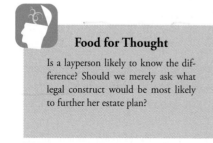

Food for Thought

Is a layperson likely to know the difference? Should we merely ask what legal construct would be most likely to further her estate plan?

Even if the Court were to find the testator had manifested an intent to create a trust and were to imply a trustee (*see e.g. Matter of Sicular*, N.Y.L.J., Aug. 22, 1997, at 27, col. 2), but not fabricate additional terms now proposed by petitioner (*see e.g. Matter of Nowak*, N.Y.L.J., June 17, 2002, at 21, col. 6), it would be unavailing. A trust involving no active duties on the part of the trustee is only a passive trust (*Jacoby v. Jacoby*, 188 N.Y. 124, 129, 80 N.E. 676). By operation of law, title to property bequeathed to the trustee of a passive trust vests in the beneficiary (*Matter of Gagliardi*, 55 N.Y.2d 109, 113, 447 N.Y.S.2d 902, 432 N.E.2d 774; *Ward v. Saranac Lake Federal Savings & Loan Assn.*, 48 A.D.2d 337, 339, 369 N.Y.S.2d 540; *Matter of Alexander*, 20 Misc.2d 983, 984, 189 N.Y.S.2d 495; *Matter of Gansil*, N.Y.L.J., Feb. 23, 1993, at 22, col. 6; *see* EPTL 7–1.2).

There being no valid testamentary trust, the net residuary estate vests in the testator's two nephews.

Matter of Maliszewski

42 A.D.3d 737 (N.Y. Ct. App. 2007)

Before: Mercure, J.P., Carpinello, Rose, Lahtinen and Kane, JJ.

Mercure, J.P.

Appeal from an order of the Surrogate's Court of Schenectady County (Kramer, S.), entered August 17, 2006, which construed paragraph four of decedent's last will and testament.

Petitioners commenced this proceeding to construe the fourth paragraph of decedent's last will and testament. That paragraph provided that if any part of decedent's estate vested "absolute ownership in a person under the age of [25]," then decedent's fiduciary was authorized "to hold the property so vested in a separate fund for the benefit of such person and to invest and reinvest the same." The fiduciary was also directed to apply so much of the net income or principal necessary for the "care, support, maintenance and education of said person" until he or she reached age 25, at which point the accumulated income, as well as the unexpended principal, would be paid to him or her. According to petitioners, the fourth paragraph was meant to establish trusts for the benefit of any beneficiaries who were under age 25 at the time of decedent's death. Surrogate's Court disagreed and concluded that this paragraph did not set up a valid trust, prompting this appeal.

At issue are the specific bequests of stocks in a separate paragraph of decedent's will that passed to individuals who were under the age of 25 at the time of decedent's death. Petitioners argue that it was decedent's intent that the stocks would be held in trust until the legatees attain the age of 25. We agree.

To constitute a valid trust, there must be a designated beneficiary, a designated trustee, an identifiable res and delivery with the intent of vesting legal title in a trustee (*see Matter of Marcus Trusts*, 2 A.D.3d 640, 641, 769 N.Y.S.2d 56 [2003]).

Surrogate's Court found that there was no showing of delivery with the intent of vesting legal title in the trustee; instead, the court determined that legal title was granted to the listed legatees by virtue of the language "vest in absolute ownership." The will also provided, however, that if

> ### Take Note
>
> It is often said that trusts will not fail for want of trustee. One can be appointed by the court. If a trustee is not appointed but the creator intended to create a trust, the creator can be regarded as the implied trustee or if the trust is testamentary the creator's executor can fill that role.

the legatee was under age 25, the fiduciary was to hold the property "so vested" in a separate fund and to invest it and reinvest it as above set forth until the legatee reached 25 years of age. Thus, contrary to the findings of Surrogate's Court, even given the "so vested" language, the fiduciary did in fact gain legal title to the assets so as to be considered a trustee (*see Orentreich v. Prudential Ins. Co. of Am.*, 275 A.D.2d 685, 685–686, 713 N.Y.S.2d 330 [2000]).

It is well settled that the "cardinal rule of construction of a will is to carry out the intent of the testator" (*Matter of Ramdin*, 11 A.D.3d 698, 699, 783 N.Y.S.2d 643 [2004]). The intent of the testator is not to be found "from a single word or phrase but from a sympathetic reading of the will as an entirety and in view of all the facts and circumstances under which [its] provisions . . . were framed" (*Matter of Fabbri*, 2 N.Y.2d 236, 240, 159 N.Y.S.2d 184, 140 N.E.2d 269 [1957]. While the "vested" language is suggestive of an absolute gift, the remainder of the language of the will demonstrates that decedent intended to establish a trust for each legatee. Specifically, by naming a "fiduciar[y]" for each legatee and directing him or her to hold the property in a separate fund and to invest it, as well as to apply the "net income . . . or . . . principal to the care, support, maintenance and education" of the legatee until the age of 25, decedent manifested his intent to create a trust for each legatee.

> ### Practice Pointer
>
> Perhaps the scrivener could have removed all doubt by clearer, more unequivocal language. Redraft.

Accordingly, this Court construes the fourth paragraph of the will as establishing trusts for the benefit of each legatee who was under 25 years of age at the time of decedent's death (*see Matter of Bay*, 178 Misc. 737, 738, 36 N.Y.S.2d 916 [1942]).

ORDERED that the order is reversed, on the law, without costs, and matter remitted to the

Surrogate's Court of Schenectady County for further proceedings not inconsistent with this Court's decision.

Carpinello, Rose, Lahtinen and Kane, JJ., concur.

Points for Discussion

1. *Distinguishing the indistinguishable*

a. Can you distinguish *Mannara* from *Maliszewski*? Are they distinguished by the language used in the documents or by each court's distinctive approach to gleaning the intent of the property owner from the words used therein? Which decision do you think is preferable and why?

b. Would the Surrogate's opinion in *Mannara* have been different if the testator had bequeathed all of her assets to Pelaghias "in trust for the education of my two nephews"?

2. *Passive trusts*

A passive trust is one in which the trustee has no fiduciary duties to perform. If the trustee has no such duties, the trust will never commence or it will terminate when active duties cease. In either case the beneficiary will assume full outright ownership of the trust corpus. The distinction between the two types of trusts is historic, and harks back to the Statute of Uses enacted in England 1535 during the reign of Henry VIII. In simple terms, the statute "executed" trusts (then called "uses") that required that the trustee do nothing more than allow the beneficiary to use the trust property: in fact most of the uses that had hitherto been created. However, trusts in which the trustee had an active role to perform continued to exist. Although the Statute was abolished in England in 1925, it persists in some jurisdictions in the United States as part of the common law or in some sort of statutory formulation. In New York the principle of the statute is contained in NY EPTL § 7–1.2 which requires that a disposition of property be made directly "to the person to whom the right to possession and income is intended to be vested" and not to another in trust. Realize that if a person has both legal possession of property (title) and owns the income from it (the beneficial interest), there is no separation of equitable and legal title, and therefore no trust.

Problem 8-1

Can ambiguous language create "active trusts"? Consider the following examples.

Example 1: A will contains the following language: "I give devise and bequeath all my property to my wife, and I recommend to her the care and protection of my mother and sister, and request her to make such . . . provision for them as in her judgment will be best." Is a trust created? What are court's choices? A trust to be sure. Although the court so decided, it is arguable that the property was transferred absolutely with a non-enforceable moral obligation that the transferee consider the needs of the named family members. These non-trusts are confusingly referred to as **precatory trusts**. The categorization turns on the court's interpretation of the language. The question parsed is whether the words should be regarded as a request rather than an imperative, non-binding rather than a binding legal obligation. Lesson for the practitioner: clarity, not obfuscation.

Example 2: Suppose our testatrix used the following language instead: 'I give devise and bequeath all my property to my wife, asking that she pay $100,000 to my mother and sister.' Binding or non-binding? Was a trust created? What are a court's choices? A precatory trust? Unlikely; though not a bad choice. When a sum certain is limited, the language is generally interpreted to create what the law refers to as an equitable charge, a security interest in the estate, which the executor is bound to satisfy.

B. The Need for a Trustee

Although courts routinely include the nomination of a trustee as a trust requisite, it is textbook law that a trust will not fail for want of a trustee. The "trust" in the *Mannara* case did not (and would not) fail because the creator of the trust did not name a trustee. A court can always appoint a trustee in order to fulfill the creator's intent to create a trust. Similarly, if the creator does name a trustee and that trustee dies or resigns, and the trust instrument does not name a successor trustee, the appropriate court can name a new trustee. (*See* Restatement Third, Trusts § 31; there is an exception to this general rule where the creator of the trust has manifested an intention to create a trust only if a specific person will act as trustee, *id.*, comment *b*). A well-drafted instrument, of course, will name someone to become successor trustee should one be necessary.

The requirements established for individuals to be a trustee are similar to those for executors. Only natural persons and banks with trust powers may be trustees, although in some limited circumstances other entities may act as trustee, an exception that usually applies to charities as trustees of trusts for their own benefit.

Because the duties of a trustee are demanding, no one can be forced to be trustee. The correlative to that rule is that a trustee must accept the trusteeship before duties are enforceable. A testamentary trustee must apply for letters of trusteeship at the time the will is offered for probate, and a well-drafted instrument creating a lifetime trust will require the trustee's signature and state that by signing the instrument the trustee accepts obligations under the trust. Absent the requirement of signing the trust instrument, whether or not a trustee has accepted is a matter of intent.

Jimenez v. Lee

547 P. 2nd 126 (Or. 1976)

O'CONNELL, CHIEF JUSTICE.

This is a suit brought by plaintiff against her father to compel him to account for assets which she alleges were held by defendant as trustee for her.

Plaintiff appeals from a decree dismissing her complaint.

Plaintiff's claim against her father is based upon the theory that a trust arose in her favor when two separate gifts were made for her benefit. The first of these gifts was made in 1945, shortly after plaintiff's birth, when her paternal grandmother purchased a $1,000 face value U.S. Savings Bond which was registered in the names of defendant 'and/or' plaintiff 'and/or' Dorothy Lee, plaintiff's mother. It is uncontradicted that the bond was purchased to provide funds to be used for plaintiff's educational needs. A second gift in the amount of $500 was made in 1956 by Mrs. Adolph Diercks, one of defendant's clients. At the same time Mrs. Diercks made identical gifts for the benefit of defendant's two other children. The $1,500 was deposited by the donor in a savings account in the names of defendant and his three children.

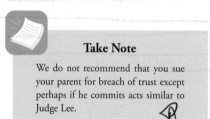

Take Note

We do not recommend that you sue your parent for breach of trust except perhaps if he commits acts similar to Judge Lee.

In 1960 defendant cashed the savings bond and invested the proceeds in common stock of the Commercial Bank of Salem, Oregon. Ownership of the shares was registered as 'Jason Lee, Custodian under the Laws of Oregon for Betsy Lee (plaintiff).' At the same time, the joint savings account containing the client's gifts to defendant's children was closed and $1,000 of the proceeds invested in Commercial Bank stock. Defendant also took title to this stock as 'custodian' for his children.

The trial court found that defendant did not hold either the savings bond or the savings account in trust for the benefit of plaintiff and that defendant held the shares of the Commercial Bank stock as custodian for plaintiff under the Uniform Gift to Minors Act (ORS 126.805–126.880). Plaintiff contends that the gifts for her educational needs created trusts in each instance and that the trusts survived defendant's investment of the trust assets in the Commercial Bank stock.

It is undisputed that the gifts were made for the educational needs of plaintiff. The respective donors did not expressly direct defendant to hold the subject matter of the gift 'in trust' but this is not essential to create a trust relationship. It is enough if the transfer of the property is made with the intent to vest the beneficial ownership in a third person. That was clearly shown in the present case. Even defendant's own testimony establishes such intent. When he was asked whether there was a stated purpose for the gift, he replied: ' * * * Mother said that she felt that the children should all be treated equally and that she was going to supply a bond to help with Elizabeth's educational needs and that she was naming me and Dorothy, the ex-wife and mother of Elizabeth, to use the funds as may be most conducive to the educational needs of Elizabeth.'

Defendant also admitted that the gift from Mrs. Diercks was 'for the educational needs of the children.' There was nothing about either of the gifts which would suggest that the beneficial ownership of the subject matter of the gift was to vest in defendant to use as he pleased with an obligation only to pay out of his own funds a similar amount for plaintiff's educational needs.

Food for Thought

Sufficient expression manifested to create a trust? Do you think either Granny or Client understood the obligations that they were placing on Dad? Does one have to understand the nature of a trust to create one?

Defendant himself demonstrated that he knew that the savings bond was held by him in trust. In a letter to his mother, the donor, he wrote: 'Dave and Bitsie (plaintiff) & Dorothy are aware of the fact that I hold $1,000 each for Dave & Bitsie in trust for them on account of your E-Bond gifts.' It is fair to indulge in the presumption that defendant, as a lawyer, used the word 'trust' in the ordinary legal sense of that term. Defendant further contends that even if the respective donors intended to create trusts, the doctrine of merger defeated that intent because plaintiff acquired both legal and equitable title when the savings bond was registered in her name along with her parents' names and when Mrs. Diercks' gift was deposited in the savings account in the name of plaintiff and her father, brother and sister. The answer to this contention is found in II Scott on Trusts s 99.4, p. 811 (3d ed 1967):

Take Note

Might a better argument be that Dad created a trust by this writing?

'A trust may be created in which the trustees are A and B and the sole beneficiary is A. In such a case it might be argued that there is automatically a partial extinguishment of the trust, and that A holds an undivided half interest as joint tenant free of trust, although B holds a similar interest in trust for A. The better view is, however, that there is no such partial merger, and that A and B will hold the property as joint tenants in trust for A. * * * '

Take Note

Dad's off the hook if a custodianship was intended but has to account to Bitsie for expenditures if a trust was created.

Having decided that a trust was created for the benefit of plaintiff, it follows that defendant's purchase of the Commercial Bank stock as 'custodian' for plaintiff under the Uniform Gift to Minors Act was ineffectual to expand defendant's powers over the trust property from that of trustee to that of custodian. If defendant were 'custodian' of the gifts, he would have the power under the Uniform Gift to Minors Act (ORS 126.820) to use the property 'as he may deem advisable for the support, maintenance, education and general use and benefit of the minor, in such manner, at such time or times, and to such extent as the custodian in his absolute discretion may deem advisable and proper, without court order or without regard to the duty of any person to support the minor, and without regard to any other funds which may be applicable or available for the purpose.' As custodian defendant would not be required to account for his stewardship of the funds unless a petition for accounting were filed in circuit court no later than two years after the end of plaintiff's minority. ORS 126.875. As the trustee of an educational trust, however, defendant has the power to use the trust funds for educational purposes only and has the duty to render clear and accurate accounts showing the funds have been used for trust purposes. See ORS 128.010; Restatement (Second) of Trusts s 172 (1959).

Defendant's attempt to broaden his powers over the trust estate by investing the trust funds as custodian violated his duty to the beneficiary 'to administer the trust solely in the interest of the beneficiary.' Restatement (Second) of Trusts s 170, p. 364 (1959). The money from the savings bond and savings account are clearly traceable into the bank stock. Therefore, plaintiff was entitled to impose a constructive trust or an equitable lien upon the stock so acquired. Plaintiff is also entitled to be credited for any dividends or increment in the value of that part of the stock representing plaintiff's proportional interest. Whether or not the assets of plaintiff's trust are traceable into a product, defendant is personally liable for that amount which would have accrued to plaintiff had there been no breach of trust. Defendant is, of course, entitled to deduct the amount which he expended out of the trust estate for plaintiff's educational needs. However, before he is entitled to be credited for such expenditures, he has the duty as trustee to identify them specifically and prove that they were made for trust purposes. A trustee's duty to maintain and render accurate accounts is a strict one. * * *

Take Note

Trustees may be personally liable for losses occasioned by a breach of their fiduciary obligation.

The case must, therefore, be remanded for an accounting to be predicated upon a trustee's duty to account, and the trustee's burden to prove that the expenditures were made for trust purposes. There is a moral obligation and in proper cases a legal obligation for a parent to furnish his child with higher education. Where a parent is a trustee of an educational trust, as in the present case, and he makes expenditures out of his own funds, his intent on one hand may be to discharge his moral or legal obligation to educate his child or on the other hand to follow the directions of the trust. It is a question of fact in each case as to which of these two purposes the parent-trustee had in mind at the time of making the expenditures. In determining whether defendant has met this strict burden of proof, the trial court must adhere to the rule that all doubts are resolved against a trustee who maintains an inadequate accounting system.

The decree of the trial court is reversed and the cause is remanded for further proceedings consistent with this opinion.

Sankel v. Spector

33 A.D.3d 167 (N.Y. Ct. App. 2006)

JOHN T. BUCKLEY, P.J., JOSEPH P. SULLIVAN, EUGENE NARDELLI, JAMES M. MCGUIRE, JJ.

NARDELLI, J.

In this appeal, we are asked to determine, inter alia, whether the informal renouncement of his appointment by a designated co-trustee of a certain inter vivos trust was sufficiently binding to preclude his subsequent acceptance of that appointment.

On November 23, 2004, Eleanor Spector created an inter vivos trust "to provide for her own needs and the future needs of her issue," respondents/beneficiaries Linda Spector and Barbara Berlin. The trust provides that Eleanor and Linda are to be co-trustees and that upon Eleanor's death, Linda and Barbara were to receive equal monthly distributions from the trustees. Upon the death of either Linda or Barbara, the surviving beneficiary is to receive all of the income distribution. Barbara's son, Mark Pariser, is named as the remainderman and upon the death of the last remaining beneficiary, the trust would terminate and any accrued income, and the principal, would be distributed to Pariser. The corpus of the trust consisted of Eleanor's interest in the family's commercial real estate holdings at two locations in Brooklyn, New York.

Section 5.1 of the trust provides:

> "Each acting Trustee and her or his respective successor by an acknowledged writing (either before or after the Trustee making the appointment ceases to act as Trustee) delivered to the other Trustee(s) if any, and the designation may be revoked in the same manner by the person making the designation, at any time before the successor qualifies. *If ELEANOR SPECTOR or LINDA J. SPECTOR shall cease serving as Trustee without having appointed a successor, JOEL SANKEL shall act as co-Trustee in her place and stead*" (emphasis added).

Also germane to this appeal is section 2.2 of the trust, which states:

> "The Trustees (*other than either of the Settlor's daughters*) may at any time and from time to time distribute principal of the trust to either or both of LINDA or BARBARA, *equally or unequally*" (emphasis added).

It is undisputed that Barbara and Linda share an extraordinarily acrimonious relationship.

Indeed, it is apparently so hostile that, to the extent that they do communicate with each other, it is only through their respective attorneys. Sankel, on the other hand, was known to Eleanor as he had performed some legal work for her on prior occasions and, apparently at Linda's suggestion,

---

Practice Pointer

Given the known hostility between the sisters, why would a scrivener allow the creator to make one or the other or both trustee? What personal factors come in to play in trustee selection?

which was accepted by Eleanor, Sankel was delineated as a designated co-trustee. Linda maintained that Sankel was aware of the designation, whereas Sankel claims he was not.

On January 29, 2004, approximately two months after she created the trust, Eleanor died without having designated a successor trustee. Supreme Court conducted a hearing which began in July 2004 and culminated in September 2004, during which the following allegations were made concerning what transpired after Eleanor's death.

The parties agree that Linda invited Sankel to dinner at the apartment of her then fiancé and current husband, Albert Jacobs, on February 9, 2004, 11 days after her mother's death. Linda testified that while having dessert, she reminded Sankel that Eleanor had designated him successor trustee of the trust, of which Linda claimed Sankel was aware, and then requested that in view of "problems within the family and litigation with non-family members," and since Jacobs was going to "be family," she wanted Sankel to step aside and allow Jacobs to become the second trustee. Linda averred that Sankel readily agreed to step aside and was very pleased to hear about her engagement to Jacobs. Jacobs's testimony echoed that of Linda's, and he stated that "[Linda] asked [Sankel] if he would decline to serve. He said sure. He certainly would."

Sankel, in contrast, testified that when Linda asked him to withdraw, he was sympathetic to her request, but indicated that he wanted to give the matter some thought. Sankel further testified that he was unaware of his designation as a successor trustee, and that he asked Linda for a copy of the trust agreement because he had never seen it and did not know what powers were conferred on a co-trustee. Sankel stated that Linda faxed him a partial copy of the trust instrument on February 15, 2004, and that upon reviewing the portion of the document he received, he became concerned because the agreement permitted the non-beneficiary trustee to make unequal distributions of the trust principal. Sankel speculated that Linda wanted to substitute her fiancé/soon-to-be husband Jacobs in his stead as the "independent" co-trustee in order effectively to disinherit Barbara and her son.

Sankel thereafter attempted to contact Linda several times, and also requested a full copy of the trust instrument on numerous occasions, but his calls and correspondence went unreturned until March 2, 2004, by which time Linda had Jacobs execute documents purportedly appointing Jacobs as the co-trustee. Sankel, during that phone call, informed Linda that he intended to continue to act as co-trustee, at least until he spoke to Barbara, at which juncture Linda became very angry and again asked him to resign. Jacobs then got on the phone and also became very angry, threatening to use the resources of his large law firm, if necessary, to remove Sankel as co-trustee. Sankel, approximately two weeks later, was finally able to contact Barbara in Canada, where she resides, at which time Barbara pleaded with Sankel to retain his position as co-trustee in order to protect her interests. Sankel, in an effort to fulfill his duties as co-trustee, then attempted to acquire bank statements and other documents concerning the trust corpus from Linda and the properties' managing agent, but all of his efforts were thwarted by Linda and Jacobs, or simply went unanswered. On April 5, 2004, Sankel executed an acceptance of the co-trusteeship and forwarded it to Linda that same day.

Sankel subsequently commenced this proceeding on June 3, 2004, pursuant to Article 77 of the Civil Practice Law and Rules, by the service of an order to show cause and verified petition. The petition interposes two causes of action: the first cause of action seeks a permanent injunction against Linda, enjoining her from interfering or preventing Sankel from carrying out his fiduciary duties as a co-trustee of the trust, and directing her to cooperate with Sankel in the management and administration of the trust; and the second cause of action seeks an order permitting Sankel to retain his former law firm to perform legal services pertaining to the trust's administration. Barbara submitted an affidavit (incorrectly denominated an affirmation) in support of Sankel's application, and Linda cross-moved to dismiss the petition.

[The] Supreme Court, after conducting the aforementioned hearing, credited the testimony of Linda and Jacobs that Sankel initially agreed to decline the co-trusteeship at the February 9 dinner. The court found, however, that the statement was not automatically binding on Sankel and, in a thorough, well-reasoned decision, concluded, inter alia, that Sankel's:

> "informal, well-intentioned declination, spontaneously uttered out of respect and friendship for Ms. Spector . . . should not foreclose an almost immediate change of heart, upon more considered reflection, where Mr. Sankel's subsequent conduct is consistent with the acceptance of the trusteeship, where no person interested in the trust has been prejudiced and where the other trustee has not as yet entered upon the performance of the trust."

We agree and, accordingly, affirm.

Our analysis begins with the well-settled proposition that the court, in determining the intent of a grantor of an inter vivos trust, must look to the words used in the trust instrument and, once it is determined, must effectuate that intent unless it is contrary to public policy or the law (*Mercury Bay Boating Club, Inc. v. San Diego Yacht Club*, 76 N.Y.2d 256, 267, 557 N.Y.S.2d 851, 557 N.E.2d 87 [1990]; *Matter of Gilbert*, 39 N.Y.2d 663, 666, 385 N.Y.S.2d 278, 350 N.E.2d 609 [1976]; *see also Maletta v. Boczkowski*, 93 A.D.2d 828, 829, 461 N.Y.S.2d 42 [1983] [the intent of the settlor is of controlling importance and neither the court, nor a beneficiary, nor the Legislature, is competent to violate that intent and substitute its own discretion for that of the settlor]).

Moreover, it is also a firmly established principle of trust law that a trustee owes a duty of undivided loyalty to the trust, which standard "does not permit a trustee to create or to occupy a position in which he has interests to serve other than the interest of the trust estate. Undivided loyalty is the supreme test, unlimited and unconfirmed by the bounds of classified transactions" (*City Bank Farmers Trust Co. v. Cannon*, 291 N.Y. 125, 131, 51 N.E.2d 674 [1943]; *see also Pyle v. Pyle*, 137 App.Div. 568, 572, 122 N.Y.S. 256 [1910], *affd.* 199 N.Y. 538, 92 N.E. 1099 [1910] [a trustee "owes an undivided duty to his beneficiary, and

Take Note

Given these awesome responsibilities, why would an individual undertake the position?

he must not, under any circumstances, place himself in a position whereby his personal interest will come in conflict with the interest of his cestui que trust"]; *Matter of Hall*, 275 A.D.2d 979, 980, 713 N.Y.S.2d 622 [2000] ["[i]f the personal interests of a trustee conflict with her interest as a trustee, the court may remove her as a trustee"]). This inflexible duty of loyalty prohibits a trustee from even placing himself in a position of potential conflict with his or her duty to the trust (*Matter of Rothko*, 43 N.Y.2d 305, 319, 401 N.Y.S.2d 449, 372 N.E.2d 291 [1977]; *see also Birnbaum v. Birnbaum*, 73 N.Y.2d 461, 466, 541 N.Y.S.2d 746, 539 N.E.2d 574 [1989] ["[t]his is a sensitive and 'inflexible' rule of fidelity, barring not only blatant self-dealing, but also requiring avoidance of situations in which a fiduciary's personal interest possibly conflicts with the interest of those owed a fiduciary duty"]; 106 N.Y. Jur. 2d, Trusts, § 347["[t]he standard of loyalty in trust relations does not permit a trustee to create or to occupy a position in which he has interests to serve other than the interest of the trust estate. . . . The purpose sought to be served by this rule is to require a trustee to assume a position where his every act is above suspicion, and the trust estate, and it alone, can receive, not only his best services, but also his unbiased and uninfluenced judgment"]).

In this matter, the intent of the settlor can be readily gleaned from the document, not only from Eleanor's designation of Sankel, a person whom she obviously trusted, to succeed her, but also by the specific limitation, set forth in the trust instrument, that only an independent trustee, i.e., neither Barbara, nor Linda, may invade the principal and distribute it "equally or unequally." We can perceive of no view of Jacobs's appointment, nor are we presented with one, that would honor Eleanor's intent, or fulfill the obligation of a trustee to avoid placing himself in a position where not even the appearance of a conflict with his duty to the trust should exist. Indeed, Linda's rush to have her fiancé appointed as a trustee also is disquieting.

Linda's primary argument on appeal, however, is that Sankel's oral declination of the trusteeship is fully binding and cannot be reversed, or as her reply brief trumpets, "No Means No," and that Jacobs is the duly appointed co-trustee.

This matter, without doubt, presents a unique factual scenario. Moreover, there is no bright line rule, or formal methodology, by which the designated trustee of an inter vivos trust may accept or renounce that trusteeship. Initially, we note that an individual designated as a trustee cannot be compelled to act as such, or accept the burdens of the position against his or her will, and the designee is not qualified to act until he accepts the designation (*see Matter of Goldowitz*, 145 Misc. 300, 305, 259 N.Y.S. 900 [1932]; *Matter of Rivas' Trust*, 100 N.Y.S.2d 357, 360 [1950]; *Bogert*, § 150, at 78; 106 N.Y. Jur. 2d Trusts § 248). The acceptance of the position, or its renunciation, may be manifested in an abundance of ways, and can be expressed either orally or inferred from conduct (Restatement [Third] of Trusts, § 35, Comment *b*; Bogert, § 150, at 81–82).

In the case of an inter vivos trust, it has been held that once the designated trustee *has unequivocally* declined the office, he or she cannot thereafter accept it (*see Matter of Slotkin*, 191 N.J. Super. 486, 467 A.2d 803 [1983] [in which the designated co-trustee unequivocally, and formally, in court, renounced her appointment as co-trustee, only to seek to repudiate the renouncement once the court declined to appoint the individual she chose in her stead]), and that a trusteeship may likewise be renounced through the designated trustee's own inaction (*see Dunning v. Ocean Natl. Bank of the City of New York*, 61 N.Y. 497 [1875] [10-year period of dormancy by designated trustee established his refusal to accept the position]; *Matter of Robinson*, 37 N.Y. 261, 263 [1867] ["[h]is omission to qualify as trustee or to claim the trusteeship for [20 years], and permitting other persons during all that time to perform the duties without challenge, must be deemed a renunciation and refusal on his part to accept the trust"]).

It has also been observed, however, that "[a]n express disclaimer of the trust may be vitiated or rebutted by conduct which shows [the trustee] really meant to accept. When simultaneous conduct is somewhat inconsistent, the problem will be whether the predominant effect is acquiescence or rejection" (Bogert, § 150, at 84; accord Restatement [Third] of Trusts, § 35, Comment *b* ["[i]t is a question of fact in each case whether the trustee has manifested an intention to accept or to reject the trusteeship"]; Scott and Ascher on Trusts, 5th ed., Vol. 2, § 11.5.3 ["[i]n the case of an inter vivos trust, a trustee who has disclaimed cannot thereafter accept, unless . . . the court decides otherwise"])

> **Food for Thought**
>
> In reading the aforementioned authorities, is it correct to say there is a presumption that a trustee accepts the position unless she affirmatively declines?

In the matter before us, we find no reason to disturb the hearing court's conclusion that Sankel never unequivocally disclaimed the trusteeship, especially in light of his almost immediate change of heart after the ramifications of his renunciation became apparent to him; his multiple, and frustrated, attempts to secure a copy of the trust instrument from Linda; his efforts, and finally his success, in contacting Barbara, the co-beneficiary, in Canada, and, in the process, ascertaining her vigorous desire that he accept the position to protect her interests; and his numerous attempts to obtain the books, records and other relevant documentation concerning the trust property from the managing agent, all of which indicate Sankel's intention to accept the designation of co-trustee and its concomitant burdens and responsibilities (*see* Bogert, § 150, at 81–82).

Moreover, we must bear in mind that our overriding concern in this matter is the implementation of the intent of the settlor, Eleanor, who designated Sankel as her successor, and as the only trustee who could invade the principal of the trust "equally or unequally," in favor of either beneficiary. Clearly, the appointment of Jacobs does nothing to further Eleanor's interest, and would be in direct contravention of the wishes of Linda's co-beneficiary. In addition, none of the beneficiaries of the trust will be prejudiced in any manner by Sankel's assumption of the co-trusteeship. Accordingly, with a view to all of the foregoing circumstances, we find that Sankel unequivocally accepted the co-trusteeship.

Finally, we observe no obstacles to the retention of Sankel's former law firm as attorneys for the trust, and find Linda's claims of a "conflict" to be, at best, disingenuous, as she apparently finds no issue with the employment by the trust of her husband's *current* firm.

Accordingly, the judgment (denominated an order) of the Supreme Court, New York County (Harold Beeler, J.), entered on or about April 8, 2005, which granted Joel Sankel's petition and, inter alia, enjoined Linda Spector from interfering with his ability to fulfill his fiduciary duties as a co-trustee of the Eleanor Spector Trust, directed that the firm of Sankel, Skurman & McCartin could be retained by the trust for legal matters, and denied Ms. Spector's cross motion to dismiss the petition, should be affirmed, without costs.

Judgment (denominated an order), Supreme Court, New York County (HAROLD B. BEELER, J.), entered on or about April 8, 2005, affirmed, without costs.

All concur.

C. The Need for Trust Property

Linked with the issue question of whether or not the trust is passive is the requirement that there be trust property, often referred to as a corpus, trust principal, or trust res. In short, the trust must be "funded." As we have seen, however, this requirement has become attenuated in the modern world. That is because the statutes that validate "pour-over wills" eliminate any requirement that the trust be funded before the pour over funds are received from the will or before the trust receives property under a beneficiary designation such as under a life insurance policy. One way to rationalize this result in traditional terms is to focus on the trustee's duties. Instead of obligations that emanate from managing trust property, the trustee's duties arise from the obligation to make sure that the pour over or the property that is the subject of the beneficiary designation is received by the trust. Of course such rationalization is not necessary when a statute authorizes the result, but in some way the statutory authorization both reflects the development of the common law and helps to further it.

The liberalization of the requirement for trust property does not mean, however, that all questions of the existence of trust property are obsolete. One of the enduring questions involves attempts to fund trusts with future profits. The question is one of what can be described as "property" sufficient to constitute a trust res. At one end of the spectrum of possible interests are those described as "expectancies" which are emphatically not property. The classic examples are gifts contained in the will of a living person or status as an heir apparent—that is, the share of an intestate estate one would receive if the prospective decedent were to die today. (*See* Restatement Third, Trusts § 41: "An expectation or hope of receiving property in the future, or an interest that has not come into existence or has ceased to exist, cannot be held in trust.") At the other end of the same spectrum, of course, are outright ownership interests in real or personal property including future interests, no matter how contingent. Somewhere in the middle are future profits. The line is unclear.

> ***Example 1:*** B executes a declaration of trust on December 24 in which he declares himself trustee of all the profits (capital gains) he realizes from trading stocks in

the coming calendar year to pay such profits in equal shares to his mother, wife, and two children. During the subsequent year, B does indeed realize substantial profits from trading stocks and distributes those profits to the beneficiaries. Did B create a trust? Would your answer change if B's instrument declared a trust of all of his stock holdings in being on January 1 and terminating on December 31 of the coming year to pay all the dividends to himself and all of the capital gains to his mother, wife, and children? (*See Brainard v. Commissioner*, 91 F.2d 880 (7th Cir. 1937)) What if B had given a letter dated December 24 to his wife in which he stated: "I give you all the profits I realize from trading stock in the coming calendar year." Does B's wife have a legally enforceable right to the profits B realizes? What if B never gave the letter to his wife?

Example 2: Let's modernize the problem. Professor Grouchfield has been working on a casebook since the Reagan Administration. He's been gathering materials and places them in files. There is some text written. Can he create a trust of the royalties generated by the casebook? Suppose West were silly enough to have given him a contract? In the well-known case of *Speelman v. Pascal*, 178 N.E. 2d 723 (New York Court of Appeals, 1961) the court held the assignment of future royalties from a play as yet unproduced as a valid transfer of property. In that case, the assignor had a license to produce a play from the estate of the author (George Bernard Shaw) whose work (*Pygmalion*) was to be the basis of the new production, but a close reading of the case indicates that the existence of the license was not necessary to the holding.

The last variation in the problem above brings us to another question related to the existence of trust property. The requirements of a gift are intent, delivery, and acceptance. As you should recall from studying property, acceptance by the donee of a beneficial gift is implied, but there are rather complex rules regarding delivery which courts sometimes use as a way to express doubts about the intent of the donor. There are many cases and a good deal of commentary about whether a donor who fails to deliver property to a donee but whose intent to make a gift is sufficiently clear should be treated as the creator and trustee of a trust of the property for the donee. If a trust is held to exist in that situation it is a "constructive trust," that is, a trust which the law imposes in to order to prevent unjust enrichment. The sole duty of the trustee of a constructive trust is to convey title to the property involved to the beneficiary of the constructive trust, the person who in equity is entitled to the property. Another way to understand the constructive trust is to see it as an equitable device which requires that a person who holds title to property in accordance with legal rules is required to convey the property to a person who in equity has a better claim. (*See* Restatement Third, Trusts § 1 comment *e*.)

The Hebrew University Association v. Nye et al.

169 A.2d 641 (Conn. 1961)

KING, ASSOCIATE JUSTICE.

The plaintiff obtained a judgment declaring that it is the rightful owner of the library of Abraham S. Yahuda, a distinguished Hebrew scholar who died in 1951. The library included rare books and manuscripts, mostly relating to the Bible, which Professor Yahuda, with the assistance of his wife, Ethel S. Yahuda, had collected during his lifetime. Some of the library was inventoried in Professor Yahuda's estate and was purchased from the estate by his wife. There is no dispute that all of the library had become the property of Ethel before 1953 and was her property when she died on March 6, 1955, unless by her dealings with the plaintiff between January, 1953, and the time of her death she transferred ownership to the plaintiff. While the defendants in this action are the executors under the will of Ethel, the controversy as to ownership of the library is, in effect, a contest between two Hebrew charitable institutions, the plaintiff and a charitable trust or foundation to which, as hereinafter appears, Ethel bequeathed the bulk of her estate.

The pertinent facts recited in the finding may be summarized as follows: Before his death, Professor Yahuda forwarded certain of the books in his library to a warehouse in New Haven with instructions that they be packed for overseas shipment. The books remained in his name, no consignee was ever specified, and no shipment was made. Although it is not entirely clear, these books were apparently the ones which Ethel purchased from her husband's estate. Professor Yahuda and his wife had indicated to their friends their interest in creating a scholarship research center in Israel which would serve as a memorial to them. In January, 1953, Ethel went to Israel and had several talks with officers of the plaintiff, a university in Jerusalem. One of the departments of the plaintiff is an Institute of Oriental Studies, of outstanding reputation. The library would be very useful to the plaintiff, especially in connection with the work of this institute. On January 28, 1953, a large luncheon was given by the plaintiff in Ethel's honor and was attended by many notables, including officials of the plaintiff and the president of Israel. At this luncheon, Ethel described the library and announced its gift to the plaintiff. The next day, the plaintiff submitted to Ethel a proposed newspaper release which indicated that she had made a gift of the library to the plaintiff. Ethel signed the release as approved by her. From time to time thereafter she stated orally, and in letters to the plaintiff and friends, that she 'had given' the library to the plaintiff.

> **Take Note**
>
> Is that how a gift is made? What legal requirement is missing? One delivers a gift by some action not by words alone.

She refused offers of purchase and explained to others that she could not sell the library because it did not belong to her but to the plaintiff. On one occasion, when it was suggested that she give a certain item in the library to a friend, she stated that she could not, since it did not belong to her but to the plaintiff.

Early in 1954, Ethel began the task of arranging and cataloguing the material in the library for crating and shipment to Israel. These activities continued until about the time of her death. She sent some items, which she had finished cataloguing, to a warehouse for crating for overseas shipment. No consignee was named, and they remained in her name until her death. In October, 1954, when she was at the office of the American Friends of the Hebrew University, a fund raising arm of the plaintiff in New York, she stated that she had crated most of the miscellaneous items, was continuously working on cataloguing the balance, and hoped to have the entire library in Israel before the end of the year. Until almost the time of her death, she corresponded with the plaintiff about making delivery to it of the library. In September, 1954, she wrote the president of the plaintiff that she had decided to ship the library and collection, but that it was not to be unpacked unless she was present, so that her husband's ex libris could be affixed to the books, and that she hoped 'to adjust' the matter of her Beth Yahuda and her relations to the plaintiff. A 'beth' is a building or portion of a building dedicated to a particular purpose.

The complaint alleged that the plaintiff was the rightful owner of the library and was entitled to possession. It contained no clue, however, to the theory on which ownership was claimed. The prayers for relief sought a declaratory judgment determining which one of the parties owned the library and an injunction restraining the defendants from disposing of it. The answer amounted to a general denial. The only real issues raised in the pleadings were the ownership and the right to possession of the library. As to these issues, the plaintiff had the burden of proof. Kriedel v. Krampitz, 137 Conn. 532, 534, 79 A.2d 181; Holt v. Wissinger, 145 Conn. 106, 109, 139 A.2d 353. The judgment found the 'issues' for the plaintiff, and further recited that 'a trust [in relation to the library] was created by a declaration of trust made by Ethel S. Yahuda, indicating her intention to create such a trust, made public by her.' We construe this language, in the light of the finding, as a determination, that, at the luncheon in Jerusalem, Ethel orally constituted herself a trustee of the library for future delivery to the plaintiff. The difficulty with the trust theory adopted in the judgment is that the finding contains no facts even intimating that Ethel ever regarded herself as trustee of any trust whatsoever, or as having assumed any enforceable duties with respect to the property. The facts in the finding, in so far as they tend to support the judgment for the plaintiff at all, indicate that Ethel intended to make, and perhaps attempted to make, not a mere promise to give, but an executed, present, legal gift inter vivos of the library to the plaintiff without any delivery whatsoever. Obviously, if an intended or attempted legal gift inter vivos of personal property fails as such because there was neither actual nor constructive delivery, and the intent to give can nevertheless be carried into effect in equity under the fiction that the donor is presumed to have intended to constitute himself a trustee to make the necessary delivery, then as a practical matter the requirement of delivery

---

Food for Thought

Another play on trust creation: if Yahuda's intent was that the manuscripts eventually wind up in the care of the Hebrew University, why not create a trust to remedy a failed gift for want of delivery? Is the court's answer to that question convincing?

is abrogated in any and all cases of intended inter-vivos gifts. Of course this is not the law. A gift which is imperfect for lack of a delivery will not be turned into a declaration of trust for no better reason than that it is imperfect for lack of a delivery. Courts do not supply conveyances where there are none. Cullen v. Chappell, 2 Cir., 116 F.2d 1017, 1018.

This is true, even though the intended donee is a charity. Organized Charities Ass'n v. Mansfield, 82 Conn. 504, 510, 74 A. 781. The cases on this point are collected in an annotation in 96 A.L.R. 383, which is supplemented by a later annotation in 123 A.L.R. 1335. The rule is approved in 1 Scott, Trusts § 31.

> **Take Note**
>
> This is a key point. Do you think she believed that she could no longer have a change of heart about who should have custody of the library? If her grandson had told her he wanted to be a scholar like his grandfather, could she have given the library to him?

It is true that one can orally constitute himself a trustee of personal property for the benefit of another and thereby create a trust enforceable in equity, even though without consideration and without delivery. 1 Scott, op. cit. § 28; § 32.2, p. 251. But he must in effect constitute himself a trustee. There must be an express trust, even though oral. It is not sufficient that he declare himself a donor. 1 Scott, op. cit. § 31, p. 239; 4 id. § 462.1. While he need not use the term 'trustee,' nor even manifest an understanding of its technical meaning or the technical meaning of the term 'trust,' he must manifest an intention to impose upon himself enforceable duties of a trust nature. Cullen v. Chappell, supra; Restatement (Second), 1 Trusts §§ 23, 25; 1 Scott, op. cit., pp. 180, 181. There are no subordinate facts in the finding to indicate that Ethel ever intended to, or did, impose upon herself any enforceable duties of a trust nature with respect to this library.

The most that could be said is that the subordinate facts in the finding might perhaps have supported a conclusion that at the luncheon she had the requisite donative intent so that, had she subsequently made a delivery of the property while that intent persisted, there would have been a valid, legal gift inter vivos. See cases such as Bachmann v. Reardon, 138 Conn. 665, 667, 88 A.2d 391; Hammond v. Lummis, 106 Conn. 276, 280, 137 A. 767, and **645 *230 Burbank v. Stevens, 104 Conn. 17, 23, 131 A. 742. The judgment, however, is not based on the theory of a legal gift inter vivos but on that of a declaration of trust. Since the subordinate facts give no support for a judgment on that basis, it cannot stand.

* * *

There is error, the judgment is set aside and a new trial is ordered.

Points for Discussion

1. The upshot

Though it lost this battle, the Hebrew University won the war. Upon a new trial, the Hebrew University successfully maintained that Ms. Yahuda had indeed made a completed gift to the institution. The court found that her declarations coupled with her delivery of a memorandum of intent amounted to a constructive delivery of the manuscripts. It did so realizing that it was playing fast and loose with the law of gifts—the term the court used was 'abrogating'—noting that 'Rules of law must . . . serve the ends of justice, or they are worthless.' *The Hebrew University Association v. Nye*, 223 A. 2nd 397 (Superior Court, 1966). Which court made the correct decision?

2. Constructive trusts and failed gifts

The position of the Hebrew University is understandable. There are cases that go the other way, finding trusts where the donative intent is sufficiently expressed to incline the court towards leniency: disappointed donees of gifts which have failed for lack of delivery have gone to court to ask that a constructive trust be imposed on the donor (usually, actually, on the donor's estate; at the donor's death the chance of the donor completing the gift is over and this is the donee's last chance). The traditional rule stated in Restatement Third, Trusts § 16(2) is that a court *will not* turn a failed gift into a declaration of trust: 'If a property owner intends to make an outright gift inter vivos but fails to make the transfer that is required in order to do so, the gift intention will not be given effect by treating it as a declaration of trust.' However, comment *d* to that section is a lengthy meditation on all the ways in which the traditional rule can be circumvented. Moreover, Restatement Third, Property (Wills and Other Donative Transfers) § 6.2, comment *yy* adopts the position "that a gift of personal property can be perfected on the basis of donative intent alone if the donor's intent to make a gift is established by clear and convincing evidence." Given the UPC's adoption of the harmless error rule, which part of the Restatement's position is most consistent with evolving law?

D. The Need for Trust Beneficiaries

1. Indefinite Beneficiaries

A trust must have identifiable beneficiaries; someone must have the ability to hold the trustee accountable to the perform the trustee's fiduciary duties. Charitable trusts, further explored in a subsequent chapter, are an exception to this rule; the Attorneys General of the states have the obligation and the authority to enforce charitable trusts. If someone with legal capacity to sue has to be able to sue an errant trustee, what transpires if all the beneficiaries have future interests which are contingent and not vested. The rule has always been that if the contingencies will be resolved within the period allowed by the applicable version of the rule against perpetuities, if indeed there is one, the trust is valid. Of course, if the applicable contingency has not occurred at the time their interests are to become possessory, the trust will terminate, and the trust property will revert to the grantor or pass to another according to the trust's terms.

> **Example:** D's will limits property to T in trust to pay the income in T's discretion to the children of D's child, C, and at C's death to pay the trust property, including any undistributed income, to C's descendants then living by representation. Although C has no children at D's death, C's children will be born during C's lifetime and at C's death the trust property will be distributed either to C's then living descendants or to those who took the reversion from D. The trust is valid.

The beneficiaries of a trust do not have to be named individually. So long as they are described with sufficient precision, the trust is valid. For example, a trust to pay income to the creator's nieces and nephews and on the death of the last of them to die to distribute the trust property to their surviving issue is perfectly valid. We can identify the creator's nieces and nephews easily enough, and likewise their issue. Indeed, were this not the rule, class gifts would not be recognized. Broader categories of beneficiaries such as "family" or "relatives" may or may not be sufficiently definite, depending on the intent of the creator of the trust. Restatement Third, Trusts § 454 comment *d* states that in the absence of evidence of the creator of the trust's actual intent, the term "relatives" is construed as meaning the heirs of the designated person, and thus is sufficiently definite. In addition, if the trustee has the power to select among "relatives" the trustee "may select any person or persons who reasonably fit within the meaning of the term" and the trust is valid. (*Id.* comment *d*(1))

The classic indefinite class is "friends."

Clark v. Campbell

133 A. 166 (N.H. 1926)

SNOW, J.

1. The ninth clause of the will of deceased reads: "My estate will comprise so many and such a variety of articles of personal property such as books, photographic albums, pictures, statuary, bronzes, bric-a-brac, hunting and fishing equipment, antiques, rugs, scrap books, canes and masonic jewels, that probably I shall not distribute all, and perhaps no great part thereof during my life by gift among my friends. Each of my trustees is competent by reason of familiarity with the property, my wishes and friendships, to wisely distribute some portion at least of said property. I therefore give and bequeath to my trustees all my property embraced within the classification aforesaid in trust to make disposal by the way of a memento from myself, of such articles to

> **Practice Pointer**
>
> Note the elegance of the phraseology. A good example of personalizing the usually formal words of a will?

such of my friends as they, my trustees, shall select. All of said property, not so disposed of by them, my trustees are directed to sell and the proceeds of such sale or sales to become and be disposed of as a part of the residue of my estate."

The question here reserved is whether or not the enumeration of chattels in this clause was intended to be restrictive or merely indicative of the variety of the personal property bequeathed. The question is immaterial, if the bequest for the benefit of the testator's "friends" must fail for the want of certainty of the beneficiaries.

By the common law there cannot be a valid bequest to an indefinite person. There must be a beneficiary or a class of beneficiaries indicated in the will capable of coming into court and claiming the benefit of the bequest . . . Nor is the force of the precedents impaired by the fact that, of necessity, some exceptions to the application of the doctrine have been recognized, as in the case of bequests to an executor to pay funeral expenses, which have been permitted to take effect, notwithstanding the want of a beneficiary capable of invoking judicial power for their enforcement . . .

> "A gift to trustees to dispose of the same as they think fit is too uncertain to be carried out by the court." Theobald on Wills (7th Ed.) 495 . . .

That the foregoing is the established doctrine seems to be conceded, but it is contended in argument that it was not the intention of the testator by the ninth clause to create a trust, at least as respects the selected articles, but to make an absolute gift thereof to the trustees individually. It is suggested that the recital of the qualifications of the trustees may be considered as investing them with personal and nonofficial character, and that the word "trustees" is merely descriptive of the persons who had been earlier named as trustees, and was not intended to limit the capacity in which they were to act here. . . . It is a sufficient answer to this contention that the language of the ninth clause does not warrant the assumed construction. The assertion of the competency of the trustees to wisely distribute the articles in question by reason of their familiarity

> ### Make the Connection
>
> Other provisions of the will must have created at least one testamentary trust, otherwise there would be no need to have trustees named in the will.

with the testator's property, wishes and friendships seems quite as consistent with a design to clothe them with a trusteeship as with an intention to impose upon them a moral obligation only.

If, however, the recited qualifications had the significance ascribed to them the language of the bequest is too plain to admit of the assumed construction. When the clause is elided of unnecessary verbiage the testator is made to say:

> "I give to my trustee my property (of the described class) in trust to make disposal of to such of my friends as they shall select."

It is difficult to conceive of language more clearly disclosing an intention to create a trust. However, if the trust idea introduced by the words "trustees" and in "trust" were not controlling, all the evidence within the will confirms such ideas. In the first clause of the will the testator nominates three trustees, and an alternate in case of vacancy. Throughout the will these nominees are repeatedly and invariably referred to as "my trustees," whenever the testator is dealing with their trust duties. Whenever rights are conferred upon them individually, as happens in the fifth, sixth, and eighth clauses, they are as invariably severally referred to solely by their individual names.

* * *

The conclusion is inescapable that there was no intention to bestow any part of the property enumerated in the ninth clause upon the trustees for their own benefit. This necessarily follows, since the direction to make disposal is clearly as broad as the gift.

It is further sought to sustain the bequest as a power. The distinction apparently relied upon is that a power, unlike a trust is not imperative and leaves the act to be done at the will of the donee of the power. But the ninth clause by its terms imposes upon the trustees the imperative duty to dispose of the selected articles among the testator's friends. If, therefore, the authority bestowed by the testator by the use of a loose terminology may be called a power, it is not an optional power, but a power coupled with a trust, to which the principles incident to a trust so far as here involved, clearly apply. We must therefore conclude that this clause presents the case of an attempt to create a private trust, and clearly falls within the principle of well-considered authorities.* * *

Make the Connection

The court is considering whether to construe the bequest as a power of appointment in the trustees.

We find, however, no case in which our courts have sustained a gift where the testator has attempted to delegate to a trustee the arbitrary selection of the beneficiaries of his bounty through means of a private trust. Like the direct legatees in a will, the beneficiaries under a trust may be designated by class. But in such case the class must be capable of delimitation, as "brothers and sisters," "children," "issue," "nephews and nieces." A bequest giving the executor authority to distribute his property "among his relatives and for benevolent objects in such sums as in their judgment shall be for the best" was sustained upon evidence within the will that by "relatives" the testator intended such of his relatives within the statute of distributions as were needy, and thus brought the bequest within the line of charitable gifts, and excluded all others as individuals. . . . Where a testator bequeathed his stocks to be apportioned to his "relations" according to the discretion of the trustee, to be enjoyed by them after his decease, it was held to be a power to appoint amongst his relations who were next of kin under the statute of distribution. . . .

"The statute of distribution" is the intestacy statute.

In the case now under consideration the cestuis que trust are designated as the "friends" of the testator. The word "friends," unlike "relations," has no accepted statutory or other controlling limitations, and in fact has no precise sense at all. Friendship is a word of broad and varied application. It is commonly used to describe the undefinable relationships which exist, not only between those connected by ties of kinship or marriage, but as well between strangers in blood, and which vary in degree from the greatest intimacy to an acquaintance more or less casual.

* * *

It was the evident purpose of the testator to invest his trustees with the power after his death to make disposition of the enumerated articles among an undefined class with practically the same freedom and irresponsibility that he himself would have exercised if living; that is, to substitute for the will of the testator the will and discretion of the trustees. Such a purpose is in contravention of the policy of the statute which provides that—

"No will shall be effectual to pass any real or personal estate * * * unless made by a person * * * in writing, signed by the testator or by someone in his presence and by his direction, and attested and subscribed in his presence by three or more credible witnesses." P. L. c. 297, § 2.

> **Food for Thought**
>
> What is the destiny of these items? If the gift fails, the property passes to the residuary. Is that consistent with the testator's wishes? Doctrine and authorities aside, is there a reason to thwart his intent? If the disposition is upheld, would the court in reality allow others to make the testator's will for him?

Where a gift is impressed with a trust, ineffectively declared, and incapable of taking effect because of the indefiniteness of the cestui que trust, the donee will hold the property in trust for the next taker under the will, or for the next of kin by way of a resulting trust. Varrell v. Wendell, 20 N. H. 431, 438; Lyford v. Laconia, 75 N. H. 220, 223, 72 A. 1085, 22 L. R. A. (N. S.) 1062, 139 Am. St. Rep. 680; Sheedy v. Roach, 124 Mass. 472, 476, 26 Am. Rep. 680; Nichols v. Allen, 130 Mass. 211, 212, 39 Am. Rep. 445; Blunt v. Taylor, supra; Drew v. Wakefield, 54 Me. 291, 295. The trustees therefore hold title to the property enumerated in the paragraph under consideration to be disposed of as a part of the residue, and the trustees are so advised. This conclusion makes it unnecessary to answer the question reserved, and it has not been considered.

Case discharged.

All concurred.

Points for Discussion

1. *Family vs. friends*

Suppose the nameless testator in Clark had given the trustees powers to distribute property to his 'kindred.' Would the trust pass muster? While one can prove family relationship, friendship is a different matter. Recall the adage that you can pick your friends but not your relatives!

2. Friends and friends

Are "friends" always an indefinite class? Think Mr. Mark Zuckerburg: "I give devise and bequeath the aforementioned property in "Clark v. Campbell" to be distributed by my trustees to those who number amongst my friends on Facebook."

3. Trust vs. power of appointment

What is the doctrinal issue with the disposition in the above case? Is it that there is no trust if there is no individual with a beneficial interest in the trust and therefore the power to enforce the trustees' fiduciary duties? Personal property is given to *trustees* who seem to have fiduciary duties, but how can they if there is no person with the legal right to bring an action to enforce those duties? There are powers to distribute property that are non-fiduciary: a power of appointment (which we will study at length in Chapter 9). It allows the donee of the power of appointment to distribute T's property, but does not subject the donee to a fiduciary duty. So long as the individual selected is a permissible object of the power, the exercise of the power of appointment would be valid. Traditionally, courts will not construe language that transfers property to "trustees" as creating a power of appointment, although Restatement Third, Trusts § 46(2) states that power given to a trustee to distribute to an indefinite class does create a power of appointment in the trustee individually and not as "trustee." (Even though the Restatement admits there is little American authority for that result.)

2. Trusts for Domestic Animals

Clark raises a point that creates a significant problem for pet owners who want to provide for their animal companions after their own deaths. The problem is two-fold. First, the obvious issue, an animal does not have standing to enforce a trust or to take any other legal action against the trustee (or any other person for that matter). Second, one of the more bizarre aspects of the traditional rule against perpetuities is the refusal to take judicial notice of the life span of any animal. If interests in the trust are subject to conditions, the resolution of which depend on when the animal/beneficiary dies, those interests are almost certainly invalid. The former difficulty has been avoided in many cases by the application of the doctrine of the "honorary trust." That is, the person named as trustee is willing to perform the duties of trustee even though not required to do so. That willingness is enough to sustain the trust. The second problem is often insurmountable, although courts have often been quite creative in rescuing such trusts from the rule against perpetuities.

An example of court's fashioning a remedy in cases of trusts for the care of animals is *In re Searight's Estate*, 87 Ohio App. 417, 95 N.E.2d 779 (Ohio Ct. App. 1950). Testator's will gave his dog to a friend and gave $1000 to his executor as trustee directing the executor to deposit the funds in a bank and pay to the friend 75 cents a day for the support of the dog for its life. If at the dog's death any of the $1000 remained it was to be distributed among five named friends of the testator. Because the friend and the executor were willing to carry out their responsibilities, the trust was upheld as an honorary trust. However, because the contingent remainders in the friends were subject to the condition precedent of surviving the dog, the rule against perpetuities was violated because the animal cannot be a measuring life and a court cannot take judicial notice of the dog's likely lifespan. However, the pay-out rate designated by the testator would exhaust the fund, assuming that it earns 6% per annum, in a little more than four years. That is well within the perpetuities period and the gift should be upheld.

Practice Planning Problem

Brooke is unmarried, and lives in a small house with four cats. During her many absences she boards the animals at the Katkennel near her house. Its owner, Dr. Geaux, has become her personal friend, and is willing to care for the cats should Brooke die, but given the margins in veterinary service the vet requires some payment. Brooke sets up a trust for the animals with a corpus of $5,000 and with Dr. Geaux as trustee. Unhappily, they die together in a traffic accident. Brooke's will is offered for probate. The executor seeks guidance on the validity of the trust and whether she may appoint a successor trustee. The residuary beneficiaries object. Assume she lives in a jurisdiction that has adopted UPC § 2–907.

UPC § 2–907. Honorary Trusts; Trusts for Pets

(a) **[Honorary Trust.]** Subject to subsection (c), if (i) a trust is for a specific lawful noncharitable purpose or for lawful noncharitable purposes to be selected by the trustee and (ii) there is no definite or definitely ascertainable beneficiary designated, the trust may be performed by the trustee for [21] years but no longer, whether or not the terms of the trust contemplate a longer duration.

(b) **[Trust for Pets.]** Subject to this subsection and subsection (c), a trust for the care of a designated domestic or pet animal is valid. The trust terminates when no living animal is covered by the trust. A governing instrument must be liberally construed to bring the transfer within this subsection, to presume against the merely precatory or honorary nature of the disposition, and to carry out the general intent of the transferor. Extrinsic evidence is admissible in determining the transferor's intent.

(c) **[Additional Provisions Applicable to Honorary Trusts and Trusts for Pets.]** In addition to the provisions of subsection (a) or (b), a trust covered by either of those subsections is subject to the following provisions:

   (1) Except as expressly provided otherwise in the trust instrument, no portion of the principal or income may be converted to the use of the trustee or to any use other than for the trust's purposes or for the benefit of a covered animal.

   (2) Upon termination, the trustee shall transfer the unexpended trust property in the following order:

      (i) as directed in the trust instrument;

      (ii) if the trust was created in a nonresiduary clause in the transferor's will or in a codicil to the transferor's will, under the residuary clause in the transferor's will; and (iii)　if no taker is produced by the application of subparagraph (i) or (ii), to the transferor's heirs under Section 2711.

(3)　For the purposes of Section 2707, the residuary clause is treated as creating a future interest under the terms of a trust.

(4)　The intended use of the principal or income can be enforced by an individual designated for that purpose in the trust instrument or, if none, by an individual appointed by a court upon application to it by an individual.

(5)　Except as ordered by the Court or required by the trust instrument, no filing, report, registration, periodic accounting, separate maintenance of funds, appointment, or fee is required by reason of the existence of the fiduciary relationship of the trustee.

(6)　A Court may reduce the amount of the property transferred, if it determines that that amount substantially exceeds the amount required for the intended use. The amount of the reduction, if any, passes as unexpended trust property under subsection (c)(2).

(7)　If no trustee is designated or no designated trustee is willing or able to serve, a Court shall name a trustee. A Court may order the transfer of the property to another trustee, if required to assure that the intended use is carried out and if no successor trustee is designated in the trust instrument or if no designated successor trustee agrees to serve or is able to serve. A Court may also make such other orders and determinations as shall be advisable to carry out the intent of the transferor and the purpose of this section.

Points for Discussion

1. *Application of the UPC*

Would the trust described in the **Practice Planning Problem** and in *Searight* be valid in a jurisdiction that has adopted the UPC? How does the statute deal with the "no beneficiary problem" and the rule against perpetuities problem?

2. *What can go wrong?*

As a practical matter, what circumstances might arise which would bring the provisions of a honorary trust before a court in order to be enforced?

3.　Secret and Semi-Secret Trusts

Yet another way in which problems concerning the existence of trust beneficiaries is the subject of the following case which is still the leading precedent in the United States.

A page of history . . .

Eleazer Wells was a priest of the Episcopal Church who came to his vocation late in life and who founded St. Stephen's Mission to serve the poor of Boston's West End. The mission burned in the great Boston fire of 1872. Until his death in 1878 Wells worked to rebuild his mission and his ministry but was unable to do so. Ellen Donovan died in 1877.

Olliffe v. Wells

130 Mass. 221 (1881)

BILL IN EQUITY, filed December 11, 1877, alleging that the plaintiffs were the heirs at law and next of kin of Ellen Donovan, who died in Boston on May 23, 1877, and whose will, which was duly admitted to probate, after giving various legacies, contained the following clause: "13th. To the Rev. Eleazer M. P. Wells, all the rest and residue of my estate, to distribute the same in such manner as in his discretion shall appear best calculated to carry out wishes which I have expressed to him or may express to him;" and nominated said Wells to be the executor.

> **Make the Connection**
>
> Precisely how does this devise differ from the gift of tangibles in the will before the court in *Clark v. Campbell*?

The bill further alleged that Wells, who had been appointed executor by the Probate Court, claimed the right, after payment of the legacies, to dispose of the residue of the estate according to his own pleasure and discretion, and contended that he had received directions from Ellen Donovan as to the disposition of said residue; whereas, as the bill charged, the legacy of the residue of the estate had lapsed, and said residue should be distributed among the heirs at law and next of kin of the testatrix.

> **FYI**
>
> "Heirs at law" and "next of kin." When the intestacy statutes treated real property and personal property differently, real property descended to heirs and personal property was distributed to next of kin and the two groups were not necessarily the same.

The bill prayed for a discovery, an account, an order for payment of the residue to the plaintiffs, a temporary injunction against distributing the residue of the estate, and for further relief.

The answer admitted the making of the will and the appointment of the defendant as executor; left the plaintiffs to prove whether they were the heirs at law and next of kin of the testatrix; and averred that the testatrix, before and at the time of and after the execution of the will, orally expressed and made known to the defendant her wish and intention that the rest and residue of her estate should be disposed of and distributed by the defendant, as executor of her will, for charitable purposes and uses, according to his discretion and judgment, and directed the defendant so to dispose of and distribute the said rest and residue; especially expressing to the defendant her desire that the poor, aged and infirm, and the children and others in need, and worthy of charity and assistance, under the care of or connected with Saint Stephen's Mission, of Boston, and other deserving friends and deserving poor, should be aided and assisted out of said rest and residue, if the defendant in his discretion should see fit so to do; that the defendant desired and intended, unless otherwise ordered by the court, to dispose of and distribute the said rest and residue for charitable purposes and uses, according to his discretion, and especially for the benefit of the deserving poor, aged and infirm, and the children and others in need and worthy of charity and assistance, under the care of or connected with said Saint Stephen's Mission, and other deserving friends and deserving poor, as requested and directed by the testatrix; and that the testatrix, except by her will, gave to the defendant no written direction, wish or order as to the distribution of the residue of her estate remaining after the payment of the legacies.

* * *

GRAY, C. J.

> A resulting trust is not a trust but an equitable remedy, related to the constructive trust. For the nuances, see below.

Upon the face of this will the residuary bequest to the defendant gives him no beneficial interest. It expressly requires him to distribute all the property bequeathed to him, giving him no discretion upon the question whether he shall or shall not distribute it, or shall or shall not carry out the intentions of the testatrix, but allowing him a discretionary authority as to the manner only in which the property shall be distributed pursuant to her intentions. The will declares a trust too indefinite to be carried out, and the next of kin of the testatrix must take by way of resulting trust unless the facts agreed show such a trust for the benefit of others as the court can execute. *Nichols v. Allen*, 130 Mass. 211. No other written instrument was signed by the testatrix, and made part of the will by reference, as in *Newton v. Seaman's Friend Society*, 130 Mass. 91.

The decision of the case therefore depends upon the effect of the fact, stated in the defendant's answer, and admitted by the plaintiffs to be true, that the testatrix, before and at the time of and after the execution of the will, orally made known to the defendant her wish and intention that the residue should be disposed of and distributed by him as executor of her will for charitable uses and purposes, according to his discretion and judgment, and directed him so to dispose of and distribute it, especially expressing her desire as

Take Note

This is a case of first impression in Massachusetts.

to the objects to be preferred, all which objects, taking the whole direction together, may be assumed to be charitable in the legal sense.

In any view of the authorities it is quite clear, and is hardly denied by the defendant's counsel, that intentions not formed by the testatrix and communicated to the defendant before the making of the will could not have any effect against her next of kin. *Thayer v. Wellington*, 9 Allen, 283. *Johnson v. Ball*, 5 De Gex & Sm. 85. *Moss v. Cooper*, 1 Johns. & Hem. 352. But assuming, as the defendant contends, that all the directions of the testatrix set forth in the answer are to be taken as having been orally communicated to the defendant and assented to by him before the execution of the will, we are of opinion that the result must be the same. It has been held in England and in other States, although the question has never arisen in this Commonwealth, that, if a person procures an absolute devise or bequest to himself by orally promising the testator that he will convey the property to or hold it for the benefit of third persons, and afterwards refuses to perform his promise, a trust arises out of the confidence reposed in him by the testator and of his own fraud, which a court of equity, upon clear and satisfactory proof of the facts, will enforce against him at the suit of such third persons . . .

Upon like grounds, it has been held in England that, if a testator devises or bequeaths property to his executors upon trusts not defined in the will, but which, as he states in the will, he has communicated to them before its execution, such trusts, if for lawful purposes, may be proved by the admission of the executors, or by oral evidence, and enforced against them. *Crook v. Brooking*, 2 Vern. 50, 106. *Pring v. Pring*, 2 Vern. 99. *Smith v. Attersoll*, 1 Russ. 266. And in two or three comparatively recent cases it has been held that such trusts may be enforced against the heirs or next of kin of the testator, as well as against the devisee. Shadwell, V. C., in *Podmore v. Gunning*, 5 Sim. 485, and 7 Sim. 644. Chatterton, V. C., in *Riordan v. Banon*, Ir. R. 10 Eq. 469. Hall, V. C., in *Fleetwood's case*, 15 Ch. D. 594. But these cases appear to us to have overlooked or disregarded a fundamental distinction.

Where a trust not declared in the will is established by a court of chancery against the devisee, it is by reason of the obligation resting upon the conscience of the devisee, and not as a valid testamentary disposition by the deceased. *Cullen v. Attorney General*, L. R. 1 H. L. 190. Where the bequest is outright upon its face, the setting up of a trust, while it diminishes the right of the devisee, does not impair any right of the heirs or next of kin, in any aspect of the case; for if the trust were not set up, the whole property would go to the devisee by force of the devise; if the trust set up is a lawful one, it inures to the benefit of the *cestuis que trust*; and if the trust set up is unlawful, the heirs or next of kin take by way of resulting trust. *Boson v. Statham*, 1 Eden, 508; S. C. 1 Cox Ch. 16. *Russell v. Jackson*, 10 Hare, 204. *Wallgrave v. Tebbs*, 2 K. & J. 313.

Where the bequest is declared upon its face to be upon such trusts as the testator has otherwise signified to the devisee, it is equally clear that the devisee takes no beneficial interest; and, as between him and the beneficiaries intended, there is as much ground for establishing the trust as if the bequest to him were absolute on its face. But as between the devisee and the heirs or next of kin, the case stands differently. They are not excluded by the will itself. The will upon its face showing that the devisee takes the legal title only and not the beneficial interest, and the trust not being sufficiently defined by the will to take effect, the equitable interest goes, by way of resulting trust, to the heirs or next of kin, as property of the deceased, not disposed of by his will. *Sears v. Hardy*, 120 Mass. 524, 541, 542. They cannot be deprived of that equitable interest, which accrues to them directly from the deceased, by any conduct of the devisee; nor by any intention of the deceased, unless signified in those forms which the law makes essential to every testamentary disposition. A trust not sufficiently declared on the face of the will cannot therefore be set up by extrinsic evidence to defeat the rights of the heirs at law or next of kin. See Lewin on Trusts (3d ed.) 75. . . .

> ### Food for Thought
>
> A distinction without a difference? Isn't it perfectly clear from the will that the testatrix did not want her heirs to inherit her property?

Decree for the plaintiffs.

COLT & MORTON, JJ., absent.

Points for Discussion

1. Secret and semi-secret trusts

Olliffe v. Wells is widely cited in support of the distinction between "secret" and "semi-secret" trusts. The opinion, of course, involves a semi-secret trust—a bequest in a will to a person, the language of the bequest indicating that the property is not to benefit the beneficiary personally but is to be held by the beneficiary in trust for some purpose not stated in the will but communicated to beneficiary by the testator. A secret trust is a gift outright to a beneficiary in which no mention of trust appears in the will. How do we know the testamentary intent is to create a trust? Is the Reverend Wells a natural object of the testatrix's bounty? Courts will allow extrinsic evidence to prove that the gift which appears outright on the face of the will was intended to be in trust. Having admitted extrinsic evidence to so determine, the court will also entertain evidence of its terms. The secret trust can be enforced if the beneficiary/trustee is willing to carry out the testator's instruction. The semi-secret cannot. Why? What is the court's rationale for its holding? Or rather, what is the doctrinal basis for the court's holding?

2. Resulting trusts

The *Olliffe* court describes the mechanism by which the Ellen Donovan's residuary estate ends up in the hands of her heirs: as a "resulting trust." That term has two distinct meanings. First, the term describes what happens when an express trust, that is, a trust created by a person, rather than a constructive trust imposed by a court, fails to dispose of all of the trust property. The trust property not effectively settled in trust remains with the trustee on "resulting trust." The trustee's sole duty is to convey the property to whomever holds the reversionary interest in the trust, who may be the creator of the trust or the creator's successors in interest. (*See* Restatement Third, Trusts § 7). Consider a testamentary trust created by T's will to pay the income to S for life, remainder to S's descendants who survive S by representation. This limitation to S's descendants is, of course, a contingent remainder even without the express condition of survival because it is a remainder in a multi-generational class. If at S's death, there are no living issue of S, the reversion must become possessory. When S dies without living issue, the trustee holds the trust property on a resulting trust for the holder or holders of the reversion to whom the trustee must convey the property. If the trust had been created in the residuary clause of T's will, the reversion passed at the moment of T's death to T's heirs. The heirs, of course, had a transmissible interest because the death of an heir of T has nothing to do with resolving the question of whether S dies survived by issue. The trustee, therefore, may have to spend some time tracing the current holders of the reversion.

The second use of the term resulting trust has to do with the "purchase money resulting trust." If a transfer of property is made to one person but the purchase price has been paid by another, a resulting trust arises in favor of the person who paid the purchase price. The assumption, of course, is that the actual purchaser was simply a straw person and that the individual who furnished the purchase price intended to be the owner of the property. Needlessly to say, if that is the intended arrangement, it should all have been memorialized in writing. The presumption can be overcome if the person providing the purchase price exhibits the intention that a resulting trust should not arise. In addition, the presumption is reversed if the person to whom the property is transferred is the spouse, descendant or other "natural object of the bounty" of the person who provided the purchase price. In that case, the assumption is that the person who provided the purchase price intended to make a gift. (*See* Restatement Third, Trusts § 9)

3. Secret and semi-secret trusts today

The law as stated in *Olliffe v. Wells* is the law in the majority of United States jurisdictions today, in spite of attempts by the American Law Institute to change it. Both Restatement Second, Trusts § 55 comment *e* and Restatement Third, Trusts § 18 comment *c* state that in both the secret and semi-secret trust situations the beneficiary-trustee should hold the property in constructive trust for the intended beneficiaries, assuming that the terms of the trust can be proved to the appropriate degree of certainty. (What do you think the standard of proof should be?) The Reporter's Note to Restatement Third, Trusts § 18 comment *c* does admit, however, that "although supported by a substantial and growing body of authority," the rule set forth in the Restatement "probably does not reflect the current weight of authority in the 'semi-secret trust' situation . . . ."

4. How would the court enforce the bequest?

If the Massachusetts Supreme Judicial Court had decided that the bequest to Reverend Wells in Donovan's will was indeed valid, what would have become of the property? Could the court make sure that the trust was carried out?

5. A practical application

Remember when we discussed the problem of making a bequest in a will of the testator's personal property in *Clark v Campbell*? Could testator make a gift in the will to the executor of all of the personal property and stipulate that executor promise to the testator to distribute the property as the testator directs? Given what we have learned about secret and semi-secret trusts, should the will mention the executor's promise to distribute the property as the testator directs?

E.   Trusts and Creditors

1.   Introduction

Trust beneficiaries have interests in the income and principal of the trust, the nature of which are set forth in the terms of the trust. The creator of the trust has great freedom in defining those interests. This section of the materials explores the various kinds of interests beneficiaries can have.

Trusts can create interests in current beneficiaries, present possessory interests, and interests that may become possessory in the future, future interests. The present possessory interests can be interests in only the income produced by the trust property or in both the income and the trust property itself. Most of the trusts we have used in our examples have been of the simplest sort: the trustee is to pay the trust income to A and on A's death the remainder, of whatever kind, becomes possessory in a remainder beneficiary. Such a trust is a "mandatory" trust; the trustee must distribute the trust income to the income beneficiary. The trust may prescribe the frequency of payment but if it does not, state law will set a default, usually annual payment. In addition, the creator of the trust could direct the trustee to distribute a certain amount of the principal to the beneficiary each year, or allow the beneficiary to demand that the trustee pay a certain amount or percentage of the trust corpus to the beneficiary; this arrangement is regarded as a power to appointment from the trust principal to beneficiary.

Alternatively the creator may give the trustee the discretion to decide how much income is to be paid to the beneficiary. Such a trust is referred to as a discretionary trust. The trustee's discretion can also extend to distributions of trust principal to the beneficiary, the power to "invade the corpus." A power possessed by a trustee to make distributions of income or principal (or both) may be subject to a standard, like the health, education, welfare and support of the beneficiary, or it may be unfettered. The existence of a standard gives a beneficiary the ability to require the trustee to pay over income or invade the corpus if the enumerated need can be demonstrated. While an unfettered power to invade allows in the trustee the ability to exercise discretion regarding distributions, we shall see that trust law requires the exercise of discretion to be subject to a reasonableness or good faith standard.

A trust may be a hybrid. For example, a trust can provide that the trustee is to distribute all trust income to the beneficiary and to make distributions of principal for the support and maintenance of the beneficiary in her accustomed standard of living or for medical emergencies.

Again, if the trustee refuses to make a distribution requested by the beneficiary the beneficiary can try to show the appropriate court that the trustee is "abusing" the granted discretion by not making required distributions. We will take a brief look at some of the problems involved in administering discretionary trusts, but first we need to deal with the complex question of the rights of a beneficiary's creditors in the beneficiary's interest or interests in the trust.

Look carefully at Ward's trust in the estate planning chapter. Classify the interest in Ward and in June in income and trust corpus.

2. Spendthrift Trusts

A page of history . . .

Many of the fundamental principles of the common law of property and wills and trusts were developed in England prior to American independence. Some were transposed to the newly independent states. English law was of two minds on restraints upon alienation. Hark back to your course in property. Recall that free alienability was a prominent feature of the fee simple absolute. You were instructed that in the thirteenth century Parliament adopted the statute *De donis* (1285) which created the inalienable fee tail, but that long before the time of American independence its transferability had been recognized by English courts. So land held in fee tail and fee simple were both alienable by its holder. What was not related was the tedious story of the rise of family settlements and the simple fact that landed families sought ways of accomplishing what the fee tail was no longer able to achieve—the inalienability of land in the hands of an owner. The participants of this struggle over inalienability were landowners and their heirs—the owner was prepared to deprive himself of free alienation of the patrimony if his children and grandchildren were similarly disabled. It was also a struggle between creditors and landowners, because if land was inalienable, it was less likely that the land of the profligate could be sold to pay off debts. A compromise was reached in mid-seventeenth century which began the process of limiting a landowner to tying up land for about two generations setting the stage for the development of the modern rule against perpetuities.

But what of personal property held in trust? English law never recognized the inalienability of personal property. By the nineteenth century personal property became a far more important component of individual wealth, even within the ruling class, and eventually eclipsed landed wealth. Very little of the land law actually was translated to trust law. The rule against perpetuities applied to interests created in trust, but interests in trusts were freely alienable.

Now to the present and our side of the pond. To what extent may a trust creator restrain trust beneficiaries from alienating their interests in the trust? Suppose C(reator) established a support trust for spouse and daughter. The trust contains the following provisions: a life interest in S(pouse) followed by a life interest in D(aughter) with remainder to D's children at D's death. Unwisely perhaps, C has not provided the trustees the power to invade the corpus. S is ill and needs expensive medical treatment. Both S age 60 and D age 35 are prepared to transfer their life interests to an investor for a capital sum. Assume that sum is a reasonable calculation of the present value of the income interests based upon S and D's life expectancy. Absent a provision to the contrary, in the trust instrument, the trust beneficiaries can make the transfer. Is this a sensible option? Could S 'encumber' her interest, that is, assign the right to receive the income to a bank in order to receive advance payments from the bank? Suppose the law sanctioned a clause disabling interests beneficiaries to encumber or transfer their interests. Should that clause be enforceable?

In response to the latter question, the general rule is that it is possible for the creator of a trust to restrain the ability of beneficiaries to encumber or transfer their interest. We shall address policy concerns that have been raised regarding the enforceability of such a clause later. But first to doctrine. The creator may do two things to keep the trust property out of the hands of a beneficiary's creditors. The creator may prohibit the trustee from distributing any trust property to another to satisfy claims against a beneficiary, and she may also prohibit a beneficiary from transferring or assigning the beneficiary's interests in the trust. These types of restrictions are restraints on the voluntary or involuntary alienation of a beneficiary's interest. A trust that contains such restraints is called a "spendthrift trust," the "spendthrift" being the beneficiary who needs to be protected from his or her own improvidence. (*See* Restatement Third, Trusts § 58) Such trusts are valid in the United States and seem to be widely used given the amount of litigation they generate.

It is easiest to understand the operation idea of the spendthrift trust in the context of a mandatory trust. Recall that in such trusts, the trustee is required to pay the income to the beneficiary—one might conclude that the beneficiary "owns" the income, because it passes to her automatically. Arguably, it is just one more asset the beneficiary owns and should be subject to her debts. Should a creditor be able to demand that the trustee pay the creditor at the time for an income distribution rather than the beneficiary? Should a beneficiary be able to transfer her right to receive the payout? The answer to both questions is 'yes.' However, if creator subjects the income interest to a spendthrift restriction, beneficiaries may not 'anticipate" it, that is transfer it in advance of receipt and creditors may not attach the interest in the hands of the trustee. Can it apply to both present interests in the trust and future interests such as the retained interest in the above trust? Once again the answer is 'yes.'

The characteristics of a spendthrift trust can best be understood by reference to a harrowing example.

Scheffel v. Kreuger

782 A 2d 410 (N.H. 2001)

DUGGAN, J.

In 1998, the plaintiff filed suit in superior court asserting tort claims against the defendant, Kyle Krueger. In her suit, the plaintiff alleged that the defendant sexually assaulted her minor child, videotaped the act and later broadcasted the videotape over the Internet. The same conduct that the plaintiff alleged in the tort claims also formed the basis for criminal charges against the defendant. See State v. Krueger, 146 N.H. 541, ___, 776 A.2d 720 (2001). The court entered a default judgment against the defendant and ordered him to pay $551,286.25 in damages. To satisfy the judgment against the defendant, the plaintiff sought an attachment of the defendant's beneficial interest in the Kyle Krueger Irrevocable Trust (trust).

The defendant's grandmother established the trust in 1985 for the defendant's benefit. Its terms direct the trustee to pay all of the net income from the trust to the beneficiary, at least quarterly, or more frequently if the beneficiary in writing so requests.

The trustee is further authorized to pay any of the principal to the beneficiary if in the trustee's sole discretion the funds are necessary for the maintenance, support and education of the beneficiary.

The beneficiary may not invade the principal until he reaches the age of fifty, which will not occur until April 6, 2016.

The beneficiary is prohibited from making any voluntary or involuntary transfers of his interest in the trust. Article VII of the trust instrument specifically provides:

> No principal or income payable or to become payable under any of the trusts created by this instrument shall be subject to anticipation or assignment by any beneficiary thereof, or to the interference or control of any creditors of such beneficiary or to be taken or reached by any legal or equitable process in satisfaction of any debt or liability of such beneficiary prior to its receipt by the beneficiary.

Take Note

A classic spendthrift provision. No payments of income or corpus can be transferred by a beneficiary and the trustee must pay the beneficiary directly.

Asserting that this so-called spend-thrift provision barred the plaintiff's claim against the trust, the trustee defendant moved to release the attachment and dismiss the trustee defendant. The trial court ruled that under RSA 564:23 (1997), this spendthrift provision is enforceable against the plaintiff's claim and dismissed the trustee process action.

In reviewing the trial court's ruling on a motion to dismiss, we determine whether the facts as alleged establish a basis for legal relief. See DeLellis v. Burke, 134 N.H. 607, 610, 598 A.2d

203 (1991); Provencher v. Buzzell-Plourde Assoc., 142 N.H. 848, 852–53, 711 A.2d 251 (1998). "We will not disturb the findings of the trial court unless they lack evidentiary support or are erroneous as a matter of law." Key Bank of Maine v. Latshaw, 140 N.H. 634, 636, 670 A.2d 1041 (1996). [3][4] We first address the plaintiff's argument that the legislature did not intend RSA 564:23 to shield the trust assets from tort creditors, especially when the beneficiary's conduct constituted a criminal act. The plaintiff's claim presents a question of law involving the interpretation of a statute, which we review de novo. See Appeal of Rainville, 143 N.H. 624, 631, 732 A.2d 406 (1999). "We interpret legislative intent from the statute as written, and therefore, we will not consider what the legislature might have said or add words that the legislature did not include." Rye Beach Country Club v. Town of Rye, 143 N.H. 122, 125, 719 A.2d 623 (1998).

We begin by examining the language found in the statute. RSA 564:23, I, provides:

> In the event the governing instrument so provides, a beneficiary of a trust shall not be able to transfer his or her right to future payments of income and principal, and a creditor of a beneficiary shall not be able to subject the beneficiary's interest to the payment of its claim.

The statute provides two exceptions to the enforceability of spendthrift provisions. The provisions "shall not apply to a beneficiary's interest in a trust to the extent that the beneficiary is the settlor and the trust is not a special needs trust established for a person with disabilities," RSA 564:23, II, and "shall not be construed to prevent the application of RSA 545–A or a similar law of another state [regarding fraudulent transfers]," RSA 564:23, III. Thus, under the plain language of the statute, a spendthrift provision is enforceable unless the beneficiary is also the settlor or the assets were fraudulently transferred to the trust. The plaintiff does not argue that either exception applies.

Faced with this language, the plaintiff argues that the legislature did not intend for the statute to shield the trust assets from tort creditors. The statute, however, plainly states that "a creditor of a beneficiary shall not be able to subject the beneficiary's interest to the payment of its claim." RSA 564:23, I. Nothing in this language suggests that the legislature intended that a tort creditor should be exempted from a spendthrift provision. Two exemptions are enumerated in sections II and III. Where the legislature has made specific exemptions, we must presume no others were intended. See Brahmey v. Rollins, 87 N.H. 290, 299, 179 A. 186 (1935). "If this is an omission, the courts cannot supply it. That is for the Legislature to do." Id. (quotation omitted).

The plaintiff argues public policy requires us to create a tort creditor exception to the statute. The cases the plaintiff relies upon, however, both involve judicially created spendthrift law. See Sligh v. First Nat. Bank of Holmes County, 704 So.2d 1020, 1024 (Miss.1997); Elec. Workers v. IBEW-NECA Holiday Trust, 583 S.W.2d 154, 162 (Mo.1979). In this State, the legislature has enacted a statute repudiating the public policy exception sought by the plaintiff. Compare RSA 64:23, I, with Athorne v. Athorne, 100 N.H. 413, 416, 128 A.2d 910 (1957). This statutory enactment cannot be overruled, because "[i]t is axiomatic that courts do not question the wisdom or expediency of a statute." Brahmey, 87 N.H. at 298, 179 A. 186. Therefore, "[n]o rule of public policy is available to overcome [this] statutory rule." Id. The plaintiff next argues that the trust does not qualify as a spendthrift trust under RSA 564:23 because the trust document allows the beneficiary to determine the frequency of payments, to demand principal and interest after his fiftieth birthday, and to dispose of the trust assets by will. These rights, the plaintiff asserts, allow the beneficiary too much control over the trust to be recognized as a trust under RSA 564:23. Beyond the exclusion of trusts settled by the beneficiary, see RSA 564:23, II, the statute does not place any limitation on the rights

> **Food for Thought**
>
> Are the policy arguments against the application of the spendthrift provision compelling? If so, why is the legislature so misguided?

a beneficiary is granted under the trust instrument. Rather, by its plain language the statute applies where a trust's "governing instrument . . . provides, a beneficiary . . . shall not be able to transfer his or her right to future payments of income and principal, and a creditor of a beneficiary shall not be able to subject the beneficiary's interest to the payment of its claim." RSA 564:23, I. In this case, the trust instrument contains such a provision. Because the settlor of this trust is not the beneficiary, the spendthrift provision is enforceable. The legislature did not see fit to pronounce further limitations and we will not presume others were intended. See Brahmey, 87 N.H. at 299, 179 A. 186.

Finally, the plaintiff asserts that the trial court erred in denying her request that the trust be terminated because the purpose of the trust can no longer be satisfied. The plaintiff argues that the trust's purpose to provide for the defendant's support, maintenance and education can no longer be fulfilled because the defendant will likely remain incarcerated for a period of years. The trial court, however, found that the trust's purpose "may still be fulfilled while the defendant is incarcerated and after he is released." See, e.g., RSA 622:55 (Supp.2000). The record before us supports this finding.

Affirmed.

Points for Discussion

1. *The failure to create a tort creditor exception*

Whether or not a tort creditor can enforce a judgment against the tortfeasor's interest in a spendthrift trust is a controversial question. Although commentators have long advocated the recognition of such an exception, opposition has been strong. The Supreme Court of Mississippi recognized such an exception in *Sligh v. Sligh*, 704 So.2d 1020 (Miss. 1997) but the next year the legislature overturned the holding by passing the "Family Trust Preservation Act" (Miss. Code. Ann. § 53–12–28(c)). Do you support the court's view or that of the legislature?

2. Voluntary and involuntary alienation

Spendthrift restraints apply to both voluntary and involuntary alienation. The Uniform Trust Code (UTC) § 502(a) validates spendthrift restrictions only if they apply to both voluntary and involuntary alienation of a beneficiary's interest. Can you articulate a reason for this provision?

3. Exceptions to spendthrift provisions

There are some exceptions to the effectiveness of a spendthrift restriction. Uniform Trust Code § 503 creates exceptions for claims by a spouse, children or a former spouse of a beneficiary who is trying to collect support or maintenance under a judgment or court order and for a creditor whose claim comes from having provided services for the protection of the beneficiary's interest in the trust (and who might that be?). Exceptions for the claims of family members are said to be in effect in the majority of states and are also recognized in Restatement Third, Trusts § 59(a). The Restatement also recognizes exceptions for those who provide services to protect the beneficiary's interest in the trust and also for those who provide "necessaries" for the beneficiary (medical care, housing, food, clothing) (*id.*, § 59(b)). The UTC does not recognize an exception for necessaries because, according to the comment to UTC § 503 most such claims are made by government and should be handled by separate legislation that would be recognized under UTC § 503(c)'s provision that a spendthrift provision is not enforceable against a claim of a state or the federal government except to the extent a statute provides. For those who find the *Scheffel* case difficult, the comments to UTC § 503 indicate that the drafters deliberately did not create an exception for tort creditors.

3. Discretionary Trusts

A slightly different question regarding the effect of a spendthrift clause arises with discretionary trusts because the beneficiary in a discretionary trust is not entitled to receive payments from the trust, be it income or corpus, until the trustee exercises the granted discretion and makes a distribution. If there is an outstanding judgment against the beneficiary, the trustee can simply refuse to make a distribution precisely on the grounds that the recipient of trust income or corpus would be a creditor rather than the beneficiary. The general rule is that the creditor does not have a greater rights than the beneficiary; if the beneficiary cannot compel a distribution, neither can the creditor. The beneficiary's interest in a discretionary trust, therefore, may be as safe from creditor's claims as a trust with a spendthrift protection. Of course, a spendthrift provision can be added to a discretionary trust and then the trust is treated like any other spendthrift trust.

If the beneficiary's interest is not protected by a spendthrift provision, the only concession to creditors of the beneficiary is the so-called "cutting-off procedure." Sanctioned by the opinion in *Hamilton v. Drogo*, 241 N.Y. 401, 150 N.E. 496 (1926), the creditor can intercept a payment if the trustee decides to make distribution to the beneficiary during that nanosecond in which the property is actually moving from the trustee to the beneficiary. As a matter of process, the creditor levies on the beneficiary's interest so that the trustee must pay the creditor if the trustee decides to make a distribution to the beneficiary. Presumably, this situation gives the creditor some leverage over the beneficiary by preventing all distributions directly to the beneficiary (the transfer is for all intents and purposes intercepted when it passes from the trustee to the beneficiary). The possibility that the creditor can impinge on the beneficiary's enjoyment of her interest really does create an incentive on the part of the beneficiary to come to terms with the creditor and agree to pay at least some of the debt owed.

The actual wording of the trustees' mandate to support the beneficiary may be crucial. For example, if the trust allows the trustee to make distributions not only to the beneficiary but also *for the benefit of the beneficiary*, such a provision would arguably allow the trustee to pay certain creditors directly (for example, the monthly credit card bill could be delivered to the trustee who then pays the bill directly with a check drawn on the trust). Restatement Third, Trusts § 60 comment *c* extends the "cutting off procedure" to payments to or for the benefit of the beneficiary, regardless of the precise terms of the trust.

Matters become even more complicated when the trustee's discretion is subject to a standard. Traditionally, the law draws a distinction between trusts designed to support a beneficiary, that is, trusts that direct the trustee to distribute so much of the income and perhaps principal that is necessary for the beneficiary's support and maintenance or other ascertainable standards. These support trusts may be regarded as spendthrift trusts to the extent of the support need, that is, creditors of the beneficiary could only reach income and principal that exceeds the amount required to support the beneficiary.

Restatement Third, Trusts § 60 does not draw a distinction between support trusts and other discretionary trusts. However, it does direct a court to take into account a beneficiary's actual needs when satisfying her creditors out of an interest in trust "if an expressed or implied purpose of the discretionary interest is to provide for the beneficiary's support, health care or education" (*id.* comment *c*) while allowing the creditor to stand in the beneficiary's shoes and compel a distribution. Thus if a trust provision similar to the one above has been included, a doctor who has provided medical services to the beneficiary might be able to require the trustee to pay her fee. The Uniform Trust Code, however, takes a different position. It addresses the effect of standards in a discretionary trust in § 504 and provides that a creditor *cannot* compel a distribution subject to the trustee's discretion even if that discretion is subject to a standard or the trustee has abused discretion. If the trustee has not complied with a standard or has abused its discretion, a court may, however, order a distribution to satisfy a judgment or court order relating to the support or maintenance of the beneficiary's child, spouse or former spouse in an amount that is equitable under the circumstances. A distribution is not permitted to exceed that amount to which the beneficiary would be entitled if the trustee exercised its discretion properly.

4. Review: New York Law

The complex interplay between mandatory and discretionary trusts and creditor's rights can be reviewed by reference to a single state, New York. The cutting-off procedure described above was developed by New York law and continues to apply to discretionary trusts. New York law also probably maintains the distinction between support trusts and other discretionary trusts. In addition there is no barrier to the imposition of spendthrift restraints on interests in the principal of a trust (for example, remainder interests), thus barring voluntary alienation (*see In re Vought*, 25 N.Y.2d 163, 250 N.E.2d 343 (1969)) or by extension, involuntary alienation. In addition, Civil Procedure Law and Rules (CPLR) 5205(c) exempts from application to the satisfaction of a money judgment *all property* held in trust for a judgment debtor where the trust has been created by or the property has come from other than the judgment debtor. That provision, however, does not bar the creditor from seizing a remainder interest, absent a spendthrift restraint on involuntary alienation of the principal interest. Such a seizure, of course, means that when the time comes for the holder of the remainder interest to receive the trust property the creditor will collect the property rather than the beneficiary.

Income interests are a different matter. Under NY EPTL § 7–1.5(a)(1) the mandatory income interest of a beneficiary of an express trust may not be transferred "by assignment or otherwise" unless the trust instrument gives the beneficiary that power. In other words, all mandatory income interests in New York express trusts are given spendthrift protection unless the creator of the trust provides otherwise. The same section of the statute however, creates two exceptions. First, the income beneficiary may transfer any portion of the annual income of the trust in excess of $10,000 to a broad range of family members. Second, the income beneficiary may transfer or assign any or all of the income to persons the beneficiary is legally obligated to support.

Another important statutory provision is found in CPLR 5205(d)(1). That provision exempts from application to the satisfaction of a money judgment 90% of the income or other payments from a trust except such part of that 90% that a court determines is "unnecessary for the reasonable requirements of the judgment debtor and his dependents." Finally, NY EPTL § 7–3.4 subjects to the claims of creditors income in excess of sum necessary to support the beneficiary in his or her accustomed standard of living.

To sum up then, New York law makes restraint on voluntary alienation of income interests the default rule, and therefore exempts property from the claims of creditors with an exception for transfers to family and persons whom the beneficiary is legally obligated to support. But the rather harsh treatment of creditors is mitigated by statute. Involuntary alienation of income interests, that is, seizure by a creditor to satisfy a debt, is limited by the 90% rule which can be regarded as a "reasonable requirements rule," that is, all income above that reasonably required by the beneficiary and his or her dependents is subject to creditors' claims. This amount is probably greater than that that would be available to creditors under the station in life rule of NY EPTL § 7–3.4. Finally, a spendthrift restraint will not prevent the use of the beneficiary's income interest to satisfy the claims of dependents or of those who have provided necessaries to the income beneficiary.

5. Self-Settled Spendthrift Trusts

One of the long standing principles of trust law is a prohibition on creating a spendthrift trust for oneself. The Uniform Trust Code (sec 505, 2005) specifically directs that a provision in a revocable self-settled spendthrift trust, a so-called 'asset protection trust,' is not valid as against the claims of the creator's creditors. If the asset protection trust is irrevocable the creditor can reach 'the maximum amount that can be distributed to or for the settlor's benefit. (sec. 2) The Restatement (Third) of Trusts sec. 58(2) and 60 (2003) concurs. New York embodies that principle in statute. NY EPTL § 7–3.1(a) provides that "[a] disposition in trust for the use of the creator is void against the existing or subsequent creditors of the creator."

This principle, that one may not create a trust to shield oneself against one's creditors, however, has been abandoned by at least sixteen states, the most prominent being Alaska and Delaware. Statutes in these states provide that a trust in which the creator has a discretionary interest in the control of an independent trustee (usually a trust company) is not subject to the claims of the creator's creditors after the passage of a period of time, usually three years. Creditors of the creator with claims arising after the period has passed cannot levy on the trust. In Delaware, at least, these creditors even include former spouses and children of the creator or other beneficiaries (all of whom receive distributions of trust property only in the discretion of the trustee who is not guided by a standard).

What leads someone to create a self-settled spendthrift trust? Fear of litigation seems to be a prominent cause. Professionals like lawyers and doctors dread large tort judgments. Unwilling to pay substantial premiums for malpractice insurance, some opt to shelter assets in a self-settled spendthrift trust (often called an "asset protection trust") and take their chances with litigation. Another motive which at least is mentioned in the literature promoting the creation of such trusts is the desire to keep family assets out of the hands of ex-spouses of the creator's descendants. This strategy explains the provisions of the Delaware statute.

These trusts are controversial and have not yet been the subject of much litigation. They may be vulnerable to attacks on several fronts, and that discussion is beyond the scope of these materials, but probably will not be once litigation works its way through the courts.

F. Discretionary Trusts (and a Word on Principal and Income)

What are the rights of an "income beneficiary" in a trust? The answer to this question turns on the nature of the income interest which is established by the creator in the trust instrument. The rights of a beneficiary of a mandatory income interest may differ from that of a beneficiary of income subject to the exercise of the discretion of a trustee, whether or not that discretion is subject to a standard. "Income" as we have already seen, includes the interest on debt instruments held by the trust (such as bonds and deposit accounts) and dividends on the equities (stock) held by the trust and rent paid on lessees of real property owned by the trust. While some other receipts might be income, if one were to survey all the trusts in the United States, one would find that most of the income earned by those trusts consists of interest, dividends and rent.

The principal, corpus or res of the trust, the trust property, is the property to which the trustee holds legal title and which produces the income. This property consists of stocks, bonds, other debt instruments like certificates of deposit, and real property. As we have seen, of course, any kind of property can be held in trust, but again, a hypothetical survey of all United States trusts would show that the vast majority of trust property falls into those three categories. Trusts which are created as parts of sophisticated tax-driven estate plans may contain fairly exotic property such as derivatives and interests in limited liability companies and partnerships. If the trustee sells any of the trust property, the proceeds are also trust property as is the property in which the proceeds are reinvested. Remember, absent unusual trust provisions, capital gains on the sale of trust property are also trust property even though for *income tax purposes* capital gains are income. This disconnect between *trust accounting rules* and *income tax rules* is the source of much of the complication in the Internal Revenue Code provisions governing the income taxation of trusts.

Over the last few years interest rates (after 2008) have been at historic lows and the overall dividend payout rate on stocks has also been low compared to other periods (even though it has increased a bit with the creation of a preferential tax rate for "qualified dividends" in the 2001 federal tax legislation). As a consequence, the mandatory income beneficiary of a trust invested in stocks and bonds probably would feel somewhat embittered by the relatively low return on the trust property. Many creators of trusts, of course, realize that even a mandatory gift of income might not be sufficient to provide the income beneficiary with the level of benefit that the creator contemplated, and in order to enhance the level of support of a beneficiary the creator may also have given the trustee discretion to distribute principal to the beneficiary, with or without the guidance of a standard. To further enhance the interest of the income beneficiary, the creator might also give the beneficiary a presently exercisable general power of appointment to allow the beneficiary to simply demand some amount of principal every year.

The grant of discretionary power to a trustee to invade principal, even for ascertainable standards is often problematic. While there is little or perhaps no empirical evidence on which to base any trustworthy conclusions, many commentators, including practitioners, believe that many trustees are reluctant to exercise a power to invade trust property because of the fear that they will be open to criticism by the remainder beneficiaries after the income beneficiary's death if they do so. Trustees are concerned that it will be difficult to defend the decisions to invade the corpus for the support of an income beneficiary that they made perhaps many years in the past.

The following case is an example of the tension between the interests of income beneficiaries and the corpus remainder beneficiaries in a trust in which the trustees have discretion to distribute income and to invade the corpus:

Old Colony Trust Company v. Rodd

254 N.E. 2d 886 (Mass. 1970)

Kirk, J.

The respondent, a life beneficiary of a trust created by the will of George A. Sanderson, filed specifications of objection to the allowance of the fortieth and forty-first accounts of the petitioner as trustee under the will. After a hearing, the probate judge entered two decrees allowing the accounts. The respondent appeals, challenging the adequacy of the amounts paid to her by the trustee, the reasonableness of the trustee's accounting procedure, and the amount of its fees. Her attorney appeals from the denial of his petition to be allowed counsel fees from the trust assets.

Item 8 of Sanderson's will directed the trustee to pay over during the lives of designated beneficiaries "such part of the income or principal as may be necessary in its judgment for the comfortable support of any one or more of said persons, provided that in the judgment of said trustee any one or more of said persons shall need assistance and shall be worthy of the same, it being my intention hereby to carry out as far as possible the wishes of my wife's father . . . as expressed to me on many occasions, namely, that he wished to see to the comfortable support and maintenance of his descendants."

> **Practice Pointer**
>
> Specific enough guidance to the trustee regarding the exercise of discretion? As you learn further of the details of the family and their needs (and the fact that remainder beneficiary was an unnamed charity), might additional provisions have been helpful to avoid this expensive bit of litigation?

The life beneficiaries of the fund were named persons (descendants of the testator's wife's father) "and the children or grandchildren of any of the above named persons who may be living at the time of my decease and born prior to my decease" with one named exception, not here material. Item 8 further directed the trustee, at the death of the last survivor of the life beneficiaries, to transfer free of all trusts whatever remained of the fund "in such proportions as said trustee will decide will accomplish the most good, unto such charities in said Boston, said Berlin . . . [in Massachusetts] and Kingston . . . [in Rhode Island] as said trustee shall select."

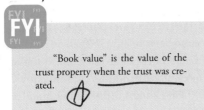

"Book value" is the value of the trust property when the trust was created.

We summarize the report of material facts made by the judge. The periods covered by the contested accounts are from November, 1963, through November, 1965. The book value of the trust, comprised of securities, is approximately $220,000, plus $30,000 in accumulated income to which a further accumulation of $3,500 in unexpended income was added during the accounting periods under consideration. The market value of the securities is approximately $423,000. During the accounting periods there were fifteen potential beneficiaries of the trust, three of whom were over eighty years of age, two between seventy-five and eighty, five between sixty and seventy-five, and the remaining five between forty and sixty.

> **Take Note**
>
> Never forget inflation. A tidy sum in 1970 when law school tuition may have reached the very low four figures in prestigious private schools; in 2019 dollars equivalent to about $2,500,000.

The trustee each year sent a questionnaire to each potential beneficiary in order to determine which if any of them required assistance. In instances where answers to the questionnaire were incomplete, the trustee made no further inquiry of the applicant in order to make an accurate determination of his net worth. The total paid to ten beneficiaries who requested assistance was $7,836 for the fortieth accounting period and $10,850 for the next period.

One of the beneficiaries, who died during the accounting periods, who owned a home without a mortgage and had no other assets, was paid $100 a month, and $1,100 for hospital and medical expenses. Two other elderly beneficiaries, with incomes of $2,540 and $3,000, received monthly payments of from $35 to $50. Another elderly beneficiary, with an annual income of $1,985, received $50 a month plus $752.70 for the payment of medical bills. Two other beneficiaries had medical and dental bills paid. An army colonel, fifty years of age, married, and stationed in Europe, with an annual salary of $13,800, exclusive of allowances, received two payments of $500 toward the educational expenses of one of his two daughters. A married woman, age forty-six, whose husband's salary was $10,000 a year, received $500 and $1,500, in the fortieth and forty-first accounting periods, respectively, toward the educational expenses of her two children, seventeen and eighteen years of age. Another married woman, age forty-five, whose husband, a college professor, earned an annual salary of $16,500, received $500 and $1,250 in the fortieth and forty-first accounting periods, respectively, for educational expenses of her two children sixteen and eighteen years of age.

The respondent, age forty-seven, is single, with no dependents. She has no resources other than her salary. During the fortieth accounting period she was employed full time, and earned a gross salary of $4,625. The trustee paid her Federal income taxes, various personal bills, and an allowance of $65 a month, for a total of $2,074. In the forty-first accounting period she earned $5,292. The trustee again paid her Federal income taxes and various personal bills. For the last seven months of the period, her allowance was raised to $115 a month; the total disbursement to her for the year was $2,131.

The trustee charged a fee of five per cent of the income of the trust, and three-tenths of one per cent of the principal.

1. The judge found no facts to support the respondent's objections to the trustee's accounting procedure, investment practice, or the amount of its fees. We agree. The trustee was not obliged to adhere strictly to the accounting form supplied by the Probate Court. General Laws c. 206, Section 2, requires only a reasonable and orderly statement of the account, and does not

require rigid adherence to any method of accounting. Hutchinson v. King, 339 Mass. 41. The respondent also argues that the trustee's filing of the two accounts at the same time, some five months after the close of the forty-first accounting period, violated G. L. c. 206, Section 1. That section provides that a trustee "shall render an account . . . at least once a year . . . until his trust is fulfilled; but the court may at his request excuse him from rendering an account in any year, if satisfied that it is not necessary or expedient that it should be rendered." In allowing the accounts, the probate judge impliedly found that it was not "necessary or expedient" for the accounts to be filed separately each year. At the most, the failure to file timely was a "mere technical breach" (Attorney Gen. v. Olson, 346 Mass. 190, 195) and done without objection at the time by any beneficiary. See Newhall, Settlement of Estates (4th ed.) Section 435. Finally, the fees allowed the trustee cannot be said to be unreasonable merely because they are apportioned between income and principal. Such apportionment is expressly permitted by G. L. c. 206, Section 16. See Old Colony Trust Co. v. Townsend, 324 Mass. 298 .

2. The judge found that the "method employed by the trustee in determining the amount of assistance required in each case to attain 'comfortable support and maintenance' was superficial. And having in mind the intent of the settlor, the amounts allocated not only to the respondent but to others of the beneficiaries were parsimonious." With these observations we emphatically agree. The ultimate conclusion of the judge was, "However, the trustee was here given broad discretion and I do not quite find that it has been abused."

This court recently said that in exercising a power of this sort a trustee is "unquestionably under an obligation to give serious and responsible consideration both as to the propriety of the amounts and as to their consistency with the terms and purposes of the trust." Holyoke Natl. Bank v. Wilson, 350 Mass. 223, 227. [A court of equity may control a trustee in the exercise of a fiduciary discretion if it fails to observe standards of judgment apparent from the applicable instrument.] Copp v. Worcester County Natl. Bank, 347 Mass. 548, 551. Old Colony Trust Co. v. Silliman, 352 Mass. 6. It is our view that, whether due to misuse of discretion or to misconception of the purpose of the trust on the part of the trustee, several of the intended primary beneficiaries of the trust are not receiving that which the settlor intended they should receive and which the trustee has the means to provide: "comfortable support and maintenance." The settlor by will expressed his intention in terms that imported a deep sense of personal obligation to fulfill the wishes of another. By providing for access to principal he provided means "to carry out as far as possible" those wishes. It is inferable that the persons who could be benefited have long since been identified and that with the passing years their number has diminished and henceforth will diminish rapidly. At the same time it is obvious that the corpus of the trust has grown. Inevitably the remainder will go to charities unspecified and unknown to anyone, except, possibly, the trustee. It is clear from the will that the gift of the remainder was of minor significance. And yet it would appear that the trustee regards the disposition of the remainder as the dominant purpose of the trust.

Practice Pointer

Should a trust instrument specify a process that the trustee must follow in order to ascertain whether a beneficiary is in need of a distribution?

The trustee has not only kept the principal inviolate but has accumulated and retained over $30,000 in income. The trustee justifies this course as reasonable and prudent in light of rising medical costs and the advancing age of the beneficiaries. However that may be, the fact remains that the book value of the trust is $220,000 and the market value, at the time of the judge's findings, double that amount. The prospect of illness in old age does not warrant a persistent policy of niggardliness toward individuals for whose comfortable support in life the trust has been established. The payments made to the respondent and several other beneficiaries, viewed in light of their assets and needs, when measured against the assets of the trust show that little consideration has been given to the "comfortable support" of the beneficiaries. Compare Holyoke Natl. Bank v. Wilson, 350 Mass. 223.

Another manifestation of the trustee's indifference to its "obligation to give serious and responsible consideration both as to the propriety of the amounts and as to their consistency with the terms and purposes of the trust" is the payment, noted above, of sums to beneficiaries to assist in the education of their children. In each of the three cases the family income was in excess of $10,000. In each case, laudable though the purpose may have been, the contribution, strictly speaking, was not for "comfortable support" nor was the actual beneficiary a designat-

ed beneficiary. Homans v. Foster, 232 Mass. 4, 6. Parker v. Lloyd, 321 Mass. 126, 134. See Boston Safe Deposit & Trust Co. v. Stebbins, 309 Mass. 282, 287. In two of the three cases referred to, the amounts given for the education of non-beneficiaries was greater than one half of the amount granted to the respondent for "comfortable support."

Food for Thought

Why was the trustee so parsimonious with Rodd and so reckless with education benefits?

The respondent asked that the payments made to her as noted in the fortieth and forty-first accounts be increased by at least fifteen per cent. We think that the request is a modest one.

3. We do not reverse the decrees. Comfort cannot be retroactively given.

Our order is that all accounts of the trustee, subsequent to the forty-first account under Item 8 of the will of George A. Sanderson, be so prepared or, if already prepared, be so modified to reflect a trusteeship that is neither superficial in its administration nor parsimonious in its spirit.

Food for Thought

Why no retroactive payments? Almost all damages are compensation for past losses.

4. We think that the probate judge, upon further proceedings, might with complete propriety allow reasonable counsel fees for the respondent's attorney payable from the trust principal. We leave the matter entirely to his discretion.

5. The decrees are affirmed. The case is remanded to the Probate Court for further proceedings consistent with this opinion.

So ordered.

Points for Discussion

1. Is the trustee being treated too leniently?

Does the court seem less than rigorous in assessing the trustees' obligation to inquire? Consider a more recent (1991) Massachusetts case, *Marsman v, Nasca*, 573 N. E. 2d 1025 in which the Massachusetts Appeals Court was more demanding. The trust beneficiary, one Cappy, had to transfer the remainder interest in a house to his stepdaughter, the remainder beneficiary of the testamentary trust set up by his wife even though the trustee was directed by the trust instrument to invade the corpus in amounts that "they shall deem advisable for his comfortable support and maintenance." The trustee made no serious effort to consider Cappy's finances even though he handled the transfer of the interest in real property. Although the court refused to require a reconveyance, it did impress a constructive trust on amounts that the trustee should have paid to Cappy. So perhaps can comfort be retroactively furnished?

2. The trustee's dilemma

Trustees often are 'parsimonious' for a variety of reasons. One reason is the 'rainy day.' As the Rodd court notes: "The prospect of illness in old age does not warrant a persistent policy of niggardliness toward individuals for whose comfortable support in life the trust has been established." How does one hedge against risk that the trust property will be dissipated before the beneficiaries die?

How did these two cases get to court. Is there some reason why a trustee might prefer to be hauled into court and be required to pay, rather than to write out a check at the beneficiary's demand? Remember that a trustee's legal fees are usually paid by the trust property even when the trustee loses the case.

In the *Rodd* case, the creator vested discretion in the 'judgment' of the trustee. The issue is information. How should a trustee inform itself as to whether it should exercise discretion? The court found the strategy used by Old Colony, the trustee, 'superficial'? What actions should a trustee take that would render their inquiry not superficial?

In *Marsman*, the trustee was vested with "sole and uncontrolled discretion." What do these terms mean? Does this formulation render the trustee a tyrant? Judge Hand though not. He wrote that "[N]o language, however strong, will entirely remove any power held in trust from the reach of a court of equity." Rationality is required. Some formulations of the mindset a trustee must have when exercising discretion are formulated 'objectively;' the trustee must act reasonably: as similarly situated trustees might act. Other formulations allow subjectivity, allowing the trustee to follow her own proclivities but nevertheless requiring the trustee to make such decisions in good faith.

3. Investing the corpus: The Prudent Investor Act

Assume, for argument sake, that trustees wished to act reasonably and in good faith in determining whether to invade the corpus for Ms. Rodd's benefit. They still faced a dilemma.

The creator in *Rodd* directed that the remainder pass to charities selected by the trustee. Odd is the person who makes a gift to charity with such indifference. The lines were more clearly drawn in *Marsman*: payments to Cappy reduced the remainder value that would eventually pass to stepdaughter. This inherent and perhaps unavoidable conflict between providing present and future benefits has long been addressed by the rule often embodied in statutes that the trustee has to treat income and remainder beneficiaries fairly. Many courts regarded the legislative directions to require the trustee to invest in such a way to pay both income to the current beneficiaries and have the potential for growth in corpus. This requirement would prohibit the holding in the trust of stocks which do not pay dividends but which have the potential for great growth in value (usually called growth stocks) and makes investments in bonds, which in the end never grow in face value (though declining interest rates may make their market price rise) sometimes problematic. To make the trustees dilemma more trying, many courts interpreted the traditional rule for making trust investments as obligating a trustee to invest as would a 'prudent person' concerned with producing income and conserving capital. Such characterization of the standard seems to make a trustee liable whenever an individual investment loses money, even if the entire trust portfolio performed well as a whole.

The entire area of trust investment law was transformed in the 1990s by the widespread adoption of the Uniform Prudent Investor Act. The basic premise of the Act is that a trustee must invest trust property to accomplish the purposes which the creator of the trust intended the trust to accomplish. Section 2 is the one most relevant to investment strategy.

UPIA § 2. Standard of care; portfolio strategy; risk and return objectives

(a) A trustee shall invest and manage trust assets as a prudent investor would, by considering the purposes, terms, distribution requirements, and other circumstances of the trust. In satisfying this standard, the trustee shall exercise reasonable care, skill, and caution.

(b) A trustee's investment and management decisions respecting individual assets must be evaluated not in isolation but in the context of the trust portfolio as a whole and as a part of an overall investment strategy having risk and return objectives reasonably suited to the trust.

(c) Among circumstances that a trustee shall consider in investing and managing trust assets are such of the following as are relevant to the trust or its beneficiaries:

(1) general economic conditions;

(2) the possible effect of inflation or deflation;

(3) the expected tax consequences of investment decisions or strategies;

(4) the role that each investment or course of action plays within the overall trust portfolio, which may include financial assets, interests in closely held enterprises, tangible and intangible personal property, and real property;

(5) the expected total return from income and the appreciation of capital;

(6) other resources of the beneficiaries;

(7) needs for liquidity, regularity of income, and preservation or appreciation of capital; and

(8) an asset's special relationship or special value, if any, to the purposes of the trust or to one or more of the beneficiaries.

(d) A trustee shall make a reasonable effort to verify facts relevant to the investment and management of trust assets.

(e) A trustee may invest in any kind of property or type of investment consistent with the standards of this [Act].

(f) A trustee who has special skills or expertise, or is named trustee in reliance upon the trustee's representation that the trustee has special skills or expertise, has a duty to use those special skills or expertise.

How anxious are you to volunteer to be a trustee?

In order to make it easier for a trust to provide for current beneficiaries without requiring the trustee to make the decision to invade principal for the current beneficiaries, the adoption of the Prudent Investor Act was accompanied in many states, including New York, by the adoption of a new definition of trust income.

Practice Planning Problem

Consider whether you would include an investment strategy in the following trust, and what form it might assume. Banks, an octogenarian, executes a will and pour-over trust. The trust is drafted to endure for the maximum period allowed by the rule against perpetuities. It directs the trustee to make discretionary distributions to all of the descendants of the creator. Should the trust instrument direct an investment strategy? Should the corpus be invested almost exclusively in a carefully chosen portfolio of stocks which will grow at least as fast as inflation. But what if the value of some of the investments tank? Why is that? Because without investment risk, the real value trust corpus will not keep pace inflation. On the other hand, a portfolio of growth stocks, however, is likely to produce insufficient income to meet the needs of current beneficiaries.

If no investment strategy is set out how would you advise a trustee to invest? Would your advice be to diversify, and not to worry about a single bad choice because the Prudent Investor Act prevents the trustee from facing liability for failed investments so long as they were prudently made and probably so long as the portfolio as a whole grows in value?

4. The Unitrust

In order to make it easier for a trust to provide for current beneficiaries without requiring the trustee to make the decision to invade principal for the current beneficiaries, the adoption of the Prudent Investor Act was accompanied in many states by the adoption of a new definition of trust income. Rather than dividends, interest, and rents, income (more precisely, what someone with a present interest in the trust is entitled to) is defined as a fixed percentage of the value of the trust calculated once a year. This fixed percentage is called a "unitrust percentage" or pay out rate and a trust administered in this way is called a "unitrust." New York even has a statute that allows the creator of a trust to define the "net income" of the trust by reference to NY EPTL § 11–2.4 which defines net income to a 4% unitrust percentage.

Example: If the value of the trust property on the yearly valuation date is $2,000,000 a "4% unitrust" would pay out $80,000 to a mandatory income beneficiary or would allow a trust with discretion to distribute "income" to distribute $80,000 to those persons with current interests in the trust. The statute provides rules for selecting the valuation date, for dealing with additions to the trust property and distributions of principal and provides that after the trust has been a unitrust for three years the unitrust percentage is applied to a three year rolling average of the annual valuations. It is also possible to vary the unitrust percentage.

The advantage of the unitrust is that growth in the value of the trust property benefits both the current "income" beneficiaries and the future beneficiaries and the trustee is therefore freed from trying to find a balance between earning income and dividends and investing for growth. There is a good deal of controversy, however, over what the "right" unitrust percentage is for a trust that is designed to last for many years and benefit several generations and there is no consensus whatsoever.

Now that we have "income" to distribute to beneficiaries how does the trustee of a discretionary trust make decisions about distributions? If the trustee's discretion is made subject to a standard, the question is somewhat easier to answer because of the existence of the standard. Even then questions arise, especially whether the trustee must take the beneficiary's other resources into account if the trust instrument is silent on that question. Cases addressing the question usually turn on the facts, and it is extremely difficult to make any generalizations. Clearly the trust instrument should answer the question.

As noted above, the trustee has a duty to determine the facts and circumstances that bear on the exercise of discretion. That duty is to inquire into the circumstances of the beneficiaries of a discretionary trust in order to make an informed decision about exercising discretion. Even if the trustee's discretion is unfettered by any standard, the trustee may not be "capricious" or "arbitrary" and must have some basis for making a decision which means that the trustee must inquire. More controversial is whether the trustee has a duty to inform the beneficiaries of a totally discretionary trust of their status. The following opinion is probably the most important opinion dealing with discretionary trusts in the last decade, if not longer.

McNeil v. McNeil

<u>798 A.2d 503 (Del. 2002)</u>

Before WALSH, HOLLAND, BERGER, STEELE, JUSTICES and HARTNETT, JUSTICE (RETIRED), constituting the COURT EN BANC.

CONSOLIDATED

WALSH, JUSTICE.

This is an appeal from a decision of the Court of Chancery which determined that the trustees of a large *inter vivos* trust had breached their fiduciary duties by ignoring the interests of a beneficiary. By way of a remedy, the court ordered a make-up distribution to the petitioner, surcharged the trustees, and removed certain of the trustees. The court rejected the beneficiary's request to further divide the trust and prevent the adoption of a unitrust formula. Upon full review of the record, we conclude that the Vice Chancellor properly exercised his discretion under applicable trust law in granting relief to the beneficiary, except with respect to the replacement of a trustee. As to that latter ruling, we conclude that the trust instrument, in the first instance, controlled the process for replacement. Accordingly, we affirm in part and reverse in part.

* * *

The trust in dispute was one of five trusts established by Henry Slack McNeil, Sr. ("McNeil, Sr.") in 1959 from the proceeds of the sale of a pharmaceutical company owned by him to Johnson and Johnson. Four of the trusts, referred to as the "Sibling Trusts," were designated for the benefit of McNeil, Sr.'s four children: Henry, Jr. ("Hank"), Barbara, Marjorie, and Robert. The fifth trust, established by McNeil, Sr. for his wife, Lois, came to be known as the Lois Trust. Each of the separate children's trusts was intended to accommodate the needs of the respective beneficiary with authorization to the trustees to afford each the means to live an affluent lifestyle. The children were quite young at the time of the creation of the trusts, ranging in age from eight to fifteen. It was not until some years later that the trustees of the Sibling Trusts were called upon to provide the children an independent source of income.

Although the children were under the impression, an impression apparently fostered by their father, that their interests in the Lois Trust were that of remaindermen, the terms of the trust provided otherwise. The trust instrument gave its trustees considerable discretion to "distribute any part or all of the income and principal of the trust to or among my lineal descendants and their spouses, and Lois." Thus, all of McNeil, Sr.'s children, and their descendants, were not remaindermen but current beneficiaries. It was the lack of such knowledge and its unequal dissemination that is at the root of the litigation between Hank and the trustees, with Hank's siblings ("The Other Siblings") also joined as defendants.

The original trustees of the Lois Trust included three individuals, George Brodhead, Robert C. Fernley, and Henry W. Gadsden, as general trustees, and Wilmington Trust Company as the administrative trustee. Later, Gadsden and Fernley were replaced by Charles E. Mather, III, a close friend of McNeil, Sr., and Provident National Bank ("PNC").

Practice Pointer

Good judgment on the part of the creator and his lawyer in their selection of fiduciaries?

There is little question that Brodhead, a close friend and attorney for McNeil, Sr., was the dominant trustee, to whom the other trustees, and all the siblings, deferred. There is also no doubt, however, that all trustees, including the administrative trustees, were aware that the McNeil siblings enjoyed the status of current beneficiaries of the Lois Trust.

At some point, Hank became estranged from his parents and his siblings. A direct result of this estrangement was that Hank received nothing under his father's will and, upon the later death of his mother, only two million dollars, a paltry sum in comparison to that received by his siblings. Hank was not without substantial wealth, however, since his own trust responded to many, but not all, of his requests for distribution. Eventually, Hank sued the trustees of his trust, who were essentially the same as the trustees of the Lois Trust, seeking a greater distribution. The trustees requested Hank's own children, Cameron and Justin, take a position on Hank's petition because, under a mirror image provision of the Lois Trust, Hank's children were also current beneficiaries. Thus, it could be argued that Hank's request for additional distributions was adverse to all of his living descendants. Prior to the trustees' notification, Cameron and Justin had been unaware of their status. The question of Hank's right to distribution under his trust, *vis-a-vis* the entitlement of his children to share a current distribution, ultimately resulted in separate litigation in the Court of Chancery. *Bishop v. McNeil*, 1999 WL 743489 (Del.Ch.1999)

Claiming to have been misled, if not deceived, by the trustees of the Lois Trust concerning his current beneficiary status, Hank filed a complaint in the Court of Chancery seeking, *inter alia*, a make-up distribution from the trust, removal of and a surcharge against the trustees, and a restructuring of the trust operation. In addition to the trustees, other interested parties joined, or were joined, in the litigation, including Hank's siblings, Cameron and Justin, and a guardian *ad litem* representing the unborn beneficiaries of the Lois Trust.

II

The Vice Chancellor ultimately concluded that Hank's "outsider" status, which began during his father's lifetime, was continued by the trustees of the Lois Trust. By contrast, however, The Other Siblings not only benefitted directly from their parents' estates, but were made privy to many aspects of the operation of all five trusts and, through their participation in a family holding company, Claneil Industries, were never "outside the loop." The Vice Chancellor further concluded that not only did the trustees rebuff Hank's efforts to learn the specifics of the Lois Trust, they acquiesced in Lois' wish, expressed strongly during her lifetime, not to invade principal. That principal consisted primarily of Johnson and Johnson stock and had appreciated substantially in value over the life of the trust.[3] The Other Siblings were content with Lois' direction to permit principal to grow but the matter came to a head upon Lois' death in 1998, when the trustees proposed to make distribution of the Lois Trust in four equal divisions. The trustees also sought to adopt a "unitrust" approach for distribution under which the beneficiaries would receive a percentage of the total value of the trust, both principal and income, each year.

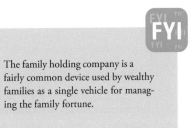

The family holding company is a fairly common device used by wealthy families as a single vehicle for managing the family fortune.

After trial, the Vice Chancellor determined that the trustees had breached their fiduciary duties by failing to inform Hank of his current beneficiary status in a timely fashion, showing partiality to The Other Siblings, and allowing the trust to operate "on autopilot." Since the trustees had considerable distribution discretion, the court recognized that it was somewhat "speculative" to fashion a remedy for the failure of the trustees to respond to requests never made, particularly given Lois' strongly expressed desire to maintain the trust corpus. Nevertheless, the court concluded that any uncertainty with respect to the appropriateness of the remedy should be resolved against the trustees, who failed to fulfill their obligation to consider the interests of different generations of the McNeil Family. A make-up distribution equal to 7.5 percent of the value of Hank's resulting trust was ordered to be shared by Hank with Cameron and Justin under the unitrust formula.

The Vice Chancellor also determined that the trustees' failure to discharge their fiduciary duties warranted some penalty. In particular, he faulted the institutional trustees, PNC and Wilmington Trust, who "failed to bring their professional expertise to bear in assisting lay trustees." PNC was removed as a trustee and all Lois Trustees were surcharged one-fifth of commissions received for the years 1987 to 1996. The Vice Chancellor declined to remove certain other individual trustees but appointed Edward L. Bishop, one of Hank's trustees, as a replacement trustee for PNC for the resulting trusts.

III

The individual and corporate trustees of the Lois Trust, John C. Bennett, Jr., Charles E. Mather, III, PNC Bank, N.A. and Wilmington Trust Company (the "Lois Trustees") have appealed from that portion of the Vice Chancellor's decision imposing a surcharge on their trustees' commission and removing PNC as a trustee. While accepting the Vice Chancellor's factual findings, they nonetheless argue that those findings do not permit the conclusion that any breach of fiduciary duty owed to Hank occurred. They point to the language of the trust instrument, which confers on the trustees extraordinarily broad authority to manage the trusts, as indicative of McNeil, Sr.'s intention to protect the trustees from personal liability and

---

3   At the time of the trial in the Court of Chancery, the Lois Trust had a value in excess of $300 million dollars.

"judicial second-guessing." The conduct of the Lois Trustees, it is contended, must be reviewed over the span of forty years, during which time they deferred to the wishes of McNeil, Sr. and his wife, and, as a consequence, the trust prospered and all beneficiaries, including Hank, ultimately benefitted.

* * * *

The Lois Trustees rely upon the express terms of the trust instrument as defining their duties. Three provisions of the Lois Trust appear to bear on this issue. Article II(a) gives the trustees wide discretion to distribute income or principal to any, all, or none of the beneficiaries as they see fit. Statements of this type are generally viewed as a definition of the trustees' powers, not as exculpatory of the liability of a trustee. *See* George Gleason Bogert, The Law of Trusts and Trustees, § 542 (1993) ("The grant of absolute or uncontrolled discretion to the trustee in the administration of the trust, without an exculpatory clause, may not relieve the trustee of liability for imprudent exercises of his powers. . ."). Further, Article III(e) of the Lois Trust specifies, "Decisions by the committee [of trustees] . . . [are] not subject to review by any court." Courts, however, flatly refuse to enforce provisions relieving a trustee of all liability. *Id.* (noting that exculpatory clauses that "provide[ ] that the trustee is not to be accountable to anyone . . . [are] not upheld"). A trust in which there is no legally binding obligation on a trustee is a trust in name only and more in the nature of an absolute estate or fee simple grant of property.

Finally, Article IV(c) states, "Any action taken by the trustees in good faith shall be proper, and I relieve the trustees of all personal liability except for gross negligence or willful wrongdoing."

Take Note

Why was this clause—a fairly standard exculpatory clause—included in the trust terms? The value and meaning of such clauses will be addressed below.

Generally, a trustee must act as the reasonable and prudent person in managing the trust.[4] Courts often permit the settlor of a trust to exculpate a trustee for failure to exercise due care, however, so long as such conduct does not rise to the level of gross negligence.[5]

A reasonable construction of these provisions, read together, is that the Lois Trustees were exculpated for ordinary negligence, but not the duty to (i) inform beneficiaries or (ii) treat them impartially. The duties to furnish information and to act impartially are not subspecies of the duty of care, but separate duties. *See* Restatement (Second) of Trusts §§ 173, 174, and 183 (1959) (devoting separate sections to a trustee's duty of care, duty to furnish information, and duty to act impartially). Whatever may have been McNeil,

---

4   *See* 12 *Del. C.* § 3302(a) (providing that a fiduciary of a trust "shall act with the care, skill, prudence and diligence under the circumstances then prevailing that a prudent person acting in a like capacity and familiar with such matters would use to attain the purposes of the account").

5   *See* Bogert, *supra*, § 542 (noting that courts enforce exculpatory clauses that "seem clearly intended to relieve the trustee from his duty to use ordinary skill and prudence").

Sr.'s intention in this regard, he did not expressly relieve the trustees of the duties which formed the basis for Hank's petition in the Court of Chancery.

There is ample record support for the Vice Chancellor's conclusion that the Lois Trustees violated their duty to provide information. It may be the case that McNeil, Sr. and Lois did not favor treating their offspring as current beneficiaries of the Lois Trust, and that it was defensible for some of the trustees who served later on to assume that notification had already been accomplished. Nevertheless, both PNC and Wilmington Trust, institutional trustees with policies of notification, should have known better. Moreover, Henry's repeated attempts to get information should have put the trustees on notice that he did not know he was a current beneficiary. A trustee has a duty to furnish information to a beneficiary upon reasonable request. Furthermore, even in the absence of a request for information, a trustee must communicate essential facts, such as the existence of the basic terms of the trust. That a person is a current beneficiary of a trust is indeed an essential fact.

The Lois Trustees, and Brodhead in particular, denied important information to Hank even after he made a reasonable request for information. PNC's representative rebuffed a similar request, and Wilmington Trust's representative even misled Henry by telling him he was a remainderman in the Lois Trust. The trustees each had a vested interest in the way they had been doing business, and giving Hank information would have forced them to re-examine that method. Although Brodhead obviously dominated the trustees and controlled their approach to Hank, each trustee was charged with an independent fiduciary obligation which did not permit them to defer to Brodhead's exclusionary views.

At the same time they were excluding Hank from knowledge of the terms of the trust and its operating results, the Lois Trustees shared that information with The Other Siblings, albeit in an indirect fashion through their participation in Claneil. This partiality precluded Hank from making distribution demands under circumstances not shared by his siblings. The trustees' claim that they distributed tens of millions of dollars to

> **Food for Thought**
>
> Is the trustees' exercise of their fiduciary duties in one of the interlinked trusts irrelevant to the handling of their obligations under the Lois Trust? If so, why?

Hank from his own trust is no defense to their blatant failure to inform him of his current beneficiary status in the Lois Trust. As the Vice Chancellor noted, Hank "was at an obvious informational disadvantage to his Siblings with regard to the Lois Trust." The record amply supports the Vice Chancellor's conclusion that the Lois Trustees failed to discharge the fiduciary duties owed to all beneficiaries of the trust. Accordingly, we affirm that ruling.

IV

A.

The Lois Trustees next contend that even if they were deficient in the discharge of their duties, the remedy ordered by the Court of Chancery was not proportionate to any harm done. In particular, they argue that in the absence of proof that the trust *res* has suffered a loss, there is no basis for an assessment of damages. In order to assess damages where none have been proved, the argument runs, a court must adopt a punitive rationale, an approach clearly not appropriate here where there has been no finding of malice or bad faith.

The Court of Chancery imposed a one-fifth surcharge against the trustees on commissions earned from 1987 to 1996, an amount which the court viewed as not "substantial." In view of our affirmance of the Vice Chancellor's findings of dereliction, we find no abuse of discretion in surcharging the trustees who had not "properly" rendered the service for which compensation was given. *See* Restatement (Second) of Trusts § 243, cmt. a (1959). The conduct in question was not isolated but resulted from a pattern of deception and neglect over a span of many years. Imposing a surcharge representing a mere fraction of the commission charged to the trust is not out of proportion and we affirm.

Food for Thought

Are the damages awarded a form of punitive damages? Given the trustees' fiduciary duties and their conduct, is the measure of damages correct?

B.

The Lois Trustees, joined by The Other Siblings, also dispute the Court of Chancery's ordering a make-up distribution of 7.5 percent of the value of Hank's resulting trust, "as part of the equitable remedy for breaches of the Lois Trust." Although he did not file a cross appeal from this portion of the Court of Chancery decision, Hank questions the source of the make-up distribution, contending that the court should have assessed the entire Lois Trust, not merely his resulting trust.

The imposition of a make-up distribution as a partial remedy in this case is, to a certain degree, speculative because it assumes that (a) Hank would have requested distribution had he known his status as a current beneficiary and (b) the trustees would have granted his request, particularly in the absence of similar requests from his siblings. There is ample reason to believe that Hank would have satisfied the demand requirement since he was continually seeking additional distribution from his own trust. Whether the trustees would have honored Hank's request is open to question but any doubt in that regard must be resolved against the trustees whose conduct led to the litigation and ultimate resolution of Hank's entitlement. Given the concerted efforts of the trustees over a long period of time to "wall-off" Hank from the operation of the trust they are ill-suited to complain about the discretionary remedy ordered here. In any event, the make-up distribution does not invade the resulting trusts of The Other Siblings and, in effect, simply provides for a partial distribution of funds to which Hank had, at least, an equitable claim in previous years. We find no abuse of discretion with respect to this aspect of the remedy. Finally, permitting Cameron and Justin to share in the make-up distribution is clearly consistent with the pattern approved in the companion litigation and was equally within the court's discretion.

V

We next address the contention of the guardian *ad litem* that the Vice Chancellor's approval of the plan to divide the Lois Trust into four resulting trusts should be reversed as contrary to the settlor's intent. The class for which the guardian *ad litem* appears consists of a projected 119 individuals, representing the anticipated descendants of McNeil, Sr. who will be living at the time the trust expires in 2060. The guardian *ad litem* complains that the Court of Chancery's approval of the plan of the trustees of the Lois Trust to divide that trust into four resulting trusts creates a "pour-over" effect for the benefit of the siblings and their living descendants to the possible detriment of future generations of lineal descendants for whom the Lois Trust would have been intact.

There is no dispute that the trustees have the power to divide the Lois Trust. Article II(a) of the trust confers on the trustees the authority to "distribute any part or all of the income and principal of the trust to or among [the settlor's] lineal descendants and their spouses, and Lois." Article II(b) allows the trustees to make such distribution either "outright to, or in trust for, any one or more of the class among which they may distribute." The trustees decision to pour-over the Lois Trust into four resulting trusts did not occur because the Court of Chancery ordered it done to remedy a perceived inequity in the trust operation. The division was the decision of the trustees, who, in effect, sought the approval of the Court of Chancery in the course of the litigation. Given the express authority conferred in the trust instrument, the Court of Chancery, or this Court on review, can disturb the trustees decision to divide the Lois Trust only if a division of the trust was unreasonable under the circumstances, *i.e.*, lacking a basis in prudence and care. 12 *Del. C.* § 3303 (stating provisions of trust instrument control absent willful misconduct); *Wilmington Trust Co. v. Coulter*, 200 A.2d 441 (Del.1964).

The Vice Chancellor approved the division of the Lois Trust as a "rational reaction" to the differing needs and desires of four different families. We agree and further add that the division will also reduce the likelihood of dispute and litigation over claims of uneven distribution. The guardian *ad litem*'s claim that the interests of future unborn beneficiaries might be at risk is not persuasive. His protest, though well intentioned, is premature. The trustees are vested with broad discretionary powers of distribution and should they exercise this power improperly in the future, redress is available, as this litigation attests. Finally, given the large size of the resulting trusts, and the unitrust distribution plan discussed hereafter, it does not appear likely that there will be a dissipation of the corpus to the detriment of unborn lineal descendants.

VI

Hank has cross-appealed from the Vice Chancellor's approval of the Lois Trustees' adoption of the Unitrust Policy, under which the trustees proposed to treat 5 percent of the trust principal as distributable on an annual basis. Hank argues that the unitrust approach is not a satisfactory substitute for the broad discretion enjoyed by the trustees to invade principal to meet the reasonable demands of the beneficiaries, himself included.

The unitrust approach is designed to preserve principal by establishing a fixed and ascertainable pay out while at the same time broadening the source of distribution in periods, as at present,

> **Take Note**
>
> The trust was not originally drafted as a unitrust; the court approved conversion to a unitrust because it allows the trustees more latitude in accommodating the interests of the income beneficiaries. Do you see why?

when income, particularly dividends, are of minor significance in measuring the growth of an equities-based trust. The Vice Chancellor approved the unitrust policy as within the discretion of the trustees in order to place the beneficiaries on notice of what distributions were available (approximately $4 million dollars annually per branch) and to encourage them to plan for such an allowance. Moreover, as the Court noted, the unitrust approach is merely a policy for distribution. The trustees continue to have the authority to invade principal to accommodate any unusual needs. We agree and add that along with the adoption of the pour-over separate trusts, the unitrust policy may also serve to redress the uncertainty and potential for friction between beneficiaries which engenders litigation.

We find no basis to disturb the Vice Chancellor's approval of the unitrust.

VII
A.

Perhaps the most contentious issue in this appeal, and one which has placed the disputants in odd alignment, is the disagreement over the Vice Chancellor's removal and/or replacement of trustees charged with administering the separate resulting trusts. We review that ruling under an abuse of discretion standard but only to the extent the Court of Chancery had full authority to select new trustees. The Lois Trustees, joined by Cameron and Justin, argue that the court should not have removed PNC. Hank supports the removal of PNC and defends the appointment of Bishop but complains that the court should also have removed Mather who participated equally in the trustees' misconduct. Cameron and Justin separately argue that the court lacked the authority to appoint Bishop to replace PNC.

The Court of Chancery has the power to remove a trustee as "ancillary to its duty to see that the trust is administered properly." *In Re Catell's Estate*, 38 A.2d 466, 469 (Del.Ch.1944). While that authority should "be exercised sparingly," the court enjoys the discretion to remove a trustee who fails to perform his duties through more than mere negligence. *Id.* at 470.

The Vice Chancellor removed PNC because it had failed in its fiduciary duties to Hank, both in its handling of his trust and as a trustee of the Lois Trust. The court felt so strongly about PNC's conduct that it suggested it also resign from Hank's trust. PNC violated its own administrative policies in failing to inform Hank that he was a current beneficiary of the Lois Trust and, in view of its role in disputing Hank's request for distribution from his own trust, it surely knew that Hank was keenly interested in securing additional distributions from any trust source. Moreover, PNC pointedly rebuffed the efforts of Hank's lawyer to gain information about the Lois Trust. Apart from the question of whether the trust, itself, was damaged by its action, PNC's studied course of conduct cannot be condoned and we find no abuse of discretion in its removal.

While removal of PNC as a trustee was clearly within the court's discretionary power, a different question arises with respect to its replacement of PNC as trustee with Edward Bishop. Cameron and Justin argue that the court's appointment of Bishop as a trustee of the Lois Trust exceeded the court's authority to the extent it contravened the intent of the settlor under the terms of the trust. This claim poses a legal question subject to *de novo* review.

Under Article III(c) of the Lois Trust, each trustee was given authority to name his own successor, and, in the event a trustee failed, or was unable to so designate, the remaining general trustees could fill the vacancies or increase or decrease the number of general trustees. PNC became a general trustee in 1978 when it was selected to replace Robert Fernley, who resigned. Unlike Wilmington Trust who functioned as an administrative trustee, PNC exercised full authority as a general trustee. Despite the explicit provisions of the trust instrument setting forth the mechanism for replacement of a trustee who resigns, or, as in this case, leaves involuntarily, the Court of Chancery did not seek the input of the trustees left in place, Mather and O'Malley, nor did it explain why it gave no consideration to the terms of the trust.

The Court of Chancery possesses undoubted authority to appoint a trustee if the trust instrument fails to do so. *Craven v. Wilmington Teachers Ass'n.*, 47 A.2d 580, 584 (Del.Ch.1946). Where the terms of the trust provide a method for filling vacancies by some method other than by appointment of the court, however, the designated method of replacement should be followed. *Scott on Trusts* (Fourth ed.) § 388. Even when a court seeks to exercise its residual authority of appointment, it should do so "only in rare circumstances," since the identity and number of the trustees is central to the structure of the trust and a key indicator of the intent of the settlor. *Schildberg v. Schildberg*, 461 N.W.2d 186, 191(Iowa 1990). *See also Matter of Guardianship of Brown*, 436 N.E.2d 877, 889 (Ind.App.1982) (holding court should defer to procedure prescribed in trust instrument "absent a showing that to do so would frustrate the purpose of the trust or be detrimental to the interests of the beneficiaries").

In selecting Bishop as a successor to PNC in the Lois Trust, the Vice Chancellor was apparently motivated by Bishop's compatibility with Hank in the operation of Hank's trust and the prospect that joint trusteeship would have some advantages. While these are worthwhile considerations, and perhaps entitled to deference were the Court of Chancery writing on a clean slate, they do not excuse disregard of the settlor's plan for replacement of trustees. In permitting Mather and O'Malley to remain as trustees, the Vice Chancellor recognized their suitability to discharge their duties as trustees. The selection of a replacement trustee is a stipulated duty under the terms of the trust. The designation of replacement trustees is a matter for the settlor's determination in the first instance and, where that intention is expressed, should not be disregarded in the absence of compelling circumstances such as the unsuitability of a designated replacement. Accordingly, we reverse that portion of the Vice Chancellor's decision designating Bishop as a replacement for PNC in the resulting trusts and remand for further consideration on this issue, taking into account the settlor's intention.

B.

With respect to the Vice Chancellor's refusal to remove Mather, of which Hank complains, we defer to the Vice Chancellor's discretion. It is true that Mather was a trustee at the time Hank was misled by PNC and Wilmington Trust, but apparently Mather did not join in that deception. Moreover, as the Vice Chancellor noted, Mather was a layperson who relied upon the institutional trustees and Brodhead, who was a lawyer. Having observed Mather in two trials, the Vice Chancellor concluded that Mather acted in good faith with "sincere concern for all Family members." Given the Vice Chancellor's advantage of personal observation we are not inclined to disturb his judgment.

VIII

Finally, we find no abuse of discretion in the refusal of the Court of Chancery to require the Lois Trustees to pay Hank's legal fees and in permitting the trustees to be reimbursed for their fees from the Lois Trust.

The American rule, which is of general application, requires each side to bear the cost of its attorney's fees. *Brice v. State Dept. of Correction*, 704 A.2d 1176, 1178 (Del.1998). The Court of Chancery may exercise its discretion to award attorneys' fees as an exception to this rule where a fund is created or, as here, the distribution of a trust is in dispute. Appropriate factors may include: (i) whether the trustees' breach of duty was fraudulent or in bad faith; (ii) the nature and extent of the wrongful conduct; and (iii) whether the action resulted in a benefit to the trust. *See Wilmington Trust v. Coulter*, 208 A.2d 677, 682 (Del.Ch.1965); *Bogert, supra*, § 871 at 191, 193. Here, Henry's suit did not benefit the trust, only him. Although the extent of the breach was serious (and extended), the Court of Chancery specifically concluded that the trustees' actions were ill considered and wrong, but not in bad faith. Finally, the Court of Chancery observed that Hank was not successful in a significant portion of the claims he asserted in the litigation.

Although the Court of Chancery imposed a surcharge on the trustees, that fact alone does not preclude the recovery of counsel fees incurred in defending the litigation since success is not the test. *Restatement (Second) of Torts*, § 188 cmt. b (1959); *Wilmington Trust Company v. Coulter*, 208 A.2d 677 (Del.Ch.1965). Here, the Vice Chancellor, in the exercise of his discretion, concluded that the conduct of the Lois Trustees, particularly the individuals, did not warrant departure from the usual rule that trustees who defend litigation against the trust are entitled to look to the trust for reimbursement of that expense. We find no basis for disturbing that discretionary ruling.

IX

In sum, we affirm all rulings of the Court of Chancery which are the subject of the appeals and cross-appeals in this matter save one: the replacement of PNC with Bishop. As to that ruling, we reverse and remand to the Court of Chancery for further proceedings consistent with this opinion.

Points for Discussion

1. *The primacy of the terms of the trust*

Why did the Supreme Court of Delaware reverse the Vice Chancellor's ruling on Hank's request for the appointment of a successor trustee? Do you see how the reversal is related to the finding that the trustees breached their fiduciary duty to keep Hank informed?

2. *The duty to inform*

The trustee's duty to keep beneficiaries informed is quite controversial. Much of the current discussion began as a reaction to UTC § 813(b)(2) that a trustee must inform the "qualified beneficiaries" within 60 days of accepting the trusteeship. UTC § 103(13) defines a qualified beneficiary as someone who is a permissible distributee of either trust income or principal. This term excludes beneficiaries with remote interests, in other words, beneficiaries would not be entitled to a distribution of income or principal if the interests of those currently entitled were to end. In addition, UTC § 813(a) requires a trustee to keep the qualified beneficiaries "reasonably informed about the administration of the trust and of the material facts necessary for them to protect their interests." Did the trustees of the Lois Trust comply with either of these requirements? Does the trustees' treatment of Hank's repeated requests give you an idea of why the duty to keep beneficiaries informed is so controversial? What was the trustees' explanation for their treatment of Hank? Is it compelling?

3. *Changing the Lois trust*

The court approves the trustees' request to divide the Lois Trust into shares. What is the doctrinal basis for that approval? Is it also at least indirectly connected to the finding that the trustees violated their duty to keep Hank informed and the court's treatment of the appointment of successor trustees? And what about the approval of the conversion of the successor trusts to unitrusts? What is the doctrinal basis of the court's approval of that request?

G. Altering the Terms of Trusts   431 - 52

1. Termination

Under American law, it is extremely difficult for the beneficiaries of a trust to terminate it, even if they all agree. The reason is the material purpose doctrine: even if all of the beneficiaries agree to terminate the trust, a court will not approve the termination if ending the trust would frustrate a material purpose for which the settlor created the trust. "Material purpose" is a term of art and its use in this context rests on an 1889 decision of the Massachusetts Supreme Judicial Court, *Claflin v. Claflin*, 149 Mass. 19, 20 N.E. 545 (1889). The case involved a testamentary trust created by the testator for one of his sons. Under the terms of the trust, the trustees were directed to distribute the trust property to the son in three stages: $10,000 at age 21, $10,000 at age 25, and the remaining trust property at age 30. When the son reached age 21 he asked the court to terminate the trust and order the trustees to distribute all of the trust property to him. He argued that his interest in the trust was indefeasibly vested, and the court agreed. Do you see why?

Despite the existence of English precedent ordering termination of the trusts in identical situations, the Massachusetts court refused the son's request. The court focused on the right of the settler to dispose of his property "with such restrictions and limitations, not repugnant to law, as he sees fits, and that his intentions ought to be carried out, unless they contravene some positive rule of law, or are against public policy." Clearly there was no violation of public policy, and the court held that the terms of the trust were not "altogether useless, for there is not the same danger that he [the beneficiary] will spend the property while it is in the hands of the trustees as there would be if it were his own."

In most termination cases, the creator of the trust is dead; the "material purpose" of the trust has to be gleaned from its terms. There are very few trust terms that are "altogether useless." Certainly an agreement only among the beneficiaries, even where the settlor is dead, as is always the case with a testamentary trust, cannot take effect if terminating the trust is inconsistent with a material purpose. The *Claflin* doctrine (a trust cannot be terminated by the beneficiaries' agreement if doing so would be inconsistent with a material purpose of the settlor in creating the trust) is generally followed in American jurisdictions, although in several it has been modified by statute or court decisions. Think about what a court might find to be a settlor's material purpose in creating a trust. In *Claflin*, the trust was not a spendthrift trust. Suppose it was? Would it have been even easier to conclude that terminating a spendthrift trust would frustrate a material purpose of the settlor? It was, however, a trust to postpone distribution of at least some of the principal until the beneficiary was older (and perhaps wiser). Would terminating the trust at 21 accomplish that end? Or does the settlor's judgment about what age is the right age to have outright ownership of wealth rule?

Consider the following case:

In re Estate of Brown

528 A.2d 752 (Vt. 1987)

GIBSON, JUSTICE.

The trustee of a testamentary trust appeals an order of the Washington Superior Court granting the petition of the lifetime and residual beneficiaries of the trust to terminate it and to distribute the proceeds to the life tenants. We reverse.

The primary issue raised on appeal is whether any material purpose of the trust remains to be accomplished, thus barring its termination.

Take Note

Claflin rules!!

The appellant/trustee also raises the closely related issue of whether all beneficiaries are before the court, i.e., whether the class of beneficiaries has closed.

Andrew J. Brown died in 1977, settling his entire estate in a trust, all of which is held by the trustee under terms and conditions that are the subject of this appeal. The relevant portion of the trust instrument provides:

> (3) The . . . trust . . . shall be used to provide an education, particularly a college education, for the children of my nephew, Woolson S. Brown. My Trustee is hereby directed to use the income from said trust and such part of the principal as may be necessary to accomplish this purpose. Said trust to continue for said purpose until the last child has received his or her education and the Trustee, in its discretion, has determined that the purpose hereof has been accomplished.

> At such time as this purpose has been accomplished and the Trustee has so determined, *the income from said trust and such part of the principal as may be necessary shall be used by said Trustee for the care, maintenance and welfare of my nephew, Woolson S. Brown and his wife, Rosemary Brown, so that they may live in the style and manner to which they are accustomed, for and during the remainder of their natural lives.* Upon their demise, any remainder of said trust, together with any accumulation thereon, shall be paid to their then living children in equal shares, share and share alike. (Emphasis added.)

The trustee complied with the terms of the trust by using the proceeds to pay for the education of the children of Woolson and Rosemary Brown. After he determined that the education of these children was completed, the trustee began distribution of trust income to the lifetime beneficiaries, Woolson and Rosemary.

On June 17, 1983, the lifetime beneficiaries petitioned the probate court for termination of the trust, arguing that the sole remaining purpose of the trust was to maintain their lifestyle and that distribution of the remaining assets was necessary to accomplish this purpose. The remaindermen, the children of the lifetime beneficiaries, filed consents to the proposed termination. The probate court denied the petition to terminate, and the petitioners appealed to the Washington Superior Court. The superior court reversed, concluding that continuation of the trust was no longer necessary because the only material purpose, the education of the children, had been accomplished. This appeal by the trustee followed.

An active trust may not be terminated, even with the consent of all the beneficiaries, if a material purpose of the settlor remains to be accomplished. This Court has invoked a corollary of this rule in a case where partial termination of a trust was at issue. *In re Bayley Trust*, 127 Vt. 380, 385, 250 A.2d 516, 519 (1969).

As a threshold matter, we reject the trustee's argument that the trust cannot be terminated because it is both a support trust and a spendthrift trust. It is true that, were either of these forms of trust involved, termination could not be compelled by the beneficiaries because a material purpose of the settlor would remain unsatisfied. See Restatement (Second) of Trusts § 337.

The trust at issue does not qualify as a support trust. A support trust is created where the trustee is directed to use trust income or principal for the benefit of an individual, but only to the extent necessary to support the individual. 2 A. Scott, Scott on Trusts § 154, at 1176; G. Bogert, Trusts and Trustees § 229, at 519 (2d ed.rev.1979). Here, the terms of the trust provide that, when the educational purpose of the trust has been accomplished and the trustee, in his discretion, has so determined, "the income . . . and such part of the principal as may be necessary shall be used by said Trustee for the care, maintenance and welfare of . . . [Rosemary and Woolson Brown] so that they may live in the style and manner to which they are accustomed. . . ." The trustee has, in fact, made the determination that the educational purpose has been accomplished and has begun to transfer the income of the trust to the lifetime

Take Note

The court's determination that the trust is not a support trust is made using the classic definition of a support trust.

beneficiaries. Because the trustee must, at the very least, pay all of the trust income to beneficiaries Rosemary and Woolson Brown, the trust cannot be characterized as a support trust.

Nor is this a spendthrift trust. "A trust in which by the terms of the trust or by statute a *valid restraint on the voluntary and involuntary transfer of the interest* of the beneficiary is imposed is a spendthrift trust." Restatement (Second) of Trusts § 152(2). (Emphasis added.) While no specific language is needed to create a spendthrift trust, *id.* at comment *c*, here the terms of the trust instrument do not manifest Andrew J. Brown's intention to create such a trust. See *Huestis v. Manley*, 110 Vt. 413, 419, 8 A.2d 644, 646 (1939).

The trustee cites *Barnes v. Dow*, 59 Vt. 530, 10 A. 258 (1887), for the proposition that a gift of support for life must be deemed a spendthrift trust. In fact, in *Barnes*, the terms of the will gave the testator's sister "support during her natural lifetime out of my estate." *Id.* at 541, 10 A. at 261. This Court construed the will as establishing a

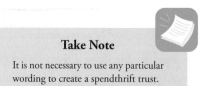

Take Note

It is not necessary to use any particular wording to create a spendthrift trust.

trust for support and held that an interest arising under such a trust is inalienable. *Id.* The mere fact that an interest in a trust is not transferable does not make the trust a spendthrift trust. See Restatement (Second) of Trusts § 154 comment *b*. In any event, *Barnes* is inapplicable here because a support trust is not at issue.

Although the issue as to whether a material purpose of the trust remains cannot be answered through resort to the foregoing formal categories traditionally imposed upon trust instruments, we hold that termination cannot be compelled here because a material purpose of the settlor remains unaccomplished. In the interpretation of trusts, the intent of the settlor, as revealed by the language of the instrument, is determinative. *In re Jones*, 138 Vt. 223, 228, 415 A.2d 202, 205 (1980) (citing *Destitute of Bennington County v. Putnam Memorial Hospital*, 125 Vt. 289, 293, 215 A.2d 134, 137 (1965)).

We find that the trust instrument at hand has two purposes. First, the trust provides for the education of the children of Woolson and Rosemary Brown. The Washington Superior Court found that Rosemary Brown was incapable of having more children and that the chance of Woolson Brown fathering more children was remote; on this basis, the court concluded that the educational purpose of the trust had been achieved.

The settlor also intended a second purpose, however: the assurance of a life-long income for the beneficiaries through the management and discretion of the trustee. We recognize that, had the trust merely provided for successive beneficiaries, no inference could be drawn that the settlor intended to deprive the beneficiaries of the right to manage the trust property during the period of the trust. *Estate of Weeks*, 485 Pa. 329, 332, 402 A.2d 657, 658 (1979) (quoting comment *f*). Here, however, the language of the instrument does more than create successive gifts. The settlor provided that the trustee must provide for the "care, maintenance and welfare" of the lifetime beneficiaries "so that they may live in the style and manner to which they are accustomed, *for and during the remainder of their natural lives.*" (Emphasis added.) The trustee must use all of

> ### Food for Thought
>
> Was it really not a support trust? Is it not a support trust because the level of payment could exceed the actual amount necessary for the day-to-day basic life of Woolson and Rosemary?

the income and such part of the principal as is necessary for this purpose. We believe that the settlor's intention to assure a life-long income to Woolson and Rosemary Brown would be defeated if termination of the trust were allowed. See 4 Scott, Scott on Trusts § 337.1, at 2261–64; see also *Will of Hamburger*, 185 Wis. 270, 282, 201 N.W. 267, 271 (1924) (court refused to terminate trust since testator desired it to continue during life of his wife).

Because of our holding regarding the second and continuing material purpose of the trust, we do not reach the question of whether the trial court erred in holding that the educational purpose of the trust has been accomplished.

Reversed; judgment for petitioners vacated and judgment for appellant entered.

2. Modification and Reformation

Courts are as reluctant to modify testamentary trusts as they are to modify wills. The traditional rule, embodied in the Restatement (Second) Trusts sec 337 (1959), requires a petitioner who seeks to modify the trust to prove two points: first, that circumstances exist that were unknown to the creator of the trust at the time it was created; and second, failure to modify will impair the accomplishment of a purpose of the trust.

Consider the following case: Grandchild is currently receiving Medicaid benefits. Medicaid is the largest state program providing a variety of medical care for the indigent. Grandchild is the remainder beneficiary of a trust created in Grandparent's will. The remainder will become possessory on the death of Grandchild's parent. Parent is now ill and parent's doctors agree that death is at the most a year away. As Grandchild's guardian, parent brings a petition in the appropriate court to modify the terms of the trust so that the remainder will not be paid outright to Grandchild but rather will be become trust property of a new supplemental needs trust (a trust in which income and corpus are used to provide enhanced care). Should the court modify the trust?

In re Trust of Stuchell 801 P. 2d 852 (Oregon Ct of Appeals, 1990) refused to allow the modification. While the court conceded that the modification would be more advantageous to the beneficiaries, it found that this fact alone was insufficient to allow modification of the trust. While the creator did not know that his grandson was disabled (so point one was met), the purposes of the trust, support for the creator's child with remainder to grandchildren could be accomplished without modification.

The *Stuchell* case illustrates the usual disposition of requests to modify trusts: they are denied. Realize that although they are often used interchangeably, the terms "reformation" and "modification" refer to different things. (See the three sections of the UTC set out after the *Rappaport* case.) Formally, there are fewer doctrinal barriers to the reformation of lifetime trusts, but as a practical matter there is probably little difference in how courts treat requests to modify either type of trusts. The following case is an example of a successful reformation proceeding.

Matter of Rappaport

866 N.Y.S.2d 483 (Surr. Ct. 2008)

John B. Riordan, J.

This is a proceeding to construe and reform the last will and testament of Rose Rappaport. Rose died on August 31, 2006 survived by four adult children: Irwin Rappaport, who is the petitioner herein, Karen Brecher, Joel Rappaport and Susan Rappaport, who is disabled. The will was admitted to probate by decree dated March 7, 2007, and Irwin, Joel and Karen were appointed as the coexecutors of the estate. Joel died in December 2007. The court has appointed Ernest T. Bartol as guardian ad litem to represent Susan's interests in this proceeding. Jurisdiction is complete. The guardian ad litem has filed his report, and the matter has been submitted for decision.

Article fourth of the will reads as follows:

"I give, bequeath and devise to my Trustees, hereinafter named, an amount equal to the Unified Credit Equivalent available at the time of my death.[5] My Trustees shall hold such amount in Trust, as a separate Trust Fund to invest and reinvest the same[,] collect the income therefrom to pay all the net income to my daughter, Susan Rappaport, during her lifetime in quarterly or more frequent installments, together with so much of the principal thereof as my Trustees shall at any time or from time to time, in their absolute discretion deem advisable to my daughter's health, support and maintenance. Upon the death of my said daughter, Susan Rappaport, my Trustees shall pay and distribute the principal then remaining together with any accrued income to such of my issue then living in equal shares, per stirpes. My Trustees shall pay all of the income of said Trust to my daughter, Susan Rappaport[,] not less than quarterly during her lifetime. Upon the death of my daughter, Susan Rappaport, my Trustees shall distribute the then principal, together with any accrued income of this Trust to my children, Joel Rappaport, Irwin E. Rappaport and Karen Brecher, share and share alike, per stirpes."

In article ninth, the decedent nominated Joel, Irwin and Karen as executors . . . . In the petition, Irwin asks that the will be reformed to . . . convert the article fourth trust to a third-party supplemental needs trust the terms of which are set forth in the proposed supplemental needs trust submitted with the petition, with Joel, Irwin and Karen as remainder persons. . . .

Take Note

A supplemental needs trust is one established by a third party to provide a person with a mental or physical disability and receiving government benefits with funds to enhance the level of care provided. The remainder can be given to whomever the creator of the trust desires.

Mr. Bartol has submitted a report in which he informs the court that after an Article 81 hearing on April 23, 2008, the Honorable Joel K. Asarch, J.S.C., rendered a decision wherein he concluded that Susan has certain deficiencies and limitations and further concluded that Irwin would be appointed as Susan's guardian with certain limited powers, which Mr. Bartol does not enumerate. As of the date of Mr. Bartol's report, an order appointing Irwin as Susan's guardian had not been signed by Judge Asarch. . . .

FYI

"Article 81" is part of the New York Mental Health Law governing the guardianship of incapacitated persons.

---

5   In 2006 the maximum amount that could fund the trust was $2,000,000.

Mr. Bartol . . . states in his report that he recommends the reformation of the decedent's will to reform the article fourth trust to create a supplemental needs trust. Mr. Bartol states that he has reviewed the proposed supplemental needs trust and concludes that it conforms to the requirements of EPTL 7–1.12.

Although the New York State Department of Health (DOH) has no current claim or pecuniary interest, it was cited and appeared in this proceeding by its attorney, the Attorney General of New York. . . . DOH opposes Irwin's request to reform the article fourth trust into a supplemental needs trust. DOH asserts that reforming the trust to create a supplemental needs trust is not necessary or appropriate given the language the decedent used in the will to pay Susan all of the net annual income of the trust without any trustee discretion or interference about how the money is to be used. DOH points out that the will postdates the enactment in 1993 of EPTL 7–1.12, the statute that authorizes the establishment of supplemental needs trusts for individuals with severe and chronic or persistent disabilities. In opposing the establishment of a supplemental needs trust, DOH points to the decedent's direction to the trustees to provide Susan with the "lifestyle that would provide for her the standard of living which she had enjoyed during [the decedent's] lifetime. I direct that my Trustees provide her with the proper residence, a full time companion, all her physical needs, recreation, support, maintenance and welfare to the fullest entend [*sic*] possible." DOH acknowledges that the payment of income from the trust to Susan will likely disqualify her from some governmental benefits. DOH argues that it is for the court or for a guardian of Susan's property to determine whether Susan's best interests are served by receiving the income payments from the article fourth trust or whether she requires the creation of a self-settled supplemental needs trust.

> **Food for Thought**
>
> Assume that the law permits a father to create a supplemental needs trust. Father did not. Is it in the best interests of the disabled individual to turn the trust in to a supplemental needs trust, or does the change merely enrich her siblings? Is modification in this case merely a way of shifting responsibility for the care of this person to the state?

In support of its position, DOH relies upon *Matter of Rubin* (4 Misc 3d 634 [Sur Ct, NY County 2004]). In *Rubin*, a decision that consolidated two proceedings, the court refused to reform various inter vivos trusts created for two disabled individuals. The court determined that reformation is available to correct mistakes, but "not . . . to change the terms of a trust to effectuate what the settlor would have done had the settler foreseen a change of circumstances that has occurred" (*id.* at 638 [citation omitted]). There is no mention in *Rubin* of whether either settlor included language in the trusts to the effect that the assets be used to supplement, rather than supplant, government benefits.

Courts are generally loathe to reform testamentary instruments and, as a rule, will not, unless reformation effectuates the testator's intent (*see Matter of Snide*, 52 NY2d 193 [1981]). When construing a will, the testator's intent is to be gleaned from a sympathetic reading of the instrument in its entirety and not from a single word or phrase (*Matter of Fabbri*, 2 NY2d 236

[1957]). It is of paramount importance that the testator's actual purpose be determined and effectuated to the extent it comports with the law and public policy (*id*. at 240). In *Matter of Escher* (94 Misc 2d 952 [Sur Ct, Bronx County 1978], *affd* 75 AD2d 531 [1st Dept 1980], *affd* 52 NY2d 1006 [1981]), the trustee of a discretionary trust established under a will brought a proceeding to judicially settle his account. The New York State Department of Mental Hygiene filed objections to the disallowance by the trustee of its claim for reimbursement from the trust for the cost of the care of the trust's lifetime beneficiary, the testator's daughter, who had been a patient at the Rockland Psychiatric Center since 1947. Surrogate's Court, Bronx County, dismissed the objections, finding that "under the terms of the trust at issue, it is not an abuse of discretion for the trustee to decline to invade corpus for the purpose advocated by objectant" (94 Misc 2d at 961). In reaching its conclusion, the court relied on the language of the testator's will and codicil, which the court found evidenced the testator's knowledge of his daughter's disabilities and his apparent intent to provide for her ongoing needs during her lifetime within the framework of a continuing trust (*id*. at 957). The court also reasoned that in recent years the view of public assistance had changed from that of a "gift" to a "right" and that the stigma attached to it had, for the most part, disappeared, particularly with respect to programs

> **Take Note**
>
> *Escher* clearly illustrates the power of the trustee of a discretionary trust. The case approves a refusal to invade principal to pay for the beneficiary's case so long as the state will pay.

> "designed to meet the astronomical cost of illness or institutional care of any sort . . . . It is divorced from the realities of life to presume that if testator were aware of the facts as they now exist, he would desire to pay the immense cost for his daughter's care in preference to having society share this burden" (id. at 959).

When the case reached the Court of Appeals, it held that, as a matter of law, the trustee did not abuse her discretion by refusing to invade the trust's corpus to reimburse the Department of Mental Hygiene (*Matter of Escher*, 52 NY2d 1006 [1981]).

Enacted in 1993, EPTL 7–1.12, in essence, codified the holding in *Escher*. The statute authorizes the creation of third-party, testamentary supplemental needs trusts when the following requirements are satisfied: (1) the person for whose benefit the trust is established suffers from a "severe and chronic or persistent disability"; (2) the trust evidences the intent that the assets be used to supplement, not supplant, government benefits; (3) the trust prohibits the trustee from using assets in any way that may jeopardize the beneficiary's entitlement to government benefits or assistance; and (4) the beneficiary does not have the power to assign, encumber, direct, distribute or authorize distribution of trust assets (EPTL 7–1.12 [a] [5] [i]–[iv]). The policy of the State of New York is to encourage the creation of supplemental needs trusts to enhance the quality of a disabled individual's life without jeopardizing Medicaid eligibility (*Matter of Newman*, 18 Misc 3d 1118[A], 2008 NY Slip Op 50127[U], *2 [Sur Ct, Bronx County 2008]; *Matter of Kamp*, 7 Misc 3d 615, 622 [Sur Ct, Broome County 2005]).

Courts have shown a willingness to reform wills to obtain the benefits of a supplemental needs trust where the testator's intent to supplement, rather than supplant, government benefits is evident from the language of the testamentary instrument and such reformation would not change the testator's dispositive plan. In deciding whether to reform a testamentary trust to create a supplemental needs trust, the

> "courts have not focused upon whether the decedent's will was executed before or after either the decision in Matter of Escher (94 Misc 2d at 952) or the enactment of EPTL 7–1.12 (see Matter of Longhine, 15 Misc 3d 1106[A] [2007] [the will was executed 12 years after the enactment of EPTL 7–1.12]; Matter of Hyman, 14 Misc 3d at 1232[A] [the will was executed the year after Matter of Escher, 94 Misc 2d at 952]). Similarly, the courts have permitted testamentary trusts to be reformed to create a [non-self-settled supplemental needs trust] notwithstanding the fact that the trusts have been operative for many years prior to the reformation application (see Matter of Kamp, 7 Misc 3d at [615], and Matter of Hyman, 14 Misc 3d at 1232[A], where the respective testamentary trust was in existence for more than 20 years prior to its reformation)."

(*Matter of Newman*, 18 Misc 3d 1118[A], 2008 NY Slip Op 50127[U], *2 [Sur Ct, Bronx County 2008].)

The proposed reformation of the article fourth trust for Susan's benefit meets the criteria first enunciated in *Escher* and later in EPTL 7–1.12. Susan, the income beneficiary, suffers from chronic disabilities. The will evidences the decedent's intention that the trust's assets be used to supplement, not supplant, government benefits. In that regard, it is significant that article eighth of the will directs that the trust "shall not in any way jeopardize any monies that she is now receiving from any government agency or that she will be entitled to receive after my death." Susan has no power to dispose of any trust assets. The requested reformation does not alter decedent's testamentary plan, and the court finds the requested reformation to be in Susan's best interests. There is no evidence that Susan is currently receiving or has received governmental benefits. Under the facts of this proceeding, the court declines to follow the restrictive analysis set forth in *Matter of Rubin* (4 Misc 3d 634 [2004]).

Accordingly, the court adopts the guardian ad litem's recommendations to construe and reform the decedent's will to . . . create a third-party supplemental needs trust in conformance with EPTL 7–1.12. The court has reviewed the proposed supplemental needs trust and is satisfied that it conforms to EPTL 7–1.12.

────────────────

Points for Discussion

1. The supplemental needs trust

Rappaport is a proceeding to turn a testamentary trust created for a single beneficiary who receives mandatory income payments and discretionary payments of principal into a supplemental needs trust. Surrogate Riordan's opinion includes a concise history of the supplemental needs trust. Remember that certain governmental welfare programs are intended for the indigent, and that there are strict limits on the amount of income a recipient of assistance can receive and on the value of assets the recipient can own. A properly structured supplemental needs trust will not affect the beneficiary's eligibility for government benefits.

The supplemental needs trust in *Rappaport* is a "third party" supplemental needs trust because the property that funds the trust did not belong to the beneficiary. A supplemental needs trust can be created with the beneficiary's own funds, often the proceeds of the settlement of a tort action. Such a trust is a "first party" supplemental needs trust, and while the trust property is not a "resource" for purposes of qualifying for governmental benefits, at the beneficiary's death, the property in the trust must first be used to reimburse the state for its expenditures for the beneficiary.

2. **Rappaport** *and* **Stuchell**

At first glance, the New York court is much more willing to allow a trust to be turned into a supplemental needs trust than did the Oregon court that decided *Stuchell*. Does that mean that a New York would decide *Stuchell* differently? Can you distinguish the two situations? Note that without altering the existing trust, the grandson beneficiary in *Stuchell* (or his guardian) could ask a court to create a first party supplemental needs trust with the remainder distributed. In *Rappaport*, the trustees could have asked the court to approve the exercise of their power to invade the trust principal to put all of the trust property into a new first party supplemental needs trust. The difference between these solutions, and the creation of a third party trust sought in both cases, is that at the death of the beneficiary of a first party trust the trust property must be used to reimburse the state before it can pass to the remainder beneficiaries. Indeed the judge in the *Rubin* case cited in *Rappaport* denied the requested reformations of two existing trusts and suggested that first party trusts be created instead. As you can see from the decision in *Rappaport*, that approach has not gotten very far in New York. So, how would a New York court decide *Stuchell*? Which decision, *Stuchell* or *Rappaport*, better comports with the basic policies of trust law? Which is sounder social policy?

Consider the following sections of the Uniform Trust Code. How would the cases be decided thereunder?

UTC § 411. Modification or termination of noncharitable irrevocable trust by consent

[(a)   [A noncharitable irrevocable trust may be modified or terminated upon consent of the settlor and all beneficiaries, even if the modification or termination is inconsistent with a material purpose of the trust.] [If, upon petition, the court finds that the settlor and all beneficiaries consent to the modification or termination of a noncharitable irrevocable trust, the court shall approve the modification or termination even if the modification or termination is inconsistent with a material purpose of the trust.] A settlor's power to consent to a trust's modification or termination may be exercised by an agent under a power of attorney only to the extent expressly authorized by the power of attorney or the terms of the trust; by the settlor's [conservator] with the approval of the court supervising the [conservatorship] if an agent is not so authorized; or by the settlor's [guardian] with the approval of the court supervising the [guardianship] if an agent is not so authorized and a conservator has not been appointed. [This subsection does not apply to irrevocable trusts created before or to revocable trusts that become irrevocable before [the effective date of this [Code] [amendment].]]

(b) A noncharitable irrevocable trust may be terminated upon consent of all of the beneficiaries if the court concludes that continuance of the trust is not necessary to achieve any material purpose of the trust. A noncharitable irrevocable trust may be modified upon consent of all of the beneficiaries if the court concludes that modification is not inconsistent with a material purpose of the trust.

[(c) A spendthrift provision in the terms of the trust is not presumed to constitute a material purpose of the trust.]

(d) Upon termination of a trust under subsection (a) or (b), the trustee shall distribute the trust property as agreed by the beneficiaries.

(e) If not all of the beneficiaries consent to a proposed modification or termination of the trust under subsection (a) or (b), the modification or termination may be approved by the court if the court is satisfied that:

(1) if all of the beneficiaries had consented, the trust could have been modified or terminated under this section; and

(2) the interests of a beneficiary who does not consent will be adequately protected.

UTC § 412. Modification or termination because of unanticipated circumstances or inability to administer trust effectively

(a) The court may modify the administrative or dispositive terms of a trust or terminate the trust if, because of circumstances not anticipated by the settlor, modification or termination will further the purposes of the trust. To the extent practicable, the modification must be made in accordance with the settlor's probable intention.

(b) The court may modify the administrative terms of a trust if continuation of the trust on its existing terms would be impracticable or wasteful or impair the trust's administration.

(c)   Upon termination of a trust under this section, the trustee shall distribute the trust property in a manner consistent with the purposes of the trust.

3.   Equitable Deviation

Another arrow in the quiver of the beneficiary who wishes to change the terms of the trust is equitable deviation. Although it is generally not acceptable to define a word by using it, equitable deviation is a change (deviation) from the terms of a trust when fairness (equity) would so require.

Matter of Carniol

861 N.Y.S.2d 587 (Surr. Ct. 2008)

JOHN B. RIORDAN, J.

This is a first and final accounting of Rhonda Carniol, the executor of the estate of David Carniol. The prayer for relief includes a request to allow the executor to modify the terms of the article fourth trust created under the will.

The decedent, David Carniol, died on March 2, 2005. The decedent's will dated August 26, 1998 was admitted to probate and letters testamentary issued to Rhonda Carniol on May 23, 2005. Article fourth of the will provides as follows:

"I give the proprietary lease or leases to, and the stock evidencing ownership of, any cooperative apartment or apartments which I own at the time of my death, together with any applicable insurance policies, including prepaid premiums, to my wife, Diane Carniol, or, if she does not survive, to my trustee, in trust, who shall retain the apartment for use by my granddaughter, Aimee Robin Carniol, if and for as long as she wishes to reside there. Payments for expenses regarding the use or preservation of the property, including maintenance, real estate taxes, insurance premiums, repairs, and interest and principal on any mortgage on any apartment or on the underlying property, and for capital improvements shall be made by my granddaughter. Neither my granddaughter nor my trustee shall be liable for loss, destruction, usage or waste of any apartment held hereunder, or for any decline in its value or its failure to appreciate in value.

"My trustee may, with the consent of my granddaughter, sell any apartment held hereunder at any time for such price and on such terms and conditions as my trustee shall determine and invest as much or all of the proceeds as my trustee shall determine in another residence, on the same terms that apply to the original residence. Any proceeds of sale in excess of the amount used to purchase another residence shall be added to the trust under article fifth.

> "Upon the death of Aimee Robin Carniol, my trustee shall sell any apartment held hereunder for such price and on such terms and conditions as my trustee shall determine and distribute the proceeds of sale to the trust under article fifth."

[The trustees of the article fifth trust are to pay the trust income to Aimee and Steven Carniol for life and also may invade principal for the beneficiaries' health, support, or maintenance. When both beneficiaries are dead the trust terminates and is distributed to the then living descendants of the decedent's brother.]

Decedent's wife Diane predeceased the decedent. Both Aimee Robin Carniol and Steven Carniol survived him. The decedent was also survived by a minor grandchild, April Carniol, who is a daughter of Norman Carniol, and, therefore, a presumptive remainderman of the article fifth trust.

The petitioner avers that inquiry was made to the Hillpark Co-op Association regarding the proposed transfer of the apartment to the trust. According to the petitioner, the co-op association advised that it would not approve a transfer to a trust and, in addition, that any person residing in the apartment needed co-op board approval, which could be granted only after all required forms are completed and the proposed resident appears before the board. To determine whether this was accurate, petitioner's counsel wrote to the attorneys for the co-op association on two separate occasions and was advised in writing both times that the board would not approve a transfer to a trust.

Petitioner further states that Paul Carniol, the trustee of the article fourth trust, obtained the required forms and sent them to Norman Carniol, Aimee's father, with a request that he assist Aimee in completing the forms. The trustee claims that he never received a response despite following up numerous times with Aimee's father, Norman. Petitioner believes that based upon Aimee's financial situation and "certain other aspects of her history," it is unlikely that the co-op board will approve her tenancy even assuming she could overcome the board's policy prohibiting transfers to a trust. Accordingly, petitioner asked Aimee if she would consent to a sale of the apartment; however, Aimee never gave a definitive response to petitioner's request.

Under these circumstances, petitioner now asks the court's permission to modify the terms of the article fourth trust to permit her either to (1) sell the cooperative apartment and to pay the proceeds, net of the existing debt on the property and expenses of sale, to the article fourth trust, or (2) transfer, with or without co-op board approval, the decedent's right, title and interest in the cooperative apartment to the article fourth trust with a direction that the trust immediately sell such apartment. Once the property is sold, either by the executor or by the trustee, petitioner asks that the trustee of the article fourth trust, at his discretion, be permitted to purchase a replacement apartment or home for Aimee and that any excess funds be used to defray the cost of housing, including rent on an apartment or home, utilities, real estate taxes and other appurtenant charges for Aimee for her lifetime, or until the trust proceeds are exhausted. The petitioner also seeks a direction from the court ordering Aimee to pay the costs of carrying the apartment until this proceeding is completed, and, if Aimee fails to meet such obligation, authorizing her to sell the cooperative apartment and apply the proceeds in the manner described above.

* * *

Initially, the court notes that the stock and proprietary lease of a cooperative together constitute ownership of the apartment (1 Warren's Heaton, Surrogate's Court Practice § 84.01 [7th ed]). A proprietary lease may provide for transfer only upon approval of the directors of the cooperative. "[S]uch a restraint cannot prevent a testator from disposing of a co-op by will (*see Application of Blakeman*, 518 F Supp 1095, 1099). It may nonetheless prevent the legatee from occupying the apartment" (*Matter of Katz*, 142 Misc 2d 1073, 1076 [Sur Ct, NY County 1989]). In *Matter of Katz*, the court held that the board's approval was not necessary in order for the owner to make a gift of the co-op even though the donee might be prohibited from taking actual possession for lack of board approval. The court found that "[a]lthough the donee may not be permitted to take possession, title will pass and the donee has the right to the monetary interest in the co-op" (*Matter of Katz*, 142 Misc 2d 1073, 1076 [1989]). Thus, the possibility that Aimee may not be permitted to take possession of the co-op does not invalidate the transfer.

Here, however, the matter is further complicated because the co-op board has a restraint on the transfer of a cooperative apartment to a trust. Accordingly, there is not only a restriction on possession in the instant case, but also a restriction on ownership since title cannot be transferred to a trust. Thus, unlike the donee in *Matter of Katz*, the trust does not have a separate monetary interest in the co-op.

It is a basic rule of reformation, that a testator's intent must be gleaned from a reading of the entire instrument (*Matter of Thall*, 18 NY2d 186 [1966]; *Matter of Fabbri*, 2 NY2d 236 [1957]). It appears from the will, in its entirety, that the testator intended for Aimee to have a place "to reside" for as long as she wishes. The testator, however, placed the burden of expenses "regarding the use or preservation of the property" upon Aimee. The

What's That?

Reformation, like modification and equitable deviation, is just another doctrinal pigeon hole classification for "changing" the terms of a document.

testator also restricted the trustee's ability to sell the property absent Aimee's consent. Absent from the will, however, is a provision considering the possibility that Aimee would fail to pay for the expenses and would also fail to consent to a sale.

Based upon the co-op board's restriction on transfer policy as evidenced in the letters from the co-op board's attorney submitted to the court, the executor is unable to transfer ownership to the article fourth trust. Aimee has failed to meet the obligation imposed on her by the terms of the will to pay the expenses of the apartment. Moreover, a sale cannot be effectuated because Aimee has not consented. For these reasons, the executor has asked the court to reform the will. The terms of the will, however, are clear as is the testator's intention to provide a place for Aimee to reside. Nevertheless, "[t]he doctrine of equitable deviation has been applied to allow trustees to depart from the terms of a trust instrument where there has been an unforeseen change in circumstances that threatens to defeat or substantially impair the purpose for which the trust was created" (*Matter of Aberlin*, 264 AD2d 775 [2d Dept 1999] [citation omitted]).

It appears that the testator did not foresee the possibility that Aimee would be unable to pay for the upkeep of the co-op apartment and withhold her consent to a sale, or that the board would not approve a transfer of the shares to a trust. Also, estate assets are being depleted to maintain the apartment, even though the testator's intention of providing this residence for Aimee cannot be realized. Thus, the circumstances of the instant case justify an equitable deviation from the literal terms of the will and the court authorizes the executor to sell the cooperative apartment and pay the proceeds, net of the existing debt on the property and expenses of sale, to the article fourth trust after repayment to the article fifth trust for those funds previously used to pay the expenses on the co-op.

> **Take Note**
>
> Does UTC § 412 authorize the court's decision? Under subsection (a) or (b) or both? Is this deviation from substantive terms or merely an administrative issue? Given the circumstances of the case, did the court have an alternative?

Concerning the request for authorization to purchase a replacement residence for Aimee, the court finds that an evidentiary hearing is necessary in order for a finding to be made as to Aimee's ability and intention to pay the expenses of upkeep. If Aimee is unable to pay these expenses, the same problem will arise in connection with a replacement residence. If the court finds that Aimee is unable to pay the expenses of upkeep on a replacement residence, the article fourth trust will be collapsed and the funds held therein will be paid over to the article fifth trust. Since one half of the income from the article fifth trust is payable to Aimee, Aimee will receive some immediate benefit in accordance with the testator's intention. . . .

Matter of Smathers

852 N.Y.S.2d 718 (Surr. Ct. 2008)

ANTHONY A. SCARPINO, JR., J.

This is a proceeding by JPMorgan Chase Bank, N.A. as trustee of the trust created under the will of Elmer Ellsworth Smathers (decedent) for construction and reformation of decedent's will and for advice and direction regarding the sale of real property held by the trust. The parties have filed a stipulation wherein they identify the papers to be considered on this application.

Decedent died testate on January 11, 1928. Under his will dated December 11, 1926, decedent disposed of his residuary estate in trust. The trust term is measured by two lives, decedent's niece-in-law, Virginia Smith Healey (who postdeceased decedent on June 22, 1945), and his grandnephew Elmer Ellsworth Smathers who is 92 years of age.[6]

During the trust term, the trustee is directed to pay from income $60,000 annually to Virginia Smith Healey or her issue. At present, there are three persons sharing such income one of whom, David Arthur Pollard (decedent's great-grand-nephew), is under a disability. The balance of the trust income is paid in specified units to numerous individuals and, upon the death of certain of such beneficiaries, to his or her surviving spouse or issue. There are approximately 100 income bene-ficiaries and nearly 200 contingent remainderpersons. James P. Reduto, Esq., was appointed as guardian ad litem for David Pollard, and J. Henry Neale, Jr., Esq., was appointed to represent the infant remainderpersons.

Take Note

A fortunate choice if the creator's intent was to postpone distribution of the trust corpus to the remainder beneficiaries.

Food for Thought

Do the difficulties of administering a trust with 100 current beneficiaries say something about the practicality of very long term trusts?

Upon the death of the second measuring life, the trustees are directed to distribute the trust assets to decedent's corporation, Elmer E. Smathers, Inc. Following such transfer, the stock of the corporation is to be distributed to the then living income beneficiaries in proportion to their respective interests in income.

The primary assets of the trust are two properties which decedent owned: 18 Broadway and 562 Fifth Avenue. The will was customized to provide for decedent's explicit direction that the trustees retain both properties. Although he granted his fiduciaries a broad power to sell and convert trust assets, decedent expressly prohibited the sale of either property as follows:

> "forty-third: As a specific exception to the power to sell real property . . . I direct that neither my Executors nor Trustees shall sell or dispose, unless required by law so to do, of the property known as No. 18 Broadway, New York, leased to the Standard Oil Company of New York, nor of the property known as the Fifth Avenue and 46th Street property. In the event that any sale of any property shall be necessary by law, I direct that the #18 Broadway property be the last to be sold or disposed of and that the said Fifth Avenue and 46th Street property be the next to the last to be sold or disposed of . . . . It is my intention that said two parcels of real estate shall remain permanent assets of the trust . . . and far as it may be legal

---

6   Under New York's rule against perpetuities as it existed at the time of the decedent's death, a trust could last for not longer than the lives of two persons alive when the trust was created. This was much more restrictive than the tradition and current New York period of lives in being plus twenty-one years.—Eds.

so to do, direct that there shall be no power on the part of either the Executors or Trustees to sell or convert said two parcels of real estate."

Under article fifty-third, decedent acknowledges that the properties will form a substantial portion of his estate and he expresses his belief that such assets are already "very favorably" invested. The disposition of the properties to the corporation was intended to avoid a premature sale of the properties in the event the trust terminated early. Should income be insufficient (an event decedent did not consider likely and which has not occurred), decedent expressed his wish under article fifty-seventh that the income beneficiaries not be allowed to change the character of the investments in order to produce additional income.

Both properties are subject to long term leases. In 1920, decedent entered into a 99-year lease (which expires in 2019) with Standard Oil Company of New York for the Broadway property at a fixed rental of $250,000 a year plus taxes, utilities, insurance and maintenance. The lease permitted Standard Oil to demolish, construct or erect a new building over the Broadway property provided that the Broadway property is "capable of being used and operated in every particular as an entirely separate building" (referred to by the parties as the separate structure clause). In 1977, the trustee entered into a lease of the Fifth Avenue property which terminates in 2011 subject to the tenant's right to extend to 2026.

Between 1921 and 1926 Standard Oil constructed a building atop of and adjoining the Broadway property which constitutes approximately 72% of the combined properties known as 26 Broadway. It is not known whether such construction violated the separate structure clause. Following an unopposed hearing held by the Landmark Preservation Commission, in September 1995, 26 Broadway was designated a landmark site. Petitioner suggests that such designation impacts whether the building is capable of being divided as contemplated by the lease, and the ultimate sale of the Broadway property.

The present application is precipitated by the sale of the adjoining property by Standard Oil to a real estate group known as the Chetrit Group, LLC. Chetrit paid $225,000,000 for the adjoining property. Initially, Chetrit offered to purchase the trust's 28% interest in 26 Broadway for $11 million. Petitioner obtained its own appraisal from Grubb & Ellis and negotiated to sell the Broadway property to Chetrit for $23,400,000 plus expenses related to the sale and this proceeding. The sales contract is conditioned upon petitioner obtaining authorization to sell.

Petitioner asks the court to reform decedent's will in order that it may: (i) deviate from the express prohibition in the will to enable consummation of the sale to Chetrit, and (ii) create a limited liability company instead of a corporation for receipt of the trust assets. Additionally, petitioner seeks advice and direction pursuant to SCPA 2107 to permit it to sell the Fifth Avenue property.

The doctrine of equitable deviation has been applied by our courts to permit deviation from the terms of a will or trust where there have been unforeseen circumstances and adherence to the instrument threatens to defeat or substantially impair the purpose of the trust. Application of the doctrine must accomplish the testator's intent which is the paramount consideration. Thus, reformation or deviation will not apply where the testator's or settlor's intention is unambiguous.

The court in *Pulitzer* (*supra*) posits several questions as a predicate to determining whether equitable deviation should apply: (i) does the fiduciary have the power to sell; (ii) where there is a prohibition, may the court utilize its equitable power to modify the terms of the trust; and (iii) do the proofs submitted justify the exercise of such power? In other words, where problems not foreseen jeopardize the trust, *Pulitzer* suggests that a court may exercise its equitable power to permit deviation in order to protect the trust. Examples are found where under the administrative powers the fiduciary was restricted to certain investments which limitation later adversely affected the purpose of the trust.

Petitioner asserts that the longevity of the second measuring life, the possible lack of severability of the building and the ability to consummate a sale with the present owner of the adjoining properties are unforeseen circumstances that warrant the application of the doctrine. The trustee further suggests that the current favorable capital gains tax rate make this an opportune time to sell. Both guardians ad litem agree and recommend that the relief be granted. The guardians also consider the likelihood that the trust will realize greater income upon the investment of the sales proceeds as a factor warranting the relief. In that regard, in the event the relief is granted, Mr. Reduto, on behalf of his ward, requests a further reformation to provide that his ward would share in the increased income in proportion to his current interest. At present, David Pollard's share is a fixed amount.

Essentially, petitioner and the guardians ad litem recommend deviation as being in the best interests of the trust beneficiaries. Not all of the beneficiaries agree.

Several beneficiaries have filed opposition to the relief, with the exception that all parties who have appeared consent to the creation of a limited liability company as the receptacle for the assets upon the termination of the trust.

Objectants maintain that petitioner has failed to demonstrate any unforeseen circumstances, and that the proposed reformation is a marked departure from decedent's will. With regard to the merits of the proposed sale, objectants have provided an appraisal of the Broadway property from Massey Knakal Realty Services in the amount of $78,083,071 or some $55 million more than the contract price.

Decedent's intent is unequivocal: "[the] two parcels of real estate shall remain permanent assets of the trust . . . ." If required by law to sell trust assets then the trustee must sell all other assets before resorting to a sale of the Broadway property. Petitioner does not allege that the trustee is required by law to sell any assets. As the courts in *Matter of Palmer* (*supra*) and *Matter of Pope, Bowes & Citibank, N.A.* (*supra*) hold, deviation should not apply where the testator's intent is unambiguous.

Moreover, the change in circumstances here cannot be characterized as unforeseen by decedent. It is more likely that decedent knew of or anticipated some of these circumstances. The long term lease was signed and the construction of the adjoining property substantially completed before decedent executed his will. Notwithstanding such facts, decedent expressed his belief that the trust income was sufficient to satisfy the terms of the trust. It appears that the income has been sufficient for some 80 years. Thus, there is no frustration of purpose.

Moreover, in the instant case, there has been no measurable change in the administration of the trust. The sale of the adjoining property has not affected the income available for distribution among the beneficiaries. Such sale and subsequent offer to buy the Broadway property is simply an opportunity which petitioner believes to be in the best interests of the trust. The test however is not "best interests"; rather, petitioner must establish that decedent's presumed intent is incapable of fulfillment. Petitioner has not met its burden. Accordingly, petitioner's request to reform the will to permit it to sell the Broadway property is denied. Based upon this determination, the court need not reach any issue concerning the particulars of the proposed contract.

Food for Thought

Best interests are irrelevant? Who's this trust for, anyway?

Equally unavailing is petitioner's request for advice and direction as to whether it should market and sell the Fifth Avenue property.

SCPA 2107 provides that a fiduciary may seek advice and direction when faced with uncertainty over the propriety of selling estate property or under extraordinary circumstances such as handling of complex valuation issues, tax elections or where a conflict exists. Absent extraordinary circumstances, the court will not intervene to substitute its judgment for the business judgment of a fiduciary.

In support of its request, petitioner relies upon the unforeseen circumstances alleged in support of the request to sell the Broadway property. The trustee seeks permission to sell the Fifth Avenue property and for the court to provide guidelines for such sale. Decedent's will clearly restricts the sale of the Fifth Avenue property. As with the Broadway property, no unforeseen factors have been presented which warrant departure from the terms of the will. Accordingly, the court declines to advise and direct.

We turn now to the request to reform decedent's will to authorize the trustee to transfer the trust assets to a limited liability company (LLC). All of the parties consent to such reformation. Here, petitioner is on stronger ground.

The general rule is that our courts will rarely reform a will to correct a mistake (*see Matter of Snide*, 52 NY2d 193 [1981]). However, an exception is made where the requested reformation seeks to cure a tax defect provided that such reformation conforms with decedent's intent.

During his lifetime decedent created the corporation. As noted, upon termination of the trust, the corporation is to receive the trust assets including the two properties. Petitioner seeks authority to form a limited liability company to be called Elmer E. Smathers, LLC and for reformation of the will to substitute the Smathers LLC for the corporation. The objective is to avoid a double income taxation by the corporation (e.g., where a tax is imposed upon the corporation and again upon the shareholders when distributions are made to them). While election as a subchapter S corporation may avoid double taxation, such entity is limited to 100 shareholders. In view of the current number of beneficiaries, it is highly unlikely that the corporation would qualify for subchapter S status.

In 1986 section 311 (b) of the United States Internal Revenue Code (26 USC) was repealed resulting in the present rule that a corporation must recognize gain on both nonliquidating and liquidating distributions of appreciated property to a shareholder. Eight years later, in 1994, New York enacted the Limited Liability Company Law which authorizes an LLC to be treated as a partnership for tax purposes. Partnership classification may be elected by checking the appropriate box on the federal tax form. The LLC may combine the corporate limitation on personal liability of the owners (called members) with the favorable pass-through tax treatment (*see* Rich, Practice Commentaries, McKinney's Cons Laws of NY, Book 32A, Limited Liability Company Law, 2007 Pamph, at 2).

Here, the proposed reformation will effectuate decedent's plan for the transfer of the trust assets to an entity whose members will consist of the income beneficiaries living at the termination of the trust. In addition, such reformation will eliminate the double taxation of the assets, a result decedent presumably intended. The court is satisfied that the proposed reformation is consistent with decedent's intent.

The Smathers LLC to be established must however parallel the corporate structure with respect to its management and control and the respective interests of the beneficiaries as its members. Accordingly, petitioner shall first provide the court and parties with a proposal for the formation of the Smathers LLC prior to this court granting authority to create the entity.

> **Food for Thought**
>
> Nobody willingly pays taxes that they can avoid; but so too nobody passes up the opportunity to realize a gain. Is there any language in the trust that allows deviation for tax benefits?

Based upon the foregoing, decedent's will is reformed to substitute an LLC, to be formed by the trustee in accordance with the foregoing, for the corporation.

Points for Discussion

1. *Three doctrines, one idea?*

What is the difference between modification, reformation, and equitable deviation? Can you come up with an explanation of why the general reluctance to reform trusts does not apply to reformations which are related to issues of taxation?

2. *Anticipation*

How well drafted were the wills involved in *Carniol* and *Smathers*? Can you suggest ways to improve the drafting of both? Is there a lack of practicality, or foresight, or could nothing be done to anticipate the problems that developed? Indeed are they really problems? Does it depend upon whether the issues are viewed from the vantage point of the beneficiaries or the trust creator?

3. Are tax questions different?

Would the results in *Carinol* or *Smathers* be different if the following provision of the UTC were the applicable law? Can you determine the "tax objectives" of the creators of these testamentary trusts?

UTC § 416. Modification to achieve settlor's tax objectives

To achieve the settlor's tax objectives, the court may modify the terms of a trust in a manner that is not contrary to the settlor's probable intention. The court may provide that the modification has retroactive effect.

Test Your Knowledge

To assess your understanding of the material in this chapter, click here to take a quiz.

CHAPTER 9

Powers of Appointment

453 - 66

A. Introduction

The power of appointment is a device that can provide for great flexibility in the disposition of trust property well after the trust has been created. For generations, powers of appointment were dubbed as "the most efficient dispositive device that the ingenuity of Anglo-American lawyers has ever worked out." A. B. A. J. 807 (1938) was largely governed by common law, though some states like New York had a rather comprehensive statutory framework (NY EPTL Article 10). In 2013, however, the National Conference of Commissioners on Uniform State Laws promulgated the Uniform Powers of Appointment Act and recommended that states adopt it. The prefatory note concedes that the aim of the act was to codify aspects of the law of powers of appointment that was 'most amenable to codification.' It relies extensively on existing law, particularly the Restatement of the Law of Property, Third.

A power of appointment is the authority to designate recipients of beneficial ownership interests in the appointive property. An owner, of course, has this authority to do so with respect to his or her property. By creating a power of appointment, the owner typically confers this authority on someone else.

The Uniform Act defines the power of appointments in Section 102 (13) as:

> a power that enables a powerholder acting in a nonfiduciary capacity to designate a recipient of an ownership interest in or another power of appointment over the appointive property. The term does not include a power of attorney.

Put more straightforwardly, a power of appointment creates or reserves in a person designated by an owner of property the authority to determine the manner (subject to limitations mandated in the power) in which the property shall be distributed.

Like most constructs in the law of wills and trusts, the power of appointment has a specialized vocabulary.

1. The *appointive property* is the property subject to the power of appointment.

2. The *donor* (usually the owner of the property subject to the power of appointment) creates the power.

3. The *donee* or *powerholder* (under the Uniform Act) is the person delegated to determine individuals who will receive the property subject to the power (the *appointive property*).

4. The *objects* or *appointee* (under the Uniform Act) means a person/s to whom a *powerholder* may make an appointment of appointive property.

In short, the power is created by the *donor* who is usually the owner of the appointive property; *donor* may set limits to how the *powerholder* can deal with the *appointive property*. In addition to selecting *objects* or *appointees*, *donor* may require that the power of appointment be exercised at a certain time and in a certain way.

Most powers of appointment delegated to a donee who is a beneficiary of trust property and the terms of the instrument allow the donee to make decisions about the disposition of the trust property after the donee ceases to be a beneficiary, usually at the powerholder's death. One of the permutations in Ward's Estate Plan was to allow the remainder interest after the death of June to pass to his issue; another would be to limit to her a power to appoint the remainder. The donor of such a power is generally the creator of the trust. Why does the donor create the power: to allow the *powerholder* to make future decisions about the disposition of the trust property, almost invariably after the death of the donor. In the typical case, the donee is the donor's spouse or child and the donor's hope is that as the spouse or child's life nears its end the *powerholder* will have a much better idea of how the donor's family can best benefit from the trust property than the donor could have had when the trust was created decades before the spouse or child's death.

Powers of appointment can be created for other reasons, of course, and they have assumed a very important role in sophisticated estate and gift tax planning.[1] Most of those uses are beyond the scope of these materials, but before we discuss the property law of powers of appointment we must make note of two points. First, the power given to a trustee by the creator of a trust to make decisions about how the trust property is to be distributed to the trust beneficiaries is sometimes classified as a power of appointment but the new Restatements of Trusts and Property exclude powers held by trustees from the definition of a power of appointment (*See* Restatement Third, Property (Wills and Donative Transfers) § 17.1, comment *g*; Restatement Third, Trusts § 50, comment *a*). The Uniform Act regards the power as non-fiduciary, therefore while the *powerholder* may exercise the power she does not do so as a fiduciary. We have discussed this distinction in *Clark v. Campbell* (above, page 390) when we considered the substantive law of trusts and of trustees' duties.

Regardless of whether the Uniform Act is adopted, the common law of powers of appointment remains in effect except as modified by statute. New York is a jurisdiction that long had statutory mandates on powers but EPTL § 10–1.1 makes it clear that the common law remains in force except to the extent that the provisions are inconsistent with common law.

---

1   Tax issues with regard to the creation and exercise of powers of appointment will be addressed in the chapter on Gift and Estate Taxation.

B. Terminology and Classification

The preceding paragraphs introduced some of the key terms involved in discussing powers of appointment: the *donor* who creates the power, the *donee or powerholder* to whom the power is given, and the *appointive property* which is subject to the power. Another important term is *object* or *appointee*, a person to whom property can be appointed by the donee. A well-drafted power of appointment will provide a *taker in default of appointment* (usually shortened to *taker in default*), a person to whom the appointive property will be distributed if the donee does not exercise the power. (Restatement (Third) of Property § 17.2, Uniform Act para 18). The designation of takers in default will avoid some recurring problems in the implementation of estate plans.

Powers of appointment come in more than one variety and the classification of powers depends on two factors: who are permissible appointees and when the donee may exercise the power?

The first factor determines whether the power of appointment is *general* or *special* (or *non-general powers*). Consider the comment to Section 102:

> Paragraphs (6) and (10) of the Uniform Act explain the distinction between general and non-general powers of appointment. A general power of appointment enables the powerholder to exercise the power in favor of one or more of the following: the powerholder, the powerholder's estate, the creditors of the powerholder, or the creditors of the powerholder's estate, regardless of whether the power is also exercisable in favor of others. A non-general power of appointment cannot be exercised in favor of the powerholder, the powerholder's estate, the creditors of the powerholder, or the creditors of the powerholder's estate. Estate planners often classify non-general powers as being either "broad" or "limited," depending on the range of permissible appointees. A power to appoint to anyone in the world except the powerholder, the powerholder's estate, and the creditors of either would be an example of a broad non-general power. In contrast, a power in the donor's spouse to appoint among the donor's descendants would be an example of a limited non-general power.

Thus, a power is general if the powerholder is among the permissible appointees. A power that allows powerholder to appoint to herself is also the definition of a general power of appointment for estate and gift tax purposes (Internal Revenue Code §§ 2041 and 2514).

The importance of the estate and gift tax definition of a general power cannot be overstated. Most obvious is the use of the tax law definition of a general power in the Uniform Act and in Restatement Third, Property § 17.3(a). While the development of the tax law definition has a complicated history, suffice it to say that the focus was on whether donee had the ability to use the appointive property for the powerholder's benefit. The tax law definition simply sums up all the ways the donee can take advantage of the appointive property for his or her own benefit. The tax effects of powers of appointment are briefly described below.

If a donee cannot take advantage of the appointive property for his or her own benefit the power of appointment is a *special* or *non-general* power of appointment (Restatement Third, Property § 17.3(b), Uniform Act 10). The permissible appointees of a non-general powers can be defined broadly; the powerholder can be given a power to appoint to anyone other than herself, her creditors, her estate or the creditors of her estate. The permissible appointees can be defined more narrowly. For example the powerholder could be given power to appoint to the powerholder's issue or to the donor's issue or to a charity or charities of the *powerholder*'s choice. In any event, the inability of the *donee* to take the economic benefit of the property for him or herself prevents the power from being general. Realize, of course, that the power to select a charitable beneficiary of a large gift might be very satisfying to the *donee* and confer on the *donee* benefits such as an enhanced reputation. The possibility of such advantages does not make the power general. Only the ability to directly receive the economic benefit of the appointive property makes the power a general power of appointment.

The other factor that determines classification is when the power can be exercised. According to the Uniform Act (and the common law)

1. A power that can be exercised only by will is a *testamentary power:*

A power is testamentary if it is not exercisable during the powerholder's life but only in the powerholder's will or in a non-testamentary instrument that is functionally similar to the powerholder's will, such as the powerholder's revocable trust that remains revocable until the powerholder's death. On the ability of a powerholder to exercise a testamentary power of appointment in such a revocable trust, see Section 304 and the accompanying Comment. See also Restatement Third of Property: Wills and Other Donative Transfers § 19.9, comment *b*.

2. A power of appointment that can be exercised by the donee at any time after its creation whether or not it is also exercisable by will is a *presently exercisable power* (sometimes called an *inter vivo* power):

A power of appointment is presently exercisable even though, at the time in question, the powerholder can only appoint an *interest* that is revocable or subject to a condition. For example, suppose that a trust directs the trustee to pay the income to the powerholder for life, then to distribute the principal by representation to the powerholder's surviving descendants. The trust further provides that, if the powerholder leaves no surviving descendants, the principal is to be distributed "to such individuals as the powerholder shall appoint." The powerholder has a presently exercisable power of appointment, but the appointive property is a remainder interest that is conditioned on the powerholder leaving no surviving descendants.

3. A power is a postponed power—sometimes known as a deferred power—if it is not yet exercisable until the occurrence of a specified event, the satisfaction of an ascertainable standard, or the passage of a specified time. A postponed power becomes presently exercisable upon the occurrence of the specified event, the satisfaction of the ascertainable standard, or the

passage of the specified time. The second sentence in paragraph (15) is modeled on Uniform Power of Attorney Act § 102(8).

Problem 9-1

Classify the following powers of appointment and identify the permissible appointees and the takers in default.

A. At the death of the last to die of my son X and his wife Y, the Trustee shall distribute the trust property as my son X shall appoint in his last will and testament duly admitted to probate. My son may appoint in such proportions as he shall decide, outright or in further trust with my trustee or other trustees, to or for the benefit of his issue. Should my said son fail to validly exercise this power of appointment in whole or in part, then upon the last to die of my said son and his said wife, the trustee shall distribute so much of the trust property not so validly appointed to my issue then living by representation.

B. At the death of my husband, A, the Trustee shall distribute the trust property in such proportions and in such manner, outright or in trust or otherwise, to or for the use of one or more or all of my and my husband's issue or the spouses of my husband's issue, or to any charitable organization as my husband may appoint by his will admitted to probate. In no event may my husband appoint the trust property or any part thereof to himself, his estate, his creditors, or the creditors of his estate. The whole or any part of such trust property not effectively appointed by my husband shall be distributed by representation to the issue of myself and my husband living at my husband's death.

Note that the language creating the power of appointment is addressed to the trustee of the trust over which the powerholder has the power of appointment. The legal concept in play is that the creator of the trust is directing the trustee on the disposition of the trust property when the trust comes to an end: the options are to follow the instructions of the powerholder, assuming they comport with the language of the power; or distribute to the takers in default if the powerholder does not validly exercise the power.

In the course of this chapter we will confront issues other than whether the power is general or special, and whether the exercise is consistent with the type of power. But classification may at times be crucial. Two very important questions depend on classification: what rights, if any, do the creditors of the powerholder have in the appointive property and what tax consequences, if any, does the power bring to the powerholder?

C. Effects of Classification

1. Rights of Creditors

Considering the right that the powerholder has in the property subject to a power of appointment, it would be doctrinally unsound if the creditors of the powerholder of a special power of appointment could somehow reach the appointive property to satisfy debts of the donee: if the powerholder of a special power cannot derive economic benefit from appointive property, why should her creditors be able to do so? That fact might lead to the conclusion that the donee's (powerholder's) creditors cannot reach the property, and that is the rule (Restatement Third, Property, § 22.1). Uniform Act Section 2–505 states: (a) Except as otherwise provided in subsections (b) and (c), appointive property subject to a non-general power of appointment is exempt from a claim of a creditor of the powerholder or the powerholder's estate. The rationale for this rule is that a non-general power of appointment is not an ownership-equivalent power, so the powerholder's creditors have no claim to the appointive assets.

General powers are treated differently consistent with the doctrinal view that a presently exercisable general power of appointment is an ownership-equivalent power. The Uniform Act draws a distinction based upon whether the general power was created by the powerholder or another. If it was created by the powerholder, Sec 2–501 allows the creditor to reach the appointive property until it has been appointed:

(a) Appointive property subject to a general power of appointment created by the powerholder is subject to a claim of a creditor of the powerholder or of the powerholder's estate to the extent provided in [cite state law on fraudulent transfers or the Uniform Fraudulent Transfers Act].

(b) Subject to subsection (b), appointive property subject to a general power of appointment created by the powerholder is not subject to a claim of a creditor of the powerholder or the powerholder's estate to the extent the powerholder irrevocably appointed the property in favor of a person other than the powerholder or the powerholder's estate.

However if the powerholder did not create the power Sec 2–502 applies. It limits the circumstances under which a creditor can reach appointive property:

(a) Except as otherwise provided in subsection (b), appointive property subject to a general power of appointment created by a person other than the powerholder is subject to a claim of a creditor of:

(1) the powerholder, to the extent the powerholder's property is insufficient, if the power is presently exercisable; and the powerholder's estate, to the extent the estate is insufficient, subject to the right of a decedent to direct the source from which liabilities are paid.

(b) Subject to Section 504(c), a power of appointment created by a person other than the powerholder which is subject to an ascertainable standard relating to an individual's health, education, support, or maintenance within the meaning of 26 U.S.C. Section 2041(b)(1)(A) or 26 U.S.C. Section 2514(c)(1), [on the effective date of this [act]][as amended], is treated for purposes of this [article] as a non-general power.

If the powerholder has insufficient assets to cover the claims of creditors, they can reach the appointive property during his lifetime or at death. However, Subsection (b) provides an exception. If the power is subject to an ascertainable standard within the meaning of 26 U.S.C. § 2041(b)(1)(A) or 26 U.S.C. § 2514(c)(1), the power is treated for purposes of this article as a non-general power, and the rights of the powerholder's creditors in the appointive property are governed by Sections 504(a) and (b).

What if the power of appointment is not presently exercisable? Suppose it is subject to a condition precedent to exercise: for example, the appointee must be at least 50 years of age. In that case, creditors cannot reach the appointive property.

Problem 9-2

Mother's will created a testamentary trust limiting property to Bank as trustee to pay the income from the trust property to Mother's Son for his life and on his death to pay the trust property to Son's descendants then living, by representation. The trust contained the following language: "Son shall have the right to withdraw from the principal of the trust once in any calendar year upon thirty (30) days written notice to the Trustee up to four percent (4%) of the market value of the entire trust principal on the date of such notice, which right shall not be cumulative." Son makes two such withdrawals, but makes none after his divorce. After the divorce Son's ex-wife obtains a judgment against Son for $15,000 representing unpaid alimony and interest. Ex-wife presents the judgment to Bank as trustee and demands payment from the trust. At the time ex-wife attempts to levy on the trust, the trust principal is worth $2,000,000. Can ex-wife prevail under the Uniform Act? Under the common law? What should be the answer? (Based on *Irwin Union Bank v. Long*, 312 N.E.2d 908 (1974).)

2. Tax Effects

In a subsequent chapter, estate and gift taxation will be sketched. However, it is worth noting that the sustentative law of powers of appointment is consistent with the tax law definition of a general power: under both sets of rules, if the donor permits the appointee to appoint to himself, his creditors, his estate or the creditors of his estate, she has a general power. The similar definitions should come as no surprise either doctrinally or practically. If the powerholder has the option to appoint the appointive property to oneself, she controls absolutely disposition of property; it is hers. One rarely turns down the opportunity to acquire cash! But even if she appoints the appointive property to another, that course may be conceptualized as an appointment of the property to the appointee with a subsequent gift over to another. As we shall see the substantive law does not accept this view: the appointment to another is said to relate back to the donor. The Uniform Acts treatment of creditors' rights is consistent with the theory that a general power presently exercisable, though not a special power, is tantamount to ownership. Similarly, estate and gift tax law regards property subject to a general power of appointment as owned by the powerholder. When the powerholder dies, the appointive property subject to a general power is part of the powerholder's estate for estate tax purposes whether or not the powerholder exercises the power. On the other hand, property subject to a non-general (special) power of appointment is not taxed in the powerholder's estate for estate tax purposes even if the donee exercises the power.

Consider the following two scenarios.

1. T creates a testamentary trust directing the trustee to pay the trust income to T's daughter D for life and to distribute the trust property on D's death as D shall appoint in her will including her creditors or her estate. D has a general power of appointment. At D's death her probate estate is worth $2,000,000 and the trust property is worth $4,000,000. Assuming that at D's death she did not have any other assets that would be subject to the federal estate tax, her gross taxable estate (before deductions) would be $6,000,000.

2. T creates a testamentary trust directing the trustee to pay the trust income to T's spouse's S for life and to distribute the trust property on S's death as S shall appoint in her will to T's issue. At S's death her probate estate is worth $2,000,000 and the trust property is worth $4,000,000. Assuming that at S's death she did not have any other assets that would be subject to the federal estate tax, her gross taxable estate (before deductions) would be $2,000,000.

Do you see why the outcomes differ?

If the general power is presently exercisable and the powerholder exercises the power to appoint property to someone other than herself, the powerholder has made a transfer which may be a taxable gift. If the powerholder has a non-general (special) power, however, appointing the property to someone other than the donee may have no gift tax effect, depending on the powerholder's other interests in the appointive property. Given these adverse tax consequences, the deliberate creation of general powers of appointment is not common, although there are circumstances in which the existence of a general power of appointment can be part of a plan to reduce taxation. An explanation of those circumstances is beyond the scope of these materials, but if you do study the estate, gift, and generation skipping transfer taxes you will learn a good deal about the role of powers of appointment in tax planning.

Recall also that a power of appointment that is limited by what the estate and gift tax statutes call an *ascertainable standard* is not a general power of appointment even though the powerholder can appoint the appointive property to herself, her estate, her creditors or the creditors of her estate. The regulations promulgated by the Department of the Treasury in connection with the statute define an ascertainable standard as one related to maintenance, education, support or health. As such, the standard limits the powerholder's access to the appointive property, and does not have the uncontrolled access to the appointive property that is the hallmark of a general power of appointment.

Powers limited by an ascertainable standard are usually created in a donee who is also the beneficiary and trustee of a trust.

Problem 9-3

Parent wants to create a trust to benefit his daughter, D, and her family for D's life. At her death the trust will terminate and be distributed to D's descendants then living by representation. Parent wants all the income from the trust to be distributed every year to D and her descendants and her spouse and also wants the trustee to be able to distribute trust principal to the same beneficiaries in the trustee's discretion. Finally, parent wants D to be the trustee. Can parent create a trust with all of these features and insure that the trust property will not be included in D's taxable estate at her death? Hint: is this a general power of appointment?

If D's power as trustee to distribute principal to the beneficiaries, a group which of course includes herself, is limited to distributing principal for the "maintenance, education, support or health" of the beneficiary, it is not a general power of appointment. If the power is not limited by such a standard, however, the trustee-beneficiary, the daughter in this example, has a general power of appointment and when the daughter dies if she is still trustee *all of the trust property will be part of her taxable estate.*

D. Creation of Powers of Appointment

An instrument can only create a power of appointment if, under applicable law, the instrument itself is valid. Thus, for example, a *will* creating a power of appointment must be valid under the law—including choice of law (see Section 103)—applicable to wills. An *inter vivos trust* creating a power of appointment must be valid under the law—including choice of law (see Section 103)—applicable to inter vivos trusts.

The Uniform Act provides:

Section 201. Creation of Power of Appointment

(a)   A power of appointment is created only if:

(1)   the instrument creating the power:

(A)   is valid under applicable law; and

(B)   except as otherwise provided . . . transfers the appointive property; and

(2)   the terms of the instrument creating the power manifest the donor's intent to create in a powerholder a power of appointment over the appointive property exercisable in favor of a permissible appointee.

Note that the act does not prescribe a specific form of words required to create a power of appointment. Careful attorneys, of course, create the powers of appointment their clients want by clearly stating that the appointive property shall be distributed as the powerholder shall appoint. But cases arise in which the express language is ambiguous, and whether a power is created is often is a matter of intent. The following cases are typical.

Matter of Weinstein

444 N.Y.S.2d 427 (Surr. Ct. 1981)

BERNARD M. BLOOM, SURROGATE.

Testatrix died January 1, 1980 leaving a will dated May 10, 1965 which has been probated. The respective litigants join in seeking a construction of article Fourth in which testatrix, after naming a niece to administer a trust of the residuary estate for the purpose of paying testatrix' husband an annuity of $100 per month plus whatever additional sums might be deemed expedient by the trustee, described the final trust purpose as follows:

> 9(c) Upon the death of my said husband, or upon my death if he has not survived me, to pay over the then remaining principal, together with all accumulated income, if any, or my entire residuary estate, as the case may be, to my cousin, JOSEPH L. BARNETT, to be distributed by him, at such time, in such manner and in such amounts, if any, as he alone shall determine, to and among his then living children, the then living children of my brother-in-law, IRVING WEINSTEIN, and of my brother, JOE BARNETT.

Petitioner, the son of Irving Weinstein, instituted this proceeding after Joseph L. Barnett, upon whom the residuary estate had devolved by reason of the predecease of testatrix' husband, announced he would exercise his purported power of appointment by distributing $500 to petitioner, while dividing the $90,000 to $125,000 balance equally among his own three children and the daughter of Joe Barnett.

Take Note

> The question is purely one of law; what do the words of the will mean. Therefore, it's a question of construction.

Petitioner characterizes this disparate treatment of the enumerated transferees as "grossly inequitable"; Joseph L. Barnett counters that it reflects the wishes of the decedent which she had communicated to him privately. The outcome of this proceeding hinges not, however, on the determination of any such question of fact, but rather upon the resolution of a single issue of law, namely, whether article Fourth, paragraph (c) creates a private express trust impressed with fiduciary obligations as urged by petitioner, or, on the other hand, a special, exclusive power of appointment, as contended by Joseph L. Barnett joined by the executrix of the estate.

The court has examined the sources of argument favorable to petitioner which could be most plausibly juxtaposed to respondents' well-articulated and ably-defended position. Prefatory to proceeding to petitioner's most cogent argument, it is first necessary to dispose of his assertion that the language in question creates an express trust in contradistinction to a power of appointment.

Paragraph (c) does not, it is true, contain the word "power" or the word "appointment"; on the other hand, neither does "trust" or any derivative of that term appear therein. Since no particular semantic formula is necessary to create either a trust (*Steinhardt v. Cunningham*, 130 N.Y. 292, 29 N.E. 100 [1891]; *Matter of Grutz*, 203 Misc. 110, 114 N.Y.S.2d 206 [Sur.Ct. Kings Co. 1952] or a power of appointment (*Matter of Thompson*, 274 A.D. 49, 80 N.Y.S.2d 1 [1st Dep't.1948]; *In re Hilliard's Estate*, 86 N.Y.S.2d 158 [Surr.Ct.N.Y.C.1948]), and as both may be created by implication (E.P.T.L. § 10–4.1[a][3]; *Robert v. Corning*, 89 N.Y. 226 [1882]; *Matter of Thompson, supra*; *Matter of Jackson*, 57 Misc.2d 896, 293 N.Y.S.2d 982 [Surr.Ct.N.Y.Co.1968]), we must ascertain the intention of the testatrix as expressed in her will as an entirety (*Matter of Fabbri*, 2 N.Y.2d 236, 159 N.Y.S.2d 184, 140 N.E.2d 269 [1957]), giving its terms their natural and ordinary meaning (*Matter of Gautier*, 3 N.Y.2d 502, 169 N.Y.S.2d 4 [1957]).

In so doing, it is evident from a comparison of the dichotomous language used in paragraphs (a) and (b) of article Fourth, on the one hand, and paragraph (c), on the other, that no trust was intended to be created or continued once Joseph L. Barnett received the funds. In paragraphs (a) and (b), testatrix directed in explicit and unmistakable terms that should she be survived by her husband, the residuum was to be held "in trust" for his benefit. Administration of the trust was committed to "my Trustee" (named in article Sixth) and specific trust duties to hold, manage, invest and reinvest the corpus and to pay the cestui que trust a monthly annuity and such further sums as were deemed expedient were enumerated. Paragraph (c) does set forth a trust duty insofar as it requires the trustee to pay over the rest to Joseph L. Barnett upon the death of the trust beneficiary (or upon testatrix's death if her husband had predeceased her). But there the trust was to end. The failure of testatrix to characterize Barnett as a fiduciary, the want of denomination of the payment over to him as made "in trust" and the lack of ascription of trust purposes and duties, none of which are necessarily determinative in themselves, furnish in the aggregate a marked contrast to the use of customary trust terminology in the paragraphs immediately preceding. Moreover, but for the absence of the word "appoint", the phrasing of the disposition—"to pay over [the corpus] to my cousin, Joseph L. Barnett, to be distributed by him, at such time, in such manner and in such amounts, if any, as he alone shall determine, to and among [described individuals]"—takes one of the classic forms of a special power of appointment. . . . [For the remainder of this opinion see page 486 *below*.]

Matter of Ramdin

11 A.D.3d 698 (N.Y. Ct. App. 2004)

GAIL PRUDENTI, P.J., GABRIEL M. KRAUSMAN, THOMAS A. ADAMS, and ROBERT A. SPOLZINO, JJ.

In a will construction proceeding, Bhanmattie Hulasiya, the executrix of the estate of Sidney Ramdin, appeals, as limited by her brief, from so much of a decree of the Surrogate's Court, Queens County (Nahman, S.), dated February 24, 2003, as denied that branch of her motion which was, in effect, to vacate that portion of a Referee's report (Loukides, R.), dated June 24, 2002, which found that article THIRD (b) of the will was a defective disposition of the decedent's property, and confirmed that portion of the Referee's report.

ORDERED that the decree is reversed insofar as appealed from, on the law, with costs, that branch of the motion which was, in effect, to vacate that portion of the Referee's report which found that article THIRD (b) of the will was a defective disposition of the decedent's property is granted, and that portion of the Referee's report is disaffirmed.

The appellant, Bhanmattie Hulasiya, the decedent's sister, is the executrix of the estate. The petitioners, the decedent's two sons, requested, inter alia, that the Surrogate's Court determine the construction and validity of article THIRD (b) of their father's will, and the Surrogate's Court referred the matter to a Referee to hear and report. Article THIRD (b) provided, in pertinent part:

> "I hereby direct that [an interest in real property] shall be distributed in the absolute joint discretion of my sisters Bhanmattie Hulasiya and Rajmattie Jailall to whomsoever they jointly deem fit to distribute same and that their joint decision shall be unimpecable (sic) for all purposes."

The Referee found in her report that this provision was a defective disposition of the decedent's property, and the Surrogate's Court confirmed the report. The appellant challenges this finding and contends that article THIRD (b) of the will was a valid disposition of the decedent's property. We agree and reverse the decree insofar as appealed from.

The cardinal rule of construction of a will is to carry out the intent of the testator (*see Matter of Walker*, 64 N.Y.2d 354, 486 N.Y.S.2d 899, 476 N.E.2d 298; *Matter of Fabbri*, 140 N.E.2d 269; *Matter of Sprinchorn*, 151 A.D.2d 27; *Matter of Bellows*, 103 A.D.2d 594, *affd.* 483 N.E.2d 130. All rules of interpretation are subordinated to the requirement that the actual purpose of the testator is sought and effectuated as far as is consonant with principles of law and public policy (*see Matter of Fabbri, supra* at 239–240, 140 N.E.2d 269). "Intent is not to be gleaned by focusing upon any one particular word, sentence or provision; rather, it must be ascertained from a perusal of the entire will by a reader mindful of the particular facts and circumstances under which the provisions of the instrument were framed" (*Matter of Bellows, supra* at 597,

480 N.Y.S.2d 925; *see Matter of Carmer*, 71 N.Y.2d 781, 525 N.E.2d 734; *Matter of Thall*, N.E.2d 397).

It is clear from the language of the will, when read in conjunction with the deposition testimony of the drafter, that the deceased, as donor, intended to give his sisters, as donees, absolute control over the appointive property. Such an absolute grant of power created a general power of appointment (*see Manion v. Peoples Bank of Johnstown*, 55 N.E.2d 46; *see also* EPTL 10–3.2[b]). "The effect of conferring [such power] is to invest its doneee with a power of disposition as broad as though she was disposing of her own property" (*Isham v. New York Assn. for Improving the Condition of the Poor*, 223, 69 N.E. 367). Accordingly, there is no basis for finding the power invalid due to the deceased's decision not to identify a particular appointee (*cf. Tilden v. Green*, 28 N.E. 880; *Read v. Williams*, 26 N.E. 730).

Make the Connection

The case is about construction of the words of the will, but note that the court takes into account extrinsic evidence without any discussion of what sort of ambiguity is involved.

Points for Discussion

1. Do you think that both cases come to the correct results? In other words, did both testators intend to create powers of appointment?

2. The absence of fiduciary duties is critical to the creation of a power of appointment. A fiduciary is bound by duties to the beneficiaries of the property which the fiduciary controls; the powerholder is not. The very essence of being an executor, administrator or trustee is the existence of fiduciary duties owed to the beneficiaries of the estate or trust. The powerholder of a power of appointment owes nothing (no binding obligation under the law of trusts) to the persons to whom the property can be appointed. This means, of course, that when the trustee of the trust over which the powerholder has the power of appointment distributes the appointive property all the trustee has to confirm is that the power was properly exercised. The trustee's duty is to follow the powerholder's instructions in exercising the power. And of course the powerholder of a non-general power of appointment must appoint the property to the permissible appointees articulated by the donor in the instrument which created the power. Does this mean that the powerholder of any power of appointment can dispose of the appointive property with the same freedom as can an outright owner?

E. Exercise of Powers of Appointment

In the exercise of most powers of appointment, there is usually no question whether or not a powerholder has properly exercised it. A presently exercisable power (one not subject to a condition precedent before the powerholder can exercise it) must be exercised by a writing. An instrument purporting to exercise a power of appointment must be a valid one. Thus for a will to exercise a power it must conform to the formalities of due execution in the jurisdiction in which it was executed. An *inter vivos trust* created by an powerholder which purports to exercise a power of appointment must be properly executed in accordance with the law of the jurisdiction in which the trust is created.

The Uniform Act mandates:

Section 301. Requisites for Exercise of Power of Appointment

A power of appointment is exercised only:

(1)   if the instrument exercising the power is valid under applicable law;

(2)   if the terms of the instrument exercising the power:

(A)   manifest the powerholder's intent to exercise the power; and

(B)   subject to Section 304, satisfy the requirements of exercise, if any, imposed by the donor; and

(3)   to the extent the appointment is a permissible exercise of the power.

Issues arise when the purported exercise does not specifically mention the power. The Comment to the above section addresses this issue:

Paragraph (2) requires the terms of the instrument exercising the power of appointment to manifest the powerholder's intent to exercise the power of appointment. Whether a powerholder has manifested an intent to exercise a power of appointment is a question of construction. See generally Restatement Third of Property: Wills and Other Donative Transfers § 19.2. For example, a powerholder's disposition of appointive property may manifest an intent to exercise the power even though the powerholder does not refer to the power. See Restatement Third of Property: Wills and Other Donative Transfers § 19.3. Paragraph (2) also requires that the terms of the instrument exercising the power must, subject to Section 304, satisfy the requirements of exercise, if any, imposed by the donor.

Language expressing an intent to exercise a power is clearest if it makes a specific reference to the creating instrument and exercises the power in unequivocal terms and with careful attention to the requirements of exercise, if any, imposed by the donor.

The recommended method for exercising a power of appointment is by a specific-exercise clause, using language such as the following: "I exercise the power of appointment conferred upon me by [my father's will] as follows: I appoint [fill in details of appointment]."

Not recommended is a blanket-exercise clause, which purports to exercise "any" power of appointment the powerholder may have, using language such as the following: "I exercise any power of appointment I may have as follows: I appoint [fill in details of appointment]." Although a blanket-exercise clause does manifest an intent to exercise any power of appointment the powerholder may have, such a clause raises the often-litigated question of whether it satisfies the requirement of specific reference imposed by the donor in the instrument creating the power.

The issue of exercise most frequently arises with respect to testamentary powers. The preferred mode of exercising a power is by employing express language that refers to the power, and exercises it in unequivocal terms according to the mandate on exercise imposed by the donor in the instrument which created the power.

The Comment to Section 301 notes:

"The recommended method for exercising a power of appointment is by a specific-exercise clause, using language such as the following: "I exercise the power of appointment conferred upon me by [my father's will] as follows: I appoint [fill in details of appointment]."

Not all powerholders are so punctilious. Suppose powerholder has the following clause in her will: "All the residue of my estate, including the property over which I have a power of appointment under my mother's will, I devise as follows . . ." This so-called blending clause purports to blend the appointive property with the powerholder's own property in a common disposition. It should be deemed to exercise the power.

But suppose the residuary clause does not include even the vague mention of the power in the previous example: "All the residue of my estate I devise as follows" does the residuary (which the Uniform Act refers to as a garden-variety residuary clause) exercise the power? At common law, the residuary clause in the powerholder's will was deemed to exercise the power even if it made no reference to the power if the power was general. Why was that? Think about the "property law" formulation of the power. Because the powerholder of a general power of appointment is regarded as the owner of the appointive property, the testamentary disposition of "all" of the appointee's property should also dispose of property subject to a general power of appointment. The Uniform Act narrows the circumstances in which a general power is exercised by the residuary:

Section 302. Intent to Exercise: Determining Intent from Residuary Clause

(b)   A residuary clause in a powerholder's will, or a comparable clause in the powerholder's revocable trust, manifests the powerholder's intent to exercise a power of appointment only if:

(1)   the terms of the instrument containing the residuary clause do not manifest a contrary intent;

(2)   the power is a general power exercisable in favor of the powerholder's estate;

(3)   there is no gift-in-default clause or the clause is ineffective; and

(4)   the powerholder did not release the power.[2]

Under Section 302, then, a residuary clause in the powerholder's will is treated as manifesting an intent to exercise a general power in limited circumstances if the instrument creating the power permits exercise through the appointee's estate: *not* if the powerholder specifically excludes the exercise of the general power; *not* if there is a taker in default; or *not* if the powerholder released the power.

Given the fact the exercise follows the "property law" characterization, how should non-general powers be treated? The Comment to Section 301 makes clear that:

> Under no circumstance does a residuary clause manifest an intent to exercise a non-general power. A residuary clause disposes of the powerholder's own property, and a non-general power is not an ownership-equivalent power. Similarly, a residuary clause does not manifest an intent to exercise a general power which is general only because it is exercisable in favor of the creditors of the powerholder or the creditors of the powerholder's estate. The rule of this section is consistent with, and this Comment draws on, Restatement Third of Property: Wills and Other Donative Transfers § 19.4 and the accompanying Commentary.

This position is broadly in accord with UPC § 2–608 which allows a general residuary clause to exercise a power of appointment if it is a general power of appointment and there are no takers in default or if the will manifests an intention to include the appointive property. The Comment to § 2–608 gives as an illustration of the manifestation of an intention to include appointive property in a residuary clause which refers to all of the rest of the testator's estate "including any property over which I have a power of appointment." The Restatement makes it clear that the residuary clause need not mention powers of appointment at all, that is, it conforms to the traditional common law rule and gives as an example of a residuary clause that can exercise a general power the following: "All of my estate, I devise to . . . ." (Restatement Third, Property (Wills and Donative Transfers) § 19.4, comment *a*). But the Restatement then echoes the UPC by going on to state that the residuary clause will exercise a general power only if there are no takers in default.) (*Id.*)

The Uniform Act Section 304 allows the donor to impose specific requirements for the exercise of the power to be valid. For example, the donor of the power can dictate that the powerholder exercise the power by a specific reference to the power. The Comment to the Uniform Act notes that whether the powerholder complied with those requirements should be assessed with respect to their purpose:

---

2   The Uniform Act 402 permits releases under the following limitation: A powerholder may release a power of appointment, in whole or in part, except to the extent the terms of the instrument creating the power prevent the release.—Eds.

Whenever the donor imposes formal requirements with respect to the instrument of appointment that exceed the requirements imposed by law, the donor's purpose in imposing the additional requirements is relevant to whether the powerholder's attempted exercise satisfies the rule of this section. To the extent the powerholder's failure to comply with the additional requirements will not impair the accomplishment of a material purpose of the donor, the powerholder's attempted appointment in a manner that substantially complies with a donor-imposed requirement does not fail for lack of perfect compliance with that requirement.

What is the result if the residuary purports to exercise the power but is special and some of the residuary beneficiaries are not permissible appointees. The inclusion of impermissible appointees does not give rise to a "necessary implication" that the powerholder did not intend to exercise the power. Indeed, the necessary implication must be truly necessary in the sense of inevitable or unable to be avoided. Nor does the fact that the donee was a domiciliary of a state whose law does not allow a residuary clause to exercise a special power give rise to the necessary implication. For example, in *Matter of Block*, 157 Misc.2d 716, 598 N.Y.S.2d 668 (Sur. Ct. New York Co. 1993) the Surrogate held that the residuary clause of the will of a domiciliary of Ohio, whose law does not allow the exercise of a special power of appointment by a general residuary clause, exercised a special power of appointment over a trust governed by New York law. The residuary clause gave the testator's residuary estate to trusts for his three sons, only two of whom were permissible appointees. The appointive property passed in equal shares to the trusts for the sons who were permissible appointees.

Matter of Block illustrates another problem that sometimes arises when courts face questions of exercise of powers of appointment by will: are questions raised by the purported exercise of the power governed by the law that governs the trust which is subject to the power of appointment or the law of the state of domicile of the donee? The following case explores these interrelated questions.

Beals v. State Street Bank and Trust Co.

326 N.E.2d 896 (Mass. 1975)

WILKINS, JUSTICE.

The trustees under the will of Arthur Hunnewell filed this petition for instructions, seeking a determination of the proper distribution to be made of a portion of the trust created under the residuary clause of his will. A judge of the Probate Court reserved decision and reported the case to the Appeals Court on the pleadings and a stipulation of facts. We transferred the case here.

Arthur Hunnewell died, a resident of Wellesley, in 1904, leaving his wife and four daughters. His will placed the residue of his property in a trust, the income of which was to be paid to his wife during her life. At the death of his wife the trust was to be divided in portions, one for each then surviving daughter and one for the then surviving issue of any deceased daughter. Mrs. Hunnewell died in 1930. One of the four daughters predeceased her mother, leaving no issue. The trust was divided, therefore, in three portions at the death of Mrs. Hunnewell. The will directed that the income of each portion held for a surviving daughter should be paid to her during her life and on her death the principal of such portion should 'be paid and disposed of as she may direct and appoint by her last Will and Testament duly probated.' In default of appointment, the will directed that a daughter's share should be distributed to 'the persons who would be entitled to such estate under the laws then governing the distribution of intestate estates.'

This petition concerns the distribution of the trust portion held for the testator's daughter Isabella H. Hunnewell, later Isabella H. Dexter (Isabella). Following the death of her mother, Isabella requested the trustees to exercise their discretionary power to make principal payments by transferring substantially all of her trust share 'to the Dexter family office in Boston, there to be managed in the first instance by her husband, Mr. Gordon Dexter.' This request was granted, and cash and securities were transferred to her account at the Dexter office. The Hunnewell trustees, however, retained in Isabella's share a relatively small cash balance, an undivided one-third interest in a mortgage and undivided one-third interest in various parcels of real estate in the Commonwealth, which Isabella did not want in kind and which the trustees could not sell at a reasonable price at the time. Thereafter, the trustees received payments on the mortgage and proceeds from occasional sales of portions of the real estate. From her one-third share of these receipts, the trustees made further distributions to her of $1,900 in 1937, $22,000 in 1952, and $5,000 in 1953.

In February, 1944, Isabella, who was then a resident of New York, executed and caused to be filed in the Registry of Probate for Norfolk County an instrument which partially released her general power of appointment under the will of her father. See G.L. c. 204, ss 27–36, inserted by St.1943, c. 152. Isabella released her power of appointment 'to the extent that such power empowers me to appoint to any one other than one or more of the . . . descendants me surviving of Arthur Hunnewell.'

Make the Connection

The release turned what was a general power of appointment into a special power thus avoiding estate tax on the trust property. The release was occasioned by a change in the estate tax law that made all general powers of appointment taxable.

On December 14, 1968, Isabella, who survived her husband, died without issue, still a resident of New York, leaving a will dated May 21, 1965. Her share in the trust under her father's will then consisted of an interest in a contract to sell real estate, cash, notes and a certificate of deposit, and was valued at approximately $88,000. Isabella did not expressly exercise her power of appointment under her father's will. The residuary clause of her will provided in effect for the distribution of all 'the rest, residue and remainder of my property' to the issue per stirpes of her sister Margaret Blake, who had predeceased Isabella.[1] The Blake issue would take one-half of Isabella's trust share, as takers in default of appointment, in all events. If, however, Isabella's will should be treated as effectively exercising her power of appointment under her father's will, the Blake issue would take the entire trust share, and the executors of the will of Isabella's sister Jane (who survived Isabella and has since died) would not receive that one-half of the trust share which would go to Jane in default of appointment.[2]

In support of their argument that Isabella's will did not exercise the power of appointment under her father's will, the executors of Jane's estate contend that (1) Massachusetts substantive law governs all questions relating to the power of appointment, including the interpretation of Isabella's will; (2) the power should be treated as a special power of appointment because of its partial release by Isabella; and (3) because Isabella's will neither expresses nor implies any intention to exercise the power, the applicable rule of construction in this Commonwealth is that a general residuary clause does not exercise a special power of appointment. The Blake issue, in support of their argument that the power was exercised, contend that (1) Isabella's will manifests an intention to exercise the power and that no rule of construction need be applied; (2) the law of New York should govern the question whether Isabella's will exercised the power and, if it does, by statute New York has adopted a rule that a special power of appointment is exercised by a testamentary disposition of all of the donee's property; and (3) if Massachusetts law does apply, and the will is silent on the subject of the exercise of the power, the principles underlying our rule of construction that a residuary clause exercises a general power of appointment are applicable in these circumstances.

1. We turn first to a consideration of the question whether Isabella's will should be construed according to the law of this Commonwealth or the law of New York. There are strong, logical reasons for turning to the law of the donee's domicile at the time of death to determine whether a donee's will has exercised a testamentary power of appointment over movables. Most courts in this country which have considered the question, however, interpret the donee's will under the law governing the administration of the trust, which is usually the law of the donor's domicile.

If the question were before us now for the first time, we might well adopt a choice of law rule

> **Food for Thought**
>
> The court seems to decide against its better judgment in the interest of consistency. Is that a good reason not to do the right thing?

---

1   The significant portion of the residuary clause reads as follows: 'All the rest, residue and remainder of my property of whatever kind and wherever situated (including any property not effectively disposed of by the preceding provisions of this my will and all property over which I have or may have the power of appointment under or by virtue of the last will and testament dated November 27, 1933 and codicils thereto dated January 7, 1935 and January 8, 1935 of my husband, the late Gordon Dexter) . . . I give, devise, bequeath and appoint in equal shares to such of my said nephew GEORGE BATY BLAKE and my said nieces MARGARET CABOT and JULIA O. BEALS as shall survive me and the issue who shall survive me of any of my said nephew or nieces who may predecease me, such issue to take per stirpes.'

2   The parties agree that in these circumstances the intestate recipients, and the proportion due to each, are the same under the laws governing the distribution of intestate estates in Massachusetts and New York.

which would turn to the substantive law of the donee's domicile, for the purpose of determining whether the donee's will exercised a power of appointment. However, in a field where much depends on certainty and consistency as to the applicable rules of law, we think that we should adhere to our well established rule. Thus, in interpreting the will of a donee to determine whether a power of appointment was exercised, we apply the substantive law of the jurisdiction whose law governs the administration of the trust.

2. Considering the arguments of the parties, we conclude that there is no indication in Isabella's will of an intention to exercise or not to exercise the power of appointment given to her under her father's will. A detailed analysis of the various competing contentions would not add to our jurisprudence.[6] In the absence of an intention disclosed by her will construed in light of circumstances known to her when she executed it, we must adopt some Massachusetts rule of construction to resolve the issue before us. The question is what rule of construction. We are unaware of any decided case which, in this context, has dealt with a testamentary general power, reduced to a special power by action of the donee.

3. We conclude that the residuary clause of Isabella's will should be presumed to have exercised the power of appointment. We reach this result by a consideration of the reasons underlying the canons of construction applicable to general and special testamentary powers of appointment. Considered in this way, we believe that a presumption of exercise is more appropriate in the circumstances of this case than a presumption of nonexercise.

When this court first decided not to extend to a special power of appointment the rule of construction that a general residuary clause executes a general testamentary power (unless a contrary intent is shown by the will), we noted significant distinctions between a general power and a special power. Fiduciary Trust Co. v. First Natl. Bank, supra, 344 Mass. at 6–10, 181 N.E.2d 6. A general power was said to be a close approximation to a property interest, a 'virtually unlimited power of disposition' (9), while a special power of appointment lacked this quality (10). We observed that a layman having a general testamentary power over property might not be expected to distinguish between the appointive property and that which he owns outright, and thus 'he can reasonably be presumed to regard this appointive property as his own' (9). On the other hand, the donee of a special power would not reasonably regard such appointive property as his own: '(h)e would more likely consider himself to be, as the donor of the power intended, merely the person chosen by the donor to decide who of the possible appointees should share in the property (if the power is exclusive), and the respective shares of the appointees' (10).

Food for Thought

If the trust had not allowed the trustee to distribute the trust property to Isabella, would this case be decided in the same way?

Considering the power of appointment given to

---

6 Clearly Isabella had only a special power of appointment after she partially released the general power given to her under her father's will. See Jeffers Estate, 394 Pa. 393, 398–399, 147 A.2d 402 (1959); Mearkle Estate, 23 Pa.D. & C.2d 661, 665 (1960). And, of course, if she had totally released the power of appointment, her will could have had no effect on the devolution of 'her' portion of the trust under her father's will.

Isabella and her treatment of that power during her life, the rationale for the canon of construction applicable to general powers of appointment should be applied in this case. This power was a general testamentary power at its inception. During her life, as a result of her request, Isabella had the use and enjoyment of the major portion of the property initially placed in her trust share. Prior use and enjoyment of the appointive property is a factor properly considered as weighing in favor of the exercise of a power of appointment by a will. Fiduciary Trust Co. v. First Natl. Bank, supra, at 10, 181 N.E.2d 6. Isabella voluntarily limited the power by selecting the possible appointees. In thus relinquishing the right to add the trust assets to her estate, she was treating the property as her own. Moreover, the gift under her residuary clause was consistent with the terms of the reduced power which she retained. In these circumstances, the partial release of a general power does not obviate the application of that rule of construction which presumes that a general residuary clause exercises a general power of appointment.

4. A decree shall be entered determining that Isabella H. Dexter did exercise the power of appointment, partially released by an instrument dated February 25, 1944, given to her by art. Fourth of the will of Arthur Hunnewell and directing that the trustees under the will of Arthur Hunnewell pay over the portion of the trust held under art. Fourth of his will for the benefit of Isabella H. Dexter, as follows: one-third each to George Baty Blake and Julia O. Beals; and one-sixth each to Margaret B. Elwell and to the estate of George B. Cabot. The parties shall be allowed their costs and counsel fees in the discretion of the probate court.

So ordered.

QUIRICO, JUSTICE (with whom TAURO, CHIEF JUSTICE, joins), concurring in the result.

I concur in the court's conclusion that the general residuary clause in the will of Isabella H. Dexter exercised the power of appointment given to her by art. Fourth of the will of Arthur Hunnewell. However, I would reach that result without regard to whether the power of appointment was, either when it was created or when it was exercised, a general power of appointment or a special power of appointment, and without perpetuating the distinction made between the two types of powers in our decision in Fiduciary Trust Co. v. First Natl. Bank, 181 N.E.2d 6–8 (1962). I would hold that the 'settled canon of construction that a general residuary clause will operate as an execution of a general testamentary power unless a contrary intent is shown by the will' (Fiduciary Trust Co. case, 5, 181 N.E.2d), quoting from Second Bank-State St. Trust Co. v. Yale Univ. Alumni Fund, 156 N.E.2d 57 (1959), which has been a part of the case law of this Commonwealth at least since our decision in Amory v. Meredith, 7 Allen 397 (1863), applies equally to the execution of a special power of appointment, provided, of course, that (a) the residuary clause includes any beneficiary within the scope of the special power of appointment, (b) the instrument creating the special power does not prohibit its exercise by a general residuary clause, and (c) the residuary clause includes no disclaimer of intent to exercise the special power.

It is with reluctance that I advocate a departure from the holding in the Fiduciary Trust Co. case which was decided in 1962 by a quorum of distinguished Justices of this court, but I am persuaded to do so by the policy considerations discussed below. The Fiduciary Trust Co. case itself represented a departure from views expressed, by way of dicta, in several cases which preceded it. In Stone v. Forbes, 75 N.E. 141, 143 (1905), we said: 'If it were necessary to determine the question we should hesitate to follow the . . . (distinction drawn in the English cases between the exercise of general and special powers by a residuary clause). There is certainly less reason for doing so since Amory v. Meredith than before. There would seem to be no good reason why the question whether a special power of appointment had been exercised should not be determined by the same rules that are applied in other cases to the construction or interpretation of wills.' In several other cases the opportunity to rule that a general residuary clause does not ordinarily exercise a special power of appointment was also declined. Worcester Bank & Trust Co. v. Sibley, 192 N.E. 31 (1934); Pitman v. Pitman, 50 N.E.2d 69 (1943). Frye v. Loring, 113 N.E.2d 595 (1953). In the last cited case we referred to Am.Law of Property, s 23.40(a) (1952). That source provides: 'The reasoning supporting the Massachusetts presumption that a residuary clause was intended to exercise powers of appointment applies with equal force whether the power in question is general or special.'

The basic judicial objective in this and similar cases is to ascertain the testamentary intent of the donee of the power. I am unable to accept the proposition that a testator who subscribes to a will which includes a residuary clause in substantially the common form, broadly covering 'all the rest, residue and remainder of my property' does not thereby express quite clearly an intention to dispose of all of the property and estate which can be the subject of testamentary disposition by him. Neither am I able to accept the proposition that such language, reasonably construed, permits any inference that the testator intended, by the use of such broad language, to exercise a general power of appointment but not a special one.

In its decision in the Amory case, supra, from which there evolved the 'settled canon of construction that a general residuary clause will operate as an execution of a general testamentary power unless a contrary intent is shown by the will,' this court first reviewed the development of the law of England on this subject. It cited several English cases which had held that a will would not operate to execute a power of appointment unless it referred expressly to the power or to the subject of the power, and that 'a mere residuary clause gave no sufficient indication of intention to execute a power' (399). This court then noted criticism of the English rule, particularly because of its emphasis on the distinction between 'power' and 'property,' stating that 'the refinements and subtleties to which this distinction leads are great and perplexing' (398). It then noted that the rule was changed by a statute (St. 7 Will. IV and 1 Vict. c. 26, s 27) [1837], declaring 'that a general devise of real or personal estate, in wills thereafter made, should operate as an execution of a power of the testator over the same, unless a contrary intention should appear on the will'; and then quoted the comment of Judge Story (1 Story R. 458, note), to the effect that as a result of the statute, '(t)he doctrine, therefore, has at last settled down in that country (England) to what would seem to be the dictate of common sense, unaffected by technical niceties' (400). For further discussions and citations of cases on the development of the law on this subject in England and in this country, see Restatement: Property, s 343(1), comment *d* (1940); Am.Law of Property, s 23.40 (1952); 104 Trusts and

Estates 814 (1965); 51 Cornell L.Q. 1, 9–10 (1965); 16 A.L.R.3d 911, 920–924 (1967); 62 Am.Jur.2d, Powers, ss 51–52 (1972).

It is apparent that in the case of Fiduciary Trust Co. v. First Natl. Bank, 344 Mass. 1, 181 N.E.2d 6 (1962), the court distinguished general powers and special powers in part on the basis of the distinction between powers and property.[1] The latter is the same distinction of which this court said in the Amory case, supra: '(T)he refinements and subtleties to which this distinction leads are great and perplexing' (7 Allen 398). Indeed, the case now before us represents one of the perplexities resulting from a rule based on such a distinction. These unnecessary 'refinements and subtleties' inevitably breed litigation initiated either by competing claimants or by a fiduciary, often a professional fiduciary, seeking to avoid or minimize the risk of liability to himself by obtaining the protection of a judicial declaration, usually at considerable expense to the intended beneficiaries. We should, if possible, develop and apply rules of law which will eliminate the occasion for such litigation. One stop in that direction would be to hold that a general residuary clause in a will is equally competent to execute a special power of appointment as it is to exercise a general power. See Bostwick & Hurstel, ___ Mass. ___, 304 N.E.2d 186 (1973).

> **Food for Thought**
>
> Are you as confident as Justice Quirico that the New York rule reduces litigation? Should the reduction of litigation be a goal when courts "develop and apply" rules of law?

Points for Discussion

1. Choice of law

The choice of law problem in *Beals* is not uncommon and is probably becoming more so given the mobility of the population. The likelihood that the powerholder will live in a state other than the state whose law governs the trust over which the powerholder has a power of appointment is probably greater than it has ever been. Remember that the trust in *Beals* was a testamentary trust created by the will of Isabella Hunnewell's father and under the traditional rule was governed by the law of Massachusetts where the will was admitted to probate. The arguments against the traditional rule, although they do not move the Massachusetts court have won over the ALI: Restatement Third Property § 19.1 comment *e* states "In the absence of a provision in the instrument creating the power, the law of the donee's (powerholder's)

---

1   The court said, 344 Mass. at 9, 181 N.E.2d at 11: 'We think that, unlike a general power, a special power is not 'a close approximation to a property interest . . .'. It is our opinion that the traditional common law distinction between 'property' and 'powers' . . . which with regard to general powers has in effect been overridden in cases cited above, persists with undiminished validity in the case of special powers and would alone serve as a sufficiently sound rationale for the nonapplicability of the canon in question to special powers.'

domicile governs whether the donee has effectively exercised a power of appointment," and cites Restatement Second, Conflict of Laws § 275 comment *c* in support.

Conflicts is a notoriously complex area of law and the complexities that can arise when powers of appointment are involved are well illustrated by *Matter of Chappell*, 25 Misc.3d 704, 883 N.Y.S.2d 857 (Sur. Ct. New York Co. 2009) which involved the question of whether the will of a Connecticut domiciliary exercised powers of appointment over three lifetime trusts created by a Connecticut domiciliary. Each trust had a provision stating that the trust was to be governed by New York law. The Surrogate held that New York law would indeed apply, but that "New York law" included New York's choice of law rules under which Connecticut law would apply; Connecticut was the state with the "paramount interest" in the matter because the creator of the trusts who was the donor of the power of appointment, the donee, and all but one of the potential takers were residents of Connecticut.

2. Taxation again

Beals also reminds us how important taxation is to the law of powers of appointment. In 1944 Isabella Dexter partially released her general power of appointment turning it into a special power because of a major change in the federal estate and gift tax law. Until 1942 property subject to a general power of appointment was taxed in the estate of the donee only if the donee exercised the power. When Congress changed the law so that property subject to a general power of appointment is included in the taxable estate of the donee (powerholder) whether or not the power is exercised by the donee, it also gave donees (powerholders) a break. The legislation changing the rule for taxation of property subject to a general power included a provision providing that if state law allowed, the donee of a general power could partially release the power and turn it into a special power and the transformation would be effective for estate tax purposes. A donee (powerholder) releases a general power of appointment by giving up either completely or partially the ability to appoint it to herself, her estate, or her creditors. In response to Congress's invitation, all of the states passed legislation allowing donees (powerholders) of general powers of appointment to release the power. Many donees of general powers of appointment, including Isabella Dexter, took advantage of the opportunity to partially release their general powers of appointment and turn them into special powers of appointment.

3. To exercise or not to exercise by residuary clause

After the decision in *Beals*, the Massachusetts legislature provided a statutory rule governing exercise of a power of appointment by a residuary clause: Mass. Gen. Laws Ann. ch. 191 § 1A(4): "4. No general residuary clause in a will and no will making general disposition of all of the testator's property shall exercise a power of appointment created by another instrument which does not specify a specific method of exercise unless reference is made to powers of appointment or there is some other indication of intention to exercise the power." This is actually the majority rule in the United States and the Restatement/UPC position allowing the residuary clause to exercise a general power of appointment is the minority position and New York's law allowing the residuary clause to exercise both types of powers of appointment is a minority of a minority. Which rule is better? And no matter what the rule should be, the variety of rules makes it truly imperative that every power of appointment include takers in default.

Beals voluntarily chose to release her general power and thereby created a non-general power. Presumably she did so without consideration. Suppose, however, the appointee bargains with another to exercise a power in their favor. Assume that Professor Grouchfield is the (powerholder) of a non-general power of appointment in which he can appoint to the issue of his siblings. He is, of course not a permissible appointee. But suppose he agrees with his niece Andrea to appoint the appointive property to her in return for a payment of $50,000. Is this promise binding? Suppose, they agree, he appoints and she reneges? Can he bring an action to unforce the promise? Suppose it is a testamentary power and she pays him in advance. He dies and appoints the appointive property to "the issue of my siblings, share and share alike." Does Andrea have recourse?

Consider the following case.

Seidel v. Werner

81 Misc.2d 220 (N.Y. Supreme Ct. 1975)

Plaintiffs, trustees of a trust established in 1919 by Abraham L. Werner, sue for a declaratory judgment to determine who is entitled to one half of the principal of the trust fund—the share in which Steven L. Werner, decedent (hereinafter "Steven"), was the life beneficiary and over which he had a testamentary power of appointment. The dispute concerns the manner in which Steven exercised his power of appointment and is between Steven's second wife, Harriet G. Werner (hereinafter "Harriet"), along with their children, Anna G. and Frank S. Werner (hereinafter "Anna" and "Frank") and Steven's third wife, Edith Fisch Werner (hereinafter "Edith").

Anna and Frank claim Steven's entire share of the trust remainder on the basis of a Mexican consent judgment of divorce, obtained by Steven against Harriet on December 9, 1963, which incorporated by reference and approved a separation agreement, entered into between Steven and Harriet on December 1, 1963. That agreement included the following provision: "10. The Husband shall make, and hereby promises not to revoke, a will in which he shall exercise his testamentary power of appointment over his share in a trust known as 'Abraham L. Werner Trust No. 1' by establishing with respect to said share a trust for the benefit of the aforesaid Children, for the same purposes and under the same terms and conditions, as the trust provided for in Paragraph '9' of this Agreement, insofar as said terms and conditions are applicable thereto."

Make the Connection

Is this a contract to exercise the power in the future (if so, what is the consideration?) or is it simply a present exercise?

Paragraph 9 in relevant part provides for the wife to receive the income of the trust, upon the death of the husband, for the support and maintenance of the children, until they reach 21 years of age, at which time they are to receive the principal in equal shares.

On March 20, 1964, less than four months after entry of the divorce judgment, Steven executed a will in which, instead of exercising his testamentary power of appointment in favor of Anna and Frank, he left everything to his third wife, Edith: "First, I give, devise and bequeath all of my property * * * including * * * all property over which I have a power of testamentary disposition, to my wife, EDITH FISCH WERNER."

Steven died in April, 1971 and his will was admitted to probate by the Surrogate's Court of New York County on July 11, 1973.

(1) Paragraph 10 of the separation agreement is a contract to exercise a testamentary power of appointment not presently exercisable (EPTL 10–3.3) and as such is invalid under EPTL 10–5.3, which provides as follows: "(a) The donee of a power of appointment which is not presently exercisable, or of a postponed power which has not become exercisable, cannot contract to make an appointment. Such a contract, if made cannot be the basis of an action for specific performance or damages, but the promisee can obtain restitution of the value given by him for the promise unless the donee has exercised the power pursuant to the contract."

This is a testamentary power of appointment. The original trust instrument provided in relevant part that: "Upon the death of such child [Steven] the principal of such share shall be disposed of as such child shall by its last will direct, and in default of such testamentary disposition then the same shall go to the issue of such child then surviving per stirpes".

It is not disputed that New York law is determinative of the validity of paragraph 10 of the separation agreement; the separation agreement itself provides that New York law shall govern.

The reasoning underlying the refusal to enforce a contract to exercise a testamentary power was stated by Judge Cardozo in the case of *Farmers' Loan and Trust Co. v Mortimer* (219 N.Y. 290, 293–294): "The exercise of the power was to represent the final judgment, the last will, of the donee. Up to the last moment of his life he was to have the power to deal with the share as he thought best * * * To permit him to bargain that right away would be to defeat the purpose of the donor. Her command was that her property should go to her son's issue unless at the end of his life it remained his will that it go elsewhere. It has not remained his will that it go elsewhere; and his earlier contract cannot nullify the expression of his final purpose. 'It is not, I apprehend, to be doubted,' says Rolt, L. J., in *Cooper v Martin* (LR [3 Ch App] 47, 58) 'that equity * * * will never uphold an act which will defeat what the person creating the power has

> **Food for Thought**
>
> Justice Cardozo explains why a donor might create a testamentary power. So to contract away the power during the powerholder's life was contrary to donor's intent. But could donee bargain with a permissible object at the time he writes his last will? What matters here: timing of appointment or the manner in which the appointee deals with the appointive property? Suppose his power was general? Would the case come out the same way?

declared, by expression or necessary implication, to be a material part of his intention.' " (See also, *Matter of Brown*, 33 N.Y.2d 211.)

* * *

(3) As indicated, the statute makes a promise to exercise a testamentary power in a particular way unenforceable. However, EPTL 10–5.3 (subd [b]) permits a donee of a power to release the power, and that release, if in conformity with EPTL 10–9.2, prevents the donee from then exercising the power thereafter.

Under the terms of the trust instrument, if Steven fails to exercise his power of appointment, Anna and Frank (along with the children of Steven's first marriage) take the remainder, i.e., the property which is the subject of Steven's power of appointment. Therefore, Harriet, Anna and Frank argue that at a minimum Steven's agreement should be construed as a release of his power of appointment, and that Anna and Frank should be permitted to take as on default of appointment.

There is respectable authority—by no means unanimous authority, and none binding on this court—to the effect that a promise to appoint a given sum to persons who would take in default of appointment should, *to that extent*, be deemed a release of the power of appointment. (See Restatement, Property, § 336 [1940]; Simes and Smith, Law of Future Interests, § 1016 [1956].)

This argument has the appeal that it seems to be consistent with the exception that the release statute EPTL 10–5.3 (subd [b]) carves out of EPTL 10–5.3 (subd [a]); and is also consistent with the intentions and reasonable expectations of the parties at the time they entered into the agreement to appoint, here in the separation agreement; and that therefore perhaps in these circumstances the difference between what the parties agreed to and a release of the power of appointment is merely one of form. Whatever may be the possible validity or applicability of this argument to other circumstances and situations, I think it is inapplicable to this situation because:

(a) It is clear that the parties did not intend a release of the power of appointment. (Cf. *Matter of Haskell*, 59 Misc 2d 797.) Indeed, the agreement—unlike a release of a power of appointment—expressly contemplates that something will be done by the donee of the power in the future, and that that something will be an exercise of the power of appointment. Thus, the agreement, in the very language said to be a release of the power of appointment, says (par 10, *supra*): "The Husband *shall* make * * * a will in which he *shall exercise* his testamentary power of appointment." (Emphasis added.)

(b) Nor is the substantial effect of the promised exercise of the power the same as would follow from release of, or failure to exercise the power.

(i) Under the separation agreement, the power is to be exercised so that the entire appointive property shall be for the benefit of Anna and Frank; under the trust instrument, on default of exercise of the power, the property goes to all of Steven's children (Anna, Frank and the two children of Steven's first marriage). Thus the agreement provides for appointment of a greater principal to Anna and Frank than they would get in default of appointment.

(ii) Under the trust instrument, on default of exercise of the power, the property goes to the four children absolutely and in fee. The separation agreement provides that Steven shall create a *trust*, with *income* payable to *Harriet as trustee,* for the support of Anna and Frank until they both reach the age of 21, at which time the principal shall be paid to them or the survivor; and if both fail to attain the age of 21, then the principal shall revert to Steven's estate. Thus, Anna and Frank's interest in the principal would be a defeasible interest if they did not live to be 21; and indeed at Steven's death they were both still under 21 so that their interest was defeasible.

(iii) Finally, under the separation agreement, as just noted, if Anna and Frank failed to qualify to take the principal, either because they both died before Steven or before reaching the age of 21, then the principal would go to Steven's estate. Under the trust instrument, on the other hand, on default of appointment and an inability of Anna and Frank to take, Steven's share of the principal would not go to Steven's estate, but to his other children, if living, and if not, to the settlor's next of kin.

In these circumstances, I think it is too strained and tortuous to construe the separation agreement provision as the equivalent of a release of the power of appointment. If this is a release then the exception of EPTL 10–5.3 (subd [b]) has swallowed and destroyed the principal rule of EPTL 10–5.3 (subd [a]).

Make the Connection

All is not looking good for the children: the exercise in the will is valid, the contract is not enforceable, and the contract cannot be construed to be a release leaving them as takers in default. Can any remedy ride to the rescue?

I note that in *Wood v American Security and Trust Co.* (253 F Supp 592, 594), the principal case relied upon by Harriet, Anna and Frank on this point, the court said: "The Court finds that it is significant that the disposition resulting from the agreement is in accordance with the wishes of the testator in the event the power should not be exercised."

Furthermore, the language of the instrument in that case was much more consistent with the nonexercise of the powers of appointment than in the case at bar.

Accordingly, I hold that the separation agreement is not the equivalent of a total or partial release of the power of appointment.

(4) Anna and Frank also seek restitution out of the trust fund of the value given by them in exchange for Steven's unfulfilled promise. EPTL 10–5.3 (subd [a]) provides that although the contract to make an appointment cannot be the basis for an action for specific performance or damages, "the promisee can obtain restitution of the value given by him for the promise unless the donee has exercised the power pursuant to contract."

Anna and Frank's remedy is limited, however, to the claim for restitution that they have (and apparently have asserted) against Steven's estate. They may not seek restitution out of the trust fund, even if their allegation that the estate lacks sufficient assets to meet this claim were factually supported, because the trust fund was not the property of Steven, except to the extent of his life estate, so as to be subject to the equitable remedy of restitution, but was the property of the donor of the power of appointment until it vested in someone else. (*Farmers' Loan & Trust Co. v Mortimer*, 219 N.Y. 290, 295, *supra*; 227*227 *see Matter of Rosenthal*, 283 App Div 316, 319; see, also, EPTL 10–7.1 and 10–7.4.)

Points for Discussion

1. Assume the Uniform Act is in force. Would the case be decided similarly?

Section 406. Power to Contract: Power of Appointment not Presently Exercisable

A powerholder of a power of appointment that is not presently exercisable may contract to exercise or not to exercise the power only if the powerholder:

    (1)   is also the donor of the power; and

    (2)   has reserved the power in a revocable trust.

Restatement Third of Property: Wills and Other Donative Transfers § 21.2 and the accompanying Commentary concur. According to the Comment to the Uniform Act:

> the donor of a power not presently exercisable has manifested an intent that the selection of the appointees and the determination of the interests they are to receive are to be made in the light of the circumstances that exist on the date that the power becomes exercisable. Were a contract to be enforceable, the donor's intent would be defeated.

2. Suppose the power could be exercised inter vivos? The Uniform Act reads:

Section 405. Power to Contract: Presently Exercisable Power of Appointment

A powerholder of a presently exercisable power of appointment may contract:

    (1)   not to exercise the power; or

    (2)   to exercise the power if the contract when made does not confer a benefit on an impermissible appointee.

Did Steven's contract confer a benefit on "an impermissible appointee"? Was the power "presently exercisable"?

F. Some Miscellaneous Questions

1. Lapse Statutes and Powers of Appointment

Powers of appointment are non-transferable. According to the Uniform Act (Sec. 202), the power lapses on the death of the powerholder. This position is consistent with Restatement Third of Property: Wills and Other Donative Transfers § 17.1, comment *b*. It may then be sensible to appoint successor appointees. What if the a power is exercised and the appointee predeceases the donee-testator? Does an anti-lapse statute apply to the appointee in the same way it would apply to a beneficiary of the testator's probate estate? There are few cases, but the Restatement, at least, takes a very permissive view, stating that an anti-lapse statute should apply to an appointment to deceased appointee so that the substitute takers under the anti-lapse statute (in most cases the deceased appointee's issue) should be regarded as permissible appointees. If the anti-lapse statute is limited to gifts to relatives of the testator, the statute should apply if the deceased appointee bears the necessary relationship to the donor or the donee of the power. (Restatement Third, Property (Wills and Donative Transfers) § 19.12)

> **Example:** Donor's will creates a testamentary trust to pay income to donor's spouse for life, remainder to such of the descendants of the donor's siblings and the spouse's siblings as the spouse-powerholder shall appoint by will. The powerholder's will appoints one-half the trust property to one of the donor's nephews who predeceases the powerholder and the other half to a niece of the donee who also predeceases the donee. Under the Restatement, if the applicable anti-lapse statute applied to gifts to descendants of the grandparents of the testator whose will makes a gift that has lapsed, the statute would apply to the entire appointment: one deceased appointee being a descendant of the donor's grandparents and the other a descendant of the powerholder's grandparents. One half the appointive property would pass to the nephew's issue, if any and one-half to the niece's issue, if any.

2. Allocation and Capture

Allocation is a doctrine which dictates that when a donee makes a common disposition of appointive property and other property, the appointive property should be allocated to maximize the effectiveness of the common disposition. (Restatement Third, Property (Wills and Donative Transfers) § 19.19)

Allocation is similarly treated in the Uniform Act:

Section 308. Selective Allocation Doctrine

If a powerholder exercises a power of appointment in a disposition that also disposes of property the powerholder owns, the owned property and the appointive property must be allocated in the permissible manner that best carries out the powerholder's intent.

A "common disposition" is made by a "blending clause" in the donee's will: the powerholder's own probate property and the appointive property are devised of in the same disposition. The following is a classic "blending" clause:

> I give the rest, residue, and remainder of my property, both real and personal and wheresoever situated, including any property over which I have a power of appointment, to . . . .

This clause is *not* the "garden variety" residuary clause discussed in connection with the question of whether the residuary clause exercises a power of appointment held by the testator as powerholder. The language here differs because it makes specific reference to powers of appointment but not to any one particular power. There is no question that this blending clause will exercise powers of appointment held by the testator. But there may be an exception. A blending clause probably will not exercise a power of appointment which must be exercised by specific reference to the power. The language exercising any power of appointment by the testator is referred to as "blanket exercise" language. That is, it purports to exercise any and all powers the testator may have. Such a general reference may not be regarded as a *specific* reference to any particular power. The law of wills and trusts is at times flexible, so it is not impossible that a blanket exercise clause could be construed to satisfy a requirement of exercise by specific reference, *see* Restatement Third, Property (Wills and Donative Transfers) § 19.10, comment *d*. Nevertheless, in some states, for example New York, courts strictly enforce a requirement of exercise by specific reference and a blanket exercise clause will not satisfy a specific reference requirement. (*See* Matter of Shenkman, 290 A.D.2d 374, 737 N.Y.S.2d 39 (1st Dep't. 2002).) Realize that a blending clause could make specific reference to a power of appointment: "I give all of my residuary estate, including the property subject to the power of appointment given to me under the will of my mother, X, which was admitted to probate in the Surrogate's Court of New York County on April 1, 2007 . . ."

So what happens if the testator uses a blending clause which incorporates either a blanket exercise clause or a specific reference to a power? Consider this example:

> **Example:** Parent's will creates a trust to pay the income to C for life, remainder as C shall appoint among C's issue. C's will disposes of the residue of C's estate by using a "blending clause" which disposes of the "rest, residue and remainder" of C's estate, "including any property over which I have a power of appointment" in equal shares to C's son, S, and to the widower of C's daughter, W. C's probate estate passing under the residuary clause is valued at $500,000 and the appointive property is also valued at $500,000. Assuming parent's will did not require C to exercise the power by a specific reference, the residuary clause has exercised the power. Without more, part of the appointment is ineffective because we would distribute all of C's assets ratably, that is, one-half of the probate property to each beneficiary and one-half the appointive property to each, and of course W is not a descendant of C. The doctrine of allocation provides that all of the appointive property be allocated to the permissible appointee, S, and the probate estate to W.

If the probate estate were $400,000 it would be distributed to W and the appointive property would be distributed to S.

Capture applies to ineffective or partially ineffective exercises of *general* powers of appointment. If the donee in a disposition manifests the intention to assume control of all the appointive property for all purposes and not just for the purpose of making the ineffective appointment, the property passes as part of the donee's estate rather than as unappointed property that could return to the estate of the donor. (Restatement Third, Property (Wills and Donative Transfers) § 19.22, comment *b*.) Capture usually begins with a blending clause like that in the previous example and a disposition that is partially invalid.

> **Example:** Testator is the donee of a general testamentary power of appointment. Testator's will contains a residuary clause like that in the previous example which blends the appointive property with the residuary probate estate. Such a clause traditionally is regarded as the powerholder manifesting intent to take control of the appointive property for all purposes. The residue is devised one-half to a friend who predeceased the testator and one-half to a charity.

Under the usual rules for administering estates, one-half the probate estate and one-half the appointive property would pass to each beneficiary. The gift to the friend, however, has lapsed. Assuming an anti-lapse statute does not save the bequest for the friend's issue and the no-residue-of-a-residue rule has been abolished, the probate property passing to the friend then passes to the charity. The appointive property that would have passed to the friend is now "unappointed" and, as we will see, if there is no taker in default, the appointive property reverts to the donor's estate. The doctrine of capture, however, would apply to make the appointive property part of the probate estate: the half that would otherwise be regarded as unappointed would pass to the charity whether or not there is a taker in default.

Restatement Third, Property (Wills and Donative Transfers) § 19.21 and the Uniform Act makes some changes in the traditional capture doctrine.

Section 309. Capture Doctrine: Disposition of Ineffectively Appointed Property under General Power

To the extent a powerholder of a general power of appointment, other than a power to withdraw property from, revoke, or amend a trust, makes an ineffective appointment:

(1) the gift-in-default clause controls the disposition of the ineffectively appointed property; or

(2) if there is no gift-in-default clause or to the extent the clause is ineffective, the ineffectively appointed property:

  (A) passes to:

    (i) the powerholder if the powerholder is a permissible appointee and living; or

(ii)   if the powerholder is an impermissible appointee or deceased, the powerholder's estate if the estate is a permissible appointee; or

(B)   if there is no taker under subparagraph (A), passes under a reversionary interest to the donor or the donor's transferee or successor in interest.

Accordingly, under both the Uniform Act and the Restatement, if there are takers in default, the gift to them will always take precedence over the application of the capture doctrine. Therefore, in the previous example, if the donor of the power of appointment had included a gift in default of appointment to the powerholder's issue by representation, the appointive property subject to the lapsed appointment would pass to the powerholder's issue by representation rather than to the charity. The gift in default always takes precedence, whether or not the powerholder has manifested the intent to take control of all of the appointive property, for example, by the use of a blending clause. Second, the ineffectively appointive property passes to the powerholder's estate only if there are no takers in default able to take. The decision to always give effect to the gift in default of appointment is explained by the changing use of the taker in default clause. The Restatement asserts that the "capture doctrine was developed at a time when the donor's gift-in-default clause was considered an afterthought, inserted just in case the powerholder failed to exercise the power. Today, the donor's gift-in-default clause is typically well-thought-out, carefully drafted, and intended to take effect, unless circumstances change that would cause the powerholder to exercise the power." (Restatement Third, Property (Wills and Donative Transfers) § 19.21, comment *b*.)

3.   Special Problems of Non-General Powers

Special or non-general powers of appointment raise unique problems. First, there is the question of whether the powerholder of a non-general power can appoint in further trust if the power does not expressly give the donee that authority. Traditionally, the answer was "no." Restatement Third of Property § 191.4 comment *d* departs from the traditional rule. The reasoning is as follows: if the donee of the special power can appoint so that the appointee has outright ownership of the appointive property in fee, the donee should also be able appoint a "lesser" estate, that is, an equitable life interest or remainder.

Second, there is the issue of whether the donee of a special power can create a power in an appointee. The Restatement Third of Property allows the donee of a non-general power to create a further power, but the permissible appointees of the further power must be permissible appointees of the original power. (Restatement Third, Property (Wills and Donative Transfers) § 19.14, comment *e*.). Remember that the donor of the special power can authorize the powerholder to create a further power, special or general, and to select any permissible appointees that the donee so desires.

Third, the question arises with the special power as to whether it is exclusive or non-exclusive. A special power is exclusive if it may be exercised in favor of one or more appointees to the exclusion of the others and is non-exclusive if it must be exercised in favor of all the appointees. If the power is non-exclusive, the donee must appoint to all the permissible appointees equally.

Whether a power is exclusive or non-exclusive depends on the words used to create it and courts have drawn some fine distinctions. A properly drafted power will clearly indicate the extent of the donee's discretion in exercising the power. (Restatement Third, Property (Wills and Donative Transfers) § 17.5, uses the terms "exclusionary and non-exclusionary" rather than "exclusive" and "non-exclusive.")

The consequences of determining whether a power is exclusive or non-exclusive can be complicated. Below is the second part of the opinion in *Matter of Weinstein* (*see* 462 above). The first part dealt with whether or not the testator's will created a power of appointment. The second part of the opinion deals with what kind of special power of appointment was created. The case provides a salutary reminder that a drafter should always make it clear whether a power of appointment is exclusive or non-exclusive.

Matter of Weinstein

444 N.Y.S.2d 427 (Surr. Ct. 1981)

* * * *

At this juncture the argument inviting assertion by petitioner is that the special power of appointment admittedly created by paragraph (c) is non-exclusive, that is, not properly exercisable except in favor of all objects of the power equally. Respondents, of course, take the contrary position that the power is exclusive, thereby entitling the appointor to exercise uncontrolled discretion with respect to both selection among the permissible appointees and the quantum of each share. While determination of the power's character as non-exclusive or exclusive is ultimately dependent upon the testatrix's intention as expressed in the will (*Matter of Corlias*, 201 Misc. 755, 106 N.Y.S.2d 381 [Surr.Ct.N.Y.Co.1951]), it is necessary first to consider the evolution of these complementary concepts, particularly that of the non-exclusive power, and the presumptions of law which have attached at various points in time.

At common law a non-exclusive power was defined in terms which required only that each object of the power receive some share of the appointive property, however nominal. Since this fact made a non-exclusive power the practical equivalent of an exclusive one at the opinion of the donee, equity intervened to prevent insubstantial or "illusory appointments". In 1829, the New York legislature, responding to the criticism that had been leveled at judicial attempts to establish a line of demarcation between appointments which were substantial and those which were illusory (*see* Rev. Notes to §§ 98, 99, 3 Rev. Stat. of N. Y. [2d. ed. 1836], at 592–93), abolished the common law and equitable doctrines by means of a statutory presumption that a non-exclusive power required equal appointments to all objects of the power (Rev. Stat. §§ 98, 99, part 2, ch. 1, tit. 2, art. 3, amended without substantial change by L. 1896, ch. 547, § 138 [Real Prop. Law § 158]). After a one hundred thirty-five year hiatus, the legislature reverted to the common law definition of a non-exclusive power (L.1964, ch. 864, § 151 [Real Prop. Law § 151] [effective June 1, 1965]), presumably also thereby resurrecting its concomitant, the illusory appointment doctrine. In any event, it was a short-lived revival since the Estates,

Powers and Trusts Law, which took effect on September 1, 1967, reinstated the presumption that all objects of a non-exclusive power are to be afforded identical shares (§ 10–6.5[a][2]).

This testatrix's will was executed on May 10, 1965. As has been outlined, the "modern" conception of the non-exclusive power which had been adopted in this state in 1829 was reflected in the law in effect on that date. The legislature had, however, enacted the amendment which was to restore the common law definition as of June 1, 1965, both as to non-exclusive powers created prior and subsequent thereto (Real Prop. Law § 167). But as no rights accrued under the will until the testatrix's death on January 1, 1980, the pertinent provisions (§ 10–3.2[d], [e]; § 10–6.5) of the Estates, Powers and Trusts Law govern (§ 1–1.5). Consequently, if it is determined that a non-exclusive power was created, it may be exercised only by equal appointments to all objects, assuming there is no contrary expression of intent within the will.

We now proceed to consider whether an exclusive or non-exclusive power was intended to be created in the case at bar. The operative wording of the power is "to . . . Joseph L. Barnett . . . to be distributed by him . . . *to and among*" specified persons (emphasis added). Chancellor Kent long ago recorded the view that where, as here, the power was to appoint "amongst" the named or described persons as the donee should think proper a non-exclusive power was intended while an exclusive power was conferred where the phrasing was "to such" of the individuals as he should deem proper (4 Commentaries on American Law 342–43 [1840]). This apparently remains the rule in the majority of states (Restatement of Law of Property, § 360, Comment C. Illustrations 3, 4 [1940]). Indeed, the New York statutes in effect from 1829 until June 1, 1965 (Rev.Stat. §§ 98, 99, part 2, ch. 1, tit. 2, art. 3, superseded by Real Prop. Law § 158 [effective 1896]) provided that an appointment "among" (or "to" or "between") named objects conferred a non-exclusive power unless the grant affirmatively imported that the fund was to be distributed in such manner or proportions as the donee thought proper. While most cases decided thereunder thus viewed a gift phrased "amongst", "to" or "between" the designees as sufficient to support a finding that a non-exclusive power was intended in otherwise equivocal circumstances (*Matter of Conner*, 6 A.D. 594 [1st Dept.1896], *aff'd*, 49 N.E. 1095 [1898]; *Conner v. Watson*, 1 A.D. 54 [1st Dept.1896]; *Matter of Gottfried*, 41 Misc.2d 575, 245 N.Y.S.2d 948 [Surr. Ct. N.Y.Co.1963]; *Matter of Feeney*, 123 Misc. 78, 204 N.Y.S. 399 [Surr. Ct. West.Co. 1924], their authority was not unbroken. It was ventured, for example, that a judicial preference for the exclusive power was warranted (*see Matter of Skidmore*, 148 Misc. 569, 575, 266 N.Y.S. 312, 319 [Surr. Ct. N.Y.Co. 1933]), and, in a decision of particular relevance to the case at bar, a grant of discretion to appoint among the objects "in such manner" as the donee should deem proper was held to have created an exclusive power despite lack of express authority to fix the proportions (*Matter of Corlies, supra*; but *see*

"Chancellor Kent" is James Kent (1763–1842), who was one of the most distinguished jurists in the early United States. He was chancellor (judge of the equity court) of New York (the court was abolished by the Constitution of 1846 and its jurisdiction merged into the general trial and appellate courts). His *Commentaries on American Law* is one of the first treatises on American law.

Matter of Conner, supra; Matter of Feeney, supra). At any rate, upon the recommendation of the Commission on Estates (N.Y.Legis.Doc.1964, no. 19, app. O, at 623), a statutory presumption favoring the exclusive power was engrafted onto the successor statute (Real Prop. Law § 151). While that preference was not explicitly carried over to E.P.T.L. § 10–6.5, which governs the instant case, no change in policy should be inferred (Glasser, Practice Commentary to E.P.T.L. § 10–6.5, McKinney's Consol.Laws of N.Y.Annot., Book 17B, Supp.1980–81, at 200; *Matter of Stevenson*, 68 Misc.2d 619, 327 N.Y.S.2d 768 [Surr.Ct.N.Y.Co.1971], *aff'd*, 39 A.D. 2d 1015, 333 N.Y.S.2d 985 [1st Dept.1972]). We note in passing that such a preference is deemed warranted by leading authorities as in accord with the usual intention of the modern donor to permit the donee the widest possible latitude to exercise the power in the light of circumstances existing at some future date perhaps far removed from its creation (*See* Restatement, § 360, *supra*; Simes & Smith, The Law of Future Interests, § 982, at 468 [2d ed. 1956]).

As the appearance of the word "among" is not fatal to the prospect of finding a power exclusive, which is the preferred result, we proceed to examine the remainder of paragraph (c)'s language. Joseph L. Barnett is given broad discretion to choose the time, manner and "amounts, if any" of the dispositions. The "if any" qualification of the words "amounts" requires particular scrutiny. At first glance it might appear to signify that the power of appointment was discretionary and not imperative. If so, it would have no bearing on the question whether the power was intended to be exclusive or non-exclusive, since either may be discretionary (E.P.T.L. § 10–3.4[b]). But in view of the absence of a gift over in default of appointment (*Merrill v. Lynch*, 173 Misc. 39, 13 N.Y.S.2d 514 [Sup.Ct.N.Y.Co.1939]) and the use of the phrase "shall determine" (*In re will of Seidman*, 88 Misc.2d 462, 389 N.Y.S.2d 729 [Surr.Ct. Kings Co.1976], *modified*, 58 A.D.2d 72, 395 N.Y.S.2d 674 [2d Dep't.1977]) it must be concluded that the power is imperative. Thus, the "if any" can mean only that the donee was given the power to exclude one or more of the permissible appointees.

Further evidence that an exclusive power was intended can be gleaned from subsequent provisions of the will. It is reasonable to infer from testatrix's selection of Joseph L. Barnett as successor and substitute trustee of the testamentary trust intended for the benefit of her husband that she reposed a great deal of confidence in his ability and integrity. He was authorized, should he serve in that capacity, to exercise a lengthy list of broad powers among which were the power to refrain from acting as if disinterested with respect to estate property in which he had a personal interest, to adjust debts and to hold money without receipt of interest. Testatrix specified, in addition, that his liability for loss was to be limited to acts or omissions amounting to actual fraud or willful misconduct.

There are, in summation, no contraindications that would serve to overcome the presumption in favor of an exclusive power. In fact, it would appear from the literal sense of paragraph (c) that Joseph L. Barnett was given complete discretion with respect to the timing of the power's exercise, selection among the permissible appointees and the quanta of shares.

Accordingly, the court determines that testatrix created an exclusive power of appointment. The donee may exercise it in any manner consistent with this opinion.

Points for Discussion

1. *A matter of construction*

Just like the determination of whether the will creates a power of appointment, deciding whether the power is exclusive or non-exclusive is a matter of construction. This part of the *Weinstein* opinion is an example of will construction. Do you think the court reaches the right result when it decides that the power of appointment created by the testator is indeed exclusive?

2. *. . . which should not have been necessary?*

It appears that the will in *Weinstein* was drafted by a lawyer. How good a job did the lawyer do? How would you improve on the language of the will that disposes of the trust property after the husband's death?

3. *Fraud on power*

Finally, there is the possibility that the exercise of a special power may be invalid as a fraud on the power. Fraud most commonly occurs when the powerholder appoints to one who is not an object: an impermissible appointee according to the Uniform Act:

Section 307. Impermissible Appointment

(a) Except as otherwise provided in Section 306, an exercise of a power of appointment in favor of an impermissible appointee is ineffective.

(b) An exercise of a power of appointment in favor of a permissible appointee is ineffective to the extent the appointment is a fraud on the power.

Restatement Third of Property: Wills and Other Donative Transfers §§ 19.15 and 19.16 concurs. It is the donor of a power of appointment who sets the universe of possible appointees. If the powerholder elects another, he or she is acting beyond the scope of his or her authority.

The Comment to the Uniform Act Notes:

Among the most common devices employed to commit a fraud on the power are: an appointment conditioned on the appointee conferring a benefit on an impermissible appointee; an appointment subject to a charge in favor of an impermissible appointee; an appointment upon a trust for the benefit of an impermissible appointee; an appointment in consideration of a benefit to an impermissible appointee; and an appointment primarily for the benefit of the permissible appointee's creditor if the creditor is an impermissible appointee. Each of these appointments is impermissible and ineffective.

An example of fraud on a power is *Matter of Carroll*, 274 N.Y. 288, 8 N.E.2d 864, 115 A.L.R. 923 (1937). The powerholder of a special power limited appointment to the donee's "kindred" wanted to make sure that her husband would benefit from at least a portion of the appointive property. She made an agreement with a cousin who promised that in consideration for receiving an appointment of $250,000 he would convey $100,000 of that amount to the powerholder's husband. The Court of Appeals (one judge dissenting) invalidated the entire appointment, holding that the powerholder had committed a fraud on the power by exercising it for purposes other than those for which it was created. (*See also* Restatement Third, Property (Wills and Donative Transfers) § 19.16.)

4. Failure to appoint

Every well-drafted power of appointment will include the designation of takers in default. The donor will specify how the appointive property is to be distributed if the donee fails to make an appointment. Of course not every power is well drafted. What happens if the donee does not exercise the power and there are no takers in default? The general rule is that unappointed property passes back to the donor or to the estate of the donor if the donor is deceased under a reversionary interest. Both the Uniform Act Section 310 and Restatement (Third) of Property. Section 19.22(b) provide otherwise: if the powerholder does not exercise a general power of appointment and if the donor did not provide for takers in default or if no taker in default is able to take, the appointive property passes *to the* powerholder *or the* powerholder's *estate* rather than under a reversionary interest to the donor.

Non-general powers are treated differently.

Section 311. Disposition of Unappointed Property under Released or Unexercised Nongeneral Power

To the extent a powerholder releases, ineffectively exercises, or fails to exercise a nongeneral power of appointment:

(1)   the gift-in-default clause controls the disposition of the unappointed property; or

(2)   if there is no gift-in-default clause or to the extent the clause is ineffective, the unappointed property:

    (A)   passes to the permissible appointees if:

        (i)   the permissible appointees are defined and limited; and

        (ii)   the terms of the instrument creating the power do not manifest a contrary intent; or

    (B) if there is no taker under subparagraph (A), passes under a reversionary interest to the donor or the donor's transferee or successor in interest.

In some instances, the appointive property will pass to the permissible appointees, just as if the donee had exercised the power to appoint to them. (Restatement Third, Property (Wills and Donative Transfers) § 19.23(b)). Whether or not the appointive property will be distributed to the permissible appointees depends, of course, on the intent of the donor as gleaned from the language creating the power. Some courts provide that such language creates an implied gift in default of appointment to the permissible appointees. Others do not. New York statutes, however, classify such a power as an "imperative" power which must be exercised (EPTL § 10–3.4). If a power is found to be imperative, the Surrogate's Court in the case of a will or the Supreme Court otherwise will exercise the power for the donee. (EPTL § 10–6.8) Once again, classification of the power depends on the language and a well-drafted power will clearly state what is to become of the appointive property if the donee fails to exercise the power, in other words, it will include a provision creating takers in default.

Practice Pointers

The construction of a power of appointment first and foremost must be directed by the client's intentions, the property law of powers suggests that whatever the client wants to do, the following are always relevant:

Every power of appointment should: 1) clearly indicate whether the power is general or non-general, 2) name takers in default, 3) require that the donee exercise the power by specific reference to the power and if the power is testamentary, that the reference be made in a will duly admitted to probate.

Every non-general power of appointment: 1) should clearly indicate if the power is exclusive or non-exclusive, 2) state clearly whether the donee may or may not appoint in further trust and create powers of appointment in the permissible appointees, 3) if the donee may appoint in further trust whether or not the donee may select a new trustee, 4) for testamentary powers state whether questions of whether or not the power has been exercised are to be decided by the governing law of the trust or by governing law of the donee's will.

Problem 9-4

1. Return to the powers of appointment set forth in Problem 9-1. Is there anything lacking in the drafting of these powers? Can you improve upon them?

2. Donor's will created a trust to pay the income to donee's daughter, D, for life, remainder to be distributed as D shall appoint, and in default of appointment the trust property shall be distributed to D's issue living at her death, by representation. How is the appointive property distributed under traditional law and the Uniform Act/Restatement if:

    a.   D dies testate, but her will makes no mention whatsoever of the power of appointment?

b.   D dies testate with a residuary clause that disposes of "all of the rest, residue, and remainder of my estate including any property over which I have a power of appointment" one-half to a charity and one-half to a friend who predeceases her if

i.   D is not survived by issue.

ii.   D is survived by issue.

———————————————

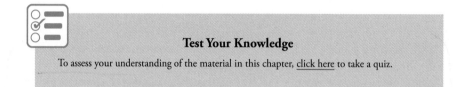

Test Your Knowledge

To assess your understanding of the material in this chapter, click here to take a quiz.

CHAPTER 10

493 — 527

Non-Probate Property

A page of history . . .

While most individuals own property at their deaths, both in the past time as in our time, most individual leave this earth without leaving a will. The precise numbers of those who wrote wills in the past is difficult to determine; historical studies of testation, matching the number of recorded deaths to the number of will probates, is not an easy task. Historians of 17th century England have done so, and a 'ball park ratio' of about one in ten seems reasonably accurate. One might have thought that it was the wealthy rather than the poor who wrote wills, but other factors were in play: type of property, number of children, religion, to name a few. Men made wills in numbers far in excess than did women, and married women could not make wills without their husband's consent. Many women died as widows and therefore women's wills do populate English will-registers.

Simply counting historical events is far easier than explaining them. Did the other 90% have too little property to bother to write a will, too few heirs to consider, or were they simply content with inheritance law? Or did our forebears like ourselves make arrangements for the passage of their property pre-mortem? Some research suggest that they did, but again in percentages that cannot be ascertained. We will never know what prevailed upon them to do so, and as you read through this chapter, ponder the same question for modern Americans who have a "wealth" of non-testamentary strategies to pass their property.

A. Typical Forms of Non-Probate Property: Will Substitutes

1. The Totten Trust

We have already recognized that some property owned or controlled by the deceased does not pass into the probate estate: so-called "nonprobate property." Our Ward Cleaver estate plan contained a revocable lifetime trust as a device to pass property at his death without it falling into his probate estate. We have also encountered nonprobate property in our discussion of the elective share. Many of the testamentary substitutes of New York law and the elements of the UPC augmented estate are forms of nonprobate property. In this section, we will examine the types of non-probate property more closely, and note the remarkable growth of the various forms of non-probate property to pass property since the mid-twentieth century. Indeed, there is talk of a "nonprobate revolution," the transmission of property through the use of "will substitutes." Why that revolution began and continues to develop is an important and complex question.

The following case should give you some idea about the reasons for this development, but it also suggests some long-term continuities: property-holders in America have over time sought to create forms of non-probate property to infuse flexibility into their inheritance strategy. The case is *Matter of Totten*, and it is one of the earliest and most important cases dealing with non-probate property. It sanctioned a type of bank account in which an individual, perhaps a parent or other relative, can deposit funds in the name of the depositor as trustee for the another: the "depositor" can deposit money as trustee for another person, the "beneficiary." Unlike a joint tenancy account, the depositor has absolute ownership and control over the account; the beneficiary will have the ability to reach the funds only upon the occurrence of an event; usually upon the death of the depositor. Arguably, when property passes upon at death, the document that directs transmission should be a will executed with the requisite testamentary formality. So should the courts allow a simple card filled out by the depositor at the bank, unwitnessed, pass property at death? The court in *Totten* seemed to think so.

Matter of Totten

71 N.E. 748 (N.Y. 1904)

APPEAL from an order of the Appellate Division of the Supreme Court in the second judicial department, entered December 30, 1903, which reversed a decree of the Kings County Surrogate's Court rejecting certain claims of the respondent herein against the estate of Fanny Amelia Lattan, deceased.

> **Take Note**
>
> Never forget inflation; today's approximate value is $46,000—a sum worth fighting over.

This is a controversy between the administrator of Fanny Amelia Lattan, deceased, and Emile R. Lattan, who presented a claim against the estate of said decedent which was duly rejected by the representative thereof. The claim was for the sum of $1,775.03, besides interest, alleged to be due "by reason of certain deposits made by" the decedent "in the Irving Savings Institution, as trustee for the said Emile R. Lattan, the moneys so deposited having been subsequently withdrawn by the said decedent." Upon the final accounting of the administrator the justice of said claim, in accordance with the stipulation of all concerned, was determined by the surrogate after a referee had reported the evidence, the facts and his conclusion. The surrogate confirmed the report and dismissed the claim upon the merits, but the decree entered accordingly was reversed by the Appellate Division "upon the law and the facts" and the claim was allowed with costs. The administrator and certain heirs and next of kin of the decedent appealed to this court.

VANN, J.

[Judge Vann first held that the Court had jurisdiction to hear the appeal because it involved a question of law.]

Beginning in 1886 the decedent and her sister Angelica each had numerous accounts in the Irving Savings Institution, the greater part in the name of the former individually, or as trustee. At various times there were sixteen of the latter class. While no single account in the name of the decedent ever exceeded $3,000 the aggregate amount of all her accounts always exceeded that sum and occasionally by several thousand dollars. At the same time many accounts were kept by her in other savings institutions, some in her own name simply and others with the addition of "trustee for" or "in trust for" some person named. It was her practice to draw from all these accounts at will, whether they were kept in her name as trustee or otherwise, and to close them and open others as she saw fit. She kept the pass books and no beneficiary named in any account ever drew therefrom except upon drafts signed by her. When she died intestate in March, 1900, accounts were outstanding in her name as trustee in favor of Emile R. Lattan and three other persons and they had the benefit thereof without controversy.

On the 2nd of January, 1886, the decedent opened an account in the Irving Savings Institution by depositing the sum of $355. A rule of the bank required the depositor to give the name of the person for whom he wished to place the money in trust, but the one making the deposit had absolute control of the account so long as he retained possession of the pass book. The pass book was numbered 42,728 and the deposit was entered thereon as well as on the books of the bank as an account with Fanny A. Lattan, trustee for Emile R. Lattan, depositor. At some time, but it does not appear when except that it was prior to May, 1893, the words "Trustee for Emile R. Lattan" were canceled by rulings in red ink. As at first entered in the ledger of the bank the account stood as at first entered on the pass book, but when carried forward to a new ledger in 1892 it stood as an account with the decedent individually. When she opened this account she had between $6,000 and $7,000 standing in her name individually and as trustee on the books of the same bank. Two other deposits were made in this account, the first of $5.10 on July 1st, 1886, and the second of $740, September 21st, 1886. Twelve drafts were drawn against it at various times. The first, dated January 27th, 1886, for $100 in favor of Lewis H. Lattan, was signed by the decedent as trustee, but all the rest, commencing with September 19th, 1890, were signed by her individually. July

> **Food for Thought**
>
> Why was the bank willing to create a multiplicity of arrangements? Does it tell you anything about what drives the financial services industry?

8th, 1898, the account was closed by her individual draft for $1,104.06 and the pass book was surrendered. With the amount thus drawn she opened two new accounts in the same bank, the first No. 66,807 in favor of Fanny A. Lattan in trust for Rosalie M. Beam for the sum of $552.03, and the other No. 66,808 in favor of Fanny A. Lattan in trust for Emile R. Lattan for the same amount. Both of these accounts remained open at the time of the decedent's death and the pass books were delivered by her administrator to the parties named who drew the money accordingly. During the existence of account No. 42,728 the decedent at all times had possession of the pass book and Emile R. Lattan received no part of the moneys deposited to the credit of that account except as already mentioned.

On the 19th of September, 1890, the decedent had ten accounts amounting to between $8,000 and $9,000 standing in her name, individually or as trustee, on the books of the Irving Savings Institution. On that day she opened account No.51,556 in that bank by depositing $462.03 in her name as trustee for Emile R. Lattan. Said amount was largely made up of sums drawn from other accounts in her name as trustee. She retained possession of the pass book, and no one, except herself and the officers of the bank, appears to have known of the existence of the account until after her death. September 19th, 1892, she deposited $100 in that account and September 13th, 1893, the further sum of $80.60. When it was closed on the 15th of November, 1894, it amounted with interest to $733.30, which she drew out and deposited in another account, in her name as trustee for Lewis H. Lattan, who after her death drew the amount thereof.

Emile R. Lattan was the son of Lewis H. Lattan, a spendthrift, who in 1884 turned over to his sisters Angelica Lattan and the decedent all his property, worth about $20,000, for their management, but without instructions as to their course in managing the same. No accounting was ever made to him with reference thereto, although he survived them both.

There was no evidence that the decedent ever spoke to anyone about any of these accounts or stated what her intention was in opening them. The accounts in question were opened with her own money and no part thereof came from her brother Lewis. Out of thirty-one accounts in seven savings banks she paid over to the alleged beneficiaries the balance left when two thereof were closed, but in both of these instances, as well as in all other cases, she treated the accounts as her own, drawing against them and making new deposits from time to time as she thought best. All the pass books with a trust heading, containing accounts which had not been closed when the decedent died, were delivered to the respective beneficiaries who drew the balance on hand. Emile R. Lattan did not know of the existence of any accounts on which he relies in this proceeding until more than a year after the decedent died. Angelica Lattan, who was appointed and qualified as administratrix, died on the 10th of April, 1901, leaving the administrator as the sole representative of the estate. The personal property of Fanny A. Lattan was inventoried at the sum of $32,950.08, but owing to increase

Food for Thought

Suppose she had told others of her 'estate plan.' Would/should her statements be admissible into evidence, and if so for what purpose?

in values the amount on hand at the date of the final decree of distribution was more than $40,000.

The most favorable view of these facts and others of like character not mentioned does not permit the inference as matter of fact that the decedent in making the deposits in question intended to establish an irrevocable trust in favor of the respondent. Aside from what took place when the deposits were made, every act of the decedent, with one exception, is opposed to the theory of a trust. That exception is the closing of one account after the words of trust had been canceled and the deposit

of part of the proceeds in the same form as the original. This is not enough when considered with the other facts to establish an irrevocable trust. (Cunningham v. Davenport, 147 N.Y. 43.) No connection was shown between any deposit and the sum held in trust by the decedent and her sister Angelica for Lewis H. Lattan, who is still living and was sworn as a witness at the trial. A deposit in favor of the son would not have satisfied the claim of the father in the absence of a request from the latter, of which there was no evidence. In view of the practice of the decedent in doing business with savings banks, the custom of many other persons in that regard, the various objects which people have in making deposits in the form of a trust, the retention of the pass book with the corresponding control of the deposits according to the rules of the bank, the subsequent history of the various accounts with the frequent withdrawals and changes, we think that the form of the deposits as they appear upon the books was not strengthened by the other evidence. There was no question of fact in the case and the Appellate Division had no power to reverse upon the facts. We find no exception in the record warranting a reversal upon the law, unless the exception to the conclusion of the referee and surrogate that the claim should be dismissed upon the merits raises reversible error. This involves the question whether upon the conceded facts, as matter of law, an irrevocable trust was established.

Savings bank trusts, as they are sometimes called, have frequently been before the courts during the past few years. When we considered the pioneer case but few instances of deposits in trust were known and a liberal rule was laid down without the limitations which later cases required. After a while when it became a common practice for persons to make deposits in that form, in order to evade restrictions upon the amount one could deposit in his own name and for other reasons, the courts became more conservative and sought to avoid unjust results by adapting the law to the customs of the people. A brief review of the cases will show how the subject has been gradually developed so as to accord with the methods of the multitude of persons who make deposits in these banks.

[The court discusses several of its early cases in which these trust accounts were held to be irrevocable trusts. In these cases, however, all the claims were for money on deposit at the death of the depositor. When the court faced claims for moneys that had been withdrawn by the depositor before death, the court began to limit the earlier decisions "in order to avoid subversion of the real intention of the depositor . . . ."]

Thus, in Beaver v. Beaver (117 N.Y. 421) the deposit was by a father of his own money in the name of his son seventeen years of age. The father retained the pass book, deposited more money to the credit of the account and drew out some. The son died over twenty years after the first deposit without knowing anything about any of the deposits. Subsequently, the father died and it was held that the facts shown would not permit the inference that either a trust or a gift was established. Judge ANDREWS said: "There was no declaration of trust in this case, in terms, when the deposit of July 5th, 1866, was made nor at any time afterwards, and none can be implied from a mere deposit by one person in the name of another. To constitute a trust there must be an explicit declaration of trust or circumstances which show beyond reasonable doubt that a trust was intended to be created. It would introduce a dangerous instability of titles if anything less was required, or if a voluntary trust inter vivos could be established in the absence of express words, by circumstances capable of another construction or consistent with a different intention * * * It may be justly said that a deposit in a savings bank by one person of his own money to the credit of another, is consistent with an intention on the part of the depositor to give the money to the other. But it does not, we think, of itself, without more, authorize an affirmative finding that the deposit was made with that intent, when the deposit was to a new account, unaccompanied by any declaration of intention, and the depositor received at the time a pass book, the possession and presentation of which by the rules of the bank known to the depositor, is made the evidence of the right to draw the deposit. We cannot close our eyes to the well-known practice of persons depositing in savings banks money to the credit of real or fictitious persons, with no intention of divesting themselves of ownership. It is attributable to various reasons; reasons connected with taxation; rules of the banks limiting the amount

> **FYI**
>
> The laws of New York governing savings banks did indeed limit the amount any one person could have on deposit. The idea was to encourage small savers, which is also the reason for the statutory provision requiring that the banks pay a higher interest rate on small accounts.

which any one individual may keep on deposit; the desire to obtain high rates of interest where there is a discrimination based on the amount of deposits, and the desire on the part of many persons to veil or conceal from others knowledge of their pecuniary condition. In most cases where a deposit of this character is made as a gift, there are contemporaneous facts or subsequent declarations by which the intention can be established, independently of the form of the deposit. We are inclined to think that to infer a gift from the form of the deposit alone would, in a great majority of cases, and especially where the deposit was of any considerable amount, impute an intention which never existed and defeat the real purpose of the depositor." . . .]

* * * * *

[Subsequent decisions by the court indicate that] [w]hen a deposit is made in trust and the depositor dies intestate leaving it undisturbed, in the absence of other evidence, the presumption seems to arise that a trust was intended in order to avoid the trouble of making a will.]

* * * * *

While we have considered we do not cite the numerous cases decided by the Supreme Court bearing upon the question, owing to the conflict in the opinions of learned justices in different appellate divisions. It is necessary for us to settle the conflict by laying down such a rule as will best promote the interests of all the people in the state. After much reflection upon the subject, guided by the principles established by our former decisions, we announce the following as our conclusion: A deposit by one person of his own money, in his own name as trustee for another, standing alone, does not establish an irrevocable trust during the lifetime of the depositor. It is a tentative trust merely, revocable at will, until the depositor dies or completes the gift in his lifetime by some unequivocal act or declaration, such as delivery of the pass book or notice to the beneficiary. In case the depositor dies before the beneficiary without revocation, or some decisive act or declaration of disaffirmance, the presumption arises that an absolute trust was created as to the balance on hand at the death of the depositor. This rule requires us to reverse the order of the Appellate Division and to affirm the decree of the surrogate, with costs to the appellants in all courts.

PARKER, CH. J., O'BRIEN, BARTLETT, MARTIN, CULLEN and WERNER, JJ., concur.

Points for Discussion

1. The doctrinal conundrum raised by will substitutes

Traditionally the only way to keep complete control of an item of property during one's life and control to whom it passes at death was to execute a document that complies with the requirements of the statute of wills: by executing and attesting a written will in accordance with due execution statutes. Any other device which purported to pass property at death that is controlled by the property owner was an invalid will substitute.

The doctrinal issue that the court was confronting was that that the savings bank account was testamentary in character unless the "in trust form" created a trust at the moment it was opened or at the very least sometime during the life of the depositor. If it was not, the beneficiary held no property interest at the time the account was opened (or alternatively during the course of the depositor's life) and the account would indeed be an attempt to make a gift at death through a device other than a will. Of course there would be no doctrinal issue if the court could regard the account as a *revocable* trust, but the general rule is that every trust is irrevocable unless the creator of the trust expressly provides that it is revocable. There was nothing in the agreement between the depositor and the bank to suggest that the account was a revocable trust.

Thus, the doctrinal problem facing the court was that (1) the depositors of these accounts almost always behave as if they are the owners of the money in the accounts during their lives; but (2) want the remaining funds in the account at the depositor's death to go to the beneficiary. In order for (2) to happen an irrevocable trust had to have been created; but if (1) is recognized the account cannot be an irrevocable trust.

2. *The Court's solution*

The New York Court of Appeals solves the doctrinal problem by simple denial, or bulldozing the issues out of the way. You might ask yourself, what is the source of the law the court applies? The court holds that these bank accounts in trust form are "tentative trusts," a novel and truly unprecedented (note that the court cites no precedents for its holding) trust. The rationale for the holding is what is important—and the rationale seems to be that the court has to find a way to allow the property owner to have this simple device for the passage of property at death. Is there danger lurking here? Is there much potential for a depositor lacking mental capacity? Is undue influence or fraud likely to be present? If any of these issues obtained, would the bank employee open the account? Denying the Totten trust's validity would be recognizing form over substance.

3. *Aftermath*

The opinion in *Totten* was generally welcomed as a benign solution to an ubiquitous problem (how to pass small quantities of property to beneficiaries without a will and probate), but it can also be roundly criticized as legislating and not adjudicating. Perhaps not surprisingly, "in trust for" bank accounts were soon the subject of legislation in several states and today are often treated by statute as just one type of payable on death account. The New York statutes dealing with Totten trust accounts are NY EPTL §§ 7–5.1 through 7–5.8.

Indeed, *Totten* was the thin edge of the wedge. *Totten* marks a critical stage in the growth of the use of will substitutes, an opening chapter in an ongoing narrative about the law's increasing comfort level with sanctioning forms of non-probate property, and a concomitant decreasing concern with testamentary formality. This trend has been driven in part at least by the same situation the Court of Appeals recognized in deciding Totten.

2. Jointly Held Property

a) Joint Tenants

There are, of course, forms of non-probate property which though will substitutes were never regarded as invalid. The common law has long recognized that property can be held jointly with right of survivorship: joint holders together own the property and when one dies, the survivor or survivors continue/s to own the property. Because the deceased joint tenant no longer has any property interest at his or her death, nothing passes through his or her estate: the deceased ownership interest in the property simply "disappears." Any attempt to dispose of one's interest in property held jointly with right of survivorship by will is therefore completely ineffective.

Strictly speaking, the term "*joint tenants* with right of survivorship" refers only to persons owning real property. Individuals who are parties to a joint and survivor bank account are often referred to as "*joint holders*" of the property. Why the difference? Joint tenants with right of survivorship own undivided interests which can be severed by unilateral action, converting the joint tenancy into a tenancy-in-common. The resulting property interests of parties to a tenancy-in-common **are** owned at the death of each co-tenant; at the death of each of the co-tenants, her share is probate property that passes by intestacy or under a will. Partition of a joint tenancy can occur even if one joint tenant provided all the consideration for the purchase of the property. Either one can then sever the joint tenancy (by executing a deed to him or herself or by first making a conveyance to a strawperson). The transaction has the effect of converting the joint tenancy into a tenancy-in-common in which each party will own an undivided one-half.

b) Joint Bank Accounts

In most states, however, the above rules, derived from English common law, do not apply to joint bank accounts. The UPC (*see* UPC § 6–211(b)) provides that while the parties to a joint account are alive, the parties own the account in proportion to their contributions to the account. Unlike joint tenants with right of survivorship in land, therefore, parties to joint bank accounts do not have undivided interests unrelated to their contributions to the amount that they deposited. Some states have different rules. In New York, for example, a joint account is treated like a joint tenancy in real property. Each joint tenant owns an undivided share of the property, called a *moiety*, no matter which individual provided what proportions of the funds. Consider the following examples.

> **Example 1:** A opens a joint and survivor bank account with B and deposits $5,000 into the account. What are B's rights in the account while B is alive?

Under the UPC the entire account belongs to A and no gift has been made to B. A's remedies against B if B withdraws money from the account without A's permission depends on "general law:" defenses such as estoppel or laches are relevant. If the depositor somehow agreed or acquiesced in the withdrawal or waited too long to assert her rights, an action against B might fail. In New York (and some other states), however, on deposit in a joint account with B, A has made *a gift* of one-half the account to B. B can therefore immediately withdraw $2,500 from the account and A has no recourse against him. Unless B withdraws more than the ½ to which B is entitled, B's right of survivorship still exists in the funds remaining in the account if A should predecease B.

That said, this rule only applies if the account was really intended to be a joint account. Whether that will be the case depends upon the interpretation of the documents used to open the account. In New York, Banking Law § 675 provides the statutory basis for a joint and survivor account, stating that an account which on its face is "to be paid or delivered to either, or the survivor" of the account owners is presumed to be a joint bank account. Unless the signature card or the savings certificate contains the word "survivorship," the presumption under Banking Law § 675 will not arise. However, even if the statutory presumption does not apply, it is still possible for the account to be considered a joint and survivor account under the common law. Clearly, the law provides a prescription for litigation, and New York has had its share.

> **Example 2:** Fearing that illness and the resulting physical disability will prevent her from paying her bills and managing her money, D decides that she needs someone to sign checks for her. D's friend F agrees to handle D's existing checking account and together they visit the bank. D explains to the bank officer that she wants F to be able to sign checks, and the bank officer suggests making the checking account a joint account on which both parties can sign checks. The new signature card clearly states that the account is joint bank account with right of survivorship. Indeed, that is the only kind of joint bank account the bank offers. All the funds in the account come from D; they represent her savings, and her Social Security benefits and her pension are automatically deposited in the account.

Arguably, the terms in the account agreement control. Even if the paperwork creating the account clearly states that the account is meant to be a joint bank account with right of survivorship, it may still be possible to show that the depositor did not intend the other party to the account to have a survivorship right. Suppose D's estate can prove that D did not intend F to have any interest in the account, but only added F's name to account as a convenience, to enable her to sign checks to pay D's bills. If the intent can be shown that the account was set up as a "convenience account" (that the other joint holder was merely intended to withdraw funds during the lifetime of the depositor) then the funds remaining in the account belongs to the estate of the deceased depositor rather than passing to the survivor.

Litigation over whether or not a joint bank account with right of survivorship was really meant to be a convenience account is depressingly common. Why? Are there no other means to accomplish the same ends? For example, the power of attorney is a well-established device for allowing someone to sign a document/s in the name of another without giving that person any interest in the property. The cases can be explained by bank practice: when customers tell a bank employee that they want to open an account on which a trusted friend can write checks the only option they are given is a joint account with right of survivorship. From the bank's point of view that's the best choice: the bank's systems are set up to deal with joint bank accounts and the law is very clear: so long as a check has the signature of one of the account holders the bank can pay it without any fear of liability.

c) Tenancy by the Entirety

Some jurisdictions have a particular permutation of the joint tenancy: the *tenancy by the entirety*. It differs from the generic joint tenancy account because it exists only between a married couple (and perhaps between couples who are parties to a civil union) but it is not recognized in every state. It does exist in New York for real property and interests in cooperative apartment corporations (that is, husband and wife may own shares in the co-op and the interest in the proprietary lease as tenants by the entirety). In a few states, Pennsylvania among them, personal property may be held by the entirety. Where the tenancy by the entirety differs fundamentally from the joint tenancy is that neither spouse may unilaterally sever the former; it ends only when the marriage terminates, either by death or dissolution. As with a joint tenancy with right of survivorship, succession by the survivor is "automatic." The great advantage of the tenancy by the entirety over the joint tenancy with right of survivorship is the protection it may provide from creditors' claims. The degree and effectiveness of that protection varies from state to state.

3. From Bank Accounts to Contracts

Matter of Totten sanctioned the so-called Totten trust, a bank account in which the funds remain under the total control of the depositor until her death at which time they are paid to a named beneficiary. The account is known as a Totten trust. We have already considered why the court in *Totten* analyzed the situation by using the word "trust," and we noted that its prototype can morph into a variety of a "payable on death" accounts (POD). Whether the POD account is regarded as just another contract with a POD designation, or a beneficiary designation, it is a useful will substitute.

The most familiar use of the latter term is in connection with life insurance contracts. There is no question that the insurance contract is testamentary in character. The insured owns the contract and usually has total discretion in changing the beneficiary designation until her death. The value in the contract passes from the insured to the beneficiary on the death of the insured. Life insurance contracts, however, have long been regarded as valid will substitutes.

The use of a wider array of contracts with POD provisions is now allowed. Once again, this development is probably the result of the law catching up with "consumer demand:" the arrangements property owners actually make for the disposition of their property. No doubt there are many different reasons for creating payable on death contracts, but perhaps the most common one is the desire to avoid probate by making a will unnecessary. Here is one case that probably exemplifies this development.

Matter of Hillowitz

238 N.E.2d 723 (N.Y. 1963)

FULD, CHIEF JUDGE.

This appeal stems from a discovery proceeding brought in the Surrogate's Court by the executors of the estate of Abraham Hillowitz against his widow, the appellant herein. The husband had been a partner in an 'investment club' and, after his death, the club, pursuant to a provision of the partnership agreement, paid the widow the sum of $2,800, representing his interest in the partnership. 'In the event of the death of any partner,' the agreement recited, 'his share will be transferred to his wife, with no termination of the partnership.' The executors contend in their petition that the above provision was an invalid attempt to make a testamentary disposition of property and that the proceeds should pass under the decedent's will as an asset of his estate. The widow maintains that it was a valid and enforceable contract. Although the Surrogate agreed with her, the Appellate Division held that the agreement was invalid as 'an attempted testamentary disposition' (24 A.D.2d 891, 264 N.Y.S.2d 868).

Food for Thought

Why was Mrs. Hillowitz not the executor of her husband's will? Assuming she was not under a disability, is there something odd here?

A partnership agreement which provides that, upon the death of one partner, his interest shall pass to the surviving partner or partners, resting as it does in contract, is unquestionably valid and may not be defeated by labeling it a testamentary disposition. We are unable to perceive a difference in principle between an agreement of this character and one, such as that before us, providing for a deceased partner's widow, rather than a surviving partner, to succeed to the decedent's interest in the partnership.

These partnership undertakings are, in effect, nothing more or less than third-party beneficiary contracts, performable at death. Like many similar instruments, contractual in nature, which provide for the disposition of property after death, they need not conform to the requirements of the statute of wills. Examples of such instruments include (1) a contract to make a will . . .

In short, members of a partnership may provide, without fear of running afoul of our statute of wills, that, upon the death of a partner, his widow shall be entitled to his interest in the firm. This type of third-party beneficiary contract is not invalid as an attempted testamentary disposition.

Make the Connection

The court looks to the law of contracts to solve the problem. Does this turn to contract law make sense in this context?

The executors may derive little satisfaction from McCarthy v. Pieret (281 N.Y. 407, 24 N.E.2d 102), upon which they heavily rely. In the first place, it is our considered judgment that the decision should be limited to its facts. And, in the second place, the case is clearly distinguishable from the one now before us in that the court expressly noted that the 'facts * * * indicate a mere intention on the part of the [party to the] mortgage to make a testamentary disposition of the property and not an intention to convey an immediate interest' and, in addition, that the named beneficiaries 'knew nothing of the provisions of the extension agreement' (p. 413, 24 N.E.2d p. 104).

Food for Thought

How effectively does the majority distinguish *McCarthy*? Why is the court so unwilling to overrule it?

The order of the Appellate Division should be reversed, with costs in this court and in the Appellate Division, and the order of the Surrogate's Court reinstated.

BURKE, SCILEPPI, BERGAN, BREITEL and JASEN, JJ., concur with FULD, J.

KEATING, J., concurs in result in the following memorandum:

I concur in reversal but find it difficult to distinguish McCarthy v. Pieret, 281 N.Y. 407, 24 N.E.2d 102, and am not prepared to overrule that authority. I prefer to rest reversal on the ground that respondent widow is entitled to interest in the partnership by right of survivorship as set forth in the second opinion of the Surrogate (51 Misc.2d 666, 273 N.Y.S.2d 607).

Points for Discussion

1. *Is there more to* Hillowitz *than at first appears?*

What is *really* at stake in *Hillowitz*? In other words, why is a dispute over $2,800 being decided by the Court of Appeals? The key to understanding the litigation therein may be the type of agreement involved. Mr. Hillowitz was part of a partnership and Mrs. Hillowitz argued that the payable on death provision in the agreement should be regarded as valid. At the time the case was decided, large law firms were organized as partnerships and it is possible that for a variety of reasons, including developments in partnership law, the time had come to establish the validity of the transfer of a partner's interest at the partner's death without testamentary formalities, that is including it in the partners will or in a trust.

2. *Third party beneficiary contracts*

Judge Keating in his concurrence is more than a little dissatisfied with the Court's attempt to distinguish *McCarthy v. Pieret*. This excerpt from the *McCarthy* opinion should help you understand why.

> Contracts made for the benefit of third parties are well recognized today, but they are executed contracts, where the promisee is unable to revoke or control the promisor in the fulfillment of the promise. The decision has nothing to do with attempts to make testamentary dispositions, and assumes that all three parties are alive.
>
> I do not say that the passing of property at death may not be provided for by contract or by deed, but the donor in such cases divests himself of all interest and vests it in the beneficiary. His intention is to establish present rights and not postpone them until death. He retains no further control over the transaction but, for a consideration or else because of relationship, establishes a present enforceable interest, postponed in enjoyment perhaps until death.

Judge Keating's reference to the right of survivorship refers to the Surrogate's finding that the money Mr. Hillowitz contributed to the partnership came from joint bank accounts with right of survivorship that he held with his wife and that the property should continue to be similarly held, that is with right of survivorship. More important, however, is the description of third party beneficiary contracts in *McCarthy*. The language in the second paragraph above, first adopts the traditional definition of an invalid will substitute, and then concedes the more modern notion of a valid will substitute. In order for the arrangement to be valid, the third party beneficiary must receive an **interest** in the property that is the subject of the contract at the time the parties enter into the contract. What **interest** did Hillowitz's spouse have in the partnership agreement?

Given the wide-ranging variety of Hillowitz-type arrangements, one could imagine a bewildering number of cases that might arise considering whether the transaction was testamentary in character and therefore would have to be recognized as a valid will substitute. Fortunately, legislatures have come to the rescue validating POD transactions. Several states have modeled their statutes on the UPC.

UPC § 6–101

A provision for a nonprobate transfer on death in an insurance policy, contract of employment, bond, mortgage, promissory note, certificated or uncertificated security, account agreement, custodial agreement, deposit agreement, compensation plan, pension plan, individual retirement plan, employee benefit plan, trust, conveyance, deed of gift, marital property agreement, or other written instrument of a similar nature is nontestamentary. This subsection includes a written provision that:

(1) money or other benefits due to, controlled by, or owned by a decedent before death must be paid after the decedent's death to a person whom the decedent designates either in the instrument or in a separate writing, including a will, executed either before or at the same time as the instrument, or later;

(2) money due or to become due under the instrument ceases to be payable in the event of death of the promisee or the promisor before payment or demand; or

(3) any property controlled by or owned by the decedent before death which is the subject of the instrument passes to a person the decedent designates either in the instrument or in a separate writing, including a will, executed either before or at the same time as the instrument, or later.

Other states limit the types of transaction that should be regarded as permissible will substitutes. Note the more limited scope of the New York statute:

New York Estates, Powers, and Trusts Law § 13–3.2. Rights of Beneficiaries of Pension and Similar Plans

(a) If a person is entitled to receive (1) payment in money, securities or other property under a pension, retirement, death benefit, stock bonus or profit-sharing plan, system or trust or (2) money payable by an insurance company or a savings bank authorized to conduct the business of life insurance under an annuity or pure endowment contract or a policy of life, group life, industrial life or accident and health insurance, or if a contract made by such an insurer relating to the payment of proceeds or avails of such insurance designates a payee or beneficiary to receive such payment upon the death of the person making the designation or another, the rights of persons so entitled or designated and the ownership of money, securities or other property thereby received shall not be impaired or defeated by any statute or rule of law governing the transfer of property by will, gift or intestacy.

(b) This section does not limit article 10 of the debtor and creditor law, articles 10–C and 26 of the tax law, or 2–1.8, 5–1.1–A or 13–3.6.[1]

(c) Paragraph (a) applies although a designation is revocable or subject to change by the person who makes it, and although the money, securities or other property receivable thereunder are not yet payable at the time the designation is made or are subject to withdrawal, collection or assignment by the person making the designation.

(d) A person entitled to receive payment includes:

(1) An employee or participant in a pension, retirement, death benefit, stock bonus or profit-sharing plan, system or trust.

(2) The owner or person purchasing an annuity, the person insured or the person effecting insurance, the person effecting a contract relating to payment of the proceeds or avails of a policy of insurance or an annuity or pure endowment contract.

(3) Any person entitled to receive payment by reason of a payee or beneficiary designation described in this section.

(e) A designation of a beneficiary or payee to receive payment upon death of the person making the designation or another must be made in writing and signed by the person making the designation and be:

(1) Agreed to by the employer or made in accordance with the rules prescribed for the pension, retirement, death benefit, stock bonus or profit-sharing plan, system or trust.

(2) Agreed to by the insurance company or the savings bank authorized to conduct the business of life insurance, as the case may be.

(f) This section applies to designations heretofore or hereafter made by persons who die on or after the date this section takes effect. This section does not invalidate any contract or designation which is valid without regard to this section.

---

1   These are references to the fraudulent transfer rules, the estate tax rules governing insurance, rules governing the payment of estate tax by persons receiving property of the taxed estate, the elective share rules, and rules allowing a fiduciary to disaffirm fraudulent acts of the decedent.—Eds.

Note that securities are not expressly provided for in the New York statute. In 2005, however, New York became one of the last states to adopt the Uniform Transfer on Death Security Registration Act (included in the UPC as §§ 6–301 through 6–311) by adding to the EPTL §§ 13–4.1 through 4.12 which became effective on January 1, 2006. These provisions allow the registration of securities in a form which allows the owner to designate a person to become the owner of the securities upon the death of the owner. Because the statute extends to brokerage accounts, it is possible to pass ownership of a brokerage account with holdings of any variety of financial products and of any value at death to a designated beneficiary without the use of a will. Absent these provisions, the only practical way to pass securities or a brokerage account at death without a will and without giving the beneficiary any rights during life similar in effect to a joint tenancy with right of survivorship was through the use of a revocable trust. To do so would require an existing trust instrument drafted by a lawyer, and the re-registration of the account in the name of the trustee. Once brokerage houses developed forms for registering POD accounts, making a transfer on death of the account holder became both far more simple and decidedly less costly.

We will examine some of the details of the new law in the next section, but for now note that the new law is explicitly based on contract law. UPC § 6–309 states that "A transfer on death resulting from a registration in beneficiary form is effective by reason of the contract regarding the registration between the owner and the registering entity [the brokerage house for example] and this part and is not testamentary." In fact, the Uniform Act goes even farther and provides that a state enacting the Uniform Transfer on Death Security Registration Act will recognize a registration in beneficiary form even when that registration is governed by the law of a jurisdiction "in which this or a similar legislation is not in force or was not in force when a registration in beneficiary form was made." Such a registration "is nevertheless presumed to be valid and authorized as a matter of contract law." (UPC § 6–303)

The law has progressed from the opinion in *McCarthy v. Pieret* with its narrow reading of contract law. In some ways, the use of contract law to validate what would otherwise be invalid will substitutes resembles the reception of contract concepts in other areas of property law. Recall the law of landlord and tenant which has long been marked by the weakening of property law related to concepts of status and its replacement by contract-related ideas of warranty and mitigation of damages. Once a binding agreement between a property owner and the custodian of property to turn over the property at the owner's death to a person whom the owner designates becomes an unexceptional use of contract principles in the law of succession to property, the will is well on its way to obsolescence.

4.   Something New: The (Valid) Transfer on Death Deed

Given the inability to pass personal property by POD transfers, it should not be surprising that it was not possible to make a "transfer on death deed:" a deed which purported to give title to Blackacre to a person or persons on the death of the person who makes the deed. That sort of deed was regarded as a classic invalid will substitute, because the purported grantor kept title to and complete control of Blackacre while alive; any legal interest in the property passed only on the grantor's death. Thus such an arrangement could only be accomplished by a will, at least under traditional law. If the deed was not executed in conformity with will execution statutes (with two witnesses to the grantor's signature) which was typically the case because deeds simply need to be signed by the transferor and notarized to be recorded. Absent 'due execution,' the deed cannot be regarded as a valid will and cannot pass the land to the intended beneficiary at death.

Nevertheless, many Americans tried to give away their real property at death using a transfer on death deed that simply could not accomplish that result.

Eventually, a small number of states passed statutes validating such deeds and in 2009 the Uniform Law Commission promulgated the Uniform Real Property Transfer on Death Act which has been incorporated into the UPC as §§ 6–401 through 415. Section 6–405 validates a transfer on death deed and § 6–409 sets out minimal requirements: the deed must "contain the essential elements of a property recordable inter vivos deed," must state that the transfer to the beneficiary is to take place at the grantor's death and the deed must be recorded in the public records. The grantor remains the owner of the real property that is the subject of the deed and § 6–412 expressly states that the beneficiary or beneficiaries designated in the deed have no legal or equitable interest in the real property until the death of the grantor.

In short, the transfer on death deed is very much like a will, although once it is recorded in the public records, it can be revoked only by a writing acknowledged in the same way as a deed and recorded in the public records. It *may not* be revoked by a provision in the grantor's will. The reason should be clear: "certainty of title is essential," in the words of the *Comment* to UPC § 4–611 and that policy invariably requires that documents dealing with title to real property be recorded.

Take note that unlike all of the other modern will substitutes we have considered, the transfer on death deed *is not* based on contract. There is no third party keeping a record of the beneficiary designation. Do you understand why the transfer on death deed must be recorded in the public records?

5. Problems Involving Coordination with Wills Rules

If contract-based testamentary substitutes can accomplish what a will can, the question arises: to what degree should the law of wills apply also to the validity of these devices? In particular, should the law of wills apply to the resolution of common problems that arise when property passes at death under POD instruments? Circumstances may have changed greatly between the time that the POD was created and when death arrives. In this section, we examine some common problems which will allow you to advise your clients when will substitutes are created.

a) Death of the Beneficiary Before the Owner of the Property Subject to a POD Designation

Perhaps the most common problem is to whom should the property pass if the designated beneficiary dies before the owner of the property subject to a POD designation. Recall the law of lapsed testamentary gifts and the elaborate anti-lapse statutes that may apply to gifts to will beneficiaries who predecease the testator. Should similar principles be applied when the beneficiary of a contract-based will substitute dies before the owner of the property?

If one views the issue solely from the perspective of contract law, the contract rights of the POD beneficiary are simply one more item that the beneficiary owns, and it seems sensible that these rights should pass through the beneficiary's estate. This analysis, however, is generally not applied with respect to contracts of insurance. Generally, insurance contracts provide for a contingent beneficiary (someone to receive the death benefit if the primary beneficiary predeceases the insured). Assuming that the insured was the owner of the policy, which is almost always the case, the death benefit passes to the estate of the insured if no contingent beneficiary has been named, and no new beneficiary is named. For an introduction to the complex history of the legal status of the beneficiary of a life insurance contract, *see* Gordon v. Portland Trust Bank, 271 P.2d 653 (1954).

The following discussion will acquaint you with basic facts about the operation of life insurance policies, as noted, a very common will substitute. The person whose death will lead to the payment of the death benefit is, of course, the *insured*. Usually the insured also is the *owner of the policy* but it is possible for another individual or a trust to own the policy. If the policy is obtained by someone other than the insured, that person must have an insurable interest in the life of the insured. Such interests are usually limited to family members. Any thoughts on why an insurable interest is required? The owner of the policy designates the *primary beneficiary* and the *contingent beneficiary*, designations which can be changed unless they have been made irrevocable. The owner can also borrow on the policy and decide whether or not to cash it in before the death of the insured. Usually the owner pays the premiums.

The two most common form of life insurance policies are:

1. *Term life policies.* Term life policies are pure life insurance. That is, in exchange for X paying a premium the insurance company will pay a death benefit to beneficiary Y, the named beneficiary on the insured's death during the term of the policy. The policy term can be one year or longer, although terms longer than five years are unusual. If the insured does not die during the term, the contract ceases. Life insurance provided to employees as a part of their benefits package is almost always term insurance, the term often being one month. Monthly payments by the employer insure that employee is covered for the entire duration of employment.

2. *Whole life policies.* Whole life policies charge higher premiums than term policies because some of the premium is invested by the insurance company and builds up a cash value in the policy against which the insured X can

borrow. Generally, the policy can be cashed in before the death of the insured for its then cash value. If X dies while the policy is in force, the death benefit will be paid to beneficiary Y.

Returning to the discussion of whether it is necessary for the beneficiary of a POD arrangement to survive the creator of these arrangements, there is no reason why the creator cannot condition the beneficiary's ability to collect the property on survival of the owner of the property since the essence of these will substitutes are contractual. If the creator does not, the beneficiary's rights should be transferable unless provisions of law mandate a different result. Under UPC § 6–212(b)(2) if the beneficiary of a POD account dies before the owner of the account (a "party" in UPC terms) the account belongs to the owner. Under the provisions of the Transfer on Death Security Registration Act (which has been incorporated into the UPC, see UPC § 6–307) the beneficiary of a TOD brokerage account must survive the owner of the account. If the beneficiary does not survive, the account belongs to the estate of the deceased owner. The UPC provision is identical to EPTL § 13–4.7 enacted as part of New York's adoption of the Uniform Act.

The UPC § 2–706 creates an anti-lapse statute for beneficiaries of life insurance and annuity policies, POD accounts, securities and brokerage accounts in TOD form, and pension and similar plans. Consistent with the UPC anti-lapse provision for wills (UPC § 2–603), a provision stating that the beneficiary must survive the owner of the account is not sufficient to override the anti-lapse provision, and in common with that same provision, it operates to save PODs in which the beneficiaries are descendants, grandparents, and descendants of grandparents of the deceased owner of the property.

Many states that have not adopted the provisions of the UPC, and therefore do not have the comprehensive anti-lapse provision of UPC § 2–706. In fact, New York has only two statutory provisions applicable when the beneficiary predeceases the owner of the property. As noted above, the New York enactment of the TOD securities registration act includes the provision of the Uniform Act that makes the account the property of the owner if the beneficiary does not survive. The only other New York statutory provision deals with Totten trust accounts. EPTL § 7–5.2(e) states "If the depositor survives the beneficiary, the trust shall terminate and title to the funds shall continue in the depositor free and clear of the trust." The rights of beneficiaries of other contractual will substitutes are governed by the terms of the contract or by the general common law which makes contract rights transmissible at death.

b) A Common Problem: Divorce Ends the Marriage of Owner and Beneficiary

As we have seen, statutes revoke wills when important "lifecycle" events take place, most commonly, divorce. UPC § 2–804 provides for revocation on divorce of all sorts of beneficiary designations of the ex-spouse and relatives of the ex-spouse (defined as anyone "related to the [ex-spouse] by blood, adoption, or affinity") as well as for revocation of gifts under wills to the ex-spouse and his or her relatives. Other jurisdictions may have slightly less broad revocation provisions. New York provides an example:

New York Estates, Powers, and Trusts Law § 5–1.4. [provisions dealing with non-probate property]

(a) Except as provided by the express terms of a governing instrument, a divorce (including a judicial separation as defined in subparagraph (f)(2)) or annulment of a marriage revokes any revocable

  (1) disposition or appointment of property made by a divorced individual to, or for the benefit of, the former spouse, including, but not limited to, a disposition or appointment by will, by security registration in beneficiary form (TOD), by beneficiary designation in a life insurance policy or (to the extent permitted by law) in a pension or retirement benefits plan, or by revocable trust, including a bank account in trust form,

* * * *

(f) For purposes of this section, the following terms shall have the following meaning and effect: . . . .

  (5) "Governing instrument" includes, but is not limited to, a will, testamentary instrument, trust agreement (including, but not limited to a Totten trust account under 7–5.1(d)), insurance policy, thrift, savings, retirement, pension, deferred compensation, death benefit, stock bonus or profit-sharing plan, account, arrangement, system or trust, agreement with a bank, brokerage firm or investment company, registration of securities in beneficiary form pursuant to part 4 of article 13 of this chapter, a court order, or a contract relating to the division of property made between the divorced individuals before or after the marriage, divorce, or annulment. ⚡

The statute became effective on July 7, 2008, and applies when the marriage ends on or after the effective date, and where the marriage ends prior to the effective date the statute applies where the disposition in favor of the former spouse takes effect on the death of the person who made that disposition and that person dies on or after the effective date. (L. 2008 ch. 173 § 2).

The major difference between the UPC § 2–804 and the New York statute is the much broader scope of the revocation under the UPC, extending, as noted above, to "relatives" of the ex-spouse. Suppose the residuary clause of the decedent's will reads:

I give, devise, and bequeath, the rest, residue, and remainder of my estate, both real and personal, to my spouse, Terry, and if he does not survive me, to Terry's descendants who survive me, by representation.

Suppose Terry and the testator divorce in New York, the residuary estate passes to Terry's descendants, by representation, but if UPC § 2–804 is the law, the residuary estate passes through intestate succession. Which result do you think is more consistent with the probable intent of the testator?

c) Changing the Beneficiary by a Provision in Owner's Will

There are many cases dealing with attempts to change the beneficiary of a contractual will substitute by a provision in the will of the owner of the property. These cases often involve attempts to change the beneficiary of a life insurance policy from the insured's ex-spouse to another, often the current spouse. Although the result in the leading New York case has been reversed by the amendment to EPTL § 5–1.4, the principles it lays down govern attempts to change beneficiaries by will and are indeed the principles that apply almost everywhere.

McCarthy v. Kapcar

704 N.E.2d 557 (N.Y. 1998)

SMITH, JUDGE.

The question raised by this appeal is whether a decedent insured may effect a change of the designation of beneficiary on a life insurance policy by means of a testamentary disposition when the policy sets out another procedure for changing beneficiaries. We hold that under the circumstances of this case, he may not.

The relevant facts are not in dispute. Plaintiff Christine McCarthy and Stephen Kapcar, the decedent, married in November 1972. At the time of their marriage, Kapcar was employed by J.C. Penney in New York and, as part of a benefit package, received a group life insurance policy issued by Aetna Life Insurance Co. Kapcar designated the plaintiff beneficiary of that Aetna policy. The policy provided that

> **Practice Pointer**
>
> Once you ascertain that a client has been divorced you must review the beneficiary designations for the client's nonprobate property in light of any property settlement agreement.

> "The amount payable by reason of the death of an employee shall be paid to the beneficiary designated by the employee. An employee, whether or not employment shall have terminated, may designate a beneficiary or change his designation of beneficiary from time to time by written request filed at the headquarters of the Policyholder or at the Home Office of the Insurance Company."

Within a year of the marriage, Kapcar was diagnosed with multiple sclerosis. He developed severe tremors, underwent brain surgery to alleviate the tremors, and became legally blind in 1974. After the couple separated in 1977, Kapcar left the marital home and took up residence with his father, Emil Kapcar, in Pennsylvania. Plaintiff and Kapcar divorced in 1978 on the ground that they had lived apart for over one year. A separation and property settlement agreement was incorporated into the divorce decree. Though neither the divorce decree nor the property settlement mentions the Aetna policy, the settlement document provided that "the WIFE forever relinquishes and releases all right, title, and interest which [she] now has or ever may have in and to the real, personal and mixed property of the HUSBAND; all right of dower; all right title and interest which she has or ever may have in and to the property or estate of the HUSBAND at his death and all right and interest to take against his will or under the intestate laws; and each and every other right, title, and interest she has or ever may have against the HUSBAND, his heirs, executors, administrators, and assigns excepting only such rights as she may have under this Agreement."

Stephen Kapcar died in 1984, having spent the last seven years of his life—unemployed—with his father in Pittsburgh. At the time of his death, he was a quadriplegic. According to the terms of a holographic will written in 1977 and entered into probate in the Commonwealth of Pennsylvania, Kapcar stated that "I will all my personal belongings, stock certificates, bank accounts, insurance benefits, and any other earthly belongings to my father. * * * This will voids my previous will bequeathing my belongings to Christine B. Kapcar." At no time did the decedent alter the named beneficiary (his ex-wife) on the Aetna policy.

After Kapcar's death his former wife Christine McCarthy commenced this action against defendant Aetna to claim the proceeds of the life insurance policy, an amount totaling approximately $16,000. Aetna interpleaded Emil Kapcar, administrator of decedent's estate, who claimed proceeds of the Aetna policy under decedent's holographic will. By court order, Aetna paid the proceeds of the policy into court and was discharged as a party in the action. The funds remain on deposit pending disposition of this appeal.

The trial court held that plaintiff was entitled to the proceeds because the decedent failed to comply with the terms of the policy delineating the manner in which the beneficiary designation could be modified. Appellate Term affirmed, one Justice dissenting, on substantially the same grounds. The Appellate Division reversed, two Justices dissenting, and awarded the insurance proceeds to decedent's father. The Court held that, under the circumstances of this case, decedent's will was a sufficient manifestation of his intent to change the beneficiary designation on the insurance policy and deny his ex-wife the proceeds of the policy. We now reverse.

Defendant asserts that the laws of Delaware should apply because the insurance contract provided that the policy was to be construed in accordance with laws of that State. Plaintiff argues that since the holographic will was probated in Pennsylvania, that State's laws apply. Because the result would be the same whether the law of Pennsylvania or Delaware is applied, we need not decide that question.

As a general rule, under Pennsylvania, Delaware and New York law, the method prescribed by the insurance contract must be followed in order to effect a change of beneficiary (*Equitable Life Assur. Socy. v. Stitzel*, 445 A.2d 523, 525; *Riley v. Wirth*, 169 A. 139; *Metropolitan Life Ins. Co. v. O'Donnell*, 102 A. 163, 165; *see also, Kane v. Union Mut. Life Ins. Co.*, 84 A.D.2d 148, *appeal dismissed* 57 N.Y.2d 956; *Matter of Jaccoma*, 142 A.D.2d 875, 877; NY EPTL 13–3.2[e] [1], [2]). Such a rule serves the paramount goals of ensuring that life insurance proceeds are disbursed consistently with an insured's stated intent and of preventing the courts and parties from engaging in rank speculation regarding the wishes of the deceased.

Strict compliance with the rule is not always required. Instead, "There must be an act or acts designed for the purpose of making the change, though they may fall short of accomplishing it" (*Aetna Life Ins. Co. v. Sterling*, 15 A.D.2d 334, 335, *affd.* 183 N.E.2d 325; *see also, Kane v. Union Mut. Life Ins. Co.*, 84 A.D.2d 148, *appeal dismissed* 57 N.Y.2d 956, *supra*; *New York Life Ins. Co. v. Lawson*, 134 F.Supp. 63, 65 [D.Del.]; *Carruthers v. $21,000*, 434 A.2d 125, 127). "The paramount factor in resolving the controversy is the intent of the insured. Mere intent, however, on the part of the insured is not enough; there must be some affirmative act or acts on [the part of the insured] to accomplish the change" (*Cable v. Prudential Ins. Co.*, 89 A.D.2d 636). Thus, if the decedent has "done all that was reasonably possible to do to show his intention" (*Carpenter v. Greene*, 396 A.2d 150, 152 [Del]; *see also, New York Life Ins. Co. v. Cannon*, 22 Del. Ch. 269, 194 A. 412, 413–414) or has made "every reasonable effort" (*Carruthers v. $21,000*, 434 A.2d, at 127, *supra*) to comply with the policy requirements, then substantial compliance with the terms of the policy will suffice to demonstrate the policyholder's intent (*New York Life Ins. Co. v. Lawson*, 134 F.Supp. 63, 65 [D.Del.], *supra* ["Delaware Courts have adopted the substantial compliance doctrine in cases involving validity of a change of beneficiary"]).

While the act or acts constituting substantial compliance may vary, they do not include general testamentary statements in a will. Indeed, "[a]s part of the [contract] bargain, the employee agrees to change the beneficiary only pursuant to the procedures outlined in the policy, and these procedures generally will either expressly prohibit a change in beneficiary by testamentary disposition or impliedly prevent such mode of change by setting forth conditions to effect the change which cannot be met by a statement in a will" (*Matter of Jaccoma, supra*, at 877, 530 N.Y.S.2d 909; *see also, Carruthers v. $21,000, supra* [holding that a bequest in a holographic will did not effect a change of a named beneficiary]). As one court has stated,

> " 'To hold that a change in beneficiary may be made by testamentary disposition alone would open up a serious question as to payment of life insurance policies. It is in the public interest that an insurance company may pay a loss to the beneficiary designated in the policy as promptly after the death of insured as may reasonably be done. If there is uncertainty as to the beneficiary upon the death of insured, in all cases where the right to change the beneficiary had been reserved there would always be a question as to whom the proceeds of the insurance should be paid. If paid to the beneficiary, a will might later be probated designating a different disposition of the fund, and it would be a risk, that few companies would be willing to take' " (*Stone v. Stephens*, 155 Ohio St. 595, 600–601, 99 N.E.2d 766, 769 [citation omitted]).

Make the Connection

Another use of the concept of substantial compliance. How does this use relate to substantial compliance with the formalities of creating a will?

In the instant case, there is no evidence that decedent made any attempt to change the beneficiary designation during the seven years between his separation from plaintiff and his death. Nor is there any record evidence that decedent was physically or mentally incapable of attempting to substantially comply with the requirements of the policy. In the absence of such evidence, the court is restrained from holding that it was the decedent's stated intention that his father receive the proceeds from the insurance policy.

We do not agree that the requirement of substantial compliance with the requirements of the insurance policy is waived where, as here, the insurance company becomes a stakeholder in an interpleader action (*cf., Kane v. Union Mut. Life Ins. Co.*, 84 A.D.2d 148, *supra*). As stated previously, although the rule serves to protect the insurer, it also serves the essential goal of preventing the courts and parties from speculating regarding the wishes of the deceased. Thus, while the insurer who has brought the proceeds of the policy into court and requested the court to adjudicate the rights of contesting claimants may no longer insist upon strict compliance with the policy provisions, that insurer may require proof of substantial compliance (*see, e.g., New York Life Ins. Co. v Lawson, supra*, at 65).

> **Make the Connection**
>
> Civil Procedure: the use of interpleader is common in disputes over entitlement to a life insurance death benefit.

Accordingly, the order of the Appellate Division should be reversed, without costs, and the judgment of Civil Court of the City of New York, New York County, reinstated. The certified question should not be answered as it is unnecessary.

KAYE, C.J., and BELLACOSA, LEVINE, CIPARICK and WESLEY, JJ., concur.

Points for Discussion

1. *Changing life insurance beneficiaries*

McCarthy requires strict compliance with the contractual terms for changing the beneficiary of a life insurance contract. The reason for that rule is stated in the opinion: to hold otherwise would greatly increase the life insurance company's administrative costs and opens up the possibility of litigation. The rule really is a rule: *McCarthy* has been held to govern a case in which the will specifically referred to the life insurance policy and made a bequest of the policy proceeds. (*See* Lincoln Life and Annuity Co. v. Caswell, 31 A.D.3d 1 (1st Dep't 2006)). Do you think the logic of the rule is sufficiently compelling to defeat intent expressed in a will?

2. *Substantial compliance*

The *McCarthy* court does state that it is possible to change the beneficiary of a life insurance contract through substantial compliance with the actual contract's requirements. Do you think that this application of substantial compliance is inconsistent with its application to issues of conformity to will execution requirements? If a successful use of substantial compliance means that "close enough is good enough," it seems that at least in the life insurance context

close should really mean **close.** The person who has the authority to select the beneficiary (the owner of the policy who is almost always the insured) should be required to do everything possible to comply with the contractual requirements. Thinking about the use of substantial compliance in this context helps us to understand why both the Restatement Third of Property and the UPC use the harmless error rule in the will context rather than the more difficult to satisfy substantial compliance doctrine.

3. *Conflicts of laws rules for wills and will substitutes*

Why did the Surrogate Court probate Mr. Kapcar's will, if New York law does not recognize holographic wills (except in limited circumstances not applicable here, EPTL § 3–2.2)? The answer is because the statute so provides:

New York Estates, Powers, and Trusts Law § 3–5.1(c). Wills Having Relation to Another Jurisdiction

> (c)   A will disposing of personal property, wherever situated, or real property situated in this state, made within or without this state by a domiciliary or non-domiciliary thereof, is formally valid and admissible to probate in this state, if it is in writing and signed by the testator, and otherwise executed and attested in accordance with the local law of:
>
> (1)   This state;
>
> (2)   The jurisdiction in which the will was executed, at the time of execution; or
>
> (3)   The jurisdiction in which the testator was domiciled, either at the time of execution or of death.

UPC § 2–506 concurs but is slightly broader in that it also recognizes the validity of a will executed in conformity with the law of the place where the testator has an abode or is a national:

> A written will is valid if executed in compliance with Section 2–502 or 2–503 or if its execution complies with the law at the time of execution of the place where the will is executed, or of the law of the place where at the time of execution or at the time of death the testator is domiciled, has a place of abode, or is a national.

The question in *McCarthy* which is not answered by the revised EPTL § 5–1.4 (or for that matter by UPC § 2–804), that is, whether a change in beneficiary can be accomplished by will, is sometimes dealt with by statutes that refer to specific will substitutes. New York has three statutes that deal with changing the beneficiary of a testamentary substitute by will. The TOD securities registration provisions provide that "A registration in beneficiary form can be revoked or amended by an express direction in the owner's will which specifically refers to such registration." (EPTL § 13–4.6(b)). The provisions dealing with revocable lifetime trusts (which we will examine more closely very shortly) provide "a revocable lifetime trust can be revoked or amended by an express direction in the creator's will which specifically refers to such lifetime trust or a particular provision thereof." (EPTL § 7–1.16) The most detailed provision, not surprisingly, involves the will substitute with the longest history, the Totten trust.

New York Estates, Powers, and Trusts Law § 7–5.2(2)

(2)   A trust can be revoked, terminated or modified by the depositor's will only by means of, and to the extent of, an express direction concerning such trust account, which must be described in the will as being in trust for a named beneficiary in a named financial institution. Where the depositor has more than one trust account for a particular beneficiary in a particular financial institution, such a direction will affect all such accounts, unless the direction is limited to one or more accounts specifically identified by account number in addition to the foregoing requirements. A testamentary revocation, termination or modification under this paragraph can be effected by express words of revocation, termination or modification, or by a specific bequest of the trust account, or any part of it, to someone other than the beneficiary. A bequest of part of a trust account shall operate as a pro tanto revocation to the extent of the bequest.

The following case describes something of the history of this provision as well as serving to introduce another important body of law that affects many will substitutes.

Eredics v. Chase Manhattan Bank, N.A.

790 N.E.2d 1166 (N.Y. 2003)

KAYE, CHIEF JUDGE.

In November 1975, plaintiff, then 38, married decedent Nick G. Nicholas, then 45. They remained together, without children, until 1990 when they separated. In June 1995, they entered into a formal separation agreement and divorced later that year. The separation agreement provided:

> "3. Except as set forth herein, each party shall own, free of any claim or right of the other, all of the items of property, real, personal or mixed, of any kind, nature or description and wheresoever situate, which are now owned by him or her, or which are now in his or her name, or to which he or she is, or may be beneficially entitled to which may hereafter belong to or come to him or her with full power to him or to her to dispose of the same as fully and effectually in all respects and for all purposes as if he or she were unmarried. * * *

> "5. * * * b. The parties agree and acknowledge that any and all bank accounts, held jointly or otherwise * * * not specifically mentioned in this agreement, have been distributed equitably and to the mutual satisfaction of the parties, prior to the execution of this agreement. * * *

Take Note

Pay close attention to the terms of the separation agreement; are they as clear as they should be?

"9. Each party hereby releases, waives and relinquishes any and all rights which he or she may now have or may hereafter acquire, as to the other party's spouse under the present or future laws of any jurisdiction * * * to share in the estate of the other party upon the latter's death * * *. This provision is intended to, and shall constitute a mutual waiver by the parties to take against each other's wills * * *."

Nicholas died December 20, 1998. His will, a one-page document dated June 15, 1998, left 60% of his estate "of whatsoever nature and wheresoever may be situate" to his brother (the executor), and the remainder to his sister.

During the marriage, decedent had deposited funds into five accounts in three banks, each "in trust for" plaintiff—an account commonly known as a Totten trust. After the parties separated, decedent continued to receive regular account statements and paid taxes on the interest generated. Decedent made no change to the accounts, which at the time of his death still named plaintiff as the beneficiary. Although at that time those accounts were worth approximately 36% of decedent's taxable estate, he made no mention of them in his will.

Plaintiff commenced this action against the three banks and decedent's estate, seeking a declaratory judgment establishing her right to the accounts. She maintained that, in the absence of a valid revocation under EPTL 7–5.2 the accounts became her property upon decedent's death, and that in fact neither she nor decedent intended the separation agreement to change her status as beneficiary. The estate counterclaimed, seeking a declaration that it owned the funds in question because plaintiff waived her right to the accounts in the separation agreement. Defendant Flushing Savings Bank, which had already turned over to the estate its share of the funds in question, cross-claimed against the estate.

Supreme Court granted plaintiff's motion for summary judgment, denied the estate's cross motion and directed entry of judgment for plaintiff against Flushing Savings Bank for the amount it had paid the estate. The court confined its analysis to the issue of revocation, concluding that the separation agreement did not amount to a revocation of the Totten trusts under EPTL 7–5.2, and rejecting the estate's waiver argument as inconsistent with the statute. As relevant here, the Appellate Division affirmed, similarly focusing exclusively on statutory revocation. Because we conclude that the separation agreement did not effect a revocation by decedent, or a waiver by plaintiff, we now affirm.

A Totten trust—born a century ago in *Matter of Totten*, 179 N.Y. 112, 71 N.E. 748 [1904]—is essentially an account which the depositor holds "in trust for" or "as trustee for" another person, the beneficiary. The trust may be revoked during the lifetime of the depositor by withdrawal of the funds or other affirmative acts, but if the depositor predeceases the beneficiary without revoking the trust, the beneficiary takes the balance of the funds at the time of the depositor's death without the funds passing through the depositor's estate. The account, in effect, is an alternative testamentary disposition.

Simple though the concept may be, in practice the Totten trust engendered substantial litigation, often with inconsistent results (*see* Preminger, Thomas, Frunzi and Hilker, Trusts and Estates Practice in New York § 2:7, at 2–14). Courts divided on such issues as whether the depositor completed the gift by giving the passbook to the beneficiary (*compare Matthews v. Brooklyn Sav. Bank*, 208 N.Y. 508, 102 N.E. 520 [1913] [not completed], *with Matter of Farrell*, 298 N.Y. 129, 81 N.E.2d 51 [1948] [completed]); the effect of oral statements of intent on modification, termination or revocation (*compare Hessen v. McKinley*, 155 App.Div. 496, 140 N.Y.S. 724 [1st Dept.1913] [no modification], *affd*. 209 N.Y. 532, 102 N.E. 1104 [1913], *with Tibbitts v. Zink*, 231 App.Div. 339, 247 N.Y.S. 300 [3d Dept.1931] [termination]); and apparent revocation in a will (*compare Matter of Krycun*, 24 N.Y.2d 710, 301 N.Y.S.2d 970, 249 N.E.2d 753 [1969] [no revocation], *with Matter of Beagan*, 112 Misc. 292, 183 N.Y.S. 941 [Sur.Ct.1920] [revocation]).

To address the inconsistency in an area of law where certainty and predictability are especially important, in 1975 the Law Revision Commission recommended, and the Legislature enacted, part 5 of EPTL article 7, specifying the means by which a depositor could revoke, terminate or modify a Totten trust (*see* L. 1975, ch. 499; Mem. of Law Rev. Commn., 1975 McKinney's Session Laws of N.Y., at 1535). Originally, EPTL 7-5.2 provided two ways to accomplish those objectives—*during the depositor's lifetime* "only by means of, and to the extent of, withdrawals from or charges against the trust account made or authorized by the depositor" (EPTL 7–5.2[1]), and *in the depositor's will* only by means of "an express direction concerning such trust account, which must be described in the will as being in trust for a named beneficiary in a named financial institution" (EPTL 7–5.2[2]). Absent such measures, the trust would terminate on a depositor's death and title to the funds remaining in the account would vest in a surviving beneficiary free and clear of the trust (EPTL 7–5.2[4]).

Food for Thought

Does this brief summary of the history of litigation over tentative trusts after the decision in *Matter of Totten* demonstrate both the difficulty of making new law through cases and about the complications of will substitutes?

In 1985, the Legislature amended the statute to permit another means of altering, or ending, a Totten trust. To relieve depositors of possible interest penalties on withdrawal resulting from federal banking regulation, the Legislature provided that a depositor could also revoke, terminate or modify the trust "by a writing which specifically names the beneficiary and the financial institution" (L. 1985, ch. 89, § 1; *see also* Sponsor's Mem, 1985 N.Y. Legis Ann, at 74). That writing, however, must be "acknowledged or proved in the manner required to entitle conveyances of real property to be recorded, and shall be filed with the financial institution wherein the account is maintained" (EPTL 7–5.2[1]).

Thus, the statute is clear and precise in prescribing the three ways by which a depositor can revoke a Totten trust: withdrawal of the funds, an express direction in a will and a qualifying writing filed with the bank.

Take Note

Is it clear to you precisely how this argument (waiver) differs from the revocation one previously dispatched?

Here, as defendants concede, there was no statutory revocation by the depositor. The funds remained on deposit; there was no mention of the accounts in decedent's will; and no document was filed with defendant banks. Defendants contend, however, that plaintiff waived her right as beneficiary in the separation agreement. We disagree. Although we conclude that a named beneficiary may waive the right to a Totten trust account, here the separation agreement is insufficient to effect that result.

Recently, in *Silber v. Silber*, 99 N.Y.2d 395, 757 N.Y.S.2d 227, 786 N.E.2d 1263 [2003], we confronted an analogous question: where no change of beneficiary is made in pension plan documents, can a designated beneficiary waive the right to her ex-husband's pension plan death benefits by an agreement incorporated into a qualified domestic relations order (QDRO)? There too the legislature—in that case, Congress, in the Employee Retirement Income Security Act of 1974 (ERISA)—had provided an explicit scheme to bring uniformity to an area of law that previously had been a patchwork of case law and statutes, including specific requirements for changing a beneficiary designation. For reasons of fairness in effectuating the clear intent of the parties to the QDRO, and following the majority of federal courts to address the issue, we concluded that a designated beneficiary can waive the right to pension plan death benefits so long as the waiver is explicit, voluntary and made in good faith. The QDRO in *Silber* met those criteria, and therefore constituted a waiver of beneficial interests in the pension funds.

> FYI
>
> A Qualified Domestic Relations Order (QDRO) is the only way to have a state court property settlement incident to divorce apply to employee benefit plans governed by federal law.

Guided by the same considerations of fairness in effectuating the clear intent of the parties, we conclude that a beneficiary also can waive rights in a Totten trust, so long as the waiver is explicit, voluntary and made in good faith. In this respect we agree with defendants that the provisions of EPTL article 7 governing *a depositor's* revocation of a Totten trust do not prevent *a beneficiary* from freely and independently waiving such rights. We are satisfied, moreover, that the legislative concern for certainty and predictability in this area is sufficiently safeguarded by the requirement that any such waiver be explicit, voluntary and made in good faith. We thus honor the unequivocal intent of the parties as well as the letter and spirit of the statute.

Here, however, the separation agreement is insufficient to effect a waiver. Defendants rest their claim largely on the broad language of paragraph 3 regarding the final division of "all of the items of property" owned by the parties, urging that the burden was on plaintiff to carve out her rights as beneficiary if she wished to preserve them. The requirement, however, is otherwise: there is no waiver of beneficiary status unless the waiver is explicitly made in the writing (*compare Matter of Maruccia*, 54 N.Y.2d 196, 205, 445 N.Y.S.2d 73, 429 N.E.2d 751 [1981]). There is no explicit waiver here, and we decline defendants' invitation to infer such a waiver from the broad language of the agreement.

The most specific language of the agreement relied upon by defendants actually undermines their waiver argument. Paragraph 5(b), dealing with "bank accounts * * * not specifically mentioned" in the agreement—which includes the Totten trust accounts—is reasonably understood to mean that it was to the parties' "mutual satisfaction" that decedent remain the owner of those accounts and plaintiff remain the beneficiary. Significantly, the separation agreement does contain several specific waivers—of plaintiff's rights to support and maintenance, life insurance, medical insurance and individual retirement accounts—but not the beneficial interest in the Totten trust. The parties' mutual waiver of claims against each other's estate in paragraph 9, furthermore, does not help defendants' position because Totten trusts pass outside the estate.

Finally, while defendants rely heavily on *Silber*, that agreement is easily distinguished from the separation agreement at issue here. In *Silber*, the divorce decree between Barbara A. Silber and Dr. Robert Silber required that she receive 25% of his retirement benefits and that he designate her as 50% beneficiary of his death benefits. Thirteen years later, Dr. Silber was still working and not receiving retirement benefits and, at the behest of Barbara A., the parties entered into a new agreement, incorporated into a QDRO, providing Barbara A. with immediate access to benefit payments. The agreement, which explicitly superseded the divorce decree, created new annuities in Barbara A.'s name (funded with 45% of the accumulations from Dr. Silber's pension plan) and provided that "[a]ll ownership and interest in the balance of the accumulations" belonged to Dr. Silber. (99 N.Y.2d at 399, 757 N.Y.S.2d 227, 786 N.E.2d 1263.) Though Dr. Silber died without changing the beneficiary designation on his pension plan, the intent of the parties was clear—to provide immediate payments out of the pension funds to Barbara A. in exchange for her waiver of any future right to the balance of the accumulations. Indeed, Barbara A. conceded that, after she entered into the QDRO, she did not expect to be a beneficiary of the pension funds.

Unlike the QDRO in *Silber*, the separation agreement in the present case broadly and generally applies to all of the parties' respective property, without addressing the accounts in dispute. There is no indication that the parties intended the agreement to affect plaintiff's right as beneficiary of the Totten trusts at all.

Accordingly, the order of the Appellate Division should be affirmed, with costs.

Judges Smith, Ciparick, Wesley, Rosenblatt, Graffeo and Read concur.

———————

Points for Discussion

1. *Effect of revocation on divorce statute*

Recognize that under UPC § 2–804 or NY EPTL § 5–1.4, the designation of the ex-spouse in *Eredics* as beneficiary of the Totten trust accounts (the UPC term is "payable on death account") would be revoked on divorce.

2. *Practical difficulties of revocation by will*

The history of EPTL § 7–5.2, the provision governing the revocation of Totten trust accounts, gives you some insight into the difficulties of revoking beneficiary designations in will substitutes by a subsequent will. The problem always is the degree of specificity required for an effective revocation. The New York statute settled on requiring an "express direction concerning such account which must be described in the will as being in trust for a named beneficiary in a named financial institution." The statute also provides that the provision may be express words of revocation, termination, or modification, or a specific bequest of the account to someone other than the beneficiary.

3. *The "superwill"*

Restatement Third, Property (Wills and Other Donative Transfers) § 7.2, comment *e* states that courts should recognize express will provisions that change the beneficiaries of all forms of nonprobate property arrangements with proper protection for those issuing the financial instruments. The problem with this so-called "superwill" is that banks and insurance companies may pay the outstanding sums to the beneficiary appearing on its records before receiving notice of the change made by the will. A "superwill "provision might read as follows: "I revoke all beneficiary designations of all my nonprobate assets and make X the beneficiary of those assets." The problem is that it is difficult to see how the financial institution, etc. will actually know of the change?

Suppose, in the absence of statute, payment is made to the former beneficiary, does the beneficiary designated in the will have a remedy? A typical remedy might be restitution through the use of a constructive trust: recipient holds for the benefit of beneficiary designated in the will. The State of Washington has a statute authorizing the revocation of beneficiary designations in will substitutes by a later will (except joint tenancies in real property, a deed "by which conveyance has been postponed until the death of the owner," property passing under a community property agreement, and an IRA), *see* Rev. Code Wash. §§ 11.11.010 and 11.11.020. Do the provisions of the New York Totten trust revocation by will provision hint at some of the problems that have to be faced in making a "superwill" work properly? Even with a statute, all may not be clear. For example, would the law give effect to a will provision that reads "I revoke all beneficiary designations of all my nonprobate assets and make X the beneficiary of those assets?" Assume that the will designates a beneficiary of "all of my Totten trust accounts." After the date of execution of the will the testator opens a new Totten trust account the beneficiary of which is not the person named in the will as beneficiary of the testator's other Totten trust accounts. Who gets the money on the testator's death?

4. *ERISA*

The *Eredics* case also mentions the effect of the Employee Retirement Income Security Act of 1974 (ERISA), 29 U.S.C.A. § 1001 et seq. on state laws effecting will substitutes subject to the federal statute. *Egelhoff v. Egelhoff,* 532 U.S.141 (2001) involved a dispute between the children of Mr. Egelhoff's first marriage and his second spouse from whom he was divorced over the proceeds of an insurance policy on father/ex-husband's life. Mr. Egelhoff was a resident of the State of Washington both at the time of his divorce from his second wife and at the time of his death two months later from injuries sustained in an automobile accident. The life insurance policy was provided by his employer as part of his employment benefits package and the insurance coverage was a "plan" subject to ERISA. Mr. Egelhoff had named the then Mrs. Egelhoff as beneficiary of the life insurance policy and had not changed that beneficiary designation before his death. Pursuant to Washington statute, however, the divorce revoked the beneficiary designation in favor of the ex-spouse.

Because Mr. Egelhoff died intestate, the revocation of the beneficiary designation meant that the death benefit was part of his probate estate and passed to his children who were his heirs. ERISA, however, has a provision which preempts state laws relating to plans subject to ERISA. In *Egelhoff*, a divided United States Supreme Court held that ERISA did indeed preempt the Washington statute and required that the beneficiary designation on file with the plan administrator be honored. The decision is controversial and it did call forth a vigorous dissent by Justice Breyer, joined by Justice Stevens.

In spite of the *Egelhoff* decision, it was possible that divorce might undo the designation of the ex-spouse as beneficiary under a qualified plan in some circumstances. In *Keen v. Weaver*, 121 S.W.3d 721 (Tex. 2003) a divided Texas Supreme Court held that the Texas revocation on divorce statute which applies to designations of an ex-spouse as beneficiary of a retirement account is indeed preempted by ERISA. However, the Court also held that federal common law governs the question of the effect of divorce on the status of the ex-spouse as beneficiary of a qualified plan and that the law "recognizes a former spouse's waiver of ERISA plan benefits in a divorce decree dividing the marital estate so long as it is specific, knowing, and voluntary." (121 S.W.3d at 727). The Court then held that the terms of the property settlement incorporated into the divorce decree in the instant case met those criteria and that the ex-spouse was therefore not entitled to the decedent's benefits under the qualified plan.

> ### Practice Pointer
>
> The lesson of this complex law on changes in beneficiary designations is straightforward. The lawyer must try to make sure that the client changes beneficiary designations when changes in circumstances make those changes appropriate.

The United States Supreme Court refused to grant *certiorari* in *Keen* (540 U.S. 1047 (2003)), but it turns out that it was waiting for the right case. In *Kennedy v. Plan Administrator for DuPont Savings and Investment Plan*, 555 U.S. 285 (2009) a unanimous court in an opinion by Justice Souter held that the governing documents of the plan subject to ERISA must control and unless they make provision for recognition of a federal common law waiver; such a wavier is not effective. The Court left open the possibility that a waiver could be consistent with the governing documents of the plan. It also refused to express any view on whether a state court could enforce the waiver once the benefits are paid to the designative beneficiary who made the wavier, in this case as in *Keen* and *Egelhoff*, the participant's ex-spouse.

Presumably, in the latter situation, the remedy would be a constructive trust imposed on the beneficiary to distribute the policy proceeds to whoever would receive them as a result of the waiver. And that is exactly what the United States Court of Appeals for the Third Circuit did in *Estate of Kensinger v. URL Pharma*, 674 F.3d 131 (2012), holding that ERISA did not prevent a court from imposing a constructive trust on an ex-spouse who made a common law waiver of the qualified plan benefits by expressly waiving those benefits in the divorce decree.

A great deal of wealth is held in the variety of will substitutes recognized. Many are subject to ERISA and litigation over the question of the effect of divorce on a beneficiary designation of the ex-spouse is always best avoided.

5. *Restatement Third of Property on applying wills rules to will substitutes*

Restatement Third, Property (Wills and Other Donative Transfers) § 7.2 is unequivocal in asserting that will doctrines should apply to will substitutes:

> Although a will substitute need not be executed in compliance with the statutory formalities required for a will, such an arrangement is, to the extent appropriate, subject to substantive restrictions on testation and to rules of construction and other rules applicable to testamentary dispositions.

The intermediate Illinois appellate court has adopted the Restatement position with respect to a funded lifetime trust intended to be a will substitute, *see Handelsman v. Handelsman*, 366 Ill.App.3d 1122, 304 Ill.Dec. 406, 852 N.E.2d 862 (Ill.App. 2 Dist. 2006).

d) Liability for the Decedent's Debts

One of the primary functions of the probate is to provide a process for paying the decedent's debts. While the details differ, all probate systems in the United States establish a procedure for the making of claims by creditors, the acceptance or rejection of a claim by the personal representative, adjudication of disputed claims, and perhaps most important, a time limit on making claims. Funds used to pay the decedent's debts come from the probate estate. With the growth in forms of non-probate property through the use of will substitutes, you may wonder whether it is possible to frustrate creditors by using nonprobate property arrangements as extensively as possible and reducing the probate estate. In general, the answer is "no," although the details of how creditors can reach nonprobate property differ from state to state.

The UPC does have provisions for making nonprobate property subject to the decedent's debts in § 6–102.

UPC § 6–102. Liability Of Nonprobate Transferees For Creditor Claims and Statutory Allowances

(a) In this section, "nonprobate transfer" means a valid transfer effective at death, other than a transfer of a survivorship interest in a joint tenancy of real estate, by a transferor whose last domicile was in this state to the extent that the transferor immediately before death had power, acting alone, to prevent the transfer by revocation or withdrawal and instead to use the property for the benefit of the transferor or apply it to discharge claims against the transferor's probate estate.

(b) Except as otherwise provided by statute, a transferee of a nonprobate transfer is subject to liability to any probate estate of the decedent for allowed claims against decedent's probate estate and statutory allowances to the decedent's spouse and children to the extent the estate is insufficient to satisfy those claims and allowances. The liability of a nonprobate transferee may not exceed the value of nonprobate transfers received or controlled by that transferee.

(c) Nonprobate transferees are liable for the insufficiency described in subsection (b) in the following order of priority:

(1) a transferee designated in the decedent's will or any other governing instrument, as provided in the instrument;

(2) the trustee of a trust serving as the principal nonprobate instrument in the decedent's estate plan as shown by its designation as devisee of the decedent's residuary estate or by other facts or circumstances, to the extent of the value of the nonprobate transfer received or controlled;

(3) other nonprobate transferees, in proportion to the values received.

(d) Unless otherwise provided by the trust instrument, interests of beneficiaries in all trusts incurring liabilities under this section abate as necessary to satisfy the liability, as if all of the trust instruments were a single will and the interests were devises under it.

(e) A provision made in one instrument may direct the apportionment of the liability among the nonprobate transferees taking under that or any other governing instrument. If a provision in one instrument conflicts with a provision in another, the later one prevails.

(f) Upon due notice to a nonprobate transferee, the liability imposed by this section is enforceable in proceedings in this state, whether or not the transferee is located in this state.

(g) A proceeding under this section may not be commenced unless the personal representative of the decedent's estate has received a written demand for the proceeding from the surviving spouse or a child, to the extent that statutory allowances are affected, or a creditor. If the personal representative declines or fails to commence a proceeding after demand, a person making demand may commence the proceeding in the name of the decedent's estate, at the expense of the person making the demand and not of the estate. A personal representative who declines in good faith to commence a requested proceeding incurs no personal liability for declining.

(h) A proceeding under this section must be commenced within one year after the decedent's death, but a proceeding on behalf of a creditor whose claim was allowed after proceedings challenging disallowance of the claim may be commenced within 60 days after final allowance of the claim.

(i)   Unless a written notice asserting that a decedent's probate estate is nonexistent or insufficient to pay allowed claims and statutory allowances has been received from the decedent's personal representative, the following rules apply:

   (1)   Payment or delivery of assets by a financial institution, registrar, or other obligor, to a nonprobate transferee in accordance with the terms of the governing instrument controlling the transfer releases the obligor from all claims for amounts paid or assets delivered.

   (2)   A trustee receiving or controlling a nonprobate transfer is released from liability under this section with respect to any assets distributed to the trust's beneficiaries. Each beneficiary to the extent of the distribution received becomes liable for the amount of the trustee's liability attributable to assets received by the beneficiary.

Because the subject it addresses is complex, the statute is detailed.

Once the will is no longer the exclusive or even the principal device to make gifts at death it was complicated to draft a statute that takes into account the treatment nonprobate property receives. Likewise, the statute has to establish a procedure that creditors can use, since the usual mechanisms for presenting a claim in the course of probate proceedings will not allow the creditor to reach nonprobate property. It also includes a statute of limitations which requires that claims be brought within one year of death (UPC § 6–102(h)). Note, too, that the statute applies only when the probate estate is insufficient to pay the decedent's debts and the allowances to the surviving spouse and children.

B. The Revocable Trust

527 - 45

1. Introduction

In our estate planning problem, Ward used a revocable trust. While Ward uses securities as the trust corpus, all types of property (including real property) can be limited in trust and therefore be nonprobate property. One might therefore regard the revocable trust as the ultimate will substitute. Not only does the creator (Ward) retain the beneficial interest in the trust for his life, he also maintains complete control over the property in the trust. Although the trust limited interests to others (June and the boys), they had no present interest in any of the property. Conceptually, as a practical matter, the remainder beneficiaries of the trust had no more interest in or control over the trust property than the beneficiaries of a will have over the testator's probate property while the testator is alive. Arguably this last sentence is somewhat of an exaggeration. Suffice it to say, that the creator of a revocable trust retains the power to defeat their interests. While the creator (or his or her delegate) with the power to revoke is competent, the analogy between the trust beneficiaries and the will beneficiaries is accurate.

Before we continue, we need to pay attention to terminology. The person who creates a trust can be identified as the *settlor*, the *grantor*, or the *creator*. The term settlor is widely used in England, where, reflecting their history, trusts, particularly those of real property, are often called *settlements*. The term grantor also is derived from the fact that trusts of land were created by a deed of trust; the person who makes a deed is a grantor. Because trusts may have both real and personal property, the term has come to be used to describe the person who transfers both real and personal property in trust. Grantor is also the term used in provisions of the Internal Revenue Code that deal with the income taxation of trusts. Given the importance of taxation, grantor has become the most widely used term. Creator is the term used in the New York's legislation on lifetime trusts, enacted in 1997. In spite of its somewhat grandiose sound, it lacks historical and doctrinal baggage, and throughout these materials we will refer to the person who creates a trust as the creator.

Revocable trusts, of course, are created by living creators; testamentary trusts are created by provisions in a will. Because it becomes effective on the death of the testator, the testamentary trust is always irrevocable (at least by the person who created them). Trusts created by living creators can also be irrevocable. Trusts created during life are often called inter vivos trusts, using Latin words that have become so common that they are seldom italicized. The New York statutes use the term lifetime trusts, and that is the term we will use in these materials. Sometimes the term "living trust" is used to refer to a revocable lifetime trust. The term is confusing and we will avoid using it.

Given what we have already learned about contract-based will substitutes, there would seem to be little difficulty in classifying the revocable trust as a valid will substitute. It certainly can be understood as a contract between the creator of the trust and the trustee to hold the property for the benefit of the beneficiaries. If only it were that simple. The trust is a very old device and the law that governs it has deep roots. The more modern view of a trust as essentially a type of contract is really quite recent and to some degree contradicts centuries-old law. We will investigate that traditional law in greater detail when we consider all types of trusts. For now, it is enough to realize that, traditionally at least, a trust cannot be created without beneficiaries who have interests which can be enforced by a court. And why is that? Quite simply, if such interests do not exist, there is no person able to hold the trustee to perform his or her duties. A simple contract between A and B to use certain property to benefit C, D, and E unless A changes the terms of the contract does not fit very well into traditional doctrinal categories. Unless the trust "beneficiaries," have an enforceable right in property rather than an "expectancy" like that of a beneficiary under the will of a living testator, there is no trust under traditional law. This concept was further explored in the chapter on trusts.

This conceptual difficulty stood in the way of the use of the revocable trust as a will substitute. If no interest passed to the beneficiaries during the lifetime of the property owner the "trust" was simply an attempt to make a gift at death without conforming to the statute of wills. Indeed, this conundrum is simply a variation on the one parsed above with respect to other will substitutes.

2. The Validation of the Revocable Trust as a Will Substitute

Modern law regards the revocable trust as a valid will substitute. Achieving that result, however, required a good deal of ink spilled in many briefs and court opinions and it was not until the mid-twentieth century that the revocable trust began to be widely accepted as a valid will substitute. The following case is one of the leading cases validating the use of a revocable trust as a will substitute.

Farkas v. Williams

125 N.E.2d 600 (Ill. 1955)

HERSHEY, JUSTICE.

This is an appeal from a decision of the Appellate Court, First District, which affirmed a decree of the circuit court of Cook County finding that certain declarations of trust executed by Albert B. Farkas and naming Richard J. Williams as beneficiary were invalid and that Regina Farkas and Victor Farkas, as coadministrators of the estate of said Albert B. Farkas, were the owners of the property referred to in said trust instruments, being certain shares of capital stock of Investors Mutual, Inc.

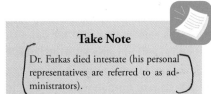

Take Note

Dr. Farkas died intestate (his personal representatives are referred to as administrators).

Said coadministrators, herein referred to as plaintiffs, filed a complaint in the circuit court of Cook County for a declaratory decree and other relief against said Richard J. Williams and Investors Mutual, Inc., herein referred to as defendants. The plaintiffs asked the court to declare their legal rights, as coadministrators, in four stock certificates issued by Investors Mutual Inc. in the name of "Albert B. Farkas, as trustee for Richard J. Williams" and which were issued pursuant to written declarations of trust. The decree of the circuit court found that said declarations were testamentary in character, and not having been executed with the formalities of a will, were invalid, and directed that the stock be awarded to the plaintiffs as an asset of the estate of said Albert B. Farkas. Upon appeal to the Appellate Court, the decree was affirmed. See 121 N.E.2d 344. We allowed defendants' petition for leave to appeal.

Albert B. Farkas died intestate at the age of sixty-seven years, a resident of Chicago, leaving as his only heirs-at-law brothers, sisters, a nephew and a niece. Although retired at the time of his death, he had for many years practiced veterinary medicine and operated a veterinarian establishment in Chicago. During a considerable portion of that time, he employed the defendant Williams, who was not related to him. On four occasions (December 8, 1948; February 7, 1949; February 14, 1950; and March 1, 1950) Farkas purchased stock of Investors Mutual, Inc. At the time of each purchase he executed a written application to Investors

Mutual, Inc., instructing them to issue the stock in his name "as trustee for Richard J. Williams." Investors Mutual, Inc., by its agent, accepted each of these applications in writing by signature on the face of the application. Coincident with the execution of these applications, Farkas signed separate declarations of trust, all of which were identical except as to dates. The terms of said trust instruments are as follows:

Investors Mutual was a major mutual fund company that regularly made the option of holding its shares in trust available to its customers.

"Declaration of Trust-Revocable. I, the undersigned, having purchased or declared my intention to purchase certain shares of capital stock of Investors Mutual, Inc. (the Company), and having directed that the certificate for said stock be issued in my name as trustee for Richard J. Williams as beneficiary, whose address is 1704 W. North Ave. Chicago, Ill., under this Declaration of Trust Do Hereby Declare that the terms and conditions upon which I shall hold said stock in trust and any additional stock resulting from reinvestments of cash dividends upon such original or additional shares are as follows:

"(1) During my lifetime all cash dividends are to be paid to me individually for my own personal account and use; provided, however, that any such additional stock purchased under an authorized reinvestment of cash dividends shall become a part of and subject to this trust.

"(2) Upon my death the title to any stock subject hereto and the right to any subsequent payments or distributions shall be vested absolutely in the beneficiary. The record date for the payment of dividends, rather than the date of declaration of the dividend, shall, with reference to my death, determine whether any particular dividend shall be payable to my estate or to the beneficiary.

"(3) During my lifetime I reserve the right, as trustee, to vote, sell, redeem, exchange or otherwise deal in or with the stock subject hereto, but upon any sale or redemption of said stock or any part thereof, the trust hereby declared shall terminate as to the stock sold or redeemed, and I shall be entitled to retain the proceeds of sale or redemption for my own personal account and use.

"(4) I reserve the right at any time to change the beneficiary or revoke this trust, but it is understood that no change of beneficiary and no revocation of this trust except by death of the beneficiary, shall be effective as to the Company for any purpose unless and until written notice thereof in such form as the Company shall prescribe is delivered to the Company at Minneapolis, Minnesota. The decease of the beneficiary before my death shall operate as a revocation of this trust.

"(5) In the event this trust shall be revoked or otherwise terminated, said stock and all rights and privileges thereunder shall belong to and be exercised by me in my individual capacity.

"(6) The Company shall not be liable for the validity or existence of any trust created by me, and any payment or other consideration made or given by the Company to me as trustee or otherwise, in connection with said stock or any cash dividends thereon, or in the event of my death prior to revocation, to the beneficiary, shall to the extent of such payment fully release and discharge the Company from liability with respect to said stock or any cash dividends thereon."

The applications and declarations of trust were delivered to Investors Mutual, Inc., and held by the company until Farkas's death. The stock certificates were issued in the name of Farkas as "trustee for Richard J. Williams" and were discovered in a safety-deposit box of Farkas after his death, along with other securities, some of which were in the name of Williams alone.

The sole question presented on this appeal is whether the instruments entitled "Declaration of Trust-Revocable" and executed by Farkas created valid inter vivos trusts of the stock of Investors Mutual, Inc. The plaintiffs contend that said stock is free and clear from any trust or beneficial interest in the defendant Williams, for the reason that said purported trust instruments were attempted testamentary dispositions and invalid for want of compliance with the statute on wills. The defendants, on the other hand, insist that said instruments created valid inter vivos trusts and were not testamentary in character.

It is conceded that the instruments were not executed in such a way as to satisfy the requirements of the statute on wills; hence, our inquiry is limited to whether said trust instruments created valid inter vivos trusts effective to give the purported beneficiary, Williams, title to the stock in question after the death of the settlor-trustee, Farkas. To make this determination we must consider: (1) whether upon execution of the so-called trust instruments defendant Williams acquired an

Make the Connection

This discussion is all about the classic test for an invalid will substitute; if Mr. Williams did not receive an "interest" when Dr. Farkas created the trusts they are invalid will substitutes.

interest in the subject matter of the trusts, the stock of defendant Investors Mutual, Inc., (2) whether Farkas, as settlor-trustee, retained such control over the subject matter of the trusts as to render said trust instruments attempted testamentary dispositions.

First, upon execution of these trust instruments did defendant Williams presently acquire an interest in the subject matter of the intended trusts?

If no interest passed to Williams before the death of Farkas, the intended trusts are testamentary and hence invalid for failure to comply with the statute on wills. Oswald v. Caldwell, 80 N.E. 131; Troup v. Hunter, 133 N.E. 56; Restatement of the Law of Trusts, section 56.

But considering the terms of these instruments we believe Farkas did intend to presently give Williams an interest in the property referred to. For it may be said, at the very least, that upon his executing one of these instruments, he showed an intention to presently part with some of the incidents of ownership in the stock. Immediately after the execution of each of these instruments, he could not deal with the stock therein referred to the same as if he owned the property absolutely, but only in accordance with the terms of the instrument. He purported to set himself up as trustee of the stock for the benefit of Williams, and the stock was registered in his name as trustee for Williams. Thus assuming to act as trustee, he is held to have intended to take on those obligations which are expressly set out in the instrument, as well as those fiduciary obligations implied by law. In addition, he manifested an intention to bind himself to having this property pass upon his death to Williams, unless he changed the beneficiary or revoked the trust, and then such change of beneficiary or revocation was not to be effective as to Investors Mutual, Inc., unless and until written notice thereof in such form as the company prescribed was delivered to them at Minneapolis, Minnesota. An absolute owner can dispose of his property, either in his lifetime or by will, in any way he sees fit without notifying or securing approval from anyone and without being held to the duties of a fiduciary in so doing.

It seems to follow that what incidents of ownership Farkas intended to relinquish, in a sense he intended Williams to acquire. That is, Williams was to be the beneficiary to whom Farkas was to be obligated, and unless Farkas revoked the instrument in the manner therein set out or the instrument was otherwise terminated in a manner therein provided for, upon Farkas's death Williams was to become absolute owner of the trust property. It is difficult to name this interest of Williams, nor is there any reason for so doing so long as it passed to him immediately upon the creation of the trust. As stated in 4 Powell, The Law of Real Property, at page 87: "Interests of beneficiaries of private express trusts run the gamut from valuable substantialities to evanescent hopes. Such a beneficiary may have any one of an almost infinite variety of the possible aggregates of an additional problem is presented here, however, for it is to be noted that the trust instruments provide: "The decease of the beneficiary before my death shall operate as a revocation of this trust." The plaintiffs argue that the presence of this provision removes the only possible distinction which might have been drawn between these instruments and a will. Being thus conditioned on his surviving, it is argued that the

"interest" of Williams until the death of Farkas was a mere expectancy. Conversely, they assert, the interest of Farkas in the securities until his death was precisely the same as that of a testator who bequeaths securities by his will, since he had all the rights accruing to an absolute owner.

Admittedly, had this provision been absent the interest of Williams would have been greater, since he would then have had an inheritable interest in the lifetime of Farkas. But to say his interest would have been greater is not to say that he here did not have a beneficial interest, properly so-called, during the lifetime of Farkas. The provision purports to set up but another "contingency" which would serve to terminate the trust. The disposition is not testamentary, and the intended

trust is valid, even though the interest of the beneficiary is contingent upon the existence of a certain state of facts at the time of the settlor's death. Restatement of the Law of Trusts, section 56, comment *f*. In an example contained in the previous reference, the authors of the Restatement have referred to the interest of a beneficiary under a trust who must survive the settlor (and where the settlor receives the income for life) as a contingent equitable interest in remainder.

This question of whether any interest passed immediately is also involved in the next problem considered, namely, the quantum of power retained by a settlor which will cause an intended inter vivos trust to fail as an attempted testamentary disposition. Therefore, much of what is said in the next part of the opinion, as well as the authorities cited, will pertain to this interest question.

Second, did Farkas retain such control over the subject matter of the trust as to render said trust instruments attempted testamentary dispositions?

In each of these trust instruments, Farkas reserved to himself as settlor the following powers: (1) the right to receive during his lifetime all cash dividends; (2) the right at any time to change the beneficiary or revoke the trust; and (3) upon sale or redemption of any portion of the trust property, the right to retain the proceeds therefrom for his own use.

> **Make the Connection**
>
> Dr. Farkas's retention of these powers makes the trust a perfect will substitute because he has practically the same relationship to the trust property as he does to his probate property.

Additionally, Farkas reserved the right to act as sole trustee, and in such capacity, he was accorded the right to vote, sell, redeem, exchange or otherwise deal in the stock which formed the subject matter of the trust.

We shall consider first those enumerated powers which Farkas reserved to himself as settlor.

It is well established that the retention by the settlor of the power to revoke, even when coupled with the reservation of a life interest in the trust property, does not render the trust inoperative for want of execution as a will. Kelly v. Parker, 54 N.E. 615; Bear v. Millikin Trust Co., 168 N.E. 349; Gurnett v. Mutual Life Ins. Co., 191 N.E. 250; Bergmann v. Foreman State Trust & Savings Bank, 273 Ill.App. 408.

The court discusses the creation of a trust by declaration of trust, a document in which the creator of the trust declares herself to be trustee of property she owns as opposed to the creation of a trust by agreement between the creator of the trust and the person who will act as trustee.

Only when it is thought that there are additional reservations present of such a substantial nature as to amount to the retention of full ownership is a court likely to invalidate an inter vivos trust by reason of its not being executed as a will. Restatement of the Law of Trusts, section (See Restatement of the Law of Trusts, section 57.) In 1 Scott, The Law of Trusts, section 57.1, the author says at pages 336–337: "It is immaterial whether the settlor reserves simply a power to revoke the whole trust at one time or whether he reserves also a power to revoke the trust as to any part of the property from time to time. It is immaterial whether the power to revoke includes a power to revoke by will as well as a power to revoke by a transaction inter vivos. It is immaterial that the settlor reserves not only a power to revoke the trust but in addition a power to alter or modify its terms."

However, it is not every so-called additional reservation of power that will be deemed sufficient to invalidate a trust of this nature. In 32 A.L.R.2d 1270, it is stated at pages 1276–1277:

> "The later cases, as do the earlier ones, justify the general conclusion that many and extensive rights and power may be reserved by a settlor, in addition to a life interest and power of revocation, without defeating the trust. The instrument is likely to be upheld notwithstanding it includes additionally the reservation of power to amend the trust in whole or in part, or extensive powers over investments, management, or administration, or power to appoint or remove trustees or to appoint interests in remainder, or the right to act as trustee or as one of the trustees, or to enjoy limited rights in the principal, or to withdraw part or all of the principal, or to possess, use, or enjoy the trust property, or to sell or mortgage the property or any of it and appropriate the proceeds."

We conclude therefore, in accordance with the great weight of authority, said powers which Farkas reserved to himself as settlor were not such as to render the intended trusts invalid as attempted testamentary dispositions.

> ### Take Note
>
> The court draws a distinction between the powers Dr. Farkas retained as creator of the trust and those he exercised as trustee. Dr. Farkas is the trustee because he wants to have control and to keep the trust completely private.

A more difficult problem is posed, however, by the fact that Farkas is also trustee, and as such, is empowered to vote, sell, redeem, exchange and otherwise deal in and with the subject matter of the trusts.

That a settlor may create a trust of personal property whereby he names himself as trustee and acts as such for the beneficiary is clear. Restatement of the Law of Trusts, section 17.

Moreover, the later cases indicate that the mere fact that the settlor in addition to making himself sole trustee also reserves a life interest and a power of revocation does not render the trust invalid as testamentary in character. 32 A.L.R.2d 1286. In 1 Scott, The Law of Trusts, it is stated at pages 353–354:

> "The owner of property may create a trust not only by transferring the property to another person as trustee, but also by declaring himself trustee. Such a declaration of trust, although gratuitous, is valid. * * * Suppose, however, that the settlor reserves not only a beneficial life interest but also a power of revocation. It would seem that such a trust is not necessarily testamentary. The declaration of trust immediately creates an equitable interest in the beneficiaries, although the enjoyment of the interest is postponed until the death of the settlor, and although the interest may be

divested by the exercise of the power of revocation. The disposition is not essentially different from that which is made where the settlor transfers the property to another person as trustee. It is true that where the settlor declares himself trustee he controls the administration of the trust. As has been stated, if the settlor transfers property upon trust and reserves not only a power of revocation but also power to control the administration of the trust, the trust is testamentary. There is this difference, however: the power of control which the settlor has as trustee is not an irresponsible power and can be exercised only in accordance with the terms of the trust." *See also* Restatement of the Law of Trusts, section 57, comment *b*.

In the instant case the plaintiffs contend that Farkas, as settlor-trustee, retained complete control and dominion over the securities for his own benefit during his lifetime. It is argued that he had the power to deal with the property as he liked so long as he lived and owed no enforceable duties of any kind to Williams as beneficiary.

It does not appear that this court has heretofore considered a trust instrument similar to those in question, but we have passed upon the validity of trust instruments wherein the settlor retained a life interest in the trust property and the power to revoke, plus other somewhat extensive powers. . . .

The case most closely analogous to the case at bar which we have seen is United Building and Loan Association v. Garrett, D.C., 64 F.Supp. 460, 461, wherein the Federal district court applying Arkansas law upheld trust instruments which in most, if not all, essentials were similar to those in question. In that case Presley F. Garrett executed an instrument entitled "Declaration of Trust", which provided that he held a certificate representing forty-five shares in a building and loan association as trustee for the benefit of named beneficiaries, reserving to himself as settlor the following: (1) the right and power to sell, assign, transfer, set over and deliver the trust property, or any part thereof, and to collect and use the dividends and proceeds therefrom for his own use and benefit; and (2) the right to revoke the trust, in whole or in part, at any time. It was further provided that the trust was to terminate one year after his death, and provision was made for the succession of interest of beneficiaries who predeceased the termination of the trust. Subsequently, Garrett purchased additional stock and executed another "Declaration of Trust" therefor identical with the first declaration, except that it provided that the trust should terminate upon the maturity of the entrusted stock certificate, but if all the beneficiaries should die prior to the termination of the trust, then the trust property was to revert to the settlor and be distributed, unless otherwise disposed of, as part of his estate. The court upheld the validity of these instruments as inter vivos trusts, rejecting the argument that they constituted testamentary dispositions.

The court pointed out in the Garrett case that the weight of authority, both in numbers and influence, support the right of the settlor to reserve the power to consume the principal of the trust res, citing an Arkansas decision which relied upon the decision of this court in the Kelly case. Regarding the interest which passed to the beneficiaries, the court said at page 465 of 64 F.Supp.: "The policy of the law favors the vesting of interests, and where possible, will construe a provision as a condition subsequent in preference to a condition precedent. The undeviating trend in cases dealing with the validity of trust declarations is to treat reservations such as those involved in this case as conditions subsequent which may operate to defeat the interest of the beneficiaries, but which, unexercised, do not prevent the vesting of equitable title."

That the retention of the power by Farkas as trustee to sell or redeem the stock and keep the proceeds for his own use should not render these trust instruments testamentary in character becomes more evident upon analyzing the real import and significance of the powers to revoke and to amend the trust, the reservation of which the courts uniformly hold does not invalidate an inter vivos trust.

It is obvious that a settlor with the power to revoke and to amend the trust at any time is, for all practical purpose, in a position to exert considerable control over the trustee regarding the administration of the trust. For anything believed to be inimical to his best interests can be thwarted or prevented by simply revoking the trust or amending it in such a way as to conform to his wishes. Indeed, it seems that many of those powers which from time to time have been viewed as "additional powers" are already, in a sense, virtually contained within the overriding power of revocation or the power to amend the trust. Consider, for example, the following: (1) the power to consume the principal; (2) the power to sell or mortgage the trust property and appropriate the proceeds; (3) the power to appoint or remove trustees; (4) the power to supervise and direct investments; and (5) the power to otherwise direct and supervise the trustee in the administration of the trust. Actually, any of the above powers could readily be assumed by a settlor with the reserved power of revocation through the simple expedient of revoking the trust, and then, as absolute owner of the subject matter, doing with the property as he chooses. Even though no actual termination of the trust is effectuated, however, it could hardly be questioned but that the mere existence of this power in the settlor is sufficient to enable his influence to be felt in a practical way in the administration of the trust. In the Garrett case, the court quoted as follows from Van Cott v. Prentice, 10 N.E. 257:

> "That language (providing that the trustee should hold the property subject to the grantor's control and direction) only repeats, in another form, the effect of the reserved power of revocation. The existence of that inevitably leaves in the settlor an absolute control, since at any moment be may end the trust and resume possession of the fund as his own. * * * Its continued existence was to be absolutely subject to the direction and control of Prentice (settlor),-a result always inevitable where a power of revocation is reserved."

In 1 Bogert, Trusts and Trustees, section 104, the author states at pages 484–485:

> "Often the grantor-settlor holds back for himself the power to manage the property directly and indirectly. He provides that he himself shall have power to sell, lease, mortgage, pay taxes, make investments, and perform other acts of trust administration, or that he shall have authority to direct the trustees how they shall perform these duties. These reservations have not generally been deemed to show that the grantor remains during his life the master of the property to such an extent as to make his gift to the cestuis testamentary. So long as the trust continues, the

'cestuis' → beneficiaries [?]

cestuis have equitable interests, no matter who acts for them in protecting those interests, whether it be trustee or settlor. If the exercise of these powers by the settlor involves the total or partial destruction of the trust, as where the settlor has power to sell the res and keep the proceeds, the power seems to be treated as practically that of revocation of the trust. It leaves an equitable interest in the cestuis till revocation. It shows a vested interest, subject to divestment, and not the lack of any interest at all."

In the case at bar, the power of Farkas to vote, sell redeem, exchange or otherwise deal in the stock was reserved to him as trustee, and it was only upon sale or redemption that he was entitled to keep the proceeds for his own use. Thus, the control reserved is not as great as in those cases where said power is reserved to the owner as settlor. For as trustee he must so conduct himself in

Food for Thought

The court is describing the constraints placed on Dr. Farkas as trustee by his fiduciary duties to the trust beneficiary. What are they?

accordance with standards applicable to trustees generally. It is not a valid objection to this to say that Williams would never question Farkas' conduct, inasmuch as Farkas could then revoke the trust and destroy what interest Williams has. Such a possibility exists in any case where the settlor has the power of revocation. Still, Williams has rights the same as any beneficiary, although it may not be feasible for him to exercise them. Moreover, it is entirely possible that he might in certain situations have a right to hold Farkas' estate liable for breaches of trust committed by Farkas during his lifetime. In this regard, consider what would happen if, without having revoked the trust, Farkas as trustee had given the stock away without receiving any consideration therefor, had pledged the stock improperly for his own personal debt and allowed it to be lost by foreclosure or had exchanged the stock for another security or other worthless property in such manner as to constitute gross impropriety and gross negligence. In such instances, it would seem in accordance with the terms of these instruments that Williams would have had an enforceable claim against Farkas' estate for whatever damage had been suffered. Contrast this with the rights of a legatee or devisee under a will. The testator could waste the property or do anything with it he wished during his lifetime without incurring any liability to those designated by the will to inherit the property. In any event, if Farkas as settlor could reserve the power to sell or otherwise deal with the property and retain the proceeds, which the cases indicate he could, then it necessarily follows that he should have the right to sell or otherwise deal with the property as trustee and retain the proceeds from a sale or redemption without having the instruments rendered invalid as testamentary dispositions.

Take Note

Suddenly the court takes a completely different tack in dealing with the question of whether the trust is an invalid will substitute.

Another factor often considered in determining whether an inter vivos trust is an attempted testamentary disposition is the formality of the transaction. Restatement of the Law of Trusts, section 57, comment *g*; Stouse v. First National Bank, Ky., 245 S.W.2d 914, 32 A.L.R.2d 1261; United Building and Loan Association v. Garrett, D.C.,

64 F.Supp. 460; In re Sheasley's Trust, 366 Pa. 316, 77 A.2d 448. Historically, the purpose behind the enactment of the statute on wills was the prevention of fraud. The requirement as to witnesses was deemed necessary because a will is ordinarily an expression of the secret wish of the testator, signed out of the presence of all concerned. The possibility of forgery and fraud are ever present in such situations. Here, Farkas executed four separate applications for stock of Investors Mutual, Inc., in which he directed that the stock be issued in his name as trustee for Williams, and he executed four separate declarations of trust in which he declared he was holding said stock in trust for Williams. The stock certificates in question were issued in his name as trustee for Williams. He thus manifested his intention in a solemn and formal manner.

For the reasons stated, we conclude that these trust declarations executed by Farkas constituted valid inter vivos trusts and were not attempted testamentary dispositions. It must be conceded that they have, in the words of Mr. Justice Holmes in Bromley v. Mitchell, 155 Mass. 509, 30 N.E. 83, a "Testamentary look." Moreover, it must be admitted that the line should be drawn somewhere, but after a study of this case we do not believe that point has here been reached.

The judgment of the Appellate Court affirming the decree of the circuit court of Cook County is reversed, and the cause is remanded to the circuit court of Cook County, with directions to enter a decree in favor of the defendants.

———————

Points for Discussion

1. Why create a revocable trust?

We don't know whether Farkas knew when he decided to use a revocable trust to implement his estate plan for his Investor Mutual shares that he was venturing into uncertain legal territory. Whether he did or not, he decided that holding the shares as trustee was advantageous. What did Farkas accomplish by creating these trusts?

2. Totten *and* Farkas

Matter of Totten turns a payable on death bank account into a valid will substitute by making it a "tentative trust." *Farkas v. Williams* permits a revocable lifetime trust of which the creator is the sole beneficiary and sole trustee during life as well as the only person with the power to revoke to be a valid will substitute by deciding the arrangement is a valid trust. In other words, the *Totten* court invents a new category while the *Farkas* court fits the arrangement in question into an existing category. Putting aside the categories, how similar are the two situations? Do the Irving Savings Institution in *Totten* and Investors Mutual in *Farkas* have a role in the legal analyses in the two cases? Another way to look at the question is to ask if Ms. Lattan could have created her will substitute without the bank and if Farkas could have created his will substitute without Investors Mutual. Aside from form is there any reason why the law should not permit these two arrangements?

3. Funded revocable trusts

The trust Farkas created was a *funded revocable trust*. That is, there was a property in the trust. The trust property is also called the *trust res*, the *trust corpus* or the *principal* of the trust. Is it possible to use a revocable trust as an estate planning vehicle without putting any property into the trust until the death of the creator of the trust? That seems impossible at first blush: no trust res, no trust, as we learned in Chapter 8 on trusts, but unfunded trusts are valid if properly created. To understand the estate planning goal that one might achieve and how such an arrangement works legally, we need to discuss the *pour-over will*, or, more precisely, what Restatement Third, Property calls *pour-over devises*. If currently curious, look at the second will executed by Ward in the estate planning problem.

4. The modern approach

The Illinois court's long and detailed analysis of the interest Williams held under the trust and of the nature of Farkas' fiduciary duties is perhaps not as important as it was when the case was decided. This is how the Uniform Trust Code deals with the fiduciary duties of the trustee of a revocable trust:

UTC § 603(a)

(a) While a trust is revocable [and the settlor has capacity to revoke the trust], rights of the beneficiaries are subject to the control of, and the duties of the trustee are owed exclusively to, the settlor.

If this statute were the law in Illinois when *Farkas* was decided, would the court have spent so much time trying to describe Dr. Farkas' duties as trustee? What does this statute, which has been widely adopted and which reflects modern case law (*see Estate of Giraldin*, 55 Cal. 4th 1058, 290 P.3d 199 (2012), *Siegel v. J.P. Morgan Chase*, 71 So.3d 935 (Fla. Dist. Ct.App. 4th Dist. 2011)) say about the modern approach to the issues surrounding the validity of a revocable trust, especially when the settlor and sole beneficiary is also trustee?

C. The Pour-Over Will

1. What Is It and Why Use It

Restatement Third, Property (Wills and Other Donative Transfers) § 3.8

(a) A "pour-over" devise is a provision in a will that (i) adds property to an inter vivos trust or (ii) funds a trust that was not funded during the testator's lifetime but whose terms are in a trust instrument that was executed during the testator's lifetime.

(b) A pour-over devise may be validated by statute, by incorporation by reference, or by independent significance.

A pour-over will, therefore, is a will that disposes of probate assets and other non-probate property by adding either to an existing lifetime (inter vivos) trust. Why might a testator, like Ward in our estate planning exercise, use a pour-over will as his estate planning mechanism? There are several possible reasons:

1. *The impossibility of adding all probate property to the trust during the testator's life.* One's possessions are constantly changing; that simple fact makes it very difficult to add property to the trust every time new property is acquired. There is no doctrine analogous to acts of independent significance applicable to revocable trusts. A will-maker can therefore devise her residuary (or make a general or specific bequest) to an existing lifetime trust. Moreover, funding the revocable lifetime trust during the lifetime of the creator of the trust may involve formalities that are complex given the type of probate property that he (Ward) or she owns.

2. *Providing coordinated management for all of the testator's various types of assets.* In addition to a bequest of probate assets to the lifetime trust in the creator's pour-over will (Ward's in our estate planning exercise), benefits under an insurance policy and other assets with beneficiary designations (for example, a POD savings account, a security registered with a TOD) can be made payable to the trust. These assets would join (or to use the current metaphor "pour over") into the trust, augmenting the corpus. In our estate planning exercise, we considered a testator (Ward) who wished to provide lifetime security for his surviving spouse (June) but also wants to give to family members the remainder interest in the trust after the partner's death (Wally and the Beaver). The testator (Ward) created a lifetime trust (but he could have created a trust that had no property as corpus) with multiple pour-over provisions. For example, the testator's will might limit the residue of the probate estate to the trust; the trust is made beneficiary of the life insurance policies the testator owns on the testator's life, and it is also made beneficiary of the testator's pension plan and IRA. Upon testator's death, all of the testator's assets are collected in one vehicle, the lifetime trust with provisions therein to implement the testator's testamentary designs. As far as dispositive provisions, testator can direct the trustee to pay all income (as did Ward) to the surviving spouse (June) or in another circumstance a partner and confer on the trustee discretion (with or without some sort of guidance in using that discretion) to use trust principal for the surviving spouse or partner. Finally, creator/testator could direct the trustee to pay the trust property remaining at the spouse or partner's death to any beneficiary (Wally and the Beaver or to the descendants of testator's parents, "then living, by representation.")

3. *The testator may wish to have trust property available for support during testator's lifetime.* While the testator for tax reasons may want to create an irrevocable trust in which he has no beneficial interest (for tax purposes that need not trouble us here), testator will want to continue to enjoy his or her probate property while alive and only commit it to the trust at death. Ward's lifetime trust so directs.

2. Pour-Over Wills and the Statute of Wills

All of the above considerations provide reasons why a testator might want to create an estate plan that disposes of probate property by adding it to an existing trust. But does the law permit such a scheme? To make a gift from a will to an existing trust may be regarded as testamentary in character, and the device is an attempt to dispose of property at death by using a document that is not executed with the formalities required by the statute of wills: the trust instrument. If it is problematic to use a lifetime trust, why not just execute the trust document as if it were a will, that is, in conformity with the statute of due execution of wills? The answer is simple: by so doing the device would then be regarded as a will and not as a trust. Does that matter? Possibly. First, the law of wills and the law of trusts traditionally are two separate doctrinal subjects, and therefore the applicable substantive law governing various issues may vary. Second, amendments to the estate plan would have to also be executed with testamentary formalities. Third, if the trust was created by a will, it would be testamentary, and therefore is, in many states, subject to probate jurisdiction throughout its existence. In some states (but not under the UPC or New York), trustees of testamentary trusts may be required by law to render an accounting of their actions to the court *every year*.

Pour-over wills were sustained initially by courts stretching traditional doctrine as we have seen with other will substitutes. Courts were also able to find ways to validate pour-overs within existing traditional law. There are two doctrines which provide ways to validate pour-over devises: incorporation by reference and acts of independent significance. Both were doctrinally problematic and had advantages and disadvantages.

First, incorporation by reference (recognized in most states, though not in New York) might be used. But recall that it requires that the document incorporated (here the lifetime trust) be in existence at the time the will is executed. The trust to be incorporated need not have any more than nominal trust property before the pour-over is received, but it could not be entirely unfunded or it would not have been valid. Moreover, subsequent amendments to the trust made after the will is executed cannot be incorporated unless the will is re-executed (or a codicil to the will is executed after the trust is amended). In addition, once it is incorporated into the will, the trust becomes a testamentary trust because it is a part of the will. As noted above, testamentary trusts can be subject to much more oversight by the probate courts than are lifetime trusts. Validating the pour-over device by using incorporation by reference, then, could negate one of the primary advantages of a lifetime trust.

Using the doctrine of acts of independent significance eliminates many of the difficulties presented by incorporation by reference. Remember that acts of independent significance are acts which have non-testamentary relevance, that is, acts not purely calculated to dispose of property at death. In order to use this doctrine, there is no requirement that the trust be in existence when the will is executed, and there is no difficulty with pouring property from the will. Amendments to the trust made after the will is executed should be effective. Under acts of independent significance, the pour-over provision is valid due to the existence of an already functioning trust (and therefore not one with purely testamentary significance) to dispose of probate property and, not from the incorporation of the very words of the trust instrument into the will. However, in order to have independent significance, the trust must be funded with more than a nominal amount of property. The trust must truly be "up and running" at the time of the testator's death, and that means that the trustee must already be managing significant amount of property.

But why, you may very well ask, would someone want to create a lifetime trust with a nominal corpus and have it lie fallow until the creator's death? There are several situations in which the creator of a trust designed to receive assets though a pour-over will might wish to create in essence an empty vessel waiting to be filled. Convenience. Consider the testator who wishes to provide for a surviving spouse or domestic partner. It may be difficult if not impossible to make the trust the owner of pension benefits, an IRA, and even an insurance policy (although trusts often do own insurance policies). In addition, the testator may wish to keep direct control of her probate assets. In addition, if the partner is the first to die, the testator might want to be able to start all over again and just ignore the trust (all that would be necessary is changing the beneficiary designations of the contract-based will substitutes).

Another example in which a pour-over arrangement is useful involves a couple with minor children. We visited this prospect when discussing the Cleaver's estate plan. Should both parents die while at least one child is a minor the couple will almost certainly want to create a trust. One way to do that is to create a testamentary trust contingent on at least one child being a minor on the death of the second of the couple to die. Recall that a testamentary trust is likely to be subject to court supervision. Even in states that have adopted the UPC and New York, where trustees of testamentary trusts need not render an accounting of their actions to the court yearly, a court order would be required to move the situs of a testamentary trust, which may be desirable if the guardian of the person of the minor lives in another state. Given these considerations, the couple might want to create a lifetime trust for the minor children but leave it nominally funded until their death and pour over probate and non-probate assets. If, at the death of the second parent to die, the children are all adults, the trust is never funded. The trust can even be drafted to terminate on the death of the second parent to die if none of the children are minors at that time. In any event, the trust will come into existence only in case of untimely death and can be easily undone should the parents live to see their children through their youth.

Why the reference to $10 or nominal funding? Lifetime trusts must have a trust res (aka trust principal, trust corpus) in order to be valid. That trust property needs to be delivered to the trustee. However, the simple recitation in the document creating the trust that property has been conveyed to the trustee is enough to sustain the creation of the trust. The trust document will often make that recitation by referring to the property listed on Schedule A attached to the document.

To some extent, the requirement that the trust be funded at least nominally in order to have property, probate assets or will substitutes, pour over into it was unnecessarily formalistic. Either the arrangement should be sanctioned or it should not. Validity should not turn on the amount of the corpus. Once again, the legislatures cut the knot by enacting statutes validating pour overs, and once again a uniform act led the way. The Uniform Testamentary Additions to Trusts Act (UTATA) has been incorporated into the UPC:

UPC § 2–511. Testamentary Additions to Trusts

(a)   A will may validly devise property to the trustee of a trust established or to be established (i) during the testator's lifetime by the testator, by the testator and some other person, or by some other person, including a funded or unfunded life insurance trust, although the settlor has reserved any or all rights of ownership of the insurance contracts, or (ii) at the testator's death by the testator's devise to the trustee, if the trust is identified in the testator's will and its terms are set forth in a written instrument, other than a will, executed before, concurrently with, or after the execution of the testator's will or in another individual's will if that other individual has predeceased the testator, regardless of the existence, size, or character of the corpus of the trust. The devise is not invalid because the trust is amendable or revocable, or because the trust was amended after the execution of the will or the testator's death.[47]

(b)   Unless the testator's will provides otherwise, property devised to a trust described in subsection (a) is not held under a testamentary trust of the testator, but it becomes a part of the trust to which it is devised, and must be administered and disposed of in accordance with the provisions of the governing instrument setting forth the terms of the trust, including any amendments thereto made before or after the testator's death.

(c)   Unless the testator's will provides otherwise, a revocation or termination of the trust before the testator's death causes the devise to lapse.

New York's statutory provision is somewhat different:

New York Estates, Powers, and Trusts Law § 3–3.7. Testamentary Additions to Trusts (Pour-Over Wills)

(a)   A testator or testatrix may by will dispose of or appoint all or any part of his or her estate to a trustee of a trust, the terms of which are evidenced by a written instrument executed by the testator or testatrix, the testator or testatrix and some other person, or some other person, including a trust established for the receipt of the proceeds of an annuity or pure endowment contract, or of a thrift, savings, pension, retirement, death benefit, stock bonus, or profit-sharing plan or system or a funded or unfunded life, group life, industrial life or accident and health insurance trust although the settlor has reserved any or all rights of ownership of the insurance contracts, regardless of the existence, size or character of the corpus of such insurance trust or other trust; provided that such trust instrument is executed in the manner provided for in 7–1.17, prior to or contemporaneously with the execution of the will, and such trust instrument is identified in such will.

(b)   The testamentary disposition or appointment is valid, even though:

    (1)   The trust instrument is amendable or revocable, or both, provided, however, that the disposition or appointment shall be given effect in accordance with the terms of the trust instrument, including an amendment thereto, as they appear in writing on the date of the testator's death and, where the testator so directs, including amendments to the trust instrument after his death, if the instrument evidencing such amendment is executed and acknowledged in the manner herein provided for executing and acknowledging the instrument which it amends.

    (2)   The right is reserved in such trust instrument (A) to exercise any power over any property transferred to or held in the trust or (B) to direct during the lifetime of the settlor or any other person, the persons and organizations to whom or in whose behalf the income shall be paid or the principal distributed.

    (3)   The trust instrument or any amendment thereto was not executed and attested in accordance with the formalities prescribed by 3–2.1.

(c)   The property so disposed of or appointed by will becomes a part of the trust to which it is given, and title thereto vests in the trustee to be administered and disposed of in accordance with the terms of the trust instrument.

(d)   Any disposition or appointment to the trustee made by a testator who died prior to the effective date of this section, which would be invalid under the applicable law of this state pre-existing the effective date of this section, shall be construed to create a testamentary trust under and in accordance with the terms of the trust instrument which the testator originally intended should embrace the property disposed of or appointed, as such terms appear in such trust instrument at the date of the testator's death.

(e)   A revocation or termination of the trust before the death of the testator shall cause the disposition or appointment to fail, unless the testator has made an alternative disposition.

Notes

1. Comparing two pour-over will statutes

Like all pour-over will statutes, UPC § 2–511 and EPTL § 3–3.7 are designed to facilitate pour-over wills by avoiding the difficulties inherent in relying for validity on the doctrines of incorporation by reference and acts of independent significance. In order to explore how that is accomplished consider the following:

1.   How are amendments of the trust treated under the two statutes?

2. Does the trust receiving the pour-over have to be more than nominally funded before the testator's death? Is the difference in language between UPC § 2–511(a), especially clause (ii) and EPTL § 3–3.7(a) significant? (*See* In re Bourcet, 175 Misc.2d 144, 668 N.Y.S.2d 329 (Sur. Ct. Nassau Co. 1997); statutory language is ambiguous but both legislative history and rules of construction indicate that EPTL § 3–3.7(a) encompasses all trusts and not just the types of trusts mentioned in the statute)

3. Does the status of the trust after the pour-over resemble the result under incorporation by reference or acts of independent significance?

2. Existing trusts as beneficiaries of certain nonprobate property arrangements

New York statutes also expressly provide for the designation of trustees as beneficiaries of certain contract-based will substitutes. EPTL § 13–3.3(a)(1) applies to the "proceeds of thrift, savings, pension, retirement, death benefit, stock bonus and profit-sharing plans, systems or trusts, of life, group life, industrial life or accident and health insurance policies and of annuity, endowment and supplemental insurance contracts" which may be made payable to trustee under an existing trust and "it shall not be necessary to the validity of any such trust agreement or declaration of trust that it have a trust corpus other than the right of the trustee as beneficiary to receive such proceeds." The statute also expressly makes the proceeds exempt from the claims of creditors to the same extent they would be if paid to the beneficiaries of the trust. (EPTL § 13–3.3(c)).

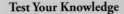

Test Your Knowledge

To assess your understanding of the material in this chapter, click here to take a quiz.

CHAPTER 11

Charitable Trusts

Much of our discussion of trusts has involved donors who use this device to benefit private individuals such as family members. But trusts can also be used to achieve broader, more public aims. Charitable trusts are one way of funding a charitable purpose. Charitable organizations hold and manage trillions of dollars each year and play a major role in the American economy. Many of the rules regarding trusts are the same for both private and charitable trusts. In this chapter, we will consider the key differences. Charitable trusts require a charitable purpose, unlike private trusts that can be created for virtually any reason. Special rules regulating modification and termination govern charitable trusts, in part because they are not subject to the rule against perpetuities and can last indefinitely. Finally, charitable trusts are enforced differently than private trusts. These differences are explored in this chapter, and the material should give you a flavor of how settlors use the charitable trust to advance particular interests.

A. Charitable Purpose

Shenandoah Valley Nat'l Bank of Winchester v. Taylor

63 S.E.2d 786 (Va. 1951)

MILLER, J., delivered the opinion of the court.

Charles B. Henry, a resident of Winchester, Virginia, died testate on the 23rd day of April, 1949. His will dated April 21, 1949, was duly admitted to probate and the Shenandoah Valley National Bank of Winchester, the designated executor and trustee, qualified thereunder.

Subject to two inconsequential provisions not material to this litigation, the testator's entire estate valued at $86,000, was left as follows:

> 'SECOND: All the rest, residue and remainder of my estate, real, personal, intangible and mixed, of whatsoever kind and wherever situate, * * *, I give, bequeath and devise to the Shenandoah Valley National Bank of Winchester, Virginia, in

trust, to be known as the 'Charles B. Henry and Fannie Belle Henry Fund', for the following uses and purposes:

'(a) My Trustee shall invest and reinvest my trust estate, shall collect the income therefrom and shall pay the net income as follows:

'(1) On the last school day of each calendar year before Easter my Trustee shall divide the net income into as many equal parts as there are children in the first, second and third grades of the John Kerr School of the City of Winchester, and shall pay one of such equal parts to each child in such grades, to be used by such child in the furtherance of his or her obtainment of an education.

'(2) On the last school day of each calendar year before Christmas my trustee shall divide the net income into as many equal parts as there are children in the first, second and third grades of the John Kerr School of the City of Winchester, and shall pay one of such equal parts to each child in such grades, to be used by such child in the furtherance of his or her obtainment of an education.'

By paragraphs (3) and (4) it is provided that the names of the children in the three grades shall be determined each year from the school records, and payment of the income to them 'shall be as nearly equal in amounts as it is practicable 'to arrange.'

Paragraph (5) provides that if the John Kerr School is ever discontinued for any reason the payments shall be made to the children of the same grades of the school or schools that take its place, and the School Board of Winchester is to determine what school or schools are substituted for it.

Under clause 'THIRD' the trustee is given authority, power, and discretion to retain or from time to time sell and invest and reinvest the estate, or any part thereof, as it shall deem to be to the best interest of the trust.

The John Kerr School is a public school used by the local school board for primary grades and had an enrollment of 458 boys and girls so there will be that number of pupils or thereabouts who would share in the distribution of the income.

The testator left no children or near relatives. Those who would be his heirs and distributees in case of intestacy were first cousins and others more remotely related. One of these next of kin filed a suit against the executor and trustee, and others challenging the validity of the provisions of the will which undertook to create a charitable trust.

Paragraph No. 10 of the bill alleges:

'That the aforesaid trust does not constitute a charitable trust and hence is invalid in that it violates the rule against the creation of perpetuities.' . . .

The sole question presented is: does the will create a valid charitable trust?

Construction of the challenged provisions is required and in this undertaking the testator's intent as disclosed by the words used in the will must be ascertained. If his dominant intent as expressed was charitable, the trust should be accorded efficacy and sustained.

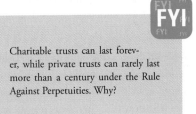

But on the other hand, if the testator's intent as expressed is merely benevolent, though the disposition of his property be meritorious and evince traits of generosity, the trust must nevertheless be declared invalid because it violates the rule against perpetuities. . . .

Charitable trusts can last forever, while private trusts can rarely last more than a century under the Rule Against Perpetuities. Why?

Authoritative definitions of charitable trusts may be found in . . . [the] Restatement of the Law of Trusts, sec. 368. . . . It is:

'Charitable purposes include:

'(a)   the relief of poverty;

'(b)   the advancement of education;

'(c)   the advancement of religion;

'(d)   the promotion of health;

'(e)   governmental or municipal purposes; and

'(f)   other purposes the accomplishment of which is beneficial to the community.' . . .

In the law of trusts there is a real and fundamental distinction between a charitable trust and one that is devoted to mere benevolence. The former is public in nature and valid; the latter is private and if it offends the rule against perpetuities, it is void. . . .

We are, however, reminded that charitable trusts are favored creatures of the law enjoying the especial solicitude of courts of equity and a liberal interpretation is employed to uphold them. . . .

Appellant contends that the gift . . . specifically fits two of those classifications, *viz.*:

'(b)   trusts for the advancement of education;

'(f)   other purposes the accomplishment of which is beneficial to the community.'

We now turn to the language of the will for from its context the testator's intent is to be derived.

In clause 'SECOND' of the will the trust is set up, and by clause 'THIRD' full power is bestowed upon the trustee to invest and reinvest the estate and collect the income for the purposes and uses of the trust. In paragraphs (1) and (2), respectively, of clause 'SECOND' in clear and definite language the discretion, power and authority of the trustee in its disposition and application of the income are specified and limited. Yearly on the last school day before

Easter and Christmas each youthful beneficiary of the testator's generosity is to be paid an equal share of the income. In mandatory language the duty and the duty alone to make cash payments to each individual child just before Easter and Christmas is enjoined upon the trustee by the certain and explicit words that it 'shall divide the net income * * * and shall pay one of such equal shares to each child in such grades.'

Without more, that language and the occasions specified for payment of the funds to the children being when their minds and interests would be far removed from studies or other school activities definitely indicate that no educational purpose was in the testator's mind. It is manifest that there was no intent or belief that the funds would be put to any use other than such as youthful impulse and desire might dictate. But in each instance immediately following the above-quoted language the sentence concludes with the words or phrase 'to be used by such child in the furtherance of his or her obtainment of an education.' It is significant that by this latter phrase the trustee is given no power, control or discretion over the funds so received by the child. Full and complete execution of the mandate and trust imposed upon the trustee accomplishes no educational purpose. Nothing toward the advancement of education is attained by the ultimate performance by the trustee of its full duty. It merely places the income irretrievably and forever beyond the range of the trust.

Appellant says that the latter phrase, 'to be used by such child in furtherance of his or her obtainment of an education', evinces the testator's dominant purpose and intent. Yet it is not denied that the preceding provision 'shall divide the net income into as many equal parts * * * and shall pay one of each equal parts to such child' is at odds with the phrase it relies upon. The appended qualification, it says, however, discloses a controlling intent that the 450 or more shares are to be used in the furtherance of education, and it was not really intended that a share be paid to each child so that he or she could during the Christmas and Easter holidays, or at any other time, use it 'without let or hindrance, encumbrance or care.' With that construction we cannot agree. In our opinion, the words of the will import an intent to have the trustee pay to each child his allotted share. If that be true,—and it is directed to be done in no uncertain language—we know that the admonition to the children would be wholly impotent and of no avail.

In construing wills, we may not forget or disregard the experiences of life and the realities of the occasion. Nor may we assume or indulge in the belief that the testator by his injunction to the donees intended or thought that he could change childhood nature and set at naught childhood impulses and desires.

Appellant asserts that literal performance of the duty imposed upon it—pay to each child his share—would be impracticable and should not be done. Its position in that respect is stated thus: 'We do not understand that under the law of Virginia a court would pay money for education into the hands of children who are incapable of handling it.' It then says that the funds could be administered by a guardian or under sec. 8–751, Code, 1950, (where the amounts are under $500), a court could direct payment to be made to the recipient's parents.

With these statements, we agree. But because the funds could be administered under applicable statutes has no bearing upon nor may that device be resorted to as an aid to prove or establish the testator's intent. We are of opinion that the testator's dominant intent appears from and is expressed in his unequivocal direction to the trustee to divide the income into as many equal parts as there are children beneficiaries and pay one share to each. This expressed purpose and intent is inconsistent with the appended direction to each child as to the use of his respective share and the latter phrase is thus ineffectual to create an educational trust. The testator's purpose and intent were, we think, to bestow upon the children gifts that would bring to them happiness on the two holidays, but that falls short of an educational trust.

If it be determined that the will fails to create a charitable trust for *educational purposes* (and our conclusion is that it is inoperative to create such a trust), it is earnestly insisted that the trust provided for is nevertheless charitable and valid. In this respect it is claimed that the two yearly payments to be made to the children just before Christmas and Easter produce 'a desirable social effect' and are 'promotive of public convenience and needs, and happiness and contentment' and thus the fund set up in the will constitutes a charitable trust. . . .

A trust from which the income is to be paid at stated intervals to each member of a designated segment of the public, without regard to whether or not the recipients are poor or in need, is not for the relief of poverty, nor is it a social benefit to the community. It is a mere benevolence—a private trust—and may not be upheld as a charitable trust. Restatement of the Law of Trusts, sec. 374:

> ' * * * if a large sum of money is given in trust to apply the income each year in paying a certain sum to every inhabitant of a city, whether rich or poor, the trust is not charitable, since although each inhabitant may receive a benefit, the social interest of the community as such is not thereby promoted.'

In 2 Bogert on Trusts, sec. 380, we find:

> 'As previously stated, gifts which are mere exhibitions of liberality and generosity, without regard to their effect upon the donees, are not charitable. There must be an amelioration of the condition of the donees as a result of the gift, and this improvement must be of a mental, physical, or spiritual nature and not merely financial. Thus, trusts to provide gifts to children, regardless of their need, or to make Christmas gifts to members of a certain class, without consideration of need or effect, are not charitable. * * *.'

> 'Gifts which are made out of mere sentiment, and will have no practical result except the satisfying of a whim of the donor, are obviously lacking in the widespread social effect necessary to a charity.' . . .

Payment to the children of their cash bequests on the two occasions specified would bring to them pleasure and happiness and no doubt cause them to remember or think of their benefactor with gratitude and thanksgiving. That was, we think, Charles B. Henry's intent. Laudable, generous and praiseworthy though it may be, it is not for the relief of the poor or needy, nor does it otherwise so benefit or advance the social interest of the community as to justify its continuance in perpetuity as a charitable trust. . . .

No error is found in the decrees appealed from and they are affirmed.

Marsh v. Frost Nat'l Bank

129 S.W.3d 174 (Tex. App. 2004)

OPINION BY JUSTICE RODRIGUEZ.

This is a declaratory judgment action. Appellants, Anna Spohn Welch Marsh, Noel Marsh, and Holly McKee, appeal from a probate order that modified a provision in the will of Charles Vartan Walker, deceased. [Appellants argued that the *cy pres* modification doctrine, which can be applied only to charitable trusts, could not be used here because the settlor lacked charitable intent.] . . .

Charles Walker died on March 13, 2000, leaving a holographic will. The will named appellee, Frost National Bank (Frost Bank), as independent executor. On July 11, 2000, Frost Bank filed an original petition for declaratory judgment for clarification of several probate matters including the construction of Article V of the Charles Walker will, the provision at issue in this appeal. Article V reads in relevant part:

> I hereby direct my Executor to sell tract 3 of the V.M. Donigan 456.80 Partition for cash and to invest the proceeds in safe and secure tax-free U.S. government bonds or insured tax-free municipal bonds. This trust is to be called the James Madison Fund to honor our fourth President, the Father of the Constitution. The ultimate purpose of this fund is to provide a million dollar trust fund for every American 18 years or older. At 6% compound interest and a starting figure of $1,000,000.00, it would take approximately 346 years to provide enough money to do this. My executor will head the Board of Trustees. . . . When the Fund reaches $15,000,000 my Executor's function will cease, and the money will be turned over to the Sec. of the Treasury for management by the federal government. The President of the U.S., the Vice President of the U.S., and the Speaker of the U.S. House of Representatives shall be permanent Trustees of the Fund. The Congress of the United States shall make the final rules and regulations as to how the money will be distributed. No one shall be denied their share because of race, religion, marital status, sexual preference, or the amount of their wealth or lack thereof. . . .

Appellants filed an answer to the petition for declaratory judgment alleging that Article V of the will is void under the rule against perpetuities. Appellee, John Cornyn, Texas Attorney General, intervened in this action pursuant to section 123.002 of the Texas Property Code, alleging that a general charitable intent could be found and that Article V of the will created a charitable trust. The Attorney General then moved for the application of the *cy pres* doctrine to Article V. After a hearing on this issue, the trial court found in relevant part that: (1) the will evidenced a general charitable intent; (2) Article V of the will established a valid charitable trust not subject to the rule against perpetuities. . . . This appeal ensued.

In their first issue, appellants argue that Article V does not show a charitable intent and therefore is not subject to reformation under the *cy pres* doctrine. . . .

In Texas, under the rule against perpetuities, an interest is not good unless it must vest, if at all, not later than twenty-one years after some life in being at the time of the creation of the interest, plus a period of gestation. Both perpetual trusts and trusts for an indefinite duration violate the rule against perpetuities and are void. The rule against perpetuities does not, however, apply to charitable trusts. Therefore, we must first address whether Article V of the will establishes a trust for a charitable purpose.

Whether or not a given purpose is "charitable" is a question of law for the court to decide. . . .

Where the question of whether a given purpose is or is not charitable arises, the words "charitable purpose" have a definite ascertainable meaning in law, and a judicial determination may be made with satisfactory certainty in every case. Legal concepts of what are "charitable purposes" are categorized in section 368 of the Restatement Second of Trusts. . . .

Article V of the will clearly states that the purpose of the fund is to provide a million dollar trust fund for every American eighteen years or older with no one being denied his share due to race, religion, marital status, sexual preference, or the amount of his wealth. Thus, it is clear from the language of Article V that if the purpose is to be found charitable, it must fall under the broad category (f) of section 368 of the Restatement; other purposes the accomplishment of which is beneficial to the community. To be included in category (f), the purpose set out in Article V must go beyond merely providing financial enrichment to the individual members of the community; the purpose must promote the social interest of the community as a whole. The Restatement provides this Court with the following illustration applicable to the facts of this case:

> [I]f a large sum of money is given in trust to apply the income each year in paying a certain sum to every inhabitant of a city, whether rich or poor, the trust is not charitable, since although each inhabitant may receive a benefit, the social interest of the community as such is not thereby promoted.

Furthermore, trusts created to distribute money out of liberality or generosity, without regard to the need of the donees and the effect of the gifts, do not have the requisite public benefit necessary to a charity. With these concepts in mind, we analyze Article V.

Charles Walker expressly states in Article V that "[t]he ultimate purpose of this fund is to provide a million dollar trust fund for every American 18 years or older." From this language, it is obvious Walker intended nothing more than to financially enrich the American public. While this act is generous and benevolent, it is not necessarily beneficial to the community. There is no evidence referenced or argument made by appellees to persuade us that the effect of the trust contemplated by Walker would promote the social interest of the community. Article V does not place restrictions or limitations on the beneficiaries of the trust, which would allow them to use the funds for any purpose, whether it be one that benefits the community or one that burdens it. The trust would provide a personal, individual benefit to each beneficiary but would fail to promote the social interest of the community as a whole. Furthermore, the trust is established without regard to the need of the beneficiaries or the effect of the trust and as a result lacks the requisite public benefit necessary to a charity. The trust created by Walker is nothing more than a generous distribution of money with no contemplation or recognition of public benefit. We conclude the trust established by Walker is devoid of any charitable intent or purpose and is therefore not charitable as defined by law.

Appellees argue that Texas courts have a long history of favoring charitable bequests and use liberal rules of construction to fulfill the intent of the testator. They also urge that where a bequest is open to two constructions, the interpretation that gives the charity effect should be adopted, and that which will defeat the charity should be rejected. In support of their arguments, appellees cite *Boyd; Blocker v. State; Taysum v. El Paso Nat'l Bank*; and *Eldridge v. Marshall Nat'l Bank*. We agree with appellees' contentions and the cases cited in support thereof. However, we find these cases distinguishable and the specific propositions stated inapplicable. In the cases cited, the courts, after finding an existing charitable intent as defined by law, used liberal rules of construction to sustain the charitable trust. In this case, however, we find no charitable intent or purpose. Therefore, these rules of law do not apply. Appellees would have us use these rules to create a charitable intent where none exists. We decline to do so.

Having concluded Article V of the will does not establish a charitable trust, the rule against perpetuities is applicable. In this case, the trust is of indefinite duration and therefore violates the rule against perpetuities. . . .

Make the Connection

Could Charles Walker have written this trust differently to make it valid? What if he had limited it to citizens who earn less than the average American?

When a noncharitable trust is in violation of the rule against perpetuities, a trial court is authorized to reform the trust pursuant to section 5.043 of the Texas Property Code. A court has the power to reform or construe the trust according to the doctrine of cy pres by giving effect to the general intent of the testator within the limits of the rule. It is clear from the language in Article V that Walker's general intent in creating the trust was to financially enrich the American public. Therefore, application of section 5.043 requires the court to reform or construe Article V within the limits of the rule against perpetuities and consistent with this intent. If reformation is not possible however, the trust is void as being in violation of the rule. . . . We remand this case to the trial court to consider the feasibility of reformation of Article V under section 5.043. . . .

Accordingly, we reverse the trial court's judgment to the extent it established a charitable trust and remand this case for further proceedings consistent with this opinion. . . .

Register of Wills for Baltimore City v. Cook

216 A.2d 542 (Md. 1966)

OPPENHEIMER, JUDGE.

This case involves the question of whether bequests to help further the passage of the proposed Equal Rights Amendment and to aid women who may be in distress or suffer any injury as a result of any inequalities in the laws of Maryland or other states or of the United States are exempt from inheritance tax under the Maryland law. The taxes involved were paid under protest and the appellees appealed to the Maryland Tax Court. The court awarded refunds; the Register of Wills appealed to the Baltimore City Court, which affirmed the Tax Court decision, and this appeal resulted.

Jessie Marjorie Cook died December 29, 1960, a resident of Baltimore City, and her will was probated in the Orphans' Court of Baltimore City. The provisions involved read as follows:

> 'TWENTY-SECOND: I give and bequeath unto Helen Elizabeth Brown and Rose S. Zetzer, attorneys at law, the sum of $10,000.00 to be held in Trust for the following purposes: to pay unto the Maryland Branch of the National Woman's Party, One Hundred ($100.) Dollars per year for a period of ten years, if said organization remains in existence and is active for that length of time; the rest and residue of said bequest in trust shall be used to help further the passage of and enactment into law of the EQUAL RIGHTS AMENDMENT to the Constitution of the United States; the said Trustees or their successors, if any, shall have absolute control of said sum of money and use the same as in their joint judgment may seem best to carry out the purposes for which this bequest is intended.

> 'TWENTY-THIRD: I give and bequeath unto Helen Elizabeth Brown and Rose S. Zetzer, attorneys at law, in Trust and to their successors, in trust, the sum of $25,000.00 for the purpose of aiding and assisting any woman who may be in distress or suffer any injury to herself or her property as a result of any inequalities in the laws of the State of Maryland or of any of the United States; said Trustees or their successors in trust shall have absolute control of said trust fund and shall use the same as in their best judgment jointly may be deemed advisable to carry out the purposes for which said bequest is intended and their decision shall be final.

> 'In the event, however, that said Trustees shall be unable to agree, each Trustee shall select one competent person who shall consider the matter and file their opinion. If these two arbitrators fail to agree, then these two shall mutually select a competent third person and the decision of any two of the three persons thus selected shall be conclusive and be accepted as final.

'TWENTY-EIGHTH: All the rest and residue of my estate, whether real, personal or mixed and wheresoever situate, which I now own, possess or to which I may be entitled to at the time of my death, or at any time thereafter, I give, devise and bequeath in Trust to my Trustees above named; viz: Helen Elizabeth Brown and Rose S. Zetzer, to be used to further the cause of equality for women in civil and economic rights and to carry on the work for women in accordance with the objectives as outlined in paragraphs Nos. 'Twenty-second' and 'Twenty-third' herein.'

Vernon Cook, Jr., the testatrix's brother and executor, filed a bill in equity to test the validity of the bequests and to determine whether his sister's will executed the power of appointment in the will of Vernon Cook, Sr., his father and the father of the testatrix. The litigation resulted in a settlement under which Mr. Cook received one-half of the residue of the trust held by Mercantile-Safe Deposit & Trust Company under the will of Vernon Cook, Sr., and the trustees under Miss Cook's will received the amounts of the specific bequests and the residue of Miss Cook's estate plus the remaining half of the residue of the Mercantile-Safe Deposit fund. The trustees under the testatrix's will received approximately $190,000 from each source, in the total amount of about $380,000, and placed the administration of the fund under the general jurisdiction of the Circuit Court.

Code Article 81, sec. 150, imposes a collateral inheritance tax of 7 1/2%, with certain exemptions. The exemption provision here involved is as follows:

' * * * And provided further that nothing in this section shall apply to property passing, in trust or otherwise, to or for the use of a corporation, trust or community chest, fund, or foundation, created or organized under the law of the United States or any state or territory or possession of the United States, organized and operated exclusively for religious, charitable, scientific, literary or educational purposes, including the encouragement of art and the prevention of cruelty to children or animals, if no part of the net earnings of which inures to the benefit of any private shareholder or individual, and (i) if a substantial part or all of the activities and work of which are carried on in the State of Maryland or in the District of Columbia, * * *.'

There is substantial, but not complete, overlap in the different kind of laws that might govern a charitable organization. Banking, tax, corporate, and trust law can all come into play.

The taxes were paid under protest and the refunds awarded by the Maryland Tax Court totaled approximately $25,000 with interest from July, 1963.

In the hearing before the Maryland Tax Court, the two trustees named in the will, Helen Elizabeth Brown and Rose S. Zetzer, both testified. In addition, various documents were offered in evidence. One exhibit was a statement of the purposes and functions of the Maryland Branch of the National Woman's Party, of which Miss Brown is a past president. The statement reads in part as follows:

'The Maryland Branch of the National Woman's Party has for its fundamental objective to secure for women complete equality under the law with respect to their property, personal, social economic and civil rights and privileges, and to that end to inform, detail and specify what rights and privileges women possess presently, and to what extent these rights and privileges are curtailed or limited. These rights and limitations of rights are brought to focus by way of public discussion and education. Furthermore, to accomplish these purposes, the National Woman's Party, Maryland Branch, whose membership consists of businesswomen, homemakers, lawyers, and civic minded women, arrange, through public meetings and discussion groups, to further the cause of equality of opportunity under the law for women in business, professions and public offices and encourage the enlightened representatives and leaders in our community to remove every vestige of discrimination which is rampant in many of our antiquated customs * * *.'

The testimony shows that the Maryland organization works for the passage of the Equal Rights Amendment, and to remove discriminations in the laws against women throughout the United States. It is a branch of the National Woman's Party, which is incorporated. At the time Miss Cook's will was probated, the Maryland Branch may not have been incorporated.

Another exhibit put into evidence was the report of the President's Commission on the Status of Women made in 1963. This report includes the following statements: 'Eight out of ten women are in paid employment outside of the home at some time during their lives * * *' 'In the face of these amendments, however [the Fifth and Fourteenth Amendments to the Federal Constitution] there remain, especially in certain State laws and official practices, distinctions based on sex which discriminate against women.' 'Lower pay rates for women doing the same work as men are not uncommon.' While in 1963 the Federal Fair Labor Standards Act of 1938 was amended to require equal pay for equal work, 'State laws should establish the principle of equal pay for comparable work.' 'In many specific areas of State law, the disabilities of married women are considerable.'

The testatrix was deeply interested in women's rights. Her trustees conceive their duties as 'educational primarily and charitable.' Miss Zetzer testified that a major legal 'discrimination' in Maryland is the wife's obligation to accept a suitable domicile selected by her husband. The trustees believe, however, that there is greater and more serious legal discrimination in other states. There was also testimony that, in Maryland, discriminations have been found in certain employment practices and that women still do not have equal pay for equal work.

There was testimony about guidelines for the administration of the trust which the trustees formulated under the title 'The Marjorie Cook Foundation.' The testimony is unclear as to whether this formulation was made prior to distribution. There was also testimony as to the scope and nature of the trusts after distribution. However, counsel agree that the legal questions involved in this appeal are to be adjudicated on the basis of the provisions made in the will, irrespective of what may or may not have been done by the trustees after distribution. . . .

The case, in our view, involves two questions. First, is the general nature of the bequest charitable under the Maryland law?; and, second, if the first question is answered in the affirmative, are the trusts exclusively for charitable purposes, in view of the right of the trustees to employ the funds to support candidates for political office who favor women's rights, to contribute to the Maryland Branch of the National Woman's Party, and to work for the passage of the Equal Rights Amendment? Counsel agree that, if the trusts are not charitable, the bequests are taxable.

The history of the statutory provision as to the exemption of charitable trusts is set forth in Second National Bank of Washington, D.C. v. Second National Bank. Many gifts for charitable uses had been declared to be invalid because of the indefiniteness of the donees. In 1931, an Act (now Code Art. 16, sec. 195) was passed declaring that henceforward the statute of 43 Elizabeth Ch. 4 applies to gifts and trusts for charitable purposes. Judge Sloan, for the Court, said:

> 'This statute did not mark the beginning of charitable uses, as courts of equity had, before it was enacted, assumed jurisdiction of charitable trusts. It made legal and enforceable trusts and gifts which had been declared invalid because indefinite and general. The courts, in states where the statute had been adopted, did not confine themselves to the charities expressly named, and many objects have been upheld as charities, which the statute neither mentions nor distinctly refers to. Thus a gift 'to the poor' generally, or to the poor of a particular town, parish, age, sex, race, or condition, or to poor emigrants, though not falling within any of the descriptions of poor in the statute, is a good charitable gift.'

The first version of the Equal Rights Amendment was drafted in 1923 by Alice Paul, founder of the National Woman's Party. The ERA was reintroduced in 1971, passed by Congress, and sent to the states for ratification. It fell three states shy of the 38 needed to become part of the Constitution. Decades after the ratification deadline expired, two additional states ratified the ERA. If one more ratifies it, the Supreme Court may be asked whether the expiration date can be waived—paving the way for the ERA to become law.

Nevertheless, strict construction does not require that an unreasonable or unusual meaning must be given to the words used in exemption statutes. We find nothing to show that the words 'charitable' and 'educational' were intended by the Legislature to have and convey other than their usual meaning in law. . . .

A purpose is charitable if its accomplishment is of such social interest to the community as to justify permitting the property to be devoted to the purpose in perpetuity. There is no fixed standard to determine what purposes are of such social interest to the community; the interests of the community vary with time and place. At common law in England and in the United States it is agreed that the relief of poverty, the advancement of education and of religion, the promotion of health, the accomplishment of governmental or municipal purposes, are of such social interest to the community as to fall within the concept of charity. As to what other purposes are of such interest to the community as to be charitable, no definite rule can be laid down. These various purposes are dealt with in the following Sections.

The bequest to the trustees in the Twenty-Second paragraph of the will is for two purposes: Payments to the Maryland Branch of the National Woman's Party and to help further the passage of the Equal Rights Amendment to the Constitution of the United States, which is designed to prohibit discrimination against women by reason of their sex. The bequest to the trustees in the Twenty-Third paragraph is for the purpose of aiding and assisting any woman who may be in distress or suffer any injury to herself or her property as a result of any inequalities in the laws of Maryland or of the United States. The residuary bequest to the trustees in the Twenty-Eighth paragraph is to further the cause of equality of women in civil and economic rights and to carry on the work for women in accordance with the objectives outlined in the Twenty-Second and Twenty-Third paragraphs.

The primary purposes of all the trusts, in our view, are the elimination of discriminations against women and to give relief to women injured by such discriminations. The passage of the Equal Rights Amendment is one of the methods set forth by the testatrix to endeavor to accomplish these objectives, both directly and by contributions to the Maryland Branch of the National Woman's Party.

Trusts to eliminate discriminations and to provide relief for the persons discriminated against have been generally upheld as charitable. "If the general purposes for which a trust is created are such as may be reasonably thought to promote the social interest of the community, the mere fact that a majority of the people and the members of the court believe that the particular purpose of the settlor is unwise or not adapted to the accomplishment of the general purposes, does not prevent the trust from being charitable. The Courts do not take sides or attempt to decide which of two conflicting views of promoting the social interest of the community is the better adapted to the purpose, even though the views are opposed to each other * * *.' Restatement, Trusts 2d § 374 comment 1.

By the great weight of authority, if a trust is essentially charitable in nature, it is still charitable even though one of its purposes is to endeavor to effectuate a change of existing law.

Restatement, Trusts 2d § 374 comment *j* reads as follows:

> '*Change in existing law.* A trust may be charitable although the accomplishment of the purpose for which the trust is created involves a change in the existing law. If the purpose of the trust is to bring about changes in the law by illegal means, such as by revolution, bribery, illegal lobbying or bringing improper pressure to bear upon members of the legislature, the purpose is illegal. See § 377. The mere fact, however, that the purpose is to bring about a change in the law, whether indirectly through the education of the electors so as to bring about a public sentiment in favor of the change, or through proper influences brought to bear upon the legislators, does not prevent the purpose from being legal and charitable.'

> 'Many American decisions and, it is submitted, the better reasoned cases, declare that trusts which seek to bring about better government by changing laws or

constitutional provisions are charitable, so long as the settlor directed that the reforms should be accomplished peaceably, by the established constitutional means, and not by war, riot, or revolution.'

'In the United States the notion that a trust for a purpose otherwise charitable is not charitable if the accomplishment of its purposes involves a change in existing laws has been pretty thoroughly rejected. Many reforms can be accomplished only by a change in the law, and there seems to be no good reason why the mere fact that they can be accomplished only through legislation should prevent them from being valid charitable purposes.'

Two Massachusetts decisions are contrary to what is admitted to be the majority view. In Jackson v. Phillips, the court held that a bequest to secure the passage of laws granting women the right to vote and all other civil rights enjoyed by men could not be sustained as a charity. Justice Gray said, for the court:

'But it is the duty of the judicial department to expound and administer the laws as they exist. And trusts whose expressed purpose is to bring about changes in the laws or the political institutions of the country are not charitable in such a sense as to be entitled to peculiar favor, protection and perpetuation from the ministers of those laws which they are designed to modify or subvert.'

The same will involved a trust designed to secure the abolition of slavery and this trust the court held charitable, even though its accomplishment would necessitate a fundamental change in the law. Jackson was followed in Bowditch v. Attorney General, which held a bequest to promote the causes of women's rights not charitable because impliedly it looked to the accomplishment of the testator's intention by legislation.

[D]ecisions from other states show that the Massachusetts doctrine had not been followed. . . .

Great as is our respect for the Massachusetts court, we believe that the majority view should be followed in this case. The provisions of the testatrix's will make it evident to us that her primary objective was to provide funds for the elimination of discriminations against women and that support of the passage of the Equal Rights Amendment and other national or state legislation to this end was merely an incidental means to the accomplishment of the general purpose. All the provisions of the will look only to legal means to effectuate the objective. The bequests to not provide in any way for contributions to a political party as such. Whatever may be the views of individuals, laymen or judges, as to the need or desirability of the passage of the Equal Rights Amendment or similar legislation, our system of government is not opposed to attempts to secure legislative changes by legal means. Indeed, the channelling of efforts to effect social or political changes to the public discussions involved in proposed constitutional amendments or legislation, rather than by possible violence or subversion, is fundamental to our democracy.

Realistically, a charitable purpose such as that of the testatrix, can often only be effectuated by legislative change. Recognition of that fact by the testatrix does not alter what we have found to be the essentially charitable nature of the bequests here involved.

Even though the bequests are charitable in nature, the exemption clause of the statute provides in effect that they are taxable unless they are exclusively for religious, charitable or similar purposes. The National Woman's Party and its Maryland Branch are non-profit organizations. In the sense that the bequests here involved do not provide for or permit personal benefit of any private shareholder or individual, except members of the designated class of beneficiaries of the fund, they are exclusively for a charitable purpose. The question remains, however, as to whether the provisions which permit the use of the funds in an endeavor to charge existing laws make the charitable purpose none-exclusive.

The Maryland law contains no provision similar to that in the federal income and estate tax statutes, which specifically provide that the deduction is to be allowed only if no substantial part of the activities of the donee or legatee is carrying on propaganda or otherwise attempting to influence legislation.

If, as we have found the purposes of the trust here involved are charitable, they are no less charitable because of the means authorized to effectuate them, when, as here, those means are legal and not against public policy. Contributions to political parties are not involved. Although efforts to bring about changes in the law are envisioned and authorized, these are only ways to effectuate the purposes; they do not make the purposes themselves less charitable in nature or dilute their nature. Had the General Assembly wished to exclude bequests otherwise charitable from the exemption if a substantial part of a bequest is used in attempts to influence legislation, it could easily have done so by incorporating in the Maryland statute a clause similar to the provisions which the Congress has had in effect for several decades. . . .

The appellant relies on federal cases construing the federal statutes in respect of charitable deductions. It is true that several earlier federal decisions take the same point of view as did the Massachusetts cases as to the effect of efforts to change the law upon the charitable nature of the organizations involved. . . .

These cases were decided before the Internal Revenue Code had been amended by the addition of the phrase 'and no substantial part of the activities of which is carrying on propaganda, or otherwise attempting, to influence legislation.' . . .

Marshall v. Commissioner of Internal Revenue held that bequests in trust to promote the theory of production for use and not for profit, to promote civil liberties and to preserve wilderness areas, were not deductible from the federal estate tax because political activity was a definite purpose of the trust. The court emphasized that the political purposes were substantial and therefore within the exception of the Internal Revenue Code. In Seasongood v. Commissioner of Internal Revenue it was held that deductions from individual income tax returns for contributions made to a local Good Government League were deductible, even though a minor portion of the time and effort of the League was devoted to activities found to be political. The court held that the statute must be liberally construed to effect its purpose and that the legislative activities of the League in relation to all its other activities were not substantial. Dulles v. Johnson, involved the deductibility under the federal estate tax law of bequests to city, county and state bar associations. Part of the work of the associations was study and report on proposed and existing legislation. Copies of the reports and resolutions were often sent to the legislative and other branches of federal and state governments. The court held that the activities of the associations in respect of impending legislation were not such a substantial part of their activities as to cause the forfeiture of their charitable status.

Taken as a whole, the trend of the federal decisions indicates to us that efforts to change the law do not necessarily affect the exclusive charitable nature of an organization, despite the restriction contained in the Internal Revenue Code, which, as we have pointed out, is not a part of the Maryland law.

We find that the bequests here involved are exclusively charitable within the meaning of the Maryland statute and therefore are deductible.

———————————

Uniform Trust Code § 405. Charitable Purposes; Enforcement

(a) A charitable trust may be created for the relief of poverty, the advancement of education or religion, the promotion of health, governmental or municipal purposes, or other purposes the achievement of which is beneficial to the community.

(b) If the terms of a charitable trust do not indicate a particular charitable purpose or beneficiary, the court may select one or more charitable purposes or beneficiaries. The selection must be consistent with the settlor's intention to the extent it can be ascertained.

(c) The settlor of a charitable trust, among others, may maintain a proceeding to enforce the trust.

Points for Discussion

1. A lasting concept

The Restatement (Third) of Trusts § 28 elected to continue with the established categories of charitable purposes, which are derived from Statute of Charitable Uses, 43 Eliz. I, c.4 (1601). Why has the definition stood the test of time so well? Are there any purposes that you think are charitable but do not fit this definition?

2. How many beneficiaries?

One of the cardinal differences between private and charitable trusts is that the former require a definite or ascertainable beneficiary, as explored in Chapter 8, but the latter do not. A definite beneficiary does not preclude a finding that the trust is charitable, but neither does a large group of unascertained beneficiaries guarantee a finding that it is charitable. A charitable trust can potentially be valid even if it ends up helping only a single person, e.g., a college scholarship that is awarded to only one student.

3. Nice versus charitable?

Why wasn't the trust in *Henry* charitable in nature? He had no connection to the children who would benefit and sought only to make young people happy for years to come. Courts might decline to uphold trusts that are expressly serving "altruistic" or "benevolent" purposes unless it is clear from language, structure, or other evidence that the settlor intended to serve one of the specific, recognized charitable purposes. One can be kind, without being charitable in the legal sense of the word. A trust to help all citizens of a community would not be valid, but a trust to help the poor members of that community likely would be.

4. Charitable discrimination?

Charitable trusts, like private trusts, must serve a purpose that is legal and not contrary to public policy. Trusts that invite or perpetuate invidious discrimination typically fail this test. How do we draw the line between a trust to serve an unpopular cause and a discriminatory one?

5. Duration of charitable crusts

Charitable trusts can last in perpetuity. Recall the technical reason why the trust in *Henry* was invalid—that it was not charitable and could not comply with the rule against perpetuities. The settlor designed it so it *would* last forever. What differences between private and charitable trusts might justify the different rules on duration? Should charitable trusts be able to last forever? Why or why not?

Problems

A. Do you have a feel for the line between charitable and non-charitable purposes? Which of the following trusts would qualify under the cases in this section? Why or why not?

(1)   A trust to search for a cure for Lou Gehrig's disease.

(2)   A trust to provide housing for the caretaker at a convent.

(3)   A trust to pay the salary of a law professor.

(4)   A trust to pay for "city beautification" projects.

(5)   A trust to educate the descendants of the settlor.

(6)   A trust to pay upkeep of a family's art collection.

(7)   A trust to provide free piano lessons for all children in a public school.

B. Would a trust that is set to provide scholarships to college students, but included the language "first priority and consideration shall be given to qualified blood relatives of the Grantor" qualify as a charitable purpose?

(1)   What is the argument for and against upholding the trust terms?

(2)   In the case, *United Bank, Inc. v. Blosser*, 218 W. Va. 378 (2005), the trustee modified the trust immediately after the death of the settlor to qualify under the tax code by eliminating the above provision. Thirty years later, the settlor's decedents sued to try and have the provision reinstated. The Supreme Court of West Virginia held that the trust qualified as a charitable trust, but state law required the trust be amended to avoid tax penalties.

(3)   Should Trustees be able to modify the terms of the trust to avoid tax penalties?

(4)   When should Trustees be allowed to modify the terms of a trust?

————

B. *Cy Pres* and Deviation

A lot can happen over time. That's why a trust that can last forever must be subject to different rules of modification and termination—it's not reasonable to assume the settlor will have foreseen or had the ability to foresee—the many changes that might affect the trust and its ability to serve the settlor's original charitable purpose. *Cy pres* translates to "as near as possible" and describes a doctrine that sometimes permits a court to redirect assets in a charitable trust when the original terms have been impossible, impracticable, or illegal. This doctrine is a necessary component of charitable trust law given that such trusts are not subject to any durational limits. The inability to shift gears would render many trusts obsolete, at least at some point, and would force trustees in many cases to engage in wasteful spending.

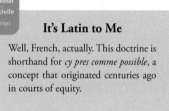

It's Latin to Me

Well, French, actually. This doctrine is shorthand for *cy pres comme possible*, a concept that originated centuries ago in courts of equity.

1.   Illegal, Impossible, or Impracticable

First Merit Bank, N.A. v. Akron Gen. Med. Cent.

116 N.E.3d 843 (Ohio Ct. App. 2018)

Wise, P.J.

Appellant DHSC, LLC dba Affinity Medical Center appeals the June 20, 2017, decision of the Stark County Probate Court's decision declaring it was not entitled to proceeds from the Kathryn L. Seymour Amended Trust.

Appellees in this matter are First Merit Bank, N.A., Massillon Rotary Foundation Trust, The Health Foundation of Greater Massillon, Akron General Medical Center and the Attorney General Mike Dewine.

STATEMENT OF THE FACTS

On April 18, 2016, Plaintiff-Appellee FirstMerit Bank, N.A. (FirstMerit), as Trustee of the Kathryn L. Seymour Revocable Trust, filed a complaint for declaratory judgment with the Stark County Court of Common Pleas, Probate Division. First Merit stated that Kathryn L. Seymour had established a Trust and among the beneficiaries of the Trust, she named Massillon Community Hospital.

In its Complaint, FirstMerit alleged that while Massillon Community Hospital was a not-for-profit hospital at the time Ms. Seymour established the trust, it subsequently was sold to a for-profit entity and became known as Affinity Medical Center. FirstMerit further alleged that the Seymour Trust was a "charitable trust" and that because her charitable intent could not be carried out, the court should apply the *cy pres* doctrine and designate the proceeds of the Trust be distributed to another charitable organization.

FirstMerit named as Defendants Akron General Medical Center, Appellant, DHSC, LLC dba Affinity Medical Center (hereinafter referred to as "Affinity"), St. John United Church of Christ, Salvation Army and the Ohio Attorney General. Thereafter, the Greater Health Foundation of Massillon and the Greater Massillon Rotary Foundation intervened as Defendants, claiming interest in the proceeds of the Trust. All parties entered answers to the Trustee's complaint. Thereafter, pursuant to Order of the Court, the parties submitted briefs in support of their respective positions.

On June 20, 2017, the Stark County Probate Court issued an Order declaring that Appellant Affinity was not entitled to the proceeds of the Trust. Instead, the court held that the *cy pres* doctrine applied and awarded the proceeds of the Trust be distributed to Defendants Health Foundation of Greater Massillon and Massillon Rotary Foundation Trust.

It is from this decision Appellant Affinity now appeals, raising the following errors for review: . . . (3) the trial court erred in applying the *cy pres* doctrine where the grantor clearly restricted the bequest to a specific limited purpose. The *cy pres* doctrine only applies where the trust language exhibits a general charitable intent." . . .

I., II., III.

In each of its assignments of error, Appellant claims the trial court erred in finding that Appellant Affinity was not entitled to the proceeds from the Trust and applying the *cy pres* doctrine. We disagree.

This case involves the Kathryn Seymour Amended Trust Agreement, which provided, *inter alia*, that upon Ms. Seymour's death, her personal and real property would be distributed to her daughter. The balance of the trust estate was to be distributed as follows:

2.   All of the rest, residue and remainder of the trust estate shall be converted to cash and distributed as follows:

a.   Fifty percent (50%) thereof to St. John's United Church of Christ presently located at 121 Tremont Ave. S.E., Massillon, Ohio, its successors or assigns. This bequest is unrestricted and the Board of Trustees or other governing body may use and expend the same for the benefit of St. John's United Church of Christ, its successors or assigns, in any manner it deems appropriate.

b.   Forty percent (40%) thereof to the Massillon Community Hospital, its successors or assigns. These funds shall be restricted so as to benefit only the facilities of said hospital at 875 Eighth Street, N.E., Massillon, Ohio. These improvements need not be limited to building renovation. Any expenditure of funds which benefit the operation of the above location shall be permitted.

c.   Ten percent (10%) thereof to the general fund of the Massillon, Ohio Branch of the Salvation Army.

Cy Pres Doctrine

The *cy pres* doctrine is a rule of construction by which charitable gifts are preserved for the public benefit. In the law of trusts it refers to a rule of construction used by courts of equity to effectuate the intention of a charitable donor "as near as may be" when it has become impossible or impractical by reason of changing conditions or circumstances to give literal effect to the donor's intention.

The *cy pres* doctrine is a saving device that permits a court to direct the application of the property held in a charitable trust to a charitable purpose different from that designated in the trust instrument.

"Roughly speaking, it is the doctrine that equity will, when the charity is originally or later becomes impossible, inexpedient, or impracticable of fulfillment, *substitute another charitable object which is believed to approach the original purpose as closely as possible.* It is the theory that equity has the power to revise a charitable trust where the settlor had a general charitable intent in order to meet unexpected emergencies or changes in conditions which threaten its existence."

At common law, Ohio courts have followed the traditional view that before the *cy pres* doctrine will be applied by a court, the following three essentials must be present:

(1)   there must be a valid charitable trust and one that is invalid will not be cured by an application of the doctrine;

(2)   it must be established that it is impossible or impractical to carry out the specific purposes of the trust;

(3)   it must be established that the donor evinced a general charitable intent.

The common-law doctrine of *cy pres* has recently been codified at R.C. § 5804.13, which provides:

(A) Except as otherwise provided in division (B) of this section, if a particular charitable purpose becomes unlawful, impracticable, or impossible to achieve, all of the following apply:

(1) The trust does not fail in whole or in part.

(2) The trust property does not revert to the settlor or the settlor's successors in interest.

(3) The court may apply *cy pres* to modify or terminate the trust by directing that the trust property be applied or distributed, in whole or in part, in a manner consistent with the settlor's charitable purposes. In accordance with section 109.25 of the Revised Code, the attorney general is a necessary party to a judicial proceeding brought under this section.

(B) A provision in the terms of a charitable trust for the distribution of the trust property to a noncharitable beneficiary prevails over the power of the court under division (A) of this section to apply *cy pres* to modify or terminate the trust.

The official comment to R.C. § 5804.13 indicates that this codification "modifies the doctrine of *cy pres* by presuming that the settlor had a general charitable intent when a particular charitable purpose becomes impossible or impracticable to achieve."

In the case *sub judice*, the trial court made the following findings:

[T]he Grantor demonstrated a charitable intent.

Due to the changing circumstances surrounding the merger of Massillon Community Hospital as a now for-profit hospital operating as Affinity Hospital, the Grantor's charitable intent has become frustrated and impossible to achieve.

A distribution of the funds to a for-profit hospital would contradict Grantor's overt charitable desires.

Based on these findings, the probate court determined that pursuant to R.C. § 5804.13, the court could apply the *cy pres* doctrine in order to save the charitable distribution and maintain Grantor's overarching charitable intent.

Upon review, we find no error in the trial court's analysis or decision in this matter. Initially, we find that the trial court's determination that the gift to Massillon Community Hospital was impossible to carry out because such entity no longer existed. The trial court then found, as do we, that DHSC dba Affinity was not an appropriate recipient of the gift because it is a for-profit entity.

> **Take Note**
>
> What kind of evidence can be used to establish or disprove general charitable intent?

The trial court then looked at the dispositive language contained in the Trust and found it to be clear and unambiguous. The court found that the Settlor had intended for her residuary estate to be distributed to only charitable organizations, i.e., a church, a non-profit hospital and the Salvation Army. The court found that such evidenced a charitable intent.

We likewise find that Ms. Seymour's intent was charitable, as evidenced by choosing only charitable organizations and in leaving approximately half of the residue and remainder of her Trust to a hospital, a health-based organization. Where a trust benefits the general promotion of health, the settlor's intent is presumed to be charitable. A trust established to generally benefit the promotion of health is a per se demonstration of the testator's charitable intent. The law favors charitable bequests, and they are liberally construed to accomplish the testator or grantor's purpose.

Finally, we find no merit in Appellant's argument that the trial court erred in considering extrinsic evidence in reaching its decision. Appellant argues that Massillon Community Hospital's status as a not-for-profit organization is not contained in Ms. Seymour's Trust agreement and therefore constitutes extrinsic evidence. The non-profit status of Massillon Community Hospital was agreed to by the parties as set forth in the Complaint and Answers thereto and was never a contested issue in this matter. DHSC dba Affinity admitted in its Answer that Massillon Community Hospital was a non-profit organization at the time Ms. Seymour amended her Trust to include such gift. As such, we do not find that the trial court considered extrinsic evidence in making its ultimate decision in this matter.

Accordingly, Appellant's assignments of error are overruled. [T]he judgment of the Court of Common Pleas . . . is affirmed.

————————

GWIN, J., and BALDWIN, J., concur.

Obermeyer v. Bank of America

140 S.W.3d 18 (Mo. 2004), as modified on denial of reh'g (Aug. 24, 2004)

EN BANC.

MICHAEL A. WOLFF, JUDGE.

When the late Dr. Joseph Kimbrough established his estate plan in 1955, Washington University had a dental school and a Dental Alumni Development Fund that existed to benefit the school. His 1955 estate plan included a trust to provide benefits for his niece and nephews during their lifetimes after Dr. Kimbrough's death. The trust provided that, upon the death of the survivor of the niece and nephews, the trust estate would be "paid over and distributed free of trust unto Washington University . . . for the exclusive use and benefit of its Dental Alumni Development Fund."

Dr. Kimbrough died in 1963. Washington University discontinued the Dental Alumni Development Fund in 1965, and the university closed its dental school in 1991. The fund no longer exists. The trust paid benefits to the niece and nephews until 2000, when the last of the three died. The death of the last survivor in 2000 was the event that triggered the clause that the trust estate be paid to Washington University for the exclusive use and benefit of the Dental Alumni Development Fund.

Louise Obermeyer and Elizabeth Salmon, the great, great-nieces of Dr. Kimbrough, brought this action for declaratory judgment and construction of Dr. Kimbrough's inter vivos trust, which was valued at approximately $2.8 million in 2000. The circuit court held that Dr. Kimbrough established the trust with a general charitable intent and applied the cy pres doctrine, ruling in favor of Washington University, and directing that the university use the funds to support two dental-related professorships in the name of Dr. Kimbrough.

The gift "free from trust" was an absolute gift to Washington University. The circuit court appropriately provided for the disposition of the trust estate. The judgment of the circuit court is affirmed.

Facts and Procedural History

Dr. Kimbrough was born in 1870. In 1890, he enrolled in the Missouri Dental College, which became a school at Washington University, a tax-exempt, educational institution. He was graduated from the Washington University Dental School in 1894. Dr. Kimbrough was a practicing dentist throughout his career, and he served on the faculty of the Washington University Dental School.

During his lifetime, Dr. Kimbrough made numerous gifts to Washington University. Nearly one-half of the gifts went to no specific college within the university and were unrestricted—meaning the university could use the money as it pleased. Dr. Kimbrough also named Washington University in his estate plan, which consisted of a will and trust.

Dr. Kimbrough established a trust in 1945 to provide income and principal encroachment rights for his niece and nephews during their lifetimes. He amended the trust in 1955 to provide for the distribution of the trust upon the death of his great-niece and great-nephews, Margaret Salmon Towles (Derrick), Oscar Kimbrough, and Harvey W. Salmon. Section two of the trust provided that following the death of the last of Dr. Kimbrough's niece and nephews, the trust shall be distributed as follows:

> Upon the death of the survivor of said niece and nephews and after the death of the Grantor, the property then constituting the trust estate shall be paid over and distributed free from trust unto Washington University, St. Louis, Missouri, for the exclusive use and benefit of its Dental Alumni Development Fund.

The trust did not contain a reversionary provision providing for an alternate disposition of the trust estate.

When the Dental Alumni Development Fund was created in 1954, contributions to it were unrestricted, allowing the deans of each school to use the funds for any purpose they deemed appropriate. The November 1954 edition of the Washington University Dental Journal announced the formation of the Dental Alumni Development Fund and reported that the purpose of the fund was to provide financial support for the dental school and improve the morale of the dental school's faculty. Dr. Kimbrough's gift to the Dental Alumni Development Fund in May 1954 was made before the published report on the establishment of the Fund in the November 1954 issue of the Dental Journal.

Dr. Kimbrough died in 1963, and his life beneficiaries received income until their respective deaths. Margaret Derrick, the last surviving life beneficiary, died in 2000. Washington University stopped using the Dental Alumni Development Fund in 1965, and began using the Annual Fund as its vehicle for the donation of unrestricted gifts. The Annual Fund still exists today. In 1991, Washington University closed the dental school and merged faculty, staff, and programs into its medical school and main campus. Dental medicine continues to be a component of education at the medical school, where maxillofacial surgery, prosthodontics, cleft palate/craniofacial deformities and pediatric dentistry are taught and performed.

Louise Obermeyer and Elizabeth Salmon, Dr. Kimbrough's great, great-nieces, filed suit claiming the trust was created with specific charitable intent, making the cy pres doctrine inapplicable, and the approximately $2.8 million fund should revert to them as Dr. Kimbrough's heirs. The named defendants in this lawsuit are Bank of America, the successor corporate trustee holding the funds of Dr. Kimborough, and Washington University, which also claimed the funds. The Attorney General was joined as a necessary party. Section 456.230. The Dental Alumni Association and a group of alumni of the dental school were granted permission to intervene, but are not part of this appeal.

Charitable trusts are subject to different enforcement rules. Think about why the alumni association was permitted to intervene in this litigation when you review the enforcement materials at the end of the chapter.

Washington University and the Attorney General agreed with the heirs that there was a charitable trust and that it was impossible or impracticable to carry out the charitable purpose in the trust because the Dental Alumni Development Fund no longer exists. They, however, claim the trust was created with general charitable intent and that, under the cy pres doctrine, the funds should be applied to Washington University for dental-related endeavors to most nearly carry out Dr. Kimbrough's charitable intent.

The circuit court held that Dr. Kimbrough established the trust with a general charitable intent and ruled in favor of Washington University. The circuit court then applied the doctrine of cy pres and ordered the assets be used to establish and maintain one or two chairs in Dr. Kimbrough's name for research and practice in cleft palate/craniofacial deformities, or for maxillofacial surgery and prosthodontics, or both. . . .

Standard of Review

This case concerns the language of a trust document and the application of the cy pres doctrine. The ultimate issue in a cy pres case is the intent of the testator. Intent is generally a question of fact, not law. The central issue of the nature of the charitable intent, however, is a matter of law.

Missouri courts apply the cy pres doctrine based on all of the relevant facts and circumstances, not simply the language of the instrument making the grant. Because this Court considers all relevant facts and circumstances, which may include evidence outside of the trust document, this case is not confined to the construction of the trust document. Upon review, the judgment of the trial court will be affirmed unless there is no substantial evidence to support it, it is against the weight of the evidence, or it erroneously declares or applies the law. The reviewing court defers to the trial court's factual findings and credibility determinations, but examines questions of law de novo. Where the circuit court applies the cy pres doctrine, this Court gives deference to that court's application of the doctrine and disposition of the funds.

Dr. Kimbrough Gave a Gift "Free From Trust" to Washington University

The parties maintain that a charitable trust is at issue. Dr. Kimbrough, instead, created a trust for life beneficiaries with the remainder as a gift "free from trust" to Washington University "for the exclusive use and benefit of its Dental Alumni Development Fund." The property was in trust during the relevant life estates, but the amendment specifically provides that the distribution to the university shall be "free from trust." Once Dr. Kimbrough's named heirs died, there was no longer a trust and the distribution was to occur in accordance with the trust instrument.

Application of the Cy Pres Doctrine

The cy pres doctrine is based on the concern of equity to protect and preserve charitable bequests. . . .

It was the policy of courts of equity "to declare valid, if possible, gifts to charity." Charitable trusts are favorites of equity, and they are "given effect wherever possible, by applying the most liberal rules of which the nature of the case will permit." . . .

The cy pres power is generally confined to charitable trusts. Missouri courts have previously applied the cy pres doctrine only to charitable trusts; this Court has held that "absent the creation of a trust, there is no room for the application of the doctrine of cy pres."

While acknowledging the historical limitation of the cy pres doctrine to trusts, the doctrine is appropriate in certain cases involving gifts to charitable corporations. At issue here is a gift with direction from the grantor indicating the intended use of the trust assets. While the cy pres power is applied to gifts in trust, other jurisdictions have applied cy pres "to absolute gifts to charitable corporations or other organizations." That view is consistent with analogous Missouri cases. This Court has held that a person may devote property to a charitable purpose by transferring it to a charitable corporation, in which case the principles applicable to charitable trusts are applicable to charitable corporations. Courts have applied the cy pres doctrine when a charitable institution that is an absolute donee has a deficiency. Such instances include: when a charitable institution cannot be identified by the name used; when impossibility arises in carrying out the intention of the donor charitable corporation, as the absolute donee ceased to exist before the gift was made, went out of existence after it received the gift, merged, or dissolved; and when the charitable corporation declines the gift, does not meet a condition precedent to the vesting of a gift, or is incompetent to take title.

Although the trust itself has ceased to exist, the gift comes from a trust. Moreover, most cy pres cases involve situations where many years have passed since the creation of a trust or other origination of the gift and the time the gift is to be given effect. Cy pres exists to conform the terms of the gift to current conditions. The money in the trust was to be "distributed free from trust unto Washington University, St. Louis, Missouri, for the exclusive use and benefit of its Dental Alumni Development Fund." Were Dr. Kimbrough's gift a charitable trust, the Court would readily apply the cy pres doctrine. Dr. Kimbrough's gift from the trust is an absolute gift to Washington University with an instruction that can no longer be observed because the fund ceased to exist in 1965. Although courts typically reserve application of the cy pres doctrine for charitable trusts, and the absolute gift to the university may not fall under the categories listed above, the cy pres analysis is adopted to carry out Dr. Kimbrough's intent.

Cy Pres Analysis

Missouri courts hold that to apply the doctrine of cy pres, three requirements must be met. First, the trust in question must be a valid charitable trust. Second, it is or becomes impossible, impracticable, or illegal to carry out the specific terms of the trust. Finally, the settlor must have established the trust with a general charitable intent. *Comfort* holds that "unless and until it is determined that a trust has failed, the question of general or specific charitable intent is irrelevant." If the settlor's intent was specific, the cy pres doctrine cannot be applied. The result would be a reversion for the settlor or the settlor's heirs.

The parties agree that a trust was created with a charitable intent and that the trust has failed because the dental school was closed and the Dental Alumni Development Fund no longer exists. The parties maintain that the issue is whether the trust was created with general or specific charitable intent.

A general charitable intent exists where there is an intent to assist a certain general type or kind of charity. General charitable intent "is an intent that a gift be continued within the limits of its general purpose and that shall not cease when a particular thing is accomplished. Unquestionably, when the intent is to apply the gift to a continuing problem, there is a general charitable intent." Gifts made to aid "education, science, literature, the poor, the sick, and so on" demonstrate general charitable intent. Because most charitable gifts are made to ameliorate a continuing problem, it must be determined whether the donor "intended to benefit all those affected by the continuing problem, or only certain of those persons." The grantor's intent is specific when the grantor intended to "aid that kind of charity only in a particular way or by a particular method or means" and further intended that, "if the particular means failed, the gift failed."

Dr. Kimbrough's gift to Washington University for the Dental Alumni Development Fund was not for a particular task to be accomplished, but to support dental medicine at Washington University, a profession of which he was deeply proud. The trust document contained no suggestion that the gift should fail if the particular fund ceased to exist.

In determining whether the charitable intent of the grantor is specific or general, the Court in *Comfort v. Higgins* set forth additional factors courts should consider.

First, *Comfort* distinguished between gifts of money and land, finding that courts have viewed gifts of land as "strong evidence of an absence of general charitable intent," while monetary gifts suggest general intent. Dr. Kimbrough gave a gift of money, not real property, thus indicating general charitable intent.

The second factor is the existence of a reverter clause associated with the gift. Use of a direction for a reversion to the settlor in the case of failure indicates specific charitable intent, while the absence of a reverter clause supports general charitable intent. Dr. Kimbrough's estate plan included reverter clauses as to the bequests for all of the individuals, which instructed the gifts to go to Washington University; however, it did not include a reverter clause as to the gift to Washington University in the will or trust.

The conclusion that a general charitable intent exists is typically reached where the heirs were either specifically excluded or had received other gifts in the will, indicating that no further gifts were included. In his last will and testament, Dr. Kimbrough granted to Margaret Derrick the rest and remainder of his estate if she were living at the time of his death. If she were deceased at the time of his death, Dr. Kimbrough granted to Washington University the rest and remainder of his estate. In his will, Dr. Kimbrough left Louise Obermeyer $5,000 and did not provide for Elizabeth Salmon in his estate plan. The lack of a reverter clause for the charitable gift and the provision for one of his great, great-nieces are indicative of Dr. Kimbrough's general charitable intent.

The third relevant factor is whether the charitable gift was made in trust or outright. A gift in trust is indicative of specific charitable intent, while a gift made outright indicates general intent. The trust provides that at the death of the survivor of the life beneficiaries, the trust is to be paid to Washington University "free from trust." Dr. Kimbrough's gift "free from trust" suggests general charitable intent.

The heirs argue that the use of the language, "for the exclusive use and benefit," requires a finding of specific charitable intent. Where the terms of a charitable trust direct a means of execution or dedicate the fund to a type of charity "forever" or "for no other purpose," or upon condition that it be applied "to no other purpose," these provisions do not necessarily demonstrate absence of a general charitable intent. In *Ramsey*, a grant for the "sole purpose of building and equipping and maintaining a City hospital" and "no other" did "not necessarily show absence of a general charitable intent." "Such provisions do not, ipso facto, show an intent that the trust should cease in the event of impossibility or impracticability of using the specified means."

Dr. Kimbrough's Charitable Intent

The question remains what Dr. Kimbrough would desire if he knew that his gift could not be used by the Dental Alumni Development Fund for the continued operation and prestige of the dental school.

> "[T]he accomplishment of the ultimate purpose of the testator is the matter of paramount importance and its achievement must be the object of any judicial permission to alter or deviate from the trust terms." The Court considers whether unforeseen circumstances have arisen that threaten the fulfillment of the charity and whether or not such circumstances warrant a court's exercise of its jurisdiction to enforce and protect charitable trusts. In discerning the intent of the grantor, the basic equitable issue is what the settlor would desire if he or she knew that the trust could not be carried out. A court is required to consider all the surrounding circumstances evidencing the grantor's intent. To adhere too strictly to the words of the testator may result in the defeat of the testator's ultimate purpose. If the testator intended to make the property useful for charitable purposes, to render it useless for such purposes defeats the testator's intention. "Under the guise of fulfilling a bequest, this is making a dead man's intentions for a single day a rule for subsequent centuries, when we know not whether he himself would have made it a rule even for the morrow." John Stuart Mill

The record repeatedly shows that Dr. Kimbrough loved dentistry and was very proud of his profession. Dr. Kimbrough graduated from the Washington University Dental School, taught at the Washington University Dental School, gave unrestricted gifts to Washington University, and left the remainder of his trust to Washington University, not to the dental school.

This Court agrees with the circuit court's conclusion that Dr. Kimbrough's charitable intent was to further education and dental medicine at Washington University. There is no evidence that Dr. Kimbrough wanted his gift so narrowly drawn and so inflexible that if it could not be used in a specifically named fund, it should lapse. The circuit court's decision to establish one or two chairs in Dr. Kimbrough's name for research and practice in dental fields is consistent with Dr. Kimbrough's charitable intent.

From 1954 to 1963, Dr. Kimbrough made 11 gifts to Washington University, including gifts to the Dental Alumni Development Fund, the Washington University School of Medicine, the Second Century Development Program, the Alumni Fund, and the Century Club. The gift in question was made to Washington University, not to the dental school. The only limitation on the gift was that it be used in the fund. The fact that Dr. Kimbrough made multiple other inter vivos gifts to Washington University that were unrelated to the dental school suggests that he had a general charitable intent to support dental education at Washington University, not only through the Dental Alumni Development Fund.

This Court also recognizes that under the tax law in effect before 1969, virtually all charitable remainder trusts provided substantial tax savings to the grantor's estate. Dr. Kimbrough's 1955 amendment to the trust, giving the remainder interest to Washington University as opposed to his heirs, was essential to the tax savings and may be evidence of his general charitable intent.

Dental Medicine Continues at Washington University

The basic aspects of dental education at Washington University Dental School were the treatment of patients, education of dental students, and research of the faculty. Applying the funds to Washington University for dental-related endeavors most nearly carries out Dr. Kimbrough's intent because treatment of patients, post-graduate dental education, and research are ongoing at Washington University.

Although the dental school has been closed and the university no longer grants the basic degree in dental medicine, some dentistry continues through the medical school. Dr. Donald E. Huebener and Dr. W. Donald Gay were both faculty members of the dental school. Dr. Huebener is a member of a team of physicians, dentists, and orthodontists at the Cleft Palate Cranial Facial Deformity Institute, of which he is a founding member. He is a pediatric dentist in the City of St. Louis and provides routine dental care to 20 to 22 children daily at the dental clinic and provides dental care to children with special health care needs and serves on the cleft palate team. Dr. Gay, a maxillofacial prosthodontist, serves as the Director of the Division of Maxillofacial Prosthetics of the Otolaryngology Department at the School of Medicine. He does primarily the same work at the School of Medicine as he did at the dental school. He fits dental prostheses for people with birth defects or who have suffered trauma or cancer. The circuit court's judgment directing one or two chairs in Dr. Kimbrough's name would support one or two such professorships.

Richard Smith, the last dean of the dental school and chairman of its orthodontics department, became a professor of anthropology at the university, where he and others educate students in dental-related topics and do research in the area of dental genetics and biomechanics of the face. The medical library at Washington University has two dental book collections. The circuit court found that "dental medicine is still a necessary component of Washington University Medical School," and remarked on the "borderline miraculous healing work" the university's professors continue to perform.

Neither the closing of the dental school nor the change in the Dental Alumni Development Fund make Dr. Kimbrough's gift useless. The trust estate can be used to continue treatment of dental patients, research, and post-graduate education in dental medicine.

Conclusion

Cy pres literally means "as near as." Dr. Kimbrough's objective was to further dental education at Washington University. The circuit court's disposition of the gift attempts to fulfill Dr. Kimbrough's intent as near as possible because it requires Washington University to use the money for dental-related education. The fact that the Dental Alumni Development Fund and the dental school no longer exist does not frustrate that objective, as the medical school at Washington University continues to teach and practice dental medicine.

There is no evidence that Dr. Kimbrough ever contemplated that the money would go to his great, great-nieces, and he did not include a provision for the reversion of the property to his heirs in the event that the fund or dental school would cease to exist.

The general purpose of Dr. Kimbrough's gift to support educational programs and projects in dental fields at Washington University can be accomplished. While the specific fund designated by the grantor to carry out this purpose no longer exists, the circuit court's disposition of the trust assets carries out Dr. Kimbrough's intent.

The judgment of the circuit court is affirmed.

2. Wasteful Trusts

In the Matter of the Estate of Beryl H. Buck

Reprinted in 21 U.S.F. L. Rev. 691 (1987)

INTRODUCTION

By resolution dated January 26, 1984, the Distribution Committee of the San Francisco Foundation, by a bare majority vote, resolved that it was "impracticable and inexpedient" to continue to spend all of the income from the Leonard and Beryl Buck Foundation ("Buck Trust") within Marin County, as required by Mrs. Buck's Will, and authorized the filing of a petition to modify the geographic restriction. The Petition for Modification asked that, after a three-year transition period, the Foundation be permitted to spend an undefined portion of Buck Trust income outside Marin County in the four other Bay Area counties served by the Foundation.

The Foundation's Petition for Modification did not contend that all charitable needs in Marin County had been met, that distributing Mrs. Buck's bequest in Marin County would be illegal or impossible, or that a condition of charitable saturation existed in Marin County. Rather, it contended that, due to the increase in the magnitude of the Buck Trust, the relative affluence of Marin County, and the relative needs in the other counties served by the Foundation, it was "impracticable," "inexpedient," and "inefficient" to comply with the Will's provision requiring all of the Trust income to be spent in Marin County.

The Foundation's Petition for Modification came before this Court for trial on February 3, 1986. Supporting the Petition for Modification were intervenors, the 46 Objector-Beneficiaries ("the Forty-Six"); opposing it were the County of Matin ("County"), the Attorney General of the State of California ("Attorney General") . . .

On July 28, 1986, after nearly six months of trial, the Foundation petitioned the Court to permit its resignation as distribution trustee of the Leonard and Beryl Buck Foundation ("the Buck Trust"). . . . On July 31, 1986, the Foundation dismissed its cy pres petition.

Notwithstanding the resignation and withdrawal of the Foundation, intervenors, the Forty-Six continue to urge this Court to apply cy pres to allow the Buck Trust income to be spent both in and outside of Marin, pursuant to the Foundation's Petition for Modification.

The Court . . . finds that cy pres is not applicable and denies the Petition for Modification.

I.
BERYL H. BUCK'S INTENT

A. Marin Limitation

Beryl H. Buck died on May 30, 1975. The Tenth Clause of her Will directed that the residue of her estate, to be known and administered as THE LEONARD AND BERYL BUCK FOUNDATION

> "shall always be held and used for exclusively non-profit charitable, religious or educational purposes in providing care for the needy in Marin County, California, and for other non-profit charitable, religious or educational purposes in that county."

Take Note

Recall the Restatement's list of recognized charitable purposes. Which one does the Buck Trust satisfy?

The terms of the Buck Trust as stated in Mrs. Buck's will are unequivocal: expenditures are to be made for charitable, religious or educational purposes in Marin County.

B. Mrs. Buck's Interests and Charitable Donations

Mrs. Buck's Will provides that the residue of her estate shall be used for charitable, religious or educational purposes in Matin County. The language of her will is consistent with Mrs. Buck's charitable donations during her lifetime.

Mrs. Buck had a strong and enduring attachment to Marin County. . . . She was concerned that a letter to the San Francisco Foundation, which accompanied one of her former wills, clearly specify the Marin County limitation she desired. . . .

She wanted to help the aged-not only the indigent-but elderly persons who lack the resources to provide for adequate care, particularly where illness or accident threatened the loss of life savings and possessions. It was her belief that with the government primarily taking care of the poor and the wealthy taking care of themselves, the middle class were often neglected in times for hardship.

Mrs. Buck also had a strong interest in religion and religious institutions in Matin County. . . . The assistance and gifts she made to these institutions reflect her attachment to them. For example, she provided scholarships, clothing, and other assistance to seminary students and their families. . . .

Mrs. Buck was also acutely interested in education as illustrated by her generous assistance to students of the San Francisco Theological Seminary. Dr. and Mrs. Buck were proud of their association with the University of California, where Dr. Buck obtained his medical degree and for 25 years had been a faculty member of the pathology department at the University of California Medical School in San Francisco, serving voluntarily without compensation. . . .

Mrs. Buck had a particular appreciation of books and libraries. Dr. Buck maintained an extensive library which Mrs. Buck donated to the University of California after his death. Both Dr. and Mrs. Buck loved books and reading.

Mrs. Buck was keenly interested in music and the arts. She attended many performances and installed a music room in her home. Dr. and Mrs. Buck also were interested in outdoor music programs at Dominican College. . . .

Mrs. Buck believed that places such as Oakland and San Francisco were better able to attract charitable dollars to meet their needs than Matin County, and she was adamant in her intent to limit her gift to Marin County. Dr. and Mrs. Buck had discussed the needs of Main County and their common desire that the Buck wealth benefit that County

II.
THE WILL

A. Mrs. Buck's Expectations. . .

The Main County limitation in Mrs. Buck's Will was her own idea. Mr. Cook [her attorney] placed the limitation in the Will at her request. Mrs. Buck never waivered in her desire to limit her gift to Main, nor did she ever indicate to Mr. Cook that the terms of her bequest were, in any way, dependent on the value of her estate. . . .

In view of the requirement that the funds be spent exclusively in Matin County, Mr. May counseled maximum flexibility in administration, and that the trust be drafted in broad language. Neither Mrs. Buck nor Mr. Cook had personal knowledge of the Foundation's so-called "variance power." Had Mr. Cook known of such claimed power, he would not have recommended the Foundation as trustee. . . .

B. Value of the Estate

The major asset, or "crown jewel," of Mrs. Buck's estate was stock in the Belridge Oil Company, a privately held company which owned rich oil reserves in Southern California. . . .

Although the exact value of the stock was not known at the time Mrs. Buck executed her Will or at the time of her death, both Mrs. Buck and her attorney believed that someday the stock would be of great value far exceeding the over-the-counter prices of the stock. . . .

In conversation, Mrs. Buck had indicated that the Belridge Oil Company field was [one of] "the largest untapped oil reserves in the United States", and that there would come a time when this asset would substantially increase in value.

Mrs. Buck never indicated any desire or willingness to sell her Belridge Oil shares. To the contrary, she cautioned that the stock should not be sold because "it was a gold mine and it would be for future generations to come.". . .

III.
ADMINISTRATION OF THE BUCK TRUST

A. The Foundation's Acceptance of the Buck Trust

Belridge Oil was purchased by the Shell Oil Company for $3.65 billion, or $3,664 per share, in late 1979. Mrs. Buck's residuary bequest was worth some $260 million on March 24, 1980 when the Final Decree was filed and the Foundation accepted the Buck Trust.

The magnitude of the Buck Trust first became apparent to the Foundation during the summer of 1979, when Shell Oil was actively bidding for the Belridge stock. . . .

By the time the Preliminary Decree was entered and the Foundation assumed its responsibilities as distribution trustee over the preliminary distribution of the Buck Trust, the Foundation knew that the value of Mrs. Buck's Belridge Oil stock that it would receive, as distribution trustee of the Buck Trust, was between $250 million and $260 million. The Foundation knew that the Trust assets were to be held and used exclusively for non-profit charitable, religious and educational purposes in Marin County. It was also aware of the demographic and geographic characteristics of Matin County, including population, housing and development trends within Marin; Marin's small population; its affluence; its "less need" than other Bay Area counties; its unemployment rate; the number of "minority" persons; its low tax base; and the nature of some of the social problems that confront the residents of Marin.

In sum, in December, 1979, when the Preliminary Decree was issued, the Foundation was fully informed concerning the magnitude of the Trust and the demographics of Matin County. However, the Foundation voiced no objections to the terms of the Trust—not to the Court, to the co-trustees or to the Trust beneficiaries. Nor did the Foundation voice any objection to the terms of the Trust in March, 1980 or declare any reservations when the Court issued the Final Decree at which time the Foundation accepted the responsibility of distributing the Buck Trust assets, including cash in the sum of nearly $260 million.

B. Subsequent Actions of the Foundation. . . .

Even before it accepted the Buck Trust, however, the Foundation had serious concerns about administration of the Buck Trust. As early as July 1979, the Foundation began to explore the possibility of modifying the geographic restriction of the Buck Trust. A legal memorandum dated July 26, 1979 directed to Mr. Harris, then Vice-Chairman of the Distribution Committee as well as counsel for the Foundation, states, in reference to "the suggested petition," that: "Although no United States Court has as yet been as liberal in its application of the cy pres doctrine as the proposed petition would require, a tenable argument could nevertheless be made for application of the doctrine." The author concluded, however, that " '[c]haritable' is so broad in scope that the San Francisco Foundation could never successfully argue on the basis of the will alone that Mrs. Buck's intentions had been fully carried out." ...

Early in its administration of the Buck Trust, the Foundation again raised the issue of modifying the geographic restriction. At its June, 1980 meeting, the Distribution Committee had a "brief discussion of the time period for seeking court relief from the provisions of the Buck Trust." The following month, at its July, 1980 meeting, the Distribution Committee discussed "(1) Marin's capacity to utilize [the Buck Trust income] indefinitely, and (2) the question of court action regarding the provisions of the trust." The Distribution Committee "agreed to follow the letter of the will until [the Foundation has] enough experience to determine that this is not feasible."

According to the Foundation's Director, the Foundation's responsibility and obligation to adhere to the terms of the Buck Trust was "not a forever commitment."

C. The Foundation's Institutional Conflict. . . .

The Foundation recognized that the concept of " 'comparative need,' suggesting that the terms of Mrs. Buck's will can be altered or ignored merely because organizations outside Marin County believe they are more in need of funding than those organizations within Marin County that presently receive funding from the Foundation . . . is not the law." The Foundation has also acknowledged that it is "inappropriate to judge the level of expenditures on some basis of 'relative' needs when that is neither what Mrs. Buck's will contemplates, nor a term which has any readily ascertainable meaning." Even so, the Foundation's Petition for Modification was based, in part, on the concept of relative need. It is based on the argument "that it is 'impracticable' and 'inexpedient' to spend the entire annual income from the Buck Trust in Marin County, given the relative needs in other counties served by the San Francisco Foundation." ...

D. No Basis for Modification

The Foundation filed its Petition without any evidence to support its request for modification. The Foundation had not secured a comprehensive needs assessment, consultant reports, or data from staff, MCA or other Trust beneficiaries to support the contentions of its Petition for Modification. . . .

[T]he Foundation has filed five annual reports on its administration of the Buck Trust. None of these reports contain any assessment of the charitable needs in Marin County, or any systematic or comprehensive assessment of the impact of its Buck grantmaking. In fact, the Foundation has insisted that such studies are neither feasible nor useful. . . .

Despite concerns expressed by the Attorney General, the Foundation filed its Petition for Modification without conducting any comprehensive study or assessment of the needs in Marin County, and without conducting any comprehensive study or assessment to determine the impact or effectiveness of its Buck Trust grantmaking. No such comprehensive needs assessment or study was presented to the Court by Petitioners.

. . .

Mr. Paley's memorandum also suggests several examples of "[i]maginative, significant project of substantial magnitude" which could be undertaken in Marin County, and "which could amply justify retention of the Buck Trust in Marin." (Id.) Mr. Paley concluded:

> "In summary, I do not believe present circumstances exist to justify our initiating partial distribution of Buck funds outside of Marin. To the contrary, I believe that the future possibilities of bold grantmaking in Matin argue against exposing the Foundation to the legal and institutional risks of partial distribution."

Notwithstanding the reservations of its Director, the Foundation hired a consultant, Stephen M. Pittel, to study whether it was "feasible to develop a sense of limits to grantmaking in Main." Mr. Paley authorized Dr. Pittel to conduct inter alia, "[a] review of literature and opinions from informed sources regarding a theoretical upper limit for beneficial charitable giving." Dr. Pittel's study concluded that:

> "1. It is unlikely that any level of charitable giving will eliminate or significantly reduce the legitimate needs of a community;" and,

> "2. It is unlikely that any level of charitable giving will necessarily have a harmful impact on a community." . . .

E. The Foundation's Policies, Priorities and Practices.

1. Policies

As described above, the terms of Mrs. Buck's Will permitted the Foundation to expend the yearly income from the trust in Marin County for virtually any charitable, educational or religious purpose. The Foundation, exercising its discretion as distribution trustee, chose to restrict these nearly infinite funding possibilities by invoking its own policies, priorities and practices to administer the Trust. These policies, priorities and practices were not required by the Will, by operation of law, by the Foundation's Resolution and Declaration of Trust, or by any generally accepted philanthropic practice. To the contrary, the Foundation was free to change its policies at any time by majority vote of the Distribution Committee.

The Foundation rejected this alternative. In fact, the Distribution Committee was "content" with existing grantmaking policies as they applied to Marin and did not, as an alternative to modification, consult with anyone outside the Foundation regarding possible alteration of those policies. In the view of one member of the Distribution Committee, the issue was one of "modify[ing] the nature of the Buck Trust to conform to and become compatible with the value [sic] and procedure [sic] of the Foundation as a whole. . ." Despite annual review of its policies and priorities and frequent criticisms and recommendations for change by grantees, the Foundation chose not to change these restrictions. Instead, it chose to seek modification of the Trust.

. . .

The Foundation has always admitted that Marin County's charitable needs have not been saturated. Changes in the Foundation's policies, priorities and practices would create a vast range of important philanthropic opportunities in Matin County and ensure the worthwhile expenditure of the Buck Trust's annual gross income far into the foreseeable future. To the extent, then, to which there have been any barriers which impeded the expenditure of Buck Trust funds in Marin County, they have resulted from the Foundation's restrictive grantmaking policies, priorities, and practices.

(i) Ongoing Operational Funding

Although it has provided funding for some charitable organizations for more than one year, the San Francisco Foundation has a general policy against providing ongoing operating support. Even with respect to its occasional multiple year funding, the Foundation has refused to fund agencies for more than three to five years at a time. Moreover, this multiple year funding was often accomplished by giving year-to-year grants with no promise of renewal, resulting in uncertainty, instability, and inability to engage in long-range planning. The Foundation frequently made multiple year grants in the form of declining awards with the implied or stated goal of forcing the agency to become independent of Foundation funding altogether.

Rather than provide continuing operating support, the Foundation preferred to act as a venture capitalist by providing short-term "seed money" grants for innovative projects. In this regard, the Foundation insisted that the Marin non-profits avoid "dependency" on the Buck Trust and achieve "self-sufficiency." However, because their clientele is needy, many agencies must charge minimal or no fees for service. Moreover, agencies serving unpopular, but nevertheless needy, clientele have limited potential for obtaining alternative sources of funds. As a result of the Foundation's emphasis on self-sufficiency, some agencies have been forced to raise fees to the point where their low income clients have had to reduce or discontinue use of a service.

In sum, the Foundation's policy prohibiting continuing operational support and its institutional preference that philanthropic dollars be used for "seed money" have artificially constricted the Foundation's ability to spend Buck Trust funds for the expansive charitable purposes permitted by the Will.

(ii) Endowments

The Foundation has had a general policy against endowment grants. Although the Foundation has reviewed this policy on several occasions since 1979, it has made no endowment grants with Buck Trust monies. The Foundation's stated rationale is that changing this policy "would tie up charitable funds that could be used, as [the Foundation] saw it, for ongoing programs for more immediate impact . . . ."

However, endowment grants are a cost effective form of philanthropy. . . . By providing a degree of financial independence, endowments help to decentralize grantmaking and increase creativity and individual initiative. By providing grantees with a stable funding base, endowments reduce the overhead expenses associated with grantmaking, thus enabling agencies to allocate greater resources to direct service. Endowments can also help agencies attract funding from other sources. . . .

Accordingly, an endowment approach could have been used in a number of areas to support agencies that have a long history of providing the kinds of services Mrs. Buck intended to support.

(iii) Religion

As a matter of policy, the Foundation will not fund religious projects. While the Foundation has revised the articulation of that policy since it received the Buck Trust, the Foundation has always required "substantial secular benefit" before it would fund a project sponsored by a religious organization. . . . This policy is antithetical to Mrs. Buck's explicit provision in her will for "religious purposes . . . in Marin County."

(iv) Medical Research

The Foundation also has a policy against using unrestricted trust funds to support medical research. Although neither the Will nor resulting Trust has any restriction on funding medical research, the Foundation has consistently refused to fund medical research from the Buck Trust. Accordingly, the only inhibition to the Foundation's use of Buck Trust funds for medical research is its own policy.

Although Martin Paley professed that the Foundation would "be happy to look at a particular project" for medical research and would be open to a presentation on why Buck Trust funds should be used for medical research, the evidence showed that: the Foundation broadly disseminated information on its prohibition against medical research; the medical community was discouraged from applying for medical research grants because of the Foundation's policy; those who did inquire or apply were told that the Foundation did not fund medical research; and the Distribution Committee itself was not receptive to suggestion that the Buck Trust assets be used for medical research. . . .

The Foundation's rationale for refusing to fund medical research from the Buck Trust was essentially two-fold. First, medical research "requires a tremendous amount of resources." The Foundation felt that "the great overwhelming amount of funds that would have to be used in order to bring off any kind of first-class medical research facility" precluded the use of Buck Trust funds. As stated by Distribution Committee member Peter Haas, "[t]here is a never ending need for medical research that private philanthropy cannot possibly fulfill" and the Foundation had "comparatively limited resources compared to those other foundations."

Second, the lack of primary benefit to Main residents was viewed as a reason against funding medical research. As former Distribution Committee member Hamilton Budge explained, "[f]unds that are spent in Matin County should focus primarily on the benefit of the people in Marin County, when what you're doing [in medical research] is having a universal or national application. That's not an appropriate expenditure of funds." (emphasis added). However, the Foundation acknowledged that its prohibition on use of Buck Trust assets was not mandated by the Will nor by its Declaration of Trust, but resulted exclusively from its own policy decisions.

(v) Government Agencies

The Foundation has been reluctant to fund programs that were traditionally the responsibility of government agencies. Furthermore, the Foundation applied an inflexible policy which, in effect, stated that it would not use philanthropic dollars to replace government services, including services curtailed by Proposition 13 or other budget limitations. Despite its recognition that the passage of Proposition 13 resulted in a reduction of programs serving the poor and needy, the Foundation's director maintained that, "what is fundamentally a government responsibility ought not to be undertaken by private philanthropy."

This policy creates an unfortunate situation. Many recipients of government services are, "by definition, the poorest of the poor." In effect, this Foundation policy excludes numerous persons who the Trust was intended to benefit, e.g., the poor and needy. Under this policy, Foundation funding is not available for many programs that serve the needy such as the poor, the elderly and the mentally ill. Furthermore, this policy is not mandated by any accepted principle of philanthropic practice.

The Foundation's policy with respect to funding of public agencies is unjustified. There are numerous instances where it would be appropriate for a foundation to fund governmental services or replace governmental tax revenues, for example, school libraries which had been closed as a result of budget cutbacks. The determining consideration should be the needs of the persons who receive the services, not the theoretical effect on government or its taxpayers. Had the Foundation modified this policy, it could have forged a partnership with government agencies to address recognized needs in an effective and productive fashion. . . .

(vii) Requirement of Primary Benefit To Marin Residents

Another grantmaking policy of the Foundation not required by the Will and, in fact, at odds with both it and Mrs. Buck's intent in certain applications, was the Foundation's requirement that all Buck Trust grants must primarily benefit Marin County and its Residents. Contrary to the Foundation's policy, Mrs. Buck intended and contemplated that, while the expenditures of the Buck Trust would be limited to Marin, its benefits would and should extend beyond Marin's borders.

The rationale for the Foundation's "primary benefit" requirement was in part to discourage "carpetbagging"—i.e., people or organizations coming to Marin to establish programs or projects there—and in part to comport with its vision of how a community foundation should act to benefit a defined, local population. However, the Foundation's primary benefit policy often resulted in the summary rejection of grant proposals clearly within the scope of the Buck Trust. For example, in 1984 the Foundation refused to fund Guide Dogs for the Blind, an organization located since 1947 in San Rafael, Matin County, which trains blind people in the use of guide dogs, on the ground that the "benefit is mainly national, not Marin or Bay Area." In 1985 the Foundation refused to support a series of television programs for children to be produced by a Main-based organization on the ground that, because it would have national distribution, it was "not a local project." This overly-restrictive policy was not required by a principle of philanthropy and inhibited the Foundation from fully realizing the enormous potential for doing good inherent in a charitable trust of over $400 million.

2. Priorities

In addition to its express policy limitations, the Foundation has imposed priorities and goals in each of its grantmaking areas. It responds more favorably to grant proposals which promote its priorities and goals, while declining otherwise worthy proposals "because they [did] not meet Foundation's priorities." The Will does not establish such priorities. . . . The Foundation admitted that its priorities and goals were ephemeral, arbitrary, and were adopted independently of consideration of the purposes of the Buck Trust and the opportunities for grantmaking in Marin County. . . .

3. Practices

In addition to its formal policies and priorities certain of the San Francisco Foundation's practices, or institutional "attitudes," also restricted opportunities for charitable spending in Marin.

Taken as a whole, the Foundation employed policies, priorities and practices that severely restricted the grantmaking choices left open by Mrs. Buck's will. These limitations reflected the Foundation's institutional preferences. They were imposed for the administrative convenience of the Foundation, and cannot be used to measure whether its grantmaking in Main was "inefficient" or "ineffective" for purposes of determining whether the Trust should be modified. . . .

F. Effect of Buck Trust Expenditures in Marin

1. Inefficiency

The Forty-Six contend that cy pres should be applied to excise the Matin limitation of the Buck Trust because adherence to that restriction results in "inefficient" or "ineffective" philanthropy. "Efficiency" is not the standard for application of the *cy pres* doctrine; however, even if it were, Petitioners failed to prove that the Foundation's expenditure of Buck Trust funds in Marin were "inefficient." . . .

[T]he evidence of "inefficiency" represents no more than the Foundation staff's current judgments of whether grants would have been recommended for funding at the time the grants were made. It in no sense represents assessments of the "efficiency" or "effectiveness" of the actual results of those grants. . . .

Given the "standards" and criteria unevenly applied to assess the "inefficiency" of the Buck Trust grants, and given the institutional constraints under which those assessments were made, "inefficiency" has not been established. As John Kreidler candidly remarked, "if I was to put myself in the place of being in another foundation, I don't think that I would find anything that I've said with respect to efficiency or wastefulness to be very persuasive." . . .

IV.
NEEDS

A. General

The Foundation conceded that charitable needs exist in Marin County. Not only do many residents of Marin currently have unmet charitable, religious and educational needs, but it is unquestioned that charitable, religious and educational needs will exist far into the foreseeable future. Barring a "miracle," Marin County's charitable needs will continue to exist forever. Serious unmet needs exist in every category that the Foundation funds. Many of these needs are pressing and several of these pressing needs (e.g., the Canal, Main City Economic Development, Open Space Acquisitions, low and moderate housing development) are independently capable of absorbing the entire Buck Trust income indefinitely.

The Foundation has determined that the entire amount of Buck Trust income available is not adequate to meet these needs, nor would ten times the amount be sufficient. It would require millions of dollars annually to feed, clothe and shelter Main County residents who live below the poverty line. In fact, there will never be enough dollars to meet even the basic needs of Matin residents. . . .

V.
The Doctrine of Cy Pres

A.   Cy Pres Applies Only Where the Purpose of a Trust Has Become Illegal, Impossible or Permanently Impracticable of Performance

The purpose of the cy pres doctrine "is to prevent the failure of valid charitable trust gifts." As explained by Professor Scott:

> "Where property is given in trust for a particular charitable purpose, the trust will not ordinarily fail even though it is impossible to carry out the particular purpose. In such a case the court will ordinarily direct that the property be applied to a similar charitable purpose." . . .

[E]minent authorities, followed by statutory and/or case law in many states, provide that where a purpose of a charitable trust becomes illegal, impossible or impracticable of fulfillment, and the testator manifested a general charitable intention, the court may direct that the property be applied to a similar charitable purpose.

Courts in California, as in other states, exercise extreme caution before they will vary the terms of a charitable trust. . . .

California courts have often quoted the language of the Restatement of Trusts and the Model Act setting forth the cy pres standard of illegality, impossibility, or impracticability. The impossibility or impracticability prerequisite, however, has been interpreted in California to require a "permanency of the impossibility or impracticability of carrying out the specific charitable purpose or purposes of the creator of the trust." . . .

In practice, cy pres has most often been applied in California in such cases-where the charitable trust purpose is or has become literally impossible to fulfill (it "cannot be accomplished")—or in cases where it has become "reasonably impossible of performance."

B. Neither Inefficiency Nor Ineffective Philanthropy Constitutes Impracticability

"Impracticability" has been defined as "impossible" as early as 1850 in Dr. Johnson's famous dictionary. Other prestigious dictionaries have defined impracticability in the same sense, e.g., "incapable of being done or carried out," "a practical impossibility"; "incapable of accomplishment"; "incapable of being performed or carried out"; "practically impossible".

California courts have never adopted a broad interpretation of the term "impracticable" in charitable trust cases. One California court, in Estate of Butin (1947), found the trust purpose to be impractical to fulfill. Estate of Butin involved a situation where there was insufficient funds to fulfill the trust purpose. The testatrix had directed the executors of her will to erect in the courthouse park at Madera, California, "a granite tower . . . to contain a carillon of eighteen bells" to be placed in the park at a reasonable cost and with a certain inscription. The testatrix' will also stated that:

> "I realize that future conditions are very uncertain and if, for any good reason, it is impractical to erect this type of memorial, my executors are then authorized to use their own discretion as to the type of memorial to be erected and the cost thereof."

The court indicated that "it appeared impractical to construct the memorial . . ." for the following reasons:

> "that a site for the tower to be located on county property could not be procured, that it would interfere with the public business conducted in the courthouse, and that it would cost more than $100,000, which is in excess of the value of the entire estate."

The court, then, actually applied the standard—i.e., impractical—set forth by the testatrix in her will. The fact situation itself, given the insufficient funds to construct the tower, essentially involved an impossibility. . . .

Like California courts, courts from other states often describe the standard for cy pres as one of "illegality, impossibility or impracticability." In many of those jurisdictions, however, "impracticability" is equated with "impossibility."

The Restatement (Second) of Trusts, (1959) section 399, comment *q* at 306, does not require a literal impossibility. Rather, it defines "impracticability" as follows:

> "The doctrine of cy pres is applicable even though it is possible to carry out the particular purpose of the settlor, if to carry it out would fail to accomplish the general charitable intention of the settlor. In such case it is 'impracticable' to carry out the particular purpose . . . ." (Emphasis added).

Ineffective philanthropy, inefficiency and relative inefficiency, that is, inefficiency of trust expenditures in one location given greater relative needs or benefits elsewhere, do not constitute impracticability under either view. Such situation is not the equivalent of impossibility; nor is there any threat that the operation of the trust will fail to fulfill the general charitable intention of the settlor. As stated by one court, "the court's power over the disposition of other people's assets is limited to removing restrictions only if they are incompatible with the testator's dominant purpose." In Wilson, although the alternative scheme proposed a gender neutral educational trust, which would have been preferable on public policy grounds, the court stated that:

> "there is another competing public policy consideration, namely, preserving the right of the testator to dispose of his property as he wishes. This rule becomes even more compelling when applied to the area of private charitable trusts, for one of the very reasons for the rule is to encourage bequests for charitable purposes."

The foregoing policy considerations fully justify the dominant tendency of courts to require a situation of illegality, impossibility or strict impracticability before they will vary the terms of a charitable trust through an application of cy pres.

The present and well-tested law that cy pres will be invoked to save a charitable bequest that has become impossible or impracticable of fulfillment where the testator has a general charitable intent provides an intermediate concept "between the well established rules of construction that a will is to be construed so as to effectuate the intent of the testator, and that a gift to charity should be effectuated whenever possible." Where both the testator's intent and the charitable gift can, in fact, be effectuated, i.e., the specified trust purpose has not become impossible or impracticable of performance, there is no justification for cy pres.

The cy pres doctrine should not be so distorted by the adoption of subjective, relative, and nebulous standards such as "inefficiency" or "ineffective philanthropy" to the extent that it becomes a facile vehicle for charitable trustees to vary the terms of a trust simply because they believe that they can spend the trust income better or more wisely elsewhere, or as in this case, prefer to do so. There is no basis in law for the application of standards such as "efficiency" or "effectiveness" to modify a trust, nor is there any authority that would elevate these standards to the level of impracticability.

C. Cy Pres May Not Be Invoked Upon The Belief That The Modified Scheme Would Be More Desirable Or Would Constitute A Better Use Of The Income

Where the income of a charitable trust can be used for the purpose specified by the testator, cy pres may not be invoked on the grounds that a different use of the income would be more useful or desirable. Several cases from other states elaborate on this principle.

The trustees in In re Oshkosh Foundation (1973), for example, sought to expand the geographical limits of the trust from the City of Oshkosh to that city plus the various townships which comprised the Oshkosh area school district. The trustees claimed that it was "impractical" to confine disbursements of trust funds to the city limits, as the city's influence extends far beyond its boundaries, and "[t]o treat [the inhabitants of the City of Oshkosh and those of the surrounding area] differently would be unfair to each group." The court held that cy pres did not apply. Indicating that an application of cy pres requires a finding that compliance with the trust's stated purpose has become impossible, unlawful or impracticable, the court stated that:

> "No argument is here made that the purpose of the trust has become either impossible or illegal. Rather it is claimed that compliance with the trust has become 'impracticable' because it has become 'unfair.' The underlined words are not synonyms. The trustee, in substance, claims only that the use of school district limits would be more useful and desirable than the use of city limits as prescribed in the trust. But cy pres does not warrant a court substituting a different plan for that set forth in the trust solely because trustee or court, or both, believe the substituted plan to be a better plan. . . ."

Similarly, in In re Petition of Downer Home (1975), the court admonished that a belief that a substituted use "would be a better use of the income" than the designated use "is not the test" for the application of cy pres.

Courts have also held that terms of a charitable trust may not be modified on the grounds that a different use would be more beneficial to the community or advantageous to the charity. . . .

Thus, cy pres may not be invoked on the grounds that it would be more "fair," "equitable" or "efficient" to spend the Trust funds in a manner different from that specified by the testator. . . .

The San Francisco Foundation did not perform its duties in conformity with Mrs. Buck's expressed wishes. It unnecessarily limited the expenditures of Buck Trust funds in Marin County in ways not contemplated by Mrs. Buck. Cy pres may not be applied to modify the terms of the Buck Trust.

Take Note

The Marin Community Foundation, which was created in the wake of this ruling, reported assets of $2.1 billion in 2018, and annual grant-making of almost $250 million.

Uniform Trust Code § 413. Cy Pres

(a) Except as otherwise provided in subsection (b), if a particular charitable purpose becomes unlawful, impracticable, impossible to achieve, or wasteful:

   (1) the trust does not fail, in whole or in part;

   (2) the trust property does not revert to the settlor or the settlor's successors in interest; and

   (3) the court may apply cy pres to modify or terminate the trust by directing that the trust property be applied or distributed, in whole or in part, in a manner consistent with the settlor's charitable purposes.

(b)   A provision in the terms of a charitable trust that would result in distribution of the trust property to a noncharitable beneficiary prevails over the power of the court under subsection (a) to apply cy pres to modify or terminate the trust only if, when the provision takes effect:

(1)   the trust property is to revert to the settlor and the settlor is still living; or

(2)   fewer than 21 years have elapsed since the date of the trust's creation.

Notes

1. A question of power

The Uniform Trust Code § 413 codifies the inherent authority of courts to apply *cy pres*. This is hardly a novel position, as courts have universally recognized their authority to authorize modifications to administrative or dispositive terms in charitable trusts. Full or partial termination can also be ordered under this power. What justifies such an expansive power of modification and termination for charitable trusts when the doctrines governing private trusts have significantly constrained these actions?

For More Information

For more on how courts use the cy pres power, read Peter Luxton, Cy-Pres and the Ghost of Things Past That Might Have Been, 47 Conv. & Prop. L. 107 (1983).

2. How charitable are most settlors?

This provision, similar to one in the Restatement (Third) of Trusts (§67), presumes that settlors have general charitable intent, which allows the redirection of assets when the trust's original purpose becomes impossible or impracticable to achieve. The presumption can be overridden by a provision in the trust instrument, but this approach flips the default in favor of allowing the trust to continue rather than fail. Before this change, courts tended to find general charitable intent in most cases, however indirectly or vaguely the settlor might have indicated it. Changing the presumption reflects the sense that most donors would rather see their trust serve a different entity or purpose than allow the trust to fail. Do you think this is correct? Might it matter why the settlor was originally motivated to establish the trust? On the reasons for this rule change, see Ronald Chester, *Cy Pres or Gift Over: The Search for Coherence in Judicial Reform of Failed Charitable Trusts*, 23 Suffolk U. L. Rev. 41 (1989).

3. Intersection of different areas of law

Cy pres originated as a trust law doctrine, but has been applied in other contexts involving charitable donations. As the drafters of §413 noted, "[u]nder longstanding and prevailing law, it would be incorrect to say, as the court did in dictum in Williams v. City of Kuttawa, 466 S.W.3d 505, 511 (Ky. App. 2015), that the "application of the cy pres doctrine is inappropriate" merely "because no trust exists."

4. A matter of waste

Section 413 expressly provides that *cy pres* may be used to redirect charitable trust assets when the original terms are producing wasteful spending. Would that have fixed the problem with the Buck Trust? Is that an appropriate expansion of the doctrine? Is it too subjective a standard? Comments to the Restatement provision explain that *cy pres* could be applied, if not precluded by the terms of the trust, if "the amount of property held in the trust exceeds what is needed for the particular charitable purpose or to such an extent that the continued expenditure of all of the funds for that purpose, although possible to do, would be wasteful. . . ." The comment continues by suggesting what should be done in such a case—a "court might broaden the purposes of the trust, direct application of the surplus funds to a like purpose in a different community, or otherwise direct the use of funds not reasonably needed for the original purpose to a different but reasonably similar charitable purpose." Can you see the shadows of the Buck Trust litigation in this new rule?

5. Deviation versus modification

The doctrine of equitable deviation, which can be used with both private and charitable trusts, permits a court to alter the administrative provisions of a trust, as opposed to the dispositive ones. This power has traditionally been used to loosen or remove restrictions on particular investments or other trustee powers, when the original trust terms would have the effect of frustrating the purpose of the trust. The difference between modification or *cy pres* and deviation can be hard to parse, and the deviation doctrine is sometimes used as a workaround when the modification rules dictate a poor result.

C. Enforcement of Charitable Trusts

The scheme for trust enforcement is different for charitable trusts than private trusts. Private trusts depend largely on beneficiaries for enforcement—they keep an eye on the trustee and have standing to sue for mismanagement and other breaches of trustee duties. But recall that charitable trusts rarely have a definite or ascertainable beneficiary and thus no one to step into that role. States, instead, provide special rules for enforcement. Primary enforcement power is given to the state's attorney general, and charitable trusts have reporting requirements that help attorneys general carry out that duty. But should enforcement powers be shared? Consider the following materials.

Carl J. Herzog Found., Inc. v. Univ. of Bridgeport

699 A.2d 995 (Conn. 1997)

NORCOTT, ASSOCIATE JUSTICE.

The sole issue in this certified appeal is whether the Connecticut Uniform Management of Institutional Funds Act (CUMIFA), General Statutes §§ 45a–526 through 45a–534, establishes statutory standing for a donor to bring an action to enforce the terms of a completed charitable gift. Because we conclude that the legislature did not intend to establish donor standing under the circumstances of this case, we reverse the judgment of the Appellate Court.

The facts and procedural history of this case are aptly set forth in the Appellate Court opinion from which this appeal ensues. "The plaintiff [Carl J. Herzog Foundation, Inc.] commenced an action against the defendant, the University of Bridgeport, seeking injunctive and other relief in connection with a gift made by it to the defendant. The plaintiff alleged in its revised complaint that prior to August 12, 1986, it made various grants to the defendant 'to provide need-based merit scholarship aid to disadvantaged students for medical related education.' On August 12, 1986, the plaintiff agreed, by letter, to participate in a matching grant program that would provide need-based merit scholarships to disadvantaged students for medical related education on a continuing basis. On September 9, 1986, the defendant wrote a letter accepting the offer of a matching grant of up to $250,000. Over a period of time, the defendant raised the necessary $250,000, which the plaintiff matched in accordance with the agreement. The plaintiff transferred $144,000 on June 26, 1987, and $106,000 on June 28, 1988, to the defendant. The grants were used to provide scholarships to students in the defendant's nursing program. On November 21, 1991, however, the plaintiff was informed that the defendant had closed its nursing school on June 20, 1991.

> "Pursuant to the provisions of CUMIFA, the plaintiff alleged that the defendant was an 'institution' within the meaning of General Statutes § 45a–527 (1), that the matching grant constituted 'institutional funds' within the meaning of § 45a–527 (2), and that the letter of August 12, 1986, which set forth the restrictions and conditions of said grant, constituted a 'gift instrument' as defined in § 45a–527 (6).
>
> "The plaintiff's alleged injury is that the funds are no longer being used for their specified purpose. . . .
>
> "The defendant moved to dismiss the action for lack of subject matter jurisdiction on the ground that the plaintiff lacked standing. The trial court held that the act did not provide a donor with the right to enforce restrictions contained in a gift instrument, and, therefore, the plaintiff lacked standing to bring the action. The trial court noted that the attorney general, pursuant to General Statutes § 3–125,could bring an action to enforce the gift, and it dismissed the action."

The Appellate Court reversed the judgment of the trial court, concluding that General Statutes § 45a–533 provides donors with standing to enforce the terms of a completed gift, even though no such right of enforcement was provided for in the gift instrument. In other words, the Appellate Court concluded that the statute, although silent on the matter, *implicitly* confers donor standing on the plaintiff. We disagree. . . .

At common law, a donor who has made a completed charitable contribution, whether as an absolute gift or in trust, had no standing to bring an action to enforce the terms of his or her gift or trust unless he or she had expressly reserved the right to do so. "Where property is given to a charitable corporation and it is directed by the terms of the gift to devote the property to a particular one of its purposes, it is under a duty, *enforceable at the suit of the [a]ttorney [g]eneral,* to devote the property to that purpose." 2 Restatement (Second), Trusts § 348, comment (f). At common law, it was established that "[e]quity will afford protection to a donor to a charitable corporation in that *the [a]ttorney [g]eneral may maintain a suit* to compel the property to be held for the charitable purpose for which it was given to the corporation." "The general rule is that charitable trusts or gifts to charitable corporations for stated purposes are [enforceable] at the instance of the [a]ttorney [g]eneral. . . . It matters not whether the gift is absolute or in trust or whether a technical condition is attached to the gift."

"The theory underlying the power of the [a]ttorney [g]eneral to enforce gifts for a stated purpose is that a donor who attaches conditions to his gift has a right to have his intention enforced." The donor's right, however, is enforceable only at the instance of the attorney general; and the donor himself has no standing to enforce the terms of his gift when he has not retained a specific right to control the property, such as a right of reverter, after relinquishing physical possession of it. As a matter of common law, when a settlor of a trust or a donor of property to a charity fails specifically to provide for a reservation of rights in the trust or gift instrument, " 'neither the donor nor his heirs have any standing in court in a proceeding to compel the proper execution of the trust, except as relators.' " "There is no such thing as a resulting trust with respect to a charity . . . . Where the donor has effectually passed out of himself all interest in the fund devoted to a charity, neither he nor those claiming under him have any standing in a court of equity as to its disposition and control." On the basis of the weight of the foregoing authorities, we conclude that it is clear that the general rule at common law was that a donor had no standing to enforce the terms of a completed charitable gift unless the donor had expressly reserved a property interest in the gift.

Having concluded that the plaintiff would have had no standing at common law, we now turn to its contention that the common law has been altered by the legislature's adoption of CUMIFA. Subsection (a) of § 45a–533 empowers the governing board of an institution to seek a release of an onerous or obsolete restriction without resort to the courts by obtaining the donor's consent. Subsection (b) of § 45a–533 empowers the board to apply to the courts for such release in the event of the donor's death, disability or other unavail-

Food for Thought

Is it wise to vest exclusive enforcement power in an attorney general? See Susan N. Gary, Regulating the Management of Charities: Trust Law, Corporate Law, and Tax Law, 21 U. Haw. L. Rev. 593, 622–24 (1999).

ability. Subsection (c) of § 45a–533 precludes the governing board from using a gift unburdened by a restriction for anything other than the "educational, religious, charitable or other eleemosynary purposes" of the institution. Subsection (d) of § 45a–533 confirms that the statute was not enacted to supplant but to supplement the doctrines of cy pres and approximation.

The plaintiff bases its statutory standing claim primarily on the language of subsection (a) of § 45a–533, which provides that "[w]ith the written consent of the donor, the governing board may release, in whole or in part, a restriction imposed by the applicable gift instrument on the use or investment of an institutional fund." On the basis of this language, the Appellate Court concluded, and the plaintiff maintains, that "[i]t would be anomalous for a statute to provide for written consent by a donor to change a restriction and then deny that donor access to the courts to complain of a change without such consent." We disagree.

The plaintiff concedes, as it must, that nothing in the plain language of § 45a–533 (a) or any other portion of CUMIFA expressly provides statutory standing for donors to charitable institutions who have not somehow reserved a property interest in the gift such as a right of reverter. In order to demonstrate that the legislature intended to abrogate the common law, therefore, the plaintiff is left only with the legislative history of CUMIFA and the circumstances surrounding its enactment. The history and background of CUMIFA, however, not only do not support the plaintiff's claim of statutory standing, they directly refute it. . . .

We agree with the defendant that the drafters of UMIFA did not intend to confer donor standing in the matter of the release of gift restrictions, and that our legislature provided no indication when it enacted CUMIFA that it intended any other result.

First, it is unmistakable that the drafters of UMIFA regarded charitable institutions, particularly colleges and universities, as the principal beneficiaries of their efforts. . . .

UMIFA, drafted in the early 1970s, was set against the backdrop of a state of flux for colleges and universities. In a time of dramatic social change that cast new light on many older charitable gift restrictions, these institutions saw their operating costs rise significantly without a similar increase in endowment funds. . . . In the late 1960s, the Ford Foundation commissioned Professors Cary and Bright "to examine the legal restrictions on the powers of trustees and managers of colleges and universities to invest endowment funds to achieve growth, to maintain purchasing power, and to expend a prudent portion of appreciation in endowment funds." UMIFA, prefatory note. It is evident that the drafters of UMIFA paid heed to the concerns expressed in the Ford Foundation report as their final draft of UMIFA attempted to offer as much relief as possible *to charitable institutions*, without any mention of concern regarding a donor's ability to bring legal action to enforce a condition on a gift. . . .

In the comment to § 7, the drafters of UMIFA expressly provided that the donor of a completed gift would not have standing to enforce the terms of the gift. "*The donor has no right to enforce the restriction*, no interest in the fund and no power to change the eleemosynary beneficiary of the fund. He may only acquiesce in a lessening of a restriction already in effect." (Emphasis added.) UMIFA, § 7, comment.

These clear comments regarding the power of a donor to enforce restrictions on a charitable gift arose in the context of debate concerning the creation of potential adverse tax consequences for donors, if UMIFA was interpreted to provide donors with control over their gift property after the completion of the gift. . . . Where there is a possibility not "so remote as to be negligible" that the charitable gift subject to a condition might fail, the tax deduction is disallowed.

In resolving these concerns, the drafters of UMIFA clearly stated their position in the commentary. "No federal tax problems for the donor are anticipated by permitting release of a restriction. *The donor has no right to enforce the restriction, no interest in the fund and no power to change the eleemosynary beneficiary of the fund.* He may only acquiesce in a lessening of a restriction already in effect." UMIFA, § 7, comment. . . . Although the comments and the prefatory note to UMIFA do recognize that a donor has an interest in a restriction, as analyzed herein, we find no support in any source for the proposition that the drafters of either UMIFA or CUMIFA intended that a donor or his heirs would supplant the attorney general as the designated enforcer of the terms of completed and absolute charitable gifts. . . .

There similarly is nothing in the history of our legislature's adoption of CUMIFA that contravenes the clear statement of the drafters of UMIFA that a "donor has no right to enforce [a] restriction. . . ." UMIFA, § 7, comment. . . .

Finally, the legislative history of CUMIFA indicates that the legislature was aware of the question of donor standing regarding restrictions, but chose not to establish it. . . .

On the basis of our careful review of the statute itself, its legislative history, the circumstances surrounding its enactment, the policy it was intended to implement, and similar common law principles governing the same subject matter, we conclude that CUMIFA does not establish a new class of litigants, namely donors, who can enforce an unreserved restriction in a completed charitable gift. . . .

The judgment of the Appellate Court is reversed and the case is remanded to that court with direction to affirm the judgment of the trial court.

In this opinion BORDEN and PALMER, Js., concurred.

McDONALD, ASSOCIATE JUSTICE, with whom BERDON, J., joins, dissenting.

I would affirm the thoughtful and well reasoned opinion of the Appellate Court.

The majority here holds that the donor itself may not enforce a restriction in a gift to an educational institution when the institution had specifically agreed to that restriction. This decision is simply an approval of a donee, in the words of the donor, "double crossing the donor," and doing it with impunity unless an elected attorney general does something about it.

This decision will not encourage donations to Connecticut colleges and universities. I fail to see why Connecticut, the home of so many respected schools that would honor their promises, should endorse such sharp practices and create a climate in this state that will have a chilling effect on gifts to its educational institutions.

Accordingly, I respectfully dissent.

————————————

Smithers v. St. Luke's-Roosevelt Hosp. Ctr.

723 N.Y.S.2d 426 (App. Div. 2001)

ELLERIN, J.

The issue before us is whether the estate of the donor of a charitable gift has standing to sue the donee to enforce the terms of the gift. We conclude that in the circumstances here present plaintiff estate does have the necessary standing.

Plaintiff Adele Smithers is the widow of R. Brinkley Smithers, a recovered alcoholic who devoted the last 40 years of his life to the treatment and understanding of the disease of alcoholism. In 1971 Smithers announced his intention to make a gift to defendant St. Luke's-Roosevelt Hospital Center (the "Hospital") of $10 million over time for the establishment of an alcoholism treatment center (the "Gift"). In his June 16, 1971 letter to the Hospital creating the Gift, Smithers stated, "Money from the $10 million grant will be supplied as needed. It is understood, however, that the detailed project plans and staff appointments must have my approval."

According to the complaint, the Hospital agreed to use the Gift to expand its treatment of alcoholism . . . .

Smithers thereafter remained involved in the management and affairs of the Smithers Center. . . .

Over the next two years, Gambuti repeatedly assured Smithers that the Hospital would strictly adhere to the terms of the Gift and carry out Smithers's intent in making it. Only when Smithers was completely satisfied of the Hospital's intentions did he agree to complete the Gift, which he accomplished in an October 24, 1983 letter, stating:

> Thanks to the cooperation of the officers and staff of the Smithers Center and St. Luke's Roosevelt Hospital Center (the "Hospital"), the Smithers Center is now in splendid shape, and I feel that the time has come for me to complete the funding of the project. . . .
>
> This final contribution is subject to the following restrictions and is to be used exclusively for the following purposes.
>
> First, it is my intention that my final contribution be set aside as an endowment fund, (the "Smithers Endowment Fund"). The income is to be used exclusively for the support of the Smithers Center, to the extent necessary for current operations,

and any unused income remaining at the end of each calendar year is to be accumulated and added to principal. Principal of the Smithers Endowment Fund is not to be expended for any purpose except for remodeling or rebuilding the administration section and out-patient floor . . . and for construction, repairs or improvements with respect to any other building space at any time used directly in connection with the Smithers Center. Such capital expenditures should be considered as secondary to the endowment function and should in no event exceed in the aggregate one half of the initial value of the Smithers Endowment Fund.

Beneath Smithers's signature is the following paragraph signed and dated by Gambuti:

The contribution of the number of shares of IBM Stock referred to above by R. Brinkley Smithers is gratefully accepted, *subject to the restrictions set forth in this letter,* in full satisfaction of any outstanding pledge or other obligation. (Emphasis added.)

The existing rehabilitation services, which Smithers included in his definition of the Smithers Center and which the Hospital's acceptance of the Gift encompassed, were housed in the free-standing Smithers building and, according to the complaint, were intended always to be housed in *a* free-standing facility.

. . . [I]n March 1995, just over a year after Smithers's death, the Hospital announced that it planned to move the Smithers Center into a hospital ward. . . .

The Hospital's announced intentions aroused Mrs. Smithers's suspicions. First, relocating the patients in a hospital ward would violate the Hospital's obligation to run the Smithers Center in a free-standing facility physically separate from the Hospital. Second, the Hospital's claim that it had to sell the building to become more competitive was inconsistent with its assurances to her husband and her through the years that the Smithers Center was operating at a profit. Mrs. Smithers notified the Hospital of her objections to the proposed relocation of the program and demanded an accounting of the Smithers Center's finances.

The Hospital at first resisted disclosing its financial records, but Mrs. Smithers persisted, and in May 1995 the Hospital disclosed that it had been misappropriating monies from the Endowment Fund since before Smithers's death, transferring such monies to its general fund where they were used for purposes unrelated to the Smithers Center. Mrs. Smithers notified the Attorney General, who investigated the Hospital's plan to sell the building and discovered that the Hospital had transferred restricted assets from the Smithers Endowment Fund to its general fund in what it called "loans." The Attorney General demanded the return of these assets and in August 1995 the Hospital returned nearly $5 million to the Smithers Endowment Fund, although it did not restore the income lost on those funds during the intervening years.

In the next three years, Mrs. Smithers tried to negotiate a resolution with the Hospital. The Attorney General participated in the negotiations, ...

In July 1998, the Attorney General entered into an Assurance of Discontinuance Pursuant to Executive Law § 63(15) with the Hospital. Under the terms of this assurance the Hospital agreed to make no more transfers or loans from Gift funds for any purpose other than the benefit of the Smithers Center and to return to the Gift fund $1 million from the proceeds of any sale of the building. The Attorney General did not require the Hospital to return the entire proceeds of such a sale, because he found that, contrary to Mrs. Smithers's contention, the terms of the Gift did not preclude the Hospital from selling the building.

Two months later, Mrs. Smithers commenced this suit to enforce the conditions of the Gift and to obtain an accounting by the Hospital of its handling of the Endowment Fund and property dedicated to the Smithers Center. The Hospital and the Attorney General were named, *inter alia*, as defendants. Mrs. Smithers had obtained Special Letters of Administration from the Nassau County Surrogate's Court appointing her the Special Administratrix of Smithers's estate for the purpose of pursuing claims by the estate against the Hospital in connection with its administration of the Smithers Center. . . .

The Hospital . . . moved to dismiss for lack of standing and for failure to state a cause of action. . . .

On appeal, the Attorney General's office, having reevaluated the matter "under the direction of the newly elected Attorney General," reversed its position and urged this Court to remand for a hearing on the merits to determine whether or not the building was subject to gift restrictions. If it were, then all proceeds of the sale would be subject to the same restrictions and could not be used for the Hospital's general purposes. The Attorney General was constrained to point out that, in that case, the Assurance of Discontinuance could not authorize the sale of the building and the application of only $1 million of the sale proceeds to the Smithers Center in the absence of the donor's release of the restrictions or a court order authorizing the release of the restrictions. He explained that he had supported Mrs. Smithers's motion before this Court for a preliminary injunction against the sale of the building because he agreed that a hearing was required to determine whether such restrictions existed. However, the Attorney General urged that the issue of Mrs. Smithers's standing to bring the suit need not, and should not, be reached in this action, since he certainly had standing and had joined with her in seeking reversal and remand.

We note that, not only did the Hospital (and the Attorney General) fail to seek court approval of the Assurance of Discontinuance, which was required by § 522 of the Not-For-Profit Corporation Law because the Assurance contemplated the sale of the building, the diversion of all the appreciation realized upon the sale, and the relocation of the rehabilitation unit out of a free-standing, non-hospital environment and into a hospital ward, all of which may have been contrary to the terms of the Gift, but also, just before signing the Assurance of Discontinuance, the Hospital had closed the in-hospital detox unit without even informing the Attorney General. The Attorney General learned of the closing a few months later from Mrs. Smithers's papers on her motion for a preliminary injunction. In his reply memorandum of law in support of the motion to dismiss, the Attorney General argued that he had not abdicated his duty by failing to prevent the closing, but had "reasonably relied on a specific representation" made by the executive vice president of the Hospital's corporate parent that the Smithers Alcoholism Center would remain at the Hospital, and that the Hospital had not advised the Attorney General of its actions "in breach of that representation." It may be observed that it was only Mrs. Smithers's vigilance that brought this to light, since apparently the Attorney General had no procedure in place by which to insure compliance by the donee. Appropriate oversight undoubtedly would have been provided had the requisite court approval been sought as statutorily required.

While this appeal was pending, the Attorney General and the Hospital reached another agreement. This agreement raised some issues for the first time, but it brought the position of the Attorney General and the Hospital on other issues into accord with Mrs. Smithers's position. For example, the Hospital agreed to allocate the entire net proceeds of the sale of the building to the restricted purposes of the Gift and to restore the income lost as a result of the transfer of Gift funds to its general fund. Reversing his position again, the Attorney General returned to his predecessor's contention that Mrs. Smithers has no standing to bring this suit, and asked this Court to modify the decision dismissing the complaint for lack of standing so as to hold only that plaintiff does not have standing as special administratrix of the donor's estate and affirm, as modified, on that narrow ground. He sought a remand of the matter, not for further proceedings on the merits, but for the court's approval and implementation of his settlement stipulation with the Hospital.

The sole issue before us is whether Mrs. Smithers, on behalf of Smithers's estate, has standing to bring this action. The Attorney General maintains that, with a few exceptions inapplicable here, standing to enforce the terms of a charitable gift is limited to the Attorney General. Most recently, the Attorney General has urged that, pursuant to the above-mentioned proposed settlement stipulation between himself and the Hospital, he has achieved all the relief that is appropriate in this case.

We begin by acknowledging that, pursuant to Article 8 of the Estates, Powers & Trusts Law governing the disposition of property for charitable purposes, "[t]he Attorney General shall represent the beneficiaries of such dispositions for religious, charitable, educational or benevolent purposes and it shall be his duty to enforce the rights of such beneficiaries by appropriate proceedings in the courts" By designating the Attorney General as the representative of undesignated beneficiaries, the Legislature provided a mechanism for enforcing charitable trusts, which for a time had been deemed invalid in New York State because they lacked certain beneficiaries who could claim their enforcement. However, while EPTL 8–1.1(f) expressly extended the Attorney General's enforcement powers to all charitable dispositions, including absolute gifts, case law had already recognized the Attorney General's power to insure that charities used absolute gifts in accordance with the donors' stated. . . .

The question of whether the donor who is living and can maintain his or her own action need rely on the protection of the Attorney General to enforce the terms of his gift . . . was addressed in *Associate Alumni of the General Theological Seminary of the Protestant Episcopal Church in the United States of America v. The General Theological Seminary of the Protestant Episcopal Church in the United States.* Alumni of a seminary had contributed money for the endowment of a professorship, on certain specified conditions, and retaining the right of nomination when the chair became vacant. When disputes arose concerning those conditions, the voluntary association of alumni formed a corporation and brought an action against the seminary. The matter was submitted upon an agreed statement of facts to the Appellate Division, which found that the corporation had standing to bring suit as successor in rights and interest of the voluntary association of alumni, the donor of the fund, and that the seminary had received the fund in trust and had breached the terms of the trust. The court directed the seminary to transfer the fund to the corporation.

The Court of Appeals affirmed the Appellate Division's determination of the rights of the respective parties, but modified the judgment to decree specific performance by the seminary of the terms of the trust, instead of directing the return of the fund to the corporation. In the event of failure to comply with the judgment, the fund would be surrendered to the court or trustees appointed by the court, after which the corporation could apply to the court for disposition of the fund.

The general rule is "If the trustees of a charity abuse the trust, misemploy the charity fund, or commit a breach of the trust, the property does not revert to the heir or legal representative of the donor unless there is an express condition of the gift that it shall revert to the donor or his heirs, in case the trust is abused, but the redress is by bill or information by the attorney-general *or other person having the right to sue*." 2 Perry on Trusts, sec. 744. The judgment below practically abrogates the trust and restores the fund to the plaintiff. To such return the plaintiff was not entitled, though as donor and possessor of the right to nominate to the professorship, it had sufficient standing to maintain an action to enforce the trust.

In dismissing Mrs. Smithers's complaint, Supreme Court relied on *Associate Alumni* to hold that, since the Gift instruments do not provide Mrs. Smithers with the right of oversight, that right is vested exclusively in the Attorney General and Mrs. Smithers has no standing to sue. However, *Associate Alumni* [does not] mandate this result. The holding of the former that the donor alumni association had standing to enforce its gift explicitly forecloses the conclusion that the Attorney General's standing in these actions is exclusive. At the same time, the Court's characterization of the association as "donor and possessor of the right to nominate to the professorship" does not necessitate the conclusion that no donor has standing without having retained such a right. In the case on which the Court relied for its holding of donor standing, the donor had not retained any rights, but, "as the founder of the charity, has a standing to appear in court to restrain the diversion of the property donated from the charitable uses for which it was given". . . .

The donor of a charitable gift is in a better position than the Attorney General to be vigilant and, if he or she is so inclined, to enforce his or her own intent. Smithers was the founding donor of the Smithers Center, which he established to carry out his vision of "first class alcoholism treatment and training." In his agreement with the Hospital he reserved to himself the right to veto the Hospital's project plans and staff appointments for the Smithers Center. He and Mrs. Smithers remained actively involved in the affairs of the Smithers Center until his death, and she thereafter. During his lifetime, when Smithers found that, as he wrote on July 31, 1978, "[c]ertain things that were definitely understood were not carried out" by the Hospital, he decided not to donate the balance of the Gift. It was only when the Hospital expressly agreed to the various restrictions imposed by Smithers that he completed the Gift. The Hospital's subsequent unauthorized deviation from the terms of the completed Gift commenced during Smithers's lifetime and was discovered shortly after he died. To hold that, in her capacity as her late husband's representative, Mrs. Smithers has no standing to institute an action to enforce the terms of the Gift is to contravene the well settled principle that a donor's expressed intent is entitled to protection and the longstanding recognition under New York law of standing for a donor such as Smithers. We have seen no New York case in which a donor attempting to enforce the terms of his charitable gift was denied standing to do so. Neither the donor nor his estate was before the court in any of the cases urged on us in opposition to donor standing. The courts in these cases were not addressing the situation in which the donor was still living or his estate still existed. *Cf., Herzog Foundation v. University of Bridgeport.*

Moreover, the circumstances of this case demonstrate the need for co-existent standing for the Attorney General and the donor. The Attorney General's office was notified of the Hospital's misappropriation of funds by Mrs. Smithers, whose accountants performed the preliminary review of the Hospital's financial records, and it learned of the Hospital's closing of the detox unit—a breach, according to the Attorney General, of a specific representation—from Mrs. Smithers's papers in this action. Indeed, there is no substitute for a donor, who has a "special, personal interest in the enforcement of the gift restriction" (Note, *Protecting the Charitable Investor: A Rationale for Donor Enforcement of Restricted Gifts.*) Mrs. Smithers herself, who the Supreme Court found had no position to lose if the Hospital altered its administration of the Gift, has her own special, personal interest in the enforcement of the Gift restrictions imposed by her husband, as is manifest from her own fundraising work on behalf of the Smithers Center and the fact that the gala that she organized and that the Hospital ultimately cancelled was to be in her honor as well as her husband's. In any event, the Attorney General's interest in enforcing gift terms is not necessarily congruent with that of the donor. The donor seeks to have his or her intent faithfully executed, which by definition will benefit the beneficiaries, and perhaps also to erect a tangible memorial to himself or herself. In the June 16, 1971 letter to the Hospital in which Smithers created the Gift, he wrote that it "is to be used to set up the Smithers Alcoholism Treatment and Training Center." As the Court of Appeals has observed, a donor's desire to perpetuate his name as a benefactor of a particular charitable institution and humankind is not a selfish one. "These desires are deeply ingrained in human nature and are effective motivating forces in donations of this character". Perpetuating the donor's good name is certainly also a profound concern of his or her estate. We conclude that the distinct but related interests of the donor and the Attorney General are best served by continuing to accord standing to donors to enforce the terms of their own gifts concurrent with the Attorney General's standing to enforce such gifts on behalf of the beneficiaries thereof. . . .

Mrs. Smithers, appointed the Special Administratrix of Smithers's estate for the purpose of pursuing claims by the estate against the Hospital

> ### Take Note
>
> There is a notable, recent trend in favor of settlor standing. Should courts or legislatures make the decision whether to recognize it?

in connection with its administration of the Smithers Center, therefore has standing to sue the Hospital for enforcement of the Gift terms.

————————

In re Declaration of Trust Creating the Avery Family Trust

402 P.3d 696 (Okla. Civ. App. 2017)

Bay Mitchell, Presiding Judge:

Petitioner/Appellant John Neel Zink (Zink) appeals from a Journal Entry of Judgment dismissing his claims against Respondents/Appellees Etta May Avery (Etta May), Nancy Ann McGill (McGill), and Mickey G. Shackelford (Shackelford) (collectively, Respondents). The court found that Zink, as a former co-trustee, did not have standing to bring his claims under 60 O.S. 2011 175.23(C) and, therefore, the court did not have jurisdiction over this action. We find Zink qualifies as a "person affected by the administration of the trust estate" under 175.23(C). The court erred by dismissing the case. Accordingly, we reverse and remand.

On April 27, 1999, Jacqueline Avery Zink created the Avery Family Trust (the Trust). The Trust was created exclusively for charitable purposes. The original trustees of the Trust were Jacqueline and her sisters, Millicent A. Ogilvie and Etta May Avery. In 2005, Jacqueline appointed Zink and Billie Coffee as successor co-trustees of the Trust. Jacqueline died soon after. Millicent died in April 2010. The remaining trustees executed an amendment to the Trust (the 2010 Amendment), which provided that "Each of the current Trustees, Etta May Avery, John Neel Zink and Billie Coffee, may continue to serve as long as she or he is willing and able to serve." The 2010 Amendment also provided that Etta May had the right to appoint persons to fill vacant trustee positions, to appoint additional trustees, or to appoint a successor trustee, but also provided that "[e]ach appointment of an individual who has not previously served as a Trustee hereunder shall be for an initial term of two years." In December of 2010, Coffee died, leaving Etta May and Zink as the only remaining trustees.

On January 14, 2014, Etta May appointed McGill and Shackelford as additional co-trustees of the Trust. On July 28, 2014, Respondents executed a new amendment to the Trust (the July 2014 Amendment). Like the 2010 Amendment, the July 2014 Amendment granted lifetime appointments to the then-serving trustees (Etta May, Zink, McGill and Shackelford). In August 2014, Respondents executed another amendment to the Trust (the August 2014 Amendment), which removed the language granting the trustees lifetime appointments, inserted language providing that only Etta May had a lifetime appointment, and granted Etta May the authority to remove any individual co-trustee from office. Zink did not sign either of the 2014 amendments. On August 14, 2014, Etta May removed Zink as co-trustee.

Zink filed suit on August 12, 2016. Zink sought a finding that the August 2014 Amendment and his removal were invalid; a determination that he was still an active co-trustee; and injunctive relief preventing the destruction of previous improvements on Trust property. Respondents filed a motion to dismiss. Respondents argued that Zink did not have standing to bring his claims under 60 O.S. 2011 175.23(C). Respondents further argued that Zink could not maintain the action because the Attorney General has the exclusive right to bring an action challenging the administration of a charitable trust. After a hearing, the court found that Zink lacked standing under 175.23 and granted Respondents' motion to dismiss. The court did not address Respondents' second ground for dismissal. . . .

Respondents argued that Zink, as a former co-trustee, did not have standing to bring his claims under 175.23. Section 175.23(A) gives the trial court the authority to construe trust instruments. Subsection (C) provides, in part, that "[a]ctions hereunder may be brought by a trustee, beneficiary, or any person affected by the administration of the trust estate." Respondents argue that a person seeking to qualify as a "person affected by the administration of the trust estate" must have interests that are "inextricably intertwined" or otherwise directly aligned with the interests of the beneficiaries. . . .

As a former trustee whose trustee status was revoked by Respondents, Zink was certainly affected by the administration of the Trust estate. Further, according to Zink, the land owned and managed by the Trust contains Zink's grandfather's grave site and residence, as well as other improvements. We fail to see how the trial court could conclude that Zink is not a person affected by the administration of the Trust. Zink has standing to bring his claims. . . .

Sagtikos Manor Historical Soc'y, Inc. v. Robert David Lion Gardiner Found., Inc.

9 N.Y.S.3d 80 (N.Y. App. Div. 2015)

. . . This controversy centers around Sagtikos Manor, a 10-acre property improved with a historic manor house located in West Bay Shore. The Manor was formerly owned by Robert David Lion Gardiner. Starting in or about 1964, Gardiner allowed the plaintiff, the Sagtikos Manor Historical Society, Inc., to give tours of the Manor and maintain the property. In 1985, Gardiner conveyed the Manor to a charitable foundation he established which came to be named the Robert David Lion Gardiner Foundation, Inc. The Foundation's stated purpose includes educating and informing the public about the history of the area of the Town of Islip and encouraging and sponsoring existing and future historical societies relevant to the area's heritage and traditions. In 2002, the Foundation sold the Manor to Suffolk County. In 2005, the Historical Society entered into a custodial agreement with the County for the maintenance and preservation of the Manor.

Gardiner died in 2004, and his will directed that his residuary estate be held in trust for the benefit of his widow, Eunice Gardiner, during her life, with the principal to be distributed to the Foundation upon her death. Eunice Gardiner died in 2011. At that time, the trust contained approximately $81,000,000. The Historical Society contacted the Foundation requesting an accounting of the charitable remainder of Gardiner's estate. By letter dated December 12, 2011, counsel for the Foundation rejected the Historical Society's request on the ground that it was not named as a beneficiary under Gardiner's will nor any trust created thereunder. The Historical Society commenced this action, inter alia, for a judgment declaring the intent of the grantor of the Foundation with respect to the Foundation's charitable purposes and beneficiaries. The Foundation and its individual trustees moved . . . to dismiss the complaint insofar as asserted against them, and the Supreme Court denied that branch of their motion.

In an action for the enforcement of a charitable trust, EPTL 8–1.1 (f) provides that "[t]he attorney general shall represent the beneficiaries of such dispositions for religious, charitable, educational or benevolent purposes and it shall be his [or her] duty to enforce the rights of such beneficiaries by appropriate proceedings in the courts." A party with a special interest in the enforcement of the trust may have standing to commence such an action; however, "one who is merely a possible beneficiary of a charitable trust, or a member of a class of possible beneficiaries, is not entitled to sue for enforcement of the trust". This "special interest" is found by looking to the trust's chartering documents to discern the purpose of the trust, and whether there is a class of intended beneficiaries that is entitled to a preference and is sharply defined and limited in number.

In support of their motion, the appellants submitted the Foundation's certificate of incorporation, as amended in 1987, which states that the Foundation's purpose includes educating the public about state and local history and encouraging and sponsoring existing and future historical societies. That document does not name the Historical Society as a beneficiary, nor does it name any beneficiary. Gardiner's will did not mention the Historical Society. Accordingly, the Historical Society was not part of a class of potential beneficiaries of the Foundation that is sharply defined and limited in number. Therefore, it lacked standing to commence this action.

In view of the foregoing, the Supreme Court should have granted that branch of the appellants' motion . . . to dismiss the complaint insofar as asserted against them on the ground of lack of standing.

In re Milton Hershey School

911 A.2d 1258 (Pa. 2006)

Justice Eakin.

In 1909, Milton and Catherine Hershey established the Milton Hershey School, a charitable institution, funded by the Milton Hershey School Trust. The deed of trust is the original agreement between the Hersheys, the Hershey Trust Company as Trustee, and the Managers of the Trust. The deed, as amended in 1976, provides that the Trust Company and the Board of Managers (which consists of members of the Board of Directors of the Trust Company), are to administer the Trust and have responsibility for all aspects of running the School and for managing the Trust's assets. The deed also states, "[a]ll children shall leave the institution and cease to be the recipients of its benefits upon the completion of the full course of secondary education being offered at the School."

In 1930, at Milton Hershey's direction, school alumni and a former superintendent formed The Milton Hershey School Alumni Association. The Association is composed mostly of School graduates, though it includes honorary and associate members. The Association is not a division of the School or Trust Company; it was not named in the deed of trust and is not an intended beneficiary of the Trust.

Around 1990, the Association believed the Trust's resources were being diverted from the purpose of helping orphaned children. The Association contacted the Attorney General, which investigated and concluded the Trust Company was not acting consistent with the Trust's intent. In 2002, the Attorney General, the School, and the Trust Company entered an agreement governing certain aspects of the administration of the Trust and the School.

In 2003, this agreement was modified, essentially rescinding the 2002 agreement. Following the modification, the Association commenced an action in the orphans' court, seeking rescission of the 2003 agreement, reinstatement of the 2002 agreement, and appointment of a guardian *ad litem* and trustee *ad litem*. The School and the Trust Company filed preliminary objections alleging the Association lacked standing to challenge the rescission of the 2002 agreement; the trial court granted the preliminary objections.

The Commonwealth Court, *en banc*, reversed in a four-to-three decision, finding the Association had a "special interest" in the complained-of actions of the Trustee that supported its standing to seek enforcement of the Trust. The court observed the Association was created at the direction of the Trust's primary settlor, with the purpose of promoting school interests and establishing and maintaining supplemental education programs and activities for students. It also summarized the Association's efforts to preserve School traditions and Trust assets, including prompting of the Attorney General to address perceived improprieties, and expending its own financial resources to aid that investigation.

The court acknowledged standing generally requires a "substantial, direct, and immediate interest" in the subject matter of the litigation. It observed in charitable trusts, courts have fashioned a "special interest" doctrine, consistent with the Restatement (Second) of Trusts. Restatement (Second) Trusts § 391 ("A suit can be maintained for the enforcement of a charitable trust by the Attorney General or other public officer, or by a co-trustee, or by a person who has a special interest in the enforcement of the charitable trust. . . ."). The court cited *Valley Forge Historical Society v. Washington Memorial Chapel* (approving standing of historical society to restrain trustees of memorial chapel from evicting society from chapel under special interest doctrine), and *Wiegand v. Barnes Foundation*. The court then implemented a five-part test to determine special interest standing in the charitable trust setting, which requires consideration of:

(1) the extraordinary nature of the acts complained of and the remedy sought; (2) the presence of fraud or misconduct on the part of the charity or its directors; (3) the attorney general's availability or effectiveness; (4) the nature of the benefited class and its relationship to the charity; and (5) subjective, case-specific circumstances.

The court found this test struck the best balance, preventing unnecessary litigation involving charities while assuring the philanthropic purposes underlying trusts are maintained.

Applying this test, the court found the circumstances here to be extraordinary, citing the need for reform administration of Trust assets, the decrease in the number of children the School served vis à vis over $5 billion in Trust assets, and the Association's instrumental role in addressing problems in the Trust's administration. The court delineated the 70-year relationship between the Association and the Trust, including their common founder, the membership's successful participation in School affairs, its ongoing bonds with students, the location of the Association's offices on Trust lands, the Association's administration of student-related activities and graduate assistance programs, and the Association's intimate knowledge of the type of care provided at the School.

The court indicated the risk of vexatious or unreasonable litigation was "virtually non-existent," as the Association only sought reasons why the 2002 agreement was supplanted, when such agreement had resulted from an extensive investigation by the Attorney General (funded in part by the Association), which concluded the Trust's charitable purposes were being impeded. *Id.* The court also found the Association's efforts neither vexatious nor unreasonable. Given the nature of the Trust and its status as the largest residential childcare charity in the world, the court concluded judicial scrutiny would advance the public interest in assuring the Trust is operating efficiently and effectively. . . .

The facts are not in dispute. The Commonwealth Court found the trial court committed an error of law by granting the preliminary objections. We are left to decide whether the Commonwealth Court committed an error of law in its standing analysis. . . .

The core concept of standing is that "a party who is not negatively affected by the matter he seeks to challenge is not aggrieved, and thus, has no right to obtain judicial resolution of his challenge." A litigant is aggrieved when he can show a substantial, direct, and immediate interest in the outcome of the litigation. A litigant possesses a substantial interest if there is a discernable adverse effect to an interest other than that of the general citizenry. It is direct if there is harm to that interest. It is immediate if it is not a remote consequence of a judgment.

Private parties generally lack standing to enforce charitable trusts. Since the public is the object of the settlor's beneficiaries in a charitable trust, private parties generally have insufficient interest in such trusts to enforce them. Those who may bring an action for the enforcement of a charitable trust include the Attorney General, a member of the charitable organization, or someone having a special interest in the trust. A person whose only interest is that interest held in common with other members of the public cannot compel the performance of a duty the organization owes to the public. The question here is whether the Association had such a special interest in the enforcement of the Trust.

In *In re Francis Edward McGillick Foundation*, the settlor directed half of a foundation's income be used to establish scholarships for Catholics, which a Catholic Bishop of Pittsburgh and his advisory board selected; the other half was to be accumulated toward the establishment of a vocational school, again with the participation of the Bishop and his advisory board. The Pittsburgh diocese sued to remove the Foundation's trustees. We held the diocese had standing to bring the action because it had an "integral involvement . . . in the awarding of scholarships and its prerogative to participate in the establishment of a vocational school under the trust create[d] an interest . . . which is immediate, direct, and substantial. . . ."

In re Francis Edward McGillick Foundation is distinguishable from the instant case on one key point; the Hershey Trust does not provide the Association with any decision-making power or administration over it. The trust in *In re Francis Edward McGillick Foundation* specifically directed the Bishop and his advisors to select scholarship recipients that were funded through the trust; thus, the diocese was directly involved in the trust's administration. Here, the Trust does not mention the Association and excludes those who would be members of the Association from benefiting from the Trust.

The Association argues *Valley Forge Historical Society* is on point. There, the Washington Memorial Chapel sought to evict the Valley Forge Historical Society from its property. Dr. W. Herbert Burk founded the Chapel and the Society, although not by a written document called a "trust." Since its inception in 1918, the Society maintained its offices and its collection in the same building as the Chapel, and claimed a right to remain there based on a trust relationship. The Society sought declaratory and injunctive relief; the Chapel argued the Society lacked standing to bring its action. We found a trust relationship existed, and the Society had special interest standing. We noted Dr. Burk intended for both the Chapel and the Society to develop patriotism, one through religion and the other through education. The Society contributed large sums of money to enlarging the Chapel, and from its origin, was a real link to the Washington Memorial in Valley Forge; thus, the Society had a special interest distinguishable from any other historical society not designated by the trust.

Valley Forge Historical Society is instructive, but distinguishable from the instant case. *Valley Forge* involved a settlor creating two foundations which shared the same building since 1918; we found a trust relationship existed. Here, the Hersheys created the Trust in 1909, but the Association was not created until 20 years later. If the Hersheys intended for the Association to have direct input on Trust affairs, they could have altered the Trust, but did not do so. The Trust has not been so amended.

More importantly, a *written* trust exists here, specifically excluding School graduates from being recipients of the Trust's benefits. The Association is not mentioned in the Trust, and the bulk of the Association's members are specifically excluded from receiving the benefits of the Trust. To give the Association "special interest" standing where the settlors of the Trust specifically denied beneficiary status to its members, would surely contravene the settlors' intent expressed through their written trust.

We find the Association did not have a special interest sufficient to vest it with standing. Nothing in this litigation would affect the Association itself; it loses nothing and gains nothing. The Association's intensity of concern is real and commendable, but it is not a substitute for an actual interest. Standing is not created through the Association's advocacy or its members' past close relationship with the School as former individual recipients of the Trust's benefits. The Trust did not contemplate the Association, or anyone else, to be a "shadow board" of graduates with standing to challenge actions the Board takes. *See In re Francis Edward McGillick Foundation*, (grave doubt as to standing of stranger to object to waste of trust assets).

The Attorney General is granted the authority to enforce charitable trusts. Current law allowed the Association, an outside group, to urge the Attorney General to enforce the Trust. However, the Association's disagreement with the Attorney General's decision to modify the 2002 agreement does not vest the Association with standing to challenge that decision in court. Ultimately, the Association's dismay is more properly directed at the Attorney General's actions and decisions; it is insufficient to establish standing here.

We hold the Association did not have standing to bring this action. Order reversed. Jurisdiction relinquished.

Russell v. Yale Univ.

737 A.2d 941 (Conn. 1999)

LAVERY, J.

The plaintiffs, an heir of the settlor of a charitable trust, alumni donors and students of the named defendant, Yale University (Yale), appeal from the judgment of dismissal rendered by the trial court in granting the Yale's motion to dismiss, which asserted that the trial court lacked subject matter jurisdiction on the ground that the plaintiffs lacked standing. On appeal, the plaintiffs claim that the trial court improperly granted Yale's motion to dismiss because, where the attorney general elects not to participate in a proceeding involving a charitable trust, a person with a "special interest" may appear on behalf of the trust to protect the interests of the beneficiaries and that the plaintiff heir, alumni donors and students have the special interest necessary to confer standing on them. We affirm the judgment of the trial court.

The following facts are necessary for our resolution of this appeal. Yale is a nonprofit corporation organized pursuant to a 1745 charter, which was reconfirmed in article eighth, § 3, of the constitution of Connecticut in 1965. The settlor, John W. Sterling, died in 1918. At that time, he left, in trust, money for the erection of a building or buildings that would constitute a fitting memorial reflecting his gratitude and affection for his alma mater, Yale. The trustees were given broad discretion in the disposition of these funds and directed, if their discretion made it advisable, to consult with Sterling's sisters with regard to the use of the funds. The will directed that the money not be used for the purchase of land or as part of Yale's general fund. In 1930, the Sterling trustees voted to contribute money for the erection and maintenance of the divinity school quadrangle that bears Sterling's name. No other restrictions existed in the will and no property rights were reserved for Sterling's heirs by the will.

The divinity school is one of Yale's graduate professional schools, which educates men and women for the Christian ministry and provides theological education for persons engaged in other professions. Prior to the commencement of this action, the president of Yale appointed a committee to undertake a comprehensive study of the divinity school and its future. In late 1996, the Fellows of the Yale Corporation approved certain recommendations, as made to them by the president and dean of the divinity school, calling for the reorganization of the divinity school, including the demolition of large portions of the Sterling Divinity Quadrangle.

The plaintiffs took exception to the reorganization and instituted this action seeking a temporary and permanent injunction enjoining Yale from carrying out the reorganization, a declaratory judgment that Yale's reorganization plan constitutes an abuse of discretion as a trustee of a public charitable trust, and an accounting of all gifts and donations Yale received for the benefit of the divinity school and of charges against the divinity school's endowment. Yale moved to dismiss the complaint on the ground that the plaintiffs lack standing to bring suit. The trial court granted the motion to dismiss and the plaintiffs appealed. Additional facts will be addressed as necessary.

> "It is a basic principle of our law . . . that the plaintiffs must have standing in order for a court to have jurisdiction to render a declaratory judgment. . . . A party pursuing declaratory relief must . . . demonstrate, as in ordinary actions, a justiciable right in the controversy sought to be resolved, that is, contract, property or personal rights . . . as such will be affected by the [court's] decision. . . . When standing is put in issue, the question is whether the person whose standing is challenged is a proper party to request an adjudication of the issue and not whether the controversy is otherwise justiciable, or whether, on the merits, the plaintiff has a legally protected interest that the defendant's action has invaded. . . .
>
> "Standing is established by showing that the party claiming it is authorized by statute to bring suit or is classically aggrieved. . . . The fundamental test for determining aggrievement encompasses a well-settled twofold determination: first, the party claiming aggrievement must successfully demonstrate a specific, personal and legal interest in [the challenged action], as distinguished from a general interest, such as is the concern of all members of the community as a whole. Second, the party claiming aggrievement must successfully establish that this specific personal and legal interest has been specially and injuriously affected by the [challenged action]. . . . The determination of aggrievement presents a question of fact for the trial court and a plaintiff has the burden of proving that fact. . . . The conclusions reached by the trial court cannot be disturbed on appeal unless the subordinate facts do not support them. . . . Where a plaintiff lacks standing to sue, the court is without subject matter jurisdiction."

> "A motion to dismiss admits all facts well pleaded and invokes any record that accompanies the motion, including supporting affidavits that contain undisputed facts. A motion to dismiss raises the question of whether a jurisdictional flaw is apparent on the record or by way of supporting affidavits."

Although *Carl J. Herzog Foundation, Inc. v. University of Bridgeport*, concerns the interpretation of a statute, in that case, our Supreme Court set out, at length, the common-law rule with regard to standing to bring suit against a charitable entity, which controls the issues here. "At common law, a donor who has made a completed charitable contribution, whether as an absolute gift or in trust, had no standing to bring an action to enforce the terms of his or her gift or trust unless he or she had expressly reserved the right to do so. Where property is given to a charitable corporation and it is directed by the terms of the gift to devote the property to a particular one of its purposes, it is under a duty, *enforceable at the suit of the [a]ttorney [g]eneral*, to devote the property to that purpose. . . . At common law, it was established that [e]quity will afford protection to a donor to a charitable corporation in that *the [a]ttorney [g]eneral may maintain a suit* to compel the property to be held for the charitable purpose for which it was given to the corporation. . . . The general rule is that charitable trusts or gifts to charitable corporations for stated purposes are [enforceable] at the instance of the [a]ttorney [g]eneral. . . . It matters not whether the gift is absolute or in trust or whether a technical condition is attached to the gift."

> "[T]he donor himself has no standing to enforce the terms of his gift when he has not retained a specific right to control the property, such as a right of reverter, after relinquishing physical possession of it. . . . As a matter of common law, when a settlor of a trust or a donor of property to a charity fails specifically to provide for a reservation of rights in the trust or gift instrument, neither the donor nor his heirs have any standing in court in a proceeding to compel the proper execution of the trust, except as relators. . . . There is no such thing as a resulting trust with respect to a charity. . . . Where the donor has effectually passed out of himself all interest in the fund devoted to a charity, neither he nor those claiming under him have any standing in a court of equity as to its disposition and control."

The trial court found the facts noted previously in this opinion and concluded that if Sterling were alive today, he would have no right to enforce conditions of his gift, and that, therefore, his heir and successor lacks standing to bring this suit, as well. We agree.

For the same reasons, the trial court also concluded that the plaintiff alumni donors also lack standing as contributors of unrestricted charitable gifts to their alma mater and nothing about the fact that they are graduates of the divinity school gives them standing. We agree with that conclusion as well.

With regard to the third group of plaintiffs, the students, the trial court determined that they also lack standing. We agree with the trial court and hold that, absent special injury to a student or his or her fundamental rights, students do not have standing to challenge the manner in which the administration manages an institution of higher education. The plaintiff students lack standing because they alleged no injuries to themselves or to any of their fundamental rights, collectively or individually.

We hold, therefore, that the trial court properly concluded that, although the plaintiffs are sincere in their efforts to maintain the divinity school as a leader in theological education and preparation for the Christian ministry and they acted in good faith based on motives that are beyond question, the plaintiffs, as a matter of law, lack standing to adjudicate the equitable remedies they seek.

The judgment is affirmed.

Points for Discussion

1. Evolving law

The Restatement (Third) of Trusts § 94 grants a settlor standing to maintain an action to enforce a charitable trust, which was not provided for in the earlier version nor by the law of most states. The Uniform Trust Code § 405(c), excerpted above, provides for it as well. Many states have adopted this rule by statute or court decision. What are the advantages and disadvantages of adding the settlor to the list of people with power to sue to enforce a charitable trust, which always includes the state attorney general and sometimes includes persons with special interests to enforce either the trust or their interests?

2. Special interests

Who should qualify for "special interest" standing? Can you make sense of the outcomes in the cases above? The Restatement (Third) of Trusts § 94 provides that a person with special interest standing must show that the person is entitled to a benefit that is greater than that available to the rest of the community. Courts typically limit this type of standing to those whose interests are mandatory rather than discretionary. Do these rules set sufficiently definite parameters?

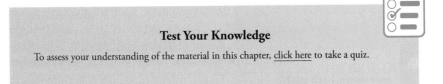

Test Your Knowledge

To assess your understanding of the material in this chapter, click here to take a quiz.

PART V

Trust Administration and Duration

CHAPTER 12

Fiduciary Administration

A page of history...

From time to time in this discourse, we have noted that wills and trusts, though clumped together in a single course, are very different instruments. We have learned that the due execution of each instrument requires adherence to different sets of rules; valid alterations and revocations may also follow different procedures. On the other hand, the line between the law of trusts and that of wills has become increasing blurred. Substantive rules originally developed for wills regarding will construction (for example, anti-lapse statutes) have been applied to trusts, and statutory revocation of a bequest to a spouse upon divorce from the testator or settlor generally applies to both documents. The spiritual, if not their physical, union of these two instrumentalities for making a gift at death, is embodied in the pour-over will. The link between these two—once separate documents—can also be seen in the areas of administration of wills and of trusts. Hence the title of this chapter and the examination of the role of the fiduciary across both subjects.

We have observed a number of times that in the past the law was different from what it is today. It should come as no surprise to you that the law of the process of property transmission is dynamic. That holds true for our own time and in the past. Initially, English law did not permit a will of most types of interests in land until 1540. Rudimentary trusts known as uses were 'raised' earlier on, and the beneficial interest (limited in the *cestui que use*) in the land therein created could pass by will. The actions of the holder of the legal title (the *feoffee to uses*) became subject to royal jurisdiction, usually the Court of Chancery, and a body of law governing the regulation of uses slowly developed. More refined arrangements, usually involving land, were created in the early modern period and called 'settlements.' Successive chancellors developed a law of equity dealing with these trusts of land. As personal property became a more prominent form of wealth-holding, trusts of personal property were fashioned and Chancery's equitable jurisdiction was extended to such trusts. The law relating to trusts (real, personal and mixed) developed a body of rules regarding trust administration outlining the appropriate conduct of the fiduciary, the trustee. We trust that this summary is a review rather than an introduction; we have been here before.

By that time, as the nascent law of trusts was developing, volumes had been written discussing the law regarding the conduct of executors. Recall that wills were usually probated in church courts in England until 1854. Prior thereto, if a dispute arose regarding land devised by will, litigation occurred in royal courts, but proof of the will's validity, matters of interpretation, and accounts were primarily a matter for the church courts and various courts in towns and rural jurisdictions called 'manors.' So while courts of equity supervised the trustee of the settlements, church courts often supervised the conduct of the executor, particularly where personal rather than real property was concerned.

Much of the distinction between the two offices has faded. Modern law regards both trustees and executors as fiduciaries. Both hold legal title to the assets of the trust or estate, for the benefit of others, the beneficiaries of the trust or the estate. Of course, the tasks of each of the types of fiduciaries differ. The role of the executor is merely to collect assets, pay debts and distribute property to the beneficiaries. The period of estate administration is likely to be less lengthy (from about 6 months in a simple estate to perhaps three years in a more complicated one) than with respect to trust administration. Trusts frequently last longer and trustees' duties are more varied. The cases we have parsed are testimony to both propositions. As we have seen, trusts can last for generations, as long as the rule against perpetuities will permit. The breadth of fiduciary duties can be (almost) as extensive as the creator mandates. Much judgment can be reposed in a trustee. As we learned with respect to discretionary trusts, a trustee of a support trust may have the responsibility to invade the corpus to pay the costs of the beneficiary's medical care, education, and support. The duties that we will explore in this chapter are more generic, that is to say, intrinsic to all trusts: the duty of loyalty, the duty to invest prudently, and the duty to account.

First, however, we consider the selection, qualification, and various aspects of the role of the fiduciary.

A. The Fiduciary: Acceptance and Qualification

As we noted in the *Sankel* case (Chapter 8), one cannot be compelled to serve as a trustee. Like Joel Sankel (or perhaps unlike Mr. Sankel, depending upon which side one is inclined to believe) most trustees are aware that they have been named in the document to serve as a fiduciary. Absent a particular requirement in the document that directs a specific process the trustee must follow to indicate assent, a trustee may accept the office of trustee by words or conduct that manifests an intent to accept the trusteeship. Thus, a trustee need not say anything to become obligated to serve. If the trustee does something, such as receiving trust property and beginning to perform the duties attendant on administering the trust, the trustee has a duty to inform the beneficiaries that the trustee has accepted the trusteeship. (See for example Fla. Stat. § 736.0813 (2019), which parallels UTC § 813). Whether the trustee must register the trust by filing in a court of competent jurisdiction differs according to state law.

Remember that the trustee of a testamentary trust must receive letters testamentary as part of the probate process in order to take up the duties of trustee. Depending on state law, if the trustee wishes to resign, the trustee might have to ask the permission of the court that issued the trustee's letters.

When someone accepts the office of trustee, that person will begin the process of locating and taking possession of trust property. If the trust has been created in the lifetime of the creator, the trustee will make certain that title to the trust property is transferred into the name of the trust. With respect to testamentary trusts, trustee will take possession as soon as the will indicates and probate permits. Trustees are liable for losses occasioned by their failure to use reasonable skill and diligence to fulfill these duties (UTC § 811).

The prudent trustee will make an account of the trust property of which the trustee takes control. Trustees should also make sure that the property held in trust is recorded as being held by the trustee 'in trust,' a process usually called 'earmarking' (UTC § 810 (c)). Earmarking guards against the co-mingling of assets under the trustee's control, with either the trustee's own property or that of another trust, and immunizes trust property from claims of the trustee or other non-beneficiaries, especially creditors of the trustee.

Once the trustee has collected the property, the trustee has a continuing duty to exercise reasonable care to safeguard trust property against loss (UTC § 809). Obviously, the steps required relate to the type of property subject to the trust: real estate should be insured; securities and other personal property kept in a safe deposit box if feasible (an antique Ferrari, for example, is slightly too large to fit in most bank vaults!). Remember, however, that today stocks and bonds rarely take physical form. Most investments in stocks and bonds exist only as electronic entries in the records of the brokerage firm where the owner has an account. Trustees regularly open brokerage accounts that hold that part of the trust property consisting of stocks and bonds and other financial investments so that trustee can buy and sell those investments. Modern statutes allow trustees to hold financial investments in such accounts without violating the duty to control and safeguard trust property. *See, e.g.,* UTC § 816(7); NY EPTL 11–1.9, 11–1.10.

Finally, the trustee, in accordance with the fiduciary obligation owed to the beneficiaries, has an obligation to defend the validity of the trust against the claims of others. A variety of individuals may have an interest in setting aside the trust. In the first place, at the death of the creator, the executor of the creator's will may have an interest in setting aside an inter vivos trust because the property constituting the trust would likely be probate assets if the trust is found to be invalid. An interesting example might be a case where the executor believes that the trust violates the Rule against Perpetuities. Creditors might to seek to have a trust set aside if the decedent's estate is not sufficiently solvent to satisfy their claims against the estate. And hark back to *Sullivan*-type trusts, suppose the surviving spouse requires trust property to satisfy the elective share? Restatement (Third) of Trusts § 76 deals with the trustee's obligation to 'defend' the trust.

In addition to claims lodged by outsiders, the trustee may have to respond to those who might impinge upon the interests of trust beneficiaries. It is axiomatic that the trustee has the obligation to carry out the expressed and implied designs of the creator. How does a trustee exercise judgment? For example, recall Ms. Rodd, one of the beneficiaries of the trust that is the subject of *Old Colony Trust Company v Rodd* that appears in Section F of Chapter 8. She comes to the trustee and demands a discretionary payment: can the trustee accede on the grounds that her request is meritorious or must the trustee seek a determination by a court? Although Ms. Rodd was a beneficiary under the trust, a disbursement to her would have an effect on the interests of other trust beneficiaries, both those entitled to income and also those entitled to corpus as remainder beneficiaries.

B. Administrative Powers

In settlements of land, the precursor to modern trusts, the duty and powers of the trustees were limited. Though not entirely so, the role of the trustee in land settlements was to protect the property from encroachment by others and to hand over the income from the land to the beneficiaries. These were not passive trusts, but by contemporary standards the trustee's role was limited. As we have seen, modern trusts frequently require the trustees' role to be more active. Powers given to the trustee by the instrument, by law or by court order allow the trustee to act, and sometimes in the trustee's discretion. There has been a tension in American statutory trust law between limiting administrative powers to those appearing in a prescribed list (the Uniform Trustees' Powers Act) and simply stating that the trustee has a broad range of powers. For an example of the latter, UTC § 815 gives the trustee powers (in addition to those stipulated in the instrument) 'which an unmarried competent owner has over individually owned property' and 'other powers appropriate to achieve the proper investment management, and distribution of the trust property.' Not to be outdone by the UTPA, the UTC also provides a lengthy list of specific powers in § 816.

So much, then for expressed powers. What about powers not delimitated, but that might arise by implication? Consider the following case.

Ward v. Nationsbank of Virginia, N.A.

507 S.E. 2d 616 (Va. 1998)

Lacy, Justice.

In this case, the beneficiaries of a trust filed a bill of complaint against the trustee alleging that the trustee breached the trust agreement by executing a purchase option, agreeing to a deed of trust on the trust property securing funds lent to the lessee/purchaser for development of the property, and subsequently conveying the trust property. Because we conclude that the trustee had the authority to grant the purchase option and exercised that authority in a prudent manner, and that the deed of trust on the trust property provided a benefit to the trust, we will affirm the judgment of the trial court.

I. FACTS

In March 1965, J.L. Hartman and Pauline H. Hartman created a trust for the benefit of their grandchildren, Lynn-Hall Ward, Robert Lee Walker, Jr., Margaret M. Martin, and Anne Walker Durrett (collectively "the Beneficiaries"). Virginia National Bank, NationsBank of Virginia, N.A.'s predecessor, was named as trustee (the Trustee). The trust property was a 29.26-acre tract of land located in Albemarle County.

In May 1969, the Trustee leased the trust property to Wendell W. Wood. The lease contained an option to purchase the property for $750,000 at the expiration of the 25-year lease term. In December 1972, Wood assigned his interest in the lease to Rio Associates Limited Partnership (Rio).

In conjunction with the assignment, the Trustee, Wood, and Rio executed an agreement (1972 agreement) in which the Trustee agreed to subordinate its fee interest in the trust property to first lien deeds of trust securing loans to Rio for development of the property. In return, Rio and Wood agreed to provide collateral security to insure performance of their obligations. The 1972 agreement further provided that when the first development loan was obtained, the lease would be amended by changing the option to purchase clause to a contract to purchase with the deed of conveyance naming Rio or its successors as the grantee.

Between 1976 and 1994, Rio developed the trust property into Albemarle Square Shopping Center. Development of the property was financed by three loans totaling over $5 million from The Life Insurance Company of Virginia (Life of Virginia). When the first loan for $4.1 million was obtained in June 1976, Rio exercised the purchase option in accordance with the 1972 agreement and agreed to close on the purchase of the trust property and pay the purchase price in December 1994 (contract of sale). Also in accordance with the 1972 agreement, the Trustee executed a subordination agreement, subordinating its fee interest to a deed of trust securing Life of Virginia's loan to Rio. Subsequent development loans were similarly secured.

In 1987, the Beneficiaries told the Trust manager, David P. Masich, that they felt the $750,000 purchase price stated in the lease was too low. Masich subsequently informed the Beneficiaries in October 1988 that the sale of the property at the end of the lease was "a done deal."

In the spring of 1994, the Beneficiaries retained E. Randall Ralston, an attorney, to represent them. Ralston told the Beneficiaries that they could file a suit to enjoin the sale of the property. One of the legal theories under consideration as a basis for such litigation was that the Trustee had breached its fiduciary duty when it entered into the purchase option. After conferring with another attorney, Ralston told the Beneficiaries that additional work necessary to analyze whether the trust agreement authorized the Trustee to enter into a purchase option required a retainer of $2,000. The Beneficiaries decided not to pursue the matter because they did not want to incur the cost associated with the additional work.

* * *

II. PROCEEDINGS

In November 1995, the Beneficiaries filed a bill of complaint against the Trustee, Rio, and Life of Virginia, alleging that the Trustee breached its fiduciary duty and the terms of the trust agreement by granting a purchase option in the 1969 lease. The Beneficiaries asked the court to void the January 1995 conveyance of the trust property from the Trustee to Rio, to void the December 1994 Deed of Trust granted by the Trustee and Rio to Life of Virginia, and to remove NationsBank as Trustee of the trust.

The Trustee, Rio, and Life of Virginia responded, denying, inter alia, any breach of fiduciary duty and asserting that the 1969 lease and option to purchase, the 1976 contract of sale, the 1994 Deed of Trust, and the 1995 deed of conveyance were valid. They also raised the affirmative defenses of consent, ratification, and affirmation of the 1995 deed by the Beneficiaries and asserted that the Beneficiaries were estopped from challenging the 1995 deed of conveyance. The Trustee sought attorney's fees. Rio and Life of Virginia filed a cross-bill for sanctions and attorney's fees under Code § 8.01–271.1.

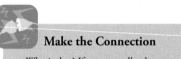

Make the Connection

Why is that? If one can sell, why cannot one contract to sell at some time in the future at a set price?

A demurrer and motions for summary judgment were filed. Prior to trial, the trial court denied the demurrer, but granted the Beneficiaries partial summary judgment, holding that the grant of the purchase option in the 1969 lease was a breach of the trust agreement because it was not expressly authorized by the agreement and could not be inferred from or implied by the language of the agreement . . . (The Trustees appealed)

III. OPTION TO PURCHASE

The trial court held that the trust agreement was not ambiguous, that it did not expressly authorize the Trustee to grant an option to purchase the trust property, and that the power to grant an option to purchase would not be implied because an option to purchase "involves much more discretion in the determination of a purchase price as in this case before the sale actually occurs under the option." The Trustee, Rio, and Life of Virginia assert that the trial court erred in holding that the power to grant an option to purchase

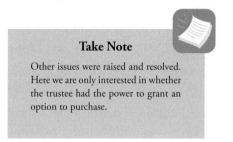

Take Note

Other issues were raised and resolved. Here we are only interested in whether the trustee had the power to grant an option to purchase.

should not be implied from the terms of the trust agreement. Alternatively, they argue that that trial court erred in holding that the trust agreement was unambiguous and denying the use of parol evidence to ascertain the intent of the grantor.

In refusing to find that the language of the trust agreement was sufficient to include an option to purchase, the trial court relied on § 190, comment *k*, of the Restatement (Second) of Trusts. Comment *k*, which the trial court described as stating "the common law rule," [which] provides that "[w]here by the terms of the trust a power of sale is conferred upon the trustee, it is ordinarily not proper for the trustee to give an option to purchase property." Restatement (Second) of Trusts § 190 cmt. *k* (1959). The trial court's reliance on this comment was misplaced in this case.

Section 190 of the Restatement is entitled "Power of Sale" and the discussion in comment *k* addresses a trustee's power to grant an option to purchase based solely upon the expressly granted power to sell the trust property. See also 3 William F. Fratcher, Scott on Trusts § 190.8, at 117–18 (4th ed. 1988). In this case, however, the trust provision expressly granting the Trustee the power to sell the trust property is not the only provision of the trust agreement which is relevant in determining whether the Trustee has the power to grant a purchase option.

In determining the scope of a trustee's powers, we seek to effectuate the intent of the grantor as expressed in the terms of the trust. Frazer v. Millington, 252 Va. 195, 199, 475 S.E.2d 811, 814 (1996). This process requires consideration of the document as a whole. Id.; Dascher v. Dascher, 209 Va. 167, 169, 163 S.E.2d 144, 146 (1968). Although not explicitly identified in the trust agreement, authority to take certain actions may be implied if the intention to create such power is evident, the power may be appropriate or necessary to carry out the purposes of the trust power, and the power is not forbidden by the trust agreement. Frazer, 252 Va. at 199, 475 S.E.2d at 814; Dascher, 209 Va. at 169, 163 S.E.2d at 147; Restatement (Second) of Trusts § 186 cmt. d.

As recognized by the trial court, the trust agreement vested very broad powers in the Trustee. Of particular relevance here is not only the power granted in Article VI of the trust agreement to sell and lease, but also the authority granted in subsection (m) of that Article 'to do all other acts and things not inconsistent with [the trust agreement which the Trustee] may deem necessary or desirable for the proper management [of the trust] in the same manner and to the same extent as an individual might or could do with respect to his own property.' (emphasis added). Any reasonable interpretation of this language would include the ability of the Trustee to grant an option to purchase. Therefore, we must determine whether an option to purchase is appropriate or necessary to carry out the purpose of the trust.

All parties agree that the purpose of this trust was to provide for the education of the grantors' grandchildren. The trust agreement states that it is the grantors' "primary concern in the creation of this trust to provide each beneficiary with an adequate and sufficient education." To effectuate this purpose, the trust agreement gave the Trustee broad discretion to manage the trust property in a way which would insure that sufficient assets would be available throughout the period needed

> **Food for Thought**
>
> If the document denies the power to create an option in trust property, one cannot be created. The settlor cannot preclude and imply a power in the same instrument. But here there is silence. How can a power be evident through silence? So is the question really one on 'appropriate' or necessary power?

to complete the grandchildren's education. The Trustee's use of an option to purchase is in no way inconsistent with this purpose. Considering all the provisions of the trust agreement, we conclude that the language of the agreement is sufficient to imply that the Trustee was given the power to grant an option to purchase and that there is no basis to exclude use of the purchase option as a mechanism for achieving the purposes of the trust.

This conclusion, however, does not end our inquiry. The authority to undertake a specific action and the proper exercise of that authority are distinct considerations. The decision to grant a purchase option is at the discretion of the Trustee and, even though a trustee's discretion is generally broadly construed, "his actions must be an exercise of good faith and reasonable judgment to promote the trust's purpose." NationsBank of Virginia, N.A. v. Estate of Grandy, 450 S.E.2d 140, 143 (Va. 1994). The trustee must "exercise the same degree of discretion in the management of the trust that a prudent man of discretion and intelligence would exercise in his own like affairs." Parsons v. Wysor, 21 S.E.2d 753, 755 (Va. 1942).

The trial court considered whether the Trustee's action in this case was prudent. Its analysis was made in the context of determining whether the Trustee's action qualified for the exception to the Restatement rule set out in § 190 comment *k*. The exception requires a finding that "the grant of the option was prudent." Regardless of the purpose for the prudence review, the analysis and the standard to be applied remain constant and, therefore, the trial court's conclusion in this regard is relevant to the inquiry before us.

The trial court concluded that the Trustee's action in granting the purchase option was prudent. Based on the evidence before it on the motions for summary judgment, the trial court found that there is no evidence that the lease with the option to Mr. Wood may not have been prudent in light of the financial analysis advanced by the [Trustee]. The lease of the property with the option to purchase appears to have rendered greater financial benefit to the beneficiaries than an outright sale of the property to Wood would have rendered.

* * *

In summary, we conclude that under the terms of the trust agreement, the Trustee had the implied power to grant an option to purchase, that an option to purchase was not inconsistent with effectuating the purpose of the trust, and that the manner in which the Trustee exercised its authority to grant the purchase option was prudent. Because the Trustee did not breach the trust agreement in granting the option to purchase, the Beneficiaries' challenge to the 1995 deed based on the 1969 purchase option as amended in 1976 must fail. Accordingly, for the reasons stated, we will affirm the trial court's decision that the 1995 deed of conveyance was valid.

Points for Discussion

Powers expressed and powers implied

1. Was the court correct in regarding the words of the trust to encompass granting an option to buy trust property? Could you regard the language as mere boilerplate? Suppose the trustee decided to mortgage the property. Could the language be construed to permit an encumbrance?

2. Powers to sell trust property are frequently implied. After all, the needs of beneficiaries may change over time demanding a greater or lesser flow of income to a beneficiary. Likewise, the income-producing ability of property moves at least in part in tandem with the economy. Thus some flexibility is necessary. Is vague guidance (like the words in the above trust) better than no guidance or is firm guidance preferable? How should a scrivener approach the issue of drafting powers? Is this an issue with which the client will have much experience?

3. Should a court allow the trustee to deviate from an express provision? Suppose the creator of a trust includes the 'home farm' as trust property and stipulates that it should not be sold. Should the power to sell be implied if it is no longer efficient to run the land as a farm? Does the following section of the UTC permit a sale?

Consider the terms of this provision of the Uniform Trust Code. Does it ride to the rescue of trustees and beneficiaries when time has rendered the provisions of the trust no longer economically efficient?

Uniform Trust Code § 412. Modification or Termination Because of Unanticipated Circumstances or Inability to Administer Trust Effectively

(a) The court may modify the administrative or dispositive terms of a trust or terminate the trust if, because of circumstances not anticipated by the settlor, modification or termination will further the purposes of the trust. To the extent practicable, the modification must be made in accordance with the settlor's probable intention.

(b) The court may modify the administrative terms of a trust if continuation of the trust on its existing terms would be impracticable or wasteful or impair the trust's administration.

C. Delegation

While a trustee cannot delegate the trustee's fiduciary responsibilities to an agent, the trustee may assign some ministerial acts to be performed by others (Restatement (Third) of Trusts § 76). Indeed, in certain circumstances the trustee may have a duty to assign special obligations to another who has the requisite technical skills. The trustee, however, does have an ongoing obligation to monitor the delegate's performance (Restatement (Third) of Trusts § 80).

Suppose, as is frequently the case, the creator of the trust has nominated multiple trustees. May the co-trustee delegate duties to another trustee and escape liability for failing to participate actively in the management of the trust?

Anton v. Anton

815 So. 2d 768 (Fl. Ct. App. 2002)

KLEIN, J.

Appellant was a co-trustee of a trust from which funds were stolen by another co-trustee. He asserts that, even though he was inattentive, the trial court should not have found him liable for the loss. We disagree and affirm.

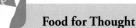

Food for Thought

Why might a trustee accept a fiduciary obligation and then fail to participate in managing the trust?

The dishonest co-trustee, who was appellant's brother and a lawyer, converted money from the trust to his personal use by having appellant sign checks on the trust bank account in blank. There was evidence showing that the co-trustee was able to carry out this scheme over a period of time because the appellant did not review bank statements, cancelled checks, or the bills which his co-trustee was allegedly paying.

Appellant, as a trustee, was under a duty to administer the trust diligently for the benefit of the beneficiary. § 737.301, Florida Statutes (1995). Where there are several trustees, each is under a duty to participate fully in the administration of the trust. *Brent v. Smathers*, 547 So.2d 683 (Fla. 3d DCA 1989). One trustee who delegates to another the administration of a trust breaches the duties of a trustee. *Id. Ball v. Mills*, 376 So.2d 1174 (Fla. 1st DCA 1979) (co-trustees are required to "maintain an attitude of vigilant concern"). The fact that the co-trustee was a lawyer does not relieve appellant from his personal responsibility to the trust. *Brent*, 547 So.2d at 686.

Appellant argues that not all of the stolen funds could be directly attributed to checks which he had signed in blank. That argument overlooks the fact that appellant paid no attention whatsoever to the manner in which the co-trustee administered the trust. Signing the blank checks was only one aspect of his failure to carry out his responsibilities as a trustee.

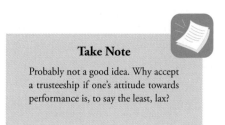

Take Note

Probably not a good idea. Why accept a trusteeship if one's attitude towards performance is, to say the least, lax?

Appellant also argues that there will be an improper double recovery for the trust in this case because the dishonest co-trustee, as a result of criminal proceedings, is making monthly restitution payments. We agree, as did appellee at oral argument, that there should not be a double recovery; however, that is not a ground for reversal of this judgment. Rather, if appellant is forced to pay this judgment, which has been stayed pending this appeal, and restitution payments from the dishonest co-trustee will result in a double recovery, appellant would be entitled to receive those payments under the doctrine of subrogation. *North v. Albee*, 155 Fla. 515, 20 So.2d 682 (1945) (subrogation arises where one having a liability pays a debt due by another under such circumstances that he is in equity entitled to the security held by the creditor whom he paid).

> **Take Note**
>
> The extent of the trustee's liability may be limited. If the dishonest trustee is judgment-proof, who suffers the loss?

Affirmed.

SHAHOOD and HAZOURI, JJ., concur.

Points for Discussion

Pondering the extent of the trustee's duty

1. In the *Anton* case, the trustees actively participated in the deception by signing blank checks. Suppose the attorney-trustee acted alone, and the co-trustee was inattentive, rather than complicit. Should the trustee still be liable?

2. If a trustee can be held harmless for acts of a co-trustee of which the co-trustee is unaware, would an incentive be created for trustees to remain oblivious? Should there be a duty to supervise the acts of a co-trustee?

D. Duty of Loyalty

The Restatement (Third) of Trusts § 90 requires trustees to use reasonable care, skill and caution. However, when the trustee is placed in a position where there might be a conflict between the trustee's personal interests (usually pecuniary) and those of the beneficiaries, a heightened standard is applied. About the governing standards of trustee conduct, as is usually the case, nobody can say it quite like Justice Cardozo. In *Meinhard v. Salmon*, 49 N.Y. 458, 164 N.E. 545 (1928), writing of a partner in a joint venture, the court observed the fiduciary relationship therein created in the following words:

> A trustee is held to something stricter than the morals of the market place. Not honesty alone, but the punctilio of an honor the most sensitive, is then the standard

of behavior. . . the level of conduct for fiduciaries [has] been kept at a level higher than that trodden by the crowd.

No other case, perhaps, raises the issue of a fiduciary's duty of loyalty quite like the litigation involving the estate of the abstract expressionist painter, Mark Rothko, albeit in the context of the executors rather than trustees. Nevertheless, the standard is similar.

Estate of Rothko

372 N.E. 2d 291 (N.Y. 1977)

COOKE, JUDGE.

Mark Rothko, an abstract expressionist painter whose works through the years gained for him an international reputation of greatness, died testate on February 25, 1970.

What's That?

Like TV news programs, the court is preparing the reader for conduct that some viewers might find 'disturbing.'

The principal asset of his estate consisted of 798 paintings of tremendous value, and the dispute underlying this appeal involves the conduct of his three executors in their disposition of these works of art. In sum, that conduct as portrayed in the record and sketched in the opinions was manifestly wrongful and indeed shocking.

Rothko's will was admitted to probate on April 27, 1970 and letters testamentary were issued to Bernard J. Reis, Theodoros Stamos and Morton Levine. Hastily and within a period of only about three weeks and by virtue of two contracts each dated May 21, 1970, the executors dealt with all 798 paintings.

Go Online

To learn more about this remarkable American artist, visit www.markroth-ko.org/.

By a contract of sale, the estate executors agreed to sell to Marlborough A.G., a Liechtenstein corporation (hereinafter MAG), 100 Rothko paintings as listed for $1,800,000, $200,000 to be paid on execution of the agreement and the balance of $1,600,000 in 12 equal interest-free

Go Online

A tidy sum. On the other hand, maybe buy and hold is the strategy; at an auction in May 2012 a Rothko sold for $87,000,000. http://www.nytimes.com/2012/05/10/arts/10iht-melikian10.html?pagewanted=all.

installments over a 12-year period. Under the second agreement, the executors consigned to Marlborough Gallery, Inc., a domestic corporation (hereinafter MNY), "approximately 700 paintings listed on a Schedule to be prepared", the consignee to be responsible for costs covering items such as insurance, storage restoration and promotion. By its provisos, MNY could sell up to 35 paintings a year from each of two groups, pre-1947 and post-

1947, for 12 years at the best price obtainable but not less than the appraised estate value, and it would receive a 50% Commission on each painting sold, except for a commission of 40% on those sold to or through other dealers.

Petitioner Kate Rothko, decedent's daughter and a person entitled to share in his estate by virtue of an election under EPTL 5–3.3, instituted this proceeding to remove the executors, to enjoin MNY and MAG from disposing of the paintings, to rescind the aforesaid agreements between the executors and said corporations, for a return of the paintings still in possession of those corporations, and for damages. She was joined by the guardian of her brother Christopher Rothko,

EPTL 5–3.3 allowed family members to set aside a testamentary gift to charity to the extent it exceeded one-half of the value of the estate after payment of debts. The provision was repealed in 1981.

likewise interested in the estate, who answered by adopting the allegations of his sister's petition and by demanding the same relief. The Attorney-General of the State, as the representative of the ultimate beneficiaries of the Mark Rothko Foundation, Inc., a charitable corporation and the residuary legatee under decedent's will, joined in requesting relief substantially similar to that prayed for by petitioner. On June 26, 1972 the Surrogate issued a temporary restraining order and on September 26, 1972 a preliminary injunction enjoining MAG, MNY, and the three executors from selling or otherwise disposing of the paintings referred to in the agreements dated May 21, 1970, except for sales or dispositions made with court permission. The Appellate Division modified the preliminary injunction order by increasing the amount of the bond and otherwise affirmed. By a 1974 petition, the Attorney-General, on behalf of the ultimate charitable beneficiaries of the Mark Rothko Foundation, sought the punishment of MNY, MAG, Lloyd and Reis for contempt and other relief.

Food for Thought

Reis and Stamos each had their own fish to fry. Whose conduct is most egregious? Would any artist, struggling or otherwise, be in the same position as Stamos? If the conflicts of interest of his co-executors were so obvious, why would Levine appear so oblivious to them? As we shall see, his lack of oversight was costly.

Following a nonjury trial covering 89 days and in a thorough opinion, the Surrogate found: that Reis was a director, secretary and treasurer of MNY, the consignee art gallery, in addition to being a coexecutor of the estate; that the testator had a 1969 inter vivos contract with MNY to sell Rothko's work at a commission of only 10% and whether that agreement survived testator's death was a problem that a fiduciary in a dual position could not have impartially faced; that Reis was in a position of serious conflict of interest with respect to the contracts of May 21, 1970 and that his dual role and planned purpose benefited the Marlborough interests to the detriment of the estate; that it was to the advantage of coexecutor Stamos as a "not-too-successful artist, financially," to curry favor with Marlborough and that the contract made by him with MNY within months after signing the estate contracts placed him in a position where his personal interests conflicted with those of the estate, especially leading to lax contract enforcement efforts by Stamos; that Stamos acted negligently and improvidently in view of his own knowledge of the conflict of interest of Reis; that the third coexecutor, Levine, while not acting in self-interest or with bad faith, nonetheless failed to exercise ordinary prudence in the performance of his assumed fiduciary obligations since he was aware of Reis' divided loyalty, believed that Stamos was also seeking personal advantage, possessed personal opinions as to the value of the paintings and yet followed the leadership of his coexecutors without investigation of essential facts or consultation with competent and disinterested appraisers, and that the business transactions of the two Marlborough corporations were admittedly controlled and directed by Francis K. Lloyd. It was concluded that the acts and failures of the three executors were clearly improper to such a substantial extent as to mandate their removal under SCPA 711 as estate fiduciaries. The Surrogate also found that MNY, MAG and Lloyd were guilty of contempt in shipping, disposing of and selling 57 paintings in violation of the temporary restraining order dated June 26, 1972 and of the injunction dated September 26, 1972; that the contracts for sale and consignment of paintings between the executors and MNY and MAG provided inadequate value to the estate, amounting to a lack of mutuality and fairness resulting from conflicts on the part of Reis and Stamos and improvidence on the part of all executors; that said contracts were voidable and were set aside by reason of violation of the duty of loyalty and improvidence of the executors, knowingly participated in and induced by MNY and MAG; that the fact that these agreements were voidable did not revive the 1969 inter vivos agreements since the parties by their conduct evinced an intent to abandon and abrogate these compacts. The Surrogate held that the present value at the time of trial of the paintings sold is the proper measure of damages as to MNY, MAG, Lloyd, Reis and Stamos. He imposed a civil fine of $3,332,000 upon MNY, MAG and Lloyd, same being the appreciated value at the time of trial of the 57 paintings sold in violation of the temporary restraining order and injunction. It was held that Levine was liable for $6,464,880 in damages, as he was not in a dual position acting for his own interest and was thus liable only for the actual value of paintings sold MNY and MAG as of the dates of sale, and that Reis, Stamos, MNY and MAG, apart from being jointly and severally liable for the same damages as Levine for negligence, were liable for the greater sum of $9,252,000 "as appreciation damages less amounts previously paid to the estate with regard to sales of paintings." The cross petition of the Attorney-General to reopen the record for submission of newly discovered documentary evidence was denied. The liabilities were held to be congruent so that payment of the highest sum would satisfy all lesser liabilities including the civil fines and the liabilities for damages were to be reduced by payment of the fine levied or by return of any of the 57 paintings disposed of, the new fiduciary to have the option in the first instance to specify which paintings the fiduciary would accept.

The Appellate Division, in an opinion by Justice Lane, modified to the extent of deleting the option given the new fiduciary to specify which paintings he would accept. Except for this modification, the majority affirmed on the opinion of Surrogate Midonick, with additional comments. Among others, it was stated that the entire court agreed that executors Reis and

Stamos had a conflict of interest and divided loyalty in view of their nexus to MNY and that a majority were in agreement with the Surrogate's assessment of liability as to executor Levine and his findings of liability against MNY, MAG and Lloyd. The majority agreed with the Surrogate's analysis awarding "appreciation damages" and found further support for his rationale in Menzel v. List, 24 N.Y.2d 91, 298 N.Y.S.2d 979, 246 N.E.2d 742. . . .

Since the Surrogate's findings of fact as to the conduct of Reis, Stamos, Levine, MNY, MAG and Lloyd and the value of the paintings at different junctures were affirmed by the Appellate Division, if there was evidence to support these findings they are not subject to question in this court and the review here is confined to the legal issues raised (CPLR 5501, subd. (b); Simon v. Electrospace Corp., 28 N.Y.2d 136, 139, 320 N.Y.S.2d 225, 227, 269 N.E.2d 21, 22; Matter of City of New York (Fifth Ave. Coach Lines), 22 N.Y.2d 613, 620–621, 294 N.Y.S.2d 502, 505–506, 241 N.E.2d 717, 719–720).

In seeking a reversal, it is urged that an improper legal standard was applied in voiding the estate contracts of May, 1970, that the "no further inquiry" rule applies only to self-dealing and that in case of a conflict of interest, absent self-dealing, a challenged transaction must be shown to be unfair. The subject of fairness of the contracts is intertwined with the issue of whether Reis and Stamos were guilty of conflicts of interest.2 Scott is quoted to the effect that "(a) trustee does not necessarily incur liability merely because he has an individual interest in the transaction * * * In Bullivant v. First Nat. Bank (246 Mass. 324, 141 N.E. 41) it was held that * * * the fact that the bank was also a creditor of the corporation did not make its assent invalid, if it acted in good faith and the plan was fair" (2 Scott, Trusts, s 170.24, p. 1384), and our attention has been called to the statement in Phelan v. Middle States Oil Corp., 220 F.2d 593, 603, 2 Cir., cert. den. sub nom. Cohen v. Glass, 349 U.S. 929, 75 S.Ct. 772, 99 L.Ed. 1260 that Judge Learned Hand found "no decisions that have applied (the no further inquiry rule) inflexibly to every occasion in which the fiduciary has been shown to have had a personal interest that might in fact have conflicted with his loyalty."

What's That?

This principle makes all self-dealing transactions entered into by the trustee per se voidable by the beneficiaries, requiring no proof that such transactions were unreasonable or harmful.

These contentions should be rejected. First, a review of the opinions of the Surrogate and the Appellate Division manifests that they did not rely solely on a "no further inquiry rule", and secondly, there is more than an adequate basis to conclude that the agreements between the Marlborough corporations and the estate were neither fair nor in the best interests of the estate. This is demonstrated, for example, by the comments of the Surrogate concerning the commissions on the consignment of the 698 paintings (see 84 Misc.2d 830, 852–853, 379 N.Y.S.2d 923, 947–948) and those of the Appellate Division concerning the sale of the 100 paintings (see 56 A.D.2d, at pp. 501–502, 392 N.Y.S.2d, at pp. 872–873). The opinions under review demonstrate that neither the Surrogate nor the Appellate Division set aside the contracts by merely applying the no further inquiry rule without regard to fairness. Rather they determined, quite properly indeed, that these agreements were neither fair nor in the best interests of the estate.

To be sure, the assertions that there were no conflicts of interest on the part of Reis or Stamos indulge in sheer fantasy. Besides being a director and officer of MNY, for which there was financial remuneration, however slight, Reis, as noted by the Surrogate, had different inducements to favor the Marlborough interests, including his own aggrandizement of status and financial advantage through sales of almost one million dollars for items from his own and his family's extensive private art collection by the Marlborough interests (see 84 Misc.2d, at pp. 843–844, 379 N.Y.S.2d at pp. 939–940). Similarly, Stamos benefited as an artist under contract with Marlborough and, interestingly, Marlborough purchased a Stamos painting from a third party for $4,000 during the week in May, 1970 when the estate contract negotiations were pending (see 84 Misc.2d, at p. 845, 379 N.Y.S.2d at p. 941). The conflicts are manifest. Further, as noted in Bogert, Trusts and Trustees (2d ed.), "The duty of loyalty imposed on the fiduciary prevents him from accepting employment from a third party who is entering into a business transaction with the trust" (§ 543, subd. (S), p. 573). "While he (a trustee) is administering the trust he must refrain from placing himself in a position where his personal interest or that of a third person does or may conflict with the interest of the beneficiaries" (Bogert, Trusts (Hornbook Series 5th ed.), p. 343). Here, Reis was employed and Stamos benefited in a manner contemplated by Bogert (see, also, Meinhard v. Salmon, 249 N.Y. 458, 464, 466–467, 164 N.E. 545, 547–548; Schmidt v. Chambers, 265 Md. 9, 33–38, 288 A.2d 356). In short, one must strain the law rather than follow it to reach the result suggested on behalf of Reis and Stamos.

Practice Pointer

Would any artist also have had a conflict? Is it surprising that Rothko chose colleagues in the same industry to execute his will? What would you have advised him?

Levine contends that, having acted prudently and upon the advice of counsel, a complete defense was established. Suffice it to say, an executor who knows that his coexecutor is committing breaches of trust and not only fails to exert efforts directed towards prevention but accedes to them is legally accountable even though he was acting on the advice of counsel (Matter of Westerfield, 32 App. Div. 324, 344, 53 N.Y.S. 25, 39; 3 Scott, Trusts (3d ed.), s 201, p. 1657). When confronted with the question of whether to enter into the Marlborough contracts, Levine was acting in a business capacity, not a legal one, in which he was required as an executor primarily to employ such diligence and prudence to the care and management of the estate assets and affairs as would prudent persons of discretion and intelligence (King v. Talbot, 40 N.Y. 76, 85–86), accented by "(n)ot honesty alone, but the punctilio of an honor the most sensitive" (Meinhard v. Salmon, 249 N.Y. 458, 464, 164 N.E. 545, 546, supra). Alleged good faith on the part of a fiduciary forgetful of his duty is not enough (Wendt v. Fischer, 243 N.Y. 439, 443, 154 N.E. 303, 304). He could not close his eyes, remain passive or move with unconcern in the face of the obvious loss to be visited upon the estate by participation in those business arrangements and then shelter himself behind the claimed counsel of an attorney (see Matter of Niles, 113 N.Y. 547,

558, 21 N.E. 687, 689; Matter of Huntley, 13 Misc. 375, 380, 35 N.Y.S. 113, 116; 3 Warren's Heaton, Surrogates' Courts (6th ed.), § 217, subd. 3, par. (b)).

Further, there is no merit to the argument that MNY and MAG lacked notice of the breach of trust. The record amply supports the determination that they are chargeable with notice of the executors' breach of duty.

The measure of damages was the issue that divided the Appellate Division (see 56 A.D.2d, at p. 500, 392 N.Y.S.2d at p. 872). The contention of Reis, Stamos, MNY and MAG, that the award of appreciation damages was legally erroneous and impermissible, is based on a principle that an executor authorized to sell is not liable for an increase in value if the breach consists only in selling for a figure less than that for which the executor should have sold. For example, Scott states:

> "The beneficiaries are not entitled to the value of the property at the time of the decree if it was not the duty of the trustee to retain the property in the trust and the breach of trust consisted merely in selling the property for too low a price" (3 Scott, Trusts (3d ed.), § 208.3, p. 1687 (emphasis added)).

> "If the trustee is guilty of a breach of trust in selling trust property for an inadequate price, he is liable for the difference between the amount he should have received and the amount which he did receive. He is not liable, however, for any subsequent rise in value of the property sold". (Id., § 208.6, pp. 1689–1690.)

A recitation of similar import appears in Comment *d* under Restatement, Trusts 2d (s 205): "d. Sale for less than value. If the trustee is authorized to sell trust property, but in breach of trust he sells it for less than he should receive, he is liable for the value of the property at the time of the sale less the amount which he received. If the breach of trust consists only in selling it for too little, he is not chargeable with the amount of any subsequent increase in value of the property under the rule stated in Clause (c), as he would be if he were not authorized to sell the property. See § 208." However, employment of "merely" and "only" as limiting words suggests that where the breach consists of some misfeasance, other than solely for selling "for too low a price" or "for too little", appreciation damages may be appropriate. Under Scott (§ 208.3, pp. 1686–1687) and the Restatement (§ 208), the trustee may be held liable for appreciation damages if it was his or her duty to retain the property, the theory being that the beneficiaries are entitled to be placed in the same position they would have been in had the breach not consisted of a sale of property that should have been retained. The same rule should apply where the breach of trust consists of a serious conflict of interest which is more than merely selling for too little.

The reason for allowing appreciation damages, where there is a duty to retain, and only date of sale damages, where there is authorization to sell, is policy oriented. If a trustee authorized to sell were subjected to a greater measure of damages he might be reluctant to sell (in which event he might run a risk if depreciation ensued). On the other hand, if there is a duty to retain and the trustee sells there is no policy reason to protect the trustee; he has not simply acted imprudently, he has violated an integral condition of the trust.

"If a trustee in breach of trust transfers trust property to a person who takes with notice of the breach of trust, and the transferee has disposed of the property (i)t seems proper to charge him with the value at the time of the decree, since if it had not been for the breach of trust the property would still have been a part of the trust estate"

(4 Scott, Trusts (3d ed.), 291.2; see, also, United States v. Dunn, 268 U.S. 121, 132, 45 S.Ct. 451, 69 L.Ed. 876). This rule of law which applies to the transferees MNY and MAG also supports the imposition of appreciation damages against Reis and Stamos, since if the Marlborough corporations are liable for such damages either as purchaser or consignees with notice, from one in breach of trust, it is only logical to hold that said executors, as sellers and consignors, are liable also pro tanto. Contrary to assertions of appellants and the dissenters at the Appellate Division, Menzel v. List, 24 N.Y.2d 91, 298 N.Y.S.2d 979, 246 N.E.2d 742, supra is authority for the allowance of appreciation damages. There, the damages involved a breach of warranty of title to a painting which at one time had been stolen from plaintiff and her husband and ultimately sold to defendant. Here, the executors, though authorized to sell, did not merely err in the amount they accepted but sold to one with whom Reis and Stamos had a self-interest. To make the injured party whole, in both instances the quantum of damages should be the same. In other words, since the paintings cannot be returned, the estate is therefore entitled to their value at the time of the decree, i.e., appreciation damages. These are not punitive damages in a true sense, rather they are damages intended to make the estate whole. Of course, as to Reis, Stamos, MNY and MAG, these damages might be considered by some to be exemplary in a sense, in that they serve as a warning to others (see Reynolds v. Pegler, 123 F.Supp. 36, 38, D.C., affd. 223 F.2d 429, 2 Cir., cert. den. 350 U.S. 846, 76 S.Ct. 80, 100 L.Ed. 754), but their true character is ascertained when viewed in the light of overriding policy considerations and in the realization that the sale and consignment were not merely sales below value but inherently wrongful transfers which should allow the owner to be made whole (see Menzel v. List, 24 N.Y.2d 91, 97, 298 N.Y.S.2d 979, 982, 246 N.E.2d 742, 744, supra; see, also, Simon v. Electrospace Corp., 28 N.Y.2d 136, 144, 320 N.Y.S.2d 225, 231, 269 N.E.2d 21, 25, supra).

Food for Thought

Are you troubled by the fact that Marlborough (a non-fiduciary) is liable for damages because of the executor's breach? Suppose Levine was the only executor, would the Gallery still have been liable?

The decree of the Surrogate imposed appreciation damages against Reis, Stamos, MNY and MAG in the amount of $7,339,464.72 computed as $9,252,000 (86 works on canvas at $90,000 each and 54 works on paper at $28,000 each) less the aggregate amounts paid the estate under the two rescinded agreements and interest. Appellants chose not to offer evidence of "present value" and the only proof furnished on the subject was that of the expert Heller whose appraisal as of January, 1974 (the month previous to that when trial commenced) on a painting-by-painting basis totaled $15,100,000. There was also testimony as to bona fide sales of other Rothkos between 1971 and 1974. Under the circumstances, it was impossible to appraise the value of the unreturned works of art with an absolute certainty and, so long as the figure arrived at had a reasonable basis of computation and was not merely speculative, possible or imaginary, the Surrogate had the right to resort to reasonable conjectures and probable estimates and to make the best approximation possible through the exercise of good judgment and common sense in arriving at that amount. This is particularly so where the conduct of wrongdoers has rendered it difficult to ascertain the damages suffered with the precision otherwise possible. Significantly, the Surrogate's factual finding as to the present value of these unreturned paintings was affirmed by the Appellate Division and, since that finding had support in the record and was not legally erroneous, it should not now be subjected to our disturbance.

* * *

We have considered the other alleged errors urged by the parties, and find those arguments to be without merit. In short, we find no basis for disturbing the result reached below.

Accordingly, the order of the Appellate Division should be affirmed, with costs to the prevailing parties against appellants, and the question certified answered in the affirmative.

BREITEL, C.J., and JASEN, GABRIELLI, JONES, WACHTLER and FUCHSBERG, JJ., concur.

Points for Discussion

1. Self-dealing

1. Suppose the sale to the Gallery by the executors was actually beneficial to the trust, would the transactions be void? Self-dealing transactions are voidable rather than void so if the transaction is beneficial the beneficiaries may allow them to stand.

2. Aside from Levine, the executors in *Rothko* all had much to gain from dealing the art through Marlborough. Suppose the benefit was more tangential? For example, may a trustee vote shares in stock held in trust in order to elect the trustee to a position in the corporation for which there is remuneration? Suppose the trustee is already an officer in a corporation, may the trustee purchase stock in the corporation which might increase the value of the corporation's stock?

3. The Uniform Trust Code's section on the duty of loyalty (§ 802(a)) requires the trustees to "administer the trust solely in the interests of the beneficiaries," but permits acts which are "a conflict between the trustee's fiduciary and personal interests" if such a transaction is approved by the court (§ 802(b)(2)). Thus, a cautious trustee should seek a court order to act if there is reason to believe that the action proposed to be undertaken might occasion a conflict of interest.

2. *The heightened duty imputed to lawyer-trustees*

Lawyer-trustees must be particularly careful to avoid breaching the duty of loyalty. Not only may it be regarded as actionable, it may violate rules of professional responsibility. See cases in McGovern, Kurtz and English, *Principles of Wills, Trusts and Estates*, 2nd ed., p. 561. An Oklahoma lawyer who drafted a trust and thereafter served as trustee was suspended from the practice of law for a year on a finding that he borrowed money from the trust and paid trustee's fees in advance. The court considered that:

> When a legal practitioner who occupies the position of trustee breaches that fiduciary obligation through mismanagement of the trust, that practitioner brings the legal profession into disrepute and, as a result, subjects himself (or herself) to bar discipline for acts contrary to prescribed standards of conduct. RGDP [Rules Governing Disciplinary Proceedings] 1.3 commands that lawyers engage in behavior that helps maintain the reputable status of the entire legal profession. Strong and unswerving commitment to the value and virtue of fiduciary loyalty is a *sine qua non* of the personal characteristics lawyers must have. A lawyer's breach of fiduciary loyalty signifies that he (or she) is incompetent to stand in the fiduciary role.

State ex rel. Oklahoma Bar Ass'n v. Clausing, 224 P.3rd 1268, 1275 (Okla. 2009).

E. The Duty to Invest Prudently

Thus far we have skirted one of the most important issues facing the trust creator: who should be selected as the trustee. As we have learned, the trustee has a variety of functions to perform, and the skill set required is multifarious. Failure to perform duties in the manner prescribed by law can lead to litigation and liability. Balance these risks with the fact that there is only a relatively modest financial incentive to serve. To be sure trustees receive fees, but the amounts are not staggeringly high. In New York, for example, a trustee of a trust with a corpus value of $2,000,000 would earn a fee of less than $10,000 per year ($9900 to be precise). (*See* SPCA 2309 which provides a sliding scale based upon trust corpus value.) If the trustee, or the trustee's firm, renders legal services to the trust and is an attorney in the state where the services are performed, legal fees can be collected in addition to trustee fees, so long as those fees are reasonable. Remember that courts often closely examine the legal fees charged by executors and trustees. So there is money to be made by serving as trustee, but it's not usually a windfall.

The creator of a trust might seek an honest individual with reasonable organizational skills to be trustee. Another trait that a creator might find desirable is financial acumen. If the trust corpus are paintings as in *Rothko*, perhaps someone who is a successful investor in stocks and bonds would not be the most qualified of fiduciaries. After all, if the trustee is empowered either expressly or by implication to exchange trust assets, to buy and sell property, some knowledge of the 'product' (the trust corpus) is essential. Suppose one does want to choose a trusted friend or relative to serve, but that person has limited financial knowledge. A financial advisor could be consulted, or a trust department of a bank. But the simple question remains what is the benchmark, what is the standard to which the trustee should be held?

Before considering the law, think about policy. What should the law demand of a trustee? Just as the person in daily life is held to the reasonable person standard, should a trustee be held to a relevant permutation of a reasonableness standard? Until the end of the twentieth century, the law required the trustee to act as a 'prudent person' would, and focused on the way in which the hypothetical prudent person would manage his or her own wealth. Today, the Uniform Prudent Investor Act (UPIA) is the law of almost all United States jurisdictions. Section 2(b) of the Act makes it clear that in selecting an investment strategy the trustee should be guided and evaluated by viewing the portfolio as a whole. The comment notes: "An investment that might be imprudent standing alone can become prudent if undertaken in sensible relation to other trust assets, or to other nontrust assets." Likewise, section 2(c) is more specific in defining precisely what a prudent investment strategy is by noting certain considerations that should be taken into account in selecting investments. Now that you have digested *Rothko*, review the guidance offered by the Uniform Act, as it is discussed and set out in Section F of Chapter 8.

We may now turn to the application of the law governing the trustee's duty of care in managing the trust property, both before and after, the adoption of the UPIA.

Estate of Janes

<u>681 N.E.2d 332 (N.Y. 1997)</u>

LEVINE, JUDGE.

Former State Senator and businessman Rodney B. Janes (testator) died on May 26, 1973, survived solely by his wife, Cynthia W. Janes, who was then 72 years of age. Testator's $3,500,000 estate consisted of a $2,500,000 stock portfolio, approximately 71% of which consisted of 13,232 shares of common stock of the Eastman Kodak Company. The Kodak stock had a date-of-death value of $1,786,733, or approximately $135 per share. Testator's 1963 will and a 1969 codicil bequeathed most of his estate to three trusts. First, the testator created a marital deduction trust consisting of approximately 50% of the estate's assets, the income of which was to be paid to Mrs. Janes for her life. In addition, it contained a generous provision for invasion of the principal for Mrs. Janes's benefit and gave her testamentary power of appointment over the remaining principal. The testator also established a charitable trust of approximately 25% of the estate's assets which directed annual distributions to selected charities. A third trust comprised the balance of the estate's assets and directed that the income therefrom be paid to Mrs. Janes for her life, with the remainder pour-

Take Note

Creator himself either had an eclectic view of diversification or was a photography buff. Should the trustee follow his lead? Does the court bear this in mind in the opinion?

ing over into the charitable trust upon her death. On June 6, 1973, the testator's will and codicil were admitted to probate. Letters testamentary issued to petitioner's predecessor, Lincoln Rochester Trust Company, and Mrs. Janes, as coexecutors, on July 3, 1973. Letters of trusteeship [were] issued to petitioner alone. By early August 1973, petitioner's trust and estate officers, Ellison Patterson and Richard Young had ascertained the estate's assets and the amount of cash needed for taxes, commissions, attorneys' fees, and specific bequests.

> **Practice Pointer**
>
> Does the scheme of the disposition suggest how the trustee should calculate an investment strategy?

In an August 9, 1973 memorandum, Patterson recommended raising the necessary cash for the foregoing administrative expenses by selling certain assets, including 800 shares of Kodak stock, and holding "the remaining issues * * * until the [t]rusts [were] funded." The memorandum did not otherwise address investment strategy in light of the evident primary objective of the testator to provide for his widow during her lifetime. In a September 5, 1973 meeting with Patterson and Young, Mrs. Janes, who had a high school education, no business training or experience, and who had never been employed, consented to the sale of some 1,200 additional shares of Kodak stock. Although Mrs. Janes was informed at the meeting that petitioner intended to retain the balance of the Kodak shares, none of the factors that would lead to an informed investment decision was discussed. At that time, the Kodak stock traded for about $139 per share; thus, the estate's 13,232 shares of the stock were worth almost $1,840,000. The September 5 meeting was the only occasion where retention of the Kodak stock or any other investment issues were taken up with Mrs. Janes.

By the end of 1973, the price of Kodak stock had fallen to about $109 per share. One year later, it had fallen to about $63 per share and, by the end of 1977, to about $51 per share. In March 1978, the price had dropped even further, to about $40 per share. When petitioner filed its initial accounting in February 1980, the remaining 11,320 shares were worth approximately $530,000, or about $47 per share. Most of the shares were used to fund the trusts in 1986 and 1987.

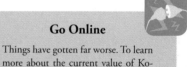

> **Go Online**
>
> Things have gotten far worse. To learn more about the current value of Kodak stock:
>
> https://finance.yahoo.com/quote/KODK/
>
> http://investor.kodak.com/

In addition to its initial accounting in 1980, petitioner filed a series of supplemental accountings that together covered the period from July 1973 through June 1994. In August 1981, petitioner sought judicial settlement of its account. Objections to the accounts were originally filed by Mrs. Janes in 1982, and subsequently by the Attorney-General on behalf of the charitable beneficiaries (collectively, "objectants"). In seeking to surcharge petitioner for losses incurred by the estate due to petitioner's imprudent retention of a high concentration of Kodak stock in the estate from July 1973 to February 1980, during which time the value of the stock had dropped to about one third of its date-of-death value, objectants asserted that petitioner's conduct violated EPTL 11–2.2(a)(1), the so-called "prudent person rule" of investment. When Mrs. Janes died in 1986, the personal representative of her estate was substituted as an objectant.

Following a trial on the objections, the Surrogate found that petitioner, under the circumstances, had acted imprudently and should have divested the estate of the high concentration of Kodak stock by August 9, 1973. The court imposed a $6,080,269 surcharge against petitioner and ordered petitioner to forfeit its commissions and attorneys' fees. In calculating the amount of the surcharge, the court adopted a "lost profits" or "market index" measure of damages espoused by objectants' expert—what the proceeds of the Kodak stock would have yielded, up to the time of trial, had they been invested in petitioner's own diversified equity fund on August 9, 1973.

The Appellate Division modified solely as to damages, holding that "the Surrogate properly found [petitioner] liable for its negligent failure to diversify and for its inattentiveness, inaction, and lack of disclosure, but that the Surrogate adopted an improper measure of damages" (Matter of Janes, 223 A.D.2d 20, 22, 643 N.Y.S.2d 972). In a comprehensive opinion by Presiding Justice M. Dolores Denman, the Court held that the Surrogate's finding of imprudence, as well as its selection of August 9, 1973 as the date by which petitioner should have divested the estate of its concentration of Kodak stock, were "well supported" by the record Id., at 29, 643 N.Y.S.2d 972. The Court rejected the Surrogate's "lost profits" or "market index" measure of damages, however, holding that the proper measure of damages was "the value of the capital that was lost"—the difference between the value of the stock at the time it should have been sold and its value when ultimately sold (Id., at 34, 643 N.Y.S.2d 972). Applying this measure, the Court reduced the surcharge to $4,065,029. We granted petitioner and objectants leave to appeal, and now affirm.

I. Petitioner's Liability

Petitioner argues that New York law does not permit a fiduciary to be surcharged for imprudent management of a trust for failure to diversify in the absence of additional elements of hazard, and that it relied upon, and complied with, this rule in administering the estate. Relying on Matter of Balfe, 152 Misc. 739, 749, 274 N.Y.S. 284, mod. 245 App.Div. 22, 280 N.Y.S. 128, petitioner claims that elements of hazard can be capsulized into deficiencies in the following investment quality factors: "(i) the capital structure of the company; (ii) the competency of its management; (iii) whether the company is a seasoned issuer of stock with a history of profitability; (iv) whether the company has a history of paying dividends; (v) whether the company is an industry leader; (vi) the expected future direction of the company's business; and (vii) the opinion of investment bankers and analysts who follow the company's stock." Evaluated under these criteria, petitioner asserts, the concentration of Kodak stock at issue in this case, that is, of an acknowledged "blue chip" security popular with investment advisors and many mutual funds, cannot be found an imprudent investment on August 9, 1973 as a matter of law. In our view, a fiduciary's duty of investment prudence in holding a concentration of one security may not be so rigidly limited.

New York followed the prudent person rule of investment during the period of petitioner's administration of the instant estate. This rule provides that "[a] fiduciary holding funds for investment may invest the same in such securities as would be acquired by prudent [persons] of discretion and intelligence in such matters who are seeking a reasonable income and the preservation of their capital" (EPTL 11–2.2[a][1]). Codified in 1970 (see, L. 1970, ch. 321), the prudent person rule's New York common-law antecedents can be traced to King v. Talbot, 40 N.Y. 76, wherein this Court stated: "[T]he trustee is bound to employ such diligence and such prudence in the care and management [of the trust], as in general, prudent men of discretion and intelligence in such matters, employ in their own like affairs.

Take Note

The 'common law' formulation. New York, subsequent to the trustees' actions in the case, adopted the Uniform Act. EPTL § 11–2.3 guides decisions made after 1/1/95.

"This necessarily excludes all speculation, all investments for an uncertain and doubtful rise in the market, and, of course, everything that does not take into view the nature and object of the trust, and the consequences of a mistake in the selection of the investment to be made. * * *

"[T]he preservation of the fund, and the procurement of a just income therefrom, are primary objects of the creation of the trust itself, and are to be primarily regarded" (id., at 85–86 [emphasis supplied]).

No precise formula exists for determining whether the prudent person standard has been violated in a particular situation; rather, the determination depends on an examination of the facts and circumstances of each case. In undertaking this inquiry, the court should engage in " 'a balanced and perceptive analysis of [the fiduciary's] consideration and action in light of the history of each individual investment, viewed at the time of its action or its omission to act' " (Matter of Donner, 82 N.Y.2d 574, 585, 606 N.Y.S.2d 137, 626 N.E.2d 922 [quoting Matter of Bank of N.Y., 35 N.Y.2d 512, 519, 364 N.Y.S.2d 164, 323 N.E.2d 700]). And, while a court should not view each act or omission aided or enlightened by hindsight, a court may, nevertheless, examine the fiduciary's conduct over the entire course of the investment in determining whether it has acted prudently. Generally, whether a fiduciary has acted prudently is a factual determination to be made by the trial court.

As the foregoing demonstrates, the very nature of the prudent person standard dictates against any absolute rule that a fiduciary's failure to diversify, in and of itself, constitutes imprudence, as well as against a rule invariably immunizing a fiduciary from its failure to diversify in the absence of some selective list of elements of hazard, such as those identified by petitioner. Indeed, in various cases, courts have determined that a fiduciary's retention of a high concentration of one asset in a trust or estate was imprudent without reference to those elements of hazard. The inquiry is simply whether, under all the facts and circumstances of the particular case, the fiduciary violated the prudent person standard in maintaining a concentration of a particular stock in the estate's portfolio of investments.

Moreover, no court has stated that the limited elements of hazard outlined by petitioner are the only factors that may be considered in determining whether a fiduciary has acted prudently in maintaining a concentrated portfolio. Again, as commentators have noted, one of the primary virtues of the prudent person rule "lies in its lack of specificity, as this permits the propriety of the trustee's investment decisions to be measured in light of the business and economic circumstances existing at the time they were made" (Laurino, Investment Responsibility of Professional Trustees, 51 St John's L Rev 717, 723 [1977] [emphasis supplied]).

Petitioner's restrictive list of hazards omits such additional factors to be considered under the prudent person rule by a trustee in weighing the propriety of any investment decision, as: "the amount of the trust estate, the situation of the beneficiaries, the trend of prices and of the cost of living, the prospect of inflation and of deflation" (Restatement [Second] of Trusts § 227, comment *e*). Other pertinent factors are the marketability of the investment and possible tax consequences (id., comment *o*). The trustee must weigh all of these investment factors as they affect the principal objects of the testator's or settlor's bounty, as between income beneficiaries and remainder persons, including decisions regarding "whether to apportion the investments between high-yield or high-growth securities" (Turano and Radigan, New York Estate Administration ch. 14, § P, at 409 [1986]).

Moreover, and especially relevant to the instant case, the various factors affecting the prudence of any particular investment must be considered in the light of the "circumstances of the trust itself rather than [merely] the integrity of the particular investment" (9C Rohan, N.Y. Civ. Prac-EPTL ¶ 11–2.2 [5], at 11–513, n. 106 [1996]). As stated in a leading treatise:

> "[t]he trustee should take into consideration the circumstances of the particular trust that he is administering, both as to the size of the trust estate and the requirements of the beneficiaries. He should consider each investment not as an isolated transaction but in its relation to the whole of the trust estate" (3 Scott, Trusts § 227.12, at 477 [4th ed]).

Our case law is entirely consistent with the foregoing authorities. Thus, in Matter of Bank of N.Y., 35 N.Y.2d 512, 364 N.Y.S.2d 164, 323 N.E.2d 700, supra, although we held that a trustee remains responsible for imprudence as to each individual investment in a trust portfolio, we stated:

> "The record of any individual investment is not to be viewed exclusively, of course, as though it were in its own water-tight compartment, since to some extent individual investment decisions may properly be affected by considerations of the performance of the fund as an entity, as in the instance, for example, of individual security decisions based in part on considerations of diversification of the fund or of capital transactions to achieve sound tax planning for the fund as a whole. The focus of inquiry, however, is nonetheless on the individual security as such and factors relating to the entire portfolio are to be weighed only along with others in reviewing the prudence of the particular investment decisions" 35 N.Y.2d, at 517, 364 N.Y.S.2d 164, 323 N.E.2d 700, supra [emphasis supplied]).

Thus, the elements of hazard petitioner relies upon as demonstrating that, as a matter of law, it had no duty to diversify, suffer from two major deficiencies under the prudent person rule. First, petitioner's risk elements too narrowly and strictly define the scope of a fiduciary's responsibility in making any individual investment decision, and the factors a fiduciary must consider in determining the propriety of a given investment.

A second deficiency in petitioner's elements of hazard list is that all of the factors relied upon by petitioner go to the propriety of an individual investment "exclusively * * * as though it were in its own water-tight compartment" (Matter of Bank of N.Y., supra, at 517, 364 N.Y.S.2d 164, 323 N.E.2d 700), which would encourage a fiduciary to treat each investment as an isolated transaction rather than "in its relation to the whole of the trust estate" (3 Scott, 53 op. cit., at 477). Thus, petitioner's criteria for elements of hazard would apply irrespective of the concentration of the investment security under consideration in the portfolio. That is, the existence of any of the elements of risk specified by petitioner in a given corporate security would militate against the investment even in a diversified portfolio, obviating any need to consider concentration as a reason to divest or refrain from investing. This ignores the market reality that, with respect to some investment vehicles, concentration itself may create or add to risk, and essentially takes lack of diversification out of the prudent person equation altogether.

Likewise, contrary to petitioner's alternative attack on the decisions below, neither the Surrogate nor the Appellate Division based their respective rulings holding petitioner liable on any absolute duty of a fiduciary to diversify. Rather, those courts determined that a surcharge was appropriate because maintaining a concentration in Kodak stock, under the circumstances presented, violated certain critical obligations of a fiduciary in making investment decisions under the prudent person rule. First, petitioner failed to consider the investment in Kodak stock in relation to the entire portfolio of the estate (see, Matter of Bank of N.Y., supra, at 517; 3, 364 N.Y.S.2d 164, 323 N.E.2d 700 Scott, op. cit.), i.e., whether the Kodak concentration itself created or added to investment risk. The objectants' experts testified that even high quality growth stocks, such as Kodak, possess some degree of volatility because their market value is tied so closely to earnings projections (cf., Turano and Radigan, op. cit., at 409). They further opined that the investment risk arising from that volatility is significantly exacerbated when a portfolio is heavily concentrated in one such growth stock.

Second, the evidence revealed that, in maintaining an investment portfolio in which Kodak represented 71% of the estate's stock holdings, and the balance was largely in other growth stocks, petitioner paid insufficient attention to the needs and interests of the testator's 72-year-old widow, the life beneficiary of three quarters of his estate, for whose comfort, support and anticipated increased medical expenses the testamentary trusts were evidently created. Testimony by petitioner's investment manager, and by the objectants' experts, disclosed that the annual yield on Kodak stock in 1973 was approximately 1.06%, and that the aggregate annual income from all estate stockholdings was $43,961, a scant 1.7% of the $2.5 million estate securities portfolio. Thus, retention of a high concentration of Kodak jeopardized the interests of the primary income beneficiary of the estate and led to the eventual need to substantially invade the principal of the marital testamentary trust.

Lastly, there was evidence in the record to support the findings below that, in managing the estate's investments, petitioner failed to exercise due care and the skill it held itself out as possessing as a corporate fiduciary (see, Matter of Donner, 82 N.Y.2d, at 578, 606 N.Y.S.2d 137, 626 N.E.2d 922, supra; Restatement [Second] of Trusts § 227, Comment on Clause [a]). Notably, there was proof that petitioner (1) failed initially to undertake a formal analysis of the estate and establish an investment plan consistent with the testator's primary objectives; (2) failed to follow petitioner's own internal trustee review protocol during the administration of the estate, which advised special caution and attention in cases of portfolio concentration of as little as 20%; and (3) failed to conduct more than routine reviews of the Kodak holdings in this estate, without considering alternative investment choices, over a seven-year period of steady decline in the value of the stock.

Since, thus, there was evidence in the record to support the foregoing affirmed findings of imprudence on the part of petitioner, the determination of liability must be affirmed (Matter of Donner, 82 N.Y.2d, at 584, 606 N.Y.S.2d 137, 626 N.E.2d 922, supra).

II. Date of Divestiture

As we have noted, in determining whether a fiduciary has acted prudently, a court may examine a fiduciary's conduct throughout the entire period during which the investment at issue was held (see, Matter of Donner, 82 N.Y.2d, at 585–586, 606 N.Y.S.2d 137, 626 N.E.2d 922, supra). The court may then determine, within that period, the "reasonable time" within which divesture of the imprudently held investment should have occurred (see, Matter of Weston, 91 N.Y. 502, 510–511). What constitutes a reasonable time will vary from case to case and is not fixed or arbitrary (see, id., at 510–511). The test remains "the diligence and prudence of prudent and intelligent [persons] in the management of their own affairs" (id., at 511 [citations omitted]). Thus, in Donner, we upheld both the Surrogate's examination of the fiduciary's conduct throughout the entire period during which the investment at issue was retained in finding liability, and the Surrogate's selection of the date of the testator's death as the time when the trustee should have divested the estate of its substantial holdings in high-risk securities (82 N.Y.2d, at 585–586, 606 N.Y.S.2d 137, 626 N.E.2d 922, supra).

Again, there is evidentiary support in the record for the trial court's finding, affirmed by the Appellate Division, that a prudent fiduciary would have divested the estate's stock portfolio of its high concentration of Kodak stock by August 9, 1973, thereby exhausting our review powers on this issue. Petitioner's own internal documents and correspondence, as well as the testimony of Patterson, Young, and objectants' experts, establish that by that date, petitioner had all the information a prudent investor would have needed to conclude that the percentage of Kodak stock in the estate's stock portfolio was excessive and should have been reduced significantly, particularly in light of the estate's over-all investment portfolio and the financial requirements of Mrs. Janes and the charitable beneficiaries.

III. Damages

Finally, as to the calculation of the surcharge, we conclude that the Appellate Division correctly rejected the Surrogate's "lost profits" or "market index" measure of damages. Where, as here, a fiduciary's imprudence consists solely of negligent retention of assets it should have sold, the measure of damages is the value of the lost capital (see, Matter of Garvin, 256 N.Y. 518, 521, 177 N.E. 24; see also, Matter of Donner, 82 N.Y.2d, at 586, 606 N.Y.S.2d 137, 626 N.E.2d 922, supra). Thus, the Surrogate's reliance on Matter of Rothko in imposing a "lost profit" measure of damages is inapposite, since in that case the fiduciary's misconduct consisted of deliberate self-dealing and faithless transfers of trust property (43 N.Y.2d, at 321–322, 401 N.Y.S.2d 449, 372 N.E.2d 291, supra).

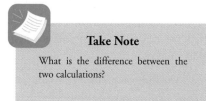

Take Note

What is the difference between the two calculations?

In imposing liability upon a fiduciary on the basis of the capital lost, the court should determine the value of the stock on the date it should have been sold, and subtract from that figure the proceeds from the sale of the stock or, if the stock is still retained by the estate, the value of the stock at the time of the accounting (see, Matter of Garvin, supra, at 521, 177 N.E. 24; Matter of Frame, 245 App.Div. 675, 686, 284 N.Y.S. 153 6 Warren's Heaton, Surrogates' Courts § 100.01[4][b][i] [misnumbered in original as § 101.01[4][b][i2], at 100–9 [6th ed. rev. 1997]). Whether interest is awarded, and at what rate, is a matter within the discretion of the trial court (see, Woerz v. Schumacher, 161 N.Y. 530, 538, 56 N.E. 72, rearg. denied 163 N.Y. 610, 57 N.E. 1128; King v. Talbot, 40 N.Y., at 95, supra; CPLR 5001[a]; SCPA 2211[1]; 6 Warren's Heaton, op. cit.; 3 Scott, op. cit., § 207, at 255–256). Dividends and other income attributable to the retained assets should offset any interest awarded (see, Matter of Garvin, supra, at 521, 177 N.E. 24).

Here, contradicted expert testimony established that application of this measure of damages resulted in a figure of $4,065,029, which includes prejudgment interest at the legal rate, compounded from August 9, 1973 to October 1, 1994. The Appellate Division did not abuse its discretion in adding to that figure prejudgment interest from October 1, 1994 through August 17, 1995, $326,302.66 previously received by petitioner for commissions and attorneys' fees, plus postjudgment interest, costs, and disbursements.

Accordingly, the order of the Appellate Division should be affirmed, without costs.

Kaye, C.J., and Titone, Bellacosa, Smith, Ciparick and Wesley, JJ., concur.

Points for Discussion

1. *Investment strategies*

1. Now that you have read the opinion and you accept that the trustees have to pay out in excess of $ 4,000,000 for their 'buy and hold' strategy, what would you advise similarly situated trustees? Sell, but buy what? Are courts really equipped to substitute their own after-the-fact judgment about proper investment strategies? There is a bewildering plethora of financial

advice spawned by the financial services industry and served up by the financial services media. Much of it is contradictory. Like those who frequent the race tracks and the slots, investment counsellors talk more frequently about their winners than they do about their losers.

2. On the other hand, diversification is easier to accomplish in the twenty-first century than it was in the twentieth. The proliferation of mutual funds and exchange traded funds allow a trustee to hold a basket of stocks and bonds. But the question of when to move from one sector or mutual fund manager to another is still an issue of judgment. Is a stock index fund always a 'prudent' choice?

2. Pursuing the creator's investment strategy?

Is it all relevant that Mr. Janes thought Kodak was a stock in which one could put all eggs in one basket? Suppose that six months after Mr. Janes's death Kodak's share price collapsed, would the trustees have been chargeable for not immediately diversifying? Recall Mr. Smathers' view of the market for New York City office real estate in Chapter 8.

With all this in mind consider a recent New York case applying the Prudent Investor Rule.

In the Matter of Michael Duffy

25 Misc.3d 901 (N.Y. Surr. Ct. 2009), aff'd 79 A.D.3d 1732, 913 N.Y.S.2d 627 (N.Y. App. Div. 2010)

EDMUND A. CALVARUSO, J.

[We have omitted the discussion of the actual investments]

* * *

Fiduciaries will not be held responsible for investment losses unless the loss was due to fiduciary negligence. Fiduciaries are not to be "insurers or guarantors", Estate of Cuddeback, 168 Misc. 698, 700, 6 N.Y.S.2d 493 (1938); they are not to be surcharged for losses stemming from unforeseeable events. Estate of Bunker, 184 Misc. 316, 56 N.Y.S.2d 746 (1944), Estate of Newhoff, 107 Misc.2d 589, 435 N.Y.S.2d 632 (1980). Because the standard of prudence looks to the fiduciary's actions, good faith is paramount, and mere errors in judgment will be free from surcharge: "The distinction between negligence and mere error of judgment must be borne in mind. Trustees acting honestly, with ordinary prudence and within the limits of their trust, are not liable for mere errors of judgment' ". Estate of Clark, 257 N.Y. 132, 137, 177 N.E. 397 (1931). See also, Estate of Bunker, supra, Estate of Cuddeback, supra, Estate of Kilmer, 18 Misc.2d 60, 186 N.Y.S.2d 120 (1959). Objectant must prove that the losses resulted from the "trustee's negligence or failure to exercise that degree of care which prudent men of discretion and intelligence in such matters employ in their own like affairs." Matter of Hahn, 93 A.D.2d 583, 586, 462 N.Y.S.2d 924 (1983). As the Hahn case holds, the proof elements of fiduciary investment liability are similar to a simple tort case. Wherein an objectant pleads that a fiduciary negligently managed the corpus, the fiduciary can be surcharged to offset the objectant's loss, provided that the objectant has proven the necessary elements of investment negligence: a breach of duty causing a loss to the beneficiary. In an accounting proceeding, the fiduciary has the primary burden to establish an account of his or her activities. This burden is met by the submission of a prima facie accounting, at which point the burden shifts to the objectant to prove that the accounting is somehow insufficient. Estate of Schnare, 191 A.D.2d 859, 594 N.Y.S.2d 827 (1993). Proof of investment negligence is therefore objectant's burden to bear. Estate of Cuddeback, 168 Misc. 698, 6 N.Y.S.2d 493 (1938).

Duty

The Prudent Investor Act, EPTL 11–2.3, guides investment decisions of fiduciaries made after January 1, 1995. It will set the standard for duty with regard to the fiduciary's investment decisions in this case. There are four primary requirements for the duty's "prudent investor standard" in EPTL 11–2.3(b)(3).

First, the fiduciary must decide within a reasonable amount of time, whether to "retain or dispose of the initial assets". EPTL 11–2.3(b)(3)(D). Second, the fiduciary must follow an investment strategy in accordance with the need to make distributions and the balance between risk and rate of return. EPTL 11–2.3(b)(3)(A). Thirdly, as a part of developing this investment strategy, the fiduciary must consider various factors, including:

> size of portfolio, nature and duration of fiduciary relationship, liquidity of estate and distribution requirements, general economic conditions, inflation/deflation, tax consequences, role of each investment within the portfolio, expected total return, needs of beneficiaries (to extent reasonably known by the fiduciary). EPTL 11–2.3(b)(3)(B)

Lastly, the Prudent Investor Act requires diversification as a default provision, though the fiduciary can elect not to diversify, if he or she "reasonably determines that it is in the interests of the beneficiaries not to diversify". EPTL 11–2.3(b)(3)(C). The statute does not, however, define "diversify".

Breach

Duffy's proof specifically addressed the components of the Prudent Investor Act. His argument spells out why he believes that his actions were in compliance with the law. He testified that he made a plan shortly after Letters were issued: to distribute the stock in kind to Stone. Decedent's Will did not restrict his investment decisions, but the stocks which were in her estate were stocks she had owned, as invested, for years. Stocks owned by the decedent undergo a somewhat softer analysis: retention of a portfolio owned by decedent may be prudent even where the independent purchase of the same stocks by the fiduciary may not. Stone, being considerably younger than his wife, was the measuring life for the investment horizon, and the stocks were kept as invested given Stone's age and Duffy's plan to distribute them in kind. The portfolio had met the income needs of Stone and the decedent for years prior to decedent's death. The portfolio itself was a varied mixture of stocks, but seventy-five percent of the corpus's value was comprised of stock from only six companies. Duffy argues that the portfolio was diversified, just aggressively invested, and not imprudent under the circumstances. Stone offered proof to suggest that the portfolio was not properly diversified without an inclusion of conservative investments, such as cash. However, Duffy countered this by showing that there were other assets present in the estate, and when the estate as a whole was reviewed, the asset mix was much broader. Duffy argued that during the time of his estate administration, the market was undergoing a lengthy and steep decline, partially due to two large external events which happened during this time, both unforeseeable and both having consequences which became difficult for investors to navigate. Fiduciaries holding stocks in times of economic stress and falling markets are to be shown "leniency". The court holds that under the totality of the circumstances, Duffy has put forth a prima facie accounting as well as prima facie evidence of compliance with the Prudent Investor Act.

Stone argues that Duffy performed little to no analysis as to the investments, communicated rarely, if ever, with Stone, and continued to ignore the portfolio even after the stock market decreased drastically during his tenure. Stone argues that the portfolio was improperly invested for a short term time horizon, which was the proper length of time for the fiduciary to consider. He argues that Duffy's nonfeasance caused a drastic loss to the estate for which he should be surcharged.

Duffy is not excused from the demonstrated lack of communication with Stone, though this complaint would appear to be a complaint against bad practice rather than imprudence under the Prudent Investor Act. Where a fiduciary has decided to retain an aggressively held portfolio for an in kind distribution to a beneficiary, the fiduciary should want to ensure that adequate communication with the ultimate beneficiary is achieved. Here, though the evidence showed that communications were infrequent and eventually antagonistic, Stone was aware of Duffy's initial plan and had no apparent objection to it until after the market began a decline. Nor did Stone take it upon himself to solicit any additional communications with Duffy or make any requests for liquidation. See, Estate of Clark, where the beneficiaries did not communicate to the fiduciary any desire for him to sell the stock, which was a consideration leading to the ultimate holding that the fiduciary was not liable.

With respect to the work performed by Duffy in evaluating the portfolio and other factors and developing an investment strategy, it is not clear how much consideration he gave to other investment strategies besides retention plus in-kind distribution. Though this court has found prima facie evidence of compliance with the Prudent Investor Act, it strongly cautions that there is a critical line between (a) deciding upon retention after considering all facts and circumstances according to the statute, and (b) merely doing nothing with respect to the assets at issue. Fiduciaries must remain "actively vigilant" in their evaluation of the investments. In Re First National Bank, 25 N.Y.S.2d 221, 225 (1941). A fiduciary's conduct is the relevant inquiry, and as long as it is within "substantial compliance", EPTL 11–2.3(b)(1), with the prudent investor standard, liability will be prevented. Duffy's evidence supporting his decades-old friendship and professional relationship with the decedent and his thorough knowledge of her finances, coupled with his decision to continue what he believed to be her goal to retain and eventually distribute in kind the stocks for the benefit of Stone, and his discussions of the stocks with a broker once the market suffered a significant loss, is sufficient to show 'substantial compliance'; and, thus, that his actions fell on the non-liability side of that line.

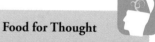

Take Note

Everyone can make better investment decisions if they knew today what would happen tomorrow. Has the court struck a balance between the beneficiary's desire to be shielded from risk and the reality that the trustee's decision on investment strategy is a complex one?

Stone's primary theory of the case for liability was that Duffy breached the duty set forth by the Prudent Investor Act because rather than retaining the stocks, he should have (a) sold the stocks "immediately", and (b), converted them to cash and kept them as such until the estate was closed. This line of reasoning comprised his entire case. It hinged upon the testimony of Duffy himself, plus an expert witness who by profession was a certified financial planner. Stone's expert witness testified that cash was the proper method of investment for short term investment horizons, defined as eighteen months or less. Stone's expert further testified since that an estate, by its nature, is a short-term investment recommendations should be applied to corpus management in estates.

Stone is correct that fiduciary investment decisions are supposed to take into account the length of time that the entity (the "estimated duration of the fiduciary relationship" EPTL 11–2.3(b)(3)(B)) will exist. On uncomplicated estates, this would suggest that, generally speaking, a more conservative approach to holding funds is warranted. Time horizon, however, is not the only factor which the Prudent Investor Act references for the fiduciary to consider. Stone's theory of the case seeks to place time horizon at the forefront of a fiduciary's considerations, to the near exclusion of the rest of the factors listed in the statute. The court does not believe that such a holding would comport with the intent of the statute. This is especially true considering that the Prudent Investor Act specifies for the first time that diversification of investments is to be the

Food for Thought

Is this law or merely common sense? Does the Uniform Act specifically prioritize the stipulated factors which the fiduciary should consider in exercising judgment?

default for fiduciaries, EPTL 11–2.3(b)(3)(D), and Stone is actually arguing here that prudence required the opposite: an all cash portfolio. If the court were to adopt Stone's approach, it would risk setting precedent under the Prudent Investor Act that uncomplicated estates should be liquidated and placed into cash accounts, a precedent which seems at odds with the intent of the statute as well as sanctioned practice. Estate of Buck, 184 Misc. 29, 52 N.Y.S.2d 294 (1944). Indeed, in times of rising markets, fiduciaries have been held liable when estate funds were invested too conservatively and provided no return. Estate of Newswander, 15 Misc.2d 148, 178 N.Y.S.2d 829 (1958). While the conversion to cash might be good practice in many estates, the court does not interpret the Prudent Investor Act to impart such a potentially unyielding requirement on all estates.

Furthermore, the court finds that Stone's assertion that Duffy should have sold the stocks "immediately" is against the weight of the evidence. Duffy's expert witness, an attorney with considerable experience in representing fiduciaries of estates, testified that it would not be prudent to sell estate assets before at least the passage of two to four months. As he testified, this time is needed to ascertain the size of the estate and its liabilities, among other considerations. Neither Stone nor his expert never defined "immediately", so the court must define it as meaning nothing other than the day that Letters Testamentary were issued to Mr. Duffy, the soonest Duffy had the power to sell. The court finds this assertion to be inherently unreasonable, an unrealistic expectation of fiduciaries. In older cases, twelve to eighteen months was seen as a reasonable time period to liquidate stock. Estate of Cuddeback, 168 Misc. 698, 6 N.Y.S.2d 493 (1938), Estate of Kent, 146 Misc. 155, 261 N.Y.S. 698 (1932), Estate of Buck, 184 Misc. 29, 52 N.Y.S.2d 294 (1944) (though parenthetically, this court believes such a timeline would be too long in many modern circumstances). Furthermore, the Fourth Department in Matter of Hahn held that there is no duty to sell as soon as possible, 93 A.D.2d 583, 462 N.Y.S.2d 924 (1983).

Stocks should not be negligently retained, but nor should they be sold rashly. Estate of Clark, 257 N.Y. 132, 177 N.E. 397 (1931). A delay in sale in and of itself will not equate to liability: "[the fiduciary] will not ordinarily beheld personally responsible if it appears, in the light of after events, that he would have displayed better judgment or have produced a more favorable result if he had sold earlier". Estate of Kent, 146 Misc. 155, 161, 261 N.Y.S. 698 (1932).

Stone's expert lacked credibility because he sought to apply his idea of prudent liquidation time lines for brokers and financial planners to an estate relationship. Duffy's expert, on the other hand, was addressing prudence solely with respect to estate administration, and as such his testimony is more relevant and due more weight. Finally, Stone's witness was a poor witness overall. Through much of his testimony he was evasive, vague or nonresponsive. Accordingly, the court disregards his testimony. Without the critical evidence from his expert, Stone's entire theory of the case becomes unsupported.

In the alternative that his "immediate conversion to cash" theory was rejected, Stone has asked for the Surrogate to select a reasonable date by which Duffy ought to have liquidated the portfolio. Though the Appellate Division overturned a sua sponte date selection in a prior fiduciary liability case, Matter of Dumont, 26 A.D.3d 824, 809 N.Y.S.2d 360 (2006), Stone has argued that this holding does not apply here because he has specifically not plead a date at all, consenting to allow the Surrogate to select one. The court does not adopt this argument. The Appellate Division's holding in Dumont was based upon concern of fairness toward the defending fiduciary, and as such, its requirement is not one which an objectant can waive.

Even if the court believed that the procedural holding in Dumont should be reconsidered, given the powers of the Surrogate discussed in Stortecky v. Mazzone, 85 N.Y.2d 518, 626 N.Y.S.2d 733, 650 N.E.2d 391 (1995), Stone is still unable to succeed. Though counsel has argued in closing papers that August 29, 2001, the date on which Duffy requested that Merrill Lynch transfer the account into an estate account, was a proper date for divestiture, this date was not proven such at trial. The proofs contain no date which the preponderance of the evidence shows to be a more reasonable date of divestiture than October 7, 2002, the date of the actual transfer.

Without any proof as to the reasonable timing of any other proposed dates of divestiture, Stone's request that the court pick a date among the various dates and corresponding valuations of the portfolio entered into the record becomes a request for a hindsight determination, and is impermissible as a basis for liability.

Causation

Though Stone did not succeed in showing that the Prudent Investor Act required Duffy to convert the estate immediately to cash, Stone's proof did show some nonfeasance on the part of Duffy, such that a brief discussion of causation is warranted. Any proof of breach advanced by the Stone cannot lead to surcharge without the establishment of a link between the fiduciary's negligence and the loss suffered by the estate. Matter of Hahn, 93 A.D.2d 583, 462 N.Y.S.2d 924 (1983). Duffy's expert, a forensic economist, offered testimony to show that decedent's portfolio (as held by the estate and later distributed to Stone) had a "beta" of .94, meaning that the portfolio's performance correlated extremely closely with the rise and fall of the market itself: "for every 1% move in the S & P 500 total return index, that portfolio would move 0.94%" (Mulcahey, Trans. Pg. 372). It is logical to conclude that the losses experienced by the estate's portfolio were due to drops in the market itself. To hold the Duffy liable for the portfolio's losses when the portfolio's valuation fluctuation almost exactly followed the market would be akin to expecting him to have had the prescience to invest and outperform the market, an unreasonable requirement the law does not expect. EPTL 11–2.3(b)(1).

> **Food for Thought**
>
> Would this statement incline a trustee to opt for an index fund? Don't we want our trustees to beat the index? Maybe we do but maybe they ought not to be chargeable if they do not.

Points for Discussion

1. What really is the standard?

1. It is probably the case that good faith on the part of the trustee in selecting investments is not sufficient to satisfy the standard under the Prudent Investor Act. According to comment *b* of the Restatement of Trusts (Third) § 77, those trustees without expertise ought to rely on 'competent guidance and assistance' to meet the standards. Does reading these two cases in which the trustee was not the trust department of a major financial institution make you more inclined to advise creator to select a corporate fiduciary? On the other hand, what does the collapse of Bear Stearns and Lehman tell you about the competence of financial services firms?

2. A problem which the 'prudent investor' must frequently address is the fact that the time horizons of the beneficiaries may differ. Do you think that that fact influenced the relative leniency of the court in *Duffy*?

2. *The particular dilemma raised by closely-held corporations/family businesses*

Some trust corpuses are comprised of controlling shares of family business or other closely held corporation. Is the prudent investor shielded from liability if she decides to maintain controlling shares at the expense of diversification? Section 3 requires diversification unless the trustee reasonably determines that, because of special circumstances, the purposes of the trust are better served without diversifying. The comment refers to family business: "Circumstances can, however, overcome the duty to diversify. . . . The wish to retain a family business is another situation in which the purposes of the trust sometimes override the conventional duty to diversify."

F.   Multiple Beneficiaries

Most trusts have more than a single beneficiary. If you recall the simple Ward Cleaver Lifetime Trust, Ward has a life interest in the trust and his interest is followed by one in June. Thereafter the corpus is subject to a remainder in their issue (or alternatively) a special power of appointment in June. Finally there is the limitation to Wally and the Beaver as takers in default of appointment. Thus, even this quite simple trust has multiple beneficiaries whose enjoyment of the trust property occurs at different times

Decisions made by the trustee may have effects upon the interests of these successive parties. For example, June has the right to receive income from the trust during her life. Suppose in order to increase the income stream the trustee buys a high yield bond with interest payments of 10% with a maturity in ten years. Even if the bond's principal is repaid at the end of the term, inflation has eroded the principal's value. The children's interest has in some sense been sacrificed for the benefit of June's interest. If the trustee bought a Treasury Bond known as TIPS for the term of the trust the interest would have been much more modest, but at the time the bond's principal would be repaid the value would have been adjusted to account for inflation. Thus, in the first example, while the bond would be repaid at its face value, the purchasing power of the sum would have declined; in the second example, the purchasing power is preserved.

This example merely scratches the surface of the varying types of financial products that a trustee might select. While the average person in accordance with Modern Portfolio Theory might strive to maximize overall return, segmenting interests presents a difficulty to trustees. What appears to be an 'overall' beneficial strategy might favor the interest of one beneficiary over another.

The interests of successive beneficiaries can conflict in ways that go beyond the choice of an investment strategy by the trustee. Consider a simple trust to pay the income generated by the trust property to A and on A's death the trust terminates and the trustee is to distribute the trust property to B. If this is not a unitrust, the "income" that is distributable to A will include dividends on equity investments (stocks, usually), interest on debt (usually bonds) and rents on real property. A trustee, however, may find that some receipts are not so easily categorized. Some typical examples are a very large, one-time, dividend paid by a corporation to its stockholders (as opposed to the regular dividends usually paid every three months). Is such a payment "income" to be distributed to the income beneficiary, or is it so large relative to the value of the corporation that it should be treated as part of the trust's investment in the corporation and should be added to the trust principal? What if the dividend is paid not in cash but in stock of the corporation? Should the stock received be added to principal—after all, it is an ownership interest in the corporation—or is it only a substitute for a cash distribution and thus its value should be distributed to the income beneficiary?

The trustee also has to pay the expense of administering the trust. There are taxes to be paid on income earned by the trust property and real estate held by the trust, fees paid to accountants and lawyers, and of course the trustee's commissions. What part of these expenses should be paid from the income received by the trust and what part by liquidating principal investments and using the cash received to pay the bills? The issue is usually described as a question of how to allocate receipts and disbursements between income and principal.

The terms of the trust may give the trustee instructions on how to deal with allocation of receipts and disbursements. Of course, if the trust is a unitrust, the problems are much less pressing. Because all beneficiaries, both present and future, benefit from an increase in the value of the trust property it matters less whether a dividend paid in stock is allocated to principal or income when the current beneficiary is entitled to a distribution of a percentage of the value of the trust property.

In the centuries-long history of the law of trusts, however, unitrusts are a new development. It is not surprising, therefore, that for many decades, state statutes have included default rules dealing with the allocation issue, almost always closely based on the Uniform Principal and Income Act (hereafter UPIA). (A new version, the Uniform Fiduciary Income and Principal Act (hereafter UFIPA) was promulgated by the Uniform Law Commission in 2018 and may come to supplant the earlier version.) The Act (and its successor) provide a long list of rules for allocating receipts and disbursements in the absence of trust terms addressing the particular problem. Not every situation will be addressed by the rules in the Act so Section 103 of the Act sets forth the general principles trustees must follow in administering trusts. The provision codifies the general law: a trustee must administer a trust impartially, at least to the extent the creator of the trust did not provide otherwise in the trust terms, and impartially means what is fair and reasonable with respect to all of the beneficiaries.

UPIA § 103. Fiduciary Duties; General Principles

    (a)   In allocating receipts and disbursements to or between principal and income, and with respect to any matter within the scope of [Articles] 2 and 3, a fiduciary:

        (1)   shall administer a trust or estate in accordance with the terms of the trust or the will, even if there is a different provision in this [Act];

        (2)   may administer a trust or estate by the exercise of a discretionary power of administration given to the fiduciary by the terms of the trust or the will, even

if the exercise of the power produces a result different from a result required or permitted by this [Act];

(3) shall administer a trust or estate in accordance with this [Act] if the terms of the trust or the will do not contain a different provision or do not give the fiduciary a discretionary power of administration; and

(4) shall add a receipt or charge a disbursement to principal to the extent that the terms of the trust and this [Act] do not provide a rule for allocating the receipt or disbursement to or between principal and income.

(b) In exercising the power to adjust under Section 104(a) or a discretionary power of administration regarding a matter within the scope of this [Act], whether granted by the terms of a trust, a will, or this [Act], a fiduciary shall administer a trust or estate impartially, based on what is fair and reasonable to all of the beneficiaries, except to the extent that the terms of the trust or the will clearly manifest an intention that the fiduciary shall or may favor one or more of the beneficiaries. A determination in accordance with this [Act] is presumed to be fair and reasonable to all of the beneficiaries.

The UPIA introduced a new concept into the law of trust administration: the power to adjust. We have already discussed in Section F.3 of Chapter 8 the difficulties trustees face in making investments that produce sufficient income as traditionally defined. One answer to that dilemma is the unitrust, described in Section F.4 of Chapter 8. The power to adjust is another device trustees can use to carry out the duty to treat income and remainder beneficiaries impartially by making decisions that are just and reasonable to all beneficiaries. The power to adjust authorizes the trustee to treat some of the appreciation in the trust principal as income and some income as trust principal if that is necessary to administer the trust impartially. The power to adjust is a default rule that can be negated by the express terms of the trust (subsection (f)). The new UFIPA also includes the power to adjust but makes it more widely available by removing the preconditions in subsection (a) below. Under UFIPA § 203(a) the power to adjust may be used if the fiduciary determines "the exercise of the power to adjust will assist the fiduciary to administer the trust or estate impartially."

Anecdotal evidence indicates the power to adjust has proven to be very popular with some corporate trustees. The same sort of evidence shows that for some corporate trustees and financial advisors, the unitrust is more popular than the power to adjust.

UPIA § 104. Trustee's Power to Adjust

(a) A trustee may adjust between principal and income to the extent the trustee considers necessary if the trustee invests and manages trust assets as a prudent investor, the terms of the trust describe the amount that may or must be distributed to a beneficiary by referring to the trust's income, and the trustee determines, after applying the rules in Section 103(a), that the trustee is unable to comply with Section 103(b).

(b)   In deciding whether and to what extent to exercise the power conferred by subsection (a), a trustee shall consider all factors relevant to the trust and its beneficiaries, including the following factors to the extent they are relevant:

(1)   the nature, purpose, and expected duration of the trust;

(2)   the intent of the settlor;

(3)   the identity and circumstances of the beneficiaries;

(4)   the needs for liquidity, regularity of income, and preservation and appreciation of capital;

(5)   the assets held in the trust; the extent to which they consist of financial assets, interests in closely held enterprises, tangible and intangible personal property, or real property; the extent to which an asset is used by a beneficiary; and whether an asset was purchased by the trustee or received from the settlor;

(6)   the net amount allocated to income under the other sections of this [Act] and the increase or decrease in the value of the principal assets, which the trustee may estimate as to assets for which market values are not readily available;

(7)   whether and to what extent the terms of the trust give the trustee the power to invade principal or accumulate income or prohibit the trustee from invading principal or accumulating income, and the extent to which the trustee has exercised a power from time to time to invade principal or accumulate income;

(8)   the actual and anticipated effect of economic conditions on principal and income and effects of inflation and deflation; and

(9)   the anticipated tax consequences of an adjustment.

(c)   A trustee may not make an adjustment:

(1)   that diminishes the income interest in a trust that requires all of the income to be paid at least annually to a spouse and for which an estate tax or gift tax marital deduction would be allowed, in whole or in part, if the trustee did not have the power to make the adjustment;

(2)   that reduces the actuarial value of the income interest in a trust to which a person transfers property with the intent to qualify for a gift tax exclusion;

(3)   that changes the amount payable to a beneficiary as a fixed annuity or a fixed fraction of the value of the trust assets;

(4)   from any amount that is permanently set aside for charitable purposes under a will or the terms of a trust unless both income and principal are so set aside;

(5)   if possessing or exercising the power to make an adjustment causes an individual to be treated as the owner of all or part of the trust for income tax purposes, and the individual would not be treated as the owner if the trustee did not possess the power to make an adjustment;

(6) if possessing or exercising the power to make an adjustment causes all or part of the trust assets to be included for estate tax purposes in the estate of an individual who has the power to remove a trustee or appoint a trustee, or both, and the assets would not be included in the estate of the individual if the trustee did not possess the power to make an adjustment;

(7) if the trustee is a beneficiary of the trust; or

(8) if the trustee is not a beneficiary, but the adjustment would benefit the trustee directly or indirectly. . . .

(f) Terms of a trust that limit the power of a trustee to make an adjustment between principal and income do not affect the application of this section unless it is clear from the terms of the trust that the terms are intended to deny the trustee the power of adjustment conferred by subsection (a).

Practice Problem

A friend has asked you to be successor trustee of the friend's revocable trust, taking office at your friend's death. The trust continues after your friend's death to pay income to the friend's surviving spouse until the spouse's death at which time the trust terminates and the trust property is distributed outright to the couple's issue by representation. At this time the couple has two children and five grandchildren. The friend's spouse is a bit younger than your friend and according to the actuarial tables will survive your friend by 10 years (you are younger than either spouse and can be expected to outlive both). Would you prefer that the trust become a unitrust after your friend's death or would you rather rely on the power to adjust?

G. Duty to Account

In the *Duffy* case, the court had to address the issue of rancor between trustee and beneficiary and in particular an alleged failure on the part of the trustee to communicate with the beneficiary. See also *McNeil v. McNeil* in Section F of Chapter 8. The court concluded that Duffy had engaged in a "bad practice." That bad practice may have violated the trustee's duty to inform. The duty to inform trust beneficiaries of actions undertaken by the trustee is essential because if the beneficiaries are not made aware of decisions of a trustee it would be very difficult for beneficiaries to hold trustees to their fiduciary obligations. On request, the trustee must furnish beneficiaries with information about past actions and contemplated future action. Under some circumstances, trustees may be required to produce documents, for example evidence of actual ownership of property said to be held in trust.

In order to satisfy the duty to inform, the trustee must keep records. Upon request, the trustee must render an account. State law differs on the extent of the obligation. The Uniform Trust Code provides a model.

UTC § 813. Duty to Inform And Report

(a) A trustee shall keep the qualified beneficiaries of the trust reasonably informed about the administration of the trust and of the material facts necessary for them to protect their interests. Unless unreasonable under the circumstances, a trustee shall promptly respond to a beneficiary's request for information related to the administration of the trust.

(b) A trustee:

   (1) upon request of a beneficiary, shall promptly furnish to the beneficiary a copy of the trust instrument;

   (2) within 60 days after accepting a trusteeship, shall notify the qualified beneficiaries of the acceptance and of the trustee's name, address, and telephone number;

   (3) within 60 days after the date the trustee acquires knowledge of the creation of an irrevocable trust, or the date the trustee acquires knowledge that a formerly revocable trust has become irrevocable, whether by the death of the settlor or otherwise, shall notify the qualified beneficiaries of the trust's existence, of the identity of the settlor or settlors, of the right to request a copy of the trust instrument, and of the right to a trustee's report as provided in subsection (c); and

   (4) shall notify the qualified beneficiaries in advance of any change in the method or rate of the trustee's compensation.

(c) A trustee shall send to the distributees or permissible distributees of trust income or principal, and to other qualified or nonqualified beneficiaries who request it, at least annually and at the termination of the trust, a report of the trust property, liabilities, receipts, and disbursements, including the source and amount of the trustee's compensation, a listing of the trust assets and, if feasible, their respective market values. Upon a vacancy in a trusteeship, unless a cotrustee remains in office, a report must be sent to the qualified beneficiaries by the former trustee. A personal representative, [conservator], or [guardian] may send the qualified beneficiaries a report on behalf of a deceased or incapacitated trustee.

(d) A beneficiary may waive the right to a trustee's report or other information otherwise required to be furnished under this section. A beneficiary, with respect to future reports and other information, may withdraw a waiver previously given.

(e) Subsections (b)(2) and (3) do not apply to a trustee who accepts a trusteeship before [the effective date of this [Code]], to an irrevocable trust created before [the effective date of this [Code]], or to a revocable trust that becomes irrevocable before [the effective date of this [Code]].

The provisions of California's law are discussed in the following case:

Salter v. Lerner

176 Cal.App.4th 1184 (2009)

POLLAK, ACTING P.J.

This action involves a dispute between appellant Glenn Lerner and his step-daughters, respondents Carin Salter and Jennifer Segal, regarding Lerner's administration of the Glenn and Elsa Lerner Trust (the trust). Lerner appeals from a determination by the probate court that a petition Segal and Salter propose to file against Lerner seeking information regarding his conduct as trustee of the trust will not violate the no contest provision of the trust. Although numerous arguments were made in the trial court, only a relatively narrow issue is raised on appeal: Does the proposed petition seek to do more than enforce Lerner's nonwaivable fiduciary duty under Probate Code section 16060 to provide reasonable information regarding the administration of the trust and, thus, violate the no contest clause of the trust? We agree with the trial court that the answer to this question is negative and that the proposed petition does not violate the no contest provision of the trust. Accordingly, we shall affirm.

> **Make the Connection**
>
> We have reviewed the applicability of no-contest clauses in our section on wills. They can appear also in trusts.

Background

The trust was created by Glenn and Elsa Lerner in April 2005. Elsa Lerner passed away on February 8, 2006. The trust agreement provides that upon Elsa's death Glenn Lerner becomes the sole trustee and the trust is to be divided into three subtrusts: the Family Trust, the Marital Trust, and the Survivor's Trust. The income of the subtrusts is to be distributed to Lerner, and Lerner has broad discretion to invade the principal of all of the subtrusts. Segal and Salter are contingent remainder beneficiaries and on Lerner's death will receive most of the remaining trust assets. The trust agreement provides that "any reports or accounts otherwise required by the California Probate Code are hereby waived to the fullest extent of the law." The agreement also contains a no contest clause prohibiting distribution to "anyone who contests or joins in . . . a contest of any provision hereof."

On December 19, 2007, respondents filed a petition pursuant to section 213203 seeking a determination of whether a further petition they proposed to file would violate the no contest clause contained in the trust.

After reviewing the proposed petition, which seeks to compel Lerner to provide information regarding the administration of the trust, the court concluded that the petition "does not implicate or run afoul of the no contest clause of the Glenn and Elsa Lerner Trust . . . because none of the relief requested constitutes an attack on the trust." Lerner filed a timely notice of appeal.

Discussion

Initially, the parties dispute the scope of the information sought by the proposed petition. Segal and Salter contend that the petition seeks only to enforce Lerner's non-waivable duty under section 16060 to provide reasonable information about the administration of the trust. Lerner contends that the scope of the petition is more expansive, seeking reports and an accounting under sections 16061 and 16062, in violation of the express waiver provision in the trust.

Section 16060 provides: "The trustee has a duty to keep the beneficiaries of the trust reasonably informed of the trust and its administration." The Law Revision Commission Comments to section 16060 explain, "The trustee is under a duty to communicate to the beneficiary information that is reasonably necessary to enable the beneficiary to enforce the beneficiary's rights under the trust or prevent or redress a breach of trust." This duty is "consistent with the duty stated in prior California case law to give beneficiaries complete and accurate information relative to the administration of a trust when requested at reasonable times." (Ibid.) Section 16061 provides: "Except as provided in section 16064, on reasonable request by a beneficiary, the trustee shall provide the beneficiary with a report of information about the assets, liabilities, receipts, and disbursements of the trust, the acts of the trustee, and the particulars relating to the administration of the trust relevant to the beneficiary's interest, including the terms of the trust." Section 16062, subdivision (a) provides: "Except as otherwise provided in this section and in section 16064, the trustee shall account at least annually, at the termination of the trust, and upon a change of trustee, to each beneficiary to whom income or principal is required or authorized in the trustee's discretion to be currently distributed." Under section 16064, "[t]he trustee is not required to report information or account to a beneficiary . . . [¶] (a) [t]o the extent the trust instrument waives the report or account. . . ." The parties agree that unlike sections 16061 and 16062, the duty imposed under section 16060 is not subject to waiver under section 16064. Likewise, "[t]he availability of information on request under [sections 16061 and 16062] does not negate the affirmative duty of the trustee to provide information under Section 16060." (Cal. Law Revision Com. com., 54A West's Ann. Prob.Code (1990 ed.) foll. § 16061, p. 52.

Here, the proposed petition alleges that Lerner has refused to provide any information about the trust. "Since his assumption of the sole trusteeship of the trust, [Lerner] has engaged in capital intensive projects with trust assets, including remodeling of a country house, at an estimated cost of between $800,000 and $1,000,000. [He] has apparently paid deposits on a Ferrari and a Bentley.

Practice Pointer

Setting aside the trustee's taste in automobiles, was it wise to make stepfather, holder of the right to income and a broad power to invade the corpus, the trustee of the trust?

[He] has also taken expensive vacations, staying at the club level of the finest hotels for extended periods of time, all at the expense of the trust. He refuses to provide any information as to whether he is subsidizing his lifestyle through expenditures of income, invasions of principal, and, if so, from what subtrust." The petition alleges further that respondents "have asked for confirmation that the trust has been divided into the three required subtrusts" and "also requested information as to the allocation of assets among the three subtrusts as required by the terms of the trust" but Lerner "has refused to provide any information" on the ground that the waiver provision of the trust gives "him the absolute right to administer the trust and the subtrusts in any way he sees fit, undeterred by the scrutiny of beneficiaries and the ability of the court to provide adequate remedies for breaches of trust." The petition asserts that respondents "are entitled to be provided with sufficient information in order to determine whether [Lerner] is faithfully discharging his fiduciary duties or, alternatively, whether [he] is abusing his position for his own benefit." The petition prays for "an order from the court requiring that [Lerner] provide them with information regarding the trust and its subtrusts, his acts and transactions with respect to the trust and its subtrusts, and his discretionary exercises of principal invasion as to the corpus of the trust and its subtrusts." The prayer requests that Lerner be instructed "to provide complete, accurate and sufficient information to [respondents] regarding trust matters and his administration of the trust for the period beginning February 8, 2006 through December 31, 2007."

Contrary to Lerner's suggestion, the petition does not expressly request a report or accounting under sections 16061 or 16062 and any implied request for such information was disavowed at the hearing. Nor does the petition challenge the trust provision that waives the report and accounting obligations. The proposed petition seeks only information that is reasonably necessary to enable Salter and Segal to enforce their rights under the trust, which Lerner is obligated to provide under section 16060.

The proposed petition is not a contest within the meaning of the no contest provision of the trust. Section 21300 defines a "contest" for purposes of a "no contest clause" as "a pleading in a proceeding in any court alleging the invalidity of an instrument or one or more of its terms." A petition to enforce a trustee's duty under section 16060 is not a direct or indirect challenge to the validity of the trust or its terms. Moreover, interpreting the no contest clause in a manner that would prevent respondents from filing the proposed petition would violate public policy. Section 21305, subdivision (b) lists 12 categories of pleadings that may not be considered "contests" as a matter of public policy, including "[a] pleading challenging the exercise of a fiduciary power" and "[a] petition to compel an accounting or report of a fiduciary, if that accounting or report is not waived by the instrument." Although not precisely enumerated, respondents' petition to compel Lerner to perform his nonwaivable, fiduciary duty under section 16060 falls within scope of the protection included in section 21305, subdivision (b).

Disposition

The judgment is affirmed. Respondents shall recover their costs on appeal.

We concur: Siggins and Jenkins, JJ.

Points for Discussion

1. Informing the beneficiaries

How does the duty to provide information differ from the duty to account? On the one hand, the petitioners have asked for clarifications regarding Lerner's handling of trust property: they "have asked for confirmation that the trust has been divided into the three required subtrusts." However, the petitioners have asked for numbers: "his acts and transactions with respect to the trust and its subtrusts, and his discretionary exercises of principal invasion as to the corpus of the trust and its subtrusts." If the latter is a mere request for 'information,' what is a request for an account? Are not the petitioners asking for the 'statement' of expenditures set out in sec. 16061?

2. Limiting the duty to account

1. Why should the creator of a trust be able to relieve the trustee of a duty to account? Should not a court of equity always be able to protect the interests of trust beneficiaries? Can such protection be afforded absent the ability to compel an accounting?

2. Section 21300 of the California Probate Code defines a contest for purposes of a "no contest clause" as "a pleading in a proceeding in any court alleging the invalidity of an instrument or one or more of its terms", would the proceeding be rightly regarded as a contest?

3. Setting aside the trustee's taste in automobiles, was it wise to make the stepfather, holder of the right to income and a broad power to invade the corpus, the trustee of the trust?

3. The "quiet trust"

Section 813(a) and (b)(2) and (3) are mandatory provisions of the UTC; that is, the terms of the trust cannot vary those provisions (UTC § 105(b)(8) and (9)). The qualified beneficiaries referred to in the section are defined in UTC § 103(13) as those beneficiaries who are at the time permissible distributees of income or principal, would be such distributees if the interests of the current distributees were to end without causing termination of the trust, or would receive the trust property were the trust to terminate. This provision of the UTC has proved to be quite controversial. It seems that there is a more or less widely held belief that the creator of a trust should be able to withhold knowledge of the trust from the beneficiaries. What do you think about the so-called "quiet trust"?

Like all good things trusts must end. It is at that point that a distribution of the trust corpus occurs and a final account is undertaken. The Uniform Trust Code provides a process for distribution.

UTC § 817. Distribution Upon Termination

(a)   Upon termination or partial termination of a trust, the trustee may send to the beneficiaries a proposal for distribution. The right of any beneficiary to object to the proposed distribution terminates if the beneficiary does not notify the trustee of an objection within 30 days after the proposal was sent but only if the proposal informed the beneficiary of the right to object and of the time allowed for objection.

(b)   Upon the occurrence of an event terminating or partially terminating a trust, the trustee shall proceed expeditiously to distribute the trust property to the persons entitled to it, subject to the right of the trustee to retain a reasonable reserve for the payment of debts, expenses, and taxes.

(c)   A release by a beneficiary of a trustee from liability for breach of trust is invalid to the extent:

    (1)   it was induced by improper conduct of the trustee; or

    (2)   the beneficiary, at the time of the release, did not know of the beneficiary's rights or of the material facts relating to the breach.

If the beneficiaries agree to a distribution, the trustees can act accordingly. In the absence of an agreed distribution the trustees may seek a court order. As the case below illustrates such a course prevents trust beneficiaries from thereafter raising objections to the trustee's accounts.

Estrada v. Arizona Bank

732 P.2d 1124 (Ariz. Ct. App. 1987)

HOWARD, PRESIDING JUDGE.

This is an appeal from the granting of a summary judgment. In February 1967, when the plaintiff was approximately two and one-half years old, his mother was killed in an automobile accident. A wrongful death action resulted in a settlement which netted plaintiff $99,161.54, which was paid into a trust established by the Cochise County Superior Court on October 18, 1968. This trust was to continue until the plaintiff reached 21 years of age. The trust instrument named the Arizona Bank as the trustee for the plaintiff, the sole beneficiary. The plaintiff's grandmother was appointed as his guardian.

In April 1976, in order to conform the trust instrument to the reduction in the age of majority in Arizona from 21 to 18, the Arizona Bank petitioned the Cochise County Superior Court for an order interpreting the trust to allow for termination and distribution of the trust assets upon plaintiff's attainment of the age of 18. On May 17, 1976, the court entered an order providing for the termination of the trust when plaintiff reached age 18 and directing the Arizona Bank to make annual accountings of the trust under the conservatorship statutes, A.R.S. §§ 14–5419 et seq.

Thereafter, in accordance with the court's order, petitions for approval of interim accountings were filed with the court each year from 1976 to 1982. The accounting for the period from May 1, 1981, to April 30, 1982, was approved by the court on August 23, 1982. The accountings fully disclosed all details of the investments, income, expenses, gains and losses from the management of the trust during each accounting period. Notice was given to the beneficiary and his guardian. No objections to these accountings were ever filed, and all were approved by the court.

> **Take Note**
>
> The facts set out standard procedure for trustee's dealing with a trust for the benefit of a minor including accounting and final distribution.

A seventh and final accounting, covering the period from April 30, 1982, through August 24, 1982, the latter date being the eighteenth birthday of the plaintiff, was filed for approval in September 1982. Notice of the petition for approval of the final accounting and of the final settlement and distribution of the trust estate was given to the plaintiff and to Joe Grajeda and Betty Grajeda, the plaintiff's successor guardians. A hearing was held on October 18, 1982, and an order approving the final accounting and proposed final distribution of trust assets was entered, again without objection.

On September 28 and October 20, 1982, the plaintiff, having attained the age of majority, signed documents acknowledging receipt from the Arizona Bank of distributions in the sums of $7,000 and $26,002.54, respectively. Following final distribution of the trust estate, the Arizona Bank filed and gave notice of a petition for final discharge of trustee for a minor. The petition was heard on or about November 15, 1982, and the court entered an order that date acknowledging that no objections to the accountings had been filed and finding that the bank's accountings were complete and correct. The order also found that the final distribution of the trust estate had been accomplished in accordance with the October 18 decree of distribution and ordered that the Arizona Bank be discharged from further claim or demand of any interested person.

On July 30, 1984, this action was commenced.

All counts of the complaint derive from the alleged mismanagement of the assets of the trust by the Arizona Bank. The complaint contains five counts. Counts one through three purport to state claims against the Arizona Bank and Arizona Bancwest Corporation, a holding company and owner of the Arizona Bank. Counts four and five attempt to state claims against Ben F. Williams, Jr., Esq.,

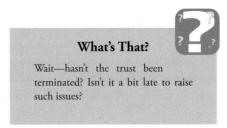

> **What's That?**
>
> Wait—hasn't the trust been terminated? Isn't it a bit late to raise such issues?

who was hired in 1970 to act as plaintiff's attorney. We are not concerned with the counts against defendant Williams because it appears from the record that he was never served with process in this case.

As against the Arizona Bank, the complaint alleges that the bank allowed the property to remain unproductive despite repeated and numerous demands upon it by plaintiff's guardians who allegedly insisted that the bank convert the trust assets to productive property. Count one of the complaint appears to be a claim for damages attributable to the bank's alleged breach of the common law or contractual fiduciary duties. Count two of the complaint alleges a claim arising out of an asserted misrepresentation by the bank to the plaintiff that it would follow the guardians' alleged demands that the trust property be invested in productive assets. Count three of the complaint asserts that the bank's alleged mismanagement amounted to a negligent failure to act as a reasonable and prudent investor. The prayer for relief sought compensatory damages in an amount not less than $63,966.69 together with punitive damages in the sum of $750,000 and $50,000 in attorney's fees. The Arizona Bank and Bancwest moved for summary judgment on the ground that the complaint was barred by res judicata. The motion was granted, and this appeal followed.

The defendants have two theories which they assert sustain the granting of summary judgment in their favor. First they rely on A.R.S. § 14–5419(D) which states:

> "An order, made upon notice and hearing, allowing an intermediate account of a conservator, adjudicates as to his liabilities concerning the matters considered in connection therewith. An order, made upon notice and hearing, allowing a final account adjudicates as to all previously unsettled liabilities of the conservator to the protected person or his successors relating to the conservatorship."

In the case of In re Estate of Terman, 135 Ariz. 453, 661 P.2d 1154 (App.1983), the son of a protected person objected to an amended inventory filed by the conservator of his father's estate. The claim was that the assets included in the inventory as sole and separate property of the protected person actually belonged to a trust in which the father and son were co-trustees. The court directed that either party desiring to contest the issues file an appropriate petition, have it set for hearing, and at that time the court would rule on the questions raised by the objection to the inventory. No such petition was filed by the son and, in the interim, orders were entered approving and settling two annual accounts filed by the conservator. Each of these accountings showed the disputed assets as belonging not to a father/son trust but rather to the conservatorship estate. The son never objected to the inclusion of the disputed assets in the inventory as the court had directed, and the question on appeal was whether res judicata, and the provisions of A.R.S. § 14–5419(D), barred the son's attempt to compel repayment of certain funds. The court held the attempt to force repayment to be precluded by the prior orders, reasoning as follows:

> "The conservator proceeded to include the questioned assets in two subsequent annual interim accountings itemizing the assets as estate property. The accounts were approved by court order, without objection from appellant. The annual accountings are final as to the matters therein determined. Approval of the annual accountings after notice and without appeal, is binding in the absence of a fraudulent concealment or misrepresentation." 135 Ariz. at 455, 661 P.2d at 1156.

Plaintiff contends that A.R.S. § 14–5419 does not apply because the bank was never appointed conservator of the plaintiff's estate, A.R.S. § 14–5419 having been enacted in 1973, subsequent to the establishment of plaintiff's trust. The defendants respond that the court's failure to appoint it as conservator is a mere technicality and that the court's order in 1976, requiring it file annual accounts in accordance with A.R.S. § 14–5419, shows that the court intended the bank to be responsible as a conservator and protected by the statutes governing conservatorships.

We agree with the plaintiff on this issue. The trust was established in this case as a court-supervised trust, not as a conservatorship and was terminated as a court-supervised trust. The court's order mandating the bank to file annual accountings in accordance with A.R.S. § 14–5419 merely expressed the court's intention to require annual accountings and was not a substitute for appointing the bank as a conservator under the conservatorship statutes.

However, defendants' second theory is viable. Defendants claim that even if A.R.S. § 14–5419(D) does not apply, the doctrine of res judicata still bars the plaintiff's claim. We agree.

A.R.S. § 14–7201 gives the court exclusive jurisdiction, inter alia, of proceedings to settle interim accounts. A.R.S. § 14–7204 sets forth the notice required for a petition to settle an interim account and in effect provides that all persons who are given such notice are bound by any order settling such an interim account. We hold that a judicial settlement of a trustee's interim accounts as to persons who receive notice and are subject to the court's jurisdiction bars subsequent litigation seeking to raise defaults or defects with respect to the matters shown or disclosed. As observed by the court in Fraser v. Southeast First Bank of Jacksonville, 417 So.2d 707 (Fla.App.1982) this is a modified kind of res judicata since matters not disclosed by the accounting, even though they might have been discovered and litigated, may be later litigated.

As observed in Fraser, the need for the conclusive effect for periodic accountings is great because the trust may continue for long periods of time. The court in Fraser quoted from In Re Van Deusen's Will, 24 Misc.2d 611, 196 N.Y.S.2d 737 (Sur.Ct.1960):

> "The application of any other Rule [than res judicata], in our judgment, would result in a maelstorm [sic] of uncertainty, lack of judicial finality and ultimate chaos. Without some safeguards, no fiduciary could ever rest secure after his supposed acquitance. Hence we cannot conceive the prior accounts, and the decrees settling them, as constituting useless gestures which may be lightly brushed aside at the caprice of interested parties years after persons involved and records required are no longer available to dispute attacks made on them." 417 So.2d at 710.

The bank complied with the notice requirements of A.R.S. § 14–7204. Plaintiff's complaint seeks to raise defaults or defects with matters which were fully disclosed. The doctrine of res judicata bars his claims for the periods covered by the annual accounts.

Plaintiff's reliance on Mims v. Valley National Bank, 14 Ariz.App. 190, 481 P.2d 876 (1971) is misplaced. Mims held that probate court orders settling the accounts of the bank as executor and as trustee were limited to in rem matters and did not terminate the personal responsibility of the bank, and an action for breach of fiduciary duty was not barred by res judicata. Mims was based on the old probate code, which was replaced by the Uniform Probate Code, effective January 1, 1974. The court no longer is limited to in rem jurisdiction. The Uniform Probate Code, specifically A.R.S. § 14–1302(A), gives the superior court jurisdiction to the full extent permitted by the constitution over all matters relating to estates of protected persons, minors and trusts. See Gonzalez v. Superior Court, 117 Ariz. 64, 570 P.2d 1077 (1977). Probate proceedings are no longer limited to proceedings in rem. Accordingly, the orders approving the annual accountings bar any claim by plaintiff as to periods covered by those accountings.

> ### Make the Connection
>
> The matter has been already been litigated and judgment entered. Is there any reason why this principle of law ought not to apply when a court has signed off on a final accounting of a trust?

3 A.R.S. § 14–7307 establishes the period of limitations for claims arising out of the final accounting of this court-supervised trust. The plaintiff was an adult when he received the bank's final account. There is no contention that there was any non-disclosure in any of the accountings, including the final account. Under A.R.S. § 14–7307, plaintiff had six months to file a claim against the defendants. He did not do so.

The plaintiff seeks to avoid the limitation period of § 14–7307, contending that it is unconstitutional because it is an unreasonably short period of time within which to assert his claim. Although this constitutional issue was never raised in the lower court, we may consider it since the question is an issue of general statewide significance. See Barrio v. San Manuel Division Hospital for Magma Copper Company, 692 P.2d 280 (Ariz. 1984). Only when a period of limitations fixed by statute is so short that it, in effect, deprives the party of equal protection of law and due process of law will it be found unconstitutional. Crawford v. Hunt, 41 Ariz. 229, 17 P.2d 802 (1932) (statute requiring state and county officers, and ex-officers, their personal representatives or assigns, claiming the right to any salary as officers or ex-officers, due by virtue of a law of the state, to bring an action therefor within 90 days after the date the said salary becomes due is not unconstitutional). Considering the fact that all the information needed by the plaintiff to discover any claim that he may have must be fully disclosed before the six months' limitation applies, we do not believe the legislature acted unreasonably or unconstitutionally in fixing the period at six months.

Affirmed.

HATHAWAY C.J., and FERNANDEZ, J., concur.

Points for Discussion

1. Are there any circumstances that you could conjure that would justify reopening the case? Absent failure to give notice to the beneficiary of the proceeding and fraud, it is well-neigh impossible to set aside a final decree on accounting.

2. The cases raises more issues in the area of guardianship law than it does in trust law. If the Bank was not a 'prudent investor' what should the guardian have done? If she did not, should the minor be able to bring an action against her? Could Estrada bring an action against the guardian 11 years after the final accounting?

———————————

Test Your Knowledge

To assess your understanding of the material in this chapter, click here to take a quiz.

CHAPTER 13

Future Interests   ↝ 𝑒𝑙𝑠 – 96

A. Introduction

1.   What's the Point?

Why study the law of future interests? The answer is simple: practically all trusts create future interests, and trusts provide a flexible estate planning device to accomplish a variety of goals from support to intergenerational transmission. And trusts with future interests are not exclusively within the dominion of the top 1%. Note the use of future interest in the Ward Cleaver Estate Plan. So coping with future interests is not simply a form of torture visited upon Property and Wills and Trusts students: no lawyer can possibly serve clients who wish to arrange for the passing of their property at death without a thorough knowledge of the modern law of future interests.

The use of "modern" in that last sentence was deliberate. The law of future interests developed deep in the English past. As such, many of its doctrines are extraordinarily complex and the subtleties can be confounding. The good news is that most of those complexities and subtleties are not relevant to practicing law in the twenty-first century. What one needs to know in order to draft trusts that accomplish one's clients' ends is overwhelming neither in extent or complexity. These materials are designed to help you understand what you need to know. There is much more to learn about future interests, some of which is of purely historical interest and which explains the reasons for some modern oddities, some of which is still relevant to dealing with future interests created in documents written decades ago. ↯

The Anglo-American law was unforgiving in its insistence on proper use of words of art. Long ago, before Windows, when one booted up a computer the so-called 'C prompt' appeared. If the user wanted the Microsoft Word Program, it was necessary to type in 'word.' A notoriously clumsy typist who typed in 'wrod' would get the following response: Bad Command or File Name. The computer was 'formalistic,' it recognized only one way for the proper program to appear. So too is the law. As you learned in Property "to A and her heirs" was the 'command' that indicated a fee simple absolute. If you meant to create one but used the limitation to A forever, a life estate was probably created: Bad Command or File Name.

Times have changed and law is more forgiving. It may help you in learning this material to remember that many of the rules are bent, and constructional rules have replaced formalism to provide a remedy for documents that have been ambiguously drafted. But never forget that the job of a trusts lawyer is to translate your clients' estate planning goals into the language of the law, words that work, that are not ambiguous, that do not seem to say one thing but actually are construed to mean another.

2. What Is a Future Interest?

A future interest is an intangible property interest regarded as a non-possessory property interest in the present and which may or may not entitle the owner of the interest to receive a possessory property interest at some time in the future. Your study of property should have already introduced you to some future interests, the most important being a remainder in land. If O conveys Blackacre to A for life, then to B, A has a life estate, a present possessory interest, and B has the remainder, a future interest. When A dies, the life estate in A terminates and the remainder becomes possessory: that is the owner of the remainder will have title to Blackacre.

One may analogize a future interest to a claim check. At some time in the future the owner of the claim check can cash it in for property. In addition, the claim check itself is property. In most instances it can be bought and sold, given away, and if held at death, pass by intestate succession or under a will. Usually the right to the property represented by the claim check is absolute; with future interests, whether the claim check can be cashed may depend upon the occurrence of an event which may or may not happen.

Perhaps this claim check metaphor will be easier to understand if you think about two other types of future interest you learned about in property: the possibility of reverter and the right of entry. The former is the interest that is left in a grantor who conveys a fee simple determinable; the latter is the interest that is left in a grantor who conveys a fee simple subject to a condition subsequent.

> **Example 1:** O conveys Whiteacre to the School Board for so long as the land is used for school purposes. The School Board has a *fee simple determinable* and the grantor has a *possibility of reverter* which is a future interest that will become possessory, that is the claim check can be cashed in, **if and when** the permitted use of Whiteacre ceases. Each estate had its own qualities: you may remember that under the common law the possibility of reverter was not devisable or alienable. That is, the owner couldn't convey it during life or dispose of it by will. It could only descend to heirs, even if the owner died testate. That rule has been changed by statute in many states.

> **Example 2:** O conveys Whiteacre to the School Board, but if the grantee ceases to use the land for school purposes, the grantor may re-enter the land. The grantor has a *right of entry* which is a future interest that will become possessory if the stated condition occurs and the grantor (or whoever owns the right of entry at the time) takes possession of the land. 🔑

How do these two estates differ? Suppose the condition is broken, what happens to the possessory interest under each limitation? Hint: does the broken condition immediately terminate the interest in the School Board in each limitation? Phraseology matters.

3. Legal and Equitable

There is one primary difference between the remainder following a life estate in land (and other future interests in land) and future interests in trusts. The former is a *legal future interest*, the latter are *equitable future interests*. Remember that the law of wills and trusts is controlled primarily by the law of equity. From the inception of the trust, issues involving trusts (whether created by inter vivos settlement or after the Statute of Wills by devise) were tried in the Chancery Court and not the common law courts (the two principal ones being King's Bench and Common Pleas). But the distinction was not always so neat because land, of course, came under the jurisdiction of the common law courts. But there might be from time to time cases in which trusts of land were heard in the common law courts. That said, the distinction remains: future interests in land are "legal" and those in trusts are "equitable."

In the modern world the rules for both legal and equitable future interests are generally the same except where oddities like the limitations on the alienability of the possibility of reverter and the right of entry have not been modified by statute. The major difference between legal future interests and equitable future interests in the modern world is the state of the title to the property which the owner of the future interest may or may not eventually possess.

Consider: A owns a life estate in Blackacre and B the remainder. Legal title to Blackacre is divided between A and B. In order to acquire good fee simple absolute title to Blackacre a prospective purchaser must acquire both the life estate and the remainder interest. If, however, O conveys Blackacre to T, in trust, to pay the income (which includes the right to live on Blackacre) to A for life, remainder on A's death to B, A has the lifetime income interest (we sometimes call that a life estate, although it would be more accurate to call it an equitable life estate to distinguish it from a legal life estate in land) and B has the remainder, but *title to Blackacre is in T as trustee*. The prospective purchaser need bargain only with T.

B. The Classification of Future Interests

The classification of future interests is the single most important aspect of future interests law. There are only six major types of future interests, classified by whether they are created in transferees or left in a transferor.

CREATED IN THE TRANSFEREE	LEFT IN THE TRANSFEROR
Fee simple determinable (a present possessory interest)	*Possibility of reverter*
Fee on a condition subsequent (a present possessory interest)	*Right of entry*
Remainders and Executory Interests (future interest)	*Reversion*

Now, if you've been reading carefully, you will ascertain five future interests in the above chart. The two conditional fees are of course present possessory interests. But there are a number of types of remainders: vested and contingent. Vested remainders, in turn, can be further subclassified in to indefeasibly vested remainders and vested remainders subject to a condition subsequent.

1. Remainders

a) A Definition

Clearly, the remainder seems to be the most important player in this system.

What is a remainder? [A remainder is a future interest that will become possessory, if it ever becomes possessory, on the expiration of all other preceding interests created in the same limitation.] Consider a limitation created in a deed or devise "to A for life then to B and his heirs." Both interests (the legal life estate in A and the remainder in B) are created simultaneously (either in a deed or by a devise in a will). When the life interest ends at the life tenant's death, the remainder person (B) will take possession of Blackacre. To return to our metaphor, the claim check will be cashed in. A life income interest in a trust and an equitable remainder work exactly the same way. Recall the Ward Cleaver trust: June has a life interest in the income, the boys a remainder. The latter is a future interest while June is alive and a possessory interest when she dies. Of course, the duration of the present possessory interest in the trust may be measured by something other than a person's life. Perhaps A is to receive the trust income for 20 years, or until reaching the age of 35 (or sooner dying), or until marriage, with the corpus to be distributed to B upon the occurrence of the event. While A's interest is possessory, B has a future interest; at the time A's interest ends, B's remainder falls in and he takes possession.

b) Remainders Described by What Interest Comes into Possession

Of what does the person who has the remainder interest take possession?

Example 3: In a conveyance of Blackacre to A for life then to B and her heirs, B (the "remainder person") will get fee simple absolute title to Blackacre at the death of A. Similarly, if the grantor creates a trust to pay the income to A for life then to distribute the trust property to B, the remainder person will get fee simple title to all the trust property at A's death. B has *a remainder in fee simple absolute* with respect to Blackacre and an equitable remainder with respect to the corpus of the trust.

Example 4: Suppose grantor conveys Blackacre to A for life, then to B for life, then to C or the grantor could create a trust to pay the income to A for life, then to pay the income to B for life then to pay the trust property to C. In both these cases, B has a *remainder in a life estate* or *in an equitable life estate in remainder,* because when the preceding interest ends, B takes possession of a stream of income that lasts for B's life.

In both **Examples 3** and **4** B has a remainder because B's interest will become possessory on the expiration of the preceding interest and both interests were created in the same instrument. The difference between the interests is in the extent of the interest B will possess. In **Example 3**, B ends up with fee simple absolute title in the land and the corpus of the trust at A's death. In **Example 4**, B ends ups up with a life estate, equitable or legal, depending on whether there is land or a trust involved. Once again, B's interest in both cases becomes possessory on the expiration of the preceding interest created in the same instrument which in both examples is a life estate or life income interest (equitable life estate).

Note that in both **Examples 3** and **4** there are no words attached to B's remainder interest which create any condition for B to fulfill in order to take possession of Blackacre or of the trust property (or of the life income stream) at the expiration of A's interest. Whoever has the claim check (B's interest is transferrable and devisable) when the preceding interest terminates will come into possession of the property.

This is the case even for the remainders created in **Example 4**.

Granted, if B does not survive A, the claim check is worthless because it entitles the holder of the claim check to income for B's life. If B is dead, a possessory interest cannot pass because in that example B's interest is a life estate. Of course, if B transferred the remainder during life and if B were living at A's death, the person to whom B had transferred the remainder would have an estate *pur autre vie* or would receive income from the trust for the remainder of B's life.

c) Indefeasibly Vested Remainders

In **Examples 3** and **4** the remainders are *indefeasibly vested*. There is no condition written into the remainder interest. On A's death, the future interest will become possessory in the owner of the remainder interest; that person will cash in the claim check (except if the remainder is a life estate in B as in **Example 4** and B does not survive A; the interest to be collected is worthless because B is not alive).

What happens in **Example 3** if B dies before A? The answer is simple: *Whoever has the claim check from B will cash it in and take possession of the property at A's death*. If B died intestate, the future interest passed to B's heirs and they will take possession of the property. If B died testate, the remainder passed under B's will. B could have made a specific bequest of the property or allowed it to pass under the residuary clause. Because the language creating the future interest does not require B to survive A or indeed to fulfill any other requirement or condition, B's interest is *transmissible* at B's death. We will return to transmissibility shortly, but for now all you need to remember is that some future interests are transmissible at the death of the person in whom the interest was created.

d) Remainders and Conditions

i)   *Remainders vested subject to divestment—conditions subsequent*

Not all remainders are indefeasibly vested. Taking possession of the property to which the future interest relates can be conditioned on the occurrence of an event. In other words, the remainder can be made subject to a condition subsequent. Recall the fee simple on a condition subsequent.

> **Example 5:** O conveys Blackacre to A, but if alcohol is ever sold on the property, O may reenter and take possession of Blackacre. If the condition is broken, O (or O's successors) may reacquire Blackacre. 🖎

The estate in **Example 5** is a fee simple subject to a **condition subsequent** because the condition (not selling alcohol on the premises) is tacked on to an otherwise absolute, unconditioned gift of Blackacre. Regard it as an afterthought—it is A's unless thereafter A does something: the selling of alcohol. O conveyed Blackacre to A but then takes it away if something happens. Exactly the same condition can be added to any otherwise absolute gift of a remainder interest.

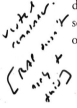

> **Example 6:** G transfers property to T as trustee to pay the income to A for life and then to pay the trust property over to B, but if B does not survive A, T shall pay the trust property to C.

The interpretation of the future interest created in B in **Example 6** is parallel to the interpretation of the conveyance in **Example 5**. The right to possession of the trust property in the future is given to B but then it is taken away if something happens, in this case, if B dies before A in which case C takes possession of the trust property. B's remainder is *vested subject to total divestment*. B has a vested remainder, but if the condition subsequent comes to pass—B not surviving A—the entire interest is taken away from B. It is divested, and passes to C. The requirement that B survive A in order to take possession of the trust property is a *condition subsequent* because the language that creates it give B's possession of the trust property in the future, but the future interest that gives the right to take possession in B will be taken away at a later time if the specified condition occurs. The interest created in C in **Example 6** is an *executory interest*. An executory interest is a future interest which divests an interest by the occurrence of a condition subsequent (if B dies before A). We will return to executory interests.

ii)   *Contingent remainders—conditions precedent*

Some remainders are limited to take effect upon the occurrence of events which may not have not happened at the time of the creation of the remainder, and indeed may not ever happen, or are created to persons not in being at the time of the grant and who indeed may never come into being.

Example 7: G transfers property to T as trustee to pay the income to A for life and then to pay the trust property over to B if B survives A, and if not T shall pay the trust property to C.

Compare **Examples 6** and **7**. *The practical results are exactly the same.* If B survives A, B takes possession of the trust property and if B does not survive A, C takes possession. The future interests that are created to give this result, however, are different.

Why? *Because the linguistic formulation of the two examples is different.* In **Example 6**, B is given future possession of the trust property but the vested remainder which represents the right to possession in the future (the claim check that can be cashed in to take possession of the property) is then taken away if B does not survive A. In **Example 7**, however, B is given a remainder which allows B to get possession of the trust property *only if B survives A*. B's future interest is a *contingent remainder*, because it is subject to a condition precedent (accent on the second syllable). The words used create a condition precedent because the right to possession of the trust property is made dependent on whether B survives A. *B cannot take possession unless B meets the condition.* Again, note the contrast in the linguistic presentation of the interest in the trust in **Example 6**: the right to take possession in the future is given to B, but then taken away should the condition occur. In **Example 7**, the linguistic formulation allows the holder of the future interest possession only upon fulfilling a condition.

How does one tell the difference between a condition subsequent and a condition precedent? In the examples we have dealt with so far, it's easy. The condition subsequent in **Example 6** comes after the creation of the remainder, separated from the words creating the remainder by a comma and introduced by the words "but if." However, in **Example 7** the condition is an integral part of the gift of the right to possession in the future, a condition precedent. The trustee is directed to pay the trust property to B if B survives A. Unlike in **Example 6**, the trustee is not directed to distribute the property to B, but then told "oh, wait a minute, if B hasn't survived A don't give B the trust property after all." The condition is not tacked on as an afterthought; it is not separated from the creation of the remainder by a comma; it is not introduced by the words "but if."

Another way to think the distinction between the condition subsequent and precedent is to compare the answers to the trustee's question: "When A is dead, what shall I do with the trust property?" In **Example 6** the answer is "Give it to B. That is, unless B isn't alive at that time. If that happens give the trust property to C." In **Example 7** the answer is "Give it to B if B is alive then and if B isn't alive give it to C."

These two examples are classic formulations of the distinctions between conditions precedent and subsequent. You've been studying law long enough to know that the real world does not produce neat examples like those in casebooks and treatises. We will spend some time studying the constructional rules courts have developed over centuries to sort out the meaning of language creating future interests. You should be able now, however, to understand the most basic constructional rule of all. The words creating the future interest are read in order. If the language first gives the right to possession in the future, but then gives an alternative should something happen (or not happen) the first interest is a vested remainder subject to divestment and the condition is a condition subsequent. If the right to possession is given only if something happens (or doesn't happen) we have a condition precedent and a contingent remainder.

What about the interest given to C in **Example 7**? It cannot be an *executory interest* because the person holding the future interest does not come into possession of the trust property because an otherwise vested interest is divested by the occurrence of a condition subsequent. Because the interest created in C will lead to possession of the trust property if a condition precedent comes to pass destroying the possibility that the person holding a contingent remainder will get possession of the trust property it is an *alternative contingent remainder*.

iii)   Contingent remainders—unascertained persons

Being subject to meeting a condition precedent is not the only way a remainder is made contingent. *A remainder is contingent if it is created in unascertained persons.*

> **Example 8:** G bequeaths property to T, in trust, T to be trustee, to pay the income to A for life then to pay the trust property to A's children. If at the time the trust is created A has no children, the remainder is contingent because it is created in unascertained persons.

Another way to understand why the remainder is contingent is to ask yourself if there is a person you can point to who possesses the remainder at the time of the creation of the grant or when the trust is created. If there is not, the remainder is contingent. Usually, of course, a remainder in unascertained persons is a remainder created in a class which does not yet have any members, but is expected to. When a class member comes into being, the remainder vests because there is now a person who possesses the remainder. Other situations involving unascertained persons may create contingent remainders even if the person is later ascertained because there is also a condition precedent.

> **Example 9:** G transfers property to T in trust to pay the income to A for life and on A's death to pay the trust property to A's surviving spouse. If at the time the trust is created, A is not married, then the remainder is created in an unascertained person and is contingent. If A is married the remainder is still contingent because in order to be A's surviving spouse one must be living at A's death. In other words, there is a condition precedent of surviving A.

Now that we have mentioned class gifts to a single generation class like a person's children, we need to consider the application of the rules that we have been considering to such classes. In **Example 8**, consider what happens if at the time the future interests are created A does not have children. G has created a contingent remainder if no person is born that fits the description, the interest in the trust will pass to someone and that someone is G because G has a reversion. Suppose after the trust is created a child is born to A? The only reason the remainder was contingent when the trust was created was because the remainder was limited to unascertained persons. Upon the birth of a class member, we can point to a person who has the remainder and therefore the remainder is now vested. G's reversion vanishes when the child is born. Technically, because when the child is born alive its legal existence relates back to the moment of conception, the reversion vanished as soon as the child was *en ventre sa mere*. This example should remind you that *future interests can change over time as relevant events occur.*

What future interest does A's newborn child (whom we'll call X) have? Clearly the remainder is vested because what rendered the remainder contingent was its limitation in unascertained persons. The holders of the remainder are no longer unascertained so the remainder must be vested. A remainder must be either vested or contingent. But upon the death of A will the trust corpus pass entirely to X? That depends. The interest is in all of A's children without any restriction. So if A is alive and has a second child, Y, Y shares in the remainder. The interest in A's children so long as there is a child of A in being and A is alive is a *vested remainder subject to open*. The class of A's children is considered by the law as "open" because the number of class members can increase. Clearly while A is alive A can have more children and the number of class members can increase and it is possible that X will have to share the property when it is distributed.

Of course, the remainder in the class can also be subject to a condition precedent.

Example 10: G bequeaths property to T, in trust, T to be trustee, to pay the income to A for life then to pay the trust property to A's children who attain the age of 21. If at the time the trust is created A has no children, the remainder is contingent because it is created in unascertained persons. If A has any number of children alive at the time the trust created all of whom are under the age of 21 the remainder is still contingent because of the age requirement which is condition precedent.

Another class whose members are unascertained and which is also subject to a condition precedent is the heirs of a living person.

Example 11: G bequeaths property to T, in trust, T to be trustee, to pay the income to A for life then to pay the trust property to B's heirs. While B is alive the remainder is contingent. Because the common law held that no one is the heir of a living person and one must be alive to be an heir, the remainder is in unascertained persons. The condition precedent is being B's heir. We cannot know who has the claim check until the death of B.

Before applying all these rules to some simple problems, there is one more rule we have to understand. Remember the chart with which we started? It included three future interests in transferors, only one of which corresponded to the creation of a remainder in a transferee: the reversion. According to the chart, the transferor has a reversion when the transferor creates a contingent remainder. And that indeed is the "rule of reversions": when a transferor creates a contingent remainder, the transferor retains a reversion. The reversion will become possessory, that is, its holder will take possession of the property involved if the contingent remainder does not vest because the condition precedent does not happen or the remainder is still in unascertained persons at the time the preceding interest ends and the future interest is ready to be "cashed in." If the transferor dies before the time for the property to come into possession of the holder of the remainder, the reversion passes through the transferor's estate either to the heirs if the transferor dies intestate or under the transferor's will. The reversion, in other words, is transmissible.

Return to ***Example 7.*** The limitation created alternative contingent remainders in B and C. If you think about it, either one or the other holder of the contingent remainders will end up taking possession of the property at A's death. (If that is so, and it absolutely is, what must happen to C's alternative contingent remainder if C dies while A and B are still living?) Does the transferor still have a reversion even though there is no chance that the property will come into the possession of the person holding the reversion? The answer is "yes." The reason the answer is yes is yet again a result of history. When the system of future interests was developed, there were many ways in which the interest preceding a remainder could end without "expiring" in the sense of that word as used in the definition. The easiest to understand example is the life tenant or life income beneficiary who committed treason and who then suffered attaint; that is, a bill of attainder would result in the guilty person being civilly dead. Consider ***Example 7*** again. If A were guilty of treason, all of A's property is disposed of as if A were dead. But because A is really alive we do not know if A has survived B so we do not know if the condition precedent has been fulfilled or not. The only solution is for the property to revert to the transferor: G's reversion becomes possessory. There were other ways in which the life interest could end before death, but they were related to the intricacies of feudal land law and really do not need to concern us. Whether civil forfeiture under modern laws such as RICO would have the same result is an open question. What is certain is if the transferor creates only contingent remainders the transferor has a reversion. If the transferor creates an indefeasibly vested remainder or a vested remainder subject to divestment, there is no reversion.

Problems

1. O conveys Blackacre to A for life, remainder to A's children. What future interests are created if

   a. At the time of the conveyance A has no children.

   b. At the time of the conveyance A has at least one living child.

2. G bequeaths property to T in trust, T as trustee is to pay the trust income to A for life, then to pay the trust property to A's children who attain 21 years of age. What future interests are created if

   a. At the time of G's death A has no children.

   b. At the time of G's death A has three children aged 10, 7, and 5.

   c. At the time of G's death A has three children aged 25, 22, and 18.

3.   G conveys property to T in trust, T as trustee to pay the income to A for life then to pay the trust property to A's children, but if no children of A survive A the trust property is to be paid to C.

    a.   What future interests are created when the trust is created if A has no children at the time the trust is created?

    b.   What are the future interests in the trust property after the birth of A's first child?

    c.   After the birth of A's second child, C dies with a valid will leaving all C's property to C's surviving spouse, D. What are the future interests in the trust property at that time?

    d.   By the time of A's death many years after creation of the trust the following events have occurred:

        A has had a total of four children. The eldest child, a son, died before A leaving a valid will giving all of his property to his widow.

        The youngest child also died before A, intestate, unmarried and without descendants.

Given these facts, how should the trustee distribute the trust property on A's death?

---

2.   Executory Interests

The executory interest has a complex history. Today, almost all executory interests are created in the context we have already seen. That is, they are interests that will allow the holder to take possession of the property if an otherwise vested remainder falls victim to a condition subsequent. Such executory interests are *shifting executory interests* because the person holding such an interest takes by divesting another transferee. Another way to say that is that the holder of the shifting executory interest takes property that otherwise another transferee would come into possession of.

> ***Example 12:*** O conveys Blackacre to A and his heirs, but if B passes the bar to B and his heirs. A has a fee simple absolute, but upon the occurrence of a specified event, the fee simple absolute shifts to B. B has an executory interest.

Other executory interests divest transferors and they are known as *springing executory interests*. The property of which the holder of the interest takes possession comes directly from the transferor who created the executory interest. There are not many examples of such interests in the modern world, but here is one that at least is possible.

> ***Example 13:*** O conveys Blackacre to A for life, then to B when B attains the age of 21. B has a contingent remainder at the time of the grant because the age requirement is a condition precedent. O therefore has a reversion. If A dies before B

is 21, the only option is that the reversion becomes possessory while we wait to see if B will fulfill the condition precedent. If B does, B will take Blackacre by divesting O, the transferor, and therefore B's interest, which was a contingent remainder when A was alive morphed into an executory interest at A's death. It is springing, because it comes into existence after the grant. If B attains the age of 21, B will be entitled to possession of Blackacre. If B dies before attaining 21, the springing executory interest will vanish and the possessory interest in O will no longer be subject to divestment. In the past, B's contingent remainder was destroyed if B did not fulfill the condition precedent before the preceding estate ended; that is, B did not reach 21 before the death of A. The common law system of estates could not cope with the idea of the transferor holding title to Blackacre under the cloud of possible divestment. There could be, it was said, no "gap in seisin." In any event, suffice it to say that the doctrine of the destructibility of contingent remainders is as dead as the proverbial doornail, but like so many dead doctrines it still casts a shadow on the modern world as we will see.

Not all jurisdictions continue to maintain the arcane distinction between contingent remainders and executory interests. For example, the term "executory interest" is not part of New York law. For one hundred and ninety years or so New York statutes have defined executory interests in the same terms as contingent remainders. Both are "future estates" subject to a condition precedent. This is the relevant statute in effect today:

New York Estates, Powers, and Trusts Law § 6–4.10. Definition of a Future Estate Subject to a Condition Precedent

A future estate subject to a condition precedent is an estate created in favor of one or more unborn or unascertained persons or in favor of one or more presently ascertainable persons upon the occurrence of an uncertain event.

Thus the statute conflates contingent remainders and executory interests. From the point of view of the holder of an executory interest the divesting condition is a condition precedent. The holder of the interest will not come into possession of the interest unless the condition is fulfilled. In keeping with older statutory terminology, the divesting condition is sometimes referred to in New York cases as a "conditional limitation" or an "executory limitation." Whatever terms are used, a New York "future estate" which is subject to a condition precedent can be in traditional future interests language a contingent remainder or an executory interest, depending on whether the fulfillment of the condition precedent means that the interest takes on the expiration of a prior interest or whether fulfillment of the condition precedent results in the divesting of an otherwise vested interest. Indeed, so dominant is the traditional terminology that New York lawyers and New York judges will sometimes refer to "executory interests."

3. Transferability

Most interests in property are freely transferable. That general rule obtains for future interests. Return to **Example 6**: G transfers property to T as trustee to pay the income to A for life and then to pay the trust property over to B, but if B does not survive A, T shall pay the trust property to C. Classify the interests in A, B and C. A has a present possessory life estate; B and C have future interests: B has a vested remainder subject to divestment and that C has an executory interest. If C dies while A and B are alive, C's executory interest will pass through C's estate to C's heirs if C died intestate or through C's will. C's death has no impact on whether the condition subsequent, B not surviving A, will or will not happen. Since C's death is irrelevant to determining who will eventually possess the trust property the interest is not destroyed by C's death. C's executory interest will pass by intestacy or under C's will like any other asset of C's probate estate.

Consider now **Example 7**: G transfers property to T as trustee to pay the income to A for life and then to pay the trust property over to B if B survives A and if B does not, T shall pay the trust property to C. Because the survival condition applicable to B is stated as a condition precedent, B and C have alternative contingent remainders. What happens if C dies while A and B are still alive? Once again, C's death does nothing to resolve the condition precedent so C's interest must continue until the condition is resolved and C's contingent remainder passes through C's estate.

Thus whether or not a future interest is transmissible on the death of the holder of the interest turns upon whether that event resolves a condition precedent or subsequent attached to the interest. If survival is a condition precedent to the enjoyment of the interest, the future interest terminates; if it is not, the interest passes through the probate estate of the deceased holder. As noted above, if the holder of the future interest dies intestate, the interest passes to heirs; if the holder of the future interest has a will, the interest passes under the terms of the will. The holder of the interest, for example, could have made a specific bequest of the interest in the will. After all, the future interest is property and can be the subject of a specific bequest like a fee simple interest in land or personal property like a painting or a watch. While there appear to be no studies of the question, most commentators believe that specific bequests of transmissible future interests are rare. The assumption behind that conclusion is that most holders of transmissible interests are not aware that they own the interest. The result is that if the holder of the interest dies testate the transmissible future interest will pass through the residuary clause. Unknowing disposition of any property can lead to problems, but they may be especially acute with future interests. Because future interest are almost always created in trusts, and many if not most private trusts are created to manage and perpetuate family wealth, having the interest pass through the residuary clause of the will of the person in whom the interest was originally created may be contrary to the intent of the creator of the trust. We will return to this topic as part of our discussion of constructional rules.

Before we go on, here are some problems to further test your understanding of the basics of future interests.

Problems

1. G bequeaths property to T in trust and T as trustee is to pay the income from the trust property to G's son, S, for his life, and on his death is to pay the property to S's children, but if no children of S survive S the trustee shall pay the trust property to G's niece, N.

   a. What future interests are created at the creation of the trust, assuming S has no children at the time of the creation of the trust?

   b. Two years after G's death a daughter, A, is born to S and his spouse. What future interests now exist in the trust property?

   c. Over the next eight years, another daughter, B, is born to S and his spouse and a son, C is also born to them. The following events then occur: A marries and has two children. B marries and has one child. S's spouse dies. C marries. C dies with a will leaving his probate estate to his surviving spouse, W. S then dies. How is the trust property distributed on S's death?

2. G bequeaths property to T in trust and T as trustee is to pay the income from the trust property to G's son, S, for his life, and on his death T is to pay the property to S's children who survive S, but if no children of S survive S, T is directed to pay the trust property to G's niece, N.

   a. What future interests are created at the creation of the trust, assuming S has no children at the time of the creation of the trust?

   b. Two years after G's death a daughter, A, is born to S and his spouse. What future interests now exist in the trust property?

   c. Over the next eight years, another daughter, B, is born to S and his spouse and a son, C is also born to them. The following events then occur: A marries and has two children. B marries and has one child. S's spouse dies. C marries and has a child. C dies with a will leaving his probate estate to his surviving spouse, W. S then dies. How should the trust property be distributed on S's death?

3. G bequeaths property to T in trust and T as trustee is required to pay the income from the trust property to G's son, S, for his life, and on his death to pay the property to S's heirs.

   a. What future interests are created at the creation of the trust, assuming S has no children at the time of the creation of the trust?

   b. Two years after G's death a daughter, A, is born to S and his spouse. What future interests now exist in the trust property?

   c. Over the next eight years, another daughter, B, is born to S and his spouse and a son, C is also born to them. The following events then occur: A marries and has two children. B marries and has one child. S's spouse dies. C marries. C dies with a will leaving his probate estate to his surviving spouse, W. S then dies. How should the trust property distributed on S's death?

4. G bequeaths property to T in trust and T as trustee is directed to pay the income from the trust property to G's son, S, for his life, and on his death to pay the property to S's children who attain the age of 21.

    a.   What future interests are created at the creation of the trust, assuming S has no children at the time of the creation of the trust?

    b.   Two years after G's death a daughter, A, is born to S and his spouse. What future interests now exist in the trust property?

    c.   When A is three years of age, another daughter, B, is born to S and his spouse. When A is six and B is three a son, C, is born to S and his spouse.

    d.   When A reaches 21, what future interests exist in the trust property?

    e.   One year after B reaches 21, C dies at the age of 19 with a will leaving his probate estate to his mother. When S dies many years later he is survived by A, B, and his surviving spouse. How is the trust property distributed?

C. Rules of Construction

The role of the estate planner is to satisfy the goals of the client. How difficult can it be, you might ask, to do so? Is it that difficult to draft a trust with a condition precedent or condition subsequent in terms that leave no doubt as to the interest created? Frankly, it is not. All that is required is making the language clear. In addition, no matter how unambiguous the language might appear, interpretation of limitations can be heavily influenced by assumptions about the intent of the creator of the interest. That means that cases often can be found that construe similar language in radically different ways.

Exploring common constructional rules used by courts to give one meaning to language which is in dispute should help you understand the consequences of deciding that one or another type of future interest is created. This exercise will in turn will help you draft language that creates future interests that will insure property is distributed according to your client's estate planning designs.

1. The Preference for Early Vesting

One of the basic constructional rules is the preference for finding interests to be vested if at all possible. The reasons for this constructional rule are clear. First and perhaps foremost, a vested interest is not subject to the rule against perpetuities. As we will see, an interest that is vested (whether indefeasibly or subject to divestment, *but not if it is subject to partial divestment*) is not subject to the rule against perpetuities. Because application of the rule against perpetuities often frustrates the intent of the creator of the future interest (indeed, the rule is supposed to frustrate intent in pursuit of a social policy) finding that an interest is vested avoids the rule and more likely follows the intent of the creator of the interest.

Another reason for the preference for vested interests was the doctrine of destructibility of contingent remainders discussed above. If the preceding, so-called supporting, estate terminated, usually because the holder of the life estate died before the condition precedent was satisfied, the contingent remainder was 'destroyed.' Avoiding the application of doctrine more likely permitted creator's estate plan to be realized.

Vested remainders had another useful quality: they could *accelerate into possession* when the preceding life estate terminated prematurely. A remainder person, B, would not meet the condition precedent at the time she was to come into possession if A, the holder of a life estate disclaimed her interest, if B's interest was limited to take effect on the death of A. Vested remainders would be saved by allowing the holder immediate possession; contingent remainders would not.

Finally, there was the issue of transferability. At common law, a vested remainder, including one subject to a condition subsequent, could be transferred during life. Contingent remainders and executory interests, however, were not transferrable inter vivos, but they were devisable and descendible. Allowing a vested remainder to be transferable allowed the sale of land, because the holder did not have to await the death of the life tenant to alienate her interest (subject of course to the life tenant's possessory interest).

These hoary doctrines have largely been abrogated. The doctrine of the destructibility of contingent remainders has been laid to rest (although perhaps not definitely so in a few states). Contingent remainders and executory interests are transferable during life, although the creator of the interest can usually prevent the transferability of remainders by attaching to them spendthrift provisions. That said, transferring a legal contingent remainder in land, is complicated by the requirement that the interest of any unborn holders of the remainder interest must be represented when a transfer of the interest is proposed. That requires a court proceeding with the appointment of guardians who are charged with protecting their interests. Consequently, estate planners usually create vested remainders in real estate. Because the trustee holds full legal title to all the trust property, title in fee simple absolute to real property held in trust can be sold by the trustee without the buyer being concerned with the equitable interests held by the beneficiaries of the trust.

The final reason for construing remainders as vested, once of overwhelming importance, is no longer as relevant. The rule against perpetuities is slowly being transformed. As many as fifteen states have abolished the rule, either outright or by creating long periods of time during which interests in trusts can remain unvested.

2. Conditions of Survival Are Not Implied

One of the most important corollaries of the preference for early vesting is the traditional rule, still widely accepted, that a condition of survival to the time of possession is not implied. If a future interest is not made expressly subject to a condition precedent of survival to the time when the holder of the future interest is to receive the property, survivorship will not be implied.

> ***Example 14:*** G bequeaths property to T, in trust, with T as trustee, to pay the income to A for life and on A's death to pay the trust property to B. The time of possession for B, sometimes called the "distribution date" or "the time of distribution," is when the future interest "takes effect in possession or enjoyment." That is the time at which the claim check can be cashed in. B has an indefeasibly vested remainder. There is no implied condition of survival to the time of A's death. If B dies before A, the future interest passes through B's estate.

The possible implications of this rule are well-illustrated by the following case:

Security Trust Co. v. Irvine

93 A.2d 528 (Del. 1953)

Complaint for instructions by Security Trust Company, a corporation of the State of Delaware, trustee under the last will and testament of James Wilson, deceased, against Samuel L. Irvine, Frazer Wilson, Jeannette A. Wilson, Grace Wilson Gearhart, Helen G. Wilson Miller, Margaret W. Hanby, Mary Hope Wilson, James Rankin Davis, executor under the last will and testament of Margaret W. Irvine, deceased, Helen G. Wilson Miller, executrix under the last will and testament of Henry Wilson, deceased, Frederick W. Kurtz, executor under the last will and testament of Mary E. Wilson, deceased, Charles C. Kurtz, executor and trustee under the last will and testament of Martha B. Wilson, deceased, and Jeannette A. Wilson, executrix or administratrix of the estate of Samuel H. Wilson, deceased.

The case was before the court for final hearing.

BRAMHALL, VICE CHANCELLOR.

In this case this court is asked to determine two issues: (1) whether or not the residuary estate left to brothers and sisters of the testator vested as of the date of his death or at the time of the death of the last life tenant; (2) if it should be decided that the residuary estate vested as of the time of the death of the testator, do the life tenants take as members of the class of brothers and sisters receiving the residuary estate?

Plaintiff is trustee under the last will and testament of James Wilson, deceased, who died on July 29, 1918, leaving a last will and testament dated October 25, 1915. After providing for certain specific bequests, testator gave and devised all his "real and mixed estate" to the Security Trust and Safe Deposit Company, now the Security Trust Company, to two sisters, Martha

B. Wilson and Mary E. Wilson, during their joint lives and during the lifetime of the survivor of them. Testator further provided that in the event that his sister, Margaret W. Irvine, should be left a widow, she should share equally with the two sisters above named in the benefits of the trust so provided. As to the remainder, testator provided as follows:

> "Upon the death of two sisters, Martha B. Wilson and Mary E. Wilson, and the survivor of them, then it is my will that all of my real and mixed estate and any proceeds that may have arisen from the sale of any part thereof, together with any unexpended income there may be, shall be equally divided among my brothers and sisters, share and share alike, their heirs and assigns forever, the issue of any deceased brother or sister to take his or her parent's share."

Testator was survived by his five brothers and sisters: Samuel H. Wilson, Margaret W. Irvine, Martha B. Wilson, Mary E. Wilson, and Henry Wilson. At the time of the execution of the will the ages of the brothers and sisters ranged from 39 to 52 years. Martha B. Wilson and Mary E. Wilson, the two life tenants, died respectively on June 9, 1928, and August 18, 1951, unmarried and without issue, the trust therefore terminating on the latter date. The other devisees all predeceased Mary E. Wilson, the surviving life tenant. Samuel H. Wilson died on October 26, 1926, leaving to survive him three children, Frazer Wilson, Jeannette A. Wilson, and Samuel H. Wilson, Jr., and Grace Wilson Gearhart, daughter of a deceased son, Francis Paul Wilson. Samuel H. Wilson, Jr. died in 1924, unmarried and without issue.

Samuel Irvine, one of the defendants, is the sole residuary legatee under the will of Margaret W. Irvine, deceased. Martha B. Wilson died testate on June 9, 1928, leaving her residuary estate to her two nieces, Margaret Gregg Wilson, now Margaret W. Hanby, and Mary Hope Wilson, each an undivided one-half interest therein.

Mary E. Wilson died testate on August 18, 1951, leaving her entire residuary estate to Margaret W. Hanby, after providing for the payment of her debts and a legacy to Mary Hope Wilson in the sum of $100.

The estate of Martha B. Wilson has been closed, the final account having been passed on February 9, 1935; the estate of Mary E. Wilson has also been closed, the final account in that estate having been passed on September 15, 1952.

I must first determine whether or not the remainder interest of the testator became vested at the time of his death or at the time of the death of the last life tenant, Mary E. Wilson, on August 18, 1951. In order to resolve this question the intention of the testator at the time of the drafting of the will must first be ascertained. If it should be clear that testator intended this provision of the will to take effect at some future date, then the intention of the testator, so far as it may be legally carried out, will prevail. However, in reaching my conclusion, I must accept certain well recognized rules of construction.

Make the Connection

Where have we heard this language before? If the will is silent on the time of vesting, how can a court in 1953 know what a testator executing a document in 1918 actually intended?

The law favors the early vesting of devised estates and will presume that words of survivorship relate to the death of the testator, if fairly capable of that construction. In the absence of a clear and unambiguous indication of an intention to the contrary, the heirs will be determined as of the date of the death of the testator and not at some future date. When the language employed by the testator annexes futurity, clearly indicating his intention to limit his estate to take effect upon a dubious and uncertain event, the vesting is suspended until the time of the occurrence of the event. See Delaware Trust Company v. Delaware Trust Company, Del.Ch., 91 A.2d 44, and cases therein cited.

The assertion that it is indicated in the will that the testator intended the residuary estate to be vested as of the date of the death of the last life tenant is based upon the contentions: (1) the fact that testator left a life estate to two of his sisters and then gave the residuary estate to his brothers and sisters indicates that testator did not intend the two sisters to share in his residuary estate and therefore the residuary estate did not vest until the date of the death of the last life tenant; (2) the use of the words "upon the death of two sisters" and the provision in the will of testator that his estate "should be equally divided among my brothers and sisters" indicates an intention that testator intended a future vesting of his residuary estate.

Whatever may be the law in other states it is well settled in this state that the fact that a life tenant is a member of a class, in the absence of any clear indication in the will to the contrary, does not prevent the life tenant from participating in the remainder of testator's estate as a part of the class. Wright v. Gooden, 6 Houst. 397. The opinion of this court in the case of Delaware Trust Company v. Delaware Trust Company, supra, is not in conflict. In the Delaware Trust Company case the testatrix, after creating several life estates, the last of which was to her only son, provided that the residue and remainder of her estate should go to her heirs-at-law. In her trust inter vivos executed at the same time, she provided that the remainder, consisting of the proceeds of the sale of some Pennsylvania real estate, should go to the heirs-at-law of her husband. In that case the only son was the only heir-at-law of both the

> **FYI**
>
> Note the presumption that we presented earlier. Early vesting; no requirement for the takers to survive unless the intention is clearly expressed. Why does this presumption make sense?

testatrix and her husband. This court decided that the intention of the testatrix as manifested by the general scheme or purpose as found in her will and in her trust agreement, was to create an estate to take effect as of the date of the death of the last life tenant. It was there stated that

> **Food for Thought**
>
> Do you agree with the court? Why should it matter who is included in the class of remainder persons in determining when the remainder vests?

the use of the words "my heirs-at-law" and "heirs-at-law of my husband", where the son was the sole heir-at-law of both, along with other circumstances therein mentioned, demonstrated the intention of the testatrix to provide for future vesting. Here the testator in his will showed only an intention to postpone the enjoyment of the remainder until after the death of the life tenants. Where the will merely postpones the time of vesting the residuary estate would vest as of the time of the death of testator. The fact that the life tenants were also members of the class to whom the remainder of testator's estate was devised, would not prevent an early vesting of the remainder estate.

As to the use of the word "upon", it is equally clear under the decisions in this state and elsewhere, that this word and other words of this nature refer only to the time of payment and not to the substance of the devise. Cann v. Van Sant, 24 Del.Ch. 300, 11 A.2d 388; In re Nelson's Estate, 9 Del.Ch. 1, 74 A. 851. Other Delaware cases are to the same effect. In any event, the use of this word, and the provision for dividing its remainder, under the circumstances of this case would not alone be sufficient to overcome the presumption of immediate vesting.

It is contended on behalf of certain defendants that even though it should be determined that the gift to the brothers and sisters vested as of the date of the death of testator, the life tenants should be excluded from membership in the class of brothers and sisters. They base their contention upon the fact that testator in another item of his will gave them a life interest in his residuary estate.

In endeavoring to ascertain the intention of testator, it is uniformly held that such a provision is not of itself sufficient to prevent the life tenant from participating in the remainder as part of the class. See cases cited in 13 A.L.R. 620. It is not sufficient to show the absence of an intention to include the life tenants; there must be some indication of a clear and unambiguous nature to exclude them. Dillman v. Dillman, 409 Ill. 494, 499, 100 N.E.2d 567; Carver v. Wright, 119 Me. 185, 109 A. 896. I can find no incongruity in the mere fact that testator provided a life estate for his two sisters and later gave the remainder to his brothers and sisters, of which the two sisters were part of the class. They were unmarried. They were no longer young. It seems to be clear from the several provisions in the will of the testator that it was his purpose to provide for them. Such provision does not indicate to me that testator did not intend that they should participate further in his estate. Certainly there is no legal inconsistency in life tenants participating in the remainder. The theory that the testator particularly desired to see that his sisters were provided for is at least as strong as the supposition that he intended to exclude them from participating in the remainder.

I conclude that the life tenants should participate in the remainder devised by testator to his brothers and sisters.

Having determined that the life tenants should participate in the provision for the brothers and sisters, I must next consider the effect of the provision that the "issue of any deceased brothers or sisters to take his or her parent's share".

As to the brothers and sisters who died leaving issue, it was specifically provided that such issue should take the interest of such brother or sister leaving issue. Their interest was thereby divested, their issue being substituted in their place. In such case, the brother or sister dying leaving issue would have no power of disposition of his or her interest in the estate. In re Nelson's Estate, supra.

The will of testator is silent as to any provision relative to any of the brothers and sisters dying without leaving issue. Martha B. Wilson, Mary E. Wilson and Margaret W. Irvine, three sisters of testator, left no issue at the time of their death. Was their interest divested by their death, even though they left no issue, or did their estates receive an absolute interest, free and clear of any conditions subsequent?

Under the will of testator, the death of the life tenants leaving issue caused their interest to be divested. I have determined that the brothers and sisters received an absolute estate, subject to the provision that the interest of any brother or sister dying prior to the death of the life tenant should go by substitution to the issue of such brother or sister. However, this provision of the will does not apply where there is no issue, since there would then be no limitation upon their estate. The decisions in this state are silent as to what would happen under such circumstances. However, the weight of authority in other states is to the effect that in the event of the death of the devisees leaving no issue, the interest of such devisees is not divested by their death. McArthur v. Scott, 113 U.S. 340, 5 S.Ct. 652, 28 L.Ed. 1015; Plitt v. Plitt, 167 Md. 252, 173 A. 35, 109 A.L.R. 1; Jacobs v. Whitney, 205 Mass. 477, 91 N.E. 1009; Rutledge v. Fishburne, 66 S.C. 155, 44 S.E. 564; Gardner v. Vanlandingham, 334 Mo. 1054, 69 S.W.2d 947. Since the estates created were absolute except for the condition subsequent, and since the subsequent condition has been removed, the estates of the sisters dying without issue would have an absolute interest unrestricted by any condition.

> **Food for Thought**
>
> Do you agree with the court's logic? Why would the testator who seems to have wanted to benefit his collateral heirs by allowing the issue of deceased issue of deceased siblings take their parent's share want to allow siblings who had no issue to essentially dispose of his property? Isn't it just as likely that he would have wanted the shares of his deceased siblings who left no issue to pass to his own heirs rather than to their devisees?

I believe that such a determination would be in accord with the plain intention of the testator. He apparently desired to provide for his own brothers and sisters and their issue. If he had desired to provide that the interest of any brother or sister dying without issue should go to the surviving brothers or sisters or had intended to make some other similar provision, it would have been easy for him to do so. The fact that he did not, indicates that he had no such intention. I concluded that the interests of Martha B. Wilson, Mary E. Wilson and Margaret W. Irvine, were not divested by their death without issue and that their interests in the estate of the testator under the residuary clause of the will should go to their respective estates.

The estates of Martha B. Wilson and Mary E. Wilson have been closed. In accordance with the opinion of this court in Cooling v. Security Trust Co., 29 Del.Ch. 286, 76 A.2d 1, their shares may be distributed by the trustee directly to the persons entitled to receive the same, the trustees first seeing that any taxes which may be due or any costs which may be incurred by reason thereof are paid.

An order will be signed on notice in accordance with this opinion.

Points for Discussion

1. It will help you to understand the case if you draw a family tree. Note especially how the testator's three sisters disposed of their estates in their wills.

2. What sort of future interest did James Wilson create? How does the court reach its conclusion?

3. The court rejects two constructional rules that would benefit the children of the testator's brother Samuel. One would prevent Martha and Mary from having a share in the remainder because they are the life income beneficiaries. Some jurisdictions recognize a constructional preference that mandates that result: if one has a life income interest one cannot also have a remainder interest in the same property. The court rejects such a rule.

The second rule is based on the use of the language "upon the death of my two sisters" and is sometimes called the "divide and pay over rule." Under that constructional preference, if the only language creating the remainder is a direction to divide and pay over the trust property at a future date, there is a condition of survival to that date. The court likewise rejects the rule and indeed most jurisdictions have repudiated it.

4. The court orders that the shares of the trust payable to the beneficiaries of the estates of Margaret, Martha, and Mary be paid to the persons entitled to possession of them. This probably does not seem to be exceptional, but in fact it is. In most jurisdictions the accepted procedure would be to reopen the estates of the deceased beneficiaries. The executors then resume their duties by collecting the trust property and then distributing the property to the persons entitled to it under the wills of the beneficiaries. If the executor cannot or will not resume the office, the court will appoint an administrator c.t.a. d.b.n. The abbreviations are the first letters of Latin words that can be translated as "with the will annexed, of goods not [yet administered]." The person that is appointed is an administrator because he or she was not nominated in the will, but distributes property according to the will rather than the intestacy statute.

5. Is the result in *Security Trust* a sound one? There are really two parts to that question. First, is the result good for Margaret, Martha, and Mary? Is it consistent with the probable intent of the testator?

6. You may be puzzled about the outcome of *Security Trust* because of a fact which seems to play no part in the opinion. Consider. The remainder is a class gift. Does it help us decide what to do with the trust property when the remainders are to come into possession? The class gift is made when the testator dies. That is the time at which class members are ascertained. Those alive at the time take whatever future interest is created. Because the principal case involved a will, it is even possible that the applicable anti-lapse statute might give a predeceased sibling's remainder interest to the sibling's issue. However, it is likely that the court believed

that the disposition in the will provided for the contingency of a deceased beneficiary. In any event, the class members who take an interest at the testator's death do not lose the interest if they die before the distribution date. (This long accepted rule is reaffirmed in Restatement Third, Property (Wills and Other Donative Transfers), § 15.4.) This treatment, however, applies only to single generation class gifts, that is, to a class in which all members are of the same generation. Here, of course, the brothers and sisters of the testator are all in the same generation. The treatment of multi-generation class gifts is different.

The refusal to imply a condition of survival to the time of possession promotes the transmissibility of future interests which in turn allows the person in whom the future interest was created to decide who will actually take possession of the property when the preceding interest terminates. The choice of a beneficiary could also have been directed through the creation of a power of appointment should a class member predecease the life tenant. The use of a power of appointment has one great advantage over the creation of a transmissible interest: the creator (*donor*) of the power of appointment can dictate who receives the property if the holder of the power of appointment (powerholder) does not expressly exercise the power. In other words, it is possible to prevent the donee from unintentionally disposing of the property. Do you think that James Wilson's sisters knew that the residuary clauses of their wills disposed of part of the trust created by their brother because the future interest they held was part of their probate property? ✍

Before considering other constructional rules, we need to assess a controversial effect of the premise discussed immediately above: that, absent express terms requiring survival in a limitation, survival will not be implied. Take, for example, a revocable lifetime trust, a will substitute, that directs the trustee on the death of the creator (grantor) of the trust to make several distributions of sums of money (the equivalent of general bequests) and to distribute the remainder of the trust property (the equivalent of the residuary estate) to "the Grantor's children, X, Y, and Z in equal shares." If X dies before the Grantor, what becomes of X's share of the trust property?

Baldwin v. Branch

888 So.2d 482 (Ala. 2004)

This case involves a dispute as to whether a disposition in a trust created by Claude H. Baldwin, Jr. ("Claude"), lapsed when the grantee died. The trial court entered a summary judgment holding that the disposition made in the Claude H. Baldwin, Jr., Revocable Trust ("the Baldwin Trust") to Claude's sister, Bernice B. Branch, did not lapse on Bernice's death. Claude H. Baldwin III ("Claude's son"), appeals. We affirm.

On September 2, 1992, Claude executed a declaration of trust creating a revocable trust. He appointed himself trustee. The declaration of trust stated that upon Claude's death or incapacity, O.W. Irwin would succeed him as trustee, that all net trust income was to be paid to Claude during Claude's lifetime, that Claude retained the right to remove assets from the trust, and that following Claude's death the successor trustee was to make certain dispositions from the trust, including one to his sister Bernice.

Bernice predeceased Claude, leaving two children, Miles Branch and Suzanne B. Ligon. Claude died testate on January 4, 2001; the trust had never been amended. On March 13, 2001, the conservator of Claude's estate filed in the probate court a final settlement of his conservatorship.[1]

On February 12, 2001, Claude's widow, Julia Watson Baldwin, filed an action in the Shelby Circuit Court seeking a judgment declaring what assets were in Claude's estate and what assets, if any, were in the Baldwin Trust. On March 16, 2001, Claude's son filed an answer and a cross-complaint in Julia's declaratory-judgment action.[2] The cross-complaint filed by Claude's son is the subject of this appeal. Claude's son argued in his cross-complaint that the distribution to be made to Bernice from the Baldwin Trust had lapsed upon Bernice's death. Bernice's children, Miles Branch ("Branch") and Suzanne Ligon ("Ligon"), filed an answer to the cross-complaint in which they argued that as Bernice's children they are entitled to her share of the Baldwin Trust. Claude's son and Branch and Ligon moved for a summary judgment. Branch and Ligon attached to their motion an affidavit by the attorney who drafted the Baldwin Trust and Claude's will; the affidavit stated that Claude had intended Bernice's children to take under the trust in the event Bernice predeceased him. Claude's son moved the trial court to strike the affidavit on the ground that the Baldwin Trust was not ambiguous and therefore parole evidence was not necessary to its interpretation; the trial court granted the motion, and on February 1, 2002, entered a summary judgment in favor of Branch and Ligon upholding their claim to Bernice's share of the Baldwin Trust.

Claude's son appeals. He states the issue on appeal as whether "a provision for a beneficiary in a revocable trust lapses if the beneficiary predeceases the settlor, for whose lifetime benefit the trust income and principal are reserved, and the trust makes no provision for the contingency." (Appellant's brief, p. 4.) Specifically, Claude's son argues that Alabama's antilapse statute, which is applicable to wills, does not apply to trusts and that a gift in a revocable trust in which the settlor is also the trustee does not vest in the beneficiary upon the creation of the trust.

We review a trial court's summary judgment de novo, giving the judgment no presumption of correctness. *Nationwide Ins. Co. v. Rhodes*, 870 So.2d 695 (Ala.2003). When a document is unambiguous, its construction and legal effect are questions of law for the court to decide. *Wheeler v. First Alabama Bank of Birmingham*, 364 So.2d 1190 (Ala.1978).

---

1   On December 9, 1996, Claude's son petitioned to have a conservator appointed for his father, who he alleged was incompetent. The probate court first appointed Claude's son as the conservator, but later amended its order to appoint James M. Tingle as Claude's conservator.

2   Julia sought to have the trust declared invalid. Claude's son moved for a summary judgment upholding the validity of the Baldwin Trust, which the trial court entered. Julia appealed. On April 25, 2003, this Court reversed the summary judgment and remanded the case to the trial court to determine the issues of material fact regarding the validity of the Baldwin Trust. *Baldwin v. Estate of Claude H. Baldwin, Jr.*, 875 So.2d 1138 (Ala.2003) ("*Baldwin I*"). This appeal, which was filed on March 12, 2002, was placed on this Court's administrative docket pending the entry of a final judgment in *Baldwin I*. On November 10, 2003, the trial court entered a consent order in which it found that the "Baldwin Trust is valid and owns the assets conveyed to it by Claude Baldwin, Jr."

Claude's son argues that the provision in the Alabama Probate Code that prevents a lapse in a will, § 43–8–224, Ala.Code 1975, does not apply to revocable trusts. The issue whether a gift in a trust may lapse has not previously been addressed by an Alabama court. While § 43–8–224, Ala.Code 1975, operates, in the case of a will, to prevent a lapse when a devisee dies before the testator, there is no similar statutory provision to prevent a lapse of a gift made in a revocable trust.

Section 43–8–224 reads:

> "If a devisee who is a grandparent or a lineal descendant of a grandparent of the testator is dead at the time of execution of the will, fails to survive the testator, or is treated as if he predeceased the testator, the issue of the deceased devisee who survive the testator by five days take in place of the deceased devisee and if they are all of the same degree of kinship to the devisee they take equally, but if of unequal degree then those of more remote degree take by representation. One who would have been a devisee under a class gift if he had survived the testator is treated as a devisee for purposes of this section whether his death occurred before or after the execution of the will."

Section 43–8–224 mentions only wills, not trusts. Therefore the plain language of § 43–8–224 indicates that it does not apply to trusts.

Claude's son argues that before the enactment of the antilapse statute, Alabama followed the common-law rule that bequests in wills lapse when the legatee or devisee predeceases the testator. *See, e.g., Morgan County Bank v. Nelson*, 244 Ala. 374, 13 So.2d 765 (1943); *First Nat'l Bank v. Hartwell*, 232 Ala. 413, 168 So. 446 (1936); and *Little v. Ennis*, 207 Ala. 111, 92 So. 167 (1922). Claude's son also notes that " '[i]t was the rule at common law that a gift in trust lapsed upon the death of the beneficiary prior to the death of the trustor' " (quoting *In re Estate of Button*, 79 Wash.2d 849, 853, 490 P.2d 731, 734 (1971)). In Alabama, "[s]tatutes in derogation or modification of the common law are strictly construed. *Cook v. Meyer*, 73 Ala. 580 (1883). Such statutes are presumed not to alter the common law in any way not expressly declared. *Pappas v. City of Eufaula*, 282 Ala. 242, 210 So.2d 802 (1968)." *Arnold v. State* 353 So.2d 524, 526 (Ala.1977). Therefore, absent an express statutory provision creating an antilapse rule for revocable trusts, no such rule exists, and Alabama continues to follow the common-law rule that gifts in trust lapse if the beneficiary predeceases the settlor.

Branch and Ligon argue that the antilapse statute should be applied to determining who takes under the Baldwin Trust. They point out that Ohio, Washington, and Virginia have held that similar statutes in those states also apply to trusts, and they cite cases from those jurisdictions in which courts have found that an antilapse statute, on its face applicable only to wills, reaches trusts as well. *See Dollar Sav. & Trust Co. of Youngstown v. Turner*, 39 Ohio St.3d 182, 529 N.E.2d 1261 (1988) (holding that Ohio's antilapse statute, which specifically refers only to wills, applies to trusts); *In re Estate of Button, supra* (applying Washington's antilapse statute to a revocable inter vivos trust); and *Hester v. Sammons*, 171 Va. 142, 198 S.E. 466 (1938) (applying Virginia's antilapse statute to a testamentary trust).

Claude's son states that those cases do not provide reliable authority for this Court to hold that Alabama's antilapse statute reaches trusts. He notes that after the Ohio court handed down its decision in *Dollar Savings & Trust*, holding that Ohio's antilapse statute applied to trusts, the Ohio Legislature amended its antilapse statute to provide that the statute refers only to "wills" and that "will does not include inter vivos trusts or other instruments that have not been admitted to probate." Ohio Rev.Code Ann. § 2107.01. *See also* Ohio Rev.Code Ann. § 2107.52. The annotation to §§ 2107.01 and 2107.52 reads:

> "In amending sections 2107.01 and 2107.52 of the Revised Code, the General Assembly hereby declares its intent to supersede the effect of the holding of the Ohio Supreme Court on October 26, 1988, in *Dollar Savings & Trust Co. of Youngstown v. Turner* (1988), 39 Ohio St.3d 182, 529 N.E.2d 1261."

When the Supreme Court of Washington held in *Estate of Button* that Washington's antilapse statute applied also to trusts, that Legislature responded by amending its antilapse statute expressly to add the word "trusts." In both cases, both state legislatures indicated by legislative amendment that the language of the statute did not comport with their courts' reading of the statute.

Claude's son also argues that *Hester v. Sammons* does not provide persuasive authority because Virginia's antilapse statute "covers every property of every kind which the decedent might have." 171 Va. at 146, 198 S.E. at 467. Therefore, Claude's son concludes, Virginia's statute by its plain wording covers trusts as well as wills.

This Court has previously expressed a reluctance to rewrite the Alabama Probate Code to accommodate the use of a revocable trust as a substitute for a will. In *Russell v. Russell*, 758 So.2d 533, 538 (Ala.1999), this Court refused to read into the Alabama Probate Code the "augmented estate concept" rejected by the Legislature in 1982 when it reenacted the Probate Code. To hold that Alabama's antilapse statute applies to trusts, this Court would have to invade the Legislature's power to amend statutes. We are not willing to do so; therefore, Branch and Ligon's argument that Alabama's antilapse statute applies to trusts fails.

Food for Thought

The threshold issue that court faces is what branch of government should make the law of wills and trusts. Is the leap from interpreting the law to making the law as great as the court implies? Is this the first instance that we have seen where law strictly speaking applicable to wills has been extended to apply to will substitutes? Follow the argument below.

Claude's son also argues that the Baldwin Trust is a special subspecies of trust-a revocable trust of which the settlor is also the trustee. Claude's son urges this Court to reject Branch and Ligon's contention that Bernice's share in the trust vested when Claude created the trust. He argues that the cases cited by Branch and Ligon do not apply to revocable trusts. Claude's son points out that Article VI of the Baldwin Trust denies a beneficiary any right of alienation prior to the actual distribution of the proceeds of the trust to the beneficiary.[4] He also notes that, in Article III, Claude retained for himself the right to revoke or to amend the Baldwin Trust, and that, in Article I, Claude retained the net income plus the unlimited power to invade the principal. Claude's son argues that the trust instrument divested Claude of nothing.

Claude's son argues that the type of revocable trust created by Claude was conceived as a means to escape probate while retaining all benefits of ownership of the trust assets until the settlor's death. In support of this argument, Claude's son calls our attention to *Russell v. Russell*, 758 So.2d at 538, which held that the assets Mr. Russell conveyed to himself as trustee before his death were not subject to probate, and, specifically, that Mr. Russell's wife was not entitled to those assets in claiming her elective share.[5]

Branch and Ligon argue that appellate courts of other jurisdictions have held that a gift in a trust to a designated beneficiary vests when the trust is created. Branch and Ligon cite *First National Bank of Bar Harbor v. Anthony*, 557 A.2d 957 (Me.1989); *Detroit Bank & Trust Co. v. Grout*, 95 Mich.App. 253, 289 N.W.2d 898 (1980); *First Galesburg National Bank & Trust Co. v. Robinson*, 149 Ill.App.3d 584, 500 N.E.2d 995, 102 Ill.Dec. 894 (1986); *Hinds v. McNair*, 413 N.E.2d 586 (Ind.Ct.App.1980); *First National Bank of Cincinnati v. Tenney*, 165 Ohio St. 513, 138 N.E.2d 15 (1956); and *Randall v. Bank of America National Trust & Savings Ass'n*, 48 Cal.App.2d 249, 119 P.2d 754 (1941), in support of the proposition that the beneficiary's interest vests at the time the settlor creates the trust, even if the trust is a revocable trust.

For example, in *First National Bank of Bar Harbor v. Anthony*, supra, the court stated that "the settlor imposed no restrictions on what his children could do with their respective shares." The court concluded:

> "The unexercised right to make a change in beneficiaries, the absence of any control over how the children might dispose of their shares, and the overall assignment

---

4   Article VI, entitled "Spendthrift Provision," reads:

"No interest in income or principal shall be alienated, encumbered, or otherwise disposed of by any beneficiary while in the possession and control of the Trustee, and if any beneficiary should attempt to alienate, incumber [sic], or dispose of all or part of the income or grants of principal before the same has been delivered to the Trustee, if of by reasons of assets remaining in the hands of the Trustee under claims of creditors or otherwise, all or any part of such income or principal might fail to be enjoyed personally by any beneficiary or might vest in or be enjoyed by some other person, then such interests shall terminate. Thereafter, the Trustee may pay to or for the benefits of such beneficiary such income or principal comprising such interest as the Trustee, in the Trustee's discretion shall deem proper until such beneficiary dies. Thereupon, the trust estate or part affected shall be held or distributed as hereinabove provided for disposition upon the death of such beneficiary; if not herein provided, distribution shall be to such persons as would take and in the proportions they would take such beneficiary's estate under the Alabama laws of descent and distribution then in effect."

5   In *Russell*, Mrs. Russell argued that Mr. Russell's transfers to his trust during his lifetime should have been set aside because they deprived her of her elective share. 758 So.2d at 538. We noted that before the adoption of the current Alabama Probate Code in 1982, the spouse's elective share was a portion of the augmented estate. *Id.* The augmented estate includes transfers of the decedent made during his lifetime. However, we concluded that because Alabama rejected the augmented-estate concept when it enacted the current Probate Code, the surviving spouse was not entitled to a share of assets that were validly transferred by the decedent during his lifetime. *Id.* We address today a different question, namely, when a transfer to a revocable trust vests in the beneficiary.

of economic benefits lead us to conclude that this plan of disposition effectively eliminated any further interest of the settlor in the trust principal unless he affirmatively chose to intervene."

557 A.2d at 959. The court then held that although the child predeceased the father who had created the trust, the child's estate would take as its share the child's share in the trust, because the child's interest vested when the trust was created.

In *First Galesburg National Bank & Trust Co. v. Robinson*, supra, the Illinois appellate court held that the interest in the trust had vested and stated the general rule for vesting of a remainder:

> " '[W]henever the person who is to succeed to the estate in remainder is in being and is ascertained, and the event which by express limitation will terminate the preceding estate is certain to happen, the remainder is vested.'
>
> . . . [T]he words such as 'at death,' 'after death,' or 'upon death' in the devise of a remainder do not refer to the time when the remainder is to vest in interest but rather to the time when the remaindermen are to take possession."

149 Ill.App.3d at 586, 500 N.E.2d at 996, 102 Ill.Dec. at 895.

Branch and Ligon also cite Uniform Probate Code § 2–707(b) (10 ed.1991 rev.), which provides:

> "If a beneficiary of a future interest under the terms of a trust fails to survive the distribution date, the following apply:
>
> "(1) Except as provided in paragraph (4), if the future interest is not in the form of a class gift and the deceased beneficiary leaves surviving descendants, a substitute gift is created in the beneficiary's surviving descendants."

In *Jolly v. Hobbs,* 80 Ala. 213, 218 (1885), this Court stated: "The earliest vesting of the remainder is favored by the law, as it prevents its liability to destruction by the immediate tenant; and when in doubt, it will be held to be vested, rather than contingent."

In *Allen v. Maxwell*, 249 Ala. 655, 660, 32 So.2d 699, 703 (1947), this Court stated:

> "A remainder is said to be vested when the estate passes out of the grantor at the creation of the particular estate, and vests in the grantee during its continuance, or eo instanti that it determines, when a present interest passes to a certain and definite person, to be enjoyed in futuro, and is said to be contingent when the estate is limited either to a dubious and uncertain person, or upon the happening of a dubious or uncertain event,-uncertainty of the right of enjoyment, as distinguished from the uncertainty of possession."

(Quoting *George v. Widemire*, 242 Ala. 579, 585, 7 So.2d 269, 272 (1942).)

> " 'Whether a remainder is vested or contingent depends on the language employed. If the conditional element is incorporated into the description of, or into the gift to, the remainderman, then the remainder is contingent; but if, after words giving a vested interest, a clause is added divesting it, the remainder is vested.' "

Brugh v. White, 267 Ala. 575, 580, 103 So.2d 800, 804 (1957), quoting J. Gray, *The Rule Against Perpetuities* § 108 (4th ed.1942).

The "Declaration of Trust" portion of the Baldwin Trust states:

> "I Claude Baldwin, Jr., of Alabama, hereby transfer the property described in Schedule A attached hereto to Claude H. Baldwin, Jr. ('Trustee'), of Pelham, Alabama, in trust to hold such securities and all substitutions therefor and additions thereto for my benefit during my lifetime, and thereafter for the benefit of others as follows. . . ."

Claude then specifically identifies his beneficiaries by name and address, including Bernice B. Branch, the mother of Branch and Ligon.

Section 2.01 of the Baldwin Trust states:

> "On my death, the Trustee shall distribute the items of Trust Estate absolutely, as follows: . . . The Trustee shall divide all the rest, residue, and remainder of the Trust Estate into three equal shares and shall distribute those shares, equally and absolutely, to Claude H. Baldwin III, Bernice Branch, and Gloria Cobb. This section is subject to the provisions of Section 2 in the event any beneficiary should then be a minor or become incapacitated."

Claude did not make a class gift; the designated remaindermen are ascertainable from the Baldwin Trust. Moreover, at the time of the creation of the Baldwin Trust the event that terminates Claude's preceding interest, that is, Claude's death, was certain to happen. Moreover, Bernice's interest was not contingent upon her surviving Claude. Therefore, Bernice retained a vested remainder interest in the Baldwin Trust; she was entitled to take possession of that interest at Claude's death. Because the interest was vested, Bernice's estate was entitled to her share of the trust upon Claude's death. Article III, the revocation and amendment provision of the Baldwin Trust, and Article VI, the spendthrift provision, do not affect the vesting of Bernice's interest; rather, they affect when and whether she will actually take possession of the vested interest upon Claude's death. *See Brugh*, 267 Ala. at 580, 103 So.2d at 804 (interpreting *Braley v. Spragins*, 221 Ala. 150, 128 So. 149 (1930)). Thus, Branch and Ligon are entitled to Bernice's share of the trust property. We affirm the trial court's summary judgment awarding Miles Branch and Susan B. Ligon Bernice's interest in the Baldwin Trust.

AFFIRMED.

HOUSTON, BROWN, JOHNSTONE, HARWOOD, WOODALL, and STUART, JJ., concur.

LYONS, JUSTICE (concurring specially).

I concur fully in the main opinion. I write specially to memorialize a unique feature of this proceeding.

Most cases, of necessity, involve at least one lawyer who will not prevail. "May the best case win" is a saying we hear from time to time around a courtroom at the beginning of the proceedings.

This enables the lawyer who ultimately does not prevail to ease the pain by telling himself, if no one else, that while the client had the best lawyer, the client did not have the best case.

I cannot apply that saying in all respects to this case because I do not want to insinuate in any way that counsel for Branch and Ligon, the prevailing party in this appeal, i.e., the party with "the best case," was in any way inferior to counsel for Claude's son. But I will carve out so much of it as is necessary to observe that it is my duty as an Associate Justice to decide cases based on my best judgment as to the proper application of the law to the facts or, put another way, based on who had "the best case." I have done so in this case, notwithstanding my awe over the fact that counsel for the unsuccessful party, D. Harry Markstein, Jr., briefed and argued this case on March 18, 2003, at the age of 90. In so doing, he probably quite easily holds the record as the oldest member of the Alabama State Bar to appear before this Court.

While he did not prevail, Mr. Markstein quite ably represented his client with zeal, clarity of thought, and legal scholarship that lawyers many years his junior would do quite well to emulate. Perhaps, on another day, we can note Mr. Markstein's eclipse of his own record with a ruling in a setting where he has "the best case."

Points for Discussion

1. If the anti-lapse statute applied to the trust in *Baldwin*, Bernice's children would take their mother's share of the trust property. Given the facts of the case Bernice either died intestate or left a will leaving her property to her children. What if Bernice's will had given her residuary estate to her surviving spouse, or to charity? Would the transmissible interest pass to the residuary beneficiary? Bernice could, of course, have made a specific bequest of her future interest in the trust, but she would have to know of its existence and her brother may not have told the beneficiaries about the existence of the trust.

2. If interests like that given Bernice Branch in her brother's revocable trust should be treated like similar gifts in wills, and the gift lost if the named beneficiary does not survive the creator of the trust, should the new rule be established by the legislature or the courts?

3. New York follows the traditional law; without an express condition of survival, a future interest is not contingent on surviving to the time of possession. *Baldwin*, therefore, would be decided the same way in New York. As you learned from the *Baldwin* opinion, however a handful of states have changed the traditional rule by statute, at least with regard to revocable trusts. (*See* Ill. Stat. Chap. 760 § 5/5.5)

Such statues usually make the interest contingent on surviving the creator of the trust, reversing the preference for early vesting. The statutes then give the interest to the issue of the beneficiary. Sometimes the substitute gift to the issue is limited to situations where the person named in the trust is related to the creator of the trust, exactly analogous to the limitations of most anti-lapse statutes to testamentary gifts to relatives of the testator.

UPC § 2–707(b) requires survivorship: "[a] future interest under the terms of a trust is contingent on the beneficiary's surviving the distribution date." In other words, under UPC § 2–707 *every future interest created by a trust is subject to a condition precedent of survival to the time the interest comes into possession or enjoyment.* This is rule of construction, however, and under the UPC § 2–701, it must give way to a contrary intention on the part of the creator of the interest. The *Comment* to the section gives two examples of language that creates a transmissible interest: " 'income to A for life, remainder in corpus to B whether or not B survives A' " and " 'income to A for life, remainder in corpus to B or B's estate.' " The examples, however, indicate that the drafters of the UPC believe that the contrary intention must be very clear and expressly negate the requirement of survivorship to the time of distribution. This is a higher standard than that embodied in the Illinois statute and further limits the rule that survivorship is not required.

Having made all future interests in trusts contingent on survival to the time of distribution, UPC § 2–707 goes on to create an anti-lapse statute for such interests. This is the simplest case:

> **Example 15:** C creates a lifetime revocable trust with herself as trustee, to pay the income to C for life and on C's death to pay the trust property to X. Under UPC § 2–707, if X dies before C, on C's death the trust property passes by representation to X's descendants who survive C. If no descendants survive, the property passes under the residuary clause of C's will if the trust involved was created by a nonresiduary gift in the will and if that rule does not apply, the property passes to C's heirs determined as if C had died at the time the property comes into possession.

UPC § 2–707 applies to situations where there is more than one gift of the property. The statutory scheme is necessarily complex, but it does work. It has not been widely adopted, however. It may be that the Illinois Code Chap. 760 § 5/5.5, which applies the rule governing the death of will beneficiaries before the testator to revocable trusts used as will substitutes, will prevail in most jurisdictions.

Whether or not UPC § 2–707 is sound doctrine is unclear. It does manifest a radical change and may lead to decisions contrary to the intent of property holders until practitioners assimilate the new rule. On the other hand, UPC § 2–707 eliminates all transmissible interests except those deliberately created. Trust property will not be disposed of unknowingly through the residuary clauses or intestate estates of beneficiaries who are unaware that they own a future interest. The beneficiary who is aware, however, is deprived of the opportunity of directing distribution if the beneficiary dies before the distribution date. If the creator of the trust wants the beneficiary to direct distribution it can easily be done by creating a power of appointment.

Perhaps the lesson is clear: the creation of transmissible future interests should be avoided, or at least should be created only where such interests are the best way to accomplish what the creator of the trust wished to do.

There is another reason to avoid transmissible remainders. The actuarial value of the remainder is part of the taxable estate of the deceased holder of the future interest. The value of the remainder included the taxable estate may not be large, but it may be significant in a trust with substantial assets. Tax liability can be avoided by use of a non-general power of appointment, which will allow the beneficiary to select the recipient of the interest *without incurring estate tax on the interest.*

There are some exceptions to the rule that conditions of survival are not implied.

The most important is widely followed: *a remainder in a multi-generational class is subject to an implied condition of survival to the time of possession.* This rule is recognized in Restatement Third, Property (Wills and Other Donative Transfers), § 15.3 and was also recognized in the previous Restatements. Of course, the rule applies only in the absence of contrary intention, but may have an effect on many trusts.

A multigenerational class is one which includes members from more than one generation: the most common examples are "my issue" or "my descendants." There is an important corollary to the multigenerational class rule: the living class members *take by representation.* (*See* Restatement Third, Property (Wills and Other Donative Transfers), § 14.4.) The common law was otherwise, requiring a per capita distribution. For example, if the remainder was given to the life income beneficiary's issue and the beneficiary was survived by three children and six grandchildren, each would receive one-sixth of the trust property.

Practice Planning Problem

Client wants to create a remainder in a multigenerational class. How should the drafter approach the issue of issue of representation? While client could want a per capita distribution treating, say children, grandchildren, and even great-grandchildren equally, lawyers who regularly draft wills and trusts report that the overwhelming desire of clients is to have property distributed to the heads of the family lines. If a member of the first generation does not survive, his or her share descends by representation.

Assuming that the client does want representational distribution, should the trust terms spell out the representational method? The answer is yes. While the current statutory rule may be known, statutes may change and the law of another state might govern the will should the client change domicile before death. Using the terms "by representation" or "per stirpes" might not be a good strategy because these terms may have different definitions in another jurisdictions. In California, for example, if the document does not specific a method of representation for a multi-generational gift, the default method is modified per stirpes (per capita with representation) (Cal. Prob. Code §§ 240, 245). If the document states that the property is to be distributed "per stirpes" or "by representation" statute dictates that the representational method to be used is what we have called strict per stirpes (Cal. Prob.Code § 246).

The drafter therefore cannot avoid including a provision which stipulates the precise representational method to be employed. Such a provision could be modeled on the statutory description of the representation scheme and would eliminate any ambiguities. The following case underscores the importance of clarity:

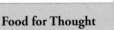

Matter of Gustafson

547 N.E.2d 1152 (N.Y. 1989)

BELLACOSA, JUDGE.

In concluding that appellants are not entitled to inherit under the relevant gift provision of this disputed will, we reaffirm two basic principles governing the adjudication of decedents' estates by courts: our primary function is to effectuate the testator's intent and the words used to express that intent are to be given their ordinary and natural meaning.

Testator executed his will in 1955 and it was admitted to probate in 1959. At issue is clause (c) of paragraph FIFTH, which bequeaths part of the residuary of one of two trusts to the "surviving child or children" of testator's brother Leonard, who predeceased the trust's life tenant, testator's widow, Elsie. A "surviving child" of Leonard, Jacqueline, is respondent before us and claims entitlement to the whole of that residuary portion. Appellants are the widow and children of Leonard's other child, Daniel (Jacqueline's brother),

> **Food for Thought**
>
> Do you agree? In the context of wills and trusts, does the word child have a plain meaning in the mind of a property owner? Do property owners consider the fact that generations do not pass on in order? The scrivener should know better.

who, like his father, predeceased the life tenant. Daniel's children, as appellants, strive to take under paragraph FIFTH'S gift provision and urge the courts to construe the word "children" to include grandchildren so that the collateral descendants of the testator, i.e., the grandnephews and grandnieces, can partake of the testamentary plan. Since they are faced with the fundamental proposition that the word "children" will be given its ordinary and natural meaning unless the will as a whole shows an unmistakable intent that different or remoter persons or classes should be included, they argue that the one-time use of the word "issue" in a different, inoperative clause of the will creates ambiguity and warrants forsaking the general rule of construction. Daniel's widow, as separate appellant, seeks to inherit on an argument that his

> **Food for Thought**
>
> By now you are seasoned observers of the law of wills and trusts. Do you agree that "children" is ambiguous?

inchoate share vested in him prior to the death of the life tenant, Elsie.

We affirm the order of the Appellate Division because a construction which would substitute for the testator's chosen word a broader, judicially applied definition is unwarranted and would be unsettling to the law of descent and distribution. Further, the relevant vesting date can be only the death of the life tenant.

Carl V.E. Gustafson was 59 years old, married and childless when he died in 1959. He disposed of virtually his entire estate through two trusts of equal size with an integrated, complementary residuary plan. The trust established in paragraph SIXTH provided that testator's brothers, Leonard and Roy, were to be equal income beneficiaries, and upon the death of either of them his one-half interest in the trust (that is, a one-fourth interest in the residuary) would pass to "his child or children". When Leonard died in 1978, his children, Jacqueline and Daniel, took equally of Leonard's share in this trust. Roy continues his life tenancy in the other portion of this trust. The half of testator's estate reflected in this trust is not involved in this case.

This case and appeal revolve around the trust created in paragraph FIFTH of the will, in which Elsie, testator's widow, held a life estate. Upon her death, testator's will directed the corpus of this trust be paid as follows:

"(a)　One-half to my brother, E. Leonard Gustafson.

"(b)　One-half to my brother, Roy L. Gustafson.

"(c)　If a brother predeceases Elsie Warren Gustafson, then his share of this Trust shall be paid over to his surviving child or children, share and share alike.

"(d)　If one of my brothers shall predecease Elsie Warren Gustafson, without issue surviving, then his part of this Trust shall be paid over to his surviving brother."

Roy survived Elsie and took his share pursuant to clause (b). This, too, is not involved in the case.

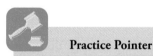

Practice Pointer

Ambiguous? How could the scrivener have been more clear?

At issue then is only the portion that would have been Leonard's one-quarter residuary share under clause (a), which, because of Leonard's predeceasing Elsie, must pass through clause (c). Leonard's son, Daniel, having also predeceased Elsie, leaves a widow and children who now seek to take a share of the residuary through this clause, though they are not "surviving child or children".

Courts construing donative instruments are governed by a threshold axiom: a testator's intent, as ascertained "from the words used in the will * * * according to their everyday and ordinary meaning", reigns supreme. In *Matter of Villalonga*, 6 N.Y.2d 477, the natural and ordinary meaning of the word at issue here was held and applied as follows: " '[c]hildren' means immediate offspring, and we reiterate the rule of the [*Matter of*] *Schaufele* [252 N.Y. 65, 67, 168 N.E. 831] case that *it will never be held to include grandchildren* 'unless the will as a whole shows that unmistakable intent.' " (Emphasis added.) The will before us cannot clear that high hurdle.

The order of testator's priorities is straightforwardly expressed in paragraph FIFTH. First, he provided for his widow as long as she lived. Then, upon her death, his brothers would benefit (para FIFTH [a], [b]). If his brother(s) predeceased his widow, then the focus of testator's beneficial intent shifted to the "surviving child or children" of his brother(s) (para FIFTH [c]), a generation proximate to himself. The final subdivision of this paragraph provides that if a brother dies "without issue surviving", the surviving brother takes all. Thus, if neither issue nor children survived one brother, the other brother (or his children or his issue) would take to prevent a lapse. Accordingly, from the four corners of the will's relevant gift provision, assigning to each word its ordinary meaning, the testamentary scheme is reasonably discernible. Carl Gustafson wanted to benefit: (1) his widow while she lived; (2) his brothers who survived his widow; and (3) if a brother did not survive his widow, then the brother's child(ren) who did so survive. Those preferences of the testator as to the order and distribution of his property are not "incoherent", "inequitable", "inconsistent" or "anomalous", but even if they were, testators are privileged to act in any way they see fit to displace the State's otherwise mandated, homogeneous distribution by intestacy, so long as they are *compos mentis*. Courts, on the other hand, are not privileged to put contrary or even additional words into a testator's actual written expression in order retrospectively to effectuate their own notions of "fair" or "equitable" distribution of estates.

Prowitt v. Rodman, 37 N.Y. 41, does not support a different result. There, an exception to the plain meaning of "children" was allowed because "the testator intended that the remote descendants should be takers * * * *if there should be a failure of the immediate offspring of [the trust life tenant]*" (*id.*, at 54 [emphasis added]; *see also, Matter of Welles*, 9 N.Y.2d 277, 280, 213 N.Y.S.2d 441, 173 N.E.2d 876 ["It seems to us that the only possible occasion justifying a more inclusive meaning (of 'children') would be to avoid failure of the estate."]). There is no failure of an estate here, which is the only justification for the exception to the paramount plain meaning rule of construction.

Nor is this case about the testator's intention to disinherit unknown, collateral descendants two generations removed from him. The law of decedents' affairs recognizes no rule requiring a testator to manifest an intent to disinherit in such circumstances. Rather, our rules relate to the testator's intent to bestow a gift and to whom. In that respect, he was plain, precise and orderly, and appellants' claim to a gift in this trust remainder by implication would wrongly extend the plainly expressed and universally understood words. Our ruling, therefore, is natural, not "narrow", and a faithful application of the holding of the governing precedent, not an "extension" of it. Simply put, children means children in the judicial construction of this will.

The nongifted parties also weave a number of speculative scenarios designed to splice themselves into this will and into this testamentary plan. The problem, however, is that none of their hypotheses materialized and are therefore neither materially helpful nor relevant to the disposition of this controversy.

We must also address the vesting date with respect to the remainder of the trust at issue. The death of the testator's life tenant, his widow, controls. Rather than "happenstance", this is the common measuring device for the orderly transferences of decedents' assets, a rule providing specificity, not serendipity. The vesting date here is arrived at by an application of well-settled principles of the law of future interests. The language of paragraph FIFTH (c) created a requirement of survival (*see*, 2A Powell, Real Property ¶ 328, at 763). When the first devisee or legatee takes a life estate, words of survivorship tend to " 'establish the time of the termination of all preceding interests as the time to which survival is required' " (*Matter of Gautier*, 3 N.Y.2d 502, 509, 169 N.Y.S.2d 4, 146 N.E.2d 771, quoting Restatement of Property § 251, at 1266). Here, the preceding interest terminated only upon the death of testator's widow, Elsie, in 1986.

Daniel's predecease in 1981 is irrelevant in this respect and precludes his heirs from asserting that any entitlements inchoately vested in him before Elsie's death to accrue later to their benefit.

As we have consistently held, the plain meaning of the testamentary language itself is the surest path to the judicial discernment of a testator's donative intent. Expanding the application of exceptions to that sound general proposition would soon swallow the rule and render less secure the effectuation of testator's relied upon, expressed intentions. Indeed, to create a new exception out of something called "paramount intent", different from the intent clearly expressed on the face of a will and in its only relevant donative provision, would be seriously unsettling because it would sacrifice predictability, an especially crucial element in the field of decedents' estates where "settled rules are necessary and necessarily relied upon" (*Matter of Eckart*, 39 N.Y.2d 493, 500, 384 N.Y.S.2d 429, 348 N.E.2d 905).

Accordingly, the order of the Appellate Division should be affirmed, with costs to all parties filing briefs payable out of the residuary trust at issue.

Hancock, Judge (dissenting).

I would modify the order of the Appellate Division and hold that the term "children" in paragraph FIFTH (c) of the will includes grandchildren and, therefore, that Leonard's share must be divided equally between his son Daniel's surviving children, collectively, and his daughter, Jacqueline.

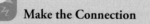

Make the Connection

A Wigmoreian? If there is an ambiguity here, is there an ambiguity everywhere? Review the sections of the casebook on the admission of extrinsic evidence.

In my view, construing "children" narrowly here and, thereby, disinheriting the lineal descendants of one of the testator's brothers is unwarranted and represents a distinct—and unfortunate—*extension* of the "unmistakable intent" rule. In *Matter of Villalonga*, 6 N.Y.2d 477, 190 N.Y.S.2d 372, 160 N.E.2d 850, where we applied that rule and declined to read "children" broadly, we emphasized that: (1) the will there was "a simple one * * * and not afflicted with the weakness of ambiguity" (*id.*, at 481, 190 N.Y.S.2d 372, 160 N.E.2d 850), (2) "[t]here [was] no interchangeable use made of the terms 'children' and 'issue' " (*id.*, at 481, 190 N.Y.S.2d 372, 160 N.E.2d 850), and (3) "[n]or [did] the general distributive scheme disclose a testamentary purpose to benefit children of predeceased immediate offspring together with surviving immediate offspring" (*id.*). Those very factors—the absence of which led our court to construe "children" narrowly in *Villalonga*—are *present* in this case.

The will here is ambiguous. The ambiguity arises, in part, from the interchangeable use of the terms "children" and "*issue*" in paragraph FIFTH. Also, the use of "issue" in paragraph FIFTH (d) manifests a clear intention to benefit a predeceasing brother's surviving lineal descendants—not just the brother's immediate offspring as a narrow reading of "children" in paragraph FIFTH (c) suggests. Moreover, the intent of the testator as indicated by the language and structure of the entire will seems straightforward: to make gifts to his brothers or their respective family lines, treating them equally. Indeed, there is nothing in the testamentary scheme to suggest that the testator wanted to disinherit the family of his brother's son (Daniel's family), in favor of that brother's other child (Jacqueline), on the seemingly unrelated and meaningless contingency of his brother's son predeceasing his widow.

Significantly, the *Villalonga* court itself reaffirmed the well-established exception to the rule it applied, viz., that where uncertainty exists, "children" should be given a broad construction to avoid an inequitable result (*id.*, at 482–483, 190 N.Y.S.2d 372, 160 N.E.2d 850). Quoting *Matter of Paton*, 111 N.Y. 480, 486, 18 N.E. 625, our court reiterated that, "[o]f course, if the language employed 'is equally susceptible of one or another interpretation, we should, on every principle of right, and within the spirit of the authorities, give it that which is *most equitable and consonant with the dictates of justice*' " (6 N.Y.2d, at 484, 190 N.Y.S.2d 372, 160 N.E.2d 850 [emphasis added]. Accordingly, we should construe "children" in paragraph FIFTH (c) as "issue" and, thereby, avoid an incoherent interpretation of paragraph FIFTH (b) and (d) and, at the same time, avoid the patent inequity which otherwise results.

The majority's attempt to reconcile paragraph FIFTH (c) and (d) avoids neither problem. Nor does it withstand scrutiny. Paragraph FIFTH (d) cannot fairly be read—as the majority contends—as providing that, "if neither issue nor children survived one brother, the other brother (*or his children or his issue*) would take to prevent a lapse." (Majority opn., at 453, at 626 of 548 N.Y.S.2d, at 1153 of 547 N.E.2d [emphasis added].) Plainly, the language of paragraph FIFTH (d) does not so provide. It does no more than give the share of the estate in question to the "surviving brother" if the other dies "without issue surviving". There is no language in paragraph FIFTH (d) itself that directs or permits "issue" (or "children") to take. Only paragraph FIFTH (c) can be read as providing for that, and then, only if "children", as used by the testator, is construed to mean "issue".

Indeed, the majority's contention, that paragraph FIFTH (d) permits a devise to a brother's "issue" under certain circumstances, plainly undercuts their position and supports the view taken here. Their contention necessarily recognizes the basic point that "issue" (i.e., children of deceased children) were intended to be beneficiaries in some situations. But because, as noted, such a disposition cannot be effected under paragraph FIFTH (d), it follows that it can only be made under paragraph FIFTH (c)—i.e., by construing "children" in paragraph FIFTH (c) broadly as permitting "issue" to take.

Similarly, other provisions in the will either make little sense or run counter to the testator's overall design if "children" is narrowly construed. For example, the distribution under paragraph SIXTH, providing for the direct gifts to the testator's two brothers,[1] would have failed if one of them had died with grandchildren or other issue, but with no surviving immediate offspring. And the very same would be true for paragraph EIGHTH—which was explicitly intended

---

1   Paragraph SIXTH (e) provides: "If a brother predeceases me, then his share of the Trust provided hereby shall be paid over to his child or children, share and share alike."

to cover any bequest elsewhere in the will that might fail.[2] Under that paragraph, as under paragraphs FIFTH and SIXTH, if "children" is read narrowly, there would be no provision for the very real contingency of a brother dying with no surviving sons or daughters, but with grandchildren or other lineal descendants still alive. Thus, paragraph EIGHTH, intended to avoid intestacy, would actually have permitted intestacy if read strictly.

I would resolve the ambiguities, and avoid the otherwise resulting inconsistencies and anomalies in the will, by broadly construing "children" to mean "issue". Such a construction would, in my view, yield the most reasonable and fair result—i.e., permitting Leonard's son's family (Daniel's family) as well as Leonard's daughter (Jacqueline) to share in the estate—and, thereby, avoid the certainly unintended inequity of depriving Daniel's children on the mere happenstance that their father died before their great uncle's widow. Finally, construing "children" broadly would, thus, give effect to the testator's paramount intent.

Wachtler, C.J., and Alexander and Titone, JJ., concur with Bellacosa, J.

Hancock, J., dissents in part and votes to modify in a separate opinion in which Simons and Kaye, JJ., concur.

———————

Points for Discussion

1. The majority opinion in *Gustafson* follows traditional future interest law, that is, the term "children" will not be read to include more distant descendants absent what the opinion calls an "unmistakable intent" on the part of the creator of the future interest to give the word an expanded meaning. This rule, of course, is a manifestation of the plain meaning rule and the refusal to "rewrite" documents, especially wills.

Many commentators, however, take a different approach. For example, and most prominently, Restatement Third, Property (Wills and Other Donative Transfers), § 11.3(c)(3) includes among the constructional preferences derived from "the foundational constructional preference" for "the construction that is more in accord with common intention than other plausible constructions" "the construction that does not disinherit a line of descent." That construction in turn is described as justifying construing "children" to mean "issue" in a wide variety of situations, discussed in § 14.1 comment *g*. The discussion of *Gustafson* in the Reporter's Notes gives the impression that the dissent had the better argument.

2. Assume that Carl Gustafson wanted his brother's grandchildren to share in the remainder. In other words, assume that the dissent correctly understood his intent. How would you have drafted the language creating the remainder to accomplish your client's intent?

———————

2   Paragraph EIGHTH provides: "If any Trust or Legacy hereunder shall be voided; or, if any intestacy develops * * * then such legacy or intestacy shall be * * * paid over to my brothers * * * or to the child or children of a deceased brother, share and share alike."

3. The requirement of survival to the time of possession makes a remainder in a multi-generational class contingent. Survival to the time of possession is clearly a condition precedent. That means, of course, that as members of the class die before the time of possession (as in *Gustafson*) they lose their interest; it is not transmissible. There are no tax consequences to the estate of the deceased class member and he or she cannot make an unknowing disposition of the interest.

3. Gifts to Heirs

If a scrivener is trying to draft a will or trust to insure that property descends to relatives there is a temptation to give the remainder to a named person's "heirs at law" or "next of kin." Most jurisdictions defined both terms and "any term of similar import" to mean the named person's distributees defined by the intestacy statute. (*See* NY EPTL § 2–1.1.) Remember that the Uniform Probate Code cuts off intestate inheritance rights at second line collateral (descendants of grandparents). Of course, such a gift may escheat to the state if the named person runs out of heirs, but with that caveat, a gift to heirs certainly insures that property will stay in the family and will also benefit a surviving spouse. Consider a gift over to another (or a charity) should the property holder die without heirs.

Recall that a remainder given to a named person's heirs (*Example 11*) is a contingent remainder until that person's death. An ancient maxim of the common law is "no one is heir of the living." Once the named person dies, however, the interests in the heir or heirs are indefeasibly vested. The only condition precedent was that they survive the named person and be the heirs designated by statute.

This is all extremely unproblematic if the named person is also the life beneficiary of the trust on whose death the remainder is to come into possession.

Example 16: G bequeaths property to T, in trust, with T as trustee, to pay the income to A for life and on A's death to pay the trust property to A's heirs. A dies unmarried, survived by two children and three children of a predeceased child. Under every representation system used in intestacy, each child is entitled to one-third the trust property and the three grandchildren are entitled to one-ninth each.

Consider the following, however.

Example 17: Testator's will creates a testamentary trust for his surviving spouse to pay the income to her for life and on her death to pay the trust property to the testator's sister "if she then survives, and if not to her heirs at law." Testator had no children, nor did his sister. Testator's sister predeceased his widow and at her death her sole heir was her surviving spouse, testator's brother-in-law. The brother-in-law also predeceased the testator's widow. He died testate and his will left his residuary estate to charity. At the death of testator's widow a niece and nephew of the testator survived (the children of another sibling). If testator's sister had died at that time, the niece and nephew would have been her heirs. The traditional rule gives the trust property to the charity. The brother-in-law's interest in the trust vested indefeasibly as soon as he became his wife's heir and it passed through the residuary clause along with the rest of his property not otherwise disposed of to the charity.

The result in **Example 17** is "correct" as a matter of legal doctrine once the preference for early vesting is applied, but may not be consistent with the intent of the testator. When faced with this circumstance, it is possible that the testator would prefer that the trust property remain in the family and that the testator believed that such an outcome would be the result of giving the alternative contingent remainder to the sister's heirs. The problem illustrated here is yet another example of the difficulties inherent in transmissible interests: the possibility of an unknowing disposition and the possibility of an increased estate tax in the heir's estate.

The problems illustrated by the examples herein, most prominently the possibility of an unknowing disposition, led to several constructional rules that stipulate that heirs of the named person should be ascertained as if the named person had died at the time the property was to come into possession or enjoyment, the time for distribution. Like so many such rules, however, their application depended first and foremost on how a court described the intent of the creator of the interest. For example, in some cases the application of the preference for early vesting and the resulting creation of a transmissible interest will result in the remainder passing to a person who is also the life beneficiary of the property. This result may be found to be contrary to the intent of the creator of the interest as it was in the following case:

Matter of Carlin

6 A.D.2d 281 (N.Y. App. 1958)

HALPERN, JUSTICE.

This is an appeal from a decree of the Surrogate's Court of Genesee County in a will construction proceeding which held that the surviving husband of the testatrix, Sarah M. Carlin, 'is the sole distributee of Sarah M. Carlin, deceased, and thereby entitled not only to the life use of the entire property of said deceased, but also to the gift and bequest of the remainder interest as well.'

The will is very short. The donative provisions are as follows:

'First. After the payment of all my just debts, funeral and testamentary expenses, I give, devise and bequeath the use of all my property, real and personal, to my husband, Walter T. Carlin and give him the privilege in case of necessity to use so much of the principal as may be necessary for his care and support.

'Upon the death of my husband, I give, devise and bequeath such of my property as shall then remain to my distributees under the laws of the State of New York.'

Analyzing these provisions, we find a clearly expressed testamentary scheme. The testatrix intended (1) to give her husband the income from her estate for life; (2) to give him a limited right to invade the principal 'in case of necessity' to provide for his care and support; (3) to give so much of the principal as remained upon his death to the testatrix' distributees.

The will was executed on March 9, 1935. The testatrix died on October 13, 1944.

Both at the time of the execution of the will and at the time of the death of the testatrix, the testatrix' husband was her closest relative under the statutory table of distribution and he would be her sole distributee, if her distributees were determined as of that time. The testatrix also left her surviving an uncle and cousins, the survivors of whom would be her distributees, if her distributees were determined as of the time of the death of her husband.

The testatrix had never had any children and, at the time of the execution of the will, there was no reason to believe that she would have any before her death;[7] she had never had brothers or sisters and her parents were dead. Therefore, there was no possibility of anyone other than her husband being her distributee, if her distributees were determined as of the time of her death, provided only that he survived her.

In this situation, the inference is inescapable that the testatrix must have intended that the remainder should go to the persons who would be her distributees at the time of the death of her husband rather than at her own death. In making a gift 'to my distributees' of what remained 'upon the death of my husband', she must have meant the persons who would be her nearest relatives as of that time. This is the only construction which is consistent with the testamentary scheme expressed in the will.

If the will were construed as requiring the determination of the distributees as of the time of the death of the testatrix, the result produced would be a wholly incongruous one. The testatrix' husband would then be the sole distributee and he would take the remainder as well as the life estate. The life estate would merge with the remainder in fee and the husband would acquire at once a present fee simple absolute, notwithstanding the clearly expressed intention of the testatrix to limit his legal interest to that of a life tenant.

Every aspect of the testamentary scheme would be frustrated if the will were construed as leaving the husband a fee simple absolute. The provision giving the husband a limited power to use the principal in case of necessity would be rendered meaningless by this construction. As the owner of the fee, the husband could, of course, expend the principal as he pleased. There would be then no need for a provision giving him a 'privilege' to use the principal. Neither would the limitation on the privilege be effective. As the sole owner of the estate, the husband would be in a position to expend or dissipate the principal at once, without regard to the amount currently needed for his support, even though this left him without any income during the rest of his life. The salutary purpose of the testatrix to protect her husband against his own improvidence would thus be defeated.

---

7   The petition for the probate of the will, which is referred to in the opinion below but is not printed in the record, shows that the testatrix was 61 years of age at the time of her death in 1944, so she was 52 years of age at the time of the execution of the will.

Furthermore, under the construction vesting the whole fee in the husband, he would be able to give or bequeath the property to relatives of his own or to strangers, thus defeating the testatrix' expressed intention that whatever remained on his death should go to 'my distributees'. Presumably, by this term she meant her own relatives. It is significant that while the husband was given the power to invade the principal during his lifetime, to the extent necessary for his care and support, he was not given any power to appoint the principal by will or, in any other manner, to dispose of the unconsumed balance of the principal on his death. This restriction would likewise be nullified by construing the will as giving the husband the whole fee.

Food for Thought

Is this will construction or simply reformation? Regardless of whether the outcome is a proper one, has the court simply added provisions to the will rather than construing existing ones?

The gift of the remainder to the testatrix' distributees is stated in the will in terms of a gift of whatever balance remains upon the husband's death after he has used as much of the principal as necessary. This formulation necessarily implies that the balance is to be paid over to someone other than the husband. Whether there will be any balance and, if so, how much, cannot be determined until the husband's death. It is therefore reasonable to infer that, under the testamentary scheme, the distributees are also to be determined as of that time.

On the other hand, it is wholly unreasonable to attribute to the testatrix an intention to give to her husband a fee by the circuitous method of giving his a life estate by name and then giving him the remainder by describing him as her 'distributees'. If the testatrix had intended to give her husband the whole fee, she could readily have so provided in a few simple words. There was no possible reason for the circumlocution.

It is hornbook law that the touchstone in all will construction cases is the intention of the testator, as ascertained from the language of the will, read as a whole in the light of the circumstances existing at the time of its execution (Spencer v. Childs, 1 N.Y.2d 103, 107, 150 N.Y.S.2d 788, 790). The testator's intent 'must be gleaned * * * from a sympathetic reading of the will as an entirety and in view of all the facts and circumstances under which the provisions of the will were framed' (Matter of Fabbri's Will, 2 N.Y.2d 236, 240, 159 N.Y.S.2d 184, 187). 'The intention of the testatrix, so long as it is not contrary to some statute or to public policy, must govern' (Salter v. Drowne, 205 N.Y. 204, 212, 98 N.E. 401, 403). Since the intention of the testatrix in this case is self-evident, the only question which need concern us is whether there is any rule of law which prevents us from carrying out her intention. We can find no such rule in the authorities.

It is true that there is a general rule to the effect that a testator's distributees are ordinarily to be determined as of the time of his death but this rule 'is not a rule of substantive law, but a rule of interpretation, which has been adopted by the courts as one means of ascertaining the intention

Make the Connection

What about the plain meaning rule?

of the testator as expressed in the will; and it never should be used to defeat what, from the whole will, appears with reasonable certainty to have been his intention' (Wills, 57 Am.Jur., § 1279, p. 848). When a gift is made to persons 'to be determined by a statute governing the intestate succession of property, then the statute is applied as of the death of the designated ancestor, unless an intent of the conveyor to have the statute applied as of some other date is found from additional language or circumstances' (3 Restatement of Property, § 308). In our case, the intent of the testatrix to postpone the determination of her distributees to the time of the death of the life tenant is readily inferable from the 'additional language' of the will in this case and from the 'circumstances' at the time of its execution.

In a comment to the section quoted, the American Law Institute takes the view that where a testator gives a life estate to a person who is presumptively his sole heir and then gives the remainder in terms to his 'heirs', the incongruity which would result from determining the heirs as of the time of the testator's death is of itself sufficient to warrant an inference of an intention to postpone the time of the determination of the testator's heirs to the death of the life tenant. '[W]hen A, by will, conveys property 'to B for life then to my heirs' and B is the sole heir of A * * * the fact that * * * B is the sole heir of A at the death of A tends to establish that A intended his heirs to be ascertained as of the death of B, so that B is prevented from sharing in the limitation to the heirs of A' (3 Restatement of Property, § 308, comment *k*). To the same effect, see 5 American Law of Property, section 22.60, pages 441–443.

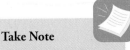

Take Note

The court is certainly fond of the word incongruity. What does the court mean by the word? Wrong result? Absurd result? Is there something to be said in favor of ignoring the result and interpreting the words employed by the scrivener?

As we have seen, in our case there is a much greater incongruity than that resulting from a construction which gives the remainder in fee to a sole heir who had theretofore been given a life estate. There is the additional incongruity which grows out of the fact that the testatrix had expressly given the life tenant a limited power to invade the principal to the extent necessary for his care and support; this provision is wholly incongruous with a construction which gives the remainder in fee to the life tenant. This basic incongruity can be escaped only by postponing the time of the determination of the testatrix' heirs to the time of the death of the life tenant.

In its recent decision in Matter of Sayre's Will, 1 A.D.2d 475, 151 N.Y.S.2d 506, affirmed 2 N.Y.2d 929, 161 N.Y.S.2d 890, this court stressed incongruity as one of the 'sound reasons for determining the class of heirs of the testator, not at his death, but at the death of the life tenant' (1 A.D.2d at page 479, 151 N.Y.S.2d at page 510). The incongruity in our case is greater than that in the Sayre case. The court pointed out in the Sayre case that if the heirs were determined in that case at the death of the testator, the estate of one of the testator's sisters would be allowed to 'qualify for a share as an heir' even though by an earlier provision a gift to the sister in fee had failed because of her predecease of the life tenant. Under this construction, the sister's estate would only take a one-sixth share as an heir but even this incongruity was held to be sufficient to militate against the construction which produced it. The court went on to say that 'for all the testator knew when he drew his will, she could have been his only heir at his death, in which case she would have received a vested remainder in fee'. 'Such an incongruity', the court concluded, 'is evidence that the testator did not intend his heirs to be determined at the time of his death' (1 A.D.2d at pages 479–480, 151 N.Y.S.2d at page 511). In our case, the testatrix knew at the time she drew her will that her husband was certain to be her sole distributee as of the time of her death, if he survived her and took the life estate. A wholly incongruous result would be produced by construing the will as giving him the remainder in fee, to take effect upon his death, as well as the life estate. This incongruity is much stronger evidence than the incongruity in the Sayre case that the 'testator [testatrix] did not intend his heirs [her distributees] to be determined at the time of his [her] death'.

It is true that the decision in the Sayre case rested not only upon the element of incongruity but also upon the fact that the remainder to the heirs was 'secondary, contingent, and substitution-al'. But it is evident from the portion of the opinion discussed above that the court recognized that complete incongruity of the type here present would of itself be sufficient to warrant an inference of an intention to postpone the time of the determination of the testator's heirs to the time of the death of the life tenant. The substitutional nature of the gift was held to be significant in the Sayre case, along with the element of incongruity, only because it furnished a clue to the intention of the testator. The ascertainment of the testator's intention was the objective of the court's inquiry in that case, as it is in all will construction cases. The factors mentioned were relied upon only as evidence of intention. If the intention to postpone the time of the determination of distributees is found, upon a reading of the whole will, it will be given effect, even if the gift to the distributees is primary and not substitutional.

The significance of the substitutional and contingent nature of the gift to the testator's heirs in the Sayre case was that it had the effect of postponing to the time of the life tenant's death, the determination of whether the heirs would take at all. This, the court held, tended to support the view that the determination of the identity of the heirs should also be postponed to that time. The provision for the invasion of the principal for the husband's benefit in the will in our case, leaving to the remaindermen only the balance of the principal remaining unexpended on the husband's death, has a similar effect. It is uncertain whether anything will be left on the husband's death. The gift of the remainder is therefore contingent in the sense that, as a practical matter, the effectiveness of the gift depends upon the husband's not using up all the principal for his support during his lifetime. Therefore, under the reasoning of the Sayre case, the determination of the distributees who are to take should also await the end of the life estate. The fact that the gift of the remainder is, in form, a primary gift and not a substitutional gift is immaterial.

Indeed, in a case such as ours, where the avoidance of an obvious incongruity is the most important consideration, the fact that the gift to the distributees is a primary gift, instead of a substitutional one, cuts against the respondent's position rather than in his favor. If the gift to distributees had been a substitutional one, it might have been argued that there was in fact no incongruity because the testator may well have intended that the life tenant should take the remainder in fee, in the event that his first choice, the gift to the primary remainderman, failed.

'If the gift were made 'to A for life, and, if B survives A, to B in fee, but if B does not survive A, then to the testator's heirs' [it] is quite conceivable that the testator might have intended to give the remainder to A if B did not survive A, and therefore the fact that A is the sole heir of the testator at testator's death does not require postponing the determination of heirs to a later date. If the limitations are simply 'to A for life, remainder to the testator's heirs,' it would be much more difficult to assume that the testator intended A to take the remainder' (2 Simes and Smith, Law of Future Interests (2d ed.), § 735, p. 210; cf. Safford v. Kowalik, 278 App. Div. 604, 101 N.Y.S.2d 876).

Furthermore, in the case of some types of substitutional gifts, it is arguable that the testator expected that in all probability the intervening primary gift would take effect and thus avoid any incongruous result and he may not have cared much that in the remote event of the substitutional gift taking effect, there might be some incongruity. But, in our case, the gift of the remainder to distributees being a primary gift, there was no possibility of the incongruity being avoided by the taking effect of an intervening gift. The incongruity was plainly foreseeable and was certain to occur if the distributees were determined as of the death of the testator. There is much stronger reason for postponing the time of the determination of the distributees in such a case than there is in a case in which the occurrence of the incongruity is a mere possibility or a matter of chance (3 Restatement of Property, § 308, comment *k*, pp. 1716–1717).

Further support for the conclusion here reached is found in Salter v. Drowne, 205 N.Y. 204, 212, 98 N.E. 401, 403; Stewart v. Giblett, 235 App.Div. 589, 257 N.Y.S. 746; Matter of Bishop's Estate, 126 Misc. 722, 215 N.Y.S. 237, affirmed 219 App.Div. 711, 219 N.Y.S. 777.

Matter of Bump's Will, 234 N.Y. 60, 65, 136 N.E. 295, 296, principally relied upon by the respondent, will be found, upon analysis, to support the appellants' view rather than the respondent's. While the court in that case reiterated the general rule that the testator's heirs are ordinarily to be determined as of the date of his death, it recognized that that rule is not applicable 'when a contrary intention appears'. In the Bump case, there was a gift of a life estate to the testator's wife with a remainder in fee to his daughter or her issue, if any, surviving the wife; if none, then a life estate to his sisters or the survivor of them, with a remainder in fee to the testator's heirs. The daughter predeceased the wife, leaving no issue. The question was who was entitled to the remainder in fee. The court found no basis in the will in that case for inferring a contrary intent and hence applied the general rule. The estate of the daughter was held to be entitled to the remainder in fee. The court pointed out, however, that this was not a completely incongruous result, since the daughter did not take as an heir the whole fee, which she would have taken if she had survived and had taken as a named devisee. 'There is first carved from it the life estate of the sisters, and only when that is exhausted does the remainder take effect' (234 N.Y. at page 64, 136 N.E. at page 296).

In another part of its opinion, the court indicated even more strongly that if the application of the general rule would have produced a complete incongruity of the type here involved, the court would have found that of itself a sufficient basis for inferring an intention contrary to the general rule. The Surrogate had chosen an intermediate course among the possible constructions of the will and had decided that the testator's heirs should be determined as of the death of the testator's wife, the primary life tenant. As of that time, the sisters were the testator's heirs but the testator had already provided for a life estate for them and it would obviously be incongruous to give them the whole fee in the face of the testator's express limitation of their interest to that of life tenants. The court therefore rejected the Surrogate's construction. 'Is it possible that he intended to designate them by the use of that word [heirs]; that in two succeeding clauses he first carefully provides for a life estate in their favor and then in addition gives them the fee? We think not' (234 N.Y. at page 64, 136 N.E. at page 296). The court thus indicated in the Bump case that it would not adopt a construction of the term 'heirs' which would produce the incongruous result of giving the whole remainder to a person whom the testator had specifically limited to a life estate.

Of course, as the incongruity is lessened in degree, the force of the reason for avoiding it diminishes (3 Restatement of Property, § 308, comment *k*, p. 1716). Thus, for example, if a life estate is devised to one of several heirs of the testator and the remainder is devised to the testator's heirs generally, there is little reason to attribute to the testator an intention to postpone the determination of the class to the time of the life tenant's death. There is little incongruity in allowing the life tenant to take a share of the remainder as one of the heirs of the testator, along with his life estate (United States Trust Company of New York v. Taylor, 193 App.Div. 153, 183 N.Y.S. 426, affirmed 232 N.Y. 609, 134 N.E. 591; 5 Am.Law of Property, § 22.60, p. 445).

Similarly, even in a case dealing with a sole heir, if the life interest given to him is not an alienable legal life estate but is a life use under a spendthrift trust, it is arguable that there is not sufficient incongruity to require rejection of a construction giving him the remainder in fee. There is no merger of the equitable life use and remainder; the life beneficiary cannot terminate the trust, even if he is the sole remainderman; the trust will still serve its intended purpose. '[T]he purpose of the testator to prevent B [the life beneficiary] from having control over the property during his lifetime is not defeated even if B is given the remainder interest' (5 Am.Law of Property, § 22.60, p. 444; Matter of Roth, 234 App.Div. 474, 255 N.Y.S. 307).

In many of the cases dealing with a gift to heirs, next of kin or distributees, the provision is an end limitation, a sort of catch-all, following a complicated set of dispositions. In that type of case, it may be said that the testator had exhausted his primary purpose and was willing to let the law take its course, if all the preceding dispositions should fail (Matter of Bump, supra, 234 N.Y. at page 66, 136 N.E. at page 296). If an incongruity should then result from the determination of the distributees as of the time of the testator's death, it might well be held that the incongruity should be disregarded on the ground that the testator had had no particular intent in mind at all with respect to the end limitation. But, in this case, the will was a simple one. The gift of the remainder to the testatrix' distributees was a part of her primary plan; it was not a catch-all expression adopted out of exhaustion of purpose or indifference, but a primary gift reflecting a specific intent in the mind of the testatrix as to the disposition of whatever remained of the principal on her husband's death. In this situation, it must be presumed that the testatrix intended to make a logically consistent disposition of her estate and not an incongruous one.

All incongruity disappears if the will is construed as providing for the determination of the testatrix' distributees as of the time of the death of the life tenant. It must be concluded that that is what the testatrix intended.

The decree of the Surrogate should be reversed and the will should be construed as giving the remainder to such persons as may answer the description of distributees of the testatrix at the time of the death of her husband.

Decree reversed on the law and facts and matter remitted to the Surrogate's Court for entry of a decree in accordance with the opinion.

All concur, except McCurn, P.J., and Kimball, J., who dissent and vote for affirmance in the following memorandum:

We all recognize that in construing a will the intent of the testator is the primary object of search. The majority in this case agree that the general rule is that distributees are to be determined as of the date of death of the testator. Here there is nothing, as we view it, which impels a departure from the general rule. The conclusion that the testatrix did not intend that her husband who survived her should take the remainder interest but that such remainder should go to relatives of the half blood, ascertainable upon her husband's death, is a pure assumption and surmise as to what the testatrix intended. She used words of a present gift of the remainder which became vested upon her death, subject only to the life use of the husband. There are, in the will, no words of a future gift as to the remainder. The gift of the remainder was direct and primary. It was not substitutional. It was not contingent upon some future event. The only uncertainty was the amount. The vesting of estate is favored by the law. The general rule 'is not affected by the fact that a life estate precedes the gift of the remainder; and, a life tenant may be the recipient of the remainder' (Safford v. Kowalik, 278 App.Div. 604, 101 N.Y.S.2d 876, 877, and cases there cited). We find nothing in the will which justifies the finding of fact as to the intent of the testatrix necessary to sustain the position taken by the majority. We prefer to adhere to the established rules which the courts of this State have established. The case of Matter of Sayre's Will in this court (1 A.D.2d 475, 151 N.Y.S.2d 506) is readily distinguishable on the facts.

> **Take Note**
>
> Obviously not the no-brainer that the majority seems to have suggested given the vigorous dissent. What interests are the dissenting judges protecting: simply mindless formalism?

On the other hand, different facts can lead to the opposite conclusion:

Matter of Erbsloh's Trust

99 N.Y.S.2d 695 (Sup. Ct. New York Co. 1950)

Hecht, Justice.

A question of construction has been raised on the intermediate settlement of accounts of two express trusts similar in language and intent. Separate trust indentures were made for the benefit of each of two daughters of the settlors. They provided that on the death of the life beneficiary the principal of the trust be paid to the surviving issue of the beneficiary, and in default of such issue the principal be divided between two other daughters of the settlors, and if both such remaindermen be dead and no issue survive either of them, then the principal 'shall be paid to the next of kin of Fanny E. Erbsloh, one of the parties hereto of the first part.'

The life beneficiaries are still alive, but Fanny E. Erbsloh has died, and the question presented is whether 'the next of kin of Fanny E. Erbsloh' are to be determined as of the date of her death or at the termination of the trust with no one present to take the remainder under the indentures except her next of kin. All persons possibly interested under either construction have been cited in this proceeding.

It is a maxim of construction that the law favors vesting of estates at the earliest possible moment, Hersee v. Simpson, 154 N.Y. 496, 48 N.E. 890, and the fact that such construction may make life tenants vested with a remainder in the estate, which can never come into actual possession of the life tenant, does not prevent application of the formula. In re Chalmer's Will, 264 N.Y. 239, 190 N.E. 476; United States Trust Co. of New York v. Taylor, 232 N.Y. 609, 134 N.E. 591. There is nothing in the trust instrument which would in the least indicate that this rule should not be applied here. In fact the whole spirit seems to be one of complete concern for the welfare of the children of the settlors. A ruling that remote collaterals would share in this estate would be repugnant to the scheme of the trusts. Consequently I hold that the next of kin of Fanny E. Erbsloh shall be determined as of the date of her death. Motion to settle account granted. Settle order.

———————

Obviously, how any particular case is decided depends to some degree on which advocate can make the most compelling argument about what the creator of the interest intended. The facts in *Example 17* are drawn from *Estate of Woodworth*, 18 Cal. App. 4th 936, 22 Cal. Rptr. 2d 676 (1993). Although the family members argued that the traditional rule was not compatible with the testator's intent in creating the testamentary trust, their lawyers never put into evidence the entire will (they proved the terms of the trust by using the decree of distribution from the probate proceeding). That omission deprived the court of the best source from which the testator's intent could be inferred. Lawyering does make a difference.

While many states, including New York, still follow the traditional rule, applying the preference for early vesting to gifts to heirs, at least a quarter of the states, including California, however, have enacted statutes directing that in situations like those that we have been considering: the heirs are determined as if the named person had died at the time of distribution. Most of these statutes are modeled on the UPC.

UPC § 2–711

If an applicable statute or a governing instrument calls for a present or future distribution to or creates a present or future interest in a designated individual's "heirs," "heirs at law," "next of kin," "relatives," or "family," or language of similar import, the property passes to those persons, including the state, and in such shares as would succeed to the designated individual's intestate estate under the intestate succession law of the designated individual's domicile if the designated individual died when the disposition is to take effect in possession or enjoyment. If the designated individual's surviving spouse is living but is remarried at the time the disposition is to take effect in possession or enjoyment, the surviving spouse is not an heir of the designated individual.

Restatement Third, Property (Wills and Other Donative Transfers), § 16.1 states that the rule set forth in UPC § 2–711 accords with the presumptive meaning of a gift to heirs.

But of course these are default rules. The client may actually want a reminder to pass to a person who dies before the reminder vests and therefore allow that person to actually dispose of the interest through a will or trust. If so, the scrivener should make that intent clear.

4. Two Special Problems of Gifts to Heirs

A page of history . . .

There are two ancient common law rules which deal with future interests created in heirs. The first, the Rule in *Shelley's Case*, dates back to the early 14th century. The rule is a rule of law, not one of construction, which may merge a present possessory life estate with a remainder under certain circumstances: IF

(1) a fee simple owner of land,

(2) transfers the land to a designated person for life, and

(3) by the same transfer also creates a remainder in the heirs of the designated person, and

(4) the life interest and the remainder are both legal or both equitable,

(5) then the transfer does not create a remainder in the heirs but instead creates a remainder in the life estate tenant.

The present possessory life estate and the contingent remainder in her heirs merge and the transferee owns the land in fee simple absolute.

As you might expect, the origins of this rule are in the English feudal system. If you are interested in the origins, logic, and operation of the Rule in *Shelley's Case* you can read the treatment of the Rule in Restatement Second, Property (Donative Transfers), § 30.1 which explains in detail the intricacies of the workings of the Rule. While the Rule was abolished in some states in the nineteenth century, widespread legislative or judicial abolition of the Rule in *Shelley's Case* is relatively recent. Indeed it is possible the Rule may still be alive in a handful of states. Restatement Third, Property (Wills and Other Donative Transfers), § 16.2 states that "[t]he Rule in Shelley's Case is not recognized as part of American law." The Reporter's Note to that section, however, cites two cases decided in the last twenty years (one in Arkansas and one in Delaware) which apply the Rule or state that it is in force.

The second doctrine affecting remainders in heirs is the Doctrine of Worthier Title. The doctrine, which was at the start a rule of law but now a rule of construction, where not abolished, gave concrete effect to the notion that to acquire property by descent was more prestigious or "worthier" than acquiring by purchase. In addition, the feudal lord received certain feudal dues (the equivalent of an estate tax) only when the heir inherited land. Originally applying only to land, the doctrine reflected these two considerations by nullifying any attempt by a grantor to create an interest in his or her heirs. The attempted creation of a life estate in the grantor, with remainder to the grantor's heirs failed to create a remainder in the heirs and left the grantor with a reversion. On grantor's death the reversion passed to his heirs.

In England, the Doctrine of Worthier Title was abolished by legislation in 1833. Most states have abolished the doctrine and, as with the Rule in Shelley's Case, Restatement Third, Property (Wills and Other Donative Transfers), § 16.3 repudiates the Doctrine of Worthier Title. But the doctrine was abolished much earlier in many states, frequently transforming it into a rule of construction. New York did so in the early twentieth century in *Doctor v. Hughes*, 225 N.Y. 305, 122 N.E. 221 (1919). The result was an unuseful invitation to litigate any creation of a remainder in the grantor's heirs if an individual would profit if the interest was deemed a reversion. The New York legislature finally abolished the doctrine in 1966 by enacting what is today NY EPTL § 6–5.9.

5. Constructional Rules and Express Conditions

Future interests created in single and multigenerational classes are a critical element of estate planning because many property holders prefer that their descendants receive the benefit of their accumulated property, even if the named class member dies before the time for distribution. Perhaps just as common, however, is the desire to condition a benefit on the occurrence of some event other than survival of the donor or to the time of distribution. The paradigmatic case is a requirement that the beneficiary reach a certain age for the interest to vest or be distributed. It is easy to explain the motives of the will-maker or trust creator in creating a threshold age. If the beneficiary is a minor and subsequently dies before reaching the age of 18, the beneficiary cannot dispose of the interest in the property by will. Thus, if a minor dies with a transmissible interest, it will most likely pass to the minor's surviving parents or parent as the minor's sole heirs. While such an outcome may not be undesirable, a donor might prefer that in such a situation that the minor's siblings benefit from the property at the time of distribution rather than the parents. Even if the beneficiary is no longer a minor, the property holder may regard a relatively young person as lacking the maturity to manage wealth prudently.

Whatever the reasons for establishing them, age contingencies are not uncommon, and there are well-established rules of construction that apply when courts are required to construe them. The most widely accepted rules in construing age contingencies have their origin in a seventeenth century decision of the English Court of Chancery. In *Clobberie's Case*, 2 Vent. 342, 86 Eng. Rep. 476 (1677), Lord Chancellor Finch (who would later become the first Earl of Nottingham and would ultimate decide The *Duke of Norfolk's Case* which set the Rule Against Perpetuities on its modern course of development) held that a bequest of a sum of money to a woman "**at her age of twenty-one years, or day of marriage, to be paid unto her with interest**" was not contingent on the woman reaching the age of 21, but rather was vested. Should she die before age 21, the property passed to her estate. He then, according to the report of the case, uttered two dicta. The first was that "if money were bequeathed to one **at** his age of twenty-one years," reaching the stated age is condition precedent. The second was that "if money be given to one **to be paid at** the age of twenty-one years" the age requirement is not a condition precedent, and if the donee dies before that age the money goes to the deceased donee's estate. Note carefully the linguistic differences in three formulations.

The first and third rules in *Clobberie's Case*, that is, the holding and the second dictum, are widely followed. Under the holding, a gift of the income of property to a person or to a class with the property itself to be paid over at a stated age is a gift of all the property. Survival to the stated age is not required.

> **Example 18:** G bequeaths property to T, in trust, T as trustee to pay the income from the property to G's nephew N until N reaches the age of 30 at which time the trust shall terminate and T shall pay the trust property to N. If N dies before reaching the age of 30 the trust property will be paid to N's estate.

The reason for the rule illustrated in **Example 18** may be explicable by the following reasoning. If N is entitled to all the income the property produces while waiting to reach the age of 30, N is the only beneficiary of the property. Under the limitation, no one other than N has any interest in the property and the income it produces other than N. N is simply waiting for the age contingency to be met to take outright possession. If N dies before reaching the stated age there is no reason not to promptly pay the property to N's estate.

The second pronouncement, dictum because it does not address the actual limitation in the case, notes that the use of the words "**to be paid at**" also create a vested gift, even if the income from the property is not given to the donee while the donee waits to attain the stated age. In this case to whom does the income pass? If it is not given to the donee, it remains with the donor. That means that if the gift was in a will, "I give $10,000 to my niece, Harriet Howard, to be paid to her when she attains the age of twenty-five years" and at the testator's death Harriet Howard is eleven years old, the income earned on the $10,000 for the next fourteen years is part of the testator's estate and passes to his residuary beneficiaries. Should the niece die before reaching the age of 25, her estate is entitled to the $10,000 *when she would have reached the age of 25.* All the income to be earned on the general bequest belongs to his residuary beneficiaries.

The second dictum, that the use of the word "**at**" means that the age requirement is a condition precedent, is not as widely accepted as the holding and the third dictum. The cases are divided.

You might think that the rules originating in *Clobberie's Case* have little application in a world where trusts are commonly created to manage property until a beneficiary is directed to receive the property outright, usually by attaining a stated age. Less than careful drafting, however, can still make these rules relevant. *Summers v. Summers*, 121 Ohio App. 3d 263, 699 N.E.2d 958 (4th Dist. 1997) involved a testamentary trust for the testator's child. The trustee had discretion to use income and principal for the child's needs until the child attained the age of 25 at which time the trust was to terminate and the principal and accumulated income was to be paid over to the child. The child died before reaching 25. The court held that the child's interest vested when the trust was created. The age requirement was not a condition precedent because the child was given all the income from the trust property. Because the child died intestate, the trust, along with the rest of the child's probate property, passed to the other parent from whom the testator had long been divorced. Perhaps not the desired outcome, but it was the logical outcome of poor drafting to be sure. The scrivener should have considered the possibility, albeit unlikely, that the beneficiary might die before reaching the age of 25. One could generalize the problem in *Summers* by simply stating that the failure to expressly state the effect on a future interest of the occurrence of an event, such as reaching a stated age, can lead to litigation about the whether the age condition is a condition precedent. The nature of the condition will decide whether the future interest will fail or be transmitted through the deceased beneficiary's estate.

good writing is vital.

Express conditions of attaining a stated age or the occurrence of some event like marriage are common, but express conditions of survival are perhaps more common still. After all, if a property holder does not want to create transmissible interests, requiring survival is the easiest way to achieve that result. The problem is that it is far too easy to use the word "surviving" in ways that are not totally clear. What should be made clear is the time or event to which the beneficiary must survive.

Example 19: G bequeaths property to T, in trust, with T as trustee to pay the income to A for life and then to pay the trust property to B, but if B does not survive A to B's surviving children. At T's death, there are two children of B living, C and D. B predeceases A and then C dies survived by two children. A then dies at which time B's only surviving child is D. To whom should the trustee distribute the trust property?

The problem is the meaning of the word "surviving." Does it mean surviving G or surviving A? The usual construction is to interpret surviving as meaning surviving to the time of distribution, that is to A's death. That construction, of course, disinherits C's children. To avoid that result, a court might construe the word "children" to mean B's "issue" (although in *Gustafson* the New York Court of Appeals would not accept a similar construction of the word "children"). Another way to include C's children in the distribution of trust property would be to construe "surviving" to refer to as surviving to G's death. This interpretation would create a transmissible interest in C that might end up in the hands of C's children. (*See* Restatement Third, Property (Wills and Other Donative Transfers), § 15.4, comment *g*.)

> **Example 20:** G bequeaths property to T, in trust, with T as trustee to pay the income to A for life and then to pay the trust property to B, but if B dies without surviving issue, to C.

The question in this hypothetical is when we decide that B has died "without surviving issue"? If B is alive at A's death, does the condition subsequent disappear and along with it C's executory interest? Or do we have to wait in that circumstance to see if B dies without issue *after* A's death? If we take the later construction, the shadow of possible divesting will always darken B's ownership of the property making it difficult for B to sell the property since any title B delivers will also be subject to possible divestment.[2] Under traditional law, if C dies while A and B are still alive, the executory interest passes through C's estate because C's death does nothing to resolve to condition subsequent. The usual modern construction is to resolve the condition subsequent at A's death.

The lesson, of course, is that scrivener must be precise. Really precise. Consider the following two cases:

Chavin v. PNC Bank

816 A.2d 781 (Del. 2003)

BERGER, JUSTICE:

In this appeal, we consider the meaning of certain trust language. The disputed provision states that, upon the death of the settlor, the trustee shall transfer the remaining trust assets to the settlor's son, "if he shall *then* be living." The sole issue on appeal is whether "then" refers to the date of the settlor's death or the date on which the trustee distributes the trust assets. We hold that, to give effect to the intent of the settlor, the trust must be construed to mean that the son had to be alive at the time of distribution in order to take under the trust. Accordingly, we reverse.

---

2   The common law regarded the limitation of failure of issue as indefinite failure of issue so that if generations hence B's lineal descendants died out the property would revert to the grantor.

Background Facts and Trial Court Decision

Florence Chavin and her husband had two sons, I. Favel and Leslie. Favel, also had two sons, Kenneth and Jeffrey. As part of their estate plan, Florence and her husband created revocable trusts. In 1998, after both her husband and Favel had died, Florence revised her trust and executed a new will, which together divided Florence's estate roughly evenly between Leslie and the two grandchildren, free of any trust. In addition, Florence made testamentary gifts totaling $9,500 to ten people, including a $1,000 gift to Harlan Miller, her husband's great nephew. Florence died on May 7, 1999, leaving an estate valued at approximately $2 million. Her son, Leslie, who was a long time resident of Brazil, was murdered in Rio de Janeiro on August 21, 1999. Leslie, who was unmarried and had no children, left his estate to Harlan. PNC Bank, Delaware, is the administrator of Leslie's estate, the executor of Florence's estate, and the trustee of her trust.

Kenneth and Jeffrey filed this declaratory judgment action against PNC Bank and Harlan seeking a determination that they are the residuary beneficiaries of the trust. The trust provides, in relevant part:

> ITEM XIII.
>
> * * *
>
> Section 4. . . . [U]pon the death of Settlor, Trustee shall pay over, transfer and convey whatever remains of the trust estate, discharged of the trust, to Settlor's son, LESLIE S. CHAVIN, if he shall then be living. If Settlor's son shall then be deceased, to Settlor's then living issue, per stirpes.

The grandchildren contend that the phrase "if he shall then be living" refers to the time when the trustee pays over the trust estate to the beneficiary. PNC Bank and Harlan argue that the phrase refers to the Settlor's date of death.

John M. Amalfitano, Esq., the attorney at PNC Bank who drafted the revised trust, provided the only evidence of Florence's dispositive intent. In his deposition, Amalfitano recalled that the most significant issue for Florence was whether she would continue to retain the assets in trust or give the assets to the beneficiaries outright. Leslie, who was visiting his mother and met with Amalfitano, told them both that he would prefer to receive the assets free of the trust, and Florence ultimately honored that preference.

Make the Connection

We have noted before the need to be wary of scrivener's recollections. They would be unnecessary if lawyers drafted instruments that addressed the issues of disposition clearly.

Amalfitano did not discuss with Florence the possibility that Leslie might survive her, but die before receiving the trust assets. He did acknowledge, however, that Leslie and the two grandsons were the only three beneficiaries that were "in the picture." Amalfitano also stated his belief, based on the discussions he had with Florence, that she would have given more of her estate to her grandsons if she had known that Leslie would die when he did.

The Court of Chancery found that the phrase "if he shall then be living" refers to the date of the settlor's death. The court viewed this as the most plausible construction because it refers to a date certain and because it results in early vesting of the estate. In addition, the trial court found its construction to be consistent with Florence's intent. The court apparently concluded that, because Florence decided to terminate her trust upon her death, she did not intend the estate assets to stay within the immediate family.

Discussion

The Court of Chancery correctly and succinctly stated the controlling legal principles:

> The cardinal rule of law in a trust case is that the intent of the settlor controls the interpretation of the instrument. "Such intent must be determined 'by considering the language of the trust instrument, read as an entirety, in light of the circumstances surrounding its creation.' " All other rules of construction must be subordinate to determining [the] settlor's intent, their value being as aids in ascertaining that intent as precisely as possible. *Chavin v. PNC Bank, Delaware*, 2002 WL 385543 at *2 (Del.Ch.) (quoting *Annan v. Wilmington Trust Co.*, 559 A.2d 1289, 1292 (Del.1989)) (Internal citations omitted.).

It appears that the trial court also correctly found that the phrase "if he shall then be living" is ambiguous as applied to the facts of this case, since that phrase is reasonably susceptible of two interpretations. *Woodward v. Farm Family Casualty Ins. Co.*, 796 A.2d 638 (Del.2002).

Thus, the question is, which interpretation will give effect to the intent of the settlor? On this point, we differ with the trial court.

The trust, by its terms, reveals Florence's intent to benefit her immediate family. It provides that certain distant relatives, like Harlan, are to receive $1,000, whereas Florence's son is to receive approximately $1 million. It also provides that, if Leslie does not take under the trust, Florence's grandsons are to receive the $1 million. Amalfitano confirmed what is apparent from this dispositive scheme-that Leslie and the two grandsons were the only beneficiaries he discussed with Florence and that she intended to give them the vast bulk of her estate.

Unfortunately, Amalfitano never discussed the possibility that Leslie might die so soon after Florence that Leslie would never receive any distribution from the trust. Even without such a conversation, however, Amalfitano believed that Florence would have wanted more of her estate to pass to her surviving grandsons, as events transpired. Amalfitano's belief was based on his discussions with Florence over several years, and seems unassailable as a matter of common sense. Florence gave virtually her entire estate to her immediate family and there is nothing in the trust or the record to suggest that she intended to change that dispositive plan in these unforeseen circumstances.

We conclude, therefore, that Florence's grandsons take under Item XIII, Section 4 of the trust. In reaching this conclusion, we are not unmindful of the fact that Florence decided to distribute her assets free of the trust-a fact that the trial court found important in reaching a contrary result. We do not think that Florence's decision to terminate the trust has any bearing on her overall intent to benefit her immediate family. Florence wanted her estate to pass to her son and grandsons, and she wanted her estate to be distributed free of the trust. Those two intentions are not contradictory and the conclusion we reach gives effect to both.

Conclusion

Based on the foregoing, the decision of the Court of Chancery is REVERSED and this matter is remanded for further action in accordance with this decision. Jurisdiction is not retained.

Bryan v. Dethlefs

959 So.2d 314 (Fla.App. 2007)

Lagoa, Judge.

Appellants, potential beneficiaries under the Revocable Living Trust ("the Trust") of Charles L. Bryan ("Bryan"), appeal from a Summary Judgment in favor of the appellee, Victoria Dethlefs ("Dethlefs") in case number 3D06–2360. For the following reasons, we affirm the entry of Summary Judgment.

I. FACTUAL HISTORY

The parties dispute which family members are entitled to inherit Bryan's assets under the Trust. Bryan executed the Trust on October 11, 2000. Article IV, Paragraph 4.1 of the Trust (the "Trust provision") states:

> Distribution to Grandson: *Upon my death*, the then balance of principal and accu-mulated income remaining in the trust fund *shall be distributed* to my Grandson, ROBERT R. BIZZELL, *if he is living at the time of distribution*. If he is not living at the time of distribution then the said trust fund shall be divided into equal shares and distributed, one share to each child who survives me and one share for each child who may then be deceased, leaving descendants then surviving, to be distributed to such descendants, per stirpes. (emphasis added).

On the same day that Bryan executed the Trust he also executed a Last Will and Testament devising the residue of his estate to the Trust.

Bryan died on September 8, 2001, and his will was admitted to probate. Bryan's grandson, Robert R. Bizzell ("Bizzell") was appointed personal representative of the estate and he, along with an accountant, became co-trustees of the Trust. Bizzell and the co-trustee began distributing assets from the Trust to Bizzell in accordance with the Trust provision. Before the distribution of the Trust assets were completed, Bizzell died intestate.

such. people die, and for various reasons.

The appellee, Dethlefs, is Bizzell's half-sister and one of the beneficiaries of Bizzell's estate. Dethlefs filed a Motion for Judgment on the Pleadings or Alternatively for Summary Judgment asserting that the Trust provision vested the Trust assets with Bizzell at the time of Bryan's death, and that those assets were therefore part of Bizzell's estate at the time of his death. The appellants argued, however, that the Trust provision was vested the Trust assets only at the time of their distribution, and thus, those assets that had yet to be distributed at the time of Bizzell's death were not part of Bizzell's estate and therefore must be distributed to them as Bryan's remaining descendants. For the foregoing reasons, we agree with Dethlefs.

II. STANDARD OF REVIEW

We review the order granting summary judgment under a *de novo* standard of review. *American Engineering & Development Corp. v. Sanchez*, 932 So.2d 1241, 1243 (Fla. 3d DCA 2006); *Merlot Commc'ns, Inc. v. Shalev*, 840 So.2d 446, 447 (Fla. 3d DCA 2003). The parties agree that the Trust provision is unambiguous and that its effect may be determined as a matter of law.[2] *See Angell v. Don Jones Ins. Agency, Inc.*, 620 So.2d 1012, 1014 (Fla. 2d DCA 1993) ("Where the determination of the issues of a lawsuit depends upon the construction of a written instrument and the legal effect to be drawn therefrom, the question at issue is essentially one of law only and determinable by entry of summary judgment.").

III. ANALYSIS

The polestar of trust or will interpretation is the settlor's intent. *Arellano v. Bisson*, 847 So.2d 998 (Fla. 3d DCA 2003); *Phillips v. Estate of Holzmann*, 740 So.2d 1, 2 (Fla. 3d DCA 1998). Intent is ascertained from the four corners of the document through consideration of "all the provisions of the will taken together, rather than from detached portions or any particular form of words. This rule prevails whether the entire will or some specific clause or part of it is being construed." *Sorrels v. McNally*, 89 Fla. 457, 462–63, 105 So. 106, 109 (1925). In construing the instrument as a whole, the court should take into account the general dispositional scheme. *Pounds v. Pounds*, 703 So.2d 487, 488 (Fla. 5th DCA 1997). The meaning applied, however, cannot lead to absurd results. *Roberts v. Sarros*, 920 So.2d 193, 196 (Fla. 2d DCA 2006).

intent, → early vesting

Additionally, the law favors the early vesting of estates. *Lumbert v. Estate of Carter*, 867 So.2d 1175, 1179 (Fla. 5th DCA 2004)(citing *Sorrels v. McNally*, 89 Fla. 457, 105 So. 106 (1925)).

---

2   In their Reply, Appellants argue that parol evidence should be considered in construing the Trust provision since both sides ascribe different meanings to the language of the Trust provision. We disagree. "The fact that both sides ascribe different meanings to the language does not mean the language is ambiguous so as to allow the admission of extrinsic evidence." See *Kipp v. Kipp*, 844 So.2d 691, 693 (Fla. 4th DCA 2003). Because we find no ambiguity in the language of the Trust provision, it would be inappropriate for this Court to consider parol evidence.

As this Court stated in *Estate of Rice v. Greenberg*, 406 So.2d 469 (Fla. 3d DCA 1981), any doubt as to whether an interest is vested or contingent should be resolved in favor of vesting:

> This Court is committed to the doctrine that remainders vest on the death of the testator or at the earliest date possible unless there is a clear intent expressed to postpone the time of vesting. It is also settled that in case of doubt as to whether a remainder is vested or contingent, the doubt should be resolved in favor of its vesting if possible, but these general rules all give way to the cardinal one that a will must be construed so as to give effect to the intent of the testator.

406 So.2d at 473 (quoting *Krissoff v. First Nat. Bank of Tampa*, 159 Fla. 522, 32 So.2d 315 (1947)). Accordingly, no estate should be held to be contingent "unless very decided terms are used" and "unless there is a clear intent to postpone the vesting." *Sorrels*, 89 Fla. at 467, 105 So. at 110. Indeed, "[t]he presumption that a legacy was intended to be vested applies with far greater force, where a testator is making provision for a child or grandchild, than where the gift is to a stranger or to a collateral relative." *Sorrels*, 89 Fla. at 467, 105 So. at 110.

Finally, if a trust vests at the settlor's death, then "the death of the beneficiary before it becomes payable does not cause the legacy or devise to lapse." *Sorrels*, 89 Fla. at 465, 105 So. at 110. Similarly, where a settlor intends a trust to vest upon the testator's death, benefits accrue to the beneficiaries from the time of the death, not the subsequent time that the trust was funded. *In re Bowen's Will*, 240 So.2d 318, 320 (Fla. 3d DCA 1970).

Given these legal principles, we find that the language of the Trust provision can only have the legal effect of vesting the trust assets in Bizzell upon Bryan's death. The Trust provision mandates distribution "[u]pon my death." The last clause of the sentence, "if he is living at the time of distribution," must be interpreted in the context of the entire sentence and can only lead to the conclusion that the time of distribution intended by Bryan was at his death. The clause "if he is living at the time of distribution" does not establish a requirement that the assets be distributed before Bizzell's right vested.

Moreover, the Trust provision does not require that some other event, such as an age requirement, occur before the devise vests. Contrary to the appellants' contention that the distribution is the event which vests the assets in Bizzell, the provision can be read only to require that Bizzell be living at the time of Bryan's death in order for the assets to vest. There is no doubt in this case that Bizzell met the testator's explicit survival requirements.[3] Therefore, Bizzell's death did not divest his estate of its interest in the assets of the Trust that remained to be distributed. *Sorrels*, 89 Fla. at 465, 105 So. at 110. Accordingly, we affirm the summary judgment entered below and affirm the non-final order entered below ordering the liquidation of an asset of the Bryan estate.

Affirmed.

———————————————

3   Paragraph 8.1 of the Trust provides for a 90 day survivorship requirement for any beneficiary.

Points for Discussion

1.   Can you distinguish these cases? In other words, if the exact facts of *Chavin* occur in Florida, can you argue for the result of *Chavin*? In your view, which court came to the correct result if their goal was to follow the intent of the testator?

2.   If Florence Chavin truly wanted to benefit only her "immediate family," how should the trust have been drafted?

3.   You represent the remainder person of a Delaware trust which creates a remainder using the same words which appear in ITEM XIII, Section 4 of the Chavin trust, that is the remainder is given to your client if "then living" and if not living at that time the remainder should pass to the descendants of the creator of the trust, a class which includes children of your client's sibling who died some years ago. At the death of the life beneficiary, your client, who is childless, is seriously ill. Your client's will divides her estate between her domestic partner and charity. What do you do to protect your client's interests?

6.   What Does Survival Mean?

As you can see, the problem in *Chavin* really is not the creation of a transmissible future interest; the remainder is not transmissible. The problem is that the remainder person died too soon after the life income beneficiary. He really did not have the opportunity to enjoy the property, making the gift to him meaningless—at least that seems to be one way to understand the court's opinion. It is not uncommon for a will or trust to require survival for a certain period of time after the property is to come into possession. That time for a gift in a will, of course, is the death of the testator. As we noted in Chapter 7, Section B, Note 2, there are several reasons a testator might want a beneficiary to survive the testator's death by more than a very short period of time. We also saw that those same considerations apply to gifts in trusts, even though it seems less common for trusts to include language defining a minimum period of survival in order to be entitled to enjoyment or possession of the property in which the beneficiary has a future interest. The default rules of the Uniform Simultaneous Death Act are probably more important for trusts than for wills. Remember that the Act applies to "governing instruments," a term that includes wills and trusts, and that therefore the rule requiring survival of an event by 120 hours in order to be treated as having "survived" the event is often relevant when determining in whom property has vested in possession or enjoyment. If the 120 hour rule were the default law applicable to the trust in *Chavin*, would the result be different (remember that the 120 hour rule refers to surviving an "event.")

Section 2. Requirement of Survival by 120 Hours Under Probate Code

Except as provided in Section 6, if the title to property, the devolution of property, the right to elect an interest in property, or the right to exempt property, homestead or family allowance depends upon an individual's survivorship of the death of another individual, an individual who is not established by clear and convincing evidence to have survived the other individual by 120 hours is deemed to have predeceased the other individual. This section does not apply if its application would result in a taking of intestate estate by the state.

Any statutory definition of survival, remember, is a default rule and yields to a provision in an instrument dealing with survival. Of course, in some instances it is impossible to provide a contrary rule. By definition, the statute must govern survivorship questions in intestate succession and in jointly held property arrangements where is it not possible to specify a survivorship rule.

7.　Acceleration

Vested remainders can accelerate into possession. This may occur when a preceding interest ends "unnaturally" as we noted in our discussion of the rule of reversions, when for example a life tenant disclaims. So if A holds a life estate and B a remainder, if A disclaims her interest B can come into possession of her interest immediately, even though the limitation is drafted so as to permit possession only at the **death of A**. Consider also alternative contingent remainders. To A for life but if B survives A to B but if she does not to C. A disclaims. Neither of the contingencies have occurred (neither has survived A) and the preceding estate in A has ended. Under the traditional common law, a legal contingent remainder that was not limited to come into possession when the preceding estate ended was destroyed. The destructibility rule did not apply to equitable interests, and therefore did not apply to trusts. What happens, or should happen, when an equitable remainder is not ready to come into possession when the preceding estate ends?

> ***Example 21:*** G bequeaths property to T, in trust, with T as trustee to pay the income to A for life and then to pay the trust property to A's descendants who survive A by representation, but if A dies without surviving descendants, to pay the trust property to the then living descendants of A's parents, by representation.

First, the remainder in A's descendants is contingent because the interest in the descendants is predicated on surviving A: a condition precedent. If they do not, the remainder vests and immediately becomes possessory in the descendants of A's parents. The limitation thus creates alternative contingent remainders in the two possible takers.

Second, in the normal course of events, all conditions will be resolved at A's death. Either there will be descendants of A who will survive A and will therefore take possession of the trust property, or there will not be any surviving descendants and the descendants of A's parents living at A's death will take the trust property. Should there be no descendants of A or of A's parents living at A's death, the reversion in G will become possessory.

Third, none of the interests involved are transmissible. Any descendant of A or of A's parents who dies during A's lifetime has failed to satisfy the condition precedent, and therefore has no interest to transmit.

What happens, then, if after having received income distributions for several years A decides to refuse to accept any more income from the trust? A cannot be forced to accept the income, of course, so the trustee has three alternatives. First, the reversion in G could become possessory, and the income distributed to whomever took the reversion through G's estate until A's death at which time the condition precedent would be resolved. Second, the trustee could simply accumulate the income until A's death.

Finally, the income could be paid to those persons who would take possession of the remainder were A to die right after the income payment was made.

Jurisdictions have various approaches by common law and by statute. The latter solution is the one dictated by statute in New York.

New York Estates, Powers, and Trusts Law § 9–2.3. Undistributed Income

When income is not disposed of and no valid direction is given for its accumulation it passes to the person presumptively entitled to the next eventual estate.

If at the time of the first income payment after A's refusal to accept any more income from the trust there are three living children of A and no living descendants of predeceased children, the income would be paid in equal shares to the three children. (There is an exhaustive discussion of the application of the predecessor of EPTL § 9–2.3 which is still useful in *Matter of Shupack*, 158 Misc. 873, 287 N.Y.S. 184 (Sur. Ct. Kings Co. 1936).)

However, there is an important exception to the application of acceleration statutes like EPTL § 9–2.3 which applies if as in *Example 21* A disclaims. Under the disclaimer provisions of the UPC (UPC § 2–1106) the disclaimed interest passes as if the disclaimant had died before the interest was created on G's death. Should A's disclaimer "pretend death" have the same effect as her actual death? In other words, should the trust terminate as it would when A actually passes or should the trust be established and the income somehow held by a party to the trust until A's actual death?

The answer is provided by the disclaimer statutes. They provide that future interests that follow the disclaimed interest accelerate in possession without regard to how that future interest is classified. In *Example 21*, then, if A had properly disclaimed the income interest under the applicable statute, and at the time of A's deemed death there were three living children of A, several living grandchildren, and no living descendants of pre-deceased children, the contingent remainder would accelerate, the trust would terminate and the three children would take possession of the trust property. There is no need to postpone the distribution of the property to await the actual situation that obtains on A's actual death.

This automatic acceleration rule is a default rule which takes effect only if the instrument that creates the subsequently disclaimed interest does not provide otherwise. The importance of providing otherwise is illustrated by the following example:

Example 22: T's will creates two testamentary trusts, one for each of T's two children, a son and a daughter. Both trusts direct the trustee to pay the trust income to the child for whom the trust is created and on that child's death to pay the trust property to the child's then living descendants by representation. If the child is not survived by descendants, the trust property is to be paid to the trust for the other child if it is in existence or if the other trust has already terminated, to the then living descendants of the other child, by representation, and if they are none the corpus passes to charity. At T's death, daughter and son are both living. Daughter has three living children and son has no living descendants. Son then disclaims his interest in the trust. How should the trust property be distributed? (These facts are based on *Matter of Gilbert*, 156 Misc.2d 379, 592 N.Y.S.2d 224 (Sur. Ct. New York Co. 1992).) What will happen if son later has children? Is the result what T intended and if not, how might T's will be drafted to accomplish T's intent?

D. Rules for Class Gifts

We have encountered class gifts in the materials and have observed that class gifts can be either single generation class gifts or multi-generation class gifts. One of the most important distinctions between the two varieties, of course, is that multi-generation class gifts are subject to an implied condition of survival to the time of distribution of the property to the class members. There is another aspect of class gifts which requires careful exploration. When does the class close?

The threshold is to define the meaning of the term: "close." A class closes when no more members can join the class even if they could be regarded as class members. Classes can close in two ways: *physiologically*, when no more class members can be born, and by *the rule of convenience* which "artificially" closes the class when one class member is entitled to possession of the property that is the subject of the class gift. At that time, the class must close so that the minimum amount that can be distributed to the class member entitled to payment can be calculated.

Closing the class physiologically. If a gift is made "to the children of A" then the class closes physiologically when A dies and is no longer capable of having children. Of course, "capable" may not be so easy to define. For example, if A is male, there is always a possibility that a child of A is *in ventre sa mere* at A's death. If that child is later born alive its existence relates back to the time of conception, and thus it can participate in a class gift to the children of A.

But modern reproductive technology has intervened to may allow the birth of children years after the death of our hypothetical A. Litigation has arisen and no doubt will continue to arise over the status of children conceived after their genetic parents' deaths through the use of frozen gametes and assisted reproductive techniques. The law of class gifts has yet to confront the question of the status of posthumously conceived children, and no doubt there will be litigation and proposed uniform legislation in the works until the matter is settled by statute.

Finally, the possibility of adopting children must be taken into account. Generally speaking, an adopted child is "born" for purposes of a class gift when the child is adopted.

(*See Matter of Silberman*, 23 N.Y.2d 98, 242 N.E.2d 736, 295 N.Y.S.2d 478 (1968).) The new Restatement goes even farther. Restatement Third, Property (Wills and Other Donative Transfers), § 15.1, comment *i* states that "by analogy to a child in gestation" a child in the process of being adopted is a child for purposes of determining class membership while the adoption is in process and is therefore included in the class gift "if the adoption is concluded within a reasonable time."

Closing the class by the rule of convenience. The common law takes a ruthlessly practical view of human nature. The rule of convenience is a based on the premise once a person has been given property the property will never be returned. Because the members of a class take the property that is the subject of the gift in equal shares, once at least one class member is entitled to a share of the property the minimum size of that share must be known. That calculation requires the closing of the class so that the share will not be diluted in the future.

These explanations of the class closing rules are excessively abstract and really make sense only when one can see them applied. We start with class gifts that are immediate gifts, that is, that do not create future interests in the class. The most common immediate class gift is one made in a will.

> **Example 23:** T's will makes a general bequest of $200,000 "to my brothers and sisters." At the time the will is written T has four living siblings; one sibling died before the execution of the will. Another sibling dies after the will was executed but before T's death. T's parents also die after the will is executed but before T's death.

We know that the distribution of the $200,000 is affected by more than the classification of this gift as a class gift. If an anti-lapse statute applies to the gift, issue of the predeceased siblings will take those siblings' 1/5 shares. If the bequest had been made to "my brothers and sisters who survive me" then the gift would be function like a traditional class gift and only the surviving siblings would share the $200,000.

In no event, however, do we pay much attention to the class closing rules in dealing with **Example 23**. The class is closed both physiologically because both of T's parents predeceased T and by the rule of convenience since a class member is entitled to be paid as soon as the gift is made at T's death. Of course, if T's parents had survived T the class gift would close only by the rule of convenience, but again the analysis would be the same. A clearer example of the need for class closing rules is a gift in a will to the children of a living person.

> **Example 24:** T's will makes a gift of $25,000 "to the children of my sister, B." B is living at T's death and has two living children.

The class of B's children closes on T's death because T's executor needs to know how much to give the two living children. In other words, if the class did not close on T's death so that afterborn children of B would be entitled to share in the $25,000, how would T's executor know how much to pay to the two children of B who are entitled to a share in the gift? If the executor gives them each $12,500 you can be sure that if B does have another child the executor may have a difficult time getting the older children to return a part of their gift back that their new sibling can share in the gift. If the executor decides to distribute less than the entire $25,000 to the two children of B in order to take into account the possibility of B having more children, how much should the executor hold back and for how long? Will the executor ever be able to close the estate before B's death? Again, a respect for the practicalities leads to the formulation of a rule that allows the executor to wrap up the administration of T's estate as expeditiously as possible.

> **Question 1:** T's will makes the following bequest: "I give twenty thousand dollars ($20,000) to the children of my sister, S." At T's death S is alive. S's only child died before T and is survived by three children (S's grandchildren). When does the class of S's children close for purposes of the gift in T's will? Would your answer change if the "who survive me" were added after "my sister, S"? 🅐

> **Question 2:** T's will makes the following bequest: "I give twenty thousand dollars ($20,000) to the children of my sister, S who reach the age of 21." At T's death, S is alive and has three living children aged 17, 14, and 10. Five years after T's death S has another child. When should T's executor make the first distribution in payment of the bequest? How is the $20,000 ultimately divided if two years after the birth of S's last child, the child of S who was 10 at T's death dies?

Matters are a little more complicated when the class gift follows a life estate or a life income interest in a trust. The class might be closed *physiologically* at the time the future interest in the class is created, of course, but if it is not, *the rule of convenience cannot apply until the life income interest ends*. While the trust property is paying income to the life income beneficiary the trustee cannot pay the trust property to the remainder beneficiaries. They have no interest, they cannot cash in their claim check, until the life income interest has terminated.

> **Example 25:** G bequeaths property to T, in trust, with T as trustee to pay the income to A for life and then to pay the trust property to the children of B who reach the age of 21. At G's death, B is also dead and all of B's children have reached the age of 21. At A's death T will pay the trust property to B's then living children or to the successors in interest of any children of B who have died before. Why? B's children have satisfied the condition precedent, and their interests vest and are transmissible. If the children predecease A, their interests pass through their estates.

Now consider the following variations on **Example 25**.

> **Question 3:** At G's death A and B are alive, B's three living children are under the age of 21. Three years later B's eldest child turns 21. A dies four years later. B survives A. When does the class of B's children close, and how is the trust property ultimately distributed if all of the children of B eventually reach age 21? Would your answer change if the eldest child of B died after reaching age 21 but before A's death?

> **Question 4:** At G's death A and B are alive and B has no children. After G's death three children are born to B and at A's death the eldest child of B is 14. If B survives A, when is the soonest time the class of B's children can close? How is the trust property ultimately distributed if none of B's children reach the age of 21?

Question 5: The testamentary trust in G's will requires the trustee to pay the trust income to A for life, remainder to the children of B, payable at age 21. At G's death, A and B are alive and the eldest child of B is 6. The following events then occur: B has two more children, the eldest child of B dies at age 18, A dies four years later, B has a fourth child four years after A's death, the eldest living child of B turns 21, then B's next child turns 21 and eventually B's youngest child turns 21. When does the class of B's children close and how is the trust property ultimately distributed?

As you can see, ascertaining when the class closes is absolutely necessary to determining when and how to distribute the property that is the subject of the class gift. In addition, as we will learn, the application of the Rule Against Perpetuities to class gifts requires determining when the class closes.

There are a few more rules involving class gifts that deal with unusual situations. What if T makes a general bequest "to the children of my brother, B" and at T's death B has never had any children? In other words, what does one do with a class gift to an "empty class"? The new Restatement states the "traditional rule": "unless the language or the circumstances indicate a different intent, the class remains open until it closes physiologically, despite the inconvenience to administrators and beneficiaries in doing so." Therefore, according to an illustration in the Restatement, if T's will gives the residue of T's estate to "my grandchildren" but T's only child, a son aged 22, has no children, the class remains open until the son's death. The same illustration, however, goes on to state that if the son were 62 years old, the gift would fail, it being unlikely that there would ever be grandchildren of T. (Restatement Third, Property (Wills and Other Donative Transfers), § 15.1, comment *k* and Illustration 11.) The following illustration, Illustration 12, applies the same rule to a remainder to an empty class, in that case the remainder of T's testamentary trust passes to the children of the testator's daughter who has no children at the time of the termination of the life income interest in the trust. If daughter D was 22 at that time, the class would remain open until D's death; when a child of D is born the trustee distributes trust income to that child and subsequently born children share in the income until D's death at which time the trust will terminate and the trust property distributed to D's children. If D were 62 years old at the termination of the income interest, however, the class would close at the end of the income interest and the class gift would fail.

Finally, the Restatement approves of another traditional rule concerning "specific sum" class gifts; that is, gifts of a specific sum to each member of a class. (Restatement Third, Property (Wills and Other Donative Transfers), § 15.1, comment *l*.)

Example 26: T's will gives "$10,000 to each of the children of my nephew, N." If at T's death N is alive but N has never had children, the class closes at T's death and the gift fails. If N had living children at T's death, or if a child of N had predeceased T but was covered by an anti-lapse statute, the class would close by the rule of convenience at T's death and child born to N after T's death would not share in the gift.

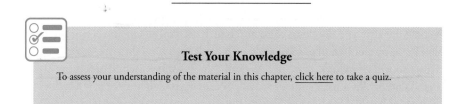

Test Your Knowledge

To assess your understanding of the material in this chapter, click here to take a quiz.

CHAPTER 14

The Rule Against Perpetuities

731.52

A. Introduction

Whether they have tackled the rule against perpetuities in Property or not, students usually enter its study in Wills and Trusts with a good deal of trepidation. Fair enough. It is often repeated tongue-in-cheek, that there is a presumption that lawyers do not understand its operation. While perhaps an overstatement, the infamous case of *Lucas v. Hamm* (364 P.2d 685 (Cal. 1961)) held that an attorney was not liable for malpractice as a matter of law for drafting a will that violated the rule. Movies, *Body Heat* being the most prominent example, reinforce that conclusion. But do not despair; all that is required to avoid embarrassment of drafting a provision that violates it is assimilating a fundamental understanding of the rule. Most family trusts have estate planning goals that do not come into conflict with the rule. Remainders in trusts are often vested, and therefore outside the rule, and if there are contingencies they vest at the death of a living person. So as you assimilate the legal doctrine and cope with some of the more outlandish rules, bear in mind that the estate plan that might come into conflict with the rule is rare indeed. Besides, like much of the legal doctrine that has been presented in this book, the rule is in the process of refinement, read, modification and tempering.

This chapter acquaints the students with the classical rule against perpetuities as it was created in the seventeenth century and refined through the following centuries. It explains first the historical context and the policy reasons why the rule was thought necessary. It illustrates how remainders were trapped within its tentacles. Finally it goes on to look at modern reform of one of the most frightening phrases in the law of property, sometimes referred to by an acronym RAP. As usual we begin with . . .

A page of history . . .

We owe the rule to the predisposition of the English landed class to assure that their estates will pass to their heirs unencumbered and intact. Aficionados of the television series *Downton Abbey* will note the succession pattern that landed the estate in Lord

731

Grantham's hands (descent from his male ancestors) and the horror that ensued because he had not produced a male heir. But the estate is to pass to a collateral male heir; a strategy crystallizes that if his daughter marries the collateral male heir the land will be kept in the family . . . good enough. Alas driving skills foil that plan.

The explanation for the desire to have land remain in the family, within a patriline, was a combination of emotion and politics. Of course economics lurked. Until the 19th century, land in England and then Britain was the paramount source of wealth; landed wealth often resulted in political control, because the self-proclaimed mother of all parliaments choose its members through a voting system that hardly complied with *Baker v. Carr*. Control of land often meant control of seats in parliament. Both the land law and conveyancers (their estate planners) allowed the landed class to keep land within the patriline.

There were, however, counterpoised interests. Britain was a commercial nation. Those successful in the world of affairs were keen to turn their personal wealth into land. In short, they aimed to sit side by side with Lord Grantham or even supplant him. The more land that was held by the landed elite and not subject to sale because it was tied up in settlements (trusts of land), the more expensive land coming on the market might be. Scarcity often impacts price. So the mercantile class favored free disposition, and the judges who made fortunes in the law and the common law also had interests in converting their fees into land.

The rule against perpetuities can be thought of as a conversation between elite members of society regarding how long a legal arrangement could restrain alienation in successor generations. It might have been easier for all concerned if the law selected a number of years that a present landowner in fee simple absolute could restrain successors from alienation thereof, say 50 years from the time of the grant. That was not the path taken. In the previous chapter, we noted the predisposition of the law was against contingent remainders; the preference was for early vesting. The battle to curtail tying-up land in lineal descendants focused on contingent remainders; if land was to pass from son to grandson, to great-grandson living at the death of the previous generation, that remainder in the lineal descendants would be eventually be contingent. Moreover, if a male lineal descendant was not produced, the preference was, like in Lord Grantham's estate, for collateral male heirs. So to limit the extent to which a remainder could be contingent after the grant was made became the focus: remoteness of vesting. After numerous cases dealing with approaches to limit remoteness of vesting, the law eventually settled on "a life in being plus 21 years." This formulation allowed a holder of land to make certain that his son and grandson would inherit his land, but thereafter the property would be freely alienable.

Thus *the common law rule against perpetuities requires that conditions precedent and conditions subsequent be resolved, one way or the other, within a fixed period of time.* If it at the time the contingent remainder or executory interest is created, it is not certain that conditions will be resolved within the period, the contingent remainder or executory interest subject to the condition is void. That fixed period of time, of course, is the well-known "lives in being plus twenty-one years and a period of gestation."

The classic formulation of the extent of that period is by Professor Gray:

'No interest is good unless it must vest if at all not later than twenty-one years after some life in being at the time of the creation of the interest.' John Chipman Grey, *The Rule Against Perpetuities* sec 201 at 191 (4th ed. 1942).

The rule is said to be one of "logical proof." Note that the rule does not say *might vest if at all*. There is no room in RAP analysis for "might." The contingent interest under observation must be certain to vest or fail to vest within the period. If there is uncertainty as to whether the contingent interest will vest, it fails. The burden is on the proponent of the interest to show that it must vest or fail to do so within the period.

And what about this "life in being at the time of the grant"? There are 7.7 billion people alive in the world today. To which life in being does the rule refer? Creator can select any life or lives that can be ascertained: so 21 years after the death of living issue of Queen Elizabeth II can be stipulated. They can be ascertained, albeit not easily. The calculation is thus made. Usually the grant itself does not establish a measuring life/lives, but one is implicit by the terms of the limitation.

B. Examples of Remote Contingencies

Just because a limitation contains a contingent remainder, do not assume it violates the rule. Many if not most contingent remainders do not violate the rule. We start with one that does not.

Example 1: O conveys Blackacre to A for life, remainder to B if B is living when the Brooklyn Bridge falls.

O has created a life estate in A, a present possessory interest, and a contingent remainder in B because the condition is a condition precedent; it must occur if B is to have possession of Blackacre. O retains a reversion. When will the condition precedent be resolved? No later than B's death. The condition precedent requires B to be living when the bridge falls, and thus the question of whether or not the contingent remainder will vest will be resolved by the time of B's death. B is the measuring life. B's contingent remainder is valid.

But some contingent remainders do not vest within the period mandated by the Rule. Consider the next example.

Example 2: O coveys Blackacre to A for life, then to B if the Brooklyn Bridge falls.

As above in ***Example 1***, O has created a life estate, a present interest in A and a contingent remainder in B because the condition is a condition precedent; it must occur if B is to have possession of Blackacre, and of course O is left with a reversion. When will the condition precedent be resolved? The short answer is, "we don't know." When A dies and if the Brooklyn

Bridge is still standing, the reversion in O will become possessory, while we wait for the condition, the bridge collapsing, to occur. Even if B has died during A's lifetime we will have to wait for the bridge to collapse because the contingent remainder O created is transmissible. B's death does nothing to resolve the condition. It is impossible to prove that the condition will be fulfilled or not within any time period. Since the time of resolution of the condition is unknown, the contingent remainder it creates is void and at A's death the reversioner takes possession of Blackacre in fee simple.

> ***Example 3:*** O conveys Blackacre to A for life, remainder to B, but if the Brooklyn Bridge falls, to C.

O has created a life estate, a present interest in A, a vested remainder subject to divestment (the language used creates a giving and a taking away, a classic condition subsequent) and therefore C has a shifting executory interest (O does not have a reversion since O created a vested remainder). When will the condition subsequent be resolved? Again, the answer is, "we don't know." Both the remainder and the executory interest are transmissible at death. Assuming the bridge is still standing when A dies, B or B's successors in interest will possess Blackacre and C or C's successor in interest will possess the executory interest. A hundred years, a thousand years later, more than a life in being plus 21 years, later, the bridge may fall. That would cause the interest in Blackacre to shift. The shifting executory interest and the condition subsequent are void because the executory interest might vest after the period stipulated in the rule. The remainder in B is valid because it cannot be divested. Contrast: if the conveyance were "to A for life, then to B, but if the Brooklyn Bridge falls *in B's lifetime* to C" the shifting executory interest would be valid because when B dies the condition subsequent will be resolved. Either the bridge will have fallen before B's death and the shifting executory interest will have divested the remainder or the bridge will be standing and we will know that the condition subsequent will never occur.

> ***Example 4:*** O conveys Blackacre to A for life, then to B for life if the Brooklyn Bridge falls.

O has created a life estate, a present possessory interest in A interest, and a contingent remainder in a life estate. O, of course, has a reversion. The difference between *2* and *4* of course, is the difference in B's remainder. In *4* the remainder is in a life estate and because B and only B can possess that life estate, B's death will resolve the question of whether the life estate will vest. When B dies, the remainder ceases to exist. The remainder is valid, but again B will probably never enjoy possession of Blackacre.

These examples of remote contingencies are not very realistic; few property owners are concerned about conditioning gifts on bridges falling. In the era in which the rule against perpetuities developed, as we noted, the question was creating gifts over to collateral male heirs of the grantor if his lineal descendants failed to produce a male heir in generations hence. The occurrence of that event could be as difficult to predict as the date of the collapse of the Brooklyn Bridge. On the other hand, these examples do show how the classification of the interests created dictate how they are subject to the rule. They also illustrate that when interests are created for purposes of the rule, or in other words, at what point must a life in being be in being. The answer: **interests are created when they are irrevocable** which means **for future interests created by will at the testator's death, for interests in irrevocable lifetime trusts at the creation of the trust and for revocable lifetime trusts when the trusts are no longer revocable which usually means at the creator's death unless the creator has released the power to revoke at an earlier time.** There are some variations on these rules when powers of appointment are involved and those variations are discussed below.

C. Contingencies Related to Persons

The illustrations above are meant to illustrate remote contingencies which are rare. Much more common in trusts are contingencies related to the lifetimes of persons. These individuals usually have some interest in the property. Whether their future interests conform to the limitations embodied in the rule is at issue. The following two examples, which on superficial examination seem to be similar but which are not, will help illustrate some aspects of the modern operation of the common law rule.

Example 5: T creates a testamentary trust. The trustee is to pay income and principal to T's living descendants in such amounts and at such times as the trustee shall determine in its discretion, without considering other resources that may be available to the beneficiaries until twenty-one years after the death of the last to die of T's descendants living at T's death. At that time the trust shall terminate and the trustee shall distribute the trust property to T's descendants then living by representation.

Example 6: T creates a testamentary trust. The trustee is to pay income and principal to T's living descendants in such amounts and at such times as the trustee shall determine in its discretion, without considering other resources that may be available to the beneficiaries until twenty-one years after the death of the last to die of T's grandchildren. At that time the trust shall terminate and the trustee shall distribute the trust property to T's descendants then living by representation.

Notice that the descriptions of terms of the two trusts differ in only a few words.

In both examples T has created a classic discretionary trust designed to provide T's family line with access to property, in the trustee's discretion of course, for many years. The present interests created in the beneficiaries for the term of the trusts are valid as we will see later. The issue is the remainders. In both examples, T has created contingent remainders, because there is a condition precedent of survival to the time of the termination of the trust. The condition is express, but even without the express statement of the condition it would be implied because T has created a remainder in a multi-generational class. For those remainders to pass muster under the rule, it must be certain that the resolution of the conditions precedent will occur within the perpetuities period.

That period, of course, is "lives in being plus twenty-one years and a period of gestation" measured from the creation of the interests subject to the condition. The starting point then is the time of T's death, as it would be for any interest created in a will. In **Example 5** the time of resolution of the condition precedent is 21 years after the death of the last to die of a group of people all of whom were living when T died. (This group, T's descendants living at T's death, includes any descendants *en ventre sa mere* who were later born alive. That is one possible application of the reference to periods of gestation in the classic statement of the rule.) The condition precedent, therefore, will be fully resolved within the perpetuities period. The descendants living at the death of T are the measuring lives. When the last of the group of lives in being dies, the trustee will continue to administer the trust for 21 more years: when the 21 year period ends the condition precedent will be resolved. T's descendants living at that time will fulfill the condition. Of course, if there are no descendants of T living at that time the condition will still be resolved, only the trust property will pass to whoever has the reversionary interest. However the condition is resolved: the rule is satisfied.

Is the remainder created in **Example 6** valid? The answer is, "it depends." It depends on whether or not children of T are living (or are *en ventre sa mere* and later born alive) at T's death. If children of T survive T it is possible that *grandchildren* of T will be born after T's death. Those "afterborn" grandchildren are not lives in being at T's death and it is possible, therefore, that the condition precedent T created could be resolved 21 years after the death of someone who was not a life in being at T's death when the contingent remainder was created. Because the condition could be resolved too late, the remainder is void from the moment of its creation. (**Question:** If the remainder is indeed void, how does the trustee distribute the trust property when the trust terminates?)

The perpetuities violation in **Example 6** occurs because the contingent remainder vests 21 years after the death of T's grandchildren. Can T's grandchildren be measuring lives? The answer is "yes" and "no". If T's children are all dead at T's death, all T's grandchildren must be alive at T's death: the class is closed, and T's grandchildren can be the measuring lives. The remainder will vest 21 years after the death of the longest living grandchild, so the answer is YES. However, if T's children are alive when T dies the answer is NO. The reason is that T's grandchildren are not a closed class. If T has children alive, another grandchild can be born. If all the grandchildren alive at the time of T's death die, the after-born grandchild could, 21 years after the death of all the lives in being that afterborn grandchild, still be alive, prolonging the resolution of the condition precedent beyond the permissible period.

To restate, if there are no children of T alive when T dies in **Example 6** the remainder is valid; if there are, it is not valid. The reason is that if T's children are dead, all of T's grandchildren who will ever exist would be lives in being at their grandparent's death. The condition precedent (surviving 21 years after the longest-living grandchildren's death) must be resolved 21 years after the death of a life in being. Alternatively, if the trust limitation provided that the trust were to terminate 21 years after the death of the last to die of T's grandchildren *living at T's death* the remainder would be valid because once again, the condition would be resolved 21 years after the death of someone who was a life in being.

Another way to think about these conditions linked to persons is to think about the remote contingency and afterborn persons. A condition that is related to the death of someone who might be born after the interests are created is dependent on a remote contingency just like the fall of the Brooklyn Bridge. We cannot be certain that the bridge will fall before the perpetuities period runs and we cannot be certain that the death of someone born after the perpetuities period begins will occur before the period runs out. The analogy is not perfect but it may be helpful.

D. The Remorseless Application of the Rule

Example 6 illustrates a very important aspect of the common law rule against perpetuities: *it is a rule of what might happen, not of what is likely to happen or of what actually happens.* In *Example 6* the mere possibility that more grandchildren could be born to T is enough to invalidate the remainder by creating the possibility, no matter how slight, that the condition precedent would be resolved (that is that the remainder would "vest") 21 years after the death of someone who was not a life in being. The resulting invalidity is *ab initio,* that is, the interest is void from the moment of creation. The remainder just isn't there.

This "what might happen" aspect of the rule really is an expression of a larger principle. The common law rule against perpetuities is remorselessly applied. There is no room for construing instruments to try to "save" interests; there is no room to consider the intent of the creator of the conditions to which the interests are tied. The whole purpose of the rule is to frustrate the intent to keep property inalienable and out of the market by postponing the resolution of conditions (that is, remember, "vesting") beyond the allowed period.

The "take no prisoners" quality of the common law rule has led to the development of several doctrines that truly are absurd. To illustrate the first, assume that in *Example 6* T is indeed survived by children: three daughters all over 70 years of age. The possibility that any one of them will have a child born after T's death is slight (even taking into account modern medical technology). Yet the question of whether the condition precedent T created will be resolved within the perpetuities period assumes that T's daughters could give birth up to the moment of their deaths. Under the common law rule against perpetuities, every person is assumed to be able to have children from the moment of birth until the moment of death. The first possibility is known as the "precocious toddler" rule and the second as the "fertile octogenarian" rule.

1. Fertile Octogenarians and Precocious Toddlers

At the beginning of the 21st century there might be some logic to the fertile octogenarian rule. Medical technology has made it possible for women to bear their genetic children (or to have their genetic children borne by another woman) beyond the traditional 'childbearing years.' And, of course, a child might be adopted at any time. Remember, however, that the fertile octogenarian rule was formulated *three hundred years ago* when human ingenuity could do nothing to extend a woman's reproductive capacity and when restrictive rules about the effect of adoption would prevent an adopted child from being a grandchild of the adoptive parent's parent. (There is no sense in the precocious toddler rule.)

Therefore, the remainders in **Example 6** are invalid if at least one child of T is living at the creation of the trust even if that child is a woman aged 70 who cannot reasonably expected to be able to conceive and bear a child. Absurd? Yes. The common law? Yes, again.

2. Unborn Widows

Another classic example of the remorseless quality of the common law rule is illustrated by the following example:

> **Example 7:** T creates a trust to pay to income to T's son S for his life, then to pay the income to S's surviving spouse, if any, and then to pay the trust property to S's issue then living by representation.

First, T has created a present interest in S, an equitable life estate, a remainder in a life estate in S's surviving spouse and of course a contingent remainder in S's issue. The requirement that issue be living on the death of S's widow (if any) is a condition precedent.

Second, when will the condition precedent be resolved? At the death of S's surviving spouse, *and S's surviving spouse might be someone who was not yet born when the trust was created.* How could that be? Suppose S is married at the time T creates the trust. It is possible that S's then spouse might die or they might divorce; some time thereafter S might marry a person who was not a life in being at the time the trust was created; that person might be S's surviving spouse.

Unlikely? Perhaps, but for purposes of the common law rule against perpetuities the only response is "well, it *might* happen." And that's enough.

This rigorous application of the common law rule is known as the "unborn widow" rule; a contingent interest limited to take effect after the death of a surviving spouse is void because the resolution of that condition is tied to the life span of someone who may not be a life in being at the time the interest was created. Realize that if the reference were to a person who is currently S's spouse the requirements of the rule would be satisfied. In **Example 7** if the remainder in a life estate had been created in "S's wife Mary, if she shall survive him" the condition precedent would be resolved on the death of someone who was alive when the interest was created. Likewise a limitation to S's spouse if the spouse is alive at T's death is valid. The unborn widow problem arises because of the reference to a "generic" surviving spouse.

In **Example 7**, of course, the contingent remainder is void and the reversion in T will eventually take possession of the trust property.

To test your understanding of the unborn widow rule, try the following questions:

> **Question 1:** T devises property in trust to pay the income to T's daughter D for life, then to pay the income to her surviving spouse, if any, and then the trust shall

terminate and the trustee shall distribute the trust property to D's children who are then living, and if none of D's children are living at the termination of the trust the trustee shall pay the trust property to T's niece, N. What interests are created by T's devise in trust? Are any of those interests void under the common law rule against perpetuities?

Question 2: T devises property in trust to pay the income to T's daughter D for life, then to pay the income to her surviving spouse, if any, and then the trust shall terminate and the trustee shall distribute the trust property to D's children, but if none of D's children are living at the termination of the trust the trustee shall pay the trust property to T's niece N. What interests are created by T's devise in trust? Are any of those interests void under the common law rule against perpetuities?

3. Administrative Contingencies

Finally, there is one more class of applications known as "administrative contingencies."

Example 8: T's will gives the residue as follows: "I give the rest, residue, and remainder of my estate, both real and personal, to my descendants living at the completion of the administration of my estate, by representation."

In many jurisdictions, this language creates a condition precedent of survival to the designated time: the time for distribution of T's estate. Because there are no human lives connected to the condition, that is the condition is not tied to the death of some person or the passage of years from the birth or death of some person, the perpetuities period by the expiration of the which the condition must be resolved is a "period in gross" of 21 years. (This is the same 21 year period we encountered when we discussed trusts for animals and found a condition precedent tied to the time of death of the animal for which the trust was created.) Since we cannot be absolutely sure that the administration of T's estate will be completed within 21 years of T's death, the residuary devise fails and the residue passes in intestacy. There are some other illustrations of administrative contingencies. For example, a bequest of the residue of the testator's estate to a charitable foundation to be organized by the executor after the testator's death might be held to be a contingent bequest and since there is no certainty that the foundation will be organized within 21 years of the testator's death the bequest is void.

E. Class Gifts and the Rule Against Perpetuities

The foregoing perpetuities "traps" can frustrate intent. There is yet another aspect of the common law rule against perpetuities that may likewise operate to make contingent remainders void: the application of the rule to class gifts. *In order to satisfy the rule, the class must close and any conditions precedent must be resolved as to all class members within the perpetuities period.*

Example 9: T creates a testamentary trust to pay the income to A for life, remainder to A's children.

The remainder in A's children is contingent if A has no children at the time T creates the trust (which is the moment of T's death). If A dies without ever having had children the remainder will simply vanish and the reversion will take possession of the trust property. This remainder is contingent but not because of the existence of a condition precedent, but simply because there is no class member alive at the time of the grant. Nevertheless, the rule does apply and is satisfied because by the time of A's death the question of whether or not A will have children will be resolved. In other words, the class of A's children will close at A's death. Note that in the modern world the statement that A cannot have children after A's death simply is not true. As we have seen, properly stored gametes can be used to conceive a child of A after A's death. The rule against perpetuities simply has not yet come to terms with the facts of modern medical technology. We apply the rule as if those techniques did not exist.

Given that deliberate ignorance of assisted conception techniques, we can be certain that the class of A's children will close at A's death. That is what the rule requires.

Example 10: T creates a testamentary trust to pay the income to A for life, remainder to A's children who reach the age of 21.

Here the remainder in A's children is subject to a condition precedent: the remainder vests in those children of A who reach 21. The rule requires that the class close and the condition precedent be resolved as to all of the class members within the perpetuities period. Will that happen here? Yes it will. The class of A's children will close at A's death. A is a life in being so the class closes in time.

Every member of the class is alive at A's death (and alive includes children *en ventre sa mere*) and within 21 years of A's death all of the class members will either reach the age of 21 of die before reaching that age. Therefore, the condition precedent will be resolved as to all class members; they will either reach 21 or die trying, within 21 years of the death of A, the life in being.

Example 11: T creates a testamentary trust to pay the income to A for life, remainder to A's children who reach the age of 25.

Once again the remainder is subject to a condition precedent: the remainder vests in those children of A who reach 25. The class will close on the death of A, a life in being. However, we cannot be certain that the condition precedent will be resolved as to every class member before the perpetuities period runs. A is the only life in being we can be sure of. That means that we have 21 years after A's death to resolve the condition, and we must know that it must be resolved, one way or the other, as to each class member if the remainder is to be valid for any of the class members. It is possible for A to have a child within 4 years of A's death. If that happens, it will take more than 21 years after A's death to determine whether that child will reach the age of 25 or not. The remainder in A's children is therefore void.

Note that if a child of A is already 25 years old at T's death the remainder is still void. The class cannot close by the rule of convenience until A dies and the income interest has terminated. The class cannot close any sooner than A's death when a demand for payment can be made and at that time it is possible that the class of A's children will include children under the age of 4.

So far we have been dealing with classes that close physiologically, but ***Example 12*** reminds us that classes can close by the rule of convenience.

> ***Example 12:*** T creates a testamentary trust to pay the income to A for life, remainder to A's grandchildren.

There is no condition precedent involved with this remainder so the issue is whether the class will close within the perpetuities period allowing the remainder to be valid. When will the class of A's grandchildren close physiologically? When the last of A's children die. The possibility of A having children after T's death with the result that the class of A's grandchildren would remain open until the death of that afterborn child of A means that the rule could be violated and the remainder is then void.

However, there are several scenarios in which the class of A's grandchildren will close by the rule of convenience at A's death. Remember that there is no condition precedent here. Once A dies and the income interest terminates, any grandchild is entitled to be paid. Thus, if at the time T creates the interest (T's death) a grandchild of A will be able to demand his or her share of the remainder at A's death, the class will close on the death of a life in being. The remainder is therefore valid.

What circumstances could exist at T's death that would lead to that conclusion?

First, if there are grandchildren of A living at T's death, the class of A's grandchildren will close at A's death because that grandchild will demand payment and close the class. Even if that grandchild dies immediately after T, there is no express condition of survival, the grandchild's interest in the remainder is transmissible, and the grandchild's successors in interest will demand payment and close the class at A's death.

Second, what if a grandchild of A was alive when T executed the will, but died before T? If the anti-lapse statute applied and if the persons designated to take the predeceased beneficiary's interest by the anti-lapse statute exist (e.g., issue of the grandchild of A were living at T's death) then those persons would close the class by the rule of convenience at A's death.

Third, suppose none of A's children were living at T's death? In that case, the class of A's grandchildren closed at T's death.

> ***Example 13:*** T creates a testamentary trust to pay the income to A for life, remainder to A's grandchildren living at A's death.

Here there is a condition precedent of survival to the time of distribution of the trust property. The remainder is valid. At A's death either there will be at least one living grandchild of A who will then close the class and be entitled to the trust property or there will be no living grandchildren of A and the remainder will fail and the interest will revert to T's estate.

There is one more doctrine related to class gifts that must be considered. Under some circumstances, it is possible to treat a gift to a class as a gift to several subclasses if that construction will validate at least some of the interests created.

Example 14: T creates a testamentary trust to pay the income to his son, S, for life then to pay the income in equal shares to S's children for their lives, and as each child of S dies, the trustee shall distribute to that child's issue, then living, by representation, the fraction of the trust property equal to the number 1 divided by the number of S's children living immediately before the death of the child to whose issue distribution is to be made. In other words, if at S's death S has six children, at the death of the first of them to die, the trustee will distribute 1/6 of the trust property to the child's descendants.

The possibility that S could have a child born after T's death would make invalid a remainder subject to the resolution of a condition precedent of surviving the last to die of S's children. The trust in *Example 14*, however, does not create one single condition precedent, rather it creates several, one tied to the death of each of S's children. Every time a child dies, a condition precedent is resolved. There are as many class gifts as there are children of S, one gift to the surviving issue of each child. For purposes of satisfying the rule each class gift can be judged separately. That means that the remainders contingent on surviving a child of S who was living at T's death are valid; the remainders contingent on surviving any child of S born after T's death are invalid.

Assume that there are three children of S living at T's death and that after T's death three more children are born to S. When S dies, all six children survive. When one of the children who was living at T's death dies, the share of the trust property resulting from the application of the formula in the trust instrument is distributed to that child's issue then living, by representation. On the death of a child of S born after T's death, the share of the trust property resulting from the application of the formula passes by resulting trust to whoever took the reversion from T's estate. That person or persons are the residuary beneficiaries or, if the trust was itself the residuary devise, then the reversion passed in intestacy. If we assume that T died unmarried, then the sole heir was S, and we have to determine who took the reversion through S's estate.

F. Powers of Appointment and the Rule

The application of the common law rule against perpetuities to powers of appointment involves some special rules. There are two questions involved in applying the rule to powers of appointment.

1. Is the Power Itself Valid?

A power of appointment is valid if it cannot be exercised beyond the perpetuities period measured from the creation of the power. This requirement is seldom violated when powers of appointment are created in individuals, because such powers are almost always created in living persons. As we have seen, the typical power is given to an income beneficiary of a trust, and enables that person to decide upon the disposition of the trust property after the income beneficiary's death. The power will be exercised no later than the appointee's death (given the rule that the exercise of a testamentary power of appointment occurs at the moment of death even though some time will elapse before the will is admitted to probate), and thus the requirements of the rule will be satisfied.

There is a problem, however, with trustees' powers to make discretionary distributions. Such powers are often regarded as non-general (special) powers of appointment. It is possible to create a trust in which no interest vests too late but which lasts too long.

> *Example 15:* T creates a testamentary trust. The trustee is to pay income and principal to T's child A for life and then is to pay income and principal to A's children in such amounts and at such times as the trustee shall determine in its discretion, without considering other resources that may be available to the beneficiaries, until the death of the last to die of A's children at which time the trust shall terminate and the trustee is to distribute the trust property to the American Cancer Society.

The interests in the trust property satisfy the rule. The class of A's children closes at A's death and A is a life in being. The remainder in the ACS is vested at the moment of creation. There is no condition precedent attached to it. Of course, if the remainder were contingent on survival to the termination of the trust it would be void. Do you understand why?

The trustee's power, however, is doubtful. A could have a child born after T's death, and while that child is alive, the trustee has a non-general power of appointment to appoint trust income to that child and any other living child of A. The power lasts as long as the life of the afterborn which of course could extend beyond the perpetuities period. There are two views about the proper treatment of such a power. One view is that the power is void from creation as with a contingent interest that does not vest within the perpetuities period. The other view is that the power may be exercised for the period in gross of 21 years. There is almost no authority for either position and we can only assume that the problem does not often arise or at least is not often noticed. Do you understand why there is no question about the validity of the trustee's power in *Example 5*?

2. The Rule and Future Interests Created by Exercise of the Power

Matters are more complicated when we consider the application of the rule against perpetuities to future interests created by the exercise of a power of appointment. The rules are:

> *A future interest created by the exercise of a presently of* a presently exercisable general power of appointment *is created for purposes of application of the rule against perpetuities at the time the power of appointment is exercised.*

> *A future interest created by the exercise of* a testamentary general power of appointment *or of* any non-general (special) power of appointment *is created for purposes of the application of the rule against perpetuities at the time the power of appointment was created.*

The second rule is called the "relation back rule." It is an expression of the doctrine that property subject to a non-general (special) power is not the property of the donee of the power but rather that of the donor. When the donee exercises the power the donee is only "filing in the blanks" in the donor's disposition. The application of the same rule to exercises of testamentary general powers is almost universal, even though property subject to a general power is for some purposes (mainly taxation) as if it belonged to the donee.

The second rule, then, really is a rule about when a life in being must be a life in being. Here is a typical example:

> **Example 16:** Father's will creates a testamentary trust with Bank as trustee. The trustee is to pay the trust income to Father's eldest child, Daughter D, for life and then to distribute the trust property as D shall appoint in her last will and testament, duly admitted to probate, which refers specifically to the power. D may appoint among her issue, outright or in further trust, with the existing trustee or another trustee, but in no event may D appoint to herself, her estate, her creditors or the creditors of her estate. D exercises the power by appointing the property in further trust with Bank as trustee to pay the income to her children for their lives and on the death of her last surviving child to pay the trust property to her descendants then living by representation.

D has created present possessory interests in her children and a contingent remainder in her descendants. The condition precedent is survival to the time of the termination of the trust which is the death of the last to die of D's children.

If D had created this trust in her own will with her probate property there would be no rule against perpetuities issue. All of D's children are lives in being at her death when the interests are created, and the condition precedent will be resolved at the death of the last of them to die, the death of a life in being.

However, because D created this trust through the exercise of a non-general power of appointment, the interests she creates are deemed to have been created in her Father's will, the instrument that created the power of appointment. For the purposes of the rule, it is as if Father's will had created a trust to pay the income to D for life, then to her children for their lives, and then to pay the trust property to D's descendants then living by representation. The condition precedent must be resolved within 21 years of the death of a life in being *at Father's death*. Because D can have a child after Father's death, the condition precedent could be resolved on the death of a child not in being when the interests subject to the condition were created, that is, on the death of an afterborn. (See **Example 6.**) The condition could be resolved after the period of the rule, rendering the contingent remainder in the D's descendants invalid. The remainder in the income interest in D's children is valid because the class of D's children will close on her death and she is a life in being when Father dies.

There is one possibility that might save the remainder in this case. Under the common law, it is possible to take a "second look." The "second look doctrine" allows us to take account of the facts that exist when the non-general (special) power of appointment or general testamentary power of appointment is exercised, and to decide whether, given the facts at that time, there is no chance that the condition precedent (or condition subsequent) created by the exercise of the power will be resolved too late. If that is not the case then the interests created by exercise of the power are valid. In this example, if at D's death all of her surviving children were also living when Father died, the remainder is valid. Because the condition precedent will be resolved (and thus the remainder will vest or fail if there are no living descendants of D) on the death of someone who was a life in being at the time the power was created the remainder is valid. There is absolutely no chance of vesting occurring after the period stipulated by the rule, because that the condition will not be resolved on the death of an afterborn. If, however, D is survived by a child who was born after Father's death, the possibility that the condition will be resolved on the death of that afterborn child makes the remainder invalid.

The application of the rule against perpetuities to exercises of powers of appointment is an important topic. Powers of appointment are relatively common aspects of estate plans and many of those powers are general testamentary powers or non-general (special) powers. Exercise of such powers to create further trusts and therefore future interests will always implicate the rule against perpetuities.

G. Perpetuities Reform

Relaxing the rigors of the rule against perpetuities has been the subject of both academic and legislative dialogue and reform for quite some time. At least fourteen states have now abolished the rule against perpetuities, at least as it applies to trusts. If the purpose of the rule is to promote alienability and to keep property from being withdrawn from the market, the application of the rule to the modern trust perhaps does not make much sense. We do not live in a legal world in which trust property is removed from the market. The modern trustee can invest in a wide range of property and is free to buy and sell whenever it is prudent to do so. The rule can be seen as directed at the trust itself, as expressing society's judgment that it is not wise to create perpetual pools of capital which can provide the material support for a dynasty of wealthy persons insulated from the need to earn a living in the marketplace.

That said, let us consider the following pathways to reform.

1. The Restatement, Third Property: Wills and Other Donative Transfers

Section 27.1 rejects the traditional rule which focuses on the vesting of an interest and simply requires that a trust must terminate at the death of individuals two generations subsequent to the creator.

27.1. Statement of the Rule Against Perpetuities

(a) A trust or other donative disposition of property is subject to judicial modification . . . to the extent that the trust or other disposition does not terminate on or before the expiration of the perpetuity period . . . .

(b)   The perpetuity period expires at the death of the last living measuring life. The measuring lives are as follows:

(1)   Except as otherwise provided in paragraph (2), the measuring lives constitute a group composed of the following individuals: the transferor, the beneficiaries of the disposition who are related to the transferor and no more than two generations younger than the transferor, and the beneficiaries of the disposition who are unrelated to the transferor and no more than the equivalent of two generations younger than the transferor.

(2)   In the case of a trust or other property arrangement for the sole current benefit of a named individual who is more than two generations younger than the transferor or more than the equivalent of two generations younger than the transferor, the measuring life is the named individual.

Consider the preceding examples in which the rule would render contingent remainder void, for examples, *Examples 6*, *7*, *8*, *11*, *12*, *14*, and *16*. Does the Restatement "rule" provide a remedy for each of these perpetuities miscues?

2.   Statutory Correctives: The Example of New York

The rule against perpetuities has had a tumultuous history in New York. Like so much of the history of the New York law of trusts and wills, the story begins with the Revised Statutes enacted in the 1830s. The Revisers were working at a time when the common law rule against perpetuities, the rule that prohibits remote vesting, was still in the process of refinement. The statute they drafted which the Legislature enacted prohibited the remote vesting only of certain interests and limited the period for which vesting could be delayed to two lives in being at the creation of the interest. What we know today as the traditional common law rule against perpetuities did not become the law of New York until 1965. That rule is now set forth in NY EPTL § 9–1.1(b):

New York Estates, Powers, and Trusts Law § 9–1.1(b)

(b)   No estate in property shall be valid unless it must vest, if at all, not later than twenty-one years after one or more lives in being at the creation of the estate and any period of gestation involved. In no case shall lives measuring the permissible period of vesting be so designated or so numerous as to make proof of their end unreasonably difficult.

Current New York law, then, embraces the rule, but there is another aspect of perpetuities in New York that is directly traceable to the nineteenth century legislation. The Revised Statutes created a second rule directed not at prohibiting remote vesting but rather directly targeted the duration of trusts. It is known as the prohibition of undue suspension of the power of alienation and today is in NY EPTL § 9–1.1(a):

New York Estates, Powers, and Trusts Law EPTL § 9–1.1(a)

(a)(1) The absolute power of alienation is suspended when there are no persons in being by whom an absolute fee or estate in possession can be conveyed or transferred.

(2) Every present or future estate shall be void in its creation which shall suspend the absolute power of alienation by any limitation or condition for a longer period than lives in being at the creation of the estate and a term of not more than twenty-one years. Lives in being shall include a child conceived before the creation of the estate but born thereafter. In no case shall the lives measuring the permissible period be so designated or so numerous as to make proof of their end unreasonably difficult.

The power of alienation is the power to reassemble full fee simple ownership of property in the hands of a single person. For example, think of the classic legal life estate created when G conveys Blackacre to A for life, then to B. So long as A can convey the life estate to C and B and convey his remainder to C, the power to alienate is not suspended because all of the sticks in the bundle of fee simple ownership can be amassed by the transfer into C's hands. Or in the statutory terms, C now has an absolute fee in possession.

The interesting aspect of the suspension of alienation rule comes in its application to trusts. Even though the trustee can convey absolutely ownership of trust property simply by selling it or distributing it out of trust, New York courts have long interpreted the suspension of alienation rule to require that trust beneficiaries be able to convey their interests so that the required absolute ownership of the trust property in a single individual would occur by the merger of the equitable interests. New York law permits the alienation of contingent interests (NY EPTL § 7–1.5(a)). So long as the holders of the interest are all ascertained they can alienate their interests. if they are minors a guardian will have to be appointed. The impediment to transfer is the statutory provision that makes income interests in express trusts inalienable unless the creator of the interest provides otherwise (NY EPTL § 7–1.5(a)(1)). So long as the creator of the trust does not override the default rule, the power to alienate is suspended for the entire duration of the income interests in a trust. The classic example is the following:

> ***Example 17:*** T creates a testamentary trust to pay the income to T's son S for life, then to pay the income to S's children for their lives, then to distribute the trust property to the American Red Cross free of trust.

Under the common law rule against perpetuities, every interest in this trust is valid. The income interest in S is a present interest. The class of S's children will close at S's death and S is a life in being. The remainder in the ARC vested at the moment it was created; it is not subject to any conditions. The problem comes from the possibility that S might have a child after T's death. (not that again!) That child of course would be an afterborn and would not be a life in being at the time of the devise/bequest. The income interest will last for that child's entire lifetime which means that the duration of the income interest would be measured by the lifespan of an afterborn child, and it therefore could last for longer than 21 years after the death of a life in being. Remember, if a child is born after the trust is created and all of the lives in being then die, the afterborn is still alive and there is nothing that requires the afterborn to die within 21 years of the death of the last life in being to die.) Because the income interest is inalienable (unless T overrides the statutory default rule which we will assume T did not) the power of alienation is suspended so long as the income interest exists which could be longer than lives in being plus 21 years. The income interest in all of S's children is invalid (remember, if a class gift is invalid as to one class member it is invalid as to all). When S dies the trust will terminate and the property be distributed to the American Red Cross. Note that if the remainder were contingent on surviving to the time of termination of the trust, the remainder would be invalid under the common law rule because the condition precedent could be resolved on the death of the afterborn child.

New York has adopted several statutory rules which blunt the force of some of the more absurd applications of what we have called the "remorseless application" of the rule. First, age contingencies are reduced to 21 years if the reduction will prevent invalidity under one or both of New York's rules against perpetuities.

New York Estates, Powers, and Trusts Law § 9–1.2

Where an estate would, except for this section, be invalid because made to depend, for its vesting or its duration, upon any person attaining or failing to attain an age in excess of twenty-one years, the age contingency shall be reduced to twenty-one years as to any or all persons subject to such contingency.

Remember **Example 10:** T creates a testamentary trust to pay the income to A for life, remainder to A's children who reach the age of 25. Under the rule, the contingent remainder in the A's children (reaching 25) is void because the only surviving child of A might be a child born after T's death and 2 years old at A's death. In New York, the class gift is valid because EPTL § 9–1.2 would reduce the age contingency to 21. The condition precedent would therefore be resolved as to all of the members of the class of A's children (a class which closed on the death of A, a life in being) within 21 years of the death A.

The second provision is NY EPTL § 9–1.3. It creates several rules of construction all of which are aimed at reducing the impact of several rules we have already considered: the fertile octogenarian (see subsection e), the unborn widow (see subsection c) and administrative contingencies (see subsection d).

New York Estates, Powers, and Trusts Law § 9–1.3

(a) Unless a contrary intention appears, the rules of construction provided in this section govern with respect to any matter affecting the rule against perpetuities.

(b) It shall be presumed that the creator intended the estate to be valid.

(c) Where an estate would, except for this paragraph, be invalid because of the possibility that the person to whom it is given or limited may be a person not in being at the time of the creation of the estate, and such person is referred to in the instrument creating such estate as the spouse of another without other identification, it shall be presumed that such reference is to a person in being on the effective date of the instrument.

(d) Where the duration or vesting of an estate is contingent upon the probate of a will, the appointment of a fiduciary, the location of a distributee, the payment of debts, the sale of assets, the settlement of an estate, the determination of questions relating to an estate or transfer tax or the occurrence of any specified contingency, it shall be presumed that the creator of such estate intended such contingency to occur, if at all, within twenty-one years from the effective date of the instrument creating such estate.

(e)(1) Where the validity of a disposition depends upon the ability of a person to have a child at some future time, it shall be presumed, subject to subparagraph (2), that a male can have a child at fourteen years of age or over, but not under that age, and that a female can have a child at twelve years of age or over, but not under that age or over the age of fifty-five years.

(2) In the case of a living person, evidence may be given to establish whether he or she is able to have a child at the time in question.

(3) Where the validity of a disposition depends upon the ability of a person to have a child at some future time, the possibility that such person may have a child by adoption shall be disregarded.

(4) The provisions of subparagraphs (1), (2) and (3) shall not apply for any purpose other than that of determining the validity of a disposition under the rule against perpetuities where such validity depends on the ability of a person to have a child at some future time. A determination of validity or invalidity of a disposition under the rule against perpetuities by the application of subparagraph (1) or (2) or (3) shall not be affected by the later occurrence of facts in contradiction to the facts presumed or determined or the possibility of adoption disregarded under subparagraphs (1) or (2) or (3).

As you can see from the language, the statute replaces the "remorseless application" first by creating a presumption that the creator of the interests intended them to be valid. The statute further resolves the unborn widow problem, to eliminate the complications of administrative contingencies, to eliminate the precocious toddler and to limit the effect of the fertile octogenarian rule as it applies to women. For example, in *Example 17*, if the first income beneficiary were T's daughter, D and the remainder in the life income interest were in her children and at T's death D were 55 years of age or older, the income interest in the children would not violate the rule against the suspension of the power of alienation or the rule against too remote vesting because it would be presumed that D can no longer have children. Thus the afterborn child cannot exist and all the children enjoying the income interest will be lives in being. What if the limitation was to his son instead?

Consider the preceding examples in which the rule would render the contingent remainder void, for examples, *Examples 6*, *7*, *8*, *11*, *12*, *14*, and *16*. Do New York statutes provide a remedy for each of these perpetuities miscues?

3. Wait and See

As we have seen, the rule invalidates interests because they can be construed to be conditioned on events that will not likely occur: fertile octogenarians; unborn widows, and excessively long probates. Instead of holding the suspect condition void because it might violate the rule, the wait-and-see approach allows the errant limitation stand until the time the contingency vests to determine whether in fact the vesting did occur outside the temporal span of the rule. Under the "wait-and-see" corrective to the rule (so-called because the contingent remains in play until the drama pays out if the interest does vest within the period of the rule), the contingent remainder is valid. Pennsylvania adopted the what might happen approach for the so-called wait-and-see approach in 1947:

> Upon the expiration of the period allowed by the common law against perpetuities measured by actual rather than possible events any interest not then vested and any interest in member of a class the membership which is then subject to increase shall be void. Pa. Stat. Ann. Tit 20 § 6104(b).

Wait-and-see won the support of Professor Barton Leach in an article in the *Harvard Law Review* (65 Harv.L.Rev. 721 (1952). There is a certain logic to the wait-and-see rule: if the evil is that an interest remotely vests, strike it down; leave those which might remotely vest, but ultimately do not stand. Detractors there were: the approach promoted uncertainty because it left errant limitations in limbo waiting to see whether what *might* happen *did* happen. If the fertile octogenarian did produce a child and that child was the one surviving at the time for vesting, or if the child married an unborn spouse who survived the child, invalidate the limitation. But do not throw the baby out with the bathwater: allow the 99.9% of limitations in which what might have happened does not to survive. The Restatement (Second) of Property embraced wait-and-see, and it is the rule that is been most widely adopted by statute and common law.

Consider the preceding examples in which the rule would render contingent remainder void, for examples, *Examples 6*, *7*, *8*, *11*, *12*, *14*, and *16*. Does "wait and see" provide a remedy for each of these perpetuities miscues?

4. The Uniform Statutory Rule Against Perpetuities

In 1986, the Uniform Law Commissioners promulgated the Uniform Statutory Rule Against Perpetuities 98A U.L.A. 103 (Supp. 1988, amended in 1990). The goal was to set a period of time that would approximate what would likely be the further reaches of the wait-and-see period. The act renders valid all "non-vested interests" for 90 years. If the interest does vest within the 90 year period, the court is empowered to reform it "in a matter that most closely approximates the transferor's manifested plan of distribution and is within the 90 years allowed [by the statute]." The same argument that was lodged against the "wait-and see" approach, uncertainty, was directed against the USRAP. In addition, it should be noted that by the time the contingency fails, 90 years after creation, all but the most robust practitioners will be no longer subject to a malpractice suit.

Consider the preceding examples in which the rule would render contingent remainder void, for examples, *Examples 6*, *7*, *8*, *11*, *12*, *14*, and *16*. Does the USRAP provide a remedy for each of these perpetuities miscues?

5. Saving Clauses

One way of dealing with potential perpetuities problems is to plan in advance for the possibility that an errant contingent remainder was inadvertently created and provide for an alternative disposition:

> . . . any trust in this instrument shall terminate, unless it has previously terminated, no later than 21 years after the death of the survivor of the beneficiaries of the trust living at the date that this instrument becomes effective. At that time, the remaining principal and undistributed income shall be distributed to the income beneficiaries in the same proportion that they were receiving income at the time of termination.

Presumably, this clause resembles a wait-and-see clause, but with a different ultimate resolution. Unless what *might* happen *does* happen, the trust operates according to the limitation. The clause only takes effect if the trust provision violates the rule, and provides an alternative method of disposition if it does. It is not necessary for the distribution to be directed to the income beneficiaries; the distribution can be directed to a charity. Does the savings clause, as drafted, really effectuate the intent of the creator? Can you suggest another?

Test Your Knowledge

To assess your understanding of the material in this chapter, click here to take a quiz.

PART VI

Transfer Taxes

CHAPTER 15

Federal Transfer Taxes at Death

A. Introduction

This chapter is an introduction to the federal wealth transfer taxes. What are they? They are excise taxes imposed by the federal government on the gratuitous transfer of wealth. An excise tax is a tax on a privilege. Taxes on the sale of tobacco and alcohol, for example, are excise taxes on the privilege of selling those things, a privilege that our society acting through our elected representatives could end. Since society, acting through government, can regulate buying and selling of these substances, government can allow the trade to continue on just about any terms it likes, including imposing taxes.

The transfer of wealth is also a privilege—at least that has been the traditional view in our legal system going back, like so many ideas that seem odd to us today, to the Norman Conquest of England. It's enough to say that these taxes on transferring wealth have long been held to be constitutional, in part because they have been in existence in one form or another for a very long time. There are three federal transfer taxes: the estate tax on transfers of property at death, the gift tax on transfers of property during life, and the generation skipping transfer tax on transfers from a person to persons more than one generation younger from the "transferor" (for example from a grandparent to a grandchild). The estate and gift taxes we have today began in the early twentieth century. The estate tax was enacted in 1916, the gift tax in 1924, repealed in 1924, and reenacted in 1932. The generation skipping transfer tax came along decades later. The first version was enacted in 1976, repealed ab initio (as if it never had been enacted) in 1986 and a new generation skipping transfer tax enacted at that time.

As with all federal taxes, the law begins with the Internal Revenue Code. Because the Code was last completely rewritten in 1986, we refer to the current version as the Internal Revenue Code of 1986, even though the statutes have been extensively amended since then. The Estate Tax is Chapter 11 of the Code, sections 2001 through 2058 (sections 2101 through 2108 deal with taxing the estates of nonresidents of the United States who are not citizens but whose estates may be subject to tax because some of the property of the estate is located in the United States and sections 2201 through 2210 deal with miscellaneous provisions generally concerned with who is liable to pay the estate tax on non-probate property). Chapter 12 is the

Gift Tax, sections 2501 through 2524 and Chapter 13 is the Generation-Skipping Transfer Tax, sections 2601 through 2664.

The provisions of the Code are supplemented by the regulations promulgated by the Secretary of the Treasury under authority given by Congress. The Regulations are an integral part of all of the system of federal taxation and provide important information on how the Treasury and the Internal Revenue Service believe the Code should be applied. Many Regulations are non-controversial and as important to the operation of the system as the Code itself. Some are controversial and from time to time the courts will invalidate a specific provision, but on the whole, no one can understand the transfer taxes without dealing with the Regulations. Finally, the Internal Revenue Service issues various forms of guidance on how the Code should apply in specific situations.

Our discussion here is only a very brief introduction to a complex system of taxation. The truth is that a truly small number of us are subject to any of these taxes because there are exemptions which are great enough that only a fraction of one-percent of the population ever needs to think about federal transfer tax planning.

The chapter discusses first the estate and gift taxes which are integrated into a single system and then the generation-skipping transfer tax (the GST tax).

B. The Estate and Gift Taxes

1. Integration of the Two Taxes

Since 1977 the estate and gift taxes have been integrated. The basic idea is that taxable transfers during life (taxable gifts) and the final taxable transfer at death are all part of one long series of gifts culminating in the final gift at death. The system allows every person to make taxable transfers at death of up to $10,000,000 (the number is indexed for inflation which means it increases every year to reflect increases in the cost of living—in 2019 the amount is $11,400,000) without paying tax. That's because we each have a unified credit against the transfer taxes which offsets the tax that would be levied on taxable transfers equal to the applicable exclusion amount. Once the applicable exclusion amount is used up the tax on taxable transfers is 40%. (Tax on lesser amounts is less than 40% and is completely offset by the credit.) The first thing to note is that part or all of the applicable exclusion amount can be used up by making taxable gifts during life.

If the taxpayer (from now on, "T") makes a $1,000,000 taxable gift in year one, the tax on that gift is offset by the unified credit and although T has to file a gift tax return (Form 709) there will be no tax due. In year 2, T makes a $2,000,000 taxable gift. Again the tax is offset by the credit and no tax is due. T can go on making taxable gifts until the total value of all of the gifts exceeds the applicable exclusion amount before T will owe any gift tax. However, using the applicable exclusion amount by making lifetime gifts will directly affect the amount of estate tax T's estate owes at T's death.

Here's how. T dies in 2019 and during life made taxable gifts valued at exactly $11,400,000. (This is a bit unrealistic because the applicable exclusion amount increases every year, but that does not affect the principle illustrated.) T's taxable estate (and more on how that is calculated in a bit) is $10,000,000. The estate tax is calculated by adding together the value of the taxable gifts and the taxable estate which gives a total of $21,400,000 and calculating the tax on that amount. The unified credit is then subtracted from that total. That means that the unified credit offsets all the tax on the taxable gifts and the $10,000,000 taxable estate is taxed at 40% which is the rate of tax for all taxable amounts greater than the applicable exclusion amount. The estate tax, therefore, is .40 × 10,000,000 = $4,000,000.

This calculation means that the tax on T's lifetime transfers subject to the estate or gift taxes of $21,400,000 are taxed *only to the extent they exceed in value the applicable exclusion amount.* Note, too, that the tax on the total amount of taxable transfers, $21,400,000 is $4,000,000 or 18.7% of the total taxable transfers and had T's taxable transfers during life and at death had not exceed $11,400,000 there would have been no tax all.

Now that we've seen how the estate and gift taxes work together, we'll examine the major features of each tax.

2. The Gift Tax

a) What Is a Gift?

The most basic question of all is: what is a gift? A *donor* makes a gift when the donor transfers property to the *donee* to the extent the donor does not receive consideration in money or money's worth, that is, the transfer is *gratuitous*. Not every gratuitous transfer is a taxable gift, however. In order to make a taxable gift the donor must relinquish dominion and control over the property. Of course, if the donor writes a check to donee the donor has clearly relinquished dominion and control when the donee cashes the check. If the donor directs the donor's broker to transfer stock in a corporation from the donor's brokerage account to the account of the donee the donor has relinquished dominion and control when the stock leaves the donor's account (that is, when the broker's records show that the stock was transferred out of the donor's account). These sorts of outright transfers of ownership are easy to understand as a relinquishing of dominion and control. The more interesting questions usually come up when the donor makes a transfer in trust.

For example, Donor transfers $5,000,000 to Trustee. The trust is irrevocable and the terms of the trust require Trustee to pay the income from the trust property to Donor for life and at Donor's death the trust ends and Trustee is to pay the trust property to issue of Donor's friend then living by representation. What's the gift?: *the value of the remainder interest.* Donor has kept the income from the property and has only relinquished dominion and control over the remainder.

If Donor had created a revocable trust however, there is no taxable gift because Donor has not relinquished dominion and control over the trust property. The trust will be part of Donor's taxable estate at death, but we'll deal with that next.

How is the gift of the remainder in the case of the irrevocable trust valued? It must be valued using actuarial principles. The value of the gift is the value today of the right to receive the $5,000,000 transferred to the trust at the end of Donor's life. Calculating that value requires that we know how long Donor is expected to live and what the discount rate is, the rate at which money is expected to increase in value over Donor' remaining life expectancy. The basic idea is that the right to receive $1 a year from now is worth the amount you have to invest today to have a dollar one year from now. So the value of the right to receive $5,000,000 at Donor's death (the future interest over which Donor relinquished dominion and control) is the amount we'd have to invest today to have $5,000,000 at the end of Donor's life expectancy. This is how it's done even if the $5,000,000 is not $5,000,000 in cash but rather property: stocks, whether publicly traded or not, bonds, real estate, or anything else.

Of course we don't know when Donor is going to die. But that's not a problem. We know what Donor's likely life expectancy is based on our experience with the lifespans of large numbers of people. This knowledge is summarized in actuarial life expectancy tables which were first created for insurance companies so they could figure out how to set the premiums on life insurance policies. Today the IRS publishes life expectancy tables that must be used in actuarial calculations involved in taxation. These tables are revised periodically based on census data. The discount rate that must be used is calculated monthly and published by the IRS. It's based on the interest rate on government bonds. If Donor makes a taxable gift of the remainder in a trust funded with property worth $5,000,000 and Donor is 60 years of age and the discount rate is 3.0%, the value of the remainder is $2,760,025. That means if we invest $2,760,025 today and it grows 3.0% a year, by the end of the Donor's actuarial life expectancy we'll have $5,000,000. The higher the discount rate the smaller the value of the remainder because the bigger the rate of growth the less we need to start with. If the discount rate is 4.0%, the value of the remainder is $2,315,500. (The actuarial tables can be found at https://www.irs.gov/retirement-plans/actuarial-tables.)

What happened to the rest of the $5,000,000? That's the value of the income interest, the value today of receiving the income on the $5,000,000, calculated at the discount rate, for the remaining years of the Donor's life expectancy. Once again, we use the discount rate to calculate the value. The value of the right to receive a dollar in income one year from now is the value which if invested at the discount rate will grow into one dollar during that year. The value of the income interest is the sum of all of those values for the number of years the income interest will last, in this case of course the number of years is Donor's actuarial life expectancy. Of course, if the Donor does not retain dominion or control of the transferred property, then the entire value of the property transferred is the value of the gift.

What happens if Donor's life expectancy is greater or less than that used to calculate the value of the gift of the remainder? Nothing. Actuarial valuation is based on average life expectancy calculated using very large numbers of persons. While individual taxpayers may have a lifetime greater or lesser than the actuarial predictions, the Department of Treasury deals with a very large number of actuarial valuations and over time the wins and losses balance out. Decades ago the United States Supreme Court approved of using actuarial valuation in taxation based on the idea that on the average the government came out even.

So many cases, problems, and discussions in this book have involved gifts to family members. You might wonder, then, why in the example above the remainder beneficiaries of the trust and therefore the donee's of Donor's gift are the descendants of Donor's friend rather than family members of Donor. There is a very good reason. If the donee of the gift of the remainder were Donor's own descendants or the descendants of Donor's spouse, or the ancestors or spouse of any of those people, or the sibling or spouse of a sibling of the Donor, the life income interest retained by Donor would be valued at zero for gift tax purposes and the value of the gift would be the entire $5,000,000 value of the property conveyed to Trustee.

That result is required by Chapter 14 of the Internal Revenue Code (§§ 2701–2704) which contains special valuation rules that apply to certain transfers between family members. For our purposes § 2702 is the most important. It provides that an interest retained by the creator of a trust (the income interest retained by Donor in our example) the creation of which transfers an interest to any of the persons described in the previous paragraph, (the remainder interest in our example) will be valued at zero for gift tax purposes unless the retained interest is an annuity interest (a fixed dollar amount) paid at least annually, or a unitrust amount, a payment at least annually of a fixed percentage of the value of the trust property determined annually. Congress enacted these provisions because it concluded that the temptation to manipulate trust investment strategy to benefit remainder beneficiaries was simply too great. Remember that the gift tax is paid on the actuarial value of the remainder when the settlor of the trust retains the income interest. Having done that, the settlor could suggest that the trustee invest to sacrifice the production of income to growth of the value of the trust property. The settlor could even be trustee and carry out this program directly. The idea is to make the value of the remainder at the distribution date exceed as much as possible the value on which the actuarial valuation was based. Requiring that the settlor retain an annuity or unitrust interest limits the ability to manipulate the ultimate value of the remainder by requiring either a minimum value for the income payments to the settlor or tying of those payments to the total value of the trust.

b) Transfers Excluded from Taxable Gifts by Statute

Some of the most important provisions of the gift tax sections of the Internal Revenue Code deal with exclusions from taxable gifts. These provisions identify transfers that even though they involve relinquishing dominion and control and are therefore taxable gifts under the general definition are not treated as taxable gifts. The most significant is the present interest exclusion (IRC § 2503(b)). Any person can make completed gifts with a total value of up to a set amount every year to any individual and not pay any gift tax. The amount is increased for increases in the cost of living in the same way as the applicable exclusion amount. In 2019 the amount is $15,000. The only requirement is that the gift be a present interest. While the case law dealing with the definition of a present interest is quite elaborate, all we need to know for now is that transfer involves a present interest if the donee can enjoy the property at the moment the transfer is complete.

Outright transfer to the donee are easy to understand. For example, in 2019 Donor directs Donor's broker to transfer 200 shares of X Corp. worth $10 per share at the time of transfer to the brokerage account of Donor's Older Child. The first $15,000 of value is excluded and the taxable gift is $5000. The Donor also directs Donor's broker to transfer 200 shares of Y Corp. worth $10 per share to Donor's Younger Child. The first $15,000 of value is excluded and the taxable gift is $5000. Total taxable gifts: $10,000.

Transfers in trust can also qualify for the present interest exclusion. For example, in 2019 Donor transfers $1,000,000 to Trustee, in trust, to pay the income to Donor's Child for life, and at Child's death the trust terminates and the Trustee is to pay the trust property free of trust to Child's issue then living by representation. The first $15,000 *of the actuarial value of the income interest* qualifies for the present interest exclusion. None of the value of the remainder qualifies because it is a future interest. The taxable gift is $985,000 (1,000,000 minus 15,000). Note that the income interest qualifies for the present interest exclusion because the trust is a mandatory trust; the trustee must pay the income to the beneficiary. If the trustee were given discretion to decide whether or not to pay income to the beneficiary there would be no present interest exclusion.

Two other statutory exclusions that are of great importance especially because both are unlimited in amount (IRC § 2503(e)). The first is for transfers to pay another person's medical bills. Any medical expense that can be deducted for income tax purposes qualifies for this exclusion, including doctor and hospital bills and insurance premiums. The second exclusion is for tuition expenses. Grandparent can pay grandchild's tuition in any amount for any level of education and not worry about making a taxable gift. (The exclusion is for tuition only; it does not include room, board, and books or other fees.) Both these exclusions are in addition to the basic present interest exclusion.

c) Deductions Allowed in Calculating the Value of the Taxable Gift

Not every transfer that involves relinquishing dominion and control by a donor results in a taxable gift. There may be a deduction available for all or part of the value of the transfer. The two most important are the marital deduction and the charitable deduction. There is no gift tax on outright transfers between spouses, and there are special rules for obtaining the marital deduction when one spouse creates a trust of which the other spouse is a beneficiary. Those rules are explained in the discussion of the estate tax because the estate tax marital deduction has the same rules. The charitable deduction is unlimited in amount. Generally, any charitable gift that can be deducted for income tax purposes also qualifies for the gift tax charitable deduction. There are special rules that govern obtaining the deduction when a trust which has both non-charitable and charitable beneficiaries, and those, too, are the same as the rules for the estate tax charitable deduction.

3. The Estate Tax

a) The Gross Estate

The most fundamental question in dealing with the estate tax is "What is the decedent's gross estate, the property subject to estate tax before deductions and credits?" It is not limited to the probate estate. If it were, the estate tax would be as toothless as an elective share limited to probate property. Although some states have never really grappled with expanding the pool of property subject to the elective share beyond the deceased spouse's probate estate, from the very beginning of the estate tax, Congress realized that limiting the taxable estate to the probate estate would make the tax meaningless. The statutory language Congress used to expand the gross estate beyond the probate the estate was the subject of frequent litigation. Today, fortunately, the meaning of these sections of the Internal Revenue Code is pretty well understood, at least as they apply to most situations.

The principle behind all of the statutory provisions is simple: if the property arrangement made by the decedent is structured so that persons other than the decedent can enjoy the economic benefits of the property only after the decedent's death than the value of the property at the decedent's death is included in the gross estate. The statutory language that defines the gross estate is found in IRC §§ 2033 through 2042. Section 2033 includes in the gross estate interests in property owned by the decedent; in other words, the decedent's probate property. Several of these sections address specific kinds of property.

§ 2042 Proceeds of life insurance. The death benefit paid because of death of the person insured under the policy is included in the insured's gross estate if the deceased insured held "incidents of ownership" in the policy. An incident of ownership is defined in the Regulations under § 2042 as any power over the policy that allows the deceased insured to obtain an economic benefit from the policy during life. Common examples are the ability to borrow against the accumulated cash value of the policy, the ability to cash the policy in, and the power to name a beneficiary. The person who owns the policy always has incidents of ownership. In many, if not most cases, the insured procured the policy and is the owner. That means that the death benefit is part of the insured's gross estate when the insured dies unless the insured disposes of the incidents of ownership by giving away ownership of the policy (which will have gift tax consequences). Note that death benefit is not taxable income in the hands of the beneficiary or beneficiaries of the policy.

§ 2041 Joint interests. This section applies to all joint arrangements with right of survivorship (including tenancy by the entirety) where the decedent was one of the joint holders of the property involved. The decedent's estate includes all of the jointly held property unless the decedent's estate can show that some or all of the property originally belonged to the other joint holder or holders. There is a special rule applicable when the other joint holder is the decedent's spouse. In that case one-half of the property is included in the decedent's gross taxable estate no matter who contributed what to acquiring the property.

For example, Decedent and Decedent's sibling, S, are joint holders with right of survivorship of a brokerage account. On Decedent's death Decedent's gross estate will include all of the property in the account unless Decedent's personal representative can show what part of the property in the account came from S. If the personal representative can show that S contributed 35% of the funds that went in to the account, Decedent's gross taxable estate will include 65% of the value of the account.

If the holders of the joint account and Decedent and Decedent's spouse, S, on the death of either Decedent or of S, the gross estate of the deceased spouse will include only one-half of the value of the property in the account no matter who contributed what.

§ 2039 Annuities. The gross estate includes the value received because of the decedent's death by a beneficiary of an annuity the decedent was receiving or had the right to receive. If the beneficiary receives an annuity rather than a lump sum the value included is calculated actuarially. At time of death Decedent was retired and receiving a pension in the form of an annuity would be paid for the longer of Decedent's life or 20 years. The decedent's sibling, S, is the beneficiary of the payments remaining, if any, to be paid after Decedent's death. Decedent's gross estate includes the present value of those payments calculated actuarially. If Decedent had lived for more than 20 years after the payment of the annuity began there would be no more payments to be made and nothing would be included Decedent's gross estate on account of the annuity.

§ 2041 Powers of Appointment. All appointive property subject to a general power of appointment held by the decedent as donee is included in the gross estate. As discussed at some length in Chapter 9, a power of appointment is general if it allows the donee to appoint to the donee, the donee's estate, the donee's creditors, or the creditors of the donee's estate. This list of potential appointees that makes a power general for tax purposes, as was noted, has also become the standard definition of a general power of appointment for property law purposes. There are exceptions to the definition of a general power of appointment, and as we also saw in Chapter 9 the most important applies to a power subject to an ascertainable standard related to maintenance, education, health, or support. Even though the permissible appointees make the power a general power, if the donee is limited by as ascertainable standard the power is not general.

The other gross estate provisions in the IRC are not limited to interests in or powers over specific kinds of property. They are generally applicable to transfers made by the decedent where the decedent retained certain interests in or powers over the transferred property. Remember that the transfer taxes are excise taxes on the privilege of transmitting property. That is how they have always been understood and indeed that is why they are constitutional. Because they are excise taxes they do not have to be apportioned among the states by population in accordance with Article I, § 2, clause 3 of the United States Constitution. The general principle explained above is directly related to this constitutional requirement. So long as the provisions including property transferred by the decedent which under the terms of the transfer other people can enjoy only after the decedent's death, the transferred property can be included in the gross estate and taxed.

Here's the classic example: Decedent transfers $5,000,000 to Trustee, in trust, and under the terms of the trust Trustee is to pay all the income from the trust property to Decedent for life, and at Decedent's death the trust terminates and the Trustee is to distribute the trust property in outright ownership to Decedent's issue then living by representation. At Decedent's death the life income interest is over. It simply vanishes and with it vanishes the Decedent's enjoyment of the economic benefits of the trust property. Decedent's death is the distribution date for the remainder interest. At that moment, of course, the remainder vests in possession and the economic benefit of the trust property passes to the remainder beneficiaries. The statute includes in Decedent's gross estate all of the property in which the Decedent had the income interest. Even though Decedent no longer had legal title to the property—that's in the trustee—and even though the Decedent had beneficial or equitable title only to the income produced by the property, the tax falls on the entire value of the property enjoyment of which passes to persons other than Decedent only at Decedent's death.

Three sections of the IRC deal with interests and powers retained by the decedent in a lifetime transfer of property.

§ 2036 Transfers with retained life estate. This section applies when decedent transfers property but retains the income from the property, an *interest* (§ 2036(a)(1)) or *the power* to designate the persons who will enjoy the property or the income from the property (§ 2036(a)(2)). (The classic example above is covered by § 2036(a)(1).)

§ 2037 Transfers taking effect at death. In spite of the broad title of this section, it applies only to an interest in property transferred by the decedent to the extent that the interest can be enjoyed only by surviving the decedent *and* the decedent had a reversionary *interest* in the property the value of which immediately before the decedent's death exceeds 5% of the value of the property. The transfers that are subject to this section can be somewhat convoluted, but this is a relatively straightforward example:

Decedent transfers property to T in trust. The terms of the trust require Trustee to pay the income produced by the trust property to B for life and at B's death the trust terminates and Trustee is to distribute the property outright to Decedent if Decedent is then living and if not to Decedent's issue then living by representation. Decedent's issue will receive possession of the trust property only if they survive Decedent because, of course, they must be alive at B's death and Decedent must have died before B if the issue's contingent remainder is going to vest in possession. If at Decedent's death during B's lifetime the actuarial value of Decedent's remainder (calculated as if Decedent were going to live out Decedent's actuarial life expectancy) exceeds 5% of the value of the trust property then the value of the trust property minus the value of B's income interest is included in Decedent's gross estate.

Section 2037 *does not* apply to a reversion in the transferor arising by operation law: the reversion that stays with the settlor of a trust when the terms of the trust create contingent remainders. If the settlor dies owning that future interest it is probate property and its actuarial value is included in the gross estate under IRC § 2033.

§ 2038 Revocable transfers. This section includes in the gross estate any property transferred by the decedent where the enjoyment of the property was subject to change at the time of the decedent's death by reason of a *power* held by the decedent to alter, amend, revoke, or terminate the terms of the transfer. (Subsection (a)(1) is applicable to transfers after June 22, 1936 and (a)(2) to transfers on or before that date. Whether there's any real difference in the provisions is a complicated story and one that is becoming ever less important as fewer and fewer persons who made transfers before June 22, 1936 and retained powers are still alive.)

Sections 2036 and 2038 will include in the gross estate just about every valid will substitute that is not included by the more specific sections, and often both sections will apply. For example, a revocable lifetime trust will be included in the settlor's gross estate under IRC § 2036(a)(1) because the settlor has retained all of the income from the property the settlor transferred in trust during life and under IRC § 2038(a)(1) because the settlor holds the power to revoke. Any sort of payable on death account or transfer on death account will also be included because the creator of the account or other arrangement almost always enjoys the income from the property involved for life and in any event has the power to revoke the arrangement.

b) Deductions from the Gross Estate

The statute allows deduction for the estate's expenses such as the cost of the decedent's funeral, executor's commissions and lawyer's fees and for the decedent's debts paid by the estate out of property that is subject to creditors' claims (IRC § 2053). As important as these deductions are, two others are even more important: the charitable deduction and the marital deduction.

Like the gift tax charitable deduction IRC § 2522, the estate tax charitable deduction, IRC § 2055, is unlimited in amount. That means that it is possible to eliminate the estate tax in any estate, no matter how large, by giving the exclusion amount not used during life (maximum $11,400,000 in 2019) to the decedent's family or to anyone else and giving the rest of the taxable estate to charity. Outright gifts to public charities (most educational institutions, religious establishments, organizations like the Red Cross) are uncomplicated. A gift to a trust to benefit only organizations that are public charities is also uncomplicated. Sometimes, however, a decedent wishes to create a trust to benefit both charity and individuals, often members of the decedent's family. These "split interest trusts," which can also be created during life and result in a gift tax charitable deduction, are subject to a complex set of rules. The basic idea, however, should be familiar to you. The purpose of the rules is to prevent manipulation of the administration of the trust to starve the charitable interest, the same worries that led Congress to later enact the special valuation rules in Chapter 14 discussed above.

The potential for manipulating the trust to disadvantage charitable beneficiaries shows how trustees' powers to allocate receipts between principal and income and to select investments can shift benefits from one set of beneficiaries to another. An important part of the trustee's fiduciary duty is the requirement that the trustee treat the beneficiaries impartially and that duty is powerful enough to prevent the application of IRC §§ 2036(a)(2) and 2038(a)(1) to these administrative powers. Congress was not willing, however, to trust fiduciary duty to ensure that trustees of split interest trusts would not attempt to shift benefits to the private beneficiaries at the expense of the charitable beneficiary. Instead, Congress decided to require that the income interest in the trust be an annuity interest, that is, a fixed sum payable at least annually, or a unitrust interest which as we saw in our discussion of principal and income and the prudent investor standard insures that both income and remainder interests will share in appreciation or depreciation of the trust property.

The marital deduction, IRC § 2055 (and the gift tax parallel provision, IRC § 2523), is unlimited in amount and can be used in conjunction with the applicable exclusion amount to eliminate estate tax in the estate of a decedent who dies survived by the decedent's spouse. The requirements for obtaining the marital deduction, however, are moderately complex. These requirements exist because of the policy behind the marital deduction. First, the property deducted in the estate of the first spouse to die must be taxed in the estate of the surviving spouse (or subject to gift tax if the surviving spouse gives it away) to the extent the property is not used up by or for the surviving spouse and, second, there must be no other beneficiary of the property during the surviving spouse's life other than the surviving spouse.

An outright gift in the will to the surviving spouse (or an outright lifetime gift to the donor's spouse) will qualify for the marital deduction. The same is true of non-probate property that passes outright to the spouse under a beneficiary designation or under the terms of a revocable trust ending at the settlor's death. If the decedent or donor wishes to make a gift to the spouse in trust, then the trust must have certain provisions required by IRC § 2056 (estate tax) or § 2523 (gift tax). Unless the remainder beneficiary of the trust is the spouse's estate (that means that the terms of the trust require the trust to end at the death of the spouse and that the trustee distribute the trust property to the spouse's executor or administrator), the spouse must be the only beneficiary of all of the income produced by the trust property during the spouse's life and no one else can be a beneficiary during the surviving spouse's life (for example, the trustee cannot have the power to distribute trust principal to anyone other than the surviving spouse) and the property held in the trust at the spouse's death must be included in the spouse's gross estate. The first requirement can be met by giving the spouse all of the rights of an income beneficiary under the law of the state that governs the trust, although many drafters include very precise language in the trust terms. The second requirement can be met by 1) making the spouse's estate the remainder beneficiary, 2) giving the spouse a general power of appointment over all of the trust property so the property is included in the spouse's gross estate under IRC § 2041, or 3) making an election on the decedent's estate tax return (Form 706) or on the gift tax return if the trust is a lifetime trust (Form 709) to treat the trust property as "qualified terminal interest property" always abbreviated as "QTIP." If that election is made, the trust property is included in the surviving spouse's gross estate under IRC § 2044 and if trust property is transferred out of the trust to anyone other than the surviving spouse the surviving spouse has made a gift under IRC § 2519. The surviving spouse can have testamentary power of appointment over the QTIP trust, but the statute does not require it.

The marital deduction is very often used in the estate planning of a married person. Most married couples seem to assume that at the death of the first to die, the survivor's wealth should not be diminished by estate tax. And as noted above, the estate of a married person need not pay any estate tax, no matter how valuable the taxable estate by using the marital deduction. Decedent's estate plan can create a trust to be funded with the available applicable exclusion amount the beneficiaries of which can be anyone including the surviving spouse and then give the rest of the taxable estate outright to the surviving spouse or to a properly structured trust that qualifies for the marital deduction. Giving all of the taxable estate to the surviving spouse would be not wise because it would waste the deceased spouse's applicable exclusion amount. That is, that was the rule until 2010 when IRC § 2010 was amended to allow a decedent to transfer to the decedent's surviving spouse the decedent's applicable exclusion amount not used during the decedent's life. The decedent's executor or administrator makes an election on the estate tax return to make the transfer. The surviving spouse then has an applicable exclusion amount equal to that received from the decedent plus the surviving spouse's own amount. Note that if the surviving spouse remarries and that spouse dies, the surviving spouse is the surviving spouse for these purposes only of the second spouse and any applicable exclusion amount received from the survivor's first spouse can no longer be used.

C. The Generation Skipping Transfer (GST) Tax

The third wealth transfer tax is the GST tax. The policy behind the tax is that the transfer of wealth should be taxed in each generation. That is, if Grandparent makes a gift to Grandchild, the gift should be subject to tax twice, just as if Grandparent had made a gift to Child who then made a gift to Grandchild. The same principle applies to a trust. Grandparent creates a trust under the terms of which Trustee is to pay income to Child for life and on Child's death the trust terminates and the trust property is distributed to Child's descendants then living by representation. The creation of the trust will be subject to gift tax if it is a lifetime trust or to estate tax if it is a testamentary trust. But on Child's death there is no gift or estate tax liability. Child is not the donor and unless the trust is included in Child's gross estate (for example, Child was given a general power of appointment over the trust property) there will be no estate tax. In GST tax terms, the person making the gift, creating trust, or making a gift at death through a will or non-probate property arrangement is a "transferor."

The GST tax applies in both these situations. The first, the outright gift to a person or at trust for the benefit of a person or persons at least two generations younger than the transferor is known as a "direct skip" and the tax is due when the transfer is made. The second is a "taxable termination" and is the tax is due at Child's death. There is a third situation where the tax applies, the "taxable distribution" which occurs when the trustee make a distribution from a trust to a beneficiary is who two or more generations younger than the settlor of the trust (think of a discretionary trust created by Grandparent for the benefit of all of Grandparent's descendants and which will terminate in a way that satisfies the Rule Against Perpetuities if necessary). While at least one child of the settlor is alive the trustee makes a distribution to a grandchild. That's a taxable distribution and tax is due when the distribution is made. When all of the settlor's children die that is a type of taxable termination and tax is due then, too.

After that event, distributions to the settlor's grandchildren will not be taxable distributions but distributions to great-grandchildren are.

What if the donees or beneficiaries are not related to the transferor? Section 2651 has rules for assigning persons to generation based on the number of years between their births and that of the transferor. The transferor's spouse is always the same generation as the transferor so the GST tax does not apply to transfers to spouses and relatives of the spouse are assigned to generations based on the spouse being the same generation as the transferor. Thus the spouse's nieces and nephews are one generation younger than the transferor no matter what the difference in ages.

The tax is a "flat tax," that is there is only one tax rate and it is equal to the highest estate and gift tax rate, currently 40%. So in the example of the trust created by Grandparent to pay income to Child for life, remainder to Child's descendants living at Child's death, Child's death is a taxable termination and there will be a tax equal to 40% of the value of the trust property at Child's death. If that value is $10,000,000 after allowable deductions for things like trustee's commissions, legal fees and accounting fees in connection with the termination, the tax is $4,000,000. The GST tax will not apply if the estate tax does, so if Child had a general power of appointment over the trust property the property will be part of Child's gross estate and the taxable termination is ignored. If Child's taxable estate including the trust property is less than the available applicable exclusion amount, there will be no GST tax and no estate tax payable in connection with the trust.

The GST tax certainly seems to be pretty robust; after all, 40% of all the property involved in the taxable event—direct skip, taxable termination, or taxable distribution—is not insignificant. However, just as everyone has an applicable exclusion amount for estate and gift tax purposes, everyone as a GST tax exemption amount which is equal to the applicable exclusion amount which in 2019 is $11,400,000. Therefore, everyone can make up to $11,400,000 of direct skips without paying GST tax (only the estate or gift tax applies). But there is a much better use for the exemption. Let's say that Grandparent created the trust for Child for life, remainder to Child's descendants by transferring $5,000,000 to the trustee. By allocating $5,000,000 of Grandparent's GST tax exemption to the transfer, the GST tax will never apply to the trust no matter how large the value of the trust property involved in a taxable distribution or termination. Never. Ever. Therefore, if the trust is governed by the law of a state that has repealed the Rule Against Perpetuities and allows perpetual trusts, the trust could theoretically continue forever without paying any transfer taxes beyond the gift or estate tax involved in the creation of the trust.

The statutory mechanism for using the exemption to eliminate the GST tax is a bit complex. Under IRC §§ 2641 and 2642, the amount of tax due because of a direct skip, taxable termination, or taxable distribution is determined by multiplying the maximum estate and gift tax rate (currently 40%) by the *inclusion ratio* which is determined by subtracting the *applicable fraction* from the number 1. All of that is not as complicated as it looks. The applicable fraction is a fraction the denominator of which the value of the property funding the generation skipping trust or involved in the direct skip and the numerator is the amount of exemption allocated. In our example using Grandparent's trust, if Grandparent (if a lifetime trust) or Grandparent's executor (if a testamentary trust) allocates $5,000,000 of Grandparent's exemption to the $5,000,000 of property that funds the trust

1. The applicable fraction is 5,000,000/5,000,000 = 1.

2. The inclusion ratio then is 1 – 1 = 0.

3. The applicable rate is (maximum estate and gift tax rate) × 0 = 0.

For the entire duration of the trust the applicable rate of GST tax will always be 0. Not a bad result for the taxpayer.

D. Summary

The three wealth transfer taxes today are of no importance to the vast majority of the American people. The number of persons whose wealth exceeds the applicable exclusion amount is quite small. For example, in a total population of more than 325,000,000 people, most estimates find that fewer than 5,000 decedents are subject to estate tax each year. Nevertheless, the estate tax in particular has been the subject of much political controversy and there has been agitation for its repeal for decades, although the only result has been a greatly increased applicable exclusion amount, last increased in 2017 to $10,000,000 which as noted is adjusted upwards every year in rough alignment with the cost of living. That increase to the base amount of $10,000,000 will end on December 31, 2026, however, and revert to the prior amount of $5,000,000 adjusted for inflation from 2010 when the $5,000,000 amount became law unless Congress acts. In the meantime, the taxes will continue to be a source of a good deal of legal work and of political controversy.

Test Your Knowledge

To assess your understanding of the material in this chapter, <u>click here</u> to take a quiz.

Index

References are to page numbers.